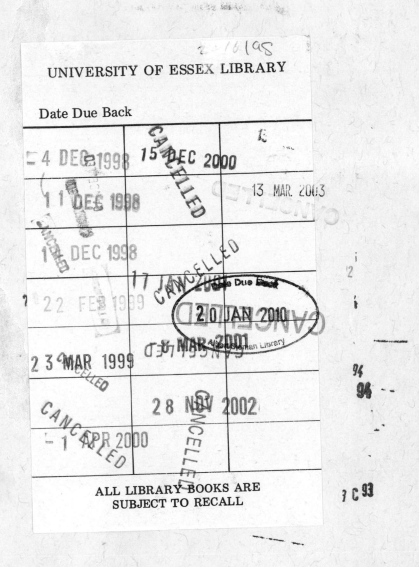

# CASES AND COMMENTARY
# ON THE
# LAW OF TRUSTS

AUSTRALIA
The Law Book Company
Sydney

CANADA
The Carswell Company
Toronto, Ottawa

INDIA
N.M. Tripathi (Private) Ltd.
Bombay
*and*
Eastern Law House (Private) Ltd.
Calcutta
MPP House
Bangalore
Universal Book Traders
Delhi

ISRAEL
Steimatzky's Agency Ltd.
Tel Aviv

PAKISTAN
Pakistan Law House
Karachi

# HAYTON AND MARSHALL

# CASES AND COMMENTARY
# ON THE
# LAW OF TRUSTS

*NINTH EDITION*

by

## DAVID J. HAYTON, LL.D.
*of the Inner Temple and Lincoln's Inn, Barrister*
*Professor of Law, Kings College,*
*London University*

LONDON
SWEET & MAXWELL/STEVENS
1991

First edition 1939 by J. A. Nathan
Second edition 1951 by O. R. Marshall
Third edition 1955 by O. R. Marshall
Fourth edition 1961 by O. R. Marshall
Second impression 1966 by O. R. Marshall
Fifth edition 1967 by O. R. Marshall
Second impression 1971 by O. R. Marshall
Sixth edition 1975 by D. J. Hayton
Seventh edition 1980 by D. J. Hayton
Eighth edition 1986 by D. J. Hayton
Second impression 1988 by D. J. Hayton
Third impression 1989 by D. J. Hayton
Ninth edition 1991 by D. J. Hayton

Published by
Sweet & Maxwell/Stevens
of South Quay Plaza
183 Marsh Wall, London
Phototypeset by L.B.J. Enterprises Limited,
Chilcompton and Tadley
Printed by Richard Clay Limited,
Bungay, Suffolk

A CIP catalogue record
for this book is available
from The British Library

ISBN 0 420 48240 7

# PREFACE

This combined textbook and casebook is for those who intend to be in the top half of successful examinees and so seek to develop a good understanding of English trust law. To help this, questions and problems are posed at the end of relevant sections as an integral part of the book. After all, "To read without reflecting is like eating without digesting," as someone once said. With the assistance of lengthy excerpts from cases, articles, White Papers, Charity Commissioners' reports and Attorney-General's Guidelines, the book aims to expound the law clearly and succinctly, to provide insights into the operation of trust law and how it might develop, and to encourage readers to develop their analytical faculties and to think for themselves. To this end, reference is made to some illuminating Commonwealth cases and statutes. There is detailed investigation of those grey areas so enjoyed by examiners. University and professional examinations are catered for, whilst practitioners should find the book useful for keeping in touch with modern developments.

It should be easy to use the book in conjunction with the introductory book, Hayton: *The Law of Trusts,* and the practitioners' book, Underhill & Hayton: *The Law of Trusts and Trustees.*

In up-dating the book it is surprising how developments have caused much to be re-written. Moreover, a new section on Pension Fund Trusts has been inserted as section 9 of Chapter 9 to deal with the trust concept in contemporary practical perspective: I gratefully acknowledge the valuable assistance of Miss J Donohue of Barlow, Lyde and Gilbert, Solicitors in providing the material on which this section was based.

Major re-writing of Chapter 7 on Constructive Trusts had to be done to deal with potentially far-reaching developments involving the liability of fiduciaries and of strangers to the trust, the prevention of unconscionable conduct, and beneficiaries' proprietary and personal remedies. Much re-writing has occurred in covering the following topics: the rules against remoteness and inalienability, gifts to unincorporated associations, attempts to defraud creditors, religious and miscellaneous charitable purposes, the investment of trust funds and investment management problems, control of trustees' discretions and exemption clauses.

Excerpts from the following cases have been inserted: *R. v. District Auditor ex p. W. Yorkshire Metropolitan CC., Agip (Africa) Ltd* v.

*Jackson, Ashburn Anstalt* v. *Arnold, Grant* v. *Edwards, Lloyds Bank* v. *Rosset, Stokes* v. *Anderson, Knocker* v. *Youle, Boe* v. *Alexander, Imperial Group Pension Trust Ltd. Imperial Tobacco Co* and *Davis* v. *Richards & Wallington Ltd.* Excerpts from the following cases have been deleted: *Re Densham, Burns* v. *Burns, Allen* v. *Snyder, Eves* v. *Eves, Midland Bank* v. *Dobson, Baden Delvaux & Lecuit* v. *Societe Generale, Williams-Ashman* v. *Price, Re Brockbank, Re Whitehead's W T, Shaw* v. *Cates, Re Walker, Khoo Tek Kheong* v. *Chng Too Neoh, Re Holt's Settlement, Re Evans' WT, Re Chaytor, Hardoon* v. *Belilios, Perrins* v. *Bellamy* and *Re Stuart.*

I am delighted to express my heartfelt appreciation to the publishers for their thoroughness in producing this edition and for producing the index and tables of cases and statutes. I am especially grateful to Miss Debra Cossey for typing all the extra text for this new edition.

The book is based on sources available in January 1991 but at proofs stage up-dating has been possible to take account, *inter alia*, of the bold acceptance of the general defence of change of position by the House of Lords in *Lipkin Gorman* v. *Karpnale*, so that it is hoped that the law is accurately stated as at July 1, 1991.

*King's College London*
*St Swithin's Day 1991*                                          David Hayton

# ACKNOWLEDGMENTS

*The author and publishers wish to thank the following for permission to reprint material from the books and the periodicals indicated:*

Barry Rose Publishers Ltd.:
  *Keeton's Law of Trusts* (11th edition)
Butterworths Law Publishers Ltd.:
  *The All England Law Reports*
  *Underhill and Hayton on the Law of Trusts*
Crown Copyright ©
  Various Acts
Green:
  "Grey, Oughtred and Vandervell—A Contextual Reappraisal"
  (1984) 47 M.L.R. 385
Her Majesty's Stationery Office:
  *The Charity Commissions Annual Reports*
  *Recommendations from Efficiency, Scrutiny of the Supervision of
    Charities*
Incorporated Council of Law Reporting for England & Wales:
  *Appeal Cases*
  *Chancery Division Cases*
  *Weekly Law Reports*
Jones:
  "Delegation by Trustee: A Reappraisal" (1959) 22 M.L.R. 381
Little Brown & Co. (Boston):
  Scott *Abridgment of the Law of Trusts* (3rd ed. 1960)
Stevens & Sons Ltd.:
  Various extracts from Law Quarterly Review
Weidenfeld & Nicolson Ltd. and the author:
  M. R. Chesterman *Charities, Trusts and Social Welfare*

# CONTENTS

# TABLE OF CASES

# TABLE OF STATUTES

# ABBREVIATIONS

Ford & Lee: Ford & Lee, *Principles of the Law of Trusts* (1st ed.).

Goff & Jones: Goff & Jones, *The Law of Restitution* (3rd ed.).

Hanbury: Hanbury & Maudsley, *Modern Equity* (13th ed.).

Heydon, Gummow & Austin: Heydon, Gummow & Austin, *Cases & Materials on Equity & Trusts* (1st ed.).

Lewin: Lewin, *Trusts* (17th ed.).

Meagher, Gummow & Lehane: Meagher, Gummow & Lehane, *Equity: Doctrines & Remedies* (2nd ed.).

Megarry & Wade: Megarry & Wade, *Law of Real Property* (5th ed.).

Oakley: Oakley, *Constructive Trusts* (2nd ed.).

Pettit: Pettit, *Equity & the Law of Trusts* (6th ed.).

Snell: Snell, *Equity* (29th ed.).

Underhill: Underhill & Hayton, *Law of Trusts* (14th ed.).

Waters: Waters, *Law of Trusts in Canada* (2nd ed.).

Wolstenholme & Cherry: Wolstenholme & Cherry, *Conveyancing Statutes* (13th ed.).

# Chapter 1

## INTRODUCTION

A trust arises where property is transferred by a person to trustees to be managed for the benefit of beneficiaries or a charitable purpose. Usually, the transfer is by way of gift but it may be pursuant to a contract. The law of trusts is thus concerned with the utilisation of wealth, whether in the form of pension funds, unit trusts, charitable funds, union funds, club funds or family funds. It is about settling property on trustees so as to minimise liability to the various taxes. Much of trust law has so far developed in regard to the preservation of family wealth, tying up property so that it can be enjoyed by successive generations, protecting the family from the depredations of creditors and of particular relatives with extravagant reckless dispositions, providing secretly for mentally defective relatives, for mistresses, for illegitimate children or for causes with which an open association is not desired. Modern case law is still much concerned with family trusts or trusts for employees of family companies where the funds are a small fraction of the total value of all funds held on trust, though a few problems are now surfacing in respect of union funds and pension funds. That toast of the legal profession, the testator who draws up his own will, is also responsible for much case law.

The trust concept is extremely flexible and can be used to achieve almost any lawful end except that it cannot directly provide for abstract non-charitable purposes.[1] Some rules of trust law make it difficult to give property to unincorporated associations on trust, though the courts now avoid this difficulty where possible by construing such gifts as out-and-out accretions to the association's funds subject to the contractual rights thereto of the members of the association under its constitution.[2] The trust concept has proved particularly useful in conveyancing so that whenever land is owned by two or more persons that land must be held on trust for sale.[3] Maitland has quite rightly characterised the trust concept as "the greatest and most distinctive achievement performed by Englishmen in the field of jurisprudence."[4] No lawyer can claim to provide a proper service for his clients without a thorough grasp of trust law and its potentialities.

---

[1] See pp. 185–197, *infra*. By devious devices it may indirectly be possible to achieve abstract non-charitable ends: pp. 188–189, *infra*.

[2] See pp. 191–197 *infra*.

[3] ss.34–36 of the Law of Property Act 1925. Trustees hold property as joint tenants so that on the death of one trustee the property automatically passes to the surviving trustees by virtue of the *ius accrescendi*. On the death of the last surviving trustee his personal representatives take over his function until the appointment of new trustees: Trustee Act 1925, ss.18, 36.

[4] *Selected Essays*, p. 129.

Trusts are used not only for pension schemes, collective investment schemes (unit trusts), trade union funds, charitable purposes and for minimising the impact of tax on family wealth. Ownership of a family business can be transferred to trustees so as to prevent ownership becoming fragmented by inheritance and then, perhaps, passing to outsiders. Assets can be held by trustees to protect minors, persons of unsound mind, spendthrifts or young adults who might fall under the influence of an unscrupulous lover or religious guru. Persons can have transactions conducted anonymously, *e.g.* in a politically sensitive country by having trustees use their assets. The trust instrument revealing the names of beneficiaries does not have to be filed on any public register and is a private document which normally remains confidential between the trustees and the beneficiaries. Indeed, the names of beneficiaries do not always appear on the face of the trust instrument because the trustees, with the settlor's consent, may have power to make anyone in the world a member of the class of beneficiaries.

A settlor can use a trust as a substitute for a will by transferring all his significant assets to trustees (of whom he may be one). On his death the assets remain in the surviving trustee(s) subject to the terms of the trust: no public grant of probate is required before those assets can be dealt with. If resident in a politically unstable country a person can transfer assets to trustees in some stable country so that the assets are beyond the reach of some new regime in his country of residence.

As part of some comprehensive financing scheme the voting rights attached to shares or other securities can be vested in trustees to be managed as a block. As an independent security device there is the trust for debenture holders where a company mortgages property to trustees and confers rights on them to be held on trust for large numbers of debenture holders who actually lend money to the company in return for debenture stock. In the company sphere there are also tax-efficient employee share ownership plans under which the company gives moneys to trustees to purchase shares in the company itself for the ultimate benefit of company employees.

A good lawyer can tailor a trust for any particular purpose not in contravention of the beneficiary principle[5] or the perpetuity and accumulation rules[6] or otherwise contrary to public policy or illegal.

What then is a trust? It is impossible to define such a flexible concept. However, four quasi-definitions are now set out to provide a rough and ready introduction to trust law.

**Scott, Trusts, 3rd ed., paras. 2, 3**

"Even if it were possible to frame an exact definition of a legal concept, the definition would not be of great practical value. A definition cannot properly

---

[5] See Chap. 3, section 5, *infra*.
[6] See Chap. 3, section 4, *infra*.

be used as though it were a major premise so that rules governing conduct can be deduced from it. Our law, at least, has not grown in that way. When the rules have been arrived at from other sources, it may be possible to attempt to frame a definition. But the definition results from the rules, and not the rules from the definition.

All that one can properly attempt to do is to give such a description of a legal concept that others will know in a general way what one is talking about. It is possible to state the principal distinguishing characteristics of the concept so that others will have a general idea of what the writer means. With this in mind, those responsible for the Restatement of Trusts proposed the following definition or description of an express trust. It is 'a fiduciary relationship with respect to property, subjecting the person by whom the title to property is held to equitable duties to deal with the property for the benefit of another person, which arises as a result of a manifestation of an intention to create it.' In this definition or description the following characteristics are to be noticed: (1) a trust is a relationship; (2) it is a relationship of a fiduciary character; (3) it is a relationship with respect to property, not one involving merely personal duties; (4) it involves the existence of equitable duties imposed upon the holder of the title to the property to deal with it for the benefit of another; and (5) it arises as a result of a manifestation of an intention to create the relationship."

**Underhill & Hayton's Law of Trusts, 14th ed., p. 1**

"A trust is an equitable obligation binding a person (who is called a trustee) to deal with property over which he has control (which is called the trust property), for the benefit of persons (who are called beneficiaries or *cestuis que trust*), of whom he may himself be one,[7] and any one of whom may enforce the obligation. Any act or neglect on the part of a trustee which is not authorised or excused by the terms of the trust instrument, or by law, is called a breach of trust."[8]

**Keeton's Law of Trusts, 11th ed., p. 2**

"A trust . . . is the relationship which arises wherever a person called the trustee is compelled in equity to hold property, whether real or personal, and whether by legal or equitable title, for the benefit of some persons (of whom he may be one and who are termed beneficiaries) or for some object permitted by law, in such a way that the real benefit of the property accrues, not to the trustee, but to the beneficiaries or other objects of the trust."

**Hague Convention on the Law Applicable to Trusts and on their Recognition**

ARTICLE 2

"For the purposes of this Convention, the term 'trust' refers to the legal relationships created—*inter vivos* or on death—by a person, the settlor, when

---

[7] Unless he takes as a secret trustee on the face of a will when evidence not complying with the Wills Act 1837 is inadmissible to contradict the apparently exclusive status of trustee on the face of the will: *Re Rees's W.T.* [1950] Ch. 204. The definition is not intended to cover charitable purpose trusts.

[8] Approved by Cohen J. in *Re Marshall's Will Trusts* [1945] Ch. 217, 219 and by Romer L.J. in *Green* v. *Russell* [1959] 2 Q.B. 226, 241.

assets have been placed under the control of a trustee for the benefit of a beneficiary or for a specified purpose.

A trust has the following characteristics—

*a*  the assets constitute a separate fund and are not a part of the trustee's own estate;
*b*  title to the trust assets stands in the name of the trustee or in the name of another person on behalf of the trustee;
*c*  the trustee has the power and the duty, in respect of which he is accountable, to manage, employ or dispose of the assets in accordance with the terms of the trust and the special duties imposed upon him by law.

The reservation by the settlor of certain rights and powers, and the fact that the trustee may himself have rights as a beneficiary, are not necessarily inconsistent with the existence of a trust."

### The trustees' position

It will thus be seen that the trust property is vested in the trustees (or their nominees) to be managed wholly for the benefit of the beneficiaries. Because the opportunities for trustees to take advantage of their position are so great equity has imposed very strict rigorous duties or disabilities upon trustees.[9] Indeed, so onerous have these duties become that properly drawn trust instruments greatly relax the standards that equity would otherwise demand: were it not for such relaxation few individuals or companies would be prepared to act as trustees. It should be noted that as long as illegality or public policy or uncertainty[10] does not intervene then draftsmen of trust instruments have a free hand to vary or negative trust principles, *e.g.* to allow the trustees to delegate to a professional discretionary portfolio manager the management of investments.[11] In so far as the draftsman has not made the consent of someone other than the trustees requisite before certain things are done the trustees have an independent, unfettered discretion in their decisions though, of course, the income and capital managed by the trustees must be held according to the terms of the trust for the relevant beneficiaries.

The interests of the beneficiaries are paramount and the trustees must do their best to hold the balance evenly between those beneficiaries (with life interests) interested in income and those beneficiaries (with absolute interests in remainder) interested in capital.[12] Indeed, the trustees have a paternalistic function of protecting each beneficiary against himself. Even if all the beneficiaries interested in a particular trust are each *sui juris* and wish the trustees to do a certain thing the trustees can refuse if they consider that some of the beneficiaries are

---

[9] See Chap. 9, *infra*.
[10] See Chap. 3, *infra*.
[11] See Chap. 9, section 4, *infra*.
[12] See Chap. 9, *infra*.

not objectively acting in their own best interests[13]: however, if all the beneficiaries are between them absolutely entitled to the trust property and are each *sui juris* then under the *Saunders* v. *Vautier*[14] principle, the beneficiaries can call for the trust property to be vested in them (or their nominees) by the trustees, so terminating the trust.

Since the beneficiaries' interests are paramount the trustees cannot (in the absence of authorisation in the trust instrument) invest trust moneys as they might invest their own: they have to play "safe" and invest in a limited, "safe" portion of the securities market as set out in the Trustee Investments Act 1961.[15] Even if they have a broad express power of investment they cannot speculate because they have to exercise as much care as a prudent man of business would exercise if investing for persons for whom he would be morally obliged personally to support if anything went wrong.[16] On the other hand, whilst trustees when selling their own houses might feel bound to honour the commercial morality code and reject out of hand a higher offer when they had orally agreed, subject to contract, to sell to a purchaser who had just submitted his part of the contract to them, trustees, when selling trust property in such circumstances, must not reject the higher offer without probing it with a view to acceptance.[17] Any authority given by the trust instrument to the trustees is deemed to exclude ordinary trust law as little as possible and will be presumed not to allow the trustees to act in a way detrimental to the beneficiaries.

A trust, unlike a company,[18] has no legal personality: thus, it cannot own property or enter into contracts, sue or be sued. It is the trustees who own the trust property, enter into contracts, sue or are sued. A trustee as such has no distinct legal personality in his representative capacity separate from himself in his personal capacity.[19] Thus, he is personally liable to the extent of his whole personal fortune for debts contracted in managing the trust fund,[20] whether contracting in his own name or as trustee,[21] unless he makes it clear that he is to be liable only to the extent that the trust fund is available to him to satisfy the liability.[22] To discharge liabilities properly incurred by him as trustee he has a right of indemnity against the trust fund[23] (subject to any countervailing equities of the beneficiaries for breach of trust[24]) and

---

13 *Re Brockbank* [1949] Ch. 206.
14 *Saunders* v. *Vautier* (1841) 4 Beav. 115, *infra*, p. 651; *Re Smith* [1928] Ch. 915, *infra*, p. 261.
15 See Chap. 9, *infra*.
16 See pp. 611 *infra*.
17 *Buttle* v. *Saunders* [1950] W.N. 255.
18 A company needs to be created formally and registered under the Companies Act 1985. A trust can be created informally: see Chap. 2.
19 However, for some taxation purposes trustees are considered a single continuing body of persons distinct from the actual individuals who are from time to time trustees: Capital Gains Tax Act 1979, s.52(1), *Bond* v. *Pickford* [1983] S.T.C. 517.
20 *Fraser* v. *Murdoch* (1881) 6 App.Cas. 855, 874; *Staniar* v. *Evans* (1886) 34 Ch.D. 470, 477.
21 *Watling* v. *Lewis* [1911] 1 Ch. 414, 423–424; *Burt, Boulton & Hayward* v. *Bull* [1895] 1 Q.B. 276, 285.
22 *Lumsden* v. *Buchanan* (1865) 4 Macq. 950, 955; 13 L.T. 174; *Muir* v. *City of Glasgow Bank* (1879) 4 App.Cas. 337, 355, 388.
23 *Re Blundell* (1888) 40 Ch.D. 370, 377; *Re Exhall Coal Co. Ltd.* (1886) 35 Beav. 449, 453.
24 *Jacubs* v. *Rylance* (1874) L.R. 17 Eq. 341; *Doering* v. *Doering* (1889) 42 Ch.D. 203.

creditors may be subrogated to this right.[25] Thorny problems arise where it is a worthless company with limited liability that is personally liable as trustee and where the creditors find that the liabilities incurred were not within the trustee's powers or that the trust fund is worthless, either because it has been distributed to (foreign) beneficiaries or because it only consisted of borrowed moneys.[26]

Generally, one can say that the external aspects of a trust are governed by common law rules whilst the internal aspects are governed by rules of equity.[27] Thus, before turning the spotlight from the trustees to the beneficiaries one needs to have an astronaut's-eye view of the development of equity and the trust so that one can then consider the nature of the interest of a beneficiary under a trust.

*The development of equity and the trust*

A trust is the creature of equity and not of the common law so what is "equity?" In this context equity can only be described as the body of rules which evolved from those rules applied and administered by the Court of Chancery before the Judicature Act 1873. Since that Act came into force on November 1, 1875 the rules of equity and the rules of common law have been concurrently applied and administered in all Courts.[28]

The Court of Chancery grew out of the residuum of justice left in the King where his common law courts for some special reason brought about an unjust result, *e.g.* because they provided no remedy or because a party could not obtain the appropriate remedy because of the power or wealth of the other party.[29] An aggrieved person would petition the King who would refer it to his Chancellor as his right-hand man. The Chancellor, who was an ecclesiastic, learned in civil law and canon law, first advised the King and his Council, but towards the end of the fifteenth century began making decrees on his own authority. He was concerned with affording relief in hard cases and acted *in personam* against defendants who were imprisoned for contempt if they did not observe his decrees. At first, equity varied according to the Chancellor's conscience—or the size of the Chancellor's foot as Selden remarked.[30] The work of hearing petitions led to increasing

---

[25] *Re Johnson* (1880) 15 Ch.D. 548; *Re Firth* [1902] 1 Ch. 342; *Re Raybould* [1900] 1 Ch. 199; *Re Suco Gold Pty. Ltd.* (1983) 7 Australian C.L.R. 873.

[26] See pp. 747–749 *infra*. Criminal sanctions exist.

[27] The trustee having legal ownership could enforce his legal rights against third parties in the common law courts. The beneficiary having only equitable rights could enforce these against the trustee in the Court of Chancery. If the trustee wrongfully refused to exercise his legal rights the beneficiary could be authorised to take legal proceedings in the trustee's name as plaintiff. Since 1875 in such a case the beneficiary will be plaintiff and will merely join the trustee as a co-defendant to ensure that all necessary parties will be bound by the decision in the case: *Parker-Tweedale* v. *Dunbar Bank plc* [1990] 2 All E.R. 577, 583.

[28] Supreme Court of Judicature Act 1873, ss.24, 25, now Supreme Court Act 1981, s.49.

[29] For fuller accounts see Holdsworth's *History of English Law*, Vol. 1, pp. 395 *et seq.*; Potter's *Historical Introduction to English Law* (4th ed.), pp. 152 *et seq.*; Milsom's *Historical Foundations of the Common Law* (2nd ed.), pp. 82 *et seq.*; J. H. Baker's *Introduction to English Legal History* (2nd ed.), Chap. 6.

[30] *Table Talk of John Selden* (ed. Pollock, 1927), p. 43.

judicial activity of the Chancellor in what came to be known as the Court of Chancery. Lawyers, instead of ecclesiastics, became Chancellors and began systematically developing a body of rules of equity. The Chancellor, Lord Eldon, observed in 1818,[31] "Nothing would inflict on me greater pain than the recollection that I had done anything to justify the reproach that the equity of this Court varies like the Chancellor's foot." In 1972 Bagnall J. remarked[32] "In the field of equity the length of the Chancellor's foot has been measured or is capable of measurement. This does not mean that equity is past child-bearing; simply that its progeny must be legitimate—by precedent out of principle."

There are three aspects to the relationship between equity and the common law. First, equity recognises and enforces rights and duties known to the common law but then goes further in recognising and enforcing other rights and duties. The classic example is the trust, *e.g.* where property is vested in trustees for A for life, remainder to B absolutely. The common law protects the trustees' title to the property and facilitates their dealing with third parties but if A or B wishes to enforce his rights then it is equity that governs the position. Hence the trustees' rights are legal rights and the beneficiaries' rights are equitable rights.

The trust derives from the mediaeval practice of a "feoffor" conveying a legal estate in land to a "feoffee to uses" to hold it to the use of a "*cestui que use*." This was done to enable a knight to go off to the Crusades, leaving someone to safeguard his land for himself and his family,[33] or to enable some body to benefit as a "*cestui que use*" which could not directly benefit as a feoffee owing to the Mortmain Statutes[34] or vows of poverty.[35] Indeed, "uses" could be exploited as a tax avoidance device to avoid burdensome feudal incidents.[36] Accordingly, the Statute of Uses 1535, "executed" the use so that the legal estate vested automatically in the *cestui que use* and not the feoffee to uses. What happened if a legal estate was purportedly conveyed to A to the use of B to the use of C? At first, B held the legal estate as his own property, the first use being executed and the second use being void as repugnant to the first use. However, by the middle of the seventeenth century the second use came to be enforced and it came to be known as a trust to distinguish it from the first use. The drafting formula became "Unto and to the use of B and his heirs in trust for C and his heirs" and C came to be known as the *cestui que trust*. Over

---

[31] *Gee* v. *Pritchard* (1818) 2 Swans. 402, 414.

[32] *Cowcher* v. *Cowcher* [1972] 1 All E.R. 943, 948.

[33] To protect the land a "real" action to recover the land (the "*rem*") had to be brought by an adult male "seised" of the land by virtue of feoffment with livery of seisin.

[34] The Mortmain Statutes prevented land being conveyed without a royal licence into the "dead hand" of a corporation (not liable to the feudal dues payable on marriage, death or the heir being under age).

[35] *e.g.* the Order of Franciscan Friars.

[36] The number of trustees could be kept up so that there was never a death of a sole surviving trustee to provoke the levy of feudal dues on death of the estate owner.

the years C's equitable interest came to be enforced in the Court of Chancery not just against the trustee or a donee of the legal estate from the trustee but against anyone having the legal estate, other than a bona fide purchaser for value of it without notice ("equity's darling"). Notice comprised actual knowledge and knowledge which a person should have had if he had made reasonable inquiries and inspections ("constructive notice"); such actual or constructive notice of a purchaser's agent would be imputed to the purchaser ("imputed notice").

The second aspect is that common law and equity may provide different remedies but each leave the plaintiff free to enjoy whatever remedy was allowed by the other. Where the common law only allows damages for breach of contract or for nuisance equity may decree specific performance or grant an injunction. A contract relating to land may be void at law for lack of writing required by the Law of Property (Miscellaneous Provisions) Act 1989 but in equity the land may be held on constructive trust for the purchaser to prevent the unconscionable enrichment of the vendor.[37] A voluntary *i.e.* gratuitous covenant under seal enables the covenantee to obtain common law damages for breach thereof[38] but equity will not decree specific performance since "equity will not assist a volunteer *i.e.* a donee."

Thirdly, there are some very rare cases where the rules of equity and of common law actually conflict. In 1616[39] it was held that equity prevailed because the Court of Chancery could effectively issue common injunctions restraining parties successful in common law courts from enforcing their judgments or restraining parties from continuing with a common law action. Now the Supreme Court Act 1981, s.49 (replacing the Judicature Act 1873, s.25(11) and the Judicature Act 1925, s.44) states, "Every Court exercising jurisdiction in England or Wales in any civil cause or matter shall continue to administer law and equity on the basis that, wherever there is any conflict or variance between the rules of equity and the rules of common law with reference to the same matter, the rules of equity shall prevail."

Examples of conflict are cases where in an action on a deed at law it was no defence for a defendant to plead a written variation for value not in a deed but such a defendant could obtain a common injunction in equity.[40] Similarly, if a legal estate owner purportedly granted a lease exceeding three years in writing, instead of by deed, and the document contained a term enabling the landlord to claim a year's rent in advance then at law the landlord (only being entitled to rent in arrear at law) could not sue for such rent or levy distress for such rent, so he could be liable to the tenant for illegal distress. Since equity

---

[37] See *infra*, pp. 52, 507.
[38] *Cannon* v. *Hartley* [1949] Ch. 213, *infra*, p. 236.
[39] *Earl of Oxford's Case* (1615) 1 Rep. Ch. 1.
[40] *Berry* v. *Berry* [1929] 2 K.B. 316.

would be prepared to decree specific performance so as to have a legal lease by deed executed, the landlord could obtain a common injunction in respect of the tenant's action for legal distress.[41] An example of variance arises where a plaintiff seeks contribution from sureties where one of them is insolvent. At law if A, B and C are sureties for £30,000 and A becomes insolvent then B and C are only liable for £10,000 each. In equity B and C are liable for £15,000 each.[42] The plaintiff receives less at law than in equity so no question arose before 1875 of a defendant seeking a common injunction as happened in cases of conflict.

## The fusion fallacy

The Judicature Act 1873 enabled the one Court concurrently to administer the rules of common law and the rules of equity. It did not provide for the fusion of these two systems of principle; it only provided for the fusion of the Courts administering the two systems. As Sir George Jessel M.R. stated in *Salt* v. *Cooper*,[43] having himself as Solicitor General piloted the Act through the Commons, the main object of the Act "has been sometimes inaccurately called 'the fusion of Law and Equity'; but it is not any fusion, or anything of the kind; it was the vesting in one tribunal the administration of Law and Equity in every cause, action or dispute which should come before that tribunal." After all, section 25(11) of the 1873 Act and its statutory replacements assume the continued existence of two separate systems for otherwise there would be no need to provide for the resolution of conflicts between them. In Ashburner's vivid metaphor,[44] "the two streams of jurisdiction though they run in the same channel run side by side and do not mingle their waters."

Surprisingly, Lord Diplock in *obiter dicta* has stated[45]:

"My Lords, by 1977 this metaphor has in my view become both mischievous and deceptive. The innate conservatism of English lawyers may have made them slow to recognise that by the Judicature Act 1873 the two systems of substantive and adjectival law formerly administered by Courts of Law and Courts of Chancery were fused. As at the confluence of the Rhone and Saone, it may be possible for a short distance to discern the

---

41 *Walsh* v. *Lonsdale* (1882) 21 Ch.D. 9.

42 *Lowe & Sons* v. *Dixon & Sons* (1885) 16 Q.B.D. 455.

43 (1880) 16 Ch.D. 544, 549. In an extempore interlocutory judgment (where the right to specific performance was conceded) in *Walsh* v. *Lonsdale* (1882) 21 Ch.D. 9, 14, Jessel M.R. got carried away and erroneously said: "There are not two estates as there were formerly, one estate at common law by reason of the payment of rent from year to year and an estate in equity under the agreement. There is only one court and the equity rules prevail in it." Legal leases and equitable leases co-exist without conflict: Megarry & Wade's *Law of Real Property* (5th ed.), pp. 640–644; Meagher Gummow & Lehane, paras. 235–244.

44 *Principles of Equity* (2nd ed., 1933), p. 18.

45 *United Scientific Holdings Ltd.* v. *Burnley Borough Council* [1978] A.C. 904, 924–925. His common law colleagues all spoke in the same vein. See also Lord Denning in *Nelson* v. *Larholt* [1948] 1 K.B. 339, 343 and *Errington* v. *Errington* [1952] 1 K.B. 290, 298.

source from which each part of the combined stream came, but there comes a point at which this ceases to be possible. If Professor Ashburner's fluvial metaphor is to be retained at all, the waters of the confluent streams of law and equity have surely mingled now."

But how can law and equity be fused? In the law of trusts there is legal and equitable ownership and a beneficiary cannot sue a third party at law for negligently damaging trust property[46]; in property law there are legal and equitable rights with different effects, especially as regards third parties; equitable rights can only be enforced by equitable remedies and not by common law damages[47]; equitable defences like hardship and not affording assistance to volunteers or to those who come without "clean hands" cannot be defences to common law actions, *e.g.* for debt. It is a fallacy[48] to assume that law and equity have been fused into a new body of principles.

## The nature of a beneficiary's interest

There has been much controversy over the nature of a beneficiary's interest under a trust based upon the differences between *in personam* rights against trustees and *in rem* rights against property.[49] However, much depends on the meaning in context of *in personam* and *in rem* and whether one is dealing with a bare trust (A holds on trust for X absolutely) or a fixed trust (A holds on trust for X for life, remainder to Y for life, remainder to Z absolutely) or a discretionary trust (A holds on trust to distribute the income and capital between such of X Y or Z or their spouses and issue as he sees fit).

In all cases X has an equitable chose in action, a right *in personam* against the trustee to compel due administration of the trust: the *situs* of that chose is in the jurisdiction where the trustees reside and administer the trust. As beneficiary under a bare trust he may demand transfer of the legal title from the trustee and so obtain the trust property *in rem* for himself as legal and beneficial owner[50]; he may, instead, assign or declare a sub-trust of his equitable interest in the trust property; he may trace the trust property into the hands of third-party recipients from the trustee unless the third party is a bona fide

---

[46] *Leigh & Sillavan* v. *Aliakmon Shipping* [1986] 2 All E.R. 145, 151; *Parker-Tweedale* v. *Dunbar Bank plc* [1990] 2 All E.R. 577.

[47] Though by Supreme Court Act 1981, s.50 (replacing provisions originally in Chancery Amendment Act 1858) damages may be awarded in lieu of or in addition to specific performance or an injunction, which is how the unexplained award of damages in *Seager* v. *Copydex* (1967) 2 All E.R. 414 is explained by Slade J. in *English* v. *Dedham Vale Properties Ltd.* [1978] 1 All E.R. 382, 399.

[48] As emphasised by Holdsworth (1935) 51 L.Q.R. 142; Lord Evershed (1954) 70 L.Q.R. 326; P. V. Baker (1977) 93 L.Q.R. 529; Meagher Gummow & Lehane, paras. 220–259; Snell, 19; Pettit, 9–10; Hanbury, p. 24.

[49] Hart (1899) 15 L.Q.R. 294; Scott (1917) 17 Col.L.R. 269; Stone (1917) 17 Col.L.R. 467; Hanbury (1929) 45 L.Q.R. 198; Latham (1954) 32 Can.B.R. 520; Waters (1967) 45 Can.B.R. 219; *Baker* v. *Archer-Shee* [1927] A.C. 844.

[50] *Saunders* v. *Vautier* (1841) 4 Beav. 115; *infra*, p. 651.

purchaser of the legal title for value without notice of his equitable interest[51] or a purchaser who complies with the overreaching requirements of the Law of Property Act or the Settled Land Act.[52] Thus he has proprietary *in rem* rights in the relevant assets. However, in this last eventuality if the trustee has dissipated the proceeds of sale then X has lost his equitable proprietary interest and is left merely with his equitable chose in action against the trustee personally, which will be worthless if the trustee is bankrupt or disappears with all his assets. For tax purposes X is properly regarded as *in rem* owner of the relevant assets.

As beneficiary with a limited interest under a fixed trust X has a disposable equitable proprietary interest but he cannot claim the trust capital unless the other beneficiaries, Y and Z, are each *sui juris* and join in demanding it from the trustees so that they can then divide it between themselves as they agree. He has a right to the income produced by the trust assets and is regarded as having part of the equitable ownership of the assets themselves[53] so that if they are situate in New York State he is treated for tax purposes as interested in foreign assets, namely New York assets,[54] it being immaterial that the trustees reside in and administer the trust in England so that his equitable chose in action is English.

As beneficiary under a discretionary trust X cannot compel the trustees to pay him anything and cannot substitute another person for himself as a potential recipient of discretionary sums but he can release his rights[55] and he has *in rem* standing to trace for the benefit of all those interested under the trust.[56] However, it seems that just as personal representatives of an unadministered estate[57] and a company subject to a winding-up order[58] have ownership subject to onerous duties in circumstances where the devisees, legatees or creditors have no equitable proprietary interest but only choses in action, so trustees of a discretionary trust have ownership subject to onerous fiduciary duties in circumstances where the beneficiaries under the discretionary trust only have an equitable chose in action. Indeed, Viscount Radcliffe[59] has rejected the view that "for all purposes and at every moment of time the law requires the separate existence of two different kinds of estate or interest in property, the legal and the equitable. . . . Equity in fact calls into existence and protects equitable

---

[51] *Re Diplock* [1948] Ch. 465.
[52] L.P.A. 1925, s.27; S.L.A. 1925, s.18.
[53] *New Zealand Insurance Co. Ltd.* v. *C.P.D. (Victoria)* [1973] V.R. 659.
[54] *Baker* v. *Archer-Shee* [1927] A.C. 844; *Hamilton-Russell's Executors* v. *I.R.C.* (1943) 25 T.C. 200, 207–208; *I.R.C.* v. *Berrill* [1982] 1 All E.R. 867, 880. Where the trust is not an English trust but a New York trust then, by the New York proper law, a life tenant only has an equitable chose in action and not a proprietary interest in the trust assets: *Archer-Shee* v. *Garland* [1931] A.C. 212.
[55] *Re Gulbenkian's Settlement (No. 2)* [1970] Ch. 408.
[56] After all, a residuary beneficiary under an unadministered estate can assert "the estate's right of property": *Commissioner for Stamp Duties* v. *Livingston* [1965] A.C. 694, 714.
[57] *Commissioner for Stamp Duties* v. *Livingston* [1965] A.C. 694.
[58] *Ayerst* v. *C. & K. Constructions Ltd.* [1976] A.C. 168.
[59] [1965] A.C. 694, 712.

rights and interests in property only where their recognition has been
found to be required in order to give effect to its doctrines."[60]

To conclude, in order to understand the working operation of a trust
it is better to regard the interest of a beneficiary as an *in personam*
right to compel the trustees to perform the trust, *i.e.* as an equitable
chose in action situated where the trustees reside and administer the
trust. However, where things have gone wrong and trust property finds
its way wrongly into the hands of a third party (other than equity's
darling) then it is appropriate to regard the interest of a beneficiary, as
a result of his equitable tracing rights, as an equitable *in rem* right.[61]

Where the state is seeking to recover tax which hinges upon the *situs*
of the taxable asset the better approach (in the absence of express
statutory guidance) it is to say that if X is a bare beneficiary or a life
tenant he should in substance be regarded as having an *in rem* interest
in the trust assets wherever they may be situated. But if X is a
discretionary beneficiary then in substance he should be regarded as
having an *in personam* equitable chose in action[62] situate where the
trustees reside and administer the trust.

From a tax point of view a beneficiary's interest (leaving aside bare
trusts) will be one of two basic types. He will either have a current
fixed entitlement to such net income as remains after a proper exercise
of the trustees' administrative powers (an interest in possession,[63] *e.g.* a
life interest) or he will have no fixed entitlement to anything, merely
hoping that the trustees will from time to time give him some of the
trust income (*i.e.* he will merely be an object of a discretionary trust)[64]
or will not use their dispositive powers to divert to others the income
he would otherwise have received (*e.g.* to A for life subject to the
trustees' power within six months of income arising to pay such income
instead to B or C). Trust instruments thus begin by setting out the
sorts of interests that the beneficiaries are to have and laying down any
contingencies that beneficiaries may have to satisfy; then, they set out
any special powers of the settlor or the trustees to affect the beneficial
interests under the trusts; finally, a host of administrative powers are
conferred upon the trustees in such a way as to relax or abrogate the
rigorous duties and standards that trust law would otherwise impose.

As seeing something for yourself is so much better than any
description there now follows a trust precedent. Read it now, read it
after reading Chapter 3, section 1, and read it at later stages when the
significance of its administrative clauses will be more apparent. The

---

[60] Trustees of a charitable purpose trust would seem to be in a similar position, having ownership
subject to onerous duties enforceable by the Attorney-General: see *Att.-Gen.* v. *Cocke* [1988] Ch.
414.

[61] Unless the *lex situs* governing transfer of the relevant property was a foreign one having no concept
of equitable proprietary right in its code of property principles.

[62] *cf. Sainsbury* v. *I.R.C.* [1970] 1 Ch. 712.

[63] *Pearson* v. *I.R.C.* [1981] A.C. 753, *infra*, p. 35. The distinction between trusts with an interest in
possession and trusts where no such interest exists, is crucial for inheritance tax purposes:
Inheritance Tax Act 1984, ss.49–57, 58–85.

[64] See Chap. 4, section 2.

trust in question where no interest in possession exists usefully reveals the flexibility of a trust and common administrative clauses. It is worthwhile considering how you would explain to a lay person the effect of clauses 3 and 4 and how accountable (or free from accountability) are the trustees. Trust instruments are normally drafted so as drastically to lighten the otherwise onerous duties of trustees.

## TRUST PRECEDENT

THIS SETTLEMENT is made the —— day of —— 19—
BETWEEN —— of —— (hereinafter called "the Settlor") of the one part and —
— of —— and —— of —— (hereinafter called "the Original Trustees")[65] of the other part

WHEREAS:

(A) The Settlor is desirous of making irrevocable provision for the Specified Class as herein defined [and for charity[66]] in manner hereinafter appearing

(B) With the intention of making such provision the Settlor has prior to the execution hereof transferred to the Original Trustees the assets specified in the Second Schedule hereto and is desirous of declaring such trusts thereof as hereinafter appear

(C) The Settlor may hereafter pay or transfer further assets to or into the control of the Trustees hereof to be held by them on the trusts of this Settlement

NOW THIS DEED WITNESSETH as follows:

1. (1) THE perpetuity period applicable to this Settlement under the rule against perpetuities shall be the period of eighty years from the execution of this deed

(2) IN this Settlement and the Schedules hereto the following expressions shall have the following meanings that is to say:

(a) "the Trustees" means the Original Trustees or other the trustees or trustee for the time being of this Settlement and "Trustee" has a corresponding meaning;

(b) subject to any and every exercise of the powers conferred by Clause 5 hereof "the Specified Class" has the meaning attributed to it in the First Schedule hereto;

(c) "the Appointed Day" means the day on which shall expire the period of eighty years less three days from the execution of this Deed;

(d) "The Trust Fund" means and includes:
   (i) the said assets specified in the Second Schedule hereto;
   (ii) all assets paid or transferred to or into the control of and accepted by the Trustees as additions to the Trust Fund; and
   (iii) the assets from time to time representing the said assets specified in the Second Schedule hereto and the said additions to the Trust Fund or any part or parts thereof respectively

(e) "Spouse" means a party to a marriage which is for the time being subsisting and does not include a party to a former marriage which has terminated by death or divorce or otherwise

---

[65] As to the identity of the Trustees see clause 8(a).
[66] Delete reference to charity if settlor does not wish to benefit charity.

[(f)[67] "charity" means any institution whether corporate or not (including a trust) which is established for exclusively charitable purposes and "charities" bears a corresponding meaning]

(g) "the Nominating Beneficiaries" means such of the persons referred to in the First Schedule hereto as are for the time being members of the Specified Class and *sui juris*

2. THE Trustees shall stand possessed of the Trust Fund UPON TRUST at their discretion to retain the same (so far as not consisting of cash) in its existing form of investment or to sell the same or any part or parts thereof and to invest or apply the net proceeds of any sale and any other capital moneys in or upon any kind of investment or for any of the purposes hereinafter authorised with power at any time and from time to time to vary such investments or applications for others of any nature hereby authorised.

3. (1)[68] THE Trustees shall stand possessed of the Trust Fund and the income thereof UPON TRUST for all or such one or more exclusively of the others or other of the members of the Specified Class if more than one in such shares and either absolutely or at such age or time or respective ages or times upon and with such limitations conditions and restrictions and such trusts and powers (including discretionary trusts and powers over income and capital exercisable by any person or persons other than the Settlor or any Spouse of the Settlor whether similar to the discretionary trusts and powers herein contained or otherwise) and with such provisions (including provisions for maintenance and advancement and the accumulation of income for any period or periods authorised by law and provisions for investment and management of any nature whatsoever and provisions for the appointment of separate trustees of any appointed fund) and generally in such manner as the Trustees (being not less than two in number or being a corporate trustee) shall in their absolute discretion from time to time by any deed or deeds revocable or irrevocable appoint PROVIDED THAT:

(i) no such appointment shall invalidate any payment or application of capital or income previously made under the trusts or powers herein elsewhere contained; and

(ii) every appointment shall be made and every interest limited thereunder shall vest in interest (if at all) not later than the Appointed Day and no appointment shall be revoked later than the Appointed Day

[(2)[69] Subject to any appointment previously made by the Trustees under the powers hereinbefore contained the Trustees may in their absolute discretion and without prejudice to the generality of the said powers at any time and from time to time before the Appointed Day:

(a) pay or transfer the whole or any part or parts of the income or capital of the Trust Fund to any charity or charities or apply the same for any exclusively charitable purpose or purposes;

(b) revocably or irrevocably in writing appoint that the whole or any part or share of the income of the Trust Fund or any annual or other periodic sum out of the same income shall during any period or periods ending before the Appointed Day be paid to any charity or charities;

---

67 Delete sub-clause (f) if charities are not intended to benefit.
68 Delete numeral (1) if sub-clause (2) deleted.
69 Delete sub-clause (2) if charities are not intended to benefit.

(c) enter into any covenant or other arrangement with any charity or charities to enable or facilitate the recovery of any tax by such charity or charities in respect of any such payment transfer or appointment (as aforesaid)

PROVIDED ALWAYS that the receipt of the person purporting or appearing to be the treasurer or other proper officer of any charity or (in the case of a charitable trust) of the persons purporting or appearing to be the trustees thereof shall be a good discharge to the Trustees for any capital or income paid or transferred to such charity without the necessity for the Trustees to see further to the application thereof]

4. (1) IN default of and subject to and until any or every exercise of the powers conferred on the Trustees by the preceding clause hereof the Trustees shall until the Appointed Day hold the income of the Trust Fund upon the trusts and with and subject to the powers and provisions following namely:

(a) During the period of twenty-one years from the execution of this Deed the Trustees shall have power to pay or apply the whole or any part or parts of such income as it arises to or for the maintenance and support or otherwise for the benefit of all or such one or more exclusively of the others or other of the persons who shall for the time being be living and members of the Specified Class if more than one in such shares and in such manner as the Trustees shall in their absolute discretion without being liable to account for the exercise of such discretion think fit.

(b) Subject to any and every exercise of the last-mentioned power the Trustees shall during the said period of twenty-one years accumulate the whole or the balance (as the case may be) of the said income by investing the same in any manner hereby authorised and shall hold the accumulations so made as an accretion to the capital of the Trust Fund for all purposes.

(c) After the expiration of the same period of twenty-one years the Trustees shall until the Appointed Day pay or apply the whole of the annual income of the Trust Fund as it arises to or for the maintenance and support or otherwise for the benefit of all or such one or more exclusively of the others or other of the persons who shall for the time being be living and members of the Specified Class if more than one in such shares and in such manner as the Trustees shall in their absolute discretion without being liable to account for the exercise of such discretion think fit

(2) In default of and subject to any or every exercise of the said powers conferred on the Trustees by the preceding clause hereof the Trustees shall stand possessed of the Trust Fund on the Appointed Day UPON TRUST for such persons as shall be then living and members of the Specified Class if more than one in equal shares per capita absolutely

(3) Any income or capital of the Trust Fund which but for this present sub-clause would be undisposed of by this Deed shall be held by the Trustees Upon Trust for [[70] —— and his/her executors administrators and assigns absolutely][71] [—— and —— and their respective executors administrators and assigns in

---

[70] The beneficiaries under this ultimate trust should not be the settlor or his spouse or anyone whom he might marry or detrimental tax consequences follow.

[71] These are alternatives, so delete as appropriate.

equal shares absolutely][72] —— (as a registered charity) absolutely and in the event of the failure of this present trust then for charitable purposes generally][73]

5. THE Trustees (being not less than two in number or being a corporate trustee) may from time to time and at any time before the Appointed Day by any deed or deeds:

(a) declare that any person or class or description of person shall cease to be a member or members of the Specified Class and thereupon such person or class or description of person shall cease to be a member or members of the Specified Class in the same manner as if he she or they had originally been expressly excluded therefrom but without prejudice to any previous payment of capital or income to such person or any member of such class or description of person or application thereof for his her or their benefit PROVIDED that the removal of any such person or class or description of person as aforesaid shall not prejudice modify or affect any appointment of capital or income then already made [AND PROVIDED ALSO[74] that the removal of any such person or class or description of person as aforesaid shall not prejudice modify or affect the trust in favour of [—— and his/her executors administrators and assigns][75] [—— and —— and their executors administrators and assigns][76] contained in sub-clause (3) of the last preceding clause hereof]

(b) declare that any person or persons (not being the Settlor or a Spouse of the Settlor or one of the Trustees) previously nominated in writing in that behalf by any one or more of the Nominating Beneficiaries shall thenceforth be included in the Specified Class and thereupon such person or persons shall become a member or members of the Specified Class for all the purposes hereof PROVIDED that (subject to obtaining any necessary Exchange Control consents) the Trustees shall have an absolute discretion whether or not to make any such declaration in relation to any person or persons nominated as aforesaid and PROVIDED FURTHER that any addition of any such person or persons to the Specified Class shall not prejudice modify or affect any appointment of capital or income then already made

(c) wholly or partially release or restrict all or any of the powers and discretions conferred upon them (including this present power) whether in relation to the whole Trust Fund or any part or parts thereof or the income thereof respectively

6. WHENEVER the Trustees shall determine to apply any income for the benefit of an infant the Trustees may either themselves so apply that income or for that purpose may pay the same to any parent guardian or other person for the time being having the care or custody of such infant (other than the Settlor or any Spouse of the Settlor) without being responsible for seeing to the further application thereof

7. (1) MONEYS to be invested under this Settlement may be invested or otherwise applied on the security of or in the purchase or acquisition of real or

---

[72] *Ibid.*

[73] *Ibid.*

[74] This proviso is not required if the ultimate trust in clause 4(3) is in favour of charity.

[75] Delete as appropriate, for these are alternatives.

[76] *Ibid.*

personal property (including the purchase or acquisition of chattels and the effecting or maintaining of policies of insurance or assurance) rights or interests of whatsoever kind and wheresoever situate including any stocks funds shares securities or other investments of whatsoever nature and wheresoever whether producing income or not and whether involving liability or not or on personal loan with or without interest and with or without security to any person (other than the Settlor or any Spouse of the Settlor) anywhere in the world including loans to any member of the Specified Class and the Trustees may grant indulgence to or release any debtor (other than as aforesaid) with or without consideration and may enter into profit sharing agreements and give and take options with or without consideration and accept substitution of any security for other security or of one debtor for another debtor to the intent that the Trustees (subject as herein provided) shall have the same unrestricted powers of investing and using moneys and transposing investments and altering the user of moneys arising under these presents as if they were absolutely entitled thereto beneficially and section 6(1) of the Trustee Investments Act 1961 shall not apply to these presents

(2) IT IS HEREBY EXPRESSLY DECLARED that without prejudice to the generality of the foregoing sub-clause and without prejudice to any powers conferred by law the Trustees shall (subject to the terms of any appointment made under the powers hereinbefore contained) have the following additional powers exercisable until the Appointed Day namely:

(a) The Trustees may:

(i) at any time or times lay out any part or parts of the Trust Fund in the purchase or acquisition of and paying the expenses of purchasing or acquiring and making improvements in or repairs to or on any land and buildings of freehold leasehold or of any other tenure or interest of whatsoever description situate in any part of the world whether or not in the occupation of or intended for occupation by any member or members of the Specified Class;

(ii) at any time or times lay out any part or parts of the Trust Fund in the purchase of household furniture plate linen china cutlery and articles of household use ornament or equipment or any other chattels whatsoever for the use or enjoyment of any member or members of the Specified Class whether occupying a building purchased as aforesaid or otherwise

(b) (i) any land purchased by the Trustees shall if situate in England or Wales be assured to the Trustees upon trust for sale with power to postpone sale and if situate elsewhere be assured to the Trustees either with or without any trust for sale as the Trustees shall think fit but nevertheless with power to sell the same;

(ii) in relation to any land situate outside England and Wales the powers and indemnities given to the Trustees in relation to land in England by English law shall apply as if expressed in this Deed and the net rents and profits thereof shall be applicable in like manner as if they arose from land in England;

(iii) the Trustees shall stand possessed of any land so purchased and the net proceeds of sale thereof and other capital moneys arising under this Settlement upon the trusts and with and subject to the powers and provisions (including power to purchase land) upon with and subject to which the money laid out in the purchase of such land would have been held if the same had not been so laid out;

(iv) until the sale of any land purchased as aforesaid the Trustees may permit any member or members of the Specified Class to occupy the same upon such terms (if any) as to payment or non-payment of rent rates taxes and other expenses and outgoings and as to repair and decoration and for such period or periods before the Appointed Day as the Trustees may think fit;

(v) the Trustees shall be indemnified out of the Trust Fund against all costs rents covenants obligations and outgoings relating to any land purchased as aforesaid or for which the Trustees may be liable in respect of the said premises or the said purchase

(c) Any household furniture or other chattels purchased by the Trustees as aforesaid may be handed over to any member or members of the Specified Class for his or her or their use or enjoyment for any period before the Appointed Day upon and subject to such terms and conditions (if any) as to maintaining such inventory or inventories (if any) and as to insurance and preservation as the Trustees shall think fit

(d) (i) The Trustees shall be at liberty to borrow money (otherwise than from the Settlor or any Spouse of the Settlor) for any of the purposes of this Settlement (including the provision of money to give effect to any appointment authorised hereunder or for the purpose of effecting or maintaining any policies or purchasing or subscribing for any shares or stocks securities properties options rights or interests or other property of whatsoever description) and they may pledge or mortgage the whole or any part of the Trust Fund or the future income thereof by way of security for any such loan and no lender shall be obliged to inquire as to the purpose for which any loan is required or whether the money borrowed exceeds any such requirement

(ii) The Trustees may pledge or mortgage the whole or any part of the Trust Fund by way of principal collateral or other security or by way of guarantee to secure any bank overdraft or other moneys borrowed by any member or members of the Specified Class *Provided* that neither the Settlor nor any Spouse of the Settlor is the lender or one of the lenders in respect of or has any interest in such overdraft or other moneys and *Provided* further that no person other than a member or members of the Specified Class is liable for the repayment thereof

(e) The Trustees may at any time or times enter into any compromise or arrangement with respect to or may release all or any of their rights as shareholders stockholders or debenture stockholders or creditors of any company and whether in connection with a scheme of reconstruction or amalgamation or otherwise and may accept in or towards satisfaction of all or any of such rights such consideration as they shall in their discretion think fit whether in the form of shares stock debenture stock cash obligations or securities of the same or of any other company or companies or in any other form whatsoever

(f) (i) The Trustees may effect purchase or acquire any policy or policies assuring payment to the Trustees in the event of the death of any person of such sum as the Trustees in their absolute discretion (having regard to any prospective liability for tax that may arise in respect of the Trust Fund or any part thereof on the death of such person) may think fit or any endowment or sinking fund policy or policies of whatsoever nature and may pay any premium or premiums thereon out of income or capital

    (ii) Without prejudice to the last-mentioned powers or to any powers vested in them under the general law the Trustees may from time to time apply any part or parts of the income or capital of the Trust Fund in or towards payment of the premium or premiums on any policy or policies in which any one or more of the members of the Specified Class shall (whether under this Settlement or any other deed or otherwise) have any beneficial interest whether vested or contingent and whether indefeasible or defeasible PROVIDED ALWAYS that no person except one or more of the members of the Specified Class shall have any beneficial interest whatsoever in the said policy or policies and so that (subject to the said proviso) the Trustees shall have power if they think fit to effect any such policy or policies on any life or lives in which any one or more of the members of the Specified Class shall have an insurable interest

    (iii) PROVIDED ALWAYS that no income shall be paid or applied under the foregoing powers after the expiration of twenty-one years from the execution hereof if such payment or application would involve an accumulation of the said income

    (iv) In relation to any policy held by them hereunder the Trustees shall have all the powers of a beneficial owner including (without prejudice to the generality of such powers) power to surrender any such policy or to convert the same into a paid up policy or into any other form of assurance or otherwise or to exercise any option thereunder or to sell mortgage charge or otherwise realise or dispose of the same

(g) The Trustees may exercise all voting rights appertaining to any investments comprised in the Trust Fund in as full free and absolute a manner as if they were absolute owners of such investments and in particular but without prejudice to the generality of the foregoing provisions shall be at liberty to exercise such voting rights either by voting or by abstaining from voting so as to ensure or further the appointment or reappointment of any one or more of their number to be directors secretaries or employees of any company in which any part of the Trust Fund may for the time being be invested or of any subsidiary of any such company and any Trustee receiving from any such company or subsidiary any fees salary bonuses or commissions for services rendered to such company or subsidiary shall be entitled to retain the same for his own benefit and shall not be required to account therefor to any person interested hereunder

(h) The Trustees shall not be bound or required to interfere in the management or conduct of the affairs or business of any company in which the Trust Fund may be invested (whether or not the Trustees have the control of such company) and so long as no Trustee has knowledge of any fraud dishonesty recklessness or negligence on the part of the directors having the management of such company they may leave the same (including the payment or non-payment of dividends) wholly to such directors.

(i) The Trustees shall have the powers of appropriation and other incidental powers conferred on a personal representative by Section 41 of the Administration of Estates Act 1925 but without the necessity of obtaining the consent of any person to the exercise thereof

(j) The Trustees may apportion as they think fit any funds subject to different trusts which may have become blended and (without prejudice to the jurisdiction of the Court) may determine as they shall consider just whether any money is to be considered as capital or income and whether any expense ought to be paid out of capital or income and all other questions and matters of doubt of whatsoever description arising in the execution of the trusts of these presents and none of the Trustees and no person having formerly been one of the Trustees and no estate of any deceased Trustee shall be liable for or for the consequences of any act done or omitted to be done or for any payment made or omitted to be made in pursuance of any such determination notwithstanding that such determination shall subsequently be held to have been wrongly made

(k) The Trustees may in addition and without prejudice to any powers to employ agents or attorneys conferred by law employ and remunerate on such terms and conditions as they shall think fit any Solicitors Brokers or other agents or advisers (being in each case a person firm or corporation other than and excluding the Settlor and any Spouse of the Settlor) for the purpose of transacting all or any business of whatever nature or doing any act or giving any advice requiring to be transacted done or given in relation to the trusts hereof including any business act or advice which a trustee not being in any profession or business could have transacted done or given personally and any such Solicitor Broker or other agent or adviser shall be entitled to retain any such remuneration or his share thereof notwithstanding that he or any partner of his is a trustee or the sole trustee hereof or is a member officer or employee of or is otherwise interested in any body corporate which is a trustee or the sole trustee hereof and notwithstanding that such agent or adviser is a body corporate of which one or more of the trustees is a member officer or employee or in which one or more of the Trustees is otherwise interested. And the Trustees shall not be responsible for the default of any such Solicitor Broker or other agent or adviser or for any loss occasioned by the employment thereof in good faith

(l) The Trustees may employ and remunerate as they see fit an investment manager (who may be one of themselves or any person associated with any of themselves) so as to delegate to him full discretion to manage the Trust Fund or any part thereof within the limits and for the period stipulated by the Trustees providing his investment activities are subject to review by the Trustees no less than every six months and providing he is reasonably believed by the Trustees to be someone qualified and authorised to engage in the business of managing investments for others and the Trustees shall have authority to enter into an agreement with such investment manager on the same terms as a private person can agree for the management of his own funds and the Trustees shall not be liable for any loss resulting from the exercise of the powers herein conferred so long as they act in good faith nor for any profit made by the investment manager if a Trustee or associated with a Trustee so long as management fees and commissions do not exceed those paid by an unassociated client with a portfolio of investments of similar value to that of the Trust Fund

(m) The Trustees may deposit any moneys deed securities or investments (including shares and securities to bearer) held by them as trustees with any banker or any person firm or corporation (other than and excluding the Settlor and any Spouse of the Settlor) whether in the United Kingdom or abroad for safe custody or receipt of dividends and may pay out of the income or capital of such part of the Trust Fund as they shall think proper any sum payable for such deposit and custody

(n) Assets of the Trust may be held in the names of any two or more of the Trustees and the Trustees may vest such assets in a stakeholder or in a nominee or nominees anywhere in the world (other than the Settlor or any Spouse of the Settlor) on behalf of the Trustees and entrust or concur in entrusting the realisation and reinvestment of such assets to such stakeholder nominee or nominees upon such terms as the Trustees may deem reasonable

(o) The Trustees may (at the expense of the Trust Fund) incorporate or register or procure the incorporation or registration of any company (with limited or unlimited liability) in any part of the world for any purpose including the acquisition of the Trust Fund or any part thereof and so that (if thought fit) the consideration on the sale of the Trust Fund to any such company may consist wholly or partly of fully paid shares debentures debenture stock or other securities of the company credited as fully paid which shall be allotted to or otherwise vested in the Trustees and be capital moneys in the Trustees' hands

(p) The Trustees may embark upon or carry on whether alone or in partnership or as a joint venture with any other person or persons (except the Settlor or any Spouse of the Settlor) or corporation or corporations at the expense of the Trust Fund and the income thereof any trade or business whatsoever including (without prejudice to the generality of the foregoing) any forestry timber farming development insurance banking or other agricultural commercial industrial financial or professional trade or business whatsoever and may assist or finance to any extent the commencement or carrying on of any trade or business by any other or others (except as aforesaid)

(q) The powers of the Trustees shall extend to any and every act or omission of the Trustees which is certified by a Chancery barrister of Lincoln's Inn of at least 15 years' standing as necessary or desirable for the due execution of the trusts hereof or the protection and realisation and the due administration of the investments in the Trust Fund and the costs of and incidental to matters covered by this subclause shall be met out of income or capital of the Trust Fund or partly out of each as the Trustees may think fit

8. THE following provisions shall apply to the trusts and trusteeship hereof:

(a) The statutory powers of appointing trustees shall apply hereto and shall be exercisable by [the Settlor][77] during [his/her][78] life PROVIDED that neither the Settlor nor any Spouse of the Settlor shall be appointed a trustee of these presents

---

[77] Amend as appropriate.
[78] *Ibid.*

(b) Any person whether an individual or a body corporate may be appointed as a trustee of this settlement whether or not he or it shall be resident domiciled or incorporated in the United Kingdom and the appointment as sole trustee of a body corporate ranking as a trust corporation under the law governing its incorporation shall validly discharge the trustees from all the trusts of this settlement except those if any relating to English or Welsh land then comprised in this settlement

(c) The Trustees shall have power to carry on the administration of the trusts of this settlement in any part of the world whether inside or outside the United Kingdom and power to that end to appoint and pay agents and investment managers with general discretion as to investment and disinvestment of the whole or a specified part of the trust fund

(d) No Trustee shall be capable of being removed or replaced on the grounds that he has remained out of the United Kingdom for more than 12 months

(e) Subject to subclause (b) hereof the law according to which the trusts powers and provisions of this settlement shall for the time being be governed and administered shall be the law of England and Wales

(f) The Trustees shall have power exercisable at any time or times by deed or deeds executed before the Perpetuity Day in their absolute discretion (but during the lifetime of the Settlor not without his prior consent in writing) to declare that the law governing the validity of this settlement or the law governing the administration of this settlement shall from the date of such deed or from some later date specified therein and subject to any further exercise of this power be the law of some other State specified therein provided that such State has its own internal law of trusts and recognises the effectiveness of the exercise of this power and providing always that this power shall not be exercisable so as to render this settlement revocable or unenforceable in whole or in part or otherwise to affect the beneficial trusts and powers thereof other than the powers incorporated by Trustee Act 1925 sections 31 and 32 and analogous powers in other States and "administration" matters shall include all matters other than those governing the validity of the beneficial interests created or capable of being created under this settlement

(g) Any Trustee engaged in any profession or business shall be entitled to charge and be paid all professional or other charges made by him or his firm for business done by him or his firm in relation to the execution of the trusts hereof whether or not in the ordinary course of his profession or business and whether or not of a nature requiring the employment of a professional or business person

(h) Any corporation appointed to be a trustee hereof shall have the powers rights and benefits as to remuneration or otherwise as at or prior to its appointment may be agreed in writing between such corporation and the person or persons (or corporation or corporations) making such appointment

9. THE following provisions shall apply to the powers and discretions of the Trustees hereunder:

(1) Any Trustee may concur in exercising any such power or discretion notwithstanding that he may have a direct or other personal interest in

the mode or result of exercising the same Provided that at least one of the Trustees has no such direct or other personal interest

(2) The Trustees shall not be concerned to see to the insurance preservation repair or renewal of any freehold leasehold or other property household furniture or other chattels occupied used or enjoyed by any member of the Specified Class and in the professed execution of the trusts and powers hereof no Trustee shall be liable for any loss to the trust premises arising by reason of any improper investment or application of the Trust Fund or any part thereof made in good faith

(3) Every discretion hereby conferred upon the Trustees shall be an absolute and unfettered discretion and the Trustees shall not be required to furnish to any beneficiary hereunder any reason or justification for the manner in which any such discretion may be exercised

(4) No power or discretion hereunder to which the rule against perpetuities applies shall be exercisable after the Appointed Day

10. NOTWITHSTANDING anything hereinbefore or in the schedules hereto contained:

(a) the Trust Fund and the income thereof shall be possessed and enjoyed to the entire exclusion of the Settlor and of any benefit to the Settlor by contract or otherwise;

(b) no part of the Trust Fund or the income thereof shall be paid lent or applied for the benefit of the Settlor or any Spouse of the Settlor nor shall any power or discretion hereunder be exercised so as to confer any benefit on the Settlor or any Spouse of the Settlor in any circumstances whatsoever

11. THIS Settlement and the dispositions hereby made are intended to be and are irrevocable

IN WITNESS whereof the parties hereto have hereunto set their respective hands and seals the day and year first before written

THE FIRST SCHEDULE[79] hereinbefore referred to

The Specified Class consists (subject to any exercise of the powers contained in Clause 5 of the foregoing Deed) of the following persons namely:

[(1) the children and remoter issue of the Settlor whether living at the date hereof or born hereafter;

(2) any person (other than a Trustee) who shall (whether before or after the date hereof) have married any of such children or remoter issue of the Settlor as aforesaid (whether or not such marriage shall for the time being be subsisting);

(3) A.B. (the brother of the Settlor);

(4) the children and remoter issue of the said A.B. whether living at the date hereof or born hereafter;

(5) any person (other than a Trustee) who shall (whether before or after the date hereof) have married any of such children or remoter issue of the said A.B. as aforesaid (whether or not such marriage shall for the time being be subsisting);

---

[79] This schedule has been completed by way of example.

(6) any adopted child of the Settlor or of any of such children or remoter issue of the Settlor as aforesaid and the children and remoter issue of any such adopted child;

(7) any person (other than a Trustee) who shall (whether before or after the date hereof) have married any such adopted child or any child or remoter issue of any such adopted child as aforesaid (whether or not such marriage shall for the time being be subsisting)

Provided that for the purposes of this present definition a person shall be deemed to be the adopted child of another person only if he or she shall be recognised as the adopted child of such other person by the Law of England for the time being in force.]

THE SECOND SCHEDULE hereinbefore referred to

FISCAL CONSIDERATIONS

Just as a swimmer's environment is water so a trust's environment is a fiscal system. Necessarily, space allows of only a superficial treatment here, especially as regards those anti-avoidance provisions designed to prevent the versatile flexibility of the trust from being manipulated to obtain tax advantages. After all, in trust law a settlor may himself be a trustee and a beneficiary, may have power to add or subtract beneficiaries, may have powers of appointing income and capital amongst the beneficiaries or on new trusts, and may have power to revoke his trust, whilst the trustees may have power to accumulate income within the trust and to invest in non-income-producing assets. A trust is like a sponge capable of soaking up liquid funds and retaining them without undue leakage, yet capable of being squeezed lightly or harshly or of being totally squashed so as to yield its contents into the required hands; it can even be split up into smaller pieces having the same qualities as the whole.

*Income tax*

(1) *The settlor's position.* An individual's taxable income is taxed progressively at rates laid down annually in the Finance Act. There is a basic rate (currently 25 per cent.) up to a certain level; thereafter 40 per cent. is payable though previously progressively higher slices of taxable income were taxed at progressively higher rates (up to a top rate as high as 83 per cent.). The progressive nature of the tax is such that, in circumstances not covered by anti-avoidance provisions, a tax saving can be achieved by a wealthy person hiving off some of his income to trustees or an individual or a charity not taxable at the higher rates or at all. He can do this either by covenanting to pay income to them or by transferring the income-producing capital itself. If capital taxes have lower rates than income tax (as was the case until 1988), further tax savings can be achieved by using trustees' powers of accumulation of income to convert income into capital and eventually pass it over to beneficiaries as capital, especially when the maximum rate of tax on accumulated trust income is 35 per cent.[80] Tax-efficient

---

[80] Income and Corporation Taxes Act 1988 (I.C.T.A.), ss.686, 687.

benefits in kind (*e.g.* free loans of cash, chattels, houses) may also be conferred on beneficiaries.

Anti-avoidance provisions, however, reduce the opportunities for settlements to be used to avoid income tax. In considering whether such provisions apply one must ask four questions:

(i) Are the settlor and his spouse entirely excluded from the settled property? Where a settlor may revoke, determine or otherwise diminish the settled property and so take capital or income[81] or is a discretionary beneficiary,[82] then the trust income is treated as wholly his. Where he has an interest in capital or income then the trust income is treated as his to the extent that it is not actually distributed to other beneficiaries.[83] If a settlor receives a capital sum by way of loan from the trust or repayment of his loan to the trust, he is treated as receiving income equal to such sum grossed up at 35 per cent.[84]

(ii) Are the settlor's minor children beneficiaries? If income is actually paid[85] by the trustees to or for the benefit of the settlor's minor unmarried children such income ranks as the settlor's.[86] If income is, instead, accumulated but the settlement is revocable or the income was provided under the settlor's covenant the income ranks as the settlor's.[87] If income of an irrevocable[88] settlement of capital is accumulated, then any capital payment to or for the benefit of the unmarried minor is deemed to be a payment of income, ranking as the settlor's income, to the extent that there is accumulated income available to cover the payment.[89]

(iii) Was a covenanted payment of income (other than to charity) made pursuant to a deed made before March 15, 1988 and received by a Tax Inspector before July 1, 1988?[90] If not then the covenantor is taxed without any deduction for such payment from his taxable income. If so or in the case of a covenanted payment to charity are covenanted payments of income incapable of lasting more than six years (or three years for charitable dispositions)? If yes, the income ranks as the settlor's for tax purposes,[91] so the deed is nullified for tax purposes though enforceable under the general law by the covenantee.

(2) *The trustees' position.* The trustees are liable to basic rate tax under the appropriate income tax schedules on all the income produced by the trust fund. Such income is quite separate from their own personal income. Trust income can have no deduction against it for

---

[81] I.C.T.A., s.672.
[82] I.C.T.A., s.674.
[83] I.C.T.A., s.673.
[84] I.C.T.A., s.677.
[85] This does not cover allocating income on one side for a particular minor when subsequent income produced from such income will only be taxable as the minor's income.
[86] I.C.T.A., s.663, *Harvey* v. *Sivyer* [1986] Ch. 119.
[87] I.C.T.A., s.664(1), (2)(*a*).
[88] I.C.T.A., s.665 defines "irrevocable."
[89] I.C.T.A., s.664(2)(*b*).
[90] I.C.T.A., s.347A.
[91] I.C.T.A., s.660.

personal allowances or for expenses incurred in administering the trust.[92] It cannot be liable to higher rate tax. Much income will be received by the trustees after deduction of tax (*e.g.* dividends, building society or bank deposit interest) but in other cases (*e.g.* profits of carrying on a trade[93]) the trustees will need to pay the basic rate tax.

In an exceptional case where trust income without passing through the hands of a trustee is paid directly to an interest in possession beneficiary who has no liability to income tax because of non-residence or charitable status the trustees will not be assessed to tax.[94]

Where no one such as a life tenant has an interest in possession in the trust entitling him as of right to the income then the trustees have to pay tax at an additional 10 per cent. rate over the basic rate of 25 per cent.[95] This is because in such cases there would otherwise be too much scope for minimising liability to tax by exercising powers of accumulation or by delaying exercising discretionary powers over income until a tax-efficient beneficiary materialised. However, in the case of these accumulation trusts and discretionary trusts the expenses incurred in administering the trust which are properly chargeable to income (under the general law if ignoring express authority in the trust instrument) can be deducted from the income liable to the additional rate charge.[96]

(3) *The beneficiary's position.* A beneficiary who is currently entitled to trust income as it arises (*i.e.* who has an interest in possession like a life tenant) is liable to income tax for the year of assessment in which that income arises, even if none of the income was actually paid to him that year.[97] One should note that the effect of Trustee Act 1925, s.31[98] (which may be excluded by the trust instrument) is to convert a minor's apparent entitlement to income under a trust for him for life into a contingent interest, since it imposes a duty upon the trustees to accumulate income (so far as not needed for his maintenance, education or benefit) until his majority, and if he dies before attaining his majority the accumulated income passes with the capital, to which it has accrued, to the person entitled to capital after his death.[99] The beneficiary will be entitled to the balance after the trustees have paid basic rate tax and their administration expenses. This net sum (*e.g.* £6,000 where gross income of £10,000 has borne £2,500 basic rate tax and £1,500 expenses) is then grossed up by basic rate tax

---

[92] *Aikin* v. *Macdonald's Trustees* (1894) 3 T.C. 306.

[93] Of course, expenses incurred in earning the profits may be deducted and loss relief may be claimed.

[94] *Williams* v. *Singer* [1921] A.C. 65.

[95] F.A. 1973, ss.16, 17; *I.R.C.* v. *Berrill* [1982] 1 W.L.R. 1449. These provisions do not apply if the income is treated as the settlor's under the anti-avoidance provisions above.

[96] I.C.T.A., s.686(2)(*d*); *Carver* v. *Duncan* [1985] A.C. 1082.

[97] *Baker* v. *Archer-Shee* [1927] A.C. 844; *Hamilton-Russell's Executors* v. *I.R.C.* (1943) 25 T.C. 200; [1943] 1 All E.R. 474.

[98] *Infra*, p. 689. One should also note that a person with a contingent right, *e.g.* upon attaining 30 years of age obtains a vested right to income on attaining majority: Trustee Act 1925, s.31(1)(ii), *infra*, p. 690.

[99] *Stanley* v. *I.R.C.* [1944] 1 All E.R. 230.

$$(\pounds6,000 \times \frac{100}{100-25} = \pounds8,000)$$

to find the taxable sum to rank as part of the beneficiary's total taxable income. He is given a tax credit for the difference ($\pounds8,000 - \pounds6,000 = \pounds2,000$) so if his total income is such that he bears basic rate tax only then this credit satisfies his liability.[1] If he is not liable to tax then he can reclaim the amount of the tax credit from the Revenue; if he is liable to higher rate tax then he only has to pay the difference between the amount of such liability and the amount of the tax credit.

A beneficiary not entitled to trust income as it arises (*i.e.* who does not have an interest in possession but depends upon the discretion of the trustees) is charged[2] on what he receives. He will receive the income net of the basic and additional rate tax deducted by the trustees[3]: he obtains a tax credit for this deduction and will be able to reclaim some of this sum if his total income is such that he is assessable at some lower rate than 35 per cent. The imposition of tax at 35 per cent. on the trustees is thus not a worrying factor where the trustees distribute the income to beneficiaries liable to basic rate tax or no tax at all. However, if the income is accumulated it will suffer tax at 35 per cent. except in one case. If trust capital is so applied that it becomes *income* in the beneficiary's hands, then to the extent that the amount of capital distributed is less than the net amount of accumulated income after tax, the beneficiary will be treated as having received such gross amount of income as after deduction of tax at 35 per cent.[4] leaves the amount of the capital distributed and he will be able to claim repayment of tax if liable to tax at a lower rate than 35 per cent.

Once income has been accumulated it loses its character as income and accrues to the capital fund becoming part thereof, so payments of accumulated income will be payments of capital and will normally be receipts of capital in the beneficiary's hands and so not liable to income tax. However, if a beneficiary is given $\pounds x$ p.a. and the trustees have a duty or a power to make up that sum out of capital if trust income is less than $\pounds x$, such "topping up" payments of capital will be taxed as income in the beneficiary's hands.[5] Moreover, regular payments out of capital may be characterised as income receipts of the beneficiary if paid to enable him to keep up his standard of living.[6] However, a

---

[1] Where the trustees deduct their administration expenses the beneficiary is only entitled to gross up his net receipt *after* tax and these expenses, so his grossed-up income will be less than the trustees' gross income: *Macfarlane* v. *I.R.C.*, 1929 S.C. 453; 14 T.C. 532. If the trustees had paid him the gross £10,000 less £2,500 tax then if he were below the tax threshold he would reclaim the £2,500 and then pay the trustees their £1,500 expenses, so leaving him with £8,500 instead of £8,000 where the trustees first paid their expenses before paying him.

[2] Under Sched. D, Case III.

[3] I.C.T.A., ss.686, 687.

[4] I.C.T.A., s.687. This tax will actually have been paid earlier when the income was accumulated.

[5] *Brodies's Will Trustees* v. *I.R.C.* (1933) 17 T.C. 432; *Lindus & Horton* v. *I.R.C.* (1933) 17 T.C. 442.

[6] *Cunard's Trustees* v. *I.R.C.* [1962] 1 All E.R. 159.

disposition of capital in exercise of a power over capital will normally not rank as income in the beneficiary's hands even if used for what might be termed as an income purpose.[7]

Capital payments may involve liabilities to inheritance tax and capital gains tax.

*Inheritance tax*

(1) *The settlor's position.* When a settlor transfers assets to trustees or declares himself trustee of specific assets this amounts to a transfer of value (*i.e.* a disposition diminishing the value of the disposer's estate[8]).

A transfer of value may be chargeable, exempt or potentially exempt,[9] and on death the deceased is treated as making a transfer of value of the whole of his estate immediately before his death.[10] If a donor makes a gift on trusts (or outright) but reserves any benefit[11] then the gifted property is treated as still belonging to him so as to be taxable on his death with the rest of his estate at 40 per cent., *e.g.* if he is one of the beneficiaries of his discretionary trust or a remunerated trustee or, not being a beneficiary, retains the *de facto* use of the gifted property.

Transferring property into a discretionary trust (other than a favoured accumulation and maintenance trust) is a chargeable transfer[12] whilst transferring property into an interest in possession trust or accumulation and maintenance trust is a potentially exempt transfer[13] (so no I.H.T. is payable) ripening into an exempt transfer if the settlor survives for seven years. Inheritance tax ("I.H.T.") is charged at 40 per cent. for death transfers and those within three years of death and half that for lifetime transfers unless the transferor dies within seven years, a sliding scale operating between three and seven years of the transfer.[14] No tax is payable if the transfer falls within the nil rate band, currently £140,000, taking account of the transferor's cumulative total in the seven years immediately preceding the relevant transfer. Thus, everyone who is wealthy enough can give away £140,000 every seven years without any I.H.T. liability.

If the settlor pays the I.H.T. *inter vivos* in respect of his discretionary settlement, so diminishing his estate further, he is treated as having made a transfer of value of such amount as after payment of I.H.T. thereon leaves the value of the settled property, *i.e.* his gift is grossed

---

[7] *Stevenson* v. *Wishart* [1987] 1 W.L.R. 1204.
[8] Inheritance Tax Act 1984 (I.H.T.A.), s.3(1). A transfer will be exempt from being a chargeable transfer if within the exemption for small annual amounts (£3,000), or for normal expenditure out of income or for a transfer between spouses, or gifts in consideration of marriage, or to charities, or to political parties or for certain national purposes: I.H.T.A., ss.18–29.
[9] I.H.T.A., s.3A.
[10] I.H.T.A., s.4.
[11] Finance Act 1986, s.102.
[12] I.H.T.A., s.2.
[13] I.H.T.A., s.3A(2).
[14] I.H.T.A., s.7.

up.[15] This does not happen if the trustees pay the I.H.T. out of the trust fund.[16]

(2) *Interest in possession trusts.* The person beneficially entitled to the interest in possession (*e.g.* a life interest) is deemed to own the whole settled capital so when he disposes of his interest (*e.g.* gives it away or sells it) or his interest comes to an end[17] (other than upon his becoming absolutely entitled to the capital[18]) there is deemed to be a transfer of value equal to that of the whole settled capital. Where he sells his interest the amount of the transfer of value is reduced by the proceeds of sale.[19] His lifetime transfer of value will be potentially exempt but if he dies within seven years or died owning the interest the amount of I.H.T. payable will depend upon his cumulative total in the preceding seven years.[20] It is, however, the trustees who are primarily liable to pay the I.H.T. out of the trust property.[21]

According to an Inland Revenue Press Notice[22]:

"An interest in possession in settled property exists where the person having the interest has the immediate entitlement (subject to any prior claim by the trustees for expenses or other outgoings properly payable out of income) to any income produced by that property as the income arises; but that a discretion or power, in whatever form, which can be exercised after income arises so as to withhold it from that person negatives the existence of an interest in possession. For this purpose a power to accumulate income is regarded as a power to withhold it, unless any accumulations must be held solely for the person having the interest or his personal representatives.

On the other hand the existence of a mere power of revocation or appointment, the exercise of which would determine the interest wholly or in part (but which so long as it remains unexercised, does not affect the beneficiary's immediate entitlement to income) does not in the Board's view prevent the interest from being an interest in possession."

This Notice was needed since the legislation does not define the crucial concept "interest in possession." Since then this approach has been supported by the House of Lords in *Pearson* v. *IRC*,[23] *infra* which 3:2 rejected the traditional Chancery view that the mere existence of a

---

[15] I.H.T.A., ss.3(1), 162(3), 164.
[16] *Ibid.* and s.199(1)(*c*).
[17] I.H.T.A., s.52(1). If the interest terminates on his death then the settled capital is aggregated with his estate: ss.4(1), 49(1).
[18] I.H.T.A., s.53(2) or if the capital reverts to the settlor or passes to the beneficiary's spouse: s.53(3), (4).
[19] I.H.T.A., s.52(2).
[20] I.H.T.A., ss.51(1), 52(2), 7.
[21] I.H.T.A., ss.201(1)(*a*), 212(1). A new beneficiary with an interest in possession may also be liable though he has power to recoup the tax: ss.20(1)(*b*), 212(1), (2).
[22] [1976] B.T.R. 418.
[23] [1981] A.C. 753; [1980] 2 All E.R. 479, developed in *Re Trafford* [1985] Ch. 32.

power to accumulate or otherwise divert *income* from life tenant, L, did not prevent L having an interest in possession, L being entitled to income unless the trustees positively diverted it. Thus, a beneficiary does not have an interest in possession if the trustees have power to divert the income away from him (*e.g.* by accumulating it, so that it accrues to capital to which he has no certainty of succeeding, or by paying it or applying it for the benefit of another beneficiary). A power to terminate the interest in possession (*e.g.* a power to appoint the *capital* to X) does not prevent that interest being an interest in possession so long as the power is not exercised.

There is a distinction between *dispositive* powers, by which income can be diverted away from a beneficiary, and *administrative* powers by which income can also be so diverted. Dispositive powers enabling net income after expenses to be diverted to another beneficiary prevent an interest in possession arising. Administrative powers enabling gross income to be used for payment of expenses and other outgoings properly payable out of income[24] do not prevent an interest in possession arising in the net income. Indeed, Viscount Dilhorne in *Pearson*[25] said *obiter* that a power [perhaps ancillary and not independent] to use income to pay taxes otherwise payable out of capital was an administrative power.[26]

Interests in remainder or reversion after an interest in possession are normally excluded property so that a transfer of them occasions no charge to I.H.T.[27]: after all, the beneficiary with the interest in possession is already treated as owning the whole settled capital.[28]

(3) *Trusts with no interest in possession.* Unless these are privileged trusts (*infra*) they are liable to a periodic charge to I.H.T. every tenth anniversary[29] and it is up to the trustees to pay this out of the trust fund.[30] If during a 10-year period capital ceases to be subject to such trusts (*e.g.* because distributed to a beneficiary or because resettled or subsettled on interest in possession trusts or privileged trusts) there is an exit charge in respect of such capital.[31] Basically, the exit charge represents a proportion of the periodic charge payable on the next 10-year anniversary of the trust and depends on the time elapsed since the last such anniversary. Calculation of the tax actually payable is

---

24 For such expenses see *Carver* v. *Duncan* [1985] A.C. 1082.
25 [1981] A.C. 753, 775; [1980] 2 All E.R. 479, 486, followed in *Miller* v. *I.R.C.* [1987] S.T.C. 108.
26 Powers to allow a beneficiary to have rent-free use of a house or interest-free use of cash raise thorny problems: the Revenue treat the exercise of such powers as creating interests in possession and so occasioning an I.H.T. charge if previously no interest in possession subsisted or if causing the partial termination of an existing interest in possession. While the house remains trust property for the user to have an interest in possession in trust property, loaned cash becomes the property of the borrower absolutely and his debt is the trust property. The trust property is thus transposed from cash into a debt due to the trust and it can hardly be said that the borrower has an interest in possession in that debt that is trust property.
27 I.H.T.A., ss.47, 48. Certain exceptions exist to prevent use of such interests to avoid I.H.T.
28 I.H.T.A., s.49(1).
29 I.H.T.A., ss.61, 64.
30 I.H.T.A., ss.201(1)(*a*), 212.
31 I.H.T.A., s.65.

complex involving a hypothetical transfer of value by a hypothetical transferor with a cumulative total including that of the settlor in the seven years before creating the trust.[32] The rate of I.H.T. is calculated at 30 per cent. of the lifetime rates applicable to the hypothetical transfer,[33] so the maximum rate is 6 per cent. (30 per cent. of 20 per cent.). Thus discretionary trusts can still be useful propositions, especially if they are kept below or near to the £140,000 threshold and are made by settlors with small cumulative totals of chargeable transfers. Additions of property by the original settlor to his trust should be avoided since they will often cause more I.H.T. to be charged (at the next 10-year anniversary) than would be the case if he created a new separate settlement.[34]

If the trustees pay I.H.T. in respect of the exit charge out of property remaining in the discretionary settlement then the chargeable amount has to be grossed up.[35] This does not happen if the recipient of the capital ceasing to be subject to the discretionary trust pays the I.H.T.[36]

(4) *Privileged trusts.* For policy reasons some trusts which would otherwise fall to be taxed as trusts with no interest in possession receive privileged treatment. Accumulation and maintenance trusts for minors are the most significant privileged trusts for private tax planning. Such trusts are privileged so as not to discriminate between gifts to minors or to adults contingent upon attaining 25 years of age (which must take effect behind trusts) and outright gifts to adults of 25 years or more. No periodic or exit charges are payable and no charge arises when a beneficiary becomes entitled to the settled property.[37]

Such privileged treatment is accorded to settled property if[38]:

(1) One or more persons ("beneficiaries") *will*,[39] on or before attaining a specified age not exceeding 25,[40] become beneficially entitled to it or to an interest in possession in it; and

(2) No interest in possession subsists in it, and the income from it is to be accumulated so far as not applied for the maintenance education or benefit of a beneficiary; and

(3) Either (a) all the persons who are or have been beneficiaries are or were either (i) grandchildren of a common grandparent, or

---

[32] I.H.T.A, ss.66, 68, 69. The exit charge rate necessarily has to be calculated as a proportion of the effective rate of the last periodic charge.

[33] I.H.T.A., s.66(1).

[34] I.H.T.A., s.67.

[35] I.H.T.A., s.65(2)(*b*).

[36] I.H.T.A., s.65(2)(*a*).

[37] I.H.T.A., ss.58(1)(*b*), 71(4).

[38] I.H.T.A., s.71(1), (2).

[39] "Will" means "must under the terms of the settlement become entitled" ignoring possibilities of the beneficiary dying, becoming bankrupt, assigning his interest or losing his interest under the Variation of Trusts Act 1958: *Inglewood* v. *I.R.C* [1983] 1 W.L.R. 366.

[40] No age need be specified in the settlement or an age greater than 25 can be specified for entitlement to *capital* so long as Trustee Act 1925, s.31(1)(ii) applies to confer a vested right to *income* on a beneficiary attaining majority.

(ii) children, widows or widowers of such grandchildren who were themselves beneficiaries but died before the time when, had they survived, they would have become entitled as in (1) above, or (b) not more than 25 years have elapsed since the commencement of the settlement or, if it was later, since the time when the conditions in (1) and (2) became satisfied with respect to the property.

There are other privileged trusts which receive special treatment, *e.g.* charitable trusts and protective trusts.[41]

### Capital gains tax

(1) *The settlor's position.* On settling capital assets (other than cash[42] or his principal private residence[43]) *inter vivos* a settlor will be chargeable to C.G.T. on this disposal even if he (or his spouse) is a trustee or sole trustee or life tenant or if the settlement is revocable.[44] The chargeable gain will be the excess of the property's then market value over its March 31, 1982 value or its subsequent original acquisition (or "base") cost to the settlor.[45] However, on a transfer into a discretionary trust (a chargeable I.H.T. transfer taxable only if the nil band is exceeded) the settlor can elect that the gain be held over, the trustees taking the property over at the settlor's original base value.[46] The settlor should not settle assets on which he has made a loss since such loss can only be set off against gains on subsequent disposals to the trustees.[47] The rate of C.G.T. payable by the settlor will be the same as his income tax rate, *i.e.* 25 per cent. or 40 per cent.[48]

(2) *Actual disposals by trustees.* Normal principles apply to calculating the gain or loss on sales of chargeable assets by trustees. However, they are chargeable merely at the 25 per cent. basic rate on their gains but only have an annual exemption of half that of individuals.[49] Losses must be set off against gains of the same year or of future years.[50] Any unrelieved losses when the trust ends and a beneficiary becomes absolutely entitled to the settled property will enure for the benefit of the beneficiary.[51] Incidentally, settled property is trust property other than nominee property where the trustees are bare trustees or nomi-

---

41 I.H.T.A., ss.72–77, 86–89.
42 Capital Gains Taxes Act 1979 (C.G.T.A.), s.19(1)(*b*).
43 C.G.T.A., ss.101–103.
44 C.G.T.A., s.53. No charge to C.G.T. arises where a testator's will creates a trust since his estate is already liable to I.H.T.: the trustees (and then the legatees) take over the value of the property at the testator's death as their base value: C.G.T.A., s.49.
45 C.G.T.A., s.29A. The first £5,500 of gains are exempt and there is an indexation allowance to cope with inflation.
46 C.G.T.A., s.147A.
47 C.G.T.A., s.62(3).
48 Finance Act 1988, s.98.
49 C.G.T.A., Sched. 1, paras. 5, 6. The fraction dwindles to one-tenth if the settlor creates 10 or more settlements.
50 C.G.T.A., s.29(5).
51 C.G.T.A., s.54(2).

nees for a beneficiary (or beneficiaries between them) absolutely entitled to the trust property, subject to the trustees' lien for costs and expenses.[52] Bare trusts are ignored, the acts of the bare trustees being treated as the acts of the beneficiaries.[53]

(3) *Actual disposals of beneficiaries' equitable interests.* To prevent double taxation there is no C.G.T. charge when a beneficiary disposes of his underlying equitable interest in settled property so long as that interest had not at any time been acquired for money or money's worth (other than another interest under the settlement).[54]

(4) *Life interest in possession trusts.* On the death of a life tenant in possession where the settlement continues the trustees are deemed to dispose of and re-acquire the settled property at its then market value, but C.G.T. will not be charged.[55] After all, I.H.T. will be charged on the settled property.[56] Thus the property's base value gets a C.G.T.-free uplift. However, any held-over gain on the creation of the settlement will be chargeable, and payable by the trustees.[57]

If the life interest terminates other than on the life tenant's death but the settlement continues (*e.g.* to A for life or until remarriage, then B for life, then C absolutely and A remarries or releases her interest) there is no charge to C.G.T.[58] The original base value of the property in the trustees' hands remains unaltered.

If the life tenant dies and the settlement ends because a person becomes absolutely entitled to the settled property, the trustees are deemed to dispose of and re-acquire the settled property at its then market value, but C.G.T. will not be charged.[59] After all, I.H.T. will be charged on the property that has now become nominee property.[60] The absolutely entitled beneficiary will take over the property with its base value as at the life tenant's death. However, any held-over gain on the creation of the settlement will be chargeable at the beneficiary's expense.

If the life interest terminates other than on the life tenant's death and the settlement ends because a person becomes absolutely entitled to the settled property, such property is deemed to have been disposed of by the trustees and C.G.T. is chargeable.[61] The position is as set out in the next paragraph, except that no hold-over relief is available

---

52 C.G.T.A., ss.51, 46.
53 C.G.T.A., s.46.
54 C.G.T.A., s.58. If the trust is non-resident there will be a charge: F.A. 1981, s.88.
55 C.G.T.A., s.55.
56 I.H.T.A., ss.4, 49(1).
57 C.G.T.A., ss.56A, 48. Hold-over relief was available for transfers to trustees of interest in possession trusts until March 14, 1989: Finance Act 1989, s.124.
58 The event falls outside the charging provisions, ss.54, 55. However, I.H.T. will be payable: I.H.T.A., ss.51, 52.
59 C.G.T.A., ss.54, 56.
60 I.H.T.A., ss.4, 49(1).
61 C.G.T.A., s.54.

because the disposition will be a potentially exempt transfer for I.H.T. purposes.[62]

(5) *Trusts with no life interest in possession.* When a person becomes absolutely entitled to any settled property as against the trustees, the assets comprised in the part to which he has become entitled are deemed to have been disposed of by the trustees for market value and C.G.T. is chargeable.[63] The rate of C.G.T. where no interest in possession subsists is 35 per cent.[64] If the trustees do not pay the tax within six months then the absolutely entitled person can be assessed.[65] However, an election can be made to hold over the gain and this can extend to any held-over gain on the creation of the settlement.[66]

The charge to C.G.T. arises whether the person becoming absolutely entitled does so in his personal capacity as beneficiary or in a fiduciary capacity as trustee of another trust.[67] If trust assets wholly cease to be subject to the trusts, powers and provisions of one settlement and become subject to the trusts, powers and provisions of another settlement, there is a deemed disposal of the assets even if the trustees of the two settlements happen to be the same persons.[68] The trustees of a settlement are treated as a single continuing body of persons distinct from the actual persons who may from time to time be the trustees[69] (so that a change of trustees occasions no charge to C.G.T. or I.H.T.).

Difficult questions arise where trustees of a settlement containing a power of appointment or of allocation or of appropriation or of advancement exercise such power so that part of the settled property falls to be held by them on trusts other than those to which it was subject immediately beforehand. Does the exercise of the power create a new trust, whose trustees are absolutely entitled against the old trustees, so that there has been a deemed disposal, or does it merely create a sub-trust under the umbrella of the old original trust so that there has been no deemed disposal? If the power is in a wide form authorising an application of the trust fund freed and released from the original trusts of the settlement, so that the original trusts are replaced by other exhaustive trusts, then such an application of the trust fund will be a deemed disposal.[70] If the power is in a narrow form, *e.g.* a special power to appoint the trust fund on trusts for a class of

---

[62] Except where discretionary trustees become absolutely entitled against interest in possession trustees (not a potentially exempt transfer) when hold-over relief will be available: C.G.T.A., s.147A(2).
[63] C.G.T.A., s.54.
[64] Finance Act 1988, s.100.
[65] C.G.T.A., s.52(4).
[66] C.G.T.A., s.147A.
[67] *Hoare Trustees* v. *Gardner* [1979] Ch. 10, 13–14.
[68] *Hart* v. *Briscoe* [1979] Ch. 1, 5; *Bond* v. *Pickford* [1983] S.T.C. 517.
[69] *Roome* v. *Edwards* [1982] A.C. 279 (English trustees liable for gain on non-resident trustee's part of the trust property: see [1981] C.L.J. 240, *Bond* v. *Pickford* (*supra*).
[70] Hold-over relief will be available in respect of business or agricultural assets or if an I.H.T. charge arises because interest in possession trusts are the new trusts.

beneficiaries, their spouses and children (but with no unusual provision allowing the trustees to delegate their duties to other persons or otherwise contemplating the creation of an entirely new trust) then any appointed property will be regarded as a sub-trust within the original trust, even if the sub-trusts are exhaustive, so there will be no deemed disposal.[71]

## Review of taxation of trusts

The Inland Revenue has just produced a Consultative Document on The Income Tax and Capital Gains treatment of UK Resident Trusts because a simpler, more reasoned and principled system of taxation is required.

### PEARSON v. INLAND REVENUE COMMISSIONERS

House of Lords [1981] A.C. 753; [1980] 2 All E.R. 479 (Viscount Dilhorne, Lords Keith and Lane; Lords Salmon and Russell dissenting so that three Law Lords prevailed over six other judges who heard the case)

VISCOUNT DILHORNE: "My Lords, the only question to be decided in this appeal is whether Fiona Pilkington and her two sisters, Serena and Julia, were after they were 21 and before March 27, 1974 entitled to interests in possession in settled property. The trustees say that they were and the Crown says that they were not.

By a settlement made on November 30, 1964 the settlor, Sir Richard Pilkington, transferred to trustees 13,333 ordinary shares of £10 each in Pilkington Brothers Ltd. Clause 2 of the deed established a trust in relation to the capital and income of the trust fund under which the trustees had power to appoint capital and income for the benefit of all or any one or more of the 'discretionary objects' of the trust. 'Discretionary objects' was defined as meaning the principal beneficiaries, their children and remoter issue and the respective wives, husbands, widows and widowers of the principal beneficiaries and their children and remoter issue. The principal beneficiaries were all the children of the settlor. Clause 3 provided, *inter alia*:

> 'In default of and until and subject to any appointment made under the last foregoing clause the Trustees shall hold the capital and income of the Trust Fund upon the following trusts, that is to say: (a) During the Trust Period or the period of Twenty-one years from the execution hereof (whichever shall be the shorter period) the Trustees shall accumulate so much (if any) of the income of the Trust Fund as they shall think fit . . . (b) Subject thereto the Trustees shall hold the capital and income of the Trust Fund UPON TRUST for such of the Principal Beneficiaries as shall attain the age of Twenty one years or marry under that age and if more than one in equal shares absolutely.'

"Clause 14 read as follows:

> 'The Trustees shall in respect of any property subject to the trusts hereof have all the powers of management and exploitation of an absolute beneficial owner. . . . '

---

[71] *Bond* v. *Pickford* (*supra*). Trusts are exhaustive if the beneficial interest is fully disposed of so that there is no need to refer elsewhere to discover what happens after someone dies or fails to obtain a vested interest. See also *Swires* v *Renton* [1991] STI 652.

"Clause 21 was in the following terms:

'The Trustees may at any time or times apply any income of the Trust Fund in or towards the payment or discharge of any duties taxes costs charges fees or other outgoings which but for the provisions of this clause would be payable out of or charged upon the capital of the Trust Fund or any part thereof.'

"Fiona and her sisters had all reached the age of 21 by the end of February 1974. The position then was that, subject to the trustees' power of appointment under clause 2 and their power to accumulate income under clause 3(a) and the possibility of partial defeasance on the birth of further children to the settlor, the trust fund was held in trust for Fiona and her sisters in equal shares.

"By a deed of appointment made on March 20, 1976 the trustees appointed that £16,000 should be held on trust to pay the income thereof to Fiona during her life or during the trust period whichever should be the shorter.

"The Finance Act 1975 introduced the capital transfer tax under which tax is charged 'on the value transferred by a chargeable transfer.' Subject to certain exceptions, a transfer of value is any disposition made by a person as a result of which the value of his estate immediately after the disposition is less than it would be but for the disposition, and a chargeable transfer is any transfer of value made by an individual after March 26, 1974 (see s.20(2) and (4)).

"Schedule 5 to the Act has effect with regard to settled property. This schedule draws a distinction between what may be called fixed interest trusts and discretionary trusts. A person entitled to an interest in possession in settled property is in general treated as if he was beneficially entitled to the property in which his interest subsists. If during his life his interest in possession comes to an end, there is a charge to tax as if he had himself made a transfer of value and the value transferred had been equal to the value of the property in which his interest subsisted (see Sched. 5, para. 4(2)). If he dies and is then entitled to an interest in possession, tax is charged as if immediately before his death he had made a transfer of value equal to the value of his estate (see s.22) of which his interest in possession formed part. On the other hand, if he becomes absolutely entitled to the property in which he had an interest in possession, there is no charge to tax; nor is there if his interest in possession comes to an end but on the same occasion he becomes entitled to another interest in possession in the property (see Sched. 5, para. 4(3)).

"It follows that if Fiona had an interest in possession in the 13,333 shares settled by her father, she would not have become liable to capital transfer tax on the appointment to her of the £16,000. On the other hand, if there was no interest in possession of the settled property when the appointment was made, the position is very different. . . .

"If Fiona became entitled to the £16,000 at a time when no interest in possession subsisted in that, a capital distribution of £16,000 has to be treated as having been made. Further every 10 years from the date of the relevant transfer occurring after April 1, 1980 tax is charged at the rate of 30 per cent. of the rate which would otherwise be chargeable on the value of the property in the settlement in which no interest in possession subsists (see Sched. 5, para. 12).

"The meaning to be given to the words 'interest in possession in settled property' is thus of vital importance in ascertaining liability to capital transfer tax. . . .

"No attempt is made in the Finance Act 1975 to define 'interest in possession' apart from the definition in paragraph 11(10) and the definition for the purpose of applying the schedule to Scotland. What then should be the approach to construing those words in the Act? In my view one should first seek to determine the ordinary and natural meaning of those words and then consider whether there is anything in the context in which they are used to lead to the conclusion that the proper interpretation of them involves a departure from the ordinary and natural meaning.

"In Preston's *Elementary Treatise on Estates* (2nd ed., 1820, p. 89) an estate in possession is stated to be one which gives 'a present right of present enjoyment.' This was contrasted with an estate in remainder which it was said gave 'a right of future enjoyment.' In Fearne's *Contingent Remainders* (10th ed., 1844, Vol. 1, p. 2) it was said that an estate is vested when there is an immediate fixed right of present or future enjoyment, that an estate is vested in possession when there exists a right of present enjoyment, that an estate is vested in interest when there is a present fixed right of future enjoyment and that an estate is contingent when a right of enjoyment is to accrue on an event which is dubious and uncertain.

"In the light of these statements, it appears that in the nineteenth century the words 'an interest in possession' would have been interpreted as ordinarily meaning the possession of a right to the present enjoyment of something. The Crown in its case contends that 'a beneficiary only has an interest in possession if his interest enables him to claim the whole or an ascertainable part of the net income, if any, of the property at the moment at which it is in the hands of the trustees.' The trustees in their case contend that 'the phrase "interest in possession" simply denotes an interest which is not in reversion—a present right of present enjoyment.'

"So the parties agree that for there to be an interest in possession, there must be a present right to the present enjoyment of something, the Crown contending that it must be to the enjoyment of the whole or part of the net income of the settled property. It is not the case, and in argument the trustees did not contend that it was, that if it is established that the interest is not in remainder or reversion or contingent, it must be concluded that it is in possession. In the present case Fox J. held that 'There must be a present right of present enjoyment' [1980] Ch. 1 at 8 [1979] 1 All E.R. 273 at 277; This was endorsed by Buckley and Templeman L.JJ. in the Court of Appeal ([1980] Ch. 1 at 23, [1979] 3 All E.R. 7 at 11).

"We were referred to a considerable number of statutes in which the expression 'interest in possession' is to be found. I did not find them of any assistance in relation to the meaning to be given to that phrase in the Finance Act 1975. It suffices to say that I saw nothing in them to indicate or suggest, and I see nothing in the Act itself, to suggest, that the phrase should be given any other meaning than that of a present right of present enjoyment. In my opinion that is its meaning in the Finance Act 1975.

"The difficulty lies in its application to the facts of the present case. It is said by both parties to be one of fundamental importance. Whether or not that is the case, all we have to decide is whether on reaching 21, Fiona and her sisters acquired interests in possession in settled property. In other words had they then a present right of present enjoyment of anything?

"As to that, there are, it seems to me, two possible conclusions. The first is that, the power of appointment under clause 2 not having been exercised, the three sisters on reaching that age acquired interests in possession defeasible should the trustees decide to exercise their power to accumulate income. They were then entitled absolutely to the capital and income of the trust fund in equal shares subject to the exercise of that power. The second is that they never secured an interest in possession for they never acquired on reaching that age the right to the enjoyment of anything. Their enjoyment of any income from the trust fund depended on the trustees' decision as to the accumulation of income. They would only have a right to any income from the trust fund if the trustees decided it should not be accumulated or if they failed to agree that it should be or if they delayed a decision on this matter for so long that a decision then to accumulate and withhold income from the sisters would have been unreasonable.

"As I read their judgments, the courts below took the first view. Reluctant as I am to differ from judges so experienced in the law relating to trusts, I find myself unable to agree with them. Fox J. held that; [1980] Ch. 1 at 9; [1979] 1 All E.R. 273 at 278):

' . . . the interest of a person who is entitled to the income of property subject only to a power in the trustees to accumulate is in possession . . . it is a present interest, giving a present right to *whatever income is not accumulated*.' (My emphasis.)

"In *Gartside* v. *Inland Revenue Comrs.* [1968] A.C. 553 at 607; [1968] 1 All E.R. 121 at 128; an estate duty case, Lord Reid said:

' "In possession" must mean that your interest enables you to claim now whatever may be the subject of the interest. For instance, if it is the current income from a certain fund your claim may yield nothing if there is no income, but your claim is a valid claim, and if there is any income you are entitled to get it; but a right to require trustees to consider whether they will pay you something does not enable you to claim anything. If the trustees do decide to pay you something, you do not get it by reason of having the right to have your case considered; you get it only because the trustees have decided to give it to you.'

"That case concerned a discretionary trust where payment was made to the beneficiaries at the discretion of the trustees. Here the three sisters' entitlement to income was subject to the trustees' power to accumulate. On reaching 21 they had no valid claim to anything. If there was any income from the settled property, they were not entitled to it. Their right to anything depended on what the trustees did or did not do and the receipt of income by them appears to me to have been just as much at the discretion of the trustees as was the receipt of income by the beneficiaries in the *Gartside* case.

"It was recognised by the trustees that, if clause 3 had created a trust to accumulate subject to which the trust fund was to be held in trust for the three sisters absolutely on their attaining 21, they would not have secured an interest in possession on reaching that age. It makes all the difference, so it was said, that the trustees were not under a duty to accumulate but only had power to do so if they thought fit. I am not able to accept this for in neither case can it in my opinion be said that the sisters on attaining that age secured the right to the present enjoyment of anything.

"Fox J. in the course of his judgment distinguished *Attorney-General* v. *Power* [1906] 2 I.R. 272 and *Gartside* v. *Inland Revenue Comrs.* [1968] A.C. 553; [1968] 1 All E.R. 121 from the present case on the ground that in those cases 'the beneficiaries got nothing unless the trustees decided to give it to them' whereas in the present case the sisters 'were absolutely entitled to income unless the trustees decided to accumulate'; ([1980] Ch. 1 at 14; [1979] 1 All E.R. 273 at 281). I do not think that that is the case. I do not read the trust deed as providing that. Clause 3(a) gives the trustees power to accumulate as they think fit and the sisters' entitlement depends on whether that power is exercised. If it were the case that the deed did so provide, then I would agree that the sisters had a defeasible interest in possession. Such an interest may be terminated by the exercise of a power of revocation or of an overriding power of appointment such as that contained in clause 2 in this case. The existence of such a power does not prevent the holding of an interest in possession prior to the exercise of the power, and, until it is exercised, the holder of the interest has a present right of present enjoyment.

"A distinction has in my opinion to be drawn between the exercise of a power to terminate a present right to present enjoyment and the exercise of a power which prevents a present right of present enjoyment arising. If in this case the power of appointment under clause 2 had been exercised before the sisters became 21, it could not be said that they then got an interest in possession.

"The Crown, while contending that it made no difference in this case that the sisters' entitlement was subject to a power to accumulate as distinct from being subject to a trust to do so, contended that a distinction was to be drawn between what may be called the administrative and the dispositive powers in a trust deed . . . and in my opinion there is a very real distinction. A life tenant has an interest in possession but his interest only extends to the net income of the property, that is to say, after deduction from the gross income or expenses, etc. properly incurred in the management of the trust by the trustees in the exercise of their powers. A dispositive power is a power to dispose of the net income. Sometimes the line between an administrative and a dispositive power may be difficult to draw but that does not mean that there is not a valid distinction. In the present case the Crown contended that the power given by clause 21 to apply income towards the payment of duties, taxes, etc. which but for the provisions of the clause would be payable out of or charged on capital was a dispositive power and that this clause alone would prevent the sisters having an interest in possession on reaching 21. I do not think that this is so. I think this clause falls on the administrative side of the line and merely elucidates the meaning to be given to clause 14. . . .

"In my opinion the words 'interest in possession' in Schedule 5 should be given their ordinary natural meaning which I take to be a present right of present enjoyment and as in my view the sisters on attaining 21 did not obtain that, this appeal should succeed and paras. 1 and 2 of the commissioners' determination should be upheld. . . . "

LORD KEITH: "It is necessary to note a further argument for the trustees that Fiona's interest, subject as it was to the trustees' power of accumulation, did not differ on that account from the interest of an ordinary tenant for life, because that power was similar in principle to the ordinary administrative powers of trustees. Such powers might be exercised so as to absorb all the income received by the trustees in, for example, repairs and maintenance of the settled property, so that there was nothing left for the life tenant to enjoy. I am unable to accept this argument. I consider that a distinction is properly to be drawn between powers directed to the preservation of the trust estate for the benefit of life tenant and remainderman alike, and discretionary powers the exercise of which is intended to have an effect on the actual benefits which the beneficiaries as such became entitled, by virtue of their several interests, to receive. It is not at all appropriate, in my view, to equate a power to execute repairs with a power to distribute income at discretion among a class of beneficiaries, from the point of view of a person who is entitled to receive any income not dealt with under the power. And the considerations applicable in the case of a discretionary power to distribute income apply equally to a discretionary power of accumulation, the exercise of which in effect rolls up income for the benefit of a class of beneficiaries or objects contingently entitled.

"In the present case Fiona certainly did not have an absolute right to any income of the property as it accrued. At that moment her entitlement was qualified by the existence of the trustees' power of accumulation, to the effect that she had no immediate right to anything, but only a right to later payment of such income as the trustees, either by deliberate decision or by inaction for more than a reasonable time, did not cause to be subjected to accumulation. In my opinion a right of that nature is not a present right of present enjoyment. Further, I do not consider it to be a satisfactory state of affairs that the question whether a person has an interest in possession should turn on the distinction between the position that where his interest derives from his being the object of a discretionary power and that where his interest results in a benefit only failing the exercise of such a power. The practical results as regards the person having the interest are unlikely to be materially different in either case, and I can see no good reason why the distinction should lead to a difference of treatment for purposes of capital transfer tax. The distinction between a trust and a power may be of importance for certain other purposes (see, for example, *McPhail* v. *Doulton* [1971] A.C. 424: [1970] 2 All E.R. 228), but none of the considerations leading to that result appear to me to be applicable here. . . .

"My Lords, for the foregoing reasons I have reached the conclusion that prior to the relevant appointment in favour of Fiona, neither she nor her sisters were beneficially entitled to an interest in possession in the settled property. I would accordingly allow the appeal."

LORD RUSSELL OF KILLOWEN (dissenting): "In my opinion the provisions of clause 3 clearly constitute (i) a mere *power* in the trustees to accumulate, and (ii) subject to (*a*) that power (*b*) the clause 3 power of appointment and (*c*) (until the death of the settlor which occurred in December 1976) the possibility of partial defeasance by further children being born to him, an absolute trust as to capital and income and any accumulations for the three daughters in equal shares on attaining the age of 21 years, which as stated all three had attained by the end of February 1974. It will be observed that this is not a case of a gift of income for the benefit of a discretionary class, as was the case in *Gartside* v. *IRC* [1968] A.C. 553; Ignoring, as for present purposes may admittedly be done, factors (*b*) and (*c*), the three daughters were absolutely entitled each to one third of the income of the trust subject only to a power in the trustees to divert all or part by deciding to accumulate (during a period permitted by law) some or all of the income as it accrued. In fact the trustees accumulated all income accruing: on the one hand the appellants' claim would have been exactly the same if none had been accumulated: on the other hand the respondents' case equally is that it makes no difference that all had been accumulated: it was therefore common ground that the answer to the question posed in this appeal in no way depended upon what the trustees did or did not do by way of exercise of their power of accumulation.

"The only other clause in the settlement requiring notice was clause 21.

"The appellants contended that, even without the clause 3 power of accumulation, the clause contained a power in effect to accumulate which, though not in fact operated, had the same result in terms of the liability for capital transfer tax asserted.

"In common with my noble and learned friend Lord Keith of Kinkel I do not find any reliable guidance in this matter from the provisions of the Settled Land Acts, nor from consideration of the estate duty legislation which was superseded by the Finance Act 1975. Neither do I find it a useful exercise to compare anomalies and 'hard cases' asserted to arise on either solution: such are, I fear, only to be expected in the introduction of such a radical and complicated experiment in fiscal novelty. The crucial question, in my opinion, lies in the well known distinction between a trust and a power, a distinction recognised by this House in *Re Baden's Deed Trusts* [1971] A.C. 424 and there only regretted as a distinction which might lead in a given case to invalidity of the disposition. As I have already indicated this is clearly a case of a mere power to accumulate, as distinct from a trust to accumulate unless and to the extent to which the trustees exercised a power to pay allowances to the sisters or any of them. The sisters were able to say that as income accrued on the £16,000 they were then entitled to that income, subject to the possibility that the trustees might *subsequently divert* it from them by a decision to accumulate it. (Indeed but for the clause 2 power of appointment, and the possibility until the death of the settlor in December 1976 of the birth of further children, they were, notwithstanding the power of accumulation, entitled to claim transfer of the £16,000.) Similar considerations apply to the possibility of the exercise of the clause 21 application of the income for a capital purpose. The case is also distinguishable from the case of a discretionary trust of income among a class—as in *Gartside* [1968] A.C. 553; [1968] 1 All E.R. 121.

"These considerations persuade me that at the time of the 1976 appointment it is not correct to say that no interest in possession subsisted in the three sisters in the £16,000.

"My noble and learned friend Lord Keith of Kinkel, in forming the opposite opinion, suggests that otherwise a conclusion follows that the interest goes in and out of possession according as the trustees refrain from accumulating or decide to do so, and to the further conclusion that as the trustees did actually accumulate all the income up to the date of the 1976 appointment, the interest was never in possession. I do not recall that this proposition was advanced for the appellants, who as already indicated agreed (as did the respondents) that the exercise or non-exercise of the powers under clause 3 or clause 21 could make no difference to the outcome. I consider, with respect, that the conclusions stated above do not follow from the view which I have, supporting the courts below, formed. The fact that an interest in possession is liable to defeasance by *subsequent* exercise of the power does not deny it that description when the benefit of it is thus subsequently taken away.

"I would accordingly dismiss the appeal."

### CRUCIAL SIGNIFICANCE OF MATTERS OF CONSTRUCTION

Before a court can apply a legal rule to validate or invalidate a provision in a document or something purportedly done thereunder it is vital to construe the provision to determine exactly what it means in the context of the document as a whole and in the light of such extrinsic evidence as is admissible, *e.g.* allowing the judge to put himself in the testator's armchair.

Every provision requires minute scrutiny to see how many meanings it may have—nothing must be taken for granted. Words like "relatives" or "customers" may seem straightforward enough. But does "relatives of X" mean just those persons who would be his statutory next-of-kin taking under the intestacy rules if X were dead or does it cover the huge number who are descended like X from some common ancestor 500 or a 1,000 years ago?[72] Does "customer of the Y Co.," cover a purchaser who has not ordered any goods from the Y Co. for six months, one year, six years or more?[73] Can "small" have a meaning where a testator leaves his residuary estate on trust for "those who have only received small legacies?"[74]

It is often crucial whether words have any obligatory sense ("must") or merely a permissive sense ("may"), though complex clauses can make the distinction difficult to discern.[75] If a trustee is protected when lending on mortgage if acting upon a report as to the value of property "made by a person whom he reasonably believed to be an able practical surveyor or valuer instructed and employed independently of any owner of the property," must the valuer *in fact* be independently instructed or is the trustee's reasonable belief sufficient?[76] Does "charitable or benevolent" mean that a purpose can be charitable or instead it can be benevolent, so that the trust is void, or can it be treated as meaning that the purpose must be both charitable and benevolent so that the trust is valid?[77] If property is bequeathed to D "on condition she provides a home for her infirm sister, I," does this mean that if D takes the property she will be subject to this condition or can the apparent condition really be treated as only expressing the testator's motive.[78] Indeed, what does the condition mean? Is it certain enough to be enforceable and valid? If there is uncertainty it is likely that this will lead to the clause being treated as expressing motive only.

If a testator leaves his residuary estate "for the Hull Judeans Association in memory of my late wife to be used solely in the work of constructing the new buildings for the Association and/or improvements to the said buildings" can this be construed not as a purpose trust to endow the Association, (and so void) but as an out-and-out gift accruing to the Association's funds, subject to the contractual rights thereto of the Association members under its constitution?[79]

---

[72] *Re Baden's Deed Trusts (No. 2)* [1972] Ch. 607, *infra*, p. 159.
[73] *Sparfax (1965) Ltd.* v. *Dommett, The Times*, July 14, 1972.
[74] *Re Steel* [1978] 2 All E.R. 1026.
[75] See Chap. 3, sections 1 and 3.
[76] Contrast *Re Walker* (1890) 62 L.T. 449, 452 and *Re Somerset* [1894] 1 Ch. 231, 253 with *Re Stuart* [1897] 2 Ch. 583, 592, *Shaw* v. *Cates* [1909] 1 Ch. 389, 403 and *Re Solomon* [1912] 1 Ch. 261, 281. See p. 631, *infra*.
[77] *Chichester Diocesan Fund* v. *Simpson* [1944] A.C. 341, *infra*, p. 000.
[78] *Re Brace* [1954] 1 W.L.R. 955; *cf. Re Frame* [1939] Ch. 700.
[79] *Re Lipinski's W.T.* [1976] Ch. 235, *infra*, p. 208.

From the outset one has to be alert to the possibilities of construction. Judges are only human and once they have seen the merits of a case they may be prepared to construe a document—or even interpret circumstances[80]—in a way that one would not normally construe it—or interpret them—coming "cold" to the situation. Some judges, however, do prefer to adopt a strict approach. The rest of this book contains plenty of examples of both sorts, though the modern judicial trend is to be facilitative and uphold trustlike arrangements so far as possible.

RELEVANT ASPECTS OF THE LAW RELATING TO WILLS AND INTESTACY

In a study of trust law there are many occasions when points relating to wills or intestacies crop up. A general outline knowledge of the laws applicable thereto is thus useful before embarking on a detailed study of trust law.[81]

First, one needs to distinguish the position of personal representatives (P.R.s) winding up a deceased person's estate from the position of trustees holding the trust property. The P.R.s' function is to collect in the deceased's assets, pay off all debts, taxes and expenses and, then, to distribute the assets of those entitled under the will or intestacy. Their duty is owed to the estate as a whole so that they are under no duty to consider the effect of the exercise of their administrative powers so as to keep an even hand between those interested in income and those interested in capital.[82] Until they assent to the assets passing to the legatees or devisees the title to the assets is vested in the P.R.s.[83] The legatees or devisees have no equitable interest in such assets: they merely have a right to compel due administration of the estate though this chose in action (unlike the right of a beneficiary under a discretionary trust) can be assigned or bequeathed.[84] To assist them in their functions P.R.s have a statutory power to appropriate assets to legatees or devisees[85] and if only a sole P.R. has been appointed then, acting as such, he can give a valid receipt for capital moneys arising on a trust for sale of land.[86] P.R.s can only be appointed by will or by the court.[87] Finally, one of two or more P.R.s has full power to deal with the deceased's pure personalty[88] and, in respect of freehold or lease-

---

[80] *Re Vandervell's Trusts (No. 2)* [1974] Ch. 269, *infra*, p. 72.

[81] For further reference see *Theobald on Wills*; Parry & Clark's *Law of Succession*.

[82] *Re Hayes's W.T.* [1971] 1 W.L.R. 758. Trustees have such a duty: see p. 665, *infra*.

[83] "Whatever property come to the executor *virtute officii* comes to him in full ownership without distinction between legal and equitable interests: the whole property is his": *Commissioner for Stamp Duties* v. *Livingston* [1965] A.C. 694, 701. Thus "no legatee, devisee or next of kin has any beneficial interest in the assets being administered"; *Re Hayes's W.T.* [1971] 1 W.L.R. 758, 764. See also *Kavenagh* v. *Best* [1971] N.I. 89, 93–94.

[84] *Re Leigh's W.T.* [1970] Ch. 277; *P. V. Baker* (1970) 86 Q.L.R. 20.

[85] Administration of Estates Act 1925, s.41. Trustees only have such power if expressly conferred upon them.

[86] Law of Property Act 1925, s.27(2). *cf.* Settled Land Act 1925, s.30(3).

[87] Trustees can be appointed under Trustee Act 1925, s.36, *infra*, p. 567..

[88] *Attenborough* v. *Solomon* [1913] A.C. 76 where a P.R., three years after he had become a trustee of the deceased's silver, pledged it and this was invalid since trustees must act jointly.

hold land, can enter into a valid contract of sale (so long as he does not purport to act for the other P.R.s without their knowledge).[89] However, the land cannot be conveyed without the concurrence of the other P.R.s or an order of the court.

When P.R.s have completed administration of the deceased's estate they become trustees of the residuary estate[90] and their conduct will be sufficient to imply an assent of personalty to themselves as trustees.[91] As trustees they can exercise the statutory power that trustees have to appoint new or additional trustees.[92] Such appointment makes the new or additional trustees trustees of the trusts of the residuary estate but it does not obtain the benefit of Trustee Act 1925, s.40 so, to the extent that the residuary estate consists of land, the legal estate therein remains outstanding in the P.R.s until a written assent is executed by them (or their successors in title) in favour of the trustees,[93] no earlier implied assent being possible for legal[94] estates in land.

If a testator leaves his residuary estate on trust for A absolutely or for A for life, remainder to B absolutely, it has already been seen that no trust arises until the P.R.s have completed winding up the estate and ascertained the residue. Before then where the P.R.s dispose of assets other than to legatees C.G.T. will be payable by the P.R.s.[95] However, for I.H.T. purposes a legatee with an interest in possession in a deceased's residuary estate is treated as having such interest from the deceased's death.[96] For income tax purposes sums paid to the legatees to the extent that residuary estate income is available are taxed, but adjustments will be made as necessary when the administration has been completed and the net residue ascertained.[97]

Basically, a will (unless made by a privileged military testator) must be in writing signed at the end by the testator (or by some other person

---

[89] Administration of Estates Act 1925, ss.2(2), 3(1), 54. *Fountain Forestry* v. *Edwards* [1975] Ch. 1 where since the P.R. had purported to contract for himself and the other P.R. (when the other had no knowledge of this and had refused to ratify the contract) there was no contract to be enforced, the first P.R. only being open to an action for breach of warranty of authority.

[90] *Eaton* v. *Daines* [1894] W.N. 32; *Re Ponder* [1921] 2 Ch. 59; *Re Cockburn's W.T.* [1957] 1 Ch. 438.

[91] *Attenborough* v. *Solomon* [1913] A.C. 76; C. Stebbings [1984] Conv. 423.

[92] *Re Cockburn's W.T.* [1957] 1 Ch. 438.

[93] *Re King's W.T.* [1964] Ch. 542, criticised by Professor E. C. Ryder [1976] *Current Legal Problems* 60. The Limitation Act 1980 may remedy defects in title. Take E and F who completely administer T's estate and are to hold the residue (including Blackacre) upon trust for sale for A for life, remainder to B absolutely. Five years later E dies. Then F as surviving trustee purports to appoint G and H additional trustees with himself. Four years later F dies. G and H as trustees then sell and convey Blackacre to P. Later P contracts to sell to Q who objects to P's title. The objection is valid (unless P can prove 12 years' adverse possession). The legal estate is in F's personal representatives and not P since E and F never executed a written assent of Blackacre in favour of themselves in their new capacity as trustees. Thus they could not take advantage of Trustee Act 1925, s.40, *infra*, p. 574.

[94] An implied informal assent is possible for equitable interests if the P.R. is also beneficially entitled: *Re Edwards's W.T.* [1982] Ch. 30.

[95] *Cochrane* v. *I.R.C.* [1974] S.T.C. 335; *Prest* v. *Bettinson* [1980] S.T.C. 607; C.G.T.A., s.49. P.R.s have the annual exemption (£5,500) for the year in which the deceased died and for the next two years of assessment. Where P.R.s' gains do not exceed their losses any surplus losses cannot be passed on to the legatees unlike the position for trustees and beneficiaries under C.G.T.A., s.54(2). Assets received by legatees are taken over at their base value at the deceased's death: C.G.T.A., s.49(4).

[96] C.G.T.A., s.91.

[97] I.C.T.A. 1988, ss.695, 701.

in his presence and by his direction).[98] The testator's signature has to be made or acknowledged by him in the presence of two witnesses both with the testator at the same time. The witnesses must then sign their names in the testator's presence. The document must be intended to take effect only on the testator's death.[99] Thus, if S by deed settles £50,000 upon trust for himself for life and then for R absolutely, the formalities for a will are not applicable since S's settlement takes effect immediately, giving R a present vested interest in remainder and entitling S only to the income from the £50,000 for the rest of his life. If S had made a will bequeathing £50,000 to R absolutely S could use in his lifetime not only the income from the £50,000 but also the whole £50,000: he could also revoke his will and bequeath the £50,000 to X instead. Incidentally, personal property is said to be bequeathed to legatees and real property to be devised to devisees by will.

Gifts by will may fail to take effect by reason *inter alia* of ademption, abatement, lapse, the beneficiary being an attesting witness or the spouse thereof[1] or the beneficiary disclaiming the gift. Ademption occurs if T specifically leaves some property such as "my Ming dynasty vase" or "my house Blackacre" but no longer has the property when he dies: the legacy or devise is adeemed and the legatee or devisee receives nothing. Abatement is a little less drastic: if T's debts are such that the Ming vase and Blackacre forming part of T's estate at T's death have to be sold but that a surplus remains after using the proceeds to pay off the debts then a rateable proportion will pass to the legatee and devisee. General legacies such as "I bequeath £5,000 to A, £3,000 to B and £1,000 to C" must first abate to their entire extent before resort can be had to specific gifts.[2]

Lapse occurs if a legatee or devisee predeceases the testator unless the legatee or devisee was a child (or other issue) of the testator and left issue alive at the testator's death: in such an exceptional case the gift is effective in favour of the surviving issue *per stirpes*.[3] Where lapse occurs the gift fails and will fall into any residuary gift of the testator (*e.g.* "I leave all the residue of my property not otherwise hereinbefore disposed of to R"). Necessarily, if it is the residuary legatee, R, who has predeceased the testator and occasioned the lapse then the gifted property must be undisposed of and so pass to the next-of-kin under the intestacy rules applicable on the partial intestacy of the testator. Similarly, if a trust in a will fails, the property purportedly subject to the trust will pass under the residuary gift unless the trust was of the residuary property when the property will pass to the next-of-kin under the intestacy rules.

---

[98] Wills Act 1837, s.9, *infra*, p. 88.
[99] *Att.-Gen.* v. *Jones* (1817) 3 Price 368.
[1] Wills Act 1837, s.15 as restricted by Wills Act 1968 for which see, *infra*, p. 99.
[2] The order in which property has to be resorted to to pay debts, etc., is laid down in Part II, 1st Sched. to the Administration of Estates Act 1925.
[3] Wills Act 1837, s.33, as substituted by Administration of Justice Act 1982, s.19. Illegitimate issue count: Family Law Reform Act 1969, s.16. *Per stirpes* means through their stocks of descent so that children of a deceased child take the share their parent would have taken had he survived.

If it is uncertain whether or not a beneficiary predeceased the testator (*e.g.* where they are both killed by a bomb or in a car or plane crash) the younger is presumed to have survived the elder under the *commorientes* rule in section 184 of the Law of Property Act 1925. Exceptionally, where an intestate and his spouse die in circumstances which make it uncertain which survived the other section 184 does not apply: they are each presumed to have predeceased each other[4] for otherwise the elder intestate's property would pass to the younger's estate and thence to the younger's family, so leaving the elder's family out in the cold.

A beneficiary under a will or intestacy may disclaim the gift to him.[5] The gift then falls back into the deceased's estate and passes to whomsoever would have been entitled if the disclaiming beneficiary had predeceased the deceased.[6] Once a beneficiary has accepted the gift he cannot disclaim it[7] but he can assign it on to whomsoever he wants. This will occasion another charge to C.G.T. or I.H.T. unless this occurs within two years of the deceased's death and takes the form of a written instrument varying the will or the intestacy rules and executed by the bountiful beneficiary, who then elects for such variation to take effect as if made by the deceased in his will.[8] Unfortunately, for income tax purposes the variation is not so treated so that the bountiful beneficiary will be treated as a settlor of the benefit conferred by him.[9]

This leaves us with the intestacy rules but first it should be noted that, whilst a testator in his will can appoint "executors" to administer the testator's estate and who will obtain "probate" of the will, where a person dies intestate his closest relatives have to take out "letters of administration" and act as "administrators": the phrase "personal representatives" covers both executors and administrators. A testator's will, if professionally drafted, will, after specific gifts, usually give everything to the executors on a trust for sale, and, on an intestacy, statute[10] directs the administrators to hold the intestate's property on a trust for sale.

Where an intestate is survived by a spouse and issue[11] the spouse takes the intestate's personal chattels absolutely and the net sum of

---

4 Administration of Estates Act 1925, s.46(3).
5 *Townson* v. *Tickell* (1819) 3 B. & Ald. 31; *Re Scott* [1975] 1 W.L.R. 1260. A gift of a single whole (*e.g.* residue) must be wholly accepted or wholly disclaimed, partial acceptance amounting to whole acceptance: *Re Joel* [1943] Ch. 311; *Guthrie* v. *Walrond* (1882) 22 Ch.D. 573.
6 *Re Backhouse* [1931] W.N. 168.
7 *Re Hodge* [1940] Ch. 260.
8 I.H.T.A. 1984, s.142, C.G.T.A. 1979, s.49(6).
9 If a variation is made by a beneficiary in favour of his minor unmarried child then the income arising (unless accumulated in a capital settlement) will be assessed as that of the beneficiary: I.C.T.A. 1988, ss.663, 664, *supra*, p. 25.
10 Administration of Estates Act 1925, s.33.
11 "Issue" includes illegitimate issue: Family Law Reform Act 1987, s.1. Indeed, unless s.1 of that Act is excluded any disposition (by will or deed) referring to various relatives (*e.g.* child, nephew) covers both legitimate and illegitimate relatives.

£75,000 free of death duties and costs[12]: the residue is held on "the statutory trusts" for the issue subject to the spouse having a life interest[13] in half the residue. If the intestate is survived by a spouse and one or more of the following, that is to say, a parent, a brother or sister of the whole blood, or issue of such a brother or sister, but leaves no issue, then, the spouse takes the personal chattels absolutely and the net sum of £125,000 free of death duties and costs: half of any residue is held for the surviving spouse absolutely and the other half is held for the surviving parents or parent or, if there is no surviving parent, it is held on "the statutory trusts" for the brothers and sisters of the whole blood. If the intestate leaves a spouse and no issue and no parent or brother or sister of the whole blood and no issue of such brother or sister then the surviving spouse takes everything.

If the intestate leaves issue, but no surviving spouse, everything is held on "the statutory trusts" for the issue. If the intestate leaves no spouse and no issue any surviving parent or parents of the intestate take the assets absolutely. If, in such circumstances, there is no such surviving parent the intestate's relatives are entitled in the following order so that if any member of one class takes a vested interest he excludes all members of subsequent classes:

   (i) the brothers and sisters of the whole blood on "the statutory trusts,"

   (ii) brothers and sisters of the half blood on "the statutory trusts,"

 (iii) grandparents,

 (iv) uncles and aunts of the whole blood on "the statutory trusts,"

  (v) uncles and aunts of the half blood on "the statutory trusts." In default the Crown (or the Duchy of Lancaster or of Cornwall) takes everything as *bona vacantia*.

If property is held on the statutory trusts, *e.g.* for issue, this means that the property is held upon trust equally for all the intestate's children living at his death who have attained or subsequently attain 18 years of age or who marry under that age: if a child predeceased the intestate, but left issue living or conceived at the death of the intestate, then such issue stand in the parent's shoes and take his share if they go on to attain 18 years of age or marry thereunder.[14] Thus, if an intestate widower dies leaving a 40-year-old son (with two daughters of his own) and two grandchildren aged 20 and 15, being the children of a deceased son of the intestate, then the 40-year-old son takes one-half

---

[12] The rules are in A.E.A. 1925, s.46 and the current amount of the statutory legacies in Family Provision (Intestate Succession) Order 1987, S.I. 799. Interest of 6 per cent. is payable on unpaid statutory legacies: S.I. 1983 No. 1374.

[13] The surviving spouse has a right to have the personal representatives purchase or redeem the life interest by paying over its capital value: Administration of Estates Act 1925, s.47A. For calculation see Intestate Succession (Interest and Capitalisation) Order 1977 (No. 1491). She also has a right to compel the personal representatives to appropriate the matrimonial home at a proper valuation towards satisfaction of her interest under the intestacy: Intestates' Estate Act 1952, s.5; *Re Phelps* [1980] Ch. 275.

[14] Administration of Estates Act 1925, s.47(1).

of the intestate's property, and the two grandchildren acquire interests in the other half. The elder grandchild takes one-quarter of the property absolutely whilst the other quarter is held for the younger grandchild contingent upon his attaining 18 or marrying thereunder: if he should die before then his elder brother would then obtain the whole half share that would have passed to his father had he not predeceased the intestate.

Finally, mention may be made of the fact that if a testator's will or the intestacy rules fail to make reasonable financial provision for the testator's or intestate's dependants then an application under the Inheritance (Provision for Family and Dependants) Act 1975 can be made to the court for the court to order reasonable provision to be made. Sections 10 and 11 have special provisions to deal with dispositions within six years of death intended to defeat applications for financial provision and with contracts to leave property by will.

### Classification of trusts

Traditionally trusts have been classified as express, implied, resulting or constructive. Classification is significant in the following respects. No formalities are required for implied, resulting or constructive trusts.[15] A person who is incapable of being an express trustee may become a resulting or constructive trustee.[16] A constructive trust imposed on A, the owner of Blackacre, in favour of B as to a half interest therein may be void against A's trustee in bankruptcy under s.339 of the Insolvency Act 1986 as not being a settlement upon B for valuable consideration.[17] A resulting trust imposed on A, the owner of Blackacre, in favour of B due to B contributing half the purchase moneys will not be void against A's trustees in bankruptcy under s.339.

There is no authoritative classification of trusts but for our purposes the following classification is adopted.

*Express trust*: a trust where the settlor has positively expressed his intention to create a trust of specific property whether using the word "trust" or other informal words expressing the same idea.

*Implied trust*: a resulting or constructive trust.[18]

*Resulting trust*[19]: a *presumed* resulting trust, where A transfers property or causes property to be transferred without intending to dispose of his beneficial interest, so that if he transfers property to B gratuitously, then B is rebuttably presumed to hold such property on trust for A, or if A and B equally put up the purchase price but have Blackacre put into B's name alone, then B will hold on resulting trust for A and B equally; or an *automatic* resulting trust, where A transfers

---

15 L.P.A. 1925, s.53(2), *infra*, p. 50.
16 *Re Vinogradoff* [1935] W.N. 68.
17 *Re Densham* [1975] 3 All E.R. 726, *infra*, p. 430.
18 *Cowcher* v. *Cowcher* [1972] 1 All E.R. 943, 949, though Trustee Act 1925, s.68(17) in speaking of "implied and constructive trusts" means "resulting and constructive trusts."
19 See Chap. 6.

property to B on trusts which, for some reason, leave some or all of the beneficial interest undisposed of so B automatically holds such property on a resulting trust for A to the extent of the undisposed of beneficial interest.[20]

*Constructive trust*[21]: a trust of specific property imposed by equity on proof of special circumstances where equity considers it unconscionable for the owner of specific property to hold it purely for his own benefit. Exceptionally, a person, though not constructive trustee of specific property (so that this exception may more accurately be thought of as constructive *trusteeship*) may, through his knowing involvement with a breach of trust, be treated constructively as if he were a trustee so that he may be made personally liable to account like an express trustee, *i.e.* be personally liable to make good the loss of trust property.[22] Often a constructive trust will be imposed having regard to the express or implied intentions of the parties but sometimes it may be imposed without reference to any such intentions.

It should be noted that in some judgments "constructive trust" is sometimes used to cover automatic resulting trusts which may be said to arise as a matter of construction. "Implied trust" is sometimes used to mean informally expressed express trusts, sometimes to mean resulting trusts, sometimes to mean only presumed resulting trusts,[23] and sometimes to mean presumed resulting trusts and constructive trusts arising out of informally expressed common intentions.[24] This has created problems for parliamentary counsel.[25] Ideally, since the concept of "implied trust" has no useful function it should cease to be used, but the compendious expression "implied resulting or constructive trusts" has its attractions to judges and parliamentary counsel who act on the principle *ex abundante cautela*.

---

[20] *Re Vandervell's Trust* [1974] 1 All E.R. 47, 68–69, *infra*, p. 412. Usually the automatic resulting trust will reflect what A would have intended in such eventuality, except where, for tax reasons, it is clear that the last thing he would want is the beneficial interest which he had intended (albeit ineffectively) to dispose of.

[21] See Chap. 7.

[22] See Chap. 7, section 3.

[23] See, *e.g. Soar* v. *Ashwell* [1893] 2 Q.B. 390; *Cook* v. *Fountain* (1676) 3 Swan. 585; *Re Llanover Estates* [1926] Ch. 626; *Lloyd* v. *Spillit* (1740) Barn. Ch. 384, 388; *Allen* v. *Snyder* [1977] 2 New South Wales L.R. 685.

[24] Sir Christopher Slade, *The Informal Creation of Interests in Land* (The Childe & Co. Oxford Lecture 1984), p. 4.

[25] *e.g.* L.P.A. 1925, s.53(2), Trustee Act 1925, s.68(17).

# Chapter 2

## FORMAL REQUIREMENTS

### Section 1. Inter Vivos Trusts

THE STATUTORY PROVISIONS

*Law of Property Act 1925*

*Section* 52(1): "All conveyances of land or of any interest therein are void for the purpose of conveying or creating a legal estate unless made by deed."

*Section* 53(1): "Subject to the provisions hereinafter contained with respect to the creation of interests in land by parol:

(*a*) No interest in land can be created or disposed of except by writing signed by the person creating or conveying the same, or by his agent thereunto lawfully authorised in writing, or by will, or by operation of law;

(*b*) A declaration of trust respecting any land or any interest therein must be manifested and proved by some writing signed by some person who is able to declare such trust or by his will;

(*c*) A disposition of an equitable interest or trust subsisting at the time of the disposition, must be in writing signed by the person disposing of the same, or by his agent thereunto lawfully authorised in writing or by will.

(2) This section does not affect the creation or operation of resulting, implied or constructive trusts."

*Section* 54(1): "All interests in land created by parol and not put in writing and signed by the persons so creating the same, or by their agents thereunto lawfully authorised in writing, have, notwithstanding any consideration having been given for the same, the force and effect of interests at will only.

(2) Nothing in the foregoing provisions . . . shall affect the creation by parol of leases taking effect in possession for a term not exceeding three years at the best rent which can reasonably be obtained without taking a fine."

*Section* 55: "Nothing in the last two foregoing sections shall—

(*a*) Invalidate dispositions by will. . . .

(*d*) Affect the operation of the law relating to part performance."

*Section* 205(1): "In this Act unless the context otherwise requires, the following expressions have the meanings hereby assigned to them— . . .

(ii) 'Conveyance' includes a mortgage, charge, lease, assent, vesting declaration, vesting instrument, disclaimer, release and every other assurance of property or of an interest therein by any instrument, except a will; 'convey' has a corresponding meaning; and 'disposition' includes a conveyance and also a devise, bequest, or an appointment of property contained in a will; and 'dispose of' has a corresponding meaning. . . .

(ix) 'Land' includes land of any tenure, and mines and minerals, whether or not held apart from the surface, buildings or parts of buildings . . . and other corporeal hereditaments; also a manor, an advowson, and a rent and other incorporeal hereditaments, and an easement, right, privilege, or benefit in, over, or derived from land; but not an undivided share in land. . . .

(x) 'Legal estates' mean the estates, interests and charges, in or over land (subsisting or created at law) which are by this Act authorised to subsist or be created as legal estates; 'equitable interests' mean all the other interests and charges in or over land or in the proceeds of sale thereof."

LAW OF PROPERTY (MISCELLANEOUS PROVISIONS) ACT 1989

*Section* **2.**—(1) A contract for the sale or other disposition of an interest in land can only be made in writing and only by incorporating all the terms which the parties have expressly agreed in one document or, where contracts are exchanged, in each.

(2) The terms may be incorporated in a document either by being set out in it or by reference to some other document.

(3) The document incorporating the terms or, where contracts are exchanged, one of the documents incorporating them (but not necessarily the same one) must be signed by or on behalf of each party to the contract.

(4) Where a contract for the sale or other disposition of an interest in land satisfies the conditions of this section by reason only of the rectification of one or more documents in pursuance of an order of a court, the contract shall come into being, or be deemed to have come into being, at such time as may be specified in the order.

(5) This section does not apply in relation to—

(a) a contract to grant such a lease as is mentioned in section 54(2) of the Law of Property Act 1925 (short leases);

(b) a contract made in the course of a public auction; or

(c) a contract regulated under the Financial Services Act 1986;

and nothing in this section affects the creation or operation of resulting, implied or constructive trusts.

(6) In this section—

"disposition" has the same meaning as in the Law of Property Act 1925;

"interest in land" means any estate, interest or charge in or over land or in or over the proceeds of sale of land.

(7) Nothing in this section shall apply in relation to contracts made before this section comes into force.

(8) Section 40 of the Law of Property Act 1925 (which is superseded by this section) shall cease to have effect.

## Contracts to create trusts or dispose of equitable interests

Section 2 of the 1989 Act applies to a contract to create a trust of land or any interest in land and to a contract to dispose of an equitable interest in land, *e.g.* a life interest or a co-owner's equitable interest under a trust for sale of land. Unlike the position under Law of

Property Act 1925 section 40,[1] which it has replaced as from September 27, 1989, the contract is void if all the terms are not in one document signed by both parties or in exchanged documents signed by the exchanger (or on his behalf), though it is possible to incorporate terms set out in another document by referring to that document. Under section 40 the contract had not been required to be created by signed writing, but only to be evidenced by writing signed by or on behalf of the defendant by the time a court action was brought, and the contract was unenforceable by action,[2] but not void, until the requisite signed written evidence materialised or part performance of the contract occurred.

For a plaintiff to rely on the equitable doctrine of part performance to obtain specific performance or damages in lieu (under the equitable jurisdiction originally enshrined in Lord Cairns' Act 1858) he needed to show that he had acted to his detriment in reliance upon the inadequately evidenced contract and that his acts were such as to indicate, on a balance of probabilities, that they had been performed in reliance upon a contract with the defendant concerning land and consistent with the contract alleged.[3] The doctrine of part performance is not available in support of a void obligation but a plaintiff may, instead, rely on the imposition of a constructive trust[4] to prevent a defendant unconscionably relying upon lack of the necessary signed writing. Thus, if a defendant contracted to sell a building plot to the plaintiff for £30,000, so that the plaintiff then spent £200,000 on erecting a house on the plot, the defendant would not be able to take unconscionable advantage of the omission of some minor term from the terms of the written agreement. He would be compelled to hold the plot on constructive trust for the plaintiff, subject to payment of the £30,000 (if not already paid), so that the plaintiff would be entitled to a conveyance of the plot.[5]

A contract to create a trust of pure personalty need satisfy no special formalities as also seems to be the case for a contract to dispose of an equitable interest in pure personalty.[6]

---

[1] "(1) No action may be brought upon any contract for the sale or other disposition of land or any interest in land, unless the agreement upon which such action is brought, or some memorandum or note thereof, is in writing, and signed by the party to be charged or by some other person thereunto by him lawfully authorised.
(2) This section does not affect the law relating to part performance."

[2] A deposit could be forfeited or recovered: *Monnickendam* v. *Leanse* (1923) 39 T.L.R. 445; *Pulbrook* v. *Lawes* (1876) 1 Q.B.D. 284.

[3] *Steadman* v. *Steadman* [1976] A.C. 536 as narrowly interpreted in *Re Gonin* [1979] Ch. 16.

[4] See s.2(5) of the 1989 Act and pp. 59–61 equitable proprietary estoppel interests and Chap. 7, s.5.

[5] If D holds on trust for P who is *sui juris* then P can demand that D transfer the property to P. See *Saunders* v. *Vautier* principle p. 651, *infra*. As a short-cut the court would here direct the defendant to execute a conveyance in the plaintiff's favour: *cf. Pascoe* v. *Turner* [1979] 1 W.L.R. 431 *infra*, p. 79.

[6] See *Chinn* v. *Collins* [1981] A.C. 533, 548 and the discussion of *Oughtred* v. *I.R.C.* [1960] A.C. 206, *infra*, p. 65.

THE CREATION OF TRUSTS AND SECTION 53(1)(*b*)[7]

Transactions within section 53(1)(*b*), unlike those within section 53(1)(*a*) or within section 53(1)(*c*), need only be evidenced at some time by signed writing and do not actually have to be carried out by signed writing if they are to be effective. It would seem that section 53(1)(*a*) needs to be construed as covering the creation of equitable interests in land (*e.g.* restrictive covenants) other than equitable interests under a trust, leaving section 53(1)(*b*) to cover creation of equitable interests in land under a trust.[8] This protects a landowner and his heirs from the perils of oral evidence and enables purchasers to know whether or not to pay the purchase money to at least two trustees.

A settlor may create a trust of Blackacre either by declaring that he himself is henceforth to hold Blackacre on specified trusts or by conveying Blackacre to trustees and declaring specified trusts on which the trustees are to hold Blackacre. In both cases the declaration of the trusts must be in writing specifying the beneficiaries, the trust property and the nature of the trusts.[9] As was the case with Law of Property Act 1925, section 40 the writing may be comprised in linked documents[10] and also the trust is unenforceable, but not void, until the requisite written evidence is present.[11]

The signing must be "by some person who is able to declare such trust," *e.g.* by A where A conveys Blackacre to B and contemporaneously declares signed written trusts for C or by T1 and T2 where they hold property on trust for A for life, remainder to B but with power for the trustees to declare new trusts in favour of C or his issue. It has been assumed that the absence from section 53(1)(*b*), unlike section 53(1)(*a*) or (*c*), of an express reference to an agent precludes the settlor's agent authorised in writing from being "some person who is able to declare" a trust on the settlor's behalf. The signatory should be the person who, at the time of the signature, would seem to be the beneficial owner if the declaration of trust were ignored.[12] Such person will be A where A declares himself trustee of Blackacre for B, and such person will be B if, subsequently, B declares that he holds his equitable interest on trust for C for life, remainder to D.[13] However, if

---

[7] Replacing Statute of Frauds 1677, s.7 with fresh wording: see *Grey* v. *I.R.C.* [1960] A.C. 1.
[8] In view of L.P.A. 1925, s.52(1), s.53(1)(*a*) cannot be restricted to legal interests and so that s.53(1)(*a*) does not make s.53(1)(*b*) otiose para. (*b*) should be construed applying the maxim "*generalia specialibus non derogant.*"
[9] *Smith* v. *Matthews* (1861) 3 De G.F. & J. 139; *Morton* v. *Tewart* (1842) 2 Y. & C.Ch. Case 67.
[10] *Forster* v. *Hale* (1798) 3 Ves. 696.
[11] *Rochefoucauld* v. *Boustead* [1897] 1 Ch. 196, 206; *Gardner* v. *Rowe* (1828) 5 Russ. 258. (A granted a lease to B on oral trusts for C, and after B became bankrupt B executed a deed stating the trusts; *held* valid declaration of trust prior to B's bankruptcy so his creditors had no claim to the lease. Note under the *Rochefoucauld* doctrine, *infra*, p. 56, B was bound from the time he took the lease so if, instead, A orally declared *himself* trustee of land for C and provided written evidence only after his own bankruptcy he would not be bound by the trust until the written evidence, so his creditors would have a claim to the land, assuming C had not earlier acted to his detriment, *e.g.* by building a house on the land, in reliance on A's declaration of trust.)
[12] See T. G. Youdan [1984] C.L.J. 306, 316–320.
[13] *Tierney* v. *Wood* (1854) 19 Beav. 330; *Kronheim* v. *Johnson* (1877) 7 Ch.D. 60.

A conveys Blackacre to B and contemporaneously declares *oral* trusts for C, then subsequent written evidence of the trust signed by B satisfies section 53(1)(b)[14] though it may well be that until B signs such writing A retains the equitable interest[15] which he can dispose of as he wishes (unless C has earlier acted to his detriment, *e.g.* by building on Blackacre).

If A had conveyed land or transferred other property to B to hold to A's order and on some subsequent date told B to hold on trust for C, this would amount to A disposing of his subsisting equitable interest in C's favour: such disposition would be void under section 53(1)(c) unless in writing signed by A or his agent.[16]

Declarations of trust of property other than land or interests in land can be made orally since no special evidential or other requirements exist, but care must be taken where A purports to declare himself trustee of an equitable interest in any property for X absolutely. In substance it seems that the apparent sub-trust is a disposition of A's subsisting equitable interest within section 53(1)(c) because the head trustee, whom X can directly sue, is now holding on trust for X and not for A, who has no active duties to perform and so drops out of the picture.[17]

### DISPOSITIONS OF EQUITABLE INTERESTS AND SECTION 53(1)(c)[17]

In context the meaning of "equitable interest" must comprise interests in land or in personalty and "disposition" must comprise a disposition in writing or otherwise.[18]

The signed writing is essential to the validity of the disposition: failure to satisfy section 53(1)(c) makes the disposition void. Subsequent written evidence will be of no avail unless it can be construed as a "belt and braces" device capable of making a disposition as of its date insofar as necessary if the earlier disposition were void.[19] The signed writing may comprise linked documents.[20] Where the assignee is to hold the assigned equitable interest as trustee the writing need not contain the particulars of the trust which may thus be communicated orally,[21] though if the interest is in land some subsequent written evidence will be necessary to satisfy section 53(1)(b). If no communication of the particulars of the trust is made to the assignee, T, taking as

---

[14] *Gardner* v. *Rowe* (*supra*); *Smith* v. *Matthews* (*supra*); *Mountain* v. *Styak* [1922] N.Z.L.R. 131. If the oral trusts had been for A himself then he would have an equitable interest under a constructive trust which he could then sub-settle: *Tierney* v. *Wood* (*supra*).

[15] See p. 57, *infra*.

[16] *Grey* v. *I.R.C.* [1960] A.C. 1.

[17] See pp. 62–63.

[18] Assumed in *Grey* v. *I.R.C.* (*supra*); *Oughtred* v. *I.R.C.* [1960] A.C. 206, *Vandervell* v. *I.R.C.* [1967] 2 A.C. 291, and treated as well established in *Re Tyler's Fund Trusts* [1967] 3 All E.R. 389, 392. The context must oust L.P.A. 1925, s.205(1)(ii), (x).

[19] See *Grey* v. *I.R.C.* [1958] Ch. 690, 706–707 and B. Green (1984) 47 M.L.R. 385, 391–92.

[20] *Re Danish Bacon Co. Ltd. Staff Pension Fund* [1971] 1 W.L.R. 248.

[21] *Re Tyler's Fund Trusts* [1967] 2 All E.R. 389.

trustee, then the assigned interest will be held on resulting trust for the assignor, A, and any subsequent disposition in favour of B by the assignor will fall within section 53(1)(c). It is vital to appreciate that A's direction to T to hold the property for B, instead of A, amounts to A disposing of his subsisting equitable interest to B within section 53(1)(c): *Grey* v. *I.R.C.*, *infra* pp. 66 *et seq.*

There is no disposition of a subsisting equitable interest when a legal owner with full beneficial ownership makes a declaration of trust. He is not regarded as having two estates one legal and the other equitable: the equitable or beneficial interest is merged or subsumed in the legal estate and will pass automatically when the legal estate is transferred.[22] If he declares a trust this creates a new equitable interest so no evidential or other writing will be necessary except in the case of land within section 53(1)(b). Where trustees hold property on trust for B absolutely and, pursuant to B's direction they transfer the property to X absolutely then B's interest is extinguished and X obtains full legal and beneficial ownership so there is no separate disposition by B of his equitable interest that requires compliance with section 53(1)(c): *Vandervell* v. *I.R.C.*, *infra* pp. 63, 71. If this last example were extended one step further because X had previously agreed to hold the property on trust for Y one might think that this should make no difference. However, in substance B is responsible for disposing of his subsisting equitable interest now in the hands of Y so that section 53(1)(c) should be applicable.[23]

It would seem that there is a disposition where there is a release or a surrender of a subsisting equitable interest[24] but not where there is a disclaimer.[25] Variations of trusts under the Variation of Trusts Act 1958 escape section 53(1)(c) either by implication under the 1958 Act or by virtue of a constructive trust within section 53(2).[26]

## STATUTE MAY NOT BE USED AS AN INSTRUMENT OF FRAUD, CONSTRUCTIVE TRUSTS AND RESULTING TRUSTS

If A transfers land to B or buys land in B's name on an oral understanding with B that B is to hold the land on trust for A then prima facie A cannot prove the express trust owing to section 53(1)(b). Once the land has been vested in B without any signed writing of A evidencing the trust, it will be necessary for signed writing of B to satisfy section 53(1)(b).[27]

---

[22] *Vandervell* v. *I.R.C.* [1967] 2 A.C. 291; *D.K.L.R. Holding Co.* v. *C.S.D.(N.S.W.)* (1982) 40 Austr.L.R. 1; a person cannot hold on trust for himself: *Re Cook* [1948] Ch. 212.

[23] *cf. Grey* v. *I.R.C.* [1960] A.C. 1 where trustees held shares on trust for Mr. Hunter and he told them to hold the shares not (so to speak) in their left hands for him but in their right hands as trustees of existing trusts for his grandchildren: this ranks as a CGT disposal by one trustee to another even if the same individual is concerned: *Hoare Trustees* v. *Gardner* [1978] 1 All E.R. 791.

[24] L.P.A. 1925, s.205(1)(ii), G. Battersby [1979] Conv. 17, 20–21.

[25] *Re Paradise Motor Co. Ltd.* [1968] 1 W.L.R. 1125; disclaimer "operates by way of avoidance and not by way of disposition." See also L.P.A. 1925, s.52(2)(b).

[26] *Re Holt's S.T.* [1969] 1 Ch. 100, *infra*, p. 661.

[27] *Ambrose* v. *Ambrose* (1716) 1 P.Wms. 321; *Smith* v. *Matthews* (1861) 3 De G.F. & J. 139; *Gardner* v. *Rowe* (1828) 5 Russ. 258; *Mountain* v. *Styak* [1922] N.Z.L.R. 131.

It would be monstrous if B could plead the statute (passed to prevent fraud) so as fraudulently to keep the land for himself. Accordingly, A can have his claim to the land recognised on one of three grounds.

He can accept that section 53(1)(*b*) prevents proof of the express trust, but then he can rely on section 53(2) on the basis of either a resulting trust[28] (arising from the gratuitous circumstances) or a constructive trust[29] (imposed upon B because it would be fraudulent and unconscionable for him to keep the land for himself and so unjustly enrich himself).

Alternatively, since there is a valid trust, though unenforceable by virtue of section 53(1)(*b*), A can rely on equity estopping B from raising the issue of unenforceability under section 53(1)(*b*)[30] since otherwise B would be using statute as an instrument of fraud. The court thus enforces the express trust.

As Lindley L.J. stated in *Rochefoucauld* v. *Boustead*[31]:

> "It is a fraud on the part of a person to whom land is conveyed as a trustee and who knows it is so conveyed to deny the trust and to claim the land for himself. Consequently, notwithstanding the statute, it is competent for a person claiming land conveyed to another to prove by parol evidence that it was so conveyed upon trust for the claimant, and that the grantee, knowing the facts, is denying the trust and relying upon the form of conveyance and the statute in order to keep the land himself. . . . The trust which the plaintiff has established is clearly an express trust . . . one which the plaintiff and the defendant intended to create. The case is not one in which an equitable obligation [*i.e.* a constructive trust] arises although there may have been no intention to create a trust."[32]

This equitable principle is not confined to cases in which the conveyance was itself fraudulently obtained. "The fraud which brings the principle into play arises as soon as the absolute character of the conveyance is set up for the purpose of defeating the beneficial interest."[33] So if A sells her two adjoining cottages to B for below market value, B orally agreeing to let her live in one cottage for the rest of her days, B will be compelled to hold that cottage on trust for A for life if he subsequently changes his mind and tries to defeat her interest by relying on section 53(1)(*b*).[34]

---

[28] See p. 428, *infra*; *Hodgson* v. *Marks* [1971] Ch. 892; *Davies* v. *Otty (No. 2)* (1865) 35 Beav. 208; *Haigh* v. *Kaye* (1872) L.R. 7 Ch. 469.

[29] *Scheuerman* v. *Scheuerman* (1916) 28 D.L.R. 223; *Bannister* v. *Bannister* [1948] 2 All E.R. 133; *Binions* v. *Evans* [1972] Ch. 359.

[30] *cf.* the need for a defendant specifically to plead L.P.A. 1925, s.40.

[31] [1897] 1 Ch. 196, 206, 208.

[32] The trust was held to be an express trust for the purpose of the Statute of Limitations and such category was then broad so as to include some persons who would nowadays be classed as constructive trustees: see *Soar* v. *Ashwell* [1893] 2 Q.B. 390, 396–397. For classification of trusts see p. 48, *supra*.

[33] *Bannister* v. *Bannister* [1948] 2 All E.R. 133, 136; *Ungurian* v. *Lesnoff* [1990] Ch. 206.

[34] *Ibid.*

Where A's oral understanding with B is that B will hold the land on trust for C, B clearly cannot keep the land for himself. Can A claim beneficial entitlement if he has repented of his intention to benefit C? After all, he can argue that his failure to satisfy section 53(1)(*b*) means that there is no completely constituted trust for C and equity will not perfect imperfect gifts assuming C can make no special proprietary estoppel claim by virtue of detrimental reliance.[35] Thus B holds the land on resulting trust for A since A has failed effectively to dispose of his beneficial interest,[36] if indeed, he does not hold on constructive trust for A to prevent B's fraudulent conduct from unjustly enriching B.[37] Whilst B would be estopped from pleading section 53(1)(*b*) against A or C, A can argue that nothing should stop A from pleading section 53(1)(*b*) against C. It is true that A intended to make a gift of the beneficial interest to C but A had failed to comply with the requisite formalities, and intended donees cannot complain if the donor's original purported gift was ineffective and the donor then repents of his intentions and so refuses to perfect the gift.[38]

C can invoke the analogous case where X by will devises land to Y on the oral understanding with Y that Y is to hold the land on trust for Z. After all, the wills formalities provisions and section 53 of the Law of Property Act were originally all contained in the Statute of Frauds. It is clear that X's secret trust in favour of Z will be enforced against Y.[39] However, Y is clearly intercepting property definitively intended by X for Z, X dying happy with the secret trust, while A is alive and the last thing he wants is for C to benefit.

C might then emphasise that the oral trust of land is valid, though unenforceable due to section 53(1)(*b*),[40] so that if B wished B could carry out the trust and sign the necessary writing himself.[41] A will reply that B's authority to sign the required writing can be revoked by A's notification to him or by A's death.[42] Once A has so notified B then it would fly in the face of the statute to allow C to adduce oral evidence to establish his interest. Thus, C cannot prove any unjust deprivation to justify the imposition of a constructive trust.

After all, if A had orally declared himself trustee of Blackacre for C, C could adduce no oral evidence to establish the interest (unless taking advantage of detrimental reliance to establish an equitable proprietary claim).[43] It should make no difference that A transferred the land to B and declared oral trusts for C: if it did there would hardly be any scope

---

[35] See pp. 59–61, 225 *infra*.
[36] *Hodgson* v. *Marks* [1971] Ch. 892.
[37] *Bannister* v. *Bannister* (*supra*); *Last* v. *Rosenfeld* [1972] 2 N.S.W.L.R. 923, 937.
[38] See *Re Brooks' S.T.*, p. 232, 247 *infra*.
[39] *Ottaway* v. *Norman* [1972] Ch. 698, *infra*, p. 88.
[40] *Gardner* v. *Rowe* (1828) 5 Russ. 258; *Rochefoucauld* v. *Boustead* [1897] 1 Ch. 196, 206.
[41] *Ambrose* v. *Ambrose* (1716) 1 P.Wms. 321; *Smith* v. *Matthews* (1861) 3 De G.F. & J. 139; *Mountain* v. *Styak* [1922] N.Z.L.R. 131.
[42] *Rudkin* v. *Dolman* (1876) 35 L.T. 791; *Scheurman* v. *Scheurman* (1916) 52 S.C.R. 625, 636.
[43] *Wratten* v. *Hunter* [1978] 2 N.S.W.L.R. 367; *Midland Bank* v. *Dobson* [1986] 1 F.L.R. 171; *Gissing* v. *Gissing* [1971] A.C. 886, 905.

for the application of section 53(1)(*b*) with its cautionary and evidentiary functions.[44]

It may be argued[45] that there should be no difference between (1) A simply conveying Blackacre to B with intent manifested by oral evidence to make an outright gift to B (effective in B's favour) and (2) A conveying Blackacre to B with intent manifested by oral evidence for B to hold on trust for C. However, it does seem that section 53(1)(*b*) deliberately creates a difference in expressly requiring written evidence of trusts of land so that A's claim should prevail over C's claim, but some writers too readily assume the contrary view.

So far, we have been concerned with a gratuitous conveyance by A to B for C. However, if A sells and conveys land to B (so losing all interest therein) on the express understanding that B will hold the land on trust to give effect to an equitable interest of C or to a licence conferred by A on C, then C has enforceable rights against B.[46] B is not allowed to claim that C's rights are unenforceable against him as a purchaser because this would be fraudulent.

### AMBIT AND NATURE OF ROCHEFOUCAULD DOCTRINE

The *Rochefoucauld* doctrine is available not just against the transferee-trustee but to volunteers claiming under him[47] and to purchasers with notice. Indeed, Ungoed-Thomas J. has held[48] that it is available against a bona fide purchaser for value without notice of the trusts affecting his vendor's title, taking the view that such a purchaser is acting fraudulently if he seeks to rely on section 53(1)(*b*) once he discovers the trusts. It is difficult to see why such purchaser is acting fraudulently. Even if the trusts had originally satisfied section 53(1)(*b*) a purchaser without notice would take free from the trusts, so that even if the trusts flouting section 53(1)(*b*) are allowed to be proved under *Rochefoucauld* a purchaser without notice should still take free from the trusts.

The better view is that the trust enforced under the *Rochefoucauld* doctrine is an express trust as stated in that case by Lindley L.J.[49] However, in *Bannister* v. *Bannister* Scott L.J.[50] described the doctrine as "the equitable principle on which a constructive trust is raised against a person who insists on the absolute character of a conveyance to himself for the purpose of defeating a beneficial interest." Subse-

---

[44] J. D. Feltham [1987] Conv. 246.
[45] T. G. Youdan [1988] Conv. 267.
[46] *Ashburn Anstalt* v. *Arnold* [1989] Ch. 1; *Lyus* v. *Prowsa Developments Ltd.* [1982] 1 W.L.R. 1044.
[47] *Lincoln* v. *Wright* (1859) 4 De G. & J. 16; *Re Duke of Marlborough* [1894] 2 Ch. 133.
[48] [1971] Ch. 892, 909; [1970] 3 All E.R. 513, 522.
[49] [1897] 1 Ch. 196, 206, *supra*, p. 56; Pettit p. 82; Underhill p. 93; Snell p. 109; *Bloch* v. *Bloch* (1981) 55 A.L.J.R. 701, 706; *Lyus* v. *Prowsa Developments* [1982] 2 All E.R. 953, 962 though treating it as a constructive trust at p. 961 in applying *Bannister* v. *Bannister* [1948] 2 All E.R. 133. If secret trusts are express trusts (see *infra*, p. 105) then so should *inter vivos* trusts under the *Rochefoucauld* doctrine.
[50] [1948] 2 All E.R. 133, 136. However, the Court is recognising and enforcing a settlor's express trust so why not call a spade a spade?

quent judges[51] have blindly followed this, since it honours section 53(2), rather than embarrassingly disregarding section 53(1)(b), and it makes no difference whether the trusts in the plaintiff's favour are enforced as constructive trusts exempted by section 53(2) or as express trusts within section 53(1)(*b*) but where the defendant is estopped from raising the issue of non-compliance with section 53(1)(*b*). It seems best to regard any constructive trust declared by the court as representing "the remedy by which the plaintiff seeks to vindicate an express trust founded upon a common intention which the defendant later repudiates."[52]

As a final point on the equitable doctrine it is important to realise that where certain interests are required to be registered or protected under the Land Charges Act 1972[53] or the Land Registration Act 1925[54] or the Companies Act 1985[55] on pain of a purchaser taking free from such interests, it is not fraud for the purchaser merely to take advantage of his strict statutory rights by relying on the absence of the registration or protection stipulated for in the statute. It is fraud, however, if he positively misleads the interest owner.

EQUITABLE PROPRIETARY ESTOPPEL (BY ACQUIESCENCE OR ENCOURAGEMENT)

If O encourages or acquiesces in X acting to his detriment in the belief that O's property is X's property or that O has given or will give X the property or an interest therein, then, to prevent unconscionable behaviour, equity will estop O from asserting his full legal and beneficial ownership and from claiming that non-compliance with statutory requirements bars X's claim. Such estoppel gives rise to an equity in X's favour which may entitle him to an injunction against O[56] or an equitable lien[57] on O's property for X's expenditure[58] or for the value of X's improvements,[59] or to a decree perfecting O's imperfect gift and ordering O to convey[60] or lease[61] land to X or grant X an

---

[51] Lord Denning in *Neale* v. *Willis* (1968) 19 P. & C.R. 836 and *Binions* v. *Evans* [1972] Ch. 359; Goff J. in *Re Densham* [1975] 1 W.L.R. 1519; Dillon J. in *Lyus* v. *Prowsa Developments* (*supra*).

[52] This is the view of Samuels J. in *Allen* v. *Snyder* [1977] 2 N.S.W.L.R. 685, 699.

[53] *Hollington Bros Ltd.* v. *Rhodes* [1951] 2 T.L.R. 691; *Miles* v. *Bull (No. 2)* [1969] 3 All E.R. 1585; *Midland Bank Trust Co.* v. *Green* [1981] A.C. 513.

[54] *De Lusignan* v. *Johnson* (1973) 230 Est.Gaz. 499; *Freer* v. *Unwins Ltd.* [1976] Ch. 288; *Williams & Glyn's Bank* v. *Boland* [1981] A.C. 487.

[55] *Re Monolithic Building Co.* [1915] 2 Ch. 643.

[56] *Jackson* v. *Cator* (1800) 5 Ves. 688 or damages in lieu of an injunction: *Shaw* v. *Applegate* [1978] 1 All E.R. 123.

[57] Instead of a lien the Court may make the order for possession in favour of O conditional upon repayment to X of X's expenditure: *Dodsworth* v. *Dodsworth* (1973) 228 Est.Gaz. 1115.

[58] *Unity Joint Stock Mutual Banking Assoc.* v. *King* (1858) 25 Beav. 72; *Hussey* v. *Palmer* [1972] 1 W.L.R. 1286; *Morris* v. *Morris* [1982] 1 N.S.W.L.R. 61; *Lee-Parker* v. *Izzet (No. 2)* [1972] 2 All E.R. 800, 804–805.

[59] *Raffaele* v. *Raffaele* [1962] W.R. 238; (1963) 79 L.Q.R. 228 (D. E. Allan).

[60] *Pascoe* v. *Turner* [1979] 1 W.L.R. 431. X may even obtain O's residuary estate: *Re Basham* [1986] 1 W.L.R. 1498.

[61] *Siew Soon Wah* v. *Yong Tong Hong* [1973] A.C. 836; *Griffiths* v. *Williams* (1977) 248 E.G. 947; *Taylor Fashions Ltd.* v. *Liverpool Victoria Trustees Co.* [1982] Q.B. 133.

easement[62] or a licence as long as X uses the premises as his private residence[63] or as long as X's loan is not repaid by O.[64]

Recent Court of Appeal cases[65] (see *Pascoe* v. *Turner, infra*, p. 79) indicate that X should receive the minimum equity to do justice to him, having regard to the way in which he changed his position for the worse[66] by reason of the acquiescence and encouragement of O. This will provide a remedy intended to reverse X's detriment rather than to fulfil his expectation, unless his expectation is of less value than his detriment[67] or there are special circumstances making an expectation remedy more appropriate than a detriment remedy.[68]

Originally, the courts regarded matters from O's viewpoint so that it was considered that O had to be at fault in some way before X could claim an equity. So, if O did not know the true position and so did not know of his right to object when he either acquiesced in or encouraged X's belief then O was not estopped from subsequently asserting his rights against X.[69] This may still be the position in cases of acquiescence where O has stood by without protest while his rights were being infringed at a time when he did not realise he had such rights.[70]

In cases of encouragement the courts now regard matters from X's viewpoint. Fault on O's part is no longer crucial: attention is focused on X's position and how unconscionable it would be if he were to suffer from O enforcing his strict legal rights once O had discovered his rights.[71] Indeed, a broad approach is suggested "directed at ascertaining whether, in particular circumstances it would be unconscionable for a party to be permitted to deny that which, knowingly or unknowingly, he has allowed or encouraged another to assume to his detriment."[72] O's ignorance of the true position and of his strict rights is merely one of the relevant factors in the overall inquiry. The court considers whether it would be unconscionable for O to insist on his strict legal rights, and if it would, then the court, taking into account all circumstances to the date of the trial, qualifies, suspends or extinguishes those rights so far as necessary for X to receive the minimum equity to do justice to him.[73]

---

[62] *Ward* v. *Kirkland* [1967] Ch. 194; *Ives Investments Ltd.* v. *High* [1967] 2 Q.B. 379; *Crabb* v. *Arun D.C.* [1976] Ch. 179.

[63] *Inwards* v. *Baker* [1965] 2 Q.B. 29; *Greasley* v. *Cooke* [1980] 1 W.L.R. 1306.

[64] *Re Sharpe* [1980] 1 W.L.R. 219.

[65] *Crabb* v. *Arun D.C.* [1976] Ch. 179; *Pascoe* v. *Turner* [1979] 1 W.L.R. 431.

[66] "The person claiming must have incurred expenditure or otherwise have prejudiced himself or acted to his detriment," *per* Dunn L.J. in *Greasley* v. *Cooke* [1980] 1 W.L.R. 1306, 1313–14. See also *Att.-Gen. of Hong Kong* v. *Humphreys Estate Ltd.* [1987] A.C. 114 and *Brinnand* v. *Ewens* (1987) 19 H.L.R 415.

[67] *Crabb* v. *Arun D.C.* (*supra*).

[68] *Pascoe* v. *Turner* (*supra*).

[69] *Wilmot* v. *Barber* (1880) 15 Ch.D. 96; *Falcke* v. *Scottish Imperial Insurance Co.* (1886) 34 Ch.D. 234, 243, 253; *Re Vandervell's Trusts (No. 2)* [1974] Ch. 269, 300–301.

[70] *Taylor Fashions Ltd.* v. *Liverpool Victoria Trustees Co.* [1982] Q.B. 133, 147; *Amalgamated Investment & Property Co.* v. *Texas Commerce International Bank* [1982] Q.B. 84, 104.

[71] *Ibid.*

[72] *Taylor Fashions Ltd.* v. *Liverpool Victoria Trustees Co.* [1982] Q.B. 133, 151; approved in *Habib Bank Ltd.* v. *Habib Bank A.G. Zurich* [1981] 2 All E.R. 650, 666. Compare the approach to consents to breach of trust, *infra*, p. 782.

[73] *Ward* v. *Kirkland* [1967] Ch. 194; *Ives Investments Ltd.* v. *High* [1967] 2 Q.B. 379; *Williams* v. *Staite* [1979] Ch. 291; *Pascoe* v. *Turner* [1979] 1 W.L.R. 431.

Recently, the Australian High Court[74] analysed the English estoppel cases. Mason C.J. and Wilson J. concluded[75]:

"One may therefore discern in the cases a common thread, namely the principle that equity will come to the relief of a plaintiff who has acted to his detriment on the basis of a basic assumption in relation to which the other party to the transaction has played such a part in the adoption of the assumption that it would be unfair or unjust if he were held free to ignore it. . . . Equity comes to the relief of such a plaintiff on the footing that it would be unconscionable conduct on the part of the other party to ignore the assumption."

Brennan J. went on to emphasise[76]:

"The unconscionable conduct which it is the object of equity to prevent is the failure of a party, who has induced the adoption of the assumption or expectation and who knew or intended that it would be relied upon, to fulfil the assumption or expectation or otherwise to avoid the detriment which that failure would occasion. The object of the equity is not to compel the party bound [by the equity] to fulfil the assumption or expectation: it is to avoid the detriment which, if the assumption or expectation goes unfulfilled, will be suffered by the party who has been induced to act or to abstain from acting thereon."

In its discretionary prevention of unconscionable conduct the court tailors the remedy to fit the wrong and is not upholding crystallised rights of a proprietary nature.[77] If it does decree that O must hold his property on trust for some interest of X it seems that this trust should be a remedial constructive trust with prospective effect only.[78] Thus a purchaser, P, of a legal interest in the land (*e.g.* a mortgage) before X registered a pending action in respect of the land should take free of X's uncertain discretionary claim, unless X has some independent personal claim against P by virtue of some representation or agreement involving X and P which makes it unconscionable for P personally to deny X's claim.[79]

### IMPORTANCE OF FORMAL REQUIREMENTS

The validity and consequences of a transaction may depend on compliance with a particular form. Through not having used the

---

[74] *Waltons Stores Interstate Ltd.* v. *Maher* (1988) 62 A.L.J.R. 110.
[75] *Ibid.* 116.
[76] *Ibid.* 125. See also *Commonwealth of Australia* v. *Verwagen* (1990) 64 A.L.J.R. 540.
[77] Meagher Gummow & Lehane, p. 42 though there are dicta in cases (which can be explained on other grounds) assuming that a purchaser with notice or, at least, actual notice of the circumstances giving rise to the estoppel claim will be bound by the claim as a proprietary right: *Ives Investments Ltd.* v. *High* [1967] 2 Q.B. 379, 394; *Re Sharpe* [1980] 1 All E.R. 198, 204 criticised by C.A. in *Ashburn Anstalt* v. *Arnold* [1989] Ch. 1, 25.
[78] See *Metall und Rohstoff AG* v. *Donaldson Lufkin & Jenrette Inc.* [1990] 1 Q.B. 391, 479.
[79] *Ashburn Anstalt* v. *Arnold* [1989] Ch. 1.

requisite formalities a man, like Mr. Vandervell, may find that he has not divested himself of all interest in property settled by him so as to be liable to a large amount of tax he had intended to avoid.[80] If a disposition can be effected orally then no stamp duty will be payable: stamp duty is payable on *instruments* transferring property or interests in property and so will be escaped if the transfer is effected orally and a subsequent written instrument merely records this for the benefit of the trustees. Section 82 of the Finance Act 1985 now makes conveyances or transfers by way of gift no longer subject to ad valorem duty if made after March 25, 1985.

If stamp duty were reintroduced on such conveyances or transfers account would need to be taken of a recently developed far-reaching principle against tax avoidance. As Lord Oliver stated in *Craven* v. *White*[81]:

> "The essentials emerging from *Furniss* v. *Dawson* [1984] A.C. 474 appear to me to be four in number (1) that the series of transactions was, at the time when the intermediate transaction was entered into, pre-ordained in order to produce a given result; (2) that that transaction had no other purpose than tax mitigation; (3) that there was at that time no practical likelihood that the pre-planned events would not take place in the order ordained, so that the intermediate transaction was not even contemplated practically as having an independent life, and (4) that the pre-ordained events did in fact take place. In these circumstances the court can be justified in linking the beginning with the end so as to make a single composite whole to which the fiscal results of the single composite whole are to be applied."

### EXAMPLES OF APPLICATION OF FORMALITIES

T1 and T2 hold property on trust for A absolutely in the following five examples:

(1) *A declares that he is to hold his equitable interest on trust either for B for life, remainder to C or for such of L to Z as he or T1 and T2 may appoint.* Here A remains in the picture with active trust duties so this is a declaration of trust where the declaration may be oral if the property is pure personalty but must be evidenced in writing within section 53(1)(*b*) if the property is land.[82]

(2) *A declares himself trustee of his interest for D absolutely.* Whilst superficially a declaration of trust requiring only compliance with section 53(1)(*b*) if the property is land, this probably amounts to a disposition of A's entire equitable interest which must itself be in writing within section 53(1)(*c*) whether the property is land or pure

---

[80] *Vandervell* v. *I.R.C.* [1967] 2 A.C. 291.
[81] [1989] A.C. 398.
[82] *Onslow* v. *Wallis* (1849) 1 Mac. & G. 506 approved in *Re Lashmar* [1891] 1 Ch. 253.

personalty.[83] After all, A is a simple bare trustee with no active duties to perform so that he should drop out of the picture, T1 and T2 now holding for D instead of A: by A's action A's equitable interest has passed to D who can directly enforce his rights against T1 and T2 merely joining A as a co-defendant to the action.[84]

(3) *A directs T1 and T2 to transfer the property to E absolutely for E's own benefit.* Here, the transfer of the legal title to E automatically carries with it the equitable interest so that there is no separate disposition by A of his equitable interest that requires compliance with section 53(1)(*c*): *Vandervell* v. *I.R.C.* set out *infra*, p. 71. This is commercially convenient, *e.g.* where a stockbroker or bank as nominee holds shares for A and A directs the shares to be transferred to E it would be most inconvenient for signed writing to be required of A in addition to that of the legal transferor. However, the reasoning is not very satisfactory because in the case of a transfer by the legal and equitable owner the equitable interest is merged or subsumed in the legal interest, whereas when T holds the legal title on trust for A the legal and equitable interests are obviously separated and the issue is whether they can be joined without a separate assignment or surrender by A, so that the equitable interest is then at home with the legal interest in T and so capable of transfer by T to E. The position may be better justified on the basis that where T does transfer the legal title to E at the instigation of or with the concurrence of A, then A cannot claim there has been a breach of trust and assert his equitable interest against the new legal owner, E, so that by operation of law outside section 53(1)(*c*) A's equitable interest is extinguished, just as much as it would have been extinguished if A in signed writing had expressly surrendered his equitable interest to T so that T might then pass the legal, and thus therewith the equitable, interest to E.[85] On either basis it is the transfer to E that is crucial so it would seem that if before then A revoked his direction to T, then A would remain entitled to the equitable interest and E could not in law complain about the promised gift not materialising. In the case of shares (or registered land) the legal title is not actually transferred till the transferee becomes registered as owner (or the relevant documents are delivered to the appropriate District Land Registry) but equity treats the transfer as complete when the transferor has done everything necessary to be done by him, *e.g.* delivery of the share or land certificate and the transfer form to the transferee. Pragmatically, it is likely that once A

---

[83] *Grey* v. *I.R.C.* [1958] Ch. 375, 382, *per* Upjohn J. [1958] Ch. 690, 715, *per* Evershed M.R. *cf.* a tenant's purported sub-lease for the residue of his lease taking effect as an assignment: Megarry & Wade, *Law of Real Property* (5th ed.), p. 666.

[84] Brian Green in (1984) 47 M.L.R. 385, 396–399 prefers the declaration to be treated as a sub-trust carving out a subsidiary equitable entitlement in B's favour out of A's original equitable interest but he goes on to submit that it should fall within s.53(1)(*c*) as a part disposal of A's equitable interest, a disposal of the beneficial part of A's bundle of hitherto subsisting equitable rights.

[85] See S. M. Spencer (1967) 31 Conv. 175, G. Battersby [1979] Conv. 17. If A had directed the trustees to transfer the property to E to hold on trust for X then this is likely to be a disposition of A's subsisting equitable interest to X: see n. 23, p. 55, *supra*.

gets T to do such acts A will not be allowed to revoke his gift and claim that E on becoming registered owner holds the property on trust for A.[86]

(4) *A directs T1 and T2 to hold the property on trust for F absolutely.* This is a disposition of A's equitable interest and so must be in writing within section 53(1)(c): *Grey* v. *I.R.C.* set out *infra*, p. 66. After all, as a result of A's direction T1 and T2 hold on trust for F instead of A, so A has been responsible for his equitable interest passing from himself to F.[87]

If T1 and T2 held the property on trust for A until A *or the trustees* appointed the property amongst such of C to Z as might be seen fit, then such appointment by the trustees in favour of F absolutely would not be "a disposition of an equitable interest subsisting at the time of the disposition" within section 53(1)(c), but the creation of a new interest automatically extinguishing A's formerly subsisting equitable interest.[88] If, however, A, and not the trustees, appointed in favour of F absolutely this would seem a disposition of A's subsisting equitable interest since by virtue of A's act it passes from him to F. As Viscount Simonds stated in *Grey* v. *I.R.C.*,[89] "If the word 'disposition' is given its natural meaning it cannot be denied that a direction given by Mr. Hunter [the settlor-beneficiary] whereby the beneficial interest theretofore vested in him became vested in another is a disposition." However, in *obiter dicta* Lord Denning[90] seems to suggest that if T1 and T2 held property on a resulting trust for A until A or the trustees appointed new trusts then an appointment *by A* or the trustees should be treated as the creation of a new interest, A's equitable interest (under the resulting trust arising to plug the gap in the beneficial ownership) automatically ceasing "as soon as the gap is filled by the creation or declaration of a valid trust."[91] These dicta seem unsound where the appointment is by A: in *Re Vandervell's Trusts (No. 2)* it was surely only because *the trustees* made the appointment that there was created a valid trust to displace the resulting trust as emphasised by Stephenson L.J. (*infra*, p. 78).

---

[86] B. Green (1984) 47 M.L.R. 385, 410, and n. 9, p. 72, *infra*.

[87] An exception from the *Grey* v. *I.R.C.* principle is implicit in *Re Bowden* [1936] Ch. 31 and *Re Adlard* [1954] Ch. 29 on which see pp. 232–233. No writing seems required where S has executed a voluntary "S" settlement and therein covenanted to transfer to his trustee, *e.g.* Lloyds Bank, after-acquired property appointed to him under the "T" trust or bequeathed to him under T's will and Lloyds Bank becomes trustee of the "T" trust or of T's will when property is appointed or bequeathed to S (giving S an equitable interest) and S authorises Lloyds Bank *qua* trustee of the "T" trust or of T's will to hold the property *qua* trustee of the "S" trust. Thereafter S cannot claim the property for himself presumably on estoppel principles.

[88] *Re Vandervell's Trusts (No. 2)* [1974] Ch. 269, *infra*, p. 72, criticised on its estoppel grounds by Brian Green, *infra*, p. 83.

[89] [1960] A.C. 1, 12.

[90] [1974] Ch. 269, 320.

[91] One cannot restrict Lord Denning's views to equitable interests under *resulting* trusts, falling outside s.53(1)(c): equitable interests under *express* trusts are similarly displaced by the creation of new valid trusts. In *Re Tyler's Fund Trusts* [1967] 3 All E.R. 389, 391–392, Pennycuick J. applied s.53(1)(c) to an equitable interest under a resulting trust. In *Oughtred* v. *I.R.C.* [1960] A.C. 206, 253, Lord Denning considered s.53(1)(c) to apply to an equitable interest under a constructive trust which falls under s.53(2) like a resulting trust.

(5) *A contracts with G to transfer his equitable interest to G.* If A's equitable interest is in land, whether or not held on trust for sale, then all the terms of the contract must be in writing as required by section 2 of Law of Property (Miscellaneous Provisions) Act 1989. Otherwise, it seems writing is not required. Certainly, a contract to make a disposition of an equitable interest does not seem itself to be a disposition. However, it can be said that the constructive trusteeship imposed upon A when he enters into a specifically enforceable contract[92] to sell his equitable interest to G means that T1 and T2 hold on trust for A who holds on constructive trust for G so that if A is or becomes a simple bare trustee with no active duties to perform he disappears from the picture leaving T1 and T2 holding on trust for G. Thus A has disposed of his equitable interest and this requires writing within section 53(1)(c).[93]

Against such a conclusion is section 53(2) which states that section 53(1) is not to affect the creation or operation of constructive trusts so that without the need for any section 53(1)(c) writing G becomes owner of the equitable interest due to the constructive trust in his favour: this view has been taken by Upjohn J.,[94] Lord Radcliffe,[95] Megarry J.[96] and by Goff and Shaw L.JJ.[97] In any event as Lord Cohen has indicated[98] once G had paid the purchase price to A, A would not be able to put forward successfully any claim to the equitable interest. Furthermore, A's self-interested trusteeship in ensuring the contract is observed and the purchase price paid to him means that when the contract is first made he is not a simple bare trustee with no active duties so that the constructive trust in G's favour is a true sub-trust. The position is analogous to the case where A declares a sub-trust of his equitable interest for S for one month, remainder to T absolutely (outside section 53(1)(c)) and after a month S's interest automatically ceases and T becomes full beneficial owner (outside section 53(1)(c)).

In *Chinn* v. *Collins* the House of Lords regarded the availability of specific performance and the creation of a constructive trust immaterial in a case concerned with non-specifically enforceable contractual dealings relating to an equitable interest in shares (in an English public company held by an English private company as nominee for a Guernsey trustee). Lord Wilberforce asserted,[99] "Dealings related to the equitable interest in these [shares] required no formality. As soon as there was an agreement for their sale accompanied or followed by payment of the price, the equitable title passed at once to the

---

92 See p. 530, *infra*.
93 See Lord Denning in *Oughtred* v. *I.R.C.* [1960] A.C. 206, 233.
94 *Oughtred* v. *I.R.C.* [1958] Ch. 383.
95 *Oughtred* v. *I.R.C.* [1960] A.C. 206, 227–228.
96 *Re Holt's Settlement* [1969] 1 Ch. 100.
97 *DHN Food Distributors Ltd.* v. *Tower Hamlets London Borough Council* [1976] 1 W.L.R. 852, 865, 867.
98 *Oughtred* v. *I.R.C.* [1960] A.C. 206, 230.
99 [1981] A.C. 533, 548 without giving reasons, though the emphasis on payment of the price indicates support for Lord Cohen's view in *Oughtred* (*supra*). The other Law Lords agreed with him.

purchaser and all that was needed to perfect his title was notice to the trustee or the nominee."

## GREY v. INLAND REVENUE COMMISSIONERS

House of Lords [1960] A.C. 1; [1959] 3 W.L.R. 759; 103 S.J 896; [1959] 3 All E.R. 603; [1959] T.R. 311 (Viscount Simonds, Lords Radcliffe, Cohen, Keith of Avonholm and Reid)

On February 1, Mr. Hunter, as settlor, transferred 18,000 shares of £1 each to the appellants as nominees for himself. The appellants were the trustees of six settlements, which Mr. Hunter had previously created. On February 18, 1955, Mr. Hunter orally directed the trustees to divide the 18,000 shares into six parcels of 3,000 shares each and to appropriate the parcels to the trusts of the six settlements, one parcel to each settlement.

On March 25, 1955, the trustees executed six deeds of declaration of trust (which Mr. Hunter also executed in order to testify to the oral direction previously given by him) declaring that since February 18, 1955, they held each of the parcels of 3,000 shares on the trusts of the relevant settlement. The Commissioners of Inland Revenue assessed the deeds of declaration of trust to *ad valorem* stamp duty on the basis that the oral declaration did not effectively create trusts of the shares so that it was the subsequent deeds that created trusts of the shares and were stampable as instruments transferring an interest in property: they were not exempt as merely confirming an earlier effective transfer. The trustees appealed against this view upheld by a majority in the Court of Appeal.

LORD RADCLIFFE: "My Lords, if there is nothing more in this appeal than the short question whether the oral direction that Mr. Hunter gave to his trustees on February 18, 1955, amounted in any ordinary sense of the words to a 'disposition of an equitable interest or trust subsisting at the time of the disposition,' I do not feel any doubt as to my answer. I think that it did. Whether we describe what happened in technical or in more general terms, the full equitable interest in the eighteen thousand shares concerned, which at that time was his, was (subject to any statutory invalidity) diverted by his direction from his ownership into the beneficial ownership of the various equitable owners, present and future, entitled under his six existing settlements.

"In my opinion, it is a very nice question whether a parol declaration of trust of this kind was or was not within the mischief of section 9 of the Statute of Frauds. The point has never, I believe, been decided and perhaps it never will be. Certainly it was long established as law that while a declaration of trust respecting land or any interest therein required writing to be effective a declaration of trust respecting personalty did not. Moreover, there is warrant for saying that a direction to his trustee by the equitable owner of trust property prescribing new trusts of that property was a declaration of trust. But it does not necessarily follow from that that such a direction, if the effect of it was to determine completely or *pro tanto* the subsisting equitable interest of the maker of the direction, was not also a grant or assignment for the purposes of section 9 and therefore required writing for its validity. Something had to happen to that equitable interest in order to displace it in favour of the new interests created by the direction: and it would be at any rate logical to treat the direction as being an assignment of the subsisting interest to the new beneficiary or beneficiaries or, in other cases, a release or surrender of it to the trustee.

"I do not think, however, that that question has to be answered for the purposes of this appeal. It can only be relevant if section 53(1) of the Law of Property Act 1925 is treated as a true consolidation of the three sections of the Statute of Frauds concerned and as governed, therefore, by the general principle, with which I am entirely in agreement, that a consolidating Act is not to be read as effecting changes in the existing law unless the words it employs are too clear in their effect to admit of any other construction. But, in my opinion, it is impossible to regard section 53 of the Law of Property Act 1925 as a consolidating enactment in this sense."[1] *Appeal dismissed.*

### OUGHTRED v. INLAND REVENUE COMMISSIONERS

House of Lords [1960] A.C. 206; [1959] 3 W.L.R. 898; 103 S.J. 896; [1959] 3 All E.R. 623; [1959] T.R. 319 (Lords Keith of Avonholm, Denning and Jenkins; Lords Radcliffe and Cohen dissenting)

The trustees of a settlement held the legal title in 200,000 shares in a company called William Jackson & Son Ltd. in trust for the appellant, Mrs. Oughtred, for life and after her death for her son Peter. The appellant also owned 72,700 shares in her own right. On June 18, 1956, an oral agreement was made between the appellant and her son to the effect that on the 26th of the same month she would transfer to him the 72,700 shares and in exchange he would make her the absolute beneficial owner of the settled shares by giving up to her his beneficial reversionary interests.[2] The oral agreement was followed by the execution of three documents all dated June 26, 1956, namely, (1) a deed of release made between the appellant of the first part, Peter of the second part and the trustees of the settlement of the third part which recited that the 200,000 shares were now held in trust for the appellant absolutely and that it was intended to transfer them to her, and gave the trustees a general release in respect of their trusteeship, but was executed only by the appellant and Peter; (2) a transfer by the appellant of the 72,700 shares to nominees for Peter expressed to be made in consideration of 10s.; and (3) a deed of transfer expressed to be made in consideration of 10s. by which the trustees transferred the 200,000 shares to the appellant. The Commissioners assessed the stamp duty chargeable on the third transfer mentioned above at £663 10s., made up of £663 *ad valorem* transfer on sale duty together with the fixed duty of 10s. on the transfer of the legal interest in the 200,000 shares to the appellant.

Upjohn J. allowed the appeal, holding that the transfer in question was not chargeable with *ad valorem* duty and declaring that it was chargeable with the fixed duty of 10s. only. In his opinion a vendor under a specifically enforceable contract of sale became a constructive trustee for the purchaser. Accordingly Peter became a constructive trustee for the appellant from the date of the oral agreement on June 18, 1956. The appellant obtained an equitable interest

---

[1] Would *ad valorem* stamp duty have been avoided if (1) H had orally declared himself trustee of the shares on trust for his grandchildren; (2) H had retired as trustee in favour of the trustees of the six settlements, legal title to the shares being transferred to such trustees by instrument bearing fixed 50p duty; (3) the trustees later signed an instrument recording they hold the shares on specified trusts declared earlier by H?

[2] The idea was to save estate duty as otherwise on the appellant's death duty would be payable on the aggregated value of the settled property and the appellant's free estate. Nowadays, inheritance tax has replaced estate duty.

under the oral constructive trust. Hence there was no document to attract *ad valorem* duty. The Court of Appeal,[3] held that the transfer in question was chargeable with the *ad valorem* duty of £663, but not with the fixed duty of 10s. In their opinion, whether or not there was a constructive trust, the transfer in question was the completion of the oral contract and was liable to *ad valorem* duty for that reason. They rejected the claim to the fixed duty of 10s. on the ground that as Peter had not executed the transfer, it could not be regarded at one and the same time as the transfer on sale of Peter's equitable interest and the transfer (not on sale) of the legal interest in the shares. The appellant appealed.

LORD JENKINS: "The provisions of the Stamp Act 1891 directly relevant to the claim are these: section 1 (which contains the charge of stamp duties) provides that the stamp duties 'upon the several instruments specified in Schedule 1 to this Act shall be the several duties in the said schedule specified. . . . ' Section 54 provides as follows: 'For the purposes of this Act the expression "conveyance on sale" includes every instrument . . . whereby any property, or any estate or interest in any property, upon the sale thereof is transferred to or vested in a purchaser, or any other person on his behalf or by his direction.'

"Schedule 1 imposes under the head of charge 'Conveyance or transfer on sale of any property' (except as therein mentioned) *ad valorem* duty upon 'the amount or value of the consideration for the sale'; and under the head of charge 'Conveyance or transfer of any kind not hereinbefore described' a fixed duty of 10s."

[His Lordship referred to section 53(1)(c) and (2) of the Law of Property Act 1925, and continued:] "The question, then, is whether, upon the true construction of section 54 of the Act of 1891 and having regard to the terms and effect of the oral agreement and the nature of the interests with respect to which that agreement was made, the disputed transfer was an instrument whereby property in the shape of the settled shares or any estate or interest in that property was transferred 'upon the sale thereof' to a purchaser in the person of the appellant.

" . . . It is said, and said truly, that stamp duty is imposed on instruments, not transactions, and that a transaction of sale carried out without bringing into existence an instrument which has the effect of transferring to or vesting in the purchaser the property sold attracts no duty: see *per* Lord Esher M.R. in *Inland Revenue Commissioners* v. *Angus*, where he said[4]: 'The first thing to be noticed is that the thing which is made liable to the duty is an "instrument." If a contract of purchase and sale, or a conveyance by way of purchase and sale, can be, or is, carried out without an instrument, the case is not within the section, and no tax is imposed. It is not the transaction of purchase and sale which is struck at; it is the instrument whereby the purchase and sale are effected which is struck at. And if anyone can carry through a purchase and sale without an instrument, then the legislature have not reached that transaction. The next thing is that it is not every instrument which may be brought into being in the course of a transaction of purchase and sale which is struck at. It is the instrument "whereby any property upon the sale thereof is

---

[3] [1958] Ch. 678.
[4] (1889) 23 Q.B.D. 579, 589.

legally or equitably transferred." The taxation is confined to the instrument whereby the property is transferred. The transfer must be made by the instrument. If a transfer requires something more than an instrument to carry it through, then the transaction is not struck at, and the instrument is not struck at because the property is not transferred by it.'

"It is said further that, in the present case, the disputed transfer transferred nothing beyond a bare legal estate, because, in accordance with the well-settled principle applicable to contracts of sale between contract and completion, the appellant became under the oral agreement beneficially entitled in equity to the settled shares, subject to the due satisfaction by her of the purchase consideration, and, accordingly, the entire beneficial interest in the settled shares had already passed to her at the time of the execution of the disputed transfer, and there was nothing left upon which the disputed transfer could operate except the bare legal estate.

"The Commissioners of Inland Revenue contend that, as the agreement of June 18, 1956, was an oral agreement, it could not, in view of section 53(1)(c), effect a disposition of a subsisting equitable interest or trust, and, accordingly, that Peter's subsisting equitable interest under the trusts of the settlement, in the shape of his reversionary interest, remained vested in him until the execution of the disputed transfer, which, in these circumstances, operated as a transfer on sale to the appellant of Peter's reversionary interest and additionally as a transfer not on sale to the appellant of the legal interest in the settled shares. It was by this process of reasoning that the commissioners arrived at the opinion expressed in the case stated that the disputed transfer attracted both the *ad valorem* duty exigible on a transfer on sale of the reversionary interest and also the fixed duty of 10s. This argument is attacked on the appellant's side by reference to subsection (2) of section 53 of the Act of 1925, which excludes the creation or operation of resulting, implied or constructive trusts from the provisions of subsection (1). It is said that, inasmuch as the oral agreement was an agreement of sale and purchase, it gave rise, on the principle to which I have already adverted, to a constructive trust of the reversionary interest in favour of the appellant, subject to performance by her of her obligation to transfer to Peter the free shares forming the consideration for the sale. It is said that this trust, being constructive, was untouched by section 53(1)(c) in view of the exemption afforded by section 53(2), and that the appellant's primary argument still holds good.

"I find it unnecessary to decide whether section 53(2) has the effect of excluding the present transaction from the operation of section 53(1)(c),[5] for, assuming in the appellant's favour that the oral contract did have the effect in equity of raising a constructive trust of the settled shares for her untouched by section 53(1)(c), I am unable to accept the conclusion that the disputed

---

[5] Lord Radcliffe took the view that s.53(1)(c) was excluded whilst Lords Cohen and Denning took the view that s.53(1)(c) applied. Lord Keith merely concurred with Lord Jenkins. The relevant dicta of Lords Cohen and Denning are as follows: Lord Denning (at p. 233): "I do not think the oral agreement was effective to transfer Peter's reversionary interest to his mother. I should have thought that the wording of s.53(1)(c) clearly made a writing necessary to effect a transfer: and s.53(2) does not do away with that necessity." Lord Cohen (at p. 230): "Before your Lordships Mr. Wilberforce was prepared to agree that on the making of the oral agreement Peter became a constructive trustee of his equitable reversionary interest for the appellant, but he submitted that nonetheless s.53(1)(c) applied and accordingly Peter could not assign that equitable interest to the appellant except by a disposition in writing. My Lords, with that I agree." He went on, however, to hold that Peter could not dispute his mother's title to the formerly settled shares by reason of estoppel principles.

transfer was prevented from being a transfer of the shares to the appellant on sale because the entire beneficial interest in the settled shares was already vested in the appellant under the constructive trust, and there was, accordingly, nothing left for the disputed transfer to pass to the appellant except the bare legal estate. The constructive trust in favour of a purchaser which arises on the conclusion of a contract for sale is founded upon the purchaser's right to enforce the contract in proceedings for specific performance. In other words, he is treated in equity as entitled by virtue of the contract to the property which the vendor is bound under the contract to convey to him. This interest under the contract is, no doubt, a proprietary interest of a sort, which arises, so to speak, in anticipation of the execution of the transfer for which the purchaser is entitled to call. But its existence has never (so far as I know) been held to prevent a subsequent transfer, in performance of the contract, of the property contracted to be sold from constituting for stamp duty purposes a transfer on sale of the property in question. Take a simple case of a contract for the sale of land. In such a case a constructive trust in favour of the purchaser arises on the conclusion of the contract for sale, but (so far as I know) it has never been held on this account that a conveyance subsequently executed in performance of the contract is not stampable *ad valorem* as a transfer on sale. Similarly, in a case like the present one, but uncomplicated by the existence of successive interests, a transfer to a purchaser of the investments comprised in a trust fund could not, in my judgment, be prevented from constituting a transfer on sale for the purposes of stamp duty by reason of the fact that the actual transfer had been preceded by an oral agreement for sale.

"In truth, the title secured by a purchaser by means of an actual transfer is different in kind from, and may well be far superior to, the special form of proprietary interest which equity confers on a purchaser in anticipation of such transfer.

"This difference is of particular importance in the case of property such as shares in a limited company. Under the contract, the purchaser is, no doubt, entitled in equity as between himself and the vendor to the beneficial interest in the shares, and (subject to due payment of the purchase consideration) to call for a transfer of them from the vendor as trustee for him. But it is only on the execution of the actual transfer that he becomes entitled to be registered as a member, to attend and vote at meetings, to effect transfers on the register, or to receive dividends otherwise than through the vendor as his trustee.

"The parties to a transaction of sale and purchase may, no doubt, choose to let the matter rest in contract. But if the subject-matter of a sale is such that the full title to it can only be transferred by an instrument, then any instrument they execute by way of transfer of the property sold ranks for stamp duty purposes as a conveyance on sale, notwithstanding the constructive trust in favour of the purchaser which arose on the conclusion of the contract. . . . "
*Appeal dismissed.*[6]

## VANDERVELL v. INLAND REVENUE COMMISSIONERS

House of Lords [1967] 2 A.C. 291 (Lords Pearce, Upjohn and Wilberforce; Lords Reid and Donovan dissenting)

---

[6] This case has been said to be authority for the view that "an instrument may be liable to *ad valorem* duty as a conveyance or transfer on sale when it operates as the completion of a pre-existing bargain although the property transferred by the instrument is not the same property as that which was the subject of the earlier bargain provided that the former does in truth and in reality 'represent' the latter": *Henty & Constable Ltd.* v. *I.R.C.* [1961] 1 W.L.R. 1504, 1510 (Lord Denning M.R.).

The detailed facts appear in the judgment of Lord Denning M.R. in *Re Vandervell's Trusts (No. 2)* set out at p. 72, *infra*.

The following extracts from the speeches in the House of Lords concern the point whether the transfer by the bare trustee of the legal title to shares carried with it the equitable interest of the taxpayer beneficiary without any separate written disposition by him.

LORD UPJOHN: " . . . the object of the section, as was the object of the old Statute of Frauds, is to prevent hidden oral transactions in equitable interests in fraud of those truly entitled, and making it difficult, if not impossible, for the trustees to ascertain who are in truth the beneficiaries. When the beneficial owner, however, owns the whole beneficial estate and is in a position to give directions to his bare trustee with regard to the legal as well as the equitable estate there can be no possible ground for invoking the section where the beneficial owner wants to deal with the legal estate as well as the equitable estate.

"I cannot agree with Diplock L.J. that prima facie a transfer of the legal estate carries with it the absolute beneficial interest in the property transferred; this plainly is not so, *e.g.* the transfer may be on a change of trustee; it is a matter of intention in each case. If, however, the intention of the beneficial owner in directing the trustee to transfer the legal estate to X is that X should be the beneficial owner, I can see no reason for any further document or further words in the document assigning the legal estate also expressly transferring the beneficial interest; the greater includes the less. X may be wise to secure some evidence that the beneficial owner intended him to take the beneficial interest in case his beneficial title is challenged at a later date but it certainly cannot, in my opinion, be a statutory requirement that to effect its passing there must be some writing under section 53(1)(*c*).

"Counsel for the Crown admitted that where the legal and beneficial estate was vested in the legal owner and he desired to transfer the whole legal and beneficial estate to another he did not have to do more than transfer the legal estate and he did not have to comply with section 53(1)(*c*); and I can see no difference between that case and this.

"As I have said, that section is, in my opinion, directed to cases where dealings with the equitable estate are divorced from the legal estate and I do not think any of their Lordships in *Grey* v. *I.R.C.*[7] and *Oughtred* v. *I.R.C.*[8] had in mind the case before your Lordships. To hold the contrary would make assignments unnecessarily complicated; if there had to be assignments in express terms of both legal and equitable interests that would make the section more productive of injustice than the supposed evils it was intended to prevent. . . . "

LORD DONOVAN: " . . . If, owning the entire estate, legal and beneficial, in a piece of property, and desiring to transfer that entire estate to another, I do so by means of a disposition which *ex facie* deals only with the legal estate, it would be ridiculous to argue that section 53(1)(*c*) has not been complied with, and that therefore the legal estate alone had passed. The present case, it is true, is different in its facts in that the legal and equitable estates in the shares

---

[7] [1960] A.C. 1.
[8] [1960] A.C. 206.

were in separate ownership; but when the taxpayer, being competent to do so, instructed the bank to transfer the shares to the College, and made it abundantly clear that he wanted to pass, by means of that transfer, his own beneficial, or equitable, interest, plus the bank's legal interest, he achieved the same result as if there had been no separation of the interests. The transfer thus made pursuant to his intentions and instructions was a disposition, not of the equitable interest alone, but of the entire estate in the shares. In such a case I see no room for the operation of section 53(1)(c). . . ."

LORD WILBERFORCE: " . . . On November 14, 1958, the taxpayer's solicitor received from the bank a blank transfer of the shares, executed by the bank, and the share certificate. So at this stage the taxpayer was the absolute master of the shares and only needed to insert his name as transferee in the transfer and to register it to become the full legal owner. He was also the owner in equity. On November 19, 1958, the solicitor . . . on behalf of the taxpayer, who intended to make a gift, handed the transfer to the College, which in due course, sealed it and obtained registration of the shares in the College's name. The case should then be regarded as one in which the taxpayer himself has, with the intention to make a gift, put the College in a position to become the legal owner of the shares, which the College in fact became. If the taxpayer had died before the College had obtained registration, it is clear on the principle of *Re Rose*[9] that the gift would have been complete, on the basis that he had done everything in his power to transfer the legal interest, with an intention to give, to the College. No separate transfer, therefore, of the equitable interest ever came to or needed to be made and there is no room for the operation of the subsection. What the position would have been had there simply been an oral direction to the legal owner (*viz.*, the bank) to transfer the shares to the College, followed by such a transfer, but without any document in writing signed by the taxpayer as equitable owner, is not a matter which calls for consideration here. . . ."[10]

## RE VANDERVELL'S TRUSTS (NO. 2)

Court of Appeal [1974] Ch. 269; [1974] 3 All E.R. 205 (Lord Denning M.R., Stephenson and Lawton L.JJ.)

LORD DENNING M.R.: "During his lifetime Mr. Vandervell was a very successful engineer. He had his own private company—Vandervell Products Ltd.—'the products company,' as I will call it—in which he owned virtually all the shares. It was in his power to declare dividends as and when he pleased. In 1949 he set up a trust for his children. He did it by forming Vandervell Trustees Ltd.—'the trustee company,' as I will call it. He put three of his friends and advisers in control of it. They were the sole shareholders and directors of the trustee company. Two were chartered accountants. The other

---

[9] [1949] Ch. 78; *post*, pp. 217–222. However, in *Re Rose* the taxpayer was entitled legally and equitably to the shares and did all he could to transfer them by executing a share transfer and delivering the transfer and the share certificate to the donee. Vandervell was only equitably entitled and to say that he had done all he could to vest the shares in the College is to beg the s.53(1)(c) question of what was required of an owner of a subsisting equitable interest to achieve a disposition of that interest in the first place.

[10] See N. Strauss (1967) 30 M.L.R. 461; Gareth Jones [1966] C.L.J. 19–25; S. M. Spencer (1967) 31 Conv.(N.S.) 175–181; B. Green (1984) 47 M.L.R. 385, 410.

was his solicitor. He transferred money and shares to the trustee company to be held in trust for the children. Such was the position at the opening of the first period.

*The first period: 1958–61*

"The first period covers the three years from October 1958 to October 1961. Mr. Vandervell decided to found a chair of pharmacology at the Royal College of Surgeons. He was to endow it by providing £150,000. But he did not do it by a direct gift. In November 1958 he transferred to the Royal College of Surgeons 100,000 'A' shares in his products company. His intention was that his products company should declare dividends in favour of the Royal College of Surgeons which would amount in all to £150,000 or more. But, when that sum had been provided, he wanted to be able to regain the shares—so as to use the dividends for other good purposes. So, about the time of the transfer, on December 1, 1958, he got the Royal College of Surgeons to grant an option to the trustee company. By this option the Royal College of Surgeons agreed to transfer the 100,000 'A' shares to the trustee company for the sum of £5,000 at any time on request within the next five years. (This £5,000 was far less than the real value of the shares.) At the time when the option was granted, Mr. Vandervell did not state definitely the trusts on which the trustee company was to hold the option. He meant the trustee company to hold the option on trust—not beneficially for itself—but on trust for someone or other. He did not specify the trusts with any kind of precision. But at a meeting with the chairman of the trustee company it was proposed—and Mr. Vandervell approved—that the option should be held *either* on trust for his children (as an addition to the children's settlement) *or* alternatively on trust for the employees of his products company. He had not made up his mind which of those should benefit. But one thing he was clear about. He thought that he himself had parted with all interest in the shares and in the option. Afterwards, during the years from 1958 to 1961, he saw to it that his products company declared dividends on these 100,000 shares which were paid to the Royal College of Surgeons. They amounted to £266,000 gross (before tax), or £157,000 net (after tax). So the Royal College of Surgeons received ample funds to found the Chair of Pharmacology.

"But there were other advantages hoped for. The Royal College of Surgeons thought that, being a charity, they could claim back the tax from the Revenue. And Mr. Vandervell thought that, having parted with all interest in the shares, he was not subject to pay surtax on these dividends. The Revenue authorities, however, did not take that view. They claimed that Mr. Vandervell had not divested himself of all interest in the shares. They argued that he was the beneficial owner of the option and liable for surtax on the dividends. Faced with this demand, in October 1961, the trustee company, on the advice of counsel, and with the full approval of Mr. Vandervell, decided to exercise the option. It did it so as to avoid any question of surtax thereafter being payable by Mr. Vandervell. This ended the first period (when the option was in being) and started the second period (after the option was exercised).

*The second period: 1961–65*

"In October 1961 the trustee company exercised the option. It did it by using the money of the children's settlement. It paid £5,000 of the children's money to the Royal College of Surgeons. In return the Royal College of Surgeons, on October 27, 1961 transferred the 100,000 'A' shares to the trustee company. The intention of Mr. Vandervell and of the trustee company was that the trustee company should hold the shares (which had replaced the option) on trust for the children as an addition to the children's settlement. The trustee company made this clear to the Revenue authorities in an important letter written by its solicitors on November 2, 1961, which I will read:

> "*G. A. Vandervell, Esq.—Surtax*
>
> 'Further to our letter of the 7th September last, we write to inform you that in accordance with the advice tendered by Counsel to Vandervell Trustees Ltd., the latter have exercised the option granted to them by the Royal College of Surgeons of the 1st December 1958, and procured a transfer to them of the shares referred to in the option, with funds held by them upon the trusts of the Settlement created by Mr. G. A. Vandervell and dated the 3rd December 1959, and consequently such shares will henceforth be held by them upon the trusts of that Settlement.'

"Mr. Vandervell believed that thenceforward the trustee company held the 100,000 'A' shares on trust for the children. He acted on that footing. He got his products company to declare dividends on them for the years 1962 to 1964 amounting to the large sum of £1,256,458 gross (before tax) and £769,580 10s. 9d. (after tax). These dividends were received by the trustee company and added to the funds of the children's settlement. They were invested by the trustee company for the benefit of the children exclusively. But even now Mr. Vandervell had not shaken off the demands of the Revenue authorities. They claimed that, even after the exercise of the option, Mr. Vandervell had not divested himself of his interest in the 100,000 'A' shares and that he was liable for surtax on the dividends paid to the children's settlement. Faced with this demand Mr. Vandervell, on the advice of counsel, took the final step. He executed a deed transferring everything to the trustee company on trust for the children. This ended the second period, and started the third.

### The third period: 1965–67

"On January 19, 1965, Mr. Vandervell executed a deed by which he transferred to the trustee company all right, title or interest which he had on the option or the shares or in the dividends—expressly declaring that the trustee company was to hold them on the trusts of the children's settlement. At last the Revenue authorities accepted the position. They recognised that from January 19, 1965, Mr. Vandervell had no interest whatever in the shares or the dividends. They made no demands for surtax thenceforward.

On January 27, 1967, Mr. Vandervell made his will. It was in contemplation of a new marriage. In it he made no provision for his children. He said expressly that this was because he had already provided for them by the children's settlement. Six weeks later, on March 10, 1967, he died.

### Summary of the claims

"The root cause of all the litigation is the claim of the Revenue authorities.

"*The first period—1958–61.* The Revenue authorities claimed that Mr. Vandervell was the beneficial owner of the *option* and was liable for surtax on the dividends declared from 1958 to 1961. This came to £250,000. The claim of the Revenue was upheld by the House of Lords: see *Vandervell* v. *Inland Revenue Coms.*[11]

---

[11] [1967] 2 A.C. 291; [1967] 1 All E.R. 1.

"*The second period—1961–65.* The Revenue authorities claimed that Mr. Vandervell was the beneficial owner of the shares. They assessed him for surtax in respect of the dividends from October 11, 1961, to January 19, 1965, amounting to £628,229. The executors dispute the claim of the Revenue. They appealed against the assessments. But the appeal was, by agreement, stood over pending the case now before us. The executors have brought this action against the trustee company. They seek a declaration that, during the second period, the dividends belonged to Mr. Vandervell himself, and they ask for an account of them. The Revenue asked to be joined as parties to the action. This court did join them: see *Vandervell Trustees Ltd.* v. *White*[12]; but the House of Lords reversed the decision.[13] So this action has continued—without the presence of the Revenue—whose claim to £628,229 has caused all the trouble.

"*The third period—1965–67.* The Revenue agreed that they have no claim against the estate for this period.

### The law for the first period

"The first period was considered by the House of Lords in *Vandervell* v. *Inland Revenue Comrs.*.[14] They held, by a majority of three to two, that during this period the trustee company held the option as a trustee. The terms of the trust were stated in two ways. Lord Upjohn (with the agreement of Lord Pearce) said[15] that the proper inference was that—

> 'the trustee company should hold as trustee on such trusts as [Mr. Vandervell] or the trustee company should from time to time declare.'

Lord Wilberforce said[16] that 'the option was held [by the trustee company] on trusts not at the time determined, but to be decided on a later date.'

"The trouble about the trust so stated was that it was too uncertain. The trusts were not declared or defined with sufficient precision for the trustees to ascertain who the beneficiaries were. It is clear law that a trust (other than a charitable trust) must be for ascertainable beneficiaries: see *Re Gulbenkian's Settlement Trusts*[17] *per* Lord Upjohn. Seeing that there were no ascertainable beneficiaries, there was a resulting trust for Mr. Vandervell. But if and when Mr. Vandervell should declare any defined trusts, the resulting trust would come to an end. As Lord Upjohn said[18] 'until these trusts should be declared there was a resulting trust for [Mr. Vandervell].'

"During the first period, however, Mr. Vandervell did not declare any defined trusts. The option was, therefore, held on a resulting trust for him. He had not divested himself absolutely of the shares. He was, therefore, liable to pay surtax on the dividends.

### The law for the second period

"In October and November 1961 the trustee company exercised the option. It paid £5,000 out of the children's settlement. The Royal College of Surgeons transferred the legal estate in the 100,000 'A' shares to the trustee company.

---

12 [1970] Ch. 44; [1969] 3 All E.R. 496.
13 [1971] A.C. 912; [1970] 3 All E.R. 16.
14 [1967] A.C. 291; [1967] 1 All E.R. 1.
15 [1967] 2 A.C. at 315, 317; [1967] 1 All E.R. at 10, 11.
16 [1967] 2 A.C. at 325, 328; [1967] 1 All E.R. at 16, 17.
17 [1970] A.C. 508, 523, 524; [1968] 3 All E.R. 785 at 792, 793.
18 [1967] 2 A.C. at 317; [1967] 1 All E.R. at 11.

Thereupon the trustee company became the legal owner of the shares. This was a different kind of property altogether. Whereas previously the trustee company had only a chose in action of one kind—an option—it now had a chose in action of a different kind—the actual shares. This trust property was not held by the trustee company beneficially. It was held by the company on trust. On this occasion a valid trust was created at the time of the transfer. It was manifested in clear and unmistakable fashion. It was precisely defined. The shares were to be held on the trusts of the children's settlement. The evidence of intention is indisputable: (i) the trustee company used the children's money—£5,000—with which to acquire the shares; this would be a breach of trust unless they intended the shares to be an addition to the children's settlement; (ii) the trustee company wrote to the Revenue authorities the letter of November 2, 1961, declaring expressly that the shares 'will henceforth be held by them upon the trusts of the children's settlement'; (iii) thenceforward all the dividends received by the trustee company were paid by it to the children's settlement and treated as part of the funds of the settlement. This was all done with the full assent of Mr. Vandervell. Such being the intention, clear and manifest, at the time when the shares were conveyed to the trustee company, it is sufficient to create a trust.

"Counsel for the executors admitted that the intention of Mr. Vandervell and the trustee company was that the shares should be held on trust for the children's settlement. But he said that this intention was of no avail. He said that during the first period Mr. Vandervell had an equitable interest in the property, namely, a resulting trust; that he never disposed of this equitable interest (because he never knew he had it); and that in any case it was the disposition of an equitable interest which, under section 53 of the Law of Property Act 1925, had to be in writing, signed by him or his agent, lawfully authorised by him in writing (and there was no such writing produced). He cited *Grey* v. *Inland Revenue Comrs.*[19] and *Oughtred* v. *Inland Revenue Comrs.*[20]

"There is a complete fallacy in that argument. A resulting trust for the settlor is born and dies without any writing at all. It comes into existence wherever there is a gap in the beneficial ownership. It ceases to exist whenever that gap is filled by someone becoming beneficially entitled. As soon as the gap is filled by the creation or declaration of a valid trust, the resulting trust comes to an end. In this case, before the option was exercised, there was a gap in the beneficial ownership. So there was a resulting trust for Mr. Vandervell. But, as the option was exercised and the shares registered in the trustees' name there was created a valid trust of the shares in favour of the children's settlement. Not being a trust of land, it could be created without any writing. A trust of personalty can be created without writing. Both Mr. Vandervell and the trustee company had done everything which needed to be done to make the settlement of these shares binding on them. So there was a valid trust: see *Milroy* v. *Lord*[21] per Turner L.J.

*The law as to third period*

"The executors admit that from January 19, 1965, Mr. Vandervell had no interest whatsoever in the shares. The deed of that date operated so as to

---

[19] [1960] A.C. 1; [1959] 3 All E.R. 603.
[20] [1960] A.C. 206; [1959] 3 All E.R. 623.
[21] (1862) 4 De G.F. & J. 264, 274; [1861–73] All E.R. Rep. 783, 789.

transfer all his interest thenceforward to the trustee company to be held by them on trust for the children. I asked counsel for the executors: what is the difference between the events of October and November 1961 and the event of January 19, 1965? He said that it lay in the writing. In 1965 Mr. Vandervell disposed of his equitable interest in writing, whereas in 1961 there was no writing. There was only conduct or word of mouth. That was insufficient. And, therefore, his executors were not bound by it.

"The answer to this argument is what I have said. Mr. Vandervell did not dispose in 1961 of any equitable interest. All that happened was that his resulting trust came to an end—because there was created a new valid trust of the shares for the children's settlement.

### Estoppel

"Even if counsel for the executors were right in saying that Mr. Vandervell retained an equitable interest in the shares, after the exercise of the option, the question arises whether Mr. Vandervell can in the circumstances be heard to assert the claim against his children. Just see what happened. He himself arranged for the option to be exercised. He himself agreed to the shares being transferred to the trustee company. He himself procured his products company to declare dividends on the shares and to pay them to the trustee company for the benefit of the children. Thenceforward the trustee company invested the money and treated it as part of the children's settlement. If he himself had lived, and not died, he could not have claimed it back. He could not be heard to say that he did not intend the children's trust to have it. Even a court of equity would not allow him to do anything so inequitable and unjust. Now that he has died, his executors are in no better position. If authority were needed, it is to be found in *Milroy* v. *Lord*.[22] In that case Thomas Medley assigned to Samuel Lord 50 shares in the Bank of Louisiana on trust for his niece; but the shares were not formally transferred into the name of Samuel Lord. The bank, however, paid the dividends to Samuel Lord.[23] He paid them to the niece, and then, at Thomas Medley's suggestion, the niece used those dividends to buy shares in a fire insurance company—taking them in the name of Thomas Medley. After Thomas Medley's death, his executors claimed that the bank shares belonged to them as representing him, and also the fire insurance shares. Knight-Bruce and Turner L.JJ. held that the executors were entitled to the bank shares, because 'there is no equity in this Court to perfect an imperfect gift.' But the executors were not entitled to the fire insurance shares. Turner L.J. said[24]:

> ' . . . the settlor made a perfect gift to [the niece] of the dividends upon these shares, so far as they were handed over or treated by him as belonging to her, and these insurance shares were purchased with dividends which were so handed over or treated.'

"So here Mr. Vandervell made a perfect gift to the trustee company of the dividends on the shares, so far as they were handed over or treated by him as belonging to the trustee company for the benefit of the children. Alternatively, there was an equitable estoppel. His conduct was such that it would be quite

---

[22] 4 De G.F. & J. 264; [1861–73] All E.R.Rep. 783, *infra*, p. 217.
[23] Since he had a power of attorney from Medley authorising him to the dividends.
[24] 4 De G.F. & J. at 277; [1861–73] All E.R.Rep. at 790.

inequitable for him to be allowed to enforce his strict rights (under a resulting trust) having regard to the dealings which had taken place between the parties: see *Hughes* v. *Metropolitan Railway Co.*[25]

"I would allow the appeal and dismiss the claim of the executors."

STEPHENSON L.J.: "I have had more doubt than my brethren whether we can overturn the judgment of Megarry J.[26] in what I have not found an easy case. Indeed, treading a (to me) dark and unfamiliar path, I had parted from both my fellow-travellers and, following the windings of counsel for the executors' argument, had nearly reached a different terminus before the light which they threw on the journey enabled me to join them at the same conclusion.

"To expound my doubts would serve no useful purpose; to state them shortly may do no harm. The cause of all the trouble is what the judge called 'the ill-fated option' and its incorporation in a deed which was 'too short and simple' to rid Mr. Vandervell of the beneficial interest in the disputed shares, as a bare majority of the House of Lords held, not without fluctuation of mind on the part of one of them (Lord Upjohn), in *Vandervell* v. *Inland Revenue Comrs.*[27] The operation of law or equity kept for Mr. Vandervell or gave him back an equitable interest which he did not want and would have thought he had disposed of if he had ever known it existed. It is therefore difficult to infer that he intended to dispose or ever did dispose of something he did not know he had until the judgment of Plowman J. in *Vandervell* v. *Inland Revenue Comrs.*, which led to the deed of 1965, enlightened him, or to find a disposition of it in the exercise by the trustee company in 1961 of its option to purchase the shares. And even if he had disposed of his interest, he did not dispose of it by any writing sufficient to comply with section 53(1)(c) of the Law of Property Act 1925.

"*But Lord Denning M.R. and Lawton L.J. are able to hold that no disposition is needed because (1) the option was held on such trusts as might thereafter be declared by the trustee company or Mr. Vandervell himself, and (2) the trustee company has declared that it holds the shares in the children's settlement.*[28] I do not doubt the first, because it was apparently the view of the majority of the House of Lords in *Vandervell* v. *Inland Revenue Comrs.* I should be more confident of the second if it had been pleaded or argued either here or below and we had had the benefit of the learned judge's views on it. I see, as perhaps did counsel, difficulties in the way of a limited company declaring a trust by parol or conduct and without a resolution of the board of directors, and difficulties also in the way of finding any declaration of trust by Mr. Vandervell himself in October or November 1961, or any conduct then or later which would in law or equity estop him from denying that he made one.

"However, Lord Denning M.R. and Lawton L.J. are of the opinion that these difficulties, if not imaginary, are not insuperable and that these shares went into the children's settlement in 1961 in accordance with the intention of Mr. Vandervell and the trustee company—a result with which I am happy to agree as it seems to me to be in accordance with the justice and the reality of the case."

---

[25] (1877) 2 App.Cas. 439, 448.
[26] [1973] 3 W.L.R. 744; [1974] 1 All E.R. 47.
[27] [1967] 2 A.C. 291; [1967] 1 All E.R. 1.
[28] Editor's italics.

Lawton L.J. began with the point that it was the late Mr. Vander-vell's intention that the trustee company should hold the option on such trusts as might thereafter be declared by the trustee company or Mr. Vandervell himself and held that the trustee company declared trusts for the children in 1961. He also held that Mr. Vandervell was estopped from denying the existence of a beneficial interest for his children.

He went on to create a most unlawyerlike distinction between the option held on a resulting trust and the shares acquired upon exercising the option: he took the view that after the option had been exercised it had been extinguished, so no old equitable interest existed to be capable of assignment, so that only new equitable interests could be created! However, the option is not distinct from the shares but merely a limited right created out of the larger bundle of rights inherent in the ownership of the shares. For this very reason the House of Lords in *Vandervell* v. *I.R.C.* had held that Vandervell, the original beneficial owner of the shares, who had remained beneficial owner under a resulting trust of the option relating to the shares, had failed to divest himself absolutely of the shares which the option governed. If the right to the shares under the option was held by the trustee company under a resulting trust for Vandervell then any shares actually acquired by exercising the right should surely be similarly held under a resulting trust.

### PASCOE v. TURNER

Court of Appeal [1979] 1 W.L.R. 431; [1979] 2 All E.R. 945 (Orr, Lawton and Cumming-Bruce L.JJ.)

The plaintiff and defendant lived together for 10 years as man and wife in the plaintiff's house. In 1973 the plaintiff left the defendant and moved in with another woman nearby. He told the defendant more than once "The house is yours and everything in it." The defendant stayed on in what she now believed to be her house and spent a substantial part of her small capital on repairs and improvements. In 1976 the plaintiff sought to regain the house and its contents.

CUMMING-BRUCE L.J. [in the reserved judgment of the Court first held there had been a valid gift of the contents]: " . . . Her rights in realty are not quite so simply disposed of because of sections 53 and 54 of the Law of Property Act 1925. There was nothing in writing. The judge considered the plaintiff's declarations, and decided that they were not enough to found an express trust. We agree. But he went on to hold that the beneficial interest in the house had passed under a constructive trust inferred from words and conduct of the parties. He relied on the passage in *Snell on Equity*[29] in which the learned editors suggest a possible definition of a constructive trust. But there are difficulties in the way. The long and short of the events in 1973 is that

---

[29] (27th ed., 1973), p. 185.

the plaintiff made an imperfect gift of the house. There is nothing in the facts from which an inference of a constructive trust can be drawn. If it had not been for section 53 of the 1925 Act the gift of the house would have been a perfect gift, just as the gift of the contents was a perfect gift. In the event it remained an imperfect gift and, as Turner L.J. said in *Milroy* v. *Lord*,[30] 'there is no equity in this Court to perfect an imperfect gift.' So matters stood in 1973, and if the facts had stopped there the defendant would have remained a licensee at the will of the plaintiff.

"But the facts did not stop there. On the judge's findings the defendant, having been told that the house was hers, set about improving it within and without. Outside she did not do much: a little work on the roof and an improvement which covered the way from the outside toilet to the rest of the house, putting a new door there, and Snowcem to protect the toilet. Inside she did a good deal more. She installed gas in the kitchen with a cooker, improved the plumbing in the kitchen and put in a new sink. She got new gas fires, putting a gas fire in the lounge. She redecorated four rooms. The fitted carpets she put in the bedrooms, the stair carpeting, and the curtains and the futniture that she bought are not part of the realty, and it is not clear how much she spent on those items. But they are part of the whole circumstances. There she was, on her own after he left her in 1973. She had £1,000 left of her capital, and a pension of some kind. Having as she thought been given the house, she set about it as described. On the repairs and improvement to the realty and its fixtures she spent about £230. She had £300 of her capital left by the date of the trial, but she did not establish in evidence how much had been expended on refurbishing the house with carpets, curtains and furniture. We would describe the work done in and about the house as substantial in the sense that that adjective is used in the context of estoppel. All the while the plaintiff not only stood by and watched but encouraged and advised, without a word to suggest that she was putting her money and her personal labour into his house. What is the effect in equity?

"The cases relied on by the plaintiff are relevant for the purpose of showing that the judge fell into error in deciding that on the facts a constructive trust could be inferred. They are the cases which deal with the intention of the parties when a house is acquired. But of those cases only *Inwards* v. *Baker*[31] is in point here. For this is a case of estoppel arising from the encouragement and acquiescence of the plaintiff between 1973 and 1976 when, in reliance on his declaration that he was giving and, later, that he had given the house to her, she spent a substantial part of her small capital on repairs and improvements to the house. The relevant principle is expounded in *Snell on Equity*[32] in the passage under the heading 'Proprietary Estoppel,' and is elaborated in Spencer Bower and Turner on *Estoppel by Representation*[33] in the chapter entitled 'Encouragement and Acquiescence.' The cases in point illustrating that principle in relation to real property are *Dillwyn* v. *Llewelyn*,[34] *Ramsden* v. *Dyson*[35] and *Plimmer* v. *Mayor of Wellington*.[36] One distinction between this

---

[30] (1862) 4 De G.F. & J. 264 at 274; [1861–73] All E.R. Rep. 783 at 789.
[31] [1965] 2 Q.B. 29; [1965] 1 All E.R. 446.
[32] (27th ed., 1973), pp. 565–568.
[33] (3rd ed., 1977), Chap. 12, p. 283.
[34] (1862) 4 De G.F. & J. 517; [1861–73] All E.R. Rep. 384.
[35] (1866) L.R. 1 H.L. 129.
[36] (1884) 9 App.Cas. 699; [1881–85] All E.R. Rep. 1320.

class of case and the doctrine which has come to be known as 'promissory estoppel' is that where estoppel by encouragement or acquiescence is found on the facts those facts give rise to a cause of action. They may be relied on as a sword, not merely as a shield. In *Ramsden* v. *Dyson* the plaintiff failed on the facts, and the dissent of Lord Kingsdown was on the inferences to be drawn from the facts. On the principle, however, the House was agreed, and it is stated by Lord Cranworth L.C. and by Lord Wensleydale as well as by Lord Kingsdown. Likewise in *Plimmer's* case the plaintiff was granted a declaration that he had a perpetual right of occupation.

" . . . In *Plimmer's* case[37] the Privy Council posed the question, 'How should the equity be satisfied?' And the Board declared that on the facts a licence revocable at will become irrevocable as a consequence of the subsequent transactions. So in *Thomas* v. *Thomas*[38] the Supreme Court of New Zealand ordered the defendant to execute a proper transfer of the property.

"In *Crabb* v. *Arun District Council*[39] this court had to consider the principles on which the court should give effect to the equity: see *per* Lord Denning M.R.[40] Lawton and Scarman L.JJ. agreed with the remedy proposed by Lord Denning M.R. On the facts of that case Scarman L.J. expressed himself thus[41]:

'I turn now to the other two questions—the extent of the equity and the relief needed to satisfy it. There being no grant, no enforceable contract, no licence, I would analyse the minimum equity to do justice to the plaintiff as a right either to an easement or to a licence on terms to be agreed. I do not think it is necessary to go further than that. Of course, going that far would support the equitable remedy of injunction which is sought in this action. If there is no agreement as to terms, if agreement fails to be obtained, the court can, in my judgment, and must, determine in these proceedings on what terms the plaintiff should be put to enable him to have the benefit of the equitable right which is held to have. It is interesting that there has been some doubt amongst distinguished lawyers in the past as to whether the court can so proceed. Lord Kingsdown refers to those doubts in a passage, which I need not quote, in *Ramsden* v. *Dyson*.[42] Lord Thurlow clearly thought that the court did have this power. Other lawyers of that time did not. But there can be no doubt that since *Ramsden* v. *Dyson*[43] the courts have acted on the basis that they have to determine not only the extent of equity, but also the conditions necessary to satisfy it, and they have done so in a great number and variety of cases. I need refer only to the interesting collection of cases enumerated in *Snell on Equity*.[44] In the present case the court does have to consider what is necessary now in order to satisfy the plaintiff's equity.'

"So the principle to be applied is that the court should consider all the circumstances and, the counterclaimant having at law no perfected gift or licence other than a licence revocable at will, the court must decide what is the

---

[37] (1884) 9 App.Cas. 699; [1881–85] All E.R. Rep. 1320.
[38] [1957] N.Z.L.R. 785.
[39] [1976] Ch. 179; [1975] 3 All E.R. 865.
[40] [1976] Ch. 179 at 189; [1975] 3 All E.R. 865 at 872.
[41] [1976] Ch. 179 at 198–199; [1975] 3 All E.R. 865 at 880.
[42] (1866) L.R. 1 H.L. 129 at 171.
[43] (1866) L.R. 1 H.L. 129.
[44] (27th ed., 1973), pp. 567–568, para. 2(b).

minimum equity to do justice to her having regard to the way in which she changed her position for the worse by reason of the acquiescence and encouragement of the legal owner. The defendant submits that the only appropriate way in which the equity can here be satisfied is by perfecting the imperfect gift as was done in *Dillwyn* v. *Llewelyn*.[45]

"Counsel for the plaintiff on instructions has throughout submitted that the plaintiff is entitled to possession. . . . He made no submission on the way the equity, if there was an equity, should be satisfied save to submit that the court should not in any view grant a remedy more beneficial to the defendant than a licence to occupy the house for her lifetime.

"We are satisfied that the problem of remedy on the facts resolves itself into a choice between two alternatives: should the equity be satisfied by a licence to the defendant to occupy the house for her lifetime or should there be a transfer to her of the fee simple?

"The main consideration pointing to a licence for her lifetime is that she did not by her case at the hearing seek to establish that she had spent more money or done more work on the house than she would have done had she believed that she had only a licence to live there for her lifetime. But the court must be cautious about drawing any inference from what she did not give in evidence as the hypothesis put is one that manifestly never occurred to her. Then it may be reasonably held that her expenditure and effort can hardly be regarded as comparable to the change of position of those who have constructed buildings on land over which they had no legal rights.

"This court appreciates that the moneys laid out by the defendant were much less than in some of the cases in the books. But the court has to look at all the circumstances. When the plaintiff left her she was, we were told, a widow in her middle fifties. During the period that she lived with the plaintiff her capital was reduced from £4,500 to £1,000. Save for her invalidity pension that was all she had in the world. In reliance on the plaintiff's declaration of gift, encouragement and acquiescence she arranged her affairs on the basis that the house and contents belonged to her. So relying, she devoted a quarter of her remaining capital and her personal effort on the house and its fixtures. In addition she bought carpets, curtains and furniture for it, with the result that by the date of the trial she had only £300 left. Compared to her, on the evidence, the plaintiff is a rich man. He might not regard an expenditure of a few hundred pounds as a very grave loss. But the court has to regard her change of position over the years 1973 to 1976.

"We take the view that the equity cannot here be satisfied without granting a remedy which assures to the defendant security of tenure, quiet enjoyment and freedom of action in respect of repairs and improvements without interference from the plaintiff. The history of the conduct of the plaintiff since 9th April 1976 in relation to these proceedings leads to an irresistible inference that he is determined to pursue his purpose of evicting her from the house by any legal means at his disposal with a ruthless disregard of the obligations binding on conscience. The court must grant a remedy effective to protect her against the future manifestations of his ruthlessness. It was conceded that if she is granted a licence, such a licence cannot be registered as a land charge, so that she may find herself ousted by a purchaser for value without notice. If she has in the future to do further and more expensive repairs she may only be able to

---

[45] (1862) 4 De G.F. & J. 517; [1861–73] All E.R. Rep. 384.

finance them by a loan, but as a licensee she cannot charge the house. The plaintiff as legal owner may well find excuse for entry in order to do what he may plausibly represent as necessary works and so contrive to derogate from her enjoyment of the licence in ways that make it difficult or impossible for the court to give her effective protection.

"Weighing such considerations this court concludes that the equity to which the facts in this case give rise can only be satisfied by compelling the plaintiff to give effect to his promise and her expectations. He has so acted that he must now perfect the gift. . . .

"The plaintiff is ordered to execute a conveyance forthwith at his expense transferring the estate to the defendant." *Appeal dismissed.*

## B. GREEN (1984) 47 M.L.R. 418

"Lord Denning isolated estoppel as a basis for his decision quite separate to the declaration of new trusts ground upon which he primarily founded himself: but then complicated the picture by (i) intertwining his 'estoppel' reasoning with the 'perfect gift' approach of Turner L.J. in relation to the Louisiana Bank shares' dividends in *Milroy* v. *Lord*[46] and (ii) citing as his 'estoppel' authority *Hughes* v. *Metropolitan Railway*.[47] Lawton L.J., on the other hand, concertinaed the declaration of new trusts and estoppel arguments; and it is not clear whether in his judgment it was V's procurement of the payment of the second phase dividends or his wilful agreement to V.T.'s exercise of the option using children's settlement monies, or both factors, which achieved the estoppel result. Both judgments ignored the question of whether V (and hence his executors) were merely estopped in respect of recovery of the second phase dividends or whether estoppel extended to recovery of the shares on which the dividends had been declared as well, no doubt since that question had become otiose since V's execution of his stage (10) assignment and release upon which the second phase had terminated.

"The estoppel raised by the majority was, despite the misleading citation of *Hughes*, 'estoppel by encouragement'[48]: a genus of what is today increasingly referred to, along with the related doctrine of 'estoppel by acquiescence,' by the blanket term 'proprietary estoppel.' The difficulty here is not so much seeing how an 'estoppel by encouragement' might be made out on the facts of *Vandervell (No. 2)*, but rather as to how it could be said that the 'minimum equity' necessary to satisfy the objects of the children's settlement involved the retention of the £770,000 dividends appropriated on their behalf by V.T. It is

---

[46] (1862) 2 De G.F. & J. 264. The shares could only be transferred by complying with all due forms, but there was no such obstacle to a gift of the money dividends arising on the shares where the donor was *not* merely entitled to those dividends in equity. Had Thomas Medley only been entitled to the dividends in equity, s.9 of the Statute of Frauds 1677 would have been just as great a problem to him as was s.53(1)(c) to V. Lord Denning's use of *Milroy* v. *Lord* in the present connection begs precisely the same question as does Lord Wilberforce in *Vandervell* v. *I.R.C.* where he adopts Jenkins J. in *Re Rose*: see p. 72, *supra*, n. 9.

[47] (1877) 2 App.Cas. 439. The root authority on the waiver of contractual rights doctrine of promissory estoppel: generally seen as unconnected with the present subject-matter. (Although see the wicked treatment of this area by Robert Goff J. in *Amalgamated Investment & Property Co. Ltd.* v. *Texas Commerce International Bank Ltd.* [1981] 1 All E.R. 923, which was too much even for Lord Denning's wholesale adoption when that case reached the Court of Appeal: [1981] 3 All E.R. 577).

[48] The majority cast V in an active role: he is not alleged to have simply acquiesced but positively to have encouraged: see [1974] Ch. 269, 321A–B and 325G; *per* Denning and Lawton L.JJ. respectively.

clear that proprietary estoppels can be raised in respect of personalty just as in respect of realty.[49] Furthermore, even though it may not have been generally perceived in 1974,[50] it has now been convincingly established[51] that (whatever may be the position in regard to 'acquiescence'[52]) neither principle nor previous authority requires the person estopped in an 'encouragement' case to have known of his legal right inconsistent to that on the faith of which the person seeking to raise an equity against him acted to his detriment. And the children's settlement had incurred a certain detriment in reliance on V's encouragement, since on such facts as were emergent V.T. had considered itself honour bound to follow V's wishes and it was V's wish (on the advice of his legal advisers) that the children's settlement should exercise the option with its own monies. But even if V's encouragement of V.T.'s actions for and on behalf of the children's settlement was theoretically capable of grounding an estoppel despite V's lack of knowledge of his true rights at all material times, it is impossible to see how the comparatively trivial estoppel thereby entailed could conceivably justify the children's settlement's retention of over £¾ million. Under normal conditions it would require deeply unconscientious behaviour by a representor, which had induced an extremely substantial (if not wholly proportionate) irreversible act of detriment on the part of a representee to raise an equity of that extent.

"Yet when one searches for the villain in V, one finds an innocent. As for substantial detriment, there was no evidence whatsoever that the children's settlement had changed its position at all in the face of V's encouragement, beyond expending £5,000 in exercise of the option in the first place. The £770,000 dividends had simply been credited to the children's settlement's account, none of it had been distributed, let alone dissipated, on an assumption that V.T. was entitled to deal with it as part of the children's fund.[53] Nor does it even appear that the mechanism of estoppel was, on the facts, necessary to do justice to the objects of the children's settlement at all. The £5,000 could easily have been ordered to be repaid (with interest) by V's executors as a condition of the payment over of the dividends (with interest) to them.[54]

"The only party to the second phase transactions who had actually acted to his detriment in reliance on the property and future legal defensibility of V.T. holding the £770,000 as an accretion to the children's settlement trust fund, was V himself. He had assumed that he had adequately provided for his children *inter vivos*, and hence cut them out of his will: an act of detrimental reliance rendered irreversible by his death. One is left with the impression that

---

[49] See, *e.g. Falcke* v. *Scottish Imperial Insurance Co.* (1886) 34 Ch.D. 234.

[50] See Megarry J. in *Vandervell (No. 2)* at first instance [1974] Ch. 269, 301B espousing the conventional assumption in this regard.

[51] By Oliver J. in *Taylor Fashions Ltd.* v. *Liverpool Victoria Trustees Co. Ltd.* [1981] 1 All E.R. 897 pointing up the divergences between Cranworth L.C. and Lord Westbury in *Ramsden* v. *Dyson* (1866) L.R. 1 H.L. 129: a distinction obscured by the accessible "five probanda" of Fry J. in *Wilmot* v. *Barber* (1880) 15 Ch.D. 96, 105–106, too easily cited as a substitute for analysis for too long.

[52] Where arguably *Wilmot* v. *Barber* (1880) 15 Ch.D. 96 stands. Had V merely "acquiesced," probandum number 4 would have prevented an estoppel being raised against him as one mistaken as to his legal rights. A mistake of secondary fact, not law: *cf. Cooper* v. *Phibbs* (1867) L.R. 2 H.L. 149.

[53] *Per* Megarry J. in *Vandervell (No. 2)* at first instance: [1974] Ch. 269, 301F–G.

[54] Which is to cast *Vandervell (No. 2)* as the "trust unravelling" case it essentially should have been; with the children's settlement obtaining restitution of its £5,000 as money paid under a mistake of fact as to what it would be getting for it: *cf. Cooper* v. *Phibbs* (1867) L.R. 2 H.L. 149.

it was V's reliance on his own mistaken belief that he had successfully vested beneficial entitlement to the dividends in the children's settlement which was the real and substantial basis for raising an equity against his executors: which makes V the only person in English law ever to have stood in the shoes of both 'estopped' and 'estopper' at one and the same time."

## QUESTIONS

1. T1 and T2 hold property on trust for X. What formalities are required if:

   (i) X assigns his equitable interest to Y or to A and B on trust for Y;
  (ii) X directs T1 and T2 to hold the property on trust for Y;
 (iii) X contracts with Y to transfer his equitable interest to him;
  (iv) X declares himself a trustee of his interest for Y;
   (v) X declares himself trustee of his interest for himself for life, remainder for Y absolutely;
  (vi) X directs T1 and T2 to transfer the property to P and Q on trust for Y; what should T1 and T2 do if X died or revoked his direction before T1 and T2 had transferred the legal title?
 (vii) X directs T1 and T2 that they henceforth have power to appoint the property to such of Y, his spouse and issue as they may see fit, and a month later T1 and T2 declare they therefore hold the property on trust for Y for life, remainder to his children equally.

Does it matter if the property is land or personalty? Does it matter if the property were held on resulting trust for X?

2. All Heels' College, Durham, to which Archibald Alumnus who has just died has left all his property by will, seeks your advice on the property to which it is entitled.

On February 1, 1991 Archibald did three things:

   (i) he transferred £25,000 from his bank account into the bank account of Roger Randall;
  (ii) he executed a share transfer of his 15,000 shares in Up and Down Ltd. in favour of Simon Sharp, who in due course became registered owner of the shares;
 (iii) for no consideration he conveyed his holiday cottage, Tree-Tops, to Theodore Thin for an estate in fee simple in possession.

On March 1, Archibald orally stated, "I declare that I hold my interest in the £25,000, which I recently transferred into Roger Randall's name, upon trust for my two adult children in equal shares."

On April 1, by unsigned writing Archibald directed Simon to hold half the Up and Down Ltd. shares upon trust for Gay Gibson and to transfer the other half into the name of Maud Molesworth legally and beneficially, which Simon duly did.

As far as Tree-Tops is concerned there is cogent evidence that prior to the execution of the conveyance Theodore had orally agreed with Archibald to hold it upon trust for Wendy Williams.

3. The effect of the decision in *Pascoe* v. *Turner* was to place the plaintiff under a duty to convey the house to the defendant so that he held it on constructive trust for her. Thus the court was misguided in purporting to draw a distinction between a constructive trust and an interest arising under a proprietary estoppel unless it was merely implicitly concerned with the

distinction between bilateral common intention constructive trusts and unilateral estoppels which now seems illusory. Discuss in the light of Chap. 7
section 3.

## Section 2. Post Mortem Trusts: Secret Trusts

### I. GENERAL

The doctrine of secret trusts[55] is a product of equity not allowing
statutes to be used as an instrument of fraud.[56] It will already have
been seen that statutes prescribe certain formalities for declarations of
trust respecting land and for dispositions of equitable interests.[57] In
addition, section 9 of the Wills Act 1837 prescribes special formalities
for the validity of testamentary dispositions whilst the Administration
of Estates Act 1925 lays down rules of intestate succession. All too
often a person might be induced to die intestate leaving X as his
intestate successor[58] or to leave property by will to X on the secret oral
understanding that X was to hold the property he received on trust for
B. If X were allowed to retain the property beneficially, instead of
taking merely as trustee, then this would be allowing statutes to be
used as an instrument of fraud by X. Accordingly, equity treats X as a
trustee despite the absence of the requisite formalities.

Secret trusts most commonly concern trusts engrafted on wills and in
this context it is most important to distinguish between (1) fully secret
trusts, (2) half-secret trusts, and (3) cases where the probate doctrine
of incorporation by reference arises. Respective examples (where X
has agreed to hold on trust for B) are (1) I devise Blackacre to X
absolutely (2) I devise Blackacre to X upon trusts which I have
communicated to him and (3) I devise Blackacre to X upon trusts
which I communicated to him by letter dated November 11, 1990.
In this last example since the will refers to a written instrument,
already existing at the date of the will, in such terms that the written
instrument can be ascertained, the requirements of the doctrine of
incorporation are satisfied[59] so that the incorporated document is
admitted to probate as part of the testator's will, the will's compliance
with the requirements of section 9 of the Wills Act being sufficient to
cover the unattested written instrument referred to in the will. It will
be seen that the application of the doctrine of incorporation renders
the imposition of a secret trust unnecessary as the requisite formalities
for an express trust are present, preventing any possibility of fraud
upon X's part.

Testators, today, who do not want their testamentary wishes to
become public by admission to probate as part of their will can take

---

[55] A. J. Oakley's *Constructive Trusts*, Chap. 5.
[56] *McCormick* v. *Grogan* (1869) L.R. 4 H.L. 82, 88–89; *Blackwell* v. *Blackwell* [1929] A.C. 318,
   *infra*, p. 94; *Jones* v. *Badley* (1868) 3 Ch.App. 362, 364.
[57] Law of Property Act 1925, s.53, *supra*, pp. 53–55.
[58] *Sellack* v. *Harris* (1708) 2 Eq.Ca.Ab. 46.
[59] *In the goods of Smart* [1902] P. 238; *Re Jones* [1942] Ch. 328, restricted by *Re Edwards W.T.* [1948]
   Ch. 440.

advantage of the doctrine of secret trusts to make provision for mistresses, illegitimate children, relatives whom they do not wish to appear to be helping or organisations which they do not wish to appear to be helping. Indecisive, aged testators can also leave everything by will absolutely to their solicitors, from time to time calling upon or phoning their solicitors with their latest wishes.

Proving secret trusts can be a problem, though the standard of proof is the ordinary civil standard on a balance of probabilities unless fraud is involved when a higher standard is required.[60] A good practical precaution is for the testator to have a document signed by the intended trustee put into the possession of the secret beneficiaries.

## II. FULLY SECRET TRUSTS

A fully secret trust is one where neither the existence of the trust nor its terms are disclosed by the will.[61]

If a testator makes a valid will bequeathing or devising property to X, apparently beneficially, and communicates to X his intention that X is to hold the property on certain trusts or subject to certain conditions or charges, which X accepts either expressly by promise or impliedly by silence, oral evidence is admissible to prove both the existence and the terms of the trust or conditions or charges which, if clearly proved, X will be compelled to carry out: *Ottaway* v. *Norman, infra*. Nothing short of an express or implied acceptance by X will raise a trust (or condition or charge): *Wallgrave* v. *Tebbs, infra*. Communication and acceptance must be of a definite obligation, not of a mere hope or confidence expressed by the testator.[62] Communication and acceptance[63] may be effected at any time during the life of the testator, whether before or after the execution of the will and communication may be made through an agent.[64] It may also be made by handing to X a sealed envelope containing the terms of the trust, and requiring X not to open it until after the testator's death: *Re Keen, infra*. If X is told in the testator's lifetime that he is to hold the property on trust, but is not informed of the terms of the trust, he holds the property on a resulting trust for the testator's residuary legatee or devisee, or if there is no such person, or the property is residuary property, then for

---

[60] *Re Snowden* [1979] 2 All E.R. 172, 179, but if P has proved intent to create a trust on a balance of probabilities is it not illogical to require a higher standard of proof if the legatee is alleged to be fraudulent—see [1979] C.L.J. 260 (C. Rickett).

[61] It can also arise in cases of intestacy: *Sellack* v. *Harris* (1708) 2 Eq.Ca.Ab. 46.

[62] See *Att.-Gen.* v. *Chamberlain* (1904) 90 L.T. 581; *Re Snowden* [1979] 2 All E.R. 172. Whether the obligation is technically a trust or a condition or a charge (see p. 119, *infra*) it seems that equity will intervene.

[63] The full extent of the property to be covered by the obligation must be communicated and accepted so that where a secret trust for a £5,000 legacy has been communicated to and accepted by the trustee and the legacy is increased by £5,000 in a further codicil but nothing said to the trustee the further £5,000 is not caught by the secret trust: *Re Colin Cooper* [1939] Ch. 580 and 811. The further £5,000 is taken beneficially by the fully secret "trustee."

[64] *Moss* v. *Cooper* (1861) 1 J. & H. 352. If the agent were unauthorised but the legatee did not approach the testator to clarify the matter would this amount to acquiescence?

the testator's intestate successors[65]: *Re Boyes*.[66] If X is not so told he takes the property beneficially as is also the case if X is told that he is to take the property subject to a condition or charge but is not informed of the terms of the condition or charge.

## The Wills Act 1837

*Section 9.*[67] "No will shall be valid unless—

(*a*) it is in writing, and signed by the testator, or by some other person in his presence and by his direction; and

(*b*) it appears that the testator intended by his signature to give effect to the will; and

(*c*) the signature is made or acknowledged by the testator in the presence of two or more witnesses present at the same time; and

(*d*) each witness either—

    (i) attests and signs the will; or

    (ii) acknowledges his signature, in the presence of the testator (but not necessarily in the presence of any other witness),

but no form of attestation shall be necessary."

## OTTAWAY v. NORMAN

Chancery Division [1972] Ch. 698; [1972] 2 W.L.R. 50; [1971] 3 All E.R. 1325

A testator, Harry Ottaway, by will devised his bungalow (with fixtures, fittings and furniture) to his housekeeper Miss Hodges in fee simple and gave her a legacy of £1,500 and half the residue of his estate. It was alleged that Miss Hodges had orally agreed with the testator to leave the bungalow, etc., by her will to the plaintiffs, who were the testator's son and daughter-in-law, Mr. and Mrs. William Ottaway, and that she had also orally agreed to leave to them whatever money was left at her death. By her will Miss Hodges left all her property away from the plaintiffs, who thus brought an action against Miss Hodges' executor, Mr. Norman, for a declaration that the appropriate parts of Miss Hodges' estate were held by him on trust for the plaintiffs.

Brightman J. upheld the plaintiffs' claim except in respect of the moneys.

BRIGHTMAN J.: ". . . It will be convenient to call the person on whom such a trust is imposed the 'primary donee' and the beneficiary under that trust the 'secondary donee.' The essential elements which must be proved are: (i) the intention of the testator to subject the primary donee to an obligation in favour of the secondary donee; (ii) communication of that intention to the primary

---

[65] If X himself is the residuary beneficiary or next-of-kin it seems the court should not impose an arbitrary salutary rule removing all temptation to make self-serving statements by prohibiting X from taking *qua* residuary beneficiary or next-of-kin. Only if X appeared to be lying and it was impossible to ascertain the trust terms should public policy prevent X from obtaining any advantage from his own wrong and pass the property to the person who would have taken under the intestacy rules if X had not survived the testator; *cf. Re Sigsworth* [1935] Ch. 89.

[66] (1884) 26 Ch.D. 531.

[67] Superseding the Statute of Frauds 1677, s.5 and itself substituted by Administration of Justice Act 1982, s.17.

donee; and (iii) the acceptance of that obligation by the primary donee either expressly or by acquiescence. It is immaterial whether these elements precede or succeed the will of the donor. I am informed that there is no recent reported case where the obligation imposed on the primary donee is an obligation to make a will in favour of the secondary donee as distinct from some form of *inter vivos* transfer. But it does not seem to me that that can really be a distinction which can validly be drawn on behalf of the defendant in the present case. The basis of the doctrine of a secret trust is the obligation imposed on the conscience of the primary donee and it does not seem to me that there is any materiality in the machinery by which the donor intends that that obligation shall be carried out. . . .

"Counsel for the defendant sought at one stage to deploy an argument that a person could never succeed in establishing a secret trust unless he could show that the primary donee was guilty of deliberate and conscious wrong doing of which he said there was no evidence in the case before me. That proposition, if correct, would lead to the surprising result that if the primary donee faithfully observed the obligation imposed on him there would not ever have been a trust at any time in existence. The argument was discarded and I think rightly. Counsel then fastened on the words 'clearest and most indisputable evidence' and he submitted that an exceptionally high standard of proof was needed to establish a secret trust. I do not think that Lord Westbury's words mean more than this: that if a will contains a gift which is in terms absolute, clear evidence is needed before the court will assume that the testator did not mean what he said. It is perhaps analogous to the standard of proof which this court requires before it will rectify a written instrument, for there again a party is saying that neither meant what they have written.[68]

"I find as a fact that Harry Ottaway intended that Miss Hodges should be obliged to dispose of the bungalow in favour of the plaintiffs at her death, that he communicated that intention to Miss Hodges and that Miss Hodges accepted the obligation. I find the same facts in relation to the furniture, fixtures and fittings which passed to Miss Hodges under clause 4 of Harry Ottaway's will. I am not satisfied that any similar obligation was imposed and accepted as regards any contents of the bungalow which had not devolved on Miss Hodges under clause 4 of Harry Ottaway's will.

"I turn to the question of money. In cross-examination William Ottaway said the trust extended to the house, furniture and money:

> 'Everything my father left to Miss Hodges was to be in the trust. The trust comprised the lot. She could use the money as she liked. She had to leave my wife and me whatever money was left.'

In cross-examination Mrs. Ottaway said that her understanding was that Miss Hodges was bound to make a will giving her and her husband the bungalow, contents and any money she had left. 'She could please herself about the money. She did not have to save it for us. She was free to spend it.' It seems to me that two questions arise. First as a matter of fact what did the parties intend should be comprised in Miss Hodges's obligation? All money which Miss Hodges had at her death, including money which she had acquired before

---

[68] Now see *Re Snowden* [1979] 2 All E.R. 172, 179 applying the ordinary standard unless fraud is involved but if P has proved intent to create a trust on a balance of probabilities why require a higher standard if the legatee is also fraudulent? See C. Rickett [1979] C.L.J. 260.

Harry's death and money she acquired after his death from all sources? Or, only money acquired under Harry's will? Secondly, if such an obligation existed would it as a matter of law create a valid trust? On the second question I am content to assume for present purposes but without so deciding that if property is given to the primary donee on the understanding that the primary donee will dispose by his will of such assets, if any, as he may have at his command at his death in favour of the secondary donee, a valid trust is created in favour of the secondary donee which is in suspense during the lifetime of the primary donee, but attaches to the estate of the primary donee at the moment of the latter's death. There would seem to be at least some support for this proposition in an Australian case to which I was referred: *Birmingham* v. *Renfrew*.[69] I accept that the parties mentioned money on at least some occasions when they talked about Harry Ottaway's intentions for the future disposition of Ashcroft. I do not, however, find sufficient evidence that it was Harry Ottaway's intention that Miss Hodges should be compelled to leave all her money, from whatever source derived, to the plaintiffs. This would seem to preclude her giving even a small pecuniary legacy to any friend or relative. I do no think it is clear that Harry Ottaway intended to extract any such far-reaching undertaking from Miss Hodges or that she intended to accept such a wide obligation herself. Therefore the obligation, if any, is in my view to be confined to money derived under Harry Ottaway's will. If the obligation is confined to money derived under Harry Ottaway's will, the obligation is meaningless and unworkable unless it includes the requirement that she shall keep such money separate and distinct from her own money. I am certain that no such requirement was ever discussed or intended. If she had the right to mingle her own money with that derived from Harry, there would be no ascertainable property on which the trust could bite at her death. This aspect distinguishes this case from *Re Gardner*.[70]

"There is another difficulty. Does money in this context include only cash or cash and investments, or all moveable property of any description? The evidence is quite inconclusive. In my judgment the plaintiff's claim succeeds in relation to the bungalow and in relation to the furniture, fixtures and fittings which devolved under clause 4 of Harry Ottaway's will subject, of course, to normal wastage and fair wear and tear, but not to any other assets."

## WALLGRAVE v. TEBBS

Vice-Chancellor (1855) 2 K. & J. 313; 25 L.J.Ch. 241; 26 L.T.(o.s.) 147; 20 J.P. 84; 4 W.R. 194; 2 Jur. 83

A testator bequeathed to the defendants, Mr. Tebbs and Mr. Martin, a legacy of £12,000 as joint tenants, and also devised some freehold properties in Chelsea and a field at Earls Court "unto and to the use of Tebbs and Martin, their heirs and assigns, for ever, as joint tenants." There was oral and written evidence that the testator wanted such property used by them for purposes that contravened the Statute of Mortmain. However they knew nothing of this until after his death. They admitted that it would be proper for them to make use of the property in a manner consistent with the motives which had induced the testator to leave the property to them, but claimed to be entitled in law to hold it beneficially.

---

69 (1937) 57 C.L.R. 666, p. 110, *infra*.
70 [1920] 2 Ch. 523; [1920] All E.R.Rep. 723.

The plaintiffs (residuary beneficiaries) unsuccessfully claimed that a secret trust had been created which was rendered void by the Statute of Mortmain.

WOOD V.-C.: " . . . Where a person, knowing that a testator in making a disposition in his favour intends it to be applied for purposes other than his own benefit, either *expressly promises*, or *by silence implies*, that he will carry the testator's intention into effect, and the property is left to him *upon the faith of that promise or undertaking*, it is in effect a case of trust; and, in such a case, the court will not allow the devisee to set up the Statute of Frauds—or rather the Statute of Wills, by which the Statute of Frauds is now, in this respect, superseded; and for this reason: the devisee by his conduct has induced the testator to leave him the property; and, as Turner L.J. says in *Russell* v. *Jackson*,[71] no one can doubt, that, if the devisee had stated that he would not carry into effect the intentions of the testator, the disposition in his favour would not have been found in the will. But in this the court does not violate the spirit of the statute: but for the same end, namely, prevention of fraud, it engrafts the trust on the devise, by admitting evidence which the statute would in terms exclude, in order to prevent a party from applying property to a purpose foreign to that for which he undertook to hold it.

"But the question here is totally different. Here there has been no such promise or undertaking on the part of the devisees. Here the devisees knew nothing of the testator's intention until after his death. That the testator desired, and was most anxious to have, his intentions carried out is clear. But, it is equally clear, that he has suppressed everything illegal. He has abstained from creating, either by his will or otherwise, any trust upon which this court can possibly fix. Upon the face of the will, the parties take indisputably for their own benefit. Can I possibly hold that the gift is void? If I knew perfectly well that a testator in making me a bequest, absolute on the face of the will, intended it to be applied for the benefit of a natural child, of whom he was not known to be the father, provided that intention *had not been communicated to me during the testator's life*, the validity of the bequests as an absolute bequest to me could not be questioned.

"In the present case there is no trust created. It is impossible for the court to look upon a document which is excluded by the Statute [of Wills]; and, such evidence being excluded, the case is reduced to one in which the testator has relied solely on the honour of the devisees, who, as far as this court is concerned, are left perfectly at liberty to apply to their own purposes. . . .

"Upon the face of this will the devisees are entitled to the property in question for their own absolute benefit. The statute prevents the court from looking at the paper-writing in which the testator's intentions are expressed; and the parties seeking to avoid the devise have failed to show that during the testator's lifetime, there was any bargain or understanding between the testator and the devisees, or any communication which could be construed into a trust, that they would apply the property in such a manner as to carry the testator's intentions into effect. The devise, therefore, is a valid devise, and the bill must be dismissed."

## III. HALF-SECRET TRUSTS

A half-secret trust is one where the existence of the trust is disclosed by the will but the terms are not.

---

[71] (1852) 10 Hare 204, 211.

If a testator makes a valid will bequeathing or devising property to X on trust, without specifying in the will the objects of the trust, but communicates the objects to X *before or at the time of* the execution of the will, which states that the objects have been so communicated, and X accepts the trust then X will be compelled to carry out the trust for the specified objects[72]: *Blackwell* v. *Blackwell, infra.* If, however, the testator communicates the objects to X *after* the execution of the will, X will hold the property on trust, because the will has created a trust; but since the objects have not been effectively specified, the beneficial interest will belong to the testator's residuary legatee or devisee, or if there is no such person, or if the property is residuary property, to the testator's intestate successors[73]: *Re Keen, infra.*

The supposed justification of this is that a testator cannot, through the medium of a valid will which imposes a trust but does not create the beneficial interests of that trust, reserve to himself a power to create the beneficial interests in an informal non-testamentary manner, so giving the go-by to the requirements of the Wills Act 1837. After all, as we have seen, in the case of the probate doctrine of incorporation of documents by reference the documents must exist prior to or contemporaneously with the execution of the will, for to allow otherwise would be to give the go-by to the Wills Act. However, the doctrine of incorporation by reference operates within the ambit of the statutory formalities, whilst the whole justification for secret trusts is to impose them just where the statutory formalities have not been satisfied: they operate outside the will and independently of the Wills Act.[74] Fully secret trusts, allowing communication of the trusts between execution of the will and the testator's death, allow the go-by to be given to the Wills Act, and since a will is ambulatory, being of no effect till death, there is logically no difference between declarations of trusts before and after the will. After all, in the case of both fully and half-secret trusts communicated after the will it is fraudulent for X to deprive B of his beneficial interest which but for the testator relying on X's promise would have been secured to B by the testator altering his will. Logically, half-secret trusts in this respect should be assimilated to

---

[72] The full extent of the property to be covered by the obligation must be communicated so that if £5,000 is bequeathed on a half-secret trust accepted by the trustee and then a codicil increases that sum to £15,000 but the trustee is not informed of this increase, the surplus £10,000 will not be held on the half-secret trust but on trust for the residuary legatee or next-of-kin: *cf. Re Colin Cooper* [1939] Ch. 580 and 811. If the trustee had undertaken to hold the original legacy and anything extra that the testator might subsequently bequeath then the trustee would be bound to hold everything bequeathed on the half-secret trust.

[73] If a testator, having created a valid half-secret trust, subsequently tells the trustee not to hold for the old beneficiaries but to hold for new beneficiaries the trust for the new beneficiaries will fail by *Re Keen*, and it is possible that the revocation of the old trusts will fail on the basis that it was conditional on the creation of valid new trusts: it will succeed if construed as unconditional (*cf.* conditional revocation of wills) so the property will pass to the residuary legatee (or the statutory next-of-kin).

[74] *Re Young* [1951] Ch. 344; *Re Gardner (No. 2)* [1923] 2 Ch. 230; *Cullen* v. *Att.-Gen. for N. Ireland* (1866) L.R. 1 H.L. 190 at 198; *Blackwell* v. *Blackwell* [1929] A.C. 318, 340, 342; *Re Snowden* [1979] 2 All E.R. 172, 177.

fully secret trusts, as in Ireland[75] and most American jurisdictions,[76] rather than have a different rule based upon a misplaced analogy with the doctrine of incorporation by reference. At present, there are the following differences between half-secret trusts and the probate doctrine of incorporation;

(i) In half-secret trusts the will need not specify the type of communication with any precision; in incorporation by reference the will must refer to the document to be incorporated with sufficient precision to enable it to be identified.[77]

(ii) In half-secret trusts the communication may be oral; in incorporation by reference the document to be incorporated must be in writing.

(iii) In half-secret trusts the testator must take the intended trustee into his confidence; in incorporation by reference the intended trustee need not be told of the document to be incorporated. Indeed, incorporation by reference may be effected in cases of absolute gift as well as in cases of trust.

(iv) In half-secret trusts the names of the beneficiaries are not made public; in incorporation by reference the incorporated document is admitted to probate and so made public.

(v) A beneficiary under a half-secret trust who witnesses the will does not forfeit his beneficial interest, whereas a beneficiary named in an incorporated document who witnesses the will does.[78]

(vi) The interest of a beneficiary under a half-secret trust who predeceases the testator does not lapse (*sed quaere infra*, p. 102): in like circumstances that of a beneficiary named in an incorporated document does.[79]

One special requirement for half-secret trusts which is inapposite for fully secret trusts and is probably derived from the false analogy with the probate doctrine of incorporation, is that the communication of the trusts and the terms of the trust must not conflict with the wording of the will, for to allow otherwise would be to allow oral evidence to contradict the express words of the will: *Re Keen, infra*. Thus, leaving property to four persons "to be dealt with in accordance with my wishes which I have made known *to them*" is ineffective to create a half-secret trust unless the wishes were communicated to all four[80]: communication to less than four would only be effective if the words

---

[75] *Re Browne* [1944] Ir.R. 90; 67 L.Q.R. 413 (L. A. Sheridan). If a testator expressly specifies that Irish law shall govern the validity of any half-secret trust he creates should English law nullify such choice on public policy grounds? See Articles 6 and 18 Hague Trusts Convention pp. 817, 819, *infra*.

[76] *Restatement of Trusts*, para. 55(*c*)(*h*).

[77] *Re Edwards' W.T.* [1948] Ch. 440.

[78] *Re Young* [1951] Ch. 344, *infra*, p. 100. On the reasoning therein it would appear that a grandchild beneficiary taking under a half-secret trust in the will of his partially intestate grandfather might well not have to bring the benefit into hotchpot under s.49(1)(*a*) of the Administration of Estates Act 1925 whereas he would if benefiting under an incorporated document. Would a child beneficiary be caught by s.47(1)(iii) of the Act?

[79] *Re Gardner (No. 2)* [1923] 2 Ch. 230; *Bizzey* v. *Flight* (1876) 3 Ch.D. 269.

[80] *Re Spence* [1949] W.N. 237 following *Re Keen, infra*.

"or any one or more of them" had been added.[81] Furthermore, if property is left by will to X as trustee, evidence is not admissible to show that X was meant to have some part of that property beneficially.[82]

By way of contrast if the wording of the will gives property "to X absolutely" or "to X relying on him, but not by way of trust, to carry out my wishes . . . " then oral evidence is admissible to prove a fully-secret trust, contradicting the express words of the will, for to allow otherwise would be to allow the possibility of the perpetration of fraud: *Re Spencer's Will.*[83]

Should there really be such distinctions between fully- and half-secret trusts if their basis[84] is that whilst the will must first operate to vest the property in the secret trustee thereafter the secret trusts themselves arise outside the will for equity "makes him do what the will in itself has nothing to do with; it lets him take what the will gives him and then makes him apply it as the court of conscience directs, and it does so in order to give effect to the wishes of the testator which would not otherwise be effectual"? Is it not illogical in the case of half-secret trusts for the court to concern itself so strictly with the wording of the will and to require communication of the trust in accordance therewith before or at the time of the will?

## BLACKWELL v. BLACKWELL

House of Lords [1929] A.C. 318; 98 L.J.Ch. 251; 140 L.T. 444; 45 T.L.R. 208;
    73 S.J. 92; affirming Chancery Division [1928] Ch. 614; 97 L.J.Ch. 257;
    139 L.T. 200; 44 T.L.R. 521; 73 S.J. 318 (Lord Hailsham L.C., Viscount
    Sumner, Lords Buckmaster, Carson and Warrington)

A testator by a codicil bequeathed a legacy of £12,000 to five persons upon trust to invest according to their discretion and "to apply the income . . . for the purposes indicated by me to them." Before the execution of the codicil the objects of the trust were communicated in outline to four of the legatees and in detail to the fifth, and the trust was accepted by all of them. The legatee to whom the communication had been made in detail also made a memorandum, on the same day as (though a few hours after) the execution of the codicil, of the testator's instructions. The plaintiffs (the residuary legatees) now claimed a declaration that no valid trust in favour of the objects so communicated had been created, on the ground principally that parol evidence was inadmissible to establish the purposes indicated by the testator: *Johnson* v. *Ball.*[85]

---

[81] "to them or either of them" was used in *Re Keen, infra.*
[82] *Re Rees* [1950] Ch. 204; *Re Tyler* [1967] 1 W.L.R. 1269; *Re Pugh's W.T.* [1967] 1 W.L.R. 1262; *Re Baillie* (1886) 2 T.L.R. 660. *Aliter* if property given under a fully secret trust when the possibilities of trust, conditional gift and equitable charge have to be examined: *Irvine* v. *Sullivan* (1869) L.R. 8 Eq. 673; *Re Foord* [1922] 2 Ch. 519.
[83] (1887) 57 L.T. 519; *Re Williams* [1933] 1 Ch. 244; *Irvine* v. *Sullivan (supra)*; *cf. Re Falkiner* [1924] 1 Ch. 88; *Re Stirling* [1954] 1 W.L.R. 763.
[84] *Blackwell* v. *Blackwell* [1929] A.C. 318, 335; *Re Young* [1951] Ch. 344; *Re Snowden* [1979] 2 All E.R. 172, 177.
[85] (1851) 5 De G. & Sm. 85.

Eve J. held, following *Re Fleetwood*,[86] that the evidence was admissible, and here proved a valid secret trust for the persons named by the testator in his instructions to the legatees. The Court of Appeal affirmed the decision of Eve J. The appellants appealed unsuccessfully.

VISCOUNT SUMNER: " . . . In itself the doctrine of equity, by which parol evidence is admissible to prove what is called 'fraud' in connection with secret trusts, and effect is given to such trusts when established, would not seem to conflict with any of the Acts under which from time to time the legislature has regulated the right of testamentary disposition. A court of conscience finds a man in the position of an absolute legal owner of a sum of money, which has been bequeathed to him under a valid will, and it declares that, on proof of certain facts relating to the motives and actions of the testator, it will not allow the legal owner to exercise his legal right to do what he will with his own. This seems to be a perfectly normal exercise of general equitable jurisdiction. The facts commonly, but not necessarily, involve some immoral and selfish conduct on the part of the legal owner. The necessary elements, on which the question turns, are intention, communication and acquiescence. The testator intends his absolute gift to be employed as he and not as the donee desires; he tells the proposed donee of this intention and, either by express promise or by the tacit promise, which is satisfied by acquiescence, the proposed donee encourages him to bequeath the money in the faith that his intentions will be carried out. The special circumstance that the gift is by bequest only makes this rule a special case of the exercise of a general jurisdiction, but in its application to a bequest the doctrine must in principle rest on the assumption that the will has first operated according to its terms. It is because there is no one to whom the law can give relief in the premises that relief, if any, must be sought in equity. So far, and in the bare case of a legacy absolute on the face of it, I do not see how the statute-law relating to the form of a valid will is concerned at all, and the expressions, in which the doctrine has been habitually described, seem to bear this out. For the prevention of fraud equity fastens on the conscience of the legatee a trust, a trust, that is, which otherwise would be inoperative; in other words it makes him do what the will in itself has nothing to do with; it lets him take what the will gives him and then makes him apply it as the court of conscience directs, and it does so in order to give effect to wishes of the testator which would not otherwise be effectual.

"To this, two circumstances must be added to bring the present case to the test of the general doctrine, first, that the will states on its face that the legacy is given on trust but does not state what the trusts are, and further contains a residuary bequest, and, second, that the legatees are acting with perfect honesty, seek no advantage to themselves, and only desire, if the court will permit them, to do what in other circumstances the court would have fastened it on their conscience to perform.

"Since the current of decisions down to *Re Fleetwood* and *Re Huxtable* has established that the principles of equity apply equally when these circumstances are present as in cases where they are not, the material question is

---

[86] (1880) 15 Ch.D. 594, where a testatrix by a codicil bequeathed to X all her personalty "to be applied as I have requested him to do." Before the execution of the codicil she had stated to X the trusts on which she intended the property to be held, and X made a memorandum of the details in her presence. Hall V.-C. held that external evidence was admissible to prove the terms of the uderstanding between X and the testatrix.

whether and how the Wills Act affects this case. It seems to me that, apart from legislation, the application of the principle of equity which was made in *Fleetwood's* case and *Huxtable's* case was logical, and was justified by the same considerations as in the cases of fraud and absolute gifts. Why should equity forbid an honest trustee to give effect to his promise, made to a deceased testator, and compel him to pay another legatee, about whom it is quite certain that the testator did not mean to make him the object of his bounty? In both cases the testator's wishes are incompletely expressed in his will. Why should equity, over a mere matter of words, give effect to them in one case and frustrate them in the other? No doubt the words 'in trust' prevent the legatee from taking beneficially, whether they have simply been declared in conversation or written in the will, but the fraud, when the trustee, so called in the will, is also the residuary legatee, is the same as when he is only declared a trustee by word of mouth accepted by him. I recoil from interfering with decisions of long standing, which reject this anomaly, unless constrained by statute. . . .

" . . . I think the conclusion is confirmed, which the frame of section 9 of the Wills Act seems to me to carry on its face, that the legislation did not purport to interfere with the exercise of a general equitable jurisdiction, even in connection with secret dispositions of a testator, except in so far as reinforcement of the formalities required for a valid will might indirectly limit it. The effect, therefore, of a bequest being made in terms on trust, without any statement in the will to show what the trust is, remains to be decided by the law as laid down by the courts before and since the Act and does not depend on the Act itself.

"The limits, beyond which the rules as to unspecified trusts must not be carried, have often been discussed. A testator cannot reserve to himself a power of making future unwitnessed dispositions by merely naming a trustee and leaving the purposes of the trust to be supplied afterwards, nor can a legatee give testamentary validity to an unexecuted codicil by accepting an indefinite trust, never communicated to him in the testator's lifetime: *Johnson* v. *Ball, Re Boyes,*[87] *Riordan* v. *Banon,*[88] *Re Hetley.*[89] To hold otherwise would indeed be to enable the testator to 'give the go-by' to the requirements of the Wills Act, because he did not choose to comply with them. It is communication of the purpose to the legatee, coupled with acquiescence or promise on his part, that removes the matter from the provision of the Wills Act and brings it within the law of trusts, as applied in this instance to trustees, who happen also to be legatees. . . . " *Appeal dismissed.*

## RE KEEN, EVERSHED v. GRIFFITHS

Court of Appeal [1937] Ch. 236; 106 L.J.Ch. 177; 156 L.T. 207; 53 T.L.R. 320; 81 S.J. 97; [1937] 1 All E.R. 452 (Wright M.R., Greene and Romer L.JJ.)

The testator by clause 5 of his will, dated August 11, 1932, gave to his executors and trustees, Captain Hazelhurst and Mr. Evershed, the sum of £10,000 free of duty "to be held upon trust and disposed of by them among such person, persons or charities as may be notified by me to them or either of them during my lifetime, and in default of such notification and so far as such

---

[87] (1884) 26 Ch.D. 531.
[88] (1876) 10 I.R.Eq. 469.
[89] [1902] 2 Ch. 866.

notification shall not extend I declare that the said sum of £10,000 or such part thereof as shall not be disposed of in manner aforesaid shall fall into and form part of my residuary estate." Shortly before this, on March 31, 1932, the testator had made a will containing an identical gift. He had on that date handed to Mr. Evershed a sealed envelope containing the name of the intended beneficiary, but he had not disclosed its contents to Mr. Evershed, having directed in fact that it was not to be opened until after his death. Mr. Evershed regarded himself as having undertaken and as being bound to hold the £10,000 in accordance with the directions contained in the sealed envelope. A new will was executed on August 11, 1932, but no fresh directions were given. Mr. Evershed still regarded himself as being bound by the previous communication. On the testator's death an originating summons was taken out to determine whether the £10,000 was held by Captain Hazelhurst and Mr. Evershed on trust for the intended beneficiary or whether it fell into residue. It was held by Farwell J. that it fell into residue, and his decision was affirmed by the Court of Appeal.

LORD WRIGHT M.R.: "Farwell J. . . . . decided adversely to the claims of the lady [the intended beneficiary] on the short ground that she could not prove that she was a person notified to the trustees by the testator during his lifetime within the words of clause 5 [of the will]. His opinion seems to be that the clause required the name and identity of the lady to be expressly disclosed to the trustees during the testator's lifetime, so that it was not sufficient to place these particulars in the physical possession of the trustees, or one of them, in the form of a memorandum which they were not to read till the testator's death.

"I am unable to accept this conclusion, which appears to me to put too narrow a construction on the word 'notified' as used in clause 5 in all the circumstances of the case. To take a parallel, a ship which sails under sealed orders is sailing under orders though the exact terms are not ascertained by the captain till later. I note that the case of a trust, put into writing, which is placed in the trustees' hands in a sealed envelope, was hypothetically treated by Kay J. as possibly constituting a communication in a case of this nature.[90] This, so far as it goes seems to support my conclusion. The trustees had the means of knowledge available whenever it became necessary and proper to open the envelope. I think Mr. Evershed was right in understanding that the giving of the sealed envelope was a notification within clause 5.

"This makes it necessary to examine the matter on a wider basis, and to consider the principles of law which were argued both before Farwell J. and this court, but which the judge found it merely necessary to mention. There are two main questions: first, how far parol evidence is admissible to define the trust under such a clause as this and, secondly, and in particular, how far such evidence, if admissible at all, would be excluded on the ground that it would be inconsistent with the true meaning of clause 5?

"It is first necessary to state what, in my opinion, is the true construction of the words of the clause.

"These words, in my opinion, can only be considered as referring to a definition of trusts which have not yet, at the date of the will, been established and which, between that date and the testator's death, may or may not be

---

[90] *Re Boyes* (1884) 26 Ch.D. 531, 536.

established. Mr. Roxburgh[91] has strenuously argued, basing himself in particular on the word 'may,' that the clause, even though it covers future dispositions, also includes a disposition antecedent to or contemporaneous with the execution of the will. I do not think that even so wide a construction of the word 'may' would enable Mr. Roxburgh's contention to succeed, but, in any case, I do not feel able to accept it. The words of the clause seem to me to refer only to something future and hypothetical, to something as to which the testator is reserving an option whether to do or not to do it.

" . . . The principles of law or equity relevant in a question of this nature have now been authoritatively settled or discussed by the House of Lords in *Blackwell* v. *Blackwell*[92] [in the case of half-secret trusts and *McCormick* v. *Grogan*[93] in the case of fully secret trusts. The Master of the Rolls then analysed the facts and decisions in those cases, and continued:] As, in my judgment, clause 5 should be considered as contemplating future dispositions, and as reserving to the testator the power of making such dispositions without a duly attested codicil, simply by notifying them during his lifetime, the principles laid down by Lord Sumner [in *Blackwell* v. *Blackwell*] must be fatal to the appellant's claim. Indeed, they would be equally fatal even on the construction for which Mr. Roxburgh contended, that the clause covered both anterior or contemporaneous notifications and future notifications. The clause would be equally invalid, but as already explained I cannot accept that construction. In *Blackwell* v. *Blackwell*,[94] *Re Fleetwood*[95] and *Re Huxtable*[96] the trusts had been specifically declared to some or all of the trustees, at or before the execution of the will, and the language of the will was consistent with that fact. There was, in these cases, no reservation of a future power to change the trusts, in whole or in part. Such a power would involve a power to change a testamentary disposition by an unexecuted codicil, and would violate section 9 of the Wills Act. This was so held in *Re Hetley*.[97] *Johnson* v. *Ball*[98] is, again, a somewhat different example of the rule against dispositions made subsequently to the date of the will in cases where the will in terms leaves the property on trust, and shows that the position may be different from the position where the will in terms leaves the gift absolutely. The trusts referred to, but undefined in the will, must be described in the will as established prior to, or at least contemporaneously with, its execution.

"But there is a still further objection which, in the present case, renders the appellant's claim unenforceable: the trusts which it is sought to establish by parol evidence would be inconsistent with the express terms of the will. That such an objection is fatal appears from the cases already cited, such as *Re Huxtable*. In that case, an undefined trust of money for charitable purposes was declared in the will, as in respect of the whole corpus and, accordingly, evidence was held inadmissible that the charitable trust was limited to the legatee's life, so that he was free to dispose of the corpus after his death. Similarly in *Johnson* v. *Ball* the testator by the will left the property to trustees, upon the uses contained in a letter signed 'by them and myself': it was

---

[91] Counsel for the appellant.
[92] [1929] A.C. 318; *supra*, p. 94.
[93] (1869) L.R. 4 H.L. 82.
[94] [1929] A.C. 318.
[95] (1880) 15 Ch.D. 594.
[96] [1902] 2 Ch. 793.
[97] [1902] 2 Ch. 866.
[98] (1851) 5 De G. & Sm. 85.

held that that evidence was not admissible to show that, though no such letter was in existence at the date of the will, the testator had made a subsequent declaration of trust; the court held that these trusts could not be enforced. Lord Buckmaster in *Blackwell's* case[99] described *Johnson* v. *Ball* as an authority pointing 'to a case where the actual trusts were left over after the date of the will to be subsequently determined by the testator.' That, in his opinion, would be a contravention of the Wills Act. I know of no authority which would justify such a contravention. Lord Buckmaster also quotes[1] the grounds on which Parker V.-C. based his decision as being both 'that the letter referred to in the will had no existence at the time when the will was made and that, supposing it referred to a letter afterwards signed, it is impossible to give effect to it as a declaration of the trusts since it would admit the document as part of the will and it was unattested.'

"In the present case, while clause 5 refers solely to a future definition, or to future definitions, of the trust, subsequent to the date of the will, the sealed letter relied on as notifying the trust was communicated (as I find the facts) before the date of the will. That it was communicated to one trustee only, and not to both, would not, I think, be an objection (see Lord Warrington's observation in the *Blackwell* case).[2] But the objection remains that the notification sought to be put in evidence was anterior to the will, and hence not within the language of clause 5, and inadmissible simply on that ground, as being inconsistent with what the will prescribes. . . . " *Appeal dismissed.*[3]

## IV. THE BASIS OF SECRET TRUSTS

Before dealing with the basis of secret trusts it is as well to examine certain unusual secret trust situations since they will shed light thereon.

### (i) *Attestation of will by secret beneficiary*

Section 15 of the Wills Act 1837: "If any person shall attest the execution of any will to whom or to whose wife or husband any beneficial devise, legacy, estate, interest, gift, or appointment, of or affecting any real or personal estate (other than and except charges and directions for the payment of any debt or debts), shall be thereby given or made, such devise, legacy, estate, interest, gift, or appointment shall, so far only as concerns such person attesting the execution of such will, or the wife or husband of such person, or any person claiming under such person or wife or husband, be utterly null and void, and such person so attesting shall be admitted as a witness to prove the execution of such will, or to prove the validity or invalidity thereof, notwithstanding such devise, legacy, estate, interest, gift, or appointment mentioned in such will."

---

[99] [1929] A.C. 318, 331.
[1] *Ibid.* 330.
[2] *Ibid.* 341.
[3] In *Re Bateman's W.T.* [1970] 1 W.L.R. 1463; [1970] 3 All E.R. 817, *Re Keen* was followed without argument where a testator had directed his trustees to set aside £24,000 and pay the income thereof "to such persons and in such proportions *as shall* be stated by me in a sealed letter to my trustees": "[The direction] clearly imports that the testator may, in the future after the date of the will, give a sealed letter to his trustees. It is impossible to confine the words to a sealed letter already so given. If that be the true construction of the wording it is not in dispute that the direction is invalid": *per* Pennycuick V.-C. at pp. 1468 and 820, respectively.

Section 1 of the Wills Act 1968: "For the purposes of section 15 of the Wills Act 1837 the attestation of a will by a person to whom or to whose spouse there is given or made any such disposition as is described in that section shall be disregarded if the will is duly executed without his attestation and without that of any other such person."

*Re Young* [1951] Ch. 344 (Danckwerts J.): bequest by a testator to his wife with a direction that on her death she should leave the property for the purposes which he had communicated to her. Before execution of will, direction given and accepted by wife that she would leave a legacy of £2,000 to testator's chauffeur. The chauffeur had witnessed the testator's will. *Held* that the chauffeur had not forfeited his legacy under section 15 of the Wills Act 1837 for "the whole theory of the formulation of a secret trust is that the Wills Act has nothing to do with the matter because the forms required by the Wills Act are entirely disregarded, since the persons do not take by virtue of the gift in the will, but by virtue of the secret trusts imposed upon the beneficiary who does in fact take under the will."

*Sed quaere* whether the secret beneficiary does not obtain an interest in the testator's property (or rights against the secret trustee) at the date of the testator's death by virtue of the gift in the will. Why should the attesting secret beneficiary be allowed to benefit if the function of section 15 is to ensure there is an impartial witness with nothing to gain or lose by his testimony? He may know he is a beneficiary at the time of attestation. He could be lying if he said he did not know: for this reason a beneficiary taking on the face of a will is subject to section 15 even if, in fact, he just witnessed the signature at the end of the will and so did not know he was a beneficiary.

It seems likely that persons taking under a fully secret trust would receive nothing if the trustee taking absolutely beneficially on the face of the will had witnessed the will[4] though some might argue that the admission of oral evidence to establish the trusteeship would carry the day: half-secret trustees taking as trustees on the face of the will clearly cannot infringe section 15 of the Wills Act 1837.

## (ii) *Trustee predeceasing testator*

Generally, a gift by will to X is said to lapse if X predeceases the testator and the gift fails.[5] If, however, the gift is to X on trust for B and B survives the testator then despite X's predecease the gift will not lapse for equity will not allow a trust to fail for want of a trustee: the testator's personal representative will take over as trustee.[6]

---

[4] See n. 7 and n. 9, *infra*.

[5] Exceptionally, if issue predecease a testator leaving issue of their own surviving the testator the gift takes effect in favour of the surviving issue: Wills Act 1837, s.33. The persons benefiting from this exception will not be able to disregard the deceased legatee-trustee's undertaking: *cf. Huguenin* v. *Baseley* (1807) 14 Ves. 273.

[6] *Sonley* v. *Clock Makers' Company* (1780) 1 Bro.C.C. 81; *Mallott* v. *Wilson* [1903] 2 Ch. 494; *Re Smirthwaite's Trusts* (1871) L.R. 11 Eq. 251; *Re Armitage* [1972] Ch. 438. See p. 580, *infra*.

According to dicta of Cozens-Hardy L.J. in *Re Maddock*,[7] a case concerning a fully secret trust, "if the legatee renounces and disclaims, or dies in the lifetime of the testator,[8] the persons claiming under the memorandum [*i.e.* the secret trusts] can take nothing." This is based upon the view that the secret trusts only arise when the property intended to be the subject-matter of the trust vests in someone under the terms of the will.[9] It follows that if for some reason the property does not so vest then no trust arises.

(iii) *Trustee disclaiming after testator's death*

A beneficiary under a will can always disclaim a legacy or devise before acceptance and a person can always disclaim the office of trustee before acceptance.[10] If a person named as a half-secret trustee disclaimed the office then it would seem that the testator's personal representative would hold on the trusts for the secret beneficiaries. Where disclaimer by fully secret trustees is concerned although Cozens-Hardy L.J. opined in *Re Maddock* (*supra*) that no trusts would arise in such a case there are contrary dicta of Lord Buckmaster and Lord Warrington in *Blackwell* v. *Blackwell*[11]: "In the case where no trusts are mentioned the legatee might defeat the whole purpose by renouncing the legacy and the breach of trust would not in that case inure to his own benefit, but I entertain no doubt that the court having once admitted the evidence of the trust, would interfere to prevent its defeat." Lord Buckmaster's dicta presuppose the existence of a trust whereof the legatee is in breach and apply the maxim that equity will not allow a trust to fail for want of a trustee. Whether the trusts arose on the testator's death or at an earlier time is not stated by Lord Buckmaster. By analogy with mutual wills the testator's death might be the appropriate time, it being immaterial whether or not gifts were disclaimed.[12] Disclaimer might, however, be material if the testator's orally communicated intentions to the legatee were construed not as imposing trusts but as conferring a gift subject to a personal condition.[13]

(iv) *Trustee revoking acceptance before the testator's death*

Compare the three following examples:

---

[7] [1902] 2 Ch. 220, 231.

[8] For a contrary view see *Inchiquin* v. *French* (1745) 1 Cox Eq.Cas. 1.

[9] "The obligation can be enforced if the donee becomes entitled": *per* Romer J. in *Re Gardner* [1923] 2 Ch. 230, 232. "The doctrine must, in principle, rest on the assumption that the will has first operated according to its terms": *per* Viscount Sumner [1929] A.C. 318, 334. "The whole basis of secret trusts is that they operate outside the will, changing nothing that is written in it and allowing it to operate according to its tenor, but then fastening a trust on to the property in the hands of the recipient": *per* Megarry V.-C. *Re Snowden* [1979] 2 All E.R. 172, 177.

[10] *Re Sharman's W.T.* [1942] Ch. 311.

[11] [1929] A.C. 318, 328, 341.

[12] *cf. Re Hagger, infra*; see also *Blackwell* v. *Blackwell* [1929] A.C. 318, 341, *per* Lord Warrington: "It has long been settled that if a gift be made to a person in terms absolutely but in fact upon a trust communicated to the legatee and accepted by him, the legatee would be bound to give effect to the trust, on the principle that the gift may be presumed to have been made on the faith of his acceptance of the trust, and a refusal after the death of the testator to give effect to it would be a fraud on the part of the legatee." See also (1972) 36 Conv.(N.S.) 113 (R. Burgess).

[13] See p. 119, *infra*.

(a) Testator, T, bequeaths £10,000 to X absolutely, having told X that he wants X to hold the money on trust for Y and Z. A year later X tells T that he is no longer prepared to hold the money on trust for anyone. Five years later T dies without having changed his will;

(b) The bequest as before but X tells T that he is no longer prepared to hold the money on trust for anyone only three days before T dies of a week-long illness;

(c) The bequest as before but T is incurably insane when informed by X as before and T remains so till his death.

Does X take the £10,000 beneficially in each case? Is X under any obligations before T's death? What if the trust had been half secret?

### (v) *Secret beneficiary predeceasing testator*

If T by will left property to X on trust expressly for B and B predeceased T the gift to B would lapse just as an *inter vivos* trust for B fails if B is not alive when the trust is created.[14] One would have imagined that the result would be the same if T, having asked X to hold on trust for B, left property "to X absolutely" or "to X upon trusts that I have communicated to him." However, in *Re Gardner (No. 2)*[15] Romer J. held that B's interest did not lapse as B obtained an interest as soon as T communicated the terms of the trust to X and X accepted the trust. B's interest derived not from T's will (to which the rules regarding lapse would have applied) but under the agreement between T and X. "The rights of the parties appear to me to be exactly the same as though the husband (X), after the memorandum had been communicated to him by the testatrix (T) in the year 1909 had executed a declaration of trust binding himself to hold any property that should come to him upon his wife's (T's) partial intestacy upon trust as specified in the memorandum."[16] Such a declaration, however, does not create a properly constituted trust since the subject-matter is future property.[17] It may be that Romer J. considered that the vesting of the property in X completely constituted the trust[18] but on the terms of the memorandum. However, the interests of those taking under the memorandum only became vested proprietorial interests after T's death: until then the so-called interests only amounted to mere *spes* that T would not change her mind and make a new will or die insolvent

---

[14] *Re Corbishley's Trusts* (1880) 14 Ch.D. 846; *Re Tilt* (1896) 74 L.T. 163, both concerned with personalty where a gift to B gave B an absolute interest: for realty a gift by will after 1837 to B gave an absolute interest whilst till 1925 a gift by deed to B gave B only a life interest in the absence of proper words of limitation.

[15] [1923] 2 Ch. 230.

[16] *Ibid.* at 233. Here Romer J. may have been thinking that if B had an absolute vested interest in a 1909 settlement then funds accruing under a will taking effect in 1919 would be treated as an accretion to the 1909 settlement rather than as comprised in a separate 1919 referential settlement: see *Re Playfair* [1951] Ch. 4.

[17] *Re Ellenborough* [1903] 1 Ch. 697; *Re Northcliffe* [1925] Ch. 651; *Williams* v. *C.I.R.* [1965] N.Z.L.R. 395, *infra*, p. 252; *Brennan* v. *Morphett* (1908) 6 C.L.R. 22.

[18] *cf. Re Ralli's W.T.* [1964] Ch. 288; *Re Adlard* [1954] Ch. 29.

and that X would not revoke his acceptance, so that ultimately X would receive property to hold on trust for them. Just as an *inter vivos* trust constituted by X in 1919 declaring himself trustee of certain property for the benefit of A, B and C equally would give B no interest, if at that date B were dead and so no longer an existing legal entity, so the trust arising in *Re Gardner* after T's death in 1919 could give B no interest, B being dead by that date. It makes no difference that whilst B was alive he might have had some sort of *spes* that if he lived long enough a trust might come into existence for his benefit at a later date. The authority of *Re Gardener* is thus very doubtful indeed.

(vi) *Bequest to two on a promise by one*

The orthodox position is laid down in *Re Stead*[19] by Farwell J.:

"If A induced B either to make, or to leave unrevoked, a will leaving property to A and C as tenants in common, by expressly promising or tacitly consenting, that he and C will carry out the testator's wishes and C knows nothing of the matter until after the testator's death, A is bound, but C is not bound: *Tee* v. *Ferris*[20]; the reason stated being, that to hold otherwise would be to enable one beneficiary to deprive the rest of their benefits by setting up a secret trust. If, however, the gift were to A and C as joint tenants, the authorities have established a distinction between those cases in which the will is made on the faith of an antecedent promise by A and those in which the will is left unrevoked on the faith of a subsequent promise. In the former case the trust binds both A and C: *Russell* v. *Jackson*[21]; *Jones* v. *Bradley*,[22] the reason stated being that no person can claim an interest under a fraud committed by another; in the latter case A and not C is bound: *Burney* v. *Macdonald*[23] and *Moss* v. *Cooper*,[24] the reason stated being that the gift is not tainted with any fraud in procuring the execution of the will. Personally, I am unable to see any difference between a gift made on the faith of an antecedent promise and a gift left unrevoked on the faith of a subsequent promise to carry out the testator's wishes; but apparently a distinction has been made by the various judges who have had to consider the question. I am bound, therefore, to decide in accordance with these authorities. . . . "

However, Bryn Perrins in (1972) 88 L.Q.R. 225 examines these authorities to different effect, persuasively concluding that the only

---

[19] [1900] 1 Ch. 231, 247. The principles here discussed apply only to fully secret trusts. In the case of half-secret trusts, if the will permits communication to be made to one only of several trustees, a communication made before or at the time of the execution of the will to one only of the trustees binds all of them, the trust being a joint office: *Blackwell* v. *Blackwell* [1929] A.C. 318; *Re Spence* [1949] W.N. 237; *Ward* v. *Duncombe* [1893] A.C. 369; *Re Gardom* [1914] 1 Ch. 662, 673.

[20] (1856) 2 K. & J. 357.

[21] (1852) 10 Hare 204.

[22] (1868) L.R. 3 Ch. 362.

[23] (1845) 15 Sim. 6.

[24] (1861) 1 J. & H. 352.

question to be asked is: was the gift to C induced by A's promise? If yes, C is bound; if no, he is not:

### BRYN PERRINS (1972) 88 L.Q.R. 225

"The reasons stated by Farwell J. in *Re Stead* are at first sight contradictory. One consideration is that a person must not be allowed, by falsely setting up a secret trust, to deprive another of his benefits under the will. Apparently this is decisive if the parties are tenants in common but not if they are joint tenants. On the other hand one person must not profit by the fraud of another. Apparently this is decisive only if the parties are joint tenants and not if they are tenants in common. Yet again it is apparently only fraud in procuring the execution of a will that is relevant, and not fraud in inducing a testator not to revoke a will already made. All very confusing, but add *Huguenin* v. *Baseley*[25] and the whole picture springs into focus and the confusion disappears. Returning to A and C, whether they are tenants in common or joint tenants, C is not bound *if his gift was not induced by the promise of A* because to hold otherwise would be to enable A to deprive C of his benefit by setting up a secret trust; but C is bound *if his gift was induced by the promise of A* because he cannot profit by the fraud of another; and if the trust was communicated to A after the will was made, then C takes free *if this gift was not* induced by the promise of A because if there is no inducement there is no fraud affecting C.

This, it is submitted, is what was decided by the cases cited in Farwell J.'s judgment."

## CONCLUSIONS

In the light of the foregoing discussion of unusual secret trust situations it will be seen that the title of a beneficiary under a fully secret and a half-secret trust arises outside the will and is not testamentary.[26] It seems that, except in the case of disclaimer by a fully secret trustee after the testator's death, such a trust is conditional and dependent upon the gift by will taking effect according to its terms. Section 9 of the Wills Act 1837 is nowadays seen to be irrelevant to the validity of the secret trust since it operates outside the will and depends on the equitable obligation binding the trustee's conscience in accordance with the principles already considered.[27]

The equitable principle that equity will not allow a statute to be used as an instrument of fraud was the basis for not allowing the Statute of Frauds 1677 to be invoked by persons intended to be secret trustees of

---

[25] (1807) 14 Ves. 273. This is authority for the principle, "No man may profit by the fraud of another." A widow was persuaded by Rev. Baseley, who managed her property, to settle some of it on him and his family. Later, she married Mr. Huguenin and sought to set aside the conveyance for undue influence. She succeeded, for Lord Eldon held that the Rev. Baseley's wife and children, though innocent, were not purchasers but volunteers who could not profit from Baseley's fraud and retain their vested interests.

[26] *e.g. Re Gardner* [1923] 2 Ch. 230; *Re Young* [1951] Ch. 344; see n. 9, p. 101, *supra*. For unorthodox views on half-secret trusts see [1979] Conv. 360 (P. Matthews) which it is submitted are satisfactorily rebutted in [1980] Conv. 341, 349–350 (D. R. Hodge).

[27] Since secret trusts operate outside the will it is illogical in the case of a half-secret trust not to allow communication after the date of the will but before the testator's death and claim that otherwise the Wills Act would be avoided: see p. 92 (*supra*).

testamentary gifts or to be trustees of inter vivos trusts of land.[28] The provisions of the 1677 Statute are now to be found in the Wills Act 1837 and the Law of Property Act 1925. The equitable principle applies since there is fraud when the secret trustee attempts to rely on the statute to defeat a beneficial interest which he had led the testator to believe would belong to another. There is not just a fraud on the testator in betraying the testator's confidence but there is a fraud on the secret beneficiary who would be deprived of the benefit which, but for the trustee agreeing to carry out the testator's wishes, would have been secured to him by other means.[29] Thus, in a fully secret trust and in a half-secret trust the trustee holds the testator's property not on resulting or constructive trust for the testator's residuary legatee (or next of kin as the case may be) but on the express trust for the beneficiary: the trustee is not allowed to raise issues on the Wills Act 1837 (though, nowadays, the beneficiary is, anyhow, treated as taking outside the will and the Wills Act) or the Law of Property Act 1925, s.53(1)(*b*), for that would enable statute to be used as an instrument of fraud. Thus, C can enforce his interest where A devises land by will to B on an oral trust for C.[30]

The same result can be achieved if one treats such trusts as constructive trusts—exempted from L.P.A., s.53(1) by s.53(2)—on the ground that such trusts, unlike ordinary express trusts, depend crucially upon the trustee's express or tacit promise to honour the trust in favour of the secret beneficiary.[31] Moreover, there is a modern erroneous trend to treat the equitable principle of not allowing statutes to be used as an instrument of fraud as itself creating a constructive trust favoured under L.P.A., s.53(2).[32]

### Section 3. Post Mortem Trusts: Mutual Wills[33]

The term "mutual wills" is used to describe documents of a testamentary character made as the result of an agreement between husband and wife, or other persons, to create irrevocable interests in favour of ascertainable beneficiaries. The revocable nature of the wills under which the interests are created is fully recognised by the court of probate[34]; but, in certain circumstances, the court of equity will protect

---

[28] *McCormick* v. *Grogan* (1868) L.R. 4 H.L. 82, 88–89; *Jones* v. *Badley* (1868) 3 Ch.App. 362, 364; *Wallgrave* v. *Tebbs* (1855) 2 K. & J. 313, 321–322; *Rochefoucauld* v. *Boustead* [1897] 1 Ch. 196; R. Blumenstein (1978) 36 U. Toronto F.L.R. 108.

[29] D. R. Hodge [1980] Conv. 341. This point seems overlooked by B. Perrins in [1985] Conv. 248.

[30] *Ottaway* v. *Norman* [1972] Ch. 698 (L.P.A. 1925, s.53(1)(*b*) assumed inapplicable *sub silentio*) and see pp. 56–59 (*supra*). In *Re Baillie* (1886) 2 T.L.R. 660, 661 a half-secret trust of land failed for not complying with the predecessor of s.53(1)(*b*) but it should have been saved under the equitable principle appearing in *Rochefoucauld* v. *Boustead* [1897] 1 Ch. 196 as explained p. 56–59 (*supra*).

[31] In *Re Cleaver* [1981] 2 All E.R. 1018, 1024 Nourse J. categorised secret trusts as constructive trusts, but since the court is recognising and enforcing a testator's express trust why not call a spade a spade?

[32] *Bannister* v. *Bannister* [1948] 2 All E.R. 133 and p. 59 (*supra*). In *Hodgson* v. *Marks* [1971] Ch. 892, however, the equitable principle and constructive trusts were treated as separate pleas.

[33] See Oakley's *Constructive Trusts*, Chap. 5; (1979) Univ. Toronto L.J. 390 (T. G. Youdan); (1989) 105 L.Q.R. 534 (C. E. F. Rickett).

[34] *Re Heys* [1914] P. 192.

and enforce the interests created by the agreement despite the revocation of the will by one party after the death of the other without having revoked his will.

A typical case of mutual wills arises in the following circumstances: H(usband) and W(ife) agree to execute mutual wills (or a joint will) leaving their respective properties to the survivor of them for life, with remainder to the same ultimate beneficiary (B). H dies, W makes a fresh will leaving her property away from B to her second husband (S).

In these circumstances, H's will (or the joint will) is admitted to probate on his death and, under it, W gets a life interest and B an interest in remainder. On W's death, her second will is admitted to probate. Under it her property vests in her personal representatives upon trust, not for S, but to give effect to the terms of the agreement upon which the mutual wills were made, *i.e.* upon trust for B.

B's interest in W's property arises as soon as H dies. It prevails over the interest of S therein by virtue of the maxim that "where the equities are equal the first in time prevails." Indeed, if B survives H but predeceases W his interest in W's property does not lapse but is payable to his personal representatives, and forms part of his estate: *Re Hagger, infra.* The better opinion is that B's interest arises irrespective of whether W disclaims her benefit under H's will.[35] It is the death[36] of H, no longer having the opportunity to revoke his own will, which concludes performance of the contract and renders the will of W irrevocable in equity, though, it is always revocable at law.

The courts will not infer a trust merely because mutual wills are made in almost identical terms. There must be evidence of an agreement to create interests under the mutual wills which are intended to be irrevocable after the death of the first to die. Where there is no such evidence the fact that the survivor takes an absolute interest is a factor against the implication of an agreement: *Re Oldham.*[37] Where, however, the evidence is clear, as, for example, where it is contained in recitals in the wills themselves, the fact that each testator gave the other an absolute interest with a substitutional gift in the event of the other's prior death does not prevent a trust from arising: *Re Green.*[38]

The requirement for mutual wills sometimes expressed as the need for "an agreement not to revoke" the wills is more aptly expressed as the need for "acceptance of an obligation imposed by the other party" as the obligation may well allow the will of the survivor to be revoked so long as a new will is made giving effect to the agreed arrange-

---

[35] *Dufour* v. *Pereira* (1769) 1 Dick. 419, 421; *Stone* v. *Hoskins* [1905] P. 194, 197; *Re Hagger, infra,* p. 108; J. D. B. Mitchell (1951) 14 M.L.R. 136, 138.

[36] *Quaere*: would incurable insanity on the part of H have the same effect? Consider ss.95, 96, Mental Health Act 1983.

[37] [1925] Ch. 75.

[38] [1951] Ch. 148.

ments.[39] The acceptance of an obligation may be difficult to prove in husband and wife situations where there is less likely to be an intention to impose legal relationships, neither party making the gifts by will on the faith of a promise by the other to accept legal obligations, but instead, making the gifts without any strings attached, confidently assuming the other party will do as asked, *e.g. Gray* v. *Perpetual Trustee Co. Ltd.*[40]; *Re Oldham.*[41]

The principle is that the survivor becomes a trustee for the performance of the mutual agreement after the death of the first to die. Accordingly, if the agreement is too vague to be enforced, there will be no trust. Subject to this, however, the agreement can define the property, which is to be subject to the trust, in any way it pleases. The trust may just give the survivor a life interest in all or a specific part of the deceased's property or it may also provide for him to have a life interest in all or a specific part of his own property at the date of death of the deceased.[41a] The life interest may even extend to capital acquired after the deceased's death though practical problems arise if there is no broad express power of investment and no power of appointment of capital.[42] Sometimes, it may appear that the survivor is to be absolute owner of the deceased's property passing to him under the will and of his own existing and subsequently acquired property, but that he is supposed to be under some binding obligation to bequeath whatever he has left at his death to the agreed beneficiaries.[43]

A purported trust of such uncertain property would normally be void,[44] but it seems that the express contract between the parties that led the party first dying to leave his property in the agreed manner may give the ultimate beneficiaries a remedy by way of a "floating" trust, suspended during the survivor's lifetime and crystallising into a proper trust on his death: *Re Cleaver, infra*. The survivor will be under a fiduciary duty not to make *inter vivos* gifts deliberately intended to defeat the contract and, presumably, the proceeds of sale of any property within the fiduciary obligation and any property purchased with such proceeds will be subject to such obligation.[45] Perhaps the "floating" trust may develop doctrinally by analogy with the floating charge over company assets and crystallise not only on the death of the

---

[39] *cf. Re Oldham* [1925] Ch. 75 where Mrs. O after Mr. O's death had revoked her mutual will but made another in similar terms, when it was not suggested that there had been a breach of her agreement with Mr. O, the breach only allegedly occurring when she made yet another will be in different terms.

[40] [1928] A.C. 391.

[41] [1925] Ch. 75.

[41a] *Re Hagger* [1930] 2 Ch. 190.

[42] J. D. B. Mitchell (1953) 14 M.L.R. 136; R. Burgess (1972) 36 Conv. 113.

[43] Such beneficiaries may well not have vested interests liable to be divested: the parties probably intend them to benefit only if alive on the survivor's death so that if they all predecease the survivor his fiduciary obligation will cease.

[44] *Re Jones* [1898] 1 Ch. 438 and see p. 138, *infra*.

[45] The fiduciary relationship should give rise to a right to trace. The survivor might be compared to an executor who has full title to the testator's estate in which the beneficiaries have no proprietary interest (see *Commissioner for Stamp Duties* v. *Livingston* [1965] A.C. 694, 701; *Re Diplock* [1948] Ch. 465).

survivor but also when the survivor attempts to make a mala fide gift or sale at an undervalue designed to defeat his contract,[46] especially if such intent is expressed in the contract.

Before the death of the first to die the agreement is a contractual one (so distinguishing mutual wills from secret trusts) made in consideration of the mutual promises of H and W for the benefit of B, who neither is a party to the contract nor supplies consideration.[47] Whether H would be in breach of the contract if he told W that he no longer intended to give effect to their arrangement, or if his will was automatically revoked by remarriage to someone else after divorcing W, or if he revoked his will without informing W but predeceased W, depends on the construction of the contract. The contract might be construed as a contract not to depart from the terms of the arrangement without *inter vivos* notice to the other party *prima facie* if H makes a new will containing new arrangements without informing W, but predeceases W, it seems that W can sue H's executors for damages which will amount to H's whole estate if W was supposed to be sole beneficiary.[48]

If H died first, by his will carrying into effect the mutual arrangement, then, in order to protect B and to prevent W repudiating her obligations, a constructive trust is imposed since B is unable to bring an action for specific performance[49] of the express terms of the contract. If the contract relates not just to whatever assets might be owned at death but to interests in land then equity will not allow L.P.A. 1925, s.40 or now Law of Property (Miscellaneous Provisions) Act 1989, s.2 to be pleaded since this would be to use the statute as an instrument of fraud.[50]

It would seem that the principles underlying mutual wills could extend to an agreement subsequent to the making of the wills[51] and to an agreement between joint tenants not to sever their interest on terms that the survivor will dispose of the asset in an agreed manner.

### RE HAGGER, FREEMAN v. ARSCOTT

Chancery Division [1930] 2 Ch. 190; 99 L.J.Ch. 492; 143 L.T. 610

A husband and wife made a joint will in 1902 by which, after reciting *that there was to be no alteration or revocation except by agreement*, they gave the whole of their estate at the death of the first spouse to die to their trustees to

---

[46] *cf. Re Manuwera Transport* [1971] N.Z.L.R. 909.
[47] *Dufour* v. *Pereira* (1769) 1 Dick. 419, 421; *Lord Walpole* v. *Lord Orford* (1797) 3 Ves. 402; *Gray* v. *Perpetual Trustee Co.* [1928] A.C. 391; *Birmingham* v. *Renfrew* (1937) 57 C.L.R. 666.
[48] *cf. Bigg* v. *Queensland Trustees Ltd.* [1990] 2 Qd.R. 11, (1991) 54 M.L.R.581; *Dufour* v. *Pereira, supra* at 420; *Stone* v. *Hoskins* [1905] P. 194, 197; *Re Marsland* [1939] Ch. 820.
[49] *Birmingham* v. *Renfrew* (1937) 57 C.L.R. 666. In view of *Beswick* v. *Beswick* [1968] A.C. 58, specific performance might be available to the estate of the party first dying against the survivor if the personal representative were so minded (which he would not be if himself the survivor). It will be advisable to make the beneficiary executor of both wills.
[50] *Birmingham* v. *Renfrew* (1937) 57 C.L.R. 666, 690.
[51] *Re Fox* [1951] Ontario R. 378.

pay debts, expenses and legacies, and to pay the income to the survivor for life. By another clause they gave their property at Wandsworth on trust after the death of the survivor to sell the same, and to divide the proceeds in certain shares between nine beneficiaries, including Eleanor Palmer. They gave their residuary estate on trust after the death of the survivor for two other beneficiaries.

The wife died in 1904, and the husband, who died in 1928 (and had since 1904 received the income of the whole estate), by his will made in 1921 gave "everything of which he was able to dispose" to his executors on trust for various persons, of whom some were not mentioned in the joint will. The court was asked to determine the effect of the two wills, probate having been granted to both.

Eleanor Palmer had died in 1923. Her personal representatives argued that the parties to the joint will had clearly intended the whole of their estate to be impressed with a trust on the first death, so that beneficiaries took under the joint will and not under the husband's will; hence the interest of Eleanor Palmer had not lapsed.

CLAUSON J.: "To my mind *Dufour* v. *Pereira*[52] decides that where there is a joint will such as this on the death of the first testator the position as regards that part of the property which belongs to the survivor is that the survivor will be treated in this court as holding the property on trust to apply it so as to carry out the effect of the joint will. As I read Lord Camden's judgment in *Dufour* v. *Pereira*, that would be so, even though the survivor did not signify his election to give effect to the will by taking benefits under it.[53] But in any case it is clear that Lord Camden has decided that if the survivor takes a benefit conferred on him by the joint will he will be treated as a trustee in this court, and he will not be allowed to do anything inconsistent with the provisions of the joint will. It is not necessary for me to consider the reasons on which Lord Camden based his judgment. The case must be accepted in this court as binding. Therefore I am bound to hold that from the death of the wife the husband held the property, according to the tenor of the will, subject to the trusts thereby imposed upon it, at all events if he took advantage of the provisions of the will. In my view he did take advantage of those provisions.

"The effect of the will was that the husband and wife agreed that the property should on the death of the first of them to die pass to trustees to hold on trusts inconsistent with the right of survivorship, and therefore the will effected a severance of the joint interest of the husband and wife. By the will they made a provision which was inconsistent with the survivor taking by survivorship. Therefore the property at the moment when, on the wife's death, it came within the ambit of the will ceased to be held by the two jointly, and the husband had no title to the wife's interest on her dying in his lifetime, save in so far as he took a life interest under the joint will. From the moment of the wife's death the Wandsworth property was held on trust for the husband for

---

[52] (1769) 1 Dick. 419, "The instrument itself is the evidence of the agreement; and he, that dies first, does by his death carry the agreement on his part into execution. If the other then refuses, he is guilty of a fraud, can never unbind himself, and becomes a trustee of course. For no man shall deceive another to his prejudice. By engaging to do something that is in his power, he is made a trustee for the performance and transmits that trust to those that claim under him," *per* Lord Camden at 421.

[53] See also *Stone* v. *Hoskins* [1905] P. 194, 197.

life with a vested interest in remainder as to one-sixth in E. Palmer. So far as the husband's interest in the property is concerned the will operated as a trust from the date of the wife's death. There is, accordingly, no lapse by reason of Eleanor Palmer's death in the husband's lifetime, but after the wife's death."

## RE CLEAVER (DECEASED)[54]

Chancery Division [1981] 1 W.L.R. 939; [1981] 2 All E.R. 1018

The testator and testatrix married in their seventies and in 1974 made wills on the same date and in similar terms, leaving their property to each other absolutely and in default of survival to the plaintiffs. The testator died in 1975. The testatrix made a new will in 1977 and cut out the plaintiffs and died in 1978. The plaintiffs successfully claimed her executors held her estate on the terms of the 1974 will.

NOURSE J.: "I have derived great assistance from the decision of the High Court of Australia in *Birmingham* v. *Renfrew* (1936) 57 C.L.R. 666. That was a case where the available extrinsic evidence was held to be sufficient to establish the necessary agreement between two spouses. It is chiefly of interest because both Latham C.J. and more especially Dixon J. examined with some care the whole nature of the legal theory on which these and other similar cases proceed. I would like to read three passages from the judgment of Dixon J., which state, with all the clarity and learning for which the judgments of that most eminent judge are renowned, what I believe to be a correct analysis of the principles on which a case of enforceable mutual wills depends. First (at 682–683):

'I think the legal result was a contract between husband and wife. The contract bound him, I think, during her lifetime not to revoke his will without notice to her. If she died without altering her will, then he was bound after her death not to revoke his will at all. She on her part afforded the consideration for his promise by making her will. His obligation not to revoke his will during her life without notice to her is to be implied. For I think the express promise should be understood as meaning that if she died leaving her will unrevoked then he would not revoke his. But the agreement really assumes that neither party will alter his or her will without the knowledge of the other. It has long been established that a contract between persons to make corresponding wills gives rise to equitable obligations when one acts on the faith of such an agreement and dies leaving his will unrevoked so that the other takes property under its dispositions. It operates to impose upon the survivor an obligation regarded as specifically enforceable. It is true that he cannot be compelled to make and leave unrevoked a testamentary document and if he dies leaving a last will containing provisions inconsistent with his agreement it is nevertheless valid as a testamentary act. But the doctrines of equity attach the obligation to the property. The effect is, I think, that the survivor becomes a constructive trustee and the terms of the trust are those of the will which he undertook would be his last will.'

---

[54] Usefully noted in [1982] Conv. 228 by K. Hodkinson.

"Next (at 689):

> 'There is a third element which appears to me to be inherent in the nature of such a contract or agreement, although I do not think it has been expressly considered. The purpose of an arrangement for corresponding wills must often be, as in this case, to enable the survivor during his life to deal as absolute owner with the property passing under the will of the party first dying. That is to say, the object of the transaction is to put the survivor in a position to enjoy for his own benefit the full ownership so that, for instance, he may convert it and expend the proceeds if he choose. But when he dies he is to bequeath what is left in the manner agreed upon. It is only by the special doctrines of equity that such a floating obligation, suspended, so to speak, during the life-time of the survivor can descend upon the assets at his death and crystallise into a trust. No doubt gifts and settlements, *inter vivos*, if calculated to defeat the intention of the compact, could not be made by the survivor and his right of disposition, *inter vivos*, is, therefore, not unqualified. But, substantially, the purpose of the arrangement will often be to allow full enjoyment for the survivor's own benefit and advantage upon condition that at his death the residue shall pass as arranged.'

"Finally (at 690):

> 'In *In re Oldham* Astbury J. pointed out, in dealing with the question whether an agreement should be inferred, that in *Dufour* v. *Pereira* the compact was that the survivor should take a life estate only in the combined property. It was, therefore, easy to fix the corpus with a trust as from the death of the survivor. But I do not see any difficulty in modern equity in attaching to the assets a constructive trust which allowed the survivor to enjoy the property subject to a fiduciary duty which, so to speak, crystallised on his death and disabled him only from voluntary disposition *inter vivos*.'

"I interject to say that Dixon J. was there clearly referring only to voluntary dispositions *inter vivos* which are calculated to defeat the intention of the compact. No objection could normally be taken to ordinary gifts of small value. He went on:

> 'On the contrary, as I have said, it seems rather to provide a reason for the intervention of equity. The objection that the intended beneficiaries could not enforce a contract is met by the fact that a constructive trust arises from the contract and the fact that testamentary dispositions made upon the faith of it have taken effect. It is the constructive trust and not the contract that they are entitled to enforce.'

"It is also clear from *Birmingham* v. *Renfrew* that these cases of mutual wills are only one example of a wider category of cases, for example secret trusts, in which a court of equity will intervene to impose a constructive trust. A helpful and interesting summary of that wider category of cases will be found in the argument of counsel for the plaintiffs in *Ottaway* v. *Norman* [1972] Ch. 698 at 701–702. The principle of all these cases is that a court of equity will not permit a person to whom property is transferred by way of gift, but on the faith of an agreement or clear understanding that it is to be dealt with in a particular way for the benefit of a third person, to deal with that property inconsistently with that agreement or understanding. If he attempts to do so after having received the benefit of the gift equity will intervene by imposing a constructive trust on the property which is the subject-matter of the agreement or understanding. I take that statement of principle, and much else which is of assistance in this case, from the judgment of Slade J. in *Re Pearson Fund Trusts* (October 21, 1977, unreported; the statement of principle is at p. 52 of the official transcript). The judgment of Brightman J. in *Ottaway* v. *Norman* is to much the same effect.

"I would emphasise that the agreement or understanding must be such as to impose on the donee a legally binding obligation to deal with the property in the particular way and that the other two certainties, namely those as to the subject-matter of the trust and the persons intended to benefit under it, are as essential to this species of trust as they are to any other. In spite of an argument by counsel for Mr. and Mrs. Noble to the contrary, I find it hard to see how there could be any difficulty about the second or third certainties in a case of mutual wills unless it was in the terms of the wills themselves. There, as in this case, the principal difficulty is always whether there was a legally binding obligation or merely an honourable engagement.

"Before turning in detail to the evidence which relates to the question whether there was a legally binding obligation on the testatrix in the present case or not I must return once more to *Birmingham* v. *Renfrew*. It is clear from that case, if from nowhere else, that an enforceable agreement to dispose of property in pursuance of mutual wills can be established only by clear and satisfactory evidence. That seems to me to be no more than a particular application of the general rule that all claims relating to the property of deceased persons must be scrutinised with very great care. However, that does not mean that there has to be a departure from the ordinary standard of proof required in civil proceedings. I have to be satisfied on the balance of probabilities that the alleged agreement was made, but before I can be satisfied of that I must find clear and satisfactory evidence to that effect."

## QUESTIONS

1. Is a sound approach to gifts by will where secret trusts or mutual wills may be involved as follows:

(1) Appearance of (a) incorporation by reference (b) half-secret trust (c) fully secret trust (d) mutual wills?

(2) If (a) does the will refer to an ascertainable already existing document or does it attempt to incorporate a future document or an assortment of present and future documents?

(3) If (b) so that on the face of the will there really was an intent to create a binding obligation were the terms of the obligation (i) communicated before or after the will and, if before, were they (ii) communicated in accordance with the will (iii) to a person who accepted them and (iv) who does not take beneficially under the trust if the obligation was a trust and not a gift upon condition?

(4) If (c) so that there was an intention outside of the will to create a binding obligation were the terms of the obligation (i) communicated in the testator's lifetime (ii) to a person who accepted the obligation?

(5) If (d) so that the arrangements were agreed by each testator, resulting in the alike wills, was there an acceptance that the survivor would be legally obliged to carry out the arrangements?

2. In 1981 Alan made his will as follows: "Whatever I die possessed of I give to my wife Brenda." The will was witnessed by two of Alan's daughters, Diana and Edwina. Shortly afterwards, Alan asked Brenda if she would hold half the property she received under his will for their three daughters, Diana, Edwina and Freda equally. Brenda assented to this. In 1984 Freda ran away with a merchant seaman, Wayne. As a result Alan told Brenda to keep Freda's share for herself. A year ago Diana died, childless, and a week later Alan died after a long illness. How should his £150,000 estate be distributed? Would it make any difference if Brenda disclaimed all benefits due to pass to her under the will and relied, instead, upon her rights under the intestacy rules?

3. H and W make wills in identical terms *mutatis mutandis* in pursuance of an agreement that they were each to leave their estates upon trust for sale for the survivor absolutely, the survivor being obliged to leave half of the property he owned at his death to their nephews A and B equally. Each agreed not to withdraw from the arrangement without giving notice to the other. W died childless having left all her estate upon trust for sale for H absolutely.

H later married S and made a second will leaving half his property to A and B equally, one quarter to S absolutely and one quarter to S "upon trusts which have been communicated to her." In a sealed envelope given to S shortly before H made his second will there were directions that S was to hold the quarter share given to her as trustee on trust for X for life remainder to Y absolutely, whilst one month before his death H asked S to hold her absolute quarter share upon trust for Z and she agreed. H and S were involved in a bad car crash resulting in S predeceasing H by one day.

How should H's estate be distributed if the property received by H under W's will was worth £150,000 whilst the property passing under H's will was worth £100,000? Would it make any difference if two years after W's death and seven years before his own death H had created a settlement of £40,000 on trust for X for life, remainder to Y absolutely? Would the position be any different if W's estate had been worth £500,000 and she had died intestate owing to her will failing to comply with the formalities required by the Wills Act 1837?

4. A month before he died Tim conveyed his freehold estate, Longways, to Brian Bluff, having obtained Brian's oral agreement to hold it on trust for Lucy Lovejoy. Lucy first learned of this after Tim's death, she and Tim having had a major row two weeks before Tim's death so Tim then told Brian to hold Longways for Tim.

In 1990 Tim made his will in which he appointed Roger Robinson to be his executor, he gave Braeside to Bluff "to deal with as I have directed him" and he gave his residuary estate to his widow.

Tim's signature to his will was properly witnessed by Robinson and by Bluff. Tim contemporaneously handed Bluff a diskette from an Amstrad word processor saying, "This tells you what to do with Braeside after my death but you will not find the code word to its special contents until after my death, when the code word will be in my deed box at my Bank in Buty High Street." Bluff took the diskette saying, "That's fine by me."

Tim died last week in a car crash. Bluff discovered that in the deed box there were two undated slips of paper headed "Codeword," one containing the word "Scylla," the other containing the word "Charybdis." The former makes the diskette state: "Memo to B. Bluff. Please sell Braeside, invest the proceeds and pay the income to Sue Grabbitt till her death when you can have the capital." The latter makes the diskette state: "Memo to B. Bluff. Please transfer Braeside to Sue Grabbitt." Obviously, Tim had put both messages on the diskette before making his will but the codeword device left him still able to decide which message should be the binding one.

Bluff seeks your advice about entitlement to Braeside and to Longways.

5. If trustees hold property upon trust to pay or transfer the income and or capital to the settlor or his nominee in accordance with such written directions as may from time to time be received by the trustees from the settlor in his lifetime, and on his death to transfer the property remaining to X Y and Z equally (or unequally if the settlor so directs in writing in his lifetime) then is this not a bare *Saunders* v *Vautier* (*infra* p. 651) trusteeship or agency until the settlor's death (especially, if the trustees have to invest as the settlor directs or can only invest or disinvest with the settlor's consent) so that the property remains part of the settlor's disposable estate and the settlement actually amounts to a testamentary disposition requiring compliance with the Will Act 1837?

# Chapter 3

## THE ESSENTIALS OF A TRUST

To create a trust any requisite formalities for vesting property in the trustees (known as completely constituting the trust) must be complied with and the "three certainties" must be present: certainty of intention to create a trust, certainty of subject matter of the trust and certainty of objects, thereby making the trust administratively workable and capable of being "policed" by the court. To underpin the binding obligation inherent in the trust concept the trust must be directly or indirectly for the benefit of persons (individual or corporate) so that some person has *locus standi* to apply to the court to enforce the trust,[1] unless the trust is for a limited anomalous number of non-charitable purposes relating to the maintenance of animals, tombs, etc.,[2] or for charitable purposes when the Attorney-General enforces the charitable purposes. Charitable trusts, where there is a general charitable intention, are also favoured in that they do not have to satisfy the requirement of certainty of objects (so long as the objects are sufficiently certain to be classified as exclusively charitable) and they can endure for ever whilst private trusts are limited by the perpetuity rules to a perpetuity period. As charitable trusts are a special category they are dealt with in Chapter 5.

### Section 1. Certainty of Intention to Create a Trust

#### RELATIONSHIPS OTHER THAN TRUSTS

A person may deal with his property in a variety of ways. His expressed wishes have to be examined in the context of the surrounding circumstances for indications as to the consequences he expects to flow from his actions, so that these indicia may then be seen as appropriate to the creation of a trust relationship or some other relationship.

### Bailment

If an owner delivers his goods to another on condition that they will be redelivered to the owner or according to the owner's directions when the purpose of delivering the goods (*e.g.* for cleaning or for use for a year or for safe custody) has been carried out, this will be a bailment.[3] This is a common law relationship where the bailee receives

---

[1] See section 5, p. 185.
[2] See p. 189, *infra*.
[3] See A. P. Bell, *Modern Law of Personal Property*, Chap. 5. There can be sufficient fiduciary relationship between bailor and bailee to give the bailor the equitable right to trace the bailed goods and their product: *Aluminium Industries Vaasen* v. *Romalpa* [1976] 1 W.L.R. 676 but this has been much restricted as a special case: *Clough Mill Ltd.* v. *Martin, infra*, p. 120.

a special property in the goods, the general property in which remains in the bailor.

## Agency

If an owner gives money or other property to another to do things on his behalf an agency relationship will arise. The principal can direct the agent and can terminate the agency[4] (except in certain limited circumstances[5]). The agent has power to subject his principal to liability in contract and in tort.[6] The agency normally arises as a result of a contract between principal and agent.

## Equitable charges and reservation of title

To protect his financial interests as much as possible S, a supplier of materials to a manufacturer, M Ltd., may seek to retain or obtain an equitable interest (a) in the materials; (b) any products produced using his materials and (c) any proceeds of sale of the materials or the products either until the price of the particular materials is paid or even until the price of all materials from time to time supplied by S to M Ltd. is paid. If M Ltd. did hold (a), (b) and (c) on trust for S then S would be entitled to such on the insolvency of M Ltd. in priority to M Ltd.'s creditors. However, S as legal and beneficial owner of assets does not hold the legal interest on trust for himself; he simply has full ownership which passes to M Ltd. which can then grant him an equitable interest. Because such grant is by way of security it must create an equitable charge even if purporting to create an equitable interest under a trust.[7] A floating charge, allowing the chargor to deal with the materials in the ordinary course of his business, or any other charge granted by a company (other than a charge entitling the chargee to possession either of the goods or of a document of title to them) must be registered under Companies Act 1985, s.395 or it is void against creditors and the liquidator.

The alternative effective approach for S to adopt is to reserve full legal ownership in the materials supplied when there can be no question of M Ltd. granting a registrable charge because M Ltd. owns nothing out of which a grant can be made.[8] However, if S goes further and claims to obtain legal ownership of products produced using his materials with others supplied by M Ltd. or a third party this will normally be construed as giving rise to a charge on the products in S's favour: *Clough Mill Ltd.* v. *Martin, infra*, p. 120. Similarly, any clause purporting to make S owner of the proceeds of sale of such products would be construed as creating a charge.

---

[4] Neither the settlor nor beneficiaries of a trust (unless between them absolutely entitled and *sui juris* when they can terminate the trust) have such rights. A person can be a trustee but not an agent for unborn or unascertained persons: *Swain* v. *Law Society* [1981] 3 All E.R. 797, 822.

[5] See Markesinis & Munday's *Outline of Law of Agency*, Chap. 6.

[6] The trustee has no such power and is personally liable (unlike an agent contracting as agent). If the agent has a fiduciary relationship with his principal as where he has agreed to keep separate his own money or property from that obtained on his principal's behalf then the principal has an equitable right to trace: Goff & Jones, p. 71.

[7] *Re Bond Worth Ltd.* [1980] Ch. 228.

[8] *Clough Mill Ltd.* v. *Martin* [1985] 1 W.L.R. 111, *infra*, p. 120.

Where M Ltd. is simply selling goods supplied by S then the contract can contain an acknowledgment that M Ltd. is a fiduciary bailee disposing of S's goods as an agent on the basis of keeping a separate account of S's moneys arising from sale of S's goods, so that M Ltd. is validly a trustee for S of such proceeds of sale.[9] To prevent a windfall for S, S will contract to pay M Ltd. the value agreed between them for the goods supplied plus some agreed commission.

## Loans

If A gives B £50,000 towards the purchase of Blackacre for £150,000 in B's name, though intending A to have a beneficial interest therein, then A will have one-third of the equitable interest in Blackacre (under a resulting trust) which will obviously appreciate or depreciate with the value of Blackacre. If A had merely lent B the £50,000 for B to have the whole beneficial interest in Blackacre then A would merely have a personal claim against B for the debt. If the £50,000 loan had been secured by a charge on Blackacre then A would have the right to sell Blackacre to repay himself out of the proceeds of sale. A could also forgive the debt in consideration for purchasing a specified share of Blackacre.

The one arrangement cannot be both a loan and a trust since the concepts are mutually exclusive.[10] However, a loan arrangement may commence as a primary temporary trust to carry out a purpose, resulting if the purpose is performed in a pure loan relationship excluding any trust relationship, but with a secondary final trust arising in the event of non-performance of the purpose.[11] Thus where Quistclose loaned Rolls Razor Ltd. £209,000 only for the purpose of paying a dividend on July 24, and Rolls Razor went into liquidation on July 17, so preventing any dividend being paid, the House of Lords held the money was then held on trust for Quistclose.

## Prepayments

When a company goes into liquidation (or an individual becomes bankrupt) it will be crucial whether a claimant has merely a personal claim, whether contractual or quasi-contractual, or has a proprietary claim under a trust or a charge. If a customer sent money to a

---

[9] *Aluminium Industrie Vaasen BV* v. *Romalpa Aluminium Ltd.* [1976] 1 W.L.R. 676; *Pfeiffer Weinkellerei GmbH & Co.* v. *Arbuthnot Factors Ltd.* [1988] 1 W.L.R. 150 (presumption that M Ltd. is not a bailee and selling on its own account). These cases and *Clough Mill Ltd.* v. *Martin* [1985] 1 W.L.R. 111 indicate that extending a retention of title clause to cover all moneys from time to time due does not convert the clause into a charge. See R. M. Goode, *Proprietary Rights and Insolvency in Sales Transactions* (2nd ed., 1989), p. 101 and G. McCormack [1989] Conv. 92 but contrast W. Goodhart (1986) 49 M.L.R. 96.

[10] *Re Sharpe* [1980] 1 W.L.R. 219; *Spence* v. *Browne* (1988) 18 Fam. Law 291. In an exceptional case, a female not seeking repayment of her loan to a male houseowner, with whom she cohabits, nor any interest on the loan may thereby act to her detriment on the basis of a common intention that she should acquire a share of the house so that she acquires such a share: *Risch* v. *McFee*, [1991] 1 F.L.R.105.

[11] *Barclays Bank Ltd.* v. *Quistclose Investments Ltd.* [1970] A.C. 567; *Carreras Rothmans Ltd.* v. *Freeman Mathews Treasure Ltd.* [1985] 1 All E.R. 155; *Re EVTR Ltd.* [1987] B.C.L.C. 646.

company for goods and the company went into liquidation before supplying the goods the customer with his personal claim will be a mere unsecured creditor. If the customer in his letter had stipulated that his money was to be held in trust for him till he received title to the goods, then he would have an equitable interest giving him priority over the company's creditors in so far as it was possible to trace such money. If the company, fearful of liquidation, had opened a trust bank account in which it had deposited customers' payments then, again, such a customer would have an equitable interest. It is possible to take the view as in *Re Kayford Ltd., infra*, p. 126 that the company's unilateral declaration of trust prevents the customers from becoming creditors by making them beneficiaries under a trust,[12] as in the case where the customers themselves create the trust. However, there is much to be said for the view[13] that the company's unilateral declaration of trust is a voidable preference of the customers as creditors. The customer would expect to be a mere creditor, having done nothing to prevent his payment going into the ordinary bank account of the company to be available to creditors generally. The company's voluntary act preferred the customers' interests above those of ordinary creditors, and this is a voidable preference resulting in the customers being relegated to the position of ordinary creditors.

*Privity of contract*

If A gives property to B as consideration for B's promise to do something that benefits C, then B will not hold the property on trust for C but will be under a contractual obligation to A. Only the parties to a contract can sue upon it so C will have no right to sue in respect of the contract between A and B.[14] If, exceptionally,[15] A and B[16] had positively intended to contract on the basis that A was to be trustee of the benefit of B's promise (a chose in action capable of being the subject-matter of a trust) for C, then there would be a trust which could be enforced by C against B, so long as he joined A as a party to be bound by the judgment.[17] This trust where A is settlor and trustee

---

12 *Re Kayford Ltd.* [1975] 1 W.L.R. 279. Also see *Re Chelsea Cloisters Ltd.* (1980) 41 P.&C.R. 98 (tenants' damage deposit account moneys held on trust by company landlord in liquidation).

13 Goodhart & Jones (1980) 43 M.L.R. 489, 496–498 cogently querying whether Kayford's unilateral voluntary declaration of trust contravened the Companies Act 1948, ss. 302, 320, now Companies Act 1985, ss. 597, 615.

14 See the chapters on "Privity of Contract" in textbooks like Treitel's *Law of Contract* and Cheshire & Fifoot's *Law of Contract*.

15 The courts have become increasingly reluctant to find an intention to create a trust for C if only because this renders the contract between A and B incapable of variation without C's consent, a result not often contemplated by A or B. See *Re Engelbach's Estate* [1924] 2 Ch. 48; *Vandepitte* v. *Preferred Accident Insurance Co.* [1933] A.C. 70; *Re Sinclair's Life Policy* [1938] Ch. 799; *Re Schebsman* [1944] Ch. 83; *Green* v. *Russell* [1959] 2 Q.B. 226; *Beswick* v. *Beswick* [1966] Ch. 538 (the L.P.A. 1925, s. 56 point was rejected by the Lords [1968] A.C. 58). The trust argument is usually a transparent device to try to evade the doctrine of privity of contract. The intent to create a trust must be affirmatively proved: *West* v. *Houghton* (1879) L.R. 4 C.P.D. 197, 203.

16 The promisor's intent is relevant since the measure of his liability may depend on whether there is a trust: *Re Schebsman* [1944] Ch. 83, 89, 104.

17 *Vandepitte* v. *Preferred Accident Insurance Co.* [1933] A.C. 70, 79. It matters not that C is a volunteer, *i.e.* gave no consideration. Consideration is not required for a trust: it is very rare except in marriage settlements. A trust may be regarded as the equitable equivalent of a common law gift.

of B's promise is unusual in that the trust property (the chose in action constituted by B's promise) comes into existence only when the trust is created. A further rarer instance is where A settles the benefit of his own promise on trust for C by covenanting (a promise in a deed) with B to pay £60,000 to B to the intent that B shall be a trustee holding the benefit of such covenant upon trust for C.[18]

*Possibilities of construction*

If a testator by will leaves property to B and requires B to make some payment to C or perform some obligation in favour of C, there are five possible constructions open to a court. The testator's words may be treated as:

(i) Merely indicating his motive, so that B takes an absolute beneficial interest, *e.g.* "to my wife, B, so that she may support herself and the children according to their needs" or "to my daughter B, on condition she provides a home for my handicapped daughter, C."[19]

(ii) Creating a charge on the property given to B, so that B takes the property beneficially subject to the charge for securing payment of money to C,[20] *e.g.* "my office block, Demeter House, to my son, B, subject to paying thereout £10,000 p.a. to my widow, C."

(iii) Creating a trust in favour of C,[21] *e.g.* "my office block, Demeter House, to B absolutely but so that he must pay the rents and profits therefrom to my widow C for the rest of her life."

(iv) Creating a personal obligation binding B to C when if B accepts the property he must perform the obligation in C's favour[22] (even if it costs him more than the value of the property[23]) *e.g.* "my leasehold cottage currently subleased to X I hereby devise to B absolutely on condition that he agrees to pay my widow C £3,500 p.a. for the rest of her life."

(v) Creating a condition subsequent that affects the property in B's hands making B liable to forfeit the property if the condition is broken,[24] *e.g.* "my 500,000 £1 shares in Fantabulous Co. Ltd. to B Charity Co. on condition that it pays my widow, C, an annuity of £10,000 for her life and properly maintains my family burial vault, and upon any failure to observe this condition then the R.S.P.C.A. shall become entitled to the shares."

## CLOUGH MILL LTD. v. MARTIN

Court of Appeal [1984] 3 All E.R. 982 [1985] 1 W.L.R. 111.

---

[18] *Fletcher* v. *Fletcher* (1844) 4 Hare 67, *infra*, p. 238.
[19] *Re Brace* [1954] 1 W.L.R. 955; *cf. Re Frame* [1939] Ch. 700.
[20] *Re Oliver* (1890) 62 L.T. 533. B is under no personal obligation to make up any deficiency caused by insufficiency of the property charged.
[21] *e.g. Irvine* v. *Sullivan* (1869) L.R. 8 Eq. 673.
[22] *Re Lester* [1942] Ch. 324.
[23] *Re Hodge* [1940] Ch. 260.
[24] *Att.-Gen.* v. *Cordwainers' Company* (1833) 3 My. & K.; 40 E.R. 203; *Re Oliver* (1890) 62 L.T. 533; *Re Tyler* [1891] 3 Ch. 252.

ROBERT GOFF L.J.: "This appeal is concerned with what is sometimes called 'a retention of title clause', but more frequently nowadays a 'Romalpa clause.' The appellants, Clough Mills Ltd., carry on business as spinners of yarn. Under four contracts entered into between December 1979 and March 1980 they contracted to supply yarn to a company called Heatherdale Fabrics Ltd. (which I shall refer to as 'the buyers'), which carried on business as manufacturers of fabric. When the appellants entered into these contracts, they knew that the yarn to be supplied under them was to be used by the buyers for such manufacture. Each of the contracts incorporated the appellants' standard conditions. These included a condition (condition 12) entitled 'Passing of title'; this is the Romalpa clause, with the construction and effect of which this case is concerned. It is convenient that I should immediately set out the terms of condition 12. It is a continuous clause, but I will, for convenience of reference, segregate the four sentences of which the condition is comprised into separate paragraphs. It reads as follows:

'However the ownership of the material shall remain with the Seller, which reserves the right to dispose of the material until payment in full for all the material has been received by it in accordance with the terms of this contract or until such time as the Buyer sells the material to its customers by way of bona-fide sale at full market value.

If such payment is overdue in whole or in part the Seller may (without prejudice to any of its other rights) recover or re-sell the material or any of it and may enter upon the Buyer's premises by its servants or agents for that purpose.

Such payments shall become due immediately upon the commencement of any act or proceeding in which the Buyer's solvency is involved.

If any of the material is incorporated in or used as material for other goods before such payment the property in the whole of such goods shall be and remain with the Seller until such payment has been made, or the other goods have been sold as aforesaid, and all the Seller's rights hereunder in the material shall extend to those other goods.'

On March 11, 1980 the respondent, Geoffrey Martin, was appointed receiver of the buyers under the terms of a debenture granted in favour of Lloyds Bank. On that date the buyers still owed to the appellants part of the purchase price due under each of the four contracts, and the buyers retained at their premises 375 kg of unused yarn supplied under those contracts and still unpaid for. So on March 11, 1980 the appellants wrote to the receiver expressing their intention to repossess the unused yarn, and on March 19 their solicitors wrote a further letter to the same effect, invoking the appellants' standard conditions, and requesting the receiver to stop using the unused yarn in the manufacture of fabric. On the following day the solicitors acting for the receiver replied that the appellants' retention of title clause was invalid for, inter alia, non-registration under section 95 of the Companies Act 1948 and that the receiver would therefore continue to allow the yarn to be used and would refuse the appellants admission to collect it. The receiver has since allowed the buyers to use the yarn in its manufacturing process, but the balance of the price has not been paid. The appellants therefore commenced proceedings, claiming damages from the receiver for conversion of the yarn. His Honour Judge O'Donoghue ([1984] 1 W.L.R. 1067 [1984] 1 All E.R. 721), sitting as a judge of the High Court, dismissed the claim, holding that, on its true construction, condition 12 created a charge on the yarn and that such charge was void for non-registration under section 95. It is against that decision that the appellants now appeal to this court.

"There has been a spate of decisions in recent years concerning these so-called Romalpa clauses. But it is of great importance to bear in mind that these cases have been concerned with different clauses, very often in materially different terms, that different cases have raised different questions for decision and that the decision in any particular case may have depended on how the matter was presented to the court, and in particular may have depended on a material concession by counsel. So this is a field in which we have to be particularly careful in reading each decision in the light of the facts and issues before the court in question. So, for example, the original Romalpa case, *Aluminium Industrie Vaasen BV* v. *Romalpa Aluminium Ltd.* [1976] 1 W.L.R. 676 [1976] 2 All E.R. 552, was concerned with the question whether sellers of aluminium foil under contracts containing a Romalpa clause could trace their title into money which was the proceeds of sale by the buyers of aluminium foil supplied by the sellers. That question (which was answered in the affirmative) was considered on the basis that, as was admitted by the buyers, title to the foil itself had been retained by the sellers and that the buyers became bailees of the foil on delivery to them. By contrast, the question in the present case is whether, under condition 12, the appellants did indeed retain their title to the yarn or (as the judge held) thereby became chargees of the yarn, a point which did not fall for decision in the *Romalpa* case. Again, in *Re Bond Worth Ltd.*; [1980] Ch. 228 [1979] 3 All E.R. 919, a case on which the judge in the present case placed particular reliance, Slade J. had to consider, in relation to facts of considerable complexity, a clause which provided not simply that 'the ownership' in the goods should be retained by the sellers, but that 'equitable and beneficial ownership' should remain with the sellers until full payment had been received or until prior resale, in which case their 'beneficial entitlement' should attach to the proceeds of sale. In that case, therefore, it was never suggested that the sellers retained the legal title to the goods; the only two possibilities were the creation of a trust or of a charge, and Slade J. held that it was a charge which had been created. Finally, in *Borden (UK) Ltd.* v. *Scottish Timber Products Ltd.* [1981] Ch. 25 [1979] 3 All E.R. 961 the question at issue was whether, under a contract of sale of resin containing a Romalpa clause, the sellers could trace their title into chipboard in which resin supplied by the sellers had been incorporated during its manufacture by the buyers. This court held that they could not do so, the manufacture of the chipboard having amalgamated the resin and other ingredients into a new product by an irreversible process, so that the resin ceased to exist and the title in it must also have ceased to exist. However, in that case Templeman L.J. made certain observations about the general effect of the Romalpa clause in the contract then before the court which have been of assistance to me in considering the question in the present case.

"I approach that question as follows. We have to construe condition 12 as a whole, and in its contractual context; but it is convenient to start with the opening sentence of the condition, on which the appellants particularly rely. In that sentence, it is provided:

' . . . the ownership of the material shall remain with the Seller, which reserves the right to dispose of the material until payment in full for all the material has been received by it in accordance with the terms of this contract or until such time as the Buyer sells the material to its customers by way of bona-fide sale at full market value.'

"Now there are various points to notice about this sentence. The first is that what is reserved by the seller is the ownership of the material, the material being the material supplied under the particular contract (see condition 1(a)(ii)). Prima facie, in a commercial document such as this, ownership means, quite simply, the property in the goods. The second point is that the reservation of the right to dispose of the material is expressed to be until a certain event, *viz.* until payment in full for all the material received by the buyer or until resale by the buyer. This shows the purpose for which the right of disposal is reserved, which is to provide the seller with security for any unpaid and overdue purchase price payable under the contract. It is obvious from the third sentence that the possibility of insolvency is a matter which is particularly in contemplation. It also appears from the first sentence that the buyer has power to sell the material to his customers; and we know from the fourth sentence that it is also contemplated that the buyer has power to consume the material in the manufacture of goods, mixing it with other material in the process, the function of the last sentence being to provide for the rights of the seller in, and in respect of, any such manufactured goods. The second sentence empowers the seller to recover to resell the material or any of it, and to enter on the buyer's premises for that purpose.

"The submission of counsel for the appellants as to the nature of the appellants' retention of title under the first sentence of the condition was extremely simple. Under the Sale of Goods Act 1979 a seller of goods is fully entitled, after delivery of the goods to the buyer, to retain title in the goods until he has been paid: see section 19(1) of that Act. That is precisely what the appellants have done by condition 12. The appellants' title did not derive from the contract; on the contrary, it was simply retained by them, though under the contract power was conferred on the buyers both to sell the goods and to use them in manufacturing other goods. As the buyers never acquired any title to the unused yarn in question, they could not charge the yarn to the appellants. So the appellants were, quite simply, the owners of the yarn; and there was no question of there being any charge on the yarn in their favour, which was void if unregistered.

"This attractively simple approach was challenged by counsel for the receiver. He submitted, first of all, that, if the first sentence of condition 12 is read literally, as counsel for the appellants suggested it should be read, the buyers can only have had possession of the yarn in a fiduciary capacity, whether as bailees or as fiduciary agents. But, he said, the power conferred on the buyers under the contract, not merely to sell the material but also to mix it with other materials in the manufacture of goods, was inconsistent with the existence of any fiduciary capacity in the buyers, or indeed with the appellants' unqualified ownership of the yarn. In support of this submission, he relied in particular on a proposition derived from the judgment of Slade J. in *Re Bond Worth Ltd.* [1980] Ch. 228 at 261 [1979] 3 All E.R. 919 at 949, when he said:

' . . . where an alleged trustee has the right to mix tangible assets or moneys with his own other assets or moneys and to deal with them as he pleases, this is incompatible with the existence of a *presently* subsisting fiduciary relationship in regard to such particular assets or moneys.' (Slade J.'s emphasis.)

"Now this is a submission which I am unable to accept. In every case, we have to look at the relevant documents and other communications which have passed between the parties, and to consider them in the light of the relevant surrounding circumstances, in order to ascertain the rights and duties of the parties *inter se*, always paying particular regard to the practical effect of any conclusion concerning the nature of those rights and duties. In performing this task, concepts such as bailment and fiduciary duty must not be allowed to be our masters, but must rather be regarded as the tools of our trade. I for my part can see nothing objectionable in an agreement between parties under which A, the owner of goods, gives possession of those goods to B, at the same time conferring on B a power of sale and a power to consume the goods in manufacture, though A will remain the owner of the goods until they are either sold or consumed. I do not see why the relationship between A and B, pending sale or consumption, should not be the relationship of bailor and bailee, even though A has no right to trace the property in his goods into the proceeds of sale. If that is what the parties have agreed should happen, I can see no reason why the law should not give effect to that intention. I am happy to find that both Staughton and Peter Gibson J.J. have adopted a similar approach in the recently reported cases of *Hendy Lennox (Industrial Engines) Ltd.* v. *Grahame Puttick Ltd.* [1984] 1 W.L.R. 485 [1984] 2 All E.R. 152 and *Re Andrabell Ltd.* [1984] 3 All E.R. 407.

"Even so, it is necessary to examine counsel for the appellants' construction in a little more detail. If, under this condition, retention of title applied only to goods not yet paid for, I can see that his construction could be given effect to without any problem. But the difficulty with the present condition is that the retention of title applies to material, delivered and retained by the buyer, until payment in full for *all* the material delivered under the contract has been received by the seller. The effect is therefore that the seller may retain his title in material still held by the buyer, even if part of that material has been paid for. Furthermore, if in such circumstances the seller decides to exercise his rights and resell the material, questions can arise concerning (1) whether account must be taken of the part payment already received in deciding how much the seller should be entitled to sell and (2) whether, if he does resell, he is accountable to the buyer either in respect of the part payment already received, or in respect of any profit made on the resale by reason of a rise in the market value of the material. . . .

"To me, the answer to these questions lies in giving effect to the condition in accordance with its terms, and on that approach I can discern no intention to create a trust. The condition provides that the seller retains his ownership in the material. He therefore remains owner; but, during the subsistence of the contract, he can only exercise his powers as owner consistently with the terms, express and implied, of the contract. On that basis, in my judgment, he can during the subsistence of the contract only resell such amount of the material as is needed to discharge the balance of the outstanding purchase price; and, if he sells more, he is accountable to the buyer for the surplus. However, once the contract has been determined, as it will be if the buyer repudiates the contract and the seller accepts the repudiation, the seller will have his rights as owner (including, of course, his right to sell the goods) uninhibited by any contractual restrictions; though any part of the purchase price received by him and attributable to the material so resold will be recoverable by the buyer on the ground of failure of consideration, subject to any set-off arising from a cross-claim by the seller for damages for the buyer's repudiation.

" . . . If this approach is right, I can see no reason why the retention of title in the first sentence of condition 12 should be construed as giving rise to a charge on the unused material in favour of the seller. In the course of his

argument counsel for the receiver prayed in aid another proposition culled
from the judgment of Slade J. in *Re Bond Worth Ltd.* [1980] Ch. 228 at 248
[1979] 3 All E.R. 919 at 939 when he said:

> 'In my judgment, any contract which, by way of security for payment
> of a debt, confers an interest in property defeasible or destructible on
> payment of such debt, or appropriates such property for the discharge of
> the debt, must necessarily be regarded as creating a mortgage or charge,
> as the case may be. The existence of the equity of redemption is quite
> inconsistent with the existence of a bare trustee-beneficiary
> relationship."

"However, so far as the retention of title in unused materials is concerned, I
see no difficulty in distinguishing the present case from that envisaged by Slade
J. Under the first sentence of the condition, the buyer does not, by way of
security, *confer* on the seller an interest in property defeasible on the payment
of the debt so secured. On the contrary, the seller *retains* the legal property in
the material.

"There is however one further point which I must consider. Counsel for the
receiver relied, in support of his argument, on the fourth sentence of the
condition. It will be remembered that this reads as follows:

> 'If any of the material is incorporated in or used as material for other
> goods before such payment the property in the whole of such goods shall
> be and remain with the Seller until such payment has been made, or the
> other goods have been sold as aforesaid, and all the Seller's rights
> hereunder in the material shall extend to those other goods.'

"The submission of counsel for the receiver was that the effect of this
provision is to confer on the seller an interest in the buyer's property and so
must have been to create a charge; and he further submitted that, having
regard to the evident intention that the seller's rights in goods in which the
material provided by him has been incorporated shall be the same as his rights
in unused material, the seller's rights in unused material should likewise be
construed as creating a charge.

"Now it is no doubt true that, where A's material is lawfully used by B to
create new goods, whether or not B incorporates other material of his own, the
property in the new goods will generally vest in B, at least where the goods are
not reducible to the original materials (see Bl. Com. (14th ed. pp. 404–405).
But it is difficult to see why, if the parties agree that the property in the goods
shall vest in A, that agreement should not be given effect to. On this analysis,
under the fourth sentence of the condition as under the first, the buyer does
not *confer* on the seller an interest in property defeasible on the payment of
the debt; on the contrary, when the new goods come into existence the
property in them *ipso facto* vests in the seller, and he thereafter retains his
ownership in them, in the same way and on the same terms as he retains his
ownership in the unused material. However, in considering the fourth sentence, we have to take into account not only the possibility that the buyer may
have paid part of the price for the material, but also that he will have borne
the cost of manufacture of the new goods, and may also have provided other
materials for incorporation into those goods; and the condition is silent, not
only about repaying such part of the price for the material as has already been
paid by the buyer, but also about any allowance to be made by the seller to the
buyer for the cost of manufacture of the new goods, or for any other material

incorporated by the buyer into the new goods. Now, no injustice need arise from the exercise of the seller's power to resell such goods provided that, having applied the price received from the resale in satisfaction of the outstanding balance of the price owed to him by the buyer, he is bound to account for the remainder to the buyer. But the difficulty of construing the fourth sentence as simply giving rise to a retention by the seller of title to the new goods is that it would lead to the result that, on the determination of the contract under which the original material was sold to the buyer, the ownership of the seller in the new goods would be retained by the seller uninhibited by any terms of the contract, which had then ceased to apply; and I find it impossible to believe that it was the intention of the parties that the seller would thereby gain the windfall of the full value of the new product, deriving as it may well do not merely from the labour of the buyer but also from materials that were his, without any duty to account to him for any surplus of the proceeds of sale above the outstanding balance of the price due by him to the seller. It follows that the fourth sentence must be read as creating either a trust or a charge. In my judgment, however, it cannot have been intended to create a trust. Those who insert Romalpa clauses in their contracts of sale must be aware that other suppliers might do the same; and the prospect of two lots of material, supplied by different sellers, each subject to a Romalpa clause which vests in the seller the legal title in a product manufactured from both lots of material, is not at all sensible. Accordingly, consistent with the approach of Vinelott J. to a similar provision in *Re Peachdart Ltd.* [1984] Ch. 131 [1983] 3 All E.R. 204, I have come to the conclusion that, although it does indeed do violence to the language of the fourth sentence of the condition, that sentence must be read as giving rise to a charge on the new goods in favour of the seller.

"Even so, I do not see why the presence of the last sentence in the condition should prevent us from giving effect to the first sentence in accordance with its terms. The fact that I feel driven to do violence to the language of the fourth sentence of the condition is not of itself enough to persuade me that further violence must be done to the language of the first. The provision in the first sentence is perfectly clear. The concept of retention of title, or reservation of the right of disposal, pending payment of the price is, and has for very many years been, well known in commerce as section 19(1) of the Sale of Goods Act 1979 clearly demonstrates. For my part I cannot see why, if the law should require that the fourth sentence, expressed to be a retention of title, must nevertheless take effect as a charge, we should be required to impose a meaning on the first sentence which conflicts with the natural and ordinary meaning of the words there used.

"I recognise that, on the view which I have formed of the retention of title in the first sentence of condition 12 in this case, its effect is very similar to that of a charge on goods created by the buyer in favour of the seller. But the simple fact is that under the first sentence of the condition the buyer does not in fact confer a charge on his goods in favour of the seller: on the contrary, the seller retains his title in his goods, for the purpose of providing himself with security. I can see no reason in law why a seller of goods should not adopt this course, and, if the relevant contractual term is effective to achieve that result, I can see no reason why the law should not give effect to it in accordance with its terms."

## RE KAYFORD LTD.

Chancery Division [1975] 1 W.L.R. 279 [1975] 1 All E.R. 604

The company conducted a mail order business. Customers either paid the full price for goods in advance, or paid a deposit. Its suppliers got into difficulties and Kayford could not meet orders. Its accountants advised the company to open a separate "customers' trust deposit account" and pay into it all money received from customers for goods not yet delivered, withdrawing money only upon delivery of goods. The object was to allow the company fully to refund payments to customers should the company go into liquidation. The company accepted this advice except that the money was paid into a dormant account in the company's name, the title of the account being changed later. When the company went into liquidation, the liquidators sought a declaration as to the ownership of the sums of money paid into the account.

MEGARRY J.: "I may say at the outset that on the facts of the case counsel for the joint liquidators was unable to contend that any question of a fraudulent preference arose. If one leaves on one side any case in which an insolvent company seeks to declare a trust in favour of creditors, one is concerned here with the question not of preferring creditors but of preventing those who pay money from becoming creditors, by making them beneficiaries under a trust.

" . . . I feel no doubt that the intention was that there should be a trust. There are no formal difficulties. The property concerned is pure personalty, and so writing, though desirable, is not an essential. There is no doubt about the so-called 'three certainties' of a trust. The subject-matter to be held on trust is clear, and so are the beneficial interests therein, as well as the beneficiaries. As for the requisite certainty of words, it is well settled that a trust can be created without using the words 'trust' or 'confidence' or the like: the question is whether in substance a sufficient intention to create a trust has been manifested.

"In *Re Nanwa Gold Mines Ltd.* [1955] 1 W.L.R. 1080 [1955] 1 All E.R. 219, the money was sent on the faith of a promise to keep it in a separate account, but there is nothing in that case or in any other authority that I know of to suggest that this is essential. I feel no doubt that here a trust was created. From the outset the advice (which was accepted) was to establish a trust account at the bank. The whole purpose of what was done was to ensure that the moneys remained in the beneficial ownership of those who sent them, and a trust is the obvious means of achieving this. No doubt the general rule is that if you send money to a company for goods which are not delivered, you are merely a creditor of the company unless a trust has been created. The sender may create a trust by using appropriate words when he sends the money (though I wonder how many do this, even if they are equity lawyers), or the company may do it by taking suitable steps on or before receiving the money. If either is done, the obligations in respect of the money are transformed from contract to property, from debt to trust. Payment into a separate bank account is a useful (though by no means conclusive) indication of an intention to create a trust, but of course there is nothing to prevent the company from binding itself by a trust even if there are no effective banking arrangements.

" . . . In cases concerning the public, it seems to me that where money in advance is being paid to a company in return for the future supply of goods or services, it is an entirely proper and honourable thing for a company to do what this company did, on skilled advice, namely, to start to pay the money into a trust account as soon as there begin to be doubts as to the company's ability to fulfil its obligations to deliver the goods or provide the services. I wish that, sitting in this court, I had heard of this occurring more frequently; and I can only hope that I shall hear more of it in the future."

## TRUSTS AND POWERS

Special attention has to be given to the distinction between trusts and powers which is complicated by the fact that the trustees will in many cases not just have trusts which they *must* carry out but also dispositive (as opposed to administrative) powers which they *may or may not* exercise. Furthermore, in construing a clause in a trust deed there may be a fine (and perhaps artificial) distinction between (a) a power of distribution of income coupled with a trust to dispose of the undistributed surplus and (b) a trust for distribution coupled with a power to withhold a portion and accumulate it or otherwise dispose of it, (*e.g.* (a) on trust to pay or apply the income to or for the benefit of such of my family company's employees, ex-employees and their relatives and dependants as my trustees may see fit but so that my trustees shall pay or apply any income not so paid or applied within three months of receipt by my trustees to or for the benefit of such of my issue as my trustees shall see fit and (b) on trust to pay or apply the income to or for the benefit of such of my family company's employees, ex-employees and their relatives and dependants as my trustees shall see fit but so that my trustees may pay or apply any income within three months of receiving it to or for the benefit of such of my issue as my trustees may see fit).

A trustee *must*[25] act in accordance with the terms of the trust and whilst such terms may leave him no discretion (*e.g.* if holding on trust for A for life, remainder to B when he must pay the income to A and then on A's death pay the capital to B) sometimes such terms may afford him some discretion, as in the case of a discretionary trust (*e.g.* on trust to distribute the income and capital as he sees fit between such of A, B, C, D and E and their spouses and issue as he may choose). Lack of someone to enforce a trust is fatal to its validity.[26]

A power, which is the authority to deal with property which one does not own, may be legal where it is a statutory power of attorney[27] or a mortgagee's statutory power of sale,[28] but it is usually a power to choose who are to be the beneficial recipients of property and such power is equitable[29] and will arise under a trust. Such a power will be a special power unless the donee can himself appoint to himself when it will be a general power.[30] Where a special power is exercisable in favour of everyone but a small excepted class (*e.g.* the settlor and his spouse and past and present trustees) it is often referred to as a hybrid

---

[25] If he does not then the court will intervene to ensure that the trusts are carried out: *McPhail* v. *Doulton* [1971] A.C. 424, 457, *infra*, p. 158.
[26] Except in limited anomalous cases: p. 189, *infra*.
[27] Powers of Attorney Act 1971.
[28] Law of Property Act 1925, ss. 88, 101, 104.
[29] *Ibid.* s. 1(7).
[30] *Re Penrose* [1933] Ch. 793, Perpetuities Act 1964, s. 7.

or intermediate power.[31] The validity of a power does not depend upon the existence of someone capable of supervising its exercise.[32]

The donee of a special power will usually be a trustee but, as far as the power is concerned, the donee *may or may not* exercise it as he chooses, *e.g.* where he holds on trust with power to distribute income amongst such of V, W, X, Y, Z as he sees fit but in default of appointment upon trust for A for life, remainder to B absolutely. Here, he can choose whether or not to pay income to V, W, X, Y, Z but, if he does not so choose or does not exercise his discretion in respect of particular income within a reasonable time so that his discretion is extinguished,[33] then the income in question must be paid to A. A trustee with a special power must ask two interrelated questions: (1) "Shall I exercise the power?" (2) "If so, how shall I exercise it?" A trustee of a discretionary trust just asks "How shall I exercise my duty to distribute income amongst the beneficiaries?"

### *Powers are fiduciary or personal*

Whilst the donee of a power need not exercise it he will, if a trustee, be under an obligation bona fide to consider exercising the power and to this end to take reasonable steps to discover the identities and needs of objects of the power.[34] Someone who is donee of a special power in a personal, as opposed to a fiduciary, capacity is not under the obligation to consider exercising the power (*e.g.* where a testator's will trusts have E and F as trustees but the widow is given power to appoint a certain maximum amount of property between grandchildren). The personal donee of a special power can release it unlike a fiduciary donee who can only do so if authorised by the trust instrument.[35] Powers vested in trustees as such are fiduciary (unless there is express contrary intent in the trust instrument).

### *Position of beneficiaries*

Beneficiaries under a discretionary trust and objects of a special power held by trustees have much in common.[36] Both have a right to retain any sums properly paid by the trustees in exercise of their discretion; both have a right to prevent certain kinds of conduct on the part of the trustees, *e.g.* trustees distributing to persons outside the class of beneficiaries or objects or trustees acting mala fide; both have a right to be considered by the trustees with a view to a distribution in their favour, though the trustees' duty of inquiry of possible recipients is higher where they have to carry out discretionary trusts than where they merely have to consider whether or not to exercise a power.[37]

---

[31] *Re Hay's Settlement* [1982] 1 W.L.R. 202.
[32] *Re Douglas* (1887) 35 Ch.D. 472, *Re Shaw* [1957] 1 W.L.R. 729.
[33] *Re Allen-Meyrick's W.T.* [1966] 1 W.L.R. 499; *Re Gulbenkian's S.T. (No. 2)* [1970] Ch. 408.
[34] *McPhail* v. *Doulton* [1971] A.C. 424; *Re Manisty* [1974] Ch. 17; *Re Hay's S.T.* [1982] 1 W.L.R. 202, *infra*, p. 163.
[35] *Re Wills's Trust Deeds* [1964] Ch. 219. See further, p. 146, *infra*.
[36] *Vestey* v. *I.R.C.* [1979] 2 All E.R. 225, 235–236.
[37] *McPhail* v. *Doulton* [1971] A.C. 424.

However, where under discretionary trusts income has to be distributed year by year (an exhaustive discretionary trust)[38] amongst a discretionary class then if all members of such class are ascertained and of full capacity they can, if unanimous, call for the income and so have a collectively enforceable right: they can have a similar right if also similarly interested in capital.[39] The collective objects of a special power can have no such right. Furthermore, discretionary trusts over income remain exercisable despite the passing of time, though only in favour of such persons as would have been possible beneficiaries if the discretion had been exercised within a reasonable time, whilst if powers over income are not exercised within a reasonable time the discretion is extinguished and the default beneficiaries are entitled.[40]

Problems can arise in ascertaining the intentions of a testator. He may intend to leave property to his executors and trustees on trust for W for life with:

(1) a mere power for her to appoint the capital amongst such of their children as she may see fit, so that if the power is not exercised the capital is held on a resulting trust for the testator's estate[41];

(2) a mere power for her to appoint the capital amongst such of their children as she may see fit, but in default of appointment remainder for their children equally[42];

(3) a mere power for her to appoint the capital amongst such of their children as she may see fit, but in default of appointment for such of their children and in such shares as his executors and trustees shall select in their absolute discretion[43];

(4) a "trust" power whereby she must exercise the power to appoint the capital (vested in the executors and trustees) amongst such of their

---

38 A discretionary trust is "exhaustive" where the trustees must distribute the income amongst class "A" and "non-exhaustive" where the trustees must distribute the income amongst class "A" *only* if they fail to exercise a power to withhold the income for some purpose such as accumulating it or using it for class "B." There is a fine line between the latter situation and a trust for accumulation or for benefiting discretionary class "B" with a power to benefit discretionary class "A." See *Sainsbury* v. *I.R.C.* [1970] 1 Ch. 712; *McPhail* v. *Doulton* [1971] A.C. 424, 448.

39 *Re Smith* [1928] Ch. 915; *Saunders* v. *Vautier* (1841) Cr. & Ph. 240. Rights to capital are often contingent upon being alive at the "closing date" of the trust, so preventing a *Saunders* v. *Vautier* right arising.

40 *Re Locker's S.T.* [1977] 1 W.L.R. 1323; *Re Allen-Meyrick's W.T.* [1966] 1 W.L.R. 499.

41 *Re Weekes's Settlement* [1897] 1 Ch. 289, *infra*, p. 131; *Re Combe* [1925] 1 Ch. 210 (after life interest, "in trust for such persons as my said son shall by will appoint but such appointment must be confined to relations of mine of the whole blood": held resulting trust when no appointment made); *Re Poulton's W.T.* [1987] 1 All E.R. 1068.

42 *Wilson* v. *Duguid* (1883) 24 Ch.D. 244 (trust for A for life, remainder to such of his children as he should by any writing appoint: held children had vested interests, liable to be divested by exercise of power, since there was an *implied* gift to the children equally in default of appointment). If A's power had only been exercisable by will then the implied gift in default of appointment would have been only to those children alive at A's death, since any appointment could only have been in favour of those children: *Walsh* v. *Wallinger* (1830) 2 Russ. & M. 78, 81. One should note that "to W for life, remainder to our children equally, but so that W may instead appoint the capital between our children in such shares as she may see fit" is equivalent to "to W for life, with power for her to appoint the capital amongst our children as she sees fit, but in default of appointment for our children equally": the children in both cases have immediate vested interests liable to be divested. See *Re Llewellyn's Settlement* [1921] 2 Ch. 281; *Re Arnold* [1947] Ch. 131.

43 This gift on discretionary trust in default of appointment will need to be express, whereas a gift to beneficiaries equally in default of appointment may well be implied. If the trustees do not select beneficiaries then new trustees can be appointed or the court may order equal distribution in the absence of a more appropriate basis for distribution: *McPhail* v. *Doulton* [1971] A.C. 424, 457.

children as she sees fit.[44] If the discretionary trust power is unexercised at her death then the court will order equal division on the basis that equality is equity[45] unless some other basis for distribution appears more appropriate[46] (which may well be the case if the class of objects is broader, *e.g.* my children and my nephews and nieces and the children of such persons).

Where the class of objects is so large that they cannot all be listed then, obviously, there can be no question of equal division under an implied gift in default of appointment. Thus, in welfare trusts for employees, ex-employees and their relations and dependants where the trustees are empowered to make grants to such persons, the question that arises is whether the relevant clause in the trust deed is a mere power or a "trust" power.[47] Where the person with the "trust" power has the trust property vested in him it has become the modern usage simply to say that he holds the property on discretionary trust.[48]

The similarities between discretionary trusts and powers have led to the certainty test being the same for both: both are valid if it can be said with certainty of any given beneficiary or object that he is or is not a member of the class of beneficiaries or objects.[49] For a fixed trust for equal division, however, since it is necessary to know the exact number of beneficiaries to arrange for equal arithmetical division, the trust will only be valid if a comprehensive list of all the beneficiaries can be drawn up.

In reading cases and textbooks it is necessary to be aware of the fact that discretionary trusts are sometimes referred to as trust powers or powers in the nature of a trust, and that the situation where, after a power, there is implied a trust in default for persons equally, is sometimes referred to as a trust power or a power in the nature of a trust or a power coupled with a trust.

In ascertaining whether or not only a mere power and no more is intended the following propositions[50] can be stated:

---

[44] *Brown* v. *Higgs* (1803) 8 Ves. 561; M. C. Cullity (1976) 54 Can.B.R. 229.

[45] In *Wilson* v. *Duguid* (1883) 24 Ch.D. 244, 249 Chitty J. adverts to the distinction between a trust power and a trust in default of appointment under a mere power. Where the class is small like "children," then the class members take equally on either view (*e.g. Burrough* v. *Philcox* (1840) 5 My. & Cr. 72) so why create the paradoxical concept of a trust power as inquired by M. G. Unwin (1962) 26 Conv. 92? See also [1984] Conv. 227 (Bartlett and Stebbings). However, unequal division is possible in the case of a trust power and this may be appropriate where the class is larger, *e.g.* my children and my nephews and nieces and their issue. Moreover, even where the class is as small as children it may be that the class includes children who predeceased W and the court may prefer to divide the capital only between those alive at W's death. If the class is children or grandchildren it is likely the gift to grandchildren will be treated as a substitutionary gift in the event of predeceasing children, so the children will take *per stirpes* like the statutory trusts on intestacy: p. 47, *supra*.

[46] *McPhail* v. *Doulton* [1971] A.C. 424, *infra*, p. 154.

[47] *Ibid*.

[48] *e.g. Re Baden's Deed Trusts (No. 2)* [1973] Ch. 9, *infra*, p. 159; *Re Hay's S.T.* [1982] 1 W.L.R. 202, *infra*, p. 163.

[49] *McPhail* v. *Doulton* [1971] A.C. 424, *infra*, p. 154.

[50] It should be noted that general powers of appointment are never considered to be in the nature of trusts, since there is no class of persons in whose favour the trust could operate. The question, therefore, arises only in connection with special powers of appointment.

(1) If there is a gift over in default of appointment, the power is a mere power,[51] even where the gift over is void for some reason.[52]

(2) A residuary gift in favour of the donee of the power is not a gift over for this purpose.[53]

(3) To cause a power to be treated as a mere power only, the gift over must be in default of appointment, and not for any other event. Thus in the absence of a gift in default of appointment, a gift over on the failure of the appointees or any of them to reach a specified age will not necessarily prevent the power from being treated as a discretionary trust or prevent the implication of a trust for the objects equally in default of appointment.[54]

(4) Where there is no gift over in default of appointment, the power may be only a mere power, or a power coupled with an implied trust in default of appointment, or a trust power or discretionary trust, according to the true intention of the settlor.[55]

### RE WEEKES' SETTLEMENT

Chancery Division [1897] 1 Cj. 289; 66 L.J.Ch. 179; 76 L.T. 112.

A testatrix gave a life interest in property to her husband with a "power to dispose of all such property by will amongst our children in accordance with the power granted to him as regards the other property which I have under my marriage settlements."[56] There was in her will no gift over in default of appointment, and the husband died intestate without having exercised the power. The surviving children of the marriage claimed the property in equal shares, on the ground that there was an implied gift to them in default of appointment.

ROMER J.: " . . . The husband did not exercise the power of appointment, and the question is whether the children take in default of appointment.

"Now, apart from the authorities, I should gather from the terms of the will that it was a mere power that was conferred on the husband, and not one coupled with a trust that he was bound to exercise. I see no words in the will to justify me in holding that the testatrix intended that the children should take if her husband did not execute the power.

"This is not a case of a gift to the children with power to the husband to select, or to such of the children as the husband should select by exercising the power.

"If in this case the testatrix really intended to give a life interest to her husband and a mere power to appoint if he chose, and intended if he did not think fit to appoint that the property should go as in default of appointment according to the settlement, why should she be bound to say more than she has said in this will?

---

[51] *e.g. Re Mills* [1930] 1 Ch. 654.
[52] *Re Sprague* (1880) 43 L.T. 236; *Re Sayer* [1957] Ch. 423.
[53] *Re Brierley* [1894] 43 W.R. 36.
[54] *Re Llewellyn's Settlement* [1921] 2 Ch. 281.
[55] *Burrough* v. *Philcox* (1840) 5 My. & Cr. 72; *Re Weekes's Settlement, infra; Re Combe* [1925] Ch. 210; *Re Perowne* [1951] Ch. 785; *Re Scarisbrick* [1951] Ch. 622; *Re Arnold's Trusts* [1947] Ch. 131; *McPhail* v. *Doulton* [1971] A.C. 424.
[56] There were gifts over in default of appointment in those settlements.

"I come to the conclusion on the words of this will that the testatrix only intended to give a life interest and a power to her husband—certainly she has not said more than that.

"Am I then bound by the authorities to hold otherwise? I think I am not. The authorities do not show, in my opinion, that there is a hard-and-fast rule that a gift to A for life with a power to A to appoint among a class and nothing more must, if there is no gift over in the will, be held a gift by implication to the class in default of the power being exercised. In my opinion the cases show (though there may be found here and there certain remarks of a few learned judges which, if not interpreted by the facts of the particular case before them, might seem to have a more extended operation) that you must find in the will an indication that the testatrix did intend the class or some of the class to take—intended in fact that the power should be regarded in the nature of a trust, only a power of selection being given, as, for example, a gift to A for life with a gift over to such of a class as A shall appoint. . . . "

*Held*, the power was a mere power only so the children were therefore not entitled in default of appointment.

### THE NECESSARY LANGUAGE TO REVEAL INTENT TO CREATE A TRUST

No technical expressions are necessary to create a trust so long as some imperative formula is used to indicate that the person with the property in question is to be subject to a legally binding obligation to hold and manage the property for others (or himself and others). Wills often create problems where a testator expresses his confidence, wish, hope or request that a particular legatee should use the legacy in a certain way. Originally, the courts[57] were only too ready to treat such precatory words as creating a trust and as James L.J. said in *Lamb* v. *Eames*[58] "the officious kindness of the Court of Chancery in interposing trusts where in many cases the father of the family never meant to create trusts, must have been a very cruel kindness indeed." Since the 1870s the courts have not allowed precatory words to create a trust unless on the consideration of the will as a whole it was clearly the intention of the testator to create a trust.[59] By Administration of Justice Act 1982, section 21 extrinsic evidence, including evidence of the testator's intention, may be admitted to assist in its interpretation (a) in so far as any part of the will is meaningless (b) in so far as the language used in any part of it is ambiguous on the face of it and (c) in so far as evidence, *other than evidence of the testator's intention*, shows that the language used in any part of it is ambiguous in the light of the surrounding circumstances.

The following clauses have been held, in context, not to create a trust: "feeling confident that she will act justly to our children in

---

[57] *Eade* v. *Eade* (1820) 5 Madd. 118, 121; *Palmer* v. *Simmonds* (1854) 2 Drew 221; *Gully* v. *Cregoe* (1857) 24 Beav. 185.

[58] (1871) 6 Ch.App. 597.

[59] *Lamb* v. *Eames* (1871) 6 Ch.App. 597; *Re Adams and Kensington Vestry* (1884) 27 Ch.D. 394. In *Re Steele's W.T.* [1948] Ch. 603 an unusual precatory formula for disposing of jewellery which Page-Wood V.-C. in *Shelley* v. *Shelley* (1868) L.R. 6 Eq. 540, had held created a trust was also apt to create a trust since it was likely the professional draftsman had the earlier formula in mind: (1968) 32 Conv. 361 (P. St. J. Langan).

dividing the same when no longer required by her,"[60] "it is my desire that she allows A.G. an annuity of £25 during her life,"[61] "I wish them to bequeath the same equally between the families of O and P,"[62] "in the fullest trust and confidence that she will carry out my wishes in the following particulars,"[63] "I request that C on her death leave her property to my four sisters."[64] Nowadays, Administration of Justice Act 1982, section 22 states, "Except where a contrary intent is shown, it shall be presumed that if a testator devises or bequeaths property to his spouse in terms which in themselves would give an absolute interest to the spouse but by the same instrument purports to give his issue an interest in the same property, the gift to the spouse is absolute notwithstanding the purported gift to the issue", *e.g.* "all my property to my wife and after her death to our children."

In *Comiskey* v. *Bowring-Hanbury*[65] a testator left to his wife "the whole of my real and personal estate in full confidence that she will make such use of it as I should have made myself and that at her death she will devise *it* to such one or more of my nieces as she may think fit and in default of any disposition by her thereof by her will I hereby *direct* that all my estate and property acquired by her under this my will *shall* at her death be equally divided among the surviving said nieces." The House of Lords (Lord Lindley dissenting) held a trust had been created: the widow could have the use of the property (*e.g.* income, occupation of the house) and could manage it (she was Settled Land Act tenant for life) but the capital had to pass on her death to the nieces equally if not passed to them in other shares by her will.

Recently the Court of Appeal[66] has not been as strict as formerly in requiring clear evidence of an intent to create a trust, but it does recognise that a settlor does not actually need to know that it is technically a trust that he is creating: he is taken to intend the legal consequences that would be apparent to a lawyer.[67]

## PAUL v. CONSTANCE

Court of Appeal [1977] 1 W.L.R. 527; [1977] 1 All E.R. 195 (Scarman, Bridge and Cairns L.JJ.)

SCARMAN L.J.: "Mr. Dennis Albert Constance was a wage earner living in Cheltenham until he died on March 9, 1974. He was married to Bridget

---

[60] *Mussoorie Bank Ltd.* v. *Raynor* (1882) 7 App.Cas. 221.
[61] *Re Diggles* (1888) 39 Ch.D. 253.
[62] *Re Hamilton* (1895) 2 Ch. 370.
[63] *Re Williams* [1897] 2 Ch. 12.
[64] *Re Johnson* [1939] 2 All E.R. 458.
[65] [1905] A.C. 84.
[66] *Paul* v. *Constance, infra*; *Re Vandervell's Trusts (No. 2)* [1974] Ch. 269, *supra*, p. 72.
[67] See also Buckley L.J. on the creation of an equitable charge in *Swiss Bank Corporation* v. *Lloyds Bank* [1980] 2 All E.R. 419, 426: "notwithstanding that the matter depends on the intention of the parties, if on the true construction of the relevant documents in the light of any admissible evidence as to surrounding circumstances the parties have entered into a transaction the legal effect of which is to give rise to an equitable charge, the fact that they may not have realised this consequence will not mean that there is no charge. They must be presumed to intend the consequences of their acts." Also *Clough Mill Ltd.* v. *Martin, supra*, pp. 120–125.

Frances Constance, the defendant in this action. But they parted in June 1965. In 1967 Mr. Constance met Mrs. Doreen Grace Paul, who is the plaintiff in this action. The two of them set up house together in December of that year, and they lived to all appearances as man and wife up to the date of Mr. Constance's death. The house in which they lived was 42 Larput Place, St. Pauls, Cheltenham, and it was the property of the plaintiff.

"In August 1969 Mr. Constance, who was employed as a fitter in or near Cheltenham, was injured at his work. He claimed damages against his employers and ultimately, in early 1973, his claim was disposed of after he had initiated legal proceedings, by the payment to him of a sum of £950. This money he received by cheque early in 1973. He discussed with the plaintiff what to do with the money, and the evidence is clear that they decided it was to go into a bank account. The two of them went to see the manager of the St. George's Square branch of Lloyds Bank in Cheltenham, and there they had a discussion about opening a bank account. According to the notes of evidence which the trial judge made, the two of them had a discussion with the bank manager. He explained to them the different sorts of accounts which they could open, and the decision was taken to open a deposit account. At that stage Mr. Constance revealed that they were not married. It is perhaps of some significance in understanding this interview if one recalls the evidence that was given by a Mr. Thomas, a fellow employee of Mr. Constance's, who said that he knew that they were not married but most people did not. After Mr. Constance had told the manager that they were not married the manager said: 'Well, it will be in your name only then?' Mr. Constance said: 'Yes.' Then Mr. Constance asked the manager what was to happen if the plaintiff wanted to draw on the account, or if he wanted the plaintiff to draw on it, and the manager said that that could be done if she used a note with Mr. Constance's signature on it authorising her to draw on the account.

"The account that was opened on that day in February 1973 is at the very heart of this case. The account was maintained in Mr. Constance's name from that date until the date of his death. Over the period between 1973 and his death, some 13 months later in 1974, further sums were paid into the account including, in particular, some sums which represented 'bingo' winnings. It is clear from the evidence that Mr. Constance and the plaintiff did play 'bingo,' and they played it really as a joint venture. They did have winnings from time to time, and at any rate three of such winnings—none of them very great— were paid into the account. It is clear from the plaintiff's evidence that they thought of those winnings as 'their winnings': neither hers nor his alone, but theirs. Nevertheless, when the account was closed on the death of Mr. Constance the ultimate balance, after the addition of interest, consisted largely of the initial sum of £950 representing Mr. Constance's damages as a result of his injury at work. There was one withdrawal during this period, a sum of £150, and the evidence was that that money was divided between the two of them after part of it had been used for buying Christmas presents and some food.

"The plaintiff began her action after the death of Mr. Constance against his lawful wife, the defendant, who took out letters of administration for his estate since he died intestate. The plaintiff claims in the action that the bank account in his name, to which I have referred, was held by him on trust for the benefit of himself and the plaintiff jointly. She claims that it was an express trust declared orally by him on numerous occasions. The defendant, as administratrix closed the account, and she maintains that the whole fund contained in the account was the beneficial property of the deceased at the time of his death, and, as such, became part of his estate after death.

"The matter came on for trial before His Honour Judge Rawlins in August 1975 and on August 12 the judge found in favour of the plaintiff. He found the existence of an express trust, a trust for the benefit of the plaintiff and the deceased jointly, and he ordered that the sum of £499.21 be paid to the plaintiff as representing one half share of the fund to which she was beneficially entitled.

"The only point taken by the defendant on her appeal to this court goes to the question whether or not there was, in the circumstances of this case, an express declaration of trust. It is conceded that if there was the trust would be enforceable.

"Counsel for the defendant drew the attention of the court to the so-called three certainties that have to be established before the court can infer the creation of a trust. He referred us to Snell's *Principles of Equity*[68] in which the three certainties are set out. We are concerned only with one of the three certainties, and it is this:

> 'The words [that is the words of the declaration relied on] must be so used that on the whole they ought to be construed as imperative. [A little later on the learned author says:] No particular form of expression is necessary for the creation of a trust, if on the whole it can be gathered that a trust was intended. "A trust may well be created, although there may be an absence of any expression in terms imposing confidence." A trust may thus be created without using the word "trust," for what the court regards is the substance and effect of the words used.'

"Counsel for the defendant has taken the court through the detailed evidence and submits that one cannot find anywhere in the history of events a declaration of trust in the sense of finding the deceased man, Mr. Constance, saying: 'I am now disposing of my interest in this fund so that you, Mrs. Paul, now have a beneficial interest in it.' Of course, the words which I have just used are stilted lawyers' language, and counsel for the plaintiff was right to remind the court that we are dealing with simple people, unaware of the subtleties of equity, but understanding very well indeed their own domestic situation. It is right that one should consider the various things that were said and done by the plaintiff and Mr. Constance during their time together against their own background and in their own circumstances.

"Counsel for the defendant drew our attention to two cases, and he relies on them as showing that, though a man may say in clear and unmistakable terms that he intends to make a gift to some other person, for instance his child or some other member of his family, yet that does not necessarily disclose a declaration of trust; and, indeed, in the two cases to which we have been referred the court held that, though there was a plain intention to make a gift, it was not right to infer any intention to create a trust.

"The first of the two cases is *Jones* v. *Lock*.[69] In that case Mr. Jones, returning home from a business trip to Birmingham, was scolded for not having brought anything for his baby son. He went upstairs and came down with a cheque made out in his own name for £900 and said, in the presence of

---

[68] (27th ed., 1973), p. 111.
[69] (1865) 1 Ch.App. 25.

his wife and nurse: 'Look you here, I give this to the baby,' and he then placed the cheque in the baby's hand. It was obvious that he was intending to make a gift of the cheque to his baby son but it was clear, as Lord Cranworth L.C. held, that there was no effective gift then and there made of the cheque; it was in his name and had not been endorsed over to the baby. Other evidence showed that he had in mind to go and see his solicitor, Mr. Lock, to make proper provision for the baby boy, but unfortunately he died before he could do so. *Jones* v. *Lock* was a classic case where the intention to make a gift failed because the gift was imperfect. So an attempt was made to say: 'Well since the gift was imperfect, nevertheless, one can infer the existence of a trust.' But Lord Cranworth L.C. would have none of it.

"In the other case to which counsel for the defendant referred us, *Richards* v. *Delbridge*,[70] the facts were that a Mr. Richards, who employed a member of his family in his business, was minded to give the business to the young man. He evidenced his intention to make this gift by endorsing on the lease of the business premises a short memorandum to the effect that[71]:

> 'This deed [*i.e.* the deed of leasehold] and all thereto belonging I give to Edward . . . [*i.e.* the boy] from this time forth with all stock in trade.'

"Jessel M.R. who decided the case, said that there was in that case the intention to make a gift, but the gift failed because it was imperfect; and he refused from the circumstances of the imperfect gift to draw the inference of the existence of a declaration of trust or the intention to create one. The *ratio decidendi* appears clearly from the report.[72] It is a short passage, and because of its importance I quote it:

> 'In *Milroy* v. *Lord*[73] Lord Justice Turner, after referring to the two modes of making a voluntary settlement valid and effectual, adds these words: "The cases, I think, go further, to this extent, that if the settlement is intended to be effectuated by one of the modes to which I have referred, the Court will not give effect to it by applying another of those modes. If it is intended to take effect by transfer, the Court will not hold the intended transfer to operate as a declaration of trust, for then every imperfect instrument would be made effectual by being converted into a perfect trust." It appears to me that that sentence contains the whole law on the subject.'

"There is no suggestion of a gift by transfer in this case. The facts of those cases do not, therefore, very much help the submission of counsel for the defendant, but he was able to extract from them this principle: that there must be a clear declaration of trust, and that means there must be clear evidence from what is said or done of an intention to create a trust, or as counsel for the defendant put it, 'an intention to dispose of a property or a fund so that somebody else to the exclusion of the disponent acquires the beneficial interest in it.' He submitted that there was no such evidence.

"When one looks to the detailed evidence to see whether it goes as far as that—and I think that the evidence does have to go as far as that—one finds

---

[70] (1874) L.R. 18 Eq. 11.
[71] L.R. 18 Eq. 11.
[72] L.R. 18 Eq. 11, 15.
[73] (1862) 4 De. G.F. & J. 264, 274, 275.

that from the time that Mr. Constance received his damages right up to his death he was saying, on occasions, that the money was as much the plaintiff's as his. When they discussed the damages, how to invest them or what to do with them, when they discussed the bank account, he would say to her: 'The money is as much yours as mine.' The judge, rightly treating the basic problem in the case as a question of fact, reached this conclusion. He said:

> 'I have read through my notes, and I am quite satisfied that it was the intention of [the plaintiff] and Mr. Constance to create a trust in which both of them were interested.'

"In this court the issue becomes: was there sufficient evidence to justify the judge reaching that conclusion of fact? In submitting that there was, counsel for the plaintiff draws attention first and foremost to the words used. When one bears in mind the unsophisticated character of Mr. Constance and his relationship with the plaintiff during the last few years of his life, counsel for the plaintiff submits that the words that he did use on more than one occasion namely: 'This money is as much yours as mine,' convey clearly a present declaration that the existing fund was as much the plaintiff's as his own. The judge accepted that conclusion. I think he was well justified in doing so and, indeed, I think he was right to do so. There are, as counsel for the plaintiff reminded us, other features in the history of the relationship between the plaintiff and Mr. Constance which support the interpretation of those words as an express declaration of trust. I have already described the interview with the bank manager when the account was opened. I have mentioned also the putting of the 'bingo' winnings into the account, and the one withdrawal for the benefit of both of them.

"It might, however, be thought that this was a borderline case, since it is not easy to pin-point a specific moment of declaration, and one must exclude from one's mind any case built on the existence of an implied or constructive trust; for this case was put forward at the trial and is now argued by the plaintiff as one of express declaration of trust. It was so pleaded, and it is only as such that it may be considered in this court. The question, therefore, is whether in all the circumstances the use of those words on numerous occasions as between Mr. Constance and the plaintiff constituted an express declaration of trust. The judge found that they did. For myself, I think he was right so to find. I therefore would dismiss the appeal."[74]

### Section 2. Certainty of Subject-matter

Certainty of subject-matter requires that the property to be held on trust must be certain and the beneficial interests to be taken by the beneficiaries must be certain.[75] However, where a court is imposing a

---

[74] Why was Mrs. Paul not entitled to the whole £998.42 as surviving joint tenant? *cf. Re Osoba* [1979] 2 Ali E.R. 393. Ought it not to be possible to identify a declaration of trust at a particular time, *e.g.* to know when Mrs. Paul's right commenced for limitation purposes, or for entitlement to interest?

[75] *Palmer* v. *Simmonds* (1854) 2 Drew. 221, 227 ("the bulk of my residuary estate" cannot satisfy the certainty requirement though "my residuary estate" can); *Re London Wine Co. (Shippers) Ltd.* [1986] *Palmer's Company Cases* 121 (settlor cannot declare itself trustee of unascertained 20 out of 80 bottles of Lafite 1970 in its cellar though it could declare it held its holding of 80 bottles on trust as for three-quarters for itself and one-quarter for X); *Boyce* v. *Boyce* (1849) 16 Sim. 476 where T devised four houses on trust to convey whichever one she chose to Maria and to convey the others to Charlotte; and upon Maria predeceasing T so that she could not choose any house it was held the trust in favour of Charlotte was void for uncertainty.

constructive trust to prevent fraudulent or unconscionable behaviour of a defendant trying to take advantage of uncertainty it will circumvent problems of uncertainty.[76]

### SPRANGE v. BARNARD

Master of the Rolls (1789) 2 Bro.C.C. 585

A testatrix provided as follows: "This is my last will and testament at my death, for my husband Thomas Sprange, to bewill to him the sum of £300, which is now in the joint stock annuities, for his sole use; and, at his death, *the remaining part of what is left, that he does not want for his own wants and use*, to be divided between my brother John Crapps, my sister Wickenden, and my sister Bauden, to be equally divided between them." The stock being vested in trustees, Thomas Sprange applied to them for payment, but they refused; whereupon he filed this bill.

ARDEN M.R.: " . . . The words are a bequest of the £300 South Sea annuities to his [Thomas Sprange's] sole use; and ' . . . at his death, the remaining part of what is left, that he does not want for his own wants,' to the brother and sisters. The husband has taken out administration and filed his bill for the sum. It is contended, for the persons to whom it is given in remainder, that he shall only have it for his life, and that the words are strictly mandatory on him to dispose of it in a certain way; but it is only to dispose of what he has no occasion for: therefore the question is whether he may not call for the whole; and it seems to be perfectly clear on all the authorities that he may. I agree with the doctrine in *Pierson* v. *Garnet*[77] following the cases of *Harland* v. *Trigg*[78] and *Wynne* v. *Hawkins*[79] that the property, and the person to whom it is to be given, must be certain in order to raise a trust. Now here the property is wasting, as it is only what shall remain at his death. . . . [80] It is contended that the court ought to impound the property; but it appears to me to be a trust which would be impossible to be executed. I must therefore declare him to be absolutely entitled to the £300, and decree it to be transferred to him. The costs to come out of the £300."[81]

### UNDERHILL & HAYTON ON TRUSTS 14TH ED., P. 44

*"Floating" (or suspended) trusts*

It used to be thought that if property were bequeathed essentially to X to pass on whatever was left at his death to Y, then this would normally be

---

[76] *Pallant* v. *Morgan* [1953] Ch. 43; *Gissing* v. *Gissing* [1971] A.C. 886, 909 ("fair" share); *Eves* v. *Eves* [1975] 3 All E.R. 768, 772; *Passee* v. *Passee* [1988] 1 F.L.R. 263, 271.

[77] (1787) 2 Bro.C.C. 226.

[78] (1782) 1 Bro.C.C. 142.

[79] (1782) 1 Bro.C.C. 179.

[80] This should read: "Now here the property, so far from being certain, is only what shall remain at his death": 29 E.R. 322.

[81] See also *In the Estate of Last* [1958] P. 137; bequest to the testatrix' brother of "everything I have. . . . At his death anything that is left, that came from me to go to my late husband's grandchildren." Held by Karminski J. that in spite of the words "anything that is left" the testatrix intended to give a life interest only to her brother, with the result that on his death the grandchildren were entitled. *Quaere* whether the result would have been the same if during his lifetime the brother had applied to the court for the determination of the question whether the bequest to him was absolute; *Re Golay* [1965] 2 All E.R. 660; 81 L.Q.R. 48 (R.E.M.); bequest of "a reasonable income" sufficiently certain. *Cf.* "reasonable price" or "reasonable rent" or "reasonable valuation" in *Talbot* v. *Talbot* [1968] Ch. 1; *Smith* v. *Morgan* [1971] 1 W.L.R. 803; *Brown* v. *Gould* [1972] A.C. 53; *Kings Motors Ltd.* v. *Lax* [1970] 1 W.L.R. 426; *Ponsford* v. *H.M.S. Aerosols Ltd.* [1978] 2 All E.R. 837; *Sudbrooke Trading Estate Ltd.* v. *Eggleton* [1983] 1 A.C. 444.

treated as an absolute gift to X[82] but, in an exceptional case, the court in context might be able to find the property had to be held on trust for X for life, remainder to Y absolutely.[83]

There is now a third possibility, *where the testator and X have reached an agreement*, since Brightman J. in *Ottaway* v. *Norman* stated[84]:

> "I am content to assume for present purposes, but without so deciding, that if property is given to [X] on the understanding that [X] will dispose by his will of such assets, if any, as he may have at his command at his death in favour of [Y], a valid trust is created in favour of [Y] which is in suspense during the lifetime of [X] but attaches to the estate of [X] at the moment of [X's] death."

Further elucidation is present in an earlier Australian case, *Birmingham* v. *Renfrew*, where Dixon J. (as he then was) stated[85]:

> "The purpose must often be to enable the survivor during his life to deal as absolute owner with the property passing under the will of the party first dying. The object is to put the survivor in a position to enjoy for his own benefit the full ownership so that he may convert it and expend the proceeds if he choose. But when he dies he is to bequeath what is left in the manner agreed upon. It is only by the special doctrines of equity that such a floating obligation, suspended, so to speak, during the lifetime of the survivor can descend upon the assets at his death and crystallise into a trust. No doubt, gifts and settlements inter vivos, if calculated to defeat the intention of the compact, could not be made by the survivor and his right of disposition inter vivos is therefore not qualified."

Where this third possibility arises it thus seems that X has an absolute interest subject to an equitable fiduciary obligation during his lifetime neither to transfer the property nor to contract to transfer the property with destructive intent to prevent the property passing to Y.[86] The obligation is rather nebulous so that a well-advised testator should leave the property to trustees for X for life, remainder to Y but give X and the trustees a joint power to appoint capital to X.

### Section 3. Certainty of Objects and Administrative Workability

*The comprehensive list test*

Prior to the radical decision in *McPhail* v. *Doulton*, *infra*, a distinction had to be drawn between trusts and powers for certainty purposes. Since trusts, even if discretionary, *have* to be carried out by

---

[82] *Sprange* v. *Barnard* (1789) 2 Bro.C.C. 585.
[83] *Re Last* [1958] P. 137; [1958] 1 All E.R. 316.
[84] [1972] Ch. 698, 713. The need for X's express or implied agreement should restrict floating trusts to secret trusts and mutual wills: it is this agreement that makes it unconscionable for him to claim the property absolutely after the testator's death.
[85] (1937) 57 C.L.R. 666, 689, endorsed by *Re Cleaver* [1981] 2 All E.R. 1018, *supra*, p. 110.
[86] It would seem that Y should have a right to trace and that Y should have a right to ensure that X kept a separate account of the property received by him subject to the fiduciary obligation. Presumably, if Y predeceased X then X's fiduciary obligation would cease. Further, see *Palmer* v. *Bank of New South Wales* (1975) 7 Austr. L.R. 671, 113 C.L.R. 150.

trustees it must be possible in default for the courts to enforce and control the trust: for this reason there must be no linguistic or semantic uncertainty, otherwise known as conceptual uncertainty, in the expression of the objects nor can the objects be such that the trust is administratively unworkable. It was considered that if trustees failed to carry out a discretionary trust then since it would be individious and injudicial for the courts to distinguish between the possible discretionary beneficiaries the court would have to act on the maxim "Equality is equity" and distribute the trust assets equally. It followed that for an equal division it must be possible to draw up a comprehensive list of the beneficiaries. Accordingly, trusts failed for uncertainty if such a list could not be drawn up.[87] This must still be the position for "fixed" trusts which require equal division amongst the beneficiaries. Thus a trust for "my relations in equal shares," has to be construed as for "my statutory next-of-kin in equal shares" to save it from being void for uncertainty.[88]

### The conceptually clear criteria test

On the other hand, where powers are concerned,[89] so long as the trustees consider whether or not to exercise the powers and do not go beyond the scope of the powers the courts cannot intervene unless the trustees can be shown to have acted mala fide or capriciously, *i.e.* for reasons which are irrational, perverse or irrelevant to any sensible expectation of the settlor. It is purely up to the trustees whether or not they exercise the powers so all that is required is that they are in a proper position to consider the exercise of the powers, *i.e.* if they can say with certainty of any given person that he is or is not within the scope of the power: *Re Gulbenkian's S.T., infra*, rejecting the view expressed in the Court of Appeal that it suffices if the trustees can say of any *one* person with certainty that he is within the scope of the power though uncertainty may exist in respect of other persons. Accordingly, a power fails for uncertainty only if the court cannot with certainty determine whether any given individual is or is not within the scope of the power.

In *McPhail* v. *Doulton, infra*, the House of Lords held by a 3:2 majority that the *Gulbenkian* test for powers is also the appropriate test for discretionary trusts as it was possible for the court to carry out a discretionary trust by distributing the trust assets not equally amongst all possible beneficiaries (surely the last thing the settlor ever intended) but in such proportions as appropriate in the circumstances "so as to give effect to the settlor's or testator's intentions. It may do so by appointing new trustees or authorising or directing representative persons of the classes of beneficiaries to prepare a scheme of distribu-

---

[87] *I.R.C.* v. *Broadway Cottages Trust* [1955] Ch. 20.
[88] *Re Ganslosev's W.T.* [1952] Ch. 30; *Re Poulton's W.T.* [1987] 1 All E.R. 1068 since it is impossible to establish all persons related by blood, however remotely.
[89] For the distinction between trusts and powers see pp. 127–130, *supra*.

tion, or even, should the proper basis for distribution appear, by itself directing the trustees so to distribute."[90] This seems to be creating a jurisdiction not that far removed from the *cy-près* jurisdiction for charitable trusts, a jurisdiction denied to ordinary trusts according to *Re Astor*[91] and *Re Denley*.[92] The case was then remitted to the High Court for determination whether on the new test the trust was valid or void for uncertainty.

### Application of test

In *Re Baden's Deed Trusts (No. 2), infra*, on appeal from the High Court the Court of Appeal unanimously held the trust valid. Stamp L.J. considered the court must be able to say of any given postulant that he definitely is a member of the beneficiary class or he definitely is *not* such a member, *i.e.* the name of a postulant must be capable of being put either in a "Yes" box or a "No" box. Thus a discretionary trust would be void if some postulants' names had to go into a "Don't know" box: if "relatives" meant descendants of a common ancestor there would be a very large number of persons, neither known to be relatives nor to be non-relatives, needing to be placed within the "Don't know" box so invalidating a discretionary trust for relatives. However, Stamp L.J. was prepared to treat relatives as meaning "next-of-kin" in which case any postulant would fall within the "Yes" box or the "No" box, so validating the trust.

Sachs and Megaw L.JJ., however, held the trust valid with "relatives" bearing its broadest meaning. Sachs L.J. took the robust practical view that if a postulant could not prove that his name should go into the "Yes" box then it went into the "No" box. Megaw L.J. treated Stamp L.J.'s view that a discretionary trust will fail if it cannot be shown of any individual that he definitely is or *definitely is not* a member of the class is to contend "in substance and reality that it does fail simply because it is impossible to ascertain every member of the class"[93] and draw up a comprehensive list thereof, a contention rejected by *McPhail* v. *Doulton*. However, in ascertaining whether *any* (as opposed to every) individual is or is not a class member it is surely not necessary to ascertain *every* class member and draw up a comprehensive list. Be that as it may, Megaw L.J. considered the "is or is not" test satisfied if "as regards a substantial number of objects it can be said with certainty that they fall within the trust, even though as regards a substantial number of other persons the answer would have to be not 'they are outside the trust' but 'it is not proven whether they are in or out.' What is a substantial number may well be a question of common sense and of some degree in relation to the particular trust."[94]

---

90 [1971] A.C. 424, 457.
91 [1952] Ch. 534.
92 [1969] 1 Ch. 373, 388.
93 [1973] Ch. 9, 23.
94 *Ibid.* 24.

However, is it so wrong for Stamp L.J. to emphasise the need to ascertain those who are *not* class members when a person alleging a breach of trust will need to prove that the trustees distributed to an individual who was *not* a class member? There is also obvious uncertainty in the word "substantial," *e.g.* in trusts similar to *Re Astor*[95] where clause 7(b) was for the relief or benefit of persons, or families or dependants thereof, actually or formerly engaged in journalism or the newspaper business or any branch thereof. What, indeed, if to a class like that in *McPhail* v. *Doulton* there was added a conceptually uncertain clause such as "any of my company's customers" or any of my old friends."[96] Moreover, the "substantial" view is only a question of degree removed from the view rejected by the Lords in *Re Gulbenkian* in relation to powers, and so in relation to trusts by *McPhail* v. *Doulton*, namely the view[97] that a power or discretionary trust is valid if it can be said with certainty of any one or a few persons[98] that he or they are within the scope of the power or discretionary trust though uncertainty exists as to whether other persons are within or without the power or discretionary trust.

The crux of the matter is how the court will deal with B's allegation that the trustees committed a breach of trust by paying income to X, who is alleged to be not a relative of A. There is no evidence capable of proving that X is or is not such a relative. Does this mean that, since B has not discharged the burden of proving that X is not a relative of A, B's action fails? If so, then the trustees are free to pay income to X and, indeed, to any Tom, Dick or Harry, since it is in practice impossible to prove that anyone is not a relative of A, for anyone might well be if we could go back far enough, *e.g.* to 4,000 B.C.. However, if, although the *legal* burden of proving such a breach of trust lies on B, the *evidential* burden of proving payment to a beneficiary lies on the trustees once B has provided prima facie evidence that the payee is not a beneficiary, then B's action will succeed. If so, then the trustees will be under an enforceable duty to pay only those who can produce the relevant birth and marriage certificates or other sufficient evidence to prove relationship. Sachs[99] and Megaw L.JJ. expressly agreed with the judge of first instance, Brightman J., for the reasons he gave and these can justify the pragmatic majority view in the Court of Appeal. He said[1]:

---

[95] [1952] Ch. 534.

[96] Is there scope for the court to develop a power to strike out an offending concept and sever it from the valid concepts within the class or classes of beneficiaries?: *Re Leek* [1969] 1 Ch. 563, 586; *Re Gulbenkian's Settlement* [1968] Ch. 126, 138. Just in the House of Lords.

[97] *Re Gulbenkian's Settlement* [1968] Ch. 126 (C.A.).

[98] Megaw L.J. in *Re Baden (No. 2)* [1973] Ch. 9, 24, treats the rejected view as concerning one person but Lord Upjohn in *Re Gulbenkian's Settlement* [1970] A.C. 508, 524, in his example of two or three individuals being clearly "old friends" treats the rejected view as concerning one or a few persons.

[99] Sachs L.J. considered that if a postulant is not proved to be within the beneficial class then he is outside it, so placing the evidential burden on the trustees to prove the payee is a relative. See *Cross on Evidence*, Chap. 4 on legal and evidential burdens of proof.

[1] [1971] 3 All E.R. 985, 995.

"In practice, the use of the expression 'relatives' cannot cause the slightest difficulty. A supposed relative to whom a grant is contemplated would, in strictness, be bound to produce the relevant birth and marriage certificates or other sufficient evidence to prove his or her relationship. If the relationship is sufficiently proved the trustees will be entitled to make the grant. If no sufficient evidence can be produced the trustees would have no option but to decline to make a grant."

On this basis the trustees ultimately must discharge the evidential burden of proving payment to a relative.

### Conceptual certainty, evidential certainty, ascertainability and administrative workability

As Carl Emery has emphasised,[2] questions concerning "certainty" of objects may relate to one or more of the following:

"(a) 'Conceptual uncertainty': this refers to the precision of language used by the settlor to define the classes of persons whom he intends to benefit.

(b) 'Evidential uncertainty': this refers to the extent to which the evidence available in a particular case enables specific persons to be identified as members of those classes—and so as beneficiaries or potential beneficiaries.

(c) 'Ascertainability': this refers to the extent to which 'the whereabouts or continued existence' of persons identified as beneficiaries or potential beneficiaries can be ascertained.

(d) 'Administrative workability': this refers to the extent to which it is practicable for trustees to discharge the duties laid upon them by the settlor towards beneficiaries or potential beneficiaries."

Evidential uncertainty does not invalidate a discretionary trust or a power since if a person is not proved to be within the beneficial class then he is outside it.[3] Ascertainability problems (*e.g.* over the whereabouts or continued existence of a relative, A, or an ex-employee, B) do not invalidate a discretionary trust or a power because such problems are valid reasons for trustees deciding not to exercise their discretions or powers, and because, in the case of a trust, the court may give leave to distribute the trust fund on the basis that X is dead[4] or may direct a scheme for distribution amongst ascertained beneficiaries.[5]

---

[2] (1982) 98 L.Q.R. 551, 552.

[3] *Re Baden's Deed Trust (No. 2)* [1973] Ch. 9, 20, *per* Sachs L.J. [1972] Ch. 607, 626, *per* Brightman J. The minority view of Stamp L.J. was to the effect that the evidential uncertainty (which he considered could not be resolved so simplistically) converted the apparent black and white certainty of concept into an uncertain grey concept.

[4] *Re Benjamin* [1902] 1 Ch. 723.

[5] *McPhail* v. *Doulton* [1971] A.C. 424, 457; *Re Hain* [1961] 1 W.L.R. 440 and *Muir* v. *I.R.C.* [1966] 3 All E.R. 38, 44 show that a trust will not be invalidated because some of the class of beneficiaries may have disappeared or become impossible to find or it has been forgotten who they were.

If a discretionary trust is not conceptually certain or not administratively workable then the express trust fails and the property will be held on resulting trust for the settlor. If a trust is not conceptually certain then it cannot be administratively workable, *e.g.* a discretionary trust "for such persons as have moral claims upon me,"[6] "for my old friends[7] and business associates," "for worthy causes,"[8] "for those of my friends and relations who are good citizens," "for my fans" (unless restricted to members of a particular fan club), "for Cambridge students" (unless restricted to students from time to time studying as junior members of the University of Cambridge). As Lord Hailsham emphasised in *I.R.C.* v. *McMullen*,[9] "Where it is claimed that there is an ambiguity, a benignant construction should be given if possible. This was the maxim of the civil law: *semper in dubiis benigniora praeferenda sunt*. There is a similar maxim in English law: *ut res magis valeat quam pereat*. It applied where a gift is capable of two constructions one of which would make it void and the other effectual."

In a very rare case a discretionary trust may be conceptually certain but, nonetheless, may be administratively unworkable, *e.g.* "for everyone in the world except the settlor, his spouse and past and present trustees"[10] or even "for the benefit of any or all or some of the inhabitants of the County of West Yorkshire."[11] Such a "trust" would not be justiciable, and a court must act judicially according to some criteria, expressly or impliedly provided by the trust instrument or by extrinsic admissible evidence, so that it may control or execute the trusts: it cannot resort to pure guesswork for such is a non-justiciable function. If you were trustee of a discretionary trust for everyone but five persons, how on earth would you begin to try to decide what to do?

However, trustees' *powers* to add anyone in the world (excepting the settlor, his spouse, past and present trustees) to the class of discretionary trust beneficiaries and trustees' powers to appoint capital or income to anyone in the world (excepting the above small class) have been upheld by judges of first instance as not capable of being invalidated by the test of administrative workability which has been restricted to trusts.[12] The basis for this distinction is that in the case of a discretionary trust a trustee is under more extensive obligations which

---

[6] *Re Leek* [1969] 1 Ch. 563.
[7] *Brown* v. *Gould* [1972] 53, 57; *Re Barlow's W.T.* [1979] 1 All E.R. 296.
[8] *Re Atkinson* [1978] 1 All E.R. 1275.
[9] [1981] A.C. 1, 11, [1980] 1 All E.R. 884, 890, *infra*, p. 308.
[10] *Re Hay's S.T.* [1982] 1 W.L.R. 202, *infra*, p. 163; *Yeap Cheo Neo* v. *Ong Chen Neo* (1875) L.R. 6 P.C. 381; *Blausten* v. *I.R.C.* [1972] Ch. 256, 266, 271, 272. The question of conceptual certainty and of administrative workability must be determined at the date of creation of the trust: *Re Baden's Deed Trust (No. 2)* [1972] Ch. 607.
[11] *R.* v. *District Auditor, ex p. West Yorkshire County Council* (1985) 26 R.V.R. 24: there were 2,500,000 potential beneficiaries.
[12] *Re Manisty's Settlement* [1974] Ch. 17; *Re Hay's S.T.* [1982] 1 W.L.R. 202, *infra*, p. 163, *Re Beatty's W.T.* [1990] 3 All E.R. 844. In *Re Denley's Trust Deed* [1969] 1 Ch. 373 Goff J. with little discussion upheld the power of trustees to allow any persons other than the trust beneficiaries to use the sports ground primarily intended for the beneficiaries' use.

the beneficiaries can enforce and which may lead to the court seeing to the carrying out of the trusts. In the case of powers a trustee only need consider periodically whether or not he should exercise the power, taking into account the range of objects of the power and the appropriateness of possible individual appointments; the only control exercisable by the court in the words of Templeman J.[13] "is the removal of the trustees and the only 'due administration' which can be 'directed' is an order requiring the trustees to consider the exercise of the power, and, in particular a request from a person within the ambit of the power." However, he also accepted[14] that the court must be able to intervene if a wide power is exercised capriciously, *i.e.* for reasons which are irrational, perverse or irrelevant to any sensible expectation of the settlor.

But if this is the case, then for the trustees' power to be justiciable the settlor's expectations must somehow be discerned.[15] If they cannot be discerned so that the power is not justiciable then it cannot be a fiduciary power, yet a power exercisable *virtute officii* can only be a fiduciary power.[16] The object of a fiduciary power has, like a beneficiary in default of exercise of the power, a right to seek the court's removal of the trustees for exercising the power for reasons which are irrational, perverse or irrelevant to any sensible expectation of the settlor. If such expectation cannot be discerned then the court cannot adjudicate on the matter and cannot determine rights and duties. Thus, Buckley L.J. considered *obiter*[17] that a power to add anyone in the world to a class of trust beneficiaries (and, presumably, by parity of reasoning a power to appoint to anyone in the world) would be void. Templeman J.[18] and Megarry V.-C.[19] have rejected this, considering[20] that "dispositions ought, if possible, to be upheld and the court ought not to be astute to find grounds on which a power can be invalidated."

The need for justiciability underlies the requirement of administrative workability yet the High Court has created a distinction between trusts where there is positive and negative justiciability and fiduciary powers where there is only negative justiciability. The distinction may well be disputed in an appellate court.[21]

---

[13] [1974] Ch. 17, 27–28.

[14] [1974] Ch. 17, 26. But the court exercised a power in *Mettoy Pension Trustees* v. *Evans* [1991] 2 All E.R. 517.

[15] In *Re Manisty's Settlement* [1974] Ch. 17, 24–25 Templeman J. significantly stated, "In the present case if the settlement is read as a whole the expectations of the settlor are not difficult to discern."

[16] *Re Gulbenkian's S.T.* [1970] A.C. 508, 518, *per* Lord Reid, unless the trust instrument expressly states that the powers are to be regarded as personal and not fiduciary.

[17] *Blausten* v. *I.R.C.* [1972] Ch. 256, 273 and Orr and Salmon L.J.J. agreed with him at 274 and 175. The moral is to couch the power as a power for the trustees to add to the class of beneficiaries anyone from a list submitted to them by any existing beneficiary: see trust precedent p. 16, *supra.*

[18] *Re Manisty's S.T.* [1974] Ch. 17.

[19] *Re Hay's S.T.* [1982] 1 W.L.R. 202, applied in *I.R.C.* v. *Schroder* [1983] S.T.C. 480.

[20] *Ibid.* 212. So long as conceptual certainty is present it does not matter that in substance the testator is effectively delegating his function of choosing legatees to another: *Re Abraham's W.T.* [1969] 1 Ch. 463: *Re Park* [1932] 1 Ch. 580; *Re Nicholls* (1987) 34 D.L.R. (4th) 321; *Re Beatty's WT* [1990] 3 All E.R. 844.

[21] In *McPhail* v. *Doulton* [1971] A.C. 424 discretionary trusts and fiduciary powers were regarded as so similar in substance that the same certainty test should apply to both so why only have administrative workability apply to discretionary trusts?

*Fiduciary powers and personal powers*

There is a crucial distinction between powers vested in trustees *qua* trustees ("fiduciary powers") and powers vested in individuals *qua* individuals ("personal powers"). As already seen, trustees are under certain duties with regard to making inquiries and considering whether or not to exercise their fiduciary powers and they cannot release such powers since they are not theirs to release.[22] An individual is unhampered by any fiduciary duties since the power is his to do with as he wishes, whether he formally releases it or merely decides never to bother to consider exercising it or exercises it capriciously without taking into account the range of objects. The only restriction, of course, is that he cannot go outside the class of objects of the power but such class may be vast since "there is nothing in the number of persons to whom an appointment may be made which will invalidate it."[23] There is no scope for administrative unworkability to vitiate a personal power.

There seems no reason why a personal power should have to satisfy the test for conceptual certainty of fiduciary powers. Instead of the concept being certain enough to enable the court to say of any given postulant that he definitely is or is not an object of the power, it should suffice that the court can say of one or more persons that they are within the "core" meaning of the concept (*e.g.* "old friends") even if the penumbra may be so uncertain that the court cannot say of many persons whether they qualify or not.[24] Thus, a widow's personal power should be valid where her husband leaves his residuary estate to trustees upon particular discretionary trusts, but gives his widow power to appoint thereout up to 10 separate sums of £2,000 to up to 10 friends of the testator not otherwise benefited by his will, or power to appoint up to £20,000 thereout between business associates of the testator not otherwise benefited by his will as she might see fit. After all, this is not so different from a testator leaving his residuary estate to trustees upon discretionary trusts "for my old friends, A, B, C, and D, and for my good business associates, V, W, X and Y, with power for my widow to add as beneficiaries anyone else (apart from herself or past and present trustees) but particularly any of my other friends or business associates as she may see fit." This last power would enable her to benefit the testator's friends and business associates by making them eligible to benefit from the exercise of the trustees' discretion.

---

[22] *Re Wills's Trust Deeds* [1964] Ch. 219, A. J. Hawkins (1968) 84 L.Q.R. 64. Only if the trust instrument authorises trustees to release their powers can this effectively be done. Cross J. in *Re Abraham's W.T.* [1969] 1 Ch. 463, 474–475 uses "fiduciary power" in the sense used in the text. Also Vinelott J. in *I.R.C.* v. *Schroder* [1983] S.T.C. 480.

[23] *Re Hay's S.T.* [1982] 1 W.L.R. 202, 208. Such a vast power impliedly allows him to escape the rule "*delegatus non potest delegare*": *Re Triffit's Settlement* [1958] Ch. 852. The court cannot take a personal power away from an individual: *Re Park* [1932] 1 Ch. 580. The fraud on a power doctrine applies to personal powers: p. 714, *infra*.

[24] See C. T. Emery (1982) 98 L.Q.R. 551, 582 where he uses the expression "bare power" to distinguish a personal power from a fiduciary power. Exercise of the personal power would be effective so long as confined to those within the "core" meaning of the concept. Query whether it should be effective unless in favour of some person clearly outside the penumbra of meaning, *e.g.* where the alleged old friend had never met or corresponded with the testator: see p. 151, *infra*.

*Conditions subsequent and conditions precedent*

Trusts may contain conditions subsequent or conditions precedent. If property is held subject to a condition subsequent so that the beneficiary's vested interest will be liable to forfeiture on the subsequent happening of the proscribed event, the condition must be such that the court can see from the outset precisely and distinctly upon the happening of what event the interest is to be forfeited.[25] The circumstances involving forfeiture must be clearly known in advance so that the beneficiary knows precisely where he stands.

Where property is held on trust for persons subject to the fulfilment of a condition so that it is up to them positively to show that they satisfy such condition precedent then a less strict standard of certainty is usually required. If the trust is a fixed trust for equal division amongst all those who can satisfy a particular condition then the condition must be certain enough to enable a complete list to be drawn up of those who satisfy the condition.[26] However, if instead of a fixed trust for a class there is a discretionary trust or a fiduciary power for a class of people who can satisfy a particular condition, then the condition must contain conceptually clear criteria so that it can be said of any given postulant that he is or is not a member of the class.[27]

Where property is held on trust not for distribution between qualifying members of a class but to enable qualifying individuals to benefit to a specified extent (*i.e.* not "£100,000 to be distributed between such of my relatives as marry persons of the Jewish faith and of Jewish parentage as my trustees may see fit" but "£5,000 to each of my relatives as marry persons of the Jewish faith and of Jewish parentage" or "£25,000 to my daughter Naomi if she marries a person of the Jewish faith and of Jewish parentage") Browne-Wilkinson J. has held[28] that the qualifying condition is valid if it is possible to say of one or more persons that he or they undoubtedly qualify, even though it may be impossible to say of others whether or not they qualify.

In *Re Barlow* Browne-Wilkinson J. was faced with a testatrix who directed her executor "to allow any member of my family and any friends of mine who may wish to do so to purchase" particular paintings in the testatrix's estate at a low 1970 valuation. He held that the disposition was properly to be regarded as a series of individual gifts to persons answering the description friends or blood relations of the testatrix, since the effect of the disposition was to confer on such persons a series of options to purchase. It was not necessary to

---

[25] *Clavering* v. *Ellison* (1859) 7 H.L.Cas. 707; *Blathwayt* v. *Lord Cawley* [1976] A.C. 397, 429.
[26] *e.g.* the case of a trust for my relatives in equal shares as envisaged in *Re Barlow's W.T.* [1979] 1 W.L.R. 278.
[27] *McPhail* v. *Doulton* [1971] A.C. 424.
[28] *Re Barlow's W.T.* [1979] 1 W.L.R. 278, *infra*, p. 169. This was the test suggested by Lord Denning in *Re Gulbenkian's S.T.* [1968] Ch. 126, 134 for judging certainty of powers and rejected by the House of Lords on appeal. "Jewish faith and parentage" was held void for uncertainty in *Clayton* v. *Ramsden* [1943] A.C. 320 but in *Re Tepper's W.T.* [1987] Ch. 358 Scott J. was reluctant to find "Jewish faith" uncertain and so adjourned the case to see if evidence of the Jewish faith as practised by the testator would clarify the matter. Both cases involved conditions subsequent.

discover who all the friends or relations were: all that was required was
for the executors to be able to say of any individual coming forward
that he had proved that he was a friend or relation.[29] He justified this
on the basis of *Re Allen*[30] where the Court of Appeal had upheld a
devise "to the eldest of the sons of A who shall be a member of the
Church of England and an adherent to the doctrine of that Church,"
so allowing the eldest son to seek to establish that he qualified, even if
the conditions were conceptually uncertain so that it would be impossible to say of others whether or not they qualified. He considered *Re
Allen* still to be good law after *McPhail* v. *Doulton* since the Court of
Appeal in *Re Tuck's S.T.*[31] had mentioned it approvingly (but only in
the context of revealing a distinction between conditions precedent and
conditions subsequent, which he overlooked).

He was much impressed by Lord Evershed's dictum[32] that a gift to A
if he is a tall man will be valid, enabling A if he is 6ft. 6ins. to claim
the gift. Where there is one ascertained individual, who is the only
possible beneficiary, then one can accept his entitlement if he can
prove he comes within the "core" meaning of the qualifying condition,
even if the penumbra is so conceptually uncertain that it may often be
impossible to judge whether the condition is satisfied.[33] This exception
will cover several ascertained beneficiaries where each is the only
possible beneficiary, *e.g.* "£15,000 to each of my sons A, B, C and D if
he is tall."

However, one ought not to extend the exception beyond individuals
whose identity is ascertained from the outset to individuals whose
identity can only be ascertained after deciding whether or not others
have satisfied a particular condition which is conceptually uncertain,
*e.g.* £20,000 to my first daughter to marry (or to the eldest of my
daughters who shall marry) a tall adherent to the doctrine of the
Church of England. If the eldest daughter, A, marries someone within
the penumbra of the conceptually uncertain condition so that it is
impossible to say whether she qualifies or not then it cannot help B,
the second eldest, if she is within the "core" of the condition by
marrying a 6ft. 6ins. Church of England vicar. Whether B satisfies the
condition depends on the *ex hypothesi* insoluble question whether or
not A has satisfied the condition.[34] The condition would fail more

---

[29] *Re Baden's Deed Trusts (No. 2)* [1973] Ch. 9 enables relations to be ascertained on the basis that
he who does not prove he is a relation is not a relation, the concept of descendant of a common
ancestor being clear. The concept of friendship is not clear. If one picture was particularly good
and available at a particularly low price, so that everyone wanted this best bargain, would the
purchaser have to be found by putting all possible names into a hat and drawing out one name?
But would not this be impossible since the uncertain penumbra of meaning of friendship would
make it impossible for the executor or the court to decide whether many persons were friends or
not?

[30] [1953] Ch. 810.

[31] [1978] Ch. 49.

[32] [1953] Ch. 810, 817.

[33] L. McKay [1980] Conv. 263, 277; C. T. Emery (1982) 98 L.Q.R. 551, 564.

[34] C. T. Emery (1982) 98 L.Q.R. 551, 564–565. The Court of Appeal in *Re Allen* [1953] Ch. 810 did
not face up to this when dealing with a claim by the eldest son (or rather, his executor).

clearly if the gift had been to "my first female friend to marry a tall adherent to Church of England doctrine" since "friend" is a highly imprecise concept.

Browne-Wilkinson J. considered that "a gift of £10 to each of my friends" was valid, whilst accepting that a discretionary trust or power for "my friends" would be void.[35] Such a less strict approach seems anomalous and illogical. After all, a trustee or executor directed to make payments to qualifying beneficiaries has a duty to make such payments which may be enforced by each qualifying beneficiary, unlike the weaker position of beneficiaries or objects under discretionary trusts or powers. Furthermore, the person entitled to the fund after payment thereout of the sums to the "friends" must have a clear right to sue the trustee or executor for paying sums out to persons not ranking as "friends." To protect themselves the trustees or executors must have a right to obtain the court's directions as to whom to make the payments. "Friends" gives rise not just to evidential uncertainty but to conceptual uncertainty having an uncertain penumbra making it impossible in many instances for the court to say whether a person is or is not a friend. If, pragmatically, one is to have Browne-Wilkinson J.'s exception for persons within the "core" meaning of friend why not allow discretionary trusts and powers to be validly exercised in favour of persons within the "core" meaning of friend, though House of Lords authority[36] is against this?

*Resolution of uncertainty*

Questions of evidential uncertainty can be resolved by the court in the last resort, though it is possible for the trust instrument to contain a clause empowering someone like the trustees[37] or the testator's widow, or the testator's business partner or the Chief Rabbi[38] to resolve any evidential uncertainty.

Apparent conceptual uncertainty may not be such if the court restrictively construes the concept, *e.g.* restricts "Cambridge students" to students from time to time studying as junior members of the University of Cambridge or restrict "fans of Elvis Presley" to members of Elvis Presley fan clubs or restricts a residuary bequest to "those beneficiaries who have only received small amounts" to those who had received legacies of £25, £50 and £100 where other legatees had received legacies of £200 and £250.[39] A proviso that in cases of doubt the decision of the Registrary of the University of Cambridge or of the secretaries of official Elvis Presley fan clubs shall be conclusive may assist the court restrict the concept so that it is actually certain.

---

[35] *Re Barlow's W.T.* [1979] 1 W.L.R. 278, 281, *infra*, p. 169.
[36] *Re Gulbenkian's S.T.* [1970] A.C. 508, *infra*, p. 151; *McPhail* v. *Doulton* [1971] A.C. 424, *infra*, p. 154.
[37] *Dundee General Hospital Board* v. *Walker* [1952] 1 All E.R. 896.
[38] *Re Tuck's S.T.* [1978] Ch. 49. In *Re Tepper's W.T.* [1987] Ch. 358 Scott J. considered "Jewish faith" could be evidentially certain.
[39] *Re Steel* [1978] 2 All E.R. 1026, 1032.

However, actual conceptual uncertainty cannot be resolved by such provisos.[40] If the concept is "my tall relations" or "my old friends" or "my good business associates," and the testator's trustees are given power to resolve any doubts as to whether any persons qualify or not then since *ex hypothesi* the court cannot resolve the uncertainty caused by the conceptual uncertainty it is difficult to see how the trustees can. There are no clear conceptual criteria to guide them or, indeed, the court if their exercise of the power is challenged. An inherently irresolvable issue is just that: it cannot be resolved, whether by a judge or anyone else.

If the concept is "persons whom my trustees consider to be my tall relatives or my old friends or my good business associates" the concept still seems uncertain. As Jenkins J. said in *Re Coxen*[41]:

"If the testator had insufficiently defined the state of affairs on which the trustees were to form their opinion he would not have saved the condition from invalidity on the ground of uncertainty merely by making their opinion the criterion, although the declaration by the trustees of this or that opinion would be an event about which in itself there could be no uncertainty."

This view was followed in *Re Jones*[42] and more recently in *Re Wright's W.T.*[43] where a gift of property to trustees "to use the same at their absolute discretion for such people and institutions as they think have helped me or my late husband" failed for conceptual uncertainty. How can the trustees consider someone to have helped a testatrix or to be a tall relative or old friend or good business associate without knowing what exactly they are supposed to consider as criteria justifying their conclusion? If their conclusion is challenged how can the court adjudicate upon the matter?[44]

If a power to resolve conceptual uncertainty is given not as a fiduciary power but as a personal power, for example, to the testator's widow, might this validate a prima facie uncertain trust? What if a testator left his residuary estate to his executors and trustees on discretionary trust for his old friends but stated that if any doubts or disputes arose as to membership of such class then his widow's decision was to be final unless it was unreasonable, as rejecting a person clearly within the "core" meaning of "old friends" or admitting a person

---

[40] *Re Coxen* [1948] Ch. 747, 761–762; *Re Jones* [1953] Ch. 125; *Re Wright's W.T.* [1981] L.S.Gaz. 841. Lord Denning's dicta to the contrary in *Re Tuck's S.T.* [1978] Ch. 49, 60, 62 are out of line and seem based on a misinterpretation of *Dundee General Hospital Board* (*supra*) as Eveleigh L.J. indicates [1978] Ch. 49, 66. See also P. Matthews (1983) 133 New L.J. 915.

[41] [1948] Ch. 747, 761–762.

[42] [1953] Ch. 125: "if at any time B shall in the uncontrolled opinion of the trustee have social or other relationship with C."

[43] [1981] L.S.Gaz. 841.

[44] The jurisdiction of the court cannot be ousted: *Re Raven* [1915] 1 Ch. 673: *Re Wynn's W.T.* [1952] Ch. 271. One should note that a court could well construe a discretionary trust "for my old friends but so that my trustees shall have power to resolve any doubts as to whether anyone is or is not an old friend of mine" as being a discretionary trust for "persons whom my trustees consider to be my old friends" so that the position should be the same on either construction.

clearly outside the "penumbra" of meaning of "old friend," like someone whom the testator had never met or corresponded with?[45] It would seem unreasonable for a court not to accept the validity of such a power with the above express or implied limitation that it may not be exercised unreasonably. But if one concedes the validity of such power of the widow why should one not concede the validity of such power if vested in trustees?[46] If such power was *expressly* limited as above the court might well accept it as conferring dispositive leeway on the trustees, just as much as on the widow, but the court would be reluctant to find such validating *implied* limitation on the power vested in the trustees as such.

### Absence of certainties

If there is no intention to create a trust the alleged settlor or his estate retains the relevant property. If there is uncertainty of subject-matter then the alleged trust is ineffective since there is nothing for the alleged trust to "bite" on. If certainty of intention and of subject-matter are present but there is uncertainty of objects then the trustee holds the property on a resulting trust for the settlor or the testator's estate as the case may be.

If property is given by will or other instrument to someone absolutely and subsequently in that instrument trusts are imposed on that absolute interest then if these trusts fail for uncertainty or otherwise the donee takes the property for himself absolutely.[47]

### RE GULBENKIAN'S SETTLEMENT TRUSTS

House of Lords [1970] A.C. 508; [1968] 3 W.L.R. 1127; [1968] 3 All E.R. 785.

Settlements were made including a special power for trustees to appoint in favour of Nubar Gulbenkian "and any wife and his children or remoter issue . . . and any person . . . in whose house or apartment or in whose company or under whose care or control or by or with whom [he] may from time to time be employed or residing," and with trusts in default of appointment.

The House of Lords unanimously upheld the power and (Lord Donovan reserving his opinion though "inclined to share" Lord Upjohn's views) rejected *obiter* the broad view that a power was valid if any one person clearly fell within the scope of the power. The House construed the clause as meaning "and any person or persons by whom Nubar may from time to time be employed and any person or persons with whom N from time to time is residing whether in the house or apartments of such person or persons or

---

[45] This is narrower than taking advantage of *Re Hay's S.T.* [1982] 1 W.L.R. 202, *infra*, p. 163 to give the widow power to add to the class of beneficiaries anyone else (apart from herself or past or present trustees) but particularly anyone she considers to be an old friend of the testator. Also see *Re Coates* [1955] Ch. 495.

[46] Perhaps this may have been at the back of Harman L.J.'s mind in *Re Leek* [1969] 1 Ch. 563, 579 when, whilst accepting that a discretionary trust for such persons as have moral claims on the settlor would be void for conceptual uncertainty, he uttered unorthodox dicta to the effect that if the trustees were arbiters of the class of beneficiaries, being such persons as the trustees considered to have a moral claim on the settlor, the trust would be valid.

[47] *Hancock* v. *Watson* [1902] A.C. 14: *Re Burton's S.T.* [1955] Ch. 348.

whether in the company or under the care and control of such person or persons" and held that it could be said with certainty whether any given individual was or was not a member of that class so that the power was valid.

LORD UPJOHN: "My lords, that is sufficient to dispose of the appeal, but the reasons of two members of the Court of Appeal went further and so must be examined.

"Lord Denning M.R.,[48] propounded a test in the case of powers collateral, namely, that if you can say of one particular person meaning thereby, apparently, any one person only that he is clearly within the category the whole power is good though it may be difficult to say in other cases whether a person is or is not within the category, and he supported that view by reference to authority. Winn L.J. said[49] that where there was not a complete failure by reason of ambiguity and uncertainty the court would give effect to the power as valid rather than hold it defeated since it will not have wholly failed, which put—though more broadly—the view expressed by Lord Denning M.R. Counsel for the respondents in his second line of argument relied on these observations as a matter of principle but he candidly admitted that he could not rely on any authority. Moreover, Lord Denning M.R. expressed the view[50] that the different doctrine with regard to trust powers should be brought into line with the rule with regard to conditions precedent and powers collateral. So I propose to make some general observations on this matter.

"If a donor (be he a settlor or testator) directs trustees to make some specified provision for 'John Smith,' then to give effect to that provision it must be possible to identify 'John Smith.' If the donor knows three John Smiths then by the most elementary principles of law neither the trustees nor the court in their place can give effect to that provision; neither the trustees nor the court can guess at it. It must fail for uncertainty unless of course admissible evidence is available to point to a particular John Smith as the object of the donor's bounty.

"Then, taking it one stage further, suppose the donor directs that a fund, or the income of a fund, should be equally divided between members of a class. That class must be as defined as the individual; the court cannot guess at it. Suppose the donor directs that a fund be divided equally between 'my old friends,' then unless there is some admissible evidence that the donor has given some special 'dictionary' meaning to that phrase which enables the trustee to identify the class with sufficient certainty, it is plainly bad as being too uncertain. Suppose that there appeared before the trustees (or the court) two or three individuals who plainly satisfied the test of being among 'my old friends' the trustees could not consistently with the donor's intentions accept them as claiming the whole or any defined part of the fund. They cannot claim the whole fund for they can show no title to it unless they prove they are the only members of the class which of course they cannot do, and so, too, by parity of reasoning they cannot claim any defined part of the fund and there is no authority in the trustees or the court to make any distribution among a smaller class than that pointed out by the donor. The principle is, in my opinion, that the donor must make his intention sufficiently plain as to the object of his trust and the court cannot give effect to it by misinterpreting his

---

[48] [1968] Ch. 126, 133, 134.
[49] [1968] Ch. 126, 138.
[50] *Ibid.*

intentions by dividing the fund merely among those present. Secondly, and perhaps it is the most hallowed principle, the Court of Chancery, which acts in default of trustees, must know with sufficient certainty the objects of the beneficence of the donor so as to execute the trust. Then, suppose the donor does not direct an equal division of his property among the class but gives a power of selection to his trustees among the class; exactly the same principles must apply. The trustees have a duty to select the donees of the donor's bounty from among the class designated by the donor; he has not entrusted them with any power to select the donees merely from among known claimants who are within the class, for that is constituting a narrower class and the donor has given them no power to do this.

"So if the class is insufficiently defined the donor's intentions must in such cases fail for uncertainty. Perhaps I should mention here that it is clear that the question of certainty must be determined as of the date of the document declaring the donor's intention (in the case of a will, his death). Normally the question of certainty will arise because of the ambiguity of definition of the class by reason of the language employed by the donor, but occasionally owing to some of the curious settlements executed in recent years it may be quite impossible to construct even with all the available evidence anything like a class capable of definition (*Re Sayer Trust*[51]), though difficulty in doing so will not defeat the donor's intentions (*Re Hain's Settlement*[52]). But I should add this: if the class is sufficiently defined by the donor the fact that it may be difficult to ascertain the whereabouts or continued existence of some of its members at the relevant time matters not. The trustees can apply to the court for directions to pay a share into court.

"But when mere or bare powers are conferred on donees of the power (whether trustees or others) the matter is quite different. As I have already pointed out, the trustees have no duty to exercise it in the sense that they cannot be controlled in any way. If they fail to exercise it then those entitled in default of its exercise are entitled to the fund. Perhaps the contrast may be put forcibly in this way: in the first case it is a mere power to distribute with a gift over in default; in the second case it is a trust to distribute among the class defined by the donor with merely a power of selection within that class. The result is in the first case even if the class of appointees among whom the donees of the power may appoint is clear and ascertained and they are all of full age and *sui juris*, nevertheless they cannot compel the donees of the power to exercise it in their collective favour. If, however, it is a trust power, then those entitled are entitled (if they are of full age and *sui juris*) to compel the trustees to pay the fund over to them, unless the fund is income and the trustees have power to accumulate for the future.

"Again the basic difference between a mere power and a trust power is that in the first case trustees owe no duty to exercise it and the relevant fund or income falls to be dealt with in accordance with the trusts in default of its exercise, whereas in the second case the trustees *must* exercise the power and in default the court will.

"So, with all respect to the contrary view, I cannot myself see how, consistently with principle, it is possible to apply to the execution of a trust power the principles applicable to the permissible exercise by the donees, even

---

[51] [1957] Ch. 423.
[52] [1961] 1 All E.R. 848.

if the trustees of mere powers; that would defeat the intention of donors completely.

"But with respect to mere powers, while the court cannot compel the trustees to exercise their powers, yet those entitled to the fund in default must clearly be entitled to restrain the trustees from exercising it save among those within the power. So the trustees, or the court, must be able to say with certainty who is within and who is without the power. It is for this reason that I find myself unable to accept the broader position advanced by Lord Denning M.R. and Winn L.J., mentioned earlier, and agree with the proposition as enunciated in *Re Gestener*[53] and the later cases.

"My lords, I would dismiss these appeal." *Appeals dismissed.*

## McPHAIL v. DOULTON

House of Lords [1971] A.C. 424; [1970] 2 W.L.R. 1110; [1970] 2 All E.R. 228.

The facts and the issues appear clearly in the following speech of Lord Wilberforce with which Lord Reid and Viscount Dilhorne concurred though dissenting speeches were delivered by Lords Hodson and Guest.

LORD WILBERFORCE: "My Lords, this appeal is concerned with the validity of a trust deed dated July 17, 1941, by which Mr. Bertram Baden established a fund for the benefit, broadly, of the staff of the respondent company Matthew Hall & Co. Ltd.

The critical clauses are as follows:

'9. (a) The Trustees shall apply the net income of the Fund in making at their absolute discretion grants to or for benefit of any of the officers and employees or ex-officers or ex-employees of the Company or any relatives or dependants of any such persons in such amounts at such times and on such conditions (if any) as they think fit and any such grant may at their discretion be made by payment to the beneficiary or to any institution or person to be applied for his or her benefit and in the latter case the Trustees shall be under no obligation to see to the application of the money.

'(b) The Trustees shall not be bound to exhaust the income of any year or other period in making such grants as aforesaid and any income not so applied shall be dealt with as provided by clause 6(a) hereof enabling moneys to be placed with any Bank or to be invested.

'(c) The Trustees may realise any investments representing accumulations of income and apply the proceeds as though the same were income of the Fund and may also (but only with the consent of all the Trustees) at any time prior to the liquidation of the Fund realise any other part of the capital of the Fund which in the opinion of the Trustees it is desirable to realise in order to provide benefits for which the current income of the Fund is insufficient.

'10. All benefits being at the absolute discretion of the Trustees, no person shall have any right title or interest in the Fund otherwise than pursuant to the exercise of such discretion, and nothing herein contained shall prejudice the right of the Company to determine the employment of any officer or employee.'

[53] [1953] Ch. 672.

"Clause 11 defines a perpetuity period within which the trusts are, in any event, to come to an end and clause 12 provides for the termination of the fund. On this event the trustees are directed to apply the fund in their discretion in one or more of certain specified ways of which one is in making grants as if they were grants under clause 9(a) . . .

"In this House, the appellants contended that the provisions of clause 9(a) constitute a trust and not a power. If that is held to be the correct result both sides agree that the case must return to the Chancery Division for consideration, on this footing, whether this trust is valid. But here comes a complication. In the present state of authority, the decision as to validity would turn on the question whether a complete list (or on another view a list complete for practical purposes) can be drawn up of all possible beneficiaries. This follows from the Court of Appeal's decision in *Inland Revenue Comrs.* v. *Broadway Cottages Trust*[54] as applied in later cases by which, unless this House decides otherwise, the Court of Chancery would be bound. The respondents invite your Lordships to review this decision and challenge its correctness. So the second issue which arises, if clause 9(a) amounts to a trust, is whether the existing test for its validity is right in law and if not, what the test ought to be.

"Before dealing with these two questions some general observations, or reflections, may be permissible. It is striking how narrow and in a sense artificial is the distinction, in cases such as the present, between trusts or as the particular type of trust is called, trust powers, and powers. It is only necessary to read the learned judgments in the Court of Appeal[55] to see that what to one mind may appear as a power of distribution coupled with a trust to dispose of the undistributed surplus, by accumulation or otherwise, may to another appear as a trust for distribution coupled with a power to withhold a portion and accumulate or otherwise dispose of it. A layman and, I suspect, also a logician, would find it hard to understand what difference there is.

"It does not seem satisfactory that the entire validity of a disposition should depend on such delicate shading. And if one considers how in practice reasonable and competent trustees would act, and ought to act, in the two cases, surely a matter very relevant to the question of validity, the distinction appears even less significant. To say that there is no obligation to exercise a mere power and that no court will intervene to compel it, whereas a trust is mandatory and its execution must be compelled, may be legally correct enough, but the proposition does not contain an exhaustive comparison of the duties of persons who are trustees in the two cases. A trustee of an employees' benefit fund, whether given a power or a trust power, is still a trustee and he would surely consider in either case that he has a fiduciary duty; he is most likely to have been selected as a suitable person to administer it from his knowledge and experience, and would consider he has a responsibility to do so according to its purpose. It would be a complete misdescription of his position to say that, if what he has is a power unaccompanied by an imperative trust to distribute, he cannot be controlled by the court if he exercised it capriciously, or outside the field permitted by the trust (*cf. Farwell on Powers*[56]). Any trustee would surely make it his duty to know what is the permissible area of selection and then consider responsibly, in individual cases, whether a con-

---

[54] [1955] Ch. 20.
[55] [1969] 2 Ch. 388.
[56] (3rd ed., 1916), p. 524.

templated beneficiary was within the power and whether, in relation to other possible claimants, a particular grant was appropriate.

"Correspondingly a trustee with a duty to distribute, particularly among a potentially very large class, would surely never require the preparation of a complete list of names, which anyhow would tell him little that he needs to know. He would examine the field, by class and category; might indeed make diligent and careful enquiries, depending on how much money he had to give away and the means at his disposal, as to the composition and needs of particular categories and of individuals within them; decide on certain priorities or proportions, and then select individuals according to their needs or qualifications. If he acts in this manner, can it really be said that he is not carrying out the trust?

"Differences there certainly are between trusts (trust powers) and powers, but as regards validity should they be so great as that in one case complete, or practically complete ascertainment is needed, but not in the other? Such distinction as there is would seem to lie in the extent of the survey which the trustee is required to carry out; if he has to distribute the whole of a fund's income, he must necessarily make a wider and more systematic survey than if his duty is expressed in terms of a power to make grants. But just as, in the case of a power, it is possible to underestimate the fiduciary obligation of the trustee to whom it is given, so, in the case of a trust (trust power), the danger lies in overstating what the trustee requires to know or to enquire into before he can properly execute his trust. The difference may be one of degree rather than of principle; in the well-known words of Sir George Farwell (*Farwell on Powers*[57]) trusts and powers are often blended, and the mixture may vary in its ingredients.

"With this background I now consider whether the provisions of clause 9(a) constitute a trust or a power. Naturally read, the intention of the deed seems to me clear: clause 9(a), whose language is mandatory ('shall'), creates, together with a power of selection, a trust for distribution of the income, the strictness of which is qualified by clause 9(b) which allows the income of any one year to be held up and (under clause 6(a)) either placed, for the time, with a bank, or, if thought fit, invested. Whether there is, in any technical sense an accumulation, seems to me in the present context a jejune enquiry; what is relevant is that clause 9(c) marks the difference between 'accumulations' of income and the capital of the fund: the former can be distributed by a majority of the trustees, the latter cannot. As to clause 10, I do not find in it any decisive indication. If anything it seems to point in favour of a trust, but both this and other points of detail are insignificant in the face of the clearly expressed scheme of clause 9. I therefore agree with Russell L.J. and would to that extent allow the appeal, declare that the provisions of clause 9(a) constitute a trust and remit the case to the Chancery Division for determination whether on this basis clause 9 is (subject to the effects of section 164 of the Law of Property Act 1925) valid or void for uncertainty.

"This makes it necessary to consider whether, in so doing, the court should proceed on the basis that the relevant test is that laid down in the *Broadway Cottages* case[58] or some other test. That decision gave the authority of the Court of Appeal to the distinction between cases where trustees are given a

---

[57] *Ibid.* p. 10.
[58] [1955] Ch. 20.

*power* of selection and those where they are bound by a *trust* for selection. In the former case the position, as decided by this House, is that the power is valid if it can be said with certainty whether any given individual is or is not a member of the class and does not fail simply because it is impossible to ascertain every member of the class. (The *Gulbenkian* case.[59]) But in the latter case it is said to be necessary, for the trust to be valid, that the whole range of objects (I use the language of the Court of Appeal) should be ascertained or capable of ascertainment.

"The respondents invited your Lordships to assimilate the validity test for trusts to that which applies to powers. Alternatively, they contended that in any event the test laid down in the *Broadway Cottages* case was too rigid, and that a trust should be upheld if there is sufficient practical certainty in its definition for it to be carried out, if necessary with the administrative assistance of the court, according to the expressed intention of the settlor. I would agree with this, but this does not dispense from examination of the wider argument. The basis for the *Broadway Cottages* case principle is stated to be that a trust cannot be valid unless, if need be, it can be executed by the court, and (though it is not quite clear from the judgment where argument ends and decision begins) that the court can only execute it by ordering an equal distribution in which every beneficiary shares. So it is necessary to examine the authority and reason for this supposed rule as to the execution of trusts by the court.

"Assuming, as I am prepared to do for present purposes, that the test of validity is whether the trust can be executed by the court, it does not follow that execution is impossible unless there can be equal division. As a matter of reason, to hold that a principle of equal division applies to trusts such as the present is certainly paradoxical. Equal division is surely the last thing the settlor ever intended; equal division among all may, probably would, produce a result beneficial to none. Why suppose that the court would lend itself to a whimsical execution? And as regards authority, I do not find that the nature of the trust, and of the court's powers over trusts, calls for any such rigid rule. Equal division may be sensible and has been decreed, in cases of family trusts for a limited class, here there is life in the maxim 'equality is equity,' but the cases provide numerous examples where this has not been so, and a different type of execution has been ordered, appropriate to the circumstances.

[His Lordship then dealt with the following examples of unequal division; *Moseley* v. *Moseley*[60]; *Clarke* v. *Turner*[61]; *Warburton* v. *Warburton*[62]; *Richardson* v. *Chapman*.[63]]

"So I came to *Inland Revenue Comrs.* v. *Broadway Cottage Trusts*.[64] This was certainly a case of trust, and it proceeded on the basis of an admission, in the words of the judgment, 'that the class of "beneficiaries" is incapable of ascertainment.' In addition to the discretionary trust of income, there was a trust of capital for all the beneficiaries living or existing at the terminal date. This necessarily involved equal division and it seems to have been accepted that it was void for uncertainty since there cannot be equal division among a

---

[59] [1970] A.C. 508.
[60] (1673) Rep.temp. Finch 53.
[61] (1694) Freem.Ch. 198.
[62] (1702) 4 Bro.Parl.Cas. 1.
[63] (1760) 7 Bro.Parl.Cas. 318.
[64] [1955] Ch. 20.

class unless all the members of the class are known. The Court of Appeal[65]
applied this proposition to the discretionary trust of income, on the basis that
execution by the court was only possible on the same basis of equal division.
They rejected the argument that the trust could be executed by changing the
trusteeship, and found the relations cases of no assistance as being in a class by
themselves. The court could not create an arbitrarily restricted trust to take
effect in default of distribution by the trustees. Finally they rejected the
submission that the trust could take effect as a power, a valid power could not
be spelt out of an invalid trust.

"My Lords, it will have become apparent that there is much in this which I
find out of line with principle and authority, but before I come to a conclusion
on it, I must examine the decision of this House in *Re Gulbenkian's Settlement
Trusts* on which the appellants placed much reliance as amounting to an
endorsement of the *Broadway Cottages* case. But is this really so? [No, he
concluded after considering *Re Gulbenkian*.]

"So I think we are free to review the *Broadway Cottages* case.[66] The
conclusion which I would reach, implicit in the previous discussion, is that the
wide distinction between the validity test for powers and that for trust powers,
is unfortunate and wrong, that the rule recently fastened on the courts by the
*Broadway Cottages* case ought to be discarded, and that the test for the validity
of trust powers ought to be similar to that accepted by this House in *Re
Gulbenkian's Settlement Trusts* for powers, namely that the trust is valid if it
can be said with certainty that any given individual is or is not a member of the
class.

"Assimilation of the validity test does not involve the complete assimilation
of trust powers with powers. As to powers, I agree with my noble and learned
friend Lord Upjohn in *Re Gulbenkian's Settlement* that although the trustees
may, and normally will, be under a fiduciary duty to consider whether or in
what way they should exercise their power, the court will not normally compel
its exercise. It will intervene if the trustees exceed their powers, and possibly if
they are proved to have exercised it capriciously. But in the case of a trust
power, if the trustees do not exercise it, the court will; I respectfully adopt as
to this the statement in Lord Upjohn's opinion.[67] I would venture to amplify
this by saying that the court, if called on to execute the trust power, will do so
in the manner best calculated to give effect to the settlor's or testator's
intentions. It may do so by appointing new trustees, or authorising or directing
representative persons of the classes of beneficiaries to prepare a scheme of
distribution, or even, should the proper basis for distribution appear, by itself
directing the trustees so to distribute. The books give many instances where
this has been done and I see no reason in principle why they should not do so
in the modern field of discretionary trusts (see *Brunsden* v. *Woolredge,*[68]
*Supple* v. *Lowson,*[69] *Liley* v. *Hey*[70] and Lewin on Trusts[71]). Then, as to the
trustees' duty of enquiry or ascertainment, in each case the trustees ought to
make such a survey of the range of objects or possible beneficiaries as will

---

[65] [1968] Ch. 126.
[66] [1955] Ch. 20.
[67] [1970] A.C. 508, 525.
[68] (1765) Amb. 507.
[69] (1773) Amb. 729.
[70] (1842) 1 Hare 580.
[71] (16th ed., 1964), p. 630.

enable them to carry out their fiduciary duty (*cf. Liley* v. *Hey*). A wider and more comprehensive range of enquiry is called for in the case of trust powers than in the case of powers.

"Two final points: first, as to the question of certainty, I desire to emphasise the distinction clearly made and explained by Lord Upjohn,[72] between linguistic or semantic uncertainty which, if unresolved by the court, renders the gift void, and the difficulty of ascertaining the existence or whereabouts of members of the class, a matter with which the court can appropriately deal on an application for directions. There may be a third case where the meaning of the words used is clear but the definition of beneficiaries is so hopelessly wide as not to form 'anything like a class' so that the trust is administratively unworkable or in Lord Eldon L.C.'s words one that cannot be executed (*Morice* v. *Bishop of Durham*[73]). I hesitate to give examples for they may prejudice future cases, but perhaps 'all the residents of Greater London' will serve. I do not think that a discretionary trust for 'relatives' even of a living person falls within this category. . . . "

*Appeal allowed. Declaration that the provisions of clause 9(a) constituted a trust. Case remitted for determination whether on this basis clause 9 was (subject to the effects of section 164 of the Law of Property Act 1925) valid or void for uncertainty.*

## RE BADEN'S DEED TRUSTS (NO. 2)

Court of Appeal [1973] Ch. 9; [1972] 3 W.L.R. 250; [1972] 2 All E.R. 1304.

Upon remittance Brightman J.[74] and the Court of Appeal held the trust valid but there was a difference of approach in applying the test for certainty, Stamp L.J. not being prepared to hold the trust valid if relatives meant descendants of a common ancestor and not merely statutory next-of-kin.

SACHS L.J.: " . . . Once the class of persons to be benefited is conceptually certain it then becomes a question of fact to be determined on evidence whether any postulant has on enquiry been proved to be within it; if he is not so proved then he is not in it. That position remains the same whether the class to be benefited happens to be small (such as 'first cousins') or large (such as 'members of the X Trade Union' or 'those who have served in the Royal Navy'). The suggestion that such trusts could be invalid because it might be impossible to prove of a given individual that he was *not* in the relevant class is wholly fallacious—and only the persuasiveness of counsel for the defendant executors has prevented me from saying that the contention is almost unarguable."

MEGAW L.J.: " . . . The main argument of counsel for the defendant executors was founded on a strict and literal interpretation of the words in which the decision of the House of Lords in *Re Gulbenkian's Settlement Trust*[75] was expressed. That decision laid down the test for the validity of powers of selection. It is relevant for the present case, because in the previous excursion of this case to the House of Lords[76] it was held that there is no relevant

---

[72] [1970] A.C. 508, 524.
[73] (1805) 10 Ves. at 527.
[74] [1972] Ch. 607.
[75] [1970] A.C. 508.
[76] [1971] A.C. 424.

difference in the test of validity, whether the trustees are given a power of selection or, as was held by their Lordships to be the case in this trust deed, a trust for selection. The test in either case is what may be called the *Gulbenkian* test. The *Gulbenkian* test, as expressed by Lord Wilberforce[77] (and again in almost identical words in a later passage[78]) is this:

> ' . . . the power is valid if it can be said with certainty whether any given individual is or is not a member of the class and does not fail simply because it is impossible to ascertain every member of the class.'

"The executors' argument concentrates on the words 'or is not' in the first of the two limbs of the sentence quoted above: 'if it can be said with certainty whether any given individual is *or is not* a member of the class.' It is said that those words have been used deliberately, and have only one possible meaning; and that, however startling or drastic or unsatisfactory the result may be—and counsel for the defendant executors does not shrink from saying that the consequence is drastic—this court is bound to give effect to the words used in the House of Lords' definition of the test. It would be quite impracticable for the trustees to ascertain in many cases whether a particular person was *not* a relative of an employee. The most that could be said is: 'There is no proof that he is a relative.' But there would still be no 'certainty' that such a person was not a relative. Hence, so it is said, the test laid down by the House of Lords is satisfied, and the trust is void. For it cannot be said with certainty, in relation to any individual, that he is not a relative.

"I do not think it was contemplated that the words 'or is not' would produce that result. It would, as I see it, involve an inconsistency with the latter part of the same sentence: 'does not fail simply because it is impossible to ascertain every member of the class.' The executors' contention, in substance and reality, is that it *does* fail 'simply because it is impossible to ascertain every member of the class.'

"The same verbal difficulty, as I see it, emerges also when one considers the words of the suggested test which the House of Lords expressly rejected. That is set out by Lord Wilberforce in a passage[79] immediately following the sentence which I have already quoted. The rejected test was in these terms: ' . . . it is said to be necessary . . . that the whole range of objects . . . shall be ascertained or capable of ascertainment.' Since that test was rejected, the resulting affirmative proposition, which by implication must have been accepted by their Lordships, is this: a trust for selection will not fail simply because the whole range of objects cannot be ascertained. In the present case, the trustees could ascertain, by investigation and evidence, many of the objects; as to many other theoretically possible claimants, they could not be certain. Is it to be said that the trust fails because it cannot be said with certainty that such persons are not members of the class? If so, is that not the application of the rejected test; the trust failing because 'the whole range of objects cannot be ascertained?'

"In my judgment, much too great emphasis is placed in the executors' argument on the words 'or is not.' To my mind, the test is satisfied if, as regards at least a substantial number of objects, it can be said with certainty

---

[77] [1971] A.C. 424, 450.
[78] [1971] A.C. 424, 454.
[79] [1971] A.C. 424, 450. See p. 157, *supra*.

that they fall within the trust; even though, as regards a substantial number of other persons, if they ever for some fanciful reason fell to be considered, the answer would have to be, not 'they are outside the trusts,' but 'it is not proven whether they are in or out.' What is a 'substantial number' may well be a question of common sense and of degree in relation to the particular trust: particularly where, as here, it would be fantasy, to use a mild word, to suggest that any practical difficulty would arise in the fair, proper and sensible administration of this trust in respect of relatives and dependants.

"I do not think that this involves, as counsel for the defendant executors suggested, a return by this court to its former view which was rejected by the House of Lords in the *Gulbenkian* case.[80] If I did so think, I should, however reluctantly, accept his argument and its consequences. But as I read it, the criticism in the House of Lords of the decision of this court in that case related to this court's acceptance of the view that it would be sufficient if it could be shown that *one single person* fell within the scope of the power or trust. The essence of the decision of the House of Lords in the *Gulbenkian* case, as I see it, is *not* that it must be possible to show with certainty that any given person is *or is not* within the trust; but that it is not, or may not be, sufficient to be able to show that one individual person is within it. If it does not mean that, I do not know where the line is supposed to be drawn, having regard to the clarity and emphasis with which the House of Lords has laid down that the trust does not fail because the whole range of objects cannot be ascertained. I would dismiss the appeal."

STAMP L.J.: " . . . Counsel for the defendant executors, fastening on those words, 'if it can be said with certainty that any given individual is or is not a member of the class,' submitted in this court that a trust for distribution among officers and employees or ex-officers or ex-employees or any of their relatives or dependants does not satisfy the test. You may say with certainty that any given individual is or is not an officer, employee, ex-officer or ex-employee. You may say with certainty that a very large number of given individuals are relatives of one of them; but, so the argument runs, you will never be able to say with certainty of many given individuals that they are not. I am bound to say that I had thought at one stage of counsel's able argument that this was no more than an exercise in semantics and that the phrase on which he relies indicated no more than that the trust was valid if there was such certainty in the definition of membership of the class that you could say with certainty that some individuals were members of it; that it was sufficient that you should be satisfied that a given individual presenting himself has or has not passed the test and that it matters not that having failed to establish his membership— here his relationship—you may, perhaps wrongly, reject him. There are, however, in my judgment serious difficulties in the way of a rejection of counsel's submission.

"The first difficulty, as I see it, is that the rejection of counsel's submission involves holding that the trust is good if there are individuals—or even one—of whom you can say with certainty that he is a member of the class. That was the test adopted by and the decision of the Court of Appeal in the *Gulbenkian* case[81] where what was under consideration was a power of distribution among a class conferred on trustees as distinct from a trust for distribution: but when

---

[80] [1970] A.C. 508.
[81] [1968] Ch. 126.

the *Gulbenkian* case came before the House of Lords that test was decisively rejected and the more stringent test on which counsel for the defendant executors insists was adopted. Clearly Lord Wilberforce in expressing the view that the test of validity of a discretionary trust ought to be similar to that accepted by the House of Lords in the *Gulbenkian* case did not take the view that it was sufficient that you could find individuals who were clearly members of the class; for he himself remarked, towards the end of his speech as to the trustees' duty of enquiring or ascertaining, that in each case the trustees ought to make such a survey of the range of objects or possible beneficiaries as will enable them to carry out their fiduciary duty. It is not enough that trustees should do nothing but distribute the fund among those objects of the trust who happen to be at hand or present themselves. Lord Wilberforce, after citing that passage which I have already quoted from the speech of Lord Upjohn in the *Gulbenkian* case,[82] put it more succinctly by remarking that what this did say (and he agreed) was that the trustees must select from the class, but that passage did not mean (as had been contended) that they must be able to get a complete list of all possible objects. I have already called attention to Lord Wilberforce's opinion that the trustees ought to make such a survey of the range of objects or possible beneficiaries as will enable them to carry out their fiduciary duty, and I ought perhaps to add that he indicated that a wider and more comprehensive range of enquiry is called for in the case of what I have called discretionary trusts than in the case of fiduciary powers. But, as I understand it, having made the appropriate survey, it matters not that it is not complete or fails to yield a result enabling you to lay out a list or particulars of every single beneficiary. Having done the best they can, the trustees may proceed on the basis similar to that adopted by the court where all the beneficiaries cannot be ascertained and distribute on the footing that they have been: see, for example, *Re Benjamin*.[83] What was referred to as 'the complete ascertainment test' laid down by this court in the *Broadway Cottages* case[84] is rejected. So also is the test laid down by this court in the *Gulbenkian* case. Validity or invalidity is to depend on whether you can say of any individual—and the accent must be on that word 'any,' for it is not simply the individual whose claim you are considering who is spoken of—that he 'is or is not a member of the class,' for only thus can you make a survey of the range of objects or possible beneficiaries.

"If the matter rested there, it would in my judgment follow that, treating the word 'relatives' as meaning descendants from a common ancestor, a trust for distribution such as is here in question would not be valid. Any 'survey of the range of objects or possible beneficiaries' would certainly be incomplete, and I am able to discern no principle on which such a survey could be conducted or where it should start or finish. The most you could do, so far as regards relatives, would be to find individuals who are clearly members of the class—the test which was accepted in the Court of Appeal, but rejected in the House of Lords, in the *Gulbenkian* case. The matter does not however, rest there . . . *Harding* v. *Glyn*[85] is authority endorsed by the decision of the House of Lords[86] that a discretionary trust for 'relations' was a valid trust to be executed by the

---

[82] [1970] A.C. 508, 524.
[83] [1902] 1 Ch. 723.
[84] [1955] Ch. 20.
[85] (1739) 1 Atk. 469.
[86] [1971] A.C. 424, 452.

court by distribution to the next-of-kin. The class of beneficiaries thus becomes a clearly defined class and there is no difficulty in determining whether a given individual is within it or without it.

"Does it then make any difference that here the discretionary trust for relations was a reference not to the relations of a deceased person but of one who was living? I think not. The next-of-kin of a living person are as readily ascertainable at any given time as the next-of-kin of one who is dead."

*Appeal dismissed. Leave to appeal to the House of Lords refused.*

## RE HAY'S SETTLEMENT TRUSTS

Chancery Division [1982] 1 W.L.R. 202; [1981] 3 All E.R. 786

By clause 4 of Lady Hay's settlement made in 1958, trustees held the trust fund "on trust for such persons or purposes for such interests and with such gifts over and (if for persons) with such provisions for their respective maintenance or advancement at the discretion of the Trustees or of any other persons as the Trustees shall by any deed or deeds revocable or irrevocable (but if revocable not after the expiration of 21 years from the date hereof) executed within 21 years from the date hereof appoint . . . and in default of such appointment in trust for the nieces and nephews of the Settlor now living in equal shares." A proviso precluded any appointment being made to the settlor, any husband of her, and any trustee or past trustee. For the first five years income was to be accumulated and then the income was to be held on discretionary trusts for the nieces and nephews or charities until the clause 4 power of appointment was exercised or ceased to be exercisable (by expiry of the 21 years).

In 1969 a deed of appointment was executed, clause 1 conferring a power of appointment on the trustees (exercisable till expiry of the 21-year period in the 1958 settlement) to hold "the trust fund and the income thereof on trust for such persons and such persons as shall be appointed." Clause 2 directed that the undisposed-of income (until full exercise of the clause 1 power) be held on discretionary trusts for the benefit of any persons whatsoever (the settlor, any husband of her, any existing or former trustee excepted) or for any charity.

Was the vast power of appointment in the 1958 settlement valid or not? If valid was its exercise void in creating a vast discretionary trust that could be said to infringe the rule "*delegatus non potest delegare*" or the rule that a trust must be administratively workable?

MEGARRY V.-C.: " . . . The starting point must be to consider whether the power created by the first limb of clause 4 of the settlement is valid. . . . The essential point is whether a power for trustees to appoint to anyone in the world except a handful of specified persons is valid. Such a power will be perfectly valid if given to a person who is not in a fiduciary position: the difficulty arises when it is given to trustees, for they are under certain fiduciary duties in relation to the power, and to a limited degree they are subject to the control of the courts. At the centre of the dispute there are *Re Manisty's Settlement Trusts*; [1974] Ch. 17 [1973] 2 All E.R. 1203 (in which Templeman J. differed from part of what was said in the Court of Appeal in *Blausten* v. *Inland Revenue Comrs.*; [1972] Ch. 256 [1972] 1 All E.R. 41; *McPhail* v. *Doulton*; [1971] A.C. 424 [1970] 2 All E.R. 228 (which I shall call *Re Baden* (*No. 1*)); and *Re Baden's Deed Trusts* (*No. 2*); [1973] Ch. 9 [1972] 2 All E.R. 1304, which I shall call *Re Baden* (*No. 2*). Counsel for the defendants, I may say, strongly contended that *Re Manisty's Settlement* was wrongly decided.

"In *Re Manisty's Settlement* a settlement gave trustees a discretionary power to apply the trust fund for the benefit of a small class of the settlor's near relations, save that any member of a smaller 'excepted class' was to be excluded from the class of beneficiaries. The trustees were also given power at their absolute discretion to declare that any person, corporation or charity (except a member of the excepted class or a trustee) should be included in the class of beneficiaries. Templeman J. held that this power to extend the class of beneficiaries was valid. In *Blausten* v. *Inland Revenue Comrs.* which had been decided some eighteen months earlier, the settlement created a discretionary trust of income for members of a 'specified class' and a power to pay or apply capital to or for the benefit of members of that class, or to appoint capital to be held on trust for them. The settlement also gave the trustees power 'with the previous consent in writing of the settlor' to appoint any other person or persons (except the settlor) to be included in the 'specified class.' The Court of Appeal decided the case on a point of construction; but Buckley L.J.; ([1972] Ch. 256 at 271 [1972] 1 All E.R. 41 at 49) also considered a contention that the trustees' power to add to the 'specified class' was so wide that it was bad for uncertainty, since the power would enable anyone in the world save the settlor to be included. He rejected this contention on the ground that the settlor's prior written consent was requisite to any addition to the 'specified class'; but for this, it seems plain that he would have held the power void for uncertainty. Orr L.J. simply concurred, but Salmon L.J. expressly confined himself to the point of construction, and said nothing about the power to add to the 'specified class.' In *Re Manisty's Settlement*; [1974] Ch. 17 at 29 [1973] 2 All E.R. 1203 at 1213, Templeman J. rejected the view of Buckley L.J. on this point on the ground that *Re Gestetner (deceased)*; [1953] Ch. 672 [1953] 1 All E.R. 1150, *Re Gulbenkian's Settlement Trusts*; [1970] A.C. 508 [1968] 3 All E.R. 785 and the two *Baden* cases did not appear to have been fully explored in the *Blausten* case, and the case did not involve any final pronouncement on the point. In general, I respectfully agree with Templeman J.

"I propose to approach the matter by stages. First, it is plain that if a power of appointment is given to a person who is not in a fiduciary position, there is nothing in the width of the power which invalidates it per se. The power may be a special power with a large class of persons as objects; the power may be what is called a 'hybrid' power, or an 'intermediate' power, authorising appointment to anyone save a specified number or class of persons; or the power may be a general power. Whichever it is, there is nothing in the number of persons to whom an appointment may be made which will invalidate it. The difficulty comes when the power is given to trustees as such, in that the number of objects may interact with the fiduciary duties of the trustees and their control by the court. The argument of counsel for the defendants carried him to the extent of asserting that no valid intermediate or general power could be vested in trustees.

"That brings me to the second point, namely, the extent of the fiduciary obligations of trustees who have a mere power vested in them, and how far the court exercises control over them in relation to that power. In the case of a trust, of course, the trustee is bound to execute it, and if he does not, the court will see to its execution. A mere power is very different. Normally the trustee is not bound to exercise it, and the court will not compel him to do so. That, however, does not mean that he can simply fold his hands and ignore it, for normally he must from time to time consider whether or not to exercise the power, and the court may direct him to do this.

"When he does exercise the power, he must, of course (as in the case of all trusts and powers) confine himself to what is authorised, and not go beyond it. But that is not the only restriction. Whereas a person who is not in a fiduciary position is free to exercise the power in any way that he wishes, unhampered by any fiduciary duties, a trustee to whom, as such, a power is given is bound by the duties of his office in exercising that power to do so in a responsible manner according to its purpose. It is not enough for him to refrain from acting capriciously; he must do more. He must 'make such a survey of the range of objects or possible beneficiaries' as will enable him to carry out his fiduciary duty. He must find out 'the permissible area of selection and then consider responsibly, in individual cases, whether a contemplated beneficiary was within the power and whether, in relation to the possible claimants, a particular grant was appropriate': per Lord Wilberforce in *Re Baden (No. 1)*; [1971] A.C. 424 at 449, 457 [1970] 2 All E.R. 228 at 240, 247. . . .

"That brings me to the third point. How is the duty of making a responsible survey and selection to be carried out in the absence of any complete list of objects? This question was considered by the Court of Appeal in *Re Baden (No. 2)*. That case was concerned with what, after some divergences of judicial opinion, was held to be a discretionary trust and not a mere power; but plainly the requirements for a mere power cannot be more stringent than those for a discretionary trust. The duty, I think, may be expressed along the following lines: I venture a modest degree of amplification and exegesis of what was said in *Re Baden (No. 2)*; [1973] Ch. 9 at 20, 27; [1972] 2 All E.R. 1304 at 1310, 1315. The trustee must not simply proceed to exercise the power in favour of such of the objects as happen to be at hand or claim his attention. He must first consider what persons or classes of persons are objects of the power within the definition in the settlement or will. In doing this, there is no need to compile a complete list of the objects, or even to make an accurate assessment of the number of them: what is needed is an appreciation of the width of the field, and thus whether a selection is to be made merely from a dozen or, instead, from thousands or millions. . . . Only when the trustee has applied his mind to 'the size of the problem' should he then consider in individual cases whether, in relation to other possible claimants, a particular grant is appropriate. In doing this, no doubt he should not prefer the undeserving to the deserving; but he is not required to make an exact calculation whether, as between deserving claimants, A is more deserving than B: see *Re Gestetner (deceased)*; [1953] Ch. 672 at 688 [1953] 1 All E.R. 1150 at 1155, approved in *Re Baden (No. 1)*; [1971] A.C. 424 at 453 [1970] 2 All E.R. 228 at 243–244.

"If I am right in these views, the duties of a trustee which are specific to a mere power seem to be threefold. Apart from the obvious duty of obeying the trust instrument, and in particular of making no appointment that is not authorised by it, the trustee must, first, consider periodically whether or not he should exercise the power; second, consider the range of objects of the power; and third, consider the appropriateness of individual appointments. I do not assert that this list is exhaustive; but as the authorities stand it seems to me to include the essentials, so far as relevant to the case before me.

"On this footing, the question is thus whether there is something in the nature of an intermediate power which conflicts with these duties in such a way as to invalidate the power if it is vested in a trustee. The case that there is rests in the main on *Blausten* v. *Inland Revenue Comrs.* which I have already summarised. The power there was plainly a mere power; and it authorised the trustees, with the settlor's previous consent in writing, to add any other person or persons (except the settlor) to the specified class.

"In that case, Buckley L.J. referred to the power as being one the exercise of which the trustees were under a duty to consider from time to time, and said; ([1972] Ch. 256 at 272 [1972] 1 All E.R. 41 at 50):

> 'If the class of persons to whose possible claims they would have to give consideration were so wide that it really did not amount to a class in any true sense at all no doubt that would be a duty which it would be impossible for them to perform and the power could be said to be invalid on that ground. But here, although they may introduce to the specified class any other person or persons except the [settlor], the power is one which can only be exercised with the previous consent in writing of the [settlor]. . . . Therefore on analysis the power is not a power to introduce anyone in the world to the specified class, but only anyone proposed by the trustees and approved by the [settlor]. This is not a case in which it could be said that the [settlor] in this respect has not set any metes and bounds to the beneficial interests which he intended to create or permit to be created under this settlement.'

"After referring to *Re Park* [1932] 1 Ch. 581 at 583; [1931] All E.R. Rep. 633 at 634, Buckley L.J. went on; ([1972] Ch. 256 at 273 [1972] 1 All E.R. 41 at 50):

> ' . . . this is not a power which suffers from the sort of uncertainty which results from the trustees being given a power of so wide an extent that it would be impossible for the court to say whether or not they were properly exercising it and so wide that it would be impossible for the trustees to consider in any sensible manner how they should exercise it, if at all, from time to time. The trustees would no doubt take into consideration the possible claims of anyone having any claim in the beneficence of the [settlor]. That is not a class of persons so wide or so indefinite that the trustees would not be able rationally to exercise their duty to consider from time to time whether or not they should exercise the power.'

"It seems quite plain that Buckley L.J. considered that the power was saved from invalidity only by the requirement for the consent of the settlor. The reason for saying that in the absence of such a requirement the power would have been invalid seems to be twofold. First, the class of persons to whose possible claims the trustees would be duty-bound to give consideration was so wide as not to form a true class, and this would make it impossible for the trustees to perform their duty of considering from time to time whether to exercise the power.

"I feel considerable difficulty in accepting this view. First, I do not see how mere numbers can inhibit the trustees from considering whether or not to exercise the power, as distinct from deciding in whose favour to exercise it. Second, I cannot see how the requirement of the settlor's consent will result in any 'class' being narrowed from one that is too wide to one that is small enough. Such a requirement makes no difference whatever to the number of persons potentially included: the only exclusion is still the settlor. Third, in any case I cannot see how the requirement of the settlor's consent could make it possible to treat 'anyone in the world save X' as constituting any real sort of a 'class,' as that term is usually understood.

"The second ground of invalidity if there is no requirement for the settlor's consent seems to be that the power is so wide that it would be impossible for the trustees to consider in any sensible manner how to exercise it, and also impossible for the court to say whether or not they were properly exercising it. With respect, I do not see how that follows. If I have correctly stated the extent of the duties of trustees in whom a mere power is vested, I do not see what there is to prevent the trustees from performing these duties. It must be remembered that Buckley L.J., though speaking after *Re Gulbenkian's Settlement* and *Re Baden (No. 1)* had been decided, lacked the advantage of considering *Re Baden (No. 2)*, which was not decided until some five months later. He thus did not have before him the explanation in that case of how the trustees should make a survey and consider individual appointments in cases where no complete list of objects could be compiled. I also have in mind that the settlor in the present case is still alive, though I do not rest my decision on that.

"From what I have said it will be seen that I cannot see any ground on which the power in question can be said to be void. Certainly it is not void for linguistic or semantic uncertainty; there is no room for doubt in the definition of those who are or are not objects of the power. Nor can I see that the power is administratively unworkable. The words of Lord Wilberforce in *Re Baden (No. 1)* [1971] A.C. 424 at 457 [1970] 2 All E.R. 228 at 247 are directed to discretionary trusts, not powers. Nor do I think that the power is void as being capricious. In *Re Manisty's Settlement* [1974] Ch. 17 at 27 [1973] 2 All E.R. 1203 at 1211 Templeman J. appears to be suggesting that a power to benefit 'residents in Greater London' is void as being capricious 'because the terms of the power negative any sensible intention on the part of the settlor.' In saying that, I do not think that the judge had in mind a case in which the settlor was, for instance, a former chairman of the Greater London Council, as subsequent words of his on that page indicate. In any case, as he pointed out earlier, this consideration does not apply to intermediate powers, where no class which could be regarded as capricious has been laid down. Nor do I see how the power in the present case could be invalidated as being too vague, a possible ground of invalidity considered in *Re Manisty's Settlement* [1974] Ch. 17 at 24 [1973] 2 All E.R. 1203 at 1208. Of course, if there is some real vice in a power, and there are real problems of administration or execution, the court may have to hold the power invalid: but I think that the court should be slow to do this. Dispositions ought if possible to be upheld, and the court ought not to be astute to find grounds on which a power can be invalidated. Naturally, if it is shown that a power offends against some rule of law or equity, then it will be held to be void: but a power should not be held void on a peradventure. In my judgment, the power conferred by clause 4 of the settlement is valid.

"With that, I turn to the discretionary trust of income under clause 2 of the deed of appointment. Apart from questions of the validity of the trust per se, there is the prior question whether the settlement enabled the trustees to create such a trust, or, for that matter, the power set out in clause 1 of the deed of appointment. The power conferred by clause 4 of the settlement provides that the trustees are to hold the trust fund on trust 'for such persons or purposes for such interests and with such gifts over and (if for persons) with such provision for their respective maintenance or advancement at the discretion of the Trustees or any other persons as the trustees shall appoint. Clause 2 of the deed of appointment provides that the trustees are to hold the trust fund on trust to pay the income 'to or for the benefit of any person or persons whatsoever . . . or to any charity' in such manner and shares and proportions as the trustees think fit. I need say nothing about purposes or charities as no question on them has arisen. The basic question is whether the appointment has designated the 'persons' to whom the appointment is made.

"Looked at as a matter of principle, my answer would be 'No.' There is no such person to be found in clause 2 of the deed of appointment: instead, there is merely the mechanism whereby a person or persons may be ascertained from time to time by the exercise of the discretion given to the trustees. If that mechanism is operated, then persons may emerge who will be entitled: but they will emerge not by virtue of any exercise of the power in the settlement but by virtue of the exercise of the discretion in the deed of appointment. That seems to me to be a plain case of delegation: the power in the settlement is not being exercised by appointing the persons who are to benefit but by creating a discretionary trust under which the discretionary trustees will from time to time select those who will benefit. I can see nothing whatever in the power conferred by the settlement which even contemplates that an appointment should designate no appointees but instead should set up a discretionary trust under which the trustees could determine who should benefit.

"Counsel for the defendants relied on *Re Hunter's Will Trusts* [1963] Ch. 372 [1962] 3 All E.R. 1050 [and *Re Morris' S.T.* [1951] 2 All E.R. 528] as supporting his contention that clause 2 of the deed of appointment was void.

"Now it is clear that in these authorities the rule delegatus non potest delegare was in issue. Does this rule apply to intermediate powers? This was not explored in argument, but I think that it is clear from *Re Triffitt's Settlement* [1958] Ch. 852 [1958] 2 All E.R. 299 that the rule does not apply to an intermediate power vested in a person beneficially. Here, of course, the power is an intermediate power, but it is vested in trustees as such, and not in any person beneficially; and the rule is that 'trustees cannot delegate unless they have authority to do so': *per* Viscount Radcliffe in *Re Pilkington's Will Trusts* [1964] A.C. 612 at 639 [1962] 3 All E.R. 622 at 630. Accordingly, I do not think that the fact that the power is an intermediate power excludes it from the rule against delegation. On the contrary, the fact that the power is vested in trustees subjects it to that rule unless there is something in the settlement to exclude it. I can see nothing in the settlement which purports to authorise any such appointment or to exclude the normal rule against delegation. In my judgment, both on principle and on authority clause 2 of the deed of appointment is void as being an excessive execution of the power.

"That, I think, suffices to dispose of the case. I have not dealt with the submission which counsel for the defendants put in the forefront of his argument. This was that even if the power had been wide enough to authorise the creation of the discretionary trust, that trust was nevertheless as bad as being a trust in favour of 'so hopelessly wide' a definition of beneficiaries 'as not to form anything like a class so that the trust is administratively unworkable': see *per* Lord Wilberforce in *Re Baden (No. 1)*; [1971] A.C. 424 at 457 [1970] 2 All E.R. 228 at 247. I do not propose to go into the authorities on this point. I consider that the duties of trustees under a discretionary trust are more stringent than those of trustees under a power of appointment (see *Re Baden (No. 1)*; [1971] A.C. 424 at 457 [1970] 2 All E.R. 228 at 247), and as at present advised I think that I would, if necessary, hold that an intermediate trust such as that in the present case is void as being administratively unworkable. In my view there is a difference between a power and a trust in this respect. The essence of that difference, I think, is that beneficiaries under a trust have rights of enforcement which mere objects of a power lack. But in this difficult branch of the law I consider that I should refrain from exploring without good reason any matters which do not have to be decided. In my opinion, the question whether an appointment is within a power is anterior to the question whether, if the an appointment is within the power, it is inherently good or bad; and having decided the first question against the validity of the appointment, I leave the second question undecided. . . . "

[He then held that the nieces and nephews living at the date of the settlement had become entitled to the trust fund on the expiration of 21 years from the date of the settlement by virtue of the gift over in default of any valid appointment within the 21 years.]

## RE BARLOW'S WILL TRUSTS

Chancery Division [1979] 1 W.L.R. 278; [1979] 1 All E.R. 296.

BROWNE-WILKINSON J. read the following judgment: "This summons raises a number of questions on the will of Helen Alice Dorothy Barlow, who died on September 16, 1975. She had a valuable collection of paintings.

"By clause 4 of her will, dated September 8, 1970, she made specific bequests of a number of them. Then by clause 5(a) she provided as follows:

> 'I GIVE AND BEQUEATH all my pictures not hereby specifically disposed of unto the Corporation [I interpose to say that that is the executor] upon trust to distribute any which may be specified in written instructions placed with this my Will among the persons or bodies named in such instructions subject thereto upon trust for sale but I DIRECT the Corporation to allow any members of my family and any friends of mine who may wish to do so to purchase any of such pictures at the prices shown in Mr. Fry's catalogue or at the values placed upon them by valuation for Probate purposes at the date of my death, whichever shall be the lower. The Corporation shall hold the net proceeds of sale of such pictures as are sold by them as part of my residuary estate.'

"The written instructions referred to in the first part of clause 5(a) were not admitted to probate. Therefore, apart from the pictures specifically bequeathed, the rest of the testatrix's pictures are directed by clause 5(a) to be sold subject to the rights of the testatrix's family and friends to purchase them at valuation.

"The pictures passing under clause 5(a) are of considerable quality, though not of outstanding importance. Mr. Fry's catalogue referred to in the clause was made in 1970. Mr. Fry also made the valuation for probate purposes, when he put a total value of £28,310 on the pictures in question. The values for probate purposes of most of the pictures are substantially greater than the values appearing in the 1970 catalogue. The present day value of the pictures must certainly be greater still. Therefore, the right to purchase conferred by clause 5(a) on the testatrix's family and friends is a beneficial right of some value.

"The main questions which arise for my decision are (a) whether the direction to allow members of the family and friends to purchase the pictures is void for uncertainty since the meaning of the word 'friends' is too vague to be given legal effect and (b) what persons are to be treated as being members of the testatrix's family. I will deal first with the question of uncertainty.

"Those arguing against the validity of the gift in favour of the friends contend that, in the absence of any guidance from the testatrix, the question 'who were her friends?' is incapable of being answered. The word is said to be 'conceptually uncertain' since there are so many different degrees of friendship and it is impossible to say which degree the testatrix had in mind. In support of this argument they rely on Lord Upjohn's remarks in *Re Gulbenkian's Settlement Trusts, Whishaw* v. *Stephens*[87] and the decision of the House of Lords in *McPhail* v. *Doulton*[88] (on appeal from *Re Baden's Deed Trusts*[89]) to the effect that it must be possible to say who is within and who without the class of friends. They say that since the testatrix intended all her friends to have the opportunity to acquire a picture it is necessary to be able to ascertain with certainty all the members of that class.

"Counsel for the fourth defendant, who argued in favour of the validity of the gift, contended that the tests laid down in the *Gulbenkian* case[90] and *McPhail* v. *Doulton* were not applicable in this case. The test, he says, is that laid down by the Court of Appeal in *Re Allen*[91] as appropriate in cases where the validity of a condition precedent or description is in issue, namely that the gift is valid if it is possible to say of one or more persons that he or they undoubtedly qualify even though it may be difficult to say of others whether or not they qualify.

"The distinction between the *Gulbenkian* test and the *Re Allen* test is, in my judgment, well exemplified by the word 'friends.' The word has a great range of meanings; indeed, its exact meaning probably varies slightly from person to person. Some would include only those with whom they had been on intimate terms over a long period; others would include acquaintances whom they liked. Some would include people with whom their relationship was primarily business; others would not. Indeed, many people, if asked to draw up a complete list of their friends, would probably have some difficulty in deciding whether certain of the people they knew were really 'friends' as opposed to 'acquaintances.' Therefore, if the nature of the gift was such that it was legally necessary to draw up a complete list of 'friends' of the testatrix, or to be able to say of any person that 'he is not a friend,' the whole gift would probably fail even as to those who, by any conceivable test, were friends. But in the case of a gift of a kind which does not require one to establish all the members of the class (*e.g.* 'a gift of £10 to each of my friends'), it may be possible to say of some people that, on any test, they qualify. Thus in *Re Allen*[92] Evershed M.R. took the example of a gift to X 'if he is a tall man'; a man 6 feet 6 inches tall could be said on any reasonable basis to satisfy the test, although it might be impossible to say whether a man, say 5 feet 10 inches high satisfied the requirement.

"So in this case, in my judgment, there are acquaintances of a kind so close that, on any reasonable basis, anyone would treat them as being 'friends.' Therefore, by allowing the disposition to take effect in their favour, one would certainly be giving effect to part of the testatrix's intention even though as to others it is impossible to say whether or not they satisfy the test.

"In my judgment, it is clear that Lord Upjohn in *Re Gulbenkian*[93] was considering only cases where it was necessary to establish all the members of

87 [1970] A.C. 508, 523–524.
88 [1971] A.C. 424.
89 [1969] 2 Ch. 388.
90 [1970] A.C. 508.
91 [1953] Ch. 810.
92 [1953] Ch. 810, 817.
93 [1970] A.C. 508, 524.

the class. He made it clear that the reason for the rule is that in a gift which requires one to establish all the members of the class (*e.g.* 'a gift to my friends in equal shares') you cannot hold the gift good in part, since the quantum of each friend's share depends on how many friends there are. So all persons intended to benefit by the donor must be ascertained if any effect is to be given to the gift. In my judgment, the adoption of Lord Upjohn's test by the House of Lords in *McPhail* v. *Doulton* is based on the same reasoning, even though in that case the House of Lords held that it was only necessary to be able to survey the class of objects of a power of appointment and not to establish who all the members were. But such reasoning has no application to a case where there is a condition or description attached to one or more individual gifts; in such cases, uncertainty as to some other persons who may have been intended to take does not in any way affect the quantum of the gift to persons who undoubtedly possess the qualification. Hence, in my judgment, the different test laid down in *Re Allen*. The recent decision of the Court of Appeal in *Re Tuck's Settlement Trust*[94] establishes that the test in *Re Allen* is still the appropriate test in considering such gifts, notwithstanding the *Gulbenkian* and *McPhail* v. *Doulton* decisions: see *per* Lord Russell of Killowen.[95]

"Accordingly, in my judgment, the proper result in this case depends on whether the disposition in clause 5(a) is properly to be regarded as a series of individual gifts to persons answering the description 'friend' (in which case it will be valid), or a gift which requires the whole class of friends to be established (in which case it will probably fail).

"The effect of clause 5(a) is to confer on friends of the testatrix a series of options to purchase. Although it is obviously desirable as a practical matter that steps should be taken to inform those entitled to the options of their rights, it is common ground that there is no legal necessity to do so. Therefore, each person coming forward to exercise the option has to prove that he is a friend; it is not legally necessary, in my judgment, to discover who all the friends are. In order to decide whether an individual is entitled to purchase, all that is required is that the executors should be able to say of that individual whether he has proved that he is a friend. The word 'friend,' therefore, is a description or qualification of the option holder.

"It was suggested that by allowing undoubted friends to take I would be altering the testatrix's intentions. It is said that she intended all her friends to have a chance to buy any given picture, and since some people she might have regarded as friends will not be able to apply, the number of competitors for that picture will be reduced. This may be so, but I cannot regard this factor as making it legally necessary to establish the whole class of friends. The testatrix's intention was that a friend should acquire a picture. My decision gives effect to that intention.

"I therefore hold, that the disposition does not fail for uncertainty, but that anyone who can prove that by any reasonable test he or she must have been a friend of the testatrix is entitled to exercise the option. Without seeking to lay down any exhaustive definition of such test, it may be helpful if I indicate certain minimum requirements: (a) the relationship must have been a long-standing one; (b) the relationship must have been a social relationship as opposed to a business or professional relationship; (c) although there may have

---

[94] [1978] Ch. 49.
[95] [1978] Ch. 49, 65.

been long periods when circumstances prevented the testatrix and the applicant from meeting, when circumstances did permit they must have met frequently. If in any case the executors entertain any real doubt whether an applicant qualifies, they can apply to the court to decide the issue.

"Finally on this aspect of the case I should notice two further cases to which I was referred. The first is *Re Gibbard*,[96] in which Plowman J. upheld the validity of a power to appoint to 'any of my old friends.' It is not necessary for me to decide whether that decision is still good law, in that it applied the *Re Allen* test to powers of appointment. But it does show that, if the *Re Allen* test is the correct test, the word 'friends' is not too uncertain to be given effect. Secondly, in *Re Lloyd's Trust Instruments*[97] (unreported but extracts from which are to be found in *Brown* v. *Gould*,[98]) Megarry J. stated:

> 'If there is a trust for "my old friends," all concerned are faced with uncertainty as to the concept or idea enshrined in those words. It may not be difficult to resolve that "old" means not "aged" but "of long standing"; but then there is the question of how long is "long." Friendship, too, is a concept with almost infinite shades of meaning. Where the concept is uncertain, the gift is void. Where the concept is certain, then mere difficulty in tracing and discovering those who are entitled normally does not invalidate the gift.'

"The extract that I have read itself shows that the judge was considering a trust for 'my old friends' (which required the whole class to be ascertained) and not such a case as I have to deal with. In my judgment, that dictum was not intended to apply to such a case as I have before me.

"I turn now to the question, who are to be treated as 'members of my family?' It is not suggested that this class is too uncertain. The contest is between those who say that only the next-of-kin of the testatrix are entitled and those who say that everyone related by blood to the testatrix is included." [He held that everyone related by blood to the unmarried testatrix was included.]

### R. v. DISTRICT AUDITOR, ex p. WEST YORKSHIRE METROPOLITAN COUNTY COUNCIL

Divisional Court (1985) 26 R.V.R. 24.

To spend money under Local Government Act 1972, section 137 just before its abolition the Metropolitan Council resolved to create a trust (to which £400,000 would be transferred), in which the capital and income had to be spent within 11 months, "for the benefit of any or all or some of the inhabitants of the County of West Yorkshire" in any one of four specified ways: (i) to assist economic development in the county in order to relieve unemployment and poverty, (ii) to assist bodies concerned with youth and community problems, (iii) to assist and encourage ethnic and other minority groups, (iv) to inform all interested and influential persons of the consequences of the proposed abolition of the Council (and other metropolitan councils). Was the trust administratively workable?

[96] [1967] 1 W.L.R. 42.
[97] (June 24, 1970) unreported.
[98] [1972] Ch. 53, 57.

LLOYD L.J. (with whom Taylor J. concurred): "Counsel for the county council did not seek to argue that the trust is valid as a charitable trust, though he did not concede the point in case he should have second thoughts in a higher court. His case was that the trust could take effect as an express private trust. For the creation of an express private trust three things are required. First, there must be a clear intention to create the trust. Secondly there must be certainty as to the subject matter of the trust; and thirdly there must be certainty as to the persons intended to benefit. Two of the three certainties, as they are familiarly called, were present here. Was the third? He argued that the beneficiaries of the trust were all or some of the inhabitants of the county of West Yorkshire. The class might be on the large side, containing as it does some two and a half million potential beneficiaries. But the definition, it was said, is straightforward and clear cut. There is no uncertainty as to the concept. If anyone were to come forward and claim to be a beneficiary, it could be said of him at once whether he was within the class or not.

"I cannot accept counsel for the county council's argument. I am prepared to assume in favour of the council, without deciding, that the class is defined with sufficient clarity. I do not decide the point because it might, as it seems to me, be open to argument what is meant by 'an inhabitant' of the county of West Yorkshire. But I put that difficulty on one side. For there is to my mind a more fundamental difficulty. A trust with as many as two and a half million potential beneficiaries is, in my judgment, quite simply unworkable. The class is far too large. In *Re Gulbenkian's Settlements* [1970] A.C. 508 Lord Reid said at 518:

> 'It may be that there is a class of case where, although the description of a class of beneficiaries is clear enough, any attempt to apply it to the facts would lead to such administrative difficulties that it would for that reason be held to be invalid.'

[His Lordship quoted Lord WILBERFORCE'S final paragraph in *McPhail* v. *Doulton* [1971] A.C. 424 at 457, p. 159, *supra*, and continued]:

"It seems to me that the present trust comes within the third case to which Lord Wilberforce refers. I hope I am not guilty of being prejudiced by the example which he gave. But it could hardly be more apt, or fit the facts of the present case more precisely.

"I mention the subsequent decisions in *Re Baden's Deed Trusts (No. 2)* [1972] Ch. 607 and on appeal [1973] Ch. 9, p. 159, *supra*, and *Re Manisty's Settlement* [1974] Ch. 17, with misgiving, since they were not cited in argument. The latter was a case of an intermediate power, that is to say, a power exercisable by trustees in favour of all the world, other than members of an excepted class.

"After referring to *Gulbenkian* and the two *Baden* cases, Templeman J. (as he then was) said:

> 'I conclude . . . that a power cannot be uncertain merely because it is wide in ambit.'

"A power to benefit, for example, the residents of Greater London might, he thought, be bad, not on the ground of its width but on the ground of capriciousness, since the settlor could have no sensible intention to benefit 'an accidental conglomeration of persons' who had 'no discernible link with the settlor.' But that objection could not apply here. The council had every reason for wishing to benefit the inhabitants of West Yorkshire.

"Lord Wilberforce's dictum has also been the subject of a good deal of academic comment and criticism, noticeably by L. McKay (1974) 38 Conv. 269 and C. T. Emery (1982) 98 L.Q.R. 551. I should have welcomed further argument on these matters, but through no fault of counsel for the county council this was not possible. So I have to do the best I can.

"My conclusion is that the dictum of Lord Wilberforce remains of high persuasive authority, despite *Re Manisty. Manisty's* case was concerned with a power, where a function of the court is more restricted. In the case of a trust, the court may have to execute the trust. Not so in the case of a power. That there may still be a distinction between trusts and powers in this connection was recognised by Templeman J. himself in the sentence immediately following his quotation of Lord Wilberforce's dictum, when he said:

> 'In these guarded terms Lord Wilberforce appears to refer to trusts which may have to be executed and administered by the court and not to powers where the court has a very much more limited function.'

"There can be no doubt that the declaration of trust in the present case created a trust and not a power. Following Lord Wilberforce's dictum, I would hold that the definition of the beneficiaries of the trust is 'so hopelessly wide' as to be incapable of forming 'anything like a class.' I would therefore reject counsel for the county council's argument that the declaration of trust can take effect as an express private trust.

"Since, as I have already said, it was not argued that the trust can take effect as a valid charitable trust, it follows that the declaration of trust is ineffective. What we have here, in a nutshell, is a non-charitable purpose trust. It is clear law that, subject to certain exceptions, such trusts are void: see *Lewin on Trusts* (16th ed.), pp. 17–19. The present case does not come within any of the established exceptions. Nor can it be brought within the scope of such recent decisions as *Re Denley's Trust Deed* [1969] 1 Ch. 373, p. 202, *infra* and *Re Lipinski's Will Trusts* [1976] Ch. 235, p. 208, *infra*, since there are, for the reasons I have given, no ascertained or ascertainable beneficiaries."

## Section 4. Compliance with the Rules against Perpetuity

Reference is often made to a trust offending the perpetuity rule without it being made clear whether the trust infringes the rule against remoteness of vesting, directed at interests vesting at too remote a time, or infringes the rule against inalienability, directed at immediately vested interests which can go on for too long, so tying up trust property for too long. The two rules are mutually exclusive, the former applying to "people" trusts and the latter to "purpose" trusts.

THE RULE AGAINST REMOTENESS[1]

*The common law rule*

Where capital is set on one side to be kept intact ("endowment" capital) with only the income thereof being used, this cannot last

---

[1] See Morris & Leach, *The Rule against Perpetuities* (2nd ed.), Megarry & Wade, Chap. 7 but in the light of J. Dukeminier (1986) 102 L.Q.R. 250 on relevant lives in being.

indefinitely. A settlor cannot be allowed to rule the living from his grave for thousands of years nor to compel capital to be used for ever as "safe" trust capital instead of absolutely owned capital available for risky entrepreneurial ventures. Thus, where a settlor created successive interests a future interest (contingent on birth or whatever) was, under the common law rule, void unless *at the creation of the trust* it was *absolutely certain* that the contingency would be satisfied—and so the interest would become "vested in interest"—within the perpetuity period.

The perpetuity period cannot exceed 21 years from the death of some expressly or impliedly relevant life in being at the creation of the trust. A settlor can expressly stipulate that his beneficiaries are only those described by him who take a vested interest before the expiry of 21 years from the death of the last survivor of all the descendants of King George VI living at the date of the settlement (a "royal lives" clause). If T died, leaving his estate on trust for his widow, W, for life, remainder to S, his only child, for life, remainder to such of his grandchildren who attained 21 years of age, all the trusts are valid. W has a life interest "vested in possession" (a present right of present enjoyment), S has a life interest "vested in interest" (a present right to future enjoyment), while grandchildren under 21 have contingent interests (a contingent right to future enjoyment), which must become vested in interest within 21 years of the deaths of S and his spouse. The grandchildren's parents' lives are impliedly causally relevant in restricting the period within which the contingent interests inevitably must, if at all, become vested interests.

*The 1964 Act "wait and see" rule*

If, by any stretch of the imagination, a contingent interest might possibly not become vested in interest within the perpetuity period, it was void. To mitigate this harshness the Perpetuities and Accumulations Act 1964 radically reformed the rule against remoteness. Where a contingent future interest would have been void at common law one now "waits and sees" what actually happens in a statutory perpetuity period.[2] The interest is valid until it becomes clear that it must vest in interest (if at all) outside the period prescribed by statute, which replaces causally relevant common law lives by a list of statutory lives in being[3] and, as an alternative, expressly allows a specified period of years not exceeding 80 to be chosen as the perpetuity period.[4] Modern practice is to use the 80-year period because one then knows in advance exactly when the trust will terminate.

The 1964 Act only affects settlements created after July 16, 1964 but in the case of settlements made in the exercise of a special power of

---

[2] 1964 Act, s.3(1), (2), (3), *infra*, p. 181.
[3] *Ibid*. s.3(5), *infra*, p. 182.
[4] *Ibid*. s.1.

appointment only applies where the head-settlement containing the special power was created after July 16, 1964.[5] The reason for this exception is that the perpetuity period for special powers runs not from the date the power is exercised but from the date of the head-settlement creating the power.[6]

### Discretionary trusts

The rule against remoteness originated in dealing with contingent, life or absolute, interests in remainder. How did it deal with the validity of discretionary trusts? It dealt with them by regarding them as trust *powers* and so, like special powers of appointment, they were void unless they were absolutely bound to be completely exercised within the perpetuity period so that all the trust property became absolutely owned by some of the discretionary beneficiaries within the period.[7] Under the 1964 Act discretionary trusts and special powers of appointment that would have been void at common law are valid to the extent that the trustees actually exercise their fiduciary powers within the statutory perpetuity period.[8] Thereafter, there will be a resulting trust of the property in favour of the settlor[9] (unless, exceptionally, there is a gift over to a person with a vested interest[10]).

### Class gifts

The 1964 Act deals specifically with class gifts,[11] particularly where beneficiaries have to attain an age greater than 21 years. Thus, if a testator, T, left property to his only child, C, for life, remainder to such of his grandchildren as attained 25 years of age this remainder would have been wholly void at common law because a grandchild might theoretically attain 25 years of age more than 21 years after the death of impliedly relevant lives in being.[12] The 1964 Act reduces the age from 25 years to 24 years if the youngest grandchild is only three years old at the death of the last statutory life in being, so that in the next 21 years, if at all, the grandchild will obtain a vested interest, so the remainder is valid.

Where the problem relates not to attaining a specified age outside the perpetuity period but to persons by birth, or marriage or otherwise, becoming members of a class outside the period the Act provides

---

5 *Ibid.* s.15(5).
6 *Pilkington* v. *I.R.C.* [1964] A.C. 612.
7 *Re Coleman* [1936] Ch. 528.
8 1964 Act, ss.3(3), 15(2).
9 1964 Act, s.4(4), like the rest of s.4, only seems applicable to fixed trusts in favour of a class and not discretionary trusts, "class" gifts traditionally being restricted to cases where the property is divisible into shares varying according to the number of persons in the class and the "class-closing" rule in *Andrews* v. *Partington* (1791) 3 Bro. C.C. 401 applying when the first member of the class becomes entitled to claim his share.
10 1964 Act, s.6.
11 See note 9, *supra*, 1964 Act, s.4.
12 A class gift could not be partly valid and partly void: the size of the benefit of each member of the class had to be certain before expiry of the perpetuity period so the possibility of the number of members increasing outside the period made the gift to the class wholly void.

a statutory guillotine. At the end of the period such persons will be excluded from the class of beneficiaries so the property will then be held absolutely for the then existing beneficiaries.[13] Thus, if a testator leaves his cricket ground and pavilion thereon to the persons who are at his death the Chairman and Treasurer of the Slogworthy Cricket Club to hold the same on trust solely for present and future members of the club one waits and sees if the club is dissolved within the period of statutory lives plus 21 years, because the then members would divide the property (or, rather, its proceeds of sale) equally between themselves. Otherwise, because at the end of the period persons can still become members and so obtain an interest in the property, the 1964 Act applies to exclude such future persons from the class of beneficiaries. Those happening to be members at the end of the period will become absolutely entitled to the property. Hopefully, they will agree (after buying out the relevant shares of any dissentients) that the property should then be vested in four club members on a bare trust to be administered for current members according to the rules of the club.

### Re Denley-type locus standi purpose trusts

As will be seen in the next section, *Re Denley*[14] upheld a trust of land to be maintained and used as a recreation or sports ground for the benefit of employees from time to time of a particular company, while in *Wicks* v. *Firth*[15] the House of Lords assumed that there can be a valid trust to award scholarships to assist in the education of children of employees of a company from time to time. Both trusts were limited expressly to a valid perpetuity period but what would have happened if such trusts were left open-ended to last indefinitely?

This category of trust has only become apparent since 1968 so there is no case law directly in point, but it seems likely that for perpetuity purposes such a trust would be regarded as analogous to a discretionary trust. Thus, because the powers of the trustees to benefit the beneficiaries were not bound to have been exhaustively exercised within the common law perpetuity period the trusts would have been void. However, under the 1964 Act the trusts are valid to the extent that the trustees exercise their fiduciary powers within the statutory perpetuity period.[16] At the end of such period the property will be held on resulting trust for the settlor.[17] This would seem to be the position today if, for example, a testator left £50,000 and his cricket ground and pavilion thereon to his executors and trustees on trust to enable the villagers of Slogworthy to play cricket there forever.

An alternative approach is to say that *Re Denley*-type purpose trusts should be treated like other permitted non-charitable purpose trusts[18]

---

[13] 1964 Act, s. 4(4).
[14] [1969] 1 Ch. 373.
[15] [1983] A.C. 214.
[16] 1964 Act, s. 3(3).
[17] See note 9, *supra*.
[18] See p. 189, *infra*.

and so be subject not to the rule against remoteness but to the rule against inalienability. This will make them void unless at the outset it is certain that by the end of the perpetuity period the purpose trust will end so that the trust fund will be wholly alienable by someone.[19] Because of the modern, praiseworthy, judicial tendency to facilitate, rather than frustrate, the intentions of settlors and testators it seems likely that the courts will not invoke the harsh application of the rule against inalienability.

### THE RULE AGAINST INALIENABILITY (OR PERPETUAL PURPOSE TRUSTS)

The common law rule against remoteness ensured that endowment trusts for persons were void unless one could be absolutely sure from the outset that by the end of the perpetuity period the beneficiaries would have obtained vested interests enabling them to deal with the trust fund as they wished. Under the rule in *Saunders* v. *Vautier*[20] if trustees hold property on trust for A absolutely or for B for life, remainder to C absolutely then (assuming each is *sui juris*) A or B and C, as the case may be, can direct the trustees how to deal with the property, *e.g.* vest it in A absolutely or divide it absolutely between B and C in the shares agreed by B and C. Persons like B must obtain vested interests before the end of the perpetuity period but there is no requirement that their interests must terminate within the perpetuity period.[21] Thus, if at the end of the period B has a life interest the trust continues till C acquires the property on B's death.

The rule against inalienability makes permitted[22] non-charitable endowment purpose trusts void unless from the outset they are certain to terminate by the end of the perpetuity period,[23] 21 years from the death of the last survivor of any causally relevant lives in being.[24] Such a rule was necessary because purposes unlike individuals can last forever and because a rule against remoteness of vesting is inappropriate when interests cannot vest in purposes as opposed to persons. Thus, testamentary trusts to erect and then maintain a sepulchral monument, to say private masses for the testator and to maintain the testator's horse or cat are void unless restricted to a specified perpetuity period, which will be 21 years unless, say, a royal lives clause is used.

What about *Re Denley* purpose trusts? Take a gift of endowment capital to trustees to assist in their discretion in the education of a testator's issue or of children of employees of a particular company. The educational purpose is intended to last indefinitely and because

---

[19] See next sub-heading.

[20] (1841) 4 Beav. 115, p. 651, *infra*.

[21] *Re Chardon* [1928] Ch. 464; *Re Gage* [1898] 1 Ch. 506; *Wainwright* v. *Miller* [1897] 2 Ch. 255.

[22] See p. 189, *infra*.

[23] *Leahy* v. *Att.-Gen. for New South Wales* [1959] A.C. 457, *Cocks* v. *Manners* (1871) L.R. 12 Eq. 574.

[24] *Re Astor's S.T.* [1952] Ch. 534; *Re Khoo Cheng Teow* [1932] Straits Settlement Reports 226. The statutory period of 80 years is available only for the rule against remoteness: see note 28, *infra*.

the beneficiaries are a fluctuating class of people there is no question of the beneficiaries ever being all ascertained (quite apart from every one being *sui juris*) so as to be able to terminate the trust under the rule in *Saunders* v. *Vautier* and divide the property between themselves.[25] Thus, the rule against inalienability seems more appropriate than the rule against remoteness.

However, the harsh results of such a conclusion will probably be avoided by the court invoking the wording of Perpetuities and Accumulation Act 1964, section 3(3)[26] and implicitly restricting to fixed interest class gifts the application of section 4 thereof,[27] while restricting section 15(4) thereof[28] (enacted before *Re Denley*-type purpose trusts were appreciated) to permitted non-charitable purpose trusts other than *Re Denley*-type purpose trusts.

### Alienability of trust assets but inalienability of trust fund

Whatever happen from time to time to be the particular trust *assets* comprised in the trust *fund* will be alienable under the Trustee Investments Act 1961, the Settled Land Act 1925 or the Law of Property Act 1925. However, if trust income has to be used for a particular purpose then the trust fund producing that income must be kept intact for as long as the income is required for that purpose. The inalienability of the trust income inevitably leads to the inalienability of the trust fund. The rule against inalienability is concerned to ensure that the length of time for which trustees must retain the trust fund (in whatever assets it is from time to time invested) does not exceed the perpetuity period.

### Only endowment trusts are subject to rule

If the trustees do not have to keep the capital intact and use only the income thereof but can spend trust money on the trust purposes without the need to consider whether or not the money represents capital or income and whether the purpose is a "capital" or "income" type of purpose, then the rule against inalienability has no applica-

---

[25] *Re Levy* [1960] Ch. 346, 363; *Re Westphal* [1972] N.Z.L.R. 792, 794–795.
[26] The settlor's disposition confers powers on the trustees which, like the fiduciary powers of trustees under discretionary trusts, would have been void at common law on the ground that they could have been exercised at too remote a time to give trust property to the issue or children. See text to notes 16 and 17, *supra*.
[27] See note 9, *supra*.
[28] s.15(4), *infra*, p. 185 is oddly worded. In context "the rule of law rendering void for remoteness" is the rule against inalienability (which the draftsman considers to make purpose trusts void if they can continue till too remote a time). The draftsman in s.1 uses "the rule against perpetuities" when referring to the rule against remoteness of vesting and allowing the 80-year period expressly to be specified. One should add implicitly to the end of s.15(4) "applicable to the relevant disposition under such rule of law."

tion.[29] Usually, the settlor will make it clear that the trustees are to hold his property on trust only to use the income within a specified perpetuity period for particular purposes and at the end of the period to distribute the capital to beneficiaries. Exceptionally, he may make it clear that his property is to be used without distinction between capital and income until fully consumed. A trust, whether or not by way of endowment, must also satisfy the beneficiary principle (dealt with in the next section) but a purpose trust can be valid if benefiting persons in such fashion that they have *locus standi* to enforce the trust or if falling within an exceptional, anomalous class of testamentary trusts.

*The rule against accumulations*

If a trust is concerned with a trust or power to accumulate it is crucial to restrict the accumulation to one of the six periods allowed by section 164 of the Law of Property Act 1925 and section 13 of the 1964 Act unless section 31 of the Trustee Act 1925 allows accumulations during a beneficiary's minority:

(a) the life of the grantor or settlor;

(b) twenty-one years from the death of the grantor, settlor or testator;

(c) the duration of the minority or respective minorities of any person(s) living or *en ventre sa mère* at the death of the grantor, settlor or testator;

(d) the duration of the minority or respective minorities only of any person(s) who under the limitations of the instrument directing the accumulations would, for the time being, if of full age, be entitled to the income directed to be accumulated;

(e) twenty-one years from the date of the making of the disposition;

(f) the duration of the minority or respective minorities of any person(s) in being at that date.

If an excessive accumulation infringes the perpetuity period it is void *in toto*.[30] If within the perpetuity period it is cut down to the nearest appropriate period of the six permitted, and only the excess is void.[31]

Indirectly, "excessive" accumulation may be provided for by empowering trustees to transfer trust assets to a company formed by them in return for shares in the company: the company can then retain profits and not declare dividends. Indeed, the company can settle

---

[29] *Re Lipinski's W.T.* [1976] Ch. 235, 245, p. 208, *infra*; *Re Drummond* [1914] 2 Ch. 90, 98; *Re Prevost* [1930] 2 Ch. 383, 388; *Re Price* [1943] Ch. 422, 428, 430; *Re Macaulay's Estate* [1943] Ch. 435, 436 (H.L.); R. H. Maudsley, *The Modern Law of Perpetuities*, p. 173. In *Leahy* v. *Att.-Gen. for New South Wales* [1959] A.C. 457, 483 *infra*, p. 197 Viscount Simonds doubted whether a society's liberty to spend the capital and income of a gift as it saw fit saved a gift on trust to the society unless its members are treated as the immediate beneficiaries capable of disposing of the gifted property. This is too restrictive a view of the beneficiary principle: there can be *Re Denley*-type purpose trusts benefiting individuals who have no right to make the trust property their own but do have a right to ensure that the property is used for their benefit.

[30] *Curtis* v. *Lukin* (1842) 5 Beav. 147.

[31] *Re Watt's W.T.* [1936] 2 All E.R. 1555, 1562; *Re Ransome* [1957] Ch. 348, 361.

assets on accumulation trusts without being bound by the statute which only applies to natural persons.[32] It seems likely that a settlor can expressly choose a foreign law to govern accumulations without offending English public policy.[33]

## Perpetuities and Accumulations Act 1964

### 1. Power to specify perpetuity period

(1) Subject to section 9(2) of this Act and subsection (2) below, where the instrument by which any disposition is made so provides, the perpetuity period applicable to the disposition under the rule against perpetuities, instead of being of any other duration, shall be of a duration equal to such number of years not exceeding eighty as is specified in that behalf in the instrument.

(2) Subsection (2) above shall not have effect where the disposition is made in exercise of a special power of appointment, but where a period is specified under that subsection in the instrument creating such a power the period shall apply in relation to any disposition under the power as it applies in relation to the power itself.

### 3. Uncertainty as to remoteness

(1) Where, apart from the provisions of this section and sections 4 and 5 of this Act, a disposition would be void on the ground that the interest disposed of might not become vested until too remote a time, the disposition shall be treated, until such time (if any) as it becomes established that the vesting must occur, if at all, after the end of the perpetuity period, as if the disposition were not subject to the rule against perpetuities; and its becoming so established shall not affect the validity of anything previously done in relation to the interest disposed of by way of advancement, application of intermediate income or otherwise.

(2) Where, apart from the said provisions, a disposition consisting of the conferring of a general power of appointment would be void on the ground that the power might not become exercisable until too remote a time, the disposition shall be treated, until such time (if any) as it becomes established that the power will not be exercisable within the perpetuity period, as if the disposition were not subject to the rule against perpetuities.

(3) Where, apart from the said provisions, a disposition consisting of the conferring of any power, option or other right would be void on the ground that the right might be exercised at too remote a time, the disposition shall be treated as regards any exercise of the right within the perpetuity period as if it were not subject to the rule against perpetuities and, subject to the said provisions, shall be treated as void

---

[32] *Re Dodwell & Co.'s Trust Deed* [1979] Ch. 301.
[33] Consider Articles 6 and 18 of Hague Convention on Trust and problem p. 828 *infra*.

for remoteness only if, and so far as, the right is not fully exercised within that period.

(4) Where this section applies to a disposition and the duration of the perpetuity period is not determined by virtue of section 1 or 9(2) of this Act, it shall be determined as follows:—

(*a*) where any persons falling within subsection (5) below are individuals in being and ascertainable at the commencement of the perpetuity period the duration of the period shall be determined by reference to their lives and no others, but so that the lives of any description of persons falling within paragraph (*b*) or (*c*) of that subsection shall be disregarded if the number of persons of that description is such as to render it impracticable to ascertain the date of death of the survivor;

(*b*) where there are no lives under paragraph (*a*) above the period shall be twenty-one years.

(5) The said persons are as follows:—

(*a*) the person by whom the disposition was made;

(*b*) a person to whom or in whose favour the disposition was made, that is to say—

   (i) in the case of a disposition to a class of persons, any member or potential member of the class;

   (ii) in the case of an individual disposition to a person taking only on certain conditions being satisfied, any person as to whom some of the conditions are satisfied and the remainder may in time be satisfied;

   (iii) in the case of a special power of appointment exercisable in favour of members of a class, any member or potential member of the class;

   (iv) in the case of a special power of appointment exercisable in favour of one person only, that person or, where the object of the power is ascertainable only on certain conditions being satisfied, any person as to whom some of the conditions are satisfied and the remainder may in time be satisfied;

   (v) in the case of any power, option or other right, the person on whom the right is conferred;

(*c*) a person having a child or grandchild within sub-paragraphs (i) to (iv) of paragraph (*b*) above, or any of whose children or grandchildren, if subsequently born, would by virtue of his or her descent fall within those sub-paragraphs;

(*d*) any person on the failure or determination of whose prior interest the disposition is limited to take effect.

## 4. Reduction of age and exclusion of class members to avoid remoteness

(1) Where a disposition is limited by reference to the attainment by any person or persons of a specified age exceeding 21 years, and it is

apparent at the time the disposition is made or becomes apparent at a subsequent time—

(*a*) that the disposition would, apart from this section, be void for remoteness, but

(*b*) that it would not be so void if the specified age had been twenty-one years,

the disposition shall be treated for all purposes as if, instead of being limited by reference to the age in fact specified, it had been limited by reference to the age nearest to that age which would, if specified instead, have prevented the disposition from being so void.

(2) Where in the case of any disposition different ages exceeding 21 years are specified in relation to different persons—

(*a*) the reference in paragraph (*b*) of subsection (1) above to the specified age shall be construed as a reference to all the specified ages, and

(*b*) that subsection shall operate to reduce each such age so far as is necessary to save the disposition from being void for remoteness.

(3) Where the inclusion of any persons, being potential members of a class or unborn persons who at birth would become members or potential members of the class, prevents the foregoing provisions of this section from operating to save a disposition from being void for remoteness, those persons shall thenceforth be deemed for all the purposes of the disposition to be excluded from the class, and the said provisions shall thereupon have effect accordingly.

(4) Where, in the case of a disposition to which subsection (3) above does not apply, it is apparent at the time the disposition is made or becomes apparent at a subsequent time that, apart from this subsection, the inclusion of any persons, being potential members of a class or unborn persons who at birth would become members or potential members of the class, would cause the disposition to be treated as void for remoteness, those persons shall, unless their exclusion would exhaust the class, thenceforth be deemed for all the purposes of the disposition to be excluded from the class.

(5) Where this section has effect in relation to a disposition to which section 3 above applies, the operation of this section shall not affect the validity of anything previously done in relation to the interest disposed of by way of advancement, application of intermediate income or otherwise.

**Saving and acceleration of expectant interests**

**6.** A disposition shall not be treated as void for remoteness by reason only that the interest disposed of is ulterior to and dependent upon an interest under a disposition which is so void, and the vesting of an interest shall not be prevented from being accelerated on the failure of a prior interest by reason only that the failure arises because of remoteness.

### Powers of appointment

7. For the purposes of the rule against perpetuities, a power of appointment shall be treated as a special power unless—

(a) in the instrument creating the power it is expressed to be exercisable by one person only, and

(b) it could, at all times during its currency when that person is of full age and capacity, be exercised by him so as immediately to transfer to himself the whole of the interest governed by the power without the consent of any other person or compliance with any other condition, not being a formal condition relating only to the mode of exercise of the power:

Provided that for the purpose of determining whether a disposition made under a power of appointment exercisable by will only is void for remoteness, the power shall be treated as a general power where it would have fallen to be so treated as if exercisable by deed.

### Administrative powers of trustees

8.—(1) The rule against perpetuities shall not operate to invalidate a power conferred on trustees or other persons to sell, lease, exchange or otherwise dispose of any property for full consideration, or to do any other act in the administration (as opposed to the distribution) of any other property, and shall not prevent the payment to trustees or other persons of reasonable remuneration for their services.

(2) Subsection (1) above shall apply for the purpose of enabling a power to be exercised at any time after the commencement of this Act notwithstanding that the power is conferred by an instrument which took effect before that commencement.

### Short title, interpretation and extent

15.—(1) This Act may be cited as the Perpetuities and Accumulations Act 1964.

(2) In this Act—

"disposition" includes the conferring of a power of appointment and any other disposition of an interest in or right over property, and references to the interest disposed of shall be construed accordingly;

"in being" means living or en ventre sa mere;

"power of appointment" includes any discretionary power to transfer a beneficial interest in property without the furnishing of valuable consideration;

"will" includes a codicil;

and for the purposes of this Act a disposition contained in a will shall be deemed to be made at the death of the testator.

(3) For the purposes of this Act a person shall be treated as a member of a class if in his case all the conditions identifying a member of the class are satisfied, and shall be treated as a potential member if in his case some only of those conditions are satisfied but there is a possibility that the remainder will in time be satisfied.

(4) Nothing in this Act shall affect the operation of the rule of law rendering void for remoteness certain dispositions under which property is limited to be applied for purposes other than the benefit of any person or class of persons in cases where the property may be so applied after the end of the perpetuity period.

(5) The foregoing sections of this Act shall apply (except as provided in section 8(2) above) only in relation to instruments taking effect after the commencement of this Act, and in the case of an instrument made in the exercise of a special power of appointment shall apply only where the instrument creating the power takes effect after that commencement:

Provided that section 7 above shall apply in all cases for construing the foregoing reference to a special power of appointment.

(6) This Act shall apply in relation to a disposition made otherwise than by an instrument as if the disposition had been contained in an instrument taking effect when the disposition was made.

## Section 5. The Beneficiary Principle

Over the past 25 years an offshoot of the principle that the courts of equity will not recognise as valid any trust which they cannot properly administer has taken on a particularly lively lease of life. This requirement can be stated as, "There must be somebody in whose favour the court can decree performance"[34] or "A gift on trust must have a *cestui que trust* and there being here no *cestui que trust* the gift must fail."[35] A settlor as such has no *locus standi* to enforce the terms of his trust or gift.[36] It follows that a trust for purposes (other than charitable purposes when the Attorney-General can sue: see later) is invalid as emphasised in *Re Astor's S.T.*,[37] in *Re Endacott*,[38] where the Court of Appeal warmly endorsed *Re Astor's S.T.*, in *Re Shaw*[39] and in *Leahy* v. *Att.-Gen for New South Wales, infra*,[40] unless the attainment of the trust purposes is sufficiently for the benefit of individuals that they have *locus standi* to apply to the court to enforce the trust: *Re Denley's Trust Deed, infra*.[41] In this last case Goff J. opined that the

---

[34] Sir William Grant M.R., *Morice* v. *Bishop of Durham* (1804) 9 Ves. 399, 405.
[35] Harman J. in *Re Wood* [1949] Ch. 498, 501. He need not be alive and ascertained so long as he will be by the end of the perpetuity period and so then able to bring the trustees to account.
[36] *Re Astor's S.T.* [1952] Ch. 534, 542; *Bradshaw* v. *University College of Wales* [1987] 3 All E.R. 200, 202.
[37] [1952] Ch. 534.
[38] [1960] Ch. 232.
[39] [1957] 1 W.L.R. 729.
[40] p. 197.
[41] p. 202, endorsed in *Re Lipinski's W.T.* [1976] Ch. 235, *infra*, p. 208.

beneficiary principle only invalidates purpose trusts which are abstract
or impersonal. Unfortunately, he failed to deal adequately with *Leahy*
v. *Att.-Gen. for New South Wales* (though he could have dealt
adequately with it on the footing that there was no restriction to the
perpetuity period and that the trust was for the pure abstract purpose
of enabling a contemplative Catholic order of nuns fulfil a Catholic
devout function whilst *Denley* was for earthly employees to use a
sports ground for a limited period). However, in so far as his judgment
suggests that a factual interest in performance of a trust may suffice for
*locus standi* it appears to conflict with *Shaw* v. *Lawless*[42] and *Gandy* v.
*Gandy*.[43] The employees in *Denley* could have been explained to have
*locus standi*, it is submitted, as licensees under a deed (analogous to
contractual licensees) sufficing to give them standing to seek a court
order compelling performance of the trust, if the trustees happened to
refuse to carry out the trust, and authorising persons to draw up
regulations for use of the land.[44]

However, in *Denley*, Goff J. clearly[45] treated the trust of land to be
maintained and used as and for the purpose of a recreation or sports
ground for the benefit of the employees of a company for a limited
period as a trust for a purpose, which incidentally benefited persons
with sufficient selfish interest to justify a *locus standi* positively to
enforce the trust. This has subsequently been accepted in various
cases[46] and may explain some earlier cases[47] where no point was taken
on the beneficiary principle.

Recently, the beneficiary principle has been considered in relation to
the *Quistclose* type of trust where A lends money to B under a primary
temporary trust to use the money to pay off C, resulting if the purpose
is performed in a pure loan relationship between A and B (excluding
any trust relationship), but with a secondary final trust arising in A's
favour in the event of non-performance of the purpose.[48] It has been
held[49] that A has an interest under the secondary final trust and C,
though having no beneficial interest, has an equitable right to compel
B to administer the loaned moneys properly, analogous to the right of
beneficiaries entitled to residue under a will to compel the executor to
administer the deceased's assets properly.

---

42 (1838) 5 Cl. & Fin. 129, 155 (school owner).
43 (1885) 30 Ch.D. 57. See McKay (1973) 37 Conv.(N.S.) 420, 426–427. Enforcement is not available
  to the owner of a school where a trust provides for the education of X at the school or to a settlor
  who would feel benefited and fulfilled if his purpose were carried out: *Re Astor's S.T.* [1952] Ch.
  534, 542.
44 *McPhail* v. *Doulton* [1971] A.C. 424, 457, Lord Wilberforce.
45 In *Re Grant's W.T.* [1979] 3 All E.R. 359, 368 Vinelott J. suggests that *Re Denley* simply
  concerned a discretionary trust for beneficiaries but Goff J.'s judgment lengthily considered the
  beneficiary principle surely because he did not believe he was faced with a mere discretionary
  trust.
46 *Re Northern Developments Holdings Ltd.* October 6, 1978; *Re Lipinski's W.T.* [1976] Ch. 235; *R.*
  v. *District Auditor, ex p. West Yorkshire Metropolitan C.C.* (1986) 26 R.V.R. 24.
47 *Re Abbott Fund Trusts* [1900] 2 Ch. 326; *Re Gillingham Bus Disaster Fund* [1959] Ch. 62.
48 See p. 117, *supra* and *Re EVTR* [1987] B.C.L.C. 646.
49 *Carreras Rothmans Ltd.* v. *Freeman Mathews Treasure Ltd.* [1985] 1 All E.R. 155, 166 applying the
  unreported decision of Megarry V.-C. in *Re Northern Developments Holdings Ltd.*, October 6,
  1978.

Peter Millett Q.C. has preferred to analyse the situation more traditionally as follows[50]:

"It is submitted that the *Quistclose* trust does not involve any departure from well-settled principles of trust law, and certainly does not call for the recognition of a new kind of enforceable purpose trust, a new kind of trust which the settlor can enforce, or a new situation in which the beneficial interest in the trust fund is in suspense. The answer to the question raised at the beginning of this article depends upon A's intention, to be collected from the language used, the conduct of the parties, and the circumstances of the case. The following, it is suggested, may be regarded as suitable guidelines by which A's intention may be ascertained:

1. If A's intention was to benefit C, or his object would be frustrated if he were to retain a power of revocation, the transaction will create an irrevocable trust in favour of C, enforceable by C but not by A. The beneficial interest in the trust property will be in C.

2. If A's intention was to benefit B (though without vesting a beneficial interest in him), or to benefit himself by furthering some private or commercial interest of his own, and not (except incidentally) to benefit C, then the transaction will create a trust in favour of A alone, and B will hold the trust property in trust to comply with A's directions. The trust will be enforceable by A but not by C. The beneficial interest will remain in A.

3. Where A's object was to save B from bankruptcy by enabling him to pay his creditors, the prima facie inference is that set out in paragraph 2 above. Wherever that is the correct inference:

 (i) Where A has an interest of his own, separate and distinct from any interest of B, in seeing that the money is applied for the stated purpose, B will be under a positive obligation, enforceable by A, to apply it for that purpose. Where A has no such interest, B will be regarded as having a power, but no duty, to apply it for the stated purpose, and A's remedy will be confined to preventing the misapplication of the money.

 (ii) Prima facie, A's directions will be regarded as revocable by him; but he may contract with B not to revoke them without B's consent.

 (iii) Communication to C of the arrangements prior to A's revocation will effect an assignment of A's equitable interest to C, and convert A's revocable mandate into an irrevocable trust for C."

---

50 (1985) 101 L.Q.R. 269, 290.

### VOID ABSTRACT IMPERSONAL PURPOSE TRUSTS

It would appear that the beneficiary principle, like the certainty principle, is intended to enable the courts positively to carry out trusts if the trustees fail to do so, so that someone with a positive interest in seeing trusts properly performed will have *locus standi* to satisfy the beneficiary principle, whilst someone having a negative interest in preventing trust moneys from being misapplied and in hoping that earlier trusts will not be performed will not have *locus standi* to satisfy the beneficiary principle. After all, there will almost always[51] be some living person in the background (*e.g.* a residuary legatee or the next-of-kin) with a negative interest in applying to the courts in the case of failure on the part of trustees to carry out abstract impersonal purposes, but his existence will not validate such purpose trusts.[52]

Some examples may help to illustrate the line between unenforceable, abstract, impersonal purpose trusts (void) and enforceable purpose trusts benefiting persons sufficiently for them to have *locus standi* to enforce the valid trusts. Impersonal void trusts are those to further the interests of a political party[53] or a non-charitable religious order[54] or to maintain good relations between nations and preserve the independence of newspapers[55] or to research and develop a new 40-letter English alphabet in place of the present one[56] or to erect a statue of the testator in a village square[57] or to prevent vivisection.[58]

Enforceable *Re Denley*-type purpose trusts include trusts to further the education of children of employees of a company through the discretionary provision of scholarships,[59] or trusts to provide pensions, in the discretion of directors of a company (or of trustees), for ex-employees[60] or, presumably, to provide holidays (sporting or otherwise) for such employees and their families as the directors of the company (or trustees) see fit.

### VALIDITY OF ABSTRACT IMPERSONAL POWERS

It does appear that powers (as opposed to trusts) to carry out abstract impersonal purposes can be valid,[61] though the courts refuse to allow a trust to take effect as though it were a power in order to enable the

---

51 In a rare case he might not be currently ascertainable, *e.g.* he might be unborn or the person who is Warden of All Souls College 80 years from the creation of the trust.
52 *e.g. Re Astor's S.T.* [1952] Ch. 534; *Re Shaw* [1957] 1 W.L.R. 729; *Leahy* v. *Att.-Gen. for N.S.W.* [1959] A.C. 457; *Re Endacott* [1960] Ch. 232.
53 *Re Grant's W.T.* [1979] 3 All E.R. 359; *Bacon* v. *Pianta* (1966) 114 C.L.R. 634.
54 *Leahy* v. *Att.-Gen. for New South Wales* [1959] A.C. 457.
55 *Re Astor's S.T.* [1952] Ch. 534.
56 *Re Shaw* [1957] 1 W.L.R. 729.
57 *cf. Re Endacott* [1960] Ch. 232.
58 *cf. National Anti-Vivisection Society* v. *I.R.C.* [1948] A.C. 31. For gifts to unincorporated societies, see pp. 191–197, *infra.*
59 *Wicks* v. *Firth* [1983] A.C. 214.
60 *cf. Re Saxone Shoe Co.'s Trust Deed* [1962] 1 W.L.R. 943 where the old fixed list test invalidated the discretionary trusts which should now be valid after *McPhail* v. *Doulton* [1971] A.C. 424.
61 *Re Douglas* (1887) 35 Ch.D. 472; *Goff* v. *Nairne* (1876) 3 Ch.D. 278; *Re Shaw* [1957] 1 W.L.R. 729.

purposes to be carried out.[62] Although a strong case[63] can be made out against such a refusal, especially when some purpose trusts represent desirable social experiments falling outside the realm of charity and when, in principle, equity should give effect to a settlor's intentions unless they are capricious, harmful or illegal, it is likely[64] that the House of Lords would endorse the conventional view and leave it to Parliament to change the law if it wishes.[65]

It is thus up to draftsmen to carry out their clients' intentions by using powers, in the hope that the chosen trustees will be likely to exercise the powers. Otherwise, a company can be created with the pure abstract purposes as its objects, and funds can be given outright to the company. Alternatively, funds may be given as an accretion to the funds of an unincorporated association subject to the contractual rights and liabilities of the members *inter se* but subject to no trusts.[66]

### ANOMALOUS VALID TESTAMENTARY PURPOSE TRUSTS

The Court of Appeal[67] has accepted that there are some anomalous cases, not to be extended, where testamentary trusts infringing the beneficiary principle have been held valid. These anomalous cases are:

(1) trusts for the maintenance of particular animals[68];
(2) trusts for the erection or maintenance of graves and sepulchral monuments[69];
(3) trusts for the saying of masses in private[70];
(4) trusts for the promotion and furtherance of fox-hunting.[71]

These trusts are sometimes referred to as trusts of imperfect obligation[72] since the trustees are not obliged to carry out the trusts in

---

[62] *Re Shaw* [1957] 1 W.L.R. 729, 746; *Re Endacott* [1960] Ch. 232, 246.
[63] Ames (1892) 5 Harv.L.R. 389; Scott (1945) 58 Harv.L.R. 548; Morris & Leach's *Perpetuities* (2nd ed.), pp. 319–321; Hackney, *Understanding Equity & Trusts*, pp. 75–82.
[64] *Cf.* the refusal to treat trusts like powers for certainty purposes: *I.R.C.* v. *Broadway Cottages Trust* [1955] Ch. 20, 36.
[65] *e.g.* as in s.16 of the Ontario Perpetuities Act 1966, *infra*, p. 214 or the Bermudan Trusts (Special Provisions) Act 1989, ss.12–16 requiring the settlor to appoint an enforcer and provide for appointment of successors.
[66] *Re Recher's W.T.* [1972] Ch. 526, *infra*, p. 206.
[67] *Re Endacott* [1960] Ch. 232 (residuary gift to a parish council "for the purpose of providing some useful memorial to" the testator held void for uncertainty and for infringing the beneficiary principle).
[68] *Pettingall* v. *Pettingall* (1842) 11 L.J. Ch. 176; *Re Dean* (1889) 41 Ch.D. 552. Many trusts for animals generally are charitable: *Re Wedgwood* [1915] 1 Ch. 113.
[69] *Re Hooper* [1932] Ch. 38; *Mussett* v. *Bingle* [1876] W.N. 170; *Pirbright* v. *Salwey* [1896] W.N. 86; *Trimmer* v. *Danby* (1856) 25 L.J. Ch. 424. The maintenance of private graves may be possible for 99 years under the Parish Council and Burial Authorities (Miscellaneous Provisions) Act 1970, s.1. If the construction is part of the fabric of a church the trust is charitable and valid: *Hoare* v. *Osborne* (1866) L.R. 1 Eq. 585.
[70] *Bourne* v. *Keane* [1919] A.C. 815, 874–875. Gifts for the saying of masses in public are charitable because of the public benefit in assisting in the endowment of priests but not for the saying of masses in private: *Re Hetherington* [1989] 2 All E.R. 129 (but the endowment ground seems applicable in both cases). In Malaysia and Singapore trusts for ancestor worship (Sin Chew or Chin Shong ceremonies) have been held valid anomalous non-charitable purpose gifts if restricted to the perpetuity period: *Tan* v. *Tan* (1946) 12 M.L.J. 159.
[71] *Re Thompson* [1934] Ch. 342, but the default beneficiary, a charity, only objected *pro forma*. If any of these anomalous cases is to be overruled this seems the prime candidate: it certainly should not be extended to other forms of sport. The furtherance of sport in the context of schools and universities will be charitable: *I.R.C.* v. *McMullen*, *infra*, p. 308.
[72] Snell's *Equity*, p. 102.

the absence of a beneficiary able to apply to the court to enforce the trust. The trusts are subject to the rule against inalienability and so must be restricted directly or indirectly[73] to the common law perpetuity period. If the trustees do not take advantage of what, in substance, amounts to a power to carry out a purpose, then the person otherwise entitled to the trust property will be able to claim it.

### Purposes as mere motives of trusts for beneficiaries

*Re Denley*-type purpose trusts typically involve a large fluctuating class of beneficiaries never intended to have, and never capable[74] of having, absolute ownership of the trust property, and only having a positive right to the performance of the trustee's duties in the form prescribed by the settlor. What of the cases, however, where there is a small class of identified beneficiaries who could be intended to have absolute ownership of the trust property, though the settlor purportedly qualifies this by requiring the property to be used for a specified purpose?

Take the case of a trust fund set up for the education of the seven children of a deceased clergyman, once their formal education is over. Kekewich J.[75] held this to be an absolute gift with the reference to education expressing merely the motive of the gift. He applied the well-established, and difficult to rebut,[76] presumption of construction,[77] "If a gross sum be given, or if the whole income of property be given, and a special purpose be assigned for this gift this court regards the gift as absolute and the purpose merely as the motive of the gift, and therefore holds that the gift takes effect as to the whole sum or the whole income as the case may be."

This was applied by the Court of Appeal in *Re Osoba*[78] where a bequest to the testator's widow upon trust "for her maintenance and for the training of my daughter, Abiola, up to university grade and for the maintenance of my aged mother" was held to be a trust for the three females absolutely as joint tenants. In *Re Bowes*[79] a trust to spend £5,000 on planting trees for shelter on the Wemmergill Estate was held to be a trust for the estate owners absolutely with the motive of having trees planted, so the owners could have the £5,000 to spend as they wished.

---

[73] If a will restricts a bequest expressly "so far as the law allows" this is construed as restricting the period to 21 years so satisfying the rule against inalienability: *Re Hooper* [1932] Ch. 38. The court will not imply such a term: *Re Compton* [1946] 1 All E.R. 117. If the legacy does not have to be kept intact as endowment capital but can be spent as soon as practicable on the purpose then the rule against inalienability has no application: *Trimmer* v. *Danby* (1856) 25 L.J.Ch. 424; *Mussett* v. *Bingle* [1876] W.N. 170.

[74] A fluctuating class can never exercise *Saunders* v. *Vautier* rights to make the trust property their own: *Re Levy* [1960] Ch. 346, 363; *Re Westphal* [1972] N.Z.L.R. 792, 764–765.

[75] *Re Andrew's Trust* [1905] 2 Ch. 48.

[76] *Re Abbott Fund Trust* [1900] 2 Ch. 326: fund subscribed for maintenance of two deaf and dumb ladies (so not of normal capacity) held after their deaths to pass to subscribers under resulting trust and not to survivor's estate.

[77] *Re Sanderson's Trusts* (1857) 3 K. & J. 497 and see *Re Skinner* (1860) 1 J. & H. 102, 105.

[78] [1979] 2 All E.R. 393.

[79] [1896] 1 Ch. 507.

A problem arises over the application of the rule in *Saunders* v. *Vautier*[80] if a settlor purports to create a *Re Denley*-type purpose trust for identified *sui juris* beneficiaries by making it clear that the purpose is not to be construed as a motive but is the integral central function of the trust, *e.g.* "In order that my son does not use the money for his own purposes I bequeath £50,000 to my trustees on trust annually to use the annual income for the purpose of providing holidays and no other purpose whatsoever for my son, L, during his life and subject thereto for the R.S.P.C.C. absolutely." By the rule in *Saunders* v. *Vautier* L can claim all the income as of right if he is *sui juris* and absolutely entitled thereto, *i.e.* he must have an absolute and indefeasible vested interest in the relevant income as opposed to a contingent or defeasible interest. A court could well take the view that *Re Denley* did not intend indirectly to oust the fundamental *Saunders* v. *Vautier* principle, so that L must be considered, as a matter of law, to have an absolute life interest which the settlor cannot fetter because this would be repugnant to the absolute nature of the life interest granted. Thus, *Re Denley* purpose trusts are valid only in favour of fluctuating classes of beneficiaries where the rule in *Saunders* v. *Vautier* can have no application. A narrower strained approach would be to hold that A, in effect, has a defeasible life interest, in that income so far as not used for holidays because of his non-participation must pass to the R.S.P.C.C., so that the rule in *Saunders* v. *Vautier* cannot apply.

#### GIFTS TO UNINCORPORATED BODIES

Unincorporated bodies, whether called associations, clubs or societies, raise special problems since an unincorporated body, unlike a corporate body, is not a legal person capable of owning property or entering into contracts or of being the subject of legal rights and duties.[81] Tax legislation tackles an unincorporated body formed for business purposes as a partnership with tax liability attributed to the individual partners, but if not formed for business purposes then the unincorporated body is regarded as a beneficiary under a bare trust, so making the trustees liable for corporation tax or, until its recent abolition, development land tax.[82]

The body's property will be vested in trustees under a bare trust for the members of the body (except to the extent that statute may prevent members of certain bodies from winding up the body and dividing its property between themselves[83]). The trustees or other

---

[80] (1841) 4 Beav. 115, p. 651, *infra*.

[81] Trade unions are unincorporated associations (if not incorporated as a special register body) but by the Trade Union and Labour Relations Act 1974, s.2 they can make contracts in their own names, may sue or be sued in their own names, judgments can be enforced against them as if they were bodies corporate, and property may be vested in trustees on trust "for the union."

[82] *Conservative Central Office* v. *Burrell* [1982] 1 W.L.R. 522; *Frampton* v. *I.R.C.* [1985] S.T.C. 186, Income and Corporation Tax Act 1970, s.155. Development Land Tax Act 1976, s. 47, Interpretation Act 1978, s.5 and Sched. 1 defining person to include a body corporate or incorporate.

[83] *e.g.* Literary and Scientific Institutions Act 1854, s.30; *Re Bristol Athenaeum* (1899) 43 Ch.D. 236.

organ under the body's constitution may enter into contracts, thereby putting the body's property at risk *vis-à-vis* the claims of creditors, and may even be authorised to declare trusts binding the body's property.[84] To the extent such valid trusts have not been declared the body's property belongs to the members, subject to their contract *inter se* under the body's constitution and subject to any claims that third parties may have resulting from contracts made by the trustees.[85]

A member or his spouse (or anyone) may give property *inter vivos* or by will to the officers of the body as trustees upon certain trusts that are germane to the purpose of the body. In a rare case such trusts may be to use the property as soon as convenient in payment of everyday expenses so that the property is treated as part of the body's general assets. However, normally such trust property is not intended to become the body's property to be spent as part of its general assets. The trust property is intended to be held under a separate endowment account and managed separately from the body's general assets: neither the body's constitution nor the agreement of its members can then change the trustees' obligations as trustees of the trust property.

### Associations with no unifying contract

An unincorporated body has the following features:

(1) it is composed of two or more persons bound together for a common purpose;
(2) these persons have mutual rights and duties arising from a contract between them;
(3) the body has rules to determine (a) who controls the body and its funds and (b) the terms on which such control is exercisable;
(4) the body can be joined or left at will.

For lack of the second and third features the Conservative Party was held not to be an unincorporated association liable to corporation tax.[86] The Revenue had argued that the party was an unincorporated association since members' contributions surely took effect as an accretion to the funds which were the subject-matter of a contract which such members had made *inter se*. How else could there be a legal relationship between a contributor and the recipient of the contribution so as to safeguard the contributor's interest?

Vinelott J.[87] suggested that the answer is that the contributor enters into a contract with the treasurer whereby in consideration of payment

---

[84] Anything they do may be ratified by the membership since unincorporated associations have no capacity to be limited and so unlike companies cannot act *ultra vires*.

[85] *Re Bucks Constabulary Fund Friendly Society (No. 2)* [1979] 1 All E.R. 623, *infra*, p. 419.

[86] *Conservative Central Office* v. *Burrell* [1982] 1 W.L.R. 522. The fourth feature was not in issue but it seems too restrictive since an association may well have restrictions on new membership or rules curtailing the freedom of members to leave at will.

[87] *Conservative Central Office* v. *Burrell* [1980] 3 All E.R. 42. He appears to suggest as an alternative that the treasurer by accepting the subscription comes under a special equitable obligation similar to an executor.

of the subscription the treasurer undertakes to apply the subscription towards the association's purposes: breach of this undertaking can be enjoined on normal contractual principles at the suit of the contributor. On appeal,[88] Brightman L.J. opined that the contributor, by way of mandate or agency, gives his contribution to the treasurer to add it to the general funds of the association. Once that has been done the mandate[89] becomes irrevocable but the contributor will have a remedy to restrain or have made good a misapplication of the mixed fund, unless it appeared on ordinary accounting principles that his own contribution had already been properly expended.

A gift for purposes (whether of an unincorporated body or otherwise[90]) may thus take effect by way of contract or of mandate (which may be gratuitous) if the donor is to retain some measure of control. Effect cannot be given to a testator's bequests in such fashion since one cannot imply a contract or mandate between a deceased person and another,[91] though a deceased may authorise or direct his personal representatives to enter into a contract or mandate. A deceased may also in his lifetime contract to leave property by will to someone for a purpose, and if he does die, leaving such a will, then his rights under the contract will vest in his personal representatives who will be able to enforce the contractual undertakings given to him.

There is no need for any of the above artificial reasoning in the case of gifts for unincorporated associations as Brightman L.J. has emphasised,[92] since *inter vivos* or testamentary gifts can validly take effect "as an accretion to the funds which are the subject-matter of the contract which the members [of the unincorporated association] have made *inter se.*"[93]

### Different constructions of gifts to unincorporated bodies

Before the 1964 Perpetuities and Accumulations Act there were particular legal obstacles confronting gifts to unincorporated bodies. The gift could not be an absolute gift to such a body because such a body has no legal personality. It could not be a valid gift if construed as a gift to the present and future members of the body because the intent to ensure benefiting future members required the capital to be kept intact and held on trust for only the income to be used, so that the capital would remain available for the benefit of future members.[94] This rendered the gift void for infringing the rule against remoteness,

---

[88] [1982] 1 W.L.R. 522, and see [1983] Conv. 150 (P. Creighton) and (1983) 133 New L.J. 87 (C. T. Emery). Brightman L.J. made no comment on Vinelott J.'s views.
[89] Brightman L.J. was probably thinking in terms of a gratuitous rather than a contractual mandate but he does not make it clear.
[90] *e.g.* a disaster appeal committee in a situation like that in *Re Gillingham Bus Disaster Fund* [1958] Ch. 300.
[91] As accepted by Vinelott J. and Brightman L.J. in the *Conservative Central Office* case, also *Re Wilson* [1908] 1 Ch. 839.
[92] *Conservative Central Office* v. *Burrell* [1982] 2 All E.R. 1, 7.
[93] *Ibid.*
[94] *Leahy* v. *Att.-Gen. for New South Wales* [1959] A.C. 457.

though since the 1964 Act such a gift would be valid for the statutory
perpetuity period.[95] If the gift were construed as a gift to the body on
trust for carrying out purposes, with the gift being an endowment fund
to be used for those purposes only, and not to be used without
distinction between capital and income nor to be capable (on dissolution of the body) for sharing out between the then members, then such
a purpose trust was void for infringing the rule against inalienability,
unless it was a charitable purpose trust. The 1964 Act has not affected
this.[96]

The gift would be valid if construed as an absolute gift to the persons
happening to be current members of the body, so that any such person
could claim his proportionate share. This might not be quite what the
deceased donor wished but, at least, his gift was not void. There thus
developed a sophisticated construction, more likely to give effect to a
testator's intention to benefit future members, but without imposing a
trust to benefit future members with the attendant void for remoteness
problem before the 1964 Act.

The sophisticated construction construes the gift as an absolute gift
to the current members beneficially, but as an accretion to the body's
property held subject to the terms of the contract which the members
are subjected to by virtue of their membership of the body. This
contract determines how the body's assets are to be enjoyed and what
are the rights of the members in respect of such assets, while the
treasurer or other worthy members will hold the assets on a bare trust
for current members to be dealt with according to the contract (the
constitution of the body).

*Possible constructions to consider*

1. The gift is a valid absolute gift (and not a trust except to the
   extent a testator's executors may be under a trust duty to give
   effect to the intended absolute gift) to the persons currently
   members of the unincorporated body, so that any such person
   can claim his proportionate share.[97]
2. The gift is a valid absolute gift (and not a trust except to the
   extent a testator's executors may be under a trust duty to give
   effect to the intended absolute gift) to the current members,
   taking effect as an accretion to the body's funds which are to be
   dealt with (under a bare trust) according to the rules of the
   body by which the members are all contractually bound.[98] The
   donor/testator is not providing endowment capital but giving his

[95] See p. 175, *supra*.
[96] See s.15(4) of 1964 Act, p. 179, *supra*.
[97] *Cocks* v. *Manners* (1871) L.R. 12 Eq. 574; *Re Smith* [1916] 1 Ch. 937; *Re Ogden* [1933] Ch. 678; *Re Clarke* [1901] 2 Ch. 110.
[98] *Re Recher's W.T.* [1972] Ch. 526, *infra*, p. 206; *Re Lipinski's W.T.* [1976] Ch. 235, *infra*, p. 208; *Universe Tankships Inc. of Monrovia* v. *International Transport Workers Federation* [1983] A.C. 366; *News Group Ltd.* v. *Sogat* [1986] I.C.R. 716; *Re Bucks Constabulary Fund (No. 2)* [1979] 1 All E.R. 623, *infra*, p. 419.

property to be freely spent[99] on day-to-day expenses or something of a more lasting nature, or to be divided up and pocketed
by the members if the contractual rules allow this on dissolution
or otherwise. It ought not to matter that because of some
statute or subordination to some outside legal entity the members are unable to wind up the body and pocket its assets.[1] The
gift in augmentation of the body's general assets is wholly
alienable: it can be totally consumed in supporting the body's
purposes directly or indirectly benefiting the members who all
have *locus standi* to sue. The gift does not have to be kept intact
as endowment capital, so no trust rules concerning remoteness
or inalienability can be applicable. However, if the testator
knew that it was impossible or very difficult in practice for
members to wind up the body and pocket its assets, so that the
body was designed to carry on indefinitely, his bequest could
well be construed as intending to set up endowment capital so
that the income would benefit members from time to time
indefinitely as under construction 3.[2]

3. The gift is intended to ensure that present and future members
are either directly benefited or indirectly benefited by the
carrying out of the purposes of the body to which they belong.
Thus, the gift is of endowment capital to be held upon trust
(separate from the body's general assets available to be spent
like current income) so that the income will always be available
for the members from time to time or for purposes benefiting
such members.

At one extreme, one could have a fixed trust (or, even, a
discretionary trust) for whoever happen each year to be members of The Athenaeum. Normally, however, a gift will be to,
say, The Athenaeum to ensure that it continues to fulfil its
general purposes or to ensure that it continues to fulfil a
particular purpose within its various purposes. Such an endowment gift before the 1964 Perpetuities and Accumulation Act
would have been void for infringing the rule against remoteness
(if regarded as a trust for persons) or the rule against alien-
ability (if regarded as a non-charitable purpose trust). Nowadays, the trend[3] is to stretch matters to hold that there is no

---

[99] *Re Macaulay's Estate* [1943] Ch. 435; *Re Price* [1943] Ch. 422; *Re Lipinski* [1976] Ch. 235; *Re Drummond* [1914] 2 Ch. 90, 97–98; *Re Prevost* [1930] 2 Ch. 383.
[1] The suggestion of Vinelott J. in *Re Grant's W.T.* [1979] 3 All E.R. 359 that a "necessary characteristic" of any gift within this second construction is the members' power to alter the rules and divide the assets between them seems unsound. It surely suffices that the gifted property is not endowment capital but can be freely spent on purposes benefiting the members. The members' contractual rights to enforce spending the property for their benefit suffices even if they cannot personally "pocket" the property: their position is *a fortiori* that of beneficiaries with *locus standi* to enforce purpose trusts directly benefiting them even if they have no *Saunders* v. *Vautier* right to "pocket" the trust property.
[2] *Carne* v. *Long* (1860) 2 De G.F. & J. 75; *Bacon* v. *Pianta* (1966) 114 C.L.R. 634 (to the Communist Party of Australia "for its sole use and benefit"); *Re Grant's W.T.* [1979] 3 All E.R. 359.
[3] See note 98, *supra*.

endowment capital, so that there is an absolute gift accruing to the body's assets under the second construction above.

If the court cannot so hold then, where the members can wind up the body and make its capital assets (including the gifted capital) their own, the court will wait and see if the members do so within the statutory perpetuity period of statutory lives in being plus 21 years. If the members do not, then section 4(4) of the 1964 Act should close the class of members so as to exclude persons becoming members outside the perpetuity period. The current members at the end of that period should between them be absolutely entitled to the gifted capital. No doubt, in practice, they will be happy to transfer it to trustees as an accretion to the club's funds but a member could claim his proportionate share (at the risk of not having his membership renewed).

Where the members cannot make the club assets their own because statute prohibits this[4] or because on dissolution the assets must pass to another body[5] then the trust will be a purpose trust and be dealt with under constructions 4, 5 and 6, *infra*.

4. The gift is intended to be of endowment capital to be held on trust for the income to be applied to a charitable purpose. This is a valid charitable trust (exempt from the beneficiary principle and the rule against inalienability) whose funds will need to be kept separate from the non-charitable funds of the body and will remain subject to the charitable purpose, even after dissolution of the body.[6]

5. The gift is intended to be of endowment capital to be held on trust for the income to be applied for a non-charitable purpose within the *Re Denley* type of valid purpose trusts, *e.g.* if T leaves a cricket ground and £100,000 to the Chairman and Treasurer of the ICI plc Social Club to be held on trust for providing and maintaining cricket facilities for the benefit of the club members and the inhabitants of Billingham.[7] The better view is that such a trust should be subject to the rule against remoteness and so be valid under the 1964 Act until expiry of the statutory perpetuity period, after which there will be a resulting trust in favour of the settlor.[8] However, a case can be made out for subjecting such a trust to the rule against inalienability, so that the trust is void from the outset.[9]

---

[4] *e.g.* Literacy and Scientific Institutions Act 1854, s.30. *Re Bristol Athenaeum* (1889) 43 Ch.D. 236.

[5] *e.g. Re Grant's W.T.* [1979] 3 All E.R. 359.

[6] *Brooks* v. *Richardson* [1986] 1 All E.R. 952; *Re Finger's W.T.* [1972] Ch. 300 revealing the predisposition of the court to treat a gift to an unincorporated charitable body as a trust for purposes, so as to prevent the gift lapsing if the body had been earlier dissolved and the second construction had been applied.

[7] *Cf. Re Denley's Trust Deed* [1969] 1 Ch. 373.

[8] See p. 177, *supra*.

[9] See pp. 178–179, *supra*.

6. The gift is intended to be of endowment capital to be held on trust for the income to be applied for pure non-charitable purposes where any benefit for persons is so indirect or intangible that no person has *locus standi* to apply for enforcement of the trust. The trust will be void for infringing the beneficiary principle[10] unless it is one of the anomalous permitted testamentary purpose trusts,[11] but even these must be restricted to the common law perpetuity period if they are not to infringe the rule against inalienability.[12]

In *Re Grant's W.T.*[13] a testator left his estate "to the Labour Party Property Committee for the benefit of the Chertsey Headquarters of the Chertsey and Walton Constituency Labour Party" ("C.L.P.") providing that if the headquarters ceased to be in the Chertsey UDC area (1972) his estate should pass to the National Labour Party ("N.L.P.") absolutely. The C.L.P. constitution subordinated it to the N.L.P., who could direct changes in the constitution and prevent the C.L.P. changing its constitution without N.L.P. approval. Vinelott J. held that the estate was meant to be kept intact as endowment capital on trust for Labour Party purposes and so was void for infringing the beneficiary principle and the rule against inalienability.

At this stage it is worth noting that these matters of construction are also relevant in determining the destination of donations or legacies to an unincorporated body when the body dissolves itself or becomes moribund after the date of the donation or legacy or had earlier dissolved itself or become moribund.[14]

## LEAHY v. ATTORNEY-GENERAL FOR NEW SOUTH WALES

Privy Council [1959] A.C. 457; [1959] 2 All E.R. 300 (Viscount Simonds, Lords Morton of Henryton, Cohen, Somervell of Harrow and Denning)

By clause 3 of his will the testator, Francis George Leahy, provided as follows: "As to my property known as 'Elmslea' situated at Bungendore aforesaid and the whole of the land comprising the same and the whole of the furniture contained in the homestead thereon upon trust for such order of nuns of the Catholic Church or the Christian Brothers as my executors and trustees shall select and I again direct that the selection of the order of nuns or brothers as the case may be to benefit under this clause of my will shall be in the sole and absolute discretion of my said executors and trustees."

Counsel for the trustees argued that the disposition made thereby was good as it stood. Once the trustees selected the recipient of the gift, whether an

---

[10] *Leahy v. Att.-Gen. for New South Wales* [1959] A.C. 457.

[11] See p. 189, *supra.*

[12] *Ibid.*

[13] [1979] 3 All E.R. 359. *Obiter dicta* overlook the impact of the 1964 Perpetuities and Accumulations Act and the significance of *Re Denley's Trust Deed* [1969] 1 Ch. 373 and *Re Lipinski's W.T.* [1976] Ch. 235. See further (1980) 39 Camb.L.J. 88 (C. E. F. Rickett) and (1980) 44 M.L.R. 459 (B. Green).

[14] See pp. 416–417, *infra.*

order of nuns or the Christian Brothers, the selected body became absolutely entitled to the gift. No question of uncertainty or perpetuity was therefore involved and the gift was valid. It should be observed that this argument, if successful, would enable the trustees to select as the recipient an order of nuns which was not charitable in the legal sense of that term. The phrase "order of nuns" included "contemplative" as well as "active" orders, the former of which were not charitable.[15] Counsel for the trustees, accordingly, argued, in the alternative, that, if the disposition made by clause 3 was not valid as it stood, it was nevertheless saved from invalidity by section 37D of the Conveyancing Act 1919–54.[16] That section provided as follows:

"(1) No trust shall be held to be invalid by reason that some non-charitable and invalid purpose as well as some charitable purpose is or could be deemed to be included in any of the purposes to or for which an application of the trust funds or any part thereof is by such trust directed or allowed. (2) Any such trust shall be construed and given effect to in the same manner in all respects as if no application of the trusts funds or any part thereof to or for any such non-charitable and invalid purpose had been or could be deemed to have been so directed or allowed." It should be observed that this argument, if successful, would not enable the trustees to select as the recipient a "contemplative," and therefore non-charitable, order of nuns. The area of choice would be restricted to "active" orders.

The High Court of Australia affirmed the order of Myers J. in regard to the disposition made by clause 3, holding (by a majority) that an absolute gift was thereby established in favour of the selected beneficiary and (unanimously) that in any case it was saved by section 37D.

The testator's widow and children appealed to Her Majesty in Council.

VISCOUNT SIMONDS: "The disposition made by clause 3 must now be considered. As has already been pointed out, it will in any case be saved by the section so far as orders other than contemplative orders are concerned, but the trustees are anxious to preserve their right to select such orders. They can only do so if the gift is what is called an absolute gift to the selected order, an expression which may require examination.

"Upon this question there has been a sharp division of opinion in the High Court. Williams and Webb JJ. agreed with Myers J. that the disposition by clause 3 was valid. They held that it provided for an immediate gift to the particular religious community selected by the trustees and that it was immaterial whether the order was charitable or not because the gift was not a gift in perpetuity. 'It is given,' they said (and these are the significant words), 'to the individuals comprising the community selected by the trustees at the date of the death of the testator. It is given to them for the benefit of the community.' Kitto J. reached the same conclusion. He thought that the selected order would take the gift immediately and absolutely, and could expend immediately the whole of what is received. 'There is,' he said, 'no attempt to create a perpetual endowment.' A different view was taken by the Chief Justice and McTiernan J. After an exhaustive examination of the problem and of the relevant authorities, they concluded that the provision made by clause 3 was intended as a trust operating for the furtherance of the

15 See *Gilmour* v. *Coats* [1949]; *infra*, p. 333.
16 New South Wales. See also M. C. Cullitty (1967) 16 I.C.L.Q. 464–490.

purpose of the order as a body of religious women or, in the case of the Christian Brothers, as a teaching order. 'The membership of any order chosen,' they said, 'would be indeterminate and the trust was intended to apply to those who should become members at any time. There was no intention to restrain the operation of the trust to those presently members or to make the alienation of the property a question for the governing body of the order chosen or any section or part of that order.' They therefore held that unless the trust could be supported as a charity it must fail.

"The brief passages that have been cited from the judgments in the High Court sufficiently indicate the question that must be answered and the difficulty of solving it. It arises out of the artificial and anomalous conception of an unincorporated society which, though it is not a separate entity in law, is yet for many purposes regarded as a continuing entity and, however inaccurately, as something other than an aggregate of its members. In law a gift to such a society simpliciter (*i.e.*, where, to use the words of Lord Parker in *Bowman* v. *Secular Society Ltd.*,[17] neither the circumstances of the gift nor the directions given nor the objects expressed impose on the donee the character of a trustee) is nothing else than a gift to its members at the date of the gift as joint tenants or tenants in common. It is for this reason that the prudent conveyancer provides that a receipt by the treasurer or other proper officer of the recipient society for a legacy to the society shall be a sufficient discharge to executors. If it were not so, the executors could only get a valid discharge by obtaining a receipt from every member. This must be qualified by saying that by their rules the members might have authorised one of themselves to receive a gift on behalf of them all.

"It is in the light of this fundamental proposition that the statements, to which reference has been made, must be examined. What is meant when it is said that a gift is made to the individuals comprising the community and the words are added 'it is given to them for the benefit of the community?' If it is a gift to individuals, each of them is entitled to his distributive share (unless he has previously bound himself by the rules of the society that it shall be devoted to some other purpose). It is difficult to see what is added by the words 'for the benefit of the community.' If they are intended to import a trust, who are the beneficiaries? If the present members are the beneficiaries, the words add nothing and are meaningless. If some other persons or purposes are intended, the conclusion cannot be avoided that the gift is void. For it is uncertain and beyond doubt tends to a perpetuity.

"The question then appears to be whether, even if the gift to a selected order of nuns is prima facie a gift to the individual members of that order, there are other considerations arising out of the terms of the will, or the nature of the society, its organisation and rules, or the subject-matter of the gift, which should lead the court to conclude that though prima facie the gift is an absolute one (absolute both in quality of estate and in freedom from restriction) to individual nuns, yet it is invalid because it is in the nature of an endowment and tends to a perpetuity or for any other reason. This raises a problem which is not easy to solve as the divergent opinions in the High Court indicate.

"The prima facie validity of such a gift (by which term their Lordships intend a bequest or demise[18]) is a convenient starting-point for the examination

---

[17] [1917] A.C. 406, 437.
[18] This appears to be a misprint for "devise."

of the relevant law. For, as Lord Tomlin (sitting at first instance in the Chancery Division) said in *Re Ogden*,[19] a gift to a voluntary association of persons for the general purposes of the association is an absolute gift and prima facie a good gift. He was echoing the words of Lord Parker in *Bowman's* case[20] that a gift to an unincorporated association for the attainment of its purposes 'may . . . be upheld as an absolute gift to its members.' These words must receive careful consideration, for it is to be noted that it is because the gift can be upheld as a gift to the individual members that it is valid, even though it is given for the general purpose of the association. If the words 'for the general purposes of the association' were held to import a trust, the question would have to be asked, what is the trust and who are the beneficiaries? A gift can be made to persons (including a corporation) but it cannot be made to a purpose or to an object: so, also, a trust may be created for the benefit of persons as *cestuis que trust* but not for a purpose or object unless the purpose or object be charitable. For a purpose or object cannot sue, but, if it be charitable, the Attorney-General can sue to enforce it. . . . " [He then considered *Cocks* v. *Manners* (1871) L.R. 12 Eq. 574, *Re Smith* [1914] 1 Ch. 937, *Re Clarke* [1901] 2 Ch. 110, *Re Drummond* [1914] 2 Ch. 90, *Re Taylor* [1940] Ch. 481, *Re Price* [1943] Ch. 422, *Re Prevost* [1930] 2 Ch. 383 and *Re Ray's W.T.* [1936] Ch. 520.]

"The cases that have been referred to (and many others might have been referred to in the courts of Australia, England and Ireland) are all cases in which gifts have been upheld as valid either on the ground that, where a society has been named as legatee, its members could demand that the gift should be dealt with as they should together think fit; or on the ground that a trust has been established (as in *Re Drummond*) which did not create a perpetuity. It will be sufficient to mention one only of the cases in which a different conclusion has been reached, before coming to a recent decision of the House of Lords which must be regarded as of paramount authority. In *Carne* v. *Long*[21] the testator devised his mansion-house after the death of his wife to the trustees of the Penzance Public Library to hold to them and their successors for ever, for the use, benefit, maintenance and support of the said library. It appeared that the library was established and kept on foot by the subscriptions of certain inhabitants of Penzance, that the subscribers were elected by ballot and the library managed by officers chosen from amongst themselves by the subscribers, that the property in the books and everything else belonging to the library was vested in trustees for the subscribers and that it was provided that the institution should not be broken up so long as ten members remained. It was argued that the gift was to a number of private persons and there were in truth no other beneficiaries. But Campbell L.C. rejected the plea in words which, often though they have been cited, will bear repetition[22]: 'If the devise had been in favour of the existing members of the society, and they had been at liberty to dispose of the property as they might think fit, then it might, I think, have been a lawful disposition and not tending to a perpetuity. But looking to the language of the rules of this society, it is clear that the library was intended to be a perpetual institution, and the testator must be presumed to have known what the regulations were.' This

---

19 [1933] Ch. 678, 681.
20 [1917] A.C. 406, 442.
21 (1860) 2 De G.F. & J. 75.
22 *Ibid.* 79.

was, perhaps, a clear case where both from the terms of the gift and the nature of the society a perpetuity was indicated.

"Their Lordships must now turn to the recent case of *Re Macaulay's Estate*,[23] which appears to be reported only in a footnote to *Re Price*.[24] There the gift was to the Folkestone Lodge of the Theosophical Society absolutely for the maintenance and improvement of the Theosophical Lodge at Folkestone. It was assumed that the donee 'the Lodge' was a body of persons. The decision of the House of Lords in July 1933, to which both Lord Buckner and Lord Tomlin were parties, were that the gift was invalid. A portion of Lord Buckmaster's speech may well be quoted. He had previously referred to *Re Drummond* and *Carne* v. *Long*. 'A group of people,' he said, 'defined and bound together by rules and called by a distinctive name can be the subject of gift as well as any individual or incorporated body. The real question is what is the actual purpose for which the gift is made. There is no perpetuity if the gift is for the individual members for their own benefit, but that, I think, is clearly not the meaning of this gift. Nor again is there a perpetuity if the society is at liberty in accordance with the terms of the gift to spend both capital and income as they think fit. . . . If the gift is to be for the endowment of the society to be held as an endowment and the society is according to its form perpetual, the gift is bad: but, if the gift is an immediate beneficial legacy, it is good.' In the result he held the gift for the maintenance and improvement of the Theosophical Lodge at Folkestone to be invalid. Their Lordships respectfully doubt whether the passage in Lord Buckmaster's speech in which he suggests the alternative ground of validity, *viz.*, that the society is at liberty in accordance with the terms of the gift to spend both capital and income as they think fit, presents a true alternative. It is only because the society, *i.e.*, the individuals constituting it, are the beneficiaries that they can dispose of the gift. Lord Tomlin came to the same conclusion. He found in the words of the will 'for the maintenance and improvement' a sufficient indication that it was the permanence of the Lodge at Folkestone that the testatrix was seeking to secure and this, he thought, necessarily involved endowment. Therefore a perpetuity was created. A passage from the judgment of Lord Hanworth M.R. (which has been obtained from the records) may usefully be cited. He said: 'The problem may be stated in this way. If the gift is in truth to the present members of the society described by their society name so that they have the beneficial use of the property and can, if they please, alienate and put the proceeds in their own pocket, then there is a present gift to individuals which is good: but if the gift is intended for the good not only of the present but of future members so that the present members are in the position of trustees and have no right to appropriate the property or its proceeds for their personal benefit, then the gift is invalid. It may be invalid by reason of there being a trust created, or it may be by reason of the terms that the period allowed by the rule against perpetuities would be exceeded.'

"It is not very clear what is intended by the dichotomy suggested in the last sentence of the citation, but the penultimate sentence goes to the root of the matter. At the risk of repetition their Lordships would point out that if a gift is made to individuals, whether under their own names or in the name of their society, and the conclusion is reached that they are not intended to take

---

[23] [1943] Ch. 435n.
[24] [1943] Ch. 422.

beneficially, then they take as trustees. If so, it must be ascertained who are the beneficiaries. If, at the death of the testator, the class of beneficiaries is fixed and ascertained or ascertainable within the limit of the rule against perpetuities, all is well. If it is not so fixed and not so ascertainable, the trust must fail.

"It must now be asked, then, whether in the present case there are sufficient indications to displace the prima facie conclusion that the gift made by clause 3 of the will is to the individual members of the selected order of nuns at the date of the testator's death so that they can together dispose of it as they think fit. It appears to their Lordships that such indications are ample.

"In the first place, it is not altogether irrelevant that the gift is in terms upon trust for a selected order. It is true that this can in law be regarded as a trust in favour of each and every member of the order. But at least the form of the gift is not to the members, and it may be questioned whether the testator understood the niceties of the law. In the second place, the members of the selected order may be numerous, very numerous perhaps, and they may be spread over the world. If the gift is to the individuals it is to all the members who were living at the death of the testator, but only to them. It is not easy to believe that the testator intended an 'immediate beneficial legacy' (to use the words of Lord Buckmaster) to such a body of beneficiaries. In the third place, the subject-matter of the gift cannot be ignored. It appears from the evidence filed in the suit that Elmslea is a grazing property of about 730 acres, with a furnished homestead containing twenty rooms and a number of outbuildings. With the greatest respect to those judges who have taken a different view, their Lordships do not find it possible to regard all the individual members of an order as intended to become the beneficial owners of such a property. Little or no evidence has been given about the organisation and rules of the several orders, but it is at least permissible to doubt whether it is a common feature of them that all their members regard themselves or are to be regarded as having the capacity of (say) the Corps of Commissionaires (see *Re Clarke*) to put an end to their association and distribute its assets. On the contrary it seems reasonably clear that, however little the testator understood the effect in law of a gift to an unincorporated body of persons by their society name, his intention was to create a trust not merely for the benefit of the existing members of the selected order but for its benefit as a continuing society and for the furtherance of its work.

" . . . Their Lordships, therefore, humbly advise Her Majesty that the appeal should be dismissed, but that the gift made by clause 3 of the will is valid by reason only of the provisions of section 37D of the Conveyancing Act 1919–54, and that the power of selection thereby given to the trustees does not extend to contemplative orders of nuns."

*Appeal dismissed.*

## RE DENLEY'S TRUST DEED

Chancery Division [1969] 1 Ch. 373; [1968] 3 W.L.R. 457; [1968] 3 All E.R. 65.

In 1936 land was conveyed by a company to trustees so that until the expiration of 21 years from the death of the last survivor of certain specified persons the land should under clause 2(c) of a trust deed "be maintained and used as and for the purpose of a recreation or sports ground primarily for the benefit of the employees of the company and secondarily for the benefit of such other person or persons (if any) as the trustees may allow to use the same." Various questions arose as to this clause and other clauses so the trustees took out an originating summons to have them resolved. The main question was dealt with as follows in a reserved judgment:

GOFF J.: "It was decided in *Re Astor's Settlement Trusts, Astor* v. *Scholfield*[25] that a trust for a number of non-charitable purposes was not merely unenforceable but void on two grounds; first that they were not trusts for the benefit of individuals, which I refer to as 'the beneficiary principle,' and, secondly, for uncertainty.

"Counsel for the first defendant has argued that the trust in clause 2(c) in the present case is either a trust for the benefit of individuals, in which case he argues that they are an unascertainable class and therefore the trust is void for uncertainty, or it is a purpose trust, that is a trust for providing recreation, which he submits is void on the beneficiary principle, or alternatively it is something of a hybrid having the vices of both kinds.

"I think that there may be a purpose or object trust, the carrying out of which would benefit an individual or individuals, where that benefit is so indirect or intangible or which is otherwise so framed as not to give those persons any locus standi to apply to the court to enforce the trust, in which case the beneficiary principle would, as it seems to me, apply to invalidate the trust, quite apart from any question of uncertainty or perpetuity. Such cases can be considered if and when they arise. The present is not, in my judgment, of that character, and it will be seen that clause 2(d) of the trust deed expressly states that, subject to any rules and regulations made by the trustees, the employees of the company shall be entitled to the use and enjoyment of the land.

"Apart from this possible exception, in my judgment the beneficiary principle of *Re Astor*,[26] which was approved in *Re Endacott (decd.), Endacott* v. *Corpe*,[27] see particularly by Harman L.J.,[28] is confined to purpose or object trusts which are abstract or impersonal. The objection is not that the trust is for a purpose or object *per se*, but that there is no beneficiary or cestui que trust. The rule is so expressed in *Lewin on Trusts* (16th ed.), p. 17, and, in my judgment, with the possible exception which I have mentioned, rightly so. In *Re Wood, Barton* v. *Chilcott*,[29] Harman J. said:

> 'There has been an interesting argument on the question of perpetuity, but it seems to me, with all respect to that argument, that there is an earlier obstacle which is fatal to the validity of this bequest, namely, that a gift on trust must have a cestui que trust, and there being here no cestui que trust the gift must fail.'

"Again, in *Leahy* v. *Att.-Gen. of New South Wales*,[30] Viscount Simonds, delivery the judgment of the Privy Council, said:

> 'A gift can be made to persons (including a corporation) but it cannot be made to a purpose or to an object: so, also [and these are the

---

[25] [1952] Ch. 534.
[26] [1952] Ch. 534.
[27] [1960] Ch. 232.
[28] [1960] Ch. 232, 250.
[29] [1949] Ch. 498, 501.
[30] [1959] A.C. 457, 478.

important words] a trust may be created for the benefit of persons as
cestuis que trust but not for a purpose or object unless the purpose or
object be charitable. For a purpose or object cannot sue, but, if it be
charitable, the Attorney-General can sue to enforce it.'

"Where, then, the trust, though expressed as a purpose, is directly or
indirectly for the benefit of an individual or individuals, it seems to me that it is
in general outside the mischief of the beneficiary principle.

"I am fortified in this conclusion by the dicta of Lord Evershed M.R. and
Harman L.J. in *Re Harpur's Will Trusts, Haller* v. *Att.-Gen.*[31] It was urged that
section 2 of the Charitable Trusts (Validation) Act 1954 clearly envisages a
valid 'imperfect trust provision,' and that there could not be any such valid
provision unless the word 'purposes' in the definition in section 1(1) were so
construed as to include institutions.[32] Lord Evershed M.R. said that if the
premise were right he would be strongly disposed so to construe the section,
but he rejected the premise, saying this:

> 'But the argument in this court has satisfied me that there may well be
> provisions for purposes, as distinct from provisions for distribution
> among institutions, which would be imperfect trust provisions with the
> definition but which, none the less, being valid, could be saved by
> section 2(1) from the impact of section 1(2). An illustration was given of
> a gift upon trust to apply income during a limited period of, say, ten
> years for certain named purposes such as the trustees think fit, some of
> the purposes being charitable and some not charitable. It seems to me
> that such a gift would by the ordinary law be valid. It is no less clear, as I
> think, that a provision in that form would be an imperfect trust provision
> within the definition of the section. It, therefore, is, as I think, no longer
> true to say that failure to bring a gift of this class into the scope of
> section 1 is inevitably to give no effect to section 2.'

"The passage in the judgment of Harman L.J. is perhaps not quite as
reinforced, because he would not (as he described it) have twisted the
language of section 1(1) even if the premise were right, but still he too rejected
it, and he said[33]:

> 'I do not feel impressed by that argument because, in my judgment,
> there are gifts to objects which would be hit by section 1(1) although
> perfectly valid and which, therefore, need the protection of section 2(1).
> That being so, the motive for the suggested restating of the language
> does not seem to me to have any particular force.'

"Read without any qualification, these observations would, I think, with the
greatest respect, be too wide, because 'named purposes' or 'objects' would
cover abstract objects, which would be void under the operation of the
beneficiary principle, but it is difficult to think that those two learned judges,
and in particular Harman L.J., who had in 1959 in *Re Endacott*[34] applauded the
orthodox sentiments expressed by Roxburgh J. in *Re Astor*,[35] were in 1962

---

[31] [1962] Ch. 78, 91, 96.
[32] [1962] Ch. 78, 91.
[33] [1962] Ch. 78, 96.
[34] [1960] Ch. 232, 250.
[35] [1952] Ch. 534.

unmindful of the beneficiary principle. In my judgment, therefore, these dicta, and especially that of Harman L.J., clearly show that in their view there are purpose or object trusts which escape the operation of that principle.

"Some further support for my conclusion is, I think, to be found in *Re Aberconway's Settlement Trusts*[36] where it was assumed that a trust for the upkeep and development of certain gardens which were part of a settled estate was valid.

"I also derive assistance from what was said by North J. in *Re Bowes*.[37] That was a bequest of a sum of money on trust to expend the same in planting trees for shelter on certain settled estates. It happened that there was a father and a son of full age, tenant for life in possession and tenant in tail in remainder respectively; so that, subject to the son disentailing, they were together absolutely entitled, and the actual decision was that they could claim the money, but North J. said[38]:

> 'If it were necessary to uphold it, the trees can be planted upon the whole of it until the fund is exhausted. Therefore, there is nothing illegal in the gift itself . . . ';

and[39]: 'I think there clearly is a valid trust to lay out money for the benefit of the persons entitled to the estate.'

"The trust in the present case is limited in point of time so as to avoid any infringement of the rule against perpetuities and, for the reasons which I have given, it does not offend against the beneficiary principle; and unless, therefore, it be void for uncertainty, it is a valid trust.

"There is, however, one other aspect of uncertainty which has caused me some concern; that is, whether this is in its nature a trust which the court can control, for, as Lord Eldon L.C. said in *Morice* v. *Bishop of Durham*[40]:

> 'As it is a maxim that the execution of a trust shall be under the control of the court, it must be of such a nature that it can be under that control; so that the administration of it can be reviewed by the court; or, if the trustee dies, the court itself can execute the trust: a trust, therefore, which, in case of maladministration could be reformed; and a due administration directed; and then, unless the subject and the objects can be ascertained upon principles familiar in other cases, it must be decided that the court can neither reform maladministration nor direct a due administration.'

"The difficulty which I have felt is that there may well be times when some of the employees wish to use the sports club for one purpose while others desire to use it at the same time for some other purpose of such nature that the two cannot be carried on together. The trustees could, of course, control this by making rules and regulations under clause 2(d) of the trust deed, but they might not. In any case, the employees would probably agree amongst themselves but I cannot assume that they would. If there were an impasse, the court could not resolve it, because it clearly could not either exercise the trustees' power to make rules or settle a scheme, this being a non-charitable trust: see *Re Astor*.[41]

---

[36] [1953] Ch. 647.
[37] [1896] 1 Ch. 507.
[38] [1896] 1 Ch. 507, 510.
[39] [1896] 1 Ch. 507, 511.
[40] (1805) 10 Ves. 522, 539.
[41] [1952] Ch. 534. [But see now *McPhail* v. *Doulton* [1971] A.C. 424, 457, *per* Lord Wilberforce cited p. 158, *supra*).

"In my judgment, however, it would not be right to hold the trust void on this ground. The court can, as it seems to me, execute the trust both negatively by restraining any improper disposition or use of the land, and positively by ordering the trustees to allow the employees and such other persons (if any) as they may admit to use the land for the purpose of a recreation or sports ground. Any difficulty there might be in practice in the beneficial enjoyment of the land by those entitled to use it is, I think, really beside the point. The same kind of problem is equally capable of arising in the case of a trust to permit a number of persons—for example, all the unmarried children of a testator or settlor—to use or occupy a house or to have the use of certain chattels; nor can I assume that in such cases agreement between the parties concerned would be more likely, even if that be a sufficient distinction, yet no one would suggest, I fancy, that such a trust would be void.

"In my judgment, therefore, the provisions of clause 2(c) are valid."

## RE RECHER'S WILL TRUSTS

Chancery Division [1972] Ch. 526; [1971] 3 W.L.R. 321; [1971] 3 All E.R. 401.

By will dated May 23, 1957, T gave a share of her residue to what the judge interpreted as "The London and Provincial Anti-Vivisection Society" which had ceased to exist on January 1, 1957. T died in 1962. In a reserved judgment consideration was first given to the question whether the gift would have been valid if the unincorporated society had existed at T's death:

BRIGHTMAN J.: "Having reached the conclusion that the gift in question is not a gift to the members of the London and Provincial Society at the date of death, as joint tenants or tenants in common so as to entitle a member as of right to a distributive share, nor an attempted gift to present and future members beneficially, and is not a gift in trust for the purpose of the society, I must now consider how otherwise, if at all, it is capable of taking effect.

"As I have already mentioned, the rules of the London and Provincial Society do not purport to create any trusts except insofar as the honorary trustees are not beneficial owners of the assets of the society, but are trustees on trust to deal with such assets according to the directions of the committee.

"A trust for non-charitable purposes, as distinct from a trust for individuals, is clearly void because there is no beneficiary. It does not, however, follow that persons cannot band themselves together as an association or society, pay subscriptions and validly devote their funds in pursuit of some lawful non-charitable purpose. An obvious example is a members' social club. But it is not essential that the members should only intend to secure direct personal advantages to themselves. The association may be one in which personal advantages to the members are combined with the pursuit of some outside purpose. Or the association may be one which offers no personal benefit at all to the members, the funds of the association being applied exclusively to the pursuit of some outside purpose. Such an association of persons is bound, I would think, to have some sort of constitution; *i.e.* the rights and liabilities of the members of the association will inevitably depend on some form of contract *inter se*, usually evidenced by a set of rules. In the present case it appears to me clear that the life members, the ordinary members and the associate members of the London Provincial Society were bound together by a contract *inter se*. Any such member was entitled to the rights and subject to the liabilities defined by the rules. If the committee acted contrary to the rules, an individual member would be entitled to take proceedings in the courts to compel observance of the rules or to recover damages for any loss he had suffered as a result of the breach of contract. As and when a member paid his subscription to the association, he would be subjecting his money to the disposition and expenditure thereof laid down by the rules. That is to say, the member would be bound to permit, and entitled to require, the honorary trustees and other members of the society to deal with that subscription in accordance with the lawful directions of the committee. Those directions would include the expenditure of that subscription, as part of the general funds of the association, in furthering the objects of the association. The resultant situation, on analysis, is that the London and Provincial Society represented an organisation of individuals bound together by a contract under which their subscriptions became, as it were, mandated towards a certain type of expenditure as adumbrated in rule 1. Just as the two parties to a bipartite bargain can vary or terminate their contract by mutual assent, so it must follow that the life members, ordinary members and associate members of the London and Provincial Society could, at any moment of time, by unanimous agreement (or by majority vote if the rules so prescribe), vary or terminate their multipartite contract. There would be no limit to the type of variation or termination to which all might agree. There is no private trust or trust for charitable purposes or other trust to hinder the process. It follows that if all members agreed, they could decide to wind up the London and Provincial Society and divide the net assets among themselves beneficially. No one would have any locus standi to stop them so doing. The contract is the same as any other contract and concerns only those who are parties to it, that is to say, the members of the society.

"The funds of such an association may, of course, be derived not only from the subscriptions of the contracting parties but also from donations from non-contracting parties and legacies from persons who have died. In the case of a donation which is not accompanied by any words which purport to impose a trust, it seems to me that the gift takes effect in favour of the existing members of the association as an accretion to the funds which are the subject-matter of the contract which such members have made *inter se*, and falls to be dealt with in precisely the same way as the funds which the members themselves have subscribed. So, in the case of a legacy. In the absence of words which purport to impose a trust, the legacy is a gift to the members beneficially, not as joint tenants or as tenants in common so as to entitle each member to an immediate distributive share, but as an accretion to the funds which are the subject-matter of the contract which the members have made *inter se*.

"In my judgment the legacy in the present case to the London and Provincial Society ought to be construed as a legacy of that type, that is to say, a legacy to the members beneficially as an accretion to the funds subject to the contract which they had made *inter se*. Of course, the testatrix did not intend the members of the society to divide their bounty between themselves, and doubtless she was ignorant of that remote but theoretical possibility. Her knowledge or absence of knowledge of the true legal analysis of the gift is irrelevant. The legacy is accordingly in my view valid, subject only to the effect of the events of January 1, 1957.

"A strong argument has been presented to me against this conclusion and I have been taken through most, if not all, of the cases which are referred to in *Leahy's* case[42] as well as later authorities. It has been urged upon me that if the

---

[42] [1959] A.C. 457.

gift is not a purpose gift, there is no half-way house between, on the one hand, a legacy to the members of the London and Provincial Society at the date of death, as joint tenants beneficially, or as tenants in common beneficially, and, on the other hand, a trust for members which is void for perpetuity because no individual member acting by himself can ever obtain his share of the legacy. I do not see why the choice should be confined to these two extremes. If the argument were correct it would be difficult, if not impossible, for a person to make a straightforward donation, whether *inter vivos* or by will, to a club or other non-charitable association which the donor desires to benefit. This conclusion seems to me contrary to common sense.

"Finally, I cite and gratefully adopt the following passage which forms part of the judgment of Cross J. in *Neville Estates Ltd.* v. *Madden*.[43] [This is summarised in *Re Lipinski, infra.* He went on to hold that the gift lapsed owing to the dissolution of the society on January 1, 1957.]

## RE LIPINSKI'S WILL TRUSTS

Chancery Division [1976] Ch. 235; [1977] 1 All E.R. 33; [1976] 3 W.L.R. 522.

The testator bequeathed his residuary estate to trustees on trust "as to one half thereof for the Hull Judeans (Maccabi) Association in memory of my late wife to be used solely in the work of constructing the new buildings for the association and/or improvements to the said buildings." Was this valid?

OLIVER J.: "I approach question 1 of the summons, therefore, on the footing that this is a gift to an unincorporated non-charitable association. Such a gift, if it is an absolute and beneficial one, is of course perfectly good: see, for instance, the gift to the Corps of Commissionaires in *Re Clarke*.[44] What I have to consider, however, is the effect of the specification by the testator of the purposes for which the legacy was to be applied. The principles applicable to this type of case were stated by Cross J. in *Neville Estates Ltd.* v. *Madden*[45] and they are conveniently summarised in *Tudor on Charities*, where it is said[46]:

'In *Neville Estates Ltd.* v. *Madden* Cross J. expressed the opinion (which is respectfully accepted as correct) that every such gift might, according to the actual words used, be construed in one of three quite different ways: (*a*) As a gift to the members of the association at the date of the gift as joint tenants so that any member could sever his share and claim it whether or not he continues to be a member. (*b*) As a gift to the members of the association at the date of the gift not as joint tenants, but subject to their contractual rights and liabilities towards one another as members of the association. In such a case a member cannot sever his share. It will accrue to the other members on his death or resignation, even though such members include persons who become members after the gift took effect. If this is the effect of the gift, it will not be open to objection on the score of perpetuity or uncertainty unless there is something in its terms or circumstances or in the rules of the association which precludes the members at any given time from dividing the subject

---

43 [1962] Ch. 832, 849.
44 [1901] 2 Ch. 110.
45 [1962] Ch. 832.
46 (6th ed., 1967), p. 150.

of the gift between them on the footing that they are solely entitled to it in equity. (c) The terms or circumstances of the gift or the rules of the association may show that the property in question—*i.e.* the subject of the gift—is not to be at the disposal of the members for the time being but is to be held in trust for or applied for the purposes of the association as a quasi-corporate entity. In this case the gift will fail unless the association is a charitable body.'

"That summary may require, I think, a certain amount of qualification in the light of subsequent authority, but for the present purposes I can adopt it as a working guide. Counsel for the next-of-kin argues that the gift in the present case clearly does not fall within the first category, and that the addition of the specific direction as to its employment by the association prevents it from falling into the second category. This is, therefore, he says, a purpose trust and fails both for that reason and because the purpose is perpetuitous. He relies on this passage from the judgment of the board in *Leahy* v. *Attorney-General for New South Wales*[47]:

'If the words "for the general purposes of the association" were held to import a trust, the question would have to be asked, what is the trust and who are the beneficiaries? A gift can be made to persons (including a corporation) but it cannot be made to a purpose or to an object: so also, a trust may be created for the benefit of persons as *cestuis que trust* but not for a purpose or object unless the purpose or object be charitable. For a purpose or object cannot sue, but, if it be charitable, the Attorney-General can sue to enforce it.'

"Counsel for the next-of-kin points out, first, that the gift is in memory of the testator's late wife (which, he says, suggests an intention to create a permanent memorial or endowment); secondly, that the gift is *solely* for a particular purpose (which would militate strongly against any suggestion that the donees could wind up and pocket the money themselves, even though their constitution may enable them to do so); and, thirdly, that the gift contemplates expenditure on 'improvements,' which connotes a degree of continuity or permanence. All this, he says, shows that what the testator had in mind was a permanent endowment in memory of his late wife.

"For my part, I think that very little turns on the testator's having expressed the gift as being in memory of his late wife. I see nothing in this expression which suggests any intention to create a permanent endowment. It indicates merely, I think, a tribute which the testator wished to pay, and it is not without significance that this self-same tribute appeared in the earlier will in which he made an absolute and outright gift to the association. The evidential value of this in the context of a construction summons may be open to doubt, and I place no reliance on it. It does, however, seem to me that nothing is to be derived from these words beyond the fact that the testator wished the association to know that his bounty was a tribute to his late wife.

"I accept, however, the submission of counsel for the next-of-kin that the designation of the sole purpose of the gift makes it impossible to construe the gift as one falling into the first of Cross J.'s categories, even if that were otherwise possible. But I am not impressed by the argument that the gift shows

[47] [1959] A.C. 457, 478, 479.

an intention of continuity. Counsel prays in aid *Re Macaulay*[48] where the gift
was for the 'maintenance and improvement of the Theosophical Lodge at
Folkestone.' The House of Lords held that it failed for perpetuity, the donee
being a non-charitable body. But it is clear from the speeches of both Lord
Buckmaster and Lord Tomlin that their Lordships derived the intention of
continuity from the reference to 'maintenance.' Here it is quite evident that
the association was to be free to spend the capital of the legacy. As Lord
Buckmaster said in *Re Macaulay*[49]:

> 'In the first place it is clear that the mere fact that the beneficiary is an
> unincorporated society in no way affects the validity of the gift. . . . The
> real question is what is the actual purpose for which the gift is made.
> There is no perpetuity if the gift were for the individual members for
> their own benefit, but that, I think, is clearly not the meaning of this gift.
> Nor again is there a perpetuity if the Society is at liberty, in accordance
> with the terms of the gift, to spend both capital and income as they think
> fit.'

"*Re Price*[50] itself is authority for the proposition that a gift to an unincorporated non-charitable association for objects on which the association is at
liberty to spend both capital and income will not fail for perpetuity, although
the actual conclusion in that case has been criticised, the point that the trust
there (the carrying on of the teachings of Rudolf Steiner) was a 'purpose trust'
and thus unenforceable on that ground was not argued. It does not seem to
me, therefore, that in the present case there is a valid ground for saying that
the gift fails for perpetuity.

"But that is not the end of the matter. If the gift were to the association
*simpliciter*, it would, I think, clearly fall within the second category of Cross
J.'s categories. At first sight, however, there appears to be a difficulty in
arguing that the gift is to members of the association subject to their
contractual rights *inter se* when there is a specific direction or limitation sought
to be imposed on those contractual rights as to the manner in which the
subject-matter of the gift is to be dealt with. This, says counsel for the next-of-
kin, is a pure 'purpose trust' and is invalid on that ground, quite apart from
any question of perpetuity. I am not sure, however, that it is sufficient merely
to demonstrate that a trust is a 'purpose' trust. With the greatest deference, I
wonder whether the dichotomy postulated in the passage which I have referred
to in the judgment of the board in *Leahy* v. *Attorney-General for New South
Wales*[51] is not an oversimplification. Indeed, I am not convinced that it was
intended as an exhaustive statement or to do more than indicate the broad
division of trusts into those where there are ascertainable beneficiaries
(whether for particular purposes or not) and trusts where there are none.
Indeed, that this is the case, as it seems to me, is to be derived from a later
passage[52] of the report, which is in these terms:

> 'If a gift is made to individuals, whether under their own names or in
> the name of their society and the conclusion is reached that they are not

intended to take beneficially, then they take as trustees. If so, it must be ascertained who are the beneficiaries. If, at the death of the testator, the class of beneficiaries is fixed and ascertained or ascertainable within the limit of the rule against perpetuities, all is well. If it is not so fixed and not so ascertainable, the trust must fail. Of such a trust, no better example could be found than a gift to an order for the benefit of a community of nuns once it is established that the community is not confined to living and ascertained persons. A wider question is opened if it appears that the trust is not for persons but for a non-charitable purpose. As has been pointed out, no one can enforce such a trust. What follows? *Ex hypothesi*, the trustees are not themselves the beneficiaries yet the trust fund is in their hands, and they may, or may not, think fit to carry out their testator's wishes. If so, it would seem that the testator has imperfectly exercised his testamentary power; he has delegated it, for the disposal of his property lies with them, not with him. Accordingly, the subject-matter of the gift will be undisposed of or fall into the residuary estate as the case may be.'

"There would seem to me to be, as a matter of common sense, a clear distinction between the case where a purpose is described which is clearly intended for the benefit of ascertained or ascertainable beneficiaries, particularly where those beneficiaries have the power to make the capital their own, and the case where no beneficiary at all is intended (for instance, a memorial to a favourite pet) or where the beneficiaries are unascertainable (as for instance in *Re Price*[53]). If a valid gift may be made to an unincorporated body as a simple accretion to the funds which are the subject-matter of the contract which the members have made *inter se*, and *Neville Estates* v. *Madden*[54] and *Re Recher's Will Trusts*[55] show that it may, I do not really see why such a gift, which specifies a purpose which is within the powers of the unincorporated body and of which the members of that body are the beneficiaries, should fail. Why are not the beneficiaries able to enforce the trust or, indeed, in the exercise of their contractual rights, to terminate the trust for their own benefit? Where the donee body is itself the beneficiary of the prescribed purpose, there seems to me to be the strongest argument in common sense for saying that the gift should be construed as an absolute one within the second category, the more so where, if the purpose is carried out, the members can by appropriate action vest the resulting property in themselves, for here the trustees and the beneficiaries are the same persons.

"Is such a distinction as I have suggested borne out by the authorities? The answer is, I think, 'Not in terms,' until recently. But the cases appear to me to be at least consistent with this. For instance, *Re Clarke*[56] (the case of the Corps of Commissionaires), *Re Drummond*[57] (the case of the Old Bradfordians) and *Re Taylor*[58] (the case of the Midland Bank Staff Association), in all of which the testator had prescribed purposes for which the gifts were to be used, and in all of which the gifts were upheld, were all cases where there were ascertainable beneficiaries; whereas in *Re Wood*[59] and *Leahy* v. *Attorney-General for*

---

[53] [1943] Ch. 422.
[54] [1962] Ch. 832.
[55] [1972] Ch. 526.
[56] [1901] 2 Ch. 110.
[57] [1914] 2 Ch. 90.
[58] [1940] Ch. 481.
[59] [1949] Ch. 498.

*New South Wales*[60] (where the gifts failed) there were none. *Re Price* is perhaps
out of line, because there was no ascertained beneficiary and yet Cohen J. was
prepared to uphold the gift even on the supposition that (contrary to his own
conclusion) the purpose was non-charitable. But as I have mentioned, the
point about the trust being a purpose trust was not argued before him.

"A striking case which seems to be not far from the present is *Re
Turkington*,[61] where the gift was to a masonic lodge 'as a fund to build a
suitable temple in Stafford.' The members of the lodge being both the trustees
and the beneficiaries of the temple, Luxmoore J. construed the gift as an
absolute one to the members of the lodge for the time being. Directly in point
is the more recent decision of Goff J. in *Re Denley's Trust Deed*,[62] where the
question arose as to the validity of a deed under which land was held by
trustees as a sports ground:

> ' . . . primarily for the benefit of the employees of [a particular]
> company and secondarily for the benefit of such other person or persons
> . . . as the trustees may allow to use the same'

the latter provision was construed by Goff J. as a power and not a trust. The
same deed conferred on the employees a right to use and enjoy the land
subject to regulations made by the trustees. Goff J. held that the rule against
enforceability of non-charitable 'purpose or object' trusts was confined to those
which were abstract or impersonal in nature where there was no beneficiary or
*cestui que trust*. A trust which, though expressed as a purpose, was directly or
indirectly for the benefit of an individual or individuals was valid provided that
those individuals were ascertainable at any one time and the trust was not
otherwise void for uncertainty. Goff J. said[63]:

> 'I think there may be a purpose or object trust, the carrying out of
> which would benefit an individual or individuals, where that benefit is so
> indirect or intangible or which is otherwise so framed as not to give those
> persons any *locus standi* to apply to the court to enforce the trust, in
> which case the beneficiary principle would, as it seems to me, apply to
> invalidate the trust, quite apart from any question of uncertainty or
> perpetuity. Such cases can be considered if and when they arise. The
> present is not, in my judgment, of that character, and it will be seen that
> clause 2(d) of the trust deed expressly states that, subject to any rules
> and regulations made by the trustees, the employees of the company
> shall be entitled to the use and enjoyment of the land. Apart from this
> possible exception, in my judgment the beneficiary principle of *Re Astor*,
> which was approved in *Re Endacott*; see particularly by Harman L.J.[64]; is
> confined to purpose or object trusts which are abstract or impersonal.
> The objection is not that the trust is for a purpose of object *per se*, but
> that there is no beneficiary or *cestui que trust* . . . Where, then, the trust,
> though expressed as a purpose, is directly or indirectly for the benefit of
> an individual or individuals, it seems to me that it is in general outside
> the mischief of the beneficiary principle.'

60 [1959] A.C. 457.
61 [1937] 4 All E.R. 501.
62 [1969] 1 Ch. 373, 375.
63 [1969] 1 Ch. 373, 382–384.
64 [1960] Ch. 232, 250.

I respectfully adopt this, as it seems to me to accord both with authority and with common sense.

"If this is the right principle, then on each side of the line does the present case fall? Counsel for the Attorney-General has submitted in the course of his argument in favour of charity that the testator's express purpose 'solely in the work of constructing the new buildings for the association' referred and could only refer to the youth centre project, which was the only project for the erection of buildings which was under consideration at the material time. If this is right, then the trust must, I think, fail, for it is quite clear that that project is ultimately conceived embraced not only the members of the association, but the whole Jewish community in Hull, and it would be difficult to argue that there was any ascertainable beneficiary. I do not, however, so construe the testator's intention. The evidence is that the testator knew the association's position and that he took a keen interest in it. I infer that he was kept informed of its current plans. The one thing that is quite clear from the minutes is that from 1965 right up to the testator's death there was great uncertainty about what was going to be done. There was a specific project for the purchase of a house in 1965. By early 1966 the youth centre was back in favour. By October 1966 it was being suggested that the association should stay where it was in its rented premises. The meeting of March 21, is, I think, very significant because it shows that it was again thinking in terms of its own exclusive building and that the patrons (of whom the testator was one) would donate the money when it was needed. At the date of the will, the association had rejected the youth centre plans and was contemplating again the purchase of premises of its own; and thereafter interest shifted to the community centre. I am unable to conclude that the testator had any specific building in mind; and, in my judgment, the reference to '*the* . . . buildings for the association' means no more than whatever buildings the association may have or may choose to erect or acquire. The reference to improvements reflects, I think, the testator's contemplation that the association might purchase or might, at his death, already have purchased an existing structure which might require improvement or conversion or even that it might, as had at one time been suggested, expend money in improving the premises which it rented from the Jewish Institute. The association was to have the legacy to spend in this way for the benefit of its members.

"I have already said that, in my judgment, no question of perpetuity arises here, and accordingly the case appears to me to be one of the specification of a particular purpose for the benefit of ascertained beneficiaries, the members of the association for the time being. There is an additional factor. This is a case in which, under the constitution of the association, the members could, by the appropriate majority, alter their constitution so as to provide, if they wished, for the division of the association's assets among themselves. This has, I think, a significance. I have considered whether anything turns in this case on the testator's direction that the legacy shall be used 'solely' for one or other of the specified purposes. Counsel for the association has referred me to a number of cases where legacies have been bequeathed for particular purposes and in which the beneficiaries have been held entitled to override the purpose, even though expressed in mandatory terms.

"Perhaps the most striking in the present context is the case of *Re Bowes*,[65] where money was directed to be laid out in the planting of trees on a settled

---

[65] [1896] 1 Ch. 507.

estate. That was a 'purpose' trust, but there were ascertainable beneficiaries, the owners for the time being of the estate; and North J. held that the persons entitled to the settled estate were entitled to have the money whether or not it was laid out as directed by the testator. He said[66]:

> 'The owners of the estate now say "It is a very disadvantageous way of spending this money; the money is to be spent for our benefit, and that of no one else; it was not intended for any purpose other than our benefit and that of the estate. That is no reason why it should be thrown away by doing what is not for our benefit, instead of being given to us, who want to have the enjoyment of it." I think their contention is right. I think the fund is devoted to improving the estate, and improving the estate for the benefit of the persons who are absolutely entitled to it.'

"I can see no reason why the same reasoning should not apply in the present case simply because the beneficiary is an unincorporated non-charitable association. I do not think the fact that the testator has directed the application 'solely' for the specified purpose adds any legal force to the direction. The beneficiaries, as members of the association for the time being, are the persons who could enforce the purpose and they must, as it seems to me, be entitled not to enforce it or, indeed, to vary it.

"Thus, it seems to me that whether one treats the gift as a 'purpose' trust or as an absolute gift with a superadded direction or, on the analogy of *Re Turkington*,[67] as a gift where the trustees and the beneficiaries are the same persons, all roads lead to the same conclusion.

"In my judgment, the gift is a valid gift."

# REFORM?

## Section 16 of the Ontario Perpetuities Act 1966

(1) A trust for a specific non-charitable purpose that creates no enforceable equitable interest in a specific person shall be construed as a power to appoint the income or the capital, as the case may be, and, unless the trust is created for an illegal purpose or a purpose contrary to public policy, the trust is valid so long as, and to the extent that it is exercised either by the original trustee or his successor, within a period of twenty-one years, notwithstanding that the limitation creating the trust manifested any intention, either expressly or by implication, that the trust should or might continue for a period in excess of that period, but, in the case of such a trust that is expressed to be of perpetual duration, the court may declare the limitation to be void if the court is of opinion that by so doing the result would more closely approximate to the intention of the creator of the trust than the period of validity provided by this section.

(2) To the extent that the income or capital of a trust for a specific non-charitable purpose is not fully expended within a period of twenty-one years, or within any annual or other recurring period within which the limitation creating the trust provided for the expenditure of all or a specified portion of the income or the capital, the person or persons, or his or their successors, who would have been entitled to the property comprised in the trust if the trust

66 [1896] 1 Ch. 507, 511.
67 [1937] 4 All E.R. 501.

had been invalid from the time of its creation, are entitled to such unexpended income or capital.

## QUESTIONS

1. A testator who died a month ago by his will made the following bequests:

(i) £10,000 to Alan and at his death the remaining part of what is left that he does not want for his own use to be divided equally between Xerxes and Yorick;

(ii) £50,000 to my trustees Tom and Tim to distribute amongst such of the inhabitants of Cambridge as they shall in their unfettered discretion think fit;

(iii) £100,000 to my said trustees to distribute amongst Brian, Charles, David, Ellen, Oswald, Peter, Quentin and Roger and such of my other business associates and old friends as they shall see fit;

(iv) £100,000 to my said trustees to use the income for 80 years from my death as the applicable perpetuity period or such other period as the law allows if less for providing holidays for employees and ex-employees their spouses and relatives of I.C.I. plc and of companies on whose boards of directors, directors of I.C.I. plc sit, and thereafter to use the income for the education of my relatives;

(v) residue to my son Simon trusting that he will see to it that my old friends shall have the contents of my wine cellar; and in case of any doubts he shall have power to designate who are my business associates and old friends.

Consider the validity of these bequests, the testator having lived in Cambridge all his life.

2. "If the practical distinctions between discretionary trusts and fiduciary powers are so slight as to justify the decision in *McPhail* v. *Doulton* it cannot be right to have one but not the other subject to the test of administrative workability; nor, in light of *McPhail* v. *Doulton*, can *Re Barlow's W.T.* be justified." Discuss.

3. Simon Small, who was only 4 feet 11 inches tall, has just died. In his home-made will, he directed his executors:

"(a) to pay £2,000 to each of my small relatives;

(b) to distribute £8,000 as they see fit amongst such persons as they consider to be friends of mine;

(c) to hold my residuary estate on trust to pay the income therefrom to my four daughters equally in their respective lifetimes but if a daughter marries a supporter of Watford Football Club the share of such daughter shall accrue to the other daughters, as shall also be the case on the death of a daughter, but on the death of my last surviving daughter they shall distribute the capital within one year amongst such persons connected with me who have been benefited by me in my lifetime as they shall see fit."

Advise on the validity of the above bequests.

4. By his will Tony left:

(a) "£50,000 to the Treasurer of the Cambridge University Law Society to deal with it as the Society wishes";

(b) "£500,000 to the Treasurer of the Manchester Literary and Philosophical Society on trust to apply the income for the benefit of its members";

(c) "the proceeds of sale of my residuary estate to the Treasurer of the Manchester Real Tennis Club to apply half the income for the purposes of the Club and half the income for providing educational assistance to the children of Club members."

Statute prevents the members of the "Lit. and Phil." Society from winding up the Society and dividing its assets between themselves, while this is possible in the case of the Real Tennis Club only if membership falls below five, though the rules can be changed by a 90 per cent. majority vote.

Advise on the validity of the above bequests.

5. Kim appointed his wife and Charles to be executors and trustees of his will. He left his residuary estate to "my executors and trustees upon trust, so far as the law allows, to distribute annually half the income between the men they consider to be the ten best-dressed men of British nationality and half the income between the women they consider to be the ten most beautiful women of British nationality, providing that no one may receive a distribution more than once and providing that my widow's opinion shall prevail in cases of doubt."

Advise Kim's widow, who, as next-of-kin, is seeking to obtain the residuary estate for herself. (*Cf. Chaplin* v. *Hicks* [1911] 2 KB 786).

# Chapter 4

## EXPRESS PRIVATE TRUSTS

### Section 1. Completely and Incompletely Constituted Trusts[1]

THERE are two ways of completely constituting an *inter vivos* trust: (1) by the settlor transferring the property intended to be the subject-matter of the trust to persons as trustees upon certain trusts declared by him or (2) by the settlor declaring that he himself will hold certain of his property as trustee upon certain trusts.

There is no room for such a distinction in the case of testamentary trusts nor in such case is there any scope for the rule in *Milroy* v. *Lord*[2] that applies to incomplete gifts. So long as the three certainties are present[3] a testamentary trust will be constituted though the named trustee disclaims or is unable to take the property through incapacity or predeceasing the testator.[4] Whoever succeeds to the legal title takes subject to the trust, for equity will not allow a trust to fail for want of a trustee.

### I. CREATION OF EXPRESS TRUSTS BY AN EFFECTUAL TRANSFER UPON TRUST

A voluntary transfer of legal title is ineffectual both at law and in equity where something remains to be done by the transferor in order to render the transfer effectual. When, however, the transferor has done everything which it is obligatory for him to do to render the transfer of legal title effectual, but something remains to be done by a third party, the transfer, though invalid at law, is nevertheless valid in equity.

### MILROY v. LORD

Court of Appeal in Chancery (1862) 4 De G.F. & J. 264; 31 L.J.Ch. 798; 7 L.T. 178; 8 Jur. 806 (Turner and Knight-Bruce L.JJ.)

Thomas Medley executed what was treated as a voluntary deed[5] purporting to assign 50 shares in the Louisiana Bank to Samuel Lord upon trust for the

---

[1] For the formalities required for the creation of trusts, see Chap. 2.

[2] (1862) 4 De G.F. & J. 264.

[3] See Chap. 3. On death insolvent no property is subject to the trust.

[4] *Sonley* v. *Clock Makers' Company* (1780) 1 Bro.L.L. 81; *Re Smirthwaite's Trusts* (1871) L.R. 11 Eq. 251; *Re Armitage* [1972] Ch. 438, 445 (where it is pointed out that very exceptionally, the trust will fail if the personality of the named trustee is vital to the carrying out of the trust).

[5] The deed (apparently executed in Louisiana) was expressed to be made in consideration of one dollar. In *Mountford* v. *Scott* [1975] Ch. 258, the Court of Appeal treated £1 as valuable consideration enabling specific performance to be ordered. If a transfer or grant of a legal title for consideration fails (*e.g.* a purported legal lease is not granted by deed) equity will treat this as a contract to transfer or grant the legal title properly, and if the contract is specifically enforceable equity will treat it as having been carried out, so that the transfer or grant is effective to create an equitable interest: *Walsh* v. *Lonsdale* (1882) 21 Ch.D. 9.

benefit of the plaintiffs. The shares were transferable only by entry in the books of the bank; *but no such transfer was ever made*. Samuel Lord held at the time a general power of attorney authorising him to transfer Thomas Medley's shares, and Thomas Medley, after the execution of the settlement, gave him a further power of attorney authorising him to receive the dividends on the bank shares. Thomas Medley lived three years after the execution of the deed, during which period the dividends were received by Samuel Lord and remitted by him to the plaintiffs, sometimes directly and sometimes through Thomas Medley. There was thus a perfect gift of the dividends.

Shortly after the execution of the deed, the settlor had delivered to Samuel Lord the certificates for the shares; and on the death of the settlor, Samuel Lord gave up the certificates to the settlor's executor. The shares stood in the settlor's name before and at the time of his death.

Stuart V.-C. held that a trust had been created for the plaintiffs but was reversed upon an appeal by the executor.

TURNER L.J.: "Under the circumstances of this case, it would be difficult not to feel a strong disposition to give effect to this settlement to the fullest extent, and certainly I have spared no pains to find the means of doing so, consistently with what I apprehend to be the law of the court; but, after full and anxious consideration, I find myself unable to do so. *I take the law of this court to be well settled, that, in order to render a voluntary settlement valid and effectual, the settlor must have done everything which, according to the nature of the property comprised in the settlement, was necessary to be done in order to transfer the property and render the settlement binding upon him. He may, of course, do this by actually transferring the property to the persons for whom he intends to provide, and the provision will then be effectual, and it will be equally effectual if he transfers the property to a trustee for the purposes of the settlement, or declares that he himself holds it in trust for those purposes*[6]*; and if the property be personal, the trust may, as I apprehend, be declared either in writing or by parol; but, in order to render the settlement binding, one or other of these modes must, as I understand the law of this court, be resorted to, for there is no equity in this court to perfect an imperfect gift. The cases, I think, go further to this extent: that if the settlement is intended to be effectuated by one of the modes to which I have referred, the court will not give effect to it by applying another of those modes. If it is intended to take effect by transfer, the court will not hold the intended transfer to operate as a declaration of trust,*[7]* for then every imperfect instrument would be made effectual by being converted into a perfect trust. These are the principles by which, as I conceive, this case must be tried.*

"Applying, then, these principles to the case, there is not here any transfer either of the one class of shares or of the other[8] to the objects of the settlement, and the question therefore must be whether a valid and effectual trust in favour of those objects was created in the defendant Samuel Lord or in the settlor himself as to all or any of these shares. Now it is plain that it was not the purpose of this settlement, or the intention of the settlor, to constitute himself a trustee of the bank shares. The intention was that the trust should be vested in the defendant Samuel Lord, and I think therefore that we should not be justified in holding that by the settlement, or by any parol declaration made

---

[6] See section 1(II), *infra*.
[7] See section 1(III), *infra*.
[8] A similar question arose in the case with reference to a second set of shares.

by the settlor, he himself became a trustee of these shares for the purposes of the settlement. By doing so we should be converting the settlement or the parol declaration to a purpose wholly different from that which was intended to be effected by it and, as I have said, creating a perfect trust out of an imperfect transaction. . . .

"The more difficult question is whether the defendant Samuel Lord did not become a trustee of these shares. Upon this question I have felt considerable doubt; but in the result, I have come to the conclusion that no perfect trust was ever created in him. The shares, it is clear, were never legally vested in him; and the only ground on which he can be held to have become a trustee of them is that he held a power of attorney under which he might have transferred them into his own name; but he held that power of attorney as the agent of the settlor; and if he had been sued by the plaintiffs as trustee of the settlement for an account under the trust, and to compel him to transfer the shares into his own name as trustee, I think he might well have said: 'These shares are not vested in me; I have no power over them except as the agent of the settlor, and without his express directions I cannot be justified in making the proposed transfer, in converting an intended into an actual settlement.' A court of equity could not, I think, decree the agent of the settlor to make the transfer, unless it could decree the settlor himself to do so, and it is plain that no such decree could have been made against the settlor. In my opinion, therefore, this decree cannot be maintained as to the fifty Louisiana Bank shares. . . . "

## RE ROSE, ROSE v. INLAND REVENUE COMMISSIONERS[9]

Court of Appeal [1952] Ch. 499; [1952] 1 T.L.R. 1577; [1952] 1 All E.R. 1217; [1952] T.R. 175; 31 A.T.C. 138 (Evershed M.R., Jenkins and Morris L.JJ.)

The transferor, Eric Hamilton Rose, was the registered owner of a number of shares in a company known as Leweston Estates Co. On March 30, 1943, he executed two transfers[10] in respect of two blocks of these shares, one in favour of his wife, and the other in favour of his wife and another person to be held by them upon certain trusts. The transfers were registered by Leweston Estates Co. on June 30, 1943. The transferor died more than five years after executing the instruments of transfer but less than five years after the transfers were registered. The question was whether in these circumstances the two blocks of shares should be taken into account for the purpose of assessing estate duty. If the shares were taken under a voluntary disposition made by a person more than five years before his death and purporting to operate as an immediate gift, no duty would be leviable.

Roxburgh J.[11] decided the case adversely to the Inland Revenue Commissioners, who appealed unsuccessfully to the Court of Appeal.

EVERSHED M.R. "The burden of the case presented by the Crown may be briefly put as it was formulated by counsel. This document, he said, on the face of it, was intended to operate and operated, if it operated at all, as a transfer. If for any reason it was at its date incapable of so operating it is not legitimate, either by reference to the expressed intention in the document or on well-

---

[9] See L. McKay (1976) 40 Conv. 139.
[10] One was a gratuitous transfer, and the other was expressed to be for a nominal consideration.
[11] [1951] 2 All E.R. 959.

established principles of law, to extract from it a wholly different transaction, *i.e.* to make it take effect, not as a transfer, but as a declaration of trust. Now I agree that on the face of the document it was obviously intended (if you take the words used) to operate, and operate immediately, as a transfer . . . of rights. To some extent at least, it is said, it could not possibly do so. To revert to the illustration which has throughout been taken, if the company had declared a dividend during his interregnum, it is not open to question that the company must have paid that dividend to the donor. So that *vis-à-vis* the company this document did not and could not operate to transfer to Mrs. Rose the right against the company to claim and receive that dividend. Shares, it is said by counsel for the Crown, are property of a peculiar character consisting, as it is sometimes put, of a bundle of rights, *i.e.* rights against or in the company. It has followed from counsel's argument that, if such a dividend had been paid, Mr. Rose could, consistently with the document to which he has set his hand and seal, have retained that dividend, and if he had handed it over to his wife it would have been an independent gift. I think myself that such a conclusion is startling. Indeed, I venture to doubt whether to anybody but a lawyer such a conclusion would even be comprehensible, at least without a considerable amount of explanation. That again is not conclusive, but I confess that I approach a matter of this kind with a preconceived notion that a conclusion that offends common sense so much as this would prima facie do ought not to be the right conclusion.

[His Lordship then examined *Milroy* v. *Lord*[12] and after quoting the passage from that case italicised *supra*, p. 218 continued:] Those last few sentences form the gist of the Crown's argument, and on it is founded the broad, general proposition that if a document is expressed as, and on the face of it intended to operate as, a transfer, it cannot in any respect take effect by way of trust—so far I understand the argument to go. In my judgment, that statement is too broad and involves too great a simplification of the problem, and is not warranted by authority. I agree that if a man purporting to transfer property executes documents which are not apt to effect that purpose, the court cannot then extract from those documents some quite different transaction and say that they were intended merely to operate as a declaration of trust which *ex facie* they were not; but if a document is apt and proper to transfer the property—is, in truth, the appropriate way in which the property must be transferred—then it does not seem to me to follow from the statement of Turner L.J. that, as a result, either during some limited period or otherwise, a trust may not arise, for the purpose of giving effect to the transfer. The simplest case will, perhaps, provide an illustration. If a man executes a document transferring all his equitable interest, say, in shares, that document, operating and intended to operate as a transfer, will give rise to and take effect as a trust, for the assignor will then be a trustee of the legal estate in the shares for the person in whose favour he has made an assignment of his beneficial interest. And for my part I do not think that *Milroy* v. *Lord* is an authority which compels this court to hold that in this case, where, in the terms of Turner L.J.'s judgment, the settlor did everything which, according to the nature of the property comprised in the settlement, was necessary to be done by him in order to transfer the property, the result necessarily negatives the conclusion that, pending registration, the settlor was a trustee of the legal interest for the transferee.

---

12 (1862) 4 De G.F. & J. 264.

"The view of the limitations of *Milroy* v. *Lord* which I have tried to express was much better expressed by Jenkins J. in the recent case which also bears the name of *Re Rose*[13] (though that is a coincidence). It is true that the main point, the essential question to be determined, was whether there had been a transfer *eo nomine* of certain shares within the meaning of a will. The testator in that case, Rose, by his will had given a number of shares to one Hook, but the gift was subject to this qualification: 'If such . . . shares have not been transferred to him previously to my death.' The question was: Had the shares been transferred to him in these circumstances? He had executed (as had this Mr. Rose) a transfer in appropriate form, and handed the transfer and the certificate to Hook, but, at the time of his death, the transfer had not been registered. It was said, therefore, that there had been no transfer, and (following the argument of counsel for the Crown) there had been no passing to Hook of any interest, legal or beneficial, whatever, by the time the testator died. If that view were right, then, of course, Hook would be entitled to the shares under the will. But Jenkins J. went a little more closely into the matter because it was obvious that on one view of it, if it were held that there was a 'transfer' within the terms of the will, though the transfer was inoperative in the eye of the law and not capable of being completed after the death, then Mr. Hook suffered the misfortune of getting the shares neither by gift *inter vivos* nor by testamentary benefaction. Therefore Jenkins J. considered *Milroy* v. *Lord* and in regard to it he used this language[14]: 'I was referred on that to the well-known case of *Milroy* v. *Lord* and also to the recent case of *Re Fry*.[15] Those cases, as I understand them, turn on the fact that the deceased donor had not done all in his power, according to the nature of the property given, to vest the legal interest in the property in the donee. In such circumstances it is, of course, well settled that there is no equity to complete the imperfect gift. If any act remains to be done by the donor to complete the gift at the date of the donor's death, the court will not compel his personal representatives to do that act and the gift remains incomplete and fails. In *Milroy* v. *Lord* the imperfection was due to the fact that the wrong form of transfer was used for the purpose of transferring certain bank shares. The document was not the appropriate document to pass any interest in the property at all.' Then he refers to *Re Fry*, which is another illustration, and continued: 'In this case, as I understand it, the testator had done everything in his power to divest himself of the shares in question to Mr. Hook. He had executed a transfer. It is not suggested that the transfer was not in accordance with the company's regulations. He had handed that transfer together with the certificate to Mr. Hook. There was nothing else the testator could do.'

"I venture respectfully to adopt the whole of the passage I have read which, in my judgment, is a correct statement of the law. If that be so, then it seems to me that it cannot be asserted on the authority of *Milroy* v. *Lord*, and I venture to think it also cannot be asserted as a matter of logic and good sense or principle, that because, by the regulations of the company, there had to be a gap before Mrs. Rose could, as between herself and the company, claim the rights which the shares gave her *vis-à-vis* the company, Mr. Rose was not in the meantime a trustee for her of all his rights and benefits under the shares.

---

[13] [1949] Ch. 78.
[14] *Ibid.* 89.
[15] [1946] Ch. 312. For inessential irregularities see *Re Paradise Motor Co.* [1968] 1 W.L.R. 1125.

That he intended to pass all those rights, as I have said, seems to me too plain for argument. I think the matter might be put, perhaps, in a somewhat different fashion though it reaches the same end. Whatever might be the position during the period between the execution of this document and the registration of the shares, the transfers were on June 30, 1943, registered. After registration, the title of Mrs. Rose was beyond doubt complete in every respect, and if Mr. Rose had received a dividend between execution and registration and Mrs. Rose had claimed to have that dividend handed to her, what would Mr. Rose's answer have been? It could no longer be that the purported gift was imperfect; it had been made perfect. I am not suggesting that the perfection was retroactive. But what else could he say? How could he, in the face of his own statement under seal, deny the proposition that he had, on March 30, 1943, transferred the shares to his wife? By the phrase 'transfer the shares' surely must be meant transfer to her 'the shares and all my right, title and interest thereunder.' Nothing else could sensibly have been meant. Nor can he, I think, make much of the fact that this was a voluntary settlement on his part. Being a case of an unlimited company, as I have said, Mrs. Rose had herself to undertake by covenant to accept the shares subject to their burdens—in other words to relieve Mr. Rose of his liability as a corporator. I find it unnecessary to pursue the question of consideration, but it is, I think, another feature which would make exceedingly difficult, and sensibly impossible, the assertion on Mr. Rose's part of any right to retain any such dividend. . . . "

*Held,* therefore, that the transfer was valid and effectual in equity from March 30, 1943, and accordingly the shares were not assessable for estate duty. *Appeal dismissed.*

## Note

A gift of shares is, therefore, valid in equity if (1) the transferor has executed the form of transfer required by the company's articles[16] and (2) has done everything else, *e.g.* delivered the share certificate which it is obligatory for *him* to do to make the transfer effective and binding upon him.[17] The gift is effective at law when registration of the transfer is made, and until this is done a transferor who complies with (1) and (2) above is a trustee for the transferee.

The identical principle applies to a gift of a debt or other legal chose in action. If, therefore, the donor makes an absolute written assignment of the debt,[18] the gift is good in equity, though it will not be valid

---

[16] In *Milroy* v. *Lord* (*supra*) the form used was a deed poll; in *Antrobus* v. *Smith* (1805) 12 Ves. 39, unsealed writing, both of which were inappropriate forms according to the company's articles. Under Companies Act 1989, s. 207 the Secretary of State for Trade and Industry has power to make regulations for enabling securities to be evidenced and transferred without a written instrument but he has not yet exercised this power.

[17] In *Re Fry* [1946] Ch. 312 although the American donor had sent the necessary forms to obtain Treasury exchange control consent no consent had been obtained before his death. If the gift was imperfect because such consent had not been obtained why was the gift in *Re Rose* not imperfect because the directors' consent to register the shares had not been obtained at the relevant time? Is it because the directors' consent is the ultimate consent and is a negative requirement in that transfers must automatically be registered within two months unless the directors' discretion to refuse is exercised within the two months: Companies Act 1985, s. 183(5), *Re Swaledale Cleaners Ltd.* [1968] 1 W.L.R. 1710?

[18] As required by s. 136 of the Law of Property Act 1925.

at law until written notice is received by the debtor whether from the assignor or the assignee.[19] A voluntary oral assignment on the other hand would be ineffective both at law and in equity.[20]

In the case of a gift of an equitable interest statute[21] requires action only by the donor so that there is no scope for *Milroy* v. *Lord*. If the donor has made a written assignment, whether of the whole or a part of the equitable interest, the gift is good. This was so in *Kekewich* v. *Manning*,[22] where the donor made a voluntary assignment by deed of his equitable interest in a trust fund. A voluntary *promise* to assign an equitable interest is unenforceable even if in signed writing since it is not an assignment and the absence of consideration means the promisee is a volunteer whom equity will not assist.[23]

Legal estates in freehold or leasehold property must be transferred by deed or in the case of registered land by a transfer form which is subsequently registered. Delivery by the registered proprietor to the transferee of the executed transfer form and the land certificate will satisfy the *Re Rose* principle.[24]

Personal chattels must be transferred by delivery or by deed of gift. It is noteworthy that money is not effectively given by the donor giving his cheque for the money[25] for a cheque is merely a revocable authority or mandate. A bill of exchange must be transferred by endorsement[26] and copyright by writing.[27]

As will be seen (p. 228, *infra*), existing rights to have property now or in the future and whether or not such rights are conditional (*e.g.* on marrying or attaining 25 years) or defeasible (*e.g.* by exercise of a power of appointment) are capable of being gratuitously assigned: a *spes* is not (*e.g.* a hope of receiving property if a power of appointment is exercised or a hope of inheriting property under T's will).

II. CREATION OF AN EXPRESS TRUST BY AN EFFECTUAL DECLARATION OF TRUST

In each case where a declaration of trust is relied on the court must be satisfied that a *present binding* declaration of trust has been made complying with the requisite formalities,[28] though the trust interest may be defeasible upon exercise of a power of appointment or a power of revocation.[29]

---

19 *Holt* v. *Heatherfield Trust* [1942] 2 K.B. 1; *Norman* v. *F.C.T.* (1963) 109 C.L.R. 28.
20 *Olsson* v. *Dyson* (1969) 120 C.L.R. 365; *cf. Tibbits* v. *George* (1836) 5 A. & E. 107.
21 s. 53(1)(c) of the Law of Property Act 1925.
22 (1851) 1 De G.M. & G. 176; such an assignment may take the form of a written direction to the trustees to hold on trust for the third party; *Grey* v. *I.R.C.*, *supra*, p. 66
23 *Re McArdle* [1951] Ch. 669.
24 *Re Ward* [1968] W.A.R. 33; *Scoones* v. *Galvin* [1934] N.Z.L.R. 1004; *Brunker* v. *Perpetual Trustee Co.* (1937) 57 C.L.R. 555; *Mascall* v. *Mascall* (1984) 49 P. & C.R. 119.
25 *Re Swinburne* [1926] Ch. 38; *Re Owen* [1949] W.N. 201; [1949] 1 All E.R. 901.
26 Bills of Exchange Act 1882, s. 31; Cheques Act 1957, ss. 1, 2.
27 Copyright Designs and Patents Act 1988, s. 90(3).
28 Neville J. in *Re Cozens* [1913] 2 Ch. 478, 486; Romilly M.R. in *Grant* v. *Grant* (1865) 34 Beav. 623, 626.
29 *Copp* v. *Wood* [1962] 2 D.L.R. 224; Underhill, p. 105, *Young* v. *Sealey* [1949] Ch. 278, 284, 294.

A declaration of trust, to be effectual, need not be literal. It is not necessary for an intending declarant to say: "I declare myself a trustee." What is necessary is some form of expression which shows clearly that he intended to constitute himself trustee or to constitute another a beneficiary, see *Paul* v. *Constance, supra*, pp. 133–137.

Neville J., in *Re Cozens*,[30] referred to a "present irrevocable declaration of trust." The distinction is apparently between these declarations: "I declare a trust for X to be entitled on my death" and "I declare that on my death I will declare a trust for X." The latter is a mere promise to create a trust in the future, an example being *Bayley* v. *Boulcott*.[31] The former could operate as a declaration of trust in favour of the declarant for life, remainder to X, an example being *Kelly* v. *Walsh*.[32]

An interesting example of a declaration of trust occurred in *Re Ralli's Will Trusts*.[33] H, the owner of a reversionary interest under the will of her deceased father covenanted with the trustees of her marriage settlement to settle, as soon as circumstances would admit, all her existing and after-acquired property upon certain trusts (which failed) and ultimately upon trusts for the benefit of the children of H's sister who were volunteers. A clause in the marriage settlement declared that all property comprised within the terms of the covenant should be subject in equity to the trusts of the settlement pending transfer to the trustees. H never assigned the reversionary interest to the trustees before she died. Buckley J. held that the reversionary interest being existing property of H at the time of her declaration of trust there was a valid trust of the interest. It would appear that if her reversionary interest had only been acquired by her subsequently to her settlement so as to be after-acquired property then no trust of the interest would have arisen as declarations of trust in respect of after-acquired property are ineffective at law and in equity.[34]

III. INEFFECTUAL TRANSFERS NOT SAVED BY BEING REGARDED AS EFFECTUAL DECLARATIONS

No matter how clearly there may have been an intention to create a voluntary trust by transfer, if the intending transferor has used an ineffectual method of transfer, this will not be construed into a declaration of trust. *Milroy* v. *Lord, supra*, pp. 217–219 and *Paul* v. *Constance, supra*, pp. 133–137, show that the attempted out-and-out *transfer* to trustees is the clearest evidence that the donor did not intend to *retain* the property and himself be trustee thereof.

Exceptionally, in the case of shares within the *Re Rose* principle it seems that if the directors refuse to register the share transfer then the

---

[30] [1913] 2 Ch. 478, 486.
[31] (1828) 4 Russ. 345.
[32] (1878) 1 L.R.Ir. 275; see also *Re Smith* (1890) 64 L.T. 13.
[33] [1964] Ch. 288, 298.
[34] *Williams* v. *C.I.R.* [1965] N.Z.L.R. 395, *infra*, p. 252.

transferor remains indefinitely as constructive trustee of the shares for the transferee.[35] It would further seem that if the transferee lost the transfer form or it was destroyed in a fire then the equitable interest he had acquired should justify the court requiring the transferor to execute a fresh transfer.[36]

Where the transferee disclaims the intended trust as soon as he hears of it it has been held that the transfer is not void *ab initio* but is valid until disclaimer when the legal interest, now subject to the trust, revests in the settlor.[37]

## IV. THE IMPORTANCE OF THE DISTINCTION BETWEEN COMPLETELY AND INCOMPLETELY CONSTITUTED TRUSTS

### Position of volunteers

If a will creates trusts it is immaterial that the beneficiary is a volunteer just as it is immaterial that a direct legatee is a volunteer: subject to payment of debts, expenses and liabilities the personal representatives must vest the subject-matter of the gift in the trustees or in the direct legatee.[38]

If an *inter vivos* trust is completely constituted, whether by a transfer to trustees upon trusts declared by the settlor or by the settlor himself declaring trusts of certain of his property, then the beneficiaries under the trust can enforce it despite being volunteers.[39] If the trust has not been completely constituted then the "settlor" can only be treated as having promised to make a gift on trust and so if the "beneficiary" is only a volunteer, no consideration having been supplied for the promise, he cannot enforce the promise[40]: "equity will not assist a volunteer." However, if a beneficiary who is not a volunteer seeks to enforce the promise the court will enforce the promise so that the trust becomes completely constituted and then a volunteer beneficiary will be in a position to enforce the now completely constituted trust.[41]

A person is not a volunteer if he provided value or can bring himself within a marriage consideration: *Pullan* v. *Koe, infra,* p. 236. A promise to create a trust made before and in consideration of marriage is regarded as having been made for value. If the trust is created after marriage and contains a true recital that it was made in pursuance of

---

[35] *Re Rose* [1952] Ch. 499, 510; *Tett* v. *Phoenix Property Investment Co.* [1984] B.C.L.C. 599, 619, noted (1985) 48 M.L.R. 220; A. J. Oakley, *Constructive Trusts*, p. 178.

[36] Zines, (1965) 38 Australian L.J. 344; Seddon (1974) 48 A.L.J. 13; Ford & Lee, p. 97; Trustee Act 1925, s. 51; *Mascall* v. *Mascall* (1984) 49 P. & C.R. 119.

[37] *Jones* v. *Jones* (1874) 31 L.T. 535; *Mallott* v. *Wilson* [1903] 2 Ch. 494, criticised by P. Matthews [1981] Conv. 141 but it is unlikely that this pragmatic exception will be overruled. Also see *Fletcher* v. *Fletcher* (1844) 4 Hare 67, *infra,* p. 238.

[38] Until the personal representatives appropriate the assets, having decided recourse to them will not be necessary for payment of debts, etc., or having paid off all debts, etc., the legatees only have a chose in action and not a full equitable interest: see pp. 43–44, *supra.*

[39] *Paul* v. *Paul* (1882) 20 Ch.D. 742. If the trustees refuse to sue they will be joined as co-defendants: *Harmer* v. *Armstrong* [1934] 1 Ch. 65.

[40] *Re Plumptre's Marriage Settlement* [1910] 1 Ch. 609; *Re D'Angibau* (1880) 15 Ch.D. 228.

[41] *Davenport* v. *Bishopp* (1843) 2 Y. & C.C.C. 451, affd. (1846) 1 Ph. 698.

an ante-nuptial promise to create the trust it will be treated as having been made for value.[42] Within the scope of marriage consideration are the parties to the marriage, their children and remoter issue.[43] Old cases allowing children of a former marriage or a possible later remarriage or illegitimate children to be within the scope of marriage consideration and to enforce trust deed covenants to settle after-acquired property, can now only be supported on the basis that such children's interests were so closely interwoven with the interests of the children of the marriage that the latter could only benefit on terms allowing the former to benefit.[44]

Once a trust is completely constituted a settlor cannot "undo" it or revoke it on the basis that the beneficiaries are only volunteers[45]—unless he reserved a power to revoke at the time he created the trust. After all, if A makes a birthday or Christmas gift to B, A cannot recover the property if he subsequently falls out with B.

### Covenants to settle or transfer property

If A covenants (*i.e.* promises in a deed) to pay £11,000 or transfer 1,000 I.C.I. ordinary shares or transfer his unique fifth dynasty Ming vase to B, a volunteer, then B has a chose in action enforceable at law against A, the deed's formalities supplying the consideration.[46] However, equity does not regard the deed's formalities as considera-tion and so treats B as a volunteer and "equity will not assist a volunteer." Thus B cannot obtain specific performance of the Ming vase covenant but will have to be satisfied with common law damages, as for the £11,000 covenant or the 1,000 I.C.I. shares covenant, specific performance never being available in such cases where money compensation is itself adequate.[47] Equity, however, will not frustrate a volunteer suing at law[48] and so B may recover the £11,000 or the money equivalent of the shares or the Ming vase.

Since B has a chose in action this is property that he himself as beneficial owner can settle on trusts, whether declaring himself trustee of it or assigning it to trustees on trusts for C for life, remainder to D.

If A covenants with B to transfer £60,000 to B as trustee with express or implied intent that B shall hold the benefit of the covenant upon trust for C and D if they attain 21 years of age, then A has created a completely constituted trust of the benefit of the covenant

---

[42] *Re Holland* [1902] 2 Ch. 360.

[43] *Att.-Gen.* v. *Jacobs-Smith* [1895] 2 Y.B. 341; *Re Cook's S.T.* [1965] Ch. 902.

[44] *Mackie* v. *Herbertson* (1884) 9 App.Cas. 303, 337; *De Mestre* v. *West* [1891] A.C. 264, 270; *Rennell* v. *I.R.C.* [1962] Ch. 329, 341; *Re Cook's S.T.* [1965] Ch. 902, 914.

[45] *Re Bowden* [1936] Ch. 71; *Re Adlard* [1954] Ch. 29.

[46] *Cannon* v. *Hartley* [1949] Ch. 213, below, seals being required for deeds until August 1990.

[47] *Harnett* v. *Yielding* (1805) 2 Sch. & Lef. 549, 552; *Beswick* v. *Beswick* [1968] A.C. 58.

[48] *Cannon* v. *Hartley* [1949] Ch. 213, unless fraud, undue influence or oppressive unconscionable behaviour were involved: *Hart* v. *O'Connor* [1985] 2 All E.R. 880, 891–892, *per* Lord Brightman. To succeed at law the volunteer, if not a covenantee under a deed poll, will have to be a party to the *inter partes* deed as well as a covenantee, L.P.A. 1925, s. 56, covering only land: *Beswick* v. *Beswick* (3:2 majority view) [1968] A.C. 58, 76, 81, 87, 94, 105.

held by B as trustee, so this may be enforced by C and D, though volunteers, just as trusts are ordinarily enforceable by volunteers: *Fletcher* v. *Fletcher*,[49] *infra*, p. 238.

If A merely covenants with B to pay money or transfer property[50] to B on trust for C and D if they attain 21 the question arises whether A intended to create a trust *of the covenant* for C and D or intended only to create a trust *of the subject-matter of the covenant* if or when transferred to B. Though volunteers, C and D will be able to enforce their claims if there is a completely constituted trust of the benefit of the covenant,[51] but they will fail if A is treated as merely promising to make a gift to B of the property to which the covenant relates, for a trust will only arise when the property is effectively given to B.[52]

Originally, the courts were quite sympathetic to the claims of the likes of C and D, just as originally they were quite ready to find an intention to create a trust in precatory words like "wish," "request," "in full confidence that," etc.[53] In the twentieth century the courts have become reluctant to find an intention to create a completely constituted trust of the benefit of a covenant. This seems quite justifiable. Where in the context of a lengthy trust deed, typically a marriage settlement (wholly enforceable by the issue within the marriage consideration but not by the next-of-kin beneficiaries in default of issue so far as not completely constituted) there is a covenant by the settlor to transfer after-acquired property to the trustees, surely the settlor is only promising to make a gift of such property to the trustees, so that a completely constituted trust enforceable by next-of-kin volunteers will only arise upon the property being gifted to the trustees.[54] It would be most unusual for the settlor to intend to create a trust of the covenant forthwith enforceable by next-of-kin volunteers, so a clear express intention should be required, *e.g.* "to the intent that the benefit of this

---

[49] (1844) 4 Hare 67, where the intention was not express but implied in rather special circumstances at a time when courts were more ready to find an intent to create a trust than they now are. Other examples are *Williamson* v. *Codrington* (1750) 1 Ves.Sen. 511; *Cox* v. *Barnard* (1850) 8 Hare 310; *Watson* v. *Parker* (1843) 6 Beav. 283.

[50] M. W. Friend [1982] Conv. 280 distinguishes between covenants to settle (i) money; (ii) specific and presently existing property other than money and (iii) future or after-acquired property. For (i) a trust of the benefit of the covenant should be inferred simply because A has constituted himself the debtor of B in his capacity as trustee for C. For (ii) no debt is automatically created and B can only obtain nominal damages unless A intended to create a trust of the covenant. A covenant of type (iii) is incapable of being the subject-matter of a trust. His view on type (i) covenants is attractive but for other covenants full damages should always be available, and the covenant and damages relating thereto should be held on trust if A clearly intended such: see Feltham (1982) 98 L.Q.R. 17 and *infra*, pp. 229–230.

[51] *Fletcher* v. *Fletcher* (1844) 4 Hare 67; *Cox* v. *Barnard* (1850) 8 Hare 310 at 312, 313; *Milroy* v. *Lord* (1862) 4 De G.F. & J. 264, 278, and *Re Cavendish-Browne* [1916] W.N. 341, indicate that a covenant for further assurance may assist the court to find an intent to create a trust of a covenant to transfer property or of the covenant for further assurance itself. After all, the benefit of the covenant for further assurance can hardly be held on a resulting trust for the settlor without making the covenant futile and meaningless: see further notes 55 and 78 and text thereto.

[52] *Re Plumptre's Marriage Settlement* [1910] 1 Ch. 609.

[53] See p. 132, *supra*.

[54] *Re Plumptre's M.S.* [1910] 1 Ch. 609; *Re Pryce* [1917] 1 Ch. 234. Really the settlor intends the covenant to be for the enforceable benefit of his spouse and issue and not the next-of-kin, while any actual transfer is to be for the benefit of all the beneficiaries.

covenant shall be held by my trustees upon trust for." If a deed merely contains one covenant, *e.g.* "A covenants with B to transfer £10,000 to him on C's twenty-fifth birthday to hold on trust for C if C attains twenty-five" then since the deed would otherwise be futile[55] it seems it should be treated as creating a trust of the covenant as if it read "A covenants with B to transfer £10,000 to him on C's twenty-fifth birthday to the intent that B shall hold the benefit of this covenant on trust for C if he attains twenty-five."

It has been suggested[56] that since four[57] of the cases where there was held to be no trust of the benefit of the covenant concerned covenants to settle after-acquired property or analogous covenants, such covenants are never capable of being the subject-matter of a trust just as a *spes* or future property cannot be the subject of a trust or of an assignment. While one can *contract* to transfer not-yet-existing property one cannot *give* or transfer or declare a trust of not-yet-existing property. This calls for a digression which will show that future property is non-existent property so there is nothing for a trust to "bite" on, whilst a covenant relating to future property is an existing chose in action[58] which a trust can "bite" on.

Future property must be distinguished from existing vested or contingent rights to obtain property at some future time.[59] While a contingent equitable interest in remainder under a trust (*e.g.* to A for life, remainder to B if he attains 30 and is alive on A's death, where B has an assignable, saleable interest) is existing property, examples of future property are the hope of inheriting upon the death of some live person or of receiving property under the exercise of a power of appointment or of acquiring book-debts arising in a business or of acquiring royalties arising on a book. At law an assignment of future property is void as an assignment of nothing,[60] though, if the assignee gave valuable consideration equity will treat the assignment as a contract to assign the property when received if received,[61] the assignment being wholly inoperative if no value was given.[62] Just as an assignment of future property to trustees is void at law and inoperative in equity unless for value, a declaration of trust by S that he holds future property on trust is inoperative unless for value: *Williams* v. *C.I.R.*, *infra*, p. 252. If S covenants to assign future property, when received if received, then equity will not enforce this in favour of volunteers but only in favour of someone who provided value or is

---

[55] *cf. Fletcher* v. *Fletcher* (1844) 6 Hare 67, p. 238, *infra. Ex hypothesi* if B does not hold the benefit of the covenant on trust for C, he must hold it on resulting trust for A, and so cannot sue A for damages for breach of covenant.

[56] W. A. Lee (1969) 85 L.Q.R. 313.

[57] *Re Plumptre's M.S.* [1910] 1 Ch. 609; *Re Pryce* [1917] 1 Ch. 234; *Re Kay's Settlement* [1939] Ch. 329; *Re Cook's S.T.* [1965] Ch. 902, *infra*, p. 245.

[58] L.P.A. 1925, s. 205(1)(xx) defines property as including any thing in action.

[59] See *Re Earl of Midleton's W.T.* [1969] 1 Ch. 600, 607.

[60] *Holroyd* v. *Marshall* (1862) 10 H.L.Cas. 191, 220; *Re Tilt* (1896) 74 L.T. 163.

[61] *Ibid.*

[62] *Re Ellenborough* [1903] 1 Ch. 697.

within a marriage consideration.[63] However, at common law a covenantee can obtain full damages under a deed poll or, if also a party,
where the deed is *inter partes*. Thus, if S in a deed with B covenants to
assign to B, a volunteer, any property S may acquire under S's father's
will or intestacy B may obtain full damages at common law if S breaks
the covenant: *Cannon* v. *Hartley, infra*, p. 241.

In this case since B has the beneficial ownership of a presently
existing covenant it seems B may declare himself trustee of the
covenant for C. It follows that S when entering into the after-acquired
property covenant with B should be able intentionally to create a trust
of the covenant for C, *e.g.* "I, S, hereby covenant to assign to B any
property that I may inherit under my father's will or intestacy to the
intent that B shall immediately hold the benefit of this covenant as
trustee on trust for C." Since there is a completely constituted trust of
the covenant it is then enforceable by C though a volunteer. In
*Davenport* v. *Bishopp*[64] Knight-Bruce V.-C. indicated there could be a
completely constituted trust of a covenant to settle after-acquired
property *viz.* relating to an indefinite amount at an indefinite future
time. Further, in *Lloyd's* v. *Harper*[65] the Court of Appeal held there
was a trust of the benefit of a contractual promise to pay an uncertain
amount on an uncertain future date, which is similar to a promise to
assign an expectancy, and in *Royal Exchange Assurance* v. *Hope*[66]
Tomlin J. upheld a trust of a contractual promise to pay a sum arising
only on a person's death before a certain date which might or might
not occur. Thus, a covenant to settle after-acquired property or an
analogous covenant can itself be the subject-matter of a completely
constituted trust,[67] though where the covenant relates to future property there should be a rebuttable presumption that the settlor intended
not to create a trust of the covenant but only a trust of the property
when acquired and transferred to trustees.[68]

The elliptical judgment of Buckley J. in *Re Cook's S.T., infra*,
p. 245 is best interpreted as based on the fact that there was no
intention to create a trust of the covenant so as to be forthwith
enforceable by the children volunteers, but only an intention to create
a trust of the subject-matter of the covenant if or when it materialised
and was transferred to the trustees for the children; so only then would
the children have enforceable equitable rights, though, meanwhile, Sir
Herbert would be able to enforce the covenant, having provided
consideration therefor. It is considered that *if* the settlor had ended his
covenant with the clause, "to the intent that the benefit of this
covenant shall forthwith be held by my trustees upon the trusts hereof"

---

[63] *Ibid. Re Brooks's S.T.* [1939] Ch. 993, *infra*, p. 247.
[64] (1843) 2 Y. & C.C.C. 451, 460.
[65] (1880) 16 Ch.D. 290.
[66] [1928] Ch. 179.
[67] Further, see (1976) 92 L.Q.R. 427 (Meagher and Lehane) (though not dealing with the resulting
trust difficulty where the covenantee sues the settlor); (1975) 91 L.Q.R. 236 (J. L. Barton).
[68] See *Re Plumptre's M.S.* [1910] 1 Ch. 609.

Buckley J. surely would have upheld a trust of the covenant even though it related to a sum of money that might never arise. A good draftsman should, of course, expressly state the intention of the settlor.[69] Sir Herbert or, it seems,[70] his executors could have enforced his contractual rights and the proceeds of sale thereby placed in the trustees' hands would then be held on trust for the children volunteers. The trustees could not compel Sir Herbert or his executors to take such action nor could they join him or his executors as co-defendants in an attempt to take advantage of his contractual rights.[71]

*Can the covenantee sue?*

If A enters into a deed with B and covenants with B to transfer existing or after-acquired property to B, but breaks the covenant, then equity will not assist B as a volunteer but it will not frustrate B from obtaining damages at common law: *Cannon* v. *Hartley, infra*, p. 241. Similarly, if A covenants with X that he will transfer £20,000 to B on trust for C then A is liable at law only to X if he fails to transfer the money.[72]

If A covenants with B to transfer property to B on trust for C to the intent that B as trustee will hold the benefit of the covenant on trust for C then there is a completed constituted trust of the benefit of the covenant.[73] As with all trusts B as trustee is under a duty to get in the trust property and so enforce the covenant so as to benefit C. If B breaks his duty then C can sue A and join B as co-defendant.[74]

If A covenants with B to transfer property to B on trust for C in circumstances where there is no intention to create a trust of the covenant then A is treated as voluntarily promising to make a gift of the property referred to in the covenant, so that C will only have enforceable rights as a volunteer if A actually carries out his promise and transfers the property to B.[75]

However, cannot B sue A for damages for breach of the covenant with B[76] and recover full damages[77] to be held on trust for C? The

---

[69] Just as where the settlor intends to create a trust of the benefit of a contract: see pp. 118–119, *supra*.

[70] *Beswick* v. *Beswick* [1968] A.C. 58.

[71] Since Sir Herbert and his executors are under no obligation to the trustees or the children to exercise Sir Herbert's contractual rights, they cannot be forced against their will to become parties to an action concerning such rights.

[72] *Colyear* v. *Lady Mulgrave* (1836) 2 Keen 81.

[73] *Fletcher* v. *Fletcher, infra*, p. 238.

[74] *Vandepitte* v. *Preferred Accident Insurance Co.* [1933] A.C. 70, 79; *Wills* v. *Cooke* (1979) 76 Law Soc.Gaz. 706; *Parker-Tweedale* v. *Dunbar Bank plc (No. 1)* [1990] 2 All E.R. 577.

[75] *Re Plumptre's M.S.* [1910] 1 Ch. 609; *Re Pryce* [1917] 1 Ch. 234.

[76] Old cases tend to assume that B could be left to pursue his common law remedy without considering for whom such damages should be held: *Davenport* v. *Bishopp* (1843) 2 Y. & C.C.C. 451, 460; *Milroy* v. *Lord* (1862) 4 De G.F. & J. 264, 278; *Re Flavell* (1883) 25 Ch.D. 89, 99; *Re Plumptre's M.S.* [1910] 1 Ch. 609 (damages claim statute-barred).

[77] *Robertson* v. *Wait* (1853) 8 Exch. 299; *Lamb* v. *Vice* (1840) 6 M. & W. 862 (J. L. Barton) (1975) 91 L.Q.R. 236, 238–239 though M. W. Friend has pointed out that *Lamb* v. *Vice* concerned a bond and the bond created a debt: [1982] Conv. 280, 283; surely, at law if a covenantor did not transfer property worth £X to the covenantee then the loss was £X, the position in equity of the beneficiaries being immaterial before the Judicature Act and the position has not changed since then: *cf. Re Cavendish-Browne's S.T.* [1916] W.N. 341, though this inadequately reported case may be an example of a completely constituted trust of a covenant for further assurance.

difficulty is that *ex hypothesi* B does not hold the covenant on trust for C so that he must either hold the covenant for his own benefit or by way of resulting trust for A and it is clear that he is not intended to hold the covenant beneficially. If, therefore, the covenant and the right to damages for breach of covenant are held on resulting trust for the settlor, A, then surely so must any damages for breach of covenant.[78] Since A is, under the resulting trust, a *sui juris* absolutely entitled beneficiary he must under the *Saunders* v. *Vautier* principle[79] be able to terminate such trust and prevent the trustees from launching upon such a pointless exercise as a suit against himself for damages.[80] A further difficulty is that if B could choose to sue and so constitute a trust of the damages this would contravene the principle in *Re Brooks's S.T.*, *infra*, p. 247 that only a settlor (or his authorised agent) can completely constitute his trust, whilst for the matter to be at the whim of B whether he sues or not, not only puts B in an invidious position, it contravenes the principle that the acts, neglects or defaults of the trustees cannot be allowed to affect the rights of their beneficiaries.[81]

In practice, if a trustee like B were considering suing A to benefit C he would seek to obtain the leave of the court for, otherwise, he would be at personal risk as to costs if he sued and could not prove his costs were properly incurred.[82] It is plain that the court will direct B that he must not sue for common law damages for breach of covenant where A did not create a completely constituted trust of the benefit of the covenant.[83] Equity thus goes beyond passively not assisting volunteers by positively intervening (which can only be justified on the grounds set out in the penultimate paragraph rather than the basis mouthed by the courts that "equity will not assist a volunteer"). This negative direction is so well-established that there is no need for trustees like B to bother the court: there is a complete defence if any beneficiary like C brings a breach of trust action against B for failing to sue the covenantor for damages.[84]

If a bold trustee like B did sue (*e.g.* because married to the beneficiary or fully indemnified as to costs by the beneficiary) it is submitted such action would fail on the basis that since the settlor had

---

[78] *cf.* resulting trust of £500 in *Re Tilt* (1896) 74 L.T. 163.

[79] See p. 651.

[80] See *Hirachand Punamchand* v. *Temple* [1911] 2 K.B. 330, where plaintiff money-lenders accepted a lesser sum from the defendant's father in satisfaction of a debt and then sued the defendant for the balance. Vaughan Williams L.J. (p. 337) and Fletcher-Moulton L.J. (p. 342) held any moneys recovered would be held on trust for the father: "a court of equity would have regarded the plaintiffs as disentitled to sue except as trustees for the father and would have restrained them from suing" (p. 342).

[81] *Fletcher* v. *Fletcher* (1844) 4 Hare 67, 78; *Re Richerson* [1892] 1 Ch. 379.

[82] *Re Beddoe* [1893] 1 Ch. 547; *Re Yorke* [1911] 1 Ch. 370. Wherever trustees have reasonable doubts they may at the cost of the trust obtain directions from the court: R.S.C., Ord. 85, para. 2(5).

[83] *Re Pryce* [1917] 1 Ch. 234 (though Eve J.'s reasoning is fallacious in that the Judicature Act fusion did not make defences available to a defendant in Chancery also available to a defendant at law: *Cannon* v. *Hartley* [1949] Ch. 213; (1960) 76 L.Q.R. 100, 109, 111 (D. W. Elliot); Meagher Gummow & Lehane's *Equity: Doctrines & Remedies*, para. 234); *Re Kay's Settlement* [1939] Ch. 329, discussed by Romer J., *infra*, p. 242; *Re Cook's S.T.* [1965] Ch. 902.

[84] *Re Ralli's W.T.* [1964] Ch. 288, 301–302.

not created a trust of the voluntary covenant he must *ex hypothesi* have
reserved to himself the right, if he chooses, at a later date to constitute
a trust of the property referred to in his covenant, having lined up the
trustee as his agent to receive the property, but who meanwhile is to
hold the covenant on a resulting trust for the settlor, making any
action against the settlor groundless.

*Only the settlor (or his authorised agent) can constitute a trust*

The settlor must be responsible for the trust property becoming duly
vested in the trustees whether he or his duly authorised agent is
directly responsible.[85] This is obvious where S has created the "S"
settlement and a trustee, Y, whose daughter is life tenant, steals from
S a painting (that S has talked about transferring to the trust but as to
which S is still undecided) so that it will grace his daughter's lounge
very nicely. Equity respects the common law rule that only a donor or
his agent can make an effective gift so there is no trust of the painting.
The position would be the same if S mistakenly left the painting behind
at Y's house, having taken it there merely to show it to Y and his
daughter.

If S in his 1968 voluntary settlement has covenanted to transfer to
the trustees of his settlement after-acquired property appointed to S
under a special power in the 1966 "T" trust or devolving upon S under
T's will or intestacy, and property is appointed to S in 1991 or
bequeathed to S on T's death in 1991, what happens if, fortuitously,
the "S" trustees happen to be trustees of the "T" trust or of T's will,
not so unlikely if the "S" trustees are a trust corporation like Lloyds
Bank? Can the trustees of the "T" trust or of T's will claim to hold the
appointed or bequeathed property as trustees of the "S" settlement, so
completely constituting a trust of such property in the "S" settlement,
even though S is himself demanding the appointed or bequeathed
property? No, S is entitled to the property free from any trusts since
his voluntary obligation is unenforceable and he is in no way responsible for vesting title to the property in the "S" trustees: *Re Brooks's
S.T.*, *infra*, p. 247.

However, if S in 1991 had authorised the trustees of the "T" trust or
of T's will to hold the appointed or bequeathed property *qua* trustees
of the "S" settlement, the "S" settlement of such property would be
completely constituted and so S would not be able to claim the
property for himself.[86] Similarly, if S in his 1968 settlement had
inserted a clause authorising the "S" trustees to receive property
appointed or bequeathed to him and the "S" trustees had received
such property from the trustees of the "T" trust or of T's will then the

---

[85] *Re Brooks's S.T.* [1939] 1 Ch. 993; *Re Adlard* [1954] Ch. 29; *Milroy* v. *Lord*, p. 217, *ante*.
[86] *Re Adlard* [1954] Ch. 29. If S had been deliberately misled by the trustees telling him he was bound
    to authorise them he might have a claim if he acted promptly after finding out.

"S" settlement of such property would be completely constituted,[87] so long as the authority had not been revoked before such receipt, such authority being voluntary[88] and therefore unenforceable and revocable.[89]

In *Re Ralli's W.T.*, *infra*, p. 249 Buckley J. *obiter* took a view inconsistent with the *Re Brooks's S.T.* principle, that case not being cited to him. S voluntarily covenanted in her 1924 settlement to assign her interest in remainder under the "T" trust of 1899 to the "S" trustees as soon as circumstances might admit, but did not do so before she died in 1956. Her interest in remainder fell into possession in 1961 by which time it so happened that X, the sole surviving trustee of S's 1924 settlement (and one of the original trustees thereof) had been appointed by a third party to be a trustee of the 1899 "T" trust and was, in fact, sole surviving trustee of the "T" trust. Buckley J. considered that since X had the title to the covenanted property as sole[90] trustee of the 1899 "T" trust and was also trustee of S's 1924 settlement containing the covenant, this completely constituted S's voluntary settlement of the assets in question. However, S was in no way responsible for the assets becoming vested in X so that according to *Re Brooks's S.T.*, *infra*, p. 247 no trust of the assets within the 1924 settlement should have arisen. The position might have been different if S *herself* had appointed X to be trustee of the "T" trust or if she had appointed X to be her executor, for she would then have been responsible for X as trustee of her settlement acquiring title to the covenanted property so impliedly authorising the position. To appreciate this it is necessary to consider the rule in *Strong* v. *Bird*.

### The rule in Strong v. Bird

*Strong* v. *Bird*[91] decides that in certain circumstances equity should allow the common law position to prevail where a deceased creditor had appointed his debtor as his executor. The *common law* treated the

---

[87] *Re Bowden* [1936] Ch. 71, discussed in *Re Ralli's W.T.*, *infra*, p. 249. No L.P.A. s. 53(1)(c) writing is required for the assignment of S's interest under the "T" trust or T's will where the trustees of such are different persons from the trustees of S's settlement: see *Vandervell* v. *I.R.C.* [1967] 2 A.C. 291, as discussed at p. 55. Where the same persons are trustees it seems implicit in *Re Bowden* and *Re Adlard* [1954] Ch. 29, that there is an exception from the *Grey* v. *I.R.C.* [1960] A.C. 1 principle discussed at p. 55 where the S settlement with S's consent receives S's T property pursuant to an after-acquired property clause (whether general or specifically relating to property appointed under a special power or bequeathed under a will): it is then inequitable for S to claim the interest and so the Revenue will not be able to tax S as if the interest were still his.

[88] Or not otherwise binding as an irrevocable power of attorney or to give effect to a condition contained in a will: *Re Burton's Settlements* [1955] Ch. 82.

[89] *Re Bowden* [1936] Ch. 71, though *cf.* dicta in *Re Burton's Settlements* [1955] Ch. 82, 104.

[90] If there had been another trustee, Y, then Y would need to seek the directions of the court. Trustees hold property jointly and must act unanimously. Since Y is not a trustee-covenantee under the 1924 settlement does not Y hold the assets on trust for S's estate so that he will be liable for breach of trust if he co-operates with X to transfer the assets to X to be held on the trusts of the 1924 settlement? If this is so then X will need to co-operate with Y to transfer the assets to S's estate and X will not be liable to the 1924 settlement beneficiaries since he was never able himself to obtain the assets for the 1924 settlement.

[91] (1874) L.R. 18 Eq. 315, Waters's *Law of Trusts in Canada*, pp. 166–174; Meagher Gummow & Lehane's *Equity: Doctrines & Remedies*, paras. 2901–2908; Underhill, pp. 111–115.

appointment[92] as extinguishing or releasing the debt on the basis[93] "that a debt was no more than the right to sue for the money owing to the creditor and that a personal action was discharged when it was suspended by the voluntary act of the person entitled to bring it . . . [the true basis of the common law rule] lay in the significance attributed to the voluntary act [of appointing the executor] on the part of the testator. Once this is recognised the true character of the rule is perceived. It reflected the presumed intention of the party having the right to bring the action and was not absolute in its operation." Since administrators are not chosen by the testator the common law did not treat the court appointment of the administrator as the release of any debt due to the deceased from the administrator.[94] In *equity* the debtor (whether the deceased creditor's executor or administrator) had to account for the debt to the estate so that such moneys were available to pay off creditors of the estate or to be distributed amongst the beneficiaries.[95]

In *Strong* v. *Bird* the court of equity decided that the common law should prevail, and thus the executor did not have to account for the debt, if the testator had manifested an intent to forgive the debt in his lifetime and this intent had continued till death.

Where a donor intends to make an immediate gift of specific property but fails to satisfy the legal formalities for vesting legal title in the intended donee and goes on to appoint the donee his executor and then dies, the appointment itself is no perfect gift at law of the specific property although it is in the case of a release of a debt due from an imperfectly released debtor. However, Neville J. in *Re Stewart*[96] extended *Strong* v. *Bird*, which *negatively* left the situation as it was at law, since he *positively* treated a gift as effective though the law did not, so perfecting an imperfect gift made by the testator *inter vivos* to his wife who was one of his appointed executors. He said[97]:

> "Where a testator has expressed the intention of making a gift of personal estate to one who upon his death becomes his executor, the intention continuing unchanged, the executor is entitled to hold the property for his own benefit. The reasoning is first that the vesting of the property in the executor at the testator's death completes the imperfect gift made in the lifetime and secondly that the intention of the testator to give the beneficial interest to the executor is sufficient to countervail the equity of beneficiaries under the will, the testator having vested the legal estate in the executor."

---

[92] Taking out the grant of probate or becoming an executor *de son tort* by intermeddling sufficed and, it seems, the appointment itself, though the executor died before taking out probate or intermeddling; *Wankford* v. *Wankford* (1704) 1 Salk. 299; *Re Bourne* [1906] 1 Ch. 697, *Jenkins* v. *Jenkins* [1928] 2 K.B. 501; *Bone* v. *Stamp Duties Commissioner* (1974) 132 C.L.R. 38; *Re Applebee* [1891] 3 Ch. 422; *Williams on Wills* 15th ed., p. 717.

[93] *Per* Mason J. in *Bone* v. *Stamp Duties Commissioner* (1974) 132 C.L.R. 38, 53.

[94] *Wankford* v. *Wankford* (1704) 1 Salk. 299; *Seagram* v. *Knight* (1867) 2 Ch.App. 628; *Re Gonin* [1977] 2 All E.R. 720, 734. Now see Administration of Estates Act 1925, s. 21A added by Limitation Amendment Act 1980, s. 10.

[95] *Berry* v. *Usher* (1805) 11 Ves. 87; *Jenkins* v. *Jenkins* [1928] 2 K.B. 501.

[96] [1908] 2 Ch. 251.

[97] *Ibid.* at 254.

*Re Stewart* has been followed many times at first instance[98] and treated as good law by the Court of Appeal.[99] In *Re James*[1] Farwell J. extended *Re Stewart* to perfect an imperfect gift of real property made by a donor to his housekeeper who, on the donor's intestacy, had herself appointed by the court one of two administratrices of the deceased donor's estate, thereby obtaining legal title to the house. This extension has been doubted by Walton J. in *Re Gonin*[2]: after all, it is the voluntary act of the testator in appointing his debtor as his executor that extinguishes the debt at law, so that the fortuitous appointment by the court of an administrator who was a debtor of the intestate did not extinguish the debt, and so *Strong* v. *Bird* would have been differently decided if the defendant had been an administrator and not an executor. However, the reasoning in the above-cited dicta of Neville J. suggests that, what, perhaps, should more aptly be known as the rule in *Re Stewart* is only concerned with the acquisition of legal title like the *tabula in naufragio* doctrine.[3]

What is traditionally known as the rule in *Strong* v. *Bird* has now developed into the principle that an imperfect *immediate*[4] gift of specific[5] existing[6] real or personal property[7] will be perfected if the intended donee is appointed the testator's executor or administrator alone or with others so long as the intention to make the gift continues unchanged till the testator's death.[8] The gift is perfected *vis-à-vis* those beneficially entitled to the deceased's estate but probably not *vis-à-vis* creditors since a common law extinguishment of a debt by appointment of the debtor as executor did not avail against creditors.[9]

Where the imperfect gift is to trustees and one (or more) of them is appointed the donor's executor this should perfect the trust, the equity of the beneficiaries under the intended trust of the property being sufficient to countervail the equity of the testamentary residuary beneficiaries.[10]

With voluntary covenants, where there is no completely constituted trust of such covenants, difficulties arise in applying the rule in *Strong*

---

[98] *Re Comberback* (1929) 73 Sol.J. 403; *Re James* [1935] Ch. 449; *Re Nelson* (1967) 91 Sol.J. 533: see also *Re Ralli's W.T.* [1964] Ch. 288; *Re Gonin* [1979] Ch. 16.

[99] *Re Freeland* [1952] Ch. 110, counsel unreservedly accepting *Re Stewart*.

[1] [1935] Ch. 449.

[2] [1979] Ch. 16. The extension is acceptable to P. V. Baker (1977) 93 L.Q.R. 485 and G. Kodilinye [1982] Conv. 14.

[3] This doctrine confers priority upon later equitable interests whose owners somehow manage to obtain the legal estate: it was particularly significant before 1926 and still can have some effect: Snell's *Equity* (28th ed.), pp. 50–51; *McCarthy & Stone Ltd.* v. *Hodge* [1971] 1 W.L.R. 1547.

[4] *Re Innes* [1910] 1 Ch. 188; *Re Freeland* [1952] Ch. 110; *Re Gonin* [1979] Ch. 16; *Re Pink* [1912] 2 Ch. 528, 536, 538–539. *Re Goff* (1914) 111 L.T. 34 is out of line since the donor only intended to forgive the debt if the donor predeceased the donee.

[5] *Re Innes* [1910] 1 Ch. 188, 193.

[6] *Morton* v. *Brighouse* [1927] 1 D.L.R. 1009.

[7] *Re James* [1935] Ch. 449.

[8] It seems contrary expressions before death may be ignored if the intent to make the imperfect gift is confirmed in the will: *Re Stoneham* [1919] 1 Ch. 149, 158. For cases on contrary intention see *Re Freeland* [1952] Ch. 110; *Re Eiser's W.T.* [1937] 1 All E.R. 244; *Re Wale* [1956] 1 W.L.R. 1346; *Morton* v. *Brighouse* [1927] 1 D.L.R. 1009 (property imperfectly given to X subsequently specifically bequeathed to Y).

[9] *Bone* v. *Stamp Duties Comr.* (1974) 132 C.L.R. 38.

[10] *Re Ralli's W.T.* [1964] Ch. 288.

v. *Bird* where one of the trustee-covenantees is appointed executor of
the deceased settlor. First, the rule requires separate specific identifiable property[11] so as to be incapable of applying where S has voluntarily
covenanted to pay £20,000 or transfer shares to the value of £20,000.
Secondly, *ex hypothesi* S has neither transferred the property nor
completely constituted a trust of the covenant itself and so does not
have "a present intention to make an immediate gift"[12] of the subject-
matter, if indeed the covenant does not expressly refer to transferring
the subject-matter at a future date. The covenant is thus "an
announcement of what a man intends to do in the future and is not
intended by him as a gift in the present"[13] so as not to comply with the
requirement of a present intention to make an immediate gift. Query
whether this requirement is logically justifiable since once the pass has
been sold by equity assisting a volunteer and perfecting an imperfect
immediate gift it seems inconsistent for equity to refrain from assisting
a volunteer under an imperfect gift of specific property to be made at a
future time (other than the donor's death when testamentary formalities must be complied with[14]) once that time has arrived.[15] Thirdly,
it may be difficult to show that the settlor's intention continued
unchanged till death.

If S makes an imperfect gift to trustees of his settlement and dies, his
intention to make the gift continuing unchanged till his death, and his
executor, mistakenly believing himself legally bound to perfect the gift,
does so, Astbury J. opined[16] this would be effective against the
beneficiaries entitled under S's will. Can this really be so when an
executor does not have as much freedom as the deceased to release
debts and perfect gifts since the executor holds the estate under
fiduciary obligations owed to the will beneficiaries and not as absolute
owner like the deceased?[17] Would *Strong* v. *Bird* not have been
decided differently (and the debtor remain accountable in equity if the
executor could not personally satisfy all creditors' claims) if the debtor
had not been appointed executor but whoever was the executor had
released the debt?

### PULLAN v. KOE

Chancery Division [1913] 1 Ch. 9; 82 L.J.Ch. 37.

A marriage settlement of 1859 contained a covenant by the husband and
wife to settle the wife's after-acquired property of the value of £100 or
upwards.

---

[11] *Re Innes* [1910] 1 Ch. 188.
[12] *Re Freeland* [1952] Ch. 110, 118, the Court of Appeal assuming this to be good law since counsel
did not argue that *Re Innes* was wrong on this point.
[13] *Re Innes* [1910] 1 Ch. 188, 193.
[14] *Re Pink* [1912] 2 Ch. 528, 536, 538–539.
[15] In *Re Ralli's W.T.* [1964] Ch. 288, Buckley J. assumed a covenant to transfer property as soon as
circumstances would admit could come within the rule in *Strong* v. *Bird*. See also *Re Goff* (1914)
111 L.T. 34.
[16] *Carter* v. *Hungerford* [1917] 1 Ch. 260, 273–274.
[17] *Stamp Duties Comr.* v. *Livingstone* [1965] A.C. 694; *Re Diplock* [1948] Ch. 465.

In 1879 the wife received £285 and paid it into her husband's banking account, on which she had power to draw. Part of it was shortly after invested in two bearer bonds which remained at the bank till the husband's death in 1909 and were now in his executors' possession:

*Held*, that the moment the wife received the £285 it was specifically bound by the covenant[18] and was consequently subject in equity to a trust enforceable in favour of all persons within the marriage consideration, and therefore, notwithstanding the lapse of time, the trustees were entitled on behalf of those persons to follow and claim the bonds as trust property, though their legal remedy on the covenant was statute-barred.

SWINFEN EADY J. (in a reserved judgment): "The defence of laches and acquiescence was given up by the defendants, but they insisted that, although they still retained the bonds, they were under no liability to the plaintiffs. They put their case in this way—that the plaintiff trustees could not follow the bonds into their hands, that the only liability of the husband was upon his covenant, and the claim of the trustees was for damages only, and that as this claim accrued in 1879 it was long since barred by the Statutes of Limitation. . . .

"[The husband] received the bonds, purchased with his wife's money, with full notice of the trusts of the settlement, and knowing that the £285 and the bonds purchased with part of it were bound by the covenant, and moreover he gave no value, but is in the position of a volunteer. The trustees having traced the property into his hands are entitled to claim it from his executors.

"It was contended that the bonds never in fact became trust property, as both the wife and husband were only liable in damages for breach of covenant, and that the case was different from cases where property which has once admittedly become subject to the trusts of an instrument has been improperly dealt with, and is sought to be recovered. In my opinion as soon as the £285 was paid to the wife it became in equity bound by and subject to the trusts of the settlement. The trustees could have claimed that particular sum, could have obtained at once the appointment of a receiver of it, if they could have shown a case of jeopardy, and, if it had been invested and the investment could be traced, could have followed the money and claimed the investment.

"This point was dealt with by Jessel M.R. in *Smith* v. *Lucas*,[19] where he said: 'What is the effect of such a covenant in equity? It has been said that the effect in equity of the covenant of the wife, as far as she is concerned, is that it does not affect her personally, but that it binds the property: that is to say, it binds the property under the doctrine of equity that that is to be considered as done which ought to be done. That is in the nature of specific performance of the contract no doubt. If therefore, this is a covenant to settle the future-acquired property of the wife, and nothing more is done by her, the covenant will bind the property.'

"Again in *Collyer* v. *Isaacs*[20] Jessel M.R. said: 'A man can contract to assign property which is to come into existence in the future, and when it has come into existence, equity, treating as done that which ought to be done, fastens

---

[18] Though a covenant merely to pay money does not attract the equitable remedy of specific performance for equity to look on that as done which ought to be done and treat the money as subject to trusts so in *Stone* v. *Stone* (1869) 5 Ch.App. 74, beneficiaries, though purchasers and not volunteers, were without remedy when the action at law on a covenant to settle £1,000 had become statute-barred.

[19] 18 Ch.D. 531, 543.

[20] 19 Ch.D. 342, 351.

upon that property, and the contract to assign thus becomes a complete assignment. If a person contract for value, *e.g.* in this marriage settlement, to settle all such real estate as his father shall leave him by will, or purports actually to convey by the deed all such real estate, the effect is the same. It is a contract for value which will bind the property if the father leaves any property to his son.'

"The property being thus bound, these bonds became trust property, and can be followed by the trustees and claimed from a volunteer.

"Again the trustees are entitled to come into a Court of Equity to enforce a contract to create a trust, contained in a marriage settlement, for the benefit of the wife and the issue of the marriage, all of whom are within the marriage consideration. The husband covenanted that he and his heirs, executors, and administrators should, as soon as circumstances would admit, convey, assign, and surrender to the trustees the real or personal property to which his wife should become beneficially entitled. The trustees are entitled to have that covenant specifically enforced by a Court of Equity. In *In re D'Angibau*[21] and in *In re Plumptre's Marriage Settlement*[22] it was held that the Court would not interfere in favour of volunteers, not within the marriage consideration, but here the plaintiffs are the contracting parties and the object of the proceeding is to benefit the wife and issue of the marriage."

## FLETCHER v. FLETCHER

Vice-Chancellor (1844) 4 Hare 67; 14 L.J.Ch. 66; 8 Jur.(O.S.) 1040.

The bill was filed by Jacob, a natural son of the testator, Ellis Fletcher, demanding payment by the defendants, who were the executors of Ellis Fletcher, of the sum of £60,000 from the assets (and interest calculated from a date 12 months after the death of the testator). The claim was founded upon a voluntary deed executed by the testator some years before his death and discovered for the first time some years after his death. The deed had been retained by the testator in his own possession and, so far as appeared, he had not communicated its contents either to the trustees or to the beneficiaries.

The indenture in question was expressed to be made on September 1, 1829, between Ellis Fletcher of the one part and five trustees therein named of the other part; and it recited that Ellis Fletcher, being desirous of making provision for his two natural sons, John and Jacob, who were at that time eleven and six years old respectively, thereby covenanted for himself, his heirs, executors and administrators, with the said trustees, their heirs, executors, administrators and assigns, that if either or both of the sons should survive the testator, the latter's heirs, etc., would pay to the trustee, their heirs, etc., the sum of £60,000 within twelve months of the death of the testator to be held upon the following trusts: if both sons were alive at the testator's death and attained the age of twenty-one the trustees were to hold the money on trust for them both in equal shares as tenants in common; if only one son fulfilled these conditions the money was to be held on trust for him alone. In the event of either or both of the sons surviving the testator but neither attaining the age of twenty-one, the money was to fall back into residue.

Both sons survived the testator but John died without attaining the age of twenty-one. Jacob accordingly claimed that he had become solely entitled to

21 (1880) 15 Ch.D. 228, 242.
22 [1910] 1 Ch. 609, 616.

the £60,000 and interest under the indenture of covenant, and asked that the defendants, the executors, might be decreed to pay him what was due to him.

The executors admitted assets. The surviving trustees named in the indenture of covenant, by their answer, said that they had not accepted or acted in the trusts of the indenture; and they declined to accept or act in such trusts, unless the court should be of opinion that they were bound so to act.

At the close of the argument, Wigram V.-C. said:

"It is not denied that, if the plaintiff in this case had brought an action in the name of the trustees, he might have recovered the money; and it is not suggested that, if the trustees had simply allowed their name to be used in the action, their conduct could have been impeached. There are two classes of cases, one of which is in favour of, and the other, if applicable, against, the plaintiff's claim. The question is to which of the two classes it belongs.

"In trying the equitable question I shall assume the validity of the instrument at law. If there was any doubt of that it would be reasonable to allow the plaintiff to try the right by suing in the name of the surviving trustee. The first proposition relied upon against the claim in equity was that equity will not interfere in favour of a volunteer. That proposition, though true in many cases, has been too largely stated. A court of equity, for example, will not, in favour of a volunteer, enforce the performance of a contract *in specie*. That it will, however, sometimes act in favour of a volunteer is proved by the common case of a volunteer on a bond who may prove his bond against the assets. Again, where the relation of trustee and *cestui que trust* is constituted, as where property is transferred from the author of the trust into the name of a trustee, so that he has lost all power of disposition over it, and the transaction is complete as regards him, the trustee, having accepted the trust, cannot say he holds it, except for the purposes of the trust; and the court will enforce the trust at the suit of a volunteer. According to the authorities I cannot, I admit, do anything to perfect the liability of the author of the trust if it is not already perfect. The covenant, however, is already perfect. The covenantor is liable at law, and the court is not called upon to do any act to perfect it. One question made in argument has been whether there can be a trust of a covenant the benefit of which shall belong to a third party; but I cannot think there is any difficulty in that. Suppose, in the case of a personal covenant to pay a certain annual sum for the benefit of a third person, the trustee were to bring an action against the covenantor; would he be afterwards allowed to say he was not a trustee? If he cannot do so after once acknowledging the trust, then there is a case in which there is a trust of a covenant for another. In the case of *Clough* v. *Lambert*[23] the question arose; the point does not appear to have been taken during the argument, but the Vice-Chancellor was of opinion that the covenant bound the party; that the *cestui que trust* was entitled to the benefit of it; and that the mere intervention of a trustee made no difference. The proposition, therefore, that in no case can there be a trust of a covenant is clearly too large, and the real question is whether the relation of trustee and *cestui que trust* is established in the present case.

WIGRAM V.-C.: "The objections made to the relief sought by the plaintiff under the covenant in the trust deed of September 1829 were three: first, that the covenant was voluntary; secondly, that it was executory; and, thirdly, that

---

[23] (1839) 10 Sim. 174.

it was testamentary, and had not been proved as a will. For the purpose of considering these objections I shall first assume that the surviving trustee of the deed of September 1829 might recover upon the covenant at law; and upon that assumption the only questions will be, first, whether I shall assist the plaintiff in this suit so far as to allow him the use of the name of the surviving trustee, upon the latter being indemnified, a course which the trustee does not object to if the court shall direct it; and, secondly, whether I shall further facilitate the plaintiff's proceeding at law by ordering the production of the deed of covenant for the purposes of the trial.

"Now, with regard to the first objection, for the reasons which I mentioned at the close of the argument, I think the proposition insisted upon, that because the covenant was voluntary therefore the plaintiff could not recover in equity, was too broadly stated. I referred to the case of a volunteer by specialty claiming payment out of assets, and to the case of one claiming under a voluntary trust, where a fund has been transferred. The rule against relief to volunteers cannot, I conceive, in a case like that before me, be stated higher than this, that a court of equity will not, in favour of a volunteer, give to a deed any effect beyond what the law will give to it. But if the author of the deed has subjected himself to a liability at law, and the legal liability comes regularly to be enforced in equity, as in the cases before referred to, the observation that the claimant is a volunteer is of no value in favour of those who represent the author of the deed. If, therefore, the plaintiff himself were the covenantee,[24] so that he could bring the action in his own name, if follows, from what I have said, that in my opinion he might enforce payment out of the assets of the covenantor in this case. Then, does the interposition of the trustee of this covenant make any difference? I think it does not. Upon this part of the case I have asked myself the question, proposed by Vice-Chancellor Knight-Bruce in *Davenport* v. *Bishopp*,[25] whether, if the surviving trustee chose to sue, there would be any equity on the part of the estate to restrain him from doing so,[26] or, which is the same question, in principle, whether in a case in which the author of the deed has conferred no discretion on the trustees (upon which supposition the estate is liable at law) the right of the plaintiff is to depend upon the caprice of the trustee, and to be kept in suspense until the Statute of Limitations might become a bar to an action by the trustee. Or, in the case of new trustees being appointed (perhaps by the plaintiff himself, there being a power to appoint new trustees), supposing his own nominees to be willing to sue, the other trustees might refuse to sue. I think the answer to these and like questions must be in the negative. The testator has bound himself absolutely. There is a debt created and existing. I give no assistance against the testator. I only deal with him as he has dealt by himself, and, if in such a case the trustee will not sue without the sanction of the court, I think it is right to allow the *cestui que trust* to sue for himself, in the name of the trustee, either at law, or in this court, as the case may require. The rights of the parties cannot depend upon mere accident and caprice. Having come to this conclusion upon abstract reasoning, it was satisfactory to me to find that this view of the case is not only consistent with, but is supported by, the cases of *Clough* v. *Lambert*[27] and *Williamson* v. *Codrington*.[28] If the case, therefore, depended simply upon the

---

[24] A case of this type is *Cannon* v. *Hartley* [1949] Ch. 213.
[25] (1843) 2 Y. & C.C.C. 451.
[26] See (1960) 76 L.Q.R. 100 (Elliott).
[27] (1839) 10 Sim. 174.
[28] (1750) 1 Ves.Sen. 511.

covenant being voluntary my opinion is that the plaintiff would be entitled to use the name of the trustee at law, or to recover the money in this court, if it were unnecessary to have the right decided at law, and, where the legal right is clear, to have the use of the deed, if that use is material.

"The second question is whether, taking the covenant to be executory, the title of the plaintiff to relief is affected by that circumstance. The question is answered by what I have already said. Its being executory makes no difference, whether the party seeks to recover at law in the name of the trustee, or against the assets in this court.

"The third question is whether the plaintiff is precluded from relief in this court, on the ground suggested that this is a testamentary paper . . . There is, therefore, no ground for the argument that the interest is testamentary.

"The only other question arises from the circumstances of the instrument having been kept in the possession of the party—does that affect its legal validity? In the case of *Dillon* v. *Coppin*[29] I had occasion to consider that subject, and I took pains to collect the cases upon it. The case of *Doe* v. *Knight*[30] shows that, if an instrument is sealed and delivered, the retainer of it by the party in his possession does not prevent it from taking effect. No doubt the intention of the parties is often disappointed by holding them to be bound by deeds which they have kept back, but such unquestionably is the law. . . .

"Declare that the deed of September 1, 1829, constitutes a debt at law, and decree payment of the principal and interest on the same to the plaintiff."

## CANNON v. HARTLEY

Chancery Division [1949] Ch. 213.

By a deed of separation made on January 23, 1941, between the defendant of the first part, his wife of the second part and the plaintiff, their daughter, of the third part, the defendant covenanted, *inter alia*, "If and whenever during the lifetime of the wife or the daughter the husband shall become entitled . . . under the will or codicil . . . of either of his parents . . . to any money or property exceeding in net amount or value £1,000, he will forthwith at his own expense . . . settle one-half of such money or property upon trust for himself for life and for the wife for life after his death and subject thereto in trust for the daughter absolutely . . . " In 1944 the defendant became entitled, subject to a prior life interest therein of his mother, to a quarter share of a fund of approximately £50,000. The defendant's wife died in 1946. The defendant refused to execute a settlement in accordance with the said covenant. On a claim by the plaintiff for damages for breach of the covenant:

*Held*, that the plaintiff was entitled to damages.

ROMER J.: "The question with which I have now to deal follows on my finding that the reversionary interest to which the defendant became entitled under his father's will was caught by clause 7 of the deed of separation. It has been argued on behalf of the defendant that the plaintiff, not having given any consideration for this covenant by her father, is not only unable to apply to a court of equity for the enforcement of the covenant by way of specific performance, but that

---

[29] (1839) 4 Myl. & Cr. 647, 660.
[30] (1826) 5 B. & C. 671.

she is also disqualified from suing at common law for damages for breach of the covenant.

"It is, of course, well established that in such a case as this a volunteer cannot come to a court of equity and ask for relief which is peculiar to the jurisdiction of equity, *viz.* specific performance; but for my part I thought it was reasonably clear that, the document being under seal, the covenantee's claim for damages would be entertained, and that is still my belief. . . .

"But the defendant relies (and this appears to be the foundation of his defence) upon some observations made by Eve J. in *In re Pryce*,[31] and on the subsequent decision of Simonds J. in *In re Kay's Settlement*.[32] I think the point of the observations of Eve J. in *In re Pryce* appear sufficiently in *In re Kay's Settlement*. The headnote of that case is: 'A voluntary settlement executed by a spinster contained a covenant in the usual form to settle any after-acquired property, with certain exceptions. The settlor afterwards married and had three children. Having become entitled under a will to a legacy and a share of residue which fell within the covenant, and a share in an appointed fund, she was asked by the trustees of the settlement to settle this property, but refused to do so: Held, on an application by the trustees for directions, that the children, being volunteers, had no right to enforce the covenant, and therefore the trustees ought to be directed not to take any proceedings to enforce the covenant, by action for damages for breach or otherwise.'

"Simonds J., after referring to the facts of the case, said at p. 338:

'It is in these circumstances that the trustees have issued this summons, making as parties to it, first, the settlor herself and, secondly, her infant children, who are beneficiaries under the settlement. But, be it observed, though beneficiaries, her children are, for the purpose of this settlement, to be regarded as volunteers, there being no marriage consideration, which would have entitled them to sue, though they are parties to this application. The trustees asked whether, in the event which has happened of the settlor having become entitled to certain property, they should take proceedings against her to compel performance of the covenant or to recover damages on her failure to implement it.

'I am bound to say that that does not seem to me to be a very happy form of proceeding, though perhaps it is difficult to see how else the trustees should act. It is to be observed that one of the persons made a party is the very person as to whom the trustees ask the question whether she should be sued. She, the settlor, has appeared by Mr. Evershed and has contended, as she was entitled to contend, that the only question before the court was whether the trustees ought to be directed to take such proceedings; that is to say, she contended that the only question before the court was precisely that question which Eve J.

---

[31] [1917] 1 Ch. 234.
[32] [1939] Ch. 329, 338.

had to deal with in *In re Pryce*. She has said that the question before me is not primarily whether, if she were sued, such an action would succeed (as to which she might have a defence, I know not what), but whether, in the circumstances as they are stated to the court, the trustees ought to be directed to take proceedings against her.

'As to that, the argument before me has been, on behalf of the children of the marriage, beneficiaries under the settlement, that, although it is conceded that the trustees could not successfully take proceedings for specific performance of the agreements contained in the settlement, yet they could successfully, and ought to be directed to, take proceedings at law to recover damages for the non-observance of the agreements contained in the settlement, first, the covenant for further assurance of the appointed share of the first-mentioned £20,000 and, secondly, the covenant with regard to the after-acquired property. In the circumstances I must say that I felt considerable sympathy for the argument which was put before me by Mr. Winterbotham on behalf of the children, that there was, at any rate, on the evidence before the court today, no reason why the trustees should not be directed to take proceedings to recover what damages might be recoverable at law for breach of the agreements entered into by the settlor in her settlement. But on a consideration of *In re Pryce* it seemed to me that so far as this court was concerned the matter was concluded and that I ought not to give any directions to the trustees to take the suggested proceedings.

'In *In re Pryce* the circumstances appear to me to have been in no wise different from those which obtain in the case which I have to consider. In that case there was a marriage settlement made in 1887. It contained a covenant to settle the wife's after-acquired property. In 1904 there was a deed of gift under which certain interests in reversion belonging to the husband were assured by him absolutely to his wife. The husband was also entitled to a one-third share in certain sums appointed to him by the will of his father in exercise of a special power of appointment contained in a deed of family arrangements. The share of the £9,000 fell into possession in 1891 on the death of his father, and was paid to him, unknown to the trustees of his marriage settlement, and spent. The interests given by the husband to the wife and his share of the £4,700 came into possession in 1916 on the death of the husband's mother, and were outstanding in the trustees of his parents' settlement and of the deed of family arrangement respectively. The husband died in 1907, and there was no issue of the marriage. Subject to his widow's life interest in both funds, the ultimate residue of the wife's fund was held in trust for her statutory next-of-kin, and the husband's fund was held in trust for him absolutely. The widow was also tenant for life under her husband's will. The trustees of the marriage settlement in that case took out a summons 'to have it determined whether these interests and funds were caught by the provisions of the settlement, and, if so, whether they should take proceedings to enforce them.' In those proceedings, apparently, the plaintiffs were the trustees of the marriage settlement, and the only defendant appears to have been the widow of the settlor; that is to say, there were no other parties to the proceedings to whose beneficial interest it was to argue in favour of the enforceability and enforcement of the covenant, but the trustees no doubt argued in favour of their interests, as it was their duty to do. Eve J., in a considered judgment, held that although the interests to which I have referred were caught by the covenant of the wife and the agreement by the husband respectively, yet the trustees ought not to take any steps to recover any of them. In the case of the wife's fund he said that her next of kin were volunteers, who could neither maintain an action to enforce the covenant nor for damages for breach of it, and that the court would not give them by indirect means what they could not obtain by direct procedure; therefore he declined to direct the trustees to take proceedings either to have the covenant specifically enforced or to recover damages at law. The learned judge, as I have said, took time to consider his judgment. Many of the cases which have been cited to me, though not all of them apparently, were cited to him, and after deciding that no steps should be taken to enforce specific performance of the covenant he used these words: "The position of the wife's fund is somewhat different, in that her next of kin would be entitled to it on her death; but they are volunteers, and although the court would probably compel fulfilment of the contract to settle at the instance of any persons within the marriage consideration— see, *per* Cotton L.J. in *In re D'Angibau*[33] and in their favour will treat the outstanding property as subjected to an enforceable trust—*Pullen* v. *Koe*[34] "volunteers have no right whatever to obtain specific performance of a mere covenant which has remained as a covenant and has never been performed": see, *per* James L.J. in *In re D'Angibau*. Nor could damages be awarded either in this court, or, I apprehend, at law, where, since the Judicature Act, 1873, the same defences would be available to the defendant as would be raised in an action brought in this court for specific performance or damages."

'That is the exact point which has been urged on me with great insistence by Mr. Winterbotham. Whatever sympathy I might feel for his argument, I am not justified in departing in any way from this decision, which is now twenty-one years old. The learned judge went on: "In these circumstances, seeing that the next-of-kin could neither maintain an action to enforce the covenant nor for damages for breach of it, and that the settlement is not a declaration of trust constituting the relationship of trustee and cestui que trust between the defendant and the next of kin, in which case effect could be given to the trusts even in favour of volunteers, but is a mere voluntary contract to create a trust, ought the court now for the sole benefit of these volunteers to direct the trustees to take proceedings to enforce the defendant's covenant? I think it ought not; to do so would be to give the next of kin by indirect means relief they cannot obtain by any direct procedure, and would in effect be enforcing the settlement as against the defendant's legal right to payment and transfer from the trustees of the parents' marriage settlement." It is true that in those last words the learned judge does not specifically refer to an action for damages, but it is clear that he has in his mind directions both with regard to an action for specific performance and an action to recover damages at law—or, now, in this court. In those circumstances it appears to me that I must follow the learned judge's decision and I must direct the trustees not to take any steps either to compel performance of the covenant or to recover damages through her failure to implement it.'

---

[33] (1880) 5 Ch.D. 228, 242, 246.
[34] [1913] 1 Ch. 9.

"Now it appears to me [this is Romer J. after the lengthy citation of Simonds J.] that neither *In re Pryce*[35] nor *In re Kay's Settlement*[36] is any authority for the proposition which has been submitted to me on behalf of the defendant. In neither case were the claimants parties to the settlement in question, nor were they within the consideration of the deed. When volunteers were referred to in *In re Pryce* it seems to me that what Eve J. intended to say was that they were not within the class of non-parties, if I may use that expression, to whom Cotton L.J. recognised in *In re D'Angibau*[37] that the court would afford assistance. In the present case the plaintiff, although a volunteer, is not only a party to the deed of separation but is also a direct covenantee under the very covenant upon which she is suing. She does not require the assistance of the court to enforce the covenant for she has a legal right herself to enforce it. She is not asking for equitable relief but for damages at common law for breach of covenant.

"For my part, I am quite unable to regard *In re Pryce*, which was a different case dealing with totally different circumstances, or anything which Eve J. said therein, as amounting to an authority negativing the plaintiff's right to sue in the present case. I think that what Eve J. was pointing out in *In re Pryce* was that the next of kin who were seeking to get an indirect benefit had no right to come to a court of equity because they were not parties to the deed and were not within the consideration of the deed and, similarly, they would have no right to proceed at common law by an action for damages, as the court of common law would not entertain a suit at the instance of volunteers who were not parties to the deed which was sought to be enforced, any more than the court of equity would entertain such a suit.

"It was suggested to me in argument that in such a case as the present, where the covenant is to bring in after-acquired property, an action for damages for breach of that covenant is in effect the same as a suit for specific performance of a covenant to settle. I myself think that the short answer to that is that the two things are not the same at all. The plaintiff here is invoking no equitable relief; she is merely asking for monetary compensation for a breach of covenant.

"I shall accordingly direct an inquiry as to the damages sustained by the plaintiff for breach by the defendant of the covenant with the plaintiff contained in clause 7 of the deed of separation and the plaintiff will have her costs of the action, the costs of the inquiry to be reserved." *Judgment for the plaintiff.*

## RE COOK'S S.T.

Chancery Division [1965] Ch. 902; [1965] 2 W.L.R. 179; [1964] 3 All E.R. 898.

Sir Herbert as life tenant and his son, Sir Francis, as remainderman agreed that certain settled property (including a Rembrandt) should become Sir Francis's absolutely subject to Sir Francis resettling some of the property (not the Rembrandt) and covenanting with the trustees of the resettlement that in case any of certain pictures (including the Rembrandt) should be sold during Sir Francis's lifetime the net proceeds of sale should be paid over to the

[35] [1917] 1 Ch. 234.
[36] [1939] Ch. 329.
[37] (1880) 15 Ch.D. 228.

trustees to be held by them on the resettlement trusts in favour of Sir Francis's children. A settlement was executed pursuant to this contract.

Sir Francis gave the Rembrandt to his wife who desired to sell it. The trustees, therefore, took out a summons as to whether or not upon any sale of the Rembrandt the trustees would be obliged to take steps to enforce the covenant.

*Held*, (1) Since Sir Francis's children were volunteers they could not enforce the covenant so that the trustees would be directed not to enforce the covenant on the principles in *Re Pryce*[38] and *Re Kay*[39] but (2) that in any case the covenant operated only upon a sale by Sir Francis and not by his wife.

As to (1):

BUCKLEY J.: " . . . Counsel appearing for Sir Francis submitted that as a matter of law the covenant . . . is not enforceable against him by the trustees of the settlement. . . . [He] submits that the covenant was a voluntary and executory contract to make a settlement in a future event and was not a settlement of a covenant to pay a sum of money to the trustees. He further submits that, as regards the covenant, all the beneficiaries under the settlement are volunteers with the consequence that not only should the court not direct the trustees to take proceedings on the covenant but also that it should positively direct them not to take proceedings. He relies on *Re Pryce* and *Re Kay's Settlement*.

"Counsel for the second and third defendants have contended that, on the true view of the facts, there was an immediate settlement of the obligation created by the covenant, and not merely a covenant to settle something in the future. It was said, as counsel for the second defendant put it, that, by the agreement, Sir Herbert bought the rights arising under the covenant for the benefit of the cestuis que trust under the settlement and that, the covenant being made in favour of the trustees, these rights became assets of the trust. He relied on *Fletcher* v. *Fletcher*,[40] *Williamson* v. *Codrington*[41] and *Re Cavendish Browne's Settlement Trusts*.[42] I am not able to accept this argument. The covenant with which I am concerned did not, in my opinion, create a debt enforceable at law, that is to say, a property right, which, although to bear fruit only in the future and on a contingency, was capable of being made the subject of an immediate trust, as was held to be the case in *Fletcher* v. *Fletcher*. Nor is this covenant associated with property which was the subject of an immediate trust, as in *Williamson* v. *Codrington*. Nor did the covenant relate to property which then belonged to the covenantor, as in *Re Cavendish Browne's Settlement Trusts*. In contrast to all these cases, this covenant on its true construction is, in my opinion, an executory contract to settle a particular fund or particular funds of money which at the date of the covenant did not exist and which might never come into existence. It is analogous to a covenant

---

[38] [1917] 1 Ch. 234.
[39] [1939] Ch. 329.
[40] (1844) 4 Hare 67.
[41] (1750) 1 Ves.Sen. 511.
[42] (1916) 61 S.J. 27.

to settle an expectation or to settle after-acquired property.[43] The case, in my judgment, involves the law of contract, not the law of trusts. . . .

"Accordingly, the second and third defendants are not in my judgment entitled to require the trustees to take proceedings to enforce the covenant, even if it is capable of being construed in a manner favourable to them."

## RE BROOKS'S SETTLEMENT TRUSTS

Chancery Division [1939] 1 Ch. 993.

By the terms of a marriage settlement the income of the settled fund was directed to be paid to the wife during her life and subject to that trust the fund was to be held in trust for such of her issue as she might by deed or will appoint; in default of any such appointment the fund was to be held in trust for all her children who being sons should attain the age of twenty-one years or being daughters should attain that age or marry in equal shares. In 1929 one of her children, A.T., executed a voluntary settlement whereby he assigned to Lloyds Bank as trustees "all the part or share, parts or shares and other interest whether vested or contingent to which the settlor is now or may hereafter become entitled whether in default of appointment, or under any appointment hereafter to be made or on failure of any such appointment of and in the trust property" subject to the marriage settlement. By an appointment in pursuance of the power executed in 1939, his mother appointed him a sum of £3,517 and released her life interest. Thereupon Lloyds Bank Ltd., who had by then become trustees of the marriage settlement as well as the voluntary settlement took out a summons asking whether they should pay A.T. the £3,517.

*Held*, that A.T. was entitled to require payment of the sum appointed, and could not be compelled to permit the bank to retain the £3,517.

FARWELL J.: "When one looks at the voluntary settlement, at first sight the answer would seem to be quite clearly that the trustees' duty was to retain the sum of £3,517 as part of the funds which the son had voluntarily settled, and the language of the voluntary settlement would seem to leave no doubt on that score, because the settlor assigned to the bank 'all the part or share parts or shares and other interest whether vested or contingent to which the settlor is now or may hereafter become entitled whether in default of appointment or under any appointment hereafter to be made or on failure of any such appointment of and in the trust property which is now or may at any time hereafter become subject to the trusts of the wife's settlement.' One would say, looking at the language of the settlement, that it would be difficult to find words more apt to embrace in the voluntary settlement all the interests which the son had then or might thereafter have under the marriage settlement and that accordingly the answer should be that it is the duty of the trustees to retain this as part of the voluntary settlement fund. But, when one considers

---

[43] But could it not be argued that Sir F. was under a current obligation to pay the trustees if in future he were to sell the Rembrandt: a presently existing chose in action. See *Shepherd* v. *Commissioners of Taxes* (1965) 113 C.L.R. 385 where A granted B a licence to manufacture and sell castors for a monthly royalty of 5 per cent. of the gross sales for the preceding month and later A assigned to X all his right in and to an amount equal to 90 per cent. of the income which may accrue in the next three years from royalties payable under the licence. This was held a valid assignment of a presently existing right to bear fruit on the happening of a contingency, B making the effort to make and sell castors in the next three years.

the legal position in this matter, a different aspect seems to appear. If the matter could be tested simply as one of construction, the answer would appear to be in favour of the trustees of the voluntary settlement; but the question is not one of construction only, and I have to consider whether the attempt to assign that which the son has now become entitled to by virtue of the exercise of the power is enforceable against him.

"The legal position in the case of a special power of appointment is not in any doubt at all. Referring to *Farwell on Powers*, (3rd ed.), p. 310, I find this statement of principle, which will be found in exactly the same language in earlier editions of the book, and therefore is not in any way the creation of the editor: 'The exercise of a power of appointment divests (either wholly or partially according to the terms of the appointment) the estates limited in default of appointment and creates a new estate, and that, too, whether the property be real or personal.' Then there is a reference to a decision in the *Duke of Northumberland* v. *Inland Revenue Commissioners*,[44] where this statement was adopted by Hamilton J., as he then was. The effect of this is that in the case of a special power the property is vested in the persons who take in default of appointment, subject, of course, to any prior life interest, but liable to be divested at any time by a valid exercise of the power, and the effect of such an exercise of the power is to defeat wholly or *pro tanto* the interests which up to then were vested in the persons entitled in default of appointment and to create new estates in those persons in whose favour the appointment had been made. That being so, it is, in my judgment, impossible to say that until an appointment has been made in favour of this son the son had any interest under his mother's settlement other than an interest as one of the people entitled in default of appointment; he had an interest in that; but that interest was liable to be divested, and, if an appointment was made (as in fact it was made) in favour of the son, then to that extent the persons entitled in default were defeated and he was given an interest in the funds which he had never had before and which came into being for the first time when the power was exercised. No doubt it is quite true to say that the appointment has to be read in to the marriage settlement, but, in my judgment, that is not sufficient ground for saying that at the time when this voluntary settlement was made the son had any interest at all in the fund other than his vested interest in default of appointment; for the rest, he had nothing more than a mere expectancy, the hope that at some date his mother might think fit to exercise the power of appointment in his favour, but, until she did so choose, he had nothing other than his interest in default of appointment to which he could point and say: 'That is a fund to which I shall become entitled in future or to which I am contingently entitled.' Apart from this he was not contingently entitled at all; he had no interest whatever in the fund until the appointment had been executed.

"If that be the true view, as I believe it to be, the result must be that, whatever the language of the settlement may be, the settlor under the voluntary settlement was purporting to assign to the trustees something to which he might in certain circumstances become entitled in the future, but to which he was not then entitled in any sense at all, and if that be so, then it is plain on the authorities that the son cannot be compelled to hand over or to permit the trustees to retain this sum and that he is himself entitled to call upon them to pay it over to him.

---

44 [1911] 2 K.B. 343, 354.

"There are two cases to which I have been referred. One of them is a decision of Buckley J. (as he then was) in a case of *In re Ellenborough. Towry Law* v. *Burne.*[45] The headnote in that case is this: 'The decision in *Meek* v. *Kettlewell*[46] that the voluntary assignment of an expectancy, even though under seal, will not be enforced by a Court of Equity, has not been overruled by *Kekewich* v. *Manning.*'[47] What Buckley J. said was this: 'The question is whether a volunteer can enforce a contract made by deed to dispose of an expectancy. It cannot be and is not disputed that if the deed had been for value the trustees could have enforced it. If value be given, it is immaterial what is the form of assurance by which the disposition is made, or whether the subject of the disposition is capable of being thereby disposed of or not. An assignment for value binds the conscience of the assignor. A Court of Equity as against him will compel him to do that which ex hypothesi he has not yet effectually done. Future property, possibilities, and expectancies are all assignable in equity for value: *Tailby* v. *Official Receiver.*[48] But when the assurance is not for value, a Court of Equity will not assist a volunteer, the reason for that being, that, since it is merely a voluntary act and not an act for consideration at all, the conscience of the assignor is not affected so as in equity to prevent him from saying: "I am not going to hand over this property to which now for the first time I have become entitled." ' Then Buckley J. cites a passage from *Meek* v. *Kettlewell* and points out that that is not overruled by the latter decision of the Court of Appeal in *Kekewich* v. *Manning*, and that the rule is still binding. If that be the true view, it must follow that this particular interest, which for the first time came into being when the appointment was made, is not caught by the settlement.

"Notwithstanding the fact that the language of this voluntary settlement as a matter of construction is wide enough to comprise this interest, the principle of law which I have stated makes it impossible to enforce the settlement to that extent and prevents the settlor from being compelled by this Court to transfer or permit the trustees to retain this money as part of the funds subject thereto.

"I regret to have to come to this conclusion, because I think it is quite plainly contrary to what was intended at the date when the voluntary settlement was executed, but none the less I feel compelled by the principles to which I have referred to hold that the answer to the summons must be that the trustees ought to pay to the defendant the sum in question on the footing that that settlement does not operate as a valid assignment or declaration of trust in respect thereof. I make that declaration accordingly."

## RE RALLI'S WILL TRUSTS

Chancery Division [1964] Ch. 288; [1963] 3 All E.R. 940.

From 1899 Helen was entitled to one-half of her father's residuary estate subject to her mother's life interest. The mother died in 1961 so Helen's reversionary interest then fell into possession. In 1924 Helen in her marriage settlement had covenanted to assign to the trustees thereof as soon as circumstances would admit all her existing and after-acquired property upon

---

45 [1903] 1 Ch. 697, 700.
46 (1842) 1 Hare 464.
47 (1851) 1 De G.M. & G. 176.
48 (1888) 13 App.Cas. 523.

certain trusts for her children which failed (Helen dying a childless widow) and ultimately upon trusts for the benefit of the children of Helen's sister, Irene, who were volunteers. A subsequent clause in the marriage settlement was held on its proper construction to declare that all property comprised within the terms of the covenant should be subject in equity to the trusts of the settlement pending assignment to the trustees. Helen never assigned the reversionary interest before dying in 1956.

The plaintiff was one of the three original trustees of the 1924 marriage settlement and was sole surviving trustee thereof. It so happened that in 1946 he had also become a trustee of Helen's father's will and was indeed sole surviving trustee. He claimed Helen's reversion in half the residue was held on the trusts of the marriage settlement whilst the defendants, Helen's personal representatives, claimed her estate was entitled.

BUCKLEY J. held that the vested reversionary interest, being existing property of Helen at the time she made what he construed as an independent declaration of trust pending assignment to the trustees of her marriage settlement, was held on the trusts of the marriage settlement. He then continued:

"If this view is right, this disposes of the case, but I think I should go on to state what would be my view, if I were mistaken in the view I have expressed. The investments representing the share of residue in question stand in the name of the plaintiff. This is because he is now the sole surviving trustee of the testator's will. Therefore, say the defendants, he holds these investments primarily on the trusts of the will, that is to say, in trust for them as part of Helen's estate. The plaintiff is, however, also the sole surviving covenantee under clause 7 of the settlement, as well as the sole surviving trustee of that settlement. This, however, affords him no answer, say the defendants, to their claim under the will unless the plaintiff, having transferred the property to them in pursuance of the trusts of the will, could compel them to return it in pursuance of their obligation under the covenant, and this, they say, he could not do. In support of this last contention they rely on *Re Plumptre's Marriage Settlement*,[49] *Re Pryce*,[50] and *Re Kay's Settlement*.[51]

"The plaintiff, on the other hand, contends that, as he already holds the investments, no question of his having to enforce the covenant arises. The fund having come without impropriety into his hands is now, he says, impressed in his hands with the trusts on which he ought to hold it under the settlement; and because of the covenant it does not lie in the mouth of the defendants to say that he should hold it in trust for Helen's estate. He relies on *Re Bowden*[52] in which case a lady by a voluntary settlement purported to assign to trustees *inter alia* such property as she should become entitled to under the will of her father, who was still alive, and auhorised the trustees to receive the property and give receipts for it. In due course her father died and the property to which the lady became entitled under his will was transferred to the trustees of the settlement. Many years later the lady claimed that the property belonged to her absolutely. Bennett, J. [held] that she was not entitled to the property.

---

49 [1910] 1 Ch. 609.
50 [1917] 1 Ch. 234.
51 [1939] Ch. 329.
52 [1936] Ch. 71.

The plaintiff also relies on *Re Adlard's Settlement Trust*,[53] where Vaisey J. followed *Re Bowden*,[54] and on the observations of Upjohn J., in *Re Burton's Settlements*.[55]

"Counsel for the defendants says that *Re Bowden* and *Re Adlard's Settlement Trust* are distinguishable from the present case because in each of those cases the fund had reached the hands of the trustees of the relevant settlement and was held by them in that capacity, whereas in the present case the fund is, as he maintains, in the hands of the plaintiff in the capacity of trustee of the will and not in the capacity of trustee of the settlement. He says that *Re Burton's Settlements*,[56] the complicated facts of which I forbear to set out here, should be distinguished on the ground that, when the settlement there in question was made, the trustee of that settlement and the trustee of the settlement under which the settlor had expectations was the same, so that the settlor by her settlement gave directions to the trustee of the settlement under which she had expectations, who then already held the relevant fund.

"Counsel for the plaintiff says that the capacity in which the trustee has become possessed of the fund is irrelevant. Thus in *Strong* v. *Bird*,[57] an imperfect gift was held to be completed by the donee obtaining probate of the donor's will of which he was executor, notwithstanding that the donor died intestate as to her residue and that the donee was not a person entitled as on her intestacy. Similarly in *Re James*,[58] a grant of administration to two administrators was held to perfect an imperfect gift by the intestate to one of them, who had no beneficial interest in the intestate's estate.

"In my judgment the circumstance that the plaintiff holds the fund because he was appointed a trustee of the will is irrelevant. He is at law the owner of the fund and the means by which he became so have no effect on the quality of his legal ownership. The question is: for whom, if any one, does he hold the fund in equity? In other words, who can successfully assert an equity against him disentitling him to stand on his legal right? It seems to me to be indisputable that Helen, if she were alive, could not do so,[59] for she has solemnly covenanted under seal to assign the fund to the plaintiff and the defendants can stand in no better position. It is, of course, true that the object of the covenant was not that the plaintiff should retain the property for his own benefit, but that he should hold it on the trusts of the settlement. It is also true that, if it were necessary to enforce performance of the covenant, equity would not assist the beneficiaries under the settlement, because they are mere volunteers; and that for the same reason the plaintiff, as trustee of the settlement, would not be bound to enforce the covenant and would not be constrained by the court to do so, and indeed, it seems, might be constrained by the court not to do so. As matters stand, however, there is no occasion to invoke the assistance of equity to enforce the performance of the covenant. It is for the defendants to invoke the assistance of equity to make good their claim to the fund. To do so successfully they must show that the plaintiff cannot conscientiously withhold it from them. When they seek to do this, he

---

53 [1954] Ch. 29.
54 [1936] Ch. 71.
55 [1955] Ch. 82, 104.
56 [1955] Ch. 82.
57 (1874) L.R. 18 Eq. 315.
58 (1935) Ch. 449.
59 Is this right in view of *Re Brooks's S.T.* [1939] 1 Ch. 993, *supra*, p. 247?

can point to the covenant which, in my judgment, relieves him from any
fiduciary obligation that he would otherwise owe to the defendants as Helen's
representatives. In so doing the plaintiff is not seeking to enforce an equitable
remedy against the defendants on behalf of persons who could not enforce
such a remedy themselves: he is relying on the combined effect of his legal
ownership of the fund and his legal right to enforce the covenant. That an
action on the covenant might be statute-barred is irrelevant, for there is no
occasion for such an action.

"Had someone other than the plaintiff been the trustee of the will and held
the fund, the result of this part of the case would, in my judgment, have been
different; and it may seem strange that the rights of the parties should depend
on the appointment of the plaintiff as a trustee of the will in 1946, which for
present purposes may have been a quite fortuitous event. The result, however,
in my judgment, flows—and flows, I think, quite rationally—from the consideration that the rules of equity derive from the tenderness of a court of equity
for the consciences of the parties. *There would have been nothing unconscientious in Helen or her personal representatives asserting her equitable interests
under trusts of the will against a trustee who was not a covenantee under clause 7
of the settlement,*[60] and it would have been unconscientious for such a trustee to
disregard those interests. Having obtained a transfer of the fund, it would not
have been unconscientious in Helen to refuse to honour her covenant, because
the beneficiaries under her settlement were mere volunteers: nor seemingly
would the court have regarded it as unconscientious in the plaintiff to have
abstained from enforcing the covenant either specifically or in damages, for the
reason, apparently, that he would have been under no obligation to obtain for
the volunteers indirectly what they could not obtain directly. In such circumstances Helen or her personal representatives could have got and retained the
fund. In the circumstances of the present case, on the other hand, it is not
unconscientious in the plaintiff to withhold from Helen's estate the fund which
Helen covenanted that he should receive: on the contrary, it would have been
unconscientious in Helen to seek to deprive the plaintiff of that fund, and her
personal representatives can be in no better position. The inadequacy of the
volunteers' equity against Helen and her estate consequently is irrelevant, for
that equity does not come into play; but they have a good equity as against the
plaintiff, because it would be unconscientious in him to retain as against them
any property which he holds in consequence of the provisions of the
settlement.

"For these reasons I am of opinion that in the events which have happened
the plaintiff now holds the fund in question on the trusts of the marriage
settlement, and I will so declare."

### WILLIAMS v. COMMISSIONERS OF INLAND REVENUE

New Zealand Court of Appeal [1965] N.Z.L.R. 395.

Williams, who had a life interest under a trust, executed a voluntary deed, in
which "the assignor by way of gift hereby assigns to the assignee for the
religious purposes of the Parish of the Holy Trinity Gisborne for the four years
commencing on June 30, 1960 the first £500 of the net income which shall
accrue to the assignor personally while he lives in each of the said four years

---

[60] Author's italics.

from the Trust. . . . And the assignor hereby declares that he is trustee for the sole use and benefit of the assignee for the purpose aforesaid of so much (if any) of the said income as may not be capable of assignment (or may come to his hands)."

The question arose whether Williams had effectively divested himself of his interest in the £500 so as not to be liable for income tax on it. The New Zealand Court of Appeal held that he had not.

TURNER J. (delivering the judgment of North P. and himself) said: "Mr. Thorp, for the appellant, submitted that what was assigned by this document was a defined share in the existing life estate of the assignor in the trust property, and hence that the deed of assignment took effect, as at its date, to divest the assignor of the annual sums of £500 so that he did not thereafter derive them for taxation purposes in the years under consideration. For the respondent Commissioner it was contended that the deed was ineffective to divest the assignor of the sums, and that its effect was no more than that of an order upon the trustees still revocable by the assignor until payment.

"The life interest of the appellant in the trust was at the date of the execution of the deed an existing equitable interest. This cannot be doubted, and it was so conceded by the learned Solicitor-General. Being an existing interest, it was capable in equity of immediate effective assignment. Such an assignment could be made without consideration, if it immediately passed the equitable estate: *Kekewich* v. *Manning*.[61] There is no doubt that if the deed before us had purported to assign, not 'the first £500,' but the whole of the appellant's life interest under the trust, such an assignment would have been good in equity.

"But while equity will recognise a voluntary assignment of an existing equitable interest, it will refuse to recognise in favour of a volunteer an assignment of an interest, either legal or equitable, not existing at the date of the assignment, but to arise in the future. Not yet existing, such property cannot be owned, and what may not be owned may not be effectively assigned: *Holroyd* v. *Marshall*.[62] If, not effectively assigned, it is made the subject of an agreement to assign it, such an agreement may be good in equity, and become effective upon the property coming into existence but if, and only if, the agreement is made for consideration (as in *Spratt* v. *Commissioner of Inland Revenue*[63]), for equity will not assist a volunteer: *In re Ellenborough*.[64]

"The deed on which this appeal is founded was not made for consideration. The simple question is therefore—was that which it purported to assign (*viz.* 'the first five hundred pounds of the net income which shall accrue') an existing property right, or was it a mere expectancy, a future right not yet in existence? If the former, counsel agree that the deed was effective as an immediate assignment: if the latter, it is conceded by Mr. Thorp that it could not in the circumstances of this case have effect.

"What then was it that the assignor purported to assign? What he had was the life interest of a *cestui que trust* in a property or partnership adventure vested in or carried on by trustees for his benefit. Such a life interest exists in equity as soon as the deed of trust creating it is executed and delivered.

---

[61] (1851) 1 De G.M. & G. 176; 42 E.R. 519.
[62] (1862) 10 H.L.C. 191, 210; 11 E.R. 999, 1006, *per* Lord Westbury L.C.
[63] [1964] N.Z.L.R. 272.
[64] [1903] 1 Ch. 697.

Existing, it is capable of immediate assignment. We do not doubt that where it is possible to assign a right completely it is possible to assign an undivided interest in it. The learned Solicitor-General was therefore right, in our opinion, in conceding that if here, instead of purporting to assign 'the first £500 of the income,' the assignor had purported to assign (say) an undivided one-fourth share in his life estate, then he would have assigned an existing right, and in the circumstances effectively.

"But in our view, as soon as he quantified the sum in the way here attempted, the assignment became one not of a share or a part of his right, but of moneys which should arise from it. Whether the sums mentioned were ever to come into existence in whole or in part could not at the date of assignment be certain. In any or all of the years designated the net income might conceivably be less than five hundred pounds; in some or all of them the operations of the trust might indeed result in a loss. The first £500 of the net income, then, might or might not (judging the matter on the date of execution of the deed) in fact have any existence.

"We accordingly reject Mr. Thorp's argument that what was here assigned was a part or share of the existing equitable right of the assignor. He did not assign part of his right to income; he assigned a right to a part of the income, a different thing. The £500 which was the subject of the purported assignment was five hundred pounds *out of the net income*. There could be no such income for any year until the operations of that year were complete, and it became apparent what debits were to be set off against the gross receipts. For these reasons we are of opinion that what was assigned here was money; and that was something which was not presently owned by the assignor. He had no more than an expectation of it, to arise, it is true, from an existing equitable interest—but that interest he did not purport to assign. . . .

"It was argued in the alternative by Mr. Thorp, but somewhat faintly that if the document were not effective as an assignment it was effective as a declaration of trust, and that this result was sufficient to divest the appellant of the enjoyment of the annual sums so that he did not derive them as income. It will be recalled in this regard that the text of the deed includes an express declaration of trust. Mr. Thorp's submission was that this express declaration is effective even if the assignment fails. We agree that there may be circumstances in which a purported assignment, ineffective for insufficiency of form or perhaps through lack of notice, may yet perhaps be given effect by equity by reason of the assignor having declared himself to be a trustee; but it is useless to seek to use this device in the circumstances of the present case. Property which is not presently owned cannot presently be impressed with a trust any more than it can be effectively assigned; property which is not yet in existence may be the subject of a present agreement to impress it with a trust when it comes into the hands of the donor; but equity will not enforce such an agreement at the instance of the *cestui que trust* in the absence of consideration: *Ellison* v. *Ellison*.[65] For the same reasons therefore as apply in this case to the argument on assignment Mr. Thorp's second alternative submission must also fail."

## V. Exceptions to the Rule that Equity will not Assist a Volunteer

There seem to be three equitable and two statutory exceptions.

---

[65] (1802) 6 Ves.Jun. 656, 662, *per* Lord Eldon.

## 1. *Equitable exceptions*

(a) *The rule in* Strong *v.* Bird.[66] This has already been considered, pp. 233–236, *supra*.

(b) *Donationes mortis causa.*[67] Cases of *donationes mortis causa* sometimes provide an exception to the rule that equity will not perfect an imperfect gift. A *donatio mortis causa* must comply with the following essential requirements:

   (i) The donor must have made the gift in contemplation though not necessarily in expectation of death.

  (ii) He must have delivered the subject-matter of the gift to the donee or transferred to him the means or part of the means of getting at that subject-matter, *e.g.* a key without retaining a duplicate key.

 (iii) The circumstances must have been such as to establish that the gift was to be absolute and complete only on the donor's death so as to be revocable before then. A condition to this effect need not be expressed and will normally be implied from the fact that the gift was made when the donor was ill.[68]

Since, in the case of a chose in action, physical delivery is impossible, it follows that the title of the donee will not be completely vested at the death of the donor. The question is, therefore, whether the donee can, as a volunteer, compel the personal representatives of the donor to complete the gift. Equity will not grant its assistance to the donee in every such case; it will do so only in those cases in which the donor has delivered to the donee a document which is an index of title to the chose in action, *i.e.* a document the possession or production of which is necessary in order to entitle the possessor or producer to payment of the money as property purported to be given.[69] It is not necessary that the document should contain all the terms on which the subject-matter of the chose in action is held.[70] In the case of a bank deposit book, delivery of the book is sufficient to pass the money in the deposit account if the bank insists on production of the book before paying out. Delivery of title deeds to land or of share certificates is capable of amounting to a *d.m.c.* of the land[71] or of the shares.[72] Delivery of a donor's own cheque cannot amount to a *d.m.c.* of the sum represented by the cheque,[73] although delivery of a cheque payable to the donor can amount to a *d.m.c.*[74]

---

[66] (1874) L.R. 18 Eq. 315.

[67] See Hanbury & Maudsley, pp. 134–137, Pettit, pp. 101–106.

[68] See *Re Lillingston* [1952] 2 All E.R. 184; *Re Mustapha* (1891) 8 T.L.R. 160.

[69] *Moore* v. *Darton* (1851) 4 De G. & Sm. 517; *Re Dillon* (1890) 44 Ch.D. 76; *Birch* v. *Treasury Solicitor* [1951] Ch. 298.

[70] *Birch* v. *Treasury Solicitor* [1951] Ch. 298; disapproving dicta in *Re Weston* [1902] 1 Ch. 680 and *Delgoffe* v. *Fader* [1939] Ch. 922.

[71] *Sen* v. *Headley* [1991] 2 All E.R. 636 (under appeal to H.L.).

[72] This clearly should be the position if a share transfer form is properly executed and handed over; *Staniland* v. *Willott* (1850) 3 Mac. & G. 664; *Re Craven's Estate* [1937] Ch. 423; or if land is actually conveyed; *Cooper* v. *Seversen* (1955) 1 D.L.R. (2d) 161.

[73] *Re Beaumont* [1902] 1 Ch. 889; *Re Leaper* [1916] 1 Ch. 579.

[74] *Re Mead* (1880) 15 Ch.D. 651.

(c) *Equitable proprietary estoppel.* In some circumstances equity will prevent an owner of land, who has made an imperfect gift of some estate or interest in it, from asserting his title against the donee. The equity of the donee exists where he has expended money on the land in the mistaken belief that he has or will acquire an interest in it and the owner, knowing of the mistake, stood by and allowed the expenditure to be incurred. This type of equity has a wider sphere of operation than an estoppel of the ordinary kind, and in some cases nothing short of a conveyance of the owner's estate or interest to the donee will be sufficient to satisfy the equity.[75]

### 2. *Statutory exceptions*

The Settled Land Act 1925 provides two further exceptions to the rule.

(a) *Conveyance to an infant.* First, although after 1925 an infant cannot hold a legal estate in land, an attempt to transfer a legal estate to him is not wholly ineffective. It operates as an agreement for value by the grantor to execute a settlement in favour of the infant, and in the meantime to hold the land in trust for him.[76]

(b) *Imperfect settlement by an instrument* inter vivos. Secondly, section 4 of the Settled Land Act 1925 requires a settlement *inter vivos* to be created by a proper vesting deed and trust instrument. An instrument other than a vesting deed will not operate to pass the legal estate, but by virtue of the statute it will operate as a trust instrument. The trustees may then execute the proper vesting deed, and must do so on the request of the tenant for life or statutory owner.[77]

## PROBLEMS

1. Under A's father's will trusts property is settled on trust for W for life, remainder to his sons A and B equally, but W has express power to appoint the capital between A and B as she sees fit. If A assigns *inter alia* "All my interest under my father's will trusts to Bigg Bank on trust for" X for life, remainder to Y, advise the bank if W dies either (i) without having made an appointment so that A receives £450,000, or (ii) having appointed £500,000 to A a month before her death, so that A's half share on her death brings him assets worth £200,000.

Would your advice differ if, instead, A had assigned *inter alia* "all such assets whatsoever as shall come into my possession on my mother's death under the terms of my father's will trusts"? Would it matter if these words were followed by "but pending transfer of such assets I shall hold all my interest under my father's will trusts on the trusts applicable to such assets"?

Would any of your advice to the bank differ if unknown to A the bank happened to be trustee of his father's will trusts?

---

[75] See pp. 59–61, *supra.*
[76] Settled Land Act 1925, s. 27(1); Law of Property Act 1925, ss. 1(6), 19(4).
[77] Settled Land Act 1925, s. 9.

2. (a) Under the terms of a voluntary settlement made five years ago Prudence, a spinster, covenanted under seal with the trustees of the settlement to transfer 9,000 I.C.I. ordinary shares to the trustees on trust for any husband Prudence might marry for life, with remainder to the children of such marriage and in default thereof for Prudence's next-of-kin as if she had never married.

Two years ago Prudence married Alfonso who has now left her. Prudence has not performed these covenants and seeks your advice as the trustees have now died and Alfonso is the executor of the last surviving trustee, so having his powers under section 18(2) of the Trustee Act 1925.

(b) What is the effect if O, the object of a special power of appointment, covenants with A and B to transfer to them any property appointed to him to the intent that A and B shall hold the benefit of the covenant on trust for Y for life, remainder to Z?

3. Five years ago, 26-year-old Sheila executed a voluntary settlement whereby she assigned to Barclays Bank as her trustee all property to which she might become entitled under anybody's will or intestacy and she covenanted with the bank[78] to transfer to it upon the trusts of the settlement the sum of £30,000 to which she would become entitled under another trust if she attained 30.

Last year Sheila's mother died, by her will appointing Barclays Bank her executor and leaving £20,000 to Sheila. After receiving the £30,000 on attaining 30 Sheila, who then banked with Lloyds Bank, sent off her cheque for that sum in favour of Barclays Bank but stopped the cheque before it was met and sent off a cheque for £12,000 in its place. This cheque was cashed.

Sheila now claims to be entitled to recover this £12,000 and to be under no obligation to pay the £18,000 balance. She further demands that Barclays Bank pay her the £20,000 due to her under her mother's will. Advise the bank.

Would it make any difference if Sheila had died last month having appointed Barclays Bank executor of her will and having left everything to her husband, Barry, whom she had married last year and who persisted with her claims and demands?

4. "When it comes to Chancery judges directing trustees not to sue on covenants, that are not themselves the subject-matter of a trust, the judges cannot justify their directions simply on the negative basis that 'Equity will not assist a volunteer' because Equity is positively intervening to prevent trustees exercising their common law rights." Discuss.

5. On Albert's hundredth birthday he asked his three children to visit him in bed as he felt most unwell.

To Maud he said, "Here is a large envelope for you but don't open it till you've left me." To George he said, "Here is my share certificate for 4,000 ordinary shares in P.Q. Ltd., together with a transfer in your favour which I've signed. You can also have my car." To Emma he said, "I feel awful. If I die I want you to have everything else including this house and all my furniture. All the necessary papers are in this deed box underneath my bed. Here is the only key."

Albert died in his sleep that very night. His will appointed George his executor and left everything equally amongst his children.

---

[78] Would it have been better for the bank (and the beneficiaries under Sheila's voluntary settlement) if Sheila had, instead, expressly assigned to the bank her contingent equitable interest in £30,000 or had, additionally, declared herself trustee of such interest on the trusts of her voluntary settlement?

In Maud's envelope were a cheque for £2,000 and the deeds of some freehold land and on the last conveyance to Albert he had written, "I hold this for Maud." In the deed box Emma found several share certificates, Albert's Trustee Savings Bank passbook showing a balance of £1,000, and a receipt acknowledging that the bank had the safe custody of the title deeds to the house. George was unable to get himself registered in respect of the 4,000 shares as the directors refused to register him and were entitled to do so under the company's articles.

Advise Albert's executor on the distribution of Albert's estate.

6. Is the following approach to completely and incompletely constituted trusts a sound one?

(1) Has a trust been completely constituted by a declaration of trust by S himself or by property having been effectively given by him to trustees, bearing in mind that the strict rules as to gifts have been attenuated by *Strong* v. *Bird* principles and *donatio mortis causa* principles and that if the intent is clear there may be a completely constituted trust of a covenant?

(2) If a trust is incompletely constituted is the beneficiary seeking to enforce the trust
   (a) a covenanting party,
   (b) someone who gave consideration for the settlor's covenant,
   (c) someone within the marriage consideration if the settlement was made in consideration of marriage?

(3) If a beneficiary cannot enforce the trust can the trustees as covenantees sue at common law and hold the damages on trust—but for whom?[79]

### Section 2. Discretionary and Protective Trusts[80]

If a settlor wishes to provide for B by creating a trust for the benefit of B (*e.g.* conferring a life interest upon B) he ought to consider whether his intention will best be carried out by conferring a distinct fixed interest upon B. After all, if B becomes bankrupt his life interest like his other property will pass to his trustee in bankruptcy for the benefit of his creditors. Moreover, B himself could sell his life interest and lose the proceeds on a gambling holiday so as then to be unprovided for.

If, however, B were merely an object of a discretionary trust[81] B would have no right to any of the trust income: he would merely have a hope that the trustees' discretion would be exercised in his favour. The essence of a discretionary trust is, of course, the complete discretion of the trustees as to the amount of income, if any, to be paid to the various objects of the trust. If the trustees have no power to

---

[79] If the trustee-covenantee assigned the benefit of the covenant to the person beneficially claiming the subject-matter of the covenant should the covenant not still be held on resulting trust for the settlor? Similarly, if the trustee resigned on appointing the alleged beneficiary to be trustee.

[80] See generally Sheridan, "Discretionary Trusts" (1957) 21 Conv.(N.S.) 55; "Protective Trusts," *Ibid.* 110; A. J. Hawkins (1967) 31 Conv.(N.S.) 117.

[81] For the nature of an interest under a discretionary trust see *Gartside* v. *I.R.C.* [1968] A.C. 553; *Re Weir's Settlement* [1969] 1 Ch. 657 (reversed [1971] Ch. 145 on grounds not affecting these principles); *McPhail* v. *Doulton* [1971] A.C. 424. For an example of a draft discretionary settlement see *supra*, p. 13.

retain income for accumulation the whole income[82] has to be distributed though only amongst such of the objects and in such proportions as the trustees see fit.[83] Only if all the objects of the discretionary trust are each *sui juris* and between themselves absolutely entitled to the income and capital of the trust and call for the trustees to transfer the trust property to them (or to their nominee) do the trustees' discretions determine: *Re Smith, infra.* Till then neither individually nor collectively do the beneficiaries have an interest in possession.[84]

If B is made an object of a discretionary trust and then sells his interest or becomes bankrupt his assignee or trustee in bankruptcy has no more right than he to demand payment from the trustees. If the trustees do exercise their discretion in favour of B by paying money to him or delivering goods to him then B's assignee or trustee in bankruptcy is entitled to the money or goods.[85] Indeed, where the trustees have had notice of the assignment or bankruptcy but have still paid money to B they have been held liable to his assignee or trustee in bankruptcy for the money so paid.[86] It seems, however, that if the trustees spend trust money on the maintenance of B by paying third parties for food, clothes or accommodation for B then the assignee or trustee in bankruptcy will have no claim.[87]

Discretionary trusts thus have the advantage of protecting beneficiaries from themselves besides the obvious advantages of flexibility. However, there is the corresponding disadvantage that such trusts create uncertainty for a beneficiary since he has no fixed entitlement as he would have, say, if he had a life interest.

To tackle this disadvantage there arose the protective trust[88] conferring upon B a life (or lesser) interest determinable upon the bankruptcy of B or upon any other event which would deprive B of the right to receive all the income of the trust, whereupon a discretionary trust springs up in favour of B and his spouse and issue. It has long been established that whilst a condition or proviso for forfeiture of an interest on bankruptcy or attempted alienation of the interest is void a determinable limitation of an interest to last until bankruptcy or attempted alienation is valid.[89] The justification for such a distinction[90]

---

[82] An "exhaustive" discretionary trust: *Sainsbury* v. *I.R.C.* [1970] 1 Ch. 712.

[83] *Re Gourju's W.T.* [1943] Ch. 24; *Re Gulbenkian's Settlements (No. 2)* [1970] Ch. 408; *Re Allen Meyrick's W.T.* [1966] 1 W.L.R. 499.

[84] *Re Trafford* [1984] 1 All E.R. 1108; *Vestey* v. *I.R.C. (No. 2)* [1979] 2 All E.R. 225, 235–236.

[85] *Re Coleman* (1888) 39 Ch.D. 443. The assignment must be for value if the assignment of what B hopes to receive from an exercise of the trustees' discretion is to be enforceable once B has actually received property from the trustees; see p. 228, *supra*.

[86] *Re Neil* (1890) 62 L.T. 649; *Re Bullock* (1891) 60 L.J.Ch. 341 though *Re Ashby* [1892] 1 Q.B. 872 has created some uncertainty by indicating that an assignee or a trustee in bankruptcy can only claim to the extent to which sums paid are in excess of the amount necessary for B's maintenance: see Hardingham & Baxt's *Discretionary Trusts*, p. 144.

[87] *Re Coleman* (1888) 39 Ch.D. 443, 451; *Re Allan-Meyrick's W.T.* [1966] 1 W.L.R. 499.

[88] See the statutory form invoked by use of the phrase "protective trusts" set out in the Trustee Act 1925, s. 33, *infra*, p. 262. They have favoured treatment for inheritance tax purposes: Inheritance Tax Act 1984, s. 88.

[89] *Brandon* v. *Robinson* (1811) 18 Ves. 429; *Rochford* v. *Hackman* (1852) 9 Hare 475; *Re Leach* [1912] 2 Ch. 422.

[90] Generally see *Megarry & Wade*, pp. 67–75; Glanville Williams (1943) 59 L.Q.R. 343.

is that a limitation merely sets a natural limit to an interest whilst a condition or proviso cuts down an interest before it reaches its natural limit: if such a condition or proviso is void for being contrary to a course of devolution prescribed by law, in cutting down the natural length of an interest to prevent creditors obtaining the benefit of the interest, or for being repugnant to the nature of the alienable interest granted, then the whole natural interest is available for creditors and for alienation. A limitation, however, creates a determinable interest lasting until the limiting event happens and such interest itself is the whole natural interest. The conceptual difference between conditional and determinable interests may be stated as the difference between giving someone a 12-inch ruler subject to being cut down to a six-inch ruler in certain conditions and giving someone a six-inch ruler in the first place.

Protective trusts are now normally created by use of the shorthand phrase "protective trusts" which invokes the detailed trusts set out in section 33 of the Trustee Act 1925, *infra*. It is also quite common in the cause of fiscal flexibility to insert some express provision enabling the protected life tenant during the currency of his determinable life interest, if he obtains the written approval of the trustees, to enter into arrangements with the other beneficiaries under the settlement for dividing up the trust funds or otherwise rearranging the beneficial interests as if he had an absolute life interest. Indeed, the protected life tenant (especially, if he is the settlor) may be given a general power of appointment exercisable only with the written consent of the trustees (for this purpose being a trust corporation or not less than two persons other than or in addition to the protected life tenant) so as to be able to vary the beneficial or administrative provisions of the settlement or even completely to revoke the settlement.[91] For the reasons set out in an extract *infra* from a case note by R.E.M. on *Re Richardson's W.T.*, *infra* it has also become not uncommon to create a series of protective trusts, *e.g.* one set until a beneficiary is 30, another from 30 to 40, a third from 40 to 50 and another for the rest of his life.

As will be seen upon examining section 33 of the Trustee Act 1925 a protective trust contains three parts: (1) a life or lesser interest determinable on certain events; (2) a forfeiture clause specifying the determining events; (3) a discretionary trust which arises after forfeiture.

### RE SMITH, PUBLIC TRUSTEE v. ASPINALL

Chancery Division [1928] Ch. 915; 97 L.J.Ch. 441; 140 L.T. 369.

The testator by his will directed his trustees to stand possessed of one-fourth of his residuary estate upon trust during the life of the defendant Mrs. Aspinall

---

[91] Such a general power falls to be treated as a special power for perpetuity purposes so that the perpetuity period runs not from the date of the exercise of the power of appointment but from the date of the settlement creating the power: *Re Earl of Coventry's Indentures* [1974] Ch. 77; Perpetuities and Accumulations Act 1964, s. 7.

at their absolute discretion and in such manner as they should think fit "to pay or apply the whole or any part of the annual income of such one-fourth and the investments thereof or if they shall think fit from time to time any part of the capital thereof unto or for the maintenance and personal support or benefit of the said Lilian Aspinall or as to the income thereof but not as to the capital for the maintenance education support or benefit of all or any one or more of the children of the said Lilian Aspinall and either themselves so to apply the same or to pay the same for that purpose to any other person or persons without seeing to the application thereof. And during the period of twenty-one years from my death if the said Lilian Aspinall shall live so long to accumulate the surplus if any of such income at compound interest by investing the same and the resulting income thereof in any of the investments aforesaid by way of addition to the capital of such fund as aforesaid and so as to be subject to the same trusts as are hereby declared concerning the same. And after the death of the said Lilian Aspinall as regards both capital and income both original and accumulated in trust for the child or children of the said Lilian Aspinall who either before or after her decease shall being a son or sons attain the age of twenty-one years or being a daughter or daughters attain that age or marry and if more than one in equal shares." Mrs. Aspinall had three children, all of whom attained the age of twenty-one years, and one of whom died before the proceedings in this summons. Mrs. Aspinall was of an age when it was quite impossible that she should have any further issue. In those circumstances Mrs. Aspinall, the two surviving children and the legal personal representatives of the deceased child all joined in executing a mortgage to the defendants the Legal and General Assurance Company, which took the form of an assignment to the assurance company of all the interests that Mrs. Aspinall and the three children took under the will in any event.

ROMER J.: "The question I have to determine is whether the Legal and General Assurance Company are now entitled to call upon the trustees to pay the whole of the income to them. It will be observed from what I have said that the whole of this share is now held by the trustees upon trusts under which they are bound to apply the whole income and eventually pay over or apply the whole capital to Mrs. Aspinall and the three children or some or one of them. So far as the income is concerned they are obliged to pay it or apply it for her benefit or to pay it or apply it for the benefit of the children. So far as regards the capital, they have a discretion to pay it, and to apply it for her benefit and subject to that, they must hold it upon trust for the children. Mrs. Aspinall, the two surviving children and the representatives of the deceased child are between them entitled to the whole fund. In those circumstances it appears to me, notwithstanding the discretion which is reposed in the trustees, under which discretion they could select one or more of the people I have mentioned as recipients of the income, and might apply part of the capital for the benefit of Mrs. Aspinall and so take it away from the children, that the four of them, if they were all living, could come to the court and say to the trustees: 'Hand over the fund to us.' It appears to me that that is in accordance with the decision of the Court of Appeal in a case of *Re Nelson*,[92] of which a transcript of the judgments has been handed to me, and is in accordance with principle. What is the principle? As I understand it it is this. Where there is a

---

[92] [1928] Ch. 920n.

trust under which trustees have a discretion as to applying the whole or part of a fund to or for the benefit of a particular person, that particular person cannot come to the trustees, and demand the fund; for the whole fund has not been given to him but only so much as the trustees think fit to let him have. But when the trustees have no discretion as to the amount of the fund to be applied, the fact that the trustees have a discretion as to the method in which the whole of the fund shall be applied for the benefit of the particular person does not prevent that particular person from coming and saying: 'Hand over the fund to me.' That appears to be the result of the two cases which were cited to me: *Green* v. *Spicer*[93] and *Younghusband* v. *Gisborne*.[94]

"Now this third case arises. What is to happen where the trustees have a discretion whether they will apply the whole or only a portion of the fund for the benefit of one person, but are obliged to apply the rest of the fund, so far as not applied for the benefit of the first-named person, to or for the benefit of a second-named person? There, two people together are the sole objects of the discretionry trust and, between them, are entitled to have the whole fund applied to them or for their benefit. It has been laid down by the Court of Appeal in the case to which I have referred that, in such a case as that, you treat all the people put together just as though they formed one person, for whose benefit the trustees were directed to apply the whole of a particular fund. The case before the Court of Appeal was this: A testator had directed his trustees to stand possessed of one-third of his residuary estate upon trust during the lifetime of the testator's son Arthur Hector Nelson: 'to apply the income thereof for the benefit of himself and his wife and child or children or of any of such persons to the exclusion of the others or other of them as my trustees shall think fit.' What happened was something very similar to what happened in the case before me. Hector Nelson, his wife and the only existing child of the marriage joined together in asking the trustees to hand over the income to them, and it was held by the Court of Appeal that the trustees were obliged to comply with the request, in other words, to treat all those persons who were the only members of the class for whose benefit the income could be applied as forming together an individual for whose benefit a fund has to be applied by the trustee without any discretion as to the amount so to be applied.

"There will, consequently, be a declaration that, in the events which have happened, the plaintiff is bound to pay the whole of the income of the one-fourth to the defendant society during the lifetime of Mrs. Aspinall, or until the mortgage is discharged."

### The Trustee Act 1925

Section 33.—(1) Where any income, including an annuity or other periodical income payment, is directed to be held on protective trusts for the benefit of any person[95] (in this section called "the principal beneficiary") for the period of his life or for any less period, then, during that period (in this section called the "trust period") the said income shall, without prejudice to any prior interest, be held on the following trusts, namely:

> (i) Upon trust for the principal beneficiary during the trust period or until he, whether before or after the termination of any prior interest, does

---

93 (1830) 1 Russ. & My. 395.
94 (1844) 1 Coll.C.C. 400.
95 Person means a human being and not a company: *IRC* v. *Brandenburg* [1982] S.T.C. 555, 565, 569.

or attempts to do or suffers any act or thing, or until any event happens, other than an advance under any statutory or express power,[96] whereby, if the said income were payable during the trust period to the principal beneficiary absolutely during that period, he would be deprived of the right to receive the same or any part thereof, in any of which cases, as well as on the termination of the trust period, whichever first happens, this trust of the said income shall fail or determine;

(ii) If the trust aforesaid fails or determines during the subsistence of the trust period, then, during the residue of that period, the said income shall be held upon trust for the application thereof[97] for the maintenance or support, or otherwise for the benefit, of all or any one or more exclusively of the other or others of the following persons (that is to say)—

  (a) the principal beneficiary and his or her wife or husband, if any, and his or her children or more remote issue, if any; or

  (b) if there is no wife or husband or issue of the principal beneficiary in existence, the principal beneficiary and the persons who would, if he were actually dead, *be entitled to the trust property or the income thereof* or to the annuity fund, if any, or arrears of the annuity, as the case may be; as the trustees in their absolute discretion, without being liable to account for the exercise of such discretion, think fit.

(2) This section does not apply to trusts coming into operation before the commencement of this Act, and has effect subject to any variation[98] of the implied trusts aforesaid contained in the instrument creating the trust.

(3) Nothing in this section operates to validate any trust which would, if contained in the instrument creating the trust, be liable to be set aside.[99]

## RE RICHARDSON'S WILL TRUSTS

Chancery Division [1958] Ch. 504; [1958] 2 W.L.R. 414; 102 S.J. 176; [1958] 1 All E.R. 538.

By his will the testator gave £2,000 to his trustees to hold the income on protective trusts for the benefit of his grandson Douglas William Llewellyn Evans during his life and until he attained the age of thirty-five in accordance with section 33 of the Trustee Act 1925. If, on attaining that age, the grandson had not attempted to do or suffer any act or thing or no event had happened

---

[96] See *Re Hodgson* [1913] 1 Ch. 34; *Re Shaw's Settlement* [1951] Ch. 833; *Re Rees* [1954] Ch. 202; *cf. Re Stimpson's Trusts* [1931] 2 Ch. 77, which should now be confined to its own facts, that is where an express advancement clause is lacking and where no use is made of s. 33 of the Trustee Act. Even so, it must be regarded as of doubtful authority.

[97] The income must be distributed: *Re Gourju's W.T.* [1934] Ch. 24.

[98] See, *e.g. Re Wittke* [1944] Ch. 166: bequest of residue upon protective trusts for testatrix's sister, no period being specified, but trustees being given a power to pay capital to the sister from time to time. *Held* by Vaisey J. that a protected life interest had been created, for, had an absolute interest been given, it would have been open to the sister to call for an immediate transfer of the capital, which would have been inconsistent with the power given to the trustees.

[99] This preserves *inter alia* the rule that although a settlor may validly create in favour of another person a life interest determinable by bankruptcy, such a limitation in favour of himself is void against his trustee in bankruptcy. See *Re Burroughs-Fowler* [1916] 2 Ch. 251; *Re Detmold* (1889) 40 Ch.D. 585 (where a determining event, other than bankruptcy, occurred, and it was held that the life interest determined). See Sect. 3, *infra*.

(other than any advance under any statutory or express power) whereby he would then or at any time thereafter have been deprived of the right to receive the capital or income or any part thereof, he was to receive the capital absolutely. If, on the other hand, he had made such attempt or sufferance or such event had happened, then he was to receive the income on protective trusts for the rest of his life. If he died before attaining the age of thirty-five or the protective trusts for his benefit after his attaining that age came into operation, then on his death the capital was to go to his children, who attained the age of twenty-one, if more than one in equal shares.

On November 15, 1954, the grandson's wife obtained a decree absolute of divorce against him. On June 3, 1955, an order was made in the Probate, Divorce and Admiralty Division charging the grandson's interest under the will with a payment of £50 per annum interim maintenance in favour of his wife. On October 24, 1955, the grandson attained the age of thirty-five. On August 27, 1956, he was adjudicated bankrupt.

The Public Trustee (who was the sole trustee of the will) took out a summons to have determined (1) whether the capital (a) vested in the grandson, Douglas William Llewellyn Evans, on his attaining the age of thirty-five (in which case his trustee in bankruptcy would now be entitled to it) or (b) by reason of the order of June 3, 1955, the grandson forfeited his interest therein; (2) if the grandson had forfeited his interest in the capital, whether the capital was held (a) during the remainder of his life on the discretionary trusts provided for in section 33(1)(ii) of the Trustee Act 1925 and after his death on the trusts in the testator's will expressed to take effect in the event of the protective trusts for his benefit after his attaining the age of thirty-five having come into operation, or (b) upon some other trusts.

DANCKWERTS J.: "In considering whether there has been a forfeiture, the first question is: What was the effect of the order of June 3, 1955, on the footing that it was never completed by the execution of any deed? The matter has been very well argued before me, and I have been taken through a number of cases. I am satisfied, upon three decisions, that clearly the effect of that order in itself was to create an equitable charge, if that were possible, upon the interest of Douglas William Llewellyn Evans under his grandfather's will. The cases in question are *Waterhouse* v. *Waterhouse*,[1] *Maclurcan* v. *Maclurcan*[2] and *Hyde* v. *Hyde*.[3]

"That being so, the next thing to consider is: What was the effect of that order which created that equitable charge? There are two portions of the will which involve the question of forfeiture. First of all, there is the part which invokes section 33 of the Trustee Act 1925 before the grandson had attained the age of thirty-five, and then the part which describes what is to happen upon his attaining that age. As to the first part, the trusts of the will before he attains the age of thirty-five years must be taken to be expressed in this form: 'Upon trust for the principal beneficiary'—that is, the grandson—'during the trust period or until he . . . does or attempts to do or suffers any act or thing, or until any event happens (other than any advance under any statutory or express power) whereby, if the said income were payable during the trust period to the principal beneficiary absolutely during that period, he would be

---

[1] [1893] P. 284.
[2] (1897) 77 L.T. 474.
[3] [1948] P. 198.

deprived of the right to receive the same or any part thereof.' It seems to me that the effect of the order was to create, or attempt to create, an equitable charge on his interest under the testator's will. When this order was made, if he had been absolutely entitled, he would have been deprived of the right to receive part of the income, because part of the income was to be payable to his former wife to the extent of £50 a year. Consequently, it seems to me that there was a forfeiture at that date; but in any case under the express terms of the will he never succeeded in attaining his absolute interest, and the protective trusts which were to take effect during the rest of his life in accordance with section 33 of the Trustee Act 1925 came into effect because the direction was, if such event had happened, that the protective trusts were to come into effect, and the fund in question is referred to as the fund of which 'he would then or at any time thereafter be deprived of the right to receive the capital or income or any part thereof.' When, therefore, the order of the Divorce Division was made on June 3, 1955, an event happened whereby he would either then or at some time thereafter 'be deprived of the right to receive the capital or income' or any part of it.

"Consequently, I have come to the conclusion that, in the events which have happened in this case, by the time that Douglas William Llewellyn Evans became bankrupt his interest under the will had been forfeited, and a discretionary trust had come into effect. Consequently, the trustee in bankruptcy cannot take anything under the testator's will.

"I will make a declaration that by reason of the order dated June 3, 1955, the life interest of Douglas William Llewellyn Evans under the terms of the testator's will was determined, and that he did not become entitled to an absolute interest upon the attainment by him of thirty-five years, and that on the true construction of the will, and in the events which have happened, during the life of Douglas William Llewellyn Evans, the plaintiff as trustee holds the property during the rest of the life of Douglas William Llewellyn Evans and the income thereof upon the discretionary trusts laid down in section 33(1)(i) of the Trustee Act 1925, and after the death of the said Douglas William Llewellyn Evans as to the capital and income thereof upon the trusts in the testator's said will expressed then to take effect if the protective trusts for his benefit after his attaining the age of thirty-five years should come into operation."

### R. E. Megarry (1958) 74 L.Q.R. 184

"This sequence of events points a moral for draftsmen. Hitherto the normal course of drafting has been to give a life interest simply 'on protective trusts,' with or without variations. The result is that a single mistaken act by the beneficiary may deprive him of his determinable life interest and reduce him for the rest of his life to the status of merely one of the beneficiaries of a discretionary trust. *Re Richardson* suggests that there may be advantages in setting up a series of protective trusts, *e.g.* one set until the beneficiary is twenty-five, another from twenty-five to thirty-five, a third from thirty-five to forty-five, and another for the rest of his life. The result would be that a youthful indiscretion at, say, twenty-two, would not irretrievably condemn the beneficiary to the mere hopes of a beneficiary under a discretionary trust, dependent upon the exercise of the trustees' discretion, but would give him a fresh start when he was twenty-five. Again, a bankruptcy at the age of thirty would not *per se* mean that when he was twice that age he would still have not an income as of right, but a mere hope of a well-exercised discretion. Indeed, instead of relating the stages to the age of the beneficiary, they might be related to a period of time (*e.g.* five years) after the occurrence of any event which had made the initial trust pass from Stage 1 to Stage 2. England lacks the device of the spendthrift trust in the American sense, but it is far from clear that the fullest possible use is being made of the existing machinery of protective and discretionary trusts." [The American spendthrift trust is a result of most American jurisdictions allowing inalienable beneficial interests to be created.]

### Forfeiting Events

Whether the interest of the beneficiary is determined in the events which have happened is a question of construction of the forfeiture clause in each particular case. It is sometimes said that forfeiture clauses should be construed in favour of the principal beneficiary, but it must be remembered that he is not the sole object of the testator's bounty, and that there are other persons upon whom the testator intended to confer a benefit.[4] It is only if, after construing the clause, a doubt remains that this should be resolved in favour of the principal beneficiary, for "the burden is upon those who allege a forfeiture to satisfy the court that a forfeiture has occurred."[5]

The forfeiture clause contained in section 33 of the Trustee Act 1925 is very wide, for it includes not only the acts and omissions of the principal beneficiary, but also the happening of any event which deprives him of his right to receive the income or any part thereof. Such an event was the Trading with the Enemy Act 1939 and orders made thereunder, whereby the property of those resident in enemy territory vested in the Custodian of Enemy Property.[6] It was otherwise with express forfeiture clauses which were drafted in narrower terms. Thus in *Re Hall, Public Trustee* v. *Montgomery*[7] forfeiture was to occur "if the annuitant should alienate or charge her annuity or become bankrupt or do or suffer any act or thing whereby the said annuity or any part thereof would or might become vested in or payable to any other person." It was held by Uthwatt J. that the clause was directed to the forfeiture of the annuity in the event of the annuitant doing *personally* certain classes of things whereby she would be deprived of her annuity. Accordingly, the Trading with the Enemy Act 1939 did not bring about a forfeiture.

Apart from these special cases, involving the application of the Trading with the Enemy Act to protective trusts, the following events have been held to cause a forfeiture:

*Re Balfour's Settlement*[8]: the impounding by the trustees of part of the income of the principal beneficiary to repair a breach of trust

---

4 *Re Sartoris's Estate* [1892] 1 Ch. 11, 16.
5 *Re Baring's Settlement Trusts* [1940] Ch. 737 (Morton J.).
6 *e.g.* Trading with the Enemy (Custodian) Order 1939 (S.R. & O. 1939 No. 1198). Later orders contained a proviso that vesting in the custodian should not take place if it would cause a forfeiture (*e.g.* S.R. & O. 1945 No. 887).
7 [1944] Ch. 46; so too *Re Furness, Wilson* v. *Kenmare (No. 1)* [1944] 1 All E.R. 575; *Re Harris* [1945] Ch. 316; *Re Pozot's Settlement Trusts* [1952] Ch. 427.
8 [1938] Ch. 928.

committed by them in paying part of the trust fund to him at his own instigation.

*Re Walker*[9]: the bankruptcy of the principal beneficiary, even if this had occurred before the trust first came into operation.

*Re Baring's Settlement Trusts*[10]: an order of sequestration of the income for contempt of court, even though the contempt is subsequently purged.

*Re Dennis's Settlement Trusts*[11]: the execution by the principal beneficiary of a deed of variation relinquishing his right to part of the income in certain events.

*Re Richardson's W.T.*,[12] *supra*: an order of the court attempting to impose a charge which though ineffectual for that purpose was sufficient to bring about a forfeiture.

On the other hand no forfeiture occurred in the following cases:

*Re Tancred's Settlement*[13]: the appointment by the principal beneficiary of an attorney to receive the income, even though the attorney's expenses are to be deducted from the income, and the balance paid over to the principal beneficiary.

*Re Mair*[14]: the making by the court of an order under section 57 of the Trustee Act 1925 authorising capital moneys to be raised to enable the principal beneficiary to pay certain pressing liabilities: section 57 is an overriding section whose provisions are read into every settlement. cf. *Re Salting*,[15] where the scheme sanctioned by the court under section 57 involved the doing of certain acts by the principal beneficiary—and *his* omission to do them caused a forfeiture. The scheme provided for the life tenant to pay premiums on insurance policies with a proviso that the trustees were to pay the premiums out of his income if the premiums were not duly paid: his failure to pay was held to create a forfeiture.

*Re Westby's Settlement*[16]: the charge of a lunacy percentage upon the estate of a lunatic under section 148(3) of the Lunacy Act 1890 (now Mental Health Act 1983, s.106(6)), since the fees payable were to be regarded as management expenses, and, even if a charge was created by the section, it was not such an incumbrance as was contemplated by the forfeiture clause.[17]

9 [1939] Ch. 974.
10 [1940] Ch. 737.
11 [1942] Ch. 283; see (1942) 58 L.Q.R. 312.
12 See also *Edmonds* v. *Edmonds* [1965] 1 W.L.R. 58 (attachment of earnings order to secure former wife's maintenance held to cause forfeiture of husband's protected interest in pension fund).
13 [1903] 1 Ch. 715.
14 [1935] Ch. 562.
15 [1932] 2 Ch. 57.
16 [1950] Ch. 296; overruling *Re Custance's Settlements* [1946] Ch. 42; see also *Re Oppenheim's Will Trusts* [1950] Ch. 633 (appointment of receiver of person of unsound mind did not effect a forfeiture).
17 The same result was then achieved, independently of the cases, by the Law Reform (Miscellaneous Provisions) Act 1949, s. 8.

*Re Longman*[18]: a testatrix left the income of her residiary estate on certain trusts for her son under which he would forfeit his interest if he should "commit permit or suffer any act default or process whereby the said income or any part thereof would or might but for this present proviso become vested in or payable to any other person." The son authorised the trustee to pay his creditors specified sums out of a particular future dividend due on shares forming part of the residiary estate. The son later withdrew this authority, and the company afterwards did not declare a dividend. It was held by Danckwerts J. that the withdrawal of authority would not by itself prevent forfeiture[19]; but the failure to declare a dividend did, since the income of the residiary estate never included anything to which the authority could possibly have attached.

*General Accident Fire and Life Assurance Corporation Ltd.* v. *I.R.C.*[20]: order of the court diverting income from husband to wife and taking effect in priority to the protective trusts was held by the Court of Appeal not to create a forfeiture. Although the case turned on a narrow ground of construction of section 33 it seems better to treat it on the same basis as *Re Mair, supra* (order under section 57 of the Trustee Act): all protective trusts must be read as subject to the court's jurisdiction to make orders under section 57 of the Trustee Act and sections 24 and 31 of the Matrimonial Causes Act 1973.

An order of the court may sometimes do more than cause a forfeiture: it may destroy the protected life interest and discretionary trusts altogether. This happened in *Re Allsopp's Marriage Settlement Trusts*,[21] where an express protective trust was created by a marriage settlement in 1916 with discretionary trusts after forfeiture. In 1928 on the dissolution of the marriage the court made an order varying the marriage settlement by *extinguishing* the rights of the husband as if he were already dead. Vaisey J. held that the husband's protected life interest was extinguished for all purposes and the discretionary trusts were so closely connected with the life interest that they also were destroyed.

The effect of the forfeiture is to determine the principal beneficiary's life interest and to bring the discretionary trusts into operation. Thus in *Re Gourju's Will Trusts*,[22] the Trading with the Enemy Act 1939 and orders made thereunder having brought about a forfeiture of the principal beneficiary's interests, and the discretionary trusts having arisen, it was held by Simonds J. that income which had accrued due before the forfeiture was payable to the Custodian of Enemy Property, but income which accrued due after that event was to be held on the discretionary trusts for the benefit of the objects, and that since the

---

18 [1955] 1 W.L.R. 197.
19 See *Re Baker* [1904] 1 Ch. 157.
20 [1963] 1 W.L.R. 1207; (1963) 27 Conv.(N.S.) 517 (F. R. Crane).
21 [1959] Ch. 81.
22 [1943] Ch. 24.

Act contemplated a continuous benefit to those objects, the trustees were not to retain the income, but were to apply it for the objects as and when it came in, subject to such reasonable exceptions as the exigencies of the case demanded.[23] Thus the trustees could not accumulate the income so as to pay it at the end of the war to the principal beneficiary (a woman marooned in German-occupied Nice).

### Section 3. Attempts by a Settlor to Deprive his Creditors

Although a settlor may validly create in favour of another person a life interest determinable upon bankruptcy such a limitation in favour of himself is void against his trustee in bankruptcy though effective between himself and the other beneficiaries under the settlement; *Re Burroughs-Fowler, infra.* Where there are several determinable events including bankruptcy then the occurrence before bankruptcy of some other determinable event is, however, valid against the trustee in bankruptcy.[24] A settlement upon discretionary trusts where the settlor is one of the discretionary objects is prima facie valid but may be impeached under section 423 of the Insolvency Act 1986 (replacing section 172 of the Law of Property Act 1925) or sections 339 and 341 of the Insolvency Act 1986 (replacing section 42 of the Bankruptcy Act 1914).

### *INSOLVENCY ACT 1986, SECTIONS 423-425, 339-342*

These sections are broad enough to catch many dispositions by a settlor in favour of third parties. Section 423, *infra,* p. 272 operates independently of any bankruptcy of the settlor and covers all voluntary settlements and settlements in consideration of marriage (whenever made) if the settlor made the settlement *"for the purpose (a)* of putting assets beyond the reach of a person who is making, or may at some time make, a claim against him, or *(b)* of otherwise prejudicing the interests of such a person in relation to the claim which he is making or may make."

Sections 339 and 341, *infra,* pp. 273-275 only apply if the settlor is adjudged bankrupt (and apply only in favour of the trustee in bankruptcy) and only if the settlement was not created more than five years before the bankruptcy, but no purposive intent to defraud creditors is required: merely entering into a transaction at an undervalue suffices. This creates difficulties for purchasers of property gifted to their vendor if five years have not elapsed from the date of the gift. The purchaser will have notice of the relevant circumstances, namely a transaction at an undervalue, and so will not be protected by section 342(2).

Section 423, replacing Law of Property Act 1925 section 172 (itself replacing a statute of 1571) probably encapsulates in modern language the effect of the

---

[23] If the trustees fail to exercise their discretion, the discretionary trusts over income remain exercisable despite the passing of time though only in favour of such persons as would have been objects of the discretion had it been exercised within a reasonable time: *Re Locker's S.T.* [1978] 1 All E.R. 216.

[24] *Re Detmold* (1889) 40 Ch.D. 585.

old case law. The section clearly extends to "present" creditors (with existing enforceable claims) and "subsequent" creditors (identifiable persons who have claims that may reasonably be anticipated to mature into existing enforceable claims, *e.g.* holders of guarantees executed by the donor, or persons who had issued writs or informed the donor that they would be issuing a writ or would have so informed the donor if they had his knowledge, such as his knowledge of his negligence in relation to them).

In some circumstances the section seems capable of extending to "potential future" creditors, *viz.* presently unidentifiable persons, who may or may not surface in the future to bring presently unascertainable claims of indeterminate amounts against the donor.

In *Re Butterworth*[25] Butterworth, who had been a successful baker for many years, decided to expand and buy a grocery business, a trade in which he had no experience. He therefore settled most of his property on his family just before buying the grocery business. It was not a success but Butterworth was able to sell it six months later for the same price he had paid. He continued with his bakery until it failed three years later. The Court of Appeal held that the settlement was made "with intent to defraud" under the 1571 Statute of Elizabeth and so could be upset by the creditors of the bakery.

Jessel M.R. said,[26] "The principle of *Mackay* v. *Douglas* is this, that a man is not entitled to go into a hazardous business, and immediately before doing so settle all his property voluntarily, the object being this: 'If I succeed in business, I make a fortune for myself. If I fail, I leave my creditors unpaid. They will bear the loss.' That is the very thing which the Statute of Elizabeth was meant to prevent. The object of the settlor was to put his property out of the reach of his future creditors. He contemplated engaging in this new trade and he wanted to preserve his property from his future creditors. That cannot be done by a voluntary settlement. That is, to my mind, a clear and satisfactory principle."

In these days when lawyers, accountants and doctors may find that they can only insure themselves against negligence up to a ceiling of £x, but that they may possibly become liable for £2x, what can they do? They can, of course, settle their property on their families, but can one distinguish their activities as professions and not hazardous trades so as to fall outside Jessel M.R.'s statement of principle? Should it matter whether a business is a trade or a profession in these days when there should be no room for class distinction? Can section 423(3) be treated as changing the law through speaking of "putting assets beyond the reach of *a* person who may at some time make a claim" rather than "*any* person," so that it could be said to contemplate only an identifiable person rather than any future potential creditors?[27]

If not, then an asset protection trust should be set up in some jurisdiction like the Cayman Islands with its Fraudulent Dispositions Law 1989 which protects a settlor against potential future creditors (and also introduces a limitation period where present and subsequent creditors are concerned).[28]

The burden of proving the settlor's purpose is on the applicant while the burden of proving exemption under section 425(2) is on the transferee who

---

[25] (1882) 19 Ch.D. 588.
[26] *Ibid.* 598, also see Lindley L.J. p. 60 and *Cadogan* v. *Cadogan* [1977] 1 W.L.R. 1041.
[27] A question posed by Moffat & Chesterman, *Trusts Law: Text & Materials*, p. 283. After all, a prospective hazardous trader can form a company with limited liability to engage in the trade (though creditors may well insist on him personally guaranteeing company debts).
[28] Assets situated in England would still be at risk of s. 423.

seeks exemption.[29] Proving the settlor's purpose is a question of fact and the surrounding circumstances may be capable of establishing a rebuttable presumption that the requisite purpose was present, *e.g.* where the settlor settles virtually all his assets, or settles so much of his assets that his liabilities then exceed what he has left, or makes the settlement secretly and hastily.[30]

## Dispositions to defeat spouses

Under section 37 of the Matrimonial Causes Act 1973 the Family Division has jurisdiction to set aside certain dispositions made with the intention of defeating a spouse's claim to financial relief[31] and made within three years of the application to the court. Such intent is rebuttably presumed where a disposition actually has the effect of defeating such claim: section 37(5).

## Dispositions to defeat heirs

Under the Inheritance (Provision for Family and Dependants) Act 1975 the court has power to make various orders in relation to dispositions effected by a deceased, other than for full valuable consideration, and made with the intention of defeating applications for financial provision.[32] Section 10 applies to dispositions made less than six years before the deceased's death but not including appointments made in exercise of a special power of appointment.

### RE BURROUGHS-FOWLER

Chancery Division [1916] 2 Ch. 251.

By an ante-nuptial settlement dated March 24, 1905, freeholds and leaseholds belonging to W. J. Fowler, the intended husband, were conveyed to the trustees upon trust to sell with the consents therein mentioned and "to pay the rents profits and income thereof to the said W. J. Fowler or to permit him to receive the same during his life or until he shall be outlawed or be declared bankrupt or become an insolvent debtor within the meaning of some Act of Parliament for the relief of insolvent debtors or shall do or suffer something whereby the said rents profits and income or some part thereof respectively might if absolutely belonging to him become vested in or payable to some other person or persons. And from and immediately after the death of the said W. J. Fowler or other the determination of the trust for his benefit in his lifetime to pay the said rents profits and income unto the" wife if she should survive him during her life for her separate use without power of anticipation, and after the death of the survivor upon the usual trusts for the children of the marriage.

After the marriage the husband took the name of Burroughs-Fowler.

---

[29] *Lloyds Bank Ltd.* v. *Marcan* [1974] 1 W.L.R. 370 on s. 172 L.P.A. 1925 but similar principles seem applicable to s. 423.

[30] *Re Wise* (1886) 17 Q.B.D. 290; *Freeman* v. *Pope* (1870) 5 Ch.App. 538; *Re Sinclair* (1884) 26 Ch.D. 319; *Lloyds Bank Ltd.* v. *Marcan* [1974] 1 W.L.R. 370, though the decision in this last case would now be different due to s. 423(1)(c) excluding a transaction for full value, *e.g.* a lease which has a depreciating effect on the freehold value.

[31] *e.g. Kemmis* v. *Kemmis* [1988] 1 W.L.R. 1307.

[32] *e.g. Re Dawkins* [1986] 2 F.L.R. 360.

On May 13, 1915, the husband was adjudicated bankrupt. The official receiver at Oxford was appointed trustee in the bankruptcy and offered for sale the husband's life interest under the settlement, but the intending purchaser objected that the debtor's life interest remained defeasible if the debtor should do or suffer any of the other specified acts of forfeiture.

PETERSON J.: "Now the limitation until the settlor is declared bankrupt is void against the trustee in bankruptcy, and therefore, so far as the trustee in bankruptcy is concerned, the words relating to the bankruptcy and insolvency of the settlor must be treated as if they were omitted altogether from the clause. But on the other hand the provision as to bankruptcy and insolvency is not void as between the husband and the wife; for it was decided in *In re Johnson*[33] that, while the provision for the cessation of the life interest on bankruptcy was void as against the trustee in bankruptcy, it was effective for the purpose of producing a forfeiture as between the person who had the protected life interest and the persons interested in remainder. What, then, is the result? It is said that the result may be that the trustee in bankruptcy will be in a position to dispose of more than was vested in the bankrupt himself. That would be so in any case, because, so far as the trustee is concerned, the provisions for terminating the protected life interest upon bankruptcy are void. It seems to me that the true view is that, so far as the trustee in bankruptcy is concerned, the provisions as to bankruptcy and insolvency must be treated as excluded from the settlement, and the trustee is therefore in a position to deal with the interest of the husband under the settlement, whatever it may be, as if those provisions were excluded. So far, however, as the wife is concerned the forfeiture by reason of the bankruptcy has already taken place, and, therefore, it is no longer possible for the husband hereafter to do or suffer something which would determine his interest. The result is that the trustee in bankruptcy is in possession of the life interest of the bankrupt, which is now incapable of being affected by any subsequent forfeiture."

*Insolvency Act 1986*

**423. Transactions defrauding creditors.**—(1) This section relates to transactions entered into at an undervalue; and a person enters into such a transaction with another person if—

    (*a*)  he makes a gift to the other person or he otherwise enters into a transaction with the other on terms that provide for him to receive no consideration;

    (*b*)  he enters into a transaction with the other in consideration of marriage; or

    (*c*)  he enters into a transaction with the other for a consideration the value of which, in money or money's worth, is significantly less than the value, in money or money's worth, of the consideration provided by himself.

(2) Where a person has entered into such a transaction, the court may, if satisfied under the next subsection, make such order as it thinks fit[34] for—

    (*a*)  restoring the position to what it would have been if the transaction had not been entered into, and

---

[33] [1904] 1 K.B. 134.
[34] s. 425(1) sets out specific orders "without prejudice to the generality of s. 423."

(*b*) protecting the interests of persons who are victims of the transaction.

(3) In the case of a person entering into such a transaction, an order shall only be made if the court is satisfied that it was entered into by him for the purpose—

(*a*) of putting assets beyond the reach of a person who is making, or may at some time make, a claim against him, or

(*b*) of otherwise prejudicing the interests of such a person in relation to the claim which he is making or may make. . . .

(5) In relation to a transaction at an undervalue, references here and below to a victim of the transaction are to a person who is, or is capable of being, prejudiced by it; and in the following two sections the person entering into the transaction is referred to as "the debtor."

**424. Those who may apply for an order under s.423.**—(1) An application for an order under section 423 shall not be made in relation to a transaction except—

(*a*) in a case where the debtor has been adjudged bankrupt or is a body corporate which is being wound up or in relation to which an administration order is in force, by the official receiver, by the trustee of the bankrupt's estate or the liquidator or administrator of the body corporate or (with the leave of the court) by a victim of the transaction. . . .

(*c*) in any other case, by a victim of the transaction.

(2) An application made under any of the paragraphs of subsection (1) is to be treated as made on behalf of every victim of the transaction.

**425. Provision which may be made by order under s.423.**—(2) An order under section 423 may affect the property of, or impose any obligation on, any person whether or not he is the person with whom the debtor entered into the transaction; but such an order—

(*a*) shall not prejudice any interest in property which was acquired from a person other than the debtor and was acquired in good faith, for value and without notice[35] of the relevant circumstances, or prejudice any interest deriving from such an interest, and

(*b*) shall not require a person who received a benefit from the transaction in good faith, for value and without notice of the relevant circumstances to pay any sum unless he was a party to the transaction.

(3) For the purposes of this section the relevant circumstances in relation to a transaction are the circumstances by virtue of which an order under section 423 may be made in respect of the transaction.

**339. Transactions at an undervalue.**—(1) Subject as follows in this section and sections 341 and 342, where an individual is adjudged bankrupt and he has at a relevant time (defined in section 341) entered into a transaction with any person at an undervalue, the trustee of the bankrupt's estate may apply to the court for an order under this section.

(2) The court shall, on such an application, make such order as it thinks fit for restoring the position to what it would have been if that individual had not entered into that transaction.

---

[35] Notice will include constructive notice: *Lloyds Bank Ltd.* v. *Marcan* [1973] 1 W.L.R. 339, 345.

(3) For the purposes of this section and sections 341 and 342, an individual enters into a transaction with a person at an undervalue if—

    (*a*) he makes a gift to that person or he otherwise enters into a transaction with that person on terms that provide for him to receive no consideration,

    (*b*) he enters into a transaction with that person in consideration of marriage, or

    (*c*) he enters into a transaction with that person for a consideration the value of which, in money or money's worth, is significantly less than the value, in money or money's worth, of the consideration provided by the individual.

**341. "Relevant time" under ss.339, 340.**—(1) Subject as follows, the time at which an individual enters into a transaction at an undervalue . . . is a relevant time if the transaction is entered into or the preference given—

    (*a*) in the case of a transaction at an undervalue at a time in the period of 5 years ending with the day of the presentation of the bankruptcy petition on which the individual is adjudged bankrupt . . .

(2) Where an individual enters into a transaction at an undervalue . . . at a time mentioned in paragraph (*a*) . . . of subsecton (1) (not being, in the case of a transaction at an undervalue, a time less than 2 years before the end of the period mentioned in paragraph (*a*)), that time is not a relevant time for the purposes of section 339 . . . unless the individual—

    (*a*) is insolvent at that time, or

    (*b*) becomes insolvent in consequence of the transaction . . . but the requirements of this subsection are presumed to be satisfied, unless the contrary is shown, in relation to any transaction at an undervalue which is entered into by an individual with a person who is an associate of his (otherwise than by reason only of being his employee).

(3) For the purposes of subsection (2), an individual is insolvent if—

    (*a*) he is unable to pay his debts as they fall due, or

    (*b*) the value of his assets is less than the amount of his liabilities, taking into account his contingent and prospective liabilities.

**342. Orders under ss.339, 340.**—(2) An order under section 339 or 340 may affect the property of, or impose any obligation on, any person whether or not he is the person with whom the individual in question entered into the transaction . . . but such an order—

    (*a*) shall not prejudice any interest in property which was acquired from a person other than that individual and was acquired in good faith, for value and without notice of the relevant circumstances, or prejudice any interest deriving from such an interest, and

    (*b*) shall not require a person who received a benefit from the transaction . . . in good faith, for value and without notice of the relevant circumstances to pay a sum to the trustee of the bankrupt's estate, except where he was a party to the transaction . . .

(4) For the purposes of this section the relevant circumstances, in relation to a transaction . . . are—

    (*a*) the circumstance by virtue of which an order under section 339 or 340 could be made in respect of the transaction . . . if the

individual in question were adjudged bankrupt within a particular period after the transaction is entered into or . . . and
(b) if that period has expired, the fact that the individual has been adjudged bankrupt within that period.

## PROBLEMS

1. Sharp transferred various assets to trustees to be held on trust for Sharp himself for life or until he should become bankrupt or his property should otherwise become available to his creditors. On any such event occurring the trustees were directed to pay the income to Sharp's wife for her life. Subject to those trusts the trustees were to hold on trust for Sharp's children absolutely in equal shares.

Four years after making the settlement Sharp was adjudicated bankrupt when he had a wife and two adult children.

Advise Sharp's trustee in bankruptcy as to the position if he wishes (1) to sell or (2) to retain Sharp's interest under the settlement. What consequences might ensue in the event of Sharp being discharged from bankruptcy after (a) his interest was sold or (b) his interest was retained?

2. Valiant has just been asked to become a partner in the ten partner firm of solicitors, "Chance & Hope." He knows that the firm has not been able to obtain sufficient insurance cover in respect of negligence claims, so the partners would then be personally liable for any excess claims which might amount to £20 million. He owns a £¼ million house and has just inherited £380,000. His wife is likely to be elected a local councillor in the next election. Her party is likely to win and impose financial policies contravening the law, so that she could be surcharged by the District Auditor and be bankrupted if unable to pay. They have twin sons, aged two years.

He seeks your advice on what they can do to safeguard their assets, and mentions the possibility that his wife's involvement with politics might lead them to divorce, ultimately.

3. "Tradesmen, like Mr. Butterworth of *Re Butterworth* fame, can avoid his problems by forming a limited liability company and lending it money (secured by a charge) to purchase or start up a business: *Saloman* v. *Saloman* [1897] A.C. 22. Solicitors and accountants who are precluded from operating as such companies are thereby much disadvantaged." Discuss.

# Chapter 5

# CHARITABLE (OR PUBLIC) TRUSTS[1]

## Section 1. The Advantages of Charity

*Tax advantages*

United Kingdom[2] charities do not pay income tax on their investment income which is applicable to charitable purposes only and is in fact applied solely for those purposes.[3] They can recover basic rate or corporation tax paid by donors in respect of four year covenants drawn up in their favour.[4] Where trading income is concerned, however, they are only exempt from tax if either the trade is exercised in the course of the actual carrying out of a primary purpose of the charity or the work in connection with the trade is mainly carried out by beneficiaries of the charity.[5]

Charities do not pay capital gains tax in respect of gains made upon disposals by them[6] and individuals are encouraged to make *inter vivos* gifts to charities since no charge to capital gains tax arises upon such gifts.[7] Where inheritance tax is concerned transfers to charities are exempt.[8] Charities can obtain 80 per cent. relief as of right in respect of non-domestic rates for premises wholly or mainly used for charitable purposes and some discretionary relief in respect of the rest.[9] Charities are also exempt in respect of stamp duty[10] but only have a few reliefs from value added tax[11] in prescribed circumstances.

The fiscal advantages of charities are such that in 1988 terms over £500 million tax is lost to the Exchequer each year and probably over

---

[1] *Tudor on Charities* and Picarda's *The Law and Practice to Charities* are the authoritative legal works. Keeton and Sheridan's *Modern Law of Charities* can also be useful. Goodman Committee: Charity Law and Voluntary Organisations (1976); Wolfenden Committee: The Future of Voluntary Organisations: Chesterman: *Charities, Trusts and Social Welfare*; F. Gladstone, *Charity Law and Social Justice*; 16th Report of Committee of Public Accounts 1987–88; Charities: A Framework for the future (1989) Cm. 694 (Government White Paper).
[2] *Camille and Henry Dreyfus Foundation Inc.* v. *I.R.C.* [1956] A.C. 39.
[3] Income and Corporation Taxes Act 1988, ss.505, 506. See *I.R.C.* v. *Educational Grants Association Ltd.* [1967] Ch. 123 *infra*, p. 324.
[4] I.C.T.A. 1988, ss.660, 683, Finance Act 1989, ss.56, 59. Single gifts to charity of £600 or more also attract reliefs: Finance Act 1990, ss.25, 26, 27. Up to £600 p.a. can also be given (with tax relief) by employees under a payroll deduction scheme: I.C.T.A. 1988, s.202, Finance Act 1990, s.24.
[5] I.C.T.A. 1988, s.505; G. N. Glover [1972] B.T.R. 346. If substantial trading is being carried on which is not within the exemption the charity may form a company to run the trade and have the company covenant to pay its net profits to the charity for a period capable of exceeding 3 years: the company then deducts the payment as a charge on income for the purposes of corporation tax: I.C.T.A. 1988, s.338(5)(6)(8). By concession the Revenue do not charge tax in respect of profits from occasional fund-raising bazaars, jumble sales, etc.
[6] I.C.T.A. 1970, s.345(2); Capital Gains Tax Act 1979, s.145.
[7] *Ibid.* s.146.
[8] Inheritance Tax Act 1984, s.23.
[9] Local Government Finance Act 1988, ss.47, 64.
[10] F.A. 1974, s.49(2).
[11] Value Added Tax Act 1983, Sched. 5, Group 16; Sched. 6 Groups 6, 7, 8, 10, 11.

£120 million rates is lost to the rating authorities each year.[12] By making up the loss the taxpayer and the ratepayer are subsidising all sorts of charities and so have a direct personal interest in the integrity and efficiency of charities: as one-man's philanthropy is another man's tax burden it is only right that legal safeguards should exist to ensure that there is proper philanthropy properly carried out. It is estimated that the annual turnover of the charitable sector is over £13,000 million. There are over 165,000 registered charities and about 100,000 excepted or exempt from registration. Positive Government funding (directly or indirectly) of charities amounts to over £2,000 million a year, quite apart from the tax subsidy.

## Trust law advantages

Charities have further advantages in that they are not subject to the rule against inalienability[13] and they enjoy one limited exemption from the rule against remoteness. At common law a gift over from one person to another that might possibly take effect outside the perpetuity period was void.[14] However, a gift over from one charity to another charity was valid, the property being treated as belonging to charity throughout so as not to be caught by the rule against remoteness.[15] If the gift were a gift over from a charity to a non-charity[16] or from a non-charity to a charity[17] then the rule against remoteness applied. Since the Perpetuities and Accumulations Act 1964 came into force it is now possible in these two latter instances to wait and see[18] when the gift over takes effect: if it takes effect within the perpetuity period then it is good, if not it is bad and the first gift becomes absolute, no longer subject to defeasance or determination.[19] Of course, the validity of gifts over from one charity to another charity is unaffected by the 1964 Act.

Furthermore, a charitable trust is valid though a pure purpose trust because the Attorney-General can enforce it, and the trust requirement of certainty of objects is satisfied so long as the settlor manifested a general charitable intention to enable a *cy-près* scheme to be formulated for giving effect to his intention as nearly as possible.[20]

---

12 See White Paper: Charities:– A Framework for the Future (1989) Ch. 694, para. 1.
13 *e.g. Re Banfield* [1968] 1 W.L.R. 846 compared with *Re Warre's W.T.* [1953] 1 W.L.R. 725 or *Re Gwyon* [1930] 1 Ch. 255.
14 *Re Frost* (1889) 43 Ch.D 246.
15 *Christ's Hospital* v. *Grainger* (1849) 1 Mac. & G. 460; *Re Tyler* [1891] 3 Ch. 252.
16 *Re Bowen* [1893] 2 Ch. 491.
17 *Re Dalziel* [1943] Ch. 277; *Re Peel's Release* [1921] 2 Ch. 218.
18 Perpetuities and Accumulations Act 1964, s.3.
19 P.A.A. 1964, s.12 treats determinable interests in the same way as conditional interests.
20 The court has inherent jurisdiction to resolve any problems of administrative unworkability so long as the settlor has manifested a general charitable intention. If the trust is one the administration of which the court could not undertake and control and no exclusively charitable intent appears so as to found a *cy-près* scheme then the trust fails: *Re Hummultenberg* [1923] 1 Ch. 237 (legacy to the treasurer of the London Spiritualistic Alliance for the purpose of establishing a college for the training of suitable persons as mediums); *Re Koeppler's W.T.* [1984] 2 All E.R. 111 (legacy to trustees for the formation of an informed international public opinion and the promotion of greater co-operation in Europe and the West, though held charitable in the Court of Appeal [1985] 2 All E.R. 869 *infra*, p. 292).

Thus a trust "for world-wide charitable purposes" or "for poor persons" or "for the following religious societies" without specifying any is valid whilst a discretionary trust for everyone in the United Kingdom is void. The *cy-près* doctrine is peculiar to charitable trusts and will be dealt with at the end of this chapter. Finally, charitable trustees can act by a majority instead of unanimously which is the position for private trusts unless the trust deed authorises majority decisions.[21]

CHARITABLE COMPANIES

At this stage it might usefully be noted that a charity will often take the form of a charitable trust with individual or corporate trustees but it may take the form of a company incorporated under the Companies Act 1985, but limited by guarantee (not by shares), with the charitable provisions in its memorandum of association. Such provisions will not be trusts in the strict equitable sense but will be trusts for the purposes of the Charities Act 1960 (concerned with the proper administration of charities) by virtue of section 46 thereof. Section 45 defines a charity as "any institution, corporate or not, which is established for charitable purposes and is subject to the control of the High Court in the exercise of the court's jurisdiction with respect to charities." A gift to a company which is incorporated under the Companies Acts, so that its general property is held for charitable purposes without the intervention of trusts, is usually treated as intended to be held as an addition to the company's general property and not upon trusts unless the donor uses express words importing a trust.[22] Although a company can always change its objects clause in its memorandum under section 4 of the Companies Act 1985 it cannot do so without the prior written consent of the Charity Commissioners.[23] Of course, where property was gifted upon express trust then the company must always give effect to those trusts unless and until a *cy-près* scheme is finalised. A charitable company's own general property is also subject to the court's *cy-près* jurisdiction, *e.g.* on its winding up.[24] In the rare case where the Commissioners may allow a company to change its objects so as to cease to be a charity this cannot affect the application of any property acquired other than for full consideration or any property representing property so acquired or the income from any such property.[25]

---

[21] *Re Whiteley* [1910] 1 Ch. 600, 608. Yet another distinction is that the six year limitation period in Limitation Act 1980, s.21(3) applies to an action by a beneficiary under a trust but not an action by the Att.-Gen.: *Att.-Gen.* v. *Cocke* [1988] 2 All E.R. 391.

[22] *Re Finger's W.T.* [1972] 1 Ch. 286 and see Charity Commissioners' Report for 1971, paras. 22–30.

[23] Charities Act 1960, s.30A(2) substituted by Companies Act 1989, s.111.

[24] *Liverpool and District Hospital* v. *Att.-Gen.* [1981] Ch. 193.

[25] Charities Act 1960, s.30A(1) substituted by Companies Act 1989, s.111.

## Section 2. The Scope of Charity

### 1. INTRODUCTORY

*The spirit and intendment of the 1601 preamble*

Before the Statute of Charitable Uses 1601, the Court of Chancery exercised jurisdiction in matters relating to charity, but notions of what was a charity were imprecise. The preamble to that statute contained a list of charitable objects which the courts used as "an index or chart" for the decision of particular cases, with the result that, in addition to the objects enumerated in the preamble, other objects analogous to them or within the spirit and intendment of the preamble came to be regarded as charitable: *see Scottish Burial Reform and Cremation Society* v. *Glasgow Corporation, infra*, p. 285 holding the provision of crematoria charitable by analogy with the provision of burial grounds by analogy with the upkeep of churchyards by analogy with the repair of churches. This enables the courts to avoid direct assessment of the social worth of putative charitable trusts and to avoid overt value judgments.

The 1601 statute was enacted as part of a comprehensive poor law code and provided for commissioners to be appointed to investigate misappropriations of charity property. Its preamble commenced: "Whereas lands, chattels, money have been given by sundry well disposed persons: some for the relief of aged, impotent and poor people; the maintenance of sick and maimed soldiers and mariners, schools of learning, free schools, and scholars in universities; the repair of bridges, ports, havens, causeways, churches, sea banks and highways; the education and preferment of orphans; the relief, stock, or maintenance for houses of correction; the marriage of poor maids; the supportation aid and help of young tradesmen, handicraftsmen and persons decayed; the relief or redemption of prisoners or captives; the aid or ease of any poor inhabitants concerning payment of fifteens, setting out of soldiers and other taxes; which lands, chattels and money have not been employed according to the charitable intent of the givers by reason of frauds, breaches of trust and negligence."

The Statute of Charitable Uses 1601 was repealed by the Mortmain and Charitable Uses Act 1888, but section 13(2) of the latter Act expressly preserved the preamble to the former statute, and on the basis of its continued existence Lord Macnaghten in *Commissioners of Income Tax* v. *Pemsel* enunciated his famous fourfold classification of charity: "Charity in its legal sense comprises four principal divisions: trusts for the relief of poverty; trusts for the advancement of education; trusts for the advancement of religion; and trusts for other purposes beneficial to the community, not falling under any of the preceding heads."

The Mortmain and Charitable Uses Act 1888, and with it the preamble to the Statute of Charitable Uses 1601, were repealed by section 38(1) of the Charities Act 1960, section 38(4) of which went on to provide: "Any reference in any enactment or document to a charity within the meaning, purview and interpretation of the Charitable Uses Act 1601, or of the preamble to it, shall be construed as a reference to a charity within the meaning which the word bears as a legal term according to the law of England and Wales."

This provision is not free from obscurity,[26] but the courts treat the somewhat ossificatory classification to which the preamble gave rise as still surviving in the decided cases.[27]

*Historical overview*

It seems that the 1601 Act was intended to be almost wholly confined to purposes which would operate for the benefit of the public as a whole, rich and poor, by reducing the burden of parish poor relief and other parochial obligations.[28] If gifts for the specified purposes were properly employed they should relieve poverty and so reduce the burden of poor rates.

Worries about testators disinheriting their families in favour of charity by wills or gifts made within 12 months of death (so as to curry favour with their Maker) led to the Mortmain and Charitable Uses Act 1736 (now repealed) which made void most of such charitable trusts of land. These same sentiments led to the legal requirement that if a gift of personalty to charity was initially impossible or impracticable to take effect then the property reverted to the testator's estate (for his family's benefit) unless there was a clear general charitable intention evinced, when the property would be applied *cy-près* for closely allied purposes.[29]

To favour families and make charitable trusts of land void under the 1736 Act the courts divorced the enumerated objects from the pre-amble and the 1601 legislative and historical context.[30] The argument that charity involved something in the nature of a relief was rejected.[31] It sufficed that public benefit existed and this could exist where any section of the community benefited even if not poor. Thus, while the words in the preamble were originally thought to cover free schools only,[32] they became used to uphold a bequest to establish a school for educating the sons of gentlemen.[33] Providing schools, hospitals[34] and sheltered accommodation for the elderly[35] albeit at a cost came to be

---

26 See Marshall (1961) 24 M.L.R. 444.
27 *e.g. Incorporated Council of Law Reporting* v. *Att.-Gen.*, *infra*, p. 314; *I.R.C.* v. *McMullen*, *infra*, p. 308.
28 See Francis Moore's (1607) Reading on the 1601 Statute, G. H. Jones, *History of Charity Law 1532–1827*, p. 27.
29 See pp. 393–410.
30 *e.g. Townley* v. *Bedwell* (1801) 6 Ves. 194, *Thornton* v. *Howe* (1862) 31 Beav. 14.
31 *Trustees of the British Museum* v. *White* (1826) 2 Sim. & Stu. 594, 596.
32 *Att.-Gen.* v. *Hewer* (1700) 2 Vern. 387.
33 *Att.-Gen.* v. *Lord Lonsdale* (1827) 1 Sim. 105.
34 *Re Resch's W.T.* [1969] 1 A.C. 514.
35 *Rowntree Memorial Trust Housing Association* v. *Att.-Gen.* [1983] Ch. 159.

charitable objects so long as the profits are ploughed back into the enterprise and not distributed. However, it became established[36] that purposes will not qualify for charitable status if they are substantially political in the broad sense of seeking to change or preserve the law or government policy.

Concern over the negligent or fraudulent mismanagement of charitable funds led to the establishment of the Charity Commission under the Charitable Trusts Acts 1853, 1855 and 1860 to supervise the administration of charities. Similar concerns in the 1980s led to reports[37] resulting in the Government White Paper[38] "Charities: A Framework for the Future" (May 1989). Extensive new powers are to be given to the Commission which is taking advantage of new information technology to have more accurate up-to-date records. The Government intends to implement virtually all the Woodfield Report recommendations (pp. 390–393, *infra*). It goes one significant step further. The Commission is to have powers, corresponding to and concurrent with those possessed by the Attorney-General, to go directly to the courts for the enforcement of obligations against defaulting trustees and others. The Commission will have the leading role in enforcement litigation but will be required to obtain the Attorney-General's consent before commencing proceedings.[39]

*Public benefit*

A valid charitable trust must also promote some public benefit unless it is within Lord Macnaghten's first category of trusts for the relief of poverty.[40] This exception is anomalous but well established in the House of Lords: *Dingle* v. *Turner, infra*, p. 296.

The public benefit test requires the trust to confer a tangible benefit[41] directly or indirectly upon the public but does not require a benefit available to all the public: it suffices that the possibility of benefiting is conferred upon some section of the public such that the trust is a public one as opposed to a private one. The House of Lords in *Oppenheim* v. *Tobacco Securities Trust Co. Ltd., infra*, p. 318, used the personal nexus test put forward in *Re Compton*[42] to distinguish between public trusts and private trusts: they held that except in "poverty" trusts no class of beneficiaries can constitute a section of the public if the distinguishing quality which links them together is relationship to a particular individual either through a common ancestor or a common employer. Thus a trust for the education of children

---

[36] *Bowman* v. *Secular Society Ltd.* [1917] A.C. 406, 442, *National Anti-Vivisection Society* v. *I.R.C.* [1948] A.C. 31, *McGovern* v. *Att.-Gen.* [1982] Ch. 321.
[37] 16th Report of Committee of Public Accounts 1987–88; Sir Philip Woodfield Efficiency Scrutiny of the Supervision of Charities (1987).
[38] Cm. 694.
[39] Cm. 694 paras. 5.29 and 5.30.
[40] *Oppenheim* v. *Tobacco Securities Trust Co. Ltd., infra*, p. 318; *Gilmour* v. *Coats, infra*, p. 333; *I.R.C.* v. *Baddeley* [1955] A.C. 572.
[41] *Gilmour* v. *Coats, infra*, p. 333, *Re Pinion* [1965] Ch. 85.
[42] [1945] Ch. 123.

of employees or former employees of British American Tobacco Co. Ltd. or any of its subsidiary or allied companies was not a valid charitable trust though there were over 110,000 current employees. If the trust had been for the education of children of those employed or formerly employed in the tobacco industry it would have been valid as it would if confined to children of those engaged in the tobacco industry in a particular county or town.[43]

The weaknesses of the personal nexus test are revealed in the dissenting speech of Lord MacDermott in *Oppenheim, infra,* and with whose broad approach the House of Lords were in agreement obiter in *Dingle* v. *Turner, infra,* where Lord Cross indicated that whether or not the potential beneficiaries can fairly be said to constitute a section of the public is a question of degree in all the circumstances of the case and that much must depend upon the purpose of the trusts.[44] If charity of purpose and benefit to the public are not separate, but interrelated, issues then there can be no universal test of public benefit. Indeed, the cases reveal that minute public benefit is required for religious trusts,[45] a substantial amount of public benefit is required for educational trusts[46] and slightly more public benefit still is required for trusts for other purposes beneficial to the community.[47] This is dealt with when examining these categories of trusts.

Owing to the conflicting views expressed in the Lords in *Oppenheim* and in *Dingle* v. *Turner* lower courts will face an unenviable dilemma when the case arises that compels a choice between the two views. In its favour the broad approach at least concerns itself with the substance of the matter and is not unduly preoccupied with form as is the narrow personal nexus approach. The narrow formal approach, though conducive to certainty, also leads to artificial manipulation of the legal forms so as to obtain fiscal advantages, *e.g.* in the case of a trust for the education of children of inhabitants of Bournville which might be invalidated under the broad approach as in substance a trust benefiting employees of Cadbury-Schweppes Ltd.[48]

Indeed, the law of charitable trusts is bedevilled by the fact that such trusts enjoy not just immunity from the rules against uncertainty and inalienability but also automatically fiscal privileges. The two questions of the validity of the trust and of exemption from rates and taxes are

---

43 [1951] A.C. 297, 318; *Re Morgan* [1955] 1 W.L.R. 738, similarly, on this basis a trust for the education of children of inhabitants of Bournville will be valid but not a trust for the education of children of employees of Cadbury-Schweppes Ltd.: *I.R.C.* v. *Educational Grants Association* [1967] Ch. 993, 1009.

44 D. J. Hayton (1972) 36 Conv.(N.S.) 209; Gareth Jones (1974) C.L.J. 63. For comments of Lord Cross see *Carter* v. *Race Relations Board* [1973] A.C. 868, 907.

45 *Re Watson* [1973] 1 W.L.R. 1472; *Thornton* v. *Howe* (1862) 31 Beav. 14; *Dingle* v. *Turner, infra,* pp. 296–303, *Neville Estates Ltd.* v. *Madden* [1962] Ch. 832 (members for the time being of the Catford Synagogue).

46 *Oppenheim* v. *Tobacco Securities Trust., infra,* p. 318; *I.R.C.* v. *Educational Grants Association Ltd., infra.,* p. 324.

47 *I.R.C.* v. *Baddeley* [1955] A.C. 572; *Williams' Trustees* v. *I.R.C., infra,* p. 347.

48 In tax matters the courts nowadays take a broad approach: see *Furniss* v. *Dawson* [1984] A.C. 474, *Craven* v. *White* [1989] A.C. 398.

joined together in an unholy and unnatural union. It is most noticeable that in "Chancery" cases, where the validity of a trust is attacked by the residuary legatee or next of kin, there are many doubtful first instance cases in favour of charity, whereas in "Revenue" cases, where exemption from taxes is the real bone of contention, there are many appellate cases restricting the scope of charity.[49] Is it too much to ask that fresh consideration should be given to the recommendations of the Radcliffe Commission on Taxation[50] that the question whether a trust should be regarded as a charitable trust for the purpose of general validity as a trust should be separated from the question whether it should enjoy any fiscal privileges?[51] It is noteworthy that in *Dingle* v. *Turner* the Lords disagreed over the influence of fiscal considerations in an application of a broad public benefit test. It would seem that Lords Simon and Cross thought that fiscal considerations would require a case like *Oppenheim* to be decided the same way today on the basis that it was not sufficiently altruistic to merit tax exemptions, merely providing a perquisite to attract and retain employees.

Most charities have to be registered with the Charity Commissioners under the Charities Act 1960[52] so that in the vast majority of instances it is the Charity Commissioners who alone determine the issue of charity or not though they do consult the Inland Revenue. They produce Annual Reports showing what their practice is in interpreting the case law. As to be expected they feel it their duty to err on the side of a conservative restrictive interpretation. This has brought them much criticism especially from recently established philanthropic bodies which to a greater or lesser extent pursue political ends. However, some of the criticism would be better directed at the anomalous state of the law for as the Commissioners write in their defence, "The Law is, of course, what it is and we cannot change it."[53]

*Trusts with political purposes*

Trusts for political purposes are non-charitable trusts on the basis that the courts have no means of judging whether a proposed change in the law would or would not be for the public benefit,[54] and the law could not stultify itself by holding that it was for the public benefit that the law itself should be changed.[55] Political purposes comprise not only

---

[49] See Cross (1956) 72 L.Q.R. 187 though *I.R.C.* v. *McMullen* [1981] A.C. 1 is an exception to this trend.

[50] (1955) Cmd. 9474.

[51] See [1989] Conv. 28 (S. Bright).

[52] s.4; appeal to the courts is possible under s.5(3) though the cost of appeal is a deterrent: between 1960 and 1971 only one appeal resulted from 1,380 refusals of charitable status (*New Law Journal Annual Charities Review* 1974, p. 34).

[53] 1971 Report, para. 10.

[54] *Bowman* v. *Secular Society* [1917] A.C. 406, 442, *per* Lord Parker.

[55] *National Anti-Vivisection Society* v. *I.R.C.*, *infra*, p. 344. See also *Bonar Law Memorial Trust* v. *I.R.C.* (1933) 49 T.L.R. 220 (Conservative); *Re Ogden* [1933] Ch. 678 (Liberal); *Re Hopkinson* [1949] W.N. 29 (Socialist); *Re Strakosch* [1949] Ch. 529 (appeasing racial feeling); *Re Bushnell* [1975] 1 All E.R. 721; (1975) 38 M.L.R. 471. (furthering socialised medicine in a socialist state); C.J. Forder [1984] Conv. 263.

attempts to change the law by legislation but also attempts to influence government foreign policy: see *Re Koeppler's Will Trusts, infra*, p. 292. Thus the following bodies are not registered as charities: the National Anti-Vivisection Society, National Council for Civil Liberties, Campaign against Racial Discrimination, Martin Luther King Fund, Anti-Apartheid Movement, Human Rights Society, South African Defence and Aid Fund, United Nations Association, Amnesty International, and the Disablement Income Group. However, if a body, particularly a long established one, which exists for much wider charitable purposes,[56] incidentally puts pressure on the public and politicians this does not affect the charitable status of the body, *e.g.* the RSPCA fighting vivisection, the British Legion fighting for better pensions for ex-servicemen, Guide Dogs for the Blind resisting VAT on dog food, the National Association for Mental Health in their MIND campaign organising and presenting a petition to Parliament. Certain registered charities such as the Child Poverty Action Group and Shelter have been walking the tightrope so precariously as to lead the Charity Commissioners to publish some guidance in their 1969 Annual Report paras. 10–16 and their 1981 Annual Report, *infra*, p. 290.

Since Parliament in the Race Relations Act 1976 has decided that promoting good race relations, endeavouring to eliminate discrimination on racial grounds and encouraging equality of opportunity between persons of different racial groups are for the public benefit, the Charity Commissioners in their 1983 Annual Report now consider such purposes as charitable. Previously they had not been so considered on the authority of *Re Strakosch*[57] where the appeasement of racial feelings (between the Dutch and English speaking South Africans) had been held to be a political and, therefore, non-charitable purpose.

Since the essence of any living law and of any healthy democracy is change, it is difficult to see why trusts for political purposes should not be capable of being valid charitable trusts, though whether trusts for purely party political purposes should attract fiscal advantages is rather doubtful and raises wider issues. Relaxation or abrogation of the vitiating political factor could usefully be part and parcel of reforms separating the fiscal advantages of charities from their other advantages.

For the present, bodies that are sufficiently hard-pressed to need relief on rates and taxes are not prepared to risk the costs of fighting

---

[56] These purposes do not in practice have to be much wider in the case of respectable long established charities like the Anti-Slavery Society, the Lords Day Observance Society and the Howard League for Penal Reform. By way of contrast the Humanist Trust, the National Secular Society and the Sexual Law Reform Society are not charities. The Upper Teesdale Defence Fund was registered as a charity, though its *raison d'être* seemed to be oppose a private Bill in Parliament, since the Commissioners take the view that virtually all private Bills are free from the taint of political activity: see 1969 Annual report, para. 15.

[57] [1949] Ch. 529.

the decisions of the Charity Commissioners in the Law Courts, especially when it is possible to hive off part of their funds for such activities as are certainly charitable, *e.g.* Amnesty with its Prisoners of Conscience Fund for relieving the poverty of such prisoners and their families, the National Council for Civil Liberties with its Cobden Trust for educational activities, the Martin Luther King Fund with its Martin Luther King Foundation for educational activities; UNA and the Anti-Apartheid Movement also have their own separate educational trusts.

### Profit-making trusts

A trust can make a profit by charging fees (*e.g.* for educational, medical or housing purposes) and still be a charitable trust so long as the profits are not distributed to benefit individuals but used for the purposes of the trust.[58]

## SCOTTISH BURIAL REFORM AND CREMATION SOCIETY LTD. v. GLASGOW CORPORATION

House of Lords [1968] A.C. 138; [1967] 3 W.L.R. 1132; [1968] 3 All E.R. 215.

The appellants were a non-profit-making limited company with a main object of promoting inexpensive and sanitary methods of disposal of the dead, in particular promoting cremation. For rating purposes they claimed a declaration that they were a charity, it being common ground that English law determined the issue. The Society charged fees but was non-profit-making.[59]

On appeal from the Court of Session the House of Lords held that the appellants were a charity within Lord Macnaghten's fourth category of charitable purposes and indicated the approach adopted by the courts as follows:

LORD REID: " . . . The appellants must also show, however, that the public benefit is of a kind within the spirit and intendment of the statute of Elizabeth. The preamble specifies a number of objects which were then recognised as charitable. But in more recent times a wide variety of other objects have come to be recognised as also being charitable. The courts appear to have proceeded first by seeking some analogy between an object mentioned in the preamble and the object with regard to which they had to reach a decision. Then they appear to have gone farther, and to have been satisfied if they could find an analogy between an object already held to be charitable and the new object claimed to be charitable. This gradual extension has proceeded so far that there are few modern reported cases where a bequest or donation was made or an institution was being carried on for a clearly specified object which was for the benefit of the public at large and not of individuals, and yet the object was held not to be within the spirit and intendment of the statute of Elizabeth. Counsel in the present case were invited to search for any case having even the remotest resemblance to this case in which an object was held to be for the

---

[58] *Re Resch's W.T.* [1969] 1 A.C. 514, *Re Rowntree Memorial Trust Housing Association* [1983] Ch. 159, *Customs & Excise Commissioners* v. *Bell Concord Education Trust Ltd.* [1989] 2 All E.R. 217.

[59] Organisations out to make a profit for their members are obviously not charitable: *Re Smith's W.T.* [1962] 2 All E.R. 563. *Re Girls Public Day School Trust* [1951] Ch. 400.

public benefit but not yet to be within that spirit and intendment; but no such case could be found.

"There is, however, another line of cases where the bequest did not clearly specify the precise object to which it was to be applied, but left a discretion to trustees or others to choose objects within a certain field. There the courts have been much more strict, so that if it is possible that those entrusted with the discretion could, without infringing the testator's direction, apply the bequest in any way which would not be charitable (for example, because it did not benefit a sufficiently large section of the public) then the claim that the bequest is charitable fails. That line of cases, however, can have no application to the present case, and it is easy to fall into error if one tries to apply to a case like the present judicial observations made in a case where there was a discretion which could go beyond objects strictly charitable. In the present case the appellants make a charge for the services which they provide. It has never been held, however, that objects, otherwise charitable, cease to be charitable if beneficiaries are required to make payments for what they receive. It may even be that public demand for the kind of service which the charity provides becomes so large that there is room for a commercial undertaking to come in and supply similar services on a commercial basis; but no authority and no reason has been put forward for holding that when that state is reached the objects and activities of the non-profit earning charitable organisation cease to be charitable.

"If, then, all that is necessary to bring the objects and activities of the appellants within the spirit and intendment of preamble to the statute of Elizabeth is to find analogous decided cases, I think that there is amply sufficient analogy with the series of cases dealing with burial.[60] I would therefore allow this appeal."

### *Charity Commissioners' Annual Report 1966*

36. Some of our non-legal correspondents have questioned the justification for the importance which the law attaches to the words used rather than to the institution's activities. It is felt by such correspondents that it should be enough to examine the activities of the institution to decide whether it is a charity and that two organisations both doing the same things should be equally qualified for registration. But this fails to take account of the fact that the law must be concerned principally with the obligation imposed on the institution to pursue certain objects. It is this obligation which established it as a charity; and so long as an institution is free to pursue any activities it wishes it cannot be treated as an established charity however much its current activities may resemble those of other recognised charities.

37. The problem of interpreting words presents a somewhat different aspect when we are asked to consider draft documents intended to set up proposed charities. It is not unusual to find an attempt to dress up the purposes of the proposed institution in words which it is hoped will be accepted as charitable even though the purposes, so phrased, are quite remote from the true intentions of the promoters. We are convinced that this is a highly unsatisfactory course and that the governing instrument of every institution should show unequivocally what the institution really sets out to achieve. Three particular devices call for comment.

---

[60] See also *Incorporated Council of Law Reporting v. Att.-Gen.* [1972] Ch. 73, 88, *per* Russell L.J.; p. 349, *infra*.

38. The first is the over-working of the word "education." Ingenious draftsmen have found it possible to embrace within this word a vast variety of activities, mainly propagandist, which do not come within the meaning of the "advancement of education" as it is used in charity law. A purpose which is not charitable cannot be made charitable merely by representing it to be a form of education.

39. The second device is the use of very wide general terms. It is of course true that there are some founders of charities, particularly those who are settling part of their own personal fortune, who genuinely expect to apply the settled property for all manner of charitable purposes; in such a case the general words are not intended to conceal a more limited true purpose. But, nonetheless, they may be difficult to interpret and it is undesirable that they should be used in any case where the proposed charity has a more limited purpose, particularly if the charity is intending to appeal to the public and not be merely the vehicle for the founder's own benevolence.

40. The third device is that of enumerating a number of objects, some perhaps charitable and others less obviously so, and then declaring that the institution is to be confined to carrying out such of the listed objects as are charitable. We have already commented on this device in paragraph 25 of our report for 1964. This approach begs the question, prevents the real purpose of the institution from being readily recognised and quite unnecessarily introduces difficulty in construing and acting upon the documents in which it is used. If a proposed charity shows us a draft instrument incorporating such a phrase we consider ourselves entitled to enquire what are intended to be its activities, with a view to seeing whether those activities can be authorised in terms of clearly defined charitable purposes.

55. Difficulties which arise with continuing funds of the kind in question [disaster relief funds] are frequently the result of unsuitably worded appeals and inappropriate drafting of trust deeds. One danger is that, if the purposes of the fund are not worded satisfactorily, persons within the beneficial class may be entitled as of right to claim a proportionate share of the capital and income, thus preventing the fund from being recognised as a charity. The more usual difficulty, however, is that the persons who come within the class to be benefited have been, or can be, ascertained, and having regard to the decided cases, it appears that the class does not form a sufficient section of the public to take the fund out of the category of private funds and so make it charitable. This difficulty would not arise if the purpose of the fund were clearly to relieve poverty among the victims of their dependants, which would make it charitable. But more often than not there is no direct mention of the relief of poverty in the original appeal or, where one has been executed, in the subsequent trust deed. Nonetheless, it seems to us reasonable to take the view that a fund raised by public subscription for a class known to the subscribing public only as "dependants of the victims of the accident" should be presumed to have a charitable rather than a private nature. Accordingly, in such cases we have considered whether we are justified in taking other factors into account and inferring from them a trust for the relief of poverty.

56. We have taken advice on this problem and, after giving the whole matter long and careful consideration, we have come to the conclusion that the court would readily accept as charities those funds where a poverty qualification could reasonably be inferred, and that we may quite properly do likewise. In many of the cases examined we have found that it was perfectly reasonable to infer that the funds were in fact for the relief of poverty although this was not

specifically stated in the trusts, and we have accordingly registered those funds as charities. Pointers to a fund being for the relief of poverty can to our mind be found in the use of such words as "relief," "distress," and "making due provision," and in provision for the payment to the beneficiaries of small weekly sums, while a provision for the application to charitable purposes of any surplus remaining after the proper claims of beneficiaries have been met is in cases of this nature some indication of a general charitable intention. Each case must, of course, be considered on its merits.

### Disaster Appeals—Attorney-General's Guidelines

*The Making of the Appeal*

Those who use these guidelines must remember that no two appeals can ever be quite the same, and should do all they can to ensure that their own appeal is appropriate to the particular circumstance of their case, and runs into no unforeseen difficulties, whether personal, administrative, or fiscal. Amongst the most important and urgent decisions which must be made will be whether or not a charitable appeal is called for, and it may well be desirable to take advice on such question before the appeal is issued. Generally speaking, the terms of the appeal will be all-important in deciding the status and ultimate application of the fund. Once the terms are agreed, it will generally be desirable to publish the appeal as soon as possible, and as widely as appropriate in the circumstances.

Sometimes gifts may be sent before publication of the appeal. If there are more than can be acknowledged individually, the published appeal should indicate that gifts already made will be added to the appeal fund unless the donors notify the organisers (say within ten days) that this is not their wish.

*Pros and Cons of the Types of Appeal*

*Charitable funds* attract generous tax reliefs; donations to them may do so (and in particular will be exempt from inheritance tax). But charitable funds, being essentially public in their nature, cannot be used to give individuals benefits over and above those appropriate to their needs; and the operation of a charitable trust will be subject to the scrutiny of the Charity Commissioners.

*Non-charitable funds* attract no particular tax reliefs. However, for example, for inheritance tax it is unlikely in practice that tax will actually be payable, either on donations to, or payments out of, the trust fund. But under a non-charitable trust there is no limit on the amount which can be paid to individual beneficiaries if none has been imposed by the appeal, and only the court acting on behalf of the beneficiaries will have control over the trust, which will not be subject to scrutiny by the Charity Commissioners.

The terms of the non-charitable appeal must be prepared with particular care to ensure that there is no doubt who is to benefit, whether or not their benefit is to be at the discretion of the trustees, and whether or not the entire benefit is to go to the beneficiaries, and if not, for example because specific purposes are laid down and the funds may be more than is required for those purposes, or because the beneficiaries are only to take as much as the trustees think appropriate, what is to happen to any surplus. If specific purposes are laid down, and after they have been fulfilled a surplus remains for which no use has been specified, the surplus will belong to the donors, which may lead to expensive and wasteful problems of administration.

## Forms of Appeal

If a *charitable* fund is intended then the appeal could take the following form:

"This appeal is to set up a charitable fund to relieve distress caused by the accident/disaster at . . . . . . . . . . . on . . . . . . . . . . . . The aim is to use the funds to relieve those who may be in need of help (whether now or in the future) as a result of this tragedy in accordance with charity law. Any surplus after their needs have been met will be used for charitable purposes designed: (i) To help those who suffer in similar tragedies. (ii) To benefit charities with related purposes. (iii) To help the locality."

If a *non-charitable* fund is intended and those affected are to take the entirety of the fund in such shares as the trustees think fit the appeal could take the following form:

"This appeal is to set up a fund, the entire benefit of which will be used for those injured or bereaved in the accident/disaster at . . . . . . . . . . . . on . . . . . . . . . . . . or their families and dependants as the trustees think fit. This fund will not be a charity."

A non-charitable fund in which the trustees would have a discretion to give as much as they think fit to those who have suffered with any surplus going to charity could be set up on the basis of the following form:

"This appeal is to set up a fund for those injured or bereaved in the accident/disaster at . . . . . . . . . . . . on . . . . . . . . . . . . and their families and dependants. The trustees will have a discretion how and to what extent to benefit individual claimants: the fund will not itself be a charity but any surplus will be applied for such charitable purposes as the trustees think most appropriate to commemorate those who died."

## Appeals for Individuals

It sometimes happens that publicity given to individual suffering moves people to give. In such a case it is particularly desirable for those who make appeals to indicate whether or not the appeal is for a charitable fund. It is also desirable for those who give to say whether their gift is meant for the benefit of the individual, or for charitable purposes including helping the individual so far as that is charitable; if no such intention is stated, then the donation should be acknowledged with an indication how it will be used if the donor does not dissent. Those who make appeals should bear in mind the possibility that a generous response may produce more than is appropriate for the needs of the individual and should be sure to ask themselves what should be done with any surplus.

Thus, if a child suffers from a disease, there are two alternatives: to appeal for the benefit of the child, or to appeal for charitable purposes relating to the suffering of the child, such as may help him and others in the same misfortune, for example by helping find a cure. It may be that the child will not live long, and so may not be able to enjoy generosity to him as an individual; alternatively, he may be intended to receive as much as possible because he faces a lifetime's suffering. Once again, the pros and cons of setting up a charitable fund or a non-charitable fund should be considered before the appeal is made and the appeal should indicate which alternative is intended; once again, even if a non-charitable appeal is made, it may be thought right to make it on terms that any surplus can be used for charity.

*Generally*

The suggestions made in this memorandum are only examples of forms which can be used; and before making an appeal it is always wise to seek advice on what form to use. The Charity Commissioners will always be ready as a matter of urgency to advise on the terms of any intended charitable appeal, or to consider whether a proposed appeal is likely to be charitable and if so to advise on the likely consequences.

In conclusion, the Attorney-General would like to emphasise that those organising an appeal should do all they can to make sure that the purpose of the appeal is clear and that donors know how their gifts will be used. This will do much to reduce the risk of confusion and distress. It is considered undesirable to make a general appeal postponing until the size of the fund is known decisions on whether the fund ought to be charitable and whether those affected should take the entire benefit; this can all too easily lead both donors and beneficiaries to form the view that the ultimate result is not what was intended, as well as giving rise to legal problems. [On Penlee Lifeboat Disaster, see (1982) 132 New L.J. 223].

*Charity Commissioners' Annual Report 1981*

53. The implications for charity trustees of the present state of the law—as confirmed by the Amnesty case—may be summarised as:

(i) Trustees who stray too far into the field of political activity:
   (a) risk being in breach of trust;
   (b) risk being held personally liable to repay to the charity the funds spent on such activity; and
   (c) risk losing some tax relief for their charity, since this may be claimed only in respect of income applied to charitable purposes.

(ii) Political activity by the trustees would not necessarily affect the charitable status of the institution or be a reason for removing it from the Central Register of Charities; *but*

(iii) If the trustees could validly claim that the expressed purposes of the institution were wide enough to cover political activities, doubt would arise whether those purposes were exclusively charitable and, if the institution was registered as a charity, upon the correctness of the registration.

54. The following guidelines may be of help for the general guidance of charity trustees:

(i) A charity should undertake only those activities which can reasonably be said to be directed to achieving its purposes and which are within the powers conferred by its governing instrument;

(ii) To avoid doubt being cast on the claim of an institution to be a charity, its governing instrument should not include power to exert political pressure except in a way that is merely ancillary to a charitable purpose. Whether a particular provision in the governing instrument of an institution is a substantive object or an ancillary object or power is a matter of the construction of the instrument. In general, what is ancillary is that which furthers the work of the institution, not something that will procure the performance of similar work by, for example, the Government of the day.

(iii) The powers and purposes of a charity should not include power to bring pressure to bear on the Government to adopt, alter, or maintain a particular line of action. It is permissible for a charity, in furtherance of its purposes, to help the Government to reach a decision on a particular issue by providing information and argument, but the emphasis must be on rational persuasion.

(iv) A charity can spend its funds on the promotion of public general legislation only if in doing so it is exercising a power which is ancillary to and in furtherance of its charitable purposes.

(v) If a charity's objects include the advancement of education, care should be taken not to overstep the boundary between education and propaganda in promoting that object: for example, the distribution of literature urging the Government to take a particular course, or urging sympathisers to apply pressure to Members of Parliament for that purpose, would not be education in the charitable sense.

(vi) A charity which includes the conduct of research as one of its objects must aim for objectivity and balance in the method of conducting research projects; and in publishing the results of the research must aim to inform and educate the public, rather than to influence political attitudes or inculcate a particular attitude of mind.

(vii) Charities, whether they operate in this country or overseas, must avoid:

> (*a*) Seeking to influence or remedy those causes of poverty which lie in the social, economic and political structures of countries and communities.

> (*b*) Bringing pressure to bear on a government to procure a change in policies or administrative practices (for example, on land reform, the recognition of local trade unions, human rights, etc.).

> (*c*) Seeking to eliminate social, economic, political or other injustice.

55. Unless its governing instrument precludes it from doing so, a charity may, generally speaking, freely engage in activities of the following kinds:

(i) Where the Government or a governmental agency is considering or proposing changes in the law and invites comments or suggestions from charities, they can quite properly respond.

(ii) Where a Green or White Paper is published by the Government, a charity may justifiably comment.

(iii) Where a Parliamentary Bill has been published, a charity is justified in supplying to Members of either House such relevant information and arguments to be used in debate as it believes will assist the furtherance of its purposes.

(iv) Where a Bill would give a charity wider powers to carry out its purposes, it can quite properly support the passage of the Bill; and it can support or oppose any Private Bill relevant to its purposes since private legislation does not normally have a political character.

(v) Where a question arises as to whether a Government grant is to be made or continued to a particular charity, the charity is entitled to seek to persuade Members of Parliament to support its cause.

(vi) Where such action is in furtherance of its purposes, a charity may present to a Government Department a reasoned memorandum advocating changes in the law.

56. In suggesting these guidelines to trustees, we are not purporting to say that certain activities are morally, socially, or politically wrong or undesirable or that they ought not to be done; but that it is not permissible for them to be carried out by a charity, according to our understanding of the law. We are concerned only with the law and must seek to ensure that funds and other property impressed with charitable trusts are used for the purposes of those trusts and not for purposes which the law does not accept as charitable. We are always willing to give further advice on any specific problem a charity may have in this connection; for example, on the distinction between education and propaganda, or between an ancillary purpose and a main purpose, and to consider the drafts of any publications such as advertisements, appeals, newsletters, etc, on which trustees have doubts.

## RE KOEPPLER'S WILL TRUSTS

Court of Appeal (O'Connor, Slade and Robert Goff L.JJ.) [1986] Ch. 423

By his will, Sir Heinrich Koeppler left a substantial share of his estate "for the Warden . . . of the institution known as Wilton Park . . . for the benefit . . . of the said institution as long as Wilton Park remains a British contribution to the formation of an informed international public opinion and to the promotion of greater co-operation in Europe and the West in general. . . . " Wilton Park had been created by the testator who for many years organised and directed its work. When he made his will in 1972 and at his death in 1979 that work centred on a series of conferences which enabled participants from member nations of the major western organisations to exchange views on political, economic and social issues of common interest. The conferences did not conform to any particular political viewpoint. They were financed partly by participants' fees and partly by the Foreign Office which provided premises and facilities.

At the time of the testator's death there was no legal entity by the name of "Wilton Park" nor a "Warden" of Wilton Park. The executor and trustee of the will applied to the court for the determination of the validity of the gift. Peter Gibson J. held that the gift failed because the purposes of Wilton Park, namely the formation of informed international public opinion and the promotion of greater co-operation in Europe and the West, were too vague and uncertain to constitute a valid charitable trust. The Attorney-General appealed successfully to the Court of Appeal.

SLADE L.J.: . . . "the gift in favour of 'Wilton Park' is expressed to be conditional on Wilton Park remaining a British contribution to two ends, namely (i) the formation of an informed international public opinion (the 'formation end') and (ii) the promotion of greater co-operation in Europe and the West in general (the 'promotion end') . . .

"It is next necessary to consider what is meant by 'the institution known as Wilton Park' which was designated by the testator as the intended beneficiary. One important feature of this case is that though Wilton Park was described by the testator as an 'institution,' it is not a body corporate or even an unincorporated association in the ordinary sense of that term, that is to say an association of persons bound together by identifiable rules and having an identifiable membership. . . . Accordingly, there is not, and never has been, an entity which is capable of receiving the gift beneficially, The gift, therefore, must have been intended, and can only be construed as, a gift for *purposes* of one kind or another. . . .

"It is by no means unusual for a testamentary gift expressed as a gift to an unincorporated body to be construed as a gift for the furtherance of the work of the body in question (see *e.g. Re Vernon's Will Trusts* [1971] 3 All E.R. 1061 and *Re Fingers' Will Trust* [1971] 3 All E.R. 1050 when Goff J. referred to the trust in question as a 'purpose trust'). *A fortiori*, in my opinion, this approach is the correct one in the present case where the so-called 'institution' referred to by the testator was not an association of persons bound together by identifiable rules and having an identifiable membership. The gift thus, in my opinion, falls to be construed as one *for the furtherance of the work of the Wilton Park project* . . . I think that to construe this gift as being one simply for the purposes of the formation end and the promotion end was erroneous. . . . Concluding therefore, as I do, that the gift falls to be construed as a 'purpose trust' for the furtherance of the work of the Wilton Park project, in the form which that work took at the date of the death, were those purposes of an exclusively charitable nature?

" . . . The organisation and conduct of the conferences, which had been held since 1950 at Wiston House, were clearly the central features of the Wilton Park project. The 'specific aspects' dealt with at each conference covered a wide range of topics . . . those specific themes are self-evidently matters on which persons of differing political persuasions might have differing views and some of the speakers invited to speak at plenary sessions of the conferences were politicians. However, the judge found ([1984] 2 All E.R. 111 at 117) that 'it is clear that Wilton Park has taken pains to avoid inculcating any particular political viewpoint.' There is therefore no question of the Wilton Park conferences being intended to further the interests of a particular political party.

"No one would suggest that the mere organisation and conduct of conferences, albeit dealing with topics of public interest, would necessarily constitute a charitable activity. If such activities are to be charitable, they must be shown to be for the benefit of the public, or the community, in a sense or manner within the intendment of the preamble to the Statute of Elizabeth I (the Charitable Uses Act 1601). The possibly relevant head of charity in the present case is that of the advancement of education . . . counsel for the next of kin conceded that if, on the true construction of the will, the purpose of the gift is the futherance of the Wilton Park project, then that is an educational purpose and the gift is of a charitable nature. . . . I think that this concession made by counsel was rightly made. As the judge said ([1984] 2 All E.R. 111 at 125): 'the concept of education is now wide enough to cover the intensive discussion process adopted by Wilton Park in relation to a somewhat special class of adults, persons influencing opinion in their own countries, designed (as I was told Sir Heinrich put it) to dent opinions and to cross-fertilise ideas.' . . . As to the element of public benefit, the participants in the courses appear to have been selected from widely drawn categories, as persons likely to influence opinion in their own country. Like the judge, I find little difficulty in inferring that not only they themselves are likely to benefit from the courses but are likely to pass on such benefits to others.

"There are two particular points which have caused me to hesitate before finally concluding that his gift is of a charitable nature. First, I have already mentioned the wide range of topics which are discussed at Wilton Park conferences, some of which could be said to have a political flavour. We were referred to a decision of my own in *McGovern* v. *Attorney-General* [1981] 3 All E.R. 493 where I held (*inter alia*) that though certain trusts, declared in a trust deed, for research into the observance of human rights and the dissemination of the results of such research would have been charitable if they had stood alone, they failed because, read in their context, they were merely adjuncts to the political purposes declared by the earlier provisions of the deed. However, in the present case, as I have already mentioned, the activities of Wilton Park are not of a party political nature. Nor, so far as the evidence shows, are they designed to procure changes in the laws or governmental policy of this or any other country; even when they touch on political matters, they constitute, so far as I can see, no more than genuine attempts in an objective manner to ascertain and disseminate the truth. In these circumstances I think that no objections to the trust arise on a political score, similar to those which arose in the *McGovern* case. The trust is, in my opinion, entitled to what is sometimes called 'benignant construction,' in the sense that the court is entitled to presume that the trustees will only act in a lawful and proper manner appropriate to the trustees of a charity and not, for example, by the propogation of tendentious political opinions, any more than those running the Wilton Park project so acted in the 33 years preceding the testator's death: *cf. McGovern* v. *Att.-Gen.* [1981] 3 All E.R. 493 at 519.

Finally, in considering whether the purpose of furthering the Wilton Park project is of an exclusively charitable nature, one cannot disregard the fact that in the forefront of the mind of the testator, both as the founder and, during his life, the moving spirit of the Wilton Park project, were the aims and aspirations referred to in this judgment as the formation end and the promotion end. Does the vague and accordingly non-charitable nature of these aims and aspirations prevent the gift from taking effect as charitable? If their nature were to be such as to be contrary to the policy of the law, the answer to this question must have been Yes. In the present case, however, there is no public policy objection whatever to the aims and aspirations of the testator, expressed by him as the formation end and the promotion end; the judge himself had no doubt that the work of Wilton Park was both 'admirable and worthwhile.' The sole objection, if any, lies in their vagueness and lack of definition.

"That objection proved fatal in *Re Strakosch* [1949] 2 All E.R. 6 . . .

"In the present case I accept the submission of counsel for the Attorney-General that there is no sufficient reason why the wide and vague scope of the testator's stated ultimate aims in doing the work which he did, should be held to destroy the otherwise admittedly educational nature of that work and that gift. There seems to have been no vagueness about the nature of the work itself. For the reasons which I have given, I consider that the true purpose of that gift was the furtherance of the work of the Wilton Park project and that that purpose was charitable as being for the advancement of education.

"I would accordingly allow this appeal and declare that the gift in question was a valid charitable gift."

O'CONNOR and ROBERT GOFF L.JJ. agreed.

*Appeal allowed.*

## II. TRUSTS FOR THE RELIEF OF POVERTY

This group of charitable trusts has its origins in that part of the preamble to the Statute of Charitable Uses 1601 which speaks of "the relief of aged, impotent and poor people." It has been held that these words must be read disjunctively so that a trust is charitable if the beneficiaries are either elderly or ill or poor.[61] The word "relief" implies that the persons in question have a need attributable to their condition as aged, ill or poor persons which requires alleviating and which those persons could not alleviate or would find difficulty in alleviating themselves from their own resources. The word "relief" is not synonymous with "benefit."[62] A trust for aged millionaires of Mayfair would thus not be charitable.[63]

"Poverty" is a relative term and the expression "poor people" is not necessarily confined to the destitute poor[64]: it includes persons who have to "go short" in the ordinary acceptation of that term, due regard being had to their station in life and so forth[65]; but the "working classes" do not *ipso facto* constitute a section of the poor.[66] However in *Niyazi's* W.T.[67] a gift of residue worth about £15,000 for "the construction of or as a contribution towards the construction of a working men's hostel" in Famagusta was held charitable. The size of the gift, the grave housing shortage in Famagusta, and the term "working men's hostel" provided a sufficient connotation of poverty to make the gift charitable.

If a trust may be brought under any of the other three heads, then it is no objection that it may incidentally benefit the rich as well as the poor; but if it cannot be brought under any head save that of the relief of poverty, then the benefits contemplated by the trust must be directed exclusively to that end: *Re Gwyon*,[68] where clothing for boys would benefit rich and poor boys.

Trusts for the relief of poverty (but not for the relief of elderly[69] or ill persons[70]) form an exception to the principle that every charitable trust must be for the public benefit. The exception covers both the poor relations of a named person[71] and the poor employees of a particular employer and their families: *Dingle* v. *Turner, infra*. However, there must be a primary intent to relieve poverty, though amongst a

---

[61] Age: *Re Robinson* [1951] Ch. 198; *Re Glyn's* W.T. [1950] 2 All E.R. 1150n.; *Re Bradbury* [1950] 2 All E.R. 1150n.; *Rowntree Memorial Trust Housing Association* v. *Att.-Gen.* [1983] Ch. 159; impotence: *Re Elliott* (1910) 102 L.T. 528; *Re Hillier* [1944] 1 All E.R. 480; *Re Lewis* [1955] Ch. 104.

[62] *Rowntree Memorial Trust* [1983] Ch. 159, *per* Peter Gibson J.

[63] See (1951) 67 L.Q.R. 164 (R.E.M.); (1955) 71 L.Q.R. 16 (R.E.M.); (1958) 21 M.L.R. 140–141 (Atiyah); *Rowntree Memorial Trust* [1983] Ch. 159.

[64] See 78 S.J. 377; 82 S.J. 882.

[65] *Re Coulthurst* [1951] Ch. 661, 666 (Evershed M.R.); *I.R.C.* v. *Baddeley* [1955] A.C. 572, 585 (Lord Simonds). Thus gifts for "distressed gentlefolk" and for "any members of the Savage Club who have fallen on evil days" have been held charitable: *Re Young* [1951] Ch. 344, *Re Young* [1953] 3 All E.R. 689.

[66] *Re Sanders'* W.T. [1954] Ch. 265, ("dwellings for the working classes and their families resident in the area of Pembroke Dock or within a radius of 5 miles therefrom" held not charitable).

[67] [1978] 3 All E.R. 785.

[68] [1930] 1 Ch. 255.

[69] *Re Dunlop* [1984] N.I. 408 (trust to found a home for old Presbyterian persons held to be for sufficient section of public to be charitable under fourth head of charity).

[70] *Re Resch's* W.T. [1969] 1 A.C. 514.

[71] *Re Scarisbrick* [1951] Ch. 662.

particular class of person. If the primary intent is to benefit particular persons (*e.g.* A, B, C and their children for their relief in needy circumstances) the trust is a private one and not charitable.[72]

## DINGLE v. TURNER

House of Lords [1972] A.C. 601; [1972] 2 W.L.R. 523; [1972] 1 All E.R. 878.

The facts sufficiently appear in Lord Cross' speech, *infra*.

VISCOUNT DILHORNE: "My Lords, I agree with Lord Cross that this appeal should be dismissed and with the reasons he gives for that conclusion.

"With Lord MacDermott, I too do not wish to extend my concurrence to what my noble and learned friend Lord Cross has said with regard to the fiscal privileges of a legal charity. Those privileges may be altered from time to time by Parliament and I doubt whether their existence should be a determining factor in deciding whether a gift or trust is charitable."

LORD MACDERMOTT: "My Lords, the conclusion I have reached on the facts of this case is that the gift in question constitutes a public trust for the relief of poverty which is charitable in law. I would therefore dismiss the appeal.

"I do not find it necessary to state my reasons for this conclusion in detail. In the first place, the views which I have expressed at some length in relation to an educational trust in *Oppenheim* v. *Tobacco Securities Trust Co. Ltd.*[73] seem to me to apply to this appeal and to mean that it fails. It would, of course, be otherwise if the case just cited purported to rule the point now in issue. But that is not so, for it clearly left that point undecided and open for further consideration. And, secondly, I have had the advantage of reading the opinion prepared by my noble and learned friend, Lord Cross of Chelsea, and find myself in agreement with his conclusion for the reasons he has given. In particular, I welcome his commentary on the difficulties of the phrase 'a section of the public.' But I would prefer not to extend my concurrence to what my noble and learned friend goes on to say respecting the fiscal privileges of a legal charity. This subject may be material on the question whether what is alleged to be a charity is sufficiently altruistic in nature to qualify as such, but beyond that, and without wishing to express any final view on the matter, I doubt if these consequential privileges have much relevance to the primary question whether a given trust or purpose should be held charitable in law."

LORD HODSON: "My Lords, I agree with my noble and learned friend, Lord Cross of Chelsea, that this appeal should be dismissed and with his reasons for that conclusion. With this reservation: that I share the doubts expressed by my noble and learned friends, Lord MacDermott and Viscount Dilhorne, as to the relevance of fiscal considerations in deciding whether a gift or trust is charitable."

LORD SIMON OF GLAISDALE: "My Lords, I have had the advantage of reading the opinion of my noble and learned friend, Lord Cross of Chelsea, with which I agree."

---

[72] *Re Scarisbrick* [1951] Ch. 662; *Re Cohen* [1973] 1 W.L.R. 415.
[73] [1951] A.C. 297. See pp. 318–324, *infra*.

LORD CROSS OF CHELSEA: "My Lords, by his will Frank Hanscomb Dingle (whom I will call 'the testator') made the following—among other—dispositions. . . . Clause 8(e) was in the following terms:

'(e) To invest the sum of ten thousand pounds in any of the investments for the time being authorised by law for the investment of trust funds in the names of three persons (hereinafter referred to as "the Pension Fund Trustees") to be nominated for the purpose by the persons who at the time at which my Executors assent to this bequest are directors of E. Dingle & Company Limited and the Pension Fund Trustees shall hold the said sum and the investments for the time being representing the same (hereinafter referred to as "the Pensions Fund") UPON TRUST to apply the income thereof in paying pensions to poor employees of E. Dingle & Company Limited or of any other company to which upon any reconstruction or amalgamation the goodwill and the assets of E. Dingle & Company Limited may be transferred who are of the age of Sixty years at least or who being of the age of Forty five years at least are incapacitated from earning their living by reason of some physical or mental infirmity PROVIDED ALWAYS that if at any time the Pension Fund Trustees shall for any reason be unable to apply the income of the Pensions Fund in paying such pensions to such employees as aforesaid the Pension Fund Trustees shall hold the Pensions Fund and the income thereof UPON TRUST for the aged poor in the Parish of St. Andrew, Plymouth.'

Finally by clause 8(g) the testator directed his trustees to hold the ultimate residue of his estate on the trusts set out in clause 8(e).

"The testator died on January 10, 1950. His widow died on October 8, 1966, having previously released her testamentary power of appointment over her husband's shares in E. Dingle & Co. Ltd., which accordingly fell into the residuary estate. When these proceedings started in July 1970, the value of the fund held on the trusts declared by clause 8(e) was about £320,000 producing a gross income of about £17,800 per annum.

"E. Dingle and Co. Ltd. was incorporated as a private company on January 20, 1935. Its capital was owned by the testator and one John Russell Baker and it carried on the business of a departmental store. At the time of the testator's death the company employed over 600 persons and there was a substantial number of ex-employees. On October 23, 1950, the company became a public company. Since the testator's death its business has expanded and when these proceedings started it had 705 full-time and 189 part-time employees and was paying pensions to 89 ex-employees.

"The trustees took out an originating summons asking the court to determine whether the trust declared by clause 8(e) were valid and if so to determine various subsidiary questions of construction—as, for example, whether part-time employees or employees of subsidiary companies were eligible to receive benefits under the trust. To this summons they made defendants (1) representatives of the various classes of employees or ex-employees, (2) those who would be interested on an intestacy if the trusts failed, and (3) Her Majesty's Attorney-General. It has been common ground throughout that the trust at the end of clause 8(e) for the aged poor in the Parish of St. Andrew Plymouth is dependent on the preceding trust for poor employees of the company so that although it will catch any surplus income which the trustees do not apply for the benefit of poor employees it can have no application if the preceding trust is itself void.

"The contentions of the appellant and the respondents may be stated broadly as follows. The appellant says that in the *Oppenheim* case this House decided that in principle a trust ought not to be regarded as charitable if the benefits under it are confined either to the descendants of a named individual or individuals or the employees of a given individual or company and that although the 'poor relations' cases may have to be left standing as an anomalous exception to the general rule because their validity has been recognised for so long, the exception ought not to be extended to 'poor employees' trusts which had not been recognised for long before their status as charitable trusts began to be called in question. The respondents, on the other hand, say, first, that the rule laid down in the *Oppenheim* case with regard to educational trusts ought not to be regarded as a rule applicable in principle to all kinds of charitable trust and, secondly, that in any case it is impossible to draw any logical distinction between 'poor relations' trusts and 'poor employees' trusts, and, that as the former cannot be held invalid today after having been recognised as valid for so long, the latter must be regarded as valid also.

"By a curious coincidence within a few months of the decision of this House in the *Oppenheim* case the cases on gifts to 'poor relations' had to be considered by the Court of Appeal in *Re Scarisbrick, Cockshott* v. *Public Trustee*.[74] Most of the cases on this subject were decided in the eighteenth or early nineteenth centuries and are very inadequately reported but two things at least were clear. First, that it never occurred to the judges who decided them that in the field of 'poverty' a trust could not be a charitable trust if the class of beneficiaries was defined by reference to descent from a common ancestor. Secondly, that the courts did not treat a gift or trust as necessarily charitable because the objects of it had to be poor in order to qualify, for in some of the cases the trust was treated as a private trust and not a charity. The problem in *Re Scarisbrick* was to determine on what basis the distinction was drawn. Roxburgh J.—founding himself on some words attributed to Sir William Grant M.R. in *Att.-Gen.* v. *Price*[75]—had held that the distinction lay in whether the gift took the form of a trust under which capital was retained and the income only applied for the benefit of the objects, in which case the gift was charitable, or whether the gift was one under which the capital was immediately distributable among the objects, in which case the gift was not a charity. The Court of Appeal rejected this ground of distinction. They held that in this field the distinction between a public or charitable trust and a private trust depended on whether as a matter of construction the gift was for the relief of poverty amongst a particular description of poor people or was merely a gift to particular poor persons. The fact that the gift took the form of a perpetual trust would no doubt indicate that the intention of the donor could not have been to confer private benefits on particular people whose possible necessities he had in mind; but the fact that the capital of the gift was to be distributed at once did not necessarily show that the gift was a private trust.

[His Lordship then reviewed the earlier cases leading up to *Gibson* v. *S. American Stores*.]

"The facts in *Gibson* v. *South American Stores (Gath & Chaves) Ltd.*[76]—the case followed by Megarry J. in this case—were that a company had vested in

---

[74] [1951] Ch. 622.
[75] [1803–13] All E.R. Rep. 467; (1810) 17 Ves. 371.
[76] [1950] Ch. 177.

trustees a fund derived solely from its profits to be applied at the discretion of the directors in granting gratuities, pensions or allowances to persons—

> 'who . . . are or shall be necessitous and deserving and who for the time being are or have been in the company's employ . . . and the wives widows husbands widowers children parents and other dependants of any person who for the time being is or would if living have been himself or herself a member of the class of beneficiaries.'

The Court of Appeal held that this trust was a valid charitable trust but it did so without expressing a view of its own on the question of principle involved, because the case of *Re Laidlaw*[77] which was unearthed in the course of the hearing showed that the Court of Appeal had already accepted the decision in *Re Gosling*[78] as correct.

"In *Oppenheim* v. *Tobacco Securities Trust Co. Ltd.*[79] this House had to consider the principle laid down by the Court of Appeal in *Re Compton*.[80] There the trustees of a fund worth over £125,000 were directed to apply its income and also if they thought fit all or any part of the capital—

> 'in providing for or assisting in providing for the education of children of employees or former employees of British-American Tobacco Co., Ltd. . . . or any of its subsidiary or allied companies. . . . '

"There were over 110,000 such employees. The majority of your Lordships—namely Lord Simonds (in whose judgment Lord Oaksey concurred), Lord Normand and Lord Morton of Henryton—in holding that the trust was not a valid charitable trust gave unqualified approval to the *Compton* principle. They held, that is to say, that although the 'poverty' cases might afford an anomalous exception to the rule, it was otherwise a general rule applicable to all charitable trusts that no class of beneficiaries can constitute a 'section of the public' for the purpose of the law of charity if the distinguishing quality which links them together is relationship to a particular individual either through common descent or common employment. My noble and learned friend, Lord MacDermott, on the other hand, in his dissenting speech, while not challenging the correctness of the decisions in *Re Compton* or in the *Hobourn Aero* case[81] said that he could not regard the principle stated by Lord Greene M.R. as a criterion of general applicability and conclusiveness. He said[82]:

> ' . . . I see much difficulty in dividing the qualities or attributes which may serve to bind human beings into classes into two mutually exclusive groups, the one involving individual status and purely personal, the other disregarding such status and quite impersonal. As a task this seems to me no less baffling and elusive than the problem to which it is directed, namely, the determination of what is and what is not a section of the public for the purposes of this branch of the law.'

He thought that the question whether any given trust was a public or a private trust was a question of degree to be decided in the light of the facts of the

---

[77] (January 11, 1935) unreported, the decision (and not the reasoning) only being available.
[78] (1900) 48 W.R. 300.
[79] [1951] A.C. 297.
[80] [1945] Ch. 123.
[81] [1946] Ch. 194.
[82] [1951] A.C. 297, 317.

particular case and that viewed in that light the trust in the *Oppenheim* case
was a valid charitable trust.

" . . . I turn to consider the arguments advanced by the appellant in support
of the appeal. For this purpose I will assume that the appellant is right in
saying that the *Compton*[83] rule ought in principle to apply to all charitable
trusts and that the 'poor relations' cases, the 'poor members' cases and the
'poor employees' cases are all anomalous—in the sense that if such cases had
come before the courts for the first time after the decision in *Re Compton* the
trusts in question would have been held invalid as 'private' trusts.

"Even on that assumption—as it seems to me—the appeal must fail. The
status of some of the 'poor relations' trusts as valid charitable trusts was
recognised more than 200 years ago and a few of those then recognised are still
being administered as charities today. In *Re Compton*[84] Lord Greene M.R. said
that it was 'quite impossible' for the Court of Appeal to overrule such old
decisions and in the *Oppenheim case*[85] Lord Simonds in speaking of them
remarked on the unwisdom of—

> '[casting] doubt on decisions of respectable antiquity in order to intro-
> duce a greater harmony into the law of charity as a whole.'

"Indeed counsel for the appellant hardly ventured to suggest that we should
overrule the 'poor relations' cases. His submission was that which was accepted
by the Court of Appeal in Ontario in *Re Cox (decd.)*[86]—namely that while the
'poor relations' cases might have to be left as long standing anomalies there
was no good reason for sparing the 'poor employees' cases which only date
from *Re Gosling*[87] decided in 1900 and which have been under suspicion ever
since the decision in *Re Compton* in 1945. But the 'poor members' and the
'poor employees' decisions were a natural development of the 'poor relations'
decisions and to draw a distinction between different sorts of 'poverty' trusts
would be quite illogical and could certainly not be said to be introducing
'greater harmony' into the law of charity. Moreover, although not as old as the
'poor relations' trusts, 'poor employees' trusts have been recognised as
charities for many years; there are now a large number of such trusts in
existence; and assuming, as one must, that they are properly administered in
the sense that benefits under them are only given to people who can fairly be
said to be, according to current standards, 'poor persons' to treat such trusts as
charities is not open to any practical objection. So as it seems to me it must be
accepted that wherever else it may hold sway the *Compton* rule had no
application in the field of trusts for the relief of poverty and that there the
dividing line between a charitable trust and a private trust lies where the Court
of Appeal drew it in *Re Scarisbrick*.[88]

"The *Oppenheim* case was a case of an educational trust and although the
majority evidently agreed with the view expressed by the Court of Appeal in
the *Hobourn Aero* case,[89] that the *Compton* rule was of universal application
outside the field of poverty, it would no doubt be open to this House without

---

[83] [1945] Ch. 123.
[84] [1945] Ch. 123, 139.
[85] [1951] A.C. 297, 309.
[86] [1951] O.R. 205.
[87] (1900) 48 W.R. 300.
[88] [1951] Ch. 622.
[89] [1946] Ch. 194.

overruling *Oppenheim* to hold that the scope of the rule was more limited. If ever I should be called on to pronounce on this question—which does not arise in this appeal—I would as at present advised be inclined to draw a distinction between the practical merits of the *Compton* rule and the reasoning by which Lord Greene M.R. sought to justify it. That reasoning—based on the distinction between personal and impersonal relationships—has never seemed to me very satisfactory and I have always—if I may say so—felt the force of the criticism to which my noble and learned friend Lord MacDermott subjected it in his dissenting speech in the *Oppenheim* case.[90] For my part I would prefer to approach the problem on far broader lines. The phrase 'a section of the public' is in truth a phrase which may mean different things to different people. In the law of charity judges have sought to elucidate its meaning by contrasting it with another phrase 'a fluctuating body of private individuals.' But I get little help from the supposed contrast for as I see it one and the same aggregate of persons may well be describable both as a section of the public and as a fluctuating body of private individuals. The ratepayers in the Royal Borough of Kensington and Chelsea, for example, certainly constitute a section of the public; but would it be a misuse of language to describe them as a 'fluctuating body of private individuals'? After all, every part of the public is composed of individuals and being susceptible of increase or decrease is fluctuating. So at the end of the day one is left where one started with the bare contrast between 'public' and 'private.' No doubt some classes are more naturally describable as sections of the public than as private classes while other classes are more naturally describable as private classes than as sections of the public. The blind, for example, can naturally be described as a section of the public; but what they have in common—their blindness—does not join them together in such a way that they could be called a private class. On the other hand, the descendants of Mr. Gladstone might more reasonably be described as a 'private class' than as a section of the public, and in the field of common employment the same might well be said of the employees in some fairly small firm. But if one turns to large companies employing many thousands of men and women most of whom are quite unknown to one another and to the directors the answer is by no means so clear. One might say that in such a case the distinction between a section of the public and a private class is not applicable at all or even that the employees in such concerns as ICI or GEC are just as much 'sections of the public' as the residents in some geographical area. In truth the question whether or not the potential beneficiaries of a trust can fairly be said to constitute a section of the public is a question of degree and cannot be by itself decisive of the question whether the trust is a charity. Much must depend on the purpose of the trust. It may well be that, on the one hand, a trust to promote some purpose, prima facie charitable, will constitute a charity even though the class of potential beneficiaries might fairly be called a private class and that, on the other hand, a trust to promote another purpose, also prima facie charitable, will not constitute a charity even though the class of potential beneficiaries might seem to some people fairly describable as a section of the public.

"In answering the question whether any given trust is a charitable trust the courts—as I see it—cannot avoid having regard to the fiscal privileges accorded to charities. As counsel for the Attorney-General remarked in the course of

---

[90] [1951] A.C. 297. [See also G. Cross, as he then was, (1956) 72 L.Q.R. 187].

the argument the law of charity is bedevilled by the fact that charitable trusts enjoy two quite different sorts of privilege. On the one hand, they enjoy immunity from the rules against perpetuity and uncertainty and although individual potential beneficiaries cannot sue to enforce them the public interest arising under them is protected by the Attorney-General. If this was all there would be no reason for the courts not to look favourably on the claim of any 'purpose' trust to be considered as a charity if it seemed calculated to confer some real benefit on those intended to benefit by it whoever they might be and if it would fail if not held to be a charity. But that is not all. Charities automatically enjoy fiscal privileges which with the increased burden of taxation have become more and more important and in deciding that such and such a trust is a charitable trust the court is endowing it with a substantial annual subsidy at the expense of the taxpayer. Indeed, claims of trusts to rank as charities are just as often challenged by the Revenue as by those who would take the fund if the trust was invalid. It is, of course, unfortunate that the recognition of any trust as a valid charitable trust should automatically attract fiscal privileges, for the question whether a trust to further some purpose is so little likely to benefit the public that it ought to be declared invalid and the question whether it is likely to confer such great benefits on the public that it should enjoy fiscal immunity are really two quite different questions. The logical solution would be to separate them and to say—as the Radcliffe Commission proposed—that only some charities should enjoy fiscal privileges. But as things, are, validity and fiscal immunity march hand in hand and the decisions in the *Compton*[91] and *Oppenheim*[92] cases were pretty obviously influenced by the consideration that if such trusts as were there in question were held valid they would enjoy an undeserved fiscal immunity. To establish a trust for the education of the children of employees in a company in which you are interested is no doubt a meritorious act; but however numerous the employees may be the purpose which you are seeking to achieve is not a public purpose.[93] It is a company purpose and there is no reason why your fellow taxpayers should contribute to a scheme which by providing 'fringe benefits' for your employees will benefit the company by making their conditions of employment more attractive. The temptation to enlist the assistance of the law of charity in private endeavours of this sort is considerable—witness the recent case of the Metal Box scholarships—*Inland Revenue Comrs.* v. *Educational Grants Association Ltd.*[94]—and the courts must do what they can to discourage such attempts. In the field of poverty the danger is not so great as in the field of education—for while people are keenly alive to the need to give their children a good education and to the expense of doing so, they are generally optimistic enough not to entertain serious fears of falling on evil days much before they fall on them. Consequently the existence of company 'benevolent funds,' the income of which is free of tax does not constitute a very attractive 'fringe benefit.' This is a practical justification—although not, of course, the historical explanation—for the special treatment accorded to poverty trusts in charity law. For the same sort of reason a trust to promote some religion among the employees of a company might perhaps safely be held to be charitable provided that it was clear that the benefits were to be purely

---

91 [1945] Ch. 123.
92 [1951] A.C. 297.
93 For a critical view of this approach see T. G. Watkin [1978] Conv. 277.
94 [1967] Ch. 993, *infra*, p. 324.

spiritual. On the other hand, many 'purpose' trusts falling under Lord Macnaghten's fourth head if confined to a class of employees would clearly be open to the same sort of objection as educational trusts. As I see it, it is on these broad lines rather than for the reasons actually given by Lord Greene M.R. that the *Compton* rule can best be justified.

"My Lords, I would dismiss this appeal." *Appeal dismissed.*

### III. TRUSTS FOR THE ADVANCEMENT OF EDUCATION

*Educational purposes*

This group of charitable trusts has its origins in those parts of the preamble to the Statute of Charitable Uses 1601 which speak of "the maintenance of schools of learning, free schools and scholars in universities" and "the education and preferment of orphans." It is now clear that trusts endowing fee-paying schools are charitable if the school is non-profit-making or if, though profit-making, its profits are used for school purposes only.[95]

Education is not confined to matters formally taught in schools and universities. It includes the promotion or encouragement of the arts and graces of life: see *Re Shaw's Will Trusts*[96] ("the teaching, promotion and encouragement in Ireland of self-control, elocution, oratory, deportment, the arts of personal contact, of social intercourse, and the other arts of public, private, professional and business life"); *Royal Choral Society* v. *I.R.C.*[97] (choral singing in London); *Re Levien*[98] (organ music); *Re Delius*[99] (the music of the composer Delius); *Re Dupree's Deed Trusts*[1] (encouragement of chess-playing among young people in Portsmouth); and *Re South Place Ethical Society*[2] (the study and dissemination of ethical principles and the cultivation of a rational religious sentiment).

The decision of Harman J. in *Re Shaw*[3] (where George Bernard Shaw had bequeathed funds for pursuing inquiries into a new 40 letter alphabet) appeared to render doubtful the validity of trusts for the advancement of research, at any rate where no element of teaching was involved; but the decision of Wilberforce J. in *Re Hopkins' Will Trusts, infra*[4] removes most of the doubts. In *McGovern* v. *Att.-Gen.*[5] Slade J. summarised the principles as follows:

"(1) A trust for research will ordinarily qualify as a charitable trust if, but only if (a) the subject matter of the proposed

---

[95] *Abbey Malvern Wells Ltd.* v. *Ministry of Local Government* [1951] Ch. 728; *Customs & Excise Commissioners* v. *Bell Concord Education Trust* [1989] 2 All E.R. 217.
[96] [1952] Ch. 163.
[97] [1943] 2 All E.R. 101; contrast *Associated Artists Ltd.* v. *I.R.C.* [1956] 1 W.L.R. 752 (production of artistic dramatic works).
[98] [1955] 1 W.L.R. 964.
[99] [1957] Ch. 299; contrast *Re Pinion* [1965] Ch. 85 (bequest of worthless works of art to found a museum); *Sutherland's Trustees* v. *Verschoyle*, 1968 S.L.T. 43.
[1] [1945] Ch. 16.
[2] [1980] 1 W.L.R 1565.
[3] [1957] 1 W.L.R. 729.
[4] See (1965) 29 Conv.(N.S.) 368 (Newark and Samuels).
[5] [1982] Ch. 321, 352.

research is a useful subject of study; and (b) it is contemplated that knowledge acquired as a result of the research will be disseminated to others; and (c) the trust is for the benefit of the public, or a sufficiently important section of the public. (2) In the absence of a contrary context, however, the court will be readily inclined to construe a trust for research as importing subsequent dissemination of the results thereof. (3) Furthermore, if a trust for research is to constitute a valid trust for the advancement of education, it is not necessary either (a) that a teacher/pupil relationship should be in contemplation, or (b) that the persons to benefit from the knowledge to be acquired should be persons who are already in the course of receiving 'education' in the conventional sense."

The promotion of sport as such is not a charitable object: see *Re Nottage*[6] (yacht-racing); *Re Clifford*[7] (angling); *Re Patten*[8] (cricket); *Re King*[9] (general sport); *Re Birchfield Harriers*[10] (athletics for both sexes from 10 years old); *I.R.C.* v. *Baddeley*[11] (moral, social and physical training and recreation). In certain circumstances trusts for similar objects may now be charitable by virtue of being a recreational trust for the public within the fourth head of charitable trusts,[12] or of the Recreational Charities Act 1958, *infra*.[13] On the other hand, where the promotion of sport is ancillary to a charitable object, it will itself be charitable: *Re Mariette*[14] (sport in a school—educational), *Re Gray*[15] (sport in a regiment—general public benefit in promoting the efficiency of the Army), *London Hospital Medical College* v. *I.R.C.*[16] (athletic, social and cultural activities of Students Union charitable as furthering educational purposes of College). *I.R.C.* v. *McMullen, infra*, p. 308 (soccer and other sports in the physical education and development of pupils at schools and universities).

### Public benefit

The promotion of a particular type of political education[17] is not charitable; and some other forms of education may also not be for the public benefit: *Re Hummeltenberg*[18] (training of spiritualistic mediums).

---

6 [1885] 2 Ch. 649.
7 (1911) 106 L.T. 14.
8 [1929] 2 Ch. 276.
9 [1931] W.N. 232.
10 [1989] Report of Charity Commissioners, paras. 48–55, *infra*, p. 356.
11 [1955] A.C. 572.
12 pp. 338–340, *infra*, *Re Morgan* [1955] 2 All E.R. 632, *Re Oxford Ice Skating Rink* [1984] Report of Charity Commissioners, paras. 19–25.
13 pp. 352–358.
14 [1915] 2 Ch. 284, *Re Geere's W.T.* [1954] C.L.Y. 388 (swimming bath at Marlborough College).
15 [1925] Ch. 362; but this has been doubted in *I.R.C.* v. *City of Glasgow Police Athletic Association* [1953] A.C. 380, 391, 401.
16 [1976] 2 All E.R. 113, *Att.-Gen.* v. *Ross* [1985] 3 All E.R. 334 (N. London Polytechnic Students' Union charitable).
17 *Bonar Law Memorial Trust* v. *I.R.C.* (1933) 49 T.L.R. 220; *Re Hopkinson* [1949] 1 All E.R. 346; cf. *Re Scowcroft* [1898] 2 Ch. 638 which nowadays should be regarded as of doubtful authority; and see *Re McDougall* [1957] 1 W.L.R. 81 (study of methods of government is a charitable object).
18 [1923] 1 Ch. 237.

The court and not the settlor determines whether public benefit is present so that a testator cannot set up a charitable museum of his artistic collection if it has no artistic merit.[19] The fact that it is by means of an educational process that non-charitable purposes are to be achieved does not render such purposes charitable.[20]

A trust for the education of beneficiaries who are ascertained by reference to some personal tie (*e.g.* of blood or contract), such as the relations of a particular individual, the members of a particular family, the employees of a particular firm, or the members of a particular trade union, lacks the element of public benefit and is not charitable: *Oppenheim* v. *Tobacco Securities Trust Co. Ltd., infra,* p. 318, though this may require reconsideration in the light of *Dingle* v. *Turner*[21] where large-scale trusts are concerned. A trust to educate residents of a town[22] or children of members of a particular profession[23] or to provide "closed" scholarships from a specified school to a specified Oxbridge College will be valid.[24]

Merely creating a clearly valid charitable trust, *e.g.* "for the advancement of the education of children in the United Kingdom" will not confer tax advantages if the trustees run the trust as a private trust for certain associated persons: *I.R.C.* v. *Educational Grants Association, infra,* p. 324. Indeed, the trustees will be acting *ultra vires* and can be liable for breach of trust.

If a trust for a broad charitable class of beneficiaries gives the trustees a power, without being under any duty, to prefer a certain private class within the broader public class this does not vitiate the validity of the trust as a charitable trust.[25] However, payments to members of the private class will have unfortunate tax consequences if regarded as of such significance that they ought fairly to be considered as misuse of public funds for a private purpose. Rather than put the tax inspector on his mettle some settlors may omit the preference from the trust deed and rely on the sensible selection of beneficiaries by trustees.

If the trust for the broad charitable class imposes a duty upon the trustees to use the whole, if possible, or an uncertain part of the funds for a specified private class then the trust cannot be a valid charitable trust.[26] If only a maximum specified part of the fund was directed to be

---

[19] *Re Pinion* [1965] Ch. 85.
[20] *Re Koeppler's W.T.* [1984] 2 All E.R. 111 though reversed by the Court of Appeal [1985] 2 All E.R. 869 since the purpose was held charitable.
[21] [1972] A.C. 601, set out at p. 296, *supra.*
[22] *Re Tree* [1945] Ch. 325: a restriction to Methodists or members of the Church of England would seem valid.
[23] *Hall* v. *Derby Sanitary Authority* (1885) 16 Q.B.D. 163 approved in *Oppenheim* v. *Tobacco Securities Trust Co.* [1951] A.C. 297, *infra,* p. 318.
[24] Picarda *Law & Practice Relating to Charities* (1st ed.), p. 49.
[25] *Re Koettgen* [1954] Ch. 252; *Caffoor* v. *Comr. of Income Tax, Colombo* [1961] A.C. 584; *I.R.C.* v. *Educational Grants Association* [1967] Ch. 123, dealing with above cases at p. 326, *infra.*
[26] *Re Martin* (1977) 121 Sol.J. 828, *Times,* November 17, 1977. An anomalous exception exists for the ancient English institution of educational provision for Founder's Kin in certain schools and colleges "though there seems to be virtually no direct authority as to the principle on which they rested and they should probably be regarded more as belonging to history than to doctrine": *Caffoor* v. *Comr. of Income Tax* [1961] A.C. 584, at p. 602.

used for the private class then whilst such part should not be charitable the remainder, presumably, should be severed as charitable since it can be used for exclusively charitable purposes. However, in *Re Koettgen*[27] (doubted in *I.R.C.* v. *Educational Grants Association*[28] *infra*, p. 327) Upjohn J. in a brief extempore judgment held that if there was a broad primary class that was charitable the trust remained charitable despite an imperative direction imposing a duty to prefer a private class for up to a maximum of 75 per cent. of the trust income. This is difficult to justify logically, but pragmatically it validates the trust, whilst leaving it open to the Revenue to charge tax if the trust is operated as a private trust and enabling charitable purposes to be carried out to the extent it is impossible or impracticable to benefit the preferred class. The Charity Commissioners have accepted *Re Koettgen* as good law.[29]

## RE HOPKINS' WILL TRUSTS

Chancery Division [1965] Ch. 669; [1964] 3 W.L.R. 840; [1964] 3 All E.R. 46.

By her will dated the testatrix bequeathed a part of her residuary estate on trust for the Francis Bacon Society Inc., of 50A, Old Brompton Road, London, S.W.7, "to be earmarked and applied towards finding the Bacon-Shakespeare manuscripts. . . . " The society's main objects both at the date of her will and when she died were: "(1) to encourage the study of the works of Francis Bacon as philosopher, lawyer, statesman and poet; also his character, genius and life; his influence on his own and succeeding times, and the tendencies and results of his writings; (2) to encourage the general study of the evidence in favour of Francis Bacon's authorship of the plays commonly ascribed to Shakespeare, and to investigate his connection with other works of the Elizabethan period." A summons was taken to determine *inter alia* whether the bequest was held on valid charitable trusts.

WILBERFORCE J. [After rejecting the argument that the bequest was made for a purpose so manifestly futile that it did not even qualify for consideration as a possible charitable gift.[30]]

"Accepting, as I have the authority of Lord Simonds for so doing, that the court must decide each case as best it can, on the evidence available to it, as to benefit, and within the moving spirit of decided cases, it would seem to me that a bequest for the purpose of search, or research for the original manuscripts of England's greatest dramatist (whoever he was) would be well within the law's conception of charitable purposes. The discovery of such manuscripts, or of one such manuscript, would be of the highest value to history and to literature. It is objected, against this, that as we already have the text of the plays, from an almost contemporary date, the discovery of a manuscript would add nothing worth while. This I utterly decline to accept. Without any undue exercise of the imagination, it would surely be a reasonable expectation that the revelation of a manuscript would contribute, probably decisively, to a solution of the authorship problem, and this alone is benefit enough. It might also lead to improvements in the text. It might lead to more accurate dating.

---

[27] [1954] Ch. 252.
[28] [1967] Ch. 123.
[29] [1978] Annual Report, paras. 86, 89.
[30] *cf. Re Pinion* [1965] Ch. 85.

"Is there any authority, then, which should lead me to hold that a bequest to achieve this objective is not charitable? For the next-of-kin, much reliance was placed on the decision on Bernard Shaw's will, the '*British Alphabet*' case (*Re Shaw, decd.*[31]). Harman J. held that the gift was not educational because it merely tended to the increase of knowledge and that it was not within the fourth charitable category because it was not itself for a beneficial purpose but for the purpose of persuading the public by propaganda that it was beneficial. The gift was very different from the gift here. But the judge did say this[32]: 'If the object be merely the increase of knowledge, that is not in itself a charitable object unless it be combined with teaching or education'; and he referred to the House of Lords decision *Whicker* v. *Hume*,[33] where, in relation to a gift for advancement of education and learning, two of the Lords read 'learning' as equivalent to 'teaching,' thereby in his view implying that learning, in its ordinary meaning, is not a charitable purpose.

"This decision certainly seems to place some limits upon the extent to which a gift for research may be regarded as charitable. Those limits are that either it must be 'combined with teaching or education,' if it is to fall under the third head, or it must be beneficial to the community in a way regarded by the law as charitable, if it is to fall within the fourth category. The words 'combined with teaching or education,' though well explaining what the judge had in mind when he rejected the gift in *Shaw's* case,[34] are not easy to interpret in relation to other facts. I should be unwilling to treat them as meaning that the promotion of academic research is not a charitable purpose unless the researcher were engaged in teaching or education in the conventional meaning; and I am encouraged in this view by some words of Lord Greene M.R. in *Re Compton*.[35] The testatrix there had forbidden the income of the bequest to be used for research, and Lord Greene M.R. treated this as a negative definition of the education to be provided. It would, he said, exclude a grant to enable a beneficiary to conduct research on some point of history or science. This shows that Lord Greene M.R. considered that historic research might fall within the description of 'education.' I think, therefore, that the word 'education' as used by Harman J. in *Re Shaw, decd.*,[36] must be used in a wide sense, certainly extending beyond teaching, and that the requirement is that, in order to be charitable, research must either be of educational value to the researcher or must be so directed as to lead to something which will pass into the store of educational material, or so as to improve the sum of communicable knowledge in an area which education may cover—education in this last context extending to the formation of literary taste and appreciation (compare *Royal Choral Society* v. *Inland Revenue Commissioners*[37]). Whether or not the test is wider than this, it is, as I have stated it, amply wide enough to include the purposes of the gift in this case.

"As regards the fourth category, Harman J. is evidently leaving it open to the court to hold, on the facts, that research of a particular kind may be beneficial to the community in a way which the law regards as charitable,

---

[31] [1957] 1 W.L.R. 729.
[32] *Ibid.* 737.
[33] (1858) 7 H.L.C. 124 (H.L.).
[34] [1957] 1 W.L.R. 729.
[35] [1945] Ch. 123, 127.
[36] [1957] 1 W.L.R. 729.
[37] [1943] 2 All E.R. 101 (C.A.).

'beneficial' here not being limited to the production of material benefit (as through medical or scientific research) but including at least benefit in the intellectual or artistic fields.

"So I find nothing in this authority to prevent me from finding that the gift falls under either the third or fourth head of the classification of charitable purposes.

"On the other side there is *Re British School of Egyptian Archaeology*,[38] also a decision of Harman J., a case much closer to the present. The trusts there were to excavate, to discover antiquities, to hold exhibitions, to publish works and to promote the training and assistance of students—all in relation to Egypt. Harman J. held that the purposes were charitable, as being educational. The society was one for the diffusion of a certain branch of knowledge, namely, knowledge of the ancient past of Egypt; and it also had a direct educational purpose, namely, to train students. The conclusion reached that there was an educational charity was greatly helped by the reference to students, but it seems that Harman J. must have accepted that the other objects—those of archaeological research—were charitable, too. They were quite independent objects on which the whole of the society's funds could have been spent, and the language 'the school has a direct educational purpose, namely, to train students' seems to show that the judge was independently upholding each set of objects.

"Mr. Fox correctly pointed out that in that case there was a direct obligation to diffuse the results of the society's research and said that it was this that justified the finding that the archaeological purposes were charitable. I accept that research of a private character, for the benefit only of the members of a society, would not normally be educational—or otherwise charitable—as did Harman J.,[39] but I do not think that the research in the present case can be said to be of a private character, for it is inherently inevitable, and manifestly intended, that the result of any discovery should be published to the world. I think, therefore, that the *British School of Egyptian Archaeology* case[40] supports the society's contentions.

"One final reference is appropriate: to *Re Shakespeare Memorial Trust*.[41] The scheme there was for a number of objects which included the performance of Shakespearian and other classical English plays, and stimulating the art of acting. I refer to it for two purposes, first, as an example of a case where the court upheld the gift either as educational or as for purposes beneficial to the community—an approach which commends itself to me here—and, secondly, as illustrative of the educational and public benefit accepted by the court as flowing from a scheme designed to spread the influence of Shakespeare as the author of the plays. This gift is not that, but it lies in the same field, for the improving of our literary heritage, and my judgment is for upholding it. . . . "

## INLAND REVENUE COMMISSIONERS v. McMULLEN

House of Lords [1981] A.C. 1; [1980] 1 All E.R. 884.

LORD HAILSHAM: "Four questions arose for decision below. In the first place neither the parties nor the judgments below were in agreement as to the

---

[38] [1954] 1 W.L.R. 546.
[39] *Ibid.* 551.
[40] *Ibid.* 546.
[41] [1923] 2 Ch. 398.

proper construction of the trust deed itself. Clearly this is a preliminary debate which must be settled before the remaining questions are even capable of decision. In the second place the trustees contend and the Crown disputes that, on the correct construction of the deed, the trust is charitable as being for the advancement of education. Thirdly, the trustees contend and the Crown disputes that if they are wrong on the second question the trust is charitable at least because it falls within the fourth class of Lord Macnaghten's categories as enumerated in *Income Tax Special Purposes Comrs.* v. *Pemsel*[42] as a trust beneficial to the community within the spirit and intendment of the preamble to the statute 43 Eliz. I, c. 4.[43] Fourthly, the trustees contend and the Crown disputes that, even if not otherwise charitable, the trust is a valid charitable trust as falling within section I of the Recreational Charities Act 1958, that is as a trust to provide or to assist in the provision of facilities for recreation or other leisure time occupation provided in the interests of social welfare.

"Since we have reached the view that the trust is a valid educational charity their Lordships have not sought to hear argument nor, therefore, to reach a conclusion on any but the first two disputed questions in the dispute. Speaking for myself, however, I do not wish my absence of decision on the third or fourth points to be interpreted as an indorsement of the majority judgments in the Court of Appeal nor as necessarily dissenting from the contrary views contained in the minority judgment of Bridge L.J. For me at least the answers to the third and fourth questions are still left entirely undecided.

"I now turn to the question of construction, for which it is necessary that I reproduce the material portions of the deed. . . .

'The objects of the Trusts are:—

'(a) to organise or provide or assist in the organisation and provision of facilities which will enable and encourage pupils of Schools and Universities in any part of the United Kingdom to play Association Football or other games or sports and thereby to assist in ensuring that due attention is given to the physical education and development of such pupils as well as to the development and occupation of their minds and with a view to furthering this object (i) to provide or assist in the provision of Association Football or games or sports equipment of every kind for the use of such pupils as aforesaid (ii) to provide or assist in the provision of courses lectures demonstrations and coaching for pupils of Schools and Universities in any part of the United Kingdom and for teachers who organise or supervise playing and coaching of Association Football or other games or sports at such Schools and Universities as aforesaid (iii) to promote provide or assist in the promotion and provision of training colleges for the purpose of training teachers in the coaching of Association Football or other games or sports at such Schools and Universities as aforesaid (iv) to lay out manage equip and maintain or assist in the laying out management equipment and mainte- nance of playing fields or appropriate indoor facilities or accommodation (whether vested in the Trustees or not) to be used for the teaching and playing of Association Football or other sports or games by such pupils as aforesaid

'(b) to organise or provide or assist in the organisation or provision of facilities for physical recreation in the interests of social welfare in any

---

[42] [1891] A.C. 531 at 583: [1891–94] All E.R.Rep. 28 at 55.
[43] Charitable Uses Act 1601.

part of the United Kingdom (with the object of improving the conditions of life for the boys and girls for whom the same are provided) for boys and girls who are under the age of twenty-one years and who by reason of their youth or social and economic circumstances have need of such facilities.'

I pause here only to say that no question arises as to clause 3(b) above which clearly corresponds to the language of the Recreational Charities Act 1958. Controversy therefore revolves solely around clause 3(a), since it is obvious that, if this cannot be shown to be solely for charitable purposes, the whole trust ceases to be a charitable trust. . . .

"I agree with [the judgment of Bridge L.J.] . . . that what the deed means is that the purpose of the settlor is to promote the physical education and development of pupils at schools and universities as an addition to such part of their education as relates to their mental education by providing the facilities and assistance to games and sports in the manner set out at greater length and in greater detail in the enumerated sub-clauses of clause 3(a) of the deed. . . .

"On a proper analysis, therefore, I do not find clause 3(a) ambiguous. But, before I part with the question of construction, I would wish to express agreement with a contention made on behalf of the trustees and of the Attorney-General, but not agreed to on behalf of the Crown, that in construing trust deeds the intention of which is to set up a charitable trust, and in others too, where it can be claimed that there is an ambiguity, a benignant construction should be given if possible. This was the maxim of the civil law: semper in dubiis benigniora praeferenda sunt. There is a similar maxim in English law: ut res magis valeat quam pereat. It certainly applies to charities when the question is one of uncertainty (*Weir* v. *Crum-Brown*[44]) and, I think, also where a gift is capable of two constructions one of which would make it void and the other effectual (*cf. Bruce* v. *Deer Presbytery*,[45] *Houston* v. *Burns*[46] and *Re Bain, Public Trustee* v. *Ross*[47]). In the present case I do not find it necessary to resort to benignancy in order to construe the clause, but, had I been in doubt, I would certainly have been prepared to do so. . . .

"I must now turn to the deed, construed in the manner in which I have found it necessary to construe it, to consider whether it sets up a valid charitable trust for the advancement of education.

"It is admitted, of course, that the words 'charity' and 'charitable' bear, for the purposes of English law and equity, meanings totally different from the senses in which they are used in ordinary educated speech, or for instance, in the Authorised Version of the Bible (contrast, for instance, the expression 'cold as charity' with the Authorised Version of I Corinthians 13 and both of these with the decisions in *Incorporated Council of Law Reporting for England and Wales* v. *Attorney-General*,[48] *Inland Revenue Comrs.* v. *Yorkshire Agricultural Society*,[49] *Brisbane City Council* v. *Attorney-General for Queensland*[50]). But I do not share the view, implied by Stamp and Orr L.JJ. in the instant case,[51] that the words 'education' and 'educational' bear, or can bear, for the

---

[44] [1908] A.C. 162 at 167.
[45] (1867) L.R. 1 Sc. & Div. 96 at 97.
[46] [1918] A.C. 337 at 341–342.
[47] [1930] 1 Ch. 224 at 230.
[48] [1972] Ch. 73.
[49] [1928] 1 K.B. 611.
[50] [1979] A.C. 411.
[51] [1979] 1 W.L.R. 130 at 135, 139.

purposes of the law of charity, meanings different from those current in present day educated English speech. I do not believe that there is such a difference. What has to be remembered, however, is that, as Lord Wilberforce pointed out in *Re Hopkins' Will Trusts*[52] and in *Scottish Burial Reform and Cremation Society Ltd.* v. *Glasgow City Corpn*,[53] both the legal conception of charity, and within it the educated man's ideas about education are not static, but moving and changing. Both change with changes in ideas about social values. Both have evolved with the years. In particular in applying the law to contemporary circumstances it is extremely dangerous to forget that thoughts concerning the scope and width of education differed in the past greatly from those which are now generally accepted.

"In saying this I do not in the least wish to cast doubt on *Re Nottage*,[54] which was referred to in both courts below and largely relied on by the Crown here. Strictly speaking *Re Nottage* was not a case about education at all. The issue there was whether the bequest came into the fourth class of charity categorised in Lord Macnaghten's classification of 1891.[55] The mere playing of games or enjoyment of amusement or competition is not per se charitable, nor necessarily educational, though they may (or may not) have an educational or beneficial effect if diligently practised. Neither am I deciding in the present case even that a gift for physical education per se and not associated with persons of school age or just above would necessarily be a good charitable gift. That is a question which the courts may have to face at some time in the future. But in deciding what is or is not an educational purpose for the young in 1980 it is not irrelevant to point out what Parliament considered to be educational for the young in 1944 when, by the Education Act of that year in sections 7 and 53 (which are still on the statute book), Parliament attempted to lay down what was then intended to be the statutory system of education organised by the state, and the duties of the local education authorities and the Minister in establishing and maintaining the system. Those sections are so germane to the present issue that I cannot forbear to quote them both. Section 7 provides (in each of the sections the emphasis being mine):

'The statutory system of public education shall be organised in three progressive stages to be known as primary education, secondary education, and further education; and it shall be the duty of the local education authority for every area, so far as their powers extend, to contribute towards *the spiritual, moral, mental, and physical development of the community by securing that efficient education throughout those stages shall be available to meet the needs of the population of their area*'

and in section 53 of the same Act it is said:

'(1) It shall be the duty of every local education authority to secure that the facilities for primary, secondary and further education provided for their area include adequate facilities for recreation *and social and physical training*, and for that purpose a local education authority, with the approval of the Secretary of State, may establish maintain and manage, or assist the establishment, maintenance, and management of

[52] [1965] Ch. 669 at 678.
[53] [1968] A.C. 138 at 154.
[54] [1895] 2 Ch. 649.
[55] See *Income Tax Special Purposes Comrs.* v. *Pemsel* [1891] A.C. 531 at 583.

*camps, holiday classes, playing fields, play centres and other places
(including playgrounds, gymnasiums, and swimming baths not appropriated to any school or college), at which facilities for recreation and for
such training as aforesaid are available for persons receiving primary,
secondary or further education, and may organise games, expeditions and
other activities for such persons, and may defray or contribute towards the
expenses thereof.*

"There is no trace in these sections of an idea of education limited to the
development of mental, vocational or practical skills, to grounds or facilities
the special perquisite of particular schools, or of any schools or colleges, or
term time, or particular localities, and there is express recognition of the
contribution which extra-curricular activities and voluntary societies or bodies
can play even in the promotion of the purely statutory system envisaged by the
Act. In the light of section 7 in particular I would be very reluctant to confine
the meaning of education to formal instruction in the classroom or even the
playground, and I consider them sufficiently wide to cover all the activities
envisaged by the settlor in the present case. One of the affidavits filed on the
part of the Crown referred to the practices of ancient Sparta. I am not sure
that this particular precedent is an entirely happy one, but from a careful
perusal of Plato's Republic I doubt whether its author would have agreed with
Stamp L.J. in regarding 'physical education and development' as an elusive
phrase, or as other than an educational charity, at least when used in
association with the formal education of the young during the period when
they are pupils of schools or in statu pupillari at universities.

"It is, of course, true that no authority exactly in point could be found which
is binding on your Lordships in the instant appeal. Nevertheless, I find the first
instance case of *Re Mariette*,[56] a decision of Eve J., both stimulating and
instructive. Counsel for the Crown properly reminded us that this concerned a
bequest effectively tied to a particular institution. Nevertheless, I cannot
forbear to quote a phrase from the judgment, always bearing in mind the
danger of quoting out of context. Eve J. said[57]:

'No one of sense could be found to suggest that between those ages
[10 to 19] any boy can be properly educated unless at least as much
attention is given to the development of his body as is given to the
development of his mind.'

"Apart from the limitation to the particular institution I would think that
these words apply as well to the settlor's intention in the instant appeal as to
the testator's in *Re Mariette*, and I regard the limitation to the pupils of schools
and universities in the instant case as a sufficient association with the provision
of formal education to prevent any danger of vagueness in the object of the
trust or irresponsibility or capriciousness in application by the trustees. I am
far from suggesting either that the concept of education or of physical
education even for the young is capable of indefinite extension. On the
contrary, I do not think that the courts have as yet explored the extent to
which elements of organisation, instruction or the disciplined inculcation of
information, instruction or skill may limit the whole concept of education. I

---

[56] [1915] 2 Ch. 284.
[57] [1915] 2 Ch. 284 at 288.

believe that in some ways it will prove more extensive, in others more restrictive than has been thought hitherto. But it is clear at least to me that the decision in *Re Mariette*[58] is not to be read in a sense which confines its application for ever to gifts to a particular institution. It has been extended already in *Re Mellody*[59] to gifts for annual treats for schoolchildren in a particular locality (another decision of Eve J), to playgrounds for children (*Re Chester*,[60] possibly *not* educational, but referred to in *Inland Revenue Comrs. v. Baddeley*[61]); to a children's outing (*Re Ward's Estate*[62]), to a prize for chess to boys and young men resident in the City of Portsmouth (*Re Dupree's Deed Trusts*,[63] a decision of Vaisey J.) and for the furthering of the Boy Scouts' movement by helping to purchase sites for camping, outfits, etc (*Re Webber*,[64] another decision of Vaisey J.).

"It is important to remember that in the instant appeal we are dealing with the concept of physical education and development of the young deliberately associated by the settlor with the status of pupillage in schools or universities (of which, according to the evidence, about 95 per cent are within the age-group 17 to 22). We are not dealing with adult education, physical or otherwise, as to which some considerations may be different. Whether one looks at the statute or the cases, the picture of education when applied to the young which emerges is complex and varied, but not, to borrow Stamp L.J.'s epithet, 'elusive'. It is the picture of a balanced and systematic process of instruction, training and practice containing, to borrow from section 7 of the 1944 Act, both spiritual, moral, mental and physical elements, the totality of which, in any given case, may vary with, for instance, the availability of teachers and facilities, and the potentialities, limitations and individual preferences of the pupils. But the totality of the process consists as much in the balance between each of the elements as of the enumeration of the thing learned or the places in which the activities are carried on. I reject any idea which would cramp the education of the young within the school or university syllabus, confine it within the school or university campus, limit it to formal instruction, or render it devoid of pleasure in the exercise of skill. It is expressly acknowledged to be a subject in which the voluntary donor can exercise his generosity, and I can find nothing contrary to the law of charity which prevents a donor providing a trust which is designed to improve the balance between the various elements which go into the education of the young. That is what in my view the object of the instant settlement seeks to do.

"I am at pains to disclaim the view that the conception of this evolving, and therefore not static, view of education is capable of infinite abuse or, even worse, proving void for uncertainty. Quite apart from the doctrine of the benignant approach to which I have already referred, and which undoubtedly comes to the assistance of settlors in danger of attack for uncertainty, I am content to adopt the approach of my predecessor Lord Loreburn L.C. in *Weir v. Crum-Brown*,[65] to which attention was drawn by counsel for the Attorney-

---

58 [1915] 2 Ch. 284.
59 [1918] 1 Ch. 228.
60 (July 25, 1934) unreported.
61 [1955] A.C. 572 at 596.
62 (1937) 81 S.J. 397.
63 [1945] Ch. 16.
64 [1954] 1 W.L.R. 1500.
65 [1908] A.C. 162 at 167.

General, that if the bequest to a class of persons, is as here capable of application by the trustees, or, failing them, the court, the gift is not void for uncertainty. Lord Macnaghten also said[66]:

'The testator has taken pains to provide competent judges. It is for the trustees to consider and determine the value of the service on which a candidate may rest his claim to participate in the testator's bounty.'

"Mutatis mutandis, I think this kind of reasoning should apply here. Granted that the question of application may present difficulties for the trustees, or, failing them, for the court, nevertheless it is capable of being applied, for the concept in the mind of the settlor is an object sufficiently clear, is exclusively for the advancement of education, and, in the hands of competent judges, is capable of application.

"My Lords, for these reasons I reach the conclusion that the trust is a valid charitable gift for the advancement of education, which, after all, is what it claims to be. The conclusion follows that the appeal should be allowed."

Lords Diplock and Salmon merely concurred while Lords Russell and Keith concurred and gave brief speeches.

### INCORPORATED COUNCIL OF LAW REPORTING FOR ENGLAND AND WALES v. ATTORNEY-GENERAL

Court of Appeal [1972] Ch. 73; [1971] 3 W.L.R. 853; [1971] 3 All E.R. 1029

The Charity Commissioners refused to register the Council as a charity so it appealed to the courts under section 5(3) of the Charities Act 1960. Foster J. held that the Council was a charity within Lord Macnaghten's fourth category but not his second category.

On appeal, Sachs and Buckley L.JJ. affirmed the charitable status of the Council but as falling within the second category. Russell L.J. considered that the second category was inapplicable but that the fourth category was applicable. Sachs and Buckley L.JJ. stated that if they had not found the second category to be applicable then they would have found the fourth category applicable. The judgment of Sachs L.J. follows immediately whilst the judgment of Russell L.J. follows later in this chapter at p. 340.

Sachs L.J.: . . . "It is convenient at the outset to mention some points which have often been repeated in those judgments. First the word 'charity' is 'of all words in the English Language . . . one which more unmistakeably has a technical meaning in the strictest sense of the term . . . peculiar to law' (*per* Lord Macnaghten in *Pemsel's* case),[67] one that is 'wide and elastic' (*per* Lord Ashbourne),[68] and one that can include something quite outside the ordinary meaning the word has in popular speech (*cf.* Lord Cozens-Hardy M.R., *Re Wedgwood*)[69] It is thus necessary to eliminate from one's mind a natural allergy, stemming simply from the popular meaning of 'charity,' to the idea that law reporting might prove to be a charitable activity. Secondly, it is clear that the mere fact that charges on a commercial scale are made for services rendered by an institution does not of itself bar that institution from being held

---

66 [1908] A.C. 162 at 169.
67 [1891] A.C. 531, 581.
68 In *Re Cranston, Webb* v. *Oldfield* [1898] 1 I.R. 431, 442.
69 [1915] 1 Ch. 113, 117.

to be charitable—so long, at any rate, as all the profits must be retained for its purposes and none can enure to the benefit of its individual members (*cf. Scottish Burial Reform and Cremation Society Ltd.* v. *Glasgow City Corpn.*).[70] Thirdly, that there have, over at any rate the past century, been a number of references to the oddity that the tests by which the courts decide whether an institution is charitable depend entirely on the preamble of the Statute of Elizabeth I. The most recent is one opining that this state of affairs was 'almost incredible to anyone not familiar with this branch of the English law' (*per* Lord Upjohn in the *Scottish Burial* case).[71] To this I will return later.

"Turning now to the points of substance argued before us, there came *in limine* the question as to what material we were entitled to look at to determine whether the purposes of the council were charitable. Counsel for the Crown contended that in substance the court could and should only look at paragraph 3 of the memorandum of association and in particular at its important first sub-paragraph:

'The Objects for which the Association is established are:
1. The preparation and publication, in a convenient form, at a moderate price, and under gratuitous professional control, of Reports of Judicial Decisions of the Superior and Appellate Courts in England.'

This contention involved the proposition that we could neither look at any of the facts to which the trial judge[72] referred under the heading of 'the historical background' nor at any available evidence as to what at any time since July 1870 had been the use to which the Law Reports are put. That in effect would mean looking at paragraph 3(1) as if it were situate in a vacuum. That cannot be right.

"Moreover he went on to submit that (a) the courts cannot look at the motives of the founders in order to show the purposes of an institution—at any rate, when those purposes as otherwise ascertained might be shown not to be charitable, and (b) the absence in the opening phrase of paragraph 3 of general words such as 'for the purpose of the advancement and promotion of the science of law' was fatal to the council's claim even if on the facts it was shown that that was the exclusive purpose of their activities and that that purpose was charitable. Whilst the first of those submissions was correct (*cf. Keren Kayemeth Le Jisroel Ltd.* v. *Inland Revenue Comrs.*),[73] the second was not. The courts look at the substance of what is being effected.

"A further question discussed was whether the use of the words 'is established' in the section 45(1) definition of 'charity' is to bind the court to look only at facts as existing at the date the 1960 Act came into force, or whether the court could or should look at the facts as at the date of the incorporation of the council. It makes no practical difference in the present case whether one looks at the circumstances of 1870 or of 1970, but to my mind it is the foundation date that matters when considering whether an institution is established for charitable purposes.

"Whilst appreciating what has been said as to the courts not being permitted, where plain language is used in a charter or memorandum, to admit extrinsic evidence as to its construction, it is yet plain from the course adopted

---

[70] [1968] A.C. 138.
[71] [1968] A.C. 138, 151.
[72] [1971] Ch. 626.
[73] [1931] 2 K.B. 465, 484.

by the courts in many cases that they are entitled to and do look at the circumstances in which the institution came into existence and at the sphere in which it operates to enable a conclusion to be reached on whether its purposes are charitable. Such matters were likewise regularly taken into account over the 117 years of the operation of Scientific Societies Act 1843, when the issue was whether buildings belonged 'to any Society instituted for purposes of science, literature or the fine arts exclusively'.

"As to the circumstances in which the council came into existence and the sphere in which it has since operated, the facts are admirably marshalled in the affidavit of Professor Goodhart with the accustomed lucidity of that eminent jurist. Reference can also be made to the 1853 Report[74] of the Society for Promoting the Amendment of the Law, an extract from page 4 of which is aptly cited in the judgment of Foster. J.[75] In the main the relevant circumstances and sphere are within judicial knowledge and need no detailed exposition in this judgment. The kernel of the matter is the vital function of judge-made law in relation not only to the common law and to equity, but to declaring the meaning of statutory law. No one—layman or lawyer—can have reasonably full knowledge of how the law affects what he or his neighbours are doing without recourse to reports of judicial decisions as well as to the statutes of the realm.

"What in that state of affairs is the purpose of law reports? There is in substance only one purpose. To provide essential material for the study of the law—in the sense of acquiring knowledge of what the law is, how it is developing and how it applies to the enormous range of human activities which it affects.

"At this juncture it is apposite to recall that the profession of the law is a learned profession. It was one of the earliest to be recognised as such, well before the Statute of Elizabeth I: to establish that point there is no need to have recourse to examples of this recognition such as the traditional House of Commons appellation 'honourable and *learned*' to members of the profession. Similarly it is plainly correct to speak of law as a science and of its study as a study of science in the same way as one speaks of the study of medicine or chemistry. If further exemplification were needed of the categories of learning and science the pursuit of which have been held to be charitable, one can turn to the names of the institutions listed in *Tudor on Charities*[76]: there one finds such divers names as the Royal Literary Society, the British School of Egyptian Archaeology, and the Institution of Civil Engineers. That the law is such a science happens to be illustrated by Sir Frederick Pollock's celebrated essay on 'The Science of Case-Law'[77]; but this merely provides from within the profession an authoritative view which plainly accords in principle both with the decisions affecting the above cited institutions and that under the Scientific Societies Act 1843 (see *Westminster City Council* v. *Royal United Service Institution*).[78] It may at this point be of relevance to note that Lord Macnaghten's phrase 'advancement of education' has consistently been taken to be an *enlargement* of the phrase 'advancement of learning' used by Sir Samuel Romilly for his second division of charities in *Morice* v. *Bishop of Durham*[79]: in

---

74 Law Reporting Reform.
75 [1971] Ch. 626, 640.
76 6th ed., p. 29.
77 See Pollock, *Essays in Jurisprudence and Ethics* (1882), p. 237.
78 [1938] 2 All E.R. 545, 549.
79 (1805) 10 Ves. 522, 531.

other words, there can be no question but that the latter is included in the former, as is illustrated by the authorities.

"Against that background I turn to the question whether the council's purposes are educational. It would be odd indeed and contrary to the trend of judicial decisions if the institution and maintenance of a library for the study of a learned subject or of something rightly called a science did not at least prima facie fall within the phrase 'advancement of education' whatever be the age of those frequenting it. The same reasoning must apply to the provision of books forming the raw material for that study, whether they relate to chemical data or to case histories in hospitals; and I can find no good reason for excluding case law as developed in the courts. If that is the correct approach, then when the institution is one whose individual members make no financial gain from the provision of that material and is one which itself can make no use of its profits except to provide further and better material, why is the purpose not charitable?

"On behalf of the Attorney-General the only point taken against this conclusion was that the citation of the reports in court cannot be educational—in part, at any rate, because of the theory that the judges are deemed to have complete knowledge of the law. For the Crown the main contention was that the use by the legal profession of the reports was in general (not merely when in court) a use the purpose of which was to earn professional remuneration—a use for personal profit; and that it followed that the purpose of the council was not charitable.

"Taking the latter point first, it is, of course, the fact that one of the main, if not the main, uses to which law reports are put is by members of the legal profession who study their contents so as to advise clients and plead on their behalf; those reports are as essential to them in their profession as the statutes; without them they would be ill equipped to earn professional fees. Does it follow, as submitted by counsel for the Crown, that a main purpose of the reports is the advancement of professional interests and thus not charitable? The argument put thus is attractive, not least to those who, like myself, are anxious not to favour or to seem to favour their one-time profession. But the doctor must study medical research papers to enable him to treat his patients and earn his fees; and it would be difficult indeed to say that because doctors thus earn their emoluments the printing and sale of such papers by a non-profit making institution could not be held to be for the advancement of education in medicine.

"Where the purpose of producing a book is to enable a specified subject, and a learned subject at that, to be studied, it is, in my judgment, published for the advancement of education, as this, of course, includes as regards the Statute of Elizabeth I the advancement of learning. That remains its purpose despite the fact that professional men—be they lawyers, doctors or chemists—use the knowledge acquired to earn their living. One must not confuse the results flowing from the achievement of a purpose with the purpose itself, any more than one should have regard to the motives of those who set that purpose in motion.

"As to the point that the citation of reports to the judiciary is fatal to the council's claim, this, if independent of the contention concerning professional user to earn fees, seems to turn on the suggestion that as the judges are supposed to know the law the citations cannot be educative. That, however, is an unrealistic approach. It ignores the fact that citation of authority by the Bar is simply a means by which there is brought to the attention of the judge the material he has to study to decide the matter in hand; in this country he relies on competent counsel to quote the extracts relevant to any necessary study of law on the points in issue, instead of having to embark on the time-consuming process of making the necessary researches himself. Indeed, it verges on the absurd to suggest that the courteous facade embodied in the traditional phrase 'as, of course, your Lordships know' can be used to attempt to conceal the fact that no judge can possibly be aware of all the contents of all the law reports that show the continuing development of our ever changing laws.

"For these reasons I reject the contention that the user of the Law Reports by the legal profession for earning fees of itself results in the purposes of the council not being charitable and thus return to the question whether they are charitable on the footing that their substantially exclusive purpose is to further the study of the law in the way already discussed. Such a purpose must in my judgment be charitable unless the submission that the advancement of learning is not an advancement of education within the spirit and intendment of the preamble is upheld; but for the reasons already given that submission plainly fails. Accordingly, having regard to the fact that the members of the council cannot themselves gain from its activities, its purposes in my judgment fall within the second of Lord Macnaghten's divisions.

"If, contrary to my view, the purposes of the council do not fall within the second division, they are nonetheless charitable because they would then fall within the fourth."

## OPPENHEIM v. TOBACCO SECURITIES TRUST CO. LTD.

House of Lords [1951] A.C. 297; [1951] 1 T.L.R. 118; [1951] 1 All E.R. 31 (Lord Simonds, Normand, Oaksey and Morton; Lord MacDermott dissenting)[80]

Certain investments were held by the respondents, Tobacco Securities Trust Co. Ltd., on trust to apply the income in providing for the education of children of employees or former employees of British-American Tobacco Co. Ltd. . . . or any of its subsidiary or allied companies without any limit of time being specified. The High Court and Court of Appeal held the trust void for perpetuity because it was not charitable on the ground that it lacked public benefit.

LORD SIMONDS: "In the case of trusts for educational purposes the condition of the public benefit must be satisfied. The difficulty lies in determining what is sufficient to satisfy the test, and there is little to help your Lordships to solve it.

"If I may begin at the bottom of the scale, a trust established by a father for the education of his son is not a charity. The public element, as I will call it, is not supplied by the fact that from that son's education all may benefit. At the other end of the scale the establishment of a college or university is beyond doubt a charity. 'Schools of learning and free schools, and scholars of universities' are the very words of the preamble to the [Charitable Uses Act 1601 (43 Eliz. I, c. 4)]. So also the endowment of a college, university or school by the creation of scholarships or bursaries is a charity, and nonetheless

---

[80] See also *Davies* v. *Perpetual Trustee Co.* [1959] A.C. 439; 75 L.Q.R. 292. These broad employee benefit discretionary trusts were usually void as private trusts before *McPhail* v. *Doulton* [1971] A.C. 424 liberalised the test for certainty of objects.

because competition may be limited to a particular class of persons. It is on this ground, as Lord Greene M.R. pointed out in *Re Compton*,[81] that the so-called 'founder's kin' cases can be rested. The difficulty arises where the trust is not for the benefit of any institution either then existing or by the terms of the trust to be brought into existence, but for the benefit of a class of persons at large. Then the question is whether that class of persons can be regarded as such a 'section of the community' as to satisfy the test of public benefit. These words 'section of the community' have no special sanctity, but they conveniently indicate (1) that the possible (I emphasise the word 'possible') beneficiaries must not be numerically negligible, and (2) that the quality which distinguishes them from other members of the community, so that they form by themselves a section of it, must be a quality which does not depend on their relationship to a particular individual. It is for this reason that a trust for the education of members of a family or, as in *Re Compton*, of a number of families cannot be regarded as charitable. A group of persons may be numerous, but, if the nexus between them is their personal relationship to a single *propositus* or to several *propositi*, they are neither the community nor a section of the community for charitable purposes.

"I come, then, to the present case where the class of beneficiaries is numerous, but the difficulty arises in regard to their common and distinguishing quality. That quality is being children of employees of one or other of a group of companies. I can make no distinction between children of employees and the employees themselves. In both cases the common quality is found in employment by particular employers. The latter of the two cases, by which the Court of Appeal held itself to be bound, the *Hobourn* case, is a direct authority for saying that such a common quality does not constitute its possessors a section of the public for charitable purposes. In the former case, *Re Compton*, Lord Greene M.R. had by way of illustration placed members of a family and employees of a particular employer on the same footing, finding neither in common kinship nor in common employment the sort of nexus which is sufficient. My Lords, I am so fully in agreement with what was said by Lord Greene in both cases, and by my noble and learned friend, then Morton L.J., in the *Hobourn* case, that I am in danger of repeating without improving upon their words. No one who has been versed for many years in this difficult and very artificial branch of the law can be unaware of its illogicalities, but I join with my noble and learned friend in echoing the observations which he cited[82] from the judgment of Russell L.J. in *Re Grove-Grady*,[83] and I agree with him that the decision in *Re Drummond*[84] . . . 'imposed a very healthy check upon the extension of the legal definition of charity.' It appears to me that it would be an extension, for which there is no justification in principle or authority, to regard common employment as a quality which constitutes those employed a section of the community. It must not, I think, be forgotten that charitable institutions enjoy rare and increasing privileges, and that the claim to come within that privileged class should be clearly established. With the single exception of *Re Rayner*,[85] which I must regard as of doubtful authority, no case has been brought to the notice of the House in which such a claim as

---

[81] [1945] Ch. 123.
[82] [1946] Ch. 194, 208.
[83] [1929] 1 Ch. 557, 582.
[84] [1914] 2 Ch. 90.
[85] (1920) 89 L.J.Ch. 369.

this has been made, where there is no element of poverty in the beneficiaries, but just this and no more, that they are the children of those in a common employment.

"Learned counsel for the appellant sought to fortify his case by pointing to the anomalies that would ensue from the rejection of his argument. For, he said, admittedly those who follow a profession or calling—clergymen, lawyers, colliers, tobacco-workers and so on—are a section of the public; how strange then it would be if, as in the case of railwaymen, those who follow a particular calling are all employed by one employer. Would a trust for the education of railwaymen be charitable,[86] but a trust for the education of men employed on the railways by the Transport Board not be charitable? And what of service of the Crown, whether in the civil service or the armed forces? Is there a difference between soldiers and soldiers of the King? My Lords, I am not impressed by this sort of argument and will consider on its merits if the occasion should arise, the case where the description of the occupation and the employment is in effect the same, where in a word, if you know what a man does, you know who employs him to do it. It is to me a far more cogent argument, as it was to my noble and learned friend in the *Hobourn* case, that, if a section of the public is constituted by the personal relation of employment, it is impossible to say that it is not constituted by a thousand as by 100,000 employees, and if by a thousand, then by a hundred, and, if by a hundred, then by ten. I do not mean merely that there is a difficulty in drawing the line, though that, too, is significant. I have it also in mind that, though the actual number of employees at any one moment might be small, it might increase to any extent, just as, being large, it might decrease to any extent. If the number of employees is the test of validity, must the court take into account potential increase or decrease, and, if so, as at what date?

LORD MACDERMOTT (dissenting)[87]: " . . . The question is whether it is of a public nature, whether, in the words of Lord Wrenbury in *Verge* v. *Somerville*,[88] 'it is for the benefit of the community or of an appreciably important class of the community.' The relevant class here is that from which those to be educated are to be selected. The appellant contends that this class is public in character; the respondent bank (as personal representative of the last surviving settlor) denies this and says that the class is no more than a group of private individuals.

"Until comparatively recently the usual way of approaching an issue of this sort, at any rate where educational trusts were concerned, was, I believe, to regard the facts of each case and to treat the matter very much as one of degree. No definition of what constituted a sufficient section of the public for the purpose was applied, for none existed; and the process seems to have been one of reaching a conclusion on a general survey of the circumstances and considerations regarded as relevant rather than of making a single, conclusive test. The investigation left the course of the dividing line between what was and what was not a section of the community unexplored, and was concluded when it had gone far enough to establish to the satisfaction of the court whether or not the trust was public; and the decision as to that was, I think, very often reached by determining whether or not the trust was private.

---

[86] As to this see *Hall* v. *Derby Sanitary Authority* (1885) 16 Q.B.D. 163.
[87] See (1951) 67 L.Q.R. 162 (R. E. M.); *ibid.* 164 (A. L. G.) and the support in *Dingle* v. *Turner* [1972] A.C. 601 set out p. 296, *infra*.
[88] [1924] A.C. 496, 499.

"If it is still permissible to conduct the present inquiry on these broad if imprecise lines, I would hold with the appellant. The numerical strength of the class is considerable on any showing. The employees concerned number over 110,000, and it may reasonably be assumed that the children, who constitute the class in question, are no fewer. The large size of the class is not, of course, decisive but in my view it cannot be left out of account when the problem is approached in this way. Then it must be observed that the *propositi* are not limited to those presently employed. They include former employees (not reckoned in the figure I have given) and are, therefore, a more stable category than would otherwise be the case. And, further, the employees concerned are not limited to those in the service of the 'British American Tobacco Co. Ltd. or any of its subsidiary or allied companies'—itself a description of great width—but include the employees, in the event of the British American Tobacco Co. Ltd. being reconstructed or merged on amalgamation, of the reconstructed or amalgamated company or any of its subsidiary companies. No doubt the settlors here had a special interest in the welfare of the class they described, but, apart from the fact that this may serve to explain the particular form of their bounty, I do not think it material to the question in hand. What is material, as I regard the matter, is that they have chosen to benefit a class which is, in fact, substantial in point of size and importance and have done so in a manner which, to my mind, manifests an intention to advance the interests of the class described as a class rather than as a collection or succession of particular individuals. . . .

"The respondent bank, however, contends that the inquiry should be of quite a different character to that which I have been discussing. It advances as the sole criterion a narrower test derived from the decisions of the Court of Appeal in *In re Compton*,[89] and in *In re Hobourn*.[90] The basis and nature of this test appear from the passage in the judgment of the court in *In re Compton*,[91] where Lord Greene M.R., says: 'In the case of many charitable gifts it is possible to identify the individuals who are to benefit, or who at any given moment constitute the class from which the beneficiaries are to be selected. This circumstance does not, however, deprive the gift of its public character. Thus, if there is a gift to relieve the poor inhabitants of a parish the class to benefit is readily ascertainable. But they do not enjoy the benefit, when they receive it, by virtue of their character as individuals but by virtue of their membership of the specified class. In such a case the common quality which unites the potential beneficiaries into a class is essentially an impersonal one. It is definable by reference to what each has in common with the others, and that is something into which their status as individuals does not enter. Persons claiming to belong to the class do so not because they are A.B., C.D. and E.F., but because they are poor inhabitants of the parish. If, in asserting their claim, it were necessary for them to establish the fact that they were the individuals A.B., C.D. and E.F., I cannot help thinking that on principle the gift ought not to be held to be a charitable gift, since the introduction into their qualification of a purely personal element would deprive the gift of its necessary public character. It seems to me that the same principle ought to apply when the claimants, in order to establish their status, have to assert and

---

[89] [1945] Ch. 123.
[90] [1946] Ch. 194.
[91] [1945] Ch. 123, 129–30.

prove, not that they themselves are A.B., C.D., and E.F., but that they stand in some specified relationship to the individuals A.B., C.D., and E.F., such as that of children or employees. In that case, too, a purely personal element enters into and is an essential part of the qualification, which is defined by reference to something, *i.e.*, personal relationship to individuals or an individual which is in its essence non-public.'

"The test thus propounded focuses upon the common quality which unites those within the class concerned and asks whether that quality is essentially impersonal or essentially personal. If the former, the class will rank as a section of the public and the trust will have the element common to and necessary for all legal charities; but, if the latter, the trust will be private and not charitable. It is suggested in the passage just quoted, and made clear beyond doubt in *In re Hobourn*,[92] that in the opinion of the Court of Appeal employment by a designated employer must be regarded for this purpose as a personal and not as an impersonal bond of union. In this connection and as illustrating the discriminating character of what I may call 'the *Compton*[93] test' reference should be made to that part of the judgment of the learned Master of the Rolls in *In re Hobourn*,[94] in which he speaks of the decision in *Hall* v. *Derby Borough Urban Sanitary Authority*.[95] The passage runs thus:

'That related to a trust for railway servants. It is said that if a trust for railway servants can be a good charity, so too a trust for railway servants in the employment of a particular railway company is a good charity. That is not so. The reason, I think, is that in the one case the trust is for railway servants in general and in the other case it is for employees of a particular company, a fact which limits the potential beneficiaries to a class ascertained on a purely personal basis.'

"My Lords, I do not quarrel with the result arrived at in the *Compton* and *Hobourn* cases, and I do not doubt that the *Compton* test may often prove of value and lead to a correct determination. But, with the great respect due to those who have formulated this test, I find myself unable to regard it as a criterion of general applicability and conclusiveness. In the first place I see much difficulty in dividing the qualities or attributes, which may serve to bind human beings into classes, into two mutually exclusive groups, the one involving individual status and purely personal, the other disregarding such status and quite impersonal. As a task this seems to me no less baffling and elusive than the problem to which it is directed, namely, the determination of what is and what is not a section of the public for the purposes of this branch of the law. After all, what is more personal than poverty or blindness or ignorance? Yet none would deny that a gift for the education of the children of the poor or blind was charitable; and I doubt if there is any less certainty about the charitable nature of a gift for, say, the education of children who satisfy a specified examining body that they need and would benefit by a course of special instruction designed to remedy their educational defects.

"But can any really fundamental distinction, as respects the personal or impersonal nature of the common link, be drawn between those employed, for example, by a particular university and those whom the same university has

[92] [1946] Ch. 194.
[93] [1945] Ch. 123.
[94] [1946] Ch. 194, 206.
[95] 16 Q.B.D. 163

put in a certain category as the result of individual examination and assessment? Again, if the bond between these employed by a particular railway is purely personal, why should the bond between those who are employed as railway men be so essentially different? Is a distinction to be drawn in this respect between those who are employed in a particular industry before it is nationalized and those who are employed therein after that process has been completed and one employer has taken the place of many? Are miners in the service of the National Coal Board now in one category and miners at a particular pit or of a particular district in another? Is the relationship between those in the service of the Crown to be distinguished from that obtaining between those in the service of some other employer? Or, if not, are the children of, say, soldiers or civil servants to be regarded as not constituting a sufficient section of the public to make a trust for their education charitable?

"It was conceded in the course of the argument that, had the present trust been framed so as to provide for the education of the children of those engaged in the tobacco industry in a named county or town, it would have been a good charitable disposition, and that even though the class to be benefited would have been appreciably smaller and no more important than is the class here. That concession follows from what the Court of Appeal has said. But if it is sound and a personal or impersonal relationship remains the universal criterion I think it shows, no less than the queries I have just raised in indicating some of the difficulties of the problem, that the *Compton* test is a very arbitrary and artificial rule. This leads me to the second difficulty that I have regarding it. If I understand it aright it necessarily makes the quantum of public benefit a consideration of little moment; the size of the class becomes immaterial and the need of its members and the public advantage of having that need met appear alike to be irrelevant. To my mind these are considerations of some account in the sphere of educational trusts for, as already indicated, I think the educational value and scope of the work actually to be done must have a bearing on the question of public benefit.

"Finally, it seems to me that, far from settling the state of the law on this particular subject, the *Compton* test is more likely to create confusion and doubt in the case of many trusts and institutions of a character whose legal standing as charities has never been in question. I have particularly in mind gifts for the education of certain special classes such, for example, as the daughters of missionaries, the children of those professing a particular faith or accepted as ministers of a particular denomination, or those whose parents have sent them to a particular school for the earlier stages of their training. I cannot but think that in cases of this sort an analysis of the common quality binding the class to be benefited may reveal a relationship no less personal than that existing between an employer and those in his service. Take, for instance, a trust for the provision of university education for boys coming from a particular school. The common quality binding the members of that class seems to reside in the fact that their parents or guardians all contracted for their schooling with the same establishment or body. That the school in such a case may itself be a charitable foundation seems altogether beside the point and quite insufficient to hold the *Compton* test at bay if it is well founded in law.

"My Lords, counsel for the appellant and for the Attorney-General adumbrated several other tests for establishing the presence or absence of the necessary public element. I have given these my careful consideration and I do not find them any more sound or satisfactory than the *Compton* test. I therefore return to what I think was the process followed before the decision in *Compton's* case, and, for the reasons already given, I would hold the present trust charitable and allow the appeal. I have only to add that I recognize the imperfections and uncertainties of that process. They are as evident as the difficulties of finding something better. But I venture to doubt if it is in the power of the courts to resolve those difficulties satisfactorily as matters stand. It is a long cry to the age of Elizabeth and I think what is needed is a fresh start from a new statute." *Appeal dismissed.*

## I.R.C. v. EDUCATIONAL GRANTS ASSOCIATION LTD.

Chancery Division [1967] Ch. 123; [1966] 3 W.L.R. 724; [1966] 3 All E.R. 708

The Revenue appealed from a decision of the Special Commissioners of Income Tax that the respondents were a charity entitled to exemption from income tax under section 447(1)(*b*) of the Income Tax Act 1952 (now section 360(1)(*c*) of the Income and Corporation Taxes Act 1970).

The respondents were a company limited by guarantee formed for the advancement of education. However, the promoters of the company and its management were very much connected with Metal Box Ltd. Virtually all the income came from a seven-year deed of covenant executed by Metal Box Ltd. Care was taken that details of the company's objects did not leak out except to the higher ranks of Metal Box employees and their associates. Between 75 and 85 per cent. of payments were for the benefit of children of Metal Box employees.

The Revenue conceded that the respondents were established for charitable purposes only and so the case turned upon whether or not the payments had been applied to charitable purposes only.

Pennycuick J. allowed the appeal holding that the absence of public benefit had the consequence that the payments had not been applied to charitable purposes only. The Court of Appeal[96] in short extempore judgments affirmed his decision but without pursuing his doubts over *Re Koettgen*. The reserved judgment of Pennycuick J. appears below as illuminating the issues more clearly than the Court of Appeal decision.

PENNYCUICK J.: "I will next read the relevant part of section 447 of the Income Tax Act 1952.[97]

'(1) Exemption shall be granted . . . (*b*) . . . from tax chargeable under Sch. D in respect of any yearly interest or other annual payment, forming part of the income of any body of persons or trust established for charitable purposes only, or which, according to the rules or regulations established by Act of Parliament, charter, decree, deed of trust or will, are applicable to charitable purposes only, and so far as the same are applied to charitable purposes only.'

"It will be observed that the subsection imposes two distinct requirements: (i) the income must form part of the income of a body of persons or trust established for charitable purposes only, or must, according to the rules established by the relevant instrument, be applicable to charitable purposes

---

only; and (ii) the exemption is available only so far as the income is applied to charitable purposes only. The first requirement depends on the construction of the relevant instrument; the second requirement depends on what is in fact done with the income as it arises from time to time. I will, for convenience, consider these requirements in their application to a corporate body, since that is the case now before me. They apply equally, mutatis mutandis, in the case of a trust created by a will or settlement.

"The objects of the corporation, in order that they may be exclusively charitable, must be confined to objects for the public benefit. Equally, the application of the income, if it is to be within those objects, must be for the public benefit. Conversely, the application of income otherwise than for the public benefit must be outside the objects and *ultra vires*. For example, under an object for the advancement of education, once that is accepted as an exclusively charitable object, the income must be applied for the advancement of education by way of public benefit. An application of income for the advancement of education by way of private benefit would be *ultra vires*, and nonetheless so by reason that, in the nature of things, the members of a private class are included in the public as a whole. This may perhaps explain the repetition of the words 'for charitable purposes only' in the second require-ment of the subsection.

"Counsel for the taxpayers advanced a simple and formidable argument: *viz*. (i) the taxpayers are established for specified educational purposes; (ii) those purposes are admittedly charitable purposes, so the first requirement is satisfied; (iii) the income has been applied for the specified educational purposes; and (iv) therefore the income has been applied for charitable purposes, and the second requirement is satisfied. It seems to me that this argument leaves out of account the element of public benefit. It is true that it is claimed by the taxpayers and admitted by the Crown that the educational purposes specified in the taxpayers' memorandum are charitable purposes, but this by definition implies that the purposes are for the public benefit. In order that the second requirement may be satisfied, it must equally be shown that their income has been applied not merely for educational purposes as expressed in the memorandum but for those educational purposes by way of public benefit. An application of income by way of private benefit would be *ultra vires*. It is not open to the taxpayers first to set up a claim which can only be sustained on the basis that the purposes expressed in the memorandum are for the public benefit, and then, when it comes to the application of the income, to look only to the purposes expressed in the memorandum, leaving the element of public benefit out of account. This point may be illustrated by considering the familiar example of a case in which a fund is settled on trust for the advancement of education in general terms and the income is applied for the education of the settlor's children. Counsel for the taxpayer does not shrink from the conclusion that such an application comes within the terms of the trust and satisfies the second requirement of the subsection. I think that it does neither.

"I understand from counsel for the taxpayers that he advanced the foregoing contention—and, I think, only this contention—before the Special Commis-sioners, although it is not very clearly reflected in their findings. The Special Commissioners were evidently much preoccupied by the case of *Re Koettgen*,[98] to which I shall refer in a moment.

---

[98] [1954] Ch. 252.

"Counsel for the Crown based his argument on construction broadly on the lines which I have indicated above as being correct. He devoted much of his argument to repelling the application of the *Koettgen* case to the present one. In the *Koettgen* case a testatrix bequeathed her residuary estate on trust 'for the promotion and furtherance of commercial education. . . . ' The will provided that

> 'The persons eligible as beneficiaries under the fund shall be persons of either sex who are British born subjects and who are desirous of educating themselves or obtaining tuition for a higher commercial career but whose means are insufficient or will not allow of their obtaining such education or tuition at their own expense. . . . '

The testatrix further directed that in selecting the beneficiaries

> 'It is my wish that the . . . trustees shall give a preference to any employees of J.B. & Co. (London), Ltd., or any members of the families of such employees; failing a sufficient number of beneficiaries under such description then the persons eligible shall be any persons of British birth as the . . . trustees may select provided that the total income to be available for benefiting the preferred beneficiaries shall not in any one year be more than seventy-five per cent. of the total available income for that year.'

In the event of the failure of those trusts there was a gift over to a named charity. It was admitted that the trust was for the advancement of education, but it was contended for the charity that having regard to the direction to prefer a limited class of persons the trusts were not of a sufficiently public nature to constitute valid charitable trusts. It was held that the gift to the primary class from whom the trustees could select beneficiaries contained the necessary element of benefit to the public, and that it was when that class was ascertained that the validity of the trust had to be determined; so that the subsequent direction to prefer, as to 75 per cent. of the income, a limited class did not affect the validity of the trust, which was accordingly a valid and effective charitable trust. *Oppenheim* v. *Tobacco Securities Trust Co. Ltd.*,[99] was distinguished.

"The other case considered by the Special Commissioners was *Caffoor (Trustees of the Abdul Gaffoor Trust)* v. *Comr. of Income Tax, Colombo*[1] in the Privy Council. In that case by the terms of a trust deed executed in Ceylon in 1942 the trust income after the death of the grantor was to be applied by the board of trustees, the appellants, in their absolute discretion for all or any of a number of purposes, which included '(2)(b) the education instruction or training in England or elsewhere abroad of deserving youths of the Islamic Faith' in any department of human activity. The recipients of the benefits were to be selected by the board 'from the following classes of persons and in the following order: (i) male descendants along either the male or female line of the grantor or of any of his brothers or sisters' failing whom youths of the Islamic Faith born of Muslim parents of the Ceylon Moorish community permanently resident in Colombo or elsewhere in Ceylon. It was held that in view of what was in effect the absolute priority to the benefit of the trust

---

[99] [1951] A.C. 297.
[1] [1961] A.C. 584.

income which was conferred on the grantor's own family by clause 2(b)(i) of the trust deed this was a family trust and not a trust of a public character solely for charitable purposes, and the income thereof was accordingly not entitled to the exemption claimed. In his speech, Lord Radcliffe, giving the decision of the Privy Council, made the following comments[2] on the *Koettgen* case:

> 'It was argued with plausibility for the appellants that what this trust amounted to was a trust whose general purpose was the education of deserving young people of the Islamic Faith, and that its required public character was not destroyed by the circumstances that a preference in the selection of deserving recipients was directed to be given to members of the grantor's own family. Their Lordships go with the argument so far as to say that they do not think that a trust which provides for the education of a section of the public necessarily loses its charitable status or its public character merely because members of the founder's family are mentioned explicitly as qualified to share in the educational benefits or even, possibly, are given some kind of preference in the selection. They part with the argument, however, because they do not consider that the trust which is now before them comes within the range of any such qualified exception.'

Lord Radcliffe went on to say that, there, the grantor's own family had, in effect, absolute priority. Then he said of the *Koettgen* case[3]:

> 'It is not necessary for their Lordships to say whether they would have put the same construction on the will there in question as the learned judge did, or whether they regard the distinction which he made as ultimately maintainable. The decision edges very near to being inconsistent with *Oppenheim's* case, but it is sufficient to say that the construction of the gift which was there adopted does not tally with the construction which their Lordships are bound to place on the trust which is now before them. Here, the effect of the wording of para. 2(b)(i) is to create a primary disposition of the trust income in favour of the family of the grantor.'

I am not concerned with the construction placed by Upjohn J. on the particular will before him in the *Koettgen* case. I will assume that the effect of the will was as he construed it, *i.e.*, that it constituted a primary public class and then directed that the trustees should give preference to employees of a named company and their families, those employees being necessarily members of the whole public class. Upjohn J., held the trust to be charitable. In the *Caffoor* case, Lord Radcliffe gave a very guarded and qualified assent to that principle. The decision in *Koettgen's* case is concerned with the character of a trust on the construction of the relevant instrument, and not with the application of income. Its relevance in the latter connection is presumably that, if in the instrument creating a trust for a public class a private class whose members are included in the public class can be mentioned specifically and accorded a preference, then a preferential application of income for the benefit of a private class whose members are comprised in a public class is a proper execution of a trust for the public class. This is a long step, and I do not feel obliged to take it.

---

2 [1961] A.C. 297, 603.
3 [1961] A.C. 297, 604.

"For myself I find considerable difficulty in the *Koettgen* decision. I should have thought that a trust for the public with preference for a private class comprised in the public might be regarded as a trust for the application of income at the discretion of the trustees between charitable and non-charitable objects. However, I am not concerned here to dispute the validity of the *Koettgen* decision. I only mention the difficulty which I feel as affording some additional reason for not applying the *Koettgen* decision by analogy in connection with the second requirement of the subsection.

"I return now to the present case. The taxpayers have claimed that the purposes of the taxpayers are exclusively charitable, which imports that the purposes must be for the public benefit. The Crown have admitted that claim. I have then to consider whether the taxpayers have applied their income within their expressed objects and by way of public benefit. There is no doubt that the application has been within their expressed objects, but has it been by way of the public benefit? In order to answer this question, I must, I think, look at the individuals and institutions for whose benefit the income has been applied, and seek to discern whether these individuals and institutions possess any, and if so, what, relevant characteristics by virtue of which the income has been applied for their benefit. One may for this purpose look at the minutes of the council, circular letters and so forth. Counsel for the Crown at one time appeared to suggest that one might look at the actual intention of the members of the council. I do not think that that is so.

"When one makes this enquiry, one finds that between 75 per cent. and 85 per cent. of the income of the taxpayers has been expended on the education of children connected with Metal Box Co. Ltd. The taxpayers are intimately connected with Metal Box Co. Ltd., in the many respects found in the Case Stated. They derive most of their income from Metal Box Co. Ltd. The council of management, as the Special Commissioners found, has followed a policy of seeking applications for grants from employees and ex-employees of Metal Box Co. Ltd., though these applications are not, of course, always successful. The inference is inescapable that this part of the taxpayer's income—*i.e.* 75 per cent. to 85 per cent.—has been expended for the benefit of these children by virtue of a private characteristic: *i.e.*, their connection with Metal Box Co. Ltd. Such an application is not by way of public benefit. It is on all fours with an application of 75 per cent. to 85 per cent. of the income of a trust fund on the education of a settlor's children. It follows, in my judgment, that, as regards the income which has been applied for the education of children of Metal Box Co. Ltd's. employees, the taxpayers have failed to satisfy the second requirement in the subsection, and that the claim for relief fails. No reason has been suggested why the taxpayers should not obtain relief in respect of income applied for the benefit of institutions and outside individuals; see the words 'so far as' in the section.

"I recognise that this conclusion involves a finding that the council of management has acted *ultra vires* in applying the income of the taxpayers as it has done, albeit within the expressed objects of the taxpayers' memorandum. This conclusion follows from the basis on which the taxpayers have framed their objects and based their claim. It is of course open to a comparable body to frame its objects so as to make clear that its income may be applied for private as well as public purposes, but in that case it may not obtain tax relief. It does not seem to me that such a body can have it both ways. I propose, therefore, to allow this appeal." *Appeal allowed.*

IV. TRUSTS FOR THE ADVANCEMENT OF RELIGION

*Religious purposes*

This category of charitable trusts has its origin in the preamble to the 1601 Statute which speaks of "the repair of churches" but the courts soon held that the equity of the Statute extended to trusts advancing orthodox religion. With increasing religious toleration "the present position is that any religious body is entitled to charitable status so long as its tenets are not morally subversive and so long as its purposes are directed to the benefit of the public."[4] In rejecting the claim of an ethical society to charitable status Dillon J. said[5]:

"Religion is concerned with man's relations with God, and ethics are concerned with man's relations with man. The two are not the same, all are not made the same by sincere inquiry into the question: what is God? If reason leads people not to accept Christianity or any known religion, but they do believe in the excellence of qualities, such as truth, beauty and love, or believe in the platonic concept of the ideal, their beliefs may seem to them to be the equivalent of a religion, but viewed objectively they are not religion. . . . It seems to me that two of the essential attributes of religion are faith and worship: faith in a god and worship of that god. The Oxford English Dictionary gives as one of the definitions of religion: 'A particular system of faith and worship.' Then: 'Recognition on the part of man of some higher unseen power as having control of his destiny, and as being entitled to obedience, reverence and worship.' "

No distinction is drawn between monotheistic and polytheistic religions. Charitable trusts have been registered for the advancement of the Church of England, Catholic,[6] Baptist,[7] Quaker,[8] Exclusive Brethren,[9] Jewish,[10] Sikh, Islamic, Buddhist and Hindu[11] religions. The Unification Church (the "Moonies") has registered charitable status[12] but not the Church of Scientology, founded by Ron Hubbard, because the element of worship is lacking.[13] However, in Australia[14] Scientology

---

[4] Charities: A Framework for the Future (1989) Cm. 694, para. 2.20.
[5] *Re South Place Ethical Society* [1980] 1 W.L.R. 1565, 1571.
[6] *Bradshaw v. Tasker* (1834) 2 Myl. & K. 221.
[7] *Re Strickland's W.T.* [1936] 3 All E.R. 1027.
[8] *Re Manser* [1905] 1 Ch. 68.
[9] *Holmes v. Att.-Gen.*, *The Times*, February 12, 1981.
[10] *Neville Estates Ltd.* v. *Madden* [1962] Ch. 832 but not a trust for the settlement of Jews in Palestine: *Keren Kayemeth Le Jisroel* v. *I.R.C.* [1932] A.C. 650.
[11] See (1989) Cm. 694, para. 2.19, [1962] S.I. 1421, [1963] S.I. 2074.
[12] [1982] Charity Commissioners Annual Report paras. 36–38. The Att.-Gen. dropped his action to deprive them of charitable status: Hansard February 3, 1988, p. 977.
[13] *R. v. Registrar General ex p. Segerdal* [1970] 2 Q.B. 697. Its creed was more of a philosophy of the existence of man rather than a religion; such creed was described as "dangerous material" (*per* Lord Denning in *Hubbard* v. *Vosper* [1972] 2 Q.B. 84, 96) and as "pernicious nonsense" (*per* Goff J. in *Church of Scientology* v. *Kaufman* [1973] R.P.C. 635, 658).
[14] *Church of the New Faith* v. *Commissioner of Pay-roll Tax* [1982–1983] 154 C.L.R. 120. The broad Australian view has been applied in New Zealand: *Centrepoint Community Growth Trust* v. *I.R.C.* [1985] 1 N.Z.L.R. 673.

(as exemplified by the Church of New Faith) has been accepted as a charitable religion.

Mason A.C.J. and Brennan J. in the Australian High Court said[15]:

"We would hold that the criteria of religion are twofold: first, belief in a supernatural Being, Thing or Principle; and, second, the acceptance of canons of conduct in order to give effect to that belief, though canons of conduct which offend against the ordinary law are outside the area of any immunity, privilege or right conferred on the grounds of religion. Those criteria may vary in their comparative importance, and there may be a different intensity of belief or of acceptance of canons of conduct among religions or among the adherents to a religion. . . . Variations in emphasis may distinguish one religion from other religions, but they are irrelevant to the determination of an individual's or a group's freedom to profess and exercise the religion of his or their choice."

Wilson and Deane JJ. stated[16]:

"One of the more important indicia of 'religion' is that the particular collection of ideas and/or practices involves belief in the supernatural, that is to say, belief that reality extends beyond that which is capable of perception by the senses. If that be absent it is unlikely that one has a 'religion.' Another is that the ideas relate to a man's nature and place in the universe and his relation to things supernatural. A third is that the ideas are accepted by adherents as requiring or encouraging them to observe particular standards or codes of conduct or to participate in specific practices having supernatural significance. A fourth is that, however loosely knit and varying in beliefs and practices adherents may be, they constitute an identifiable group or groups. A fifth, and perhaps more controversial, indicium is that the adherents themselves see the collection of ideas and/or practices as constituting a religion. . . . No one of the above indicia is necessarily determinative of the question whether a particular collection of ideas of and/or practices should be objectively characterised as a 'religion.' They are no more than aids in determining that question. . . . All of those indicia are, however, satisfied by most or all leading religions."

Public anxiety has been expressed about some religious movements that may cause dissension in, and a break-up of, family life but the question is usually not whether their *objects* are contrary to morality or the public interest but whether *conduct* of the movement causes harm. Here the Government has recently emphasised that the Charity

15 [1982–1983] 154 C.L.R. 120, 136.
16 *Ibid.* 174.

Commissioners have powers of inquiry available to them under section 6 of the 1960 Charities Act and stated[17]:

> "Where conduct is in breach of trust or is marginal to the pursuit of an organisation's objects, action can generally be taken to restrain the trustees or their agents. Action of this kind does not affect an organisation's charitable status. But in exceptional circumstances where from a careful examination of all the circumstances the activities complained of appeared to them to be directly and essentially expressive of the objects and tenets of a particular movement, the Commissioners might conclude that the pursuit of those objects was not beneficial, and hence not therefore being directed to charitable purposes. Should they reach this conclusion the Commissioner could remove the organisation from the register of charities under section 4(3) of the 1960 Act. Under section 5(3) the Att.-Gen. can appeal against any decision of the Commissioners to remove or not to remove an organisation from the register."

The Freemasons[18] and the Oxford Group[19] (as originally formed) are not religious charities, though a trust for the publication of the writings of Joanna Southcott (who claimed to be with child by the Holy Ghost and so about to give birth to a new Messiah) was held to be charitable[20] (and so void under the 1736 Mortmain and Charitable Uses Act). Indeed, a trust "for the continuance of the work of God as it has been maintained by H and myself since 1942" was held charitable[21] where the work consisted mainly in the free distribution of fundamentalist Christian tracts written by H, though the tracts were of no intrinsic merit except in confirming the beliefs of H's circle.

Trusts for adding to or repairing the fabric of a church[22] or for the upkeep of a churchyard[23] are charitable but not for the erection or upkeep of a particular tomb in a churchyard.[24] If a gift is made to an ecclesiastic in his official name and by virtue of his office then if no purposes are expressed in the gift the gift is for charitable religious purposes inherent in the office.[25] However, if the purposes are expressed in terms not confining them to exclusively charitable purposes then the charitable character of the trustee will not make the gift charitable.[26] A trust for religious purposes will be treated as for

---

[17] (1989) Cm. 694, para. 2.32.
[18] *United Grand Lodge of Freemasons* v. *Holborn B.C.* [1957] 1 W.L.R. 1080.
[19] *Re Thackrach* [1939] 2 All E.R. 4, *Oxford Group* v. *I.R.C.* [1949] 2 All E.R. 537.
[20] *Thornton* v. *Howe* (1862) 31 Beav. 14.
[21] *Re Watson* [1973] 1 W.L.R. 1472.
[22] *Re Raine* [1956] Ch. 417, *Hoare* v. *Osborne* (1866) L.R. 1 Eq. 585.
[23] *Re Douglas* [1905] 1 Ch. 279, *Re Vaughan* (1866) 33 Ch.D. 187, 192.
[24] *Lloyd* v. *Lloyd* (1852) 2 Sim. (N.S.) 225, *Re Hooper* [1932] 1 Ch. 38; see Parish Councils and Burial Authorities Miscellaneous Provisions Act 1970, s.1 (a burial or local authority may contract to maintain a grave or memorial for not exceeding 99 years).
[25] *Re Rumball* [1956] Ch. 105.
[26] *Re Simson* [1946] Ch. 299 (gift to vicar "for his work in the parish" charitable), *Farley* v. *Westminster Bank* [1939] A.C. 430 (gift to vicar "for parish work" not charitable).

charitable religious purposes[27] but a trust for religious institutions will not be a charitable trust because some religious institutions (like a purely contemplative order of nuns) lack the necessary public benefit for a charitable trust.[28]

### Public benefit

A trust for the advancement of religion (in the sense previously discussed) is presumed to be for the public benefit unless there is evidence to the contrary.[29] This presumption reflects the reluctance of the courts to enter into questions of the comparative worth of different religions. However, in *Gilmour* v. *Coats* p. 333 the House of Lords held that a trust for a contemplative order of nuns who did not leave their cloisters was not charitable. The benefits of their edifying example and their intercessory prayers were too vague and incapable of being proved to be of tangible benefit for the public. The court does not have to accept as proved whatever a particular religion believes. Nonetheless, in *Neville Estates Ltd.* v. *Madden*[30] Cross J. upheld as charitable a trust for the members from time to time of the Catford Jewish Synagogue because[31] "the court is entitled to assume that some benefit accrues to the public from the attendance at places of worship of persons who live in this world and mix with their fellow citizens." Recently, the Charity Commissioners[32] registered as charitable The Society of the Precious Blood. This was an enclosed society of Anglican Nuns but their activities included public religious services, religious and secular education of the public and the relief of suffering, sickness, poverty and distress through their counselling service.

Is the saying of masses for the public benefit? According to *Re Hetherington, infra,* p. 336, only if the masses are said in public and not in private yet the judge's justification that trusts for public masses endow the priesthood (who advance Catholicism) seems equally applicable to private masses.[33] Are not a good part of a priest's activities necessarily undertaken in private?

### GILMOUR v. COATS

House of Lords [1949] A.C. 426; [1949] 1 All E.R. 848 (Lords Simonds, du Parcq, Normand, Morton and Reid)

---

[27] *MacLaughlin* v. *Campbell* [1906] I.R. 588 to trustees "for such Roman Catholic purposes in the parish of Coleraine or elsewhere as they deem fit" void because possibility of Catholic political economic or social purposes, while there and in *Re White* [1893] 2 Ch. 41 it was accepted that a gift for "religious purposes" means impliedly "charitable religious purposes."

[28] *Gilmour* v. *Coats* [1949] A.C. 426.

[29] 1989 Cm. 694, para. 2.26, [1973] 1 W.L.R. 1472, 1482.

[30] *Neville Estates Ltd.* v. *Madden* [1962] Ch. 832. Clearly, the benefited class was small, and in *Dingle* v. *Turner* [1972] A.C. 601, 625 Lord Cross said, "A trust to promote some religion among the employees of a company might perhaps be held to be charitable, provided it was clear that the benefits were to be purely spiritual."

[31] *Ibid.* 853; *Re Warre's W.T.* [1953] 1 W.L.R. 725 (retreat house not charitable) is of dubious authority.

[32] [1989] Annual Report paras. 56–62.

[33] [1990] Conv. 34 (C. E. F. Rickett) *Nelan* v. *Downes* (1917) 23 C.L.R. 546, *Carrigan* v. *Redwood* (1910) 30 N.Z.L.R. 244.

The income of a trust fund was to be applied to the purposes of a Carmelite convent, if those purposes were charitable. The convent was comprised of an association of strictly cloistered and purely contemplative nuns who were concerned with prayers and meditation, and who did not engage in any activities for the benefit of people outside the convent. In the view of the Roman Catholic Church, however, their prayers and meditation caused the intervention of God for the benefit of members of the public, and their life inside the convent provided an example of self-denial and concentration on religious matters which was beneficial to the public. All courts held that the trust was not a charitable one.

LORD SIMONDS: " . . . I need not go back beyond the case of *Cocks* v. *Manners*,[34] which was decided nearly eighty years ago by Wickens V.-C. In that case the testatrix left her residuary estate between a number of religious institutions, one of them being the Dominican convent at Carisbrooke, a community not differing in any material respect from the community of nuns now under consideration. The learned judge used these words,[35] which I venture to repeat, though they have already been cited in the courts below: 'On the Act [the statute of Elizabeth] unaffected by authority I should certainly hold that the gift to the Dominican convent is neither within the letter nor the spirit of it; and no decision has been referred to which compels me to adopt a different conclusion. A voluntary association of women for the purpose of working out their own salvation by religious exercises and self-denial seems to me to have none of the requisites of a charitable institution, whether the word "charitable" is used in its popular sense or in its legal sense. It is said, in some of the cases, that religious purposes are charitable, but that can only be true as to religious services tending directly or indirectly towards the instruction or the edification of the public; an annuity to an individual, so long as he spent his time in retirement and constant devotion, would not be charitable, nor would a gift to ten persons, so long as they lived together in retirement and performed acts of devotion, be charitable. Therefore the gift to the Dominican convent is not, in my opinion, a gift on a charitable trust.'

"Apart from what I have called the final argument, which I will deal with later, the contention of the appellant rests, not on any change in the lives of the members of such a community as this, nor, from a wider aspect, on the emergence of any new conception of the public good, but solely on the fact that for the first time certain evidence of the value of such lives to a wider public together with new arguments based on that evidence has been presented to the court. Never before, it was urged, has the benefit to be derived from intercessory prayer and from edification been brought to the attention of the court; if it had been, the decision in *Cocks* v. *Manners* would, at least should, have been otherwise.

"My Lords, I would speak with all respect and reverence of those who spend their lives in cloistered piety, and in this House of Lords spiritual and temporal, which daily commences its proceedings with intercessory prayers, how can I deny that the Divine Being may in His Wisdom think fit to answer them? But, my Lords, whether I affirm or deny, whether I believe or disbelieve, what has that to do with the proof which the court demands that a particular purpose satisfies the test of benefit to the community? Here is

[34] (1871) L.R. 12 Eq. 574.
[35] *Ibid.* p. 585.

something which is manifestly not susceptible of proof. But, then it is said, this is a matter not of proof but of belief, for the value of intercessory prayer is a tenet of the Catholic faith, therefore, and in such a prayer there is benefit to the community. But it is just at this 'therefore' that I must pause. It is, no doubt, true that the advancement of religion is, generally speaking, one of the heads of charity, but it does not follow from this that the court must accept as proved whatever a particular church believes. The faithful must embrace their faith believing where they cannot prove: the court can act only on proof. A gift to two or ten or a hundred cloistered nuns in the belief that their prayers will benefit the world at large does not from that belief alone derive validity any more than does the belief of any other donor for any other purpose. The importance of this case leads me to state my opinion in my own words but, having read again the judgment of the learned Master of the Rolls, I will add that I am in full agreement with what he says on this part of the case.

"I turn to the second of the alleged elements of public benefit, edification by example, and I think that this argument can be dealt with very shortly. It is, in my opinion, sufficient to say that this is something too vague and intangible to satisfy the prescribed test. The test of public benefit has, I think, been developed in the last two centuries. Today it is beyond doubt that that element must be present. No court would be rash enough to attempt to define precisely or exhaustively what its content must be. But it would assume a burden which it could not discharge if now for the first time it admitted into the category of public benefit something so indirect, remote, imponderable and, I would add, controversial as the benefit which may be derived by others from the example of pious lives.

"I must now refer to certain cases on which the appellant relied. They consist of a number of cases in the Irish courts and *Re Caus*,[36] a decision of Luxmoore J. A consideration of the Irish cases shows that it has there been decided that a bequest for the saying of masses, whether in public or in private, is a good charitable bequest: see, *e.g.*, *Att.-Gen.* v. *Hall*[37] and *O'Hanlon* v. *Logue*.[38] And in *Re Caus* Luxmoore J. came to the same conclusion. I would expressly reserve my opinion on the question whether these decisions should be sustained in this House. So important a matter should not be decided except on a direct consideration of it. It is possible that, particularly in regard to the celebration of masses in public, good reason may be found for supporting a gift for such an object as both a legal and a charitable purpose. But it follows from what I have said in the earlier part of this opinion that I am unable to accept the view, which at least in the Irish cases is clearly expressed, that in intercessory prayer and edification that public benefit which is the condition of legal charity is to be found. Of the decision of Luxmoore J. in *Re Caus*, I would only say that his *ratio decidendi* is expressly stated to be,[39] 'first, that it (*i.e.*, a gift for the saying of masses) enables a ritual act to be performed which is recognised by a large proportion of Christian people to be the central act of their religion, and, secondly, that it assists in the endowment of priests whose duty it is to perform the ritual act.' The decision, therefore, does not assist the appellant's argument in the present case and I make no further comments on it.

---

36 [1934] Ch. 162.
37 [1897] 2 I.R. 426.
38 [1906] 1 I.R. 247.
39 [1934] Ch. 162, 170.

"It remains, finally, to deal with the argument that the element of public benefit is supplied by the fact that qualification for admission to membership of the community is not limited to any group of persons but is open to any woman in the wide world who has the necessary vocation. Thus, it is said, just as the endowment of a scholarship open to public competition is a charity, so also a gift to enable any woman (or, presumably, any man) to enter a fuller religious life is a charity. To this argument, which, it must be admitted, has a speciously logical appearance, the first answer is that which I have indicated earlier in this opinion. There is no novelty in the idea that a community of nuns must, if it is to continue, from time to time obtain fresh recruits from the outside world. That is why a perpetuity is involved in a gift for the benefit of such a community, and it is not to be supposed that, to mention only three masters of this branch of the law, Wickens V.-C., Lord Lindley or Lord Macnaghten failed to appreciate the point. Yet, by direct decision or by way of emphatic example, a community such as this is by them regarded as the very type of religious institution which is not charitable. I know of no consideration applicable to this case which would justify this House in unsettling a rule of law which has been established so long and by such high authority. But that is not the only, nor, indeed, the most cogent reason why I cannot accede to the appellant's argument. It is a trite saying that the law is life, not logic. But it is, I think, conspicuously true of the law of charity that it has been built up, not logically, but empirically. It would not, therefore, be surprising to find that, while in every category of legal charity some element of public benefit must be present, the court had not adopted the same measure in regard to different categories, but had accepted one standard in regard to those gifts which are alleged to be for the advancement of religion, and it may be yet another in regard to the relief of poverty. To argue by a method of syllogism or analogy from the category of education to that of religion ignores the historical process of the law. Nor would there be lack of justification for the divergence of treatment which is here assumed. For there is a legislative and political background peculiar to so-called religious trusts, which has, I think, influenced the development of the law in this matter. Thus, even if the simple argument that, if education is a good thing, then the more education the better, may appear to be irrefutable, to repeat that argument substituting 'religion' for 'education' is to ignore the principle, which I understand to be conceded, that not all religious purposes are charitable purposes. Upon this final argument I would add this observation. I have stressed the empirical development of the law of charity and your Lordships may detect some inconsistency in an attempt to rationalise it. But it appears to me that it would be irrational to the point of absurdity, on the one hand, to deny to a community of contemplative nuns the character of a charitable institution, but, on the other, to accept as a charitable trust a gift which had no other object than to enable it to be maintained in perpetuity by recruitment from the outside world."[40] *Appeal dismissed.*

### RE HETHERINGTON (DECEASED)

Chancery Division [1989] 2 All E.R. 129 [1990] Ch. 1

---

[40] The Nathan Committee on Charitable Trusts rejected the suggestion of the representatives of the Roman Catholic Church that trusts for the advancement of religion should be defined to include "the advancement of religion by those means which that religion believes and teaches are means by which it does advance it": (1952) Cmnd. 8710, paras. 129–130.

By will the testatrix left £2,000 to the Roman Catholic Bishop of Westminster for "masses for the repose of the souls of my husband and my parents and my sisters and myself." Was the bequest a valid charitable trust?

BROWNE-WILKINSON V.-C.: "I turn then to *Re Caus* [1934] Ch. 162, [1933] All E.R. Rep. 818. In that case there were two gifts for foundation Masses for the repose of souls. Foundation Masses are perpetual income trusts. It was argued that the trusts for Masses for the repose of souls were not charitable and that accordingly the gifts were void for perpetuity. Luxmoore J. held that the trusts were charitable. He noted that the earlier decisions in *West* v. *Shuttleworth* (1835) 2 My. & K. 684, and *Heath* v. *Chapman* (1854) 2 Drew 417, that such trusts were illegal, had been overruled by *Bourne* v. *Keane*. However, he treated those two earlier decisions as still subsisting authority on the queston whether trusts for Masses were or were not charitable.

"He distinguished the earlier cases on the basis that the evidence before him (which is the evidence I have already read) showed that the earlier decisions proceeded on an erroneous assumption of fact. He decided that the gifts were charitable on the following grounds ([1934] Ch. 162 at 170):

' . . . first, that it enables a ritual act to be performed which is recognised by a large proportion of Christian people to be the central act of their religion, and, secondly, because it assists in the endowment of priests whose duty it is to perform that ritual act.'

"Earlier in his judgment, however, after quoting the evidence which I have read, he said ([1934] Ch. 162 at 168):

'On that evidence, apart from the decisions in *West* v. *Shuttleworth* and *Heath* v. *Chapman*, could there be any real doubt but that a gift for Masses was charitable in the sense which is derived [from the Charitable Uses Act 1601], because the object must necessarily be one which is not only for the public benefit, but for the advancement of religion.'

It is that statement that it must necessarily be for the public benefit that gave rise to difficulty in the later House of Lords decision of *Gilmour* v. *Coats* [1949] A.C. 426. *Re Caus* has stood now for over 50 years and I would certainly follow it unless it has been undermined by the decision of the House of Lords in *Gilmour* v. *Coats*.

"In the latter case there was gift on trust to apply income for the purposes of a Roman Catholic community of cloistered nuns who devoted their lives to prayer, contemplation, penance and self-sanctification within their convent, from which the public was wholly excluded. The nuns did not engage in any work outside their convent. The House of Lords held that the trusts were not valid charitable trusts since they lacked any element of public benefit. The only benefits alleged to accrue to the public at large were said to accrue through the effects of intercessory prayer, which the House of Lords said were incapable of proof, or by edification by example which the House of Lords held to be too intangible.

"In argument before the House of Lords *Re Caus* was relied on. Lord Simonds pointed out that the actual grounds for decision in *Re Caus* did not rely on the public benefiting by means of intercessory prayer and example (see [1949] A.C. 426 at 447–448). He reserved the question whether the decision in *Re Caus* was itself right on other grounds. Lord du Parcq also reserved the same question. Lord Reid pointed out that there were grounds, other than the alleged public benefit by means of prayer, on which it could be argued that *Re Caus* was rightly decided, but he too expressed no opinion on the point (see [1949] A.C. 426 at 460).

"In my judgment *Gilmour* v. *Coats* does not impair the validity of the decision in *Re Caus*. Certainly the passage from the judgment of Luxmoore J. which I have quoted which suggests that public benefit can be shown from the mere celebration of a religious rite is no longer good law. The same in my judgment is true of Luxmoore J.'s first ground of decision, if it suggests that the performance *in private* of a religious ritual act is charitable as being for the public benefit. But in my judgment there is nothing in the House of Lords decision which impugns Luxmoore J.'s second ground of decision, namely that the public benefit was to be found in the endowment of the priesthood. Therefore the decision in *Re Caus* is still good law and I must follow it.

"I do so without reluctance because it accords with my own views on the matter, though the reasoning by which I reach that conclusion is rather different.

"The grounds on which the trust in the present case can be attacked are that there is no *express* requirement that the Masses for souls which are to be celebrated are to be celebrated in public. The evidence shows that celebration in public is the invariable practice but there is no requirement of canon law to that effect. Therefore it is said the money could be applied to saying Masses in private which would not be charitable since there would be no sufficient element of public benefit.

"In my judgment the cases establish the following propositions. (1) A trust for the advancement of education, the relief of poverty or the advancement of religion is prima facie charitable and assumed to be for the public benefit: see *National Anti-Vivisection Society* v. *I.R.C.* [1948] A.C. 31 at 42, 65. This assumption of public benefit can be rebutted by showing that in fact the particular trust in question cannot operate so as to confer a legally recognised benefit on the public, as in *Gilmour* v. *Coats*. (2) The celebration of a religious rite in public does confer a sufficient public benefit because of the edifying and ⤳ improving effect of such celebration on the members of the public who attend. As Lord Reid said in *Gilmour* v. *Coats* [1949] A.C. 426 at 459:

> 'A religion can be regarded as beneficial without it being necessary to assume that all its beliefs are true, and a religious service can be regarded as beneficial to all those who attend it without it being necessary to determine the spiritual efficacy of that service or to accept any particular belief about it.'

(3) The celebration of a religious rite in private does not contain the necessary element of public benefit since any benefit by prayer or example is incapable of proof in the legal sense, and any element of edification is limited to a private, not public, class of those present at the celebration: see *Gilmour* v. *Coats* itself; *Yeap Cheah Neo* v. *Ong Cheng Neo* (1875) L.R. 6 P.C. 381 and *Hoare* v. *Hoare* (1886) 56 L.T. 147. (4) Where there is a gift for a religious purpose which could be carried out in a way which is beneficial to the public (*i.e.* by public Masses) but could also be carried out in a way which would not have sufficient element of public benefit (*i.e.* by private Masses) the gift is to ⤳ be construed as a gift to be carried out only by the methods that are charitable, all non-charitable methods being excluded: see *Re White, White* v. *White* [1893] 2 Ch. 41 at 52–53 and *Re Banfield (decd.)* [1968] 1 W.L.R. 846.

"Applying those principles to the present case, a gift for the saying of Masses is prima facie charitable, being for a religious purpose. In practice, those Masses will be celebrated in public, which provides a sufficient element of public benefit. The provision of stipends for priests saying the Masses, by relieving the Roman Catholic Church pro tanto of the liability to provide such stipends, is a further benefit. The gift is to be construed as a gift for public Masses only on the principle of *Re White*, private Masses not being permissible since it would not be a charitable application of the fund for a religious purpose.

"I will therefore declare that both gifts are valid charitable trusts for the saying of Masses in public."

## V. Trusts for Other Purposes Beneficial to the Community

### Other beneficial purposes which are charitable

This group of charitable trusts has its origin in the remaining charitable purposes enumerated in the preamble to the Statute of Charitable Uses 1601, and like the other groups it includes purposes within the spirit and intendment of those enumerated.

This category is limited to purposes not falling within the previous three categories but which are beneficial to the community in a way recognised by the law to be charitable. In 1972 the Court of Appeal[41] indicated that the proper approach after a finding that a purpose is beneficial to the community is to hold it charitable unless there are grounds for holding it outside the equity of the 1601 Statute. However, Dillon J. has taken the justifiable view[42] (adopted by the Charity Commissioners[43] and the Australian High Court[44]) that this ignores House of Lords decisions,[45] so that the proper approach remains that of analogy from the statutory preamble or from decided cases. It is the opinion of the court and not of the settlor that determines whether or not a trust is beneficial to the community: *National Anti-Vivisection Society v. I.R.C. infra*, p. 344.

The following types of activities are charitable: the relief of the aged[46] or sick[47] or disabled[48]; providing public works and public amenities[49]; protecting human life, the environment and property[50];

---

[41] *Incorporated Council of Law Reporting v. I.R.C.* [1972] Ch. 73, 88 *infra*, p. 349.

[42] *Re South Place Ethical Society* [1980] 1 W.L.R. 1565 *infra*, p. 351, and see *Brisbane City Council v. Att.-Gen. for Queensland* [1978] 3 All E.R. 30, 33 (Lord Wilberforce), *I.R.C. v. McMullen* [1979] 1 All E.R. 588, 592 (Stamp L.J.).

[43] [1985] Annual Report paras. 5, 26.

[44] *Royal National Agricultural Association v. Chester* (1974) 48 A.L.J.R. 304.

[45] *e.g. Williams Trustees v. I.R.C.* [1947] A.C. 447 *infra*, p. 347.

[46] *Re Dunlop* [1984] N.I. 408 (Home for elderly Presbyterians), *Rowntree Memorial Trust Housing Association v. Att.-Gen.* [1983] Ch. 159 (sheltered accommodation for elderly for payment).

[47] *Re Resch's W.T.* [1969] 1 A.C. 514 (private hospital for fee-paying patients).

[48] *Re Lewis* [1955] Ch. 104 (the blind). "Relief" is not synonymous with "benefit": a trust for aged or blind millionaires will not relieve a need of theirs as aged or blind persons: *Rowntree* [1983] Ch. 159, 171.

[49] *Att.-Gen. v. Shrewsbury Corp.* (1843) 6 Beav. 220 (repair, improvement of town's bridges, towers and walls), *Scottish Burial Reform and Cremation Society v. Glasgow Corp.* [1968] A.C. 138 (crematorium) *Re Hadden* [1932] 1 Ch. 133 and *Re Morgan* [1955] 1 W.L.R. 738 (public recreation ground) *Re Oxford Ice Skating Association Ltd.* [1984] Annual Report of Charity Commissioners paras. 19–25 (public ice-skating rink), *Goodman v. Saltash Corporation* (1882) 7 App.Cas. 633 (for benefit of inhabitants of particular locality) but anomalous and not to be extended: *Williams Trustees v. I.R.C.* [1947] A.C. 447, 459–460, see next section on Recreational Charities Act 1958.

[50] *Re Wokingham Fire Brigade Trusts* [1951] Ch. 373, *Johnston v. Swann* (1818) 3 Madd. 457 (lifeboat service), *Re Upper Teesdale Defence Fund* [1969] Annual Report of Ch. Comms. paras. 23–24 (preservation of flora and fauna of Upper Teesdale), The National Trust.

providing for social rehabilitation and welfare[51]; protecting or benefiting animals so long as this benefits, or promotes the moral improvement of, the community[52]; promoting patriotic purposes.[53] Notions of charity change with the times so that early cases may become unreliable as authorities.[54] There was some authority that trusts within this fourth category are not charitable if carried out overseas unless there is some benefit, albeit indirectly, for the United Kingdom community, *e.g.* cancer research abroad.[55] It may be that a recent Canadian lead[56] may be followed so that a trust within the fourth category could be charitable even if solely benefiting a foreign community.

In considering proposed new charitable trusts the Commissioners and the court will be particularly concerned to see that the purposes are not tainted by politics in the broad sense,[57] that any profits from charging fees are reapplied to charitable purposes and not distributed privately,[58] and that the purposes do not benefit too narrow a class to be a sufficient section of the public.[59]

## Public benefit

The trust must provide some tangible benefit for a sufficient section of the community which must not be defined by reference to a personal nexus with a named propositus,[60] *e.g.* an individual or a corporate employer. This creates problems for dependants of particular victims

---

[51] *e.g.* rehabilitation of drug addicts and criminals, crime victim support schemes, family conciliation services, provision for "latch-key" children, but a trust for the welfare of children and young persons is too wide to be charitable: *Att.-Gen. of Bahamas* v. *Royal Trust Co.* [1986] 1 W.L.R. 1001 (P.C.).

[52] *Re Wedgwood* [1915] 1 Ch. 113, 122: "A gift for the benefit and protection of animals tends to promote and encourage kindness towards them, to discourage cruelty, and thus to stimulate humane and generous sentiments in man towards the lower animals, and by these means promote feelings of humanity and morality generally, repress brutality and thus elevate the human race." But in *Re Grove-Grady* [1929] 1 Ch. 557 C.A. held a trust to set up an animal refuge safe from human interference not charitable. Animal sanctuaries involving the public can be charitable and, with the increasing recognition nowadays of the need to preserve wild life, a non-public animal sanctuary might now be held charitable, certainly if some element of education from films taken by the warden were incorporated: *cf. Att.-Gen. (N.S.W.)* v. *Sawtell* [1978] 2 N.S.W. L.R. 200.

[53] A gift "for patriotic purposes" is not necessarily charitable, and so void: *Att.-Gen.* v. *Nat Provincial Bank* [1924] A.C. 262 but some particular patriotic purposes are charitable: trusts for helping defence of the realm *Re Stratheden* [1895] 3 Ch. 265, *Re Corbyn* [1941] Ch. 400, *Re Gray* [1925] Ch. 362; gifts to the National Revenue *Nightingale* v. *Goulburn* (1848) 2 Ph. 594 or to erect a statue of Earl Mountbatten [1981] Annual Report of Ch. Comms. paras. 68–70.

[54] *e.g. Re Strakosch* [1949] Ch. 529 appeasement of racial feelings between Dutch- and English-speaking South Africans too political to be charitable but Charity Commissioners' Annual Report 1983 paras. 18–20 reveals that "promoting good race relations, endeavouring to eliminate discrimination on grounds of race and encouraging equality of opportunity" are charitable purposes in light of Race Relations Act 1976.

[55] [1963] Annual Report of Ch. Comms. paras. 72–73, *Camille & Henry Dreyfuss Foundation Inc.* v. *I.R.C.* [1954] Ch. 672, 684, *McGovern* v. *Att.-Gen.* [1981] 3 All E.R. 493, 507 *cf. Re Jacobs* (1970) 114 So.Jo. 515 (upholding trust to plant trees in Israel but unclear whether overseas point argued).

[56] *Re Levy Estate* (1989) 58 D.L.R. (4th) 375: Ontario C.A. upheld bequest to State of Israel for charitable purposes only (likely to be restricted to Israel).

[57] *National Anti-Vivisection Society* v. *I.R.C.* [1948] A.C. 31.

[58] *Re Resch's W.T.* [1969] 1 A.C. 514.

[59] *I.R.C.* v. *Baddeley* [1955] A.C. 572.

[60] *Re Hobourn Aero Components Ltd.'s Air Raid Disaster Fund* [1946] Ch. 194 (fund limited to employees so not charitable), *Re Mead* [1981] 1 W.L.R. 1244 (limited to trade union members so convalescent home non-charitable).

of a disaster, so disaster relief funds, if charitable, are restricted to relieving needs within the poverty category of charitable trust.[61]

The degree of benefit required for this residual category is very much greater than that required for religion and greater than that required for education. In *I.R.C.* v. *Baddeley infra*, p. 340, Lords Simonds and Somervell opined[62] that a residual category trust involving recreational facilities for Methodists resident in West Ham and Leyton was not for a sufficient section of the public. They constituted "a class within a class" because they were "a class of persons not only confined to a particular area but selected from within it by reference to a particular creed." However, a trust to establish a school for the children of Methodists resident in West Ham and Leyton would be a charitable educational trust.[63]

The Law Lords pointed out that a trust to build a bridge only for the use of Methodists would not be charitable. Here, one can understand that there must be a sensible relationship between the benefit conferred and the group chosen to receive it. To restrict use of a recreation ground to Methodists seems eccentric and not for the benefit of the public. However, a trust to establish a home for old Presbyterian persons is sensibly restricted to a sufficient section of the public to be charitable.[64]

The *ratio* of *I.R.C.* v. *Baddeley* was that the social element in the recreational purposes prevented the purposes from being charitable in nature. This led to the Recreational Charities Act 1958 discussed in the next section.

### INLAND REVENUE COMMISSIONERS v. BADDELEY

House of Lords [1955] A.C. 572; [1955] 1 All E.R. 525

By the first conveyance, land was conveyed to trustees on trust to permit it to be used by certain Methodist leaders "for the promotion of the religious social and physical well-being of persons resident in . . . West Ham and Leyton . . . *by the provision of facilities for religious services and instruction and for the social and physical training and recreation of such aforementioned persons* who for the time being are in the opinion of such leaders members or likely to become members of the Methodist Church and of insufficient means otherwise to enjoy the advantages provided by these presents and by the provision of facilities for religious social and physical training and education and by promoting and encouraging all forms of such activities as are calculated to contribute to the health and well-being of such persons." The second conveyance was in the same terms but with the omission of the italicized words. The conveyances were held not to be charitable and so not exempt from stamp duty.

---

61 Following suggestions of Charity Commissioners: Annual Reports, 1965, paras. 54–58, 1966, paras. 9–12.
62 [1955] A.C. 572, 592.
63 *cf. Commissioner of Income Tax* v. *Pemsel* [1991] A.C. 531, *Re Tree* [1945] Ch. 325 and valid charitable trust for specific C. of E. or Methodist schools.
64 *Re Dunlop* [1984] N.I. 408, [1987] Conv. 114 (N. Dawson).

VISCOUNT SIMONDS: "This brings me to another aspect of the case, which was argued at great length and to me at least presents the most difficult problems in this branch of the law. Suppose that, contrary to the view that I have expressed that the social element prevented the trust being charitable, the trust would be a valid charitable trust, if the beneficiaries were the community at large or a section of the community defined by some geographical limits, is it the less a valid trust if it is confined to members or potential members of a particular church within a limited geographical area?

"The starting point of the argument must be, that this charity (if it be a charity) falls within the fourth class in Lord Macnaghten's classification. It must therefore be a trust which is, to use the words of Sir Samuel Romilly in *Morice* v. *Bishop of Durham* (1805) 10 Ves. 522 at 532, of 'general public utility,' and the question is what these words mean. It is, indeed, an essential feature of all 'charity' in the legal sense that there must be in it some element of public benefit, whether the purpose is educational, religious or eleemosynary . . . and, as I have said elsewhere, it is possible, particularly in view of the so-called 'poor relations' cases,' the scope of which may one day have to be considered, that a different degree of public benefit is requisite according to the class in which the charity is said to fall. But it is said that if a charity falls within the fourth class, it must be for the benefit of the whole community or at least of all the inhabitants of a sufficient area. And it has been urged with much force that, if, as Lord Greene said in *Re Strakosch* [1949] Ch. 529, this fourth class is represented in the preamble to the Statute of Elizabeth by the repair of bridges, etc., and possibly by the maintenance of Houses of Correction, the class of beneficiaries or potential beneficiaries cannot be further narrowed down. Some confusion has arisen from the fact that a trust of general public utility, however general and however public, cannot be of equal utility to all and may be of immediate utility to few. A sea wall, the prototype of this class in the preamble, is of remote, if any, utility to those who live in the heart of the Midlands. But there is no doubt that a trust for the maintenance of sea walls generally or along a particular stretch of coast is a good charitable trust. Nor, as it appears to me, is the validity of a trust affected by the fact that by its very nature only a limited number of people are likely to avail themselves, or are perhaps even capable of availing themselves, of its benefits. It is easy, for instance, to imagine a charity which has for its object some form of child welfare, of which the immediate beneficiaries could only be persons of tender age. Yet this would satisfy any test of general public utility. It may be said that it would satisfy the test because the indirect benefit of such a charity would extend far beyond its direct beneficiaries, and that aspect of the matter has probably not been out of sight. Indirect benefit is certainly an aspect which must have influenced the decision of the 'cruelty to animal' cases. But, I doubt whether this sort of rationalization helps to explain a branch of the law which has developed empirically and by analogy upon analogy.

"It is, however, in my opinion, particularly important in cases falling within the fourth category to keep firmly in mind the necessity of the element of general public utility, and I would not relax this rule. For here is a slippery slope. In the case under appeal the intended beneficiaries are a class within a class; they are those of the inhabitants of a particular area who are members of a particular church: the area is comparatively large and populous and the members may be numerous. But, if this trust is charitable for them, does it cease to be charitable as the area narrows down and the numbers diminish? Suppose the area is confined to a single street and the beneficiaries to those whose creed commands few adherents: or suppose the class is one that is determined not by religious belief but by membership of a particular profession or by pursuit of a particular trade. These were considerations which influenced the House in the recent case of *Oppenheim*. That was a case of an educational trust, but I think that they have even greater weight in the case of trusts which by their normal classification depend for their validity upon general public utility.

"It is pertinent, then, to ask how far your Lordships might regard yourselves bound by authority to hold the trusts now under review valid charitable trusts, if the only question in issue was the sufficiency of the public element . . .

"In [*Verge* v. *Somerville* [1924] A.C. 496 at 499] in which the issue was as to the validity of a gift 'to the trustees of the Repatriation Fund or other similar fund for the benefit of New South Wales returned soldiers,' Lord Wrenbury, delivering the judgment of the Judicial Committee, said that, to be a charity, a trust must be 'for the benefit of the community or of an appreciably important class of the community. The inhabitants,' he said, 'of a parish or town or any particular class of such inhabitants, may, for instance, be the objects of such a gift, but private individuals, or a fluctuating body of private individuals, cannot.' Here, my Lords, are two expressions: 'an appreciably important class of the community' and 'any particular class of such inhabitants,' to which in any case it is not easy to give a precise quantitative or qualitative meaning. But I think that in consideration of them the difficulty has sometimes been increased by failing to observe the distinction, at which I hinted earlier in this opinion, between a form of relief accorded to the whole community yet by its very nature advantageous only to the few and a form of relief accorded to a selected few out of a larger number equally willing and able to take advantage of it. Of the former type repatriated New South Wales soldiers would serve as a clear example. To me it would not seem arguable that they did not form an adequate class of the community for the purpose of the particular charity that was being established. It was with this type of case that Lord Wrenbury was dealing, and his words are apt to deal with it. Somewhat different considerations arise if the form, which the purporting charity takes, is something of general utility which is nevertheless made available not to the whole public but only to a selected body of the public—an important class of the public it may be. For example, a bridge which is available for all the public may undoubtedly be a charity and it is indifferent how many people use it. But confine its use to a selected number of persons, however numerous and important: it is then clearly not a charity. It is not of general public utility: for it does not serve the public purpose which its nature qualifies it to serve.

"Bearing this distinction in mind, though I am well aware that in its application it may often be very difficult to draw the line between public and private purposes, I should in the present case conclude that a trust cannot qualify as a charity within the fourth class . . . if the beneficiaries are a class of persons not only confined to a particular area but selected from within it by reference to a particular creed. The Master of the Rolls in his judgment cites a rhetorical question asked by Mr. Stamp in argument [1953] Ch. 504 at 519: 'Who has ever heard of a bridge to be crossed only by impecunious Methodists?' The *reductio ad absurdum* is sometimes a cogent form of argument, and this illustration serves to show the danger of conceding the quality of charity to a purpose which is not a public purpose. What is true of a bridge for Methodists is equally true of any other public purpose falling within the fourth class and of the adherents of any other creed.

"The passage that I have cited from *Verge* v. *Somerville* refers also (not, I think for the first time) to 'private individuals' or a 'fluctuating body of private individuals' in contradistinction to a class of the community or of the inhabitants of a locality. This is a difficult conception to grasp: the distinction between a class of the community and the private individuals from time to time composing it is elusive. But, if it has any bearing on the present case, I would suppose that the beneficiaries, a body of persons arbitrarily chosen and impermanent, fall more easily into the latter than the former category . . . "

LORD REID [dissenting, and disagreeing with Viscount Simonds on the "public" point] "But your Lordships are bound by a previous decision in this House, and it appears to me to be unquestionable that in *Goodman* v. *Mayor of Saltash* (1882) 7 App. Cas. 633 this House decided that there was a valid charitable trust where there was no question of poverty or disability or of education or religion, and where the beneficiaries were not by any means all the inhabitants of any particular area. . . . [If] the members of a religious denomination do not constitute a section of the public (or the community) then a trust solely for the advancement of religion or of education would not be a charitable trust if limited to members of a particular church. Of course, the appellants do not contend that that is right: they could not but admit that the members of a church are a section of the community for the purpose of such trusts. But they maintain that they cease to be a section of the community when it comes to trusts within the fourth class . . . Poverty may be in a special position but otherwise I can see no justification in principle or authority for holding that when dealing with one deed for one charitable purpose the members of the Methodist or any other church are a section of the community, but when dealing with another deed for a different charitable purpose they are only a fluctuating body of private individuals. I therefore reject this argument and on the whole matter I am of opinion that this appeal ought to be dismissed."

LORD SOMERVELL OF HARROW: "I agree with the Court of Appeal in rejecting the argument that as a matter of law a trust to qualify under Lord Macnaghten's fourth class must be analgous to the repair of 'bridges portes havens causwaies seabankes and highewaies,' being the examples given in the preamble outside the three main categories of poverty, religion and education . . . I think, however, that a trust to be valid under this head would normally be for the public or all members of the public who needed the help or facilities which the trust was to provide. The present trust is not for the public.

"I cannot accept the principle submitted by the respondents that a section of the public sufficient to support a valid trust in one category must as a matter of law be sufficient to support a trust in any other category. I think that difficulties are apt to arise if one seeks to consider the class apart from the particular nature of the charitable purpose. They are, in my opinion, interdependent. There might well be a valid trust for the promotion of religion benefiting a very small class. It would not at all follow that a recreation ground for the exclusive use of the same class would be a valid charity, though it is clear from the Mortmain and Charitable Uses Act 1888, that a recreation ground for the public is a charitable purpose."

[LORDS PORTER AND TUCKER expressed no opinion on the "public" point.]

## NATIONAL ANTI-VIVISECTION SOCIETY v. INLAND REVENUE COMMISSIONERS

House of Lords [1948] A.C. 31; 177 L.T. 226; [1947] L.J.R. 1112; 63 T.L.R. 424; [1947] 2 All E.R. 217 (Lords Simon, Wright, Simonds and Normand; Lord Porter dissenting)

The question was whether the appellant society was a body established for charitable purposes only within the meaning of section 37 of the Income Tax Act 1918 and accordingly entitled to exemption from income tax upon the income of its investments. The Special Commissioners for the purposes of the Income Tax Acts held that they were so entitled, but this decision was reversed by Macnaghten J.,[65] whose judgment was upheld by the Court of Appeal[66] (Mackinnon and Tucker L.JJ., Greene M.R. dissenting). The society appealed unsuccessfully.

LORD SIMONDS: " . . . The first point is whether a main purpose of the society is of such a political character that the court cannot regard it as charitable. The second point is whether the court, for the purpose of determining whether the object of the society is charitable, may disregard the finding of fact that any assumed public benefit in the direction of the advancement of morals and education was far outweighed by the detriment to medical science and research and, consequently, to the public health, which would result if the society succeeded in achieving its objects, and that, on balance, the object of the society, so far from being for the public benefit, was gravely injurious thereto.

"My Lords, on the first point the learned Master of the Rolls cites in his judgment[67] a passage from the speech of Lord Parker in *Bowman* v. *Secular Society Ltd.*[68]: ' . . . a trust for the attainment of political objects has always been held invalid, not because it is illegal . . . but because the court has no means of judging whether a proposed change in the law will or will not be for the public benefit . . . ' Lord Parker is here considering the possibility of a valid charitable trust, and nothing else, and when he says 'has always been held invalid' he means 'has always been held not to be a valid charitable trust.' The learned Master of the Rolls found this authoritative statement upon a branch of the law, with which no one was more familiar than Lord Parker, to be inapplicable to the present case for two reasons, first, because he felt difficulty in applying the words to 'a change in the law which is in common parlance a "non-political" question' and, secondly, because he thought they could not in any case apply when the desired legislation is 'merely ancillary to the attainment of what is *ex hypothesi* a good charitable object.'

"My Lords, if I may deal with this second reason first, I cannot agree that in this case an alteration in the law is merely ancillary to the attainment of a good charitable object. In a sense, no doubt, since legislation is not an end in itself, every law may be regarded as ancillary to the object which its provisions are intended to achieve. But that is not the sense in which it is said that a society has a political object. Here the finding of the commissioners is itself conclusive. 'We are satisfied,' they say, 'that the main object of the society is the total abolition of vivisection . . . and (for that purpose) the repeal of the Cruelty to Animals Act 1876, and the substitution of a new enactment prohibiting vivisection altogether.' This is a finding that the main purpose of the society is the compulsory abolition of vivisection by Act of Parliament. What else can it mean? And how else can it be supposed that vivisection is to be abolished?

---

65 [1945] 2 All E.R. 529.
66 [1946] K.B. 185.
67 [1946] K.B. 185, 207.
68 [1917] A.C. 406, 442.

Abolition and suppression are words that connote some form of compulsion. It can only be by Act of Parliament that that element can be supplied. Upon this point I must with respect differ both from the learned Master of the Rolls and from Chitty J., whose decision in *Re Foveaux*[69] I shall later consider. Coming to the conclusion that it is a main object, if not the main object, of the society to obtain an alteration of the law, I ask whether that can be a charitable object, even if its purposes might otherwise be regarded as charitable.

"My Lords, I see no reason for supposing that Lord Parker, in the cited passage, used the expression 'political objects' in any narrow sense or was confining it to objects of acute political controversy. On the contrary, he was, I think, propounding familiar doctrine, nowhere better stated than in a textbook which has long been regarded as of high authority, but appears not to have been cited for this purpose to the courts below (as it certainly was not to your Lordships), *Tyssen on Charitable Bequests*. The passage[70] is worth repeating at length: 'It is a common practice for a number of individuals amongst us to form an association for promoting some change in the law, and it is worth our while to consider the effect of a gift to such an association. It is clear that such an association is not of a charitable nature. However desirable the change may really be, the law could not stultify itself by holding that it was for the public benefit that the law itself should be changed. Each court in deciding on the validity of a gift must decide on the principle that the law is right as it stands. On the other hand, such a gift could not be held void for illegality.'

"Lord Parker uses slightly different language, but means the same thing, when he says that the court has no means of judging whether a proposed change in the law will or will not be for the public benefit. It is not for the court to judge and the court has no means of judging. The same question may be looked at from a slightly different angle. One of the tests, and a crucial test, whether a trust is charitable lies in the competence of the court to control and reform it. I would remind your Lordships that it is the King as *parens patriae* who is the guardian of charity, and that it is the right and duty of his Attorney-General to intervene and inform the court if the trustees of a charitable trust fall short of their duty. So too is it his duty to assist the court, if need be, in the formulation of a scheme for the execution of a charitable trust. But, my Lords, is it for a moment to be supposed that it is the function of the Attorney-General, on behalf of the Crown, to intervene and demand that a trust shall be established and administered by the court, the object of which is to alter the law in a manner highly prejudicial, as he and His Majesty's Government may think, to the welfare of the state? This very case would serve as an example if upon the footing that it was a charitable trust it became the duty of the Attorney-General on account of its maladministration to intervene. There is, undoubtedly, a paucity of judicial authority on this point. It may fairly be said that *De Themmines* v. *De Bonnevale*,[71] to which Lord Parker referred in *Bowman's* case, turned on the fact that the trust there in question was held to be against public policy. In *Commissioners of Inland Revenue* v. *Temperance Council*[72] the principle was clearly recognised by Rowlatt J. as it was in *Re Hood*.[73] But in truth the reason of the thing appears to me so clear that I

[69] [1895] 2 Ch. 501.
[70] (1st ed., 1898), p. 176.
[71] (1828) 5 Russ. 288.
[72] (1926) 136 L.T. 27.
[73] [1931] 1 Ch. 240, 250, 252.

neither expect nor require much authority. I conclude upon this part of the case that a main object of the society is political and for that reason the society is not established for charitable purposes only. I would only add that I would reserve my opinion upon the hypothetical example of a private enabling Act, which was suggested in the course of the argument. I do not regard *Re Villers-Wilkes*[74] as a decision that a legacy which had for its main purposes the passing of such an Act is charitable.

"The second question raised in this appeal . . . is of wider importance, and I must say at once that I cannot reconcile it with my conception of a court of equity, that it should take under its care and administer a trust, however well intentioned its creator, of which the consequence would be calamitous to the community. [His Lordship made a brief review of the origin of the equitable jurisdiction in matters of charity, and continued:]

"My Lords, this then being the position, that the court determined 'one by one' whether particular named purposes were charitable, applying always the overriding test whether the purpose was for public benefit, and that the King as *parens patriae* intervened *pro bono publico* for the protection of charities, what room is there for the doctrine, which has found favour with the learned Master of the Rolls, and has been so vigorously supported at the Bar of the House, that the court may disregard the evils that will ensue from the achievement by the society of its ends? It is to me a strange and bewildering idea that the court must look so far and no farther, must see a charitable purpose in the intention of the society to benefit animals, and thus elevate the moral character of men, but must shut its eyes to the injurious results to the whole human and animal creation. I will readily concede that, if the purpose is within one of the heads of charity forming the first three classes in the classification which Lord Macnaghten borrowed from Sir Samuel Romilly's argument in *Morice* v. *Bishop of Durham*,[75] the court will easily conclude that it is a charitable purpose. But even here to give the purpose the name of 'religious' or 'educational' is not to conclude the matter. It may yet not be charitable if the religious purpose is illegal or the educational purpose is contrary to public policy. Still there remains the overriding question: Is it *pro bono publico*? It would be another strange misreading of Lord Macnaghten's speech in *Pemsel's* case[76] to suggest that he intended anything to the contrary. I would rather say that, when a purpose appears broadly to fall within one of the familiar categories of charity, the court will assume it to be for the benefit of the community and therefore charitable unless the contrary is shown, and further that the court will not be astute in such a case to defeat upon doubtful evidence the avowed benevolent intention of a donor. But, my Lords, the next step is one that I cannot take. Where upon the evidence before it the court concludes that, however well intentioned the donor, the achievement of his object will be greatly to the public disadvantage, there can be no justification for saying that it is a charitable object. If and so far as there is any judicial decision to the contrary, it must, in my opinion, be regarded as inconsistent with principle and be overruled." *Appeal dismissed.*

## WILLIAMS' TRUSTEES v. INLAND REVENUE COMMISSIONERS

House of Lords [1947] A.C. 447; 176 L.T. 462; 63 T.L.R. 352; [1947] 1 All E.R. 513 (Lords Simon, Wright, Porter, Simonds and Normand)

---

[74] (1895) 72 L.T. 323.
[75] (1805) 10 Ves. 522.
[76] [1891] A.C. 531, *supra*.

A trust was established for the purpose of maintaining an institute "for the benefit of Welsh people resident in or near or visiting London with a view to creating a centre in London for promoting the moral, social, spiritual and educational welfare of Welsh people, and fostering the study of the Welsh language and of Welsh history, literature, music and art."[77] The trust property, consisted of two blocks of property, one of which was let out to tenants, and the other occupied by the London Welsh Association Ltd. This association had been incorporated for substantially the same purposes as those contained in the deed of trust which are set out above. The trustees applied the rents of the first block and made certain gifts to the association intending that they should be directed to the following purposes: public lectures and debates, a music club, literary and educational classes, the maintenance of the headquarters' premises, badminton and table-tennis clubs, dances, whist- and bridge-drives, an annual dinner and garden-party, a weekly social and dance, and the provision of a central information bureau. The trustees admitted that the purposes of the association were not exclusively charitable, but contended that they themselves were trustees of a trust established for charitable purposes only, and that in applying the rents of the first block of trust property to the purposes of the association they had applied them to charitable purposes only and that accordingly they were entitled to exemption from income tax in respect of the rents of that property.

The Court of Appeal held[78] that on the true construction of the trust deed the property was not vested in the trustees for charitable purposes only, and on the facts the rents applied to the purpose of the association were not applied for charitable purposes only. The trustees appealed unsuccessfully.

LORD SIMONDS: "Lord Cave said 'Lord Macnaghten did not mean that all trusts for purposes beneficial to the community are charitable, but that there were certain beneficial trusts which fell within that category: . . . it is not enough to say that the trust in question is for public purposes beneficial to the community; you must also show it to be a charitable trust.' See *Att.-Gen.* v. *National Provincial Bank* [1924] A.C. 262, 265. But . . . it is just because the purpose of the trust deed in this case is said to be beneficial to the community or a section of the community, and for no other reason, that its charitable character is asserted. It is not alleged that the trust is (1) for the benefit of the community and (2) beneficial in a way which the law regards as charitable. Therefore, as it seems to me, in its mere statement the claim is imperfect and must fail.

"My Lords, the cases in which the question of charity has come before the courts are legion, and no one who is versed in them will pretend that all the decisions, even of the highest authority, are easy to reconcile, but I will venture to refer to one or two of them . . . In *Houston* v. *Burns*[79] the question was as to the validity of a gift 'for such public benevolent or charitable purposes in connection with the parish of Lesmahagow or the neighbourhood'

---

[77] These purposes might today be regarded as charitable by the Recreational Charities Act 1958, *infra*, p. 352. It would still be necessary to prove the existence of the other criterion, namely, an element of public benefit. *Williams' Trustees* v. *I.R.C.* remains an important authority on the latter requirement. The Charitable Trusts (Validation) Act 1954 (pp. 363–366, *infra*) has been applied to validate the *Williams* trusts: see Charity Commissioners Annual Report 1977, paras. 71–80, considering the beneficial class to be a sufficient section of the public.

[78] [1945] 2 All E.R. 236.

[79] [1918] A.C. 337.

as might be thought proper. This was a Scottish case, but upon the point now under consideration there is no difference between English and Scottish law. It was argued that the limitation of the purpose to a particular locality was sufficient to validate the gift, that is to say, though purposes beneficial to the community might fail, yet purposes beneficial to a localised section of the community were charitable. That argument was rejected by this House. If the purposes are not charitable *per se*, the localisation of them will not make them charitable. It is noticeable that Lord Finlay L.C. expressly overrules a decision or dictum of Lord Romilly to the contrary effect in *Dolan* v. *MacDermot*.[80] . . .

"My Lords, I must mention another aspect of this case. It is not expressly stated in the preamble to the statute, but it was established in the Court of Chancery and, so far as I am aware, the principle has been consistently maintained, that a trust to be charitable must be of a public character. It must not be merely for the benefit of particular private individuals. If it is it will not be in law a charity, though the benefit taken by those individuals is of the very character stated in the preamble. The rule is thus stated by Lord Wrenbury in *Verge* v. *Somerville*[81] 'To ascertain whether a gift constitutes a valid charitable trust so as to escape being void on the ground of perpetuity, a first inquiry must be whether it is public—whether it is for the benefit of the community or of an appreciably important class of the community. The inhabitants of a parish or town, or any particular class of such inhabitants, may for instance be the objects of such a gift, but private individuals, or a fluctuating body of private individuals, cannot.' It is, I think, obvious that this rule, necessary as it is, must often be difficult of application, and so the courts have found. Fortunately, perhaps, though Lord Wrenbury put it first, the question does not arise at all if the purpose of the gift, whether for the benefit of a class of inhabitants or of a fluctuating body of private individuals, is not itself charitable. I may, however, refer to a recent case in this House which in some aspects resembles the present case. In *Keren* v. *Inland Revenue Commissioners*[82] a company had been formed which had as its main object (to put it shortly) the purchase of land in Palestine, Syria or other parts of Turkey in Asia and the peninsula of Sinai for the purpose of settling Jews on such lands. In its memorandum it took numerous other powers which were to be exercised only in such a way as should, in the opinion of the company, be conducive to the attainment of the primary object. No part of the income of the company was distributable among its members. It was urged that the company was established for charitable purposes for numerous reasons, with only one of which I will trouble your Lordships, namely, that it was established for the benefit of the community or of a section of the community, whether the association was for the benefit of Jews all over the world, or of the Jews repatriated in the Promised Land. Lord Tomlin,[83] dealing with the argument that I have just mentioned on the footing that if benefit to a 'community' could be established the purpose might be charitable, proceeded to examine the problem in that aspect and sought to identify the community. He failed to do so, finding it neither in the community of all Jews throughout the world nor in that of the Jews in the region presented for settlement. It is perhaps unnecessary to pursue the matter. Each case must be judged on its own facts

---

[80] (1867) L.R. 5 Eq. 60, 62.
[81] [1924] A.C. 496, 499.
[82] [1932] A.C. 650.
[83] *Ibid*. 659.

and the dividing-line is not easily drawn, but the difficulty of finding the community in the present case, when the definition of 'Welsh people' in the first deed is remembered, would not, I think, be less than that of finding the community of Jews in *Keren's* case."

## INCORPORATED COUNCIL OF LAW REPORTING FOR ENGLAND AND WALES v. ATTORNEY-GENERAL

Court of Appeal [1972] Ch. 73; [1971] 3 W.L.R. 853; [1971] 3 All E.R. 1029

This decision turned primarily upon Lord Macnaghten's secondary category but the following extract from the judgment of Russell L.J. reveals a new approach to Lord Macnaghten's fourth category which Sachs L.J. agreed with.

RUSSELL L.J.: " . . . I come now to the question whether, if the main purpose of the Association is (as I think it is) to further the sound development and administration of the law in this country, and if (as I think it is) that is a purpose beneficial to the community or of general public utility, that purpose is charitable according to the law of England and Wales. On this point the law is rooted in the Statute of Elizabeth, a statute whose object was the oversight and reform of abuses in the administration of property devoted by donors to purposes which were regarded as worthy of such protection as being charitable. The preamble to the statute listed certain examples of purposes worthy of such protection. These were from an early stage regarded merely as examples, and have through the centuries been regarded as examples or guide-posts for the courts in the differing circumstances of a developing civilisation and economy. Sometimes recourse has been had by the courts to the instances given in the preamble in order to see whether in a given case sufficient analogy may be found with something specifically stated in the preamble, or sufficient analogy has been found. Of this approach perhaps the most obvious example is the provision of crematoria by analogy with the provision of burial grounds by analogy with the upkeep of churchyards by analogy with the repair of churches. On other occasions a decision in favour or against a purpose being charitable has been based in terms on a more general question whether the purpose is or is not within 'the spirit and intendment' of the Elizabethan statute and in particular its preamble. Again (and at an early stage in development) whether the purpose is within 'the equity' or within 'the mischief' of the statute. Again whether the purpose is charitable 'in the same sense' as purposes within the purview of the statute. I have much sympathy with those who say that these phrases do little of themselves to elucidate any particular problem. 'Tell me' they say, 'what you define when you speak of spirit, intendment, equity, mischief, the same sense, and I will tell you whether a purpose is charitable according to law. But you never define. All you do is sometimes to say that a purpose is none of these things. I can understand it when you say that the preservation of sea walls is for the safety of lives and property, and therefore by analogy the voluntary provision of lifeboats and fire brigades are charitable. I can even follow you as far as crematoria. But these other generalities teach me nothing.' I say I have much sympathy for such an approach; but it seems to me to be unduly and improperly restrictive. The Statute of Elizabeth was a statute to reform abuses; in such circumstances and in that age the courts of this country were not inclined to be restricted in their implementation of Parliament's desire for reform to particular examples given by the statute, and they deliberately kept open their ability to intervene when they thought necessary in cases not specifically mentioned, by applying as the test whether any particular case of abuse of funds or property was within the 'mischief' or the 'equity' of the statute.

"For myself I believe that this rather vague and undefined approach is the correct one, with analogy its handmaid, and that when considering Lord Macnaghten's fourth category in *Pemsel's* case[84] of 'other purposes beneficial to the community' (or as phrased by Sir Samuel Romilly[85] 'objects of general public utility') the courts, in consistently saying that not all such are necessarily charitable in law, are in substance accepting that if a purpose is shown to be so beneficial or of such utility it is prima facie charitable in law, but have left open a line of retreat based on the equity of the statute in case they are faced with a purpose (*e.g.* a political purpose) which could not have been within the contemplation of the statute even if the then legislators had been endowed with the gift of foresight into the circumstances of later centuries.

"In a case such as the present, in which in my view the object cannot be thought otherwise than beneficial to the community and of general public utility, I believe the proper question to ask is whether there are any grounds for holding it to be outside the equity of the statute; and I think the answer to that is here in the negative. I have already touched on its essential importance to our rule of law. If I look at the somewhat random examples in the preamble to the statute I find in the repair of bridges, havens, causeways, sea banks and highways examples of matters which if not looked after by private enterprise must be a proper function and responsibility of government, which would afford strong ground for a statutory expression by Parliament of anxiety to prevent misappropriation of funds voluntarily dedicated to such matters. It cannot I think be doubted that if there were not a competent and reliable set of reports of judicial decisions, it would be a proper function and responsibility of government to secure their provision for the due administration of the law. It was argued that the specific topics in the preamble that I have mentioned are all concerned with concrete matters, and that so also is the judicially accepted opinion that the provision of a court house is a charitable purpose. But whether the search be for analogy or for the equity of the statute this seems to me to be too narrow or refined an approach. I cannot accept that the provision, in order to facilitate the proper administration of the law, of the walls and other physical facilities of a court house is a charitable purpose, but that the dissemination by accurate and selective reporting of knowledge of a most important part of the law to be there administered is not.

"In my judgment accordingly the purpose for which the Association is established is exclusively charitable in the sense of Lord Macnaghten's fourth category."

## RE SOUTH PLACE ETHICAL SOCIETY

Chancery Division [1980] 1 W.L.R. 1565; [1980] 3 All E.R. 918

DILLON J.: . . . "The fourth category developed from the matters specified in the preamble to the . . . Charitable Uses Act 1601 but it has long been recognised that it is not limited to those matters actually listed in the preamble which do not fall within Lord Macnaghten's other three categories of the relief

---

[84] [1891] A.C. 531, 583.
[85] In *Morice* v. *Bishop of Durham* (1805) 10 Ves. 522, 531.

of poverty, the advancement of education and the advancement of religion. It is also clear, as stated in *Tudor on Charities* (6th Ed., 1967, pp. 85, 120) that the fourth category can include trusts for certain purposes tending to promote the mental or moral improvement of the community. It is on the basis of mental or moral improvement of the community that animal welfare trusts have been supported. But it is plain that not all objects which tend to promote the moral improvement of the community are charitable.

"Again, as Wilberforce J. pointed out in *Re Hopkins' Will Trusts* [1965] Ch. 669 at 680–681, beneficial in the fourth category is not limited to the production of material benefit, but includes at least benefit in the intellectual or artistic fields.

"In *Incorporated Council of Law Reporting for England and Wales* v. *Attorney General* [1972] Ch. 73 at 88–89, Russell L.J. seems to have taken the view that the court can hold that there are some purposes 'so beneficial or of such utility' to the community that they ought prima facie to be accepted as charitable. With deference, I find it difficult to adopt that approach in view of the comments of Lord Simonds in *Williams' Trustees* v. *Inland Revenue Commissioners* [1947] A.C. 447 at 455 where, in holding that the promotion of the moral, social, spiritual and educational welfare of the Welsh people was not charitable, he pointed out that it was really turning the question upside down to start with considering whether something was for the benefit of the community. He said:

> 'My Lords, there are, I think, two propositions which must ever be borne in mind in any case in which the question is whether a trust is charitable. The first is that it is still the general law that a trust is not charitable and entitled to the privileges which charity confers unless it is within the spirit and intendment of the preamble to 43 Eliz., c. 4, which is expressly preserved by section 13(2) of the Mortmain and Charitable Uses Act 1888. The second is that the classification of charity in its legal sense into four principal divisions by LORD MACNAGHTEN in *Pemsel's* case ([1891] A.C. 583) must always be read subject to the qualification appearing in the judgment of LINDLEY L.J. in *Re Macduff* ([1896] 2 Ch. 446): "Now SIR SAMUEL ROMILLY did not mean, and I am certain that LORD MACNAGHTEN did not mean to say, that every object of public general utility must necessarily be a charity. Some may be and some may not be." This observation has been expanded by VISCOUNT CAVE L.C. in this House in *A.G.* v. *National Provincial Bank* [1924] A.C. 265 in these words: "LORD MACNAGHTEN did not mean that all trusts beneficial to the community are charitable, but that there were certain beneficial trusts which fall within that category: and accordingly to argue that because a trust is for a purpose beneficial to the community it is therefore a charitable trust is to turn round his sentence and to give it a different meaning. So here it is not enough to say that the trust in question is for public purposes beneficial to the community or is for the public welfare; you must also show it to be a charitable trust." '

"Therefore it seems to me that the approach to be adopted in considering whether something is within the fourth category is the approach of analogy from what is stated in the preamble to the Statute of Elizabeth or from what has already been held to be charitable within the fourth category.

"The question is whether the trust is within the spirit and intendment of the preamble, and the route that the courts have traditionally adopted is the route of precedent and analogy as stated by Lord Wilberforce in *Brisbane City Council* v. *Att. Gen.* [1979] A.C. 411 at 422."

## VI. THE PROVISION OF FACILITIES FOR RECREATION IN THE INTERESTS OF SOCIAL WELFARE

### *The Recreational Charities Act 1958*[86]

Section 1.—(1) Subject to the provisions of this Act, it shall be and be deemed always to have been charitable to provide, or assist in the provision of, facilities for recreation or other leisure-time occupation, if the facilities are provided in the interests of social welfare:

Provided that nothing in this section shall be taken to derogate from the principle that a trust or institution to be charitable must be for the public benefit.

(2) The requirement of the foregoing subsection that the facilities are provided in the interests of social welfare shall not be treated as satisfied unless—

    (*a*) the facilities are provided with the object of improving the conditions of life for the persons for whom the facilities are primarily intended; and

    (*b*) either—

        (i) those persons have need of such facilities as aforesaid by reason of their youth, age, infirmity or disablement, poverty or social and economic circumstances; or

        (ii) the facilities are to be available to the members or female members of the public at large.

(3) Subject to the said requirement, subsection (1) of this section applies in particular to the provision of facilities at village halls, community centres and women's institutes, and to the provision and maintenance of grounds and buildings to be used for purposes of recreation or leisure-time occupation, and extends to the provision of facilities for those purposes by the organising of any activity.

[Section 2 makes special provision for trusts for miners' welfare; section 3 makes it clear that the Act does not restrict the purposes which are charitable independently of the Act.]

### *Note*

The Act was passed to remedy a defect in the law revealed by the House of Lords in *I.R.C.* v. *Baddeley.*[87] The objects of the trusts were "the moral, social and physical well-being of persons resident in West Ham and Leyton who for the time being were or were likely to become members of the Methodist Church and who were of insufficient means otherwise to enjoy the advantages provided." The method by which the objects were to be attained was "by the provision of facilities for

---

[86] See S. G. Maurice, "Recreational Charities" (1959) 23 Conv.(N.S.) 15; (1958) 21 M.L.R. 534 (L. Price). There is a Northern Ireland Recreational Charities Act 1958 in similar terms.

[87] [1955] A.C. 572 *supra*, p. 332. The provision of a recreation ground for the inhabitants of a particular area is, however, charitable: *Re Morgan* [1955] 1 W.L.R. 738. See also *Brisbane City Council* v. *Att.-Gen. for Queensland* [1978] 3 All E.R. 30.

moral, social and physical training and recreation and by promoting and encouraging all forms of such activities." The House of Lords by a majority (Lord Reid dissenting) held that the objects were not exclusively charitable. The word "social" included worthy objects of benevolence which were not charitable in the legal sense and the trust accordingly failed.[88] Lord Simonds also held[89] that "a trust cannot qualify as a charity within the fourth class in *Pemsel's* case (*i.e.* as being of general public utility) if the beneficiaries are a class of persons not only confined to a particular area but selected from within it by reference to a particular creed." Lord Somervell appeared to agree with this. Lords Porter and Tucker expressed no opinion on the point and Lord Reid dissented.[90]

The Act established two criteria for the validity of a recreational charity: first, the trust must be for the public benefit; and, secondly, the facilities must be provided in the interests of social welfare. The second criterion itself has two elements: the first is constant, namely, that the object of providing the facilities must be to improve the conditions of life of the beneficiaries; but the second may be satisfied in alternative ways—by showing *either* that the beneficiaries have need of the facilities by reason of the factors enumerated in the Act, *or* that the facilities are available to the members or female members of the public at large.

The Act is not free from difficulties of interpretation. For example, what is the test of "public benefit" to be applied? If it is Lord Simonds' test for trusts of general public utility, a trust like that in *I.R.C.* v. *Baddeley* would still not be charitable. Moreover, the "social welfare" criterion would not be satisfied in that the beneficiaries did not have need of the facilities by reason of the factors comprised in the Act. Similarly, *Williams* v. *I.R.C.*[91] may be unaffected on the footing that the London Welsh factor is not a sufficient qualifying factor. There would even be some difficulty forcing *I.R.C.* v. *Glasgow Police Athletic Association*[92] (encouragement and promotion of "all forms of athletic sports and general pastimes" for Glasgow Police held not charitable) within the Act as police are not normally considered as persons needing recreational facilities by reason of age or social and economic circumstances.

In *Wynn and Others* v. *Skegness U.D.C.*[93] a convalescent home and holiday centre for North Derbyshire mineworkers was conceded to be

---

88 See *Williams' Trustees* v. *I.R.C.* [1947] A.C. 447, *supra*, p. 347.
89 [1955] A.C. 572, 592. See discussion at p. 340, *supra*.
90 Citing *Verge* v. *Somerville* [1924] A.C. 496; and *Goodman* v. *Mayor of Saltash* (1882) 7 App.Cas. 633.
91 [1947] A.C. 447, *supra*. However, the Charity Commissioners have treated the Charitable Trusts (Validation) Act 1954, as applying to such trusts as benefiting a sufficient section of the public: [1977] Annual Report, paras. 71–80.
92 [1953] A.C. 380 regarded as really a trust for the private advantage of members. Trusts for promoting the efficiency of the police or the armed forces are valid: [1953] A.C. 380, 409.
93 [1967] 1 W.L.R. 52. The 1984 Annual Report of the Charity Commissioners, para. 25 shows they treated the provision of a public ice-skating rink in Oxford as within the 1958 Act.

within the terms of the Act but Ungoed-Thomas J. discussed some of the difficulties inherent in the Act. More recently in *I.R.C.* v. *McMullen, infra,* Stamp and Orr L.JJ., took a strict view on the application of the Act whilst Bridge L.J. took a liberal approach. On appeal the House of Lords left the point undecided but Lord Hailsham said that this should not be interpreted as an endorsement of the majority C.A. judgments nor as dissenting from Bridge L.J. The Charity Commissioners and the Court of Session apply the view of Bridge L.J.: see *Re Birchfield Harriers infra,* and *Guild* v. *I.R.C.* [1991] STC 281.

## I.R.C. v. McMULLEN

Court of Appeal [1979] 1 All E.R. 588. For the House of Lords decision see
    p. 308, *supra,* where the terms of the trust deed are set out.

STAMP L.J.: " . . . I will assume, as I think did the judge in the court below, that the trust declared by clause 3(a) of the trust deed is a trust to provide facilities for recreation and that there is in it the necessary element of public benefit spoken of in section 1(1) of the 1958 Act. The question then turns on whether the facilities to be provided satisfy the requirement that they are to be provided 'in the interests of social welfare.'

"Even if the phrase 'in the interests of social welfare' fell to be construed without the limitation imposed by section 1(2) I would take the view, reading the provisions of the trust deed as a whole, that it could not be said of it that the facilities provided, or to be provided, pursuant to clause 3(a) are provided in the interests of 'social welfare.' No doubt the funds could, consistently with the terms of the trust, be applied in such a way that they did, and were intended to, promote the interests of social welfare. The purchase of a playing field in part of a great town where there were no facilities for fresh air or recreation to be used by the public at large for the playing of games might well qualify. But an application of the funds in encouraging the pupils of what I may call a 'rugger' school to play 'soccer' would on the one hand be authorised by clause 3(a) and on the other hand could hardly satisfy the social welfare requirement of section 1(1) of the 1958 Act. Similarly, to provide facilities for one or other of the sports which I have mentioned would hardly be an application of the trust fund for the promotion of social welfare. When one comes to the limitation of the meaning of the phrase 'the facilities are provided in the interests of social welfare' found in section 1(2), and finds that to satisfy that requirement the facilities must be provided 'with the object of improving the conditions of life for the persons for whom the facilities are primarily intended,' the difficulty of fitting the instant trust into the Act is underlined. One has to ask the question: who are the persons for whom the facilities are primarily intended? If the answer be that the facilities are primarily intended for pupils of schools and universities in any part of the United Kingdom, and I can think of no other answer, it cannot in my judgment with any show of reason be argued that the facilities are provided with the object of improving the conditions of life for the pupils of such schools and universities. Of course they are not. The facilities are to be provided for those of them who are persuaded to, or do, play football or some other game or sport quite irrespective of their conditions of life.

"I must add this. The Act does not validate trust deeds but merely provides that the provision of facilities which might not otherwise be regarded as charitable shall be so regarded. It does not validate trusts which embrace other objects which are not charitable or which authorise the application of the trust fund for non-charitable purposes. Accordingly if it be correct that on the true construction of the deed in the instant case the trustees could, consistently with the terms of the trust deed, utilise the trust fund in providing facilities for fox hunting, for example, which if there be such a thing as 'physical education and development' would be a fine sport to promote it, then the trust could only be saved by the Act if the fox hunting had to be provided 'in the interests of social welfare. . . . ' "

[ORR L.J. agreed with Stamp L.J.]

BRIDGE L.J.: "I turn therefore to consider whether the object defined by clause 3(a) is charitable under the express terms of section 1 of the Recreational Charities Act 1958. Are the facilities for recreation contemplated in this clause to be 'provided in the interests of social welfare' under section 1(1)? If this phrase stood without further statutory elaboration, I should not hesitate to decide that sporting facilities for persons undergoing any formal process of education are provided in the interests of social welfare. Save in the sense that the interests of social welfare can only be served by the meeting of some social need, I cannot accept the judge's view[94] that the interests of social welfare can only be served in relation to some 'deprived' class. The judge found this view reinforced by the requirement of section 1(2)(*a*) that the facilities must be provided 'with the object of improving the conditions of life for the persons for whom the facilities are primarily intended.' Here again I can see no reason to conclude that only the deprived can have their conditions of life improved. Hyde Park improves the conditions of life for residents in Mayfair and Belgravia as much as for those in Pimlico or the Portobello Road, and the village hall may improve the conditions of life for the squire and his family as well as for the cottagers. The persons for whom the facilities here are primarily intended are pupils of schools and universities, as defined in the trust deed, and these facilities are in my judgment unquestionably to be provided with the object of improving their conditions of life. Accordingly the ultimate question on which the application of the statute to this trust depends, is whether the requirements of section 1(2)(*b*)(i) are satisfied on the ground that such pupils as a class have need of facilities for games or sports which will promote their physical education and development by reason either of their youth or of their social and economic circumstances, or both. The overwhelming majority of pupils within the definition are young persons and the tiny minority of mature students can be ignored as *de minimis*. There cannot surely be any doubt that young persons as part of their education do need facilities for organised games and sports both by reason of their youth and by reason of their social and economic circumstances. They cannot provide such facilities for themselves but are dependent on what is provided for them. There is overwhelming evidence that for the class as a whole the facilities available to meet the need are wholly inadequate: see the Report of the Wolfenden Committee on Sport[95]; the Second Report of the House of Lords Select Committee on Sport and Leisure[96]; and the White Paper on Sport and Recreation.[97]

---

[94] [1978] 1 W.L.R. 664, 675.
[95] Sport and the Community (Central Council for Physical Recreation (1960)).
[96] (1960) Cmnd. 193–I.
[97] (1975) Cmnd. 6200.

"Accordingly I have reached the clear conclusion that all the requirements of the statute are here satisfied. . . . "

## RE BIRCHFIELD HARRIERS

48. Birchfield Harriers are, in the words of their solicitors, "the leading athletics club in Birmingham." Their objects are "to encourage and promote interest in athletics for both sexes from the age of 10 years upwards." Founded in 1877, the Harriers had about 1300 members at the end of 1988, 800 of whom were under 18. It was said that roughly 600 lived within three miles of the Harriers' premises in Perry Barr, near the inner city areas of Handsworth, Lozells, Witton, Aston and Gravelly Hill and that many of the members were unemployed and from the ethnic minorities. Letters in support of the Harriers' application placed much emphasis on the perceived social value of the Harriers' activities, both in promoting good relations between people of different ethnic origins and in promoting young peoples' personal development and sense of social responsibility through the discipline of organised sport. The Harriers' solicitors claimed that, although the rules required prospective ordinary and junior members to be proposed and seconded, and details of their applications were displayed on the club notice-board, in practice no prospective member in recent years had, to the Harriers' knowledge, experienced difficulty in finding a proposer and seconder. In addition, no prospective member was ever refused membership save on grounds of bad character, a breach of the rules of the Amateur Athletics Association or a need to restrict numbers for reasons of safety. Although the membership application form asked for details of performances to date, it was said that no one was ever refused membership on the grounds of lack of attainment of any specific level of performance.

49. Apart from competing against each other or against set times and distances, members of the Harriers were said to participate, both as individuals and on a team basis, in external competitions, including competitions at the highest national and international levels. Members had, with one exception, been selected to compete in every Olympic Games since 1908, and had on occasion won medals. Nationally, in the ranking list of amateur athletics clubs prepared by the National Union of Track Statisticians, the Harriers were listed in both 1986 and 1987 as first for women and second for men. It was conceded that some members did come from far afield because they found the atmosphere "more competitive" and were, as a result, assisted to attain higher standards of performance. It was said that while the Harriers did not go out of their way to recruit top sports people they did not decline to accept them as members. In effect, we were being asked to treat this element in the Harriers' membership as insignificant in determining the question of their charitable status. The overwhelming impression given by the documentary evidence, however, was that the Harriers saw their success, not in terms of the provision of recreational facilities to a wide cross section of society, but in terms of results achieved in external competitions, particularly at national and international level.

50. Their solicitors contended that the Harriers' activities furthered purposes which were charitable at common law both because their activities promoted physical education and health and because the facilities they provided, meant that they fell within the principles established by *Re Hadden* [1932] 1 Ch. 133 and *Re Morgan* [1955] 2 All E.R. 632. They also contended that the Harriers'

activities furthered purposes which were charitable under the Recreational Charities Act 1958.

51. It is clearly established (see Lindley L.J. in *In Re Nottage* [1895] 2 Ch. 649 at page 656) that the encouragement of "mere sport" is not charitable unless it is part of a wider purpose which is itself charitable, such as the promotion of the efficiency of the armed forces (*Re Gray* [1925] Ch. 362) or the promotion of the efficiency of the police (*Inland Revenue Commissioners* v. *City of Glasgow Police Athletic Association* [1953] A.C. 380) or the promotion of education (*Inland Revenue Commissioners* v. *McMullen* [1981] A.C. 1).

52. We took the view that the claim of the Harriers to charitable status under the second head of Lord Macnaghten's classification, on the ground that their purposes were directed for the advancement of physical education, should be rejected since there was an insufficient element of education in the activities of the Harriers to support it. The coaching in athletics given to members was only one aspect of the Harriers' activities and the informal educational opportunities offered by contact between young people of different ages, races and cultures must be regarded as incidental.

53. We also rejected the Harriers' claim for charitable status under the fourth head of Lord Macnaghten's classification, on the ground that they promoted health and wellbeing. The Harriers placed reliance on the Ontario decision in *Re Laidlaw Foundation* [1984] 48 OR (2d) 549, where it was held by the Surrogate Court judge, and confirmed by the Ontario High Court, that the promotion of amateur athletic sports, under controlled conditions, was itself a charitable purpose in that it promoted health. *Re Laidlaw*, based on a Canadian statute, is not binding on the English courts and, in our view, the decision paid insufficient regard to the decision in *In Re Nottage* and in particular to the words of Lindley L.J. when he said (at page 655):

> "Now, I should say that every healthy sport is good for the nation—cricket, football, fencing, yachting or any other healthy exercise and recreation; but if it had been the idea of lawyers that a gift for the encouragement of such exercise is therefore charitable, we should have heard of it before now."

In that case Lopes L.J. also based his decision on a wider ground than the mere rejection of the particular benefit alleged by The Yacht Racing Association, making it clear that although the promotion of sport may have certain beneficial side effects (including the promotion of health) it was not a charitable purpose.

54. We also rejected the claim of the Harriers to charitable status under the principle of *Re Hadden*. Although it might be difficult to draw the line in certain cases, there is a thin, but discernible, line between a gift whose dominant purpose is to improve the health of the public by providing facilities where they can take healthy recreational exercise (*Re Hadden; Re Morgan*), and cases where the dominant purpose is to encourage competitive sport for the benefit of the spectators or the enjoyment of the participants (*Re Nottage*). In the case of the Oxford Ice Skating Association Limited (see paragraphs 19 to 25 of our report for 1984) we had decided that the provision of an ice skating rink to be open to the public at large was a charitable purpose by analogy with *Re Hadden* and *Re Morgan*. However, the nature of the facilities provided by the Harriers pointed firmly in the direction of competitive sport, so placing them on the other side of the line from the Oxford Ice Skating case. A further difficulty to the Harriers' claim for charitable status on the basis of

*Re Hadden* lay in the fact that the facilities provided by the Harriers were available only to members and, in view of the restrictive membership provisions, it was difficult to see that the membership constituted a sufficient section of the public to satisfy the public benefit requirement. Membership of another club affiliated to the Amateur Athletics Association would be sufficient to preclude membership of the Harriers.

55. In order to qualify under the Recreational Charities Act 1958 a trust or institution must, under section 1(1) of the Act, be for the public benefit. The Harriers did not at present satisfy the test of public benefit because of the restrictive membership provisions contained in their Rules. Apart from the issue of public benefit the Harriers would, in order to attain charitable status, still need to satisfy the requirements of subsection 1(2) of the 1958 Act by showing that the facilities were provided "in the interests of social welfare." We did not accept the suggestion made by Walton J. at first instance in *I.R.C. v. McMullen* that the persons for whom the facilities are primarily intended must be to some extent and in some way deprived persons. We preferred the liberal approach of Bridge L.J. in the Court of Appeal in that case which required us to consider objectively whether the facilities are of a type which were capable of improving the conditions of life for the recipients. The facilities provided by the Harriers were, however, neither provided for any of the special classes mentioned in section 1(2)(*b*)(i) of the Act nor, because of the restrictive membership requirements, for the benefit of the public at large within section 1(2)(*b*)(ii) of the Act.

## VII. No Unlawful Discrimination

### Race Relations Act 1976

It is not against public policy or unlawful in a private trust to discriminate on grounds of race, religion, nationality or colour.[98] However, the Race Relations Act 1976 prohibits discrimination *against* persons on the ground of colour, race, nationality, or ethnic or national origins in the case of charitable trusts, though it allows discrimination in *favour* of persons of a class defined by reference to race, nationality or ethnic or national origins,[99] though not by reference to colour. The colour qualification is disregarded even where favourable discrimination is concerned.[1] Thus, a trust to educate "black youngsters of West Indian origin in Brixton" would have the word "black" deleted. In exceptional circumstances the removal of any discriminatory provision unacceptable to the original trustees is possible under the *cy-près* jurisdiction.[2]

### Sex Discrimination Act 1975

Sexually discriminating provisions in private trusts are valid. Where a charitable trust contains a provision for benefiting persons of one sex only it is valid,[3] *e.g.* Boy Scouts, Girl Guides, retired schoolmasters,

---

[98] *Re Lysaght* [1986] Ch. 191; *Re Dominion Students' Hall Trusts* [1947] Ch. 183.
[99] s.34(2)(3).
[1] s.34(1).
[2] See *Re Lysaght* [1966] Ch. 191; *Re Woodhams* [1981] 1 W.L.R. 493; *Infra* p. 394 n.73.
[3] Sex Discrimination Act 1975, s.43.

research fellowships available for men only.[4] In the case of an educational charity, however, the trustees can apply to the Secretary of State for Education to make the trust's benefits open to both sexes. He will make the order if satisfied that to do so would conduce to the advancement of education without sex discrimination and 25 years have elapsed since creation of the trust, unless the donor (or his personal representatives) or the personal representatives of the testator have consented in writing.[5]

VIII. THE PURPOSE OF THE TRUST MUST BE EXCLUSIVELY CHARITABLE

If, consistently with its terms, a trust may be applied exclusively for purposes which are not charitable, it is a non-charitable trust notwithstanding that, consistently with its terms, it may be applied exclusively for purposes which are charitable. Thus a trust to apply income to "registered charities or to such bodies as in the opinion of the trustees have charitable objects" is not charitable since the final clause does not state "*exclusively* charitable objects" and, even if it did, bodies *in the opinion of the trustees* having exclusively charitable objects might not be regarded by the courts as having exclusively charitable objects.[6] More obviously, the following trusts are not exclusively charitable and so are void: "for worthy causes," "for benevolent purposes," for "charitable or benevolent purposes," for purposes connected with the education and welfare of children."[7]

**CHICHESTER DIOCESAN FUND AND BOARD OF FINANCE (INCORPORATED) v. SIMPSON**

House of Lords [1944] A.C. 341; [1944] 2 All E.R. 60 (Viscount Simon, Lords Macmillan, Porter and Simonds; Lord Wright dissenting)

The testator, Caleb Diplock, left his residuary estate to the executors of his will upon trust "for such charitable institution or institutions or other charitable or benevolent object or objects as his executors might in their absolute discretion select." The testator's next-of-kin claimed that the residuary gift was void for uncertainty and the Court of Appeal agreed. The charities appealed unsuccessfully to the House of Lords.

LORD PORTER: "My Lords, it is common ground and undoubted law that, in construing a will, the object of the court is to try to ascertain the intention of the testator, but it is the expressed intention which must govern. The principle is succinctly expressed by Lindley L.J., as he then was, in *Re Morgan*[8]: 'Now, I do not see why, if we can tell what a man intends, and can give effect to his

---

[4] *Hugh-Jones* v. *St. John's College Cambridge* (1979) 123 So.Jo. 603.
[5] 1975 Act, s.78.
[6] *Re Wootton's W.T.* [1968] 2 All E.R. 618. In poverty cases the courts seem ready to restrict the opinion of trustees as to persons in needy circumstances or special need to such persons that the law recognises as within the poverty head of charity: *Re Scarisbrick* [1951] Ch. 622; *Re Cohen* [1973] 1 All E.R. 889.
[7] *Att.-Gen. of the Bahamas* v. *Royal Trust Co.* [1986] 1 W.L.R. 1001 (welfare purposes not restricted to educational welfare purposes so as to qualify as charitable).
[8] [1893] 3 Ch. 222, 227, 228.

intention *as expressed*, we should be driven out of it by other cases or decisions in other cases.' The italics are mine. In construing what the testator has said, it is permissible to consider that he did not intend to die intestate: see *per* Lord St. Leonards in *Grey* v. *Pearson*.[9] But technical words must be interpreted in their technical sense and 'charity' or 'charitable' are technical words in English law and must be so construed unless it can be seen from the wording of the will as a whole that they are used in some sense other than their technical sense. For this purpose and in order to discover the testator's intention it is the duty of the court to take into consideration the whole of the terms of the will and not to confine itself to the disputed words or their immediate context.

"In the present case the words whose interpretation is contested are 'charitable or benevolent.' It is admitted on behalf of the appellants that, if the word 'benevolent' stood alone, it would be too vague a term and the gift would be void: see *James* v. *Allen*[10]; but it is said that, when coupled with the word 'charitable' even by the disjunctive 'or,' it either takes its colour from its associate, or is merely exegetical, and the phrase is used as implying either that 'charitable' and 'benevolent' are the same thing or that 'benevolent' qualifies 'charitable' so as to limit the gift to objects which are both charitable and benevolent.

"In my view, the words so coupled do not naturally bear any of the meanings suggested. The addition of 'benevolent' to 'charitable' on the face of it suggests an alternative purpose and I do not see why in this collocation 'benevolent' should be read as 'charitable benevolent.' Nor do I think that it can be said to be merely exegetical. Prima facie, these are alternative objects, and, even if they were not, the word 'charitable,' to be exegetical of 'benevolent,' should follow and not precede it. The wording should be 'benevolent or charitable,' meaning 'benevolent, *i.e.*, charitable,' not 'charitable or benevolent,' meaning 'charitable, *i.e.*, benevolent.' In the latter case the gift might still be said to be given to too wide a class, that is, to benevolent and not to charitable objects. In truth, however anxious though one may be to strain the language used so as to benefit charities only, the weight of authority is too great to be readily overthrown.

"The various tribunals in England which have expressed their views have all tended the same way. So long ago as 1836 Lord Cottenham L.C. expressed the opinion in *Ellis* v. *Selby*[11] that a gift to 'charitable or other purposes' was void. Similar opinions are to be found in *Houston* v. *Burns*,[12] and in *Attorney-General for New Zealand* v. *New Zealand Insurance Co. Ltd.*[13] Indeed, in *Williams* v. *Kershaw*[14] a bequest of property for benevolent charitable and religious purposes was held void because it was considered that the testator could not have intended the recipient purposes to be benevolent and charitable and religious all at the same time, and, therefore, that 'and' must be read disjunctively. I need not refer at length to the numerous cases decided in courts of first instance and in the Court of Appeal expressing a view similar to that contained in those quoted. If, however, the authorities be extended beyond those decided in a final court of appeal, the exact combination

---

[9] (1857) 6 H.L.C. 61, 99.
[10] (1817) 3 Mer. 17.
[11] (1836) 1 My. & Cr. 286, 299.
[12] [1918] A.C. 337, 341.
[13] (1936) 53 T.L.R. 37.
[14] (1835) 5 Cl. & F. 111n.

'charitable or benevolent' is to be found and was held void in *Re Jarman's Estate*.[15] Nor is the force of these and the many other authorities to the same effect weakened by the fact that a bequest for charitable *and* benevolent purposes has been held a valid gift: see *Re Best*,[16] since the conjunction in that case is effected by using 'and,' not 'or.' Nor by the decisions in *Attorney-General for New Zealand* v. *Brown*,[17] where the wording was 'charitable benevolent religious and educational institutions societies associations and objects,' and in *Re Bennett*,[18] where the wording was 'for the benefit of the schools, and charitable institutions, and poor, and other objects of charity or any other public objects.' In each of these last two cases it was held the complex phrases used must properly be construed so that 'benevolent' or 'public,' as the case might be, took its colour from charitable and must be read as *ejusdem generis* with it. In so complex a form of words the *ejusdem generis* rule might well be prayed in aid, whereas in a simpler form it might be inapplicable.

"In truth, however, the terms in which other wills are framed are but a loose guide to the construction of that in question. Each will must be interpreted in the light of its own wording. No doubt, the testator in the present case wished his estates to go to objects of a benevolent character or, as Goddard L.J. has it,[19] to 'charity in the popular sense': but 'charity' in that sense is not coterminous with 'charity' in the technical sense, and I can find nothing in the wording of the will to lead to a different result."

### Note

There are some exceptions to the rule that a trust cannot be charitable unless its purposes are exclusively charitable.

### (i) *Incidental Purposes*

If the main purpose of a corporation or trust is charitable and the only elements in its constitution and operations, which are non-charitable, are merely incidental to the effective promotion of that main purpose, the corporation and trust are established for charitable purposes only.[20] If the non-charitable object is itself a main object, neither the corporation nor the trust is established for charitable purposes only; but there is this difference between them: the corporation remains validly constituted, but the trust is void.[21] As Slade J. states,[22] "The distinction is between (a) those non-charitable activities authorised by the trust instrument which are merely incidental or subsidiary to a charitable purpose and (b) those non-charitable activities so authorised which themselves form part of the trust purpose. In the latter but not

---

15 (1878) 8 Ch.D. 584.
16 [1904] 2 Ch. 354.
17 [1917] A.C. 393.
18 [1920] 1 Ch. 305.
19 [1941] Ch. 253, 267.
20 *Royal College of Surgeons of England* v. *National Provincial Bank Ltd.* [1952] A.C. 631; *Re Coxen* [1948] Ch. 747; *London Hospital Medical College* v. *I.R.C.* [1976] 1 W.L.R. 613; N. Gravells [1978] Conv. 92.
21 *Oxford Group* v. *I.R.C.* [1949] W.N. 343; *Chichester Diocesan Fund and Board of Finance (Incorporated)* v. *Simpson* [1944] A.C. 341; *Associated Artists Ltd.* v. *I.R.C.* [1956] 1 W.L.R. 752.
22 *McGovern* v. *Att.-Gen.* [1981] 3 All E.R. 493, 510.

the former case the reference to non-charitable activities will deprive the trust of its charitable status."

(ii) *Apportionment*

Where a trustee is directed to apportion between charitable and non-charitable objects the trust is always good as to the charitable objects. The trust will be valid *in toto* if the non-charitable objects are certain and valid,[23] and, in the absence of apportionment by the trustee, the court will divide the fund equally between both classes of objects in accordance with the maxim that "equality is equity."[24] If the non-charitable objects are uncertain, the trust will be good as to the charitable objects only[25] so long as defined sufficiently enough to reveal a general charitable intention.[26]

If there is no direction to apportion, and if the trust is partly for a non-charitable purpose, and then to apply the remainder to a charitable purpose, some cases decide that where the court is satisfied that an inquiry is practicable as to the portion required for the non-charitable purpose, it will direct such an inquiry and uphold the charitable part of the gift.[27] If, on the other hand, such an inquiry is impracticable, it will divide the fund into equal shares, the share applicable to non-charitable purposes falling into residue.[28] Other cases, however, have held that the whole of the gift goes to charity, independently of the question whether the portion which would otherwise have been required for the non-charitable purpose is ascertainable.[29] Yet another case decides that if the non-charitable part of the gift cannot be carried out without also performing the charitable part the whole gift will be valid.[30]

In *Re Coxen*,[31] Jenkins J. (as he then was) emphasised that, where the amount applicable to the non-charitable purpose cannot be quantified, the whole gift fails for uncertainty. He pointed out, however, that there were two exceptions to this general rule: first, an exception of a general character to the effect that, where, as a matter of construction, the gift to charity was a gift of the entire fund subject to the payments thereout required for the non-charitable purpose, the amount set free by the failure of the non-charitable gift was caught by,

---

[23] *Re Douglas* (1887) 35 Ch.D. 472.
[24] *Salusbury* v. *Denton* (1857) 3 K. & J. 529.
[25] *Re Clarke* [1923] 2 Ch. 407.
[26] The *cy-près* doctrine is available if required.
[27] *Re Rigley* (1867) 36 L.J.Ch. 147; *Re Vaughan* (1886) 33 Ch.D. 187. The distinction between the invalid "charitable or benevolent purposes" cases and the apportionment cases is made by Page-Wood V.-C. in *Salusbury* v. *Denton* (1857) 3 K. & J. 529, 539. "It is one thing to direct a trustee to give a *part* of a fund to one set of objects and the *remainder* to another, and it is a distinct thing to direct him to give either to one set of objects or to another."
[28] *Adnam* v. *Cole* (1843) 6 Beav. 353; *Hoare* v. *Osborne* (1866) L.R. 1 Eq. 585; *cf. Fowler* v. *Fowler* (1864) 33 Beav. 616, where the whole gift failed.
[29] *Fisk* v. *Att.-Gen.* (1867) L.R. 4 Eq. 521; *Hunter* v. *Bullock* (1872) L.R. 14 Eq. 45; *Dawson* v. *Small* (1874) L.R. 18 Eq. 114; *Re Williams* (1877) 5 Ch.D. 735; *Re Birkett* (1878) 9 Ch.D. 576; *Re Rogerson* [1901] 1 Ch. 715; *cf. Re Porter* [1925] Ch. 746.
[30] *Re Eighmie* [1935] Ch. 524.
[31] [1948] Ch. 747, 752.

and passed under, the charitable gift[32]; and, secondly, an exception of a more limited character, applicable in the "tomb" cases, to the effect that where there is a primary trust (imposing a merely honorary obligation[33]) to apply the income in perpetuity to the repair of a tomb not in a church, followed by a charitable trust in terms extending only to the balance of the income, the established rule is to ignore the invalid trust for the repair of the tomb and treat the whole income as given to charity.

### (iii) *The Charitable Trusts (Validation) Act 1954*

## (a) Relevant provisions

### *Validation and modification of imperfect trust instruments*

Section 1.—(1) In this Act, "imperfect trust provision" means any provision declaring the objects for which property is to be held or applied, and so describing those objects that, consistently with the terms of the provision, the property could be used exclusively for charitable purposes, but could nevertheless be used for purposes which are not charitable.

(2) Subject to the following provisions of this Act, any imperfect trust provision contained in an instrument taking effect before the sixteenth day of December, nineteen hundred and fifty-two,[34] shall have, and be deemed to have had, effect in relation to any disposition or covenant to which this Act applies—

(a) as respects the period before the commencement of this Act,[35] as if the whole of the declared objects were charitable; and

(b) as respects the period after that commencement as if the provision had required the property to be held or applied for the declared objects in so far only as they authorise use for charitable purposes.

(3) A document inviting gifts of property to be held or applied for objects declared by the document shall be treated for the purposes of this section as an instrument taking effect when it is first issued.

(4) In this Act, "covenant" includes any agreement, whether under seal or not, and "covenantor" is to be construed accordingly.

### *Dispositions and covenants to which the Act applies*

Section 2.—(1) Subject to the next following subsection, this Act applies to any disposition of property to be held or applied for objects declared by an imperfect trust provision, and to any covenant to make such a disposition, where apart from this Act the disposition or covenant is invalid under the law of England and Wales, but would be valid if the objects were exclusively charitable.

[Subsection (2) excepts from the operation of the Act any disposition under which property or income therefrom was paid or distributed before December 16, 1952, on the footing that the imperfect trust provision was void.]

---

[32] *Cf. Hancock* v. *Watson* [1902] A.C. 14; *infra*, p. 415.

[33] *Re Morton's W.T.* [1948] 2 All E.R. 842; *Re Dalziel* [1943] Ch. 277, 278; *Tudor on Charities*, (7th ed.), pp. 486–490; *Picarda on Charities*, pp. 145–146.

[34] The date on which the Report of the Nathan Committee on Charitable Trusts was presented to Parliament. The Act gives effect to certain recommendations of that Committee (Cmnd. 8710 (1952); Chap. 12).

[35] July 30, 1954.

(3) A disposition in settlement or other disposition creating more than one interest in the same property shall be treated for the purposes of this Act as a separate disposition in relation to each of the interests created.

## (b) Comment

The effect of the Act may be summarised as follows: Where consistently with the terms of a trust which took effect before December 16, 1952, the trust property could be used exclusively for charitable purposes, but could, nevertheless, be used for purposes which are not charitable, then for the period before July 30, 1954, the trust is deemed to have had effect as if all the declared objects were charitable, and for the period after that date, the trust is deemed to require the property to be applied for the declared objects in so far only as they are charitable. The provisions of such trusts are called "imperfect trust provisions" and the Act applies to dispositions of property held under such trusts, where apart from the Act the disposition would be invalid, but would be valid if the objects were exclusively charitable. But the Act does not apply if before December 16, 1952, the property has been disposed of in favour of persons entitled by reason of the invalidity of the trust. The Act is limited in effect, but may still concern the construction of trusts of reversionary interests created before, but falling into possession after, December 16, 1952, *e.g.* where H died in 1951 leaving his estate to his widow for life and then on imperfect trust provisions, and the widow has just died.

The language of the Act is more complicated and obscure than similar legislation from other Commonwealth countries, which is generally not circumscribed by the same limitations.[36] It has given rise to the following problems:

1. Where an appeal is made for funds for three purposes, two of which are not charitable, and the third (worthy causes) includes both charitable and non-charitable objects, it is clear that section 1(1) does not apply to the fund as a whole, since it could not be used in its entirety exclusively for charitable purposes: see *Re Gillingham Bus Disaster Fund*.[37] Is there, however, a separate disposition for the third purpose within section 2(3)? At first instance Harman J. held not: the letter making the appeal was not a disposition, and, even if it were, it did not create different interests in the same property—one for each of the named purposes. On appeal Evershed M.R. and Romer L.J. considered that dispositions were made by contributors in response to

---

[36] See (New South Wales) Conveyancing Act 1938, s.37D, interpreted in *Leahy* v. *Att.-Gen. for N.S.W.* [1959] A.C. 457, 474–476; (Victoria) Property Law Act 1928, s.131; (New Zealand) Trustee Amendment Act 1935, s.2; (Western Australia) Trustees Act 1962, s.102; (Northern Ireland) Charities Act 1964, s.24; (1946) 62 L.Q.R. 23 (E. H. Coghill); *ibid.* 339 (R. Else Mitchell); (1950) 24 Austr.L.J. 239 (E. H. Coghill); M. C. Cullity (1967) 16 I.C.L.Q. 464; Ford & Lee pp. 871–879.

[37] [1958] Ch. 300 (Harman J.); affirmed [1959] Ch. 62 (C.A.); see [1959] C.L.J. 41 (S.J. Bailey); [1958] 74 L.Q.R. 190; *ibid.* 489 (P. S. Atiyah).

the appeal, but agreed with Harman J. that the dispositions did not create separate interests in the same property. Ormerod L.J. considered section 2(3) to be applicable.

2. Must the dichotomy of purposes (charitable and non-charitable) be expressed or can it be implied? In *Re Gillingham Bus Disaster Fund* Harman J. held that the failure to mention charity as one of the objects of the trust was fatal to the claim in support of validation. On appeal Evershed M.R. thought that the use of a phrase such as "worthy causes," which had within it the notion of charity, *might* come within the terms of section 1(1); Romer L.J. thought that the operation of the section was confined to cases where one, at least, of the objects was charitable, so that it would apply to the formula "charitable or benevolent," but not "philanthropic or benevolent"; and Ormerod L.J. thought that the phrase *did* come within the section since it included on its face both charitable and non-charitable purposes. In *Re Harpur's W.T.*[38] Cross J. purported to follow the view of Harman J. that the section applied only to a gift which was *expressed* to be for charitable as well as non-charitable purposes; but in *Re Wykes*[39] Buckley J., after reviewing in a classic judgment the course of the decision in *Re Gillingham Bus Disaster Fund* and the history and scope of the Act, held, following the view of Ormerod L.J. in that case, that the Act applied to a trust for the division of a fund among "benevolent or welfare purposes"; and in *Re Saxone Shoe Co. Ltd.'s Trust Deed*[40] Cross J. decided to follow Buckley J. There must, however, be a reference, express or implied, to charitable and non-charitable purposes, so that in *Buxton* v. *Public Trustee*[41] Plowman J. held the Act did not apply to trusts to promote and aid the improvement of international relations and intercourse since the trusts did not comprehend a charitable purpose.

3. Does the Act apply where the potential beneficiaries do not constitute a section of the public for the purposes of the law of charity, but a trust in their favour would nevertheless be valid if applied for the benefit of such of them as were poor: *e.g.* "a trust for welfare purposes for the benefit of the employees of a particular company"? In *Re Wykes* Buckley J. held that since, consistently with the terms of the trust, the whole fund could be applied exclusively for charitable purposes, *i.e.* the relief of poverty, the Act applied; and in *Re Mead's Trust Deed*[42] Cross J. came to the same conclusion. On the other hand, in *Re Saxone Shoe Co. Ltd.'s Trust Deed*, where there was neither an express nor an implied reference to charitable purposes (trust for any purposes the trustees should consider to be for the benefit of

---

[38] [1961] 2 Ch. 38; affirmed [1962] Ch. 78.
[39] [1961] Ch. 229.
[40] [1962] 1 W.L.R. 943.
[41] (1962) 41 T.C. 235.
[42] [1961] 1 W.L.R. 1244 (a trust to provide a convalescent home for members of a trade union and a home for poor retired members).

employees and former employees of a particular company and their
dependants), Cross J. held that the case fell outside the Act, which did
not apply to a private discretionary trust as opposed to a trust for the
promotion of quasi-charitable purposes. The Charity Commissioners
consider the trust held not charitable in *Williams* v. *I.R.C. supra*,
p. 347 to fall within the 1954 Act as benefiting a sufficient section of
the public.[43]

4. It seems clear that the Act does not apply to a trust for
institutions[44] or individuals[45] as distinct from a trust for purposes.

## IX. A NEW DEFINITION OF CHARITY?

### *Whither Charity Law?*

*M. R. Chesterman: Charities, Trusts and Social Welfare, pp. 397–409*

#### "SHOULD FISCAL AND TRUSTS LAW PRIVILEGES BE SEPARATED?

It has been contended[46] on a number of recent occasions that the linking of
fiscal and trusts law privileges to the same definition of 'charitable' produces
unsatisfactory results: in other words, that the decision in *Pemsel's* case should
be reversed. To break this link by confining the fiscal privileges to a narrower
range of purposes than those which attract the trusts law privileges would, it is
alleged, be advantageous in two respects. First, fiscal privileges would cease to
be available to a range of organizations (such as animal charities, or obscure
religious sects) which are on the periphery of 'charity' and do not really
deserve them. Secondly, purpose trusts of a public nature which presently fall
foul of the rules as to certainty of objects because fiscal pressures have
excluded them from the definition of 'charitable' would no longer be thus
deprived of the right to exist. According to one version of this argument,[47]
there would accordingly be 'charitable trusts,' privileged under both tax and
trusts law, and 'public purpose trusts,' privileged only under trusts law
provided that they could show at least a modicum of 'public benefit.'

"Reform along these lines would eliminate an unsatisfactory tension within
charity law and would accord with recent relaxations of the rules regarding
certainty of objects for discretionary trusts. There would, however, be
problems to resolve with regard to 'public purpose' trusts. Would they have
the privilege of perpetual existence as well as freedom from certainty requirements?[48] If so, would there be some procedure for *cy-près* modification of their
purposes? If, as would seem unavoidable, the Attorney-General or some other
public body such as the government department most closely concerned with

---

[43] Annual Report for 1977 paras. 71–80.
[44] *Re Harpur's W.T.* [1962] Ch. 78. For criticism see *Picarda's Charities* pp. 161–162.
[45] *Re Saxone Shoe Co. Ltd.'s Trust Deed* [1962] 1 W.L.R. 943.
[46] *Dingle* v. *Turner* [1972] A.C. 601, 624–625; (1956) 72 L.Q.R. 187, 206 (G. Cross); N. P. Gravells
(1977) 40 M.L.R. 397; Culyer, Wiseman & Posnett in *Social and Economic Administration*,
Vol. 10 (1976), p. 32.
[47] Gravells, *op. cit.*
[48] If, as has been recommended, charitable trusts were to lose their privilege on the ground that it
causes charity resources to become tied to out-of-date purposes (see *infra*) this particular issue is
more easily resolved.

their activities should be retained as a representative plaintiff to enforce them (and perhaps to instigate *cy-près* alterations of their purpose), what level of 'public benefit' would justify the necessary expenditure of public funds? Would grant-making trusts be allowed to retain the fiscal privileges attached to genuine 'charities' if they made grants to 'public purpose trusts'? These and other side-issues would have to be worked out.

"Pursuing this general line of argument, one may ask next whether the category of genuinely charitable organizations should all continue to enjoy the same 'package' of fiscal privileges? At present, some charities derive considerably more benefit than others from the operation of these privileges: for example, the covenant system discriminates in favour of longer-term charities which are supported by corporate donors and by donors who are prepared to commit money in advance. Furthermore, the policies underlying particular taxes are arguably not served by allowing all charities to claim automatic exemption from them. The provisions for relief from local rates take account of this problem to some degree, though the fifty per cent. relief enjoyed by large national or international charities still imposes a significant burden on the local authority which has to grant this exemption.[49] But the other tax reliefs are not flexible in this way, so that (for example) there is little scope to withdraw even partially the exemption from tax on investment income when a charity is both wealthy and prone to accumulate income, or to deny the exemption from capital transfer tax to a gift or bequest to such a charity on the ground that a major objective of this tax is to break down concentrations of wealth.

"The spirit of some of these recommendations is discernible in the tax policies of the United States, where actual expenditure of funds on a charity's beneficiaries is made a condition of tax relief,[50] and in Sweden, where tax relief is granted on a sliding scale according to the charity's degree of 'social merit.'[51] In these two systems, the fiscal policy underlying privileged treatment for charities is implemented with more sophistication than is to be found in the United Kingdom package of automatic reliefs. But where a system (like the Swedish system) creates 'class one charities'; 'class two charities,' etc., or where it grants different measures of relief from different groups of taxes to different groups of charities, it significantly 'fragments' the concept of charity. Within tax law, no single, comprehensive form of treatment is meted out to organisations of a legally charitable nature.

"A more far-reaching recommendation along the same lines is that automatic fiscal relief for charities should be wholly abolished and replaced by a system of discriminatory cash subsidies.[52] According to one version of this recommendation,[53] charitable status might be retained as a precondition for obtaining such a subsidy, but would not confer any entitlement to it. We have, however, seen that under present law voluntary organizations may usually obtain discretionary grants-in-aid from public funds without having to prove that their purposes are charitable. Government agencies dispensing funds in this way may decide for themselves whether the organization merits financial

---

[49] It has accordingly been suggested that the cost of mandatory rating relief should be borne by central government, *i.e.* through increases in the "rate support grant": Goodman Report, para. 132; Layfield Committee into Local Government Finance (Cmnd. 6453, 1976), pp. 167–168.

[50] B. Whitaker, *The Foundations* (1974), pp. 131, 234–235.

[51] B. Nightingale, *Charities*, pp. 66–67.

[52] Culyer, Wiseman & Posnett, *op. cit.*, pp. 44–46; S. Surrey, *Pathways to Tax Reform* (1973), pp. 223–232; *contra* the Expenditure Committee Report, paras. 90–92.

[53] Culyer, Wiseman & Posnett, *op. cit.* p. 46.

assistance without being technically bound to refuse assistance merely because it is not a charity. It would seem to follow that *either* charitable status should be made a considerably more reliable indicator of the genuine worth of an organization's welfare activities in current social conditions, *or* such status should not be a necessary condition of obtaining a subsidy under the proposed scheme. The latter recommendation, once again, threatens to deprive charitable status of legal significance; the former, as we shall see, also tends in this direction.

"A further major issue arising out of the recommendations just discussed is the reformulation of the legal definition of 'charitable' so as to comply explicitly with the demands of fiscal policy and with the consideration that charitable status facilitates access to funds from grant-making trusts, the state and the public."

## THE "DEATH OF CHARITY"?

"In the eyes of many, charity would straightway be smothered to death by bureaucracy if reform proposals along the lines considered in this chapter were ever implemented. The free exercise of a philanthropist's power to dedicate his property to the benevolent purposes of his choice and to frame these purposes within a trust; the autonomy of charity trustees to manage the funds committed to their care, free from heavy-handed state intervention; the enthusiasm of voluntary or underpaid workers giving their time and energy to a worthy cause—all these would be discouraged out of existence if an overpowering and overbearing Charity Commission were allowed to peer and pry into every corner of charitable activity.

"In a more legalistic sense, 'charity' may 'die' simply because it ceases to describe a meaningful category within any branch of the law. In the course of this chapter, it has been envisaged that charitable trusts, 'public purpose' trusts and private discretionary trusts might all become similarly regulated under trusts law, that different charities might enjoy different privileges under tax laws, that tax privileges might be replaced by a subsidy system not confined to charities, that the criteria for determining charitable status might be highly flexible and that the supervision of different classes of charity might be divided amongst different governmental bodies. Also relevant here are (a) the equivalence (more or less) of charitable and non-charitable voluntary organisations with regard to access to public subsidies and (b) the blurring of fiscal lines between these two groups of organisations. Collectively, these existing and projected trends amount to a fragmentation or dissolution of the concept of charity, in the sense that one could no longer speak of a common legal regime for 'charities.'

"If this is correct, social democratic reform of the law of charity may, in this specific sense, be ultimately destructive. By attempting to bring this branch of the law in line with the policy demands of the welfare state, reformers may simply destroy its identity. In fact, one recent proposal explicitly seeks this result. This is the recommendation of the Charity Law Reform Committee that the tax privileges associated with charity should be granted to all genuinely non-profit-distributing organisations (NPDOs). The committee put forward this idea in a leaflet entitled 'Charity Law—Only a New Start Will Do'[54]; a

---

[54] A long extract is printed as their principal "Evidence to the Expenditure Committee." See also the "Evidence of A. Steen, M.P." (Qs. 1526–1544).

better title might have been 'Charity Law Should Be Abolished.' In contending that the anomalies and inconsistences in the present legal definition of charity were so serious and so intractable that 'charity' should have no fiscal significance whatsoever, they were attempting to pluck the heart out of charity law.

"Both the fiscal wisdom of extending charity's motley array of tax privileges to all NPDOs and the likelihood in practice that distribution of profit by tax-exempt NPDOs could ever be effectively prohibited are matters of some doubt.[55] But the radical implications of the suggestion are far-reaching, particularly in the sense that English law without 'charity' would be shorn of a number of ideological notions. These suggest not only that the freedoms associated with the workings of the 'voluntary spirit' are valuable and worth preserving, but also that a number of non-egalitarian enterprises within society have a traditionally charitable nature which helps to justify their continuance with state support and that, due to the absence of any 'political' taint from 'true' charity, charitable provision of social welfare cannot have political implications least of all conservative ones. Within notions such as these, there are moral values which should not be jettisoned, at least while the principal mode of distribution of material resources within society pays homage to entitlements to wealth and property rather than to meeting the needs of society's members. Yet these notions also contribute to the perpetuation of social inequalities by helping to mask their true causes and to erect misleading justifications for them.

"The radical response to these equivocal aspects of legal 'charity' is itself equivocal. Most of the progressive recommendations discussed in this chapter are concerned to bring the law's concept of charity in line with the popular concept of charity or philanthropy by insisting, in particular, that only genuinely altruistic, redistributive and socially useful projects be labelled as charitable. But a more profoundly radical approach, based ultimately on a Marxist view of social relations, is that when charity, even thus 'purified,' exists as a systematic instrument of social welfare in society, it retards progress towards true socialism because it presupposes the inequalities which it purports to try to eliminate. When a rich individual directly or indirectly distributes welfare benefits amongst the working classes, he is simply restoring property which was stolen from them in the first place by way of the process of commodity production. He calls it a 'charitable gift' in order to conceal the element of theft. It accordingly matters not whether legal 'charity' appears genuinely altruistic: indeed, the more self-seeking it is allowed to be, the more obvious the element of pretence the whole process becomes.

"According to this argument, systematised charity would thus have no place in a truly socialist society. Yet in the meantime it continues to exhibit moral values which no society can ignore. We are back where this book began: there is a great deal of ambiguity in charity."

## CHARITIES: A FRAMEWORK FOR THE FUTURE

*Government White Paper Cm. 694 (May 1989) Development of the Law*

2.7 The loose framework, which was set by the 1601 preamble and clarified by Lord Macnaghten, has enabled the courts over the years to develop the law in

---

[55] See, *e.g.* the objections in the "Expenditure Committee Report," paras. 25–34 and in the "Evidence of the Inland Revenue" (Qs. 552–557).

a way which has been sensitive to changing needs whilst maintaining the fundamental principles on which the concept of charity rests. It has been argued that on the whole, given the increasing complexity of society, this development has been remarkably coherent and consistent. The scope of education, for example, has been gradually extended to cover not just free schooling but a whole range of objects of a broadly educational nature, such as research and information services, which are considered to be of public benefit.

2.8 The scope of charity, as it applies to organisations concerned with the advancement of religion, has been similarly widened in response to increasing religious toleration and to cultural diversity. Under the fourth head, in particular, the courts have admitted, under the umbrella of charity, a remarkable range of bodies which have been established by benefactors who have discerned new public needs and who have responded to them.

2.9 If the main lines of the law's development are clear, it is fair to say that its results in detail are not always tidy and can sometimes be confusing, even to experts. It is perhaps not surprising that, as the threads reaching back to 1601 get longer and as the analogies which the courts employ become more extended, so the rationale for decisions on charitable status should not always be immediately apparent. This has undoubtedly led to a degree of uncertainty about the interpretation of the law which can inhibit innovative bodies from seeking charitable status. Some critics, however, go further. The law, they say, is now so complex and tangled that it is bound to lead to some decisions which can only be described as illogical or capricious.

2.10 Against this background, it has been proposed from time to time, that a definition of charity should be formulated and given statutory effect. This might be achieved in one of the following ways:

(i) by listing the purposes which are deemed to be charitable;
(ii) by enacting a definition of charity based on Lord Macnaghten's classification; or
(iii) by defining "charitable purposes" as "purposes beneficial to the community."

2.11 The Government consider that an attempt to define charity by any of these means would be fraught with difficulty, and might put at risk the flexibility of the present law which is both its greatest strength and its most valuable feature. In particular, they consider that there would be great dangers in attempting to specify in statute those objects which are to be regarded as charitable.

2.12 Even if it was possible to draw up a list which could command a reasonable measure of agreement it might well lead to the exclusion of trusts which have long been treated as charitable, depriving them of any means of enforcement. A list might be inflexible and quickly outdated by changing public opinion. Listing the details in statute would not evade for long the problems which are inherent in any system of case law. Disputes would undoubtedly quickly arise on which the courts would be asked to adjudicate. There is no reason to believe that a new body of case law would be any less complex than the old.

2.13 In the Government's view, it would be scarcely less difficult to try to enact the whole of Lord Macnaghten's classification. As a classification, the formulation has proved of enduring use. As a definition, its advantages are much less compelling.

2.14 Unless it were proposed to preserve the present case law, the incorporation of Lord Macnaghten's classification into statute would throw the law into confusion and uncertainty by depriving the courts of recourse to previous decisions when they were asked to interpret the new statutory provisions. On the other hand, if some form of words were to be found which would successfully preserve the present valuable case law, it is hard to see what the new definition would achieve.

2.15 Defining "charitable purposes" as "purposes beneficial to the community" would have the merit of simplicity but this would also be open to major objections. Such a definition would allow the courts to admit to charitable status virtually any organisation which was not obviously for private benefit or profit. A definition on these simple lines, which was intended to supersede existing case law, would greatly expand the ambit of charity in ways which might be far from desirable. It would be notably subjective and would be likely to give rise to a great deal of litigation.

2.16 An attempt might be made to make clearer exactly what is meant by "public benefit" by reference to existing case law and by incorporating the other heads of charity into the general formula. The more that detail becomes added in this way, however, the fewer appear the advantages of a new definition. Instead of being simplified the law would be ossified.

2.17 There would appear, therefore, to be few advantages in attempting a wholesale redefinition of charitable status—and many real dangers in doing so.

## Section 3. Administration of Charities

Overall supervision of charities is carried on by the Charity Commissioners under the powers conferred on them by the Charities Acts 1960 and 1985: the more significant provisions of the Acts are set out *infra*, except for sections 13 and 14 which appear in the next part of this chapter concerned with the *cy-près* powers of the Commissioners and of the courts. Their Annual Reports reveal that they make about 750 *cy-près* schemes a year and contain much useful information, *e.g.* about their functions (1986, pp. 1–12, 1989, pp.1–4) trustee's responsibilities (1986, pp. 26–30) problems with trustee's political activities (1986, pp. 21–26) and problems over paying trustees for their work (1989, pp. 24–26). They are always ready to advise trustees under section 24 of the Charities Act 1960 and cannot be liable for damages if such advice negligently causes loss.[56]

In exceptional cases the Attorney-General may authorise trustees to make *ex gratia* payments out of charitable funds to persons outside the class of charitable beneficiaries and to whom it would be morally wrong to refuse such payments.[57] Normally trustees must be most careful to restrict their payments to the specific purposes of their charity as is shown by *Baldry* v. *Feintuck* discussed in the following

---

[56] *Mills* v. *Winchester Diocesan Board of Finance* [1989] 2 All E.R. 317.
[57] *Re Snowden* [1970] Ch. 700 (very substantial gift of shares by will was adeemed and its value fell into residue giving charitable residuary legatees ten times the value of their intended legacies: it was held they could make *ex gratia* payments to the adeemed legatees). Further see *Annual Report for 1969*, paras. 26–31.

extract from paragraphs 19–22 of the Commissioners' 1972 Report. Charitable trustees may act by majority, and not unanimous decision: *Re Whiteley.*[58] In the absence of a scheme, the only person competent to consent to matters affecting the beneficial interests under charitable trusts seems to be the Attorney-General.[59] From time to time he issues guidelines to assist trustees as do the Charity Commissioners. To improve supervision of charities the Government will be enacting virtually all the recommendations of the Woodfield Report *infra*, p. 390.

### 1972 Annual Report

**Baldry v. Feintuck and Others** [1972] 1 W.L.R. 552

19. Sussex University was founded by Royal Charter in 1961, its objects being to advance learning and knowledge by teaching and research and to enable students to obtain the advantages of university education. Article 15 of the charter provided that there should be a students' union of the university, the constitution, powers and functions of which should be prescribed in the ordinances. The council of the university made an ordinance in December 1967 establishing the constitution of the union. The aims of the union included: (*a*) to encourage and develop the corporate life of the union in cultural, social and athletic fields, and (*e*) to maintain and extend friendly relations with other students' unions and with the general public. The constitution also established a governing body called the council and an administrative body called the executive committee consisting of eight student officers elected by the union and one officer nominated by the senate of the university. The constitution further required that any amendments of the constitution should be carried at a council meeting and ratified at a general meeting of the union by a two-thirds majority in each case before taking effect, any such amendments being reported to the senate and the council of the university. The union had been treated by the Inland Revenue as established for exclusively charitable purposes and its charitable status was not a point in issue.

20. In the autumn of 1971 the annual general meeting of the union purported to ratify the adoption of a new constitution which had previously been approved at a meeting of the union council and also to adopt a budget for 1971–72. The objects of the union were redefined in the new constitution as being the promotion of any matter whatsoever of interest to its members. The budget in its final form included two disputed payments, a proposed contribution to War on Want and a proposed contribution to a fund for financing a political campaign of protest against the Government's policy of ending certain free milk supplies for school children.

21. The first point was whether the union had power to make such an alteration to its constitution. The Judge, Mr. Justice Brightman, said that the union was clearly an educational charity and the officers who had power to dispose of the union's funds were, clearly, trustees of those funds for charitable educational purposes. It was not, therefore, open to the union, by a purported

---

58 [1910] 1 Ch. 600.
59 *Re Freeston's Charity* [1978] 1 All E.R. 481, 490; affd. [1979] 1 All E.R. 51 but this point was left open since there had been no full consent on the part of the school governors even if their consent could be sufficient.

amendment to the union's constitution, to authorise the use of the union's funds for the purpose of promoting any object which may happen to interest the members of the union regardless of whether such object was charitable and educational or not. In his view this is what the new constitution was seeking to do but it was a result which no charitable body such as the union was capable of achieving. Accordingly, the definition of the union's objects set out in the original constitution was still subsisting, because such original objects had never been displaced. But even if that interpretation of the new constitution was erroneous and the new object was valid, the Judge considered that it must, by necessary implication, be construed in the context of the educational purposes of Sussex University, and it would still follow that the objects of the union were confined to charitable educational purposes. [Now see *Att.-Gen.* v. *Ross* [1985] 3 All E.R. 334.]

22. Regarding the two disputed payments, the Judge was unable to accept the argument that students should be able to use a reasonable amount of the union's funds in support of those views which, after discussion, they desired to advocate. The educational process included research, discussion, debate and reaching a corporate conclusion on social and economic problems, but, in the judge's view, the provision of money to finance the adoption outside the university of that corporate conclusion did not form any part of the educational process. If members of the union wished to express their views financially, the money should come from their own personal funds and not from the trust money. Thus, although War on Want was a charity, it was not an educational charity, and far less an educational charity connected with students' welfare at Sussex University, and the judge held that it was not open to one charity to subscribe to the funds of another charity unless the recipient charity is expressly or by implication a purpose or object of the donor charity.[60] With regard to the proposed Milk Campaign Fund, this was, admittedly, a political purpose and it was, therefore, inevitably not a charitable purpose, educational or otherwise, because political purposes were not charitable. It followed, therefore, that the charitable funds of the union could not lawfully be used for setting up such a fund.

### *Attorney-General's Guidelines on Expenditure by Student Unions*

" . . . It has been held in the courts that a Student Union has charitable objects if it exists to represent and foster the interests of the students at an educational establishment in such a way as to further the educational purposes of the establishment itself. The Attorney-General believes that that will be the case with the great majority of Student Unions, including those provided for in the constitutions of their parent establishments (unless those establishments do not themselves have charitable objects). If a Student Union has charitable objects it follows as a matter of law that, whatever may be stated in its constitution, those objects cannot be changed, even by unanimous vote of its members, so as to include non-charitable objects; and Union funds may be spent only on those charitable objects or for properly incidental purposes.

"The Attorney-General recognises the difficult position in which officers of Student Unions with charitable objects may find themselves. They may have no experience of charity law, and their members may believe that Union funds

---

[60] Also see *I.R.C.* v. *Helen Slater Charitable Trust Ltd.* [1981] 3 All E.R. 98 where the trust was specifically authorised to make payments to other charities.

can be spent on anything that they think to be of general interest. However, the officers are trustees of the funds, and they have a duty to see that the funds are used only for purposes permitted by charity law. The complaints which have been made in recent years contain allegations of considerable expenditure of an improper nature. Such investigation as has been undertaken confirms that there are grounds for concern. Although perhaps the items taken individually appear not to be very great, they represent in total a major abuse of charitable funds.

"In the circumstances the Attorney-General considers it right that he should issue guidelines to assist Union officers in the discharge of their responsibility for Union funds. In the event of wrongful application of funds, such officers would potentially be at personal risk to a claim that they have been party to a breach of trust, and might well find themselves bound to make good any loss to the funds of their Union at their own expense. It is therefore important that they should be aware of their responsibilities.

"The Attorney-General considers that expenditure of a Student Union's charitable funds is proper if it can be said to be appropriate for the purpose of representing and furthering the interests of the students at the relevant college (and 'college' here includes 'university') in such a way as to assist in the educational aims of the college—for example, by providing channels for the representation of student views within the college, or by improving the conditions of life of the students and in particular providing facilities for their social and physical well-being.

"It is clear, for example, that if a college is to function properly, there is a need for the normal range of clubs and societies so as to enable each student to further the development of his abilities, mental and physical. Equally, it is likely that the college will gain from the fact that the students hold meetings to debate matters of common concern, and publish some form of campus newspaper. Reasonable expenditure on such purposes is, in the view of the Attorney-General, plainly permissible for a Student Union.

"On the other hand, for the students to offer financial support to a political cause in a foreign country—as opposed to merely debating the merits of that cause—is, in the Attorney-General's view, irrelevant to the educational purpose of the college. Such expenditure must accordingly be rejected as improper.

"Between these extremes there is a wide range of cases for which the Attorney-General believes the best touchstone to be the question: does the matter in issue affect the interests of either the students *as such* or the affairs of the college *as such*? If the answer is 'no,' then the case is likely to be one on which the students may hold debates and express views but not charge expenditure to the charitable funds of the Union.

"A major area of difficulty appears to be that of political issues. While the Attorney-General recognises that it is entirely natural that students will wish to express their views on political matters, the law sets strict limits to the expenditure of charitable funds for political purposes. Such expenditure is permissible only if the political purposes are merely *incidental* to the necessarily non-political objects of the charity. Thus, for a Union to expend its charitable funds in supporting a political campaign or demonstration is extremely unlikely to be justifiable unless the issue directly affects students as students. It may be helpful to mention that in this context politics is not to be limited to party politics, but extends essentially to all aspects of the making and changing of laws. Thus it would be no less improper, in the view of the

Attorney-General, for charitable funds of a Union to be devoted to a campaign for or against the legalisation of drugs, even though this is not a matter of party political debate, than it would be for such funds to be used either in support of or opposition to a campaign concerning, say, nuclear weapons or some controversial parliamentary debate not concerned with the interests of students as such.

"Another area of difficulty appears to be that of industrial disputes. The Attorney-General accepts that students may often wish to express a view on a current dispute, particularly if it be centred upon the neighbourhood of the college of which they are students. There is, however, in his view no justification for applying charitable funds in support of either side to the dispute. It would be as wrong for charitable funds to be spent on the hire of coaches, say, for the purpose of taking demonstrators to the scene of the dispute as it would be to hire coaches to take students to a demonstration in respect of the political issues referred to in the last paragraph.

"There is, of course, no objection whatsoever to students joining together to collect their own monies for a particular purpose for which union funds cannot be used. The Attorney-General wishes to stress that the objection is not to student participation in activities outside the educational sphere, but to the use of charitable funds for purposes for which they cannot properly be applied according to the law.

"In issuing these guidelines the Attorney-General is anxious solely to assist those who may find themselves called to account for their actions as trustees of charitable monies. Officers should, of course, bear in mind that it will be amongst their most important duties to identify and keep proper accounts of all Union funds (including, for example, not merely subscriptions to the Union, but income from Union investments, and profits from Union activities, such as the running of a bar or dance at the expense of the Union and with the assistance of its employees). They have a further duty to ensure that expenditure not only is within the proper bounds within which the funds of their Union can be used, but also has been approved and recorded as the Constitution of the Union requires.

"They should also bear in mind that a trustee is at all times entitled to seek advice, if necessary at the expense of the trust fund, on any aspect of his trust which causes him doubt or concern; in particular, under section 24 of the Charities Act 1960 the Charity Commissioners are empowered on the written application of a charity trustee to give him their opinion or advice on any matter affecting the performance of his duties as such.

"The Attorney-General would add that he hopes that the senior members of the college concerned will always be willing to assist Student Union officers in considering doubtful items of expenditure. It must be borne in mind that where the parent body is itself a charitable body and thus has a duty to ensure that its funds are properly applied for purposes within, or incidental to, its own charitable educational purposes, it might well be that upon becoming aware of major items of improper expenditure by the Union it ought properly to cease to fund the Union until the position had been rectified."

*Charities Act 1960*

**The Charity Commissioners**

1.—(1) There shall continue to be a body of Charity Commissioners for England and Wales, and they shall have such functions as are conferred on them by this Act in addition to any functions under any other enactment not repealed by this Act.

(2) The provisions of the First Schedule to this Act shall have effect with respect to the constitution and proceedings of the Commissioners and other matters relating to the Commissioners and their officers and servants.

(3) The Commissioners shall (without prejudice to their specific powers and duties under other enactments) have the general function of promoting the effective use of charitable resources by encouraging the development of better methods of administration, by giving charity trustees information or advice on any matter affecting the charity and by investigating and checking abuses.

(4) It shall be the general object of the Commissioners so to act in the case of any charity (unless it is a matter of altering its purposes) as best to promote and make effective the work of the charity in meeting the needs designated by its trusts; but the Commissioners shall not themselves have power to act in the administration of a charity.

(5) The Commissioners shall, as soon as possible after the end of every year, make to the Secretary of State a report on their operations during that year, and he shall lay a copy of the report before each House of Parliament.

### The official custodian for charities[61]

**3.**—(1) There shall be an "official custodian for charities," whose function it shall be to act as trustee for charities in the cases provided for by this Act; and the official custodian for charities shall be by that name a corporation sole having perpetual succession and using an official seal, which shall be officially and judicially noticed.

(2) Such officer of the Commissioners as they may from time to time designate shall be the official custodian for charities.

(3) The official custodian for charities shall perform his duties in accordance with such general or special directions as may be given him by the Commissioners, and his expenses (except those re-imbursed to him or recovered by him as trustee for any charity) shall be defrayed by the Commissioners.

### Register of charities

**4.**—(1) There shall be a register of charities which shall be established and maintained by the Commissioners and in which there shall be entered such particulars as the Commissioners may from time to time determine of any charity there registered.

(2) There shall be entered in the register every charity not excepted by subsection (4) below; and a charity so excepted may be entered in the register at the request of the charity, but (whether or not it was excepted at the time of registration) may at any time, and shall at the request of the charity, be removed from the register.

(3) Any institution which no longer appears to the Commissioners to be a charity shall be removed from the register, with effect, where the removal is due to any change in its purposes or trusts, from the date of that change; and there shall also be removed from the register any charity which ceases to exist or does not operate.

---

61 The Government will divest the Official Custodian of his investment responsibilities in favour of the trustees of charities: Cm. 694, Chap. 8.

(4) The following charities are not required to be registered,[62] that is to say,—

    (*a*) any charity comprised in the Second Schedule to this Act (in this Act referred to as an "exempt charity");

    (*b*) any charity which is excepted by order or regulations;

    (*c*) any charity having neither any permanent endowment, nor any income from property amounting to more than fifteen pounds a year, nor the use and occupation of any land;

and no charity is required to be registered in respect of any registered place of worship.

(5) With any application for a charity to be registered there shall be supplied to the Commissioners copies of its trusts (or, if they are not set out in any extant document, particulars of them), and such other documents or information as may be prescribed or as the Commissioners may require for the purpose of the application.

(6) It shall be the duty—

    (*a*) of the charity trustees of any charity which is not registered nor excepted from registration to apply for it to be registered, and to supply the documents and information required by subsection (5) above; and

    (*b*) of the charity trustees (or last charity trustees) of any institution which is for the time being registered to notify the Commissioners if it ceases to exist, or if there is any change in its trusts, or in the particulars of it entered in the register, and to supply to the Commissioners particulars of any such change and copies of any new trusts or alterations of the trusts;

and any person who makes default in carrying out any of the duties imposed by this subsection may be required by order of the Commissioners to make good that default.

### Effect of, and claims and objections to, registration

**5.**—(1) An institution shall for all purposes other than rectification of the register be conclusively presumed to be or have been a charity at any time when it is or was on the register of charities.

(2) Any person who is or may be affected by the registration of an institution as a charity may, on the ground that it is not a charity, object to its being entered by the Commissioners in the register, or apply to them for it to be removed from the register; and provision may be made by regulations as to the manner in which any such objection or application is to be made, prosecuted or dealt with.

(3) An appeal against any decision of the Commissioners to enter or not to enter an institution in the register of charities, or to remove or not to remove an institution from the register, may be brought in the High Court by the Attorney General, or by the persons who are or claim to be the charity

---

[62] These include universities, university colleges, British Museum, Church Commissioners and institutions administered by them, societies registered under the Industrial and Provident Societies Act 1893 or Friendly Societies Act 1896. They are not subject to the Charity Commissioners' supervisory or inquisitorial jurisdiction.

trustees of the institution, or by any person whose objection or application under subsection (2) above is disallowed by the decision.

(4) If there is an appeal to the High Court against any decision of the Commissioners to enter an institution in the register, or not to remove an institution from the register, then until the Commissioners are satisfied whether the decision of the Commissioners is or is not to stand, the entry in the register shall be maintained, but shall be in suspense and marked to indicate that it is in suspense; and for the purposes of subsection (1) above an institution shall be deemed not to be on the register during any period when the entry relating to it is in suspense under this subsection.

(5) Any question affecting the registration or removal from the register of an institution may, notwithstanding that it has been determined by a decision on appeal under subsection (3) above, be considered afresh by the Commissioners and shall not be concluded by that decision, if it appears to the Commissioners that there has been a change of circumstances or that the decision is inconsistent with a later judicial decision, whether given on such an appeal or not.

### General power to institute inquiries

**6.**—(1) The Commissioners may from time to time institute inquiries with regard to charities or a particular charity or class of charities, either generally or for particular purposes:

Provided that no such inquiry shall extend to any exempt charity.

(2) The Commissioners may either conduct such an inquiry themselves or appoint a person to conduct it and make a report to them.[63]

(3) For the purposes of any such inquiry the Commissioners may by order, and a person appointed by them to conduct the inquiry may by precept, require any person (subject to the provisions of this section)—

    (*a*) to furnish accounts and statements in writing with respect to any matter in question at the inquiry, being a matter on which he has or can reasonably obtain information, or to return answers in writing to any questions or inquiries addressed to him on any such matter, and to verify any such accounts, statements or answers by statutory declaration;

    (*b*) to attend at a specified time and place and give evidence or produce documents in his custody or control which relate to any matter in question at the inquiry.

(4) For the purposes of any such inquiry evidence may be taken on oath, and the person conducting the inquiry may for that purpose administer oaths, or may instead of administering an oath require the person examined to make and subscribe a declaration of the truth of the matters about which he is examined.

### Local authority's index of local charities

**10.**—(1) The council of a county or of a borough may maintain an index of local charities or of any class of local charities in the council's area, and may publish information contained in the index, or summaries or extracts taken from it.

---

63 See *Jones* v. *Att.-Gen.* [1974] Ch. 148; 1989 Annual Report paras. 63–71.

(2) A council proposing to establish or maintaining under this section an index of local charities or of any class of local charities shall, on request, be supplied by the Commissioners free of charge with copies of such entries in the register of charities as are relevant to the index or with particulars of any changes in the entries of which copies have been supplied before; and the Commissioners may arrange that they will without further request supply a council with particulars of any such changes.

(3) An index maintained under this section shall be open to public inspection at all reasonable times.

### Reviews of local charities by local authority

**11.**—(1) The council of a county or of a borough may, subject to the following provisions of this section, initiate, and carry out in co-operation with the charity trustees, a review of the working of any group of local charities with the same or similar purposes in the council's area, and may make to the Commissioners such report on the review and such recommendations arising from it as the council after consultation with the trustees think fit.

(2) A council having power to initiate reviews under this section may co-operate with other persons in any review by them of the working of local charities in the council's area (with or without other charities), or may join with other persons in initiating and carrying out such a review.

(3) No review initiated by a council under this section shall extend to any charity without the consent of the charity trustees, nor to any ecclesiastical charity.

### Concurrent jurisdiction with High Court for certain purposes

**18.**—(1) Subject to the provisions of this Act, the Commissioners may by order exercise the same jurisdiction and powers as are exercisable by the High Court in charity proceedings for the following purposes, that is to say:—

(a) establishing a scheme for the administration of a charity;

(b) appointing, discharging or removing a charity trustee or trustee for a charity, or removing an officer or servant;

(c) vesting or transferring property, or requiring or entitling any person to call for or make any transfer of property or any payment.

(2) Where the court directs a scheme for the administration of a charity to be established, the court may by order refer the matter to the Commissioners for them to prepare or settle a scheme in accordance with such directions (if any) as the court sees fit to give, and any such order may provide for the scheme to be put into effect by order of the Commissioners as if prepared under subsection (1) above and without any further order of the court.

(3) The Commissioners shall not have jurisdiction under this section to try or determine the title at law or in equity to any property as between a charity or trustee for a charity and a person holding or claiming the property or an interest in it adversely to the charity, or to try or determine any question as to the existence or extent of any charge or trust.

(4) Subject to the following subsections, the Commissioners shall not exercise their jurisdiction under this section as respects any charity, except—

(a) on the application of the charity; or

(b) on an order of the court under subsection (2) above.

(5) In the case of a charity not having any income from property amounting to more than fifty pounds a year, and not being an exempt charity, the

Commissioners may exercise their jurisdiction under this section on the application—

(a) of the Attorney General; or

(b) of any one or more of the charity trustees, or of any person interested in the charity, or of any two or more inhabitants of the area of the charity, if it is a local charity.

(6) Where in the case of a charity, other than an exempt charity, the Commissioners are satisfied that the charity trustees ought in the interests of the charity to apply for a scheme, but have unreasonably refused or neglected to do so, the Commissioners may apply to the Secretary of State for him to refer the case to them with a view to a scheme, and if, after giving the charity trustees an opportunity to make representations to him, the Secretary of State does so, the Commissioners may proceed accordingly without the application required by subsection (4) or (5) above:

Provided that the Commissioners shall not have power in a case where they act by virtue of this subsection to alter the purposes of a charity, unless forty years have elapsed from the date of its foundation.

(7) The Commissioners may on the application of any charity trustee or trustee for a charity exercise their jurisdiction under this section for the purpose of discharging him from his trusteeship.

(8) Before exercising any jurisdiction under this section otherwise than on an order of the court, the Commissioners shall give notice of their intention to do so to each of the charity trustees, except any that cannot be found or has no known address in the United Kingdom or who is party or privy to an application for the exercise of the jurisdiction; and any such notice may be given by post and, if given by post, may be addressed to the recipient's last known address in the United Kingdom.

(9) The Commissioners shall not exercise their jurisdiction under this section in any case (not referred to them by order of the court) which, by reason of its contentious character, or of any special question of law or of fact which it may involve, or for other reasons, the Commissioners may consider more fit to be adjudicated on by the court.

(10) An appeal against any order of the Commissioners under this section may be brought in the High Court by the Attorney General.

(11) An appeal against any order of the Commissioners under this section may also, at any time within the three months beginning with the day following that on which the order is published, be brought in the High Court by the charity or any of the charity trustees, or by any person removed from any office or employment by the order (unless he is removed with the concurrence of the charity trustees or with the approval of the special visitor, if any, of the charity):

Provided that no appeal shall be brought under this subsection except with a certificate of the Commissioners that it is a proper case for an appeal or with the leave of one of the judges of the High Court attached to the Chancery Division.

(12) Where an order of the Commissioners under this section establishes a scheme for the administration of a charity, any person interested in the charity shall have the like[64] right of appeal under subsection (11) above as a charity

---

[64] See, *Childs* v. *Att.-Gen.* [1973] 1 W.L.R. 497 for the incorporation of the proviso to subs.(11).

trustee, and so also, in the case of a charity which is a local charity in any area, shall any two or more inhabitants of the area and the parish council of any rural parish comprising the area or any part of it; but a parish council shall not exercise their right of appeal without the consent of the parish meeting.

### Power to act for protection of charities

**20.**—(1) Where the Commissioners are satisfied as the result of an inquiry instituted by them under section six of this Act—

(*a*) that there has been in the administration of a charity any misconduct or mismanagement; and

(*b*) that it is necessary or desirable to act for the purpose of protecting the property of the charity or securing a proper application for the purposes of the charity of that property or of property coming to the charity;

then for that purpose the Commissioners may of their own motion do all or any of the following things:—

(i) they may by order remove any trustee,[65] charity trustee, officer, agent or servant of the charity who has been responsible for or privy to the misconduct or mismanagement or has by his conduct contributed to it or facilitated it;

(ii) they may make any such order as is authorised by subsection (1) of section sixteen of this Act with respect to the vesting in or transfer to the official custodian for charities of property held by or in trust for the charity;

(iii) they may order any bank or other person who holds money or securities on behalf of the charity or of any trustee for it not to part with the money or securities without the approval of the Commissioners;

(iv) they may, notwithstanding anything in the trusts of the charity, by order restrict the transactions which may be entered into, or the nature or amount of the payments which may be made, in the administration of the charity without the approval of the Commissioners.

(2) The references in subsection (1) above to misconduct or mismanagement shall (notwithstanding anything in the trusts of the charity) extend to the employment for the remuneration or reward of persons acting in the affairs of the charity, or for other administrative purposes, of sums which are excessive in relation to the property which is or is likely to be applied or applicable for the purposes of the charity.

(3) The Commissioners may also remove a charity trustee by order made of their own motion—

(*a*) where the trustee has been convicted of felony, or is a bankrupt or a corporation in liquidation, or is incapable of acting by reason of mental disorder within the meaning of the Mental Health Act, 1983;

(*b*) where the trustee has not acted, and will not declare his willingness or unwillingness to act;

(*c*) where the trustee is outside England and Wales or cannot be found or does not act, and his absence or failure to act impedes the proper administration of the charity.

---

65 See *Jones* v. *Att.-Gen.* [1974] Ch. 148.

(4) The Commissioners may by order made of their own motion appoint a person to be a charity trustee—

(a) in place of a charity trustee removed by them under this section or otherwise;

(b) where there are no charity trustees, or where by reason of vacancies in their number or the absence of incapacity of any of their number the charity cannot apply for the appointment;

(c) where there is a single charity trustee, not being a corporation aggregate, and the Commissioners are of opinion that it is necessary to increase the number for the proper administration of the charity;

(d) where the Commissioners are of opinion that it is necessary for the proper administration of the charity to have an additional charity trustee, because one of the existing charity trustees who ought nevertheless to remain a charity trustee either cannot be found or does not act or is outside England and Wales.

(5) The powers of the Commissioners under this section to remove or appoint charity trustees of their own motion shall include power to make any such order with respect to the vesting in or transfer to the charity trustees of any property as the Commissioners could make on the removal or appointment of a charity trustee by them under section eighteen of this Act.

(6) Any order under this section for the removal or appointment of a charity trustee or trustee for a charity, or for the vesting or transfer of any property, shall be of the like effect as an order made under section eighteen of this Act.

(7) Subsections (10) and (11) of section eighteen of this Act shall apply to orders under this section as they apply to orders under that, save that where the Commissioners have by order removed a trustee, charity trustee, officer, agent, or servant of a charity under the power conferred by subsection (1) of this section, an appeal against such an order may be brought by any person so removed without a certificate of the Commissioners and without the leave of one of the judges of the High Court attached to the Chancery Division.

(8) The power of the Commissioners under subsection (1) above to remove a trustee, charity trustee, officer, agent or servant of a charity shall include power to suspend him from the exercise of his office or employment pending the consideration of his removal (but not for a period longer than three months), and to make provision as respects the period of the suspension for matters arising out of it, and in particular for enabling any person to execute any instrument in his name or otherwise act for him and, in the case of a charity trustee, for adjusting any rules governing the proceedings of the charity trustees to take account of the reduction in the number capable of acting.[66]

(9) Before exercising any jurisdiction under this section, the Commissioners shall give notice of their intention to do so to each of the charity trustees, except any that cannot be found or has no known address in the United Kingdom; and any such notice may be given by post and, if given by post, may be addressed to the recipient's last known address in the United Kingdom.

**Power to authorise dealings with charity property, etc.**

23.—(1) Subject to the provisions of this section, where it appears to the Commissioners that any action proposed or contemplated in the administration

---

[66] The court may appoint a receiver and manager for a charity: *Att.-Gen.* v. *Schonfield* [1980] 1 W.L.R. 1182.

of a charity is expedient in the interests of the charity, they may by order sanction that action, whether or not it would otherwise be within the powers exercisable by the charity trustees in the administration of the charity; and anything done under the authority of such an order shall be deemed to be properly done in the exercise of those powers.

## Power to advise charity trustees

**24.**—(1) The Commissioners may on the written application of any charity trustee give him their opinion or advice on any matter affecting the performance of his duties as such.

(2) A charity trustee or trustee for a charity acting in accordance with the opinion or advice of the Commissioners given under this section with respect to the charity shall be deemed, as regards his responsibility for so acting, to have acted in accordance with his trust, unless, when he does so, either—

(a) he knows or has reasonable cause to suspect that the opinion or advice was given in ignorance of material facts; or

(b) the decision of the court has been obtained on the matter or proceedings are pending to obtain one.

## Taking of legal proceedings

**28.**—(1) Charity proceedings[67] may be taken with reference to a charity either by the charity, or by any of the charity trustees, or by any person interested in the charity,[68] or by any two or more inhabitants of the area of the charity, if it is a local charity, but not by any other person.

(2) Subject to the following provisions of this section, no charity proceedings relating to a charity (other than an exempt charity) shall be entertained or proceeded with in any court unless the taking of the proceedings is authorised by order of the Commissioners.

(3) The Commissioners shall not, without special reasons, authorise the taking of charity proceedings where in their opinion the case can be dealt with by them under the powers of this Act.

(4) This section shall not require any order for the taking of proceedings in a pending cause or matter or for the bringing of any appeal.

(5) Where the foregoing provisions of this section require the taking of charity proceedings to be authorised by an order of the Commissioners, the proceedings may nevertheless be entertained or proceeded with if after the order had been applied for and refused leave to take the proceedings was obtained from one of the judges of the High Court attached to the Chancery Division.

(6) Nothing in the foregoing subsections shall apply to the taking of proceedings by the Attorney General, with or without a relator.

---

[67] "Charity proceedings" as defined in s.28(8) do not cover proceedings by way of construction of a will or of a conveyance to determine whether or not the will or conveyance is effective to create a charitable trust: *Re Belling* [1967] Ch. 425; *Hauxwell* v. *Barton-upon-Humber U.D.C.* [1974] Ch. 432.

[68] In *Richmond London B.C.* v. *Rogers* [1988] 2 All E.R. 761 C.A. rejected an interested person needing either (a) to be capable of benefiting from the charity or taking some interest under the trusts or (b) to be entitled to participate in the management of the charity because this could be too wide or too narrow in some respects. If a person has an interest in securing the due administration of the trust materially greater than, or different from, that possessed by the ordinary public that interest may well qualify him as a "person interested," *e.g.* Richmond B.C. due to the close relationship between the council's welfare services and the activities of the charity and its power to appoint 3 of 11 trustees.

(7) Where it appears to the Commissioners, on an application for an order under this section or otherwise, that it is desirable for legal proceedings to be taken with reference to any charity (other than an exempt charity) or its property or affairs, and for the proceedings to be taken by the Attorney General, the Commissioners shall so inform the Attorney General, and send him such statements and particulars as they think necessary to explain the matter.

(8) In this section "charity proceedings" means proceedings in any court in England or Wales brought under the court's jurisdiction with respect to charities, or brought under the court's jurisdiction with respect to trusts in relation to the administration of a trust for charitable purposes.

### Restrictions on dealing with charity property[69]

**29.**—(1) Subject to the exceptions provided for by this section, no property forming part of the permanent endowment of a charity shall, without an order of the court or of the Commissioners, be mortgaged or charged by way of security for the repayment of money borrowed, nor, in the case of land in England or Wales, be sold, leased or otherwise disposed of.

(2) Subsection (1) above shall apply to any land which is held by or in trust for a charity and is or has at any time been occupied for the purposes of the charity, as it applies to land forming part of the permanent endowment of a charity; but a transaction for which the sanction of an order under subsection (1) above is required by virtue only of this subsection shall, notwithstanding that it is entered into without such an order, be valid in favour of a person who (then or afterwards) in good faith acquires an interest in or charge on the land for money or money's worth.

(3) This section shall apply notwithstanding anything in the trusts of a charity, but shall not require the sanction of an order—

(a) for any transaction for which general or special authority is expressly given (without the authority being made subject to the sanction of an order) by any statutory provision contained in or having effect under an Act of Parliament or by any scheme legally established; or

(b) for the granting of a lease for a term ending not more than twenty-two years after it is granted, not being a lease granted wholly or partly in consideration of a fine; or

(c) for any disposition of an advowson.

(4) This section shall not apply to an exempt charity, nor to any charity which is excepted by order or regulations.

### Manner of executing instruments

**34.**—(1) Charity trustees[70] may, subject to the trusts of the charity, confer on any of their body (not being less than two in number) a general authority, or an authority limited in such manner as the trustees think fit, to execute in the names and on behalf of the trustees assurances or other deeds or instruments for giving effect to transactions to which the trustees are a party; and any deed

---

[69] This is to be repealed and replaced by provisions requiring trustees to follow statutory procedures before selling land: Cm. 694, Chap. 7.

[70] Charities are not limited to four trustees (Trustee Act 1925, s.34) and charitable trustees may act by majority: *Re Whiteley* [1910] 1 Ch. 600.

or instrument executed in pursuance of an authority so given shall be of the same effect as if executed by the whole body.

(2) An authority under subsection (1) above—

(a) shall suffice for any deed or instrument if it is given in writing or by resolution of a meeting of the trustees, notwithstanding the want of any formality that would be required in giving an authority apart from that subsection;

(b) may be given so as to make the powers conferred exercisable by any of the trustees, or may be restricted to named persons or in any other way;

(c) subject to any such restriction, and until it is revoked, shall, notwithstanding any change in the charity trustees, have effect as a continuing authority given by and to the persons who from time to time are of their body.

(3) In any authority under this section to execute a deed or instrument in the names and on behalf of charity trustees there shall, unless the contrary intention appears, be implied authority also to execute it for them in the name and on behalf of the official custodian for charities or of any other person, in any case in which the charity trustees could do so.

(4) Where a deed or instrument purports to be executed in pursuance of this section, then in favour of a person who (then or afterwards) in good faith acquires for money or money's worth an interest in or charge on property or the benefit of any covenant or agreement expressed to be entered into by the charity trustees, it shall be conclusively presumed to have been duly executed by virtue of this section.

**Transfer and evidence of title to property vested in trustees**

**35.**—(1) Where, under the trusts of a charity, trustees of property held for the purposes of the charity may be appointed or discharged by resolution of a meeting of the charity trustees, members or other persons, a memorandum declaring a trustee to have been so appointed or discharged shall be sufficient evidence of that fact, if the memorandum is signed either at the meeting by the person presiding or in some other manner directed by the meeting, and is attested by two persons present at the meeting.

(2) A memorandum evidencing the appointment or discharge of a trustee under subsection (1) above, if executed as a deed, shall have the like operation under section forty of the Trustee Act, 1925 (which relates to vesting declarations as respects trust property in deeds appointing or discharging trustees), as if the appointment or discharge were effected by the deed.

*Settled Land Act 1925*

**Charitable and public trusts**

**29.**—(1) For the purposes of this section, all land vested or to be vested in trustees on or for charitable, ecclesiastical, or public trusts or purposes shall be deemed to be settled land, and the trustees shall, without constituting them statutory owners, have in reference to the land, all the powers which are by this Act conferred on a tenant for life and on the trustees of a settlement.

In connexion only with the exercise of those powers, and not so as to impose any obligation in respect of or to affect—

(a) the mode of creation or the administration of such trusts; or (*b*) the appointment or number of trustees of such trusts;

the statute or other instrument creating the trust or under which it is administered shall be deemed the settlement, and the trustees shall be deemed the trustees of the settlement, and, save where the trust is created by a will coming into operation after the commencement of this Act, a separate instrument shall not be necessary for giving effect to the settlement.

Any conveyance of land held on charitable, ecclesiastical or public trusts shall state that the land is held on such trusts, and, where a purchaser has notice that the land is held on charitable, ecclesiastical, or public trusts, he shall be bound to see that any consents or orders requisite for authorising the transaction have been obtained.

### Charities Act 1985

**2.**—(1) This section applies, subject to subsection (11) below, to a local charity for the relief of poverty, where—

(*a*) at least 50 years have elapsed since the date of the charity's foundation, or

(*b*) it is subject to a scheme (whether established by the court or by the Commissioners) for the joint administration of two or more charities, and in the case of each of the charities comprised in the scheme at least 50 years have elapsed since the date of its foundation.

(2) If the charity trustees are of the opinion—

(*a*) that the objects of the charity may fairly be considered obsolete or lacking in usefulness, or impossible of achievement, having regard to the period that has elapsed since the charity was founded, the social and economic changes that have taken place in that period and other circumstances (if any) relevant to the functioning and administration of the charity, and

(*b*) that an alteration of the charity's objects is required in order that the charity's resources may be applied to better effect, consistently with the spirit of the original gift.

they may (subject to the following provisions) pass a resolution that the trusts of the charity be modified by replacing the objects of the charity by other objects, being in law charitable, specified in the resolution.

(3) The objects so specified must be, in the trustees' opinion, not so far dissimilar in character to those of the original charitable gift that this modification of the charity's trusts would constitute an unjustifiable departure from the intentions of the founder of the charity, or violate the spirit of the gift.

(4) The trustees must take such steps as are reasonably open to them to secure the approval to the proposed alteration of objects of any person identifiable as having been the founder of the charity.

(5) The resolution of the trustees must be unanimous and be in the form set out in Schedule 1 to this Act, or as near to that form as circumstances may admit.

(6) having passed the resolution, the trustees shall—

(*a*) give such public notice that they have done so as they think reasonable and justified, having regard to the resources of the charity and the extent of its area of benefit, and (*b*) send copies of the resolution to the Commissioners and to the appropriate local authority, accompanied in each case by a statement of their reasons for being of the opinions specified in subsections (2) and (3) above.

The trustees need not comply with paragraph (*a*) of this subsection if they consider that, in all the circumstances, no useful purpose would be served by giving public notice of the resolution.

(7) The Commissioners may, when considering the resolution, require the trustees to provide additional information or explanation as to the circumstances in and by reference to which they have determined to act under this section or as to their compliance with this section; and the Commissioners shall take into consideration any representations made to them by the appropriate local authority and others appearing to them to be interested.

(8) The Commissioners shall, not less than six weeks or more than 3 months from the time when they receive a copy of the resolution from the trustees—

(*a*) if it appears to them that the requirements of this section are satisfied in respect of the resolution, and that the proposed alteration of objects is justified in all the circumstances (treating the trustee's opinion under subsections (2) and (3) as prima facie well-founded and not to be set aside in the absence of contrary considerations), give to the trustees notice of their concurrence with the resolution, or

(*b*) give them notice that they require further time in which to consider the case (but so that not more than an additional 6 months shall be taken for that purpose), or

(*c*) give them notice that they do not concur with the resolution.

Any notice given by the Commissioners under this subsection (including any notice of concurrence, or non-concurrence, given after they have taken further time for consideration) shall be in writing, and they shall send a copy of it to the appropriate local authority.

(9) If the Commissioners give notice of their concurrence with the resolution then, with effect from the date specified in the notice, the trusts of the charity shall, by virtue of this section, be deemed modified in accordance with the terms of the resolution, and the trust instrument shall have effect accordingly.

(10) References in this section to a charity's trust instrument include any document which for the time being lays down or regulates the manner in which the charity's property may or must be applied.

(11) This section does not apply to an exempt charity or a charity which is a company or other body corporate.

(12) Section 4(6)(*b*) of the Act of 1960 (duty to give notice etc. to the Commissioners) does not apply where the trusts of a charity are modified by virtue of this section.

**3**—(1) Subject to and in accordance with this section, the trustees of a registered charity, or a charity which is not required to be registered, may pass a resolution that the whole property of the charity be transferred to another charity, being a registered charity or a charity that is not required to be registered, to be held and applied by, and as property of, that other charity.

(2) Such a resolution shall not have effect unless in the case of the charity first-mentioned ("the transferor charity") its gross income in the preceding accounting period was £200 or less; and the trustees must, before passing such a resolution—

(a) obtain from the trustees of the other charity ("the transferee charity") written confirmation that they are willing to accept a transfer of property under this section, and

(b) have formed the opinion that the objects of the transferee charity are not so far dissimilar in character to those of the original charitable gift that the proposed transfer would constitute an unjustifiable departure from the intentions of the founder of the transferor charity or violate the spirit of the gift.

(3) The trustees must also take such steps as are reasonably open to them to secure the approval to the proposed transfer of any person identifiable as having been the founder of the charity.

(4) The resolution of the trustees must be unanimous, and must be in the form set out in Schedule 2 to this Act, or as near to that form as circumstances may admit.

(5) Having passed the resolution, the trustees shall—

(a) give such public notice that they have done so as they think reasonable and justified, having regard to the resources of the charity and the extent of its area of benefit, and

(b) send copies of the resolution to the Commissioners and, if it is a local charity for the relief of poverty, to the appropriate local authority, accompanied in each case by a statement of their reasons for wishing to effect a transfer of property under this section.

The trustees need not comply with paragraph (a) of this subsection if they consider that, in all the circumstances, no useful purpose would be served by giving public notice of the resolution.

(6) The Commissioners may, when considering the resolution, require the trustees to provide additional information or explanation as to the circumstances in and by reference to which they have determined to act under this section or as to their compliance with this section; and the Commissioners shall take into consideration any representations made to them by the appropriate local authority and others appearing to them to be interested.

(7) The Commissioners shall, not less than six weeks or more than 3 months from the time when they receive a copy of the resolution from the trustees—

(a) if it appears to them that the requirements of this section are satisfied in respect of the resolution and that it is a proper case (treating the trustees' opinion under subsection (2)(b) as prima facie well-founded and not to be set aside in the absence of contrary considerations), give to the trustees notice of their concurrence with the resolution, or

(b) give them notice that they require further time in which to consider the case (but so that not more than an additional 6 months shall be taken for that purpose), or

(c) give them notice that they do not concur with the resolution.

Any notice given by the Commissioners under this subsection (including any notice of concurrence, or non-concurrence, given after they have taken further time for consideration) shall be in writing, and if a copy of the resolution has been sent to the appropriate local authority under subsection (5)(b), they shall send a copy of any such notice to that authority.

(8) If the Commissioners give notice of their concurrence with the resolution, the trustees of the transferor charity shall on receipt of the notice make

arrangements for the transfer of the whole property of the charity to the trustees of the transferee charity, to be acquired by that charity on the terms of this section.

(9) Those terms are as follows—

(a) all property acquired from the transferor charity which was expendable as income in the hands of that charity is to be treated as expendable in the hands of the transferee charity;

(b) any property of the transferor charity which was not expendable as income, having formed part of that charity's permanent endowment, is to remain subject to the same restrictions on expenditure as applied before the transfer;

(c) the whole property acquired by the transferee charity is to be held and applied for the objects of that charity.

(10) For the purpose of enabling any property to be transferred under this section, the Commissioners shall have power, at the request of the trustees of the transferor charity to make orders vesting any property of that charity in the trustees of the transferee charity.

(11) This section does not apply to a charity falling within paragraph (g) of Schedule 2 to the Act of 1960 or a charity which is a company or other body corporate.

**6.**—(1) References in this Act to a local charity for the relief of poverty are to a registered charity, not being an ecclesiastical charity, having the following characteristics—

(a) the sole or primary object of the charity is the relief of poverty (within any meaning given to that expression under the law of charitable trusts, as applied for the time being), and

(b) it is established for purposes which are by their nature or by the trusts of the charity directed wholly or mainly to the benefit of a particular area in England and Wales (in this section referred to as "the area of benefit"), and—

(i) the area of benefit is, or falls wholly within, the area of not more than five adjoining parishes or of one county or of Greater London, or

(ii) the area that would have been the area of benefit when the charity was originally established was, or fell wholly within, the area of one or more parishes specified in the trusts.

(2) In this Act "appropriate local authority," in relation to a local charity for the relief of poverty, means any local authority for an area which is the area of benefit or within which the whole or any part of the area of benefit falls, being the council of a non-metropolitan county, metropolitan district or London borough or the Common Council of the City of London.

## RECOMMENDATIONS OF THE WOODFIELD REPORT

1. The Chief Charity Commissioner should appoint a project officer, to report directly to him, to co-ordinate Commission work on matters arising out of this report (Summary).

*The Charity Commission and other departments*

2. The Home Office and the Charity Commission should review and clarify the division of responsibilities between them; the direct accountability of the

Chief Commissioner to the Home Secretary should be preserved (paragraphs 16–20).

## Organisation and management of the Charity Commission

3. Two additional part time Commissioners should be appointed by March 1988[71] (paragraph 27).

4. The Commission should set up a top management board (paragraph 28).

5. The Commission should, in conjunction with the Treasury, consider urgently the findings of the forthcoming information technology strategy study, according particular priority to the introduction of a management information system (paragraph 32).

6. There should be more secondments of staff between the Commission and other departments; and the Commission should examine the possibility of exchanges with charitable organisations (paragraph 36).

## The Register and accounts

7. Section 4(4)(c) of the 1960 Act should be repealed, thus bringing under supervision charities with a small investment income but a large turnover of money (PL)* (paragraph 50).

8. A graded system should be introduced, if possible under existing legislative powers, for the submission of annual accounts and returns to the Commission; returns should include a narrative report and particulars of the charity trustees and correspondent (paragraphs 54–56).

9. All local charities should be required to send a copy of their accounts to the relevant local authority (PL) (paragraph 57).

10. Charities should be obliged to furnish copies of their accounts to members of the public on payment of an appropriate fee (PL) (paragraph 58).

11. The Commission should arrange suitable training for those staff who are engaged in examining annual accounts (paragraph 60).

12. The Commissioners should be enabled to deregister charities for failure to submit accounts[72] (PL) (paragraph 63).

13. The Commission should require registration as a pre-condition for dealing with any business from a registrable charity (paragraph 64).

14. The Commission's Register of charities should be computerised (paragraph 65).

## Monitoring and investigation

15. Provision should be made that no person may without the permission in writing of the Commissioners act as the trustee of a charity if (i) he has been convicted of any offence involving fraud or other dishonesty, or (ii) he has previously been removed by the Commissioners from trusteeship of a charity (PL) (paragraph 74).

16. The Commissioners should be given discretion to require that a charity has a minimum of three trustees (PL) (paragraph 75).

17. Section 20(1) of the 1960 Act should be amended to enable the Commissioners to act under (a) or (b) instead of both being required (PL) (paragraph 76).

---

[71] Implemented January 1989: 1988 Annual Report, para. 3.
* (PL)—Recommendations requiring primary legislation.
[72] Not accepted by Government Cm. 694, paras. 4.9–4.11. Failure to submit prompt accounts will lead to a public default marking.

18. The various requirements on the Commissioners to give notice to trustees, and publicity to such notices, before exercising their powers under section 20 of the 1960 Act, should be repealed (PL) (paragraph 76).

19.** The Commissioners should be able to appoint trustees additional to the number required by a charity's trust instrument (PL) (paragraph 76).

20.** The Commissioners should be able to appoint a receiver and manager (PL) (paragraph 76).

21.** The Commissioners should be able to exercise their scheme-making powers without an application of the trustees (PL) (paragraph 76).

22.** The Commissioners should be able to wind up a charity and transfer its property to another charity (PL) (paragraph 76).

23. The powers of the Commissioners in section 7(1) of the 1960 Act to call for documents and search records should be extended to allow the Commissioners to require explanations (PL) (paragraph 76).

24. The Commission should examine the scope for further clarification of section 20 of the 1960 Act and make recommendations to the Home Secretary for any necessary changes (paragraph 77).

*Advice, scheme-making, local reviews and the Charities Act 1985*

25. The Commission should continue to review the presentation and content of their leaflets, drawing up a programme to this end (paragraph 81).

26. The objectives and working methods of the Commission's Charities Division should be reviewed (paragraph 82).

27. The Commission should consult widely on possible ways of relaxing the *cy-près* doctrine and advise the Home Secretary whether legislation would be desirable (paragraph 85).

28. Section 11 of the 1960 Act should be amended to allow the Commissioners to appoint persons to review local charities (PL) (paragraph 91).

29. The Commission should as soon as practicable establish a local charity liaison section to promote and assist future local review work (paragraph 92).

30. The Charities Act 1985 should be amended to increase its use by extending its application, increasing its monetary limits and simplifying its procedures (PL) (paragraphs 93–94).

31. The second publication of notices of schemes made by the Commissioners should no longer be required (PL) (paragraph 95).

32. Where a charity does not have a properly constituted trustee body the Commissioners should be able to make a scheme of their own volition (PL) (paragraph 95).

33. The Commission should advise the Home Secretary of the outcome of discussion with interested parties on the regulation of maintenance contributions in almshouses (paragraph 95).

34. The Commission should prepare model governing instruments for wide general use by founders of new charities (paragraph 95).

*Consent to land transactions*

35. Section 29 of the 1960 Act should be repealed and replaced by provisions requiring trustees to follow statutory procedures before selling land (PL) (paragraph 98).

---

** For text, see page 390, *infra*. These recommendations are for new sanctions under section 20 of the 1960 Act, *i.e.* they would be available where an inquiry had revealed mismanagement or misconduct or the need to act to protect charity property.

36. The Trustee Investments Act 1961 should be amended to allow trustees to purchase land for investment purposes without the need for an order of the Commissioners under section 23 of the 1960 Act (PL) (paragraph 99).

37. The Commission should make every effort to reduce staff resources currently deployed on consents work (paragraph 100).

*Official Custodian for Charities*

38. The Commission should cease to encourage charities to use the services of the Official Custodian (paragraph 110).

39. The Commission should employ consultants to work out a scheme and programme for returning investments held by the Official Custodian to trustees; the specification should be drawn to make it possible for key decisions to be taken by the end of 1987. Giving effect to any changes would mean amending the 1960 Act (PL) (paragraph 110).

*Charging by the Charity Commission*

40. The Commissioners should be enabled to introduce charges for new registrations, the services of the Official Custodian if he is retained and for residual work on consents to property transactions (PL) (paragraph 112).

*Malpractice in fundraising*

41. It should be an offence for a fundraising practitioner to deduct his remuneration (however calculated) from donations received before paying them to the charity unless he can prove that his intention to do so was made clear to every donor; if such an offence is committed it should be open to the court, in addition to imposing penalties, to determine that the sums deducted be paid to such charity as the court may determine (PL) (paragraph 129).

42. Provision should be made that, whenever goods or services are advertised or offered for sale with an indication that some part of the proceeds is to be devoted to charity, there shall be specified (i) the charity or charities that are to benefit (and if more than one in what proportion), and (ii) the manner in which the sums they are to receive are to be calculated (PL) (paragraph 129).

43. A charity should be able in certain circumstances to obtain an injunction against the use of its name by a named person or organisation (PL) (paragraph 129).

44. The Home Office and the Charity Commission should review the legislation relating to public collections in consultation with representatives of the local authorities and make recommendations to the Home Secretary (paragraph 132).

### Section 4. The Cy-Près Doctrine[73]

As the next chapter shows where a private trust is initially ineffective or subsequently fails there arises a resulting trust for the settlor or his estate if he is dead. If a charitable trust is *initially* impracticable or

---

[73] See *Tudor on Charities*, Chap. 5; *Picarda on Charities*, Chap. 25 1989 Annual Report of the Ch. Commrs., paras. 73–80.

impossible and the settlor had no general charitable intention there is also a resulting trust.[74] But if the settlor had a general charitable intention, then the trust property will be applied *cy-près* under a scheme formulated by the Charity Commissioners or the court, *i.e.* it will be applied to some other charitable purposes as nearly as possible resembling the original purposes. If an effective charitable trust *subsequently* becomes impracticable or impossible then the trust property will be applied *cy-près* irrespective of the question of general charitable intention[75]: the settlor or, if he is dead, his residuary legatee or next of kin are forever excluded once the property has been effectually dedicated to charity absolutely.

Since 1960 section 14 of the Charities Act, *infra*, may be relied upon if need be in special circumstances to establish general charitable intention and section 13, *infra*, has relaxed the requirements of impracticability or impossibility.

One must appreciate that the case law reveals how much leeway a court has in determining whether there has been an initial failure of charitable purposes and, if so, whether there was a general charitable intention manifested by the testator or donor.

### Whether or not there is Initial Lapse or Failure

There are three basic ways in which a testator might bequeath property: (1) for the relief of the blind in Batley (2) for Batley Blind Home, High Street, Batley, the receipt of the treasurer for the time being to be sufficient discharge to the executors (3) for Batley Blind Home Ltd. [a company limited by guarantee under the Companies Act 1985], High Street, Batley.

No problem arises in the first case since the purpose is not initially impracticable or impossible and purposes live for ever, though particular institutions carrying out purposes may die. If the purpose had been more specific such as building a blind home at a particular site, where there was no reasonable chance of such blind home being erected whether because of planning permission problems or lack of cash (inflation eroding the will moneys in a will executed many years ago), so the purpose failed *ab initio* then the legacy would lapse unless a general charitable intention was present.[76] The time for determining

---

[74] *Re Rymer* [1895] 1 Ch. 19, *Re Stemson* [1970] Ch. 16. Gifts to particular Churches or to augment particular vicars' stipends may be saved under special legislation, *e.g.* Methodist Church Act 1976, s.15 or Endowments and Glebe Measures 1976 of the Church of England.

[75] Assuming the gift is an absolute one or made absolute by Perpetuities and Accumulations Act 1964, s.12.

[76] *Re Wilson* [1913] 1 Ch. 314 (to endow a school at a particular place where there was no reasonable chance of such a school being established); *Re Good's W.T.* [1950] 2 All E.R. 653 (funds insufficient for erection and upkeep of rest-homes); *Re Ulverston and District New Hospital Building Trusts* [1956] Ch. 622 (funds always insufficient for required purpose); *Re Mackenzie* [1962] 2 All E.R. 890 (trust to provide bursaries for education at secondary schools rendered impossible by provision of free education by state); *Re Lysaght* [1966] Ch. 191 (gift to Royal College of Surgeons on trust to provide studentships for persons not of Jewish or Catholic faith failed as the college was not prepared to act as trustees of such a trust and Buckley J., rather

whether failure has occurred is the date of the testator's death, *i.e.* when the gift vests in interest not when it vests in possession, *e.g.* after a life interest. If need be, an inquiry will be directed "whether at the date of the death of the testator it was practicable to carry his intentions into effect or whether at the said date there was any reasonable prospect that it would be practicable to do so at some future time."[77] Where a future gift is defeasible an inquiry as to its practicability should be undertaken on the basis that the gift will not be defeated but will take effect at some future time as an interest in possession.[78]

Problems arise in the second case, where an unincorporated charitable association runs the home, if the home has ceased to exist by the testator's death. Since the association is unincorporated and charitable (not being a private members' club) the gift must necessarily be construed as a gift on trust for purposes. The purposes may be (a) the relief of the blind from time to time in the Batley Blind Home and nothing more (b) the relief of the blind in Batley (c) the augmentation[79] of the endowed trust funds of the Batley Blind Home for whatever purposes such endowed trust funds might become held, *e.g.* if amalgamated with the Bury Blind Home and the Dewsbury Deaf Home.

In (a) where the gift is construed as a gift to a particular charitable institution just for its particular purposes then the gift lapses if the institution ceases to exist before the testator's death[80] unless, which is most unlikely,[81] a general charitable intention can be found to justify a *cy-près* application.[82]

In (b) where the gift is construed as a gift for a charitable purpose in circumstances where the existence of the particular institution carrying out the purpose is not material to the gift's validity, the gift does not lapse so long as the purpose can be carried out by other means which are to be determined by the court in cases of doubt.[83]

Construction (c) ensures that so long as there are funds held in trust for the named charity's purposes the gift augments such funds despite

---

remarkably, held that this was the rare type of case where the identity of the trustees was vital to the trust. He further held that a paramount charitable intent was present so that a *cy-près* scheme could be directed omitting the offending religious conditions. This reveals the flexibility of *cy-près* applications which can even provide remedies in special circumstances); *Re Woodhams* [1981] 1 W.L.R. 493 (music scholarship for British boys restricted to orphans from two institutions but the trustee, the London College of Music, would not accept the trust as so restricted so Vinelott J. removed the restrictions by *cy-près* scheme).

[77] *Re Wright* [1954] Ch. 347; *Re White* [1955] Ch. 188; *Re Martin* (1977) 121 Sol.J. 828.
[78] *Re Tacon* [1958] Ch. 447.
[79] *cf.* accretion to funds of unincorporated members' club: *Re Recher's W.T.* [1972] Ch. 526, *supra*, p. 206.
[80] *Re Rymer* [1895] 1 Ch. 19, *Re Slatter's W.T.* [1964] Ch. 512. *Re Spence's W.T.* [1979] Ch. 483. On the possible constructions see J.B.E. Hutton (1969) 32 M.L.R. 283; R.M.B. Cotterell (1972) 36 Conv. 198; J. Martin (1974) 38 Conv. 187.
[81] *Re Harwood* [1936] Ch. 285; *Re Stemson* [1970] Ch. 16, 21.
[82] As happened in *Re Finger's W.T.* [1972] 1 Ch. 286 on which Megarry V.-C. had some reservations in *Re Spence's W.T.* [1978] 3 All E.R. 92 *infra*, p. 400.
[83] *Re Watt* [1932] 2 Ch. 243; *Re Roberts* [1963] 1 W.L.R. 406; *Re Finger's W.T.* [1972] 1 Ch. 286.

any alteration in its name or constitution or any amalgamation with other charities.[84] Thus the bequest in (c) unlike (b) could be used for the Bury Blind Home and the Dewsbury Deaf Home. However, if the named charity is not to provide a fund in existence for ever devoted to charity but is liable to dissolution under its own constitution and chooses to dissolve itself, so that its surplus funds on its winding up are transferred to some other charity, the gift will lapse on the basis that the charity has ceased to exist.[85]

In the third case where the bequest is to the Batley Blind Home Ltd., High Street, Batley the bequest is presumed to be an out and out gift to the corporate institution beneficially as part of its general funds, unless there is something positive in the will to justify the bequest being treated as on trust for the purposes of the company's charitable objects. In the former case the gift will lapse if the company is wound up before the testator dies unless, which is most unlikely, a general charitable intention can be found to justify a *cy-près* application.[86] In the latter case the trust purposes will be (a) the relief of the blind from time to time in the Batley Blind Home, High Street, Batley, as run by the Batley Blind Home Ltd., or (b) the relief of the blind from time to time in premises run by the Batley Blind Home Ltd., or (c) the relief of the blind in Batley, In (a) lapse will occur if such home ceases to exist before the testator's death, in (b) lapse will occur if the company is wound up before the testator's death whilst in (c) lapse will not occur.[87]

### Where there is Initial Lapse or Failure

If matters of construction cannot save the gift then the gift lapses unless the court can find a general charitable intention present. There have been many judicial statements on the meaning of the phrase: *e.g.* Kay J. in *Re Taylor*[88]: "If upon the whole scope and intent of the will you discover the paramount object of the testator was to benefit not a particular institution but to effect a particular form of charity independently of any special institution or mode, then, although he may have indicated the mode in which he desires that to be carried out, you are to regard the primary paramount intention chiefly, and if the particular mode for any reason fails, to use the phrase familiar to us, execute that *cy-près*, that is, carry out the general paramount intention indicated without which his intention itself cannot be effected." Also Buckley J. in *Re Lysaght*[89]: "A general charitable intention . . . may be said to be a paramount intention on the part of a donor to effect some charitable

---

[84] *Re Lucas* [1948] Ch. 424 (on which see *Re Spence's W.T.* [1978] 3 All E.R. 92); *Re Faraker* [1912] 2 Ch. 488; *Re Bagshaw* [1954] 1 W.L.R. 238.
[85] *Re Stemson's W.T.* [1970] Ch. 16.
[86] *Ibid.*
[87] *Re Meyers* [1951] Ch. 534.
[88] (1888) 58 L.T. 538, 543.
[89] [1966] Ch. 191, 202, approved in *Re Woodhams* [1981] 1 All E.R. 202, 209 but see *Tudor on Charities*, p. 237.

purpose which the court can find a method of putting into operation, notwithstanding that it is impracticable to give effect to some direction by the donor which is not an essential part of his true intention—not, that is to say, of his paramount intention.

"In contrast, a particular charitable intention exists when the donor means his charitable disposition to take effect if, but only if, it can be carried into effect in a particular specified way, for example, in connection with a particular school to be established at a particular place,[90] or by establishing a home in a particular house . . . "[91]

Where the gift is to an institution described by a particular name and the institution has never existed, a general charitable intent is presumed if the name imports a charitable object[92]; but the presumption may be easily rebutted if the will also includes a residuary gift in favour of charity.[93] On the other hand, the court is assisted in discovering a general charitable intention if the gift to the non-existent institution is of a share of residue and the other residuary legatees are charities.[94]

### Subsequent Failure

If at the testator's death the designated charity existed or it was not then impossible or impracticable to carry out the designated charitable purposes then the gifted property has become charitable property to the perpetual exclusion of the testator's residuary legatee or next of kin.[95] Accordingly, the *cy-près* doctrine is available upon any subsequent failure[96]: there is no need to prove any general charitable intent.[97]

The position is the same for *inter vivos* gifts effectively dedicated to charity, whether the surplus funds are general assets of a charitable company that has been wound up[98] or assets held on charitable trusts

---

[90] *Re Wilson* [1913] 1 Ch. 314.
[91] *Re Packe* [1918] 1 Ch. 437.
[92] *Re Davis* [1902] 1 Ch. 876; *Re Harwood* [1936] Ch. 285 (though Peace Societies are probably not charitable: *Re Koeppler's W.T.* [1984] 2 All E.R. 111, 122, 124).
[93] *Re Goldschmidt* [1957] 1 W.L.R. 524; 73 L.Q.R. 166 (V.T.H. Delany).
[94] *Re Knox* [1937] Ch. 109. See also *Re Satterthwaite's W.T.* [1966] 1 W.L.R. 277, where a misanthropic testatrix left her residuary estate in nine shares to nine named institutions, seven of which were animal charities, an anti-vivisection society (once thought charitable but now in law not charitable) and the London Animal Hospital (not ascertainable): a general charitable intent was found to infect the latter two shares of residue. In *Re Jenkin's W.T.* [1966] Ch. 249 residue was divided into sevenths, six for charitable institutions and one for "the British Union for the Abolition of Vivisection to do all in its power to urge and get an Act passed prohibiting atrocious unnecessary cruelty to animals": no general charitable intent was found since there was such a clearly expressed non-charitable purpose.
[95] Assuming the gift is an absolute one or made absolute by Perpetuities and Accumulations Act 1964, s.12.
[96] Assuming the gift is an absolute one or made absolute by Perpetuities and Accumulations Act 1964, s.12.
[97] *Re Slevin* [1891] 2 Ch. 236; *Re Moon's W.T.* [1948] 1 All E.R. 300; *Re Wright* [1954] Ch. 347; *Re King* [1923] 1 Ch. 243; *Re Raine* [1956] Ch. 417; *Re Tacon* [1958] Ch. 447. Peter Luxton [1983] Conv. 107 accepts the position for simple legacies to bodies corporate or unincorporate, but submits it is open to the House of Lords to deal differently with legacies on trust for purposes which should be regarded as only disposing of the testator's equitable interest to the extent that the stated purposes are achieved. Thus, failure of the purposes after as well as before, the testator's death, should be capable of giving rise to a resulting trust unless ousted by a general charitable intention.
[98] *Liverpool & District Hospital* v. *Att-Gen* [1981] Ch. 193.

by trustees for an unincorporated association that has been dissolved or for purposes that have been carried out.[99] As Jenkins L.J. remarked,[1] "Once the charity for which the fund was raised had been effectively brought into action the fund was to be regarded as permanently devoted to charity to the exclusion of any resulting trust" for the subscribers. He endorsed[2] the decision of Danckwerts J.[3] that no general charitable intention need be proved in such cases, though there are some illogical cases[4] where the courts have gone to the lengths of excluding any resulting trust by holding that the subscribers intended to give their money out and out under a general charitable intention.

### Cy-près under Charities Act 1960, s.14

In the case of initial failure of charitable purposes section 14 *infra*, p. 409, permits a *cy-près* application as if a general charitable intention had been present. It is necessary to show that the donors cannot be traced or have executed written disclaimers. The idea is to prevent resulting trusts arising in favour of anonymous donors contributing in the course of street collections, etc., to specific charitable appeals. However, the section seems to be superfluous as pointed out by David Wilson.[5]

The problem is that the section only applies where[6] "any difficulty in applying property to those purposes makes that property or the part not applicable *cy-près* available to be returned to the donors." Thus, it applies only where under the general law the property is held on a resulting trust for donors. It does not apply where the property passes to the Crown as *bona vacantia*, as an out and out gift without any general charitable intention, nor where the property is in any event applicable *cy-près* as an out and out gift under a general charitable intention. It is clear that cash put into collection boxes is by way of out and out gift[7] so there is no scope for section 14 to apply to such cash collections.

At face value, the section purports to cover the proceeds of lotteries, competitions, entertainments or sales, but in most cases the so-called donors will have provided contractual consideration for their tickets, so there is no question of them getting their money back by way of a

---

[99] *Re Wokingham Fire Brigade Trusts* [1951] Ch. 373.
[1] *Re Ulverston & District New Hospital Building Trusts* [1956] Ch. 622, 636. To similar effect see Upjohn J. in *Re Coopers Conveyance* [1956] 1 W.L.R. 1096.
[2] *Ibid.* 637.
[3] *Re Wokingham Fire Brigade Trusts* [1951] Ch. 373.
[4] *Re Welsh Hospital (Netley) Fund* [1921] 1 Ch. 655; *Re North Devon & West Somerset Relief Fund Trusts* [1953] 1 W.L.R. 1260; *Re British School of Egyptian Archaeology* [1954] 1 W.L.R. 546; *Picarda on Charities*, pp. 238–241; *Tudor on Charities*, pp. 286–290.
[5] [1983] Conv. 40, but *cf. Beggs* v. *Kirkpatrick* [1961] V.R. 764.
[6] Charities Act 1960, s.14(5).
[7] *Re West Sussex Constabulary's Benevolent Fund Trusts* [1971] Ch. 1, *infra* p. 406; *Re Hillier* [1954] 1 W.L.R. 700 (out-and-out gift and general charitable intention imputed); *Re Ulverston & District New Hospital Building Fund* [1956] 1 Ch. 622 (out-and-out gift but *bona vacantia* since no general charitable intention imputed). In *bona vacantia* cases the Att.-Gen. normally waives the Crown's rights and has the property applied *cy-près* as emerges from *Re Ulverston* p. 634.

resulting trust,[8] so the section is inapplicable to such proceeds. If the money paid is *ex gratia* and not contractual then this will be by way of out and out gift[9] so that the section will be inapplicable.

In the case of supervening failure of charitable purposes where the property has been given out and out to charity then such property is regarded as permanently devoted to charity to the exclusion of any resulting trust[10] so that section 14 can have no scope.

### Extension of Cy-près under Charities Act 1960, s.13

Before section 13 was enacted failure justifying *cy-près* occurred when the purposes of a trust became impossible or impracticable or there was a surplus after the purposes had been carried out. "Impracticable" came to be liberally interpreted over the years so as to include "highly undesirable,"[11] but failure did not occur just because performance in another way would be more suitable or more beneficial.[12] Section 13 now extends the occasions when *cy-près* may be available but in cases of initial failure it is still necessary to show general charitable intention.[13] The section deals with difficulties over the original purposes of the trust and not over provisions as to administration of the trust, *e.g.* a provision for distribution of all capital for charitable purposes within 10 years of the settlor's death.[14] However, matters relating to administration of the trust may be dealt with under the court's inherent jurisdiction.[15]

### RE VERNON'S WILL TRUSTS

[1972] Ch. 300n., 303

BUCKLEY J.: "Every bequest to an unincorporated charity by name without more must take effect as a gift for a charitable purpose. No individual or aggregate of individuals could claim to take such a bequest beneficially. If the gift is to be permitted to take effect at all, it must be as a bequest for a purpose, *i.e.*, that charitable purpose which the named charity exists to serve. A bequest which is in terms made for a charitable purpose will not fail for lack of a trustee but will be carried into effect either under the sign manual or by means of a scheme. A bequest to a named unincorporated charity, however, may on its true interpretation show that the testator's intention to make the gift at all was dependent on the named charitable organisation being available at the time when the gift takes effect to serve as the instrument for applying

---

8 *Re West Sussex Constabulary's Benevolent Fund Trust* [1971] Ch. 1, *infra*, p. 417. Previously, the courts had overlooked this and so too, naturally, did the 1960 Act.

9 See note 4, *supra*.

10 *Re Wright* [1954] Ch. 347; *Re Ulverston* [1956] 1 Ch. 622, 636; *Re Wokingham Fire Brigade Trusts* [1951] Ch. 373.

11 *Re Dominion Students' Hall Trust* [1947] Ch. 183 (scheme removing provision restricting Hall for Dominion students to students of European origin, *i.e.* white students).

12 *Re Weir Hospital* [1910] 2 Ch. 124.

13 Charities Act 1960, s.13(2). In *Re J.W. Laing Trust* [1984] 1 All E.R. 50, 53 counsel surprisingly (and erroneously) conceded that general charitable intent was necessary for property effectively dedicated to charity in 1922.

14 *Re J.W. Laing Trust* [1984] 1 All E.R. 50.

15 *Ibid. Att.-Gen.* v. *Dedham School* (1857) 23 Beav. 350.

the subject-matter of the gift to the charitable purpose for which it is by inference given. If so and the named charity ceases to exist in the lifetime of the testator, the gift fails (*Re Ovey*[16]). A bequest to a corporate body, on the other hand, takes effect simply as a gift to that body beneficially, unless there are circumstances which show that the recipient is to take the gift as a trustee. There is no need in such a case to infer a trust for any particular purpose. The objects to which the corporate body can properly apply its funds may be restricted by its constitution, but this does not necessitate inferring as a matter of construction of the testator's will a direction that the bequest is to be held in trust to be applied for those purposes: the natural construction is that the bequest is made to the corporate body as part of its general funds, that is to say, beneficially and without the imposition of any trust. That the testator's motive in making the bequest may have undoubtedly been to assist the work of the incorporated body would be insufficient to create a trust."

*Note*

This dictum was applied by Geoff J. in *Re Finger's W.T.*[17] so as to hold a gift to a dissolved unincorporated charity, the National Radium Commission, to be a purpose trust for the sort of work carried on by the Commission so as not to lapse, whilst a gift to a dissolved corporate charity, the National Council for Maternity and Child Welfare, he held to be for such charity absolutely beneficially, so as to lapse unless a general charitable intention could be found to justify a *cy-près* application: he found such an intention enabling the gift to pass to the National Association for Maternity and Child Welfare. Earlier he had said,[18] "If the matter were *res integra* I would have thought there would be much to be said for the view that the status of the donee, whether corporate or unincorporate, can make no difference to the question whether as a matter of construction a gift is absolute or on trust for purposes. Certainly drawing such a distinction produces anomalous results."

### RE SPENCE'S WILL TRUSTS

[1979] Ch. 483; [1978] 3 All E.R. 92.; [1978] 3 W.L.R. 483

MEGARRY V.-C. read the following judgment: "The testatrix, Mrs. Spence, . . . made her will on December 4, 1968, and died on May 30, 1972. . . . She gave her residuary estate to her trustees on trust to sell it and to pay her funeral and testamentary expenses and debts, and then:

> 'to pay and divide the residue thereof equally between The Blind Home, Scott Street, Keighley and the Old Folks Home at Hillworth Lodge, Keighley for the benefit of the patients.'

The will next provided that the receipt of the treasurer for the time being of 'each of the above-mentioned institutions' should be a sufficient discharge to her trustees. Subject to the expenses of administration and to the costs of these proceedings, the net residue is now worth some £17,000. . . .

---

[16] (1885) 29 Ch.D. 560.
[17] [1972] Ch. 286.
[18] [1972] Ch. 286, 294. See also *Montefiore Jewish Home* v. *Howell* [1984] 2 N.S.W.L.R. 407.

"I shall first consider the gift to 'The Blind Home, Scott Street, Keighley . . . for the benefit of the patients.' I think it is clear that these last six words apply to the gift to the Blind Home as they apply to the gift to the Old Folks Home; and nobody contended to the contrary. The question is whether this gift carries a moiety of residue to the Keighley and District Association for the Blind and, if so, on what terms. That charity was founded in 1907 and, over the years, it has changed its name thrice. It has borne its present name for nearly 20 years and is at present governed by a trust deed dated October 25, 1963. For over 25 years it has been running a blind home at 31 Scott Street, Keighley, which provides permanent accommodation for the blind in Keighley and district. Since 1907 there have been no other premises or associations connected with the blind in Keighley. The premises in Scott Street are often called 'The Blind Home'; and a memorandum of the appointment of new trustees made on June 9, 1970, refers to the meeting for that purpose held at 'The Blind Home, Scott Street, Keighley.' Other names are used. A board on the building calls it 'The Keighley and District Home for the Blind,' and a brochure in evidence calls it 'Keighley Home for the Blind.' It seems clear beyond a peradventure that the language of the will fits the home run by the charity at these premises.

"In those circumstances, counsel for the plaintiff felt unable to advance any argument that the gift of this moiety failed and passed as on intestacy; and in this I think he was right. That, however, does not dispose of the matter, since the charity also carries on a home for the blind at Bingley, and may of course expend some or all of its funds on this or other purposes within its objects. There is therefore the question whether the moiety should go to the charity as an accretion to its endowment, and so be capable of being employed on any of its activities, or whether it is to be confined to the particular part of the charity's activities that are carried on at The Blind Home in Scott Street, Keighley. I confess that but for the decision of the Court of Appeal in *Re Lucas*[19] I should have had little hesitation in resolving this question in the latter and narrower sense, confining the moiety to the particular Blind Home in Scott Street, Keighley.

"In *Re Lucas* the testatrix made her will on October 12, 1942, and died on December 18, 1943. The will made gifts to 'the Crippled Children's Home, Lindley Moor, Huddersfield'; and it provided that the receipt of the treasurer or other officer for the time being should be a sufficient discharge. From 1916 there had been an establishment called 'The Huddersfield Home for Crippled Children' at Lindley Moor, governed by the charitable trusts established by a deed dated March 29, 1915; but according to the statement of facts in the report[20] 'On October 17, 1941, this home was closed and a scheme for the future administration of its assets was made by the charity commissioners.' Under that scheme the charity thereby created was to be known as 'The Huddersfield Charity for Crippled Children,' and the income was to be applied in sending poor crippled children to holiday or convalescent homes.

"During the argument before me the question arose (for reasons that will appear) whether the words 'On October 17, 1941,' which plainly applied to the closing of the home, also applied (as appeared to be the case) to the making of the scheme and the consequent change of the name of the charity. The matter

---

is resolved by the reports of *Re Lucas*[21] in the All England Law Reports. There, passages in the judgments which are omitted from the Law Reports explicitly state that the scheme of the Charity Commissioners was sealed on October 17, 1941. They also show that the home had been closed not on that day but some two-and-a-half years before, on April 6, 1939, when the lease had run out. The statement of facts in the Law Reports is thus wrong in this respect. When the testatrix came to make her will on October 12, 1942, the home had been closed for some three-and-a-half years, and the charity had for almost a year had a name which, in accord with its new objects, had had the word 'Home' in it replaced by 'Charity.' The All England Law Reports also show that the original name, 'The Huddersfield Home for Crippled Children,' had been given to the charity by the trust deed. The question for resolution in *Re Lucas* was thus whether the gifts to 'the Crippled Children's Home, Lindley Moor, Huddersfield' took effect as gifts to 'The Huddersfield Charity for Crippled Children,' or whether they were gifts for the upkeep of a particular home for crippled children which had ceased to exist before the will had been made, so that they failed.

"At first instance, Roxburgh J. held that the latter was the correct view: *Re Lucas*.[22] On appeal, Lord Greene M.R. delivered the reserved judgment of himself, Somervell L.J. and Jenkins J. This reversed the decision below, and held that the gifts were gifts which contributed to the endowment of the charity, and so did not fail. I have found the judgment puzzling in places. Lord Greene M.R. discussed the misdescription in the will as follows.[23]

'As to the misdescription (*i.e.* "The Crippled Children's Home" for "the Huddersfield Home for Crippled Children") the description given by the testatrix was no more an accurate description of the particular home than it was of the charity.'

Later the judgment considers the position if the testatrix 'did know the correct name of the charity (*i.e.* "The Huddersfield Home for Crippled Children").'

"I find this puzzling. My difficulty is this. Nearly a year before the will was made, the correct name of the charity had ceased to be what the judgment says it was. The 'description given by the testatrix' was 'the Crippled Children's Home, Lindley Moor, Huddersfield.' This, said the judgment, was 'no more an accurate description of the particular home [that is, the Huddersfield Home for Crippled Children which was at Lindley Moor] than it was of the charity.' Yet when the will was made the name of the charity had for nearly a year been 'The Huddersfield Charity for Crippled Children,' a name which did not include the word 'Home.' I find it difficult to see why a gift to a 'Home' does not fit an entity with 'Home' in its title better than it fits an entity without the word 'Home' in its title, but the word 'Charity,' instead. If in referring to the 'correct name' of the charity the judgment intends to refer to what had once been the correct name of the charity, I cannot see what it was that made the court reject the state of affairs when the will was made in favour of the past, particularly when there appears to have been no evidence about what the testatrix knew about the charity. I say what I say with all due humility, and a ready recognition that the fault may be an inability on my part to see what is plain to others; but, though humble, I remain puzzled.

---

[21] [1947] 2 All E.R. 773, 774; [1948] 2 All E.R. 22, 24.
[22] [1948] Ch. 175.
[23] [1948] Ch. 424, 428.

"The main factors in the decision of the Court of Appeal seem to have been that the words used in the will fitted the home that had been closed down no better than the charity which continued in existence, and that the will had omitted to make any specific reference to the upkeep or maintenance of the home which would indicate that the gifts were to be confined to the upkeep of the home. The gifts were accordingly gifts to the charity, and so did not fail. The question for me is whether on the case before me there ought to be a similar result, so that the moiety of residue would go to the Keighley and District Association for the Blind as an addition to its endowment generally, and would not be confined to the Blind Home in Scott Street, Keighley, carried on by the association.

"Counsel for the first defendant submitted that there were two substantial points of distinction between the present case and *Re Lucas*.[24] First, the words of the will fitted the Blind Home far better than they fitted the association. Indeed, although the Blind Home was from time to time described by different names, all the names used included both 'Blind' and 'Home': and, as I have mentioned, the appointment of new trustees in June 1970 uses the name 'The Blind Home, Scott Street, Keighley,' which is the precise expression used in the will. The title of the charity, 'The Keighley and District Association for the Blind,' is very different. True, it has the word 'Blind' in common with the title used in the will. There is also the word 'Keighley,' though this is used adjectively and not as part of the address. But otherwise there is nothing in common. In particular, there is not the use of the word 'Home' in both titles which the Court of Appeal in *Re Lucas* said was present in that case; and I think the words 'Home' and "Association' are different in a real and significant sense.

"Secondly, in the case before me, there are the words 'for the benefit of the patients' which follow and govern the expression 'The Blind Home, Scott Street, Keighley.' In *Re Lucas* there was no counterpart to this. Indeed, the absence of any reference to the upkeep or maintenance of the home in that case was, as I have indicated, one of the grounds on which the decision was based. Here, there is no reference to upkeep or maintenance as such: but I think 'patients' must mean 'patients of the Blind Home,' and the upkeep and maintenance of the home is an obvious means of providing a benefit for the patients in it.

"In my judgment both these distinctions are valid and substantial. It therefore seems to me that the case before me is distinguishable from *Re Lucas*, so far as I have correctly understood that case. The testatrix was making provision for the benefit of the patients for the time being at a particular home, namely, the home usually known as The Blind Home at Scott Street, Keighley. She was giving the money not to augment generally the endowment of the charity which runs that home, with the consequences that the money might be used for purposes other than the benefit of the patients at that home, but was giving the money so that it would be used exclusively for the benefit of those patients. The only way in which this can conveniently be done is to give the money to the charity but to confine its use to use for the benefit of the patients for the time being at the home. That, I think, requires a scheme; but I see no need to direct that a scheme should be settled in chambers. Instead, I think that I can follow the convenient course taken by

24 [1948] Ch. 424.

Goff J. in *Re Finger's Will Trusts*.[25] I shall therefore order by way of scheme (the Attorney-General not objecting) that the moiety be paid to the proper officer of the charity to be held on trust to apply it for the benefit of the patients for the time being of the home known as The Blind Home, Scott Street, Keighley.

"I now turn to the other moiety of residue, given by the will to 'the Old Folks Home at Hillworth Lodge, Keighley for the benefit of the patients.' Hillworth Lodge was built as a workhouse in 1858. Shortly before the outbreak of war in 1939 the West Riding County Council, in whom it had become vested, closed it down: but during the war it was used to house what were generally but inelegantly called 'evacuees.' In 1948 it became an aged persons' home under the National Assistance Act 1948, and it continued as such until January 28, 1971, when it was finally closed down. There had been between 120 and 140 residents in it as late as 1969, but the numbers were then progressively run down, until in January 1971, just before it closed, only ten residents were left; and these were transferred to another establishment in Pudsey. The aged of the area had over the years been increasingly accommodated in purpose-designed old people's homes which provided better accommodation for the aged than could the old workhouse, despite many improvements to it. Since the building ceased to house old people it has been used as Divisional Social Services Offices.

"When the testatrix made her will in 1968 the building was accordingly still in use as an old people's home run by the local authority in accordance with their duty under the National Assistance Act 1948. As an old people's home it had no assets of its own, and residents contributed towards their maintenance in accordance with the Ministry of Social Security Act 1966, Part III. When the testatrix died on May 30, 1972, the building was no longer used as an old people's home, and was being used, or was soon to be used, as offices. The home had been run neither as nor by a charity. It formerly provided homes for those living in a large area of the West Riding, and not merely Keighley; and it has not been replaced by any one home. Instead, there are many old people's homes serving the area.

"Now without looking at the authorities I would have said that this was a fairly plain case of a will which made a gift for a particular purpose in fairly specific terms. The gift was for the benefit of the patients at a particular home, namely the Old Folks Home at Hillworth Lodge, Keighley. At the date of the will there were patients at that home. When the testatrix died, there was no longer any home there, but offices instead; and so there were no longer any patients there, or any possibility of them. The gift was a gift for a charitable purpose which at the date of the will was capable of accomplishment and at the date of death was not. Prima facie, therefore, the gift fails unless a general charitable intention has been manifested so that the property can be applied *cy-près*. Buttressed by authority, counsel for the plaintiff contended that the court would be slow to find a general charitable intention where the object of the gift is defined with some particularity, as it was here.

"Against that, counsel for the Attorney-General advanced two main contentions. First, he said that as a matter of construction it was wrong to construe the gift as being merely for the benefit of patients who were actually at the Old Folks Home at Hillworth Lodge; admittedly, of course, there are none of

---

25 [1972] 1 Ch. 286, 300.

these. Instead, those who were intended to benefit included all those who would have been sent to that home if it had still existed, irrespective of the type of home in which in fact they are being or will be accommodated. He emphasised that the gift was essentially a gift for old people in Keighley, and the home was merely a means of providing a benefit for them.

"I do not think that this argument can be right. When the testatrix made her will there were patients at the Old Folks Home at Hillworth Lodge. The gift to that home 'for the benefit of the patients' is, on this construction, to be treated as being a gift for the benefit not only of the patients who successively were for the time being at the home, but of others who never go near the home but who might or would have been sent to it in certain circumstances. The words of the will were perfectly capable of being satisfied by confining their meaning to their natural sense, namely, as relating to those who are or will in the future be patients at the home. Why is there to be forced on to those words a notional extension of uncertain effect? If at the time they were being written those words could not have their natural effect, one might indeed look round for a secondary meaning; but that is not the case.

"There are further difficulties. If the notional extension is made, who are within it? As I have said, the defunct home provided for a large area of the West Riding, and not merely Keighley. How is it to be determined who can hope to benefit under the gift? Which of the occupants of the other old people's homes in such an area (the extent of which is undefined) can claim to be objects of the testatrix's bounty? Who is to decide whether any particular individual could (or would) have been sent to the defunct home had it still existed, and so would fall within the scope of the gift? I do not see how such an extension of meaning can fairly be placed on the words of the will. No doubt a scheme could cure much, but my difficulty is in seeing what on this footing, was the intention of the testatrix. For the reasons that I have given, I reject this contention.

"Counsel's other contention for the Attorney-General was that the will displayed a sufficient general charitable intention for the moiety to be applied *cy-près*. In doing this he had to contend with *re Harwood*.[26] This, and cases which apply to it, such as *Re Stemson's Will Trusts*[27] establish that it is very difficult to find a general charitable intention where the testator has selected a particular charity, taking some care to identify it, and the charity then ceases to exist before the testator's death. This contrasts with cases where the charity described in the will has never existed, when it is much easier to find a general charitable intention.

"These cases have been concerned with gifts to institutions, rather than gifts for purposes. The case before me, on the other hand, is a gift for a purpose, namely, the benefit of the patients at a particular old folks home. It therefore seems to me that I ought to consider the question, of which little or nothing was said in argument, whether the principle in *Re Harwood*, or a parallel principle, has any application to such a case. In other words, is a similar distinction to be made between, on the one hand, a case in which the testator has selected a particular charitable purpose, taking some care to identify it, and before the testator dies that purpose has become impracticable or impossible of accomplishment, and on the other hand a case where the charitable purpose has never been possible or practicable?

---

[26] [1936] Ch. 285.
[27] [1970] Ch. 16.

"As at present advised I would answer yes to that question. I do not think that the reasoning of the *Re Harwood* line of cases is directed to any feature of institutions as distinct from purposes. Instead, I think the essence of the distinction is in the difference between particularity and generality. If a particular institution or purpose is specified, then it is that institution or purpose, and no other, that is to be the object of the benefaction. It is difficult to envisage a testator as being suffused with a general glow of broad charity when he is labouring, and labouring successfully, to identify some particular specified institution or purpose as the object of his bounty. The specific displaces the general. It is otherwise where the testator has been unable to specify any particular charitable institution or practicable purpose, and so, although his intention of charity can be seen, he has failed to provide any way of giving effect to it. There, the absence of the specific leaves the general undisturbed. It follows that in my view in the case before me, where the testatrix has clearly specified a particular charitable purpose which before her death became impossible to carry out, counsel for the Attorney-General has to face that level of great difficulty in demonstrating the existence of a general charitable intention which was indicated by *Re Harwood*.

"One way in which counsel sought to meet that difficulty was by citing *Re Finger's Will Trusts*.[28] There, Goff J. distinguished *Re Harwood* and held that the will before him displayed a general charitable intention. He did this on the footing that the circumstances of the case were 'very special.' The gift that failed was a gift to an incorporated charity which had ceased to exist before the testatrix died. The 'very special' circumstances were, first, that apart from a life interest and two small legacies, the whole estate was devoted to charity, and that this was emphasised by the direction to hold the residue in trust for division 'between the following charitable institutions and funds.' Secondly, the charitable donee that had ceased was mainly, if not exclusively, a co-ordinating body, and the judge could not believe that the testatrix meant to benefit that body alone. Thirdly, there was evidence that the testatrix regarded herself as having no relatives.

"In the case before me neither of these last two circumstances applies, nor have any substitute special circumstances been suggested. As for the first, the will before me gives 17 pecuniary legacies to relations and friends, amounting in all to well over one-third of the net estate. Further, in *Re Rymer*,[29] which does not appear to have been cited, the will had prefaced the disputed gift by the words 'I give the following charitable legacies to the following institutions and persons respectively.' These words correspond to the direction which in *Re Finger's Will Trusts* was regarded as providing emphasis, and yet they did not suffice to avoid the conclusion of Chitty J. and the Court of Appeal that a gift to an institution which had ceased to exist before the testator's death lapsed and could not be applied *cy-près*. I am not sure that I have been able to appreciate to the full the cogency of the special circumstances that appealed to Goff J.; but however that may be I can see neither those nor any other special circumstances in the present case which would suffice to distinguish *Re Harwood*.

"The other way in which counsel for the Attorney-General sought to meet his difficulty was by relying on *Re Satterthwaite's Will Trusts*[30] (which he said

[28] [1972] 1 Ch. 286.
[29] [1895] 1 Ch. 19.
[30] [1966] 1 W.L.R. 277.

was his best case), and on *Re Knox*,[31] which I think may possibly be better. The doctrine may for brevity be described as charity by association. If the will gives the residue among a number of charities with kindred objects, but one of the apparent charities does not in fact exist, the court will be ready to find a general charitable intention and so apply the share of the non-existent charity *cy-près*. I have not been referred to any explicit statement of the underlying principle, but it seems to me that in such cases the court treats the testator as having shown the general intention of giving his residue to promote charities with that type of kindred objects, and then, when he comes to dividing the residue, as casting round for particular charities with that type of objects to name as donees. If one or more of these are non-existent, then the general intention will suffice for a *cy-près* application. It will be observed that, as stated, the doctrine depends, at least to some extent, on the detection of 'kindred objects' (a phase which comes from the judgment of Luxmoore J. in *Re Knox*[32] in the charities to which the shares of residue are given; in this respect the charities must in some degree be *ejusdem generis*.

"In *Re Satterthwaite's Will Trusts*[33] the residuary gift was to nine charitable bodies which were all concerned with kindness to animals; but the gifts to two of them failed as no bodies could be found which sufficiently answered the descriptions in the will. Harman L.J. said[34] that he 'felt the gravest doubts' whether a general charitable intent had been shown. However, at first instance the judge had held that in respect of one of the bodies a sufficient general charitable intention had been displayed, and as there had been no appeal as to that share, he (Harman L.J.) would reach the same conclusion in respect of the other share, which was the subject of the appeal. On the other hand, Russell L.J. had no doubt that a general charitable intention had been shown.[35] Diplock L.J. delivered a single-sentence judgment agreeing with both the other judgments. The support which this case provides for counsel for the Attorney-General accordingly seems to me to be a trifle muted.

"In *Re Knox* Luxmoore J. distilled a general charitable intention out of a residuary gift in quarters to two named infirmaries, a named nursing home and Dr. Barnardo's Homes. No institution existed which correctly answered the description of the nursing home, and it was held that the quarter share that had been given to it should be applied *cy-près*. I am not entirely sure what genus the judge had in mind as embracing the infirmaries and Dr. Barnardo's Homes when he said that 'the object of each of the other charities is a kindred object to that which is to be inferred from the name' of the nursing home: perhaps it was the provision of residential accommodation for those in need. Perhaps I should also mention *Re Hartley* (*deceased*),[36] a decision of mine in a case in which the Attorney-General was one of the parties. In that case, *Re Knox* was applied to a will when the residue was given in quarters between service charities of a benevolent nature. It was held that a general charitable intention had been shown which sufficed for the *cy-près* application of the share given to a body of that nature which did not exist at the date of the will. A body which might have answered the description in the will had existed some years earlier.

---

31 [1937] Ch. 109.
32 [1937] Ch. 109, 113.
33 [1966] 1 W.L.R. 277.
34 [1966] 1 W.L.R. 277, 284.
35 [1966] 1 W.L.R. 277, 286.
36 (March 15, 1978) unreported.

"It will be observed that these are all cases of gifts to bodies which did not exist. In such cases, the court is ready to find a general charitable intention: see *Re Davis*.[37] The court is far less ready to find such an intention where the gift is to a body which existed at the date of the will but ceased to exist before the testator died, or, as I have already held, where the gift is for a purpose which, though possible and practicable at the date of the will, has ceased to be so before the testator's death. The case before me is, of course, a case in this latter category, so that counsel for the Attorney-General has to overcome this greater difficulty in finding a general charitable intention. Not only does counsel have this greater difficulty: he also has, I think, less material with which to meet it. He has to extract the general charitable intention for the gift which fails from only one other gift: the residue, of course, was simply divided into two. In *Re Knox* and *Re Hartley* (*deceased*) the gifts which failed were each among three other gifts, and in *Re Satterthwaite's Will Trusts* there were seven or eight other gifts. I do not say that a general charitable intention or a genus cannot be extracted from a gift of residue equally between two: but I do say that larger numbers are likely to assist in conveying to the court a sufficient conviction both of the genus and of the generality of the charitable intention.

"A further point occurred to me which I think that I should mention. There are, of course, cases where there is merely a single gift, but the court is nevertheless able to see a clear general charitable intention underlying the particular mode of carrying it out that the testator has laid down. Thus in the well known case of *Biscoe* v. *Jackson*,[38] which I read in the light of *Re Wilson*,[39] the gift was to provide a soup kitchen and cottage hospital 'for the parish of Shoreditch.' Despite a considerable degree of particularity about the soup kitchen and the cottage hospital that were to be provided, the court found a general charitable intention to provide a benefit for the sick and poor of the parish. In that case, of course, there would have been no real difficulty in ascertaining those who were intended to benefit. Whatever the practical difficulties, at least the concept of those who were to be included is clear enough. The only real difficulty or impossibility lay in the particular method of carrying out that intention which the testator had specified. In the present case, on the other hand, the difficulty lies not only in the particular method but also in the very nature of the general charitable intention that is said to underlie that method. For the reasons that I have already given, I find it far from clear which 'patients' are intended to benefit once the touchstone of the Old Folks Home at Hillworth Lodge is removed. There is no geographical or other limitation to provide a guide. Where the difficulty or impossibility not only afflicts the method but also invades the concept of the alleged general charitable intention, then I think that the difficulty of establishing that the will displays any general charitable intention becomes almost insuperable.

"From what I have said it follows that I have been quite unable to extract from the will, construed in its context, any expression of a general charitable intention which would suffice for the moiety to be applied *cy-près*. Instead, in my judgment, the moiety was given for a specific charitable purpose which, though possible when the will was made, became impossible before the testatrix died. The gift of the moiety accordingly fails, and it passes as on intestacy."

---

[37] [1902] 1 Ch. 876, 884.
[38] (1887) 35 Ch.D. 460.
[39] [1913] 1 Ch. 314.

*Charities Act 1960*

*Occasions for applying property cy-près*

**13.**—(1) Subject to subsection (2) below, the circumstances in which the original purposes of a charitable gift can be altered to allow the property given or part of it to be applied *cy-près* shall be as follows[40]:

(a) where the original purposes, in whole or in part,—
   (i) have been as far as may be fulfilled; or
   (ii) cannot be carried out, or not according to the directions given and to the spirit of the gift; or
(b) where the original purposes provide a use for part only of the property available by virtue of the gift; or
(c) where the property available by virtue of the gift and other property applicable for similar purposes can be more effectively used in conjunction, and to that end can suitably, regard being had to the spirit of the gift, be made applicable to common purposes; or
(d) where the original purposes were laid down by reference to an area which then was but has since ceased to be a unit for some other purpose, or by reference to a class of persons or to an area which has for any reason since ceased to be suitable, regard being had to the spirit of the gift, or to be practical in administering the gift; or
(e) where the original purposes,[41] in whole or in part, have, since they were laid down,—
   (i) been adequately provided for by other means; or
   (ii) ceased,[42] as being useless or harmful to the community or for other reasons, to be in law charitable; or
   (iii) ceased in any other way to provide a suitable and effective method of using the property available by virtue of the gift, regard being had to the spirit of the gift.[43]

(2) Subsection (1) above shall not affect the conditions which must be satisfied in order that property given for charitable purposes may be applied *cy-près*, except in so far as those conditions require a failure of the original purposes.

(3) References in the foregoing subsections to the original purposes of a gift shall be construed, where the application of the property given has been altered or regulated by a scheme or otherwise, as referring to the purposes for which the property is for the time being applicable.

---

[40] The section is available for initial and subsequent failure, subs. (2) preserving the requirement of general charitable intention for cases of initial failure.

[41] "The original purposes" are apt to apply to the trusts as a whole where the trust is for payment of a fixed annual sum out of the income of a fund to charity A and payment of the residue of the income to charity B: the phrase is not read severally in relation to the trust for payment of the fixed annual sum and the trust for payment of residuary income: *Re Lepton's Charity* [1972] 1 Ch. 276.

[42] See Lord Simonds in *National Anti-Vivisection Society* v. *I.R.C.* [1948] A.C. 31, 64, 65. Note that once registered an institution is conclusively presumed to have been charitable when registered so *cy-près* seems available if later struck off the register.

[43] This broad head is very useful indeed. The phrase "spirit of the gift" was recommended by the Nathan Committee (Cmd. 8710, para. 365) who borrowed it from s.116 of the Education (Scotland) Act 1946 where it appears as "the spirit of the intention of the founders as embodied either (i) in the original deed constituting the endowment where it is still the governing instrument, or (ii) in any scheme affecting the endowment." See also *Re Lepton's Charity* [1972] 1 Ch. 276.

(5) It is hereby declared that a trust for charitable purposes places a trustee under a duty, where the case permits and requires the property or some part of it to be applied *cy-près*, to secure its effective use for charity by taking steps to enable it to be so applied.

*Application cy-près of gifts of donors unknown or disclaiming*

**14.**—(1) Property given for specific charitable purposes which fail shall be applicable *cy-près* as if given for charitable purposes generally, where it belongs—

(*a*) to a donor who, after such advertisements and inquiries as are reasonable,[44] cannot be identified or cannot be found; or

(*b*) to a donor who has executed a written disclaimer of his right to have the property returned.[45]

(2) For the purposes of this section property shall be conclusively presumed (without any advertisement or inquiry) to belong to donors who cannot be identified, in so far as it consists—

(*a*) of the proceeds of cash collections made by means of collecting boxes or by other means not adapted for distinguishing one gift from another; or

(*b*) of the proceeds of any lottery, competition, entertainment, sale or similar money-raising activity, after allowing for property given to provide prizes or articles for sale or otherwise to enable the activity to be undertaken.

(3) The court may by order direct that property not falling within subsection (2) above shall for the purposes of this section be treated (without any advertisement or inquiry) as belonging to donors who cannot be identified, where it appears to the court either—

(*a*) that it would be unreasonable, having regard to the amounts likely to be returned to the donors, to incur expense with a view to returning the property; or

(*b*) that it would be unreasonable, having regard to the nature, circumstances and amount of the gifts, and to the lapse of time since the gifts were made, for the donors to expect the property to be returned.

(4) Where property is applied *cy-près* by virtue of this section, the donor shall be deemed to have parted with all his interest at the time when the gift was made; but where property is so applied as belonging to donors who cannot be identified or cannot be found, and is not so applied by virtue of subsection (2) or (3) above,—

(*a*) the scheme shall specify the total amount of that property; and

(*b*) the donor of any part of that amount shall be entitled, if he makes a claim not later than twelve months after the date on which the scheme is made, to recover from the charity for which the property is applied a

---

[44] See *Re Henry Wood National Memorial Trusts* [1966] 1 W.L.R. 1601, though it is not clear how Stamp J. was able to find a resulting trust for the donor satisfying s.14(5).

[45] Apart from this provision disclaimer might have resulted in the property being *bona vacantia*, though the Att.-Gen. would normally waive the Crown's rights and have the property applied *cy-près*: *Re Ulverston & District New Hospital Building Fund* [1956] Ch. 622, 634.

sum equal to that part, less any expenses properly incurred by the charity trustees after that date in connection with claims relating to his gift; and

(c) the scheme may include directions as to the provision to be made for meeting any such claim.

(5) For the purposes of this section, charitable purposes shall be deemed to "fail" where any difficulty in applying property to those purposes makes that property or the part not applicable *cy-près* available to be returned to the donors.

(6) In this section, except in so far as the context otherwise requires, references to a donor include persons claiming through or under the original donor, and references to property given include the property for the time being representing the property originally given or property derived from it.

(7) This section shall apply to property given for charitable purposes, notwithstanding that it was so given before the commencement of this Act.

## PROBLEMS

1. Are the following trusts charitable, and, if not, are they otherwise valid?

   (i) To apply the income from £500,000 amongst such persons having the surnames Smith or Hayton, with preference so far as practicable for 50 per cent. of the income for the relatives of David Hayton, as my trustees may consider to merit educational assistance.

   (ii) £400,000 to my trustees to invest and apply the income therefrom in educating the children of needy employees or ex-employees of London Transport for 21 years whereupon the income shall be used to provide an English Public School education for such children of European origin living in Oxford as my trustees shall determine provided that in either case no person of the Roman Catholic faith shall be so assisted.

   (iii) A £10 million trust set up by I.C.I. Ltd. and Barclays Bank for the income to be used at the trustees' discretion in assisting towards the education of the children or grandchildren of any persons employed or formerly employed by I.C.I. Ltd. or Barclays Bank or any of their subsidiary or associated companies.

2. In 1990 a public appeal for funds to establish a recreation and sports centre for the City of London Police was launched. £200,000 was donated by Hank Badman, £80,000 was obtained from street collections, £110,000 profit was made out of a pop festival in aid of the appeal and £20,000 was donated anonymously. It has now proved completely impossible in view of the size of the fund to obtain any suitable site. What should be done with the moneys?[46]

3. By his will dated April 1, 1989, Oscar O'Flaherty bequeathed £60,000 to his executors to use part thereof for benevolent purposes and the remainder for charitable purposes and £50,000 to the "Torquay Home for Distressed Gentlefolk for the benefit of the needy who happen to be there." The Home, an unincorporated body, closed down six months before Oscar's death, its funds and many of its inhabitants going to the Bournemouth Home for the Handicapped. Advise Oscar's executors.

---

[46] Read the next chapter to see what would happen if the purpose was non-charitable.

4. By his will Alan left his residuary estate to Tim and Tom "upon trust to apply the income therefrom for such of the adult residents of Greater London as my Trustees in their absolute discretion shall think fit having due regard to the need to combat the stress, squalor and expense of residing in Greater London provided that my Trustees shall have power to add as further possible beneficiaries adult residents of any other city in the United Kingdom where the stress, squalor and expense are in my Trustees' absolute discretion comparable to that of Greater London provided further that one day before the expiration of the period of eighty years from my death (which period I hereby specify as the perpetuity period applicable hereto) the aforesaid Trust shall determine and the capital shall be distributed equally between United Reform Churches in West Ham and Leyton to use the income therefrom to assist in the burial or cremation of members of their congregations.

Alan has just died and Tim and Tom seek advice on the validity of the Trust.

5. During a motor race in Birmingham a car spun out of control killing the driver, a marshall and four mechanics. The Lord Mayor wants to appeal for funds for the families of the deceased and for the distressed surviving drivers, marshalls, mechanics and spectators. Advise him.

6. "In assessing the merits of putative charitable trusts the judges and the Charity Commissioners make the best of a bad job: the alternative is to go back to first principles and have a special tribunal concerned with cost-benefit analyses and value-judgments on social merits. Would you want to be a member of that tribunal (even if your decisions could not be overturned unless no reasonable person could have made such a decision)?" Discuss.

# Chapter 6

# RESULTING TRUSTS

MEGARRY J. has classified resulting trusts from the way in which they arise as either being "automatic resulting trusts" or "presumed resulting trusts": *Re Vandervell's Trusts, infra*. The former arise automatically wherever some or all of the beneficial interest has not been effectively exhausted by the express trusts. The latter are presumed to arise where property is bought by X in Y's name or gratuitously transferred by X to Y in which case Y will rebuttably be presumed to hold the property on trust for X. It is quite a useful classification though it may be argued that "automatic" resulting trusts are imposed because it is presumed that a settlor would normally expect property to result to him so far as not fully disposed of. It may also be argued that "presumed" resulting trusts arise automatically once it has been presumed that there was no intention to dispose of the beneficial interest. Resulting trusts are exempt from the formal requirements of the Law of Property Act 1925, s.53 and, in particular, take on significance where spouses or relatives contribute towards property without any writing being used to set out the respective size of each contributor's interest in the property.

## RE VANDERVELL'S TRUSTS (NO. 2)

Chancery Division [1974] Ch. 269; [1974] 1 All E.R. 47

See pp. 72 *et seq.* for the facts of the case revealing that whilst the Court of Appeal disagreed with Megarry J.'s view of the facts no adverse comment was made on his propositions on resulting trusts.

MEGARRY J. (in a reserved judgment): "It seems to me that the relevant points on resulting trusts may be put in a series of propositions as follows.

"(1) If a transaction fails to make any effective disposition of any interest it does nothing. This is so at law and in equity, and has nothing to do with resulting trusts.

"(2) Normally the mere existence of some unexpressed intention in the breast of the owner of the property does nothing: there must at least be some expression of that intention before it can effect any result. To yearn is not to transfer.

"(3) Before any doctrine of resulting trust can come into play, there must at least be some effective transaction which transfers or creates some interest in property.

"(4) Where A effectually transfers to B (or creates in his favour) any interest in any property, whether legal or equitable, a resulting trust for A may arise in two distinct classes of case. For simplicity, I shall confine my statement to cases in which the transfer or creation is made without B providing any valuable consideration, and where no presumption of advancement can arise; and I shall state the position for transfers without specific mention of the creation of new interests.

"(a) The first class of case is where the transfer to B is not made on any trust. If, of course, it appears from the transfer that B is intended to hold on certain trusts, that will be decisive, and the case is not within this category; and similarly if it appears that B is intended to take beneficially. But in other cases there is a rebuttable presumption that B holds on a resulting trust for A. The question is not one of the automatic consequences of a dispositive failure by A, but one of presumption: the property has been carried to B, and from the absence of consideration and any presumption of advancement B is presumed not only to hold the entire interest on trust, but also to hold the beneficial interest for A absolutely. The presumption thus establishes both that B is to take on trust and also what that trust is. Such resulting trusts may be called 'presumed resulting trusts.'

"(b) The second class of case is where the transfer to B is made on trusts which leave some or all of the beneficial interest undisposed of. Here B automatically holds on a resulting trust for A to the extent that the beneficial interest has not been carried to him or others. The resulting trust here does not depend on any intentions or presumptions but is the automatic consequence of A's failure to dispose of what is vested in him. Since *ex hypothesi* the transfer is on trust, the resulting trust does not establish the trust but merely carries back to A the beneficial interest that has not been disposed of. Such resulting trusts may be called 'automatic resulting trusts.'

"(5) Where trustees hold property in trust for A, and it is they who, at A's direction, make the transfer to B, similar principles apply, even though on the face of the transaction the transferor appears to be the trustees and not A. If the transfer to B is on trust, B will hold any beneficial interest that has not been effectually disposed of on an automatic resulting trust for the true transferor, A. If the transfer to B is not on trust, there will be a rebuttable presumption that B holds on a resulting trust for A."

## Section 1. Automatic Resulting Trusts

*Where they arise*

These trusts arise in favour of the settlor where he has settled his property on express trusts which fail whether for failure of marriage consideration, uncertainty, lapse, disclaimer, perpetuity, illegality, non-compliance with requisite statutory formalities, or for any other reason.[1] If the illegal purpose is effected even partially before the settlor repents this will prevent the enforcement of the resulting trust.[2] Resulting trusts also arise if settlors fail to dispose exhaustively of the

---

[1] *Hodgson* v. *Marks* [1971] Ch. 892, 933, *per* Russell L.J.; *Re Ames's Settlement* [1946] Ch. 217 though see now sections 16 and 24 of the Matrimonial Causes Act 1973. If the settlor were a testator then the property results to the testator's estate: if the property were specifically devised or bequeathed it falls into residue, whilst if the property were comprised in the residuary gift the property passes to the next-of-kin under the intestacy rules set out in the Administration of Estates Act 1925 as amended.

[2] *Symes* v. *Hughes* (1875) L.R. 9 Eq. 475; *Re Great Berlin Steamboat Co.* (1884) 26 Ch.D. 616; *Chettiar* v. *Chettiar* [1962] A.C. 294; *Perpetual Executors Association of Australia Ltd.* v. *Wright* (1917) 23 C.L.R. 185; *Petherpermal Chetty* v. *Muniandi Servai*, L.R. 35 Ind.App. 98; (1908) 24 T.L.R. 462. See p. 437, *infra*.

whole beneficial interest under their express trusts.[3] Usually, the imposition of a resulting trust creates the situation which the settlor would have intended to arise if asked—that is why the phrase "implied trust" is sometimes used in such situations. However, fiscal considerations these days often make a resulting trust in favour of the settlor in a particular eventuality the very last thing intended by the settlor.[4]

Where express trusts of funds subscribed by many settlors do not exhaust the funds there is a resulting trust in favour of the settlors rateably in proportion to the amounts subscribed by them.[5] In the case of charitable trusts that fail the funds will usually be applied *cy-près* as seen in the last chapter.

Whether or not the settlor has failed to dispose effectively of the entire beneficial interest is often a difficult matter. In *Re Abbott*[6] a fund had been subscribed for the maintenance and support of two deaf and dumb ladies and Stirling J. held, not as a matter of construction of the documents by which the subscriptions had been sought, but as an inference from all the facts, that the surplus left after both ladies died was held on a resulting trust for the subscribers. In *Re Andrew's Trust*[7] a fund was subscribed solely for the education of the children of a deceased clergyman and not for exclusive use of one child or for equal division among them but as necessary, and after the formal education of the children had been completed Kekewich J. held that the children were entitled to the balance equally. He construed "education" in the broadest sense as not being exhausted upon formal education ending and treated the reference to education as expressing merely the motive of the gift.[8] "If a gross sum be given, or if the whole income of property be given, and a special purpose be assigned for the gift this court [rebuttably] regards the gift as absolute and the purpose merely as the motive of the gift, and therefore holds that the gift takes effect as to the whole sum or the whole income as the case may be."

This was applied by the Court of Appeal in *Re Osoba*[9] holding that a bequest to the testator's widow upon trust "for her maintenance and for the training of my daughter Abiola up to university grade and for the maintenance of my aged mother" was a trust for the three females absolutely as joint tenants so that nothing resulted to the testator's estate after Abiola finished her university education, the widow and the mother having died by then, so that Abiola was absolutely entitled.

### Where there can be no resulting trust

There is no resulting trust if the donee is intended to take the property beneficially subject only to a charge for some purpose. Thus,

---

[3] *Re Gillingham Bus Disaster Fund*, [1958] Ch. 300; *Re West* [1900] 1 Ch. 84.

[4] *Re Vandervell's Trusts (No. 2)* [1974] Ch. 269 supra, p. 72.

[5] *Re British Red Cross Balkan Fund* [1914] 2 Ch. 419 (where in the absence of the Att.-Gen. a resulting trust was erroneously admitted: *Re Welsh Hospital Fund* [1921] 1 Ch. 655, 662); *Re Hobourn Aero Components Ltd.'s Air Raid Disaster Fund* [1946] Ch. 194.

[6] [1900] 2 Ch. 326. See p. 190, *supra*.

[7] [1905] 2 Ch. 48.

[8] *Ibid.* at pp. 52–53 citing Page-Wood V.-C. in *Re Sanderson's Trust* (1857) 3 K. & J. 497, 503.

[9] [1979] 2 All E.R. 393. See p. 190, *supra*.

in *Re Foord*[10] where a testator left his estate to his sister "absolutely
. . . on trust" to pay his widow an annuity and the estate income
exceeded the annuity the sister was held beneficially entitled to the
balance.

There is no resulting trust if the rule in *Hancock* v. *Watson*[11] applies.
This is the rule "that if you find an absolute gift to a legatee in the first
instance, and trusts are engrafted or imposed on that absolute interest
which fail, either from lapse or invalidity or any other reason, then the
absolute gift takes effect so far as the trusts have failed to the exclusion
of the residuary legatee or next-of-kin as the case may be."[12] The rule
is equally applicable to *inter vivos* settlements.[13]

There is no resulting trust if the doctrine of acceleration applies to
prevent there being a temporary failure to exhaust the beneficial
interest under a trust.[14] Thus, if T by will leaves property to A for life
and after A's death to B absolutely and A disclaims his interest, B's
interest is accelerated so as to take effect immediately, thereby ousting
any possible resulting trust of the income till A's death. For the
doctrine to apply the remainderman must have a vested interest and
there must be no contrary intention manifested in the trust document.[15]

There can be no resulting trust where a donor has parted with his
property in pursuance of some contract (except for the very rare case
exemplified by *Barclays Bank Ltd.* v. *Quistclose Investments Ltd.*[16]
discussed at p. 117, *ante*). Thus, in the case of a society, formed to
raise funds by subscriptions from its members for the purpose of
providing for their widows, which had surplus funds after the death of
the last widow, there could be no resulting trust for the deceased
members' estates: each member had parted absolutely with his money
in return for contractual benefits for his widow.[17] Similarly, no resulting
trust can arise where donors part absolutely with their money for
tickets contractually entitling them to participate in raffles, sweepstakes, beetle drives, whist drives, discotheques, or to watch live
entertainment, and the purposes for which such money has been raised
fail to exhaust the profits arising after deducting expenses.[18] See
further, *Davies* v. *Richards & Wallington infra* pp. 732, 737–743.

There can be no resulting trust where a donor has gifted property
not on any trusts but by way of out-and-out abandonment of all
interest in it, though it can be difficult, where money is raised for

---

[10] [1922] 2 Ch. 519. Contrast the resulting trust in *Re West* [1900] 1 Ch. 84.
[11] [1902] A.C. 14.
[12] *Ibid.* 22, *per* Lord Davey.
[13] *Att.-Gen.* v. *Lloyds Bank* [1935] A.C. 382; *Re Burton's S.T.* [1955] Ch. 348; *Watson* v. *Holland* [1985] 1 All E.R. 290.
[14] *Re Flower's S. T.* [1957] 1 W.L.R 401; *Re Davies* [1957] 1 W.L.R. 922; *Re Harker* [1969] 1 W.L.R. 1124 (rightly not following *Re Davies* on the impact of acceleration upon the class closing rules); *Re Hodge* [1963] Ch. 300; A. M. Prichard [1973] Camb.L.J. 246.
[15] *Re Scott* [1975] 2 All E.R. 1033.
[16] [1970] A.C. 567.
[17] *Cunnack* v. *Edwards* [1896] 2 Ch. 679.
[18] *Re West Sussex Constabulary's Benevolent Fund Trusts* [1971] Ch. 1, *infra*, p. 417.

certain purposes, to show that donors had a general intention to part with their money out-and-out beyond all recall rather than merely part with their money *sub modo* to the intent that the certain purposes be carried out. However, where street collections are concerned, with thousands of anonymous donors, the courts are becoming increasingly ready to find a general intention to part utterly with contributed money so as to exclude any resulting trust in favour of the donors with the result that unused moneys pass as *bona vacantia* to the Crown,[19] unless accruing to the funds of an unincorporated association[20] for whom the collections were made.

### Dissolution of unincorporated associations

When an unincorporated association is dissolved it is necessary to ascertain whether its property falls to be distributed on a resulting trust basis to persons providing such property or on a contractual basis to the association members or as *bona vacantia* to the Crown.

The old view[21] that rights to such property are founded in resulting trust has been totally discredited. It is now well established that the interests and rights of persons who are members of any type of unincorporated association are governed exclusively by contract.[22] Whilst the assets of the association are usually vested in trustees on trust for the members this is a quite separate and distinct trust bearing no relation to the claims of the members *inter se* to the surplus assets. Thus, as between a number of people contractually interested in a fund, if the terms of the contract do not provide some other method of distribution then distribution is on the basis of equality, subject only to third-party rights against the fund. Such rights will arise either by the duly authorised procedure in the association's constitution for creating contracts or express trusts or by declarations of trust imposed by a donor upon giving property to the association. However, where such a donor is concerned, since such a trust would be likely to fail for offending the rule against remoteness before the 1964 Perpetuities and Accumulations Act or the rule against inalienability or the beneficiary principle, the tendency of the courts is to validate such a gift as not imposing a trust, unless there are clear words to such effect, but as an out-and-out beneficial gift to members of the association as an accretion to the funds which are the subject-matter of the contract which the members have made between themselves, so that it falls to be dealt with in precisely the same way as the funds which the members themselves have subscribed as a matter of contract.[23]

---

[19] *Ibid*; contrast *Re Gillingham Bus Disaster Fund* [1958] Ch. 300.

[20] *Re Bucks Constabulary Fund Friendly Society (No. 2)* [1979] 1 W.L.R. 936, *infra*, p. 419.

[21] *Re Printers and Transferrers Amalgamated Trades Protection Society* [1899] 2 Ch. 184; *Re Lead Co.'s Workmen's Fund Society* [1904] 2 Ch. 196.

[22] *Tierney* v. *Tough* [1914] 1 I.R. 142; *Re St. Andrew's Allotment Association* [1969] 1 W.L.R. 229; *Re William Denby Ltd.'s Sick Fund* [1971] 1 W.L.R. 973; *Re West Sussex Constabulary's Benevolent Fund* [1971] Ch. 1; *Re Sick & Funeral Society of St. John's Sunday School* [1973] Ch. 51 (per capita basis but child members only to have a half share); *Re GKN Bolts and Nuts Ltd. Sports and Social Club* [1982] 1 W.L.R. 774; *Re Bucks Constabulary Fund Friendly Society (No. 2)* [1979] 1 All E.R. 623.

[23] *Re Recher's W.T.* [1972] Ch. 526; *Re Lipinski's W.T.* [1976] Ch. 235, discussed *ante*, pp. 194 *et seq.*

Only if the association has become moribund, as where all the members or all but one have died, will the assets be treated as *bona vacantia* and pass to the Crown.[24]

The present position is clearly apparent from the decision of Walton J. in *Re Bucks Constabulary Fund Friendly Society (No. 2), infra.* Whilst, as he pointed out, one can distinguish the decision of Goff J. in *Re West Sussex Constabulary's Benevolent Fund*[25] on the footing that it concerned a simple unincorporated association whilst *Re Bucks* concerned a friendly society affected by the Friendly Societies Act 1896, s.49(1), it is quite clear that the reasoning underlying *Re West Sussex* and distinguishing a club for members from a club of members for third parties or purposes is erroneous[26] and that Walton J. would have decided it differently in favour of the members rather than the Crown as to members' subscriptions and contributions and the proceeds of entertainment, raffles, collecting boxes, etc. Indeed, in view of the cited dicta in *Re Recher's W.T.*[27] it is likely that donations and legacies would also, if Walton J. had decided the case, have passed to the members rather than be held on resulting trust for the donors or testators.

### RE WEST SUSSEX CONSTABULARY'S BENEVOLENT FUND TRUSTS

Chancery Division [1971] Ch. 1; [1970] 2 W.L.R. 848: [1970] 1 All E.R. 544

In 1930 a fund was set up to provide for widows and orphans of deceased members. The W. Sussex Constabulary amalgamated with other forces in 1968 so that it was doubtful as to how its funds were to be dealt with. The funds came from (1) contributions of past and present members; (2) entertainments, raffles, sweepstakes; (3) collecting boxes; (4) donations and legacies.

In a reserved judgment Goff J. held that (4) were held on resulting trusts for the donors whilst (1), (2) and (3) were *bona vacantia* though these holdings are now of doubtful authority in view of the next case, *Re Bucks Constabulary Fund Friendly Society (No. 2).* However, the following dicta are good law.

GOFF J.: " . . . I must now turn to the moneys raised from outside sources. Counsel for the Attorney-General made an overriding general submission that there could not be a resulting trust of any of the outside moneys because in the circumstances it is impossible to identify the trust property. No doubt something could be achieved by complicated accounting, but this, he submitted, would not be identification but notional reconstruction. I cannot accept that argument. In my judgment in a case like the present, equity will cut the gordian knot by simply dividing the ultimate surplus in proportion to the sources from which it has arisen. . . .

---

[24] *Re Bucks Constabulary Fund Friendly Society (No. 2)* [1979] 1 All E.R. 623; *Cunnack* v. *Edwards* [1896] 2 Ch. 679; *Re West Sussex Constabulary's Benevolent Fund* [1971] Ch. 1 is probably erroneous. If under the association's rules the last member can claim the property without having to call a meeting, *e.g.* in the case of a tontine society then he or his estate will be entitled to the property.

[25] [1971] Ch. 1.

[26] See *Re Grant's W.T.* [1979] 3 All E.R. 359, 365.

[27] [1972] Ch. 526, 538–539, p. 206, *supra.*

"There may be cases of tolerable simplicity where the court will be more refined, but in general where a fund has been raised from mixed sources interest has been earned over the years and income and possibly capital expenditure has been made indiscriminately out of the fund as an entirety, and when the venture comes to an end, prematurely or otherwise, the court will not find itself baffled but will cut the gordian knot as I have said.

"Then counsel divided the outside moneys into three categories: first, the proceeds of entertainments, raffles and sweepstakes; secondly, the proceeds of collecting boxes; and thirdly, donations including legacies, if any, and he took particular objections to each. I agree that there cannot be any resulting trust with respect to the first category. I am not certain whether Harman J. meant to decide otherwise in the *Gillingham Bus Disaster* case.[28] The statement of facts[29] refers to 'street collections and so forth.' There is mention of whist drives and concerts in the argument,[30] but the judge himself did not speak of anything other than gifts. If he did, however, I must respectfully decline to follow his judgment in that regard, for whatever may be the true position with regard to collecting boxes, it appears to me to be impossible to apply the doctrine of resulting trust to the proceeds of entertainments and sweepstakes and such-like money raising operations for two reasons. First, the relationship is one of contract and not of trust. The purchaser of a ticket may have the motive of aiding the cause or he may not. He may purchase a ticket merely because he wishes to attend the particular entertainment or to try for the prize, but whichever it be he pays his money as the price of what is offered and what he receives. Secondly, there is in such cases no direct contribution to the fund at all. It is only the profit, if any, which is ultimately received, and there may even be none. In any event the first category cannot be any more susceptible to the doctrine than the second to which I now turn.

"Here one starts with the well-known dictum of P. O. Lawrence J. in *Re Welsh Hospital (Netley) Fund, Thomas v. Att.-Gen.*[31]:

'So far as regards the contributors to entertainments, street collections, etc., I have no hesitation in holding that they must be taken to have parted with their money out and out. It is inconceivable that any person paying for a concert ticket or placing a coin in a collecting box presented to him in the street should have intended that any part of the money so contributed should be returned to him when the immediate object for which the concert was given or the collection made had come to an end. To draw such an inference would be absurd on the face of it.'

This was adopted by Upjohn J. in *Re Hillier, Hillier v. Att.-Gen.*,[32] where the point was actually decided.

"[The analysis of Upjohn J.] was approved by Denning L.J. in the same case in the Court of Appeal.[33]

"In *Re Ulverston & District New Hospital Building Fund*,[34] Jenkins L.J. threw out a suggestion that there might be a distinction in the case of a person

---

[28] [1958] Ch. 300.
[29] [1958] Ch. 300, 304.
[30] [1958] Ch. 300, 309.
[31] [1921] 1 Ch. 655, 660, 661.
[32] [1954] 1 W.L.R. 9.
[33] [1954] 1 W.L.R. 700, 714.
[34] [1956] Ch. 622, 633.

who could prove that he put a specified sum in a collecting box, and in the *Gillingham* case[35] Harman J. after noting this, decided that there was a resulting trust with respect to the proceeds of collections. He said[36]:

> 'In my judgment the Crown has failed to show that this case should not follow the ordinary rule merely because there was a number of donors who, I will assume, are unascertainable. I see no reason myself to suppose that the small giver who is anonymous has any wider intention than the large giver who can be named. They all give for the one object. If they can be found by inquiry the resulting trust can be executed in their favour. If they cannot I do not see how the money could then, with all respect to Jenkins L.J., change its destination and become *bona vacantia*. It will be merely money held on a trust for which no beneficiary can be found. Such cases are common, and where it is known that there are beneficiaries, the fact that they cannot be ascertained does not entitle the Treasury Solicitor to come in and claim. The trustees must pay the money into court like any other trustee who cannot find his beneficiary. I conclude, therefore, that there must be an inquiry for the subscribers to this fund.'

It will be observed that Harman J. considered that the *Welsh Hospital* (*Netley*) case,[37] *Re Hillier*[38] and *Re Ulverston*[39] did not help him greatly because they were charity cases. It is true that they were and, as will presently appear, in my view that is very significant in relation to the third category, but I do not think it was a valid objection with respect to the second, and for my part I cannot reconcile the decision of Upjohn J. in *Re Hillier* with that of Harman J. in the *Gillingham* case. As I see it, therefore, I have to choose between them. On the one hand it may be said that Harman J. had the advantage which Upjohn J. had not of considering the suggestion made by Jenkins L.J. On the other hand that, with all respect, seems to me somewhat fanciful and unreal. I agree that all who put their money into collecting boxes should be taken to have the same intention, but why should they not all be regarded as intending to part with their money out and out, absolutely, in all circumstances? I observe that P.O. Lawrence J. used very strong words. He said any other view was inconceivable and absurd on the face of it. That commends itself to my humble judgment, and I, therefore, prefer and follow the judgment of Upjohn J. in *Re Hillier*."

## RE BUCKS CONSTABULARY FUND FRIENDLY SOCIETY (NO. 2)

Chancery Division [1979] 1 W.L.R. 936; [1979] 1 All E.R. 623

The Bucks Constabulary Fund Friendly Society was established to provide for the relief of widows and orphans of deceased members of the Bucks Constabulary. It was an unincorporated association registered under the Friendly Societies Act 1896 but it had no rules providing for the distribution of its assets in the event of it being wound up.

On being wound up the question arose whether the surplus assets were *bona vacantia* passing to the Crown or whether they should be distributed amongst

---

[35] [1958] Ch. 300.
[36] [1958] Ch. 300, 314.
[37] [1921] 1 Ch. 655.
[38] [1954] 1 W.L.R. 9.
[39] [1956] Ch. 622.

members at the date of dissolution, in which case should distribution be equally *per capita* or on some other basis?

WALTON J. read the following judgment: "There are basically two claimants to the fund, the Solicitor for the Affairs of Her Majesty's Treasury, who claims the assets as ownerless property, *bona vacantia*, and the members of the friendly society at the date of its dissolution on October 14, 1969.

"Before considering the relevant legislation, it is I think desirable to view the question of the property of unincorporated associations in the round. If a number of persons associate together, for whatever purpose, if that purpose is one which involves the acquisition of cash or property of any magnitude, then, for practical purposes, some one or more persons have to act in the capacity of treasurers or holders of the property. In any sophisticated association there will accordingly be one or more trustees in whom the property which is acquired by the association will be vested. These trustees will of course not hold such property on their own behalf. Usually there will be a committee of some description which will run the affairs of the association; though of course in a small association the committee may well comprise all the members; and the normal course of events will be that the trustee, if there is a formal trustee, will declare that he holds the property of the association in his hands on trust to deal with it as directed by the committee. If the trust deed is a shade more sophisticated it may add that the trustee holds the assets on trust for the members in accordance with the rules of the association. Now in all such cases it appears to me quite clear that, unless under the rules governing the association the property thereof has been wholly devoted to charity, or unless and to the extent to which the other trusts have validly been declared of such property, the persons, and the only persons, interested therein are the members. Save by way of a valid declaration of trust in their favour, there is no scope for any other person acquiring any rights in the property of the association, although of course it may well be that third parties may obtain contractual or proprietary rights, such as a mortgage, over those assets as the result of a valid contract with the trustees or members of the committee as representing the association.

"I can see no reason for thinking that this analysis is any different whether the purpose for which the members of the association associate are a social club, a sporting club, to establish a widows' and orphans' fund, to obtain a separate Parliament for Cornwall, or to further the advance of alchemy. It matters not. All the assets of the association are held in trust for its members (of course subject to the contractual claims of anybody having a valid contract with the association) save and except to the extent to which valid trusts have otherwise been declared of its property. I would adopt the analysis made by Brightman J. in *Re Recher's Will Trusts* [40] (set out pp. 206–208, *supra*) . . .

"All this doubtless seems quite elementary, but it appears to me to have been lost sight of to some extent in some of the decisions which I shall hereafter have to consider in detail in relation to the destination on dissolution of the funds of unincorporated associations.

"Now in the present case I am dealing with a society which was registered under the Friendly Societies Act 1896. This does not have any effect at all on the unincorporated nature of the society, or (as I have in substance already

---

[40] [1972] Ch. 526, 538–539.

indicated) on the way in which its property is held. But the latter point is in fact made very explicit by the provisions of section 49(1) of the 1896 Act which reads as follows:

> 'All property belonging to a registered society, whether acquired before or after the society is registered, shall vest in the trustees for the time being of the society, for the use and benefit of the society and the members thereof, and of all persons claiming through the members according to the rules of the society.'

"There can be no doubt, therefore, that in the present case the whole of the property of the society is vested in the trustees for the use and benefit of the society and the members thereof and of all persons claiming through the members according to the rules of the society. I do not think I need go through the rules in detail. They are precisely what one would expect in the case of an association whose main purpose in life was to enable members to make provision for widows and orphans. Members paid a contribution in exchange for which in the event of their deaths their widows and children would receive various benefits. There is a minimal benefit for which provision is made in the case of a member suffering very severe illness indeed, but, as counsel for the Treasury Solicitor was able to demonstrate from an analysis of the accounts, virtually the entire expenditure of the association was, as indeed one would expect, on the provision of widows' and orphans' benefits. But, of course, there is no trust whatsoever declared in their favour. I am not called on, I think, to decide whether they are, within the meaning of section 49(1), persons claiming through the members according to the rules of the society, or whether they are simply the beneficiaries of stipulations by the members for the benefit of third parties. All parties are agreed that accrued rights of such persons must be given full effect. There is indeed no rule which says what is to happen to surplus assets of the society on a dissolution. But in view of section 49(1) there is no need. The assets must continue to be held, the society having been dissolved, and the widows and orphans being out of the way, simply for the use and benefit of the members of the society, albeit they will all now be former members.

"This indeed appears so obvious that in a work of great authority on all matters connected with friendly societies, Baden Fuller,[41] the learned author says this:

> 'If the rules provide for the termination of the society they usually also provide for the distribution of the funds in that event, but if on the termination of a society no provision has been made by the rules for the distribution of its funds, such funds are divisible among the existing members at the time of the termination or dissolution in proportion to the amount contributed by each member for entrance fees and subscriptions, and irrespective of fines or payments made to members in accordance with the rules.'

"In my judgment this accurately represents the law, at any rate so far as the beneficiaries of the trust on dissolution are concerned, although not necessarily so far as the *quantum* of their respective interests is concerned; a matter which still remains to be argued. The effective point is that the claims of the Treasury

---

[41] *The Law of Friendly Societies* (4th ed., 1926), p. 186.

Solicitor to the funds as *bona vacantia* are unsuitable in the present case. I say 'in the present case' because there are undoubtedly cases where the assets of an unincorporated association do become *bona vacantia*. To quote Baden Fuller again[42]:

> 'A society may sometimes become defunct or moribund by its members either all dying or becoming so reduced in numbers that it is impossible either to continue the society or to dissolve it by instrument; in such cases the surplus funds, after all existing claims (if any) under the rules have been satisfied or provided for, are not divisible among the surviving members . . . or the last survivor . . . or the representative of the last survivor . . . nor is there any resulting trust in favour of the personal representatives of the members of the society . . . not even in favour of honorary members in respect of donations by them . . . but a society which, though moribund, had at a testator's death one member and three annuitant beneficiaries, was held to be existing so as to prevent the lapse of a legacy bequeathed to it by the testator . . . In these circumstances two cases seem to occur: if the purposes of the society are charitable, the surplus will be applicable *cy-près* . . . but if the society is not a charity, the surplus belongs to the Crown as *bona vacantia*.'

"Before I turn to a consideration of the authorities, it is I think pertinent to observe that all unincorporated societies rest in contract to this extent, that there is an implied contract between all of the members *inter se* governed by the rules of the society. In default of any rule to the contrary, and it will seldom if ever be that there is such a rule, when a member ceases to be a member of the association he *ipso facto* ceases to have any interest in its funds. Once again, so far as friendly societies are concerned, this is made very clear by section 49(1), that it is the members, the present members, who, alone, have any right in the assets. As membership always ceases on death, past members or the estates of deceased members therefore have no interest in the assets. Further, unless expressly so provided by the rules, unincorporated societies are not really tontine societies, intended to provide benefits for the longest liver of the members. Therefore, although it is difficult to say in any given case precisely when a society becomes moribund, it is quite clear that if a society is reduced to a single member neither he, still less his personal representatives on his behalf, can say he is or was the society and therefore entitled solely to its fund. It may be that it will be sufficient for the society's continued existence if there are two members, but if there is only one the society as such must cease to exist. There is no association, since one can hardly associate with oneself or enjoy one's own society. And so indeed the assets have become ownerless.

"I now turn to the authorities. The first case is that of *Cunnack* v. *Edwards*.[43] The association there in question was established in 1810 to raise a fund by the subscriptions, fines and forfeitures of its members, to provide annuities for the widows of its deceased members. It was later registered under the Friendly Societies Act 1829. This Act was repealed later, but its material provisions remained in force with regard to societies registered thereunder. There was no provision in that Act corresponding to section 49(1) of the 1896 Act. Sections

---

[42] *Ibid.* pp. 186–187.
[43] [1895] 1 Ch. 489; *on appeal* [1896] 2 Ch. 679.

3, 8 and 26 are material but I cannot improve on the summary thereof given by Rigby L.J. in the Court of Appeal[44] . . .

"The scheme of the 1829 Act thus was that the rules must specify all the circumstances under which any member of the society might become entitled to any part of its assets, and that on a dissolution the distribution of the assets had to conform to the general intents and purposes of the society. It is at once apparent why in that case an alteration of the rules was essential before any member could take any part of the assets, as, on their face, the rules were exclusively concerned with the provision of the relief of the widows of deceased members. There was no provision whatsoever relating to any members. In the course of time the society was reduced to two members, one an honorary member who was in fact the ultimate survivor, but who had disclaimed any interest in the society's assets, the other an ordinary member who died and whose personal representative claimed the surplus of the assets of the society after provision had been made for the payment of the last annuity to the last widow. There was a claim that the society was a charity, but with that claim we are not concerned. Now the argument for the personal representatives was first of all that the successive members of the society were entitled to its surplus assets and that the last survivor of the ordinary members was therefore entitled to them by survivorship. I have already noted that this argument is untenable because there is no idea in any such societies that they are simply tontines. The next argument was that he could have held a meeting and voted the funds to himself. It was of course necessary to put the argument in this way because of the provisions of the 1829 Act which I have read. It would not have been necessary in the case of an association which had not registered under the Act, but of course in any event the result would have been the same having regard to the tontine point. And finally as a last throw the argument was put forward that there was a resulting trust on the basis that every subscription made and fine paid by the deceased member was paid to create a trust in favour of the widows, and to the extent to which this created a fund in excess of what was required the moneys resulted back to the members. In the court of first instance Chitty J.[45] disposed of the first argument by taking the tontine point, of the second by saying that even if the last member could have held a meeting he never did, but he acceded to the third submission. He held that the members had in substance settled their subscriptions by way of trust. In my judgment the short answer to the contention put in this way ought to have been, as is pointed out in a later case, that the money was not paid to establish a trust but by way of contract so that no resulting trust came into the picture at all. In the Court of Appeal[46] the only point argued apart from the question of charity was the third, the resulting trust point, and Lord Halsbury L.C. did indeed decide against this point on the contractual basis.

"A careful examination of that case reveals that the really crucial fact was that the rules were required to state all the uses applicable to the assets of the society and they stated none in favour of members. On dissolution section 26 governed, and following on the absence of any provision in favour of members in the rules the members were not entitled to any interest in the assets. Hence the inescapable conclusion that the surplus assets had no owner and must go to

[44] [1896] 2 Ch. 679, 687–689.
[45] [1895] 1 Ch. 489.
[46] [1896] 2 Ch. 679.

the Crown. At the risk of repetition, the combined effect of the rules and the 1829 Act made it quite impossible for any argument to the effect that on dissolution the assets vested in the then members in some shares and proportions, which is the normal argument to be put forward in such a case. The case therefore did not decide that this was not the usual position in the case of an unincorporated association not then registered under the Friendly Societies Act. [The judge then referred to *Re Printers and Transferrers Amalgamated Trades Protection Society*[47]; *Braithwaite* v. *Attorney-General*[48]; *Tierney* v. *Tough*[49] and *Re St. Andrews Allotment Association's Trusts.*[50]]

"In *Re William Denby & Sons Ltd. Sick and Benevolent Fund*, Brightman J. said this[51]:

> 'One matter is common ground. It is accepted by all counsel that a fund of this sort is founded in contract and not in trust. That is to say, the right of a member of the fund to receive benefits is a contractual right and the member ceases to have any interest in the fund if and when he has received the totality of the benefits to which he was contractually entitled. In other words, there is no possible claim by any member founded on a resulting trust. I turn to the question whether the fund has already been dissolved or terminated so that its assets have already become distributable. If it has been dissolved or terminated, the members entitled to participate would prima facie be those persons who were members at the date of dissolution or termination'

Once again, this is fully in line with the principle of the cases as I see them.

"Finally, there comes a case which gives me great concern, *Re West Sussex Constabulary's Widows, Children and Benevolent (1930) Fund Trusts.*[52] The case is indeed easily distinguishable from the present case in that what was there under consideration was a simple unincorporated association and not a friendly society, so that the provisions of section 49(1) of the 1896 Act do not apply. Otherwise the facts in that case present remarkable parallels to the facts in the present case. Goff J. decided that the surplus funds had become *bona vacantia.* [See p. 417, *supra.*]

The material parts of that judgment read as follows[53]:

> 'First it was submitted that it belongs exclusively and in equal shares to all those persons now living who were members on December 31, 1967 and the personal representatives of all the then members since deceased, to all of whom I will refer collectively as "the surviving members." The argument is based on the analogy of the members' club cases. I cannot accept that as applicable, for these reasons. First, it simply does not look like it. This was nothing but a pensions or dependent relatives fund not at all akin to a club. Secondly, in all the cases where the surviving members have taken, with the sole exception of *Tierney's* case,[54] the club, society or organisation existed for the benefit of the members for

---

47 [1899] 2 Ch. 184.
48 [1909] Ch. 510.
49 [1914] I.R. 142.
50 [1969] 1 W.L.R. 229.
51 [1971] 1 W.L.R. 973, 978; [1971] 2 All E.R. 1196, 1201.
52 [1971] Ch. 1; [1970] 1 All E.R. 544.
53 [1971] Ch. 1, 8–10.
54 [1914] I.R. 142.

the time being exclusively, whereas in the present case as in *Cunnack* v. *Edwards*,[55] only third parties could benefit. Moreover, in *Tierney's* case the exception was minimal and discretionary and can, I think, fairly be disregarded. Finally, this very argument was advanced and rejected by Chitty J. in the *Cunnack* case[56] at first instance, and was abandoned on the hearing of the appeal. That judgment also disposes of the further argument that the surviving members had power to amend the rules under rule 14 and could, therefore, have reduced the fund into possession and so ought to be treated as the owners of it or the persons for whose benefit it existed at the crucial moment. They had the power but they did not exercise it, and it is now too late. Then it was argued that there is a resulting trust, with several possible consequences. If this be the right view there must be a primary division into three parts, one representing contributions from former members, another contributions from the surviving members, and the third moneys raised from outside sources. The surviving members then take the second, and possibly by virtue of rule 10 the first also. Rule 10 is as follows: "Any member who voluntarily terminates his membership shall forfeit all claim against the Fund except in the case of a member transferring to a similar Fund of another force in which instance the contributions paid by the member to the West Sussex Constabulary's Widows, Children and Benevolent (1930) Fund may be paid into the Fund of the force to which the member transfers." Alternatively, the first may belong to the past members on the footing that rule 10 is operative so long only as the fund is a going concern, or may be *bona vacantia*. The third is distributable in whole or in part between those who provide the money, or again is *bona vacantia*. In my judgment the doctrine of resulting trust is clearly inapplicable to the contributions of both classes. Those persons who remained members until their deaths are in any event excluded because they have had all they contracted for, either because their widows and dependants have received or are in receipt of the prescribed benefits, or because they did not have a widow or dependants. In my view that is inherent in all the speeches in the Court of Appeal in *Cunnack* v. *Edwards*.[57] Further, whatever the effect of rule 10 may be on the contribution of those members who left prematurely, they and the surviving members alike are also unable to claim under a resulting trust, because they put up their money on a contractual basis and not one of trust: see *Re Gillingham Bus Disaster Fund*.[58] Accordingly, in my judgment all the contributions of both classes are *bona vacantia*, but I must make a reservation with respect to possible contractual rights. In *Cunnack* v. *Edwards* and *Braithwaite* v. *Att.-Gen.*,[59] all the members had received or provision had been made for all the contractual benefits. Here the matter has been cut short. Those persons who died whilst still in membership cannot, I conceive, have any rights, because in their case the contract has been fully worked out, and on a contractual basis I would think that members who retired would be precluded from making

---

[55] [1896] 2 Ch. 679.
[56] [1895] 1 Ch. 489.
[57] [1896] 2 Ch. 679.
[58] [1958] Ch. 300, 314.
[59] [1909] 1 Ch. 510.

any claim by rule 10, although that is perhaps more arguable. The surviving members, on the other hand, may well have a right in contract on the ground of frustration or total failure of consideration, and that right may embrace contributions made by past members, though I do not see how it could apply to moneys raised from outside sources. I have not, however, heard any argument based on contract and therefore the declarations I propose to make will be subject to the reservation which I will later formulate. This will not prevent those parts of the fund which are *bona vacantia* from being paid over to the Crown as it has offered to give a full indemnity to the trustees;'

and the judge then turned to consider the destination of moneys from outside sources, with which of course I am not here concerned.

"It will be observed that the first reason given by the judge for his decision is that he could not accept the principle of the members' clubs as applicable. This is a very interesting reason, because it is flatly contrary to the successful argument of Mr. Ingle Joyce who appeared for the Attorney-General in the case Goff J. purported to follow, *Cunnack* v. *Edwards*. His argument was as follows [60]:

'This society was nothing more than a club, in which the members had no transmissible interest: *In re St. James' Club*.[61] Whatever the members, or even the surviving member, might have done while alive, when they died their interest in the assets of the club died with them';

and in the Court of Appeal[62] he used the arguments he had used below. If all that Goff J. meant was that the purposes of the fund before him were totally different from those of a members' club then of course one must agree, but if he meant to imply that there was some totally different principle of law applicable one must ask why that should be. His second reason is that in all the cases where the surviving members had taken, the organisation existed for the benefit of the members for the time being exclusively. This may be so, so far as actual decisions go, but what is the principle? Why are the members not in control, complete control, save as to any existing contractual rights, of the assets belonging to their organisation? One could understand the position being different if valid trusts had been declared of the assets in favour of third parties, for example charities, but that this was emphatically not the case was demonstrated by the fact that Goff J. recognised that the members could have altered the rules prior to dissolution and put the assets into their own pockets. If there was no obstacle to their doing this, it shows in my judgment quite clearly that the money was theirs all the time. Finally he purports to follow *Cunnack* v. *Edwards*[63] and it will be seen from the analysis which I have already made of that case that it was extremely special in its facts, resting on a curious provision of the 1829 Act which is no longer applicable. As I have already indicated, in the light of section 49(1) of the 1896 Act the case before Goff J.[64] is readily distinguishable, but I regret that, quite apart from that, I am wholly unable to square it with the relevant principles of law applicable.

---

[60] [1895] 1 Ch. 489, 494.
[61] [1852] 2 De G.M. & G. 383, 387.
[62] [1896] 2 Ch. 679.
[63] [1896] 2 Ch. 679.
[64] [1971] Ch. 1.

"The conclusion therefore is that as on dissolution there were members of the society here in question in existence, its assets are held on trust for such members to the total exclusion of any claim on behalf of the Crown. The remaining question under this head which falls now to be argued is, of course, whether they are simply held *per capita*, or, as suggested in some of the cases, in proportion to the contributions made by each. . . .

"I think that there is no doubt that, as a result of modern cases springing basically from the decision of O'Connor M.R. in *Tierney* v. *Tough*,[65] judicial opinion has been hardening and is now firmly set along the lines that the interests and rights of persons who are members of any type of unincorporated association are governed exclusively by contract, that is to say the rights between themselves and their rights to any surplus assets. I say that to make it perfectly clear that I have not overlooked the fact that the assets of the society are usually vested in trustees on trust for the members. But that is quite a separate and distinct trust bearing no relation to the claims of the members *inter se* on the surplus funds so held on trust for their benefit.

"That being the case, prima facie there can be no doubt at all but that the distribution is on the basis of equality, because, as between a number of people contractually interested in a fund, there is no other method of distribution if no other method is provided by the terms of the contract, and it is not for one moment suggested here that there is any other method of distribution provided by the contract. We are, of course, dealing here with a friendly society, but that really makes no difference to the principle. The Friendly Societies Acts do not incorporate the friendly society in any way and the only effect that it has is, as I pointed out in my previous judgment in this case, that there is a section which makes it crystal clear in the Friendly Societies Act 1896 that the assets are indeed held on trust for the members.

"Now the fact that the prima facie rule is a matter of equality has been recently laid down, not of course for the first time, in two cases to which I need do no more than refer, *Re St. Andrew's Allotment Association's Trusts*,[66] a decision of the late Ungoed-Thomas J., and *Re Sick and Funeral Society of St. John's Sunday School, Golcar,* a decision of Megarry J.[67] Neither of those cases was, however, the case of a friendly society, and there are a number of previous decisions in connection with friendly societies, and, indeed, *Tierney* v. *Tough*[68] itself is such a case, where the basis of distribution according to the subscriptions paid by the persons among whom the fund is to be distributed has been applied, and it has been suggested that perhaps those decisions are to be explained along the lines that a friendly society, or similar society, is thinking more of benefits to members, and that, thinking naturally of benefits to members, you think, on the other side of the coin, of subscriptions paid by members. But in my judgment that is not a satisfactory distinction of any description, because one is now dealing with what happens at the end of the life of the association; there are surplus funds, funds which have not been required to carry out the purposes of the association, and it does not seem to me it is a suitable method of distribution to say that one then looks to see what the purposes of the society were while the society was a going concern.

---

[65] [1914] I.R. 142.
[66] [1969] 1 W.L.R. 229.
[67] [1973] Ch. 51. Where the society's rules indicated a per capita basis of one share for each full member and one half-share for each child member.
[68] [1914] I.R. 142.

"An ingenious argument has been put by counsel for the third and fifth defendants: the members of the society are entitled in equity to the surplus funds which are distributable among them, therefore they are to be distributed among them according to equitable principles and those principles should, like all equitable principles, be moulded to fit the circumstances of the case, and in one case it would therefore be equitable to distribute in equal shares, in another case it might be equitable to distribute in proportion to the subscription that they have paid, and I suppose that in another case it might be equitable to distribute according to the length of their respective feet, following a very well known equitable precedent. Well, I completely deny the basic premise. The members are not entitled in equity to the fund; they are entitled at law. It is a matter, so far as the members are concerned, of pure contract, and, being a matter of pure contract, it is, in my judgment, as far as distribution is concerned, completely divorced from all questions of equitable doctrines. It is a matter of simple entitlement, and that entitlement must be, and can only be, in equal shares."

## Section 2. Presumed Resulting Trusts

### A. Presumption of a Resulting Trust

These trusts arise in X's favour where X purchases property but in Y's name or in the name of X and Y or where X and Y purchase property in Y's name. They may also arise in cases where X gratuitously transfers his interest in property to others. The presumption is "no more than a long-stop to provide the answer when the relevant facts and circumstances fail to yield a solution."[69] "Presumptions may be looked on as the bats of the law flitting in the twilight but disappearing in the sunrise of the actual facts."[70]

Where property is purchased with the aid of X's moneys it is vital whether X paid over the moneys as purchaser or lender. If X provided £25,000 of a £100,000 purchase price of a house put in Y's name then if X lent the £25,000 he is only entitled as a personal creditor to the £25,000 and any agreed interest, whereas if he provided the £25,000 as purchaser he is entitled to a quarter share in the house. Loan and purchase by way of resulting trust are thus mutually exclusive,[71] though in an exceptional case a loan arrangement may commence as a primary temporary trust to carry out a purpose which, if carried out, results in a pure loan relationship but which, if not carried out, gives rise to a secondary final express or resulting trust as in *Barclays Bank Ltd.* v. *Quistclose Investments Ltd.*[72] If Y alleges that X provided moneys by way of gift and not by way of loan or purchase then the onus is on Y to prove this.[73]

---

69 *Vandervell* v. *I.R.C.* [1967] 2 A.C. 291, 313, *per* Lord Upjohn.
70 *Mackowick* v. *Kansas City* (1906) 945 W. 256, 264, *per* Lamm J.
71 *Aveling* v. *Knipe* (1815) 19 Ves. 441; *Re Sharpe* [1980] 1 All E.R. 198, 201; p. 117, *supra*; *Winkworth* v. *Edward Baron Development Co.* [1987] 1 All E.R. 114, 118, *per* Lord Templeman.
72 [1970] A.C. 567 discussed *ante*, pp. 117, 186.
73 *Seldon* v. *Davidson* [1968] 1 W.L.R. 1083; *Dewar* v. *Dewar* [1975] 1 W.L.R. 1532.

A contributor to a purchase money resulting trust gets the share he pays for in a broad lay sense[74] concerned with direct and indirect financial contributions. He will obtain an interest in the property on resulting trust principles taking account of deposit payments, mortgage payments and making substantial financial contributions to joint household expenses so as to enable the other alone to keep up the mortgage payments.[75] Payments of an income (as opposed to capital) nature for the use of property (*e.g.* rent and bills for living expenses), do not give the payers any interest under a resulting trust.[76] On a strict view payments for building extensions on to a house fall foul of the rule "that if A expends money on the property of B prima facie he has no claim on such property"[77] unless there is some agreement to the contrary (or B's conduct estops B from denying A's claim). Such agreement relating to land requires to be evidenced in writing under the Law of Property Act 1925, section 53(1)(*b*) though this is not to affect the creation or operation of resulting or constructive trusts. A constructive trust may be imposed to benefit A if an agreement existed for A to acquire a specific share or a fair share in the property and it would be fraudulent or unconscionable for B to plead the lack of writing.[78] Alternatively, if the court is prepared to view the matter through a layman's eyes and treat the fee simple and the house as distinct it may consider payment for building an extension to the house as part of the acquisition cost of the property so as to afford B an interest in the property on resulting trust principles.[79]

Since resulting trusts and constructive trusts are both exempt from the formal requirements of the Law of Property Act 1925, s.53(1) it may not seem to matter which sort of trust arises. As a result judges sometimes fail to make it clear whether they are dealing with a resulting trust or a constructive trust.[80] Occasionally, a judge may even treat the terms as interchangeable[81]: they are not, and any confusion of the two types of trust may lead to a confusion of the requirements for the two types of trust. In a purchase money resulting trust "you get the share you paid for" whereas in a constructive trust "you get what was

---

[74] Mortgage payments are not strictly payment of the purchase price (already received by the vendor) but payment towards release of the charge on the house, but they are treated as part-payment of purchase moneys: *Gissing* v. *Gissing* [1971] A.C. 886, 906. Whilst, strictly, a distinction might be drawn between the capital and interest elements of mortgage payments both elements are taken into account: *Passee* v. *Passee* [1988] 1 F.L.R. 263.

[75] *Gissing* v. *Gissing* [1971] A.C. 886; *Cowcher* v. *Cowcher* [1972] 1 W.L.R. 425; *Burns* v. *Burns* [1984] 1 All E.R. 244; *Grant* v. *Edwards* [1986] Ch. 638 *infra*, p. 516. Where instead of H paying £60 per week and W paying £30 per week of a £90 per week mortgage, with H paying W £30 per week as his housekeeping share, it is agreed that H will pay all the £90 per week mortgage and let W use her money for all housekeeping purposes, then a resulting trust of the house for H and W in 2:1 proportions will arise if the house is in H's name alone. See further, p. 500.

[76] *Savage* v. *Dunningham* [1974] Ch. 181.

[77] *Pettitt* v. *Pettitt* [1970] A.C. 777, 818; *Davis* v. *Vale* [1971] 1 W.L.R. 1022, 1025.

[78] See p. 138.

[79] *Davis* v. *Vale* [1971] 2 All E.R. 1021, 1025; *Kowalczuk* v. *Kowalczuk* [1973] 2 All E.R. 1042, 1045; *Passee* v. *Passee* [1988] 1 F.L.R. 263.

[80] *Heseltine* v. *Heseltine* [1971] 1 W.L.R. 342; *Cooke* v. *Head* [1972] 2 All E.R. 38.

[81] *Hussey* v. *Palmer* [1972] 3 All E.R. 744.

agreed if you acted to your detriment in reliance on the agreement"[82] or, perhaps, less than that if this is sufficient to reverse the suffered detriment,[83] because normally equity will not perfect an imperfect gift.

*Re Densham*,[84] usefully contrasts a resulting trust with a constructive trust. A wife had contributed roughly one-ninth of the purchase price of the matrimonial home and so was held entitled to a one-ninth interest in the home on resulting trust principles. However, it was also held that she was entitled to a half share under a constructive trust since she and her husband had agreed the purchase was to be in their joint names, though her name was omitted from the transfer because of some misunderstanding, so it would be unconscionable for the husband to set up the lack of writing to defeat her intended half share. Whilst the wife's one-ninth share was valid against her husband's trustee in bankruptcy since she was a purchaser under a resulting trust, her further seven-eighteenth share under constructive trust principles was voidable under the Bankruptcy Act 1914, s.42[85] since it was a voluntary settlement made by her husband.

It is clear that an interest under a resulting trust arises as soon as the purchase moneys begin to be provided, the interest enlarging as more moneys are provided directly or indirectly: a court order does not create the interest but vindicates a pre-existing interest. It may well develop that an interest under a constructive trust arises by way of a remedy at the time of the court order[86] and so is not a pre-existing interest capable of binding third parties as an *in rem* property interest (though in an exceptional case their consciences may be bound *in personam*[87]).

## Matrimonial and quasi-matrimonial homes

Where matrimonial and quasi-matrimonial homes are concerned the law of resulting trusts was rather unsettled largely due to the desire of Lord Denning's division of the Court of Appeal to do what "is just in all the circumstances of the case."[88] Indeed it was often the constructive trust, with the consequent unsettling of the law relating to constructive trusts, that was utilised for this "just" end without it being made clear that constructive and not resulting trusts were being so utilised.[89] This unfortunate situation had arisen because the House of Lords[90] in their two leading decisions on resulting trusts and the

---

[82] *Re Densham* [1975] 1 W.L.R. 1519; *Gissing* v. *Gissing* [1971] A.C. 886.
[83] *Grant* v. *Edwards* [1986] Ch. 638, 657–658; *infra*, p. 516.
[84] [1975] 1 W.L.R. 1519.
[85] See pp. 269–271, *supra* and Insolvency Act 1985, ss. 174, 175.
[86] *Metall und Rohstoff A.G.* v. *Donaldson Lufkin* [1990] 1 Q.B. 391, 479; *infra*, pp. 493, 506; [1990] Conv. 370 (D.J.H.).
[87] *Ashburn Anstalt* v. *Arnold* [1989] Ch. 1; *infra*, p. 513.
[88] *Per* Lord Denning in *Davis* v. *Vale* [1971] 1 W.L.R. 1022, 1027. Some examples are *Heseltine* v. *Heseltine* [1971] 1 W.L.R. 342; *Hazel* v. *Hazel* [1972] 1 W.L.R. 301; *Hargrave* v. *Newton* [1971] 1 W.L.R. 1611. Mistresses are less likely to obtain a half share: *Cooke* v. *Head* [1972] 1 W.L.R. 518; *Eves* v. *Eves* [1975] 1 W.L.R. 1338; (1976) 40 Conv. 351 (M. Richards). See Murphy & Clark, *The Family Home*.
[89] *Heseltine* v. *Heseltine, supra*; *Cooke* v. *Head* [1972] 1 W.L.R. 518.
[90] *Pettitt* v. *Pettitt* [1970] A.C. 777; *Gissing* v. *Gissing* [1971] A.C. 886.

matrimonial home revealed such a diversity of approach, making the proper *rationes* difficult to ascertain, that it left the way open for Lord Denning to pay lip-service to the Lords whilst ignoring the fundamental majority views of the Lords.[91]

The position has now been clarified by the Court of Appeal in *Burns* v. *Burns*,[92] and *Grant* v. *Edwards, infra,* p. 516, in accordance with the majority view of the Lords in *Gissing* v. *Gissing.*[93]

If there is a declaration of trust in the conveyance or transfer declaring that H or H and W hold on trust for themselves jointly or equally, as the case may be, this is conclusive in the absence of proof of fraud or mistake.[94] If the conveyance or transfer does not deal with the beneficial interests, then W will need to claim by way of resulting trust or constructive trust. This will require her proving either a common intention, express or inferred, that she is to have a beneficial interest proportionate to her contribution to the purchase price (a resulting trust) or a common intention, expressed or inferred, that she is to have a specific or "fair" beneficial interest, so that she is induced to act to her detriment in the reasonable belief that by so acting she is acquiring a beneficial interest (a constructive trust, or, perhaps, an express trust, enforced despite the absence of writing since equity will not allow a statute to be used as an instrument of fraud). In both these cases it is inequitable to allow H to deny W a beneficial interest.[95] The court cannot ascribe to the parties the common intention or agreement the parties ought to have had as reasonable persons if they had directed their minds to the issue of beneficial ownership.[96] However, the court may infer from the circumstances and the conduct of the parties, including subsequent conduct, that there was an agreement or common intention.[97]

Contributions to the purchase price that give rise to a resulting trust cover not just direct financial contributions (whether out of a person's own moneys or out of pooled resources in a joint account) such as paying the deposit or mortgage instalments or paying for substantial

---

[91] *Hazell* v. *Hazell* [1972] 1 W.L.R. 301; J. M. Eekelaar (1972) 88 L.Q.R. 333; S. M. Cretney (1971) 115 S.J. 615; Bagnall J. in *Cowcher* v. *Cowcher* [1972] 1 W.L.R. 425 doing his best to lay down principles reconciling subsequent Court of Appeal decisions with the two earlier Lords' decisions. On Lord Denning's contribution to the law of trusts see Lord Denning, *The Judge and The Law* (edited by Jowell & McAuslan), Chap. 3 (D. J. Hayton).
[92] [1984] Ch. 317.
[93] [1971] A.C. 886.
[94] *Bernard* v. *Josephs* [1982] Ch. 391; *Goodman* v. *Gallant* [1986] 1 All E.R. 311.
[95] *Gissing* v. *Gissing* [1971] A.C. 886, 905. Indeed, H's unilateral conduct (without any bilateral agreement) if causing W to act to her detriment may enable W to claim an equitable estoppel interest in the home so as to reverse H's inequitable behaviour: see p. 59, *supra* and pp. 504–509, *infra.*
[96] *Ibid.* 904; *Burns* v. *Burns* [1984] 1 All E.R. 244; *Grant* v. *Edwards* [1986] Ch. 638.
[97] *Re Densham* [1975] 3 All E.R. 726, 731; *Grant* v. *Edwards* [1986] Ch. 638.

improvements[98] such as adding a garage or a conservatory. Indirect contributions, so long as referable to the acquisition of an interest in the house, also create an interest under a resulting trust as where a wife regularly pays the joint household expenses so as to enable her husband to pay the mortgage instalments out of his own money.[99] She will also acquire a proportionate (or as otherwise agreed) interest if she makes a substantial contribution in money's worth to improving the house (*e.g.* herself doing demolition or building work).[1] One may regard this payment in kind as an extension of resulting trust principles, saving her husband from having to pay for such work, or as an illustration of constructive trust principles, it being unconscionable for her husband to deny their inferred common intention that such work, referable to the improvement of the house, was to confer an interest in the house on her proportionate to the improved value thereby put on the house.

Nowadays, where section 24 of the Matrimonial Causes Act 1973[2] is available it is not necessary for the courts to ascertain the position of spouses on resulting or constructive trust principles. However, the trust "principles to be applied are in general the same whether the couple have been married or not,"[3] subject to the warning expressed by Griffiths L.J. in *Bernard* v. *Josephs*[4] where he said:

> "But the nature of the relationship is a very important factor when considering what inferences should be drawn from the way the parties have conducted their affairs. There are many reasons why a man and a woman may decide to live together without marrying, and one of them is that each values his independence and does not wish to make the commitment of marriage; in such a case it will be misleading to make the same assumptions and to draw the same inferences from their behaviour as in the case of a married couple. The judge must look most carefully at the nature of the relationship, and only if satisfied that it was intended to involve the same degree of commitment as marriage will it be legitimate to regard them as no different from a married couple."

---

[98] Matrimonial Proceedings and Property Act 1970, s.37: "It is hereby declared that where a husband or wife contributes in money or money's worth to the improvement of real or personal property in which or in the proceeds of sale of which either or both of them has or have a beneficial interest, the husband or wife so contributing shall, if the contribution is of a substantial nature and subject to any agreement between them to the contrary express or implied, be treated as having then acquired by virtue of his or her contribution a share or an enlarged share in that beneficial interest of such an extent as may have been then agreed or, in default of such agreement, as may seem in all the circumstances just." Held to be retrospective and declaratory: *Davis* v. *Vale* [1971] 2 All E.R. 1021, 1025; *Kowalczuk* v. *Kowalczuk* [1973] 2 All E.R. 1042, 1045. On assessing the share size see *Griffiths* v. *Griffiths* [1973] 3 All E.R. 1155, 1159; *Re Nicholson* [1974] 3 All E.R. 386; *Samuels* v. *Samuels* (1975) 233 Est.Gaz. 149. The section extends to engaged couples: Law Reform (Miscellaneous Provisions) Act 1970, s.2.

[99] *Burns* v. *Burns* [1984] 1 All E.R. 244, 252, 265; *Grant* v. *Edwards* [1986] Ch. 638.

[1] *Cooke* v. *Head* [1972] 1 W.L.R. 518; *Eves* v. *Eves* [1975] 1 W.L.R. 1338; Matrimonial Proceedings and Property Act 1970, s.37.

[2] See next paragraph. The section is not available where one spouse has died or where the parties have been divorced or where a spouse without the legal estate claims an equitable interest binding a mortgagee.

[3] *Per* May L.J. in *Burns* v. *Burns* [1984] 1 All E.R. 242, 256.

[4] [1982] Ch. 391, 402 endorsed by May L.J., *supra.*

Whilst strict property law and trust law should otherwise apply, on granting a decree of divorce or nullity or judicial separation the court may under section 24 of the Matrimonial Causes Act 1973 make (a) an order that a party to the marriage shall transfer to the other party, to any child of the family or to someone as trustee for the child such property as may be specified being property to which the first-mentioned party is entitled (b) an order that a party to the marriage should settle certain of his property for the benefit of the other party and of the children (c) an order varying any ante-nuptial or post-nuptial settlement[5] made on the parties to the marriage (d) an order extinguishing or reducing the interest of either of the parties under any such settlement. If at all possible applicants must have matters resolved under the discretionary jurisdiction whereby orders can be made without the need to ascertain strict property rights on resulting trust or other principles.[6] In considering what order to make the court must have regard *inter alia* to the contributions made by each of the parties to the welfare of the family, including any contributions made by looking after the home or caring for the family: section 25(2)(*f*) of the Matrimonial Causes Act 1973 as amended.

### The Types of Transactions

(a) *Purchase in the name of another*

X purchases property (real or personal) in the name of Y. Ordinarily, if X wishes to make a gift to Y, he will purchase the property in his own name and then convey it to Y. Here he has paid the purchase-money, but has required his vendor to convey to Y. Y is then presumed in equity to hold the property on a resulting trust for X.[7]

(b) *Purchase by one in joint names of himself and another*

X purchases property (real or personal) in the *joint* names of himself *and* Y. As in (a) above, X has paid the purchase-money, but instead of requiring his vendor to convey to Y alone, he takes a conveyance to himself and Y jointly. Here again equity presumes that X and Y hold the property on a resulting trust for X.[8]

(c) *Joint purchase in name of one*

X *and* Y jointly purchase property (real or personal) in the name of Y alone. Both X and Y have contributed towards the purchase-money, but the conveyance is taken in the name of Y alone. There will be a presumption that it was the intention of X and Y to constitute X a proportionate beneficiary.[9]

---

5 This covers property co-owned in equity: *Cook* v. *Cook* [1962] P. 235; *Ulrich* v. *Ulrich* [1968] 1 W.L.R. 180.
6 *Williams* v. *Williams* [1976] Ch. 278; *Fielding* v. *Fielding* [1978] 1 All E.R. 267.
7 *Dyer* v. *Dyer* (1788) 2 Cox 92; *Vandervell* v. *I.R.C.* [1967] 2 A.C. 291.
8 *Benger* v. *Drew* (1721) 1 P.Wms. 781; *Rider* v. *Kidder* (1805) 10 Ves. 360.
9 *The Venture* [1908] P. 218; *Bull* v. *Bull* [1955] 1 Q.B. 234.

Section 17 of the Married Women's Property Act 1882, which enables the court to make such orders as it thinks fit in any question between husband and wife as to the title to property, does not permit the court to vary agreed or established titles to property. It is a procedural section and does not alter substantive rights.[10] Another section that may be invoked to give effect to pure property rights under a trust for sale is the Law of Property Act 1925, s.30.[11] Neither section should be invoked if jurisdiction is available under the Matrimonial Causes Act 1973.[12]

### (d) *Transfer from one to another*

X gratuitously *transfers* property into the name of Y. In (a), (b) and (c) above the transaction was a *purchase*; here it is a *transfer*. Property already stands in the name of X, who gratuitously transfers it into the name of Y. If X is the father of Y or stands *in loco parentis* (*patris*) to Y or is husband of Y, there will be a rebuttable[13] presumption of advancement in favour of Y.[14]

But if X and Y are *strangers*, *i.e.* if there is no special relationship between them, the position before 1926 was that there was a resulting trust, it being presumed that the *paterfamilias* would not gratuitously alienate the patrimony.[15] Today it seems no resulting trust arises if the property is land, by virtue of section 60(3) of the Law of Property Act 1925, which provides[16]: "In a voluntary conveyance a resulting trust for the grantor shall not be implied merely by reason that the property is not expressed to be conveyed for the use or benefit of the grantee." By section 205(1)(ii) of the Act the expression "conveyance" includes a "mortgage, charge, lease . . . and every other assurance of property or of an interest therein by any instrument, except a will," unless the context otherwise requires; and by section 205(1)(xx) the expression "property" includes any interest in property real *or* personal, unless the context otherwise requires. The context of section 60 appears, however, to restrict the meaning of "property" in subsection (3) to land. For other property, *e.g.* stocks and shares the stranger, Y, will hold the property rebuttably upon a resulting trust for X.[17] Slight circumstances should enable the presumption to be rebutted in the case of chattels and cash where it will not be considered so likely that the donor intends to retain the beneficial interest.

---

10 *National Provincial Bank Ltd.* v. *Ainsworth* [1965] A.C. 1175; *Pettitt* v. *Pettitt* [1970] A.C. 777; *Cowcher* v. *Cowcher* [1972] 1 W.L.R. 425.

11 *Re Bailey* [1977] 2 All E.R. 26; *Burke* v. *Burke* [1974] 2 All E.R. 944; *Jones* v. *Jones* [1977] 1 W.L.R. 438. Now see Insolvency Act 1986, ss.336, 337.

12 *Williams* v. *Williams* [1976] Ch. 278; *Fielding* v. *Fielding* [1978] 1 All E.R. 267.

13 *Re Gooch* (1890) 62 L.T. 384 (shares); *Shephard* v. *Cartwright* [1955] A.C. 431.

14 *Currant* v. *Jago* (1844) 1 Coll. 261 (cash); *May* v. *May* (1863) 33 Beav. 81 (land).

15 See White and Tudor, *Leading Cases in Equity* (9th ed.), Vol. 2, p. 762; Snell, pp. 180–181.

16 In *Hodgson* v. *Marks* [1971] Ch. 892 there was oral evidence (not satisfying L.P.A. 1925, s.53(1)(*b*)) that the transferor intended to retain the equitable interest, though L.P.A. s.60(3) was not cited.

17 *Vandervell* v. *I.R.C.* [1967] 2 A.C. 291, 312; *Re Vandervell's Trusts (No. 2)* [1974] Ch. 269; *Fowkes* v. *Pascoe* (1875) 10 Ch.App. 343, 348; *Crane* v. *Davis* (1981) *The Times*, May 13; *Hepworth* v. *Hepworth* (1870) L.R. 11 Eq. 10.

(e) *Transfer into joint names of transferor and another*

X gratuitously transfers property into the *joint* names of himself and Y. As in (d) above, property already stands in the name of X, but instead of transferring it into the *sole* name of Y, he gratuitously transfers it into the *joint* names of himself and Y. There will be a presumption of a resulting trust in favour of X.[18] A modern illustration is *Young* v. *Sealey*,[19] in which X opened a joint banking account with Y, but during her life X retained complete control of the account, and Y neither paid anything into nor drew anything out of it. On X's death Y took the legal title by survivorship. Did he, however, hold it on trust for X's estate? Romer J. held that the presumption of a trust in favour of X's estate arose, but that this was rebutted by the evidence of Y as to X's intentions. Romer J. rejected the argument that the intended gift was void as an attempt to make a post-mortem gift otherwise than in accordance with the Wills Act. In his view, there were previous cases of a similar nature, in which the point had passed *sub silentio*, but it should now be taken to be settled in favour of Y. If X is Y's husband then the presumption of advancement applies unless the joint account was opened merely for conveniently managing X's affairs (*e.g.* if X is ill).[20] If it was opened with the intention of making provision for the wife, as is quite likely if X alone opened the account, then the wife will be entitled to the balance on X's death.[21]

(f) *Joint purchase and joint mortgage*

Where X and Y purchase property in their joint names though providing the money in unequal shares or jointly advance money on mortgage in their joint names, and X dies, Y takes the legal title to the whole by survivorship but will be treated as a tenant in common in equity and holds the share of the purchase or mortgage money advanced by X on trust for X's estate.[22]

### B. PRESUMPTION OF ADVANCEMENT

Where a special relationship exists between X and Y there is no presumption of resulting trust but a presumption of advancement. The principle is stated by Lord Eldon in *Murless* v. *Franklin*[23] as follows: "The general rule that on a purchase by one man in the name of another, the nominee is a trustee for the purchaser, is subject to exception where the purchaser is under a species of natural obligation to provide for the nominee."

The presumption of advancement always arises where X is the father of Y or stands *in loco parentis* (*patris*) to Y,[24] or is the husband or

---

[18] See *Owens* v. *Greene* [1932] Ir.R. 225; *Re Vinogradoff* [1935] W.N. 68.

[19] [1949] Ch. 278; *Re Reid* (1921) 50 Ont.L.R. 595; *Russell* v. *Scott* (1936) 55 C.L.R. 440.

[20] *Marshal* v. *Crutwell* (1875) L.R. 20 Eq. 328.

[21] *Re Figgis* [1969] 1 Ch. 123; see (1969) 85 L.Q.R. 530 (M. C. Cullity).

[22] *Re Jackson* (1887) 34 Ch.D. 732; *Cobb* v. *Cobb* [1955] 2 All E.R. 696 (C.A.); Law of Property Act 1925, s.111 enabling the survivor to give a good receipt.

[23] (1818) 1 Swans. 13, 17.

[24] *Shephard* v. *Cartwright* [1955] A.C. 431; *Hepworth* v. *Hepworth* (1870) L.R. 11 Eq. 10.

engaged fiancé of Y.[25] It does not arise where X is merely cohabiting with Y,[26] nor where X is the wife of Y.[27] The strength of the presumption between husband and wife is nowadays very weak.[28]

It was apparently held in *Sayre* v. *Hughes*[29] and *Re Grimes*[30] that a presumption of advancement arises also where X is the *mother* of Y, at any rate if she is a *widowed* mother. This is supported by a dictum in *Garrett* v. *Wilkinson*[31]; but *Re De Visme*[32] and *Bennet* v. *Bennet*[33] are to the opposite effect. The ground of the decision in these two cases was that whether the father is alive or not, the mother is under no equitable obligation which will raise the presumption of advancement. In *Gross* v. *French*[34] the Court of Appeal held that even if the presumption of advancement operates against a mother in favour of her child, there was sufficient evidence to rebut any such presumption: usually there will be some evidence to affirm or negative the presumption.

Modern ideas of equality indicate that the presumption of advancement should extend to mothers *vis-à-vis* their children[35] and wives *vis-à-vis* their husbands. In practice, it is easier for courts to pay lip-service to the old case law whilst being satisfied on flimsy evidence that the old-fashioned presumption has been rebutted.

## C. Rebutting the Presumptions

Both the presumption of a resulting trust and the presumption of advancement can be rebutted by evidence within the limits laid down by the House of Lords in *Shepherd* v. *Cartwright*.[36] That case reaffirms the rule that evidence of subsequent acts, though not admissible in favour of the party doing the acts, is admissible against him.[37] It appears, however, that acquiescence by a child, in whose name a purchase has been made, in the receipt by his father during his life of the rents or the income of the property does not rebut the presumption

---

25 *Tinker* v. *Tinker* [1970] P. 136; *Silver* v. *Silver* [1958] 1 W.L.R. 259; *Moate* v. *Moate* [1948] 2 All E.R. 486 (intended husband: marriage afterwards solemnised); Law Reform (Miscellaneous Provisions) Act 1970, s.2(1); *Mossop* v. *Mossop* [1988] 2 All E.R. 202.

26 *Rider* v. *Kidder* (1805) 10 Ves. 360; *Napier* v. *Public Trustee* (1980) 32 A.L.R. 153, 158; *Calverley* v. *Green* (1984) 56 A.L.R. 483.

27 *Re Curtis* (1885) 52 L.T. 244; *Mercier* v. *Mercier* [1903] 2 Ch. 98.

28 In *Pettitt* v. *Pettitt* [1970] A.C. 777 two Lords treated the presumption of advancement as applicable but two treated it as inappropriate for modern times. It is thus a weak starting point, especially if the wife makes some contribution to a house mainly purchased by the husband in his name. Usually, there will be at least circumstantial evidence to clarify the position.

29 (1868) L.R. 5 Eq. 376.

30 [1937] Ir.R. 470.

31 (1848) 2 De G. & Sm. 244, 246.

32 (1863) 2 De G.J. & S. 17.

33 (1879) 10 Ch.D. 474.

34 (1976) 238 E.G. 39. In *Sekhon* v. *Alissa* [1989] 2 F.L.R. 94 Hoffman J. presumed a resulting trust in favour of the mother which the daughter failed to rebut.

35 *Dullow* v. *Dullow* [1985] 3 N.S.W.L.R. 531.

36 [1955] A.C. 431.

37 Evidence of subsequent declarations, whether for or against the speaker, may now be admissible as a side-effect of Civil Evidence Act 1968, s.2.

of advancement,[38] at any rate where the child has not already been fully advanced[39]; for if the child is an infant it is natural that the father should receive the profits, while if the child is an adult, it is an act of good manners on his part not to dispute their reception by his father. But the retention of the title deeds by the father with a contemporaneous declaration by him that the transaction was not a gift is sufficient to rebut the presumption of advancement,[40] though retention of the title deeds without such a declaration may be insufficient.[41] Nowadays, it seems that the presumptions are readily rebutted by comparatively slight evidence.[42] Rebuttal may be partial enabling the transferee to have a life interest or to have the beneficial interest only on the transferor's death.[43]

## D. ILLEGALITY

In considering evidence offered to rebut the presumptions one must consider the maxims "he who comes to equity must come with clean hands," "*ex turpi causa actio non oritur*," "*in pari delicto potior est conditio defendentis* (or *possidentis*)." After all, a person may transfer property to another to defraud the Revenue, to defeat his creditors or to defeat his wife's claims on divorce.[44]

Where the presumption of advancement applies (*e.g.* where H transfers property to his wife, W, or son, S) the onus is on the transferor, H, to produce evidence rebutting the presumption. If he honestly transferred the property to defeat his creditors then this could not lawfully be achieved without the beneficial ownership passing with the legal title, so the presumption of advancement is strengthened that this was intended, as held in *Tinker* v. *Tinker*.[45] If he dishonestly transferred the legal title to W or S to cloak the truth and thereby defeat his creditors then he cannot rely on his illegal purpose to rebut the presumption of advancement.[46] Exceptionally, it seems that if he had no creditors at the time of the transfer (or, perhaps, even if he had) and the transferee cannot show that a creditor has been prejudiced by the transfer, then he may repent of his illegal purpose

---

[38] *Commissioner of Stamp Duties* v. *Byrnes* [1911] A.C. 386; *cf.* Wickens V.-C. in *Stock* v. *McAvoy* (1872) L.R. 15 Eq. 55, 59; *Northern Canadian Trust Co.* v. *Smith* [1947] 3 D.L.R. 135; *Re Gooch* (1890) 62 L.T. 384 (presumption of advancement rebutted where father bought shares in son's name to qualify the son to be a director, the son passed the dividends to his father and later handed over the share certificates to his father).

[39] *Grey* v. *Grey* (1677) 2 Swans. 594; and see *Hepworth* v. *Hepworth* (1870) L.R. 11 Eq. 10.

[40] *Warren* v. *Gurney* [1944] 2 All E.R. 472.

[41] *Scawin* v. *Scawin* (1841) 1 Y. & C.C.C. 65.

[42] *Pettitt* v. *Pettitt* [1970] A.C. 777, 813, 824; *Falconer* v. *Falconer* [1970] 1 W.L.R. 1333.

[43] *Napier* v. *Public Trustee* (1980) 32 A.L.R. 153; *Young* v. *Sealey* [1949] Ch. 278.

[44] But note Insolvency Act 1986, ss.339–342, 423–425; Matrimonial Causes Act 1973, s.37; Inheritance (Provision for Family and Dependants) Act 1975, s.10, *supra*, pp. 269–275.

[45] [1970] P. 136.

[46] *Gascoigne* v. *Gascoigne* [1918] 1 K.B. 223, (where there were existing creditors and where tax was paid on the basis the bungalow belonged to the wife); *Re Emery's Investment Trusts* [1959] Ch. 410 (where, it seems, American withholding tax was evaded).

(thereby washing his hands "clean") and adduce evidence of his repudiated intention so as to recover the property.[47]

Where the presumption of resulting trust applies (*e.g.* where A transfers property to his brother, B) A may plead that B holds on resulting trust for him without disclosing any illegality, merely by pleading the gratuitous transfer or a transfer apparently for a consideration but which has never been paid. On this basis once the coast is clear and the creditors have been defrauded A can recover his property as has been held in Canada.[48] Some English authority supports this,[49] though some older authorities[50] suggest that if the illegal purpose had been wholly or partly effected then the plaintiff's claim should fail if the defendant pleads the illegal purpose[51]: *in pari delicto potior est conditio defendentis*.

Indeed, to make recovery turn on whichever presumption happens to apply seems a less appropriate solution than the test of whether or not the purpose has been in any degree carried out.[52] Scott suggests[53] the test should be "whether on all the facts it appears that the conduct of the settlor was so blameworthy that it is against public policy to permit him to recover the property," irrespective of which party pleads the illegality.

If the transferor cannot recover then his personal representative is in no better position.[54] Query whether public policy should allow his trustee in bankruptcy to be in a better position.[55]

---

[47] *Symes* v. *Hughes* (1875) L.R. 9 Eq. 475; *Sekhon* v. *Alissa* [1989] 2 F.L.R. 94; *Chettiar* v. *Chettiar* [1962] A.C. 294, 302; *Petherpermal Chetty* v. *Muniandi Servai* (1908) 24 T.L.R. 462; *Perpetual Executors Association of Australia Ltd.* v. *Wright* (1917) 23 C.L.R. 185; *Martin* v. *Martin* (1959) 110 C.L.R. 297. In *Tinker* v. *Tinker* [1970] P. 136 it was suggested *obiter* that if the transfer had been made with dishonest intent then the transferor's unclean hands would prevent him evidencing such intent so as to rebut the presumption of advancement. On this basis repentance is of no assistance, but the above cases were not cited to the court, only *Gascoigne* and *Re Emery* being cited where the question of repentance before partial achievement of the unlawful purpose was not raised. In Canada fraudulent intent alone deprives the transferor of pleading that evidence in his own favour: *Scheuerman* v. *Scheuerman* (1916) 28 D.L.R. 223; *Maysels* v. *Maysels* (1975) 64 D.L.R. (3d) 765 but this has been much criticised: *Krys* v. *Krys* [1929] 1 D.L.R. 289; *Goodfriend* v. *Goodfriend* (1972) 22 D.L.R. (3d) 699; Waters, pp. 319–331.

[48] *Gorog* v. *Kiss* (1977) 78 D.L.R. (3d) 690.

[49] *Haigh* v. *Kaye* (1872) 7 Ch.App. 469. For a purported consideration not paid, H transferred land to K, who admitted he was to hold on trust for H. K did not plead it but suggested the conveyance was to protect H in case a pending lawsuit went against him. *Held*: K must reconvey to H. In *Chettiar* v. *Chettiar* [1962] A.C. 294, 301–302 the Privy Council explained that a presumption of resulting trust arose in favour of H, who therefore did not need to disclose any fraud on his part.

[50] *Cottington* v. *Fletcher* (1740) 2 Atk. 156; *Muckleston* v. *Brown* (1801) 6 Ves. 52, 68; *Davies* v. *Otty* (1866) 35 Beav. 208.

[51] Indeed, in *Haigh* v. *Kaye* (1872) 7 Ch.App. 469, 473 James L.J. pointed out that K had not pleaded the illegal arrangement he had with H, and K "must clearly put forward his own scoundrelism if he means to reap the benefit of it." Query whether this can mean that if he had put forward the illegality he would actually reap the benefit of it. Probably not, especially in view of *Chettiar* v. *Chettiar's* interpretation of it.

[52] Ford & Lee, p. 273; Grodecki (1955) 71 L.Q.R. 254, 270; *Sekhon* v. *Alissa* [1989] 2 F.L.R. 94.

[53] *Trusts* (3rd ed.), Vol. V, para. 422.5.

[54] *Ayerst* v. *Jenkins* (1873) L.R. 16 Eq. 275, 281, *per* Lord Selborne L.C. The contrary view of Lord Eldon in *Muckleston* v. *Brown* (1801) 6 Ves. 52, 68 seems unsound.

[55] *Cf. Trautwein* v. *Richardson* [1946] Argus L.R. 129, 134, *per* Dixon J.; *Ayerst* v. *Jenkins* (1873) 16 Eq. 275, 283.

# QUESTIONS

1. The Ravers Anonymous Club which is not a charitable organisation has just dissolved itself one week after having received £10,000 donated by Sir Launcelot Hellfire for the purposes of the Club and one month after having received £1,000 from certain raffles and sweepstakes and £150 from collections taken at a public meeting called to publicise the Club. What should be done with these sums?

2. The Black Sheep Club was formed in 1908 to encourage the breeding and improvement of Black Sheep and also to provide sick benefits for the widows of members. The members paid an annual subscription of £5 unless aged less than 35 years when they paid half that. Funds were also raised from annual covenants from well-wishers, from collections made at the annual show and from the profits of an annual dance and monthly beetle drives. The Club has been inactive since 1980. There are four surviving members (aged 34, 40, 50 and 60 years) and one widow of a deceased member. Its assets amount to £50,000. Advise as to the distribution of the Club's assets.

3. Six years before her death Miss Spry opened a current account with Barclays Bank in the joint names of herself and her nephew, Neal Smug. Both of them called on the manager when they came to open the joint account. Miss Spry told the manager that as she was getting frail her nephew would look after her banking matters for her. She also said that if she died before her nephew he could keep any credit balance in the account at her death. It was arranged that cheques drawn by either Miss Spry or Neal would be honoured. Although Miss Spry kept the cheque book in her desk Neal signed all the cheques.

As had been envisaged only Miss Spry contributed moneys to the joint account and at her death a credit balance of £2,000 remained. Who is entitled to this if Miss Spry by will had left everything to the RSPCA?

4. Fearing that his wife might divorce him at some time and that a new business venture might prove financially damaging, Harold transferred "Cosy Cottage" and 10,000 ICI plc shares to Simon, who agreed that when matters had resolved themselves so that it was safe to do so he would reconvey the cottage to Harold. The conveyance purported to be for £80,000 but, in fact, as agreed Simon actually paid nothing.

Advise Harold who seeks to recover the cottage. Does it matter (a) if Simon is Harold's brother or his son, or (b) if only six months have elapsed and Harold's wife is still living with him and he can pay his debts as they fall due?

5. "The presumptions of presumed resulting trusts and of advancement are today false and outmoded, so that only lip-service is paid to them in establishing where the onus of proof lies; instead, the courts should presume that the legal title reflects the intentions of the parties unless there are circumstances (not the outdated, false presumptions) which displace it in equity." Discuss.

# Chapter 7

# CONSTRUCTIVE TRUSTS[1]

It is too easy to talk of express, resulting and constructive trusts as if they are similar substantive institutions (especially in the context of cases on family homes) and as if the beneficiaries have similar rights, with the trustees having similar duties. This is often not the case.

Where there is an express or a resulting trust the court compels the trustees to give effect to the beneficiaries' rights in relation to the trust property because they are trustees of property with consequences automatically flowing therefrom. The trust instrument may explicitly state that the trustees are to be trustees not just of the original property but the investments from time to time representing the original property and also the income received from time to time in respect of such property or investments. In the absence of such a provision, the court still regards the trustees as trustees of such investments or income, whether by implying such a provision or by imposing a constructive trust to prevent a trustee from personally benefiting from the trust. If a trustee uses trust property to make a profit for himself then the profit and its exchange product (*i.e.* property in which the profit is invested) and any income produced thereby will be held on constructive trust for the beneficiaries.

Here, the constructive trust is dependent upon and ancillary to an express or a resulting trust of property. It arises and exists independently of any order of the court, just like the express or resulting trust to which it is a remedial adjunct. In other cases where a defendant may not voluntarily become trustee of a valid enforceable express or resulting trust Equity, in special limited circumstances, prevents such person from unconscionably retaining part or, sometimes, all of the beneficial interest in property vested in him by constructively treating him as if he were a trustee of the property for another. It is only because Equity compels the defendant to hold property wholly or partly for the plaintiff that the defendant is constructive trustee thereof: it is not because the defendant is a constructive trustee that he is automatically forced to hold the property for the plaintiff. The constructive trust relationship is established by order of the court which between the parties is assumed *sub silentio* to be retrospective,[2]

---

[1] See A. W. Scott, "Constructive Trusts" (1955) 71 L.Q.R. 39; Ford & Lee, Chap. 22; Waters, *Constructive Trust* (1965); Goff and Jones' *Law of Restitution*, Chap. 2; Oakley's *Constructive Trusts*; G. Elias, *Explaining Constructive Trusts*.

[2] *Lloyds Bank* v. *Rosset* [1989] Ch. 350, *Midland Bank* v. *Dobson* [1986] 1 F.L.R. 171; *Rawluk* v. *Rawluk* (1990) 65 D.L.R. (4th) 161.

though to protect third parties it is possible for a constructive trust to be prospective only,[3] as should be the case where it might make a difference even to the two parties.[4]

An express or resulting trust is always a proprietary institution, existing independently of any court order and conferring equitable interests in property upon the beneficiaries. Where a constructive trust is imposed as a remedial adjunct to an express or resulting trust it will have the same effects as such trust. Where, however, a constructive trust is established by a court order the plaintiff may retrospectively have an equitable proprietary interest or a mere equity,[5] or may only have such interest prospectively, or may merely have an *in personam* right against the defendant to occupy the defendant's property.[6] Indeed, the constructive trust may simply impose only a personal liability to account.[7]

Here, it is clearer to talk of the imposition of constructive trustee-*ship* because there is no constructive trust of any property. As a fiction[8] Equity constructively treats the defendant as if he were a trustee, so that he becomes personally liable to account for losses or profits like a trustee: thus, the plaintiff has a remedy against a defendant knowingly involved in a dishonest breach of trust or other fiduciary obligation where no remedy is otherwise available in contract or tort and even where no trust property was ever in the possession of the defendant. If the defendant is insolvent, however, this personal remedy will be of little use, unlike the case where property is subject to a proprietary constructive trust.

THE DISTINCTION BETWEEN A PROPRIETARY CONSTRUCTIVE TRUST AND
PERSONAL LIABILITY TO ACCOUNT AS A CONSTRUCTIVE TRUSTEE

Where A is trustee of an express trust of property for B, then B has an equitable proprietary right to claim such property or its exchange product and the fruits thereof. This proprietary right will prevail over A's trustee in bankruptcy and any other person deriving title from A who is not a bona fide purchaser of a legal interest for value without notice. B also has a personal claim to make A account for his trusteeship and any losses or profits resulting from breach of trust. If A is wealthy enough it does not matter whether B relies on A's proprietary liability or on A's personal liability (or on both if A has caused loss to occur). If the property has doubled in value B can claim

---

[3] *Muschinski* v. *Dodds* (1985) 160 C.L.R. 583, *Metall und Rohstoff A.G.* v. *Donaldson Lufkin* [1990] 1 Q.B. 391, 479, *LAC Minerals Ltd.* v. *International Corona Resources Ltd.* (1989) 61 D.L.R. (4th) 14, 48–51; *Atlas Cabinets* v. *National Trust Co.* (1990) 68 D.L.R. (4th) 161, 173–174.
[4] See facts of *Rawluk* v. *Rawluk* (1990) 65 D.L.R. (4th) 161 where the view of the three dissentient judges has much to commend it.
[5] Where the plaintiff has a right to set aside the transfer of property to the defendant by reason of undue influence.
[6] *Ashburn Anstalt* v. *Arnold* [1989] Ch. 1.
[7] *Re Montagu's Settlement* [1987] Ch. 264, p. 481, *infra.*
[8] *English* v. *Dedham Vale Properties Ltd.* [1978] 1 All E.R. 382, 398.

that specific property or a sum of money amounting to the value of such property, though A can then insist on handing over the specific property if he prefers. Until trial B can preserve the position by obtaining an interlocutory injunction restraining dealings with "his" trust property.

If A is insolvent then B's personal claim to make A liable to account for losses or profits will abate with the claims of all unsecured creditors. Thus B, instead, will exercise his proprietary claim and obtain an interlocutory injunction to preserve his property.

Where there is a proprietary[9] constructive trust there will similarly be a concomitant personal liability to account, though only from the time that the defendant knew[10] he was a constructive trustee. But where only constructive trusteeship is imposed the defendant is simply personally liable to account for profits or losses so that the plaintiff's claim will abate with other unsecured claims if the defendant is insolvent, and no interlocutory injunction can be obtained to restrain dealings with any property alleged to be "his."[11]

### BRIBES AND SECRET COMMISSIONS

If a trustee or other fiduciary exploits his position to take a bribe of £20,000, which he then invests in shares worth £50,000 when the beneficiary discovers what has happened, can the beneficiary recover the investments by way of a proprietary constructive trust thereof, or only the £20,000 plus interest by way of a personal claim, or the sum of £50,000 by way of a personal claim preventing the fiduciary from profiting from his position?

The leading case is *Lister & Co.* v. *Stubbs*[12] where the plaintiffs employed the defendant, their foreman, to buy materials from Messrs. Varley and the defendant accepted secret commissions from Messrs. Varley which he invested profitably. The plaintiffs moved for an interlocutory injunction pending the trial to "freeze" the investments but the Court of Appeal dismissed the motion, holding that the secret commissions were subject to a debtor-creditor relationship not to a constructive trust, since use of the fiduciary's position to obtain secret commissions for his own benefit did not deprive the plaintiffs of property which in equity belonged or ought to have belonged to the plaintiffs. Under a debtor-creditor relationship a debtor is not specifically liable for specific property but only for an amount equivalent to

---

9 See sentence to which n. 5, above refers.
10 This covers actual knowledge, "Nelsonian" knowledge and "naughty" knowledge: see p. 470, *infra* and *Re Montagu's Settlement* [1987] Ch. 264.
11 However, an interlocutory, *ex parte*, *Mareva* injunction may be obtained to freeze the defendant's assets up to the amount of the plaintiff's personal claim and legal costs in the exceptional case where there is a real risk that the defendant will dissipate or hide his assets (*e.g.* export them) so as to render the plaintiff's prospective judgment fruitless: *Rasu Maritana S.A.* v. *Perushaan* [1978] Q.B. 644, Supreme Court Act 1981, s.37(3), *Z Ltd.* v. *A–Z* [1982] Q.B. 558.
12 (1890) 45 Ch.D. 1. The Australian Courts treat the *Lister* v. *Stubbs* principle as anomalous and not to be extended: *Consul Development Pty. Ltd.* v. *D.P.C. Estates* (1975) 132 C.L.R. 373.

the money given him and is not accountable for profit derived from that money or liable for interest unless expressly or impliedly agreed between debtor and creditor.[13]

Lindley L.J. said[14]:

> "The real state of the case as between Messrs. Lister & Co. and Messrs. Varley and Stubbs is that Lister & Co. through their agent Stubbs buy goods of Messrs. Varley at certain prices and pay for them. The ownership of the goods of course is in Lister & Co.; the ownership of the money is in Messrs. Varley. Then Messrs. Varley have entered into an arrangement with Stubbs who ordered the goods to give Stubbs a commission. That is what it comes to. What is the legal position between Messrs. Varley and Stubbs? They owe him the money. He can recover it from them by an action unless the illegality of the transaction affords them a defence; but the appellants have asked us to go further and to say that Messrs. Varley were Stubbs's agent in getting his commission from Lister & Co. That appears to me to be an entire mistake. The relation between Messrs. Varley and Stubbs is that of a debtor and creditor— they pay him. Then comes the question, as between Lister & Co. and Stubbs, whether Stubbs can keep the money without accounting for it. Obviously not. I apprehend that he is liable to account for it the moment he gets it. It is an obligation to pay and account to Messrs. Lister & Co. But the relation between them is that of debtor and creditor; it is not that of trustee and *cestui que* trust. We are asked to hold that it is— which would involve consequences which I confess startle me. One consequence, of course, would be that, if Stubbs were to become bankrupt this property acquired by him with the money paid to him by Messrs. Varley would be withdrawn from the mass of his creditors and handed over bodily to Messrs. Lister & Co. Can that be right? Another consequence would be that if the appellants are right Lister & Co. could compel Stubbs to account to them, not only for the money with interest, but for all the profits which he might have made by embarking in trade with it. Can that be right? It appears to me that these consequences show that there is some flaw in the argument. If by logical reasoning from the premises conclusions are arrived at which are opposed to good sense, it is necessary to go back and look at the premises and see if they are sound—the unsoundness consisting in confounding ownership with obligation. It appears to me that the view taken of this case by Mr. Justice Stirling was correct, and that we should be doing what I conceive to be a very great mischief if we were to stretch a very sound principle to the extent to which the appellants ask us to stretch it, tempting as it is to do so as between the plaintiffs and Stubbs."

This was followed by the Court of Appeal in *Powell and Thomas* v. *Evans Jones & Co.*[15] and extended by the Court of Appeal (Criminal Division) in *Att.-Gen.'s Reference (No. 1 of 1985)*[16] to the case where an employee (*e.g.* a manager of a tied public house) makes a secret

---

13 See *Potters* v. *Loppert* [1973] 1 All E.R. 658, 661; (1976) 92 L.Q.R. 360, 371 (R. M. Goode).
14 (1890) 45 Ch.D. 1, 12–13.
15 [1905] 1 K.B. 11.
16 [1986] Q.B. 491; *Iran Shipping Lines* v. *Denby* [1987] 1 Ll.Rep. 367 also applied *Lister* v. *Stubbs*.

profit for himself by selling his own property (*e.g.* beer and sandwiches) in breach of his contract requiring him to sell only his employer's property. Because the employee received the money on his own account as a result of his private venture the circumstances were analogous to *Lister* v. *Stubbs* so that the employer had no proprietary interest in the secret profit to enable the employee to be guilty of theft under Theft Act 1968, section 5(1) or (3). It is possible that in a civil case this case could be distinguished as based on a special interpretation of section 5. After all, a "briber" knows and intends his bribe to benefit the "bribee" while the pub customers did not know or intend their money to be the employee's as opposed to the employer's. Moreover, the employee did not merely use his position: he used his employer's premises and beer-dispensing equipment.[17]

The reasoning in *Lister* v. *Stubbs* covers property bribes[18] from third parties as well as money bribes and creates a distinction between use of the position of fiduciary and use of property subject to the fiduciary relationship which is a fine one and a little difficult to justify.[19] The justification is that use of a fiduciary position to obtain a secret commission for the fiduciary's own benefit does not deprive the beneficiary of property belonging in equity to the beneficiary—but what if a fiduciary agent, upon receiving commission from a vendor, purchases goods from the vendor on his principal beneficiary's behalf at a commensurably higher price?[20] If a fiduciary employee (*e.g.* an Army sergeant)[21] uses his uniform belonging to his beneficiary employer to make a profit for himself (*e.g.* by receiving commission for sitting in a lorry with contraband so that it passes unhindered through checkpoints) does the profit arise from use of property or use of position? Should not a person clothed with a fiduciary position therefore hold on constructive trust profits obtained by use of such position and not be accountable only? After all, can one justify a distinction between the alternative circumstances in the following scenario, especially if "Equity looks to the substance and not to the form?"[22] An employee, E, is given £100,000 by his employer, H, to purchase some goods. E purchases goods from a supplier, S, on receiving a bribe of £10,000 which he invests in shares now doubled in value. In one situation E hands over H's £100,000 in a suitcase to S, who takes out £10,000 therefrom and gives it to E. In the other situation E hands over H's cheque for £100,000 and S hands over his

---

17 *Cf. Reid-Newfoundland Co.* v. *Anglo-American Telegraph Ltd.* [1912] A.C. 555, 559 where use of a telegraph wire gave rise to a constructive trust of profits made thereby.
18 But see *Eden* v. *Ridsdales Railway Lamp Co.* (1889) 23 Q.B.D. 368 where C.A. held the actual property (or its highest value) could be recovered.
19 Goff & Jones, pp. 655–657; Finn, *Fiduciary Obligations*, p. 221.
20 Indeed in *Fawcett* v. *Whitehouse* (1829) 1 Russ. & My. 132 W, on behalf of himself and his two partners, took on a burdensome lease, receiving £12,000 secretly for himself from the lessee, but Lord Lyndhurst L.C. held that immediately on receipt of the £12,000 he held it on constructive trust for himself and his two partners equally.
21 *Reading* v. *Att.-Gen.* [1951] A.C. 507.
22 See *Parkin* v. *Thorold* (1852) 16 Beav. 59, 66.

own cheque for £10,000 in favour of E. In the former situation H can trace his own £10,000 into the shares so as to have a proprietary claim, while in the latter situation by virtue of *Lister* v. *Stubbs* H can make E only personally liable to account for a sum equivalent to S's £10,000. In both cases H has paid out £100,000 for goods worth £90,000 and E has been unjustly enriched at his expense, not just to the extent of £10,000 but to the extent of £20,000 representing the current value of the shares which he would not have been able to purchase but for exploiting his fiduciary position. At the very least, to prevent E from profiting from his fiduciary position he must be personally liable for £20,000 representing the surviving enrichment value in his hands,[23] even if "nice" formal distinctions are permitted to prevent any proprietary liability from arising in the latter of the two situations discussed.

*Tracing: Its Relationship to Constructive Trusts and Personal Accountability*

If A is an express, resulting or constructive trustee of specific property, which he sells at a profit, and uses the proceeds to invest for himself in I.C.I. Ltd. shares, which he sells at a profit, and uses the proceeds to invest in Widgets Ltd. shares which have appreciated in value, the beneficiaries, besides having a right to make A personally liable to account for such value, have an equitable proprietary tracing claim entitling them to the specific Widgets shares even if A has become bankrupt. If it so happened that A had gifted the Widgets shares to X, who knew nothing of the trust, then X would be liable to the tracing claim as an innocent volunteer.[24] However, if X, before knowing of the trust, had dissipated any dividends received and had sold the shares and spent the proceeds on a world cruise there would be nothing to trace and X would not be personally liable to account as a constructive trustee since an innocent volunteer's liability only arises in respect of matters occurring after acquiring knowledge of the trust.[25] He becomes liable as a constructive trustee of the traced property for the period after but not before he acquired knowledge of the trust. If A himself had wickedly sold the shares and spent the proceeds on a world cruise he would, of course, be personally liable to account, though there could be no tracing claim against him since there would be no property of which he could be trustee.

It will be seen that the tracing claim results in someone holding the specific property to which the claim relates on constructive trust and that if there is only a mere personal liability to account, no specific property being held on trust, then no tracing claim can lie as

---

[23] See strict obligation upon fiduciary not to profit from his trust in *Regal Hastings Ltd.* v. *Gulliver* [1967] 2 A.C. 134 and in *Boardman* v. *Phipps* [1967] 2 A.C. 46 and see Birks' *Introduction to the Law of Restitution*, pp. 394–401.
[24] X would not be liable if a purchaser of a legal interest for value without notice.
[25] *Re Diplock* [1948] Ch. 465, 477–479, *Re Montagu's Settlement* [1987] Ch. 264 but query if a claim had been brought within six years whether X would have been personally liable for the amount of his unjust enrichment unless the defence of change of position were available: see p. 471, *infra*.

established in *Lister* v. *Stubbs*.[26] Where A holds specific assets or an identified fund which belong in equity to others under a trust and then wrongfully mixes such property with other property belonging to other beneficiaries the equitable tracing claim is still available, and it seems the mixed assets or mixed fund will be held on constructive trust for the beneficiary claimants in the appropriate proportionate shares just as if the beneficiaries were entitled by virtue of their contributions to an interest under a resulting trust. Exceptionally, if A wrongfully mixed beneficiaries' money with his own, and the property purchased with the mixed moneys had depreciated in value, A will hold the property subject to an equitable charge for all the money contributed by the beneficiaries: where the amount of this equitable charge exceeds the value of the property this will mean he holds the property as bare trustee for the beneficiaries.

### Section 1. The Fiduciary as Constructive Trustee of Profits

A well-established category of constructive trust arises to flesh out the obligations of a trustee or of a fiduciary. "Fiduciary" is an accordion term[27]: "the category of cases in which fiduciary obligations and duties arise from the circumstances of the case and the relationship of the parties is no more closed than the categories of negligence at common law."[28] In essence, a person will be a fiduciary in his relationship with another when and insofar as that other is entitled to expect that he will act in that other's interest (or in their joint interest)[29] so, for example, company directors,[30] partners,[31] agents,[32] discretionary portfolio managers[33] can be fiduciaries.

It is clear that a trustee is trustee not just of the original trust property and the income therefrom but also of the exchange products thereof, *i.e.* investments made from the proceeds of sale of trust property and bonus issues of shares and rights issues of shares purchased with trust money. It is probably better to regard the situation as one where the trustee is express trustee of a fund comprising whatever happens from time to time to be exchange products of the original trust property. However, the trustee can appropriately be regarded as a constructive trustee of rights issue shares purchased for himself with his own money, or of a lease renewed in favour of himself and not the trust,[34] or of the freehold reversion to a trust's lease,[35] or of shares in his own company formed

---

[26] (1890) 45 Ch.D. 1, discussed *supra*, p. 442.
[27] See P. D. Finn, "The Fiduciary Principle" in *Equity, Trusts & Fiduciary Relationships* (ed. T. G. Youdan), p. 1.
[28] *Laskin* v. *Bache* (1971) 23 D.L.R. (3d) 385, 392.
[29] See n. 27, *supra*.
[30] *Regal Hastings Ltd.* v. *Gulliver* [1967] 2 A.C. 134.
[31] *Chan* v. *Zacharia* (1984) 154 C.L.R. 178 *infra*, p. 452.
[32] *English* v. *Dedham Vale Properties Ltd.* [1978] 1 All E.R. 382.
[33] *Hewson* v. *Stock Exchange* [1968] 2 N.S.W.R. 245, 231, *Glennie* v. *McDougall* [1935] S.C.R. 257, 276.
[34] *Keech* v. *Sandford* (1726) 2 Eq.Cas.Abr. 741, *infra*, p. 450.
[35] *Protheroe* v. *Protheroe* [1968] 1 W.L.R. 519.

specially to develop trust land sold by him to the company at an undervalue,[36] or of property bought in his own name with a cheque drawn on his private account containing trust money wrongfully mixed with his own money.[37] Similarly, an agent engaged to buy property for his principal will hold it on constructive trust for his principal if he buys it for himself[38] and a director diverting to himself a profitable contract which he should have taken up on behalf of the company will hold it on constructive trust for the company.[39]

### Strict liability and its justification

A proprietary constructive trust or a personal liability to account as a constructive trustee arises as a sanction for the fundamental, strict rule that a fiduciary must not place himself where his fiduciary duty does, or may sensibly, conflict with his private interest[40]—unless duly authorised by his principal or the court. It is immaterial that the fiduciary, T, acted honestly and in his principal's best interest, that the principal could not otherwise have obtained the profit and that the profit was obtained through use of T's own assets and by virtue of T's skills,—though T will have a lien for his expenditure and, in exceptional circumstances, may obtain an allowance for his skills.[41] The rule is very strict in order to maintain confidence in the trust or other fiduciary relationship by deterring any slipping from the high standards required of trustees and other fiduciaries: just as a dishonest loss-causing defendant in the same situation would be liable for losses, so an honest profit-making defendant should be liable for profits. Equity has a strict prophylactic approach to prevent a wrong which may enrich the defendant or harm the plaintiff. To relax standards for situations where the defendant allegedly acted "properly" cannot be allowed because most of the relevant evidence will be peculiarly within the defendant's knowledge and control, so making it very difficult for the disadvantaged plaintiff beneficiaries to know whether or not they have a case for saying the defendant acted "improperly." Thus, it is *per se* improper for a defendant fiduciary to enter into transactions where there is a conflict or sensible possibility of a conflict between his fiduciary duty and his self-interest. It is up to the defendant to avoid any problems by obtaining the informed consent of his principal(s) or of the court.

He "must account . . . for any benefit or gain which has been obtained or received in circumstances where a conflict or significant possibility of conflict existed between his fiduciary duty and his

---

[36] cf. *Aberdeen Railway Co.* v. *Blaikie Bros.* (1854) 1 Macq. 461.
[37] cf. *Re Tilley's W.T.* [1967] Ch. 1179.
[38] *Longfield Parish Council* v. *Robson* (1913) 29 T.L.R. 357, *Lees* v. *Nuttall* (1834) 2 My. & K. 819.
[39] *Cook* v. *Deeks* [1916] 1 A.C. 554, *Industrial Developments Consultants Ltd.* v. *Cooley* [1972] 1 W.L.R. 443.
[40] *Phipps* v. *Boardman* [1967] 2 A.C. 46, 123, *N.Z. Netherlands Society Inc.* v. *Kuys* [1973] 1 W.L.R. 1126, 1129. See pp. 589–593 especially pp. 592–593 for defences, *infra*.
[41] *Phipps* v. *Boardman* [1967] 2 A.C. 46.

personal interest in the pursuit or possible receipt of such a benefit or gain."[42] He also "must account . . . for any benefit or gain which was obtained or received by use or by reason of his fiduciary position or of opportunity or knowledge resulting from it" where he is "actually misusing his position for his personal advantage" rather than for the advantage of his principal(s). However, if information is acquired by a fiduciary in the course of his duties and it is not classified as confidential information he is free to use the information for the benefit of himself or of another trust of which he is trustee if there is no reasonably foreseeable possibility of his needing to use that information for his original principal(s).[43] Where information acquired by a fiduciary or his "tippee" (to whom he passes the information) is confidential so that its disclosure could be prevented by a court injunction then, although such information has insufficient "property" nature for the law of theft, it may have sufficient "property" nature for profits made by use of such information to be held on constructive trust.[44]

### *Proprietary and/or personal liability*

If there is a proprietary liability because T holds specific property as constructive trustee then there is a co-extensive personal liability to account and if T is wealthy enough the plaintiffs will usually be happy enough to rely on T's personal liability and take the cash profits from him (rather than take the property upon paying T sufficient for his lien on the property for its cost to him). Thus, a House of Lords case like *Regal Hastings Ltd.* v. *Gulliver*[45] was pleaded only as a personal claim to account and in *Phipps* v. *Boardman*[46] counsel and judges concentrated upon making the wealthy Boardman personally liable to account. In *Phipps* v. *Boardman, infra,* p. 457 the plaintiff with a five-eighteenths interest under a trust claimed (i) a declaration that the defendants held five-eighteenths of the shareholding obtained by them through using information acquired by them when representing the trust as constructive trustees for him, (ii) an account of the profits made by the defendants, and (iii) an order that they should transfer to him the shares held by them as constructive trustees and should pay him five-eighteenths of profits found to be due upon taking the account. Wilberforce J. gave the plaintiff the relief requested under (i) and (ii) but adjourned (iii) having ordered an inquiry as to a liberal allowance for the defendant's work. Presumably, this was to allow the taking of accounts of profits made on sale of some of the shares and the inquiry as to the proper payment to be allowed to the defendants

---

[42] *Chan* v. *Zachariah* (1984) 154 C.L.R. 178, 199 where all the citations in this para. are to be found.
[43] *Phipps* v. *Boardman* [1967] 2 A.C. 46, 130; see p. 595, *infra.*
[44] *Nanus Asia Co. Inc.* v. *Standard Chartered Bank* [1990] Hong Kong L.R. 396 and see D. J. Hayton (1990) 11 Co. Law 97.
[45] [1967] 2 A.C. 134 *infra*, p. 457.
[46] [1967] 2 A.C. 46.

for their skilful efforts, whereupon the balance would be due to the plaintiff, who could then consider whether to call for the remaining shares subject to reimbursing the defendants for their costs in purchasing the shares. No doubt, at the end of the day the plaintiff preferred to receive all cash rather than cash plus shares, and the defendants agreed to that.

The Court of Appeal and the House of Lords, due to counsels' concentration on personal accountability, held that the defendants were constructive trustees who were liable to account for their profits but they confirmed Wilberforce J.'s order which included a proprietary declaration of constructive trust.[47]

Where the gain emanates from property entrusted to the fiduciary it is clear that the gain should be held on a proprietary constructive trust, but three[48] of the five Law Lords held that the defendants' information obtained *qua fiduciaries* was not trust property so that the shares purchased as a result of using such information did not thereby constructively become trust property. Two Law Lords[49] thought that there was no sensible possibility of conflict of duty and interest. However, the majority[50] thought that there was: the defendant as solicitor to the trustees was not in a position to give disinterested impartial advice at the stage when he was almost about to make large profits for himself and yet when he ought to have been advising the trustees to obtain wider investment powers from the court so as to enable the trust (and not himself) to make large profits. Thus, the defendants had to account for their profits on the shares because they had acquired the knowledge and the opportunity to purchase the shares while purporting to represent the trust.

The Lords did not openly consider the question of a proprietary constructive trust but the court order accepts the existence of such a trust, so that the use of position as opposed to the use of trust property seems capable of generating a proprietary constructive trust of the profit made in breach of the duty to avoid conflicts of interest. However, in *Lister* v. *Stubbs* discussed p. 442, *supra* the employee used his position to take advantage of the opportunity to take a bribe or secret commission and yet no proprietary constructive trust arose: only a personal liability to account for the amount of the bribe. Thus, a wicked fiduciary who takes a bribe of £100,000 and invests it in a flat now worth £200,000 can only be sued for £100,000 and interest which will be worthless if he is deeply insolvent. On the other hand, an honest fiduciary who makes a profit of £100,000 for himself which he invests in a flat now worth £200,000 must hand over that flat or £200,000 to the beneficiaries whose claim to such has priority if he is insolvent.

---

[47] See [1964] 2 All E.R. 187, 208; [1965] Ch. 992, 1006, 1021; (1967) 2 A.C. 46, 99, 112.
[48] Lords Cohen and Upjohn and Viscount Dilhorne.
[49] Viscount Dilhorne and Lord Upjohn.
[50] Lords Hodson, Guest and Cohen; see p. 459, *infra*.

It seems easier to support a proprietary constructive trust in *Lister* than in *Boardman*. In a bribe case is there not an incontrovertible assumption that the victim has lost property of a value at least equal to the bribe so that the bribe may justifiably be regarded as representing the victim's property. As between the victim and the fiduciary surely the victim has a better claim not only to the bribe but to the fruits thereof: the fiduciary would certainly be unjustly enriched if allowed to retain the bribe and its fruits. If he himself should not benefit from his dishonest wrongdoing why should his creditors be better off and receive a windfall if he is insolvent? According to *Eden* v. *Ridsdales Railway Lamp Co.*,[51] not cited in *Lister* v. *Stubbs*, if the bribe had been the flat and not £100,000 the victim could have recovered the flat, so there would be a proprietary constructive trust of the flat: this should be extended to money bribes.

In *Boardman* the case for a proprietary constructive trust for profits gained by use of position seems weaker. The profit, literally speaking, has not been made at the expense of the beneficiaries, though it has been made at the expense of the fiduciary not being able to give disinterested advice to the beneficiaries and so at the risk of harming the beneficiaries' interests. Does the fiduciary's wrongful breach of his duty to avoid a conflict not prevent him from denying that he acted at the beneficiaries' expense? Equity's strict prophylactic approach to prevent a wrong which may enrich the defendant or harm the plaintiff beneficiaries could well justify a proprietary constructive trust of the defendant's enrichment gained by his wrongdoing irrespective of any proof of loss by the plaintiffs. The defendant's trustee in bankruptcy should be no better off than the defendant.[52]

## KEECH v. SANDFORD[53]

Lord Chancellor (1726) 2 Eq.Cas.Abr. 741; Sel.Cas.Ch. 61

A person being possessed of a lease of the profits of a market devised his estate to a trustee in trust for his infant. Before the expiration of the term the trustee applied to the lessor for a renewal, for the benefit of the infant, which he refused, since the lease being only of the profits of a market, there could be no distress, and its enforcement must rest in covenant, by which the infant could not be bound.

The infant sought to have the lease assigned to him, and for an account of the profits, on the principle that wherever a lease is renewed by a trustee or executor it shall be for the benefit of the *cestui que use*, which principle was agreed on the other side, though endeavoured to be differenced on account of the express proof of refusal to renew to the infant.

---

[51] (1889) 23 Q.B.D. 368 *supra,* p. 444 n. 18.
[52] Further see G. Elias, *Explaining Constructive Trusts* (O.U.P. 1990), p. 77, P. Birks, *Introduction to the Law of Restitution* (O.U.P. 1985), pp. 341, 388, G. H. Jones (1968) 84 L.Q.R. 472.
[53] The rule in *Keech* v. *Sandford* is derived from the principle that a trustee must not put himself in a position where his interest conflicts with his duty: in case of conflict, duty prevails over interest. Several instances of this principle occur in the administration of express trusts: *infra*, pp. 584–610. See Hart, "The Development of the Rule in *Keech* v. *Sandford*" (1905) 21 L.Q.R. 258; Cretney (1969) 33 Conv.(N.S.) 161.

LORD KING L.C.: "I must consider this as a trust for the infant, for I very well see, if a trustee, on the refusal to renew, might have a lease to himself, few trust estates would be renewed to *cestui que use*. Though I do not say there is fraud in this case, yet he should rather have let it run out than to have had the lease to himself. This may seem hard, that the trustee is the only person of all mankind who might not have the lease; but it is very proper that the rule should be strictly pursued, and not in the least relaxed; for it is very obvious what would be the consequences of letting trustees have the lease on refusal to renew to *cestui que use*."

So decreed, that the lease should be assigned to the infant, and that the trustee should be indemnified from any covenants comprised in the lease, and an account of the profits made since the renewal.[54]

## Note

The rule applies whether the trustee obtains a renewal by virtue of a provision in the lease to that effect or whether he obtains it by virtue of the advantage which his position as sitting tenant gives him.[55] The principle applies not only to trustees and tenants for life,[56] but also to other fiduciaries such as mortgagees,[57] directors[58] and partners.[59] But unlike trustees and tenants for life the latter group of persons are not irrebuttably precluded from taking the renewal of a lease. In *Re Biss*,[60] a lease formed part of the personalty of an intestate, and after the lessor had refused to renew to the administratrix, one of her sons (helping her run the deceased's business at the premises) obtained a renewal for himself. It was held, however, to be unimpeachable, since he could show affirmatively that he acted bona fide and did not take advantage of the other persons interested. Romer L.J. said,[61] "where the person renewing the lease does not clearly occupy a fiduciary position" he "is only held to be a constructive trustee of the renewed lease if, in respect of the old lease, he occupied some special position and owed, by virtue of that position, a duty towards the other persons interested."

In *Protheroe* v. *Protheroe*[62] the Court of Appeal in a one-page extempore judgment of Lord Denning held that under the *Keech* v. *Sandford* principle there was "a long-established rule of equity" that a trustee purchasing the reversion upon a lease held by him *automatically* held the reversion upon the same trusts as the lease. *Sed quaere* as till then such constructive trusts of the reversion were only

---

[54] For a modern instance, see *Re Jarvis* [1958] 1 W.L.R. 815.
[55] *Re Knowles' Will Trusts* [1948] 1 All E.R. 866.
[56] *James* v. *Dean* (1808) 15 Ves. 236; *Lloyd-Jones* v. *Clark-Lloyd* [1919] 1 Ch. 424; ss.16, 107 of the Settled Land Act 1925.
[57] *Rushworth's Case* (1676) Freem.Ch. 13; *Leigh* v. *Burnett* (1885) 29 Ch.D. 231.
[58] *G.E. Smith Ltd.* v. *Smith* [1952] N.Z.L.R. 470; *Crittenden & Cowler Co.* v. *Cowler*, 72 New York State 701 (1901).
[59] *Featherstonhaugh* v. *Fenwick* (1810) 17 Ves. 298; *cf. Piddock* v. *Burt* [1894] 1 Ch. 343.
[60] [1903] 2 Ch. 40.
[61] *Ibid.* 61. See *Chan* v. *Zacharia infra*, p. 452.
[62] [1968] 1 W.L.R. 519; followed in *Thompson's Trustee* v. *Heaton* [1974] 1 W.L.R. 605. See (1968) 84 L.Q.R. 309; (1974) 38 Conv.(N.S.) 288; *Metlej* v. *Cavanagh* [1981] 2 N.S.W.L.R. 339, 348. *Brenner* v. *Rose* [1973] 1 W.L.R. 443 seems erroneous.

imposed where the lease was renewable by custom or contract (the purchase thus cutting off the right of renewal) or where the trustee obtained the reversion by virtue of his position *qua* leaseholder (*e.g.* a landlord offering enfranchisement to all his leaseholders).[63] The reason for the distinction is that "whereas in the case of a renewal the trustee is in effect buying a part of the trust property, in the case of a reversion this is not so; it is a separate item altogether."[64] Of course, purchasers of a reversion will fall foul of the strict principles illustrated by *Boardman* v. *Phipps, infra,* especially since the trustee would personally be the landlord of the trust tenancy.

## CHAN v. ZACHARIA

High Court of Australia (1984) 154 C.L.R. 178 (1984) 53 A.L.R. 417

DEANE J.: "There is a wide variety of formulations, of the general principle of equity requiring a person in a fiduciary relationship to account for personal benefit or gain. The doctrine is often expressed in the form that a person 'is not allowed to put himself in a position where his interest and duty conflict' (*Bray* v. *Ford*[65]) or 'may conflict' (*Phipps* v. *Boardman*[66]) or that a person is 'not to allow a conflict to arise between duty and interest': *New Zealand Netherlands Society 'Oranje' Inc.* v. *Kuys.*[67] As Sir Frederick Jordan pointed out, however (see *Chapters on Equity,* (6th ed., Stephen) (1947), p. 115, reproduced in Jordan, *Select Legal Papers* (1983), p. 115), this, read literally, represents 'rather a counsel of prudence than a rule of equity': indeed, even as an unqualified counsel of prudence, it may, in some circumstances, be inappropriate: see *e.g. Hordern* v. *Hordern*[68]; *Smith* v. *Cock.*[69] The equitable principle governing the liability to account is concerned not so much with the mere existence of a conflict between personal interest and fiduciary duty as with the pursuit of personal interest by, for example, actually entering into a transaction or engagement 'in which he has, or can have, a personal interest conflicting . . . with the interests of those whom he is bound to protect' (*per* Lord Cranworth L.C., *Aberdeen Railway Co.* v. *Blaikie Brothers*[70]) or the actual receipt of personal benefit or gain in circumstances where such conflict exists or has existed.

"The variations between more precise formulations of the principle governing the liability to account are largely the result of the fact that what is conveniently regarded as the one 'fundamental rule' embodies two themes. The first is that which appropriates for the benefit of the person to whom the fiduciary duty is owed any benefit or gain obtained or received by the fiduciary in circumstances where there existed a conflict of personal interest and

---

[63] *Bevan* v. *Webb* [1905] 1 Ch. 620; *Longton* v. *Wilsby* (1887) 76 L.T. 770; *Randall* v. *Russell* (1817) 3 Mer. 190; *Phillips* v. *Phillips* (1884) 29 Ch.D. 673; *Phipps* v. *Boardman* [1964] 1 W.L.R. 993, 1009; *Brenner* v. *Rose* [1973] 1 W.L.R. 443, 448, but *cf. Thompson's Trustee* v. *Heaton* [1974] 1 W.L.R. 605.

[64] *Phipps* v. *Boardman* (*ibid.*); *cf.* different treatment of renewals and reversions for purposes of rule against remoteness: *Woodall* v. *Clifton* [1905] 2 Ch. 257.

[65] [1896] A.C. 44, 51.

[66] [1967] 2 A.C. 46, 123.

[67] [1973] 1 W.L.R. 1126, 1129.

[68] [1910] A.C. 465, 475.

[69] (1911) 12 C.L.R. 30, 36, 37.

[70] (1854) 1 Macq. 461.

fiduciary duty or a significant possibility of such conflict: the objective is to preclude the fiduciary from being swayed by considerations of personal interest. The second is that which requires the fiduciary to account for any benefit or gain obtained or received by reason of or by use of his fiduciary position or of opportunity or knowledge resulting from it: the objective is to preclude the fiduciary from actually misusing his position for his personal advantage. Notwithstanding authoritative statements to the effect that the 'use of fiduciary position' doctrine is but an illustration or part of a wider 'conflict of interest and duty' doctrine (see, *e.g. Phipps* v. *Boardman*[71]; *N.Z. Netherlands Society 'Oranje' Inc.* v. *Kuys*,[72] the two themes, while overlapping, are distinct. Neither theme fully comprehends the other and a formulation of the principle by reference to one only of them will be incomplete. Stated comprehensively in terms of the liability to account, the principle of equity is that a person who is under a fiduciary obligation must account to the person to whom the obligation is owed for any benefit or gain (i) which has been obtained or received in circumstances where a conflict or significant possibility of conflict existed between his fiduciary duty and his personal interest in the pursuit or possible receipt of such a benefit or gain, or (ii) which was obtained or received by use or by reason of his fiduciary position or of opportunity or knowledge resulting from it. Any such benefit or gain is held by the fiduciary as constructive trustee: see *Keith Henry & Co. Pty. Ltd.* v. *Stuart Walker & Co. Pty. Ltd.*[73] That constructive trust arises from the fact that a personal benefit or gain has been so obtained or received and it is immaterial that there was no absence of good faith or damage to the person to whom the fiduciary obligation was owed. In some, perhaps most, cases, the constructive trust will be consequent upon an actual breach of fiduciary duty: *e.g.* an active pursuit of personal interest in disregard of fiduciary duty or a misuse of fiduciary power for personal gain. In other cases, however, there may be no breach of fiduciary duty unless and until there is an actual failure by the fiduciary to account for the relevant benefit or gain: *e.g.* the receipt of an unsolicited personal payment from a third party as a consequence of what was an honest and conscientious performance of a fiduciary duty. The principle governing the liability to account for a benefit or gain as a constructive trustee is applicable to fiduciaries generally including partners and former partners in relation to their dealings with partnership property and the benefits and opportunities associated therewith or arising therefrom: see *Birtchnell* v. *Equity Trustees*[74]; *Consul Development Pty. Ltd.* v. *D.P.C. Estates Pty. Ltd.*[75]

"In *Keech* v. *Sandford*[76] Lord King L.C. held that it was a 'rule' that 'should be strictly pursued, and not in the least relaxed,' that a trustee of a tenancy who obtains a renewal of the lease for himself holds the interest in the renewed lease as part of the trust estate. Lord King's admonition that the rule should be not in the least relaxed has been largely obeyed in that, in its application to the case of the ordinary trustee, the 'rule' has been accepted as being applicable regardless of whether the original lease was renewable by right or custom or whether the lessor was willing to grant a new lease for the benefit of the trust

---

71 [1967] 2 A.C. 46, 123.
72 [1973] 1 W.L.R. 1126, 1129.
73 (1958) 100 C.L.R. 342 at 350.
74 (1929) 42 C.L.R. 384, 395–397, 408–409.
75 (1975) 132 C.L.R. 373, 394.
76 (1726) Sel.Cas.t.King 61, p. 62.

or whether there would, in the circumstances, be nothing inequitable in the trustee obtaining a renewal of the lease for his own benefit. The rule has been extended, either in its strict or in a modified form, to persons under obligations arising from certain other fiduciary relationships (*e.g.* executor or agent) and to certain other relationships which are not fiduciary but are said to be special (*e.g.* tenants for life and remaindermen: mortgagee and mortgagor). In particular, it has been applied to a member of a partnership in respect of the renewal of a lease which was held on behalf of the partnership: see *Featherstonhaugh* v. *Fenwick*[77]; *Clegg* v. *Edmondson*.[78] It has, in my view correctly, been accepted as being so applicable notwithstanding that the partnership has been dissolved: see *Thompson's Trustee* v. *Heaton*,[79] *Lindley on Partnership* (144th ed., 1979), p. 430, and *Snell's Principles of Equity* (28th ed., 1982), p. 245.

"One can point to impressive support both for the view that the rule in *Keech* v. *Sandford* is an independent doctrine of equity with no more than an 'illusory' link with the general equitable principle governing the liability of a fiduciary to account for personal benefit or gain (see the discussion of both the rule and the general equitable principle in Finn, *Fiduciary Obligations* (1977), Chs. 21 and 23) and for the contrary view that that rule is no more than a manifestation of that general principle: see, *e.g.*, *per* Dixon C.J., McTiernan and Fullagar JJ., *Keith Henry & Co. Pty. Ltd.* v. *Stuart Walker & Co. Pty. Ltd.*[80] and *per* Lord Russell of Killowen, *Regal (Hastings) Ltd.* v. *Gulliver*.[81] It would plainly be futile to attempt to reconcile all that has been said in the cases as to the nature and scope of the rule in *Keech* v. *Sandford*. It is preferable to acknowledge the existence of unresolved difficulties and differences about both the precise nature of the rule and its application to persons who are not trustees. Those difficulties and differences are, however, such as to encourage rather than preclude the search in this Court for unity of principle. With all respect to those who have expressed a contrary view, I consider that the rule should not be seen as either a completely independent principle of equity or as a mere manifestation of the general principle governing the liability of a beneficiary to account for personal benefit or gain. The case itself is an illustration of that general principle: indeed, it is one of the cases which established it. The 'rule' in *Keech* v. *Sandford* is, however, a rule concerned with the operation of presumptions in the application of that general principle to particular types of property. 'In the case both of leases renewable by right or custom and of leases not so renewable the renewal is prima facie considered to have been obtained by virtue of the interest' under the prior lease: *per* Parker J., *Griffith* v. *Owen*.[82]

"In its primary application to the renewal of a lease by a trustee, the rule in *Keech* v. *Sandford*[83] 'depends partly on the nature of leasehold property and partly on' the position of special opportunity which a trustee occupies: see *per* Parker J., *Griffith* v. *Owen*,[84] and *per* Collins M.R., *In re Biss*.[85] The effect of

---

[77] (1810) 17 Ves.Jr. 298.
[78] (1857) 8 De G.M. & G. 787, 807.
[79] [1974] 1 W.L.R. 605.
[80] (1958) 100 C.L.R. 342, 350.
[81] [1967] 2 A.C. 134(n), 149–150.
[82] [1907] 1 Ch. 195, 204.
[83] (1726) Sel.Cas.t.King 61.
[84] [1907] 1 Ch. 195, 203.
[85] [1903] 2 Ch. 40, 57.

the rule in such a case is that there is an irrebuttable presumption (a presumption of law: *per* Collins M.R., *In re Biss*[86] that the lease was obtained by use of the position of advantage which the trustee enjoyed as the tenant at law, that is to say, by the use by the trustee of his fiduciary position, with the result that he holds the new lease as constructive trustee under the general principle governing the liability of a fiduciary to account for a personal benefit or gain. The presumption which the rule creates in its application to a fiduciary other than a trustee is irrebuttable or rebuttable according to the nature of the powers and obligations of the fiduciary with respect to the leasehold property and the extent to which the interposition of the fiduciary represents, as it were, a barrier between the person to whom the fiduciary duty is owed and the lessor: *cf. per* Collins M.R., *In re Biss*. In the extension, by analogy, of the rule in *Keech* v. *Sandford* to certain 'special' non-fiduciary relationships under which a person is under an obligation to advance or preserve the interests of another, the presumption would appear, at least ordinarily, to be a rebuttable one: see, *per* Romer L.J., *In re Biss*,[87] *cf.* Collins M.R.[88]

"In *In re Biss*, Collins M.R.[89] included partners in 'the class of cases' in which the relevant presumption is 'a rebuttable presumption of fact.' It has been suggested (see, *e.g.* S. Cretney, 'The Rationale of Keech v. Sandford' *The Conveyancer and Property Lawyer*, Vol. 33 (N.S.) (1969), 161, at pp. 175–176) that his comments to that effect were the result of an erroneous view that the relationship between partners is not a fiduciary one. No real basis for that suggestion is, however, to be found in the Master of the Rolls' judgment since he neither expressed the view that the partnership relationship was not fiduciary nor propounded the fiduciary nature of a relationship as determinative of whether the presumption was irrebuttable. The closest he came to seeking to identify a criterion for determining whether the presumption was irrebuttable was his reference[90] to 'possession' with 'the opportunity of renewal . . . acting upon the goodwill that accompanies it.' On the other hand, Romer L.J.[91] remarked that the relevant presumption was irrebuttable if the 'person obtaining the renewal . . . occupies a fiduciary position' and indicated his acceptance of the observation of Turner L.J. in *Clegg* v. *Edmondson*[92] that he was 'not prepared to say that in no case can a partner during the continuance of the partnership contract for a new lease to be granted to himself of property which is in lease to the partnership without the new lease being held to be subject to trusts for the benefit of the partnership.' It would seem to follow that Romer L.J. did not see the partnership relationship as a fiduciary one. Such a conclusion is difficult to reconcile, however, with his Lordship's actual references to the nature of the partnership relationship: 'in ordinary cases concerning the carrying on of the partnership business he is an agent for the partners'; 'he clearly owes a duty to his co-partners not to acquire any special advantage over them by reason of his position' and 'partners, between whom the utmost good faith is required by a Court of Equity.'[93] It may be that the solution is to be found in the difficulty which occasionally exists in determining

---

[86] [1903] 2 Ch. 40, 55.
[87] [1903] 2 Ch. 40, 61–67.
[88] [1903] 2 Ch. 40, 56–57.
[89] [1903] 2 Ch. 40, 56.
[90] [1903] 2 Ch. 40, 57.
[91] [1903] 2 Ch. 40, 60.
[92] (1857) 8 De G.M. & G. 787, 807.
[93] [1903] 2 Ch. 40, 61, 62.

whether the fiduciary obligations of a partner extend to particular property or to what is not obviously a partnership endeavour and in Romer L.J.'s distinction[94] between a case where it could be said that the person renewing the lease 'clearly occupied a fiduciary position *in the matter*' (emphasis added) and the case where it could not. Notwithstanding the difficulties and differences in and between the judgments of Collins M.R. and Romer L.J. in *In re Biss*, there are clear statements in both judgments (with each of which Cozens Hardy L.J. agreed) which support the conclusion that the presumption that a partner holds a renewed lease as constructive trustee—or, as I would enunciate the primary rule in *Keech* v. *Sandford*[95] the presumption that the renewed lease was obtained by use of the partner's fiduciary position—is a rebuttable one. Those statements are consistent with overall authority and should be accepted as correct and applicable both to the case where the renewed lease is obtained by a partner in a subsisting partnership and the case where the renewed lease is obtained by a member of a partnership which has been dissolved but whose assets are in the course of realization: see *Clegg* v. *Fishwick*[96] where Lord Cottenham L.C. held that the legal representative of a deceased partner had a 'prima facie case' to assert an interest in a renewal of a lease obtained by the surviving partners after the partnership had been dissolved by the death; *Featherstonhaugh* v. *Fenwick*[97]; *Clegg* v. *Edmondson*; *Metlej* v. *Kavanagh*[98]; but cf. *Thompson's Trustee* v. *Heaton*.[99]

"Prima facie, the rule in *Keech* v. *Sandford* has a dual operation in the present case: there is an irrebuttable presumption that any rights in respect of a new lease of the Mansfield Park premises were obtained by Dr. Chan by use of his position as a trustee of the previous tenancy and there is a rebuttable presumption of fact that any such rights were obtained by use of his position as a partner in the dissolved partnership whose assets were under receivership and in the course of realization. There is no logical inconsistency between the two presumptions in that a single benefit may well be obtained by the use of two distinct fiduciary positions. Nor is there any valid reason to preclude the dual operation of the rule to produce the two distinct presumptions. There is, however, no advantage to be gained in the present case from reliance on both presumptions or on one rather than the other since the persons to whom the relevant obligations under each fiduciary relationship were ultimately owed are the same and there is no possible basis in the facts for a finding that the presumption that any rights in respect of a new lease of the premises were obtained by Dr. Chan by use of his position as a former partner has been rebutted. Whatever presumption is relied upon, the ultimate result will be the same. Indeed, the facts of the present case are such as to make it strictly unnecessary to rely on either presumption: it is apparent that, as a matter of fact, Dr. Chan was introduced to the premises through the partnership and that he obtained any rights in respect of a new lease of the premises through the use—or misuse—of his position as a trustee of the former tenancy and as a former partner. It follows that Dr. Chan holds and will hold any rights to or under a new lease of the premises as a constructive trustee unless there be some reason for excluding the ordinary application of the general principle.

---

[94] [1903] 2 Ch. 40, 61.
[95] (1726) Sel.Cas.t.King 61.
[96] (1849) 1 Mac. & G. 294, 298–299.
[97] (1810) 17 Ves.Jr. 298.
[98] [1981] 2 N.S.W.L.R. 339, 343–345.
[99] [1974] 1 W.L.R. 605, 612–613.

"Many of the statements of the general principle requiring a fiduciary to account for a personal benefit or gain are framed in absolute terms— 'inflexible,' 'inexorably,' 'however honest and well-intentioned,' 'universal application'—which sound somewhat strangely in the ears of the student of equity and which are to be explained by judicial acceptance of the inability of the courts, 'in much the greater number of cases,' to ascertain the precise effect which the existence of a conflict with personal interest has had upon the performance of fiduciary duty: see, *per* Lord Eldon, *Ex parte James*[1]; *per* Rich, Dixon and Evatt JJ., *Furs Ltd.* v. *Tomkies*.[2] The principle is not however completely unqualified. The liability to account as a constructive trustee will not arise where the person under the fiduciary duty has been duly authorized, either by the instrument or agreement creating the fiduciary duty or by the circumstances of his appointment or by the informed and effective assent of the person to whom the obligation is owed, to act in the manner in which he has acted. The right to require an account from the fiduciary may be lost by reason of the operation of other doctrines of equity such as laches and equitable estoppel: see, *e.g. Clegg* v. *Edmondson*.[3] It may still be arguable in this Court that, notwithstanding general statements and perhaps even decisions to the contrary in cases such as *Regal (Hastings) Ltd.* v. *Gulliver*[4] and *Phipps* v. *Boardman*,[5] the liability to account for a personal benefit or gain obtained or received by use or by reason of fiduciary position, opportunity or knowledge will not arise in circumstances where it would be unconscientious to assert it or in which, for example, there is no possible conflict between personal interest and fiduciary duty and it is plainly in the interests of the person to whom the fiduciary duty is owed that the fiduciary obtain for himself rights or benefits which he is absolutely precluded from seeking or obtaining for the person to whom the fiduciary duty is owed: *cf. Peso Silver Mines Ltd. (N.P.L.)* v. *Cropper*.[6] In that regard, one cannot but be conscious of the danger that the over-enthusiastic and unnecessary statement of broad general principles of equity in terms of inflexibility may destroy the vigour which it is intended to promote in that it will exclude the ordinary interplay of the doctrines of equity and the adjustment of general principles to particular facts and changing circumstances and convert equity into an instrument of hardship and injustice in individual cases: see *Canadian Aero Service Ltd.* v. *O'Malley*[7]; Cretney, *loc. cit.*, pp. 168 *et seq.*; Oakley, *Constructive Trusts* (1978), pp. 57 *et seq.* There is 'no better mode of undermining the sound doctrines of equity than to make unreasonable and inequitable applications of them': *per* Lord Selborne L.C., *Barnes* v. *Addy*."[8]

## BOARDMAN AND ANOTHER v. PHIPPS

House of Lords [1967] 2 A.C. 46; [1966] 3 All E.R. 721 (Lords Cohen, Hodson and Guest; Viscount Dilhorne and Lord Upjohn dissenting)

The respondent, Mr. J. A. Phipps, was one of the residuary legatees under the will of his father, Mr. C. W. Phipps, who died in 1944. The residuary

---

[1] (1803) 8 Ves.Jr. 337, 345.
[2] (1936) 54 C.L.R. 583.
[3] (1857) 8 De G.M. & G. at pp. 807–810 [44 E.R. at p. 602].
[4] [1967] 2 A.C. 134.
[5] [1967] 2 A.C. 46.
[6] (1966) 58 D.L.R. (2d) 1, 8.
[7] (1973) 40 D.L.R. (3d) 371.
[8] (1874) L.R. 9 Ch.App. 244, 251.

estate included 8,000 out of 30,000 issued shares in a private company, Lester & Harris Ltd. By his will the testator left an annuity to his widow and subject thereto five-eighteenths of his residuary estate to each of his three sons and three-eighteenths to his only daughter. At the end of 1955 the trustees of the will were the testator's widow (who was senile and took no part in the affairs of the trust), his only daughter, Mrs. Noble, and an accountant, Mr. W. Fox. The first appellant, Mr. T. G. Boardman, was at all material times solicitor to the trustees and also to the children of the testator (other than the respondent). The second appellant, Mr. T. E. Phipps, was the younger brother of the respondent and in the transactions which gave rise to this action he was associated with and represented by the first appellant, Mr. Boardman.

In 1956 Mr. Boardman and Mr. Fox decided that the recent accounts of Lester & Harris Ltd. were unsatisfactory and with a view to improving the position the appellants attended the annual general meeting of the company in December 1956 with proxies obtained from two of the trustees, Mrs. Noble and Mr. Fox. They were not satisfied with the answers given at the meeting regarding the state of the company's affairs.

Shortly after this meeting the appellants decided with the knowledge of Mrs. Noble and Mr. Fox to try to obtain control of Lester & Harris Ltd. by themselves making an offer for all the outstanding shares in that company other than the 8,000 held by the trustees. The trustees had no power to invest in the shares of the company without the sanction of the court and Mr. Fox said in evidence that he would not have considered seeking such sanction. The appellants originally offered £2 5s. per share, which they later increased to £3, but by April 1957 they had received acceptances only in respect of 2,925 shares and it was clear that as things then stood they would not go through with their offer. This ended the first phase in the negotiations which ultimately led to the acquisition by the appellants of virtually all the outstanding shares in Lester & Harris Ltd. During this phase the appellants attended the annual general meeting as proxies of the two trustees and obtained information from the company as to the prices at which shares had recently changed hands; but they made the offer to purchase on their own behalf.

The second phase lasted from April 1957 to August 1958. Throughout this period Mr. Boardman carried on negotiations with the chairman of Lester & Harris Ltd. with a view to reaching agreement on the division of the assets of that company between the Harris family and the directors on the one hand and the Phipps family on the other. During this phase Mr. Boardman obtained valuable information as to the value of the company's assets and throughout he purported to act on behalf of the trustees. These negotiations proved abortive.

The third phase began in August 1958 with the suggestion by Mr. Boardman that he and Mr. T. E. Phipps should acquire for themselves the outstanding shares in the company. The widow died in November 1958 and a conditional agreement for the sale of the shares was made on March 10, 1959. On May 26, 1959, the appellants gave notices making the agreements unconditional to buy 14,567 shares held by the chairman of the company and his associates at £4 10s. per share. This, in addition to the earlier agreements to purchase 2,925 shares at £3 each and the purchase of a further 4,494 shares at £4 10s. each, made the appellants holders in all of 21,986 shares.

Thereafter the business of the company was reorganised, part of its assets was sold off at considerable profit, and substantial sums of capital, amounting in the aggregate to £5 17s. 6d. per share, were returned to the shareholders, whose shares were still worth at least £2 each after the return of capital. The appellants acted honestly throughout.

The respondent, like the other members of the Phipps family, was asked by Mr. Boardman whether he objected to the acquisition of control of the company by the appellants for themselves; but Mr. Boardman did not give sufficient information as to the material facts to succeed in the defence of consent on the part of the respondent. At first the respondent expressed his satisfaction but later he became antagonistic and issued a writ claiming (i) that the appellants held five-eighteenths of the above-mentioned 21,986 shares as constructive trustees for him[9] and (ii) an account of the profits made by the appellants out of the said shares. Wilberforce J. granted this relief[10] and his decision was affirmed by the Court of Appeal.[11] The appellants appealed to the House of Lords.

LORD COHEN: " . . . As Wilberforce J. said,[12] the mere use of any knowledge or opportunity which comes to the trustee or agent in the course of his trusteeship or agency does not necessarily make him liable to account. In the present case had the company been a public company and had the appellants bought the shares on the market, they would not, I think have been accountable. The company, however, is a private company and not only the information but also the opportunity to purchase these shares came to them through the introduction which Mr. Fox gave them to the board of the company and, in the second phase, when the discussions related to the proposed split up of the company's undertaking, it was solely on behalf of the trustees that Mr. Boardman was purporting to negotiate with the board of the company. The question is this: when in the third phase the negotiations turned to the purchase of the shares at £4 10s. a share, were the appellant debarred by their fiduciary position from purchasing on their own behalf the 21,986 shares in the company without the informed consent of the trustees and the beneficiaries?

"Wilberforce J.[13] and, in the Court of Appeal,[14] both Lord Denning M.R. and Pearson L.J. based their decision in favour of the respondent on the decision of your Lordships' House in *Regal (Hastings) Ltd.* v. *Gulliver.*[15] I turn, therefore, to consider that case. Counsel for the respondent relied on a number of passages in the judgments of the learned Lords who heard the appeal, in particular on (i) a passage in the speech of Lord Russell of Killowen where he said[16]: 'The rule of equity which insists on those, who by use of a fiduciary position make a profit, being liable to account for that profit, in no way depends on fraud, or absence of bona fides; or upon such questions or considerations as whether the profit would or should otherwise have gone to the plaintiff, or whether the profiteer was under a duty to obtain the source of the profit for the plaintiff, or whether he took a risk or acted as he did for the benefit of the plaintiff, or whether the plaintiff has in fact been damaged or benefited by his action. The liability arises from the mere fact of a profit having, in the stated circumstances, been made'; (ii) a passage in the speech of Lord Wright where he says[17]: 'That question can be briefly stated to be whether

---

[9] The appellants would, of course, have a lien for their outlay on the purchase of the shares.
[10] [1964] 1 W.L.R. 993.
[11] [1965] Ch. 992 (Lord Denning M.R., Pearson and Russell L.JJ.).
[12] [1964] 1 W.L.R. 993, 1011.
[13] *Ibid.*
[14] [1965] Ch. 992.
[15] [1942] 1 All E.R. 378.
[16] *Ibid.* 386.
[17] *Ibid.* 392.

an agent, a director, a trustee or other person in an analogous fiduciary position, when a demand is made upon him by the person to whom he stands in the fiduciary relationship to account for profits acquired by him by reason of his fiduciary position, and by reason of the opportunity and the knowledge, or either, resulting from it, is entitled to defeat the claim upon any ground save that he made profits with the knowledge and assent of the other person. The most usual and typical case of this nature is that of principal and agent. The rule in such cases is compendiously expressed to be that an agent must account for net profits secretly (that is, without the knowledge of his principal) acquired by him in the course of his agency. The authorities show how manifold and various are the applications of the rule. It does not depend on fraud or corruption.' These paragraphs undoubtedly help the respondent but they must be considered in relation to the facts of that case. In that case the profit arose through the application by four of the directors of Regal for shares in a subsidiary company which it had been the original intention of the board should be subscribed for by Regal. Regal had not the requisite money available but there was no question of it being *ultra vires* Regal to subscribe for the shares. In the circumstances Lord Russell of Killowen said[18]: 'I have no hesitation in coming to the conclusion, upon the facts of this case, that these shares, when acquired by the directors, were acquired by reason, and only by reason, of the fact that they were directors of Regal, and in the course of their execution of that office.' He went on to consider whether the four directors were in a fiduciary relationship to Regal and concluded that they were. Accordingly, they were held accountable. Counsel for the appellants argued that the present case is distinguishable. He puts his argument thus. The question one asks is whether the information could have been used by the principal for the purpose for which it was used by his agents. If the answer to that question is no, the information was not used in the course of their duty as agents. In the present case the information could never have been used by the trustees for the purpose of purchasing shares in the company; therefore purchase of shares was outside the scope of the appellants' agency and they are not accountable.

"This is an attractive argument, but it does not seem to me to give due weight to the fact that the appellants obtained both the information which satisfied them that the purchase of the shares would be a good investment and the opportunity of acquiring them as a result of acting for certain purposes on behalf of the trustees. Information is, of course, not property in the strict sense of that word and, as I have already stated, it does not necessarily follow that, because an agent acquired information and opportunity while acting in a fiduciary capacity, he is accountable to his principals for any profit that comes his way as the result of the use he makes of that information and opportunity. His liability to account must depend on the facts of the case. In the present case much of the information came the appellants' way when Mr. Boardman was acting on behalf of the trustees on the instructions of Mr. Fox, and the opportunity of bidding for the shares came because he purported for all purposes except for making the bid to be acting on behalf of the owners of the 8,000 shares in the company. In these circumstances it seems to me that the principle of the *Regal* case applies and that the courts below came to the right conclusion.

---

[18] *Ibid.* 387.

"That is enough to dispose of the case but I would add that an agent is, in my opinion, liable to account for profits which he makes out of the trust property if there is a possibility of conflict between his interest and his duty to his principal. Mr. Boardman and Mr. Tom Phipps were not general agents of the trustees, but they were their agents for certain limited purposes. The information which they had obtained and the opportunity to purchase the 21,986 shares afforded them by their relations with the directors of the company—an opportunity they got as the result of their introduction to the directors by Mr. Fox—were not property in the strict sense but that information and that opportunity they owed to their representing themselves as agents for the holders of the 8,000 shares held by the trustees. In these circumstances they could not, I think, use that information and that opportunity to purchase the shares for themselves if there was any possibility that the trustees might wish to acquire them for the trust. Mr. Boardman was the solicitor whom the trustees were in the habit of consulting if they wanted legal advice. Granted that he would not be bound to advise on any point unless he were consulted, he would still be the person they would consult if they wanted advice. He would clearly have advised them that they had no power to invest in shares of the company without the sanction of the court. In the first phase he would also have had to advise on the evidence then available that the court would be unlikely to give such sanction: but the appellants learnt much more during the second phase. It may well be that even in third phase the answer of the court would have been the same but, in my opinion, Mr. Boardman would not have been able to give unprejudiced advice if he had been consulted by the trustees and was at the same time negotiating for the purchase of the shares on behalf of himself and Mr. Tom Phipps. In other words, there was, in my opinion, at the crucial date (March 1959) a possibility of a conflict between his interest and his duty.

"In making these observations I have referred to the fact that Mr. Boardman was the solicitor to the trust. Mr. Tom Phipps was only a beneficiary and was not as such debarred from bidding for the shares, but no attempt was made in the courts below to differentiate between them. Had such an attempt been made it would very likely have failed, as Mr. Tom Phipps left the negotiations largely to Mr. Boardman, and it might well be held that, if Mr. Boardman was disqualified from bidding, Mr. Tom Phipps could not be in a better position. Be that as it may, counsel for the appellants rightly did not seek at this stage to distinguish between the two. He did, it is true, say that Mr. Tom Phipps as a beneficiary would be entitled to any information that the trustees obtained. This may be so, but nonetheless I find myself unable to distinguish between the two appellants. They were, I think, in March 1959, in a fiduciary position *vis-à-vis* the trust. That fiduciary position was of such a nature that (as the trust fund was distributable) the appellants could not purchase the shares on their own behalf without the informed consent of the beneficiaries: it is now admitted that they did not obtain that consent. They are therefore, in my opinion, accountable to the respondent for his share of the net profits which they derived from the transaction.

"I desire to repeat that the integrity of the appellants is not in doubt. They acted with complete honesty throughout, and the respondent is a fortunate man in that the rigour of equity enables him to participate in the profits which have accrued as the result of the action taken by the appellants in March 1959 in purchasing the shares at their own risk. As the last paragraph of his judgment clearly shows, the trial judge evidently shared this view. He directed an inquiry as to what sum was proper to be allowed to the appellants or either of them in respect of their or his work and skill in obtaining the said shares and the profits in respect thereof. The trial judge concluded by expressing the opinion that payment should be on a liberal scale. With that observation I respectfully agree. . . . "

LORD HODSON: " . . . The proposition of law involved in this case is that no person standing in a fiduciary position, when a demand is made on him by the person to whom he stands in the fiduciary relationship to account for profits acquired by him by reason of his fiduciary position and by reason of the opportunity and the knowledge, or either, resulting from it, is entitled to defeat the claim on any ground save that he made profits with the knowledge and assent of the other person. . . .

" . . . it is said on behalf of the appellants that information as such is not necessarily property and it is only trust property which is relevant. I agree, but it is nothing to the point to say that in these times corporate trustees, *e.g.* the Public Trustee and others, necessarily acquire a mass of information in their capacity of trustees for a particular trust and cannot be held liable to account if knowledge so acquired enables them to operate to their own advantage, or to that of other trusts. Each case must depend on its own facts, and I dissent from the view that information is of its nature something which is not properly to be described as property. We are aware that what is called 'know-how' in the commercial sense is property which may be very valuable as an asset. I agree with the learned judge[19] and with the Court of Appeal[20] that the confidential information acquired in this case, which was capable of being and was turned to account, can be properly regarded as the property of the trust. It was obtained by Mr. Boardman by reason of the opportunity which he was given as solicitor acting for the trustees in the negotiations with the chairman of the company, as the correspondence demonstrates. The end result was that, out of the special position in which they were standing in the course of the negotiations, the appellants got the opportunity to make a profit and the knowledge that it was there to be made. . . .

"*Regal (Hastings) Ltd.* v. *Gulliver* differs from this case mainly in that the directors took up shares and made a profit thereby, it having been originally intended that the company should buy these shares. Here there was no such intention on the part of the trustees. There is no indication that they either had the money or would have been ready to apply to the court for sanction enabling them to do so. On the contrary, Mr. Fox, the active trustee and an accountant who concerned himself with the details of the trust property, was not prepared to agree to the trustees buying the shares and encouraged the appellants to make the purchase. This does not affect the position. As *Keech* v. *Sandford*[21] shows, the inability of the trust to purchase makes no difference to the liability of the appellants, if liability otherwise exists. The distinction on the facts as to intention to purchase shares between this case and *Regal (Hastings) Ltd.* v. *Gulliver* is not relevant. The company (Regal) had not the money to apply for the shares on which the profit was made. The directors took the opportunity which they had presented to them to buy the shares with their own money and were held accountable. Mr. Fox's refusal as one of the trustees to

---

19 [1964] 1 W.L.R. 993, 1008–1011.
20 [1965] Ch. 992.
21 (1726) Sel.Cas.Ch. 61; *supra*, p. 450.

take any part in the matter on behalf of the trust, so far as he was concerned, can make no difference. Nothing short of fully informed consent, which the learned judge found not to have been obtained, could enable the appellants in the position which they occupied, having taken the opportunity provided by that position, to make a profit for themselves. . . .

"The confidential information which the appellants obtained at a time when Mr. Boardman was admittedly holding himself out as solicitor for the trustees was obtained by him as representing the trustees, the holders of 8,000 shares of Lester & Harris Ltd. As Russell L.J. put it[22]: 'The substantial trust shareholding was an asset of which one aspect was its potential use as a means of acquiring knowledge of the company's affairs, or of negotiating allocations of the company's assets, or of inducing other shareholders to part with their shares.' That aspect was part of the trust assets. Whether this aspect is properly to be regarded as part of the trust assets is, in my judgment, immaterial. The appellants obtained knowledge by reason of their fiduciary position, and they cannot escape liability by saying that they were acting for themselves and not as agents of the trustees. Whether or not the trust, or the beneficiaries in their stead, could have taken advantage of the information is immaterial, as the authorities clearly show. No doubt it was but a remote possibility that Mr. Boardman would ever be asked by the trustees to advise on the desirability of an application to the court in order that the trustees might avail themselves of the information obtained. Nevertheless, whenever the possibility of conflict is present between personal interest and the fiduciary position the rule of equity must be applied. . . . "

Lord Guest: " . . . I take the view that from first to last Mr. Boardman was acting in a fiduciary capacity to the trustees. This fiduciary capacity arose in phase 1 and continued into phase 2, which glided into phase 3. In saying this I do not for one moment suggest that there was anything dishonest or underhand in what Mr. Boardman did. He has obtained a clean certificate below and I do not wish to sully it; but the law has a strict regard for principle in ensuring that a person in a fiduciary capacity is not allowed to benefit from any transactions into which he has entered with trust property. If Mr. Boardman was acting on behalf of the trust, then all the information that he obtained in phase 2 became trust property. The weapon which he used to obtain this information was the trust holding; and I see no reason why information and knowledge cannot be trust property. . . . "

Lord Upjohn (dissenting): " . . . [*Regal (Hastings) Ltd.* v. *Gulliver* and *Keech* v. *Sandford* bear no relation to this case.]

"This case, if I may emphasise it again, is one concerned not with trust property or with property of which the persons to whom the fiduciary duty was owed were contemplating a purchase but, in contrast to the facts in *Regal*, with property which was not trust property or property which was ever contemplated as the subject-matter of a possible purchase by the trust. . . .

"This question whether the appellants were accountable requires a closer analysis than it has received in the lower courts.

"This analysis requires detailed consideration:

1. The facts and circumstances must be carefully examined to see whether in fact a purported agent and even a confidential agent is in a fiduciary

---

    relationship to his principal. It does not necessarily follow that he is in such a position.

2. Once it is established that there is such a relationship, that relationship must be examined to see what duties are thereby imposed on the agent, to see what is the scope and ambit of the duties charged on him.

3. Having defined the scope of those duties one must see whether he has committed some breach thereof by placing himself within the scope and ambit of those duties in a position where his duty and interest may possibly conflict. It is only at this stage that any question of accountability arises.

4. Finally, having established accountability it only goes so far as to render the agent accountable for profits made within the scope and ambit of his duty.

"Before applying these principles to the facts, however, I shall refer to the judgment of Russell L.J. which proceeded on a rather different basis. He said:

    'The substantial trust shareholding was an asset of which one aspect was its potential use as a means of acquiring knowledge of the company's affairs, or of negotiating allocations of the company's assets, or of inducing other shareholders to part with their shares. That aspect was part of the trust assets.'

My Lords, I regard that proposition as untenable.

"In general, information is not property at all. It is normally open to all who have eyes to read and ears to hear. The true test is to determine in what circumstances the information has been acquired. If it has been acquired in such circumstances that it would be a breach of confidence to disclose it to another, then courts of equity will restrain the recipient from communicating it to another. In such cases such confidential information is often and for many years has been described as the property of the donor, the books of authority are full of such references; knowledge of secret processes, 'know-how,' confidential information as to the prospects of a company or of someone's intention or the expected results of some horse race based on stable or other confidential information. But in the end the real truth is that it is not property in any normal sense, but equity will restrain its transmission to another if in breach of some confidential relationship.

"With all respect to the views of Russell L.J., I protest at the idea that information acquired by trustees in the course of their duties as such is necessarily part of the assets of trust property which cannot be used by the trustees except for the benefit of the trust. Russell L.J. referred to the fact that two out of three of the trustees could have no authority to turn over this aspect of trust property to the appellants except for the benefit of the trust; this I do not understand, for if such information is trust property not all the trustees acting together could do it for they cannot give away trust property.

"We heard much argument on the impact of the fact that the testator's widow was at all material times incapable of acting in the trust owing to disability. Of course trustees must act all of them and unanimously in matters affecting trust affairs, but they never performed any relevant act on behalf of the trust at all; I quoted Mr. Fox's answer earlier for this reason. At no time after going to the meeting in December 1956, did Mr. Boardman or Tom rely on any express or implied authority or consent of the trustees in relation to trust property. They understood rightly that there was no question of the trustees acquiring any further trust property by purchasing further shares in the company, and it was only in the purchase of other shares that they were interested.

"There is, in my view, and I know of no authority to the contrary, no general rule that information learnt by a trustee during the course of his duties is property of the trust and cannot be used by him. If that were to be the rule it would put the Public Trustee and other corporate trustees out of business and make it difficult for private trustees to be trustees of more than one trust. This would be the greatest possible pity for corporate trustees and others may have much information which they may initially acquire in connection with some particular trust but without prejudice to that trust can make it readily available to other trusts to the great advantage of those other trusts.

"The real rule is, in my view, that knowledge learnt by a trustee in the course of his duties as such is not in the least property of the trust and in general may be used by him for his own benefit or for the benefit of other trusts unless it is confidential information which is given to him (i) in circumstances which, regardless of his position as a trustee, would make it a breach of confidence for him to communicate to anyone, for it has been given to him expressly or impliedly as confidential; or (ii) in a fiduciary capacity, and its use would place him in a position where his duty and his interest might possibly conflict. Let me give one or two simple examples. A, as trustee of two settlements X and Y holding shares in the same small company, learns facts as trustee of X about the company which are encouraging. In the absence of special circumstances (such, for example, that X wants to buy more shares) I can see nothing whatever which would make it improper for him to tell his co-trustees of Y who feel inclined to sell that he has information that this would be a bad thing to do. Another example: A as trustee of X learns facts that make him and his co-trustees want to sell. Clearly he could not communicate this knowledge to his co-trustees of Y until at all events the holdings of X have been sold for there would be a plain conflict, reflected in the prices that might or might possibly be obtained.

"My Lords, I do not think for one moment that Lord Brougham in *Hamilton* v. *Wright*,[23] quoted in the speech of my noble and learned friend, Lord Guest, was saying anything to the contrary; one has to look and see whether the knowledge acquired was capable of being used for his own benefit *to injure* the trust (my italics). That test can have no application to the present. There was no possibility of the information being used to injure the trust. The knowledge obtained was used not in connection with trust property but to enhance the value of the trust property by the purchase of other property in which the trustees were not interested. . . .

"As a result of the information the appellants acquired, admittedly by reason of the trust holding, they found it worthwhile to offer a good deal more for the shares than in phase 1 of chapter 2. I cannot see that in offering to purchase non-trust shares at a higher price they were in breach of any fiduciary relationship in using the information which they had acquired for this purpose. I cannot see that they have, from start to finish, in the circumstances of this case, placed themselves in a position where there was any possibility of a conflict between their duty and interest.

---

[23] (1842) 9 Cl. & Fin. 111.

"I have dealt with the problems that arise in this case at considerable length but it could, in my opinion, be dealt with quite shortly. In *Barnes* v. *Addy*,[24] Lord Selborne L.C., said:

> 'It is equally important to maintain the doctrine of trusts which is established in this court, and not to strain it by unreasonable construction beyond its due and proper limits. There would be no better mode of undermining the sound doctrines of equity than to make unreasonable and inequitable applications of them.'

That, in my judgment, is applicable to this case.[25]

"The trustees were not willing to buy more shares in the company. The active trustees were very willing that the appellants should do so themselves for the benefit of their large minority holding. The trustees, so to speak, lent their name to the appellants in the course of prolonged and difficult negotiations and, of course, the appellants thereby learnt much which would have otherwise been denied to them. The negotiations were in the end brilliantly successful. How successful Tom was in his reorganisation of the company is apparent to all. They ought to be very grateful.

"In the long run the appellants have bought for themselves with their own money shares which the trustees never contemplated buying and they did so in circumstances fully known and approved of by the trustees. To extend the doctrines of equity to make the appellants accountable in such circumstances is, in my judgment, to make unreasonable and inequitable applications of such doctrines."

## QUESTION

Tom and Trevor, holding *inter alia* a lease with two years unexpired on trust for Brian for life, remainder for Brian's children equally, were trying to sell the lease as they were likely to receive a heavy dilapidations schedule for remedying at the expiry of the lease. They had tried to purchase the freehold reversion for the trust but the landlord had refused. Tom's friend Joe, hearing of the predicament, had relieved the trust of the lease at the proper, but low, market price. Joe happened to play golf regularly with the landlord and after persisting for four months was able to contract to purchase the freehold.

Joe, only having half the purchase price, went to see Tom and suggested that Tom put up the other half for he had been a good friend and without him Joe would never have heard of the property and obtained the opportunity to buy the freehold. Tom was only too happy to put up half the purchase price, delighted that Joe was letting him in on the deal rather than merely borrow the money from Tom or a bank. Shortly afterwards Joe and Tom sold the property with vacant possession making £25,000 profit each.

Brian seeks your advice.

### Section 2. The Stranger as Constructive Trustee

There is no question of a stranger being subject to a proprietary or personal liability as a constructive trustee where the trustees dispose of

---

[24] (1874) 9 Ch.App. 244, 251.
[25] Now see *Queensland Mines* v. *Hudson*, *infra*, p. 592.

trust property to him as authorised by law[26] or by the trust instrument. However, if a stranger, such as an agent takes it upon himself to act like a trustee in respect of trust property under his control then he cannot complain that he is liable as a constructive trustee.[27] It is also well-established that a stranger will find himself subject to a proprietary constructive trust where trust property or its traceable equivalent is found in his hands as a result of an unauthorised disposition by the trustees.[28] He will have to give up the property in his hands unless he was a bona fide purchaser of a legal interest for value without notice of the unauthorised disposition or a successor in title to such purchaser. This is the result of the property law rule that an equitable interest binds everyone but a bona fide purchaser of a legal interest for value without notice and his successors in title.[29]

If the stranger no longer has any traceable property in his hands because he has dissipated it, he cannot be personally liable in equity as a constructive trustee unless before he dissipated the property he had actual, "Nelsonian" or "naughty" knowledge that the property was not his to dissipate.[30] However, if the plaintiff's action is brought within six years the defendant may be personally liable at law for the amount of his unjust enrichment unless the defence of change of position is available to him.[31]

Where a stranger never had any trust property in his hands or only received it within the scope of his agency for the trustees before disposing of it he can still be personally liable to account as a constructive trustee if he knowingly assisted in a dishonest design of the trustees.[32]

*Positive assumption of trusteeship: trustee de son tort*

As A. L. Smith L.J. stated in *Mara* v. *Browne*,[32a] "If one, not being a trustee and not having authority from a trustee, takes upon himself to intermeddle with trust matters or to do acts characteristic of the office of trustee he may thereby make himself a trustee of his own wrong, *i.e.* a trustee *de son tort*, or as it is also termed, a constructive trustee."

A trustee *de son tort*[33] does not purport to act in his own behalf but for the beneficiaries and his assumption to act is not of itself a ground

---

[26] *e.g.* L.P.A. 1925, ss.26, 27 (overreaching sales of land by two trustees for sale).
[27] *Mara* v. *Browne* [1896] 1 Ch. 199, *Selangor United Rubber Ltd.* v. *Cradock (No. 3)* [1968] 1 W.L.R. 1555, 1579.
[28] *Re Diplock* [1948] Ch. 465.
[29] *Re Montagu's Settlement* [1987] Ch. 264 *infra* p. 481, though see text to n. 48, *infra*, p. 471.
[30] *Ibid.*; Nelsonian knowledge arises where D deliberately turns a blind eye to what would otherwise be obvious; "naughty knowledge" arises where D deliberately or recklessly refrains from making the inquiries that an honest reasonable man would make in the suspicious circumstances, so that D exhibits a "want of probity."
[31] See *infra*, p. 471; *Lipkin Gorman* v. *Karpnale* [1991] 3 W.L.R. 10 and question 9, p. 566 *infra*.
[32] [1896] 1 Ch. 199, 209, endorsed by Danckwerts L.J. in *Carl Zeiss Stiftung* v. *Herbert Smith (No. 2)* [1969] 2 Ch. 276, 289.
[32a] *Agip Africa Ltd.* v. *Jackson* [1990] Ch. 265 (Millett J.) [1991] 3 W.L.R. 116 (C.A.).
[33] Adopted from executor *de son tort* on which see Parry & Clark, *The Law of Succession* (9th ed.), pp. 408–410.

of liability (save in the sense of thereafter being liable to account and liable for any failure in the duty assumed) so that his status as trustee precedes the occurrence which may be the subject of a claim against him.[34] From the outset he will be constructive trustee of the property over which he has assumed the duties of trustee,[35] and thereafter he may be liable for any breach of these duties of administration. It matters not that the intermeddler was honest and well-intentioned.[36] However, to be a trustee *de son tort* he must have the trust property vested in him or so far under his control that he could require it to be vested in him.[37]

*The proprietary constructive trust of property or its product in the hands of a stranger*

If trust property (or other property subject to a fiduciary relationship) has been improperly disposed of and it, or its traceable equivalent,[38] is in the hands of a stranger, then such property can be claimed for the beneficiaries unless the stranger (or a person through whom he claims) was a purchaser of the legal interest therein for value without notice[39] (actual, constructive or imputed), or was protected by the overreaching provisions of the 1925 property legislation or the exceptions to the *nemo dat quod non habet* principle in the Factors Acts, the Sale of Goods Acts and the Hire Purchase Acts. This position is the result of the property law of priorities and of tracing principles.

Imputed notice is actual or constructive notice of an agent for the stranger in the relevant transaction. A person has actual notice of matters within his own knowledge and constructive notice of matters that would have come to his knowledge if such inquiries and inspections had been made as a reasonably prudent person ought to have made. What *ought* to have been done in all the circumstances and thus the nature and extent of the *duty* to make reasonable inquiries will vary according to the circumstances.[40] The duty is at its greatest where

---

[34] *Selangor United Rubber Ltd.* v. *Cradock (No. 3)* [1968] 1 W.L.R. 1555, 1579.

[35] *Lyell* v. *Kennedy* (1889) 14 App.Cas. 437; *Blyth* v. *Fladgate* [1891] 1 Ch. 337. If an agent is employed by trustees who have not been validly appointed one can argue like North J. in *Mara* v. *Browne* [1895] 2 Ch. 69, that the agent should be treated as a principal and regarded as an intermeddler so as to be liable as trustee *de son tort*, irrespective of the agent's knowledge. However, if the agent has no actual or Nelsonian knowledge (turning a blind eye) of the lack of title of the "trustees" or did not wilfully and recklessly fail to make such inquiries as an honest and reasonable man would make, should he not be in the same position as an agent of validly appointed trustees since it is surely too much to expect him to carry out a detailed inquiry into the title or authority of his trustee-principal: see *Mara* v. *Browne* [1896] 1 Ch. 199, 207, *per* Lord Herschell.

[36] *Lyell* v. *Kennedy* (1889) 14 App.Cas. 437, 459; *Life Association of Scotland* v. *Siddall* (1861) 3 De G.F. & J. 58.

[37] *Re Barney* [1892] 2 Ch. 265 (two businessmen who looked over trustee-widow's business accounts and checked expenditure, so that bank would not honour widow's cheques unless bearing their initials, not liable as trustees *de son tort* when unauthorised business failed since they had not control of the trust property).

[38] See sect. 5, *infra.*

[39] *e.g. Boursot* v. *Savage* (1866) L.R. 2 Eq. 134.

[40] *Re Diplock* [1948] Ch. 465, 478–479; *Carl Zeiss Stiftung* v. *Herbert Smith (No. 2)* [1969] 2 Ch. 276, 297.

purchases of land are concerned. In other commercial transactions the courts are most reluctant to import a duty to make inquiries, which would restrict the flow of commerce, unless the defendant knows of some suspicious circumstances and a donee is under no duty of inquiry unless he knows of suspicious circumstances.[41]

The constructive trust is imposed on the stranger holding the trust property (or property representing it on tracing principles) irrespective of his honesty or probity. His legal title is subject to a prior equitable interest. Thus, he holds property belonging to another in equity and so must restore that property itself or account for its value.

The position is different where constructive trustee*ship* is imposed on a stranger so that as a constructive trustee he may be made liable to account like an express trustee for any loss. A stranger who happens to have received trust property, but who no longer has it or property representing it, is not personally liable as a constructive trustee to restore the value of that property unless before disposing of the property he had actual, "Nelsonian" or "naughty" knowledge that it was not his to dispose of, so as to be lacking in honesty or probity.[42]

*Personal constructive trusteeship imposed on a stranger so that he may be personally liable to account like an express trustee*
The case law[43] makes a distinction between cases where the stranger received trust property beneficially (other than as agent or as a conduit pipe) and other cases where he is an accessory in the disposition of trust property. The distinction is important because the accessory's liability is limited to the case where the breach of trust was fraudulent and dishonest: the recipient's liability is not so limited.

(1) *Knowing receipt or dealing.* This head covers (a) a person who receives trust property with notice that it is trust property transferred in breach of trust or (b) a person who receives trust property with notice that it be such, but without notice of any breach of trust because there be none, and subsequently deals with the property in a manner inconsistent with the trust[44] or (c) a person who receives trust property without notice that it is trust property transferred in breach of trust (but is not a bona fide purchaser of a legal interest for value without notice) but subsequently acquires notice and yet deals with the property in a manner inconsistent with the trust.

Of course, if any such person still has the trust property or its traceable equivalent, then if he is a purchaser with actual or con-

---

[41] *Joseph* v. *Lyons* (1884) 15 Q.B.D. 280; *Manchester Trust* v. *Furness* [1895] 2 Q.B. 539; *Feuer Leather Co.* v. *Frank Johnstone & Sons* [1981] Com.L.R. 251; *Baden Delvaux & Lecuit* v. *Société Générale* [1983] B.C.L.C. 325.

[42] *Carl Zeiss Stiftung* v. *Herbert Smith (No. 2)* [1969] 2 Ch. 276 *infra*, p. 477; *Re Montagu's Settlement* [1987] Ch. 264, *infra*, p. 481. But see p. 471, *infra* and question 9, *infra*, p. 566.

[43] e.g. *Karak Rubber Co. Ltd.* v. *Burden* [1972] 1 W.L.R. 602; *Belmont Finance Ltd.* v. *Williams Furniture Ltd. (No. 2)* [1980] 1 All E.R. 393; *International Sales Ltd.* v. *Marcus* [1982] 3 All E.R. 551, *Re Montagu's Settlement* [1987] Ch. 264, *Agip (Africa) Ltd.* v. *Jackson* [1990] Ch. 265.

[44] This was added by Peter Gibson J. in *Baden Delvaux & Lecuit* v. *Société Générale* [1983] B.C.L.R. 325 to the other two categories set out in *Karak Rubber Co. Ltd.* v. *Burden* [1972] 1 W.L.R. 602 and was accepted in *Agip (Africa) Ltd.* v. *Jackson* [1989] 3 W.L.R. 1367, 1388.

structive notice, or if he is a volunteer with or without such notice, he will be liable to the proprietary constructive trust (as a matter of the property law of priorities and of tracing) so as to have to restore the property itself or account for its value. Since this is the case it is too easy to assume that such a person will also be personally liable to account as a constructive trustee without having regard to whether he no longer has the trust property or its traceable equivalent.

There can thus be found broad categorical *obiter* statements,[45] not restricted to the case where the defendant still has the trust property or its traceable equivalent, to the effect that a person who receives trust property with actual *or constructive* notice that it is transferred in breach of trust is personally liable as a constructive trustee. Of course, if when dissipating the trust property or its traceable product the defendant had actual knowledge of this or had shut his eyes to the obvious ("Nelsonian" knowledge) or had deliberately or recklessly failed to make such inquiries as an honest and reasonable man would have made in the circumstances ("naughty" knowledge) he will be personally liable to account. However, an innocent dissipating volunteer is not so liable[46] nor should a purchaser with constructive notice only from "innocent failure to make what a court may later decide to have been proper inquiry" as indicated by Sachs and Edmund Davies L.JJ. in *Carl Zeiss Stiftung infra*, p. 477.

Megarry V.-C. clarified the position in *Re Montagu's Settlement*, *infra*, p. 481. "The equitable doctrine of tracing and the imposition of a constructive trust by reason of the knowing receipt of trust property are governed by different rules and must be kept distinct. Tracing is primarily a means of determining the rights of property, whereas the imposition of a constructive trust creates personal obligations that go beyond mere property rights . . . Whether a constructive trust arises in such a case primarily depends on the knowledge of the recipient." "The cold calculus of constructive and imputed notice does not seem to me to be an appropriate instrument for deciding whether a man's conscience is sufficiently affected for it to be right to bind him by the obligations of a constructive trustee." "Knowledge is not confined to actual knowledge but includes actual knowledge that would have been acquired but for shutting one's eyes to the obvious ["Nelsonian" knowledge] or wilfully and recklessly failing to make such inquiries as a reasonable and honest man would make ["naughty" knowledge]; for in such cases there is a want of probity which justifies imposing a constructive trust."

---

[45] In *Belmont Finance Ltd.* v. *Williams Furniture (No. 2)* [1980] 1 All E.R. 393, 405, 410 and *International Sales Ltd.* v. *Marcus* [1982] 3 All E.R. 551, 557–558 where actual knowledge was held to be present. Also in *Nelson* v. *Larholt* [1948] 1 K.B. 339 where Denning J. in a short sweeping extempore judgment which he tried to justify in (1949) 65 L.Q.R. 37 held constructive notice sufficed though Sachs L.J. in *Carl Zeiss Stiftung* [1969] 2 Ch. 276, 298 thought that on the facts the defendant may well have turned a blind eye.

[46] *Re Diplock* [1948] Ch. 465, 477–479.

These views may now prevail,[47] though an alternative approach has been advocated.[48] It can be argued that receipt of trust property other than by a bona fide purchaser without notice makes the recipient a trustee holding the property on a constructive or, perhaps, a resulting trust[49] for the real beneficiaries, even though the recipient is totally unaware of the trust. When he is made aware of this, even after he has innocently dissipated the property so that it cannot be traced, he must account for the period of his unwitting trusteeship. However, he will have a defence under section 61 of the Trustee Act if he acted honestly and reasonably in parting with the trust property; indeed, section 61 has potential as a basis for developing a change of position defence.[50]

In *Re Montagu's Settlement* almost 20 years had elapsed before it was sought to make the 10th Duke personally liable to account as a constructive trustee for the chattels to which he was not entitled. Let us consider the position if fewer than six years had elapsed since sale of the chattels for, say, £30,000 and he had applied £20,000 to discharge a mortgage on Blackacre and £10,000 to discharge the bills of sundry unsecured creditors. Could the beneficiaries not have a proprietary subrogation claim[51] charged on Blackacre for £20,000 and also claim that they were subrogated to the personal claims[52] of creditors for £10,000. After all, the Duke would be unjustly enriched if the beneficiaries' claim for £30,000 did not replace the claims of the creditors paid off with their £30,000; he should have no entitlement to retain the £30,000 windfall at the expense of the beneficiaries.

There is a similar strict liability (to prevent unjust enrichment) that is well-established where an unpaid or underpaid creditor, legatee or next of kin cannot recover the money due to him from a deceased's personal representatives: he has an absolute right to such money against an overpaid creditor or a beneficiary or a stranger (*e.g.* to whom part of the estate has been mistakenly transferred).[53] An innocent recipient will have a defence of change of position available to him where he would not have indulged in exceptional irretrievable expenditure but for the windfall he had received (*e.g.* if as a result of receiving £30,000 the Duke had spent it on a special wedding reception

---

[47] *Lipkin Gorman* v. *Karpnale Ltd.* [1987] 1 W.L.R. 987.
[48] Millett J. extra-judicially in (1991) 107 L.Q.R. 71, 80–83 developing a paragraph in *Agip (Africa) Ltd.* v. *Jackson* [1989] 3 W.L.R. 1367, 1388. Also see C. Harpum (1986) 102 L.Q.R. 114 and 267, (1987) 50 M.L.R. 217.
[49] As indicated by Millett J. extra-judicially, presumably on the basis that the equitable interest remains throughout in the true beneficiaries (despite a transferor's intention to transfer the whole interest): a better view is that the express trust binding the defendant on property law principles is vindicated by a constructive trust.
[50] See G. Elias, *Explaining Constructive Trusts* (O.U.P. 1990), p. 20.
[51] *Cf. Trevillian* v. *Exeter* (1854) 5 De G.M. & G. 828, *Thurstan* v. *Nottingham* P.B.S. [1902] 1 Ch. 1 despite *Re Diplock* [1948] Ch. 465, 548 which may be distinguished, for even if the money has been used to purchase land rather than discharge a mortgage no tracing remedy would have been ordered because this could have led to sale of the land which would have been inequitable.
[52] *Wenlock* v. *River Dee Co.* (1887) 19 Q.B.D. 155.
[53] *Ministry of Health* v. *Simpson* [1951] A.C. 251, see p. 550, *infra.*

for his daughter) so that it would be inequitable to compel him to repay the money.[54]

(2) *Knowing assistance.* This head includes persons who knowingly assist in a dishonest design of the trustees, even if they have not actually received any trust property or if they have only received it within the scope of their agency for the trustees.[55] Almost invariably the dishonest design will be that of the trustees, but in an exceptional case the trustees, through ignorance or naivety, may be honest instruments of the "assistant's" dishonest design when he may be personally liable.[56] A dishonest design of the trustees is something that is more than mere misfeasance or a breach of trust falling short of dishonesty or fraud,[57] which may be described as "the taking of a risk to the prejudice of another's rights, which risk is known to be one which there is no right to take."[58]

In a "knowing assistance" case, *Baden Delvaux & Lecuit* v. *Société Générale,*[59] Peter Gibson J. held that the knowledge sufficient to impose constructive trusteeship for both "knowing receipt or dealing" and "knowing assistance" can comprise any one of five different mental states as follows[60]:

(i) actual knowledge;

(ii) wilfully shutting one's eyes to the obvious ("Nelsonian knowledge");

(iii) wilfully and recklessly failing to make such inquiries as an honest and reasonable man would make ["naughty knowledge"];

(iv) knowledge of circumstances which would indicate the facts to an honest and reasonable man (though not the morally or mentally obtuse defendant);

(v) knowledge of circumstances which would put an honest and reasonable man on inquiry (though emphasising that the courts

---

54 Geoff & Jones, Chap. 39; Millett J. as in n. 48 *supra*; see p. 549, *infra*. In *Lipkin Gorman* v. *Karpnale* [1991] 3 W.L.R. 10 the Lords held that change of position is a defence to a restitutionary claim: see p. 549 *infra*.

55 *Karak Rubber Co. Ltd.* v. *Burden* [1972] 1 W.L.R. 602; *International Sales Ltd.* v. *Marcus* [1982] 3 All E.R. 551; *Baden Delvaux & Lecuit* v. *Société Générale* [1983] B.C.L.C. 325; *Agip (Africa) Ltd.* v. *Jackson* [1990] Ch. 265.

56 *Eaves* v. *Hickson* (1861) Beav. 136 (defendant liable for loss as constructive trustee where he fraudulently induced an innocent breach of trust, merely forging a marriage certificate, so that the trustees distributed property to his illegitimate children when beneficiaries had to be legitimate children).

57 *Belmont Finance Ltd.* v. *Williams Furniture Ltd.* [1979] Ch. 250, C.A., rejecting the view of Ungoed-Thomas J. in *Selangor United Rubber Estates Ltd.* v. *Cradock (No. 3)* [1968] 2 All E.R. 1073 that morally reprehensible conduct falling short of dishonesty would suffice.

58 *Baden Delvaux & Lecuit* v. *Société Générale* [1983] B.C.L.C. 325, 406 adopting a definition in *R.* v. *Sinclair* [1968] 1 W.L.R. 1246.

59 [1983] B.C.L.C. 325 upheld on appeal without comment on the "knowledge" point. He overlooked *International Sales Ltd.* v. *Marcus* [1982] 3 All E.R. 551, 557–558 where Lawson J. considered constructive notice did not suffice for "knowing assistance."

60 pp. 408–421. After investigating the authorities he followed *Selangor United Rubber Estates Ltd.* v. *Cradock (No. 3)* [1968] 2 All E.R. 1073; *Karak Rubber Co. Ltd.* v. *Burden* [1972] 1 W.L.R. 602 and *Rowlandson* v. *National Westminster Bank* [1978] 1 W.L.R. 798, but their approach was disapproved by C.A. in *Lipkin Gorman* v. *Karpnale Ltd.* [1989] 1 W.L.R. 1340.

will not readily import a duty to inquire in the case of commercial transactions, not involving land, unless there are some grounds for suspicion).

However, having isolated the four elements for "knowing assistance" as (1) a trust (or other fiduciary relationship); (2) a dishonest design on the trustees' part; (3) assistance by the stranger in that design; and (4) the stranger's knowledge, Peter Gibson J. stated[61]:

> "It is important not to lose sight of the requirement that, taken together, those elements must leave the court satisfied that the alleged constructive trustee was a party or privy to dishonesty on the part of the trustee."

How can honest failure to know of dishonesty because of honest failure to make inquiry make one party or privy to dishonesty?

One can accept the fourth type of notice arising out of a defendants failure to recognise dishonesty when he sees it[62] (as opposed to the fifth type of notice from failure to discover dishonesty because of failure to make inquiries) as essentially being a type of actual notice to a reasonably intelligent and honest person. However, constructive notice of a dishonest design is not enough as pointed out by the Court of Appeal in *Belmont Finance Ltd.* v. *Williams Furniture*[63] and as held in *Lipkin Gorman* v. *Karpnale Ltd.*[64] and in *Agip Africa Ltd.* v. *Jackson, infra*, p. 487 where Millett J. stated[65]: "There is no sense in requiring dishonesty on the part of the principal while accepting negligence as sufficient for his assistant. Dishonest furtherance of the dishonest scheme of another is an understandable basis for liability; negligent but honest failure to appreciate that someone else's scheme is dishonest is not."

Usually, the stranger's assistance in the breach of trust renders him personally liable as constructive trustee to replace losses but what if he makes a gain? This is the obverse side of the coin of personal accountability so he should be accountable for the gain even if it may be a windfall for the trust beneficiaries.[66]

*The position of agents of trustees*

So that agents will be happy to act for trustees at a reasonable fee one must keep in mind the warnings of Lord Selborne L.C., Kay J.,[67]

---

61 [1983] B.C.L.C. 325, 404. On "privy" requiring moral complicity see *Thorne* v. *Heard* [1894] 1 Ch. 608 and *Carl Zeiss Stiftung* v. *Herbert Smith & Co. (No. 2)* [1969] 2 Ch. 264, 276, 298.

62 See Stephen J. in *Consul Development Pty. Ltd.* v. *D.P.C. Estates Ltd.* (1975) 132 C.L.R. 373, 411.

63 [1979] Ch. 250, 267, 275, approved by May L.J. in *Lipkin Gorman* v. *Karpnale Ltd.* [1989] 1 W.L.R. 1345, 1355.

64 [1987] 1 W.L.R. 987 and in *Canadian Imperial Bank of Commerce* v. *Valley Credit Union* (1990) 63 D.L.R. (4th) 632 and *Eagle Trust* v. *SBC Securities Financial, The Times*, February 5, 1991.

65 [1989] 3 W.L.R. 1367, 1389.

66 Scott's *Law of Trusts* (3rd ed.), p. 506; *DPC Estates Pty. Ltd.* v. *Consul Development Pty. Ltd.* [1974] 1 N.S.W.L.R. 443, 471–472.

67 *Williams* v. *Williams* (1881) 17 Ch.D. 437, 442.

Sachs[68] and Edmund Davies L.JJ.[69] against extending constructive trusts too far.

In *Barnes* v. *Addy* Lord Selborne said[70]:

> "Those who create a trust clothe the trustee with a legal power and control over the trust property, imposing on him a corresponding responsibility. That responsibility may no doubt be extended in equity to others who are not properly trustees if they are found either making themselves trustees *de son tort* or actually participating in any fraudulent conduct of the trustee to the injury of the *cestui que trust*. But on the other hand strangers are not to be made constructive trustees merely because they act as the agents of trustees in transactions within their legal powers, transactions, perhaps, of which a Court of Equity may disapprove, unless those agents receive and become chargeable with some part of the trust property, or unless they assist with knowledge in a dishonest and fraudulent design on the part of the trustees . . . If those principles were disregarded I know not how anyone could in transactions admitting of doubt as to the view which a Court of Equity might take of them, safely discharge the office of solicitor, of banker or of agent of any sort to the trustees. But, on the other hand, if persons dealing honestly as agents are at liberty to rely on the legal power of the trustees, are not to have the character of trustees constructively imposed upon them, then the transactions of mankind can safely be carried through; and I apprehend those who create trusts do expressly intend, in the absence of fraud and dishonesty, to exonerate such agents of all classes from the responsibilities which are expressly incumbent by reason of the fiduciary relation upon the trustees."

There, solicitors had prepared the deed necessary for a trustee to appoint X sole trustee of property held for X's wife for life, remainder to their children though they advised against such appointment. X sold the property, misapplied its proceeds and became bankrupt. It was held the solicitors could not be treated as constructive trustees so as to make them liable to account for the trust property since the solicitors had acted honestly in the course of their agency. Even where solicitors dispose of or invest trust property in ways that they ought to have known to be unauthorised they cannot be made liable as constructive trustees so long as they acted honestly and did not do acts characteristic of a trustee and outside the duties of an agent.[71]

An agent who intermeddles, taking it upon himself to act as if he were trustee, will of course be liable as a trustee *de son tort, e.g. Soar* v. *Ashwell*[72] where a solicitor paid half the trust moneys payable on redemption of a mortgage to the trustees but retained the other half and accounted for interest on it to the life tenant.

---

[68] [1969] 2 Ch. 276, 299.
[69] [1969] 2 Ch. 276, 304.
[70] (1874) L.R. 9 Ch.App. 244, 251–252.
[71] *Williams* v. *Williams* (1881) 17 Ch.D. 437, *Mara* v. *Browne* [1896] 1 Ch. 199, *Williams-Ashman* v. *Price* [1942] Ch. 219.
[72] [1893] 2 Q.B. 390, and see *Blyth* v. *Fladgate* [1891] 1 Ch. 337.

An agent will also be personally liable as constructive trustee if he receives trust moneys but deals with them in a manner inconsistent with the performance of trusts of which he is cognisant. Thus in *Lee* v. *Sankey*[73] solicitors, employed by two trustees to receive proceeds of sale did not discharge their agency by paying the proceeds over to the two trustees, but without authority paid the proceeds to one trustee, who dissipated the moneys and died insolvent: they were personally liable to the beneficiaries. Conscious impropriety in dealing with trust property under the agent's control in a manner inconsistent with the trust will thus suffice for personal liability, even in the absence of a dishonest design.[74]

In *Carl Zeiss Stiftung* v. *Herbert Smith & Co.*, Edmund Davies L.J. summarised an agent's position as follows[75]:

> "(A) A solicitor or other agent who receives money from his principal which belongs at law or in equity to a third party is not accountable as a constructive trustee to that third party unless he has been guilty of some wrongful act in relation to that money.
>
> "(B) To act 'wrongfully' he must be guilty of (i) knowingly participating in a breach of trust by his principal; or (ii) intermeddling with the trust property otherwise merely than as agent and thereby becoming a trustee *de son tort*; or (iii) receiving or dealing with the money knowing that his principal has no right to pay it over or to instruct him to deal with it in the manner indicated; or (iv) some dishonest act relating to the money. These are indeed but variants of that 'want of probity' to which I have earlier referred."

He held[76] "mere notice of a claim asserted by a third party is insufficient to render the agent guilty of a wrongful act in dealing with property derived from his principal in accordance with the latter's instructions unless the agent knows that the third party's claim is well founded and that the principal accordingly had no authority to give such instructions."

Sachs L.J.[77] cited with approval Underhill (11th ed.), p. 599, "where the agent of the trustees acts honestly and confines himself to the duties of an agent then, though he will not be accountable to the beneficiaries, they will have their remedy against the persons who are the trustees." In any event, in the circumstances of *Carl Zeiss, infra*, p. 477, the solicitor had no actual or constructive notice of the plaintiff's equitable interest; there being no duty to make inquiries into the plaintiff's allegations he could not be fixed with notice of matters discoverable if such inquiries had been made.

---

[73] (1873) L.R. 15 Eq. 204.
[74] *Agip (Africa) Ltd.* v. *Jackson* [1990] Ch. 265, 292; *Baden Delvaux & Lecuit* v. *Société Générale* [1983] B.C.L.C. 325, 403; *Carl Zeiss Stiftung* v. *Herbert Smith* [1969] 2 Ch. 276, 303–304; *Re Blundell* (1888) 40 Ch.D. 370, 381; *Consul Developments Pty. Ltd.* v. *D.P.C. Pty. Ltd.* (1975) 132 C.L.R. 373, 396; *Winslow* v. *Richter* (1989) 61 D.L.R. (4th) 549, 558.
[75] [1969] 2 Ch. 276, 303–304.
[76] *Ibid.*
[77] *Ibid.* p. 299.

Where an agent, such as a solicitor or an accountant, is worried that he might be holding fiduciary property on constructive trust for a third party or that he might be personally liable as a constructive trustee if he transferred assets to a third party he can apply by originating summons to the High Court for administration directions under Order 85 of the Rules of the Supreme Court. Where there are grounds for suspecting that his client's funds had been fraudulently obtained the court's directions can override the legal professional privilege of confidentiality to which the client was prima facie entitled.[78]

## BELMONT FINANCE LTD. v. WILLIAMS FURNITURE LTD.

Court of Appeal [1979] 1 All E.R. 118; [1978] 3 W.L.R. 712 (Buckley, Orr and Goff L.JJ.)

The court held that it was not open to Belmont on the pleadings as they stood to claim there was a constructive trust, since to claim that a person was liable to account as a constructive trustee it was necessary to plead not just the facts, but, clearly and unequivocally, that the defendant had known that the breach of trust in respect of which it was sought to make him liable was fraudulent or dishonest in a "knowing assistance" case. The following dicta are significant.

BUCKLEY L.J.: "The plaintiff has contended that in every case the court should consider whether the conduct in question was so unsatisfactory, whether it can be strictly described as fraudulent or dishonest in law, as to make accountability on the footing of constructive trust equitably just. This is admitted to constitute an extension of the rule as formulated by Lord Selborne L.C. in *Barnes* v. *Addy* (1874).[79] To depart from it now would, I think, introduce an undesirable degree of uncertainty to the law, because if dishonesty is not to be the criterion, what degree of unethical conduct is to be sufficient. So in my judgment the design must be shown to be a dishonest one, that is to say, a fraudulent one.

"The knowledge of that design on the part of the party sought to be made liable may be actual knowledge. If he wilfully shuts his eyes to dishonesty or wilfully or recklessly fails to make such enquiries as an honest and reasonable man would make, he may be found to have involved himself in the fraudulent character of the design, or at any rate to be disentitled to rely on lack of actual knowledge of the design as a defence. But otherwise, as it seems to me, he should not be held to be affected by constructive notice. It is not strictly necessary for us to decide that point; I express that opinion merely as my view at present without intending to lay it down as a final decision."

GOFF L.J.: "If Ungoed-Thomas J. intended to say that it is not necessary that the breach of trust in respect of which it is sought to make the defendant liable as a constructive trustee should be fraudulent or dishonest I respectfuly cannot accept that view. I agree it would be dangerous and wrong to depart from the safe path of the principle as stated by Lord Selborne L.C.[80] to the

---

[78] *Finers* v. *Miro* [1991] 1 All E.R. 182.
[79] L.R. 9 Ch.App. 244, 251–252. (However, see text to n. 74, *supra*, where liability is alleged not for "knowing assistance" but for "knowingly dealing" with trust property in a manner inconsistent with the performance of trusts of which the dealer knows).
[80] *Ibid.*.

uncharted sea of something not innocent (and counsel for the plaintiff conceded that mere innocence would not do) but still short of dishonesty.

"Finally, whilst wilfully shutting one's eyes to the obvious, or wilfully refraining from enquiry because it may be embarrassing is sufficient to make a person who participates in a fraudulent breach of trust without actually receiving the trust moneys, or moneys representing the same, liable as a constructive trustee there remains the question whether constructive notice in the section 199 [Law of Property Act 1925] sense will suffice.

"Ungoed-Thomas J. in the *Selangor*[81] case held that it would and Brightman J.[82] followed that decision.

"But in *Carl-Zeiss-Stiftung* v. *Herbert Smith & Co. (No. 2)*[83] Sachs and Edmund Davies L.JJ. threw great doubt on this. In *Competitive Insurance Ltd.* v. *Davies Investments Ltd.*[84] I took the view that constructive notice of the section 199 type would not be sufficient and I adhere to that view. It is however unnecessary for us to decide that particular matter."

## CARL ZEISS STIFTUNG v. HERBERT SMITH & CO. (NO. 2)

Court of Appeal [1969] 2 Ch. 276 (Danckwerts, Sachs and Edmund-Davies L.JJ.)

The East German plaintiffs alleged in legal proceedings that all the assets of a West German foundation belonged to them. The present action was for an account against the West German foundation's solicitors on the basis they had received property (*e.g.* fees and disbursements) from the West German foundation which in equity belonged to the plaintiffs. Danckwerts L.J. rejected the claim since it was clear the defendants had no notice whether actual or constructive of any equitable right of the plaintiffs.

SACHS L.J.: "[Nothing] in the statement of claim can be read as suggesting that the defendant solicitors intermeddled with the alleged trust moneys so as to make them trustees *de son tort*; nor was such intermeddling suggested in this court. . . .

"The neutral word 'cognisance' has been used by me in preference to either 'notice' or 'knowledge' because during the citation of authorities and in the course of argument it emerged that these two words were often being used as if they were interchangeable; in fact and in law, 'notice' and 'knowledge' are, of course, not necessarily the same thing, as has been recognized on more than one occasion in the past. . . .

"Firstly, and to my mind decisively, whatever be the nature of the knowledge or notice required, cognisance of what has been termed 'a doubtful equity' is not enough. This phrase is to be found in *Lewin on Trusts* (16th ed., 1964), p. 658, and *Underhill's Law Relating to Trusts and Trustees* (11th ed., 1959) p. 606: it appears first to have been used by Lord Grant M.R. in *Parker* v. *Brooke* (1804) 9 Ves. 583 at 588. The rule, as I understand it, is that no stranger can become a constructive trustee merely because he is made aware of a disputed claim the validity of which he cannot properly assess. Here it has been rightly conceded that no one can foretell the result of the litigation even if the plaintiffs were to prove all the facts they allege.

---

[81] [1968] 2 All E.R. 1073.
[82] *Karak Rubber Co. Ltd.* v. *Burden (No. 2)* [1972] 1 All E.R. 1210.
[83] [1969] 2 Ch. 276.
[84] [1975] 3 All E.R. 254, 260.

"Thus, to my mind, the plaintiffs fail at an early stage in their attempt to fix the defendant solicitors with appropriate cognisance. It seems to me, however, that in order to succeed they would also have to overcome further obstacles which are insurmountable by reason of the nature of the case and the concessions which they have rightly made earlier. . . .

"The first obstacle emerges upon an examination of the submission for the plaintiffs that to fix a stranger with the appropriate responsibility it is sufficient to show that he has notice of the type exemplified by the terms of section 199 of the Law of Property Act 1925; that is to say, to show that the existence of the trusts would have come to his knowledge if such inquiries had been made as ought reasonably to have been made by him. On the assumption that this is the right test (a point to which I will return) it is to be noticed that in many cases, and in particular in the present case, knowledge of the existence of a trust depends on knowledge first of the relevant facts and next of the law applicable to that set of facts. As to facts alleged in a statement of claim, Mr. Kerr was, to my mind, correct in submitting that a defendant's solicitor is under no duty to the plaintiffs to inquire into their accuracy for the purposes urged by Mr. Harman, nor, where there is a likelihood of a conflict of evidence between his client's witnesses and those of the plaintiffs is he under any such duty to assess the result. In coming to this conclusion, I am content to adopt the approach, albeit *obiter*, of Lush J. in *La Roche* v. *Armstrong* [1922] 1 K.B. 485 at 491 where he said:

> 'Here the solicitor has received a sum of money from his client for the purpose of his resisting on her behalf a claim by A, who says it is trust money and that the client is under a duty to return it. Under such circumstances I should be very loath to say that the solicitor, who cannot know the real truth of the matter, inasmuch as he hears one story from his client and another from A, is bound to hold the money, not for his client, but for A whose claim is not yet established.'

"That approach was correct, because the solicitor was under no duty to A either to make inquiries or to assess the results of them.

"The nature and extent of the duty to inquire when there is applicable what by way of shorthand can be referred to as the section 199 test must, of course, vary according to the facts. In the present case the defendant solicitors were thus not under a duty to the plaintiffs to inquire into the allegations of fact in the statement of claim. As to the law, they were similarly under no duty to the plaintiffs in such a complex matter either to make inquiries or to attempt to assess the result. (It has already, of course, been conceded that there was no prospect of their being able to come to a firm conclusion on the matter of law.)

"Thus the plaintiffs fail again at this point to show that the defendant solicitors should be deemed to be cognisant of the trusts. It should be added that, to my mind, they would have similarly failed in any normal case in which the relevant stranger becomes aware of a bona fide disputed claim to assets in his hands.

"The next point strongly pressed by Mr. Kerr was that in order to succeed the plaintiffs would have had to allege either fraud, or improper conduct as a solicitor, or wilful use of the moneys in breach of trust. In this behalf it has been Mr. Harman's case that once it was shown that the moneys were in law being used in breach of trust the section 199 test was once more decisive when considering whether a stranger is fixed with liability.

"It does not, however, seem to me that a stranger is necessarily shown to be both a constructive trustee and liable for a breach of the relevant trusts even if it is established that he has such notice. As at present advised, I am inclined to the view that a further element has to be proved, at any rate in a case such as the present one. That element is one of dishonesty or of consciously acting improperly, as opposed to an innocent failure to make what a court may later decide to have been proper inquiry. That would entail both actual knowledge of the trust's existence and actual knowledge that what is being done is improperly in breach of that trust—though, of course, in both cases a person wilfully shutting his eyes to the obvious is in no different position than if he had kept them open. In becoming somewhat strongly inclined to that view before the *Selangor* case was cited, I had been impressed by the recurrence of the close conjunction in textbooks and judgments of references to fraud and breach of trusts in the relevant passages. . . . Moreover, the mere fact that in *Williams* v. *Williams* (1881) 17 Ch.D. 437 (a case cited in the *Selangor* judgment [1968] 1 W.L.R. 1555) Kay J., at 445, made use of the phrase, 'If I had been satisfied that [Mr. C] had wilfully shut his eyes,' seems when taken in the context of the facts of that case once more to show that an innocent, even if negligent, failure to inquire is not enough. Indeed, these cases tend quite strongly to the conclusion that negligent, if innocent failure to make inquiry is not sufficient to attract constructive trusteeship. It is moreover to be observed that cases where upon the facts there was an obvious shutting of eyes (*e.g.* *Nelson* v. *Larholt* [1948] 1 K.B. 339) as opposed to mere lack of prudence may need careful examination lest, as in the intermeddling cases, the dicta in them may be found to go beyond what was requisite for the particular decision.

"As regards textbooks, one finds it said in *Halsbury's Laws of England*, Vol. 38 in paragraph 1447, 'in other words, he must be a party to a fraud or breach of trust on the part of the actual trustee'—a phrase repeated in paragraph 1449. Obviously the word 'knowingly' must be inserted before 'party' to make sense of 'party to a fraud,' and I am inclined to think that the word 'knowingly' (with exactly the same connotation of actual knowledge) must apply in relation to being 'a party to a breach of trust.'

"I have thus come to the conclusion that the plaintiffs could not possibly upon the allegations made in their statement of claim, as qualified in the way mentioned at the outset of this judgment, succeed in their claim against the defendant solicitors: they cannot establish that the defendant solicitors were cognizant either of the relevant trusts or of the moneys being employed in breach thereof. . . .

EDMUND DAVIES L.J.: "The concept of 'want of probity' appears to provide a useful touchstone in considering circumstances said to give rise to constructive trusts, and I have not found it misleading when applying it to the many authorities cited to this court. It is because of such a concept that evidence as to 'good faith,' 'knowledge' and 'notice' plays so important a part in the reported decisions. It is true that not every situation where probity is lacking gives rise to a constructive trust. Nevertheless, the authorities appear to show that nothing short of it will do. Not even gross negligence will suffice. Thus in *Williams* v. *Williams* (1881) 17 Ch.D. 437, where a solicitor had acted, as Kay J. found, 'with very great negligence towards his client' in dealing with trust property, the judge said at 445:

'If it were proved to me upon the evidence that he had wilfully shut his eyes, and was determined not to inquire, then the case would have been very different. . . . I do not find that anything done by [the solicitor] in the matter was done for his own benefit. . . . If he had, as I believe he

had, a bona fide conviction that there was no settlement whatever. . . . I
cannot hold that he is affected with such notice as to make him
personally liable for the purchase-moneys which passed through his
hands as solicitor.'

"In *Re Blundell* (1888) 40 Ch.D. 370, where solicitors were again absolved
in somewhat remarkable circumstances, Stirling J., after reviewing the authorities, said at 381:

'. . . solicitors cannot be made liable as constructive trustees unless
they are brought within the doctrine of the court with reference to other
strangers, who are not themselves trustees, but are liable in certain cases
to be made to account as if they were trustees. What is the general
doctrine with reference to constructive trustees of that kind? It is that a
stranger to the trust receiving money from the trustee which he knows'—
'and I stress the word "knows" '—'to be part of the trust estate is not
liable as a constructive trustee unless there are facts brought home to
him which show that to his knowledge the money is being applied in a
manner which is inconsistent with the trust; or (in other words) unless it
be made out that he is party either to a fraud, or to a breach of trust on
the part of the justice.'

"In a further passage, at 383, the judge added observations of great
pertinence to the present case:

'. . . to my mind, in order that the solicitor may be debarred from
accepting payment out of the trust estate, he must be fixed with notice
that at the time when he accepted payment the trustee had been guilty of
a breach of trust such as would preclude him altogether from resorting to
the trust estate for payment of costs, so that in fact the application of the
trust estate in payment of costs would be a breach of trust.'

"The foregoing cases are but two illustrations among many to be found in
the reports of that want of probity which, to my way of thinking, is the hall-
mark of constructive trusts, however created.

"The proposition which the plaintiffs' counsel described as fundamental to
his case was stated in these terms: that a man who receives property which he
knows (or ought to know) is trust property and applies it in a manner which he
knows (or ought to know) is inconsistent with the terms of the trust is
accountable in a suit by the beneficiaries of the trust. Although the soundness
of that proposition was from the beginning accepted without qualification by
the defendant solicitors, countless cases were cited to demonstrate its validity.
But it turned out that their citation was far from being a sleeveless errand, for
it emerged that in not one of those cases was there any room for doubt that a
trust already existed. None of them dealt with the fundamental assertion which
has here been so strongly contested, and which Pennycuick J. summarised by
saying that: 'Counsel for the [plaintiffs] contends that [the defendant solicitors]
have notice of the trust and if, at the end of the day, the trust is established in
the main action, they will be accountable as constructive trustees for all
moneys comprised in that trust which they have received from the West
German company.' But, as admittedly the West German foundation hold
nothing for the plaintiffs under an express trust, and as, even despite the 13
long years that litigation between them has been proceeding, there has been no
determination that any trust does exist, Mr. Harman has found himself

compelled to go further if this appeal is to be put on its feet. He asserts, in effect, that for present purposes claims are the same as facts. . . .

"The observation most helpful to the plaintiffs is possibly that of Fry J. in *Foxton* v. *Manchester and Liverpool District Banking Co.* (1881) 44 L.T. 406 at 408 that: 'those who know that a fund is a trust fund cannot take possession of that fund for their own private benefit, except at the risk of being liable to refund it in the event of the trust being broken by the payment of the money.' But even there knowledge of the existence of the trust and that the moneys being received are trust moneys was stressed, as opposed to knowledge of a mere claim that a trust exists. Here, in essence, nothing more than the latter is asserted, and it is conceded that the defendant solicitors cannot be expected to conjecture as to its outcome.

"Mr. Kerr gave the court a helpful distillation of the numerous authorities to which reference has already been made by my Lords. Their effect, he rightly submits, may be thus stated. (A) A solicitor or other agent who receives money from his principal which belongs at law or in equity to a third party is not accountable as a constructive trustee to that third party unless he has been guilty of some wrongful act in relation to that money. (B) To act 'wrongfully' he must be guilty of (i) knowingly participating in a breach of trust by his principal; or (ii) intermeddling with the trust property otherwise than merely as an agent and thereby becomes a trustee *de son tort*; or (iii) receiving or dealing with the money knowing that his principal has no right to pay it over or to instruct him to deal with it in the manner indicated; or (iv) some dishonest act relating to the money. These are, indeed, but variants or illustrations of that 'want of probity' to which I have earlier referred.

"Do the demands of justice and good conscience bring the present case within any of the foregoing categories? In my judgment, the question is one which demands a negative answer. The law being reluctant to make a mere agent a constructive trustee, as Lord Selborne L.C. put it in *Barnes* v. *Addy*, mere notice of a claim asserted by a third party is insufficient to render the agent guilty of a wrongful act in dealing with property derived from his principal in accordance with the latter's instructions unless the agent *knows* that the third party's claim is well-founded and that the principal accordingly had no authority to give such instructions. The only possible exception to such exemption arises where the agent is under a duty to inquire into the validity of the third party's claim and where, although inquiry would have established that it was well-founded, none is instituted. But, as it is conceded by the plaintiffs that the defendant solicitors are under no such duty of inquiry, that further matter does not now call for consideration. . . . "

## RE MONTAGU'S SETTLEMENT

Chancery Division [1987] 1 Ch. 264

SIR ROBERT MEGARRY V.-C.: " . . . What is in issue is the result of the receipt by the tenth Duke of a large number of settled chattels, and his disposal of them during his lifetime. On many matters the evidence is slender or obscure, since the tenth Duke (whom I shall call simply 'the Duke') received the chattels in the late 1940s and disposed of many of them then; he died in 1977 and others concerned have also died. What has to be resolved was whether the Duke held the chattels as a constructive trustee so that his estate is accountable for them or their proceeds.

"The issue centred on clause 14(B) of the 1923 settlement. That settlement assigned a large number of chattels to the trustees of the settlement upon certain trusts. In the events which happened, the trustees had a fiduciary duty on the death of the ninth Duke to select and make an inventory of such of the chattels as they considered suitable for inclusion in the settlement, and to hold the residue of the chattels in trust for the Duke absolutely. In the event, the trustees made no selection or inventory but instead treated all the chattels as being the absolute property of the Duke. The Duke's solicitor, Mr. Lickfold, undoubtedly knew the terms of clause 14(B) and understood its effect, and the Duke had a copy of the settlement: but the time came when Mr. Lickfold, Col. Nicholl (a solicitor advising the trustees), the trustees themselves and Mr. Gilchrist, an American lawyer advising the Duke, all seemed to have treated clause 14(B) as allowing the trustees to assent to the Duke taking any of the chattels that he wished and either keeping them or else selling them and keeping the proceeds of sale. In 1949 there were two large sales of the chattels; and many chattels were shipped out to Kenya, where the Duke was living.

"There is no suggestion that anyone concerned in the matter was dishonest. There was a muddle, but however careless it was, it was an honest muddle. Further, I do not think that the Duke was at any relevant time conscious of the fact that he was not entitled to receive the chattels and deal with them as beneficial owner. Of course, if clause 14(B) is singled out for attention and read carefully it could be seen by a reasonably intelligent layman not to empower the trustees simply to release chattels to the Duke, but to require them first to select chattels for inclusion in the settlement and to provide that only when they had done that would the chattels not selected become the Duke's property. But clause 14(B) was deeply embedded in a long and complex document, and in view of the advice and information that the Duke received from his solicitor I can see no reason why the Duke should be expected to attempt to construe the settlement himself. If expressed in terms of the doctrine of notice, I have held, ante, p. 268F–G, that the Duke 'had notice, both actual and imputed, of the terms of clause 14(B)." But I have also said, ante, pp. 271H–272A:

> 'I do not think that the tenth Duke had any knowledge at any material time that the chattels that he was receiving or dealing with were chattels that were still subject to any trust. I think that he believed that they had been lawfully and properly released to him by the trustees.'

"That brings me to the essential question for decision. The core of the question is what suffices to constitute a recipient of trust property a constructive trustee of it. I can leave on one side the equitable doctrine of tracing: if the recipient of trust property still has the property or its traceable proceeds in his possession, he is liable to restore it unless he is a purchaser without notice. But liability as a constructive trustee is wider, and does not depend upon the recipient still having the property or its traceable proceeds. Does it suffice if the recipient had 'notice' that the property he was receiving was trust property, or must he have not merely notice of this, but knowledge, or 'cognizance,' as it has been put?

"In the books and the authorities the word 'notice' is often used in place of the word 'knowledge,' usually without any real explanation of its meaning. This seems to me to be a fertile source of confusion; for whatever meaning the layman may attach to those words, centuries of equity jurisprudence have attached a detailed and technical meaning to the term 'notice,' without doing the same for 'knowledge.' The classification of 'notice' into actual notice, constructive notice and imputed notice has been developed in relation to the doctrine that a bona fide purchaser for value of a legal estate takes free from any equitable interests of which he has no notice. I need not discuss this classification beyond saying that I use the term 'imputed notice' as meaning any actual or constructive notice that a solicitor or other agent for the purchaser acquires in the course of the transaction in question, such notice being imputed to the purchaser. Some of the cases describe any constructive notice that a purchaser himself obtains as being 'imputed' to him; but I confine 'imputed' to notice obtained by another which equity imputes to the purchaser.

"Now until recently I do not think there had been any classification of 'knowledge' which corresponded with the classification of 'notice.' However, in the *Baden* case, at p. 407, the judgment sets out five categories of knowledge, or of the circumstances in which the court may treat a person as having knowledge. Counsel in that case were substantially in agreement in treating all five types as being relevant for the purpose of a constructive trust; and the judge agreed with them: p. 415. These categories are (i) actual knowledge; (ii) wilfully shutting one's eyes to the obvious; (iii) wilfully and recklessly failing to make such inquiries as an honest and reasonable man would make; (iv) knowledge of circumstances which would indicate the facts to an honest and reasonable man; and (v) knowledge of circumstances which would put an honest and reasonable man on inquiry. If I pause there, it can be said that these categories of knowledge correspond to two categories of notice: Type (i) corresponds to actual notice, and types (ii), (iii), (iv) and (v) correspond to constructive notice. Nothing, however, is said (at least in terms) about imputed knowledge. This is important, because in the case before me Mr. Taylor strongly contended that Mr. Lickfold's knowledge must be imputed to the Duke, and that this was of the essence of his case.

"It seems to me that one must be very careful about applying to constructive trusts either the accepted concepts of notice or any analogy to them. In determining whether a constructive trust has been created, the fundamental question is whether the conscience of the recipient is bound in such a way as to justify equity in imposing a trust on him. The rules concerning a purchaser without notice seem to me to provide little guidance on this and to be liable to be misleading. First, they are irrelevant unless there is a purchase. A volunteer is bound by an equitable interest even if he has no notice of it; but in many cases of alleged constructive trusts the disposition has been voluntary and not for value, and yet notice or knowledge is plainly relevant. Second, although a purchaser normally employs solicitors, and so questions of imputed notice may arise, it is unusual for a volunteer to employ solicitors when about to receive bounty. Even if he does, he is unlikely to employ them in order to investigate the right of the donor to make the gift or of the trustees or personal representatives to make the distribution; and until this case came before me I had never heard it suggested that a volunteer would be fixed with imputed notice of all that his solicitors would have discovered had he employed solicitors and had instructed them to investigate his right to receive the property.

"Third, there seems to me to be a fundamental difference between the questions that arise in respect of the doctrine of purchaser without notice and constructive trusts. As I said in my previous judgment, ante, pp. 272H–273B:

'The former is concerned with the question whether a person takes property subject to or free from some equity. The latter is concerned with whether or not a person is to have imposed upon him the personal burdens and obligations of trusteeship. I do not see why one of the touchstones for determining the burdens on property should be the same as that for deciding whether to impose a personal obligation on a man. The cold calculus of constructive and imputed notice does not seem to me to be an appropriate instrument for deciding whether a man's conscience is sufficiently affected for it to be right to bind him by the obligations of a constructive trustee.'

"I can see no reason to resile from that statement, save that to meet possible susceptibilities I would alter 'man' to 'person.' I would only add that there is more to being made a trustee then merely taking property subject to an equity.

"There is a further consideration. There is today something of a tendency in equity to put less emphasis on detailed rules that have emerged from the cases and more weight on the underlying principles that engendered those rules, treating the rules less as rules requiring complete compliance, and more as guidelines to assist the court in applying the principles. A good illustration of this approach is to be found in the judgment of Oliver J. in *Taylors Fashions Ltd.* v. *Liverpool Victoria Trustees Co. Ltd. (Note)* [1981] Q.B. 133, 145–155. This view was adopted by Robert Goff J. in *Amalgamated Investment & Property Co. Ltd.* v. *Texas Commerce International Bank Ltd.* [1982] Q.B. 84, 104, 105, and it was, I think, accepted, though not cited, by the Court of Appeal in the latter case: see at pp. 116–132. Certainly it was approved in terms by the Court of Appeal in *Habib Bank Ltd.* v. *Habib Bank A.G. Zurich* [1981] 1 W.L.R. 1265, 1285, 1287. The *Taylors Fashions* case [1981] Q.B. 133 concerned equitable estoppel and the five probanda to be found in the judgment of Fry J. in *Willmott* v. *Barber* (1880) 15 Ch.D. 96, 105; and on the facts of the case before him Oliver J. in the *Taylors Fashions* case concluded that the question was not whether each of those probanda had been satisfied but whether it would be unconscionable for the defendants to take advantage of the mistake there in question. Accordingly, although I readily approach the five categories of knowledge set out in the *Baden* case [1983] B.C.L.C. 325 as useful guides, I regard them primarily as aids in determining whether or not the Duke's conscience was affected in such a way as to require him to hold any or all of the chattels that he received on a constructive trust.

"There is one further general consideration that I should mention, and that is that 'the court should not be astute to impute knowledge where no actual knowledge exists': see the *Baden* case at p. 415, *per* Peter Gibson J. This approach goes back at least as far as *Barnes* v. *Addy* (1874) 9 Ch.App. 244, 251, 252. The view of James L.J., at p. 256, was that the court had in some cases

> 'gone to the very verge of justice in making good to cestuis que trust the consequences of the breaches of trust of their trustees at the expense of persons perfectly honest, but who have been, in some more or less degree, injudicious.'

"Of the five categories of knowledge set out in the *Baden* case [1983] B.C.L.C. 325, Mr. Chadwick, as well as Mr. Taylor, accepted the first three. What was in issue was nos. (iv) and (v), namely, knowledge of circumstances which 'would indicate the facts to an honest and reasonable man' or 'would put an honest and reasonable man on inquiry.' On the view that I take of the present case I do not think that it really matters whether or not categories (iv) and (v) are included, but as the matter has been argued at length, and further questions on it may arise, I think I should say something about it.

"First, as I have already indicated, I think that one has to be careful to distinguish the notice that is relevant in the doctrine of purchaser without notice from the knowledge that suffices for the imposition of a constructive trust. This is shown by a short passage in the long judgment of the Court of Appeal in *In re Diplock* [1948] Ch. 465, 478, 479. There, it was pointed out that on the facts of that case persons unversed in the law were entitled to assume that the executors were properly administering the estate, and that if those persons received money bona fide believing themselves to be entitled to it, 'they should not have imposed upon them the heavy obligations of trusteeship.' The judgment then pointed out:

'the principles applicable to such cases are not the same as the principles in regard to notice of defects in title applicable to transfers of land where regular machinery has long since been established for inquiry and investigation.'

"With that, I turn to the cases on constructive knowledge. Mr. Taylor relied strongly on *Selangor United Rubber Estates Ltd.* v. *Cradock (No. 3)* [1968] 1 W.L.R. 1555 and *Karak Rubber Co. Ltd.* v. *Burden (No. 2)* [1972] 1 W.L.R. 602. Each was a knowing assistance case. In the *Selangor* case at p. 1582, Ungoed-Thomas J., immediately after speaking of tracing property into the hands of a volunteer, said that equity

'will hold a purchaser for value liable as constructive trustee if he had actual or constructive notice that the transfer to him was of trust property in breach of trust . . . ";

and at p. 1583 he went on to refer to equitable rights and to say that in general 'it is equitable that a person with actual notice or constructive notice of those rights should be fixed with knowledge of them.' I find this view hard to reconcile with the passage in *In re Diplock* [1948] Ch. 465 (a case not cited to the judge) which I have just mentioned; and with all respect, it also seems to me to tend to confuse the absence of notice which shields a purchaser from liability under the doctrine of tracing, with the absence of knowledge of the trust which will prevent the imposition of a constructive trust. The judge went on to consider the meaning of 'knowledge' in various judgments, and reached a conclusion that knowledge was not confined to actual knowledge; and with this, as such, Mr. Chadwick had no quarrel. But he strongly contended that the cases cited on the extended meaning of 'knowledge' were cases within the 'wilful and reckless' head in the classification in the *Baden* case [1983] B.C.L.C. 325 (i.e. type (iii)), and that there was nothing to justify the inclusion of types (iv) an (v). The essential difference, of course, is that types (ii) and (iii) are governed by the words 'wilfully' or 'wilfully and recklessly,' whereas types (iv) and (v) have no such adverbs. Instead, they are cases of carelessness or negligence being tested by what an honest and reasonable man would have realised or would have inquired about, even if the person concerned was, for instance, not at all reasonable. Yet Ungoed-Thomas J. in his conclusion, at p. 1590, applied the standard of what would have been indicated to an honest and reasonable man, or would have put him on inquiry, and so, I think, included all five of the *Baden* types of knowledge, and not only the first three.

"In the *Karak* case [1972] 1 W.L.R. 602, Brightman J. considered this conclusion. Again *In re Diplock* [1948] Ch. 465 was not cited, but *Williams* v. *Williams* (1881) 17 Ch.D. 437, another case not cited to Ungoed-Thomas J. in the *Selangor* case [1968] 1 W.L.R. 1555, was duly examined. Brightman J. distinguished that case by pointing out that it was a knowing receipt case, whereas the case before him was a knowing assistance case; and he said, at p. 638, that *Williams* v. *Williams* had 'no relevance at all to the case before me.' In *Williams* v. *Williams* Kay J. had held that the recipient of the trust property, a solicitor, was not liable as a constructive trustee, and, at p. 445, the judge said that the case would be 'very different' if the recipient had 'wilfully shut his eyes.' He then referred to the 'very great negligence' of the solicitor, qua solicitor, in ignoring the trust, though holding that he was not liable as a constructive trustee. I do not see how Kay J. could have reached that conclusion if he had thought that knowledge of *Baden* types (iv) and (v) had sufficed; and, of course, what is before me is a case of knowing receipt, like *Williams* v. *Williams* and unlike the *Karak* case.

"There is also *In re Blundell* (1888) 40 Ch.D. 370, a case not cited in the *Selangor* case [1968] 1 W.L.R. 1555. It was cited but not mentioned in the judgment in the *Karak* case [1972] 1 W.L.R. 602, but like *Williams* v. *Williams*, 17 Ch.D. 437 and *In re Diplock* [1948] Ch. 465 it does not appear in the *Baden* case [1983] B.C.L.C. 325: all three, I may say, were duly cited in the *Carl Zeiss* case [1969] 2 Ch. 276. In *In re Blundell*, Stirling J. refused to hold that a solicitor was a constructive trustee of costs that a trustee of property had allowed him to take out of the estate, even though he knew that the trustee was guilty of a breach of trust, 'unless there are facts brought home to him which show that to his knowledge the money is being applied in a manner which is inconsistent with the trust': see p. 381. Both *Williams* v. *Williams* and *In re Blundell* figure prominently in the judgments of Sachs and Edmund Davies L.JJ. in the *Carl Zeiss* case, in support of their conclusion that negligence is not enough and that there must be dishonesty, a conscious impropriety or a lack of probity before liability as a constructive trustee is imposed.

"I should also mention certain other cases. *Consul Development Pty. Ltd.* v. *D.P.C. Estates Pty. Ltd.* (1975) 132 C.L.R. 373 is a case where from the judgments of Barwick C.J. and Gibbs and Stephen JJ. may be collected a somewhat tentative acceptance of type (iv) knowledge, but not of type (v). *Belmont Finance Corporation Ltd.* v. *Williams Furniture Ltd.* [1979] Ch. 250, 267, 275, shows Buckley and Goff L.JJ. taking the view (though not as a matter of decision) that what is required in a knowing assistance case is actual knowledge, wilful shutting the eyes to dishonesty, or wilful and reckless failure to inquire, but that other forms of constructive notice are not enough; and Orr L.J. concurred. Goff L.J. at p. 275 reaffirmed the view that he had expressed in *Competitive Insurance Co. Ltd.* v. *Davies Investments Ltd.* [1975] 1 W.L.R. 1240 that 'constructive notice of the section 199 type would not be sufficient.' I do not read the judgments of Buckley and Goff L.JJ. in *Belmont Finance Corporation Ltd.* v. *Williams Furniture Ltd. (No. 2)* [1980] 1 All E.R. 393, 405, 412, as resiling from the views that they had expressed in the earlier stages of the case.

"I shall attempt to summarise my conclusions.

(1) The equitable doctrine of tracing and the imposition of a constructive trust by reason of the knowing receipt of trust property are governed by different rules and must be kept distinct. Tracing is primarily a means of determining the rights of property, whereas the imposition of a constructive trust creates personal obligations that go beyond mere property rights.

(2) In considering whether a constructive trust has arisen in a case of the knowing receipt of trust property, the basic question is whether the conscience of the recipient is sufficiently affected to justify the imposition of such a trust.

(3) Whether a constructive trust arises in such a case primarily depends on the knowledge of the recipient, and not on notice to him; and for clarity it is desirable to use the word 'knowledge' and avoid the word 'notice' in such cases.

(4) For this purpose, knowledge is not confined to actual knowledge, but includes at least knowledge of types (ii) and (iii) in the *Baden* case [1983] B.C.L.C. 325, 407, i.e. actual knowledge that would have been acquired but for shutting one's eyes to the obvious, or wilfully and recklessly failing to make such inquiries as a reasonable and honest man would make; for in such cases there is a want of probity which justifies imposing a constructive trust.

(5) Whether knowledge of the *Baden* types (iv) and (v) suffices for this purpose is at best doubtful; in my view, it does not, for I cannot see that the carelessness involved will normally amount to a want of probity.

(6) For these purposes, a person is not to be taken to have knowledge of a fact that he once knew but has genuinely forgotten: the test (or a test) is whether the knowledge continues to operate on that person's mind at the time in question.

(7)(a) It is at least doubtful whether there is a general doctrine of 'imputed knowledge' that corresponds to 'imputed notice.' (b) Even if there is such a doctrine, for the purposes of creating a constructive trust of the 'knowing receipt' type the doctrine will not apply so as to fix a donee or beneficiary with all the knowledge that his solicitor has, at all events if the donee or beneficiary has not employed the solicitor to investigate his right to the bounty, and has done nothing else that can be treated as accepting that the solicitor's knowledge should be treated as his own. (c) Any such doctrine should be distinguished from the process whereby, under the name 'imputed knowledge,' a company is treated as having the knowledge that its directors and secretary have.

(8) Where an alleged constructive trust is based not on 'knowing receipt' but on 'knowing assistance,' some at least of these considerations probably apply; but I need not decide anything on that, and I do not do so.

"From what I have said, it must be plain that in my judgment the Duke did not become a constructive trustee of any of the chattels. I can see nothing that affected his conscience sufficiently to impose a constructive trust on him."

*Order accordingly*.

## AGIP (AFRICA) LTD. v. JACKSON

Chancery Division [1989] 3 W.L.R. 1367; [1990] Ch. 265

The plaintiff's chief accountant fraudulently altered the names of payees on cheques after they had been signed. He utilised the services of a firm of accountants, Jackson & Co., whose two partners were Mr. Jackson and Mr. Bowers, and the employee of the firm who did most of the work was Mr. Griffin. The firm formed new companies in the Isle of Man with bank accounts there. Forged cheques were paid via the accountancy firm's client account into such accounts and then paid out; and then the companies were liquidated and the accounts closed. Mr. Jackson and Mr. Griffin believed they were laundering money to assist breach of Tunisian exchange control rules or the evasion of tax and were held liable for knowing assistance in a dishonest design. Mr. Bowers was held vicariously liable for their acts.

MILLETT J.:

## "*The tracing remedy*

"The tracing claim in equity gives rise to a proprietary remedy which depends on the continued existence of the trust property in the hands of the defendant. Unless he is a bona fide purchaser for value without notice, he must restore the trust property to its rightful owner if he still has it. But even a volunteer who has received trust property cannot be made subject to a personal liability to account for it as a constructive trustee if he has parted with it without having previously acquired some knowledge of the existence of the trust: *In re Montagu's Settlement Trusts* [1987] Ch. 264.

"The plaintiffs are entitled to the money in court which rightfully belongs to them. To recover the money which the defendants have paid away the plaintiffs must subject them to a personal liability to account as constructive trustees and prove the requisite degree of knowledge to establish the liability.

### *Knowing receipt*

"In *Baden, Delvaux and Lecuit* v. *Société General pour Favoriser le Développement du Commerce et de l'Industrie en France S.A.* [1983] B.C.L.C. 325, 403, Peter Gibson J. said:

> 'It is clear that a stranger to a trust may make himself accountable to the beneficiaries under the trust in certain circumstances. The two main categories of circumstances have been given the convenient labels in *Snell's Principles of Equity* (28th ed.), pp. 194, 195, "knowing receipt or dealing" and "knowing assistance." The first category of "knowing receipt or dealing" is described in Snell, *op. cit.* at p. 194 as follows: "A person receiving property which is subject to a trust . . . becomes a constructive trustee if he falls within either of two heads, namely: (i) that he received trust property with actual or constructive notice that it was trust property and that the transfer to him was a breach of trust; or (ii) that although he received it without notice of the trust, he was not a bona fide purchaser for value without notice of the trust, and yet, after he had subsequently acquired notice of the trust, he dealt with the property in a manner inconsistent with the trust." I admit to doubt as to whether the bounds of this category might not be drawn too narrowly in *Snell*. For example, why should a person who, having received trust property knowing it to be such but without notice of a breach of trust because there was none, subsequently deals with the property in a manner inconsistent with the trust not be a constructive trustee within the "knowing receipt or dealing" category?'

I respectfuly agree. In my judgment, much confusion has been caused by treating this as a single category and by failing to differentiate between a number of different situations. Without attempting an exhaustive classification, it is necessary to distinguish between two main classes of case under this heading.

"The first is concerned with the person who receives for his own benefit trust property transferred to him in breach of trust. He is liable as a constructive trustee if he received it with notice, actual or constructive, that it was trust property and that the transfer to him was a breach of trust; or if he received it without such notice but subsequently discovered the facts. In either case he is liable to account for the property, in the first case as from the time he received the property, and in the second as from the time he acquired notice.

"The second and, in my judgment, distinct class of case is that of the person, usually an agent of the trustees, who receives the trust property lawfully and not for his own benefit but who then either misappropriates it or otherwise deals with it in a manner which is inconsistent with the trust. He is liable to account as a constructive trustee if he received the property knowing it to be such, though he will not necessarily be required in all circumstances to have known the exact terms of the trust. This class of case need not be considered further since the transfer to Baker Oil was not lawful.

"In either class of case it is immaterial whether the breach of trust was fraudulent or not. The essential feature of the first class is that the recipient must have received the property for his own use and benefit. This is why neither the paying nor the collecting bank can normally be brought within it. In paying or collecting money for a customer the bank acts only as his agent. It is otherwise, however, if the collecting bank uses the money to reduce or discharge the customer's overdraft. In doing so it receives the money for its own benefit.

"This is not a technical or fanciful requirement. It is essential if receipt-based liability is to be properly confined to those cases where the receipt is relevant to the loss. This can be demonstrated by considering the position of Mr. Bowers in the present case. He was a partner in Jackson & Co. but he played no active part in the movement of the funds. He did not deal with the money or give instructions in regard to it. He did not take it for his own benefit. He neither misapplied nor misappropriated it. It would not be just to hold him directly liable merely because Mr. Jackson and Mr. Griffin, who controlled the movement of the money from the moment it reached Baker Oil, chose on this occasion to pass it through his firm's bank account instead of through Euro-Arabian's account as previously.

"Mr. Griffin did not receive the money at all, and Mr. Jackson and Mr. Bowers did not receive or apply it for their own use and benefit. In my judgment, none of them can be made liable to account as a constructive trustee on the basis of knowing receipt.

*Knowing assistance*

"A stranger to the trust will also be liable to account as a constructive trustee if he knowingly assists in the furtherance of a fraudulent and dishonest breach of trust. It is not necessary that the party sought to be made liable as a constructive trustee should have received any part of the trust property, but the breach of trust must have been fraudulent. The basis of the stranger's liability is not receipt of trust property but participation in a fraud: *Barnes* v. *Addy* (1874) 9 Ch.App. 244, and see the explanation of the distinction between the two categories of the case given by Jacobs P. in *D.P.C. Estates Pty. Ltd.* v. *Grey* [1974] 1 N.S.W.L.R. 443.

"The authorities at first instance are in some disarray on the question whether constructive notice is sufficient to sustain liability under this head. In the *Baden* case [1983] B.C.L.C. 325, Peter Gibson J. accepted a concession by counsel that constructive notice is sufficient and that on this point there is no distinction between cases of 'knowing receipt' and 'knowing assistance.' This question was not argued before me but I am unable to agree. In my view the concession was wrong and should not have been made. The basis of liability in the two types of cases is quite different; there is no reason why the degree of knowledge required should be the same, and good reason why it should not. Tracing claims and cases of 'knowing receipt' are both concerned with rights of priority in relation to property taken by a legal owner for his own benefit; cases of 'knowing assistance' are concerned with the furtherance of fraud. In *Belmont Finance Corporation Ltd.* v. *Williams Furniture Ltd.* [1979] Ch. 250, the Court of Appeal insisted that to hold a stranger liable for 'knowing assistance' the breach of trust in question must be a fraudulent and dishonest one. In my judgment it necessarily follows that constructive notice of the fraud is not enough to make him liable. There is no sense in requiring dishonesty on the part of the principal while accepting negligence as sufficient for his assistant. Dishonest furtherance of the dishonest scheme of another is an understandable basis for liability; negligent but honest failure to appreciate that someone else's scheme is dishonest is not.

"In *In re Montagu's Settlement Trusts* [1987] Ch. 264, 285, Sir Robert Megarry V.-C. doubted whether constructive notice is sufficient even in cases of 'knowing receipt.' Whether the doubt is well founded or not (as to which I express no opinion), 'knowing assistance' is an a fortiori case.

"Knowledge may be provided affirmatively or inferred from circumstances. The various mental states which may be involved were analysed by Peter Gibson J. in *Baden's* case [1983] B.C.L.C. 325 as comprising: (i) actual knowledge; (ii) wilfully shutting one's eyes to the obvious; (iii) wilfully and recklessly failing to make such inquiries as an honest and reasonable man would make; (iv) knowledge of circumstances which would indicate the facts to an honest and reasonable man; and (v) knowledge of circumstances which would put an honest and reasonable man on inquiry.

"According to Peter Gibson J., a person in category (ii) or (iii) will be taken to have actual knowledge, while a person in categories (iv) or (v) has constructive notice only. I gratefully adopt the classification but would warn against over refinement or a too ready assumption that categories (iv) or (v) are necessarily cases of constructive notice only. The true distinction is between honesty and dishonesty. It is essentially a jury question. If a man does not draw the obvious inferences or make the obvious inquiries, the question is: why not? If it is because, however foolishly, he did not suspect wrongdoing or, having suspected it, had his suspicions allayed, however unreasonably, that is one thing. But if he did suspect wrongdoing yet failed to make inquiries because 'he did not want to know' (category (ii)) or because he regarded it as 'none of his business' (category (iii)), that is quite another. Such conduct is dishonest, and those who are guilty of it cannot complain if, for the purpose of civil liability, they are treated as if they had actual knowledge.

"In the present case, Mr. Bowers did not participate in the furtherance of the fraud and he cannot be held directly liable on this ground. Mr. Jackson and Mr. Griffin, however, clearly did. Mr. Jackson set up the arrangements and employed Mr. Griffin to carry them out. The money was under their control from the time it was paid into Baker Oil's account until the time it left Jackson & Co.'s clients' account in the Isle of Man Bank. One or other of them gave the actual instructions to the banks which disposed of the money. They plainly assisted in the fraud. The sole remaining question is: did they do so with the requisite degree of knowledge?

*The defendants' state of mind*

"I am led to the conclusion that Mr. Jackson and Mr. Griffin were at best indifferent to the possibility of fraud. They made no inquiries of the plaintiffs because they thought that it was none of their business. That is not honest behaviour. The sooner that those who provide the services of nominee companies for the purpose of enabling their clients to keep their activities secret realise it, the better. In my judgment, it is quite enough to make them liable to account as constructive trustees.

*Causation*

"Although no argument was addressed to me on this question, the judgment of Peter Gibson J. in *Baden's* case [1983] B.C.L.C. 325 contains a lengthy discussion of the position of a party who is put on inquiry but fails to inquire. He concluded that there is no presumption that, had inquiries been made, truthful answers would have been given; but that the plaintiff must prove that inquiry would have disclosed the truth, for the burden lies upon him to prove a causal connection between the failure to make inquiry and the loss.

"Peter Gibson J. was considering the question in the context of constructive notice, but a similar question appears to arise in the context of imputed knowledge of type (iii). For my part, I doubt that this is the correct approach even in cases of constructive notice, but I entirely reject it in cases of dishonesty. There is a great weight of judicial authority as well as principle against it. In my judgment, it derives from a misunderstanding of the basis of the constructive trustee's liability. He is not liable for failing to make inquiry, but for the misapplication of the plaintiff's property. He is under no duty to make inquiry. His only duty is to act honestly. If he makes inquiry, he does so for his own protection. If he does not make inquiry, the loss is not caused by his failure to do so but by his participation in the misapplication of the plaintiff's funds. He is liable only if he acted with knowledge; and this must be judged in the light of all the circumstances known to him and any explanation actually given to him. But it is not, in my view, to be judged by considering the hypothetical explanations which might have been given to him if he had sought them. If it were otherwise, his liability would depend on whether the fraudster would have been sufficiently inventive to be able to supply a plausible explanation if asked for one. In the present case, it would depend on whether the defendants should be assumed to have directed their inquiries, which ex hypothesi they did not make, to Mr. Zdiri or to his superiors. Such considerations are or ought to be irrelevant. They have been repeatedly denounced in the strongest terms: 'A more dangerous doctrine could not be laid down, nor one involving a more unsatisfactory inquiry': *Jones* v. *Williams* (1857) 24 Beav. 47, 62, *per* Sir John Romilly M.R., cited with approval by Stirling L.J. in *In re Alms Corn Charity* [1901] 2 Ch. 750, 762, and by Bankes L.J. in *A.L. Underwood Ltd.* v. *Bank of Liverpool* [1924] 1 K.B. 775, 789.

"In my judgment, the fact that a false but credible explanation would or might have been given is no defence to a party put on inquiry who makes none. Mr. Jackson and Mr. Griffin are not to be held liable for the misapplication of the plaintiffs' funds because they failed to make inquiries which would have discovered the fraud, but because they dishonestly assisted in the misapplication. Their failure to make the inquiries which honest men would have made to satisfy themselves that they were not engaged in furthering a fraud is merely the evidence from which their dishonesty is inferred.

*Mr. Bowers*

"Although Mr. Bowers cannot be held directly liable, he is vicariously liable[85] for the acts of his partner, Mr. Jackson, and his employee, Mr. Griffin." *Judgment for plaintiffs with costs.*

## QUESTIONS

1. "It is odd that a person can be liable under the 'knowing dealing' head if he deals with trust funds knowing that he is dealing with them in breach of trust, while he can only be liable under the 'knowing assistance' head if he is accessory to a *dishonest* design." Discuss.

2. "Megarry V.-C. believes that once a recipient of trust property has dissipated it he can only be personally liable to account as a constructive trustee if he had actual, Nelsonian or naughty knowledge that the property was trust property before he dissipated it. Millett J. believes that a recipient of trust property who has constructive notice that it be such—and also a donee with no constructive notice—should be accountable merely by virtue of the fact of having had (what actually was) trust property in his possession, without being a bona fide purchaser of it without notice of the trust, though defences should be available under Trustee Act 1925, s.61 or by virtue of a change of position where the recipient has parted with the trust property. The view of Megarry V.-C. based on the 'golden thread' of knowledge is simpler to follow and does not require the authority of the House of Lords for its implementation." Discuss after considering section 5, *infra*.

3. Vernon, a widower, owned a house in Wales. He married Carmen, a Spanish dancer, who spent a legacy on an extension making the house half as valuable again. He did not let Carmen or Sam, his son by his first marriage, know of each other's existence. Carmen returned to Spain temporarily to look after her terminally-ill mother.

By then Vernon was bored with Carmen. He executed a deed of gift of the house to Sam, who lived in Brussels, and gave Sam the earlier title deeds. He then sold his other possessions and destroyed Carmen's clothes and other possessions. He went to Bali taking his £19,000 savings and proceeds of sale with him.

Sam did not want the house, which he had never visited. He had estate agents sell it with vacant possession to Paul for £75,000. Sam invested the £75,000 in Superwhizz Ltd.

After four months Carmen returned to find Vernon gone and Paul occupying the house. Numb from this and her mother's death she did nothing for a further six months. It then took her two months to find exactly what had happened. On the liquidation of Superwhizz Ltd. its shares are worthless. Vernon has dissipated his £19,000 and has moved to Bangkok as a trainee Buddhist monk. Advise Carmen.

Would your advice differ if, instead of gifting the house to Sam, Vernon had sold and conveyed it to Oswald for £70,000 whilst Carmen was in Spain but in

---

[85] *cf. Re Bell's Indenture* [1980] 1 W.L.R. 1217 criticised by P. Matthews (1981) 131 New L.J. 243, P. Luxton [1981] Conv. 300 and not mentioned by Millett J. where a solicitor's partner knowingly assisted trustees to misappropriate trust funds where the trustees were clients of the firm but Vinelott J. held the partner had no implied authority to constitute himself a constructive trustee so that the solicitor was not vicariously liable for the misappropriation of which he was wholly ignorant. The distinction may be that the partner was "off on a frolic of his own" unlike Mr. Jackson and Mr. Griffin.

circumstances where Oswald had innocently failed to make a proper inquiry which should have revealed Carmen's interest in the house? Oswald had then sold and conveyed the house to Paul for £75,000 and had invested the money in Superwhizz Ltd. which went into liquidation before Oswald learned of Carmen's claim.

### Section 3: The Prevention of Fraudulent or Unconscionable Conduct

#### THE UNDERLYING RESIDUAL CATEGORY

Proprietary constructive trusts and personal constructive trusteeships are well-established in the cases of trustees and other fiduciaries and of strangers, as has just been seen. In both these cases it can be said that a constructive trust or a constructive trusteeship arises to prevent fraudulent or unconscionable conduct.

The discretionary prevention of fraudulent or unconscionable conduct underlies a miscellaneous category of cases. In some cases relief is automatic,[86] while in other cases it is very dependent on judicial discretion.[87] In some cases,[88] a constructive trust may be said to represent the remedy by which a plaintiff seeks to vindicate an express trust where the defendant cannot rely on the absence of statutory formalities because "Equity will not allow a statute to be used as an instrument of fraud." In other cases,[89] where there was no immediate declaration of trust or binding contract to create a trust, a constructive trust will be imposed to prevent the defendant acting unconscionably. The constructive trust may even be merely prospective in its effect[90] and it may confer a life interest[91] or some fractional share in property[92] or some personal right entitling the plaintiff to occupy the defendant's property for as long as he wishes or until the defendant pays him a sum of money.[93] Indeed, to reverse the defendant's unjust enrichment he may be personally liable to the plaintiff for a sum of money.[94]

The emphasis on a developing principle of unconscionability[95] may, perhaps, lead to the adoption of a general principle of liability for unjust enrichment, which may be a proprietary or a personal liability depending upon the circumstances.

Cases considered by various commentators to be instances of constructive trusts will now be considered.

---

[86] *e.g.* mutual wills, secret trusts.
[87] *e.g.* equitable proprietary estoppel interests.
[88] *e.g.* secret trusts, some common intention constructive trusts.
[89] *e.g.* some common intention constructive trusts and purchasers' undertakings.
[90] Referred to as a "remedial constructive trust" in *Metall und Rohstoff A.G.* v. *Donaldson Lufkin* [1990] 1 Q.B. 391, 479. Also see *LAC Minerals Ltd.* v. *International Corona Resources Ltd.* (1989) 61 D.L.R. (4th) 14, 48–51; *Muschinski* v. *Dodds* (1985) 160 C.L.R. 583.
[91] *Ungurian* v. *Lesnoff* [1990] Ch. 206.
[92] *Grant* v. *Edwards* [1986] Ch. 638; *Hohol* v. *Hohol* [1981] V.R. 221.
[93] *cf. Greasley* v. *Cooke* [1980] 1 W.L.R. 1306; *Inwards* v. *Baker* [1965] 2 Q.B. 29; *Re Sharpe* [1980] 1 W.R.L. 219; *Dodsworth* v. *Dodsworth* (1973) 228 Est.Gaz. 1115; *Cadman* v. *Bell* [1988] E.G.C.S. 139.
[94] *Gillies* v. *Keogh* [1989] 2 N.Z.L.R. 327, 335; *Raffaele* v. *Raffaele* [1962] W.A.R. 29; *Palachik* v. *Kiss* (1983) 146 D.L.R. (3rd) 385, 391–392, 395; *Novick Estate* v. *Lachuk Estate* (1989) 58 D.L.R. (4th) 185; *Everson* v. *Rich* (1988) 53 D.L.R. (4th) 470.
[95] See pp. 506–512, *infra*.

## MUTUAL WILLS AND SECRET TRUSTS

As we have seen,[96] under the doctrine of mutual wills the survivor of two testators is forced to observe the contract between them by the imposition of a constructive trust designed to give effect to the contract in favour of a third party. The constructive trust affecting the survivor is similar to the constructive trust which affects a vendor of Blackacre who has received the purchase price for it; the death of the predeceasing testator leaving a will in accordance with the contract corresponds to the provision of the purchase price.

In the case of secret trusts it has been seen[97] that a deceased's informally expressed wishes are effectuated where he has made his will or died intestate on the faith of an undertaking by a legatee or the next-of-kin that his wishes would be carried out. It may be better to regard a secret trust as an express trust which is enforced because "Equity will not allow a statute to be used as an instrument of fraud," but some judges[98] regard it as a constructive trust.

### EFFECTING INCOMPLETE TRANSFERS UNDER RE ROSE

A constructive trust is imposed to give effect to a donor's intentions where he has not yet assigned the legal title but he has done all that is necessary for him to do to achieve that end, so that Equity will regard the donee as beneficial owner (*e.g.* in the case of shares or land requiring registration of the new owner to transfer legal title to him).[99] Once Equity so regards the donee it becomes fraudulent or unconscionable for the donor to retain benefits, like dividends or rents, arising from the property.

### NO KILLER MAY BENEFIT FROM HIS CRIME

When Crippen murdered his wife her property did not on her intestacy pass to him and via his will to Miss Le Neve, but passed to his wife's blood relatives.[1] If the property is not intercepted before passing to the killer it seems he will hold it on constructive trust for those really entitled to it.[2] Their claims will have priority if he becomes bankrupt still owning such property, and they will have the right to trace the property or its product into the hands of anyone other than a bona fide purchaser of the legal interest for value without notice.

If one joint tenant murders another he should hold the property on constructive trust for himself and his victim in equal shares.[3] If a

---

[96] See pp. 105–112, *supra*.
[97] See pp. 86–105, *supra*.
[98] *e.g.* Nourse J. in *Re Cleaver* [1981] 1 W.L.R. 939.
[99] *Re Rose* [1952] Ch. 499, *supra*, p. 219; *Mascall* v. *Mascall* (1984) 49 P. & C.R. 119.
[1] *Re Crippen* [1911] P. 108; also see *Re Sigsworth* [1935] Ch. 89.
[2] *Schobelt* v. *Barber* (1966) 60 D.L.R. (2nd) 519; *Re Pechar* [1969] N.Z.L.R. 574; *Rasmanis* v. *Jurewitsch* [1970] N.S.W.L.R. 650; *Beresford* v. *Royal Insurance* [1938] A.C. 586, 600. See (1973) 89 L.Q.R. 235 (T. G. Youdan); (1974) 37 M.L.R. 481 (Earnshaw & Pace); Goff & Jones, Chap. 33.
[3] *Rasmanis* v. *Jurewitsch* [1970] N.S.W.L.R. 650; *Re K* [1985] 1 All E.R. 403 (if A's murder of B severs their joint tenancy A holds legal title on constructive trust for A and B's estate equally). If X, Y and Z are joint tenants and X kills Y then X should become tenant in common of one-third and Z of two-thirds. For destination of surplus endowment assurance moneys payable on death of murderer's co-owner see *Davitt* v. *Titcomb* [1990] 1 Ch. 110.

remainderman murders the life-tenant the victim should be deemed to live his actuarial life-span (except for a death-bed mercy killing), so that for the notional life-span the victim's interest should be held on constructive trust for his estate: thereafter, devolution should occur normally.[4]

Murder and manslaughter including manslaughter by reason of diminished responsibility invoke the principle, but not a finding of not guilty by reason of insanity.[5]

Except for murder cases, the Forfeiture Act 1982 now enables the court to modify the effect of the forfeiture rule where the justice of the case requires it, if the killer brings proceedings within three months of his conviction. In *Re K*[6] full relief against forfeiture was ordered in favour of a wife convicted of manslaughter of her husband. He had been violently attacking her for years. During one attack she picked up a loaded shotgun to frighten him and deter him from following her out of the room: the gun went off and killed him. The moral judgment for the judiciary to make was not too difficult here, but in other cases the task could be an unenviable one, calling for the judgment of Solomon.

PROPERTY TRANSFERRED BY UNDUE INFLUENCE OR OTHER VITIATING FACTOR

A case of undue influence "assumes a transfer of the beneficial interest, but in circumstances which entitle the transferor to recall it."[7] Thus, U, the exerciser of undue influence, receives the legal and equitable ownership as intended by O, the victim of the undue influence, but in circumstances where O has a mere equity to set aside the transfer and recover the property. U, his trustee in bankruptcy or his personal representatives, as the case may be, will be bound on demand to transfer the property[8] to O, so the position is as if they hold the property on constructive trust for O.

While O's interest is capable of being devised[9] or assigned,[10] it seems that for priority purposes such interest is a mere equity. Thus, it will only bind a third party who is a volunteer or a purchaser with notice: it will not bind a bona fide purchaser of any interest legal *or equitable* without notice.[11] There will be an equitable right to trace the property, but it seems that this right will only have the characteristics of a mere equity because the interest protected by such right is a mere equity.

The right to set aside a conveyance for fraud should be treated similarly to the right to rescind for undue influence.[12] However, where

---

4 (1973) 89 L.Q.R. 231, 250–251 (T. G. Youdan).
5 *Re Giles* [1972] Ch. 544; *Re Pitts* [1931] 1 Ch. 546.
6 [1986] Ch. 180 and see *Re H* [1990] 1 F.L.R. 441 and *Cretney* (1990) 3 Ox. J.L.S. 289.
7 *Hodgson* v. *Marks* [1971] Ch. 892, 929.
8 Including the fruits thereof and exchange products.
9 *Stump* v. *Gaby* (1852) 2 De G.M. & G. 623.
10 *Dickinson* v. *Burrell* (1866) L.R. 1 Eq. 337; *Bruty* v. *Edmunson* (1915) 85 L.J.Ch. 568.
11 *Lancashire Loans Ltd.* v. *Black* [1934] 1 K.B. 380; *Phillips* v. *Phillips* (1861) 4 De G.F. & J. 208; *Latec Investments* v. *Terrigal Pty. Ltd.* (1965) 113 C.L.R. 265.
12 *Latec Investments* (*supra*); *Ernest* v. *Vivian* (1863) 33 L.J.Ch. 513.

a fraudulent representation leads P to lend £X to Q the money is Q's to deal with as he wishes until P avoids the contract. Thus, if Q uses his investment skills to invest in property worth £2X when P avoids the contract, P can only claim the £X and the interest that he would have been entitled to if the contract of loan had been valid.[13]

Where F by mistake of fact pays G $2 million twice, instead of once, the equitable beneficial interest remains in F, so that the money is held by G on constructive trust for F, who can therefore trace the money.[14]

### TRACEABLE PROPERTY

Where P has a right to trace property and traceable property is found in the hands of D, who is not a bona fide purchaser of a legal interest therein for value without notice, it is fraudulent for D to refuse to hand over the property to P.[15] He holds the property on constructive trust for P or he may be regarded as bound involuntarily by the express trust in favour of P as a result of the property law of priorities.

### PURCHASERS' UNDERTAKINGS

Although a contractual licence to occupy a house or a flat is not an interest in land[16] and so only binds the contracting parties, a purchaser, P, may undertake to the vendor, V, that he will take the property positively subject to the rights of C, a contractual licensee. After completion of the purchase it then becomes unconscionable for P to evict C[17] by claiming that C only has contractual *in personam* rights binding V. Equity gives C an *in personam* right against P, compelling P to recognise C's rights under the contractual licence: *Ashburn Anstalt* v. *Arnold, infra,* p. 513. However, as this case also reveals, if V conveys or contracts to convey Blackacre defensively subject to whatever rights C may happen to have, so as to satisfy V's obligation to disclose all possible incumbrances and to protect him against any possible claim by P, then P is not bound by C's rights which are merely personal and not proprietary.

Where title to land is registered and C has a property interest which he has not protected by entry on the register, so that it would ordinarily be void against P, P will personally be bound by it if he has so undertaken with V or C.[18] As Brennan J. has stated[19]:

---

13 *Daly* v. *Sydney Stock Exchange* (1986) 60 A.L.J.R. 371; *Chief Constable of Leicestershire* v. *M* [1988] 3 All E.R. 1015.
14 *Chase Manhattan Bank* v. *Israel British Bank* [1981] Ch. 105; *Blacklocks* v. *J.B. Developments (Godalming) Ltd.* [1982] Ch. 183.
15 Or, if P is not the sole beneficiary, to trustees to hold for the benefit of P and the other beneficiaries according to the terms of the trust or other fiduciary relationshp affecting the property.
16 *Ashburn Anstalt* v. *Arnold* [1989] Ch. 1.
17 Indeed, from *Snelling* v. *Snelling* [1973] 1 Q.B. 87, it would seem that V could intervene in proceedings between P and C so as to have P's action stayed indefinitely and so dismissed.
18 *Lyus* v. *Prowsa Developments* [1982] 2 All E.R. 953.
19 *Bahr* v. *Nicolay (No. 2)* (1988) 62 A.L.J.R. 268, 288–289.

"A registered proprietor who has undertaken that his transfer should be subject to an unregistered interest and who repudiates the unregistered interest when his transfer is registered is, in equity's eye, acting fraudulently and he may be compelled to honour the unregistered interest. A means by which equity prevents the fraud is by imposing a constructive trust on the purchaser when he repudiates the unregistered interest. . . . The fraud which attracts the intervention of equity consists in the unconscionable attempt by the registered proprietor to deny the unregistered interest to which he has undertaken to subject his registered title."

## COMMON INTENTION CONSTRUCTIVE TRUSTS AND EQUITABLE PROPRIETARY ESTOPPEL

### Introduction

Over the last 20 years the courts have increasingly had to deal with the problems that a female[20] cohabitee, F, can face when title to the family home is in the sole name of the man, M, and the relationship has broken down. F then wants a share in the property or some compensation from M. Because they are not married she cannot claim against M under liberal divorce legislation which takes into account a wife's non-financial contributions to the welfare of her family.[21]

F will have to rely on alleging an equitable right under a resulting trust or a common intention constructive trust or an equitable estoppel claim.[22] If F directly or indirectly contributed a proportion of the purchase price of the home M will hold the legal title on resulting trust for M and F in proportion to their respective contributions.[23] Thus, F obtains only the share she paid for, though she will usually have contributed much less than M because of her lower earnings and the demands of childbirth and childcare. This limitation and the problems over what can amount to indirect financial contributions[24] have led to F claiming, instead, on common intention constructive trust principles to enable her to obtain the share expressly or implied agreed between M and F, normally a half share or, perhaps a "fair"[25] share.

Recently, problems over finding an implied agreement have led to the invocation of equitable proprietary estoppel principles to dilute the

---

[20] The same principles will apply whether the cohabitee without the legal title is male or female and even if the cohabitees are of the same sex. If the dispute is not between a husband and wife but with a third party, like a mortgagee, a spouse without the legal title may take advantage of these principles.

[21] For disputes between spouses Matrimonial Causes Act 1973, s.24 affords the courts plenty of discretion to take into account the wife's home-making and child-rearing functions.

[22] After September 27, 1989 all the terms of a contract disposing of an interest in land must actually be in writing signed by both parties or the contract will be void, and the equitable doctrine of part-performance of valid but unenforceable contracts will not be available: Law of Property (Miscellaneous Provisions) Act 1989, s.2 which does not affect interests arising under resulting or constructive trusts. Even before the 1989 Act it was difficult to establish a contract, *e.g.* because of uncertainty of terms or lack of intention to create legal relations.

[23] See pp. 428–432, *supra.*

[24] See pp. 499–501, *infra.*

[25] On a "fair" share, see *Gissing* v. *Gissing* [1971] A.C. 887, 909; *Eves* v. *Eves* [1975] 3 All E.R. 768, 772; *Passee* v. *Passee* [1988] 1 F.L.R. 263, 271; *Stokes* v. *Anderson* [1991] 1 F.L.R. 391.

requirements for a common intention constructive trust.[26] Indeed, in the light of the views of the Australian High Court,[27] English courts may ultimately come to decide that the distinction between common intention constructive trusts and equitable estoppel interests which both prevent unconscionable conduct is illusory, and that, therefore, the courts have a flexible range of remedies, whether prospective or retrospective, enabling justice to be done between M and F (perhaps even taking domestic as well as financial contributions into account), without necessarily having adverse effects on third parties who had earlier acquired interests, like mortgages, in the family home.[28]

*Common intention constructive trusts*

(a) Originally a *quid pro quo* was required. Conventionally, the common intention constructive trust requires a bilateral understanding or agreement that if F acts in a particular way[29] then she will obtain the agreed share in the family home, usually a half share (leaving the court no discretion) or a "fair" share[30] (leaving the court plenty of discretion). It can be said that Equity acts *in personam* to prevent M pleading the lack of formalities, so F gets what was agreed.[31] Her interest should date from the time she commences to act to her detriment in the contemplated manner so that it is then inequitable for M to deny her an interest. Her interest will be capable thereafter of binding a mortgagee or a purchaser if she is occupying the property.[32]

A distinction must be made[33] between cases based on evidence capable of establishing an express agreement and cases based on conduct allegedly creating an inferred agreement.

Where there is direct evidence of express discussions between the parties, however imperfectly remembered and however imprecise their terms may have been, the court may find as a fact that there was an express common intention that if F acted in a particular way she would obtain an agreed interest in the property. Whatever the agreed *quid pro quo* was (whether relating to financial contributions, labouring work on improving the property, staying at home looking after M's children by a previous marriage and any children M and F may have) it will suffice if F furnishes it.[34]

As Lord Bridge states,[35] "In sharp contrast with this situation is the very different one where there is no evidence to support a finding of an

---

[26] *Grant* v. *Edwards* [1986] Ch. 638, 657 approved by C.A. in *Lloyds Bank* v. *Rossett* [1989] Ch. 350.
[27] *Baumgartner* v. *Baumgartner* (1988) 62 A.L.J.R. 29; *Waltons Stores Interstate Ltd.* v. *Maher* (1988) 62 A.L.J.R. 110.
[28] See D. J. Hayton, "Equitable rights of cohabitees" [1990] Conv. 370.
[29] See Lord Diplock in *Gissing* v. *Gissing* [1971] A.C. 887, 905 and Lord Oliver in *Austin* v. *Keele* (1987) 61 A.L.J.R. 605, 610.
[30] See cases cited in n. 25, *supra.*
[31] Until then, there is a merely voluntary declaration of trust unenforceable for want of writing: see p. 503, *infra.*
[32] Assumed in *Midland Bank* v. *Dobson* [1986] 1 F.L.R. 171 and *Lloyds Bank* v. *Rossett* [1989] Ch. 350.
[33] Emphasised by H.L. in *Lloyds Bank* v. *Rosset* [1990] 2 W.L.R. 867.
[34] *Grant* v. *Edwards* [1986] Ch. 638.
[35] *Lloyds Bank* v. *Rosset* [1990] 1 All E.R. 1111, 1119.

agreement or arrangement to share, however reasonable it might have been for the parties to reach such an arrangement if they had applied their minds to the question, and where the court must rely entirely on the conduct of the parties both as the basis from which to infer a common intention to share the property beneficially and as the conduct relied on to give rise to a constructive trust. In this situation direct contributions to the purchase price by the partner who is not the legal owner, whether initially or by payment of mortgage instalments, will readily justify the inference necessary to the creation of a constructive trust. But, as I read the authorities, it is at least extremely doubtful whether anything less will do."

In *Lloyds Bank Ltd.* v. *Rosset*, in delivering the judgment of the House of Lords, Lord Bridge held that the facts fell within the second situation and emphasised the distinction between the shared use of assets and shared ownership, stating,[36] "Neither a common intention by spouses that a house is to be renovated as a 'joint venture' nor a common intention that the house is to be shared by parents and children as the family home throws any light on their intentions with respect to the beneficial ownership of the property."

With such common intentions H and W had decided to buy a semi-derelict farmhouse for £57,000, using money provided by trustees of a family trust who insisted the property be bought in H's name alone. Without W's knowledge, H mortgaged the property to Lloyds Bank to secure a £15,000 loan with interest. W spent some time supervising the builders doing renovatory works, did some preparatory cleaning work and did some skilful painting and decorating herself. The House of Lords held that such conduct was insufficient to justify any inference that there was a common intention for her to acquire a beneficial interest in the farmhouse capable of binding a mortgagee. The value of her work in relation to a farmhouse costing about £72,000 was trifling. More significantly,[37] "It would seem the most natural thing in the world for any wife, in the absence of her husband abroad, to spend all the time she could spare and to employ any skills she might have, such as the ability to decorate a room, in doing all she could to accelerate progress of the work, quite irrespective of any expectation she might have of enjoying a beneficial interest in the property. The judge's view that some of this work was work 'on which she could not reasonably have been expected to embark unless she was to have an interest in the house' seems to me quite untenable." Thus, the bank as mortgagee could evict her as well as H in order to be able to sell the property with vacant possession.

It is clear[38] that domestic stay-at-home contributions to the welfare of the household cannot justify the inference that the parties agreed

---

[36] *Ibid.* 1117.
[37] *Ibid.* 1118.
[38] *Gissing* v. *Gissing* [1971] A.C. 887; *Burns* v. *Burns* [1984] Ch. 317; *Lloyds Bank* v. *Rosset* [1990] 2 W.L.R. 867.

that F would obtain an agreed share in the house if she made such contributions. It is the most natural thing in the world for F to bear and rear children, to cook and clean and to sew and darn out of love for M and a desire to live in a pleasant, happy environment.[39] It is most unnatural, and therefore requires an express agreement, for F to do such things in the belief that she is thereby acquiring a beneficial interest in the home.

However, Lord Bridge probably goes too far in his *obiter dicta*[40] when he indicates that to justify an inferred agreement between M and F it is necessary to find *direct* contributions by F to the purchase price, whether initially or by payment of mortgage instalments, such financial contributions clearly representing conduct upon which F could not reasonably have been expected to embark unless she was thereby to obtain an interest in the home. Purchase-money resulting trusts will arise here in any event to enable F to have an equitable interest, the size of which will reflect her proportionate contribution to the purchase of the home[41]: the absence of any express agreement as to her obtaining, say, a half share will prevent her obtaining under the guise of a constructive trust anything larger than she would have obtained under a resulting trust.

What, then, is the position where F indirectly pays M's mortgage, *i.e.* she goes out to work and uses her earnings to pay a substantial part of the household expenses, so enabling M to pay all the mortgage instalments which he would not have been able to do and keep up their standard of living without F seeing to the other expenses? Where there is direct evidence of an express common intention that F is to have a half share in the home then F's financial contributions clearly count as detrimental conduct referable to F having an interest in the home: *Grant* v. *Edwards*, *infra*, p. 516. In the absence of direct evidence of an express common intention Fox and May L.JJ. in *Burns* v. *Burns*[42] indicate that the courts will infer from F's substantial financial contributions to household expenses, which are necessary to enable M alone to keep up the mortgage payments without affecting their standard of living, that there was a common intention for F to have an interest in the home; but, presumably, only for her to have that share which corresponds to her proportionate contribution to the purchase of the home. This should be the position under a resulting trust in any event.

Lord Bridge did not refer to *Burns* v. *Burns* but he did say[43] that F's conduct in *Grant* v. *Edwards*[44] in making substantial financial contributions to household expenses so as to enable M alone to pay the mortgage "fell far short of such conduct as would by itself have

---

[39] *e.g. Coombes* v. *Smith* [1986] 1 W.L.R. 808.
[40] See n. 35, *supra.*
[41] See p. 429, *supra.*
[42] [1984] Ch. 317, 329, 344–345. Also see *Gissing* v. *Gissing* [1971] A.C. 887, 903, 909.
[43] [1990] 1 All E.R. 1111, 1119.
[44] [1986] Ch. 638.

supported the claim in the absence of an express representation by the male partner that she was to have such an interest." These cited words also applied to F's conduct in *Eves* v. *Eves*[45] where M led F to believe she was to have a fair share in the dilapidated house, taking account of her renovatory work. She cleaned the house and did extensive decorative work and painted the brickwork on the front of the house. She wielded a 14lb sledge-hammer to demolish the concrete surface of the front garden and disposed of the rubble in a skip and prepared the front garden for turfing. She worked in the back garden and, with M, demolished an old shed and erected a new shed. The Court of Appeal held she was entitled to a quarter share in the house under a constructive trust.

In the absence of any common intention or unilateral representation Lord Bridge clearly considers that Janet Eves's conduct would have been referable to her love for Stuart Eves and a desire to live in pleasant surroundings, so that she would have obtained no interest in the home. To enable an inference to be drawn that she was to have an interest in the home, it would seem that a major capital contribution to the value of the home would be needed, such as using a £25,000 legacy to pay a building contractor's bill for an extension of a garage with a bedroom above it or herself building such extension over a six-month period. In practice, in such a case it would seem most unlikely for there not to have been some express discussion about F thereby acquiring an interest in the home, but in the absence of such discussion such conduct clearly seems conduct on which F "could not reasonably have been expected to embark unless she was to have an interest in the home."[46]

(b) Common intention without *quid pro quo*.

As Nicholls L.J. stated in *Lloyds Bank* v. *Rosset*[47]:

> "I can see no reason in principle why, if the parties' common intention is that the wife should have a beneficial interest in the property, and if thereafter to the knowledge of the husband she acts to her detriment in reliance on that common intention, the wife should not be able to assert an equitable interest against the husband just as much as she could in a case where the common intention was that, by acting in a certain way, she would acquire a beneficial interest. In each case the question is whether, having regard to what has occurred, it would be inequitable to permit the party in whom the legal estate is vested to deny the existence of the beneficial interest which they both intended should exist."

On appeal, Lord Bridge implicitly accepted this. Once there is a finding that there was a common intention for the property to be shared beneficially he stated,[48] "It will only be necessary for the partner asserting a claim to a beneficial interest against the partner

---

[45] [1975] 1 W.L.R. 1338.
[46] *Grant* v. *Edwards* [1986] Ch. 638, 648.
[47] [1989] Ch. 350, 381.
[48] [1990] 1 All E.R. 1111, 1118–1119.

entitled to the legal estate to show that he or she has acted to his or her detriment or significantly altered his or her position in reliance on the agreement in order to give rise to a constructive trust or proprietary estoppel."

This reference to proprietary estoppel is particularly significant because a proprietary estoppel claim requires only unilateral conduct by M which leads F to believe that she has an interest in the home, so that in this belief she acts to her detriment, so that it then becomes unconscionable for M to insist on his formal 100 per cent. ownership of the home.[49] Indeed, in *Grant* v. *Edwards*[50] Browne-Wilkinson V.-C. had earlier suggested that useful guidance for constructive trust cases could be obtained from the principles underlying the law of proprietary estoppel: see p. 504, *infra*.

(c) Size of F's interest.

Where the common intention is for F to have a half share it has been assumed that she will obtain the half share if she fully provides the *quid pro quo*,[51] *e.g.* contributes what she can to help with mortgage payments and household expenses, taking account of the exigencies of their family life. No court has considered what would happen if she only provided half the *quid pro quo*, *e.g.* if she held back (for her private nest-egg) half of what she could have contributed. Would she only obtain half of the half share? Indeed, what would happen if due to much unemployment F only made small financial contributions towards household expenses and holidays for two years before leaving M and running off with Roger?

The problem becomes greater where no *quid pro quo* is required, M merely carrying F over the threshold and saying, "This house is as much yours as mine" and F then acts to her detriment in reliance on the belief that she has a half share in the house. Detrimental acts may be placed on a scale of one to 99: does a tiny scale one detriment entitle F to the half share just as a colossal scale 99 detriment must so entitle F?[52]

The way forward must be that diffidently suggested by Browne-Wilkinson V.-C., namely, following guidance in the law of proprietary estoppel, *pro tanto* to prevent M unconscionably asserting his formal 100 per cent. ownership: "Equity is displayed at its most flexible."[53] Thus, in certain circumstances, instead of the promised half share, F might only obtain a quarter share, or a charge on the property to secure the sum of £2,000 representing F's contributions, or a licence to live in the property until paid the sum of £2,000.[54]

---

[49] See p. 504, *infra*.

[50] [1986] Ch. 638, 656.

[51] *Gissing* v. *Gissing* [1971] A.C. 887, 905, 908; *Midland Bank Ltd.* v. *Dobson* [1986] 1 F.L.R. 171; *Allen* v. *Snyder* [1977] 2 N.S.W.L.R. 685; *Grant* v. *Edwards* [1986] Ch. 638, 657.

[52] In *Lloyds Bank* v. *Rosset* [1990] 1 All E.R. 1111, 1118 Lord Bridge opined that Mrs. Rosset's acts would have been insufficient even if she had proved an oral declaration of trust in her favour. See also *Bothe* v. *Amos* [1976] Fam. 46, 55–56.

[53] *Grant* v. *Edwards* [1986] Ch. 638, 657.

[54] *Re Sharpe* [1980] 1 All E.R. 198, 202; *Maharaj* v. *Chand* [1986] A.C. 898; *cf. Tanner* v. *Tanner* [1975] 1 W.L.R. 1346.

(d) Impact upon third parties.

Where equity confers upon F the interest she would originally have had if M's express trust had been declared in signed writing, so that the imposition of a constructive trust arguably vindicates the express oral trust,[55] the court's decree is assumed to be retrospective.[56] However, the date of the oral declaration cannot be the relevant date because the trust is then unenforceable.[57] If there is no detrimental reliance by F before M mortgages the home to X it seems that just as M is not subject to an enforceable trust so neither is X, who derives title from M. The priority of X over F crystallises at this stage[58] so as not to be affected if F subsequently acts to her detriment or subsequently persuades M to sign a memorandum evidencing the trust within the Law of Property Act 1925, section 53(1)(*b*).[59]

What of the case where X acquires a mortgage after F has allegedly acted detrimentally and some years later F alleges that she has an interest that binds X? Courts assume without argument[60] that any interest established in due course by F will bind X. However, after F's claim the uncertainties as to inferred intention, if there is no express intention, and as to "detrimental" acts and the extent to which the circumstances are "unconscionable" enough to warrant one form of flexible equitable relief rather than another remain to be resolved by the court. F's claim is more uncertain than a claim amounting to a mere equity,[61] *e.g.* a right to have a deed rectified in a certain way. It would seem that F should have no right to have an imperfect gift in her favour perfected,[62] being merely a suitor for discretionary equitable relief. She should be regarded not as enforcing an imperfect gift or contract but as making out another cause of action,[63] namely that all the circumstances up to the date of the court decree make it unconscionable for M to be allowed to rely on the lack of formalities (or of bargained-for consideration) to assert his formal 100 per cent. ownership. The court is tailoring the remedy to fit the wrong: it should not

---

[55] See *Allen* v. *Snyder* [1977] 2 N.S.W.L.R. 685, *per* Glass J.A.; C. Harpum (1982) 2 O.J.L.S. 277, 279.
[56] *Midland Bank* v. *Dobson* [1986] 1 F.L.R. 171; *Lloyds Bank* v. *Rosset* [1989] Ch. 350. It is too easy to equate the impact of constructive trusts and resulting trusts.
[57] *Gissing* v. *Gissing* [1971] A.C. 887; *Midland Bank* v. *Dobson* [1986] 1 F.L.R. 171.
[58] *cf. London & Cheshire Insurance Co. Ltd.* v. *Laplagrene* [1971] Ch. 499.
[59] See T. G. Youdan [1984] Camb.L.J. 306, 321–322.
[60] See n. 56, *supra.*
[61] A mere equity is a right to rectify a deed conveying or creating an interest in property or a right to set aside such a deed on grounds such as fraud, undue influence or mistake. A mere equity is the weakest form of proprietary right being void against a purchaser of a legal or equitable interest for value without notice. A proprietary right must satisfy the criteria of definability, stability and identifiability as Lord Wilberforce emphasised in *National Provincial Bank* v. *Ainsworth* [1965] A.C. 1175, 1237 and see Lord Upjohn at p. 1124, "Still less can it be reasonable to make an inquiry if the answer will probably lead to no conclusion which can inform the inquirer with any certainty as to the rights of the occupant." Also see *Carl Zeiss Stiftung* v. *Herbert Smith (No. 2)* [1969] 2 Ch. 276, *supra*, p. 477 on doubtful equities.
[62] "Equity will not perfect an imperfect gift" is a most fundamental rule to which any exception requires the clearest justification: *Milroy* v. *Lord* (1862) 4 De G.F. & J. 264, 274.
[63] *cf. Pavey* v. *Paul* (1987) 69 A.L.R. 577, 583, *per* Mason C.J. and Wilson and Deane JJ. in the context of allowing a *quantum meruit* where there was an unenforceable oral contract.

be seen as upholding already-existing property rights. This, after all, is the position where she has an equitable proprietary estoppel claim[64] and any alleged distinction between constructive trusts and equitable estoppels seems illusory (see p. 506, *infra*).

Taking into account all the circumstances up to the date of the decree[65] the court may exceptionally[66] decide that to remedy M's unconscionable conduct and reverse F's detriment once and for all requires F to have all that M promised.[67] More commonly, it will suffice to let F either have a proportion of the share promised or a sum of money[68] supported by a charge on the house or the personal right to occupy the house until the money is paid to her.[69] Such a decree ought prima facie to be prospective only. However, if X, a purchaser or mortgagee, had agreed with M or F that his interest would positively be subject to F's rights then he holds his interest subject to her rights: *Ashburn Anstalt* v. *Arnold*, p. 513, *infra*. But if M had cautiously or negatively sold or mortgaged the house to X subject to the rights, if any, of F, so as to protect himself against claims by X,[70] then X should take free of F's rights based on a common intention constructive trust or an equitable estoppel. However, X would remain subject to any rights established by F under a purchase-money resulting trust. Where F is in actual occupation inquiries by X to establish whether or not such resulting trust exists could well lead to protection of her rights on *Ashburn Anstalt* v. *Arnold* principles.

*Equitable proprietary estoppels*

(a) Unilateral conduct followed by detrimental reliance. A successful equitable estoppel claim requires only unilateral conduct by M leading F to believe that she has an interest in the family home, so that she acts to her detriment in reliance thereon and it then becomes unconscionable for M to insist on his strict legal rights.[71] The court does not automatically perfect M's imperfect gift (*e.g.* of a half share where he declares "This house is as much mine as yours, share and share alike") and give the go-by to statutory formalities. It intervenes only *pro tanto* to decide what is the "minimum equity to do justice"[72] to F so as to prevent M's unconscionable conduct affecting F detrimentally: it reverses F's detriment and prevents M's unjust enrichment.

The Australian High Court recently analysed the English estoppel cases and Mason C.J. and Wilson J. in their joint judgment concluded[73]:

---

[64] See Meagher Gummow & Lehane, *Equity: Doctrine and Remedies* (2nd ed.), p. 412.
[65] *cf. Crabb* v. *Arun D.C.* [1976] Ch. 179; *Williams* v. *Staite* [1979] Ch. 291.
[66] As "the minimum equity to do justice": *Crabb* v. *Arun D.C.* [1976] Ch. 179, and see *Waltons Stores Interstate Ltd.* v. *Maher* (1988) 62 A.L.J.R. 110.
[67] *Pascoe* v. *Turner* [1979] 1 W.L.R. 431.
[68] See n. 94, p. 493, *supra*.
[69] *cf. Re Sharpe* [1980] 1 All E.R. 198, 202.
[70] As in *Ashburn Anstalt* v. *Arnold* [1989] Ch. 1.
[71] *Crabb* v. *Arun D.C.* [1976] Ch. 179.
[72] *Ibid.* 198 applied in *Pascoe* v. *Turner* [1979] 1 W.L.R. 431.
[73] (1988) 62 A.L.J.R. 110, 116. Also see *Burbery Mortgage Finance and Savings Ltd.* v. *Hindsbank Holdings Ltd.* [1989] 1 N.Z.L.R. 359.

"One may therefore discern in the cases a common thread, namely the principle that equity will come to the relief of a plaintiff who has acted to his detriment on the basis of a basic assumption in relation to which the other party has played such a part in the adoption of the assumption that it would be unfair or unjust if he were held free to ignore it. . . . Equity comes to the relief of such a plaintiff on the footing that it would be unconscionable conduct on the part of the other party to ignore the assumption."

Brennan J. emphasised[74]:

"The unconscionable conduct which it is the object of equity to prevent is the failure of a party, who has induced the adoption of the assumption or expectation and who knew or intended that it would be relied upon, to fulfil the assumption or expectation or otherwise to avoid the detriment which that failure would occasion. The object of equity is not to compel the party bound [by the claim] to fulfil the assumption or expectation; it is to avoid the detriment which, if the assumption or expectation goes unfulfilled, will be suffered by the party who has been induced to act or to abstain from acting thereon."

(b) Size of F's interest and its impact upon third parties. The "minimum equity to do justice"[75] to F and prevent M's unconsionable assertion of his strict legal rights depends upon the conduct and relationship of the parties from the date of M's original conduct till the court makes its decree—the likely outcome of F's claim may fluctuate in this period.[76] The court is tailoring the remedy to fit the wrong and is not upholding already-existing rights of a proprietary nature.[77] F cannot insist on having the expected interest: she is a supplicant for the court's discretionary assistance. Indeed, the court may award her the promised interest but it may, instead, award her a lesser interest or even merely a sum of money,[78] though it may be supported by granting F a licence to occupy the premises till the sum is paid or a charge on the property.

When the court puts an end to the great uncertainty and the effect of its decree is that M holds the house on constructive trust for F as to an equitable half share or quarter share or an equitable life interest, it seems that this should only have prospective effect so that it is what the Court of Appeal[79] recently termed a "remedial constructive trust"

---

[74] *Ibid.* 125.
[75] *Crabb* v. *Arun D.C.* [1976] Ch. 179, 198, *per* Scarman L.J.
[76] *Crabb* v. *Arun D.C.* [1976] Ch. 179; *Williams* v. *Staite* [1979] Ch. 291; *Dodsworth* v. *Dodsworth* (1973) 228 E.G. 1115; *Griffiths* v. *Williams* (1977) 248 E.G. 947.
[77] See n. 64, *supra.*
[78] See n. 94, *supra* p. 493. As Oliver L.J. stated in *Savva* v. *Costa* [1980] C.A. Transcript 723, Maudsley & Burn, *Land Law Cases & Materials* (5th ed.), p. 556, "The expenditure gives rise to an equity to which the court will give effect in such way as may be appropriate in the circumstances giving rise to the estoppel claim. It may be by injunction, it may be by declaring a trust of the beneficial interest or it may be by a declaration of lien for monies expended."
[79] *Metall und Rohstoff A.G.* v. *Donaldson Lufkin & Jenrette Inc.* [1990] 1 Q.B. 391, 479.

that arises.[80] Thus, if M had sold or mortgaged the house to X after some detrimental reliance of F (other than purchase-money resulting trust contributions) X should not be bound by F's rights unless he had agreed with M or F positively to take subject to F's rights so that it would be unconscionable for him to deny her rights on *Ashburn Anstalt* v. *Arnold* principles.[81] If F had been in actual occupation and X had inquired whether F had any resulting trust interest this could well have led to protection of her rights on *Ashburn Anstalt* v. *Arnold* principles.

*The illusory distinction between common intention constructive trusts and equitable estoppels*

Consider the following three scenarios.

(1) M says to F, "This house is as much yours as mine, so long as you contribute what you can to household expenses and mortgage payments in the exigencies of our life together." F replies, "Lovely. I'll do what I can to help out."

(2) M says to F, "This house is as much yours as mine" when asked by her whether she has a share in the house. "I'm glad you agree," she replies.

(3) Proudly carrying F over the threshold of his house, M states, "My darling, this house is as much yours as mine from this day forth." "Oh, thank you. How wonderful!" exclaims F.

It will be seen that (1) is a common intention constructive trust with a *quid pro quo*, (2) such a trust without a *quid pro quo*, while (3) is a unilateral representation upon which an estoppel claim may be based. However, all three claims hinge upon F's detrimental reliance which makes it unconscionable for M to assert his 100 per cent. formal ownership. One can see that there is not very much difference between the scenarios and that to obtain the best scenario for F there will be a heavy premium upon skilled professional assistance—or even direction—in the preparation of relevant evidence and in encouraging F to say that she acted not out of love and affection but out of an express or tacit understanding or expectation that she had a half share so long as she contributed what cash she could in the exigencies of their life together or so long as she was a good housekeeper.

One can see that the need for a *quid pro quo* requires a meeting of minds and a common intention so that scenario (1) is truly a common

---

[80] As in the Australian High Court order in *Muschinski* v. *Dodds* (1985) 160 C.L.R. 583. In the Canadian Supreme Court in *L.A.C. Minerals* v. *International Corona Resources Ltd.* (1989) 61 D.L.R. (4th) 14, 51 La Forest J. stated, "The issue of the appropriate remedy only arises once a valid restitutionary claim has been made out. The constructive trust awards a right in property but that right can only arise once a right to relief is established." However, in *Rawluk* v. *Rawluk* (1990) 65 D.L.R (4th) 161 4:3 the Canadian Supreme Court held a constructive trust of a family home to be retrospective though there seems no reason why it should not be retrospective between the parties in the exceptional case (as there) where needed between them, but it should normally be prospective where third parties are concerned.

[81] See p. 504, *supra*.

intention trust. In the other two scenarios, however, M is making a unilateral gift of half his ownership, so that it is his intention as donor that is the foundation for an estoppel claim, which then requires F to know of that intention, so that in reliance thereon she can act to her detriment and make it unconscionable for M to assert his strict legal rights. It follows that scenario (2) should be treated as an equitable estoppel claim.

Even in the case of scenario (1), is it not time that the courts and counsel moved beyond pigeon-holing circumstances into common intention constructive trusts and equitable estoppels and concentrated upon the basic principle of unconscionability underlying both doctrines? As Browne-Wilkinson V.-C. has pointed out,[82] "In both the claimant must to the knowledge of the legal owner have acted in the belief that the claimant has or will have an interest in the property. In both the claimant must have acted to his or her detriment in reliance on such belief. In both equity acts on the conscience of the legal owner to prevent him from acting in an unconscionable manner." As Megarry V.-C. has pointed out[83]: "There is today a tendency in equity to put less emphasis on detailed rules and more weight on the underlying principles that engendered those rules, treating the rules less as rules requiring complete compliance and more as guidelines to assist the court in applying the principles." Thus, the High Court of Australia in *Baumgartner* v. *Baumgartner* in dealing with a dispute between M and F where there was insufficient evidence to establish a common intention constructive trust held[84] "the appellant's assertion, after the relationship had failed, that the Leumeah property is his property beneficially to the exclusion of any interest at all on the part of the respondent, amounts to unconscionable conduct which attracts the intervention of equity and the imposition of a constructive trust at the suit of the respondent. . . . We consider that the constructive trust to be imposed should declare the beneficial interest of the parties in the proportion 55 per cent. to the appellant and 45 per cent. to the respondent."

Shortly afterwards, the Australian High Court accepted that the discretionary prevention of unconscionable conduct underlies not just constructive trust claims but also estoppel claims as apparent in the passages cited (p. 505, *supra*) from *Waltons Stores (Interstate) Ltd.* v. *Maher*.[85]

### Discretionary prevention of unconscionable conduct

Whether or not M is unconscionably asserting his 100 per cent. formal ownership and so is unconscionably retaining a benefit at F's expense may be said to turn on an apparently vague standard. For this

---

[82] *Grant* v. *Edwards* [1986] Ch. 638, 656.
[83] *Re Montagu's Settlement* [1987] Ch. 264, 278.
[84] (1987) 164 C.L.R. 137, 149.
[85] (1988) 62 A.L.J.R. 110.

reason unconscionability factors should not affect third parties as a matter of property law. As has been seen, the court's decree should not recognise any pre-existing proprietary rights but should prospectively remedy the "wrong" of unconscionable conduct. The broad flexible range of remedies should just affect M and F and to the extent that any remedy confers a proprietary right on F it should not retrospectively affect X, a third party, unless needed to prevent X's earlier unconscionable behaviour towards F on *Ashburn Anstalt* v. *Arnold* principles.[86] Thus, the courts should not be inhibited by worries about third parties in developing a flexible range of remedies as between cohabitees.

As between M and F, who have full inside knowledge of all unconscionability factors, it should matter little that there is a grey penumbra of uncertainty for which they have only themselves to blame. There should be an interpretative community of judges and lawyers who can come to a significant consensus on what is unconscionable in particular circumstances in the light of current decided cases on constructive trusts and equitable estoppels and future cases decided on unconscionability principles. Judges and lawyers already cope with whether or not a term in a mortgage[87] or a bargain with a poorly-educated member of the lower income group[88] is "unconscionable" and whether or not a landlord is "unreasonably" withholding his consent to an assignment or sub-lease.[89] Indeed, they also cope with taking a spouse's domestic contributions to family life into account in arranging financial provision on divorce.[90]

A cohabitee's domestic contributions to the welfare of the family can be taken into account in the rare case where they are the *quid pro quo* of a common intention constructive trust. More commonly, M will state that the home is as much F's as his, and F may then spend the next 10 years of her life staying at home looking after the home and M and the children they have. The key question after M and F separate is whether F would have done the acts relied upon as a detriment even if she thought she had no interest in the home: if so she cannot successfully plead that she did the acts in reliance on her belief that she had an interest in the home.

As Browne-Wilkinson V.-C. states[91]:

> "Setting up house together, having a baby, making payments to general housekeeping expenses (not strictly necessary to enable the mortgage to be paid) may all be referable to the mutual love and affection of the parties and not specifically referable to the claimant's belief that she has an interest in the house. As at present advised, once it has been shown

---

86 See p. 504, *supra*.
87 *Multiservice Bookbinding Ltd.* v. *Marden* [1979] Ch. 84.
88 *Cresswell* v. *Potter* [1978] 1 W.L.R. 255; *Watkins* v. *Watson Smith*, *The Times*, July 3, 1986.
89 *Birkel* v. *Duke of Westminster* [1977] Q.B. 517; *International Drilling Fluids Ltd.* v. *Louisville Investments (Uxbridge) Ltd.* [1986] 1 All E.R. 321.
90 Matrimonial Causes Act 1973, ss.23, 24, 25.
91 *Grant* v. *Edwards* [1986] Ch. 638, 657.

that there is a common intention that the claimant should have an interest in the house, any act done by her to her detriment relating to the joint lives of the parties is, in my judgment, sufficient detriment to qualify. The acts do not have to be inherently referable to the house . . . The holding out to the claimant that she had a beneficial interest in the house is an act of such a nature as to be part of the inducement to her to do the acts relied on. Accordingly, in the absence of evidence to the contrary, the right inference is that the claimant acted in reliance on such holding out and the burden lies on the legal owner to show that she did not do so: see *Greasley* v. *Cooke*."[92]

The Privy Council and the Court of Appeal[93] have subsequently endorsed this approach derived from proprietary estoppel and misrepresentation principles. The implication to be derived from the House of Lords in *Lloyds Bank* v. *Rosset*[94] is that once there is a finding of an express common intention or an express unilateral intention made known to F by M, then F only needs to show that she acted to her detriment or significantly altered her position in reliance on the intention to establish a constructive trust or a proprietary estoppel. This appears to leave unaffected the presumption that F did so act unless M can prove to the contrary.

If M does not so prove then the court has jurisdiction to grant F whatever remedy is necessary to undo M's unconscionable behaviour and reverse her detriment, *i.e.* to prevent M's unjust enrichment, *e.g.* give F a half share, a lesser fair share, a licence to reside in the home till the children reach adulthood or until M pays her £X compensation, crediting her for her housekeeping services and debiting her for her board and lodging benefits.[95]

Where there is no finding of an express or inferred common intention or unilateral intention made known to F by M, then it is not unconscionable for M to assert his 100 per cent. formal ownership of the property. F's domestic conduct was clearly not induced by any beliefs encouraged by M: her domestic services were provided by way of gift out of love and of liking to live in a pleasant family environment.[96] The courts have no jurisdiction to benefit F unless it is conferred by legislation along the lines of the New South Wales De Facto Relationship Act 1984.[97]

By this Act a court can "make such order adjusting the interests of the parties in the property as to it seems just and equitable having regard to:

(a) the financial and non-financial contributions made directly or indirectly by or on behalf of the de facto partners to the

---

[92] [1980] 1 W.L.R. 1306.
[93] *Maharaj* v. *Chand* [1986] A.C. 898; *Lloyds Bank* v. *Rosset* [1989] Ch. 350.
[94] [1990] 1 All E.R. 1111, 1118–1119.
[95] See n. 78, *supra*, p. 505.
[96] *e.g. Coombes* v. *Smith* [1986] 1 W.L.R. 808.
[97] For background see (1985) 48 M.L.R. 61.

acquisition, conservation or improvement of any of the property of the partners of either or them; and

(b) the contributions, including any contributions made in the capacity of homemaker or parent, made by either of the de facto partners to the welfare of the other de facto partner or to the welfare of the family constituted by the partners and one of more of the family, namely (i) a child of the partners; (ii) a child accepted by the partners or either of them into the household of the partners."

However, in the absence of such an Act, it may well be that social attitudes in England may change so as readily to lead to expectations by those within apparently stable and enduring *de facto* relationships that assets used by the family, particularly the family home, are ordinarily shared and not the exclusive property of M or of F unless it is otherwise agreed or made plain.[98] There will thus be a presumption of a common intention to share ownership of the family home and F's conduct will be presumed to have been in reliance upon such intention. Time will tell!

UNJUST ENRICHMENT

Time will also tell whether a general principle of unjust enrichment will develop in English law, probably based upon the principle of unconscionability in course of development in the cohabitation cases just discussed. Indeed, as Toohey J. pointed out in *Baumgartner* v. *Baumgartner*[99] there is really no difference between treating M as a person unconscionably retaining the property he formally owns or as a person unjustly enriched by the retention of such property, so that "the notion of unjust enrichment is as much at ease with the authorities and is as capable of ready and certain application as is the notion of unconscionable conduct." Back in 1937 the American Restatement of Restitution stated, "A person who has been unjustly enriched at the expense of another is required to make restitution to the other." At first sight this may seem a recipe for palm-tree justice just as much as would a statement made in the United Kingdom in 1930 before *Donaghue* v. *Stevenson*[1] to the effect, "A person whose negligence has harmed another is required to compensate the other." We all know how the tort of negligence has been much refined and has evolved as a workable basis for personal liability. Thus, it is possible that the principle of unjust enrichment with personal or proprietary liability may develop[2] as a workable basis for liability for currently

---

[98] As in New Zealand: *Gillies* v. *Keogh* [1989] 2 N.Z.L.R. 327. In Canada, too, F is not presumed to be making a gift of her services: *Herman* v. *Smith* (1984) 34 Alta L.R. (2nd) 90; *Everson* v. *Rich* (1988) 53 D.L.R. (4th) 470.

[99] (1988) 62 A.L.J.R. 29, 35–36.

[1] [1932] A.C. 562.

[2] Lord Diplock denied any general principle of unjust enrichment in English law in *Orakpo* v. *Manson Investments Ltd.* [1978] A.C. 95, 104.

miscellaneous cases covering constructive trusts, tracing, subjugation and quasi-contract.

In Canada,[3] though not quite yet in Australia,[4] the principle of unjust enrichment is now recognised as a general basis of liability, though its limits remain to be fully probed. As Goff J. pointed out in an English case[5]: "The principle of unjust enrichment presupposes three things:

(i) receipt by the defendant of a benefit,
(ii) at the plaintiff's expense,
(iii) in such circumstances that it would be unjust to allow the defendant to retain the benefit."

The first two requirements raise few difficulties, though a benefit may include a negative benefit, such as the savings made in not needing to employ a housekeeper because of services provided to M by F,[6] and something may be done at the plaintiff's expense where he suffers no loss but he could have been at risk of suffering a loss due to the defendant's wrongdoing.[7] The third requirement is obviously the one requiring refined development to make it clear that there is no scope for the unjust enrichment principle where the benefit was conferred by virtue of a gift or a contract or other legal obligation owed to the defendant or where the defendant did not freely accept the benefit. Two exceptionally good books deal with these matters fully and readers are referred to them: Birks, *Introduction to the Law of Restitution* (1st ed.) and Goff and Jones, *The Law of Restitution* (3rd ed.).

Prima facie, unjust enrichment leads to personal liability but it may lead to proprietary liability. In assessing whether a proprietary "constructive trust remedy is appropriate we must direct our minds to the specific question of whether the claimant reasonably expected to receive an actual interest in the property and whether the respondent was or ought reasonably to have been cognisant of that expectation."[8] So long as M, with legal title to the family home, reasonably believes that F is making a gift of her housewifely services, F obtains no interest in the home. The position thus turns upon what M led F to believe about ownership of the home and what current social attitudes should have led M and F to believe so as to place the onus of proof on the cohabitee going against such social attitudes. In England it seems that

---

[3] *Sorochan* v. *Sorochan* (1986) 29 D.L.R. (4th) 12; *Pettkus* v. *Becker* (1980) 117 D.L.R. (3rd) 259.
[4] *Baumgartner* v. *Baumgartner* (1987) 164 C.L.R. 137; *Pavey* v. *Paul* (1987) 69 A.L.R. 577.
[5] *B.P. Exploration Co. (Libya) Ltd.* v. *Hunt* [1979] 1 W.L.R. 783, 839.
[6] See *Sorochan* v. *Sorochan* (1986) 29 D.L.R. (4th), 1 approving *Hermann* v. *Smith* (1984) 34 Alta L.R. (2nd) 90 in this respect, and Birks, *Introduction to the Law of Restitution* (1st ed., 1985), p. 129.
[7] See Birks (*op. cit.*), pp. 132–139, 338–342.
[8] *Sorochan* v. *Sorochan* (1986) 29 D.L.R. (4th), 1, 12, *per* Dickson C.J.

social attitudes presume a gift[9] unlike the position in Canada[10] or New Zealand.[11]

Looking back over this chapter it will be seen that the categories of liability may be explained by reference to the underlying rationale of remedying unjust enrichment. It is likely that the courts will conservatively develop and refine these categories, taking into account such underlying rationale, but probably without replacing such categories by an apparently worryingly wide general principle of liability.[12] Counsel and the lower courts must of necessity follow the traditional categories so that it is easy for the House of Lords to deal with cases within such traditional categories, especially if the convention of having only one major speech is followed (so that it is uncontroversial enough to obtain the simple concurrences of the four other Law Lords).

## QUESTIONS

1. "Equity is not a computer. Equity operates on conscience but is not influenced by sentimentality," *per* Lord Templeman in *Winkworth* v. *Edward Baron Development Co.* [1987] 1 All E.R. 114, 118. Discuss whether or not this accurately reflects Equity's attitude to a cohabitee's rights in the family home owned by the other cohabitee.

2. Ten years ago, Martin purchased a freehold house in Shrewsbury (which was not then a compulsory registration of title area) for £100,000 of which £75,000 was borrowed by way of a legal mortgage in favour of the Greenwich BS which retained the title deeds to the house. Four years ago, he and Fiona decided to cohabit but first had a long weekend in Dublin before he carried her over the threshold of the house, saying, "This house is now as much yours as mine." "How wonderful," she replied, feeling reassured because a week earlier she had given notice to quit her protected tenancy of a flat.

She continued working as a hair tinter but used her money to buy clothes for herself and to buy holidays and restaurant dinners for herself and Martin because he refused to let her use her money to help pay the mortgage or other household outgoings. However, two years ago Martin was dismissed from his job, although within a week he obtained new employment at half his former salary.

Fiona then offered to pay half the monthly mortgage instalments but Martin refused this, telling her instead that it was simpler if he just used his money to pay the mortgage while she used her money for the other expenses of their cohabitation. Six months ago Fiona left Martin, who had been drinking and gambling too much, and moved in with Roderick. In this period Martin paid out £15,000 to cover the mortgage while Fiona paid £15,000 for other household outgoings. Of the mortgage payments £10,000 represented interest and £5,000 repayment of capital.

Martin is now bankrupt. His house is worth £300,000 but Fiona has just discovered that not only is there the original mortgage (though now only to

---

9 *Windeler* v. *Whitehall* [1990] *Family Court Reporter* 268; *Coombes* v. *Smith* [1986] 1 W.L.R. 808; *Burns* v. *Burns* [1984] Ch. 317; *Lloyds Bank* v. *Rosset* [1990] 1 All E.R. 1111, 1118.
10 *Everson* v. *Rich* (1988) 53 D.L.R. (4th) 470.
11 *Gillies* v. *Keogh* [1989] 2 N.Z.L.R. 727.
12 Unjust enrichment is accepted as the basis for actions for money had and received: *Woolwich B.S.* v. *I.R.C.* [1991] S.T.C. 364, 384, 404, 414, *Lipkin Gorman* v. *Karpnale* [1991] 3 W.L.R. 10.

secure £40,000) but there is a three-year-old legal mortgage for £150,000 in favour of Fairdeal Finance Co. and a one-year-old legal mortgage for £100,000 in favour of Martin's brother, Julian, who works in New York and made no inspection of the house. Fairdeal's surveyor inspected the house when Fiona was away on a residential course but commented to Martin on some feminine bits and pieces on a dressing table. Martin replied that he kept them as a memento of his recently-deceased wife.

Advise Fiona on her rights.

Would your answer differ if on carrying her over the threshold Martin had said, "This house is as much yours as mine so long as you'll help out as best you can with mortgage payments and household bills whenever I need it," and Fiona had replied, "Of course my darling, I'll help as much as I can"?

Would your answer differ if, instead, Martin had said, "This house is as much yours as mine so long as you give up your job and stay at home looking after me and any kids we may have" and Fiona had replied, "I'll be only too delighted to do so." She did so and so contributed no money but had his baby before leaving him and discovering the above mortgages, having been in hospital having the baby when Fairdeal's surveyor inspected the house.

### ASHBURN ANSTALT v. ARNOLD

Court of Appeal [1989] Ch. 1; [1988] 2 All E.R. 147; [1988] 2 W.L.R. 706
(Fox, Neill and Bingham L.JJ.)

FOX L.J. delivering the reserved judgment of the court: "The constructive trust principle, to which we now turn, has been long established and has proved to be highly flexible in practice. It covers a wide variety of cases from that of a trustee who makes a profit out of his trust or a stranger who knowingly deals with trust properties, to the many cases where the courts have held that a person who directly or indirectly contributes to the acquisition of a dwelling house purchased in the name of and conveyed to another has some beneficial interest in the property. The test, for the present purposes, is whether the owner of the property has so conducted himself that it would be inequitable to allow him to deny the claimant an interest in the property: see *Gissing* v. *Gissing* [1971] A.C. 886, 905, *per* Lord Diplock.

"In *Bannister* v. *Bannister* [1948] 2 All E.R. 133, on the plaintiff's oral undertaking that the defendant continue to live in a cottage rent free for as long as she wished, the defendant agreed to sell to him that and an adjacent cottage. The conveyance contained no reference to the undertaking. The plaintiff thereafter occupied the whole cottage save for one room which was occupied by the defendant. The plaintiff after a time sought to expel the defendant. The Court of Appeal held that he was not entitled to. Scott L.J., giving the judgment of the court, said, at p. 136:

'It is, we think, clearly a mistake to suppose that the equitable principle on which a constructive trust is raised against a person who insists on the absolute character of a conveyance to himself for the purpose of defeating a beneficial interest, which, according to the true bargain, was to belong to another, is confined to cases in which the conveyance itself was fraudulently obtained. The fraud which brings the principle into play arises as soon as the absolute character of the conveyance is set up for the purpose of defeating the beneficial interest. . . . Nor is it, in our opinion, necessary that the bargain on which the absolute conveyance is made should include any express stipulation that the grantee is in so many words to hold as trustee. It is enough that the bargain should have included a stipulation under which some sufficiently defined beneficial interest in the property was to be taken by another.'

"We come then to four cases in which the application of the principle to particular facts has been considered.

"In *Binions* v. *Evans* [1972] Ch. 359, the defendant's husband was employed by an estate and lived rent free in a cottage owned by the estate. The husband died when the defendant was 73. The trustees of the estate then entered into an agreement with the defendant that she could continue to live in the cottage during her lifetime as tenant at will rent free; she undertook to keep the cottage in good condition and repair. Subsequently the estate sold the cottage to the plaintiffs. The contract provided that the property was sold subject to the tenancy. In consequence of that provision the plaintiffs paid a reduced price for the cottage. The plaintiffs sought to eject the defendant, claiming that she was tenant at will. That claim failed. In the Court of Appeal Megaw and Stephenson L.JJ. decided the case on the ground that the defendant was a tenant for life under the Settled Land Act 1925. Lord Denning M.R. did not agree with that. He held that the plaintiffs took the property subject to a constructive trust for the defendant's benefit. In our view that is a legitimate application of the doctrine of constructive trusts. The estate would certainly have allowed the defendant to live in the house during her life in accordance with their agreement with her. They provided the plaintiffs with a copy of the agreement they made. The agreement for sale was subject to the agreement, and they accepted a lower purchase price in consequence. In the circumstances it was a proper inference that on the sale to the plaintiffs, the intention of the estate and the plaintiffs was that the plaintiffs should give effect to the tenancy agreement. If they had failed to do so, the estate would have been liable in damages to the defendant.

"In *D.H.N. Food Distributors Ltd.* v. *Tower Hamlets Borough Council* [1976] 1 W.L.R. 852, premises were owned by Bronze Investments Ltd. but occupied by an associated company (D.H.N.) under an informal agreement between them—they were part of a group. The premises were subsequently purchased by the council and the issue was compensation for disturbance. It was said that Bronze was not disturbed and that D.H.N. had no interest in the property. The Court of Appeal held that D.H.N. had an irrevocable licence to occupy the land. Lord Denning M.R. said, at p. 859:

> 'It was equivalent to a contract between the two companies whereby Bronze granted an irrevocable licence to D.H.N. to carry on their business on the premises. In this situation Mr. Dobry cited to us *Binions* v. *Evans* [1972] Ch. 359 to which I would add *Bannister* v. *Bannister* [1948] 2 All E.R. 133 and *Siew Soon Wah* v. *Young Tong Hong* [1973] A.C. 836. Those cases show that a contractual licence (under which a person has a right to occupy premises indefinitely) gives rise to a constructive trust, under which the legal owner is not allowed to turn out the licensee. So, here. This irrevocable licence gave to D.H.N. a sufficient interest in the land to qualify them for compensation for disturbance.'

Goff L.J. made this a ground for his decision also.

"On that authority, Browne-Wilkinson J. in *In re Sharpe (A Bankrupt), Ex parte Trustee of the Bankrupt's Property* v. *The Bankrupt* [1980] 1 W.L.R. 219

felt bound to conclude that, without more, an irrevocable licence to occupy gave rise to a property interest. He evidently did so with hesitation. For the reasons which we have already indicated, we prefer the line of authorities which determine that a contractual licence does not create a property interest. We do not think that the argument is assisted by the bare assertion that the interest arises under a constructive trust.

"In *Lyus* v. *Prowsa Developments Ltd.* [1982] 1 W.L.R. 1044, the plaintiffs contracted to buy a plot of registered land which was part of an estate being developed by the vendor company. A house was to be built which would then be occupied by the plaintiffs. The plaintiffs paid a deposit to the company, which afterwards became insolvent before the house was built. The company's bank held a legal charge, granted before the plaintiffs' contract, over the whole estate. The bank was under no liability to complete the plaintiffs' contract. The bank, as mortgagee, sold the land to the first defendant. By the contract of sale it was provided that the land was sold subject to and with the benefit of the plaintiffs' contract. Subsequently, the first defendant contracted to sell the plot to the second defendant. The contract provided that the land was sold subject to the plaintiffs' contract so far, if at all, as it might be enforceable against the first defendant. The contract was duly completed. In the action the plaintiffs sought a declaration that their contract was binding on the defendants and an order for specific performance. The action succeeded. This again seems to us to be a case where a constructive trust could justifiably be imposed. The bank were selling as mortgagees under a charge prior in date to the contract. They were therefore not bound by the contract and on any view could give a title which was free from it. There was, therefore, no point in making the conveyance subject to the contract unless the parties intended the purchaser to give effect to the contract. Further, on the sale by the bank a letter had been written to the bank's agents, Messrs. Strutt & Parker, by the first defendant's solicitors, giving an assurance that their client would take reasonable steps to make sure the interests of contractual purchasers were dealt with quickly and to their satisfaction. How far any constructive trust so arising was on the facts of that case enforceable by the plaintiffs against owners for the time being of the land we do not need to consider.

"*In re Sharpe* [1980] 1 W.L.R. 219 seems to us a much more difficult case in which to imply a constructive trust against the trustee in bankruptcy and his successors, and we do not think it could be done. Browne-Wilkinson J. did not, in fact, do so. He felt (understandably, we think) bound by authority to hold that an irrevocable licence to occupy was a property interest. In *In re Sharpe* although the aunt provided money for the purchase of the house, she did not thereby acquire any property interest in the ordinary sense, since the judge held that it was advanced by way of a loan, though, no doubt, she may have had some rights of occupation as against the debtor. And when the trustee in bankruptcy, before entering into the contract of sale, wrote to the aunt to find out what rights, if any, she claimed in consequence of the provision of funds by her, she did not reply. The trustee in bankruptcy then sold with vacant possession. These facts do not suggest a need in equity to impose constructive trust obligations on the trustee or his successors.

"We come to the present case. It is said that when a person sells land and stipulates that the sale should be "subject to" a contractual licence, the court will impose a constructive trust upon the purchaser to give effect to the licence: see *Binions* v. *Evans* [1972] Ch. 359, 368, *per* Lord Denning M.R. We do not feel able to accept that as a general proposition. We agree with the observations of Dillon J. in *Lyus* v. *Prowsa Developments Ltd.* [1982] 1 W.L.R. 1044, 1051:

> 'By contrast, there are many cases in which land is expressly conveyed subject to possible incumbrances when there is no thought at all of conferring any fresh rights on third parties who may be entitled to the benefit of the incumbrances. The land is expressed to be sold subject to incumbrances to satisfy the vendor's duty to disclose all possible incumbrances known to him, and to protect the vendor against any possible claim by the purchaser. . . . So, for instance, land may be contracted to be sold and may be expressed to be conveyed subject to the restrictive covenants contained in a conveyance some 60 or 90 years old. No one would suggest that by accepting such a form of contract or conveyance a purchaser is assuming a new liability in favour of third parties to observe the covenants if there was for any reason before the contract or conveyance no one who could make out a title as against the purchaser to the benefit of the covenants.'

The court will not impose a constructive trust unless it is satisfied that the conscience of the estate owner is affected. The mere fact that that land is expressed to be conveyed 'subject to' a contract does not necessarily imply that the grantee is to be under an obligation, not otherwise existing, to give effect to the provisions of the contract. The fact that the conveyance is expressed to be subject to the contract may often, for the reasons indicated by Dillon J., be at least as consistent with an intention merely to protect the grantor against claims by the grantee as an intention to impose an obligation on the grantee. The words 'subject to' will, of course, impose notice. But notice is not enough to impose on somebody an oblgation to give effect to a contract into which he did not enter. Thus, mere notice of a restrictive covenant is not enough to impose upon the estate owner an obligation or equity to give effect to it: *London County Council* v. *Allen* [1914] 3 K.B. 642.

"In matters relating to the title to land, certainty is of prime importance. We do not think it desirable that constructive trusts of land should be imposed in reliance on inferences from slender materials. In our opinion the available evidence in the present case is insufficient. The deputy judge, while he did not have to decide the matter, was not disposed to infer a constructive trust, and we agree with him.

"In general, we should emphasise that it is important not to lose sight of the question: 'Whose conscience are we considering?' It is the plaintiff's, and the issue is whether the plaintiff has acted in such a way that, as a matter of justice, a trust must be imposed on it. For the reasons which we have indicated, we are not satisfied that it should be." [They indicated that a "subject to" clause in a 1973 contract was a defensive protective provision only].

## GRANT v. EDWARDS

Court of Appeal [1986] Ch. 638; [1986] 3 W.L.R. 114; [1986] 2 All E.R. 426
(Sir Nicolas Browne-Wilkinson V.-C., Mustill and Nourse L.JJ.)

NOURSE L.J.: "In order to decide whether the plaintiff has a beneficial interest in 96, Hewitt Road we must climb again the familiar ground which slopes down from the twin peaks of *Pettitt* v. *Pettitt* [1970] A.C. 777 and

*Gissing* v. *Gissing* [1971] A.C. 886. In a case such as the present, where there has been no written declaration or agreement, nor any direct provision by the plaintiff of part of the purchase price so as to give rise to a resulting trust in her favour, she must establish a common intention between her and the defendant, acted upon by her, that she should have a beneficial interest in the property. If she can do that, equity will not allow the defendant to deny that interest and will construct a trust to give effect to it.

"In most of these cases the fundamental, and invariably the most difficult, question is to decide whether there was the necessary common intention, being something which can only be inferred from the conduct of the parties, almost always from the expenditure incurred by them respectively. In this regard the court has to look for expenditure which is referable to the acquisition of the house: see *per* Fox L.J. in *Burns* v. *Burns* [1984] Ch. 317, 328H–329C. If it is found to have been incurred, such expenditure will perform the twofold function of establishing the common intention and showing that the claimant has acted upon it.

"There is another and rarer class of case, of which the present may be one, where, although there has been no writing, the parties have orally declared themselves in such a way as to make their common intention plain. Here the court does not have to look for conduct from which the intention can be inferred, but only for conduct which amounts to an acting upon it by the claimant. And although that conduct can undoubtedly be the incurring of expenditure which is referable to the acquisition of the house, it need not necessarily be so . . .

"It seems therefore, on the authorities as they stand, that a distinction is to be made between conduct from which the common intention can be inferred on the one hand and conduct which amounts to an acting upon it on the other. There remains this difficult question: what is the quality of conduct required for the latter purpose? The difficulty is caused, I think because although the common intention has been made plain, everything else remains a matter of inference. Let me illustrate it in this way. It would be possible to take the view that the mere moving into the house by the woman amounted to an acting upon the common intention. But that was evidently not the view of the majority in *Eves* v. *Eves* [1975] 1 W.L.R. 1338. And the reason for that may be that, in the absence of evidence, the law is not so cynical as to infer that a woman will only go to live with a man to whom she is not married if she understands that she is to have an interest in their home. So what sort of conduct is required? In my judgment it must be conduct on which the woman could not reasonably have been expected to embark unless she was to have an interest in the house. If she was not to have such an interest, she could reasonably be expected to go and live with her lover, but not, for example, to wield a 14-lb. sledge hammer in the front garden. In adopting the latter kind of conduct she is seen to act to her detriment on the faith of the common intention.

In order to see how the present case stands in the light of the views above expressed, I must summarise the crucial facts as found, expressly or impliedly, by the judge. They are the following. (1) The defendant told the plaintiff that her name was not going onto the title because it would cause some prejudice in the matrimonial proceedings between her and her husband. The defendant never had any real intention of replacing his brother with the plaintiff when those proceedings were at an end. Just as in *Eves* v. *Eves* [1975] 1 W.L.R. 1338, these facts appear to me to raise a clear inference that there was an understanding between the plaintiff and the defendant, or a common intention, that the plaintiff was to have some sort of proprietary interest in the house; otherwise no excuse for not putting her name onto the title would have been needed. (2) Except for any instalments under the second mortgage which may have been paid by the plaintiff as part of the general expenses of the household, all the instalments under both mortgages were paid by the defendant. Between February 1970 and October 1974 the total amount paid in respect of the second mortgage was £812 at a rate of about £162 each year. Between 1972 and 1980 the defendant paid off £4,745 under the first mortgage at an average rate of £527 per year. (3) The £6 per week which the defendant admitted that the plaintiff paid to him, at least for a time after they moved into the house, was not paid as rent and must therefore have been paid as a contribution to general expenses. (4) From August 1972 onwards the plaintiff was getting the same sort of wage as the defendant, *i.e.* an annual wage of about £1,200 in 1973, out of which she made a very substantial contribution to the housekeeping and to the feeding and bringing up of the children. From June 1973 onwards she also received £5 a week from her former husband which went towards the maintenance of her two elder sons.

As stated under (1) above, it is clear that there was a common intention that the plaintiff was to have some sort of proprietary interest in 96, Hewitt Road. The more difficult question is whether there was conduct on her part which amounted to an acting upon that intention or, to put it more precisely, conduct on which she could not reasonably have been expected to embark unless she was to have an interest in the house.

From the above facts and figures it is in my view an inevitable inference that the very substantial contribution which the plaintiff made out of her earnings after August 1972 to the housekeeping and to the feeding and to the bringing up of the children enabled the defendant to keep down the instalments payable under both mortgages out of his own income and, moreover, that he could not have done that if he had had to bear the whole of the other expenses as well. For example, in 1973, when he and the plaintiff were earning about £1,200 each, the defendant had to find a total of about £643 between the two mortgages. I do not see how he would have been able to do that had it not been for the plaintiff's very substantial contribution to the other expenses. There is certainly no evidence that there was any money to spare on either side and the natural inference is to the contrary.

"In the circumstances, it seems that it may properly be inferred that the plaintiff did make substantial indirect contributions to the instalments payable under both mortgages.

"Was the conduct of the plaintiff in making substantial indirect contributions to the instalments payable under both mortgages conduct upon which she could not reasonably have been expected to embark unless she was to have an interest in the house? I answer that question in the affirmative. I cannot see upon what other basis she could reasonably have been expected to give the defendant such substantial assistance in paying off mortgages on his house. I therefore conclude that the plaintiff did act to her detriment on the faith of the common intention between her and the defendant that she was to have some sort of proprietary interest in the house.

"Finally, it is necessary to determine the extent of the plaintiff's beneficial interest in 96, Hewitt Road. Here again reference may be made to *Eves* v. *Eves* [1975] 1 W.L.R. 1338, 1345G–H, where Brightman J. regarded this question as the most difficult part of the case. Although I can understand that difficulties may arise in other cases, there is a particular feature of the present case to which we can turn for guidance. That is the crediting of the £1,037 balance of the fire insurance moneys to what the judge found was intended as a joint account. He would evidently have been more impressed by that if, as I have now held, the plaintiff had made a greater contribution than he thought. In my view it was a very significant step for the defendant to have taken. Although on the judge's findings the plaintiff did not contribute anything towards the £1,043 which had to be found in cash to complete the purchase and did not make any substantial contribution, direct or indirect, to the mortgage payments before August 1972, I nevertheless think that this act of the defendant, when viewed against the background of the initial common intention and the substantial indirect contributions made by the plaintiff to the mortgage repayments from August 1972 onwards, is the best evidence of how the parties intended that the property should be shared. I would therefore hold that the plaintiff is entitled to a half interest in the house.

MUSTILL L.J.: "I agree. For my part, I do not think that the time has yet arrived when it is possible to state the law in a way which will deal with all the practical problems which may arise in this difficult field, consistently with everything said in the cases. For present purposes it is unnecessary to attempt this. I believe that the following propositions, material to this appeal, can be extracted from the authorities. (For convenience it is assumed that the 'proprietor'—*viz.* the person who has the legal title—is male, and the 'claimant' who asserts a beneficial interest is female).

(1) The law does not recognise a concept of family property, whereby people who live together in a settled relationship ipso facto share the rights of ownership in the assets acquired and used for the purposes of their life together. Nor does the law acknowledge that by the mere fact of doing work on the asset of one party to the relationship the other party will acquire a beneficial interest in that asset.

(2) The question whether one party to the relationship acquires rights to property the legal title to which is vested in the other party must be answered in terms of the existing law of trusts. There are no special doctrines of equity, applicable in this field alone.

(3) In a case such as the present the inquiry must proceed in two stages. First, by considering whether something happened between the parties in the nature of bargain, promise or tacit common intention, at the time of the acquisition. Second, if the answer is 'Yes,' by asking whether the claimant subsequently conducted herself in a manner which was (a) detrimental to herself, and (b) referable to whatever happened on acquisition. (I use the expression 'on acquisition' for simplicity. In fact, the event happening between the parties which, if followed by the relevant type of conduct on the part of the claimant, can lead to the creation of an interest in the claimant, may itself occur after acquisition. The beneficial interests may change in the course of the relationship).

(4) For present purposes, the event happening on acquisition may take one of the following shapes. (a) An express bargain whereby the proprietor promises the claimant an interest in the property, in return for an explicit undertaking by the claimant to act in a certain way. (b) An express but incomplete bargain whereby the proprietor promises the claimant an interest in the property, on the basis that the claimant will do something in return. The parties do not themselves make explicit what the claimant is to do. The court

therefore has to complete the bargain for them by means of implication, when it comes to decide whether the proprietor's promise has been matched by conduct falling within whatever undertaking the claimant must be taken to have given sub silentio. (c) An explicit promise by the proprietor that the claimant will have an interest in the property, unaccompanied by any express or tacit agreement as to a quid pro quo. (d) A common intention, not made explicit, to the effect that the claimant will have an interest in the property, if she subsequently acts in a particular way.

(5) In order to decide whether the subsequent conduct of the claimant serves to complete the beneficial interest which has been explicitly or tacitly promised to her the court must decide whether the conduct is referable to the bargain, promise or intention. Whether the conduct satisfies this test will depend upon the nature of the conduct, and of the bargain, promise or intention.

(6) Thus, if the situation falls into category (a) above, the only question is whether the claimant's conduct is of the type explicitly promised. It is immaterial whether it takes the shape of a contribution to the cost of acquiring the property, or is of a quite different character.

(7) The position is the same in relation to situations (b) and (d). No doubt it will often be easier in practice to infer that the quid pro quo was intended to take the shape of a financial or other contribution to the cost of acquisition or of improvement, but this need not always be so. Whatever the court decides the quid pro quo to have been, it will suffice if the claimant has furnished it.

(8) In considering whether there was a bargain or common intention, so as to bring the case within categories (b) and (d) and, if there was one, what were its terms, the court must look at the true state of affairs on acquisition. It must not impute to the parties a bargain which they never made, or a common intention which they never possessed.

(9) The conduct of the parties, and in particular of the claimant, after the acquisition may provide material from which the court can infer the existence of an explicit bargain, or a common intention, and also the terms of such a bargain or intention. Examining the subsequent conduct of the parties to see whether an inference can be made as to a bargain or intention is quite different from examining the conduct of the claimant to see whether it amounts to compliance with a bargain or intention which has been proved in some other way. (If this distinction is not observed, there is a risk of circularity. If the claimant's conduct is too readily assumed to be explicable only by the existence of a bargain, she will always be able to say that her side of the bargain has been performed.)

"The propositions do not touch two questions of general importance. First, whether in the absence of a proved or inferred bargain or intention the making of subsequent indirect contributions, for instance in the shape of a contribution to general household expenses, is sufficient to found an interest. I believe the answer to be that it does not. The routes by which the members of the House reached their common conclusion in *Gissing* v. *Gissing* [1971] A.C. 886 were not, however, the same and the point is still open. Since it does not arise here, I prefer to express no conclusion upon it.

"The second question is closer to the present case: namely, whether a promise by the proprietor to confer an interest, but with no element of mutuality (*i.e.* situation (c) above) can effectively confer an interest if the claimant relies upon it by acting to her detriment. This question was not directly addressed in *Gissing* v. *Gissing* [1971] A.C. 886, although the speech of Lord Diplock, at p. 905, supports an affirmative answer. The plaintiff's case was not argued on this footing in the present appeal, and since the appeal can be decided on other grounds, I prefer not to express an opinion on this important point . . .

"Whatever the defendant's actual intention, the nature of the excuse which he gave must have led the plaintiff to believe that she would in the future have her name on the title, and this in turn would justify her in concluding that she had from the outset some kind of right to the house. The case does not fall precisely within either of categories (b), (c) or (d) above, but the defendant's conduct must now preclude him from denying that it is sufficiently analogous to these categories to make the relevant principles apply.

"Assuming therefore that the case must be approached as if the defendant had promised the plaintiff some kind of right to the house, or as if they had a common intention to this effect—and I do not think it matters which formula is chosen—what kind of right was this to be? In particular was it to be a right which was to arise only if the plaintiff gave something in exchange; and if so, what was that something to be? These are not easy questions to answer, especially since the judge never approached, or was asked to approach, the matter in this way. Nevertheless I consider it legitimate to hold that there must have been an assumption that the transfer of rights to the plaintiff would not be unilateral, and that the plaintiff would play her own part. Moreover, the situation of the couple was such that the plaintiff's part must have included a direct or indirect contribution to the cost of acquisition: for the defendant could not from his own resources have afforded both to buy their new home and to keep the joint household in existence.

"Finally, there remains the question whether the conduct of the plaintiff can be regarded as referable to the bargain or intention thus construed. On the facts as analysed by Nourse L.J. I consider that it can. Accordingly, the conditions are satisfied for the creation of an interest, and for the reasons given by Nourse L.J. I agree that the interest should be quantified at 50 per cent."

SIR NICOLAS BROWNE-WILKINSON V.-C.: "I agree. In my judgment, there has been a tendency over the years to distort the principles as laid down in the speech of Lord Diplock in *Gissing* v. *Gissing* [1971] A.C. 886 by concentrating on only part of his reasoning. For present purposes, his speech can be treated as falling into three sections: the first deals with the nature of the substantive right; the second with the proof of the existence of that right; the third with the quantification of that right.

1. *The nature of the substantive right:* [1971] A.C. 886, 905B–G
   "If the legal estate in the joint home is vested in only one of the parties ('the legal owner') the other party ('the claimant'), in order to establish a beneficial interest, has to establish a constructive trust by showing that it would be inequitable for the legal owner to claim sole beneficial ownership. This requires two matters to be demonstrated: (a) that there was a common intention that both should have a beneficial interest; (b) that the claimant has acted to his or her detriment on the basis of that common intention.

2. *The proof of the common intention*
   "(a) Direct evidence (p. 905H). It is clear that mere agreement between the parties that both are to have beneficial interests is sufficient to prove the necessary common intention. Other passages in the speech point to the admissibility and relevance of other possible forms of direct evidence of such intention: see pp. 907C and 908C.

(b) Inferred common intention (pp. 906A–908D). Lord Diplock points out that, even where parties have not used express words to communicate their intention (and therefore there is no direct evidence), the court can infer from their actions an intention that they shall both have an interest in the house. This part of his speech concentrates on the types of evidence from which the courts are most often asked to infer such intention, *viz.* contributions (direct and indirect) to the deposit, the mortgage instalments or general housekeeping expenses. In this section of the speech, he analyses what types of expenditure are capable of constituting evidence of such common intention: he does not say that if the intention is proved in some other way such contributions are essential to establish the trust.

### 3. *The quantification of the right* (pp. 908D–909)

"Once it has been established that the parties had a common intention that both should have a beneficial interest *and* that the claimant has acted to his detriment, the question may still remain 'what is the extent of the claimant's beneficial interest?' This last section of Lord Diplock's speech shows that here again the direct and indirect contributions made by the parties to the cost of acquisition may be crucially important.

"If this analysis is correct, contributions made by the claimant may be relevant for four different purposes, *viz.*: (1) in the absence of direct evidence of intention, as evidence from which the parties' intentions can be inferred; (2) as corroboration of direct evidence of intention; (3) to show that the claimant has acted to his or her detriment in reliance on the common intention: Lord Diplock's speech does not deal directly with the nature of the detriment to be shown; (4) to quantify the extent of the beneficial interest.

"I have sought to analyse Lord Diplock's speech for two reasons. First, it is clear that the necessary common intention can be proved otherwise than by reference to contributions by the claimant to the cost of acquisition. Secondly, the remarks of Lord Diplock as to the contributions made by the claimant must be read in their context.

"In cases of this kind the first question must always be whether there is sufficient direct evidence of a common intention that both parties are to have a beneficial interest. Such direct evidence need have nothing to do with the contributions made to the cost of acquisition. Thus in *Eves* v. *Eves* [1975] 1 W.L.R. 1338 the common intention was proved by the fact that the claimant was told that her name would have been on the title deeds but for her being under age. Again, in *Midland Bank Plc.* v. *Dobson* [1986] 1 F.L.R. 171 this court held that the trial judge was entitled to find the necessary common intention from evidence which he accepted that the parties treated the house as 'our house' and had a 'principle of sharing everything.' Although, as was said in the latter case, the trial judge has to approach such direct evidence with caution, if he does accept such evidence the necessary common intention is proved. One would expect that in a number of cases the court would be able to decide on the direct evidence before it whether there was such a common intention. It is only necessary to have recourse to inferences from other circumstances (such as the way in which the parties contributed, directly or indirectly, to the cost of acquisition) in cases such as *Gissing* v. *Gissing* [1971] A.C. 886 and *Burns* v. *Burns* [1984] Ch. 317 where there is no direct evidence of intention.

"Applying those principles to the present case, the representation made by the defendant to the plaintiff that the house would have been in the joint names but for the plaintiff's matrimonial disputes is clear direct evidence of a common intention that she was to have an interest in the house: *Eves* v. *Eves* [1975] 1 W.L.R. 1338. Such evidence was in my judgment sufficient by itself to establish the common intention: but in any event it is wholly consistent with the contributions made by the plaintiff to the joint household expenses and the fact that the surplus fire insurance moneys were put into a joint account.

"But as Lord Diplock's speech in *Gissing* v. *Gissing* [1971] A.C. 886, 905D and the decision in *Midland Bank Plc.* v. *Dobson* make clear, mere common intention by itself is not enough: the claimant has also to prove that she has acted to her detriment in the reasonable belief by so acting she was acquiring a beneficial interest.

"There is little guidance in the authorities on constructive trusts as to what is necessary to prove that the claimant so acted to her detriment. What 'link' has to be shown between the common intention and the actions relied on? Does there have to be positive evidence that the claimant did the acts in conscious reliance on the common intention? Does the court have to be satisfied that she would not have done the acts relied on but for the common intention, *e.g.* would not the claimant have contributed to household expenses out of affection for the legal owner and as part of their joint life together even if she had no interest in the house? Do the acts relied on as a detriment have to be inherently referable to the house, *e.g.* contribution to the purchase or physical labour on the house?

"I do not think it is necessary to express any concluded view on these questions in order to decide this case. *Eves* v. *Eves* [1975] 1 W.L.R. 1338 indicates that there has to be some 'link' between the common intention and the acts relied on as a detriment. In that case the acts relied on did inherently relate to the house (that is the work the claimant did to the house) and from this the Court of Appeal felt able to infer that the acts were done in reliance on the common intention. So, in this case, as the analysis of Nourse L.J. makes clear, the plaintiff's contributions to the household expenses were essentially linked to the payment of the mortgage instalments by the defendant: without the plaintiff's contributions, the defendant's means were insufficient to keep up the mortgage payments. In my judgment where the claimant has made payments which, whether directly or indirectly, have been used to discharge the mortgage instalments, this is a sufficient link between the detriment suffered by the claimant and the common intention. The court can infer that she would not have made such payments were it not for her belief that she had an interest in the house. On this ground therefore I find that the plaintiff has acted to her detriment in reliance on the common intention that she had a beneficial interest in the house and accordingly that she has established such beneficial interest.

"I suggest that in other cases of this kind, useful guidance may in the future be obtained from the principles underlying the law of proprietary estoppel which in my judgment are closely akin to those laid down in *Gissing* v. *Gissing* [1971] A.C. 886. In both, the claimant must to the knowledge of the legal owner have acted in the belief that the claimant has or will obtain an interest in the property. In both, the claimant must have acted to his or her detriment in reliance on such belief. In both, equity acts on the conscience of the legal owner to prevent him from acting in an unconscionable manner by defeating the common intention. The two principles have been developed separately without cross-fertilisation between them: but they rest on the same foundation and have on all other matters reached the same conclusions.

"In many cases of the present sort, it is impossible to say whether or not the claimant would have done the acts relied on as a detriment even if she thought she had no interest in the house. Setting up house together, having a baby, making payments to general housekeeping expenses (not strictly necessary to enable the mortgage to be paid) may all be referable to the mutual love and affection of the parties and not specifically referable to the claimant's belief that she has an interest in the house. As at present advised, once it has been shown that there was a common intention that the claimant should have an interest in the house, any act done by her to her detriment relating to the joint lives of the parties is, in my judgment, sufficient detriment to qualify. The acts do not have to be inherently referable to the house: see *Jones (A.E.)* v. *Jones (F.W.)* [1977] 1 W.L.R. 438 and *Pascoe* v. *Turner* [1979] 1 W.L.R. 431. The holding out to the claimant that she had a beneficial interest in the house is an act of such a nature as to be part of the inducement to her to do the acts relied on. Accordingly, in the absence of evidence to the contrary, the right inference is that the claimant acted in reliance on such holding out and the burden lies on the legal owner to show that she did not do so: see *Greasley* v. *Cooke* [1980] 1 W.L.R. 1306.

"The possible analogy with proprietary estoppel was raised in argument. However, the point was not fully argued and since the case can be decided without relying on such analogy, it is unsafe for me to rest my judgment on that point. I decide the case on the narrow ground already mentioned.

"What then is the extent of the plaintiff's interest? It is clear from *Gissing* v. *Gissing* [1971] A.C. 886 that, once the common intention and the actions to the claimant's detriment have been proved from direct or other evidence, in fixing the quantum of the claimant's beneficial interest the court can take into account indirect contributions by the plaintiff such as the plaintiff's contributions to joint household expenses: see *Gissing* v. *Gissing* [1971] A.C. 886, 909A and D–E. In my judgment, the passage in Lord Diplock's speech at pp. 909G– 910A is dealing with a case where there is no evidence of the common intention other than contributions to joint expenditure: in such a case there is insufficient evidence to prove any beneficial interest and the question of the extent of that interest cannot arise.

"Where, as in this case, the existence of some beneficial interest in the claimant has been shown, prima facie the interest of the claimant will be that which the parties intended: *Gissing* v. *Gissing* [1971] A.C. 886, 908G. In *Eves* v. *Eves* [1975] 1 W.L.R. 1338, 1345G Brightman L.J. plainly felt that a common intention that there should be a joint interest pointed to the beneficial interests being equal. However, he felt able to find a lesser beneficial interest in that case without explaining the legal basis on which he did so. With diffidence, I suggest that the law of proprietary estoppel may again provide useful guidance. If proprietary estoppel is established, the court gives effect to it by giving effect to the common intention so far as may fairly be done between the parties. For that purpose, equity is displayed at its most flexible: see *Crabb* v. *Arun District Council* [1976] Ch. 179. Identifiable contributions to the purchase of the house will of course be an important factor in many cases. But in other cases, contributions by way of labour or other unquantifiable actions of the claimant will also be relevant.

"Taking into account the fact that the house was intended to be the joint property, the contributions to the common expenditure and the payment of the fire insurance moneys into the joint account, I agree that the plaintiff is entitled to a half interest in the house."					*Appeal allowed with costs.*

## LLOYDS BANK plc v. ROSSET

House of Lords [1990] 2 W.L.R. 867; [1990] 1 All E.R. 1111 (Lords Bridge, Griffiths, Ackner, Oliver and Jauncey)

LORD BRIDGE (with whose speech the others all simply concurred) after citing the judge's findings on Mrs. Rosset's cleaning, painting and decorating: "It is clear from these passages in the judgment that the judge based his inference of a common intention that Mrs. Rossett should have a beneficial interest in the property under a constructive trust essentially on what Mrs. Rosset did in and about assisting in the renovation of the property between the beginning of November 1982 and the date of completion on 17 December 1982. Yet by itself this activity, it seems to me, could not possibly justify any such inference. It was common ground that Mrs. Rosset was extremely anxious that the new matrimonial home should be ready for occupation before Christmas if possible. In these circumstances, it would seem the most natural thing in the world for any wife, in the absence of her husband abroad, to spend all the time she could spare and to employ any skills she might have, such as the ability to decorate a room, in doing all she could to accelerate progress of the work quite irrespective of any expectation she might have of enjoying a beneficial interest in the property. The judge's view that some of this work was work 'on which she could not reasonably have been expected to embark unless she was to have an interest in the house' seems to me, with respect, quite untenable.

"On any view the monetary value of Mrs. Rosset's work expressed as a contribution to a property acquired at a cost exceeding £70,000 must have been so trifling as to be almost de minimis. I should myself have had considerable doubt whether Mrs. Rosset's contribution to the work of renovation was sufficient to support a claim to a constructive trust in the absence of writing to satisfy the requirements of s.51 of the Law of Property Act 1925 even if her husband's intention to make a gift to her of half or any other share in the equity of the property had been clearly established or if he had clearly represented to her that that was what he intended. But here the conversations with her husband on which Mrs. Rosset relied, all of which took place before November 1982, were incapable of lending support to the conclusion of a constructive trust in the light of the judge's finding that by that date there had been no decision that she was to have any interest in the property. The finding that the discussions 'did not exclude the possibility' that she should have an interest does not seem to me to add anything of significance.

"These considerations lead me to the conclusion that the judge's finding that Mr. Rosset held the property as constructive trustee for himself and his wife cannot be supported and it is on this short ground that I would allow the appeal. In the course of the argument your Lordships had the benefit of elaborate submissions as to the test to be applied to determine the circumstances in which the sole legal proprietor of a dwelling house can properly be held to have become a constructive trustee of a share in the beneficial interest in the house for the benefit of the partner with whom he or she has cohabited in the house as their shared home. Having in this case reached a conclusion on the facts which, although at variance with the views of the courts below, does not seem to depend on any nice legal distinction and with which, I understand, all your Lordships agree, I cannot help doubting whether it would contribute anything to the illumination of the law if I were to attempt an elaborate and exhaustive analysis of the relevant law to add to the many already to be found in the authorities to which our attention was directed in the course of the argument. I do, however, draw attention to one critical distinction which any judge required to resolve a dispute between former partners as to the beneficial interest in the home they formerly shared should always have in the forefront of his mind.

"The first and fundamental question which must always be resolved is whether, independently of any inference to be drawn from the conduct of the parties in the course of sharing the house as their home and managing their joint affairs, there has at any time prior to acquisition, or exceptionally at some later date, been any agreement, arrangement or understanding reached between them that the property is to be shared beneficially. The finding of an agreement or arrangement to share in this sense can only, I think, be based on evidence of express discussions between the partners, however imperfectly remembered and however imprecise their terms may have been. Once a finding to this effect is made it will only be necessary for the partner asserting a claim to a beneficial interest against the partner entitled to the legal estate to show that he or she has acted to his or her detriment or significantly altered his or her position in reliance on the agreement in order to give rise to a constructive trust or proprietary estoppel.

"In sharp contrast with this situation is the very different one where there is no evidence to support a finding of an agreement or arrangement to share, however reasonable it might have been for the parties to reach such an arrangement if they had applied their minds to the question, and where the court must rely entirely on the conduct of the parties both as the basis from which to infer a common intention to share the property beneficially and as the conduct relied on to give rise to a constructive trust. In this situation direct contributions to the purchase price by the partner who is not the legal owner, whether initially or by payment of mortgage instalments, will readily justify the inference necessary to the creation of a constructive trust. But, as I read the authorities, it is at least extremely doubtful whether anything less will do.

"The leading cases in your Lordships' House are *Pettitt* v. *Pettitt* [1969] 2 All E.R. 385, [1970] A.C. 777 and *Gissing* v. *Gissing* [1970] 2 All E.R. 780, [1971] A.C. 886. Both demonstrate situations in the second category to which I have referred and their Lordships discuss at great length the difficulties to which these situations give rise. The effect of these two decisions is very helpfully analysed in the judgment of Lord MacDermott L.C.J. in *McFarlane* v. *McFarlane* [1972] N.I. 59.

"Outstanding examples on the other hand of cases giving rise to situations in the first category are *Eves* v. *Eves* [1975] 3 All E.R. 768, [1975] 1 W.L.R. 1338 and *Grant* v. *Edwards* [1986] 2 All E.R. 426, [1986] Ch. 638. In both these cases, where the parties who had cohabited were unmarried, the female partner had been clearly led by the male partner to believe, when they set up home together, that the property would belong to them jointly. In *Eves* v. *Eves* the male partner had told the female partner that the only reason why the property was to be acquired in his name alone was because she was under 21 and that, but for her age, he would have had the house put into their joint names. He admitted in evidence that this was simply an 'excuse.' Similarly, in *Grant* v. *Edwards* the female partner was told by the male partner that the only reason for not acquiring the property in joint names was because she was involved in divorce proceedings and that, if the property were acquired jointly, this might operate to her prejudice in those proceedings. As Nourse L.J. put it ([1986] 2 All E.R. 426 at 433, [1986] Ch. 638 at 649):

'Just as in *Eves* v. *Eves*, these facts appear to me to raise a clear inference that there was an understanding between the plaintiff and the defendant, or a common intention, that the plaintiff was to have some sort of proprietary interest in the house; otherwise no excuse for not putting her name onto the title would have been needed.'

The subsequent conduct of the female partner in each of these cases, which the court rightly held sufficient to give rise to a constructive trust or proprietary estoppel supporting her claim to an interest in the property, fell far short of such conduct as would by itself have supported the claim in the absence of an express representation by the male partner that she was to have such an interest. It is significant to note that the share to which the female partners in *Eves* v. *Eves* and *Grant* v. *Edwards* were held entitled were one-quarter and one-half respectively. In no sense could these shares have been regarded as proportionate to what the judge in the instant case described as a 'qualifying contribution' in terms of the indirect contributions to the acquisition or enhancement of the value of the houses made by the female partners.

"I cannot help thinking that the judge in the instant case would not have fallen into error if he had kept clearly in mind the distinction between the effect of evidence on the one hand which was capable of establishing an express agreement or an express representation that Mrs. Rosset was to have an interest in the property and evidence on the other hand of conduct alone as a basis for an inference of the necessary common intention." *Appeal allowed.*

## STOKES v. ANDERSON

Court of Appeal (Lloyd, Nourse, Gibson L.JJ.) [1991] 1 F.L.R. 391

NOURSE L.J. (with whom Lloyd and Ralph Gibson L.JJ. agreed):

"Before *Grant* v. *Edwards* the distinction between the category of case exemplified by that decision and *Eves* v. *Eves* [1975] 1 W.L.R. 1338 on the one hand and that exemplified by *Gissing* v. *Gissing* and *Burns* v. *Burns* [1984] Ch. 317 on the other had not been clearly defined. The distinction has now been authoritatively recognised in the speech of Lord Bridge of Harwich in *Lloyds Bank PLC* v. *Rosset* [1990] 2 W.L.R. 867, at pp. 877B to 878D, a passage which is also notable for two references to conduct giving rise to 'a constructive trust or a proprietary estoppel.' Since it is necessary, in order to decide the extent of Miss Anderson's beneficial interest in Stone Cottage, to ascertain the principle on which such a decision ought to be made, a brief diversion into the burgeoning question of the relationship between the *Gissing* v. *Gissing* species of constructive trust and proprietary estoppel is here desirable.

"In *Grant* v. *Edwards* [1986] Ch. at pp. 656G and 657H, the Vice-Chancellor suggested that in cases under *Gissing* v. *Gissing* the principles underlying the law of proprietary estoppel might provide useful guidance both in regard to the conduct necessary to constitute an acting upon the common intention by the claimant and in regard to the quantification of his or her beneficial interest in the property. In *Austin* v. *Keele* (1987) A.L.J.R. 605, at p. 609, 72 A.L.R. 579, at p. 587, Lord Oliver of Aylmerton, in delivering the judgment of the Privy Council, said that in essence the doctrine of *Gissing* v. *Gissing* was an application of proprietary estoppel. The Vice-Chancellor's suggestion was echoed by Nicholls L.J. in *Lloyds Bank PLC* v. *Rosset* [1989] Ch. 350, at p. 387A–B, and it has now been adopted and enlarged upon by Professor Hayton; see [1990] Conv. 370. However, it must be emphasised that this question was only touched on in the arguments in this court in *Grant* v. *Edwards* and *Lloyds Bank PLC* v. *Rosset* and both the Vice-Chancellor and Nicholls L.J. were careful to base their decisions on conventional *Gissing* v. *Gissing* principles.

"It is possible that the House of Lords will one day decide to solve the problems presented by these cases either by assimilating the principles of *Gissing* v. *Gissing* and proprietary estoppel or even by following the recent trend in other Commonwealth jurisdictions towards more generalised principles of unconscionability and unjust enrichment. The Vice-Chancellor has identified two areas where the application of *Gissing* v. *Gissing* might be enlarged through the influence of proprietary estoppel and there is no real reason for thinking that their assimilation would be unduly hindered by their separate development out of basically different factual situations. But they have not yet been assimilated and we in this court must continue to regard cases such as the present as being governed by the principles of *Gissing* v. *Gissing*, at any rate until we come to one where we cannot be confident that their application will produce a just result. I do not lack that confidence in the present case, especially since it has given us the opportunity of putting the quantification of the claimant's beneficial interest on a more satisfactory footing, a footing which incidentally brings it nearer to proprietary estoppel.

"In regard to the quantification of Miss Anderson's beneficial interest we were referred by counsel to *Eves* v. *Eves* and *Grant* v. *Edwards*, in each of which the same question arose. But the starting point must be Lord Diplock's speech in *Gissing* v. *Gissing*, from which it is clear that this question, like the anterior one, depends on the common intention of the parties, either expressed or more usually to be inferred from all the circumstances. That does not mean that in the latter case you have to infer a common intention that the extent of the claimant's beneficial interest is to be ascertained once and for all at the date of its acquisition. Thus at [1971] A.C. 909D, Lord Diplock, in dealing with the contributions of husband and wife to mortgage instalments, said:

> 'And there is nothing inherently improbable in their acting on the understanding that the wife should be entitled to a share which was not to be quantified immediately upon the acquisition of the home but should be left to be determined when the mortgage was repaid or the property disposed of, on the basis of what would be fair having regard to the total contributions, direct or indirect, which each spouse had made by that date. Where this was the most likely inference from their conduct it would be for the court to give effect to that common intention of the parties by determining what in all the circumstances was a fair share.'

"I agree with the Vice-Chancellor in *Grant* v. *Edwards* [1986] Ch. at p. 657E, that those observations, although made only in reference to contributions to mortgage repayments, support a more general proposition that all payments made and acts done by the claimant are to be treated as illuminating the common intention as to the extent of the beneficial interest. Once you get to that stage, as Lord Diplock recognised, there is no practicable alternative to the determination of a fair share. The court must supply the common intention by reference to that which all the material circumstances have shown to be fair. I think that both *Eves* v. *Eves*, where no financial contribution was made by the claimant, and *Grant* v. *Edwards*, where the claimant had made substantial indirect contributions to the mortgage repayments and the balance of the fire insurance moneys had been equally divided, are explicable on this basis, albeit that neither was clearly expressed to be so decided.

"What is the fair result by which the common intention ought to be supplied in this case? Mr. Kaye accepted that the two payments of £5,000 and £7,000 must be taken into account. He was less happy about the £2,500, contending that there was no clear evidence that any of it was spent in any relevant way. He submitted that on any footing Miss Anderson's contribution should be valued at a maximum of £14,500 as against a gross value of £120,000, or £90,000 after deduction of the mortgage, being 12.08 per cent. in the first case and 16.11 per cent. in the second. Taking a broad view, Mr. Kaye submitted that Miss Anderson's beneficial interest in Stone Cottage did not extend to more than 15 per cent. of the whole.

"Mr. McCombe relied on the observations of Brightman J. in *Eves* v. *Eves* [1975] 1 W.L.R., at p. 1345G:

> 'There is a case for saying that in the absence of any contrary indication it can only be a joint interest in equity, leading to a half interest for each party as soon as the joint tenancy is severed. Why, it may be asked, should the interest be any different if the interest exists at all?'

Moreover, submitted Mr. McCombe, Miss Anderson's assumption, shared by the judge after seeing and hearing all the witnesses, that she was to have a half share was consistent with a fair evaluation of all the circumstances of the case. Mr. McCombe also relied on the fact that when Mrs. Linda Stokes remarried in September 1987 she apparently released Mr. Stokes from his liability to keep down the mortgage on her new house. As to that point, I cannot see that it would be right to credit Miss Anderson with a forbearance on the part of Mrs. Linda Stokes to enforce her rights against Mr. Stokes.

"It is important to bear in mind that when the first payment of £5,000 was made, Mr. Stokes was already entitled to half the beneficial interest in Stone Cottage. In order that the property might become available for the joint occupation of himself and Miss Anderson it was only necessary to acquire the other half from Mrs. Linda Stokes. How was that other half acquired? Miss Anderson put down a total of £12,000 against £3,000 put down by Mr. Stokes. Although Miss Anderson made no contribution towards the mortgage repayments on Stone Cottage, I think that Mr. McCombe was justified in relying on her provision of the major part of the necessary cash as demonstrating her instrumentality in acquiring Mrs. Linda Stokes' half share. Regard must also be had to the £2,500 which she spent on the property and to her decorating of the house and working on the grounds. Some discount must be made on the assumed value of £120,000, which seems to have been the topmost figure disclosed by the three valuations obtained at the time.

"In my judgment the judge was wrong to hold that Miss Anderson was entitled to half the beneficial interest in Stone Cottage, a result which would be markedly unfair to Mr. Stokes. On a broad approach, the only approach which can be made, I think that the fair view of all the circumstances is that Miss Anderson is entitled to a beneficial interest equivalent to one half of Mrs. Linda Stokes' half share, or one quarter of the whole, subject to the mortgage. I would therefore allow the appeal."

## Section 4. The Vendor as Constructive Trustee[14]

Once a vendor has received the purchase price for his land[15] it is clear that he holds it on constructive trust for the purchaser until he has transferred title to the purchaser. As an exceptional *sui generis* matter even when a vendor enters into a specifically enforceable contract for the sale of property he becomes a modified constructive trustee thereof for the purchaser until the contract is completed by a conveyance of the property.[16] "Equity regards as done that which ought to be done" but the doctrine of conversion does not operate until the vendor has made title in accordance with the contract or the purchaser has agreed to accept a title not in accordance with the contract. Once conversion has so occurred its operation is retrospective from the date of the contract.[17]

The vendor has to "use reasonable care to preserve the property in a reasonable state of preservation, and, so far as may be, as it was when the contract was made" or "to take reasonable care that the property is not deteriorated in the interval before completion."[18] This may be exploited by a purchaser upon whom a vendor has served a notice to complete[19] making time of the essence of the contract: the purchaser can claim that the notice was invalid because the vendor was not ready, able and willing to complete the contract owing to breach of his fiduciary duty of preservation.[20] However, if the contract goes off the vendor cannot be liable to the purchaser for failing to preserve the property.[21]

Till completion the vendor is a quasi-trustee with a highly interested trusteeship: he has a paramount right to protect his own interest.[22] He is entitled to keep the rents and profits till the date fixed for completion[23] and to retain possession of the property until the contract is completed by payment of the price.[24] If he parts with possession to the purchaser before actual completion or even conveys the land he may fall back on his equitable lien to ensure that he is paid.[25] If the

---

[14] Barnsley's *Conveyancing Law and Practice* (3rd ed.) pp. 226–238; Oakley's *Constructive Trusts*, Chap. 6.

[15] Or other property of such a special character that a contract for such property will be specifically enforceable: *Oughtred* v. *IRC* [1960] A.C. 206.

[16] *Wall* v. *Bright* (1820) 1 Jac. & W. 494, 503; *Royal British P.B.S.* v. *Bomash* (1887) 35 Ch.D. 390, 397; *Rayner* v. *Preston* (1881) 18 Ch.D. 1, 6. For conflicting views of Stamp and Goff L.JJ. on a sub-purchaser's position see *Berkeley* v. *Poulett* (1977) 241 Est.Gaz. 911; 242 Est.Gaz. 39.

[17] *Lysaght* v. *Edwards* (1876) 2 Ch.D. 499, 506–507.

[18] *Clarke* v. *Ramuz* [1891] 2 Q.B. 456, 460, 468; *Davron Estates Ltd.* v. *Turnshire* (1983) 133 New L.J. 937; risk, however, passes to the purchaser after exchange of contracts in so far as concerns anything not caused by a breach of the vendor's duties: *Rayner* v. *Preston* (1881) 18 Ch.D. 1 (affected by Law of Property Act 1925, s.47, now) unless under the contract the vendor retains the risk as under the Standard Conditions of Sale (1st ed., 1990) Condition 5.1.

[19] Standard Conditions of Sale (1st ed.) Condition 6.6.

[20] Purchasers have taken this point where squatters have managed to break into the property the subject of the contract: so far the cases appear to have been settled without the need to spend days in court arguing whether or not the vendor's precautions were reasonable.

[21] *Plews* v. *Samuel* [1904] 1 Ch. 464; *Ridout* v. *Fowler* [1904] 1 Ch. 658; [1904] 2 Ch. 93.

[22] *Shaw* v. *Foster* (1872) L.R. 5 H.L. 321, 338; *Re Watford Corporation's Contract* [1943] Ch. 82, 85.

[23] *Cuddon* v. *Tite* (1858) 1 Giff. 395.

[24] *Gedge* v. *Montrose* (1858) 26 Beav. 45; *Phillips* v. *Silvester* (1872) L.R. 8 Ch. 173.

[25] *Nives* v. *Nives* (1880) 15 Ch.D. 649; *Re Birmingham* [1959] Ch. 523; *London & Cheshire Insurance Co. Ltd.* v. *Laplagrene* [1971] Ch. 499.

vendor in breach of the constructive trust sells the property to X, the purchaser may trace the property into the proceeds of sale received by the vendor subject to accounting to the vendor for the price agreed between them. This will be useful if the contractual claim against the vendor for damages is not worthwhile, *e.g.* if he is bankrupt or more financial benefit can be obtained from the tracing claim than the damages claim.[26]

## Section 5. Beneficiaries' Proprietary Tracing Rights and Personal Remedies Against Recipients of the Trust Property[27]

### I. MEANING OF PERSONAL CLAIMS AND PROPRIETARY CLAIMS

By a personal claim is meant a claim enforceable against a defendant personally as distinct from a proprietary claim enforceable against a particular fund or a particular piece of property under the control of the defendant. In the former case the claim, if successful, will give rise to a judgment imposing a personal liability on the defendant which will be of little use if he is thoroughly insolvent. In the latter the judgment will make available to the claimant a particular fund or piece of property controlled by the defendant. It will not involve the defendant in any personal liability over and above that which is implicit in his being required to give up to the plaintiff either the entirety or a part of the fund which he has hitherto been claiming as his own.

The measure of liability in a proprietary claim amounts to the value of the "surviving enrichment" in the defendant's hands while the measure of liability in a personal claim will normally be the "value received" by the defendant, irrespective of how little value surviving there may be in his hands.[28] In an exceptional case, to prevent prejudice to third parties, there may be a personal, but not a proprietary, liability for the surviving enrichment of the defendant.[29]

### II. PROPRIETARY CLAIMS

The particular advantages of proprietary claims flow from the fact that the property in question has throughout belonged to the plaintiff. Thus the defendant's bankruptcy has no effect on the claim; neither has the barring of a personal action against the defendant under the Limitation Act. If the property has increased in value then this accrues to the plaintiff's advantage. If the property has depreciated in value then the

---

[26] *Lake* v. *Bayliss* [1974] 1 W.L.R. 1073.

[27] The personal claim against the trustee, as distinct from a recipient from the trustee, is considered, *infra*, Chap. 10. The proprietary claim considered in this Section is available against the trustee as well as a recipient of the trust property from the trustee, subject to the differences discussed *infra*, pp. 540–543.

[28] See Birks, *Introduction to the Law of Restitution* generally for development of "value received" as the first measure of restitution and "surviving enrichment" as the second measure of restitution.

[29] *e.g.* a £40,000 personal liability where a fiduciary employee takes a £25,000 bribe which he invests in shares now worth £40,000: see pp. 445, 450, *supra*.

plaintiff can have an equitable charge over the property as security for the amount of his claim against the defendant. If the plaintiff wishes to have the property preserved intact pending the hearing of his claim he has an equitable interest enabling him to obtain an injunction preserving the property under section 37(1) of the Supreme Court Act 1981.[30] If the plaintiff's money was used with the defendant's money so as to earn any interest or dividends or a capital profit the plaintiff is entitled to a proportionate share of the interest or dividends[31] or profit.[32]

### Difference between common law and equity

At common law the right to chattels was protected by the tort actions of conversion and detinue, now known as wrongful interference with goods,[33] or in quasi-contract through the action for money had and received. A person who proved a tort had been committed could waive the tort[34] and bring an action for money had and received in respect of benefits received by the tortfeasor. Otherwise, the action for money had and received lay to recover money paid by the plaintiff to the defendant under a mistake or compulsion or for a consideration which had wholly failed; the plaintiff could also recover money which the defendant had received from a third party when the defendant was accountable to the plaintiff in respect of the money.

These common law actions are actions *in personam* following upon interference with proprietary rights. "Tracing" or "following" at common law is concerned with identifying property in a changed form and in whosoever hands in order to found a personal action to support the proprietary right discovered by the "tracing" or "following" process.[35] If A's original property is in B's hands and B disposes of such property in return for the new property in such circumstances that the new property belongs to A then, if B goes bankrupt, the title to the new property does not belong to B's trustee in bankruptcy. However, if he attempts to hold on to the property he can be personally sued for wrongful interference with goods so that he must either deliver the new property to A or pay damages to their value to A. Thus A obtains priority over B's creditors.

The conventional view,[36] owing to the confused state of the case law[37] where a clear distinction has not been made between the common law

---

30 Replacing Supreme Court of Judicature Acts 1873 and 1925, ss.25(8) and 45 respectively.
31 *Re Diplock* [1948] Ch. 465, 517, 557.
32 *Re Tilleys W.T.* [1967] Ch. 1179; *Scott* v. *Scott* (1963) 109 C.L.R. 649.
33 Torts (Interference with Goods) Act 1977.
34 See Goff & Jones, Chap. 32. Waiver of tort is not based on any ratification or adoption of the wrongful acts: *United Australia Ltd.* v. *Barclays Bank* [1941] A.C. 1, 18, 28–29. For a modern view of the so-called waiver of tort doctrine see S. Hedley (1984) 100 L.Q.R. 653.
35 See M. Scott (1966) 7 W.A.L.R. 463.
36 *Banque Belge* v. *Hambrouck* [1921] 1 K.B. 321; *Re J. Leslie Engineering Co. Ltd.* [1976] 1 W.L.R. 292 both misconceiving *Taylor* v. *Plumer* (1815) 3 M. & S. 562 if as seems likely it was concerned with equitable tracing, and where Lord Ellenborough's derogatory remarks about the limitations of tracing were directed at equitable tracing owing to his ignorance of equitable developments, as pointed out by Jessel M.R. in *Re Hallett's Estate* (1880) 13 Ch.D. 696. M. Scott, *op. cit.*; R. A. Pearce (1976) 40 Conv. 277; Khurshid & Matthews (1979) 95 L.Q.R. 78; but see Goff & Jones, p. 66, n. 41. Now see Lord Goff in *Lipkin Gorman* v. *Karpnale* [1991] 3 W.L.R. 10.
37 On which see Khurshid & Matthews (1979) 95 L.Q.R. 78.

position and the equitable tracing remedy, has been that if A owns property which B without authority exchanges for cash or other property from C, then A can claim the "exchange product," either as owner or at least as having sufficient right to immediate possession to enable him to maintain a claim for conversion or, now, wrongful interference with goods, so as to bring a tort claim or waive the tort and sue in quasi-contract.

The better view[38] is that if C has not passed title to A directly via B's agency then title has passed to B so that unless B specifically appropriates the property to A, thereby passing title to A, then A has no title to the property nor sufficient right to immediate possession to enable him to bring a claim in tort. This is a significant limitation upon the common law position.

Money raises particular problems since it soon ceases to be identifiable when mixed with other money or paid into a bank account. The conventional view[39] has been that equity was far ahead of the common law in its flexible rules for tracing moneys, though mixed in bank accounts; whilst it may well have been that the common law was equally flexible.[40] However, the usefulness of equity in such situations has been such that the common law position remains unclear, *Banque Belge* v. *Hambrouck*[41] being the rather unsatisfactory decision in point when there are two ways of explaining it in a more satisfactory way.[42] The case does establish that money paid into a bank account can certainly be identified at law if not mixed with other moneys and, perhaps, even if mixed with other moneys. Recently, Millett J.[43] held that common law tracing is not possible for money transmitted by telegraphic transfer where there is no cheque or any equivalent.

The common law actions have the advantage that they are not dependent upon the presence of a fiduciary relationship, or upon any adoption by the plaintiff of the defendant's acts, or upon the continued existence or identifiability of the *res* in the defendant's hands, and bona fide purchase will rarely be a defence for wrongful interference with another's legal title to goods. Of course, a beneficiary under a trust cannot himself bring a common law action against his trustee, though where the trustees have the benefit of an action then, since this is a trust asset, the beneficiary can in equity force the trustee to take appropriate steps and nowadays can even sue at common law joining the trustees as defendants to the action.

In equity a plaintiff must base his claim on the existence of an equitable right to property which will involve a fiduciary relationship

---

[38] R. M. Goode (1976) 92 L.Q.R. 360, 367, n. 27; Khurshid & Matthews, *op. cit.*
[39] *Sinclair* v. *Brougham* [1914] A.C. 419; *Re Diplock* [1948] Ch. 465; *Banque Belge* v. *Hambrouck* [1921] 1 K.B. 321.
[40] R. M. Goode (1976) 92 L.Q.R. 360, 395–396; Khurshid & Matthews (1979) 95 L.Q.R. 78, 81–82; *Jackson* v. *Anderson* (1811) 4 Taunt. 24. Point conceded in *Lipkin Gorman* v. *Karpnale* [1991] 3 W.L.R. 10.
[41] [1921] 1 K.B. 321.
[42] R. M. Goode (1976) 92 L.Q.R. 360, 378–381; Khurshid & Matthews (1979) 95 L.Q.R. 78, 91–94.
[43] [1990] Ch. 265.

between himself and the defendant or himself and a person who transferred the property to the defendant.[44] The right of the beneficiaries to trace is based on adoption of the wrongful act, where the product of such act has increased in value so that the product is claimed, but is not based on adoption where the claim is for a charge on assets that have depreciated. Unlike the position at common law, there can be no doubt that equity regards "a composite fund as an amalgam constituted by the mixture of two or more funds, each of which . . . " is "capable, in proper circumstances, of being resolved into its component parts."[45] Moreover, equity unlike the common law can impose a charge on an amalgam. The remedy in equity is proprietary but it is not available at all against the bona fide purchaser for value without notice: it is available to a limited extent against the innocent volunteer.[46] It depends upon the continued existence of the *res* or its product.

## The right to the equitable proprietary remedy

As a product of the exclusive jurisdiction of the Court of Chancery the right to trace requires "a continuing right of property recognised in equity or its concomitant, a fiduciary or quasi-fiduciary relationship." Goulding J. stated[47] that this is the interpretation accorded to the House of Lords decision in *Sinclair* v. *Brougham*[48] by the Court of Appeal in *Re Diplock*.[49]

To allow plaintiffs a right to trace in circumstances where the court considers it to be just, the concept of fiduciary or quasi-fiduciary relationship has been stretched to the limit.[50] It covers bailor and bailee,[51] principal and agent where their relationship is not simply that of debtor and creditor,[52] directors of a company and persons making *ultra vires* deposits with the company,[53] and employer and employee,[54]

---

[44] *Chase Manhattan Bank* v. *Israel Bank* [1981] Ch. 105.

[45] [1948] Ch. 465, 520.

[46] *Infra*, pp. 546–548.

[47] [1981] Ch. 105, 119. See also *Agip (Africa) Ltd.* v. *Jackson* [1991] 3 W.L.R. 116.

[48] [1914] A.C. 398.

[49] [1948] Ch. 465.

[50] Many would like to see the removal of this requirement: Goff & Jones, pp. 71–72; Maudsley (1959) 75 L.Q.R. 234; Oakley (1975) 28 Current L.P. 64.

[51] But the presumption of a fiduciary relationship between bailor and bailee may be rebutted: *Hendy Lennox Ltd.* v. *Grahame Puttick Ltd.* [1984] 2 All E.R. 152, 162–163. Suppliers of goods to manufacturers, in order to give themselves security on the manufacturers' insolvency leaving the goods unpaid for, have tried by contract to make the manufacturer a fiduciary bailee or agent till payment, required to keep the goods and the proceeds of sale thereof separate from the manufacturers' property so that the supplier can trace the goods and the proceeds: *Aluminium Industrie Vaasen* v. *Romalpa* [1976] 1 W.L.R. 676. There are problems discussed p. 116, *supra* for the seller trying to trace into the manufactured product in which his goods are mixed and in Companies Act 1985, s.395 making equitable charges by companies void if unregistered: *Borden (U.K.) Ltd.* v. *Scottish Timber Products Ltd.* [1981] Ch. 25; *Re Bond Worth Limited* [1980] Ch. 228; *Re Andrabell Ltd.* [1984] 3 All E.R. 407; *Re Peachdart Ltd.* [1984] Ch. 131; *Clough Mill Ltd.* v. *Martin* [1984] 3 All E.R. 982, *supra*, p. 120.

[52] *Re Goode* (1974) 4 Austr.L.R. 579. Clients, who dealt with a stockbroker one transaction at a time, had full rights to trace (if vendors) their shares into a pool of shares held by the broker or to recover (if purchasers) money entrusted to the broker for settlement; clients who operated on a running account with periodic balances and settlements were in a mere debtor-creditor relationship with no tracing remedy.

[53] *Sinclair* v. *Brougham* [1914] A.C. 398.

[54] *Banque Belge* v. *Hambrouck* [1921] 1 K.B. 321; *Black* v. *Freedman* (1910) 12 C.L.R. 105.

as well as the obvious cases of solicitor and client[55] and trustee (express, resulting or constructive[56]) and beneficiary. In *Chase Manhattan Bank* v. *Israel-British Bank*[57] Goulding J. held:

> "A person who pays money to another under a factual mistake retains an equitable property in it and the conscience of that other is subjected to a fiduciary duty to respect his proprietary right . . . the equitable remedy of tracing is available, on the ground of continuing proprietary interest, to a party who has paid money under a mistake of fact."

In *A* v. *C*[58] and in *Bankers Trust Co.* v. *Shapira*[59] a bank, misled by forged cheques to credit a rogue's account with another bank, has been treated as having a right to trace its moneys into and out of the other bank and has therefore obtained an order against the other bank for discovery of all documents relating to the moneys. In these three cases the recipient of the moneys had not been in a prior fiduciary relationship with the claimant, but the very payment of the moneys to the recipient gave rise to the payer's separate equitable property right to recover his moneys which the recipient was bound to respect upon acquiring knowledge of the circumstances.

*The need for a(n equitable) proprietary interest*

As Professor Birks has pointed out,[60] a "proprietary base," rather than a fiduciary relationship, is really the fundamental requirement for a tracing claim. If P has some sort of an equitable interest or mere equity in D's property then there will be a fiduciary relationship between P and D.[61]

If P intends to transfer full legal and equitable ownership to D of property fully transferred to D then P has no tracing claim,[62] *e.g.* where D's fraudulent representations lead P to lend D £1 million at 15 per cent. interest which D invests in property now worth £2 million or where D's negligent failure to disclose his solvency position leads P to lend D £50,000 at 16 per cent. interest which D invests in property worth £40,000 when D becomes bankrupt.[63] There can be no right to trace between P and D where the relationship is creditor and debtor so that D can do what he likes with *his* property.

Thus, if D, a fiduciary employee of P, takes a £20,000 bribe, of course intended by the briber to belong wholly to D, P has no proprietary right to trace the bribe into shares now worth £35,000. In

---

[55] *Re Hallett's Estate* (1880) 13 Ch.D. 696; *Hopper* v. *Conyers* (1866) L.R. 2 Eq. 549.
[56] *Lake* v. *Bayliss* [1974] 2 All E.R. 1114 (vendor under contract of sale of land to P1 held on constructive trust for P1 so that when V sold to P2, P1 could trace those proceeds of sale).
[57] [1981] Ch. 105, 119. For another case on mistakes see *Mediterranea Reffineria Siciliani Petroli* v. *Mabanaft Gmbh* [1978] C.A.T. 816 cited in [1980] 3 All E.R. 356–357.
[58] [1980] 2 All E.R. 347.
[59] [1980] 3 All E.R. 353.
[60] Birks, pp. 378 *et seq.*
[61] *Chase Manhattan Bank* v. *Israel-British Bank* [1981] Ch. 105, 119.
[62] *Space Investments Ltd.* v. *Canadian Imperial Bank of Commerce* [1986] 1 W.L.R. 1072.
[63] See *Chief Constable of Leicestershire* v. *M* [1989] 1 W.L.R. 20, *Chief Constable of Surrey* v. *A, The Times*, October 27, 1988, and *Daley* v. *Sidney Stock Exchange* (1986) 65 A.L.R. 193.

*Lister* v. *Stubbs*,[64] the Court of Appeal held that there was only a debtor-creditor relationship for the amount of the bribe, though to prevent a fiduciary from profiting from his position, a strong case can be made for making D personally liable for the surviving unjust enrichment of £35,000. Indeed, it can be argued that equity should look to substance rather than to form so as to treat the £20,000 bribe as representing the £20,000 of P's money that must be presumed to have been overpaid to the briber in purchasing his goods or services.[65]

The need for a proprietary base of sorts appears in *Lake* v. *Bayliss*[66] which was based on the fact that a vendor, V, under a contract of sale of Blackacre to P1, holds the land (because the contract is specifically enforceable in equity and equity looks on as done that which ought to be done) on a modified constructive trust[67] for P1, who thus has some modified equitable interest in the land. It followed, when V actually sold the land to P2, that P1 could trace the proceeds of sale (*e.g.* into a profitable purchase by V). If V in breach of a non-specifically enforceable contract with P1 sells goods at a profit to P2, it seems that because P1 has no proprietary interest in the goods he cannot trace the proceeds of sale of the goods and so claim the profits. In both cases V is unjustly enriched at P1's expense[68] but until a general principle of unjust enrichment becomes part of English law technicalities will determine whether or not V's tracing claim succeeds.

Traditionally, it has been considered that a beneficial owner with legal title to goods that are stolen has no equitable right to trace the goods. The basis for this is that the right to trace arose as a part of the exclusive equitable jurisdiction[69] to protect someone with an equitable interest in property legally owned by another: it was not part of the concurrent or auxiliary equitable jurisdiction which provided new remedies or procedures to improve the enforcement of common law rights. Indeed, the legal remedies of actions for conversion or detinue or for money had and received were normally more than adequate to protect the legal owner of goods.

This indicates that the equitable remedy of tracing (like that of specific performance[70]) should not be available if the legal remedy is adequate. However, if a thief sold a car in a market overt, so that it cannot be recovered from the purchaser under an unlawful interference with goods claim, and the thief is bankrupt, why should the original legal owner not be able to trace the proceeds of sale into property purchased with such proceeds by the thief?[71] Should it really

---

[64] (1890) 45 Ch.D. 1.
[65] See pp. 445, 450, *supra*.
[66] [1974] 1 W.L.R. 1073.
[67] See p. 530, *supra*.
[68] See decision of Israel Supreme Court in *Adras Ltd.* v. *Harlow & Jones* (1988) 42(1) P.D. noted in (1988) 104 L.Q.R. 383.
[69] Where Equity enforced rights which the common law courts failed to enforce Equity alone had jurisdiction to grant relief.
[70] See Jones & Goodhart, *Specific Performance*, pp. 18–22.
[71] Ditto if the car could be recovered at law from some purchaser but worth only half its value when stolen four years earlier, and the proceeds had been invested in a painting worth more than the car's original value.

make a difference that the thief stole one car from a legal beneficial owner, O, while the other car was trust property owned by T on trust for B? Can O not argue that theft deprives him neither of his legal nor his equitable title? If O saw his car being stolen and shouted to the thief, "You must return the car to me. You hold it on trust for me," should this make a difference, especially when the thief must know that he is under a duty to return it to O even if O does not so tell him?

These considerations make it difficult to believe that an English court would nowadays deny an equitable tracing remedy against a thief were legal remedies prove inadequate.[72]

## Interlocutory injunctions

If a plaintiff does have a sufficient proprietary base to trace assets as "his" he is entitled to obtain an interlocutory injunction to preserve such assets until the trial of the action.[73] To make his tracing rights effective a court will be very ready to make ancillary orders to enable him to discover traceable assets, *e.g.* ordering a bank or the defendant to make discovery of all relevant documents, ordering a defendant to answer written interrogatories before being allowed to leave the jurisdiction. Once the plaintiff proves his tracing claim he will be entitled to the frozen assets with priority over any creditors of the defendant.

Where the plaintiff merely has a personal claim (*e.g.* for damages at common law for a tort or a breach of contract) then in an exceptional case a *Mareva*[74] interlocutory injunction may be obtained[75] to freeze assets not exceeding the amount of the plaintiff's claim and his costs. The plaintiff will need to show he has a good arguable claim justiciable in the United Kingdom or elsewhere in the European Community,[76] that the defendant has assets in the jurisdiction,[77] that there are reasonable grounds for believing that the defendant will remove the assets out of the jurisdiction or will otherwise dissipate or dispose of them, so that the court may conclude that the refusal of a *Mareva* injunction would involve a real risk that a judgment in favour of the plaintiff would not be satisfied.[78] The frozen asset is usually a bank

---

[72] See Goff & Jones, p. 72, Millett J. in "Tracing the Proceeds of Fraud" in (1991) 107 L.Q.R. 71, 76. For liberal views in Canada and Australia see, *e.g. Lennox Industries* v. *The Queen* (1986) 34 D.L.R. (4th) 304, *Black* v. *Freedman* (1910) 12 C.L.R. 105, 110 cited by Lord Templeman in *Lipkin Gorman* v. *Karpnale* [1991] 3 W.L.R. 10.

[73] See Lord Denning M.R. in *Bankers Trust* v. *Shapira* [1980] 3 All E.R. 353, 357 citing Templeman L.J. in an unreported case.

[74] [1975] 2 Lloyd's Rep. 509.

[75] It will be *ex parte* in the first instance but may be continued after an *inter partes* hearing.

[76] *Republic of Haiti* v. *Duvalier* [1989] 1 All E.R. 456.

[77] Or, in an exceptional case, assets outside the jurisdiction which the defendant in the jurisdiction ought to be compelled to preserve: *Derby* v. *Weldon* (Nos. 3 and 4) [1990] Ch. 65 which sets out a proviso to protect third parties where the *in personam* order against the defendant would otherwise have extra-territorial effect. If assets have been placed in State X to make them safe against the enforcement of an English court order the court can order the defendant in England to transfer the assets to a jurisdiction recognising an English court order: *Derby* v. *Weldon* (No. 6) [1990] 3 All E.R. 263.

[78] *Bekhor* v. *Bilton* [1981] Q.B. 923; *Z Ltd.* v. *A* [1982] Q.B. 558; *CBS United Kingdom Ltd.* v. *Lambert* [1982] 3 All E.R. 272; Supreme Court Act 1981, s.37(3). In support of a *Mareva* injunction ancillary orders may be made for disclosure of assets and for answering interrogatories: *Allied Arab Bank* v. *Hajjat* [1988] Q.B. 787.

account but it may be other types of asset.[79] However, the injunction only operates *in personam* against the defendant. It affords the plaintiff no proprietary right in the frozen asset nor priority over other creditors.[80] Indeed, the injunction may be varied to enable the frozen assets to be partly unfrozen so that the defendant may make payments in good faith in the ordinary course of business or for legal or living expenses.[81] Exceptionally, a Chief Constable has sufficient interest to obtain an injunction freezing assets such as a confidence trickster's bank account, since he has a duty to seize and detain stolen or unlawfully obtained goods for restoring them to their true owner and, by analogy, a similar duty in respect of intangible assets such as a bank account.[82]

### No need to sue trustee first

It is not considered that before a claimant can pursue his tracing claim and enforce his equitable proprietary interest against third parties he must first sue the trustee or other fiduciary responsible for the assets passing into the hands of third parties. This is an important distinction between the proprietary tracing claim and the personal claim (discussed p. 550, *infra*) available to unpaid or underpaid creditors, legatees or next of kin against recipients of a deceased's estate only after they have first exhausted their remedies against the deceased's personal representatives.

In *Re Diplock* the Court of Appeal said[83]:

> "Prima facie and subject to discussion,[84] it appears to us that the sums so recovered [£15,000 recovered from the personal representatives] ought to be credited rateably to all the charities [the third parties who had innocently received the deceased's estate] for all purposes, *i.e.* for the purposes of the claims *in rem* [the proprietary tracing claim] as well as the claim *in personam*."

In context, since it so happened that £15,000 had already been received, it was only right and proper that the claims against the charities should be reduced *pro tanto*. The case is thus not authority for the view that claims against the fiduciary must first be exhausted before any tracing claim can be pursued against third party recipients.[85]

If such view prevailed it would be most unsatisfactory. The recipients would obtain a windfall to the extent of the money extracted

---

[79] *Allen* v. *Jambo Holdings Ltd.* [1980] 1 W.L.R. 1252 (aircraft).
[80] *Iraqi Ministry of Defence* v. *Arcepey Shipping Co.* [1981] Q.B. 65.
[81] *PCW (Underwriting Agencies) Ltd.* v. *Dixon* [1983] 2 All E.R. 158.
[82] *Chief Constable of Hampshire* v. *A* [1984] 2 All E.R. 385 as restricted by *Chief Constable of Leicestershire* v. *M* [1989] 1 W.L.R. 20.
[83] [1948] Ch. 465, 556.
[84] This seems to have been inserted in case it was necessary to marshall the £15,000 in different manner, *e.g.* if charity A had dissipated all it received should any of the £15,000 have been used in reduction of the barren tracing claim against it?
[85] Significantly, in *Re Leslie Engineers Co. Ltd.* [1976] 2 All E.R. 85, 91 Oliver J., having mentioned the restriction on the personal claim, did not mention it when referring to a possible tracing claim.

from the trustee, and his creditors would be unfairly prejudiced. Usually, it will be fair that the recipients wrongfully having the trust fund should disgorge their misbegotten gains. It is, however, possible that there might be an exceptional case, where the recipient has so changed his position that it would be inequitable to make him pay rather than the trustee responsible for the recipient's unfortunate position, or where making the recipient refund to the trust fund a gift of trust moneys from the trustee would be to allow the trustee to go back on his gift, while making the trustee repay the money to the trust would regularise the gift to the recipient. For justice to be done perhaps all parties should be brought before the court as happened in *Eaves* v. *Hickson*.[86] There trustees were innocently misled by X forging his marriage certificate so as to distribute half the trust fund to his illegitimate children (when only legitimate children were beneficiaries). It was held that the illegitimate children were primarily liable, but to the extent they could not discharge their liability then X was liable,[87] but to the extent he could not discharge his liability then the trustees were liable.[88]

One may note that it is not only a beneficiary who can take advantage of the tracing remedy, *e.g.* into mixed bank accounts and claiming a charge over an amalgam of assets. A trustee may also trace where his remedies as legal owner are inadequate to safeguard his beneficiaries' interests, especially if the beneficiaries are as yet unborn or unascertained.[89]

*The scope of the equitable proprietary remedy*
Where the trust property or its product is intact, then the court will order the person having such property or product to restore it to the trustees (or to the beneficiaries if each is *sui juris* and between them they are absolutely entitled to the trust fund).[90] Thus, if in breach of trust the trustee gives a trust painting to his brother, who sells it and uses the proceeds to buy a flat for his mistress as sole beneficial owner, she will be compelled to transfer the flat to the trustees (the original trustee no doubt having resigned or having been removed from his office). If the flat is worth more than the painting it is taken over as if it had been an authorised investment. If it is worth less there is a charge on the flat for the value of the painting so that the flat is taken over and its value credited against the personal liability for breach of trust. In other words, the beneficiaries can elect to treat the flat as trust property or as security for the recouping of trust assets.

---

[86] (1861) 30 Beav. 136.
[87] His positive assistance in the breach of trust made him personally liable as a constructive trustee to replace the lost trust assets.
[88] Nowadays the trustees can claim relief under Trustee Act 1925, s.61.
[89] *Price* v. *Blakemore* (1843) 6 Beav. 507 (where the trustees let the life tenant have £8,124 of proceeds of sale of trust land and the life tenant used the money towards purchasing a £17,400 house for himself in fee simple and the trustees' tracing claim succeeded); *Carson* v. *Sloane* (1884) 13 L.R.Ir. 139.
[90] *Re Hallett's Estate* (1880) 13 Ch.D. 696; *Re Diplock* [1948] Ch. 465.

Where the trust property or its product has been mixed with other property the position is more complex.

If there is a mixture of heterogeneous goods in a manufacturing process so that the original trust property (*e.g.* resin) loses its character and what emerges is a wholly new product (*e.g.* chipboard), then in a case where the mixing had been authorised tracing has been held to be impossible because the manufacturing process is regarded as akin to the process of consumption.[91] However, if the mixing had been unauthorised it is difficult to see why the beneficiaries should not be entitled to claim every portion of the blended property that the wrongdoer cannot prove to be his own.[92]

If the goods mixed are of a homogenous character as where trust corn is mixed with a corn factor's own corn[93] or if trust shares are mixed with a trustee's private shares of the same type in the same company then the right to trace remains. Thus, if a trustee mixes 32,280 trust shares, held by him on trust for A absolutely, with 1,300 of his own shares of the same type in the same company, and then gives 17,000 to C so as to retain 16,580, he will be ordered to transfer his 16,580 to A's trustee in bankruptcy and C will be ordered so to transfer 15,700 of his 17,000 shares.[94] Similarly, if 50 tons of trust corn are mixed with 100 tons of a fiduciary bailee's own corn and the amalgam sold for £15,000 and the proceeds banked, the plaintiff may trace into the bank account moneys for £5,000. If the proceeds had been used to buy a car which was a vintage car that appreciated in value then the plaintiff could claim ownership of one third of the car, but if the car had depreciated then he would have a charge on the car for £5,000. Where the traced asset has depreciated this equitable charge or lien for the amount of the trust money is a most useful equitable device for securing the claimant beneficiaries' interests.

Usually, it is trust money that is mixed with other moneys, whether belonging to the trustee personally or as trustee of another trust or belonging to an innocent volunteer.

### Mixing of trust money with trustee's own money

If T spends £10,000 of trust money and £20,000 of his own money on a village flat worth £60,000 when the facts come to light, then the trust is entitled to a one-third interest in the flat[95] together with one-third of

---

[91] *Borden (U.K.) Ltd.* v. *Scottish Timber Products Ltd.* [1981] Ch. 25. Tracing would have been possible if there had been agreement that the supplier's interest in the resin should continue as part ownership of the product: *Coleman* v. *Harvey* [1989] 1 N.Z.L.R. 723.

[92] See *Lupton* v. *White* (1808) 15 Ves. 432 and *Southern Cross Commodities* v. *Martin* 1991 S.L.T. 83. The conscious wrongdoer could have an allowance for his personal skills and financial or other contributions: *O'Sullivan* v. *Management Agency and Music Ltd.* [1985] Q.B. 428.

[93] An example given by Bridge L.J. in *Borden (U.K.) Ltd.* (*supra*), or if crude oil is mixed with crude oil: *Indian Oil Co.* v. *Greenstone Shipping S.A.* [1987] 3 All E.R. 893.

[94] *Brady* v. *Stapleton* (1952) 88 C.L.R. 322.

[95] *Scott* v. *Scott* (1962) 109 C.L.R. 649; *B.C. Teachers' Credit Union* v. *Betterley* (1975) 61 D.L.R. (3d) 755; *Re Tilley's W.T.* [1967] Ch. 1179, *infra*, p. 556. If the trustee could not have taken advantage of the opportunity to buy the property but for the trust money query whether he should obtain a proportionate share of the profit for taking advantage of his position, *e.g.* if a development syndicate requires a minimum £100,000 contribution and T, only having £10,000 of his own uses £90,000 trust moneys. If the investment doubles should T really get £20,000 or just a return of £10,000 plus interest?

the actual or notional rent produced by the flat. If T, instead, had bought a car worth only £12,000 when the facts came to light, then the trust would be entitled to a charge on the car for £10,000 and interest, the £12,000 car being credited against T's liability for £10,000 and interest which together might amount to, say, £15,000.[96] Thus, where the value of the purchased asset appreciates the beneficiaries will claim a proportionate share but where it depreciates they will claim an equitable charge.

(a) *The Re Hallett Presumption of Honesty.* If T has a bank account which is empty until paying in £5,000 of trust money and he then pays in £3,000 of his own and he then spends the £8,000 the applicable principles are set out in the preceding paragraph. But what if he spends only £2,500 which happens to be dissipated so as to be untraceable? Can he allege this was trust money, perhaps by invoking the rule in *Clayton's* case applicable to the running account between banker and customer whereby first payments in are treated as first payments out? No, because[97] "where a man does an act which may be rightfully performed . . . he is not allowed to say against the person entitled to the property or the right that he has done it wrongfully." Thus a trustee is not allowed to deny his beneficiaries' allegation that he was rightfully withdrawing his own funds. Therefore, the beneficiaries will allege that T rightfully dissipated his own £2,500 so that the trust moneys are still intact.

(b) *The Re Oatway election of rules by beneficiaries.* However, if T had spent the £2,500 on purchasing Whizzo Ltd. shares, now worth £10,000, and had then dissipated the £5,500 balance in the account, the beneficiaries will not allege that T first rightfully withdrew his own £2,500. Moreover, T, whose wrongful mixing of trust funds with his own made them indistinguishable, "cannot maintain that the investment which remains represents his money alone and what has been spent and can no longer be traced or recovered was money belonging to the trust."[98] Thus, in *Re Oatway*[99] where the beneficiaries' £3,000 had been added to T's bank account already containing £4,077, and £2,137 was spent on shares and the rest of the moneys subsequently frittered away, the beneficiaries were entitled to a charge on the shares, then worth £2,474, as security for their £3,000 and interest claim for breach of trust against T. If the shares, for example, had appreciated to £5,000 then the beneficiaries instead of claiming a charge on the shares would have elected to adopt the unauthorised investment as purchased with their £2,137, so entitling them to the shares (and any dividends declared thereon if not dissipated) and leaving them with a personal claim for the £863 balance of trust moneys.

---

[96] *Re Hallett's Estate* (1880) 13 Ch.D. 696.
[97] *Ibid.* at 727.
[98] *Re Oatway* [1903] 2 Ch. 356, 360.
[99] [1903] 2 Ch. 356.

In *Re Oatway* it so happened that after purchase of the shares the balance of the money in the account was dissipated. In principle, it should make no difference to the beneficiaries' rights whether, fortuitously, a balance remains in the account and whether this balance is large enough to represent all the moneys due to the beneficiaries. Where a trustee amalgamates trust property with his own he cannot also control the bookkeeping and allocate profitable investments to himself. The beneficiaries are entitled to elect either to have a charge on the amalgam (consisting of bank account moneys remaining and shares or other property purchased with account moneys) as security for their claim or to adopt the purchased property as trust property.[1] In the absence of specific authority it seems that basic principle should apply as follows.

Take the case where T already has £10,000 in his bank account when he adds £10,000 of trust money to it. He spends £15,000 on shares, so leaving £5,000 in the account. The shares double in value. Clearly at least £5,000 of trust moneys must have been used in the purchase. The beneficiaries can claim that £10,000 of trust moneys were used so that they can adopt two thirds of the shares as trust property now happily worth £20,000. The trustee by virtue of his wrongful act, in creating an amalgam where it is impossible to distinguish his property from the trust property, cannot disprove the beneficiaries' claim.

If, instead, T had spent £10,000 on shares in Wonder Limited and then either left the £10,000 balance in the account or spent it on shares in Tacky Limited, the beneficiaries should still be able to claim the Wonder Limited shares which double in value rather than be left, on the word of the wrongdoing T, with the £10,000 or the shares in Tacky Limited which have halved in value. T's speculation should be at his risk and not at his beneficiaries' risk.

Essentially, the wrongdoing trustee cannot be allowed to take advantage of his own wrongdoing to put himself in the position of "Heads I win, tails you lose" whereas the wronged beneficiaries can and the trustee cannot complain. His conduct prevented proper accounts from being kept so it is up to the beneficiaries and not him to resolve the bookkeeping as they wish: "everything is presumed against him."[2]

Take the case where T pays £10,000 trust money into his bank account containing £2,000 of his own money and then draws out £5,000 (leaving £7,000) which he uses with £15,000 of a legacy to him in his building society account to purchase for £20,000 shares now worth £40,000. The beneficiaries can elect either (1) for a charge for their £10,000 and interest on the amalgam of the shares and the remaining money in the account, or (2) for one-quarter of the shares to be

---

[1] *Scott* v. *Scott* (1962) 109 C.L.R. 649; *Re Tilley's W.T.* [1967] Ch. 1179; Ford & Lee, pp. 735–740. If such property is not an authorised investment it will need to be sold (unless all the beneficiaries are *sui juris* and agree otherwise).

[2] *Gray* v. *Haig* (1855) 20 Beav. 214, 226, *per* Romilly M.R.

adopted as trust property, so satisfying their claim to the extent of £5,000 of their moneys, and for a charge for £5,000 and interest to be imposed on the moneys remaining in the account.

(c) *Necessary action for trustee to right his wrong.* A trustee, of course, may reinstate the trust fund, and so right the wrong, and thenceforward, having distinguished his own private property from the trust property, he may invest his private property profitably or unprofitably as he wishes.[3] If T mixes £10,000 of trust money with his own £10,000 to purchase £20,000 of shares, which he later sells for £40,000, he does not reinstate the trust fund by paying £10,000 into his empty account redesignated as a trust account.[4] He would only do so if he paid £20,000 into the new trust account, when he would be free to deal as he wished with the other £20,000 put into his private building society account.

(d) *Restriction to lowest intermediate balance.* If beneficiaries do seek to trace moneys remaining in a trustee's personal bank account, originally containing a mixture of their moneys and the trustee's private moneys, they cannot claim as their money an amount exceeding the lowest balance in the account since the date of mixing the moneys. Withdrawals reducing the amount of the account to a level below that of the trust money originally mixed must be withdrawals of trust money. The trust money once so reduced remains reduced despite any subsequent payments in to the account by the trustee, since payments by him into his personal account are not presumed to be repayments of trust moneys so as to remedy his misconduct.[5] Thus, if T adds £2,000 trust moneys to his private £1,000, then dissipates £2,800 and then pays in £1,200 so that his account stands at £1,400, the beneficiaries can only claim the £200 lowest intermediate balance. If T had paid £1,200 into a trust account set up for the beneficiaries then he would be treated as repaying trust money, but it might be open to attack under sections 423–425 of the Insolvency Act 1986 if effected for the purpose of prejudicing other creditors unless he could show that the £1,200 was the proceeds of sale of property purchased earlier with trust moneys in the mixed account.

(e) *The swollen assets theory.* The lowest intermediate balance rule in *Roscoe* v. *Winder*[6] means that the right to trace disappears once the balance in an account falls to nil. Thus if P's £2 million[7] is paid by D in breach of trust to D's bank account P's right to trace is worthless once the balance falls to nil. It has therefore been suggested[8] that, to

---

[3] *Re Oatway* [1903] 2 Ch. 356; *Scott* v. *Scott* (1962) 109 C.L.R. 649.
[4] *Scott* v. *Scott* (1962) 109 C.L.R. 649.
[5] *Roscoe* v. *Winder* [1915] 1 Ch. 62, 69; *Lofts* v. *Macdonald* (1974) 3 A.L.R. 404; *Re Norman Estate* [1952] 1 D.L.R. 174.
[6] [1915] 1 Ch. 62.
[7] In *Chase Manhattan Bank* v. *Israel-British Bank (London) Ltd.* [1981] Ch. 105 it seems that the $2 million ceased to be traceable.
[8] Goff & Jones, pp. 80, 116.

prevent the unjust enrichment of D at P's expense and because D's assets were swollen by the payment, the court should grant P an equitable charge over D's unencumbered assets, even though none of those assets can be identified on traditional tracing principles.

The riposte is that where D has used P's money to pay off X's debt (so that the balance falls to nil) D's assets have not been swollen. How can one say that the satisfaction of X's debt by incurring another of equal amount either decreases D's liabilities or increases his assets?[9] Thus, the general body of D's creditors does not benefit from D's wrong at P's expense.

However, Professor Jones has pointed out[10] that it should make a difference that P has come upon the scene so that, instead of a contest only between D's general creditors, the contest is now between P and the remaining general creditors of D. While the other general creditors did intend to advance credit to D and take the risk of his insolvency P never did. Thus, P should have priority over the general creditors' claim whose only possible claim is that D's payment to X was a preferential payment which should be set aside under the Insolvency Act 1986.

Lord Templeman in the Privy Council[11] has now provided some *obiter dicta* to support an equitable charge in P's favour in the above circumstances, though the force of his *dicta* are weakened by the fact that he appears to have thought that he was uttering conventional rather than heterodox (or even heretical) views. In the case, the bank trustee had lawfully (pursuant to a power in the trust instrument) deposited money as a loan with a bank (itself) which went into liquidation. The beneficiaries' claims therefore ranked as unsecured debts.

Lord Templeman contrasted this situation with the one where a bank trustee unlawfully dissipated trust moneys for its own purposes in circumstances where[12] "it is impossible for the beneficiaries to trace their money to any particular asset belonging to the trustee bank. But equity allows the beneficiaries to trace the trust money to all the assets of the bank and to recover the trust money by the exercise of an equitable charge over all the assets of the bank. . . . This priority is conferred because the customers and other unsecured creditors voluntarily accept the risk that the trustee bank might become insolvent and unable to discharge its obligations in full. On the other hand, the settlor and the beneficiaries under the trust never accept any risks involved in the possible insolvency of the bank. On the contrary, the settlor could be certain that if the trusts were lawfully administered the trustee bank could never make use of trust money for its own purposes and would always be obliged to segregate trust money . . . free from

---

[9] *Slater* v. *Oriental Mills* (1893) 27 A 443, 444.
[10] (1988) 37 King's Counsel 15, 19.
[11] *Space Investments Ltd.* v. *Canadian Imperial Bank of Commerce Trust Co.* [1986] 3 All E.R. 75.
[12] *Ibid.* pp. 76–77.

any risks involved in the possible insolvency of the trustee bank. It is therefore equitable that where the trustee bank has unlawfully misappropriated trust money by treating the trust money as though it belonged to the bank beneficially . . . then the claims of the beneficiaries should be paid in full out of the assets of the bank in priority to the claims of the customers and other unsecured creditors of the bank: 'if a man mixes trust funds with his own, the whole will be treated as the trust property' (*per* Jessel M.R. in *Re Hallett's Estate*[13])."

In these *dicta* Lord Templeman seems to be assuming that all the assets of the trustee bank constitute one colossal fund so that the totality of its assets is subject to an equitable charge once the bank treats any trust property as part of its own assets. Jessel M.R., however, was only concerned with the case where a trustee mixes £X of trust money with his own £Y and did not regard the rest of the trustee's property as affected by any equitable proprietary claim.

Professor Goode thus concludes,[14] "When the route taken by the money or property is clearly visible and leads to its dissipation, the notion that the claimant's proprietary rights are then replaced by a new equitable charge over the defendant's free assets at the expense of his unsecured creditors surely cannot be countenanced either in principle or in policy, for their infusion of funds against a defeated expectation is as much a contribution to the swelling of the debtor's estate as the infusion of the tracing claimant."

*Mixing of two or more trust funds by the trustee*

If a trustee purchases property using moneys from different trusts then the trusts will share the property in the proportions in which they contributed to the purchase, whether the property appreciates or depreciates.[15] To this equitable result there is an exception where the trust moneys had been mixed in the same bank account since by *Clayton's* case[16] payments out of an account are presumed to be made in the same order as payments in (*i.e.* first in first out) and the courts have been ready to apply this rule between banker and customer to regulate the position between beneficiary and beneficiary.[17]

Take the following payments into T's empty bank account: (i) £1,000 from Trust A (ii) £2,000 from Trust B (iii) £3,000 from Trust C. Then

---

13 (1880) 13 Ch.D. 696, 719.

14 (1987) 103 L.Q.R. 433, 447.

15 They will adopt the purchased property as trust property where it has appreciated. If it has depreciated they will claim a charge on the property as security towards their personal claim, *e.g.* if T used £10,000 cash from Trust A's account and £5,000 from Trust B's account to purchase a car now depreciated in value the car will be charged to Trust A and to Trust B in the proportion 2:1, so if sold for £9,000 Trust A will receive £6,000 and Trust B £3,000. *Lord Provost of Edinburgh* v. *Lord Advocate* (1879) 4 App.Cas. 823; *Re Diplock* [1948] Ch. 465, 533, 534, 539; *Sinclair* v. *Brougham* [1914] A.C. 398.

16 (1816) 1 Mer. 572. There must be an unbroken account between the parties, *e.g.* a current account, a solicitor's trust account, a moneylender's account: it does not apply where there are distinct and separate debts. See *The Mecca* [1897] A.C. 286; *Re Sherry* (1884) 25 Ch.D. 692, 702. The rule does not apply to entries on the same day: it is the end-of-day balance that counts: *The Mecca* at 291.

17 *Hancock* v. *Smith* (1889) 41 Ch.D. 456, 461; *Re Stenning* [1895] 2 Ch. 433; *Re Diplock* (1948) Ch. 465, 554; Fry J. in *Re Hallett's Estate* (1879) 13 Ch.D. 696, 704.

T withdraws £2,000 which he dissipates on a holiday, and on his return he purchases shares for £4,000 which are now worth £6,000. The most equitable course would be to divide the shares between Trusts A, B and C in the proportions 1:2:3 so that each trust would recover its original moneys, £1,000, £2,000 and £3,000.[18] But if *Clayton's* case is applied, the withdrawn £2,000 exhausts the funds of Trust A and reduces Trust B's funds to £1,000. Thus the £4,000 invested in shares represents £1,000 of Trust B's funds and £3,000 of Trust C's funds. Therefore, one-quarter of the shares belongs to Trust B and three-quarters to Trust C, and poor Trust A has lost all its money. If T sold a quarter of the shares this would not be treated as sale of Trust B's shares but as a sale of a shareholding made up as to one-quarter with Trust B's shares and three-quarters with Trust C's shares.[19]

*Clayton's* case can easily lead to arbitrary and inconvenient results and it is surprising to see Chancery courts happy to apply a common-law rule, as to the appropriation of payments between debtor and creditor in a running account, to the equitable proprietary rights of beneficiaries between themselves.[20] In a simple example, like that above where the proportions attributable to the possible claimants are easily ascertainable, it is difficult to see the justification for applying *Clayton's* case. Perhaps it ought to be restricted to fiduciaries who keep what are virtually banking accounts for their clients where there are so many transactions with so many clients spread over a considerable period that it would be controversial and impracticable to attempt to ascertain the amount of each client's contribution.[21] It was for such a situation that the "first in, first out" rule was developed.

Finally, if the mixed fund contains not just the money of two or more trusts but the trustee's own money as well, one must first apply the principles applicable to a trustee's own money and trust money of an amount corresponding to the aggregate value of all the mixed trust funds. Once the total entitlement of these trust funds has been determined one applies the principles just discussed to apportioning this entitlement between the funds.

*Mixing of trust money with an innocent volunteer's money*

A volunteer (*i.e.* someone who has provided no consideration) must be distinguished from a purchaser, since the equitable tracing remedy

---

[18] In *Re British Red Cross Balkan Fund* [1914] 2 Ch. 419 £28,682 was subscribed by 3,254 persons and at the end of the war £12,655 remained. If *Clayton's* case applied subscriptions before November 8, 1912 would be treated as having been withdrawn from the bank account, so that subscribers after that date would be entitled to the surplus. Astbury J. held that the surplus belonged to all 3,254 subscribers rateably, saying *Clayton's* case was "a mere rule of evidence and not an invariable rule of law." See also the rateable division of assets between depositors and shareholders in *Sinclair* v. *Brougham* [1914] A.C. 398 and between sets of beneficiaries in *Re Ontario Securities Commission* (1987) 30 D.L.R. (4th) 1 and between clients of an insolvent futures dealer who kept the clients' moneys in a separate account regarded as a trust account: *Re Eastern Capital Futures Ltd.* [1989] B.C.L.C. 223.
[19] *Re Diplock* [1948] Ch. 465, 554–555: each parcel of shares withdrawn from the whole shareholding is treated as made up of an aliquot proportion of the shareholding bought with the trust moneys.
[20] D. A. McConville (1963) 79 L.Q.R. 388.
[21] Ford & Lee, pp. 743–744; *Re Ontario Securities Commission* (1986) 30 D.L.R. (4th) 1.

fails where the property sought to be traced has reached the hands of a bona fide purchaser for value without notice of the claimant's equitable rights.[22] If, at the time of purchase or receipt, a purchaser or a volunteer has knowledge of the breach of trust, then they rank as constructive trustees[23] and so are treated as trustees if they knowingly mix their own assets with trust assets.

If an innocent volunteer happens to mix trust moneys with his own moneys and purchase property therewith,[24] then he and the trust beneficiaries will share the property in the proportions in which they contributed to the purchase, whether the property appreciates or depreciates.[25] Their position *vis-à-vis* one another is the same as that between beneficiaries of separate trust funds whose moneys have been mixed together.[26] It follows that there is the same exceptional result where the innocent volunteer's moneys and the trust moneys have been mixed in the same bank account. Prima facie the court will apply *Clayton's* case and presume that withdrawals from the account are made in the order in which moneys were first paid into the account.[27] This has already been considered and criticised. If the innocent volunteer, who has paid trust moneys into his current account, pays into an interest-bearing account designated as the trust account as soon as he learns of the trust claim, then this will be regarded as effectively unmixing the fund so that the trust claim will relate only to the money in the designated trust account.[28]

*Loss of right to trace*

(1) If property has reached the hands of a bona fide purchaser of a legal interest for value without notice,[29] though any proceeds of sale of such property may be traceable.

(2) If the plaintiff acquiesced in the wrongful mixing or distribution.[30]

---

[22] *Taylor* v. *Blakelock* (1886) 32 Ch.D. 560; *Re Diplock* [1948] Ch. 465, 539.
[23] See Chap. 7, Sect. 2, "The stranger as constructive trustee."
[24] If the moneys are dissipated the loss is borne rateably: *Re Diplock* [1948] Ch. 465; K. Hodkinson [1983] Conv. 135, 138–139.
[25] *Re Diplock* [1948] Ch. 465, 524, 539. Ideally, there should further be an allowance made to the volunteer in respect of any efforts or skills utilised in enhancing the value of the asset by analogy with *Boardman* v. *Phipps* [1967] 2 A.C. 46, *supra*, p. 457. This should be enforceable as a personal claim against the trust beneficiaries: K. Hodkinson [1983] Conv. 135.
[26] *Ibid.* Placing the innocent volunteer on a par with the trust beneficiaries does not infringe the principle that equitable rights prevail except against a bona fide purchaser of a legal interest for value without notice. Here we are concerned with the earlier identification process ascertaining in what assets the beneficiaries' equitable rights subsist and ascertaining what assets are to be treated as the volunteer's own property.
[27] *Re Diplock* [1948] Ch. 465, 554.
[28] *Re Diplock* [1948] Ch. 465, 551–552 dealing with the claim against the National Institute for the Deaf, reversed on an amended statement of facts: *ibid.* p. 559. Similarly, it would seem that if a trustee mixes two trust funds in one account and purports to withdraw a sum for a beneficiary of one trust but actually uses it for his own purposes the sum should be allocated to that particular trust: *Re Stillman and Wilson* (1950) 15 A.B.C. 68.
[29] *Re Diplock* [1948] Ch. 465, 539; *Taylor* v. *Blakelock* (1886) 32 Ch.D. 560. Purchase of an equitable interest might suffice if tracing protected the mere equity to rectify for undue influence. Except where land is purchased the concept of constructive notice is rather restricted: see pp. 469, *supra*. If the wrongdoing trustee acquired the property from such a purchaser he would be susceptible to tracing: *Barrow's* case (1880) 14 Ch.D. 432.
[30] *Blake* v. *Gale* (1886) 32 Ch.D. 571.

(3) If property has been dissipated so that tracing is physically impossible, *e.g.* trust moneys spent on world cruise, a party, extinguishing an unsecured debt.[31] Query if *Re Tilley's W.T.*, *infra*, may be explained on the basis of Mrs. Tilley purchasing property with her own line of credit with trust moneys fortuitously being used to pay off the overdraft debt.

(4) If it would be inequitable to allow the plaintiff to trace against an innocent volunteer in certain types of circumstances.[32] Thus if an innocent volunteer spends money on altering or improving his land there can be no declaration of charge and consequently no tracing for the method of enforcing a charge is by sale which would force the volunteer to exchange his land and buildings for money: an inequitable possibility, particularly if it may be that the alterations had not enhanced the value of the property. If the innocent volunteer had altered or improved his property with money borrowed for the purpose on the security of the property and subsequently repaid the loan with trust money the plaintiff beneficiary is no better off than in the previous case for the same reason. The position is allegedly the same if the innocent volunteer's property was purchased subject to a mortgage and the trust money is used to pay off the mortgage so creating an unencumbered title for otherwise the volunteer might have to submit to a sale of his interest. However, purchase of a property unlike the alteration of a property is of incontrovertible benefit to the purchaser, so why should he be allowed to benefit at the expense of the beneficiaries when he has no entitlement to the use of their money and he will be no worse off owing them the money secured by a charge on the property than he was when he owed the mortgagee that money?[33] If the volunteer knew of his wrongful receipt at the time of paying off the mortgage with trust moneys then it would be equitable to trace against such wicked volunteer and to be subrogated to his mortgagee's rights.

### Towards a general defence of change of position?

This defence of "inequitability" was closely circumscribed as the English courts[34] until 1991 refused to recognise the general defence of change of position so well established in America, namely, that if an

---

[31] *Re Diplock* [1948] Ch. 465, 521, 549.

[32] *Ibid.* 546–550. The reasons given for the special treatment afforded innocent volunteers in these circumstances are difficult to justify: R. H. Maudsley (1959) 75 L.Q.R. 240, 248–249; Ford & Lee, pp. 754–755. It is especially difficult to see why the plaintiff should not be subrogated to the position of secured creditors paid off with his money: Goff & Jones, p. 531.

[33] See (1990) 106 L.Q.R. 87, 89 (D. J. Hayton).

[34] Goff & Jones, Chap. 39; Birks, *Introduction to the Law of Restitution* (1985), pp. 410–415. *Baylis* v. *Bishop of London* [1913] 1 Ch. 127 (a defence for agents who had paid to their principal what they had received); *Ministry of Health* v. *Simpson* [1951] A.C. 251, 276; *Barclays Bank Ltd.* v. *Simms* [1980] Q.B. 677, 695, 699; *R.* v. *Tower Hamlets L.B.C.* [1988] A.C. 858, 882; *Rover International Ltd.* v. *Cannon Film Sales Ltd.* [1989] 1 W.L.R. 912, 925, 934–935.

innocent volunteer had bona fide undertaken expenditure which would not have been incurred but for the mistaken payment and which was of such a character that it would be inequitable to enforce the plaintiff's claim then the plaintiff's claim will fail. The Restatement of Restitution[35] defines the defence as follows:

"(1) The right of a person to restitution from another because of a benefit received is terminated or diminished if, after the receipt of the benefit, circumstances have so changed that it would be inequitable to require the other to make full restitution.

(2) Change of circumstances may be a defense or a partial defense if the conduct of the recipient was not tortious and he was no more at fault for his receipt, retention or dealing with the subject matter than was the claimant."

The Lords in *Lipkin Gorman* v. *Karpnale*[36] have now recognised change of position as a defence to restitutionary actions, while leaving its scope to develop on a case by case basis. "Where an innocent defendant's position has so changed that he will suffer an injustice if called upon to repay in full, the injustice of requiring him so to repay outweighs the injustice of denying the plaintiff restitution. If the plaintiff pays money to the defendant under a mistake of fact, and the defendant then, in good faith, pays the money or part of it to charity, it is unjust to require him to make restitution to the extent that he has so changed his position. Likewise, if a thief steals my money and pays it to a third party who gives it away to charity, that third party should have a good defence to an action for money had and received." This should enable a more generous approach to be taken to the recognition of the right to restitution in the knowledge that the defence is available in appropriate cases.[37]

### III. PERSONAL CLAIMS

*Improperly distributed estates of deceased persons*
The House of Lords in *Ministry of Health* v. *Simpson*[38] (where the "reasoning and conclusions" of the Court of Appeal[39] on the personal claim were said to be "unimpeachable") held that where a deceased's estate has been wrongfully distributed to persons an unpaid or underpaid creditor, legatee or next of kin has an equitable personal claim against those persons, but only after he has first exhausted his claim against the personal representatives responsible for the blunder.[40]

---

[35] Para. 142; see also para. 69.
[36] [1991] 3 W.L.R. 10.
[37] *Ibid.*, 34.
[38] [1951] A.C. 251.
[39] *Re Diplock* [1948] Ch. 468. The appeal to the Lords concerned the personal claim and not the proprietary tracing claim.
[40] It is a strict requirement that the blundering personal representatives must be sued before the innocent recipients of the property: *Re J. Leslie Engineers Ltd.* [1976] 2 All E.R. 85, 91, *Butler* v. *Broadhead* [1975] Ch. 97, 107–108. If they paid the money to the recipient under a mistake of law (as opposed to fact) they cannot recover such money (see Goff and Jones, pp. 128–129, 579) so they should take full advantage of Trustee Act 1925, s.27 and, if need be, act solely upon a court order.

Naturally, he must give credit for the money he obtains from the personal representatives. He must bring his action within 12 years of the date when the right to receive the money from the personal representative accrued.[41] His claim lies only for the principal sum due from the estate and not for any interest thereon, assuming that the wrong recipient, R, had no knowledge[42] that his receipt was wrongful. R cannot be charged interest because he is under no obligation to the claimant to make productive use of the money or property which he innocently received.[43]

The personal claim is not restricted to cases where the personal representatives' mistake was one of fact and not of law. As Lord Simonds stated[44]:

"It is difficult to see what relevance the distinction can have where a legatee [claimant] does not plead his own mistake or his own ignorance, but, having exhausted his remedy against the executor who has made the wrongful payment, seeks to recover money from him who has been wrongfully paid. To such a suit the executor was not a necessary party and there was no means by which the plaintiff could find out whether his mistake was of law or fact or, even, whether his wrongful act was deliberate or mistaken. He could guess and ask the court to guess, but he could prove nothing. I reject, therefore, the suggestion that the equitable remedy in such circumstances was thus restricted."

The executor's mistake of law was to accept the validity of a residuary bequest "for such charitable institution or institutions or other charitable or benevolent object or objects" as they should in their absolute discretion select. Such a non-charitable bequest was void for uncertainty[45] so that the next of kin were entitled to the undisposed of property. However, the executors distributed the estate between various charities whom the next of kin sued, after having first sued the executors and compromised the action with the court's approval.

The Court of Appeal held that[46]:

"persons in the position of the respondents [the charities], themselves unversed in the law, are entitled to assume that the executors are properly administering the estate, and if, as admitted in this case, they took the money bona fide believing themselves to be entitled to it, they should not have imposed on them the heavy obligations of trusteeship. We do not think it necessary or desirable to attempt an exhaustive formulation of the law applicable as regards notice in the case of payments to legatees, save to say that every case of this kind will depend

---

41 Limitation Act 1939, s.20 replaced by Limitation Act 1980, s.22.
42 Including "Nelsonian" and "naughty knowledge": see discussion pp. 470–473, *supra* of *Re Montagu's S.T.* [1987] Ch. 264.
43 If he does make productive use of it, he should account for profits actually earned: neither the "tree" nor its "fruits" should logically be his (see Ford and Lee p. 751 and *Re Diplock* [1948] Ch. 468, 517 deciding that charities which had invested moneys in interest-bearing securities should repay such investments and interest under the proprietary tracing claim).
44 [1951] A.C. 251, 270.
45 *Chichester Diocesan Fund* v. *Simpson* [1944] A.C. 341 *supra*, p. 360.
46 [1948] Ch. 465, 478–479.

on its own facts and that the principles are not the same as the principles in regard to notice of defects in title applicable to transfer of land where regular machinery has long since been established for inquiry and investigation."

The Court of Appeal then rejected the contention[47] that the jurisdiction of equity to enforce its personal remedies was subject to the limiting principle that equity acts on the conscience of the defendant which is affected only where the defendant has the necessary knowledge:

"The test as regards conscience seems rather to be whether at the time when the payment was made the legatee received anything more than, at the time, he was properly entitled to receive."[48] "It is, in our opinion, impossible to contend that a disposition which according to the law is held to be entirely invalid can yet confer on those who, *ex hypothesi*, have improperly participated under the disposition, some moral or equitable right to retain what they have received against those whom the law declares to be properly entitled."[49]

In delivering the judgment of the House of Lords, Lord Simonds based himself on the following statement of Lord Davey,[50] which he said[51] "explains the basis of the jurisdiction, the evil to be avoided and its remedy":

"The Court of Chancery in order to do justice and to avoid the evil of allowing one man to retain what is really and legally applicable to the payment of another man devised a remedy by which where the estate had been distributed without regard to the rights of a creditor, it has allowed the creditor to recover back what has been paid to the beneficiaries or the next of kin who derive title from the deceased testator or intestate."

As Lord Simonds then remarked[52]:

"It would be strange if a court of equity, whose self-sought duty it was to see that the assets of a deceased person were duly administered and came into the right hands and not into the wrong hands, devised a remedy for the protection of the unpaid creditor but left the unpaid legatee or next of kin unprotected."

*Improperly distributed trust funds*

The above reasoning of the Court of Appeal and the House of Lords would lead one to expect that if, by virtue of the trustees' mistake of law,[53] C received trust funds to which he was not entitled a court of

---

[47] *Ibid.* 482.
[48] *Ibid.* 488.
[49] *Ibid.* 476.
[50] *Harrison* v. *Kirk* [1904] A.C. 1, 7.
[51] [1951] A.C. 251, 266.
[52] *Ibid.*
[53] Money paid under a mistake of fact can be recovered by the trustees who can be compelled by the beneficiaries to take the necessary action, the beneficiaries, if need be, joining the trustees as defendants together with the recipient: *Re Robinson* [1911] 1 Ch. 502, *Re Mason* [1928] Ch. 385, *Re Blake* [1932] Ch. 54 in all of which cases the references to the analogy with the action for money had and received must be ignored in the light of *Ministry of Health* v. *Simpson* [1951] A.C. 251, 273–274 and *Re Diplock* [1948] Ch. 465, 498–502.

equity would not allow C to retain what really belonged to another, A, but would allow A a corresponding personal claim against C if no better remedy were available in the form of a proprietary tracing claim. Why should C be able to retain a windfall at A's expense, whether the windfall arises from the mistaken acts of personal representatives or of trustees? The crucial feature is surely the enrichment of C at A's expense where there is no legal justification for C's enrichment.[54]

However, Lord Simonds was careful to restrict his remarks[55] to the administration of assets of a deceased person. Nevertheless, in *G.L. Baker Ltd.* v. *Medway Building and Supplies Ltd.*[56] Danckwerts J. held that the personal claim was available in equity where funds subject to a trust of other fiduciary obligation had been improperly distributed. He refused to allow a last-minute amendment to enable the defence to switch from a defence of no knowledge of the plaintiff's claim (sufficient to defeat a constructive trusteeship claim but not the personal claim) to a defence of bona fide purchaser (sufficient to defeat the personal claim). The Court of Appeal[57] allowed the pleadings to be amended and ordered a new trial but did not otherwise say that Danckwerts J. had been wrong.

In *Butler* v. *Broadhead*[58] Templeman J. considered that "there was a sufficient analogy between the position of an executor and a liquidator to enable equity to intervene in favour of unpaid creditors [of a liquidated company] against overpaid contributories" (that is shareholders), so that he would have allowed a personal claim arising from a mistake of law but for concluding that it was ousted by the Companies Act 1948 and the Winding Up Rules made thereunder.[59] In *Re Leslie Engineers Co. Ltd.*[60] Oliver J. was ready to allow a personal claim to a liquidator claiming recovery of a company's money paid to X after commencement of the liquidation, but he rejected the claim because the liquidator had not exhausted his remedy against the fiduciary director responsible for the wrongful payment and because X had given valuable consideration.

In *Re Montagu's Settlements*[61] the trustees' mistake of law led them wrongly to transfer trust chattels to the tenth Duke of Manchester, an innocent volunteer, so that in principle there should have been a strict *in personam* liability when it transpired that it was impossible to

---

[54] See Birks, pp. 441–443 and pp. 471, 511, *supra*.

[55] [1951] A.C. 251, 266, 274–275.

[56] [1958] 1 W.L.R. 1216, 1220, 1227–1229. In *Eddis* v. *Chichester Constable* [1969] 1 W.L.R. 385, 388, however, Goff J. left open whether Danckwerts J. had been justified in extending the personal claim to trusts.

[57] [1958] 3 All E.R. 540.

[58] [1975] Ch. 97, 108.

[59] But Companies Act 1948, s.272 (now s.566 of the 1985 Act) was not cited: "Any powers by this Act conferred on the court shall be in addition to and not in restriction of any existing powers of instituting proceedings against any contributory or debtor of the company for the recovery of any call or other sum."

[60] [1976] 1 W.L.R. 292.

[61] [1987] Ch. 264 discussed p. 471, *supra*.

establish a proprietary tracing claim. However, the limitation period had expired[62] so that the plaintiffs simply pursued a non-statute-barred claim that the Duke was personally liable as a constructive trustee. Megarry V.-C. held that no such liability could be established unless the defendant had actual, "Nelsonian" or "naughty" knowledge that he had wrongly received property in breach of trust.

What ought to have happened in *Re Montagu's Settlements* if in 1948 the Duke had selected the chattels he wanted and then sold them for £30,000 and the trustees' mistake was discovered soon enough to enable an action to be brought within six years (instead of in 1979) though the money had been spent by the time of the action?

If the money had been spent on valuable traceable assets then the plaintiffs' interests would be fully satisfied by the proprietary tracing claim. If the money had been dissipated then the plaintiffs would rely on the personal claim requiring them first to sue the trustees responsible for the blunder[63] and then, to the extent not fully reimbursed by the trustees, to sue the Duke who had wrongly received the property. After all, he had received a windfall at the expense of the plaintiffs in circumstances where he had no right to the windfall.[64] However, he ought to have the defence of change of position available to him where, innocently believing the money to be his, he had been led to indulge in exceptional irretrievable expenditure, *e.g.* putting on a £30,000 wedding reception for his daughter on which he would otherwise only have spent £3,000.

## The defence of change of position

Estoppel can be a defence to personal or proprietary claims where the plaintiff made a representation to the defendant which led the defendant to act to his detriment in reliance thereon.[65] Change of position is broader[66] because it requires no representation from the plaintiff: it requires circumstances to have so changed that it would be inequitable to require the defendant to make full restitution to the plaintiff, *e.g.* if the money mistakenly paid to the defendant were stolen from his safe. The defendant can never rely on the defence if he is a wrongdoer or is otherwise at fault in purporting to rely on the apparent increase in his wealth.

The change of position defence is recognised in the United States[67] and Germany[68] and has been introduced by statute in Queensland,[69]

---

[62] See *Re Robinson* [1911] 1 Ch. 502.
[63] This is a strict requirement for the personal claim as recognised in *Re Leslie Engineers Co. Ltd.* [1976] 1 W.L.R. 292, though it will presumably be satisfied if it is impossible to sue the trustees because of an earlier valid discharge of the trustees as was actually the case in *Re Montagu's Settlements* [1987] Ch. 264.
[64] See p. 511, *supra*.
[65] See pp. 59–61, *supra*.
[66] See p. 549, *supra*, Goff and Jones, Ch. 39.
[67] Restatement of Restitution para. 142, p. 549, *supra*.
[68] S.818(*b*) BGB.
[69] Queensland Trusts Act 1973–81, s.109(3).

Western Australia[70] and New Zealand.[71] In England, if a defendant agent receives money from the plaintiff as agent for a disclosed principal and pays the money to his principal, then this prevents the plaintiff from suing the defendant.[72] He must sue the principal, having treated the agent as a conduit pipe for channelling the money to the principal. One could treat the agent's defence as a change of position, but, really, his defence is that he is the wrong defendant, the plaintiff having to be treated as if he had paid the principal directly.[73]

Eighty years ago the Court of Appeal in *Baylis* v. *Bishop of London*[74] firmly rejected any defence of change of position believing that this rested on vague notions of justice and fairness. Experience in other jurisdictions reveals that this is not the case: it does not open the floodgates. It is not easy for a defendant to discharge the onus of persuading a court that the defendant's circumstances have so changed as a result of receiving particular money or other property that it would be inequitable to require him to make restitution.

Inevitably, the House of Lords has very recently recognised the defence of change of position[75] in broad terms allowing the law on the subject to develop on a case by case basis.

*Does liability extend beyond the original recipient?*

As Goff and Jones[76] point out, the history of the personal claim in respect of wrongful distributions out of deceased person's estates suggests that the claim can only lie against the person to whom personal representatives made an assent of property. However, there are some broad *dicta*[77] of Denning J. and Danckwerts J. suggesting that any person claiming through a recipient of the estate of a deceased or of trust property should be personally liable unless he is a bona fide purchaser. It is a little surprising to find a personal receipt-based remedy extended so as to be available against a successor in title to the original recipient but one might justify it by reference to the possible proprietary tracing remedy available against the successor in title.

Take R who received £30,000 by virtue of a mistake of law made by executors or trustees and who then gave it to his son, S. If R is bankrupt[78] or can establish the defence of change of position or if the plaintiff seeks to trace the property attention focuses on S. As a practical matter he has to account for what he has done with the plaintiff's £30,000, though if he dissipated it as an innocent volunteer

---

[70] Western Australia Trustees Act 1962, s.65(8).
[71] New Zealand Judicature Act 1908, s.94B as amended.
[72] *Agip (Africa) Ltd.* v. *Jackson* [1990] Ch. 265.
[73] *Australia and New Zealand Banking Group Ltd.* v. *Westpac Banking Corporation* (1988) 78 A.L.R. 577.
[74] [1913] 1 Ch. 127.
[75] See *Lipkin Gorman* v. *Karpnale* [1991] 3 W.L.R. 10 discussed p. 549 *supra*.
[76] P. 575.
[77] *Nelson* v. *Larholt* [1948] 1 K.B. 339, 342, *G.L. Baker Ltd.* v. *Medway Building and Supplies Ltd.* [1958] 1 W.L.R. 1216, 1220–1221.
[78] And the executors or trustees are bankrupt so that first suing them is pointless.

then Megarry V.-C.[79] would hold that he cannot be personally liable as a constructive trustee. Millett J. disagrees[80] and would say that S is personally liable as a constructive trustee unless he can establish the defence of change of position. On this latter basis, it is not surprising that a successor in title to the original recipient can be personally liable.

Indeed, if one looks at the common law personal action for money had and received it seems that this personal action is available not just against the original recipient but also any transferees not being purchasers for value without notice.[81] Thus, if a dishonest employee converts his employer's cheque and pays it into his own account and then pays the money by cheque into his innocent mistress' account, the employer's claim will succeed against the employee, his mistress and her bank.[82] However, it can be argued that if the mistress then gives her money to her mother, an innocent volunteer, the mother claims not through the fraudulent employee but through his mistress who is free to dispose of her money as she sees fit, so that the mother is under no liability if she dissipates the money.[83]

The common law position requires clarification just as much as the position in equity but there is the additional problem that the common law does not have equity's ability to charge a mixed fund with repayment of money, so that common law rights are traditionally said to cease once money is mixed with other moneys, though this overlooks the common law rule in *Clayton's Case*[84] that moneys first paid in are deemed first paid out.

The greater flexibility of equity suggests that instead of trying to clarify and develop personal actions at common law the courts should develop equitable principles to make a defendant, D, personally accountable to a plaintiff, P, where D has been enriched at P's expense in circumstances where there is no legal justification (such as contract or gift) for the benefit received by D and where D cannot make out the defence of change of position.

*The need in equity to sue first the blundering fiduciary*

Currently, the law takes the strict view that it is the blundering executor or trustee who should first be personally liable because but for his act the problem would never have arisen. He should have obtained proper legal advice which should have prevented any mistake of law arising: if his lawyer were negligent then he should obtain an

---

[79] *Re Montagu's Settlements* [1987] Ch. 264.
[80] See p. 471, *supra*.
[81] Goff and Jones, p. 575, R. M. Goode (1976) 92 L.Q.R. 360, P. Birks [1989] Lloyds M.C.L.Q. 296, 338, cases cited in n. 77, *supra* and *Lipkin Gorman* v. *Karpnale* [1989] 1 W.L.R. 1340.
[82] *Banque Belge Pour L'Etranger* v. *Hambrouck* [1921] 1 K.B. 221. However, in *Agip (Africa) Ltd.* v. *Jackson* [1990] Ch. 265, 285, Millett J. suggested obiter that the claim against the subsequent recipient (the mistress) should only be to the extent of the money retained by her and not for the whole amount received by her, but see *Lipkin Gorman* v. *Karpnale* [1991] 3 W.L.R. 10.
[83] A. Burrows (1990) 106 L.Q.R. 20.
[84] See p. 541, *supra*.

indemnity from his lawyer. Otherwise, he has no remedy enabling him to recover from the recipient money paid under a mistake of law,[85] so that the innocent recipient is not so badly off. A proprietary tracing claim can first be made directly against the recipient,[86] but he will then merely have to return anything traceable retained by him, so that his liability is restricted to the surviving value left in his hands.

For the personal claim there seems some justice in the beneficiaries first having to bring a simple claim against the blundering executor or trustee. The injustice lies in the unsatisfactory distinction between mistakes of fact and of law.[87] Once the executor or trustee has compensated the beneficiaries he should be entitled to a personal claim against the recipient of the mistaken payment. Such recipient, unlike the executor or trustee, should have the defence of change of position available to him in appropriate circumstances. The executor or trustee, rather than the beneficiaries, should be at risk of the success of a change of position defence and the extra time, trouble and expense of pursuing the recipient.[88]

## RE TILLEY'S WILL TRUSTS

Chancery Division [1967] Ch. 1179; [1967] 2 W.L.R. 1533; [1967] 2 All E.R. 303

Tilley's will appointed his widow executrix and gave her a life interest in his estate with remainder to his son Charles and daughter Mabel equally. Tilley died in 1932 and his widow died in 1959 leaving £94,000, she having had a successful career as a property dealer. It so happened that she had mixed £2,237 of trust moneys with her own moneys but at all material times she had substantial moneys of her own or substantial overdraft facilities. Mabel died in 1955.

The plaintiff as Mabel's administrator claimed to be entitled to half of the profits made by the widow in respect of properties purchased originally for £2,237.

UNGOED-THOMAS J.: "The plaintiff claims that Mabel's estate should, in virtue of Mabel's half interest in the estate, subject to the widow's life interest, have half of the proportion of the profits of the purchases made by the widow to the extent to which the defendants, as her legal personal representatives, cannot show that those properties were purchased out of the widow's personal moneys. The defendants, on the other hand, say that the plaintiff is entitled only to a charge on the defendants' bank account for half the trust moneys paid into that bank account with interest, *i.e.* half the sum of £2,237, which is shown to have been paid into that bank account, and the interest on that amount.

---

[85] Goff and Jones, pp. 128–129, 574.
[86] p. 534, *supra.*
[87] See Goff and Jones, pp. 128–129, *Air Canada* v. *British Columbia* (1989) 59 D.L.R. (4th) 161, 191–192.
[88] It does not seem satisfactory for statute to reverse the law as in Western Australia and require that the beneficiaries first exhaust their remedies against the recipients before they can sue the executors or trustees.

"I come first to the law. The plaintiff relied on the statement of the law in *Lewin on Trusts* (16th ed.), at p. 223 and some of the cases cited in support of it. That statement reads:

> 'Wherever the trust property is placed, if a trustee amalgamates it with his own, his beneficiary will be entitled to every portion of the blended property which the trustee cannot prove to be his own.'

*Lupton* v. *White*,[89] is the leading case for this proposition. In that case the defendant, an accounting party, had mixed the plaintiff's lead ore of unascertainable amount with his own lead ore, and the reference to the case of *Panton* v. *Panton*[90] shows that the same principle applies where moneys are similarly mixed. The principle is thus stated[91]:

> '. . . to apply the great principle, familiar both at law and in equity, that, if a man, having undertaken to keep the property of another distinct, mixes it with his own, the whole must both at law and in equity be taken to be the property of the other, until the former puts the subject under such circumstances, that it may be distinguished as satisfactorily as it might have been before that unauthorised mixture upon his part.'

" . . . If a trustee mixes trust assets with his own, the onus is on the trustee to distinguish the separate assets and, to the extent that he fails to do so, they belong to the trust. The *Lupton* v. *White* line of cases does not appear to me to go further than this. So the proposition in Lewin, which I have read, is limited to cases where the amalgam of mixed assets is such that they cannot be sufficiently distinguished and treated separately; it is based on the lack of evidence to do so being attributable to the trustee's fault.

"The defendants relied on *Re Hallett's Estate*[92] with a view to establishing that the trustee must be presumed to have drawn out his own moneys from the bank account of mixed moneys in priority to trust moneys, with the result that property bought by such prior drawings must be the trustee's exclusive personal property. In that case the claim was against a bank balance of mixed fiduciary and personal funds, and it is in the context of such a claim that it was held that the person in a fiduciary character drawing out money from the bank account must be taken to have drawn out his own money in preference to the trust money, so that the claim of the beneficiaries prevailed against the balance of the account. *Re Oatway*[93] was the converse of this decision in *Re Hallett's Estate*.

"In that case the claim was not against the balance left in the bank of such mixed moneys but against the proceeds of sale of shares which the trustee had purchased with moneys which, as in *Re Hallett's Estate*, he had drawn from the bank account; but, unlike the situation in *Re Hallett's Estate*, his later drawings had exhausted the account, so that it was useless to proceed against the account. It was held that the beneficiary was entitled to the proceeds of sale of the shares which were more than their purchase price but less than the trust moneys paid into the account. The law is reviewed and the principles are stated by Joyce J.[94] He says:

---

[89] (1808) 15 Ves. 432.
[90] Undated, cited 15 Ves. 435, 440.
[91] *Lupton* v. *White* (1808) 15 Ves. 432.
[92] (1880) 13 Ch.D. 696.
[93] [1903] 2 Ch. 356.
[94] [1903] 2 Ch. 359–361.

'Trust money may be followed into land or any other property in which it has been invested; and when a trustee has, in making any purchase or investment, applied trust money together with his own, the *cestuis que trust* are entitled to a charge on the property purchased for the amount of the trust money laid out in the purchase or investment. Similarly, if money held by any person in a fiduciary capacity be paid into his own banking account, it may be followed by the equitable owner, who, as against the trustee, will have a charge for what belongs to him upon the balance to the credit of the account. If then, the trustee pays in further sums, and from time to time draws out money by cheques, but leaves a balance to the credit of the account, it is settled that he is not entitled to have the rule in *Clayton's Case*[95] applied so as to maintain that the sums which have been drawn out and paid away so as to be incapable of being recovered represented *pro tanto* the trust money, and that the balance remaining is not trust money, but represents only his own moneys paid into the account. *Brown* v. *Adams*[96] to the contrary ought not to be followed since the decision in *Re Hallett's Estate*. It is, in my opinion, equally clear that when any of the money drawn out has been invested, and the investment remains in the name or under the control of the trustee, the rest of the balance having been afterwards dissipated by him, he cannot maintain that the investment which remains represents his own money alone, and that what has been spent and can no longer be traced and recovered was the money belonging to the trust. In other words, when the private money of the trustee and that which he held in a fiduciary capacity have been mixed in the same banking account, from which various payments have from time to time been made, then, in order to determine to whom any remaining balance or any investment that may have been paid for out of the account ought to be deemed to belong, the trustee must be debited with all the sums that have been withdrawn and applied to his own use so as to be no longer recoverable, and the trust money in like manner be debited with any sums taken out and duly invested in the names of the proper trustees. The order of priority in which the various withdrawals and investments may have been respectively made is wholly immaterial. I have been referring, of course, to cases where there is only one fiduciary owner or set of *cestuis que trust* claiming whatever may be left as against the trustee. In the present case there is no balance left. The only investment or property remaining which represents any part of the mixed moneys paid into the banking account is the Oceana shares purchased for £2,137. Upon these, therefore, the trust had a charge for the £3,000 trust money paid into the account. That is to say, those shares and the proceeds thereof belong to the trust. It was objected that the investment in the Oceana shares was made at a time when Oatway's own share of the balance to the credit of the account (if the whole had been then justly distributed) would have exceeded £2,137, the price of the shares; that he was therefore entitled to withdraw that sum, and might rightly apply it for his own purposes; and that consequently the shares should be held to belong to his estate. To this I answer that he was never

---

95 [1814–23] All E.R. Rep. 1; (1816) 1 Mer. 572.
96 (1869) 4 Ch.App. 764.

entitled to withdraw the £2,137 from the account, or, at all events, that he could not be entited to take that sum from the account and hold it or the investment made therewith, freed from the charge in favour of the trust, unless or until the trust money paid into the account had been first restored, and the trust fund reinstated by due investment of the money in the joint names of the proper trustees, which never was done. The investment by Oatway, in his own name, of the £2,137 in Oceana shares no more got rid of the claim or charge of the trust upon the money so invested, than would have been the case if he had drawn a cheque for £2,137 and simply placed and retained the amount in a drawer without further disposing of the money in any way. The proceeds of the Oceana shares must be held to belong to the trust funds under the will of which Oatway and Maxwell Skipper were the trustees.'

So, contrary to the defendant's contention, it is not a presumption that a trustee's drawings from the mixed fund must necessarily be treated as drawings of the trustee's own money where the beneficiary's claim is against the property bought by such drawings. Further, *Re Oatway*[97] did not raise the question whether a beneficiary was entitled to any profit made out of the purchase of property by a trustee out of a fund consisting of his personal moneys which he mixed with the trust moneys, and so the judgment was not directed to, and did not deal with, that question.

"I return now to the judgments in *Re Hallett's Estate*.[98] Sir George Jessel M.R.[99] said:

> 'There is no doubt, therefore, that Mr. Hallett stood in a fiduciary position towards Mrs. Cotterill. Mr. Hallett, before his death, improperly sold the bonds and put the money to his general account at his bankers. It is not disputed that the money was at his bankers mixed with his own money at the time of his death; that is, he had not drawn out that money from his bankers. In that position of matters Mrs. Cotterill claimed to be entitled to receive the proceeds, or the amount of the proceeds, of the bonds out of the money in the hands of Mr. Hallett's bankers at the time of his death, and that claim was allowed by the learned judge of the court below, and I think was properly so allowed.'

Later Sir George Jessel said[1]:

> 'The modern doctrine of equity as regards property disposed of by persons in a fiduciary position is a very clear and well-established doctrine. You can, if the sale was rightful, take the proceeds of the sale, if you can identify them. If the sale was wrongful, you can still take the proceeds of the sale, in a sense adopting the sale for the purpose of taking the proceeds, if you can identify them. There is no distinction, therefore, between a rightful and a wrongful disposition of the property, so far as regards the right of the beneficial owner to follow the proceeds. But it very often happens that you cannot identify the proceeds. The

---

[97] [1903] 2 Ch. 356.
[98] (1880) 13 Ch.D. 696.
[99] (1880) 13 Ch.D. 708.
[1] (1880) 13 Ch.D. 708, 709.

proceeds may have been invested, together with money belonging to the person in a fiduciary position, in a purchase. He may have bought land with it, for instance, or he may have bought chattels with it. What is the position of the beneficial owner as regards such purchases? I will, first of all, take his position when the purchase is clearly made with what I will call, for shortness, the trust money, although it is not confined, as I will show presently, to express trusts. In that case, according to the now well-established doctrine of equity, the beneficial owner has a right to elect either to take the property purchased, or to hold it as a security for the amount of the trust money laid out in the purchase, or, as we generally express it, he is entitled at his election either to take the property, or to have a charge on the property for the amount of the trust money. But where a trustee has mixed the money with his own, there is the distinction that the *cestui que trust* or beneficial owner can no longer elect to take the property. . . . '

Pausing there, what is apparently meant is that a beneficiary cannot take the whole property, which is the possibility with which Sir George Jessel had just before this been dealing. He went on[2]:

' . . . because it is no longer bought with the trust money simply and purely, but with a mixed fund. He is, however, still entitled to a charge on the property purchased for the amount of the trust money laid out in the purchase, and that charge is quite independent of the amount laid out by the trustee. The moment you get a substantial portion of it furnished by the trustee, using the word "trustee" in the sense I have mentioned, as including all persons in a fiduciary relation, the right to the charge follows.'

Here, as I read this judgment, it does not exclude the right of the beneficiary to claim a proportion of the mixed fund. There was no need in that case to go further than the charge claimed in the case. So again that question was not there considered.

"In *Sinclair* v. *Brougham*[3] the decision in *Re Hallett's Estate* was considered. Lord Parker of Waddington said[4]:

'The principle on which, and the extent to which, trust money can be followed in equity is discussed at length in *Re Hallett's Estate* by Sir George Jessel M.R. He gives two instances. First, he supposes the case of property being purchased by means of trust money alone. In such a case the beneficiary may either take the property itself or claim a lien on it for the amount of the money expended in the purchase. Secondly, he supposes the case of the purchase having been made partly with the trust money and partly with money of the trustee. [I shall come back to the next sentence later.] In such a case the beneficiary can only claim a charge on the property for the amount of the trust money expended in the purchase. The trustee is precluded by his own misconduct from asserting any interest in the property until such amount has been refunded. By the actual decision in the case, this principle was held

2 (1880) 13 Ch.D. 709.
3 [1914] A.C. 398.
4 [1914] A.C. 442.

applicable when the trust money had been paid into the trustee's banking account. I will add two further illustrations which have some bearing on the present case. Suppose the property is acquired by means of money, part of which belongs to one owner and part to another, the purchaser being in a fiduciary relationship to both. Clearly each owner has an equal equity. Each is entitled to a charge on the property for his own money, and neither can claim priority over the other. It follows that their charges must rank *pari passu* according to their respective amounts [again, I emphasise this]. Further, I think that as against the fiduciary agent they could by agreement claim to take the property itself, in which case they would become tenants in common in shares proportioned to amounts for which either could claim a charge.'

It seems to me that when Lord Parker says in the sentence, to which I first called particular attention, that 'In such a case the beneficiary can only claim a charge on the property for the amount of the trust money expended in the purchase,' he is merely contrasting the charge with the right to take the whole property which is the matter with which he has just been dealing, and Lord Parker is not, as I see it, addressing his mind to the question whether the beneficiary could claim a proportion of the property corresponding to his own contribution to its purchase. This interpretation of the passage seems to me to be the only interpretation which in principle is consistent with Lord Parker's view expressed at the end of the passage which I quoted, and to which I drew particular attention, where the purchase is made by the trustee wholly out of moneys of two different beneficiaries. In that case he says that they are not limited to charges for their respective amounts, but are together entitled to the whole property. Nevertheless if each of two beneficiaries can, in co-operation with the other, take the whole property which has resulted in profit from the trustee's action in buying it with their money, why can they not do so if the trustee himself has also paid some part of the purchase price? Moreover if two beneficiaries can do so why not one? Indeed, it was conceded in argument that the passage should be so interpreted as suggested.

For the defendants it has been rightly admitted that, if a trustee wrongly uses trust money to pay the whole of the purchase price in respect of the purchase of an asset, a beneficiary can elect either to treat the purchased asset as trust property or to treat the purchased asset as security for the recouping of the trust money. It was further conceded that this right of election by a beneficiary also applies where the asset is purchased by a trustee in part out of his own money and in part out of the trust moneys, so that he may, if he wishes, require the asset to be treated as trust property with regard to that proportion of it which the trust moneys contributed to its purchase.

"Does this case fall within that principle?

"Estate properties were sold in June 1951, January and April 1952 and realised approximately £490, £750 and £735 respectively, making with the £261 already mentioned a total of approximately £2,237 trust capital received by Mrs. Tilley. It appears, however, and is not disputed, that from before the first of these sales, and at all relevant times thereafter, Mrs. Tilley's bank account was sufficiently in credit from her own personal contributions to it (without regard to any trust moneys credited to it) to pay for her later property purchases.

"The *Lupton* v. *White*[5] principle is not applicable to this bank account as the amount of trust moneys paid into the mixed bank account is distinguishable as

£2,237 and can be readily separated from the widow's personal moneys. In the circumstances of this case there would be a charge on the properties purchased by the widow out of the bank account as security for repayment of the £2,237 trust moneys paid into her bank account in accordance with the principle in *Re Oatway*,[6] but that would be immaterial as the £2,237 is readily available out of the widow's estate.

"Can the beneficiary, however, claim the proportion of the proceeds of sale of 11, Church Street which £179 approximately bears to its purchase price of £1,000 and the proportion of the proceeds of sale of 17/17A, High Street for which £82 10s. bears to the purchase price of approximately £2,050 plus costs? These trust moneys bore a small proportion to the purchase price of the properties. The widow had ample overdraft facilities to pay the purchase price without relying on these trust sums at the time of the High Street purchase, for she had an overdraft of over £22,000 apparently within her own overdraft facilities, and presumably properly secured, and this would make any contribution of £82 10s. negligible. She had throughout mixed her personal finances and those of her husband's estate, whether paying that estate's debts when it was without ready money or paying its proceeds of sale into her account. The £179 and £82 10s. were clearly not trust moneys deliberately taken by Mrs. Tilley out of the trust fund for the purpose of investing in property in her name. They merely avoided, to the extent of their amount, the use of Mrs. Tilley's ample overdraft facilities, and in the case of the £179 that advantage was lost after two months by her bank account showing a credit, although it went into debit again seventeen months later. Moreover no interest in these trust sums was lost to any other beneficiary, as the widow was herself a life tenant. All these considerations appear to me to indicate overwhelmingly that the widow was not deliberately using trust moneys to invest in or contribute towards or otherwise buy properties in her own name, and the whole course of dealing with the trust funds and the bank accounts and the properties purchased and their history, which I have mentioned, indicate that what happened was that the widow mixed the trust moneys and her own in the bank account but did not rely on the trust moneys for any of the purchases. If, as it was suggested for the defendants, the correct test whether a beneficiary is entitled to adopt a purchase by a trustee to which his trust moneys have contributed and thus claim a due proportion of its profits, is a subjective test, depending on the trustee's intention to use the trust moneys to contribute to the purchase, then in my view there was no such intention and the beneficiary is not so entitled. My conclusion about the trustee's intention, however, is based not on any direct evidence but on the circumstantial evidence which I have mentioned. If, of course, a trustee deliberately uses trust money to contribute with his own money to buy property in his own name, then I would see no difficulty in enabling a beneficiary to adopt the purchase and claim a share of any resulting profits; but the subjective test does not appear to me to be exclusive, or indeed adequate, if it is the only test. It seems to me that if, having regard to all the circumstances of the case objectively considered, it appears that the trustee has in fact, whatever his intention, laid out trust moneys in or towards a purchase then the beneficiaries are entitled to the property purchased and any profits which it produces to the extent to which it has been paid for out of the trust moneys. Even by this objective test, it

6 [1903] 2 Ch.D. 356.

appears to me, however, that the trust moneys were not in this case so laid out. On a proper appraisal of all the facts of this particular case, the trustee's breach halted at the mixing of the funds in her bank account. Although properties bought out of those funds would, like the bank account itself, at any rate if the moneys in the bank account were inadequate, be charged with repayment of the trust moneys which then would stand in the same position as the bank account, yet the trust moneys were not invested in properties at all but merely went in reduction of the trustee's overdraft which was in reality the source of the purchase moneys.

"The plaintiff's claim therefore fails and he is entitled to no more than repayment of half the sum of £2,237, interest not being in issue. £2,237 is readily available which makes the existence of any charge for its security immaterial." *Order accordingly*.

## PROBLEMS

1. In the light of the approach to causation in *Re Tilley's W.T. supra*, consider S, a sole trustee depositing a trust share certificate to secure a loan of money used by him to make a profitable investment for himself, enabling him to repay the loan, recover the certificate and make a good profit. Could S argue that the trust's share certificate was not invested at all but merely supported a loan (by overdraft or otherwise) which was in reality the source of the purchase moneys? Would it make any difference if S could easily have provided some alternative security of his own instead of the trust share certificate? Should S be allowed to claim any gain resulting as his own and any loss as the beneficiaries'?

2. Trevor, who is trustee, deposits £6,000 of trust moneys in his personal current account which is £100 in credit though he has overdraft facilities limited to £1,400. On the following day he attends an auction of paintings and buys a painting which he has always wanted for £6,500. He pays for it by a cheque drawn on his personal account. A month later he opens a trustee account into which he pays £6,000. The painting is now worth £13,000. Advise the beneficiaries. Would your advice be different if a fire had destroyed the painting?

3. Tim, trustee of a trust arising under a will of which he is executor and trustee, pays £60,000 under a mistake of law to Roger. Roger spends £20,000 on installing a swimming pool in his garden and £15,000 on a world cruise. He gave £25,000 to his daughter, Dora. Advise the beneficiaries. Would it make any difference if the trust had been an *inter vivos* trust?

4. Tricky and Ullswater are trustees of the Armitage Trust. Tricky, who had sole custody of a share certificate relating to shares belonging to the Trust, deposited the certificate by way of mortgage to secure a £6,000 loan on his own behalf. Using this loan he made a successful investment enabling him to make a profit of £4,000 and to repay the loan and recover the certificate.

He has made a further profit of £6,000 by selling shares belonging to the Barber Trust (of which he is sole trustee) when the share price was high and buying the same shares back when the price was low and pretending that the Barber Trust has had the same shares throughout.

He paid the £4,000 profit into a personal current account opened a week previously with a credit of £3,000 of his own money. A fortnight later he paid the £6,000 profit into the account.

Subsequently, last May he withdrew £4,000 and purchased some shares in Wonderwall Ltd. now worth £8,000. In June he withdrew £2,000 in order to pay his bookmaker's account. In July he withdrew £6,000 and gave it to his mistress, Michelle. She used £4,000 of this to discharge the mortgage on her flat and used the remaining £2,000, together with £1,000 of her own money, to purchase investments now worth £3,600.

Advise the beneficiaries of the two Trusts on the footing that Tricky is likely to be insolvent.

5. Bill died in 1962, having left his residuary estate to Charles and David upon trust for his sister, Samantha, for life, remainder to such of her legitimate children as attained 21 years if more than one in equal shares, but in default thereof for University College, Durham, which now seeks your advice.

Having spent a year in Italy, Samantha had returned to England in October 1954 with Romeo Mondello, pretending they had married each other in Rome on 3 September 1954. In 1955 Samantha gave birth to Luigi. In 1970 Romeo died. In 1971 Samantha had an illness which left her incapable of having further children.

In 1982 at Samantha's request the trustees were happy to advance £28,000 so that Luigi could purchase a house.

In 1984 Samantha married a wealthy Greek. She then released her life interest in the trust fund. Before transferring the trust fund to Luigi the trustees asked Samantha as a mere formality to produce her marriage certificate. Through the services of Mario an Italian hairdresser to whom she had confided her problem, Samantha managed to obtain a forged Italian marriage certificate. After seeing it the trustees transferred the trust fund, consisting of £110,000 cash and £10,000 gilt-edged securities, to Luigi.

Luigi opened a deposit account for the cash and spent £101,000 on buying an Italian restaurant. He transferred the £9,000 balance into his current account then containing £1,000. He withdrew £5,000 therefrom to buy shares in Go-go Hi-Sci Ltd. Within a year payment of bills for his restaurant put his account into overdraft.

In March 1990 Samantha told Luigi to his astonishment that he was illegitimate but that he need not worry about his inheritance since his uncle had really intended him to benefit believing he was legitimate.

Luigi then sold the gilt-edged securities and, to comfort Samantha, spent £6,000 of the proceeds on a holiday for them both, whilst spending the balance on bills for his restaurant.

At present Luigi's current account contains £2,500, though he has heavy outstanding debts in respect of his restaurant. However, the Go-go shares and Luigi's house have quadrupled in value. Mario has just won £50,000 on the football pools.

6. Two brothers, majority shareholders, in B Co. Ltd. innocently but erroneously believe they are entitled to borrow the company's money for their private purposes and without providing for payment of interest or a repayment date. Thus they contract to purchase a restaurant for £200,000 using as a deposit £20,000 borrowed, in breach of their fiduciary duty, from the company. They go into occupation for a monthly fee. A month later completion is deferred for 3 years on further payment of £20,000, similarly borrowed from the company, and on agreeing to pay a final aggregate price of £250,000. After 2½ years they complete the purchase early, taking out a mortgage on the restaurant to secure the necessary £210,000 bank loan and personally covenanting to repay the loan. Eight months later they sell out to a purchaser for £320,000, paying the loan off out of the proceeds.

Is the company entitled just to 4/25 of the profit or to all the profits? Note that the company's £40,000 gave it an equitable interest in the restaurant and the brothers then used this interest as security for the £210,000 loan which was repaid out of the proceeds of sale and not out of the brothers' moneys. See *Paul A. Davies Pty. Ltd.* v. *Davies* [1983] 1 N.S.W.L.R. 440, *Scott on Trusts* (3rd ed.), Vol. 5 at p. 3618.

7. Bill owned a picture called "Equity's Darling" and had custody as life tenant under a trust of a picture called "Devil's Advocate." Algernon Cholmondeley stole both pictures and sold them for £30,000 and £60,000 respectively. He paid the proceeds simultaneously into his current account containing £30,000, and the following day he added £90,000 from the Raffles family trust fund of which he was sole trustee.

The £30,000 originally in his account represented a legacy received under the will of his mother, Mary. However, in consideration of his marriage to Wendy, Algernon had entered into a settlement (on himself for life, remainder to Wendy for life, remainder for their children, remainder in default of children to the registered charity, The Salvation Army) in which he had covenanted with the trustees to transfer to them anything he might inherit under the will of his father or mother.

From his current account containing £210,000 Algernon first spent £30,000 on Biowhizz Ltd. shares which have since quadrupled in value. Then he spent £90,000 on a flat which has since doubled in value. Later he spent £90,000 on Solid plc shares which have since halved in value. Subsequently, he mortgaged the flat to secure a loan of £100,000 which he used to purchase a Ferrari Testarossa car, now worth £120,000, having used his own money to pay the interest on the loan.

Recently Algernon has been arrested and he is likely to be made bankrupt. Advise Bill, Wendy and the beneficiaries under the Raffles trust.

How would your answer differ if Wendy had died childless before Algernon mixed the moneys in his current account?

8. Four years ago under the terms of the Hazzard Settlement Trust the 13th Duke of Hazzard forfeited his life interest by marrying a Roman Catholic after his first wife had died. The terms of the Settlement then required the trustees to retain in the Settlement such settled chattels as they saw fit and to allow the new life tenant, the 13th Duke's son, Timon, to choose for himself absolutely any of the remaining chattels. The trustees were a solicitor, Sharp, and Colonel Bluster, who was accustomed to relying on Sharp in matters involving the Settlement.

The 13th Duke secretly gave Sharp £50,000 to let Timon have first choice of the settled chattels, so that Timon innocently took for himself chattels to the value of £380,000 and left in the Settlement chattels worth only £20,000.

Timon forthwith sold the chattels for £380,000 and spent £80,000 on the wedding reception of his only child, Ophelia and a further £200,000 on buying her a London flat in consideration of her marriage. He placed the remaining £100,000 temporarily in his current bank account into which he had paid £20,000 one day beforehand. He then spent £20,000 on Grokle plc shares now worth £80,000 and the following day he used the remaining £100,000 to pay off his mortgage on Stately Towers.

Meanwhile, Sharp had invested his £50,000 in Wizard plc shares now worth £150,000.

Six months ago Timon died and Yorick became life tenant under the Settlement. Advise him on what remedies may be available to him.

9. Is the following approach sensible for a plaintiff beneficiary?

(1) Go for a *proprietary* tracing claim, if possible.

(2) Go for *personal* liability:
  (a) of trustee or other fiduciary for breach of trust or other fiduciary obligation;
  (b) of third party who knowingly assists in a dishonest breach of trust or other fiduciary obligation and so becomes liable as constructive trustee if he has actual knowledge of the breach or exhibits a lack of probity through deliberately shutting his eyes to the obvious or deliberately or recklessly failing to make such inquiries as an honest reasonable man would make;
  (c) of third party who receives trust property for his own benefit without actual "Nelsonian" or "naughty" knowledge that this is a breach of trust or other fiduciary obligation but who no longer has the property or its traceable product and who may be personally liable to the extent that;

  (i) to prevent unjust enrichment from a windfall an action lies for money had and received: see D. J. Hayton (1990) 106 L.Q.R. 98–100, *Lipkin Gorman* v. *Karpnale* [1991] 3 W.L.R. 10;
  (ii) there is strict liability to account as trustee for (what, after all, is subsequently discovered to have been) trust property, subject to defence of change of position or s.61 Trustee Act: see Millett J. (1991) 107 L.Q.R. 80–83;
  (iii) there is strict *Ministry of Health* v. *Simpson* [1951] A.C. 251 liability not just for innocent recipients from personal representatives but also from trustees or other fiduciaries, subject to same defences as in (ii) and the need first to sue the blundering personal representatives, trustees or other fiduciaries, which probably should be incorporated in (ii) so that ultimately (ii) is subsumed in (iii).

# Chapter 8

# APPOINTMENT, RETIREMENT AND REMOVAL OF TRUSTEES

## Section 1. Appointment of Trustees

### I. APPOINTMENT UNDER THE STATUTORY POWER

#### *The Trustee Act 1925*

SECTION 36.[1]—(1) Where a trustee,[2] either original or substituted, and whether appointed by a court or otherwise, is dead, or remains out of the United Kingdom for more than twelve months,[3] or desires to be discharged from all or any of the trusts or powers reposed in or conferred on him, or refuses or is unfit to act therein, or is incapable of acting therein, or is an infant, then, subject to the restrictions imposed by this Act on the number of trustees[4]—

(a) the person or persons nominated for the purpose of appointing new trustees by the instrument, if any, creating the trust[5]; or

(b) if there is no such person, or no such person able and willing to act, then the surviving or continuing[6] trustees or trustee for the time being,

---

[1] This section reproduces, with amendments and additions, the Trustee Act 1893, s.10(1), (3) and (4). Wolstenholme & Cherry's *Conveyancing Statutes* (13th ed.), by J. T. Farrand, Vol. 4, provides a most useful commentary on all sections of the Trustee Act.

[2] "Trustee" is used as to exclude personal representatives. Accordingly, no power is conferred to appoint executors. By the Administration of Estates Act 1925, s.7, an executor of a sole or last surviving executor of a testator is the executor by representation of that testator.

[3] It does not follow that there is an absolute bar to the appointment of non-resident trustees: *Re Whitehead's W.T.* [1971] 1 W.L.R. 833.

[4] Maximum of four trustees except for charities: Trustee Act 1925, s.34.

[5] See *Re Wheeler* [1896] 1 Ch. 315: a decision on s.10(1) of the Trustee Act of 1893, which is re-enacted by s.36(1) of the Act of 1925. In that case the settlor, instead of nominating X the person to appoint new trustees generally—as in *Re Walker and Hughes* (1883) 24 Ch.D. 698— nominated X to appoint new trustees in certain specified events. One of the trustees became bankrupt and absconded, whereupon he became "unfit" to act, but not "incapable" of acting. The events specified by the settlor included the event of a trustee becoming "incapable," but not that of a trustee becoming "unfit." The question was whether the proper person to nominate a new trustee was X, as being "the person or persons nominated for the purpose of appointing new trustees by the instrument, if any, creating the trust"—s.36(1)(*a*)—or whether the proper person was the surviving or continuing trustees or trustee under s.36(1)(*b*). Kekewich J. held that if a power of appointment contained in the instrument of trust is a limited one, and the event which has actually happened is not one of the events contemplated by that power, then the nominee is not "the person or persons nominated for the purpose of appointing new trustees by the instrument, if any, creating the trust." Hence the proper person to appoint a new trustee in *Re Wheeler* was to be found in s.36(1)(*b*). *Re Wheeler* was followed, with reluctance, by Neville J. in *Re Sichel* [1916] 1 Ch. 358. The Act of 1925 does not seem to alter the position.

[6] A continuing trustee is one who is to continue to act after completion of the intended appointment: *Re Coates to Parsons* (1886) 34 Ch.D. 370.

or the personal representatives of the last surviving or continuing trustee[7];

may, by writing,[8] appoint one or more other persons[9] (whether or not being the persons exercising the power) to be a trustee or trustees in the place of the trustee so deceased, remaining out of the United Kingdom, desiring to be discharged, refusing, or being unfit or being incapable, or being an infant, as aforesaid.

(2) Where a trustee has been removed under a power contained in the instrument creating the trust, a new trustee or new trustees may be appointed in the place of the trustee who is removed, as if he were dead, or, in the case of a corporation, as if the corporation desired to be discharged from the trust, and the provisions of this section shall apply accordingly, but subject to the restrictions imposed by this Act on the number of trustees.

(3) Where a corporation being a trustee is or has been dissolved, either before or after the commencement of this Act, then, for the purposes of this section and of any enactment replaced thereby, the corporation shall be deemed to be and to have been from the date of the dissolution incapable of acting in the trusts or powers reposed in or conferred on the corporation.

(4) The power of appointment given by subsection (1) of this section or any similar previous enactment to the personal representatives of a last surviving or continuing trustee shall be and shall be deemed always to have been exercisable by the executors for the time being (whether original or by representation) of such surviving or continuing trustee who have proved the will of their testator or by the administrators for the time being of such trustee without the concurrence of any executor who has renounced or has not proved.

(5) But a sole or last surviving executor intending to renounce, or all the executors where they all intend to renounce, shall have and shall be deemed always to have had power, at any time before renouncing probate, to exercise the power of appointment given by this section, or by any similar previous enactment, if willing to act for the purpose and without thereby accepting the office of executor.

(6) Where a sole trustee, other than a trust corporation,[10] is or has been originally appointed to act in a trust, or where, in the case of any trust, there are not more than three trustees (none of them being a trust corporation) either original or substituted and whether appointed by the court or otherwise, then and in any such case—

(a) the person or persons nominated for the purpose of appointing new trustees by the instrument, if any creating the trust; or

(b) if there is no such person, or no such person able and willing to act, then the trustee or trustees for the time being;

---

[7] Persons appointed executors and trustees of wills of land must formally assent in favour of themselves *qua* trustees so as to take advantage of s.40: *Re King's W.T.* [1964] Ch. 542 discussed p. 44, *supra*. An executor who has not proved his testator's will can exercise the power but the trustee appointed in such circumstances can only prove his title by reference to a proper grant of representation so that such a grant is, in practice, vital: *Re Crowhurst Park* [1974] 1 W.L.R. 583. If a will creates trusts but the trustees predecease the testator then s.36 is inapplicable: *Nicholson* v. *Field* [1893] 2 Ch. 511.

[8] For the desirability of making the appointment by deed, see s.40 of the Trustee Act 1925, *infra*, p. 574.

[9] Not being infants: Law of Property Act 1925, s.20. Corporations may be appointed.

[10] The Law Reform Committee 1982 (Cmnd. 8733), para. 2.6 recommends that this restriction in the case of a trust corporation should be removed.

may, by writing, appoint another person or other persons[11] to be an additional trustee or additional trustees, but it shall not be obligatory to appoint any additional trustee, unless the instrument, if any, creating the trust, or any statutory enactment provides to the contrary, nor shall the number of trustees be increased beyond four by virtue of any such appointment.

(7) Every new trustee appointed under this section as well before as after all the trust property becomes by law, or by assurance, or otherwise, vested in him, shall have the same powers, authorities, and discretions, and may in all respects act as if he had been originally appointed a trustee by the instrument, if any, creating the trust.

(8) The provisions of this section relating to a trustee who is dead include the case of a person nominated trustee in a will but dying before the testator, and those relative to a continuing trustee include a refusing or retiring trustee, if willing to act in the execution of the provisions of this section.[12]

(9) Where a trustee is incapable, by reason of mental disorder within the meaning of the Mental Health Act, 1983, of exercising his functions as trustee and is also entitled in possession to some beneficial interest in the trust property, no appointment of a new trustee in his place shall be made by virtue of paragraph (*b*) of subsection (1) of this section unless leave to make the appointment has been given by the authority having jurisdiction under Part VII of the Mental Health Act 1983.[13]

Section 37.—(1) On the appointment of a trustee for the whole or any part of trust property—

    (*a*)  the number of trustees may, subject to the restrictions imposed by this Act on the number of trustees, be increased; and

    (*b*)  a separate set of trustees, not exceeding four, may be appointed for any part of the trust property held on trusts distinct from those relating to any other part or parts of the trust property, notwithstanding that no new trustees or trustee are or is to be appointed for other parts of the trust property, and any existing trustee may be appointed or remain one of such separate set of trustees, or, if only one trustee was originally appointed, then, save as hereinafter provided, one separate trustee may be so appointed; and

    (*c*)  it shall not be obligatory, save as hereinafter provided, to appoint more than one new trustee where only one trustee was originally appointed,

---

[11] It was held in *Re Power's Settlement Trusts* [1951] Ch. 1074 that while the donee of a power to appoint new trustees could appoint himself a trustee in substitution for a person ceasing to be a trustee under s.36(1) of the Trustee Act 1925, he could not appoint himself an additional trustee under s.36(6) thereof where no vacancy had arisen in the number of trustees. The reason for the difference lies in the wording of the subsections. S.36(1) authorises the appointment of "one or more other persons, whether or not being persons exercising the power." S.36(6) limits appointments of additional trustees to "another person or persons." The Law Reform Committee 1982 (Cmnd. 8733), para. 2.6 recommends the appointors should be able to appoint themselves as additional trustees.

[12] In *Re Stoneham's Settlement Trusts* [1953] Ch. 59, X and Y were the trustees of a settlement. Y remained out of the United Kingdom for a period longer than 12 months. X executed a deed retiring from the trust and appointing C and D to be trustees in place of himself and Y. Y challenged the validity of the new appointments on the ground that he was entitled to participate in making them. Danckwerts J. rejected his contention, first because he had been validly removed from the trust owing to his continuous absence from the United Kingdom for more than 12 months, even though the removal might have been against his will, and secondly because he was not a "continuing trustee" within the meaning of s.36(8) of the Act of 1925. He was not a "refusing or retiring" trustee but a trustee who had been compulsorily removed from the trust and so his concurrence in the new appointments could be dispensed with: *Re Coates to Parsons* (1886) 34 Ch.D. 370 explained.

[13] As amended by the Mental Health Act 1983, s.148 and Sched. 4, para. 4.

or to fill up the original number of trustees where more than two trustees were originally appointed, but, except where only one trustee was originally appointed, and a sole trustee when appointed will be able to give valid receipts for all capital money, a trustee shall not be discharged from his trust unless there will be either a trust corporation or at least two individuals to act as trustees to perform the trust; and

(*d*) any assurance or thing requisite for vesting the trust property, or any part thereof, in a sole trustee, or jointly in the persons who are the trustees, shall be executed or done.

(2) Nothing in this Act shall authorise the appointment of a sole trustee, not being a trust corporation where the trustee, when appointed, would not be able to give valid receipts for all capital money arising under the trust.

It should be noted that the power of appointment of trustees is a fiduciary power exercisable by the current trustees having due regard to the interests of the trust and of the conflicting interests of the beneficiaries. Indeed, the trustees' function is a paternalistic one requiring them to protect the beneficiaries from themselves.[14] Thus if the beneficiaries are all *sui juris* and between them absolutely entitled they cannot compel the trustees under section 36 to appoint their nominee: the trustees are entitled to exercise their independent judgment.[15] All that the beneficiaries can do is put an end to the existing settlement under the rule in *Saunders* v. *Vautier*[16] and then create a new settlement of which, as settlors, they will be able to appoint new trustees—but this may well have fiscal disadvantages.

### Appointment of foreign trustees

The provision in Trustee Act 1925, s.36(1) which enables a trustee who remains out of the United Kingdom for more than 12 months to be replaced does not make persons resident abroad ineligible to be appointed as trustees, as held by Pennycuick V.-C. in *Re Whitehead's W.T.*[17] However, while accepting that the appointment of non-resident trustees had been a proper valid one in the case before him, he went on to say that in the absence of special circumstances (*e.g.* the beneficiaries having taken up permanent residence in a foreign country where the newly-appointed trustees reside) the appointment of non-residents was improper (though neither void nor illegal) so that the court would be likely to interfere at the instance of the beneficiaries.[18]

This approach is now out of date where the trustees are exercising their discretion to appoint foreign trustees and are merely seeking the declaratory authorisation of the court for their own protection. In *Richard* v. *Mackay*[19] Millett J. stated:

---

[14] *Head* v. *Gould* [1898] 2 Ch. 250.
[15] *Re Brockbank* [1948] Ch. 206.
[16] *Infra*, p. 651.
[17] [1971] 1 W.L.R. 833.
[18] It thus seems that the appointment is voidable by the beneficiaries: the Revenue will have no *locus standi* to object unless the appointment was void as part of a criminal conspiracy to defraud the Revenue.
[19] Unreported except by R. Bramwell Q.C. in Volume 1, 1990, *The Offshore Tax Planning Review* 1.

"The appropriateness is for the trustees to decide, and different minds may have different views on what is appropriate in particular circumstances. Certainly, in the conditions of today when one can have an international family with international interests and where they are as likely to make their home in one country as in another and as likely to choose one jurisdiction as another for the investment of their capital, I doubt that the language of Sir John Pennycuick is really in tune with the times. In my judgment, where the trustees retain their discretion, as they do in the present case, the court should need to be satisfied only that the proposed transaction is not so inappropriate that no reasonable trustee could entertain it."

Thus, the trustees (in case United Kingdom exchange control was reintroduced) could properly transfer part of the trust fund to the trustees of a trust to be established in Bermuda with Bermudan resident trustees, Bermuda having a stable English system of law and very experienced corporate trustees, even though the beneficiaries had no connection with Bermuda. Although the proposal was not to appoint new trustees of an existing trust nothing turns on the distinction, as recognised in *Re Whitehead's W.T.*[20]

However, Millett J. contrasted cases where the court is asked to exercise a discretion of its own (*e.g.* under the Variation of Trusts Act 1958[21] or s.41[22] of the Trustee Act 1925) with cases where the trustees are exercising their own discretion. In the former situation the applicants have to make out a positive case for the court's exercise of its discretion "and the court is unlikely to assist them where the scheme is nothing more than a device to avoid tax and has no other advantages of any kind."

Tax-saving is, of course, a proper consideration for trustees[23] and where it is clear that the proposed transaction is not so inappropriate that no reasonable trustee could entertain it the appointment of foreign trustees can now proceed without seeking any confirmation from the court.

## *The foreign trust corporation trap*

Under Trustee Act 1925, s.37(1)(*c*) "a trustee shall not be discharged from his trust unless there will be either a trust corporation or at least two individuals to act as trustees to perform the trust." It is important to notice that "individuals" as opposed to the broader expression "persons" (including companies) is used and that "trust corporation" cannot cover a company that is not incorporated in a Member State of the European Community.[24]

---

20 [1971] 1 W.L.R. 833, 838.
21 See pp. 657–662, *infra, Re Weston's Settlements* [1969] 1 Ch. 223, though in *Re Chamberlain* (1976) 126 New L.J. 1034 the Court approved Guernsey trustees where the primary beneficiaries were domiciled in France and the remaindermen in Indonesia.
22 See p. 572, *infra*.
23 [1971] 1 W.L.R. 833, 839.
24 See Trustee Act 1925, s.68(18) and p. 580.

It seems that the trust instrument could expressly authorise the discharge of trustees from the trusts by replacing them with the appointment as sole trustee of a corporation ranking as a trust corporation by the law of the State of its incorporation, except for trust property consisting of land in England and Wales.[25] After all, a valid receipt for the proceeds of sale of such land can only be given by a trust corporation or two persons acting as trustees.[26]

## II. APPOINTMENT BY THE COURT

The court has power to appoint new trustees under section 41[27] of the Trustee Act 1925, *infra*, but application should not be made to the court where the power of appointing new trustees contained in section 36(1) of the Act, *supra*, can be exercised: *Re Gibbon's Trusts*.[28] The principles which guide the court in making an appointment are set out in *Re Tempest*, *infra*. If non-resident trustees are to be appointed the beneficiaries must usually[29] have a real and substantial connection with the country where the proposed trustees are resident.

### *The Trustee Act 1925*

Section 41—(1) The court, may, whenever it is expedient to appoint a new trustee or new trustees, and it is found inexpedient, difficult or impracticable so to do without the assistance of the court, make an order appointing a new trustee or trustees either in substitution for or in addition to any existing trustee or trustees, or although there is no existing trustee.

In particular and without prejudice to the generality of the foregoing provision, the court may make an order appointing a new trustee in substitution for a trustee who is incapable, by reason of mental disorder within the meaning of the Mental Health Act 1983, of exercising his functions as trustee, or is a bankrupt, or is a corporation which is in liquidation or has been dissolved.

### RE TEMPEST

Court of Appeal in Chancery (1866) L.R. 1 Ch. 485; 35 L.J.Ch. 632; 14 L.T. 688; 12 Jur.(N.S.) 539; 14 W.R. 850 (Turner and Knight-Bruce L.JJ.)

TURNER L.J.: "There are two questions. First, whether the order of the Master of the Rolls ought to be reversed in so far as it appoints Mr. Petre to be a trustee of the testator's will; and, secondly, whether, assuming that the order ought to be reversed in this respect, Lord Camoys ought to be appointed the trustee. The first of these questions has not seemed to me to be altogether free

---

[25] Trustee Act 1925, ss.69(2), 71(3).
[26] *Ibid.* s.14(2), (3), Law of Property Act 1925, s.27(2).
[27] Under the section a trustee may be displaced against his will: *Re Henderson* [1940] Ch. 764. The section authorises removal of trustees by replacement but not otherwise: *Re Harrison's S.T.* [1965] 3 All E.R. 795, 799.
[28] (1882) 30 W.R. 287; 45 L.T. 756. *Aliter*, if it is uncertain whether the power under s.36(1) of the Act is exercisable: *Re May's Will Trusts* [1941] Ch. 109.
[29] In *Re Chamberlain* [1976] 126 New Law Jo. 1034 (reported in article by J. B. Morcom) the court approved Guernsey trustees where the beneficiaries were domiciled and resident some in France some in Indonesia. See p. 571, *supra*.

from difficulty, and in my view of this case it is by no means an unimportant question. It involves, as I think, to no inconsiderable extent the principles on which this court ought to act in the appointment of new trustees.

"It was said in argument, and has been frequently said, that in making such appointments the court acts upon and exercises its discretion; and this, no doubt, is generally true; but the discretion which the court has and exercises in making such appointments is not, as I conceive, a mere arbitrary discretion, but a discretion in the exercise of which the court is, and ought to be, guided by some general rules and principles, and, in my opinion, the difficulty which the court has to encounter in these cases lies not so much in ascertaining the rules and principles by which it ought to be guided, as in applying those rules and principles to the varying circumstances of each particular case. The following rules and principles may, I think, safely be laid down as applying to all cases of appointments by the court of new trustees.

"First, the court will have regard to the wishes of the persons by whom the trust has been created, if expressed in the instrument creating the trust, or clearly to be collected from it.[30] I think this rule may be safely laid down, because if the author of the trust has in terms declared that a particular person, or a person filling a particular character, should not be a trustee of the instrument, there cannot, as I apprehend, be the least doubt that the court would not appoint to the office a person whose appointment was so prohibited, and I do not think that upon a question of this description any distribution can be drawn between express declarations and demonstrated intention. The analogy of the course which the court pursued in the appointment of guardians affords, I think, some support to this rule. The court in those cases attends to the wishes of the parents, however informally they may be expressed.

"Another rule which may, I think, safely be laid down is this—that the court will not appoint a person to be trustee with a view to the interest of some of the persons interested under the trust, in opposition either to the wishes of the testator or to the interests of others of the *cestuis que trusts*.[31] I think so for this reason, that it is of the essence of the duty of every trustee to hold an even hand between the parties interested under the trust. Every trustee is in duty bound to look to the interests of all, and not of any particular member or class of members of his *cestuis que trusts*.[32]

"A third rule which, I think, may safely be laid down is that the court in appointing a trustee will have regard to the question whether his appointment will promote or impede the execution of the trust, for the very purpose of the appointment is that the trust may be better carried into execution. . . . [33]

"There cannot, I think, be any doubt that the court ought not to appoint a trustee whose appointment will impede the due execution of the trust; but, on the other hand, if the continuing or surviving trustee refuses to act with a trustee who may be proposed to be appointed . . . I think it would be going too far to say that the court ought, on that ground alone, to refuse to appoint

---

[30] See also *Re Badger* [1915] W.N. 166; 84 L.J.Ch. 567: the court will not appoint an additional trustee against the wishes of a sole trustee appointed by the settlor, in the absence of allegations against his honesty, even at the unanimous request of the beneficiaries *in esse*, except where land is trust property since a valid receipt cannot be given by less than two trustees or a trust corporation: Law of Property Act 1925, s.27(2).

[31] This should be *cestuis que trust*: see C. Sweet (1910) 26 L.Q.R. 196.

[32] *Ibid.*

[33] A person will thus not be appointed if so to do would place him in a position in which his interest and duty would be likely to conflict: *Re Parsons* [1940] Ch. 973.

the proposed trustee; for this would, as suggested in the argument, be to give the continuing or surviving trustee a veto upon the appointment of the new trustee. In such a case, I think it must be the duty of the court to inquire and ascertain whether the objection of the surviving or continuing trustee is well founded or not, and to act or refuse to act upon it accordingly. . . . "[34]

### III. PROTECTION OF A PURCHASER OF LAND OF WHICH NEW TRUSTEES HAVE BEEN APPOINTED

#### *The Trustee Act 1925*

Section 38.—(1) A statement, contained in any instrument coming into operation after the commencement of this Act by which a new trustee is appointed for any purpose connected with land, to the effect that a trustee has remained out of the United Kingdom for more than twelve months or refuses or is unfit to act, or is incapable of acting, or that he is not entitled to a beneficial interest in the trust property in possession, shall, in favour of a purchaser of a legal estate, be conclusive evidence of the matter stated.

(2) In favour of such purchaser any appointment of a new trustee depending on that statement, and any vesting declaration, express or implied, consequent on the appointment, shall be valid.

Where an appointment is invalid the general rule is that the old trustee remains trustee with the powers and liabilities of a trustee though the invalidly appointed new trustee will become liable as trustee *de son tort* if he intermeddles with the property.[35]

### IV. VESTING OF TRUST PROPERTY IN NEW OR CONTINUING TRUSTEES

#### *The Trustee Act 1925*

Section 40.—(1) Where by a deed a new trustee is appointed to perform any trust, then—

> (*a*) if the deed contains a declaration by the appointor to the effect that any estate or interest in any land subject to the trust, or in any chattel so subject, or the right to recover or receive any debt or other thing in action so subject, shall vest in the persons who by virtue of the deed become or are the trustees for performing the trust, the deed shall operate,[36] without any conveyance or assignment, to vest in those persons as joint tenants and for the purposes of the trust the estate interest or right to which the declaration relates; and
>
> (*b*) if the deed is made after the commencement of this Act and does not contain such a declaration, the deed shall, subject to any express

---

[34] The court may postpone an order for appointment of new trustees in order to protect the interests of the existing trustees, *e.g. Re Pauling S.T. (No. 2)* [1963] Ch. 576.

[35] *Pearce* v. *Pearce* (1856) 22 Beav. 248.

[36] Even when the estate, interest or right is not vested in the person making the appointment. *Cf.* s.9 of the Law of Property Act 1925; but not as in *Re King's W.T.* [1964] Ch. 542, *supra,* p. 44, where the legal estate is held by the appointor in his capacity as personal representative, not having executed an assent in his favour as trustee. Entry on the register is needed for registered land. The practice is for the current registered proprietor(s) to execute a transfer to the new trustees as new registered proprietors: this saves the Registrar from having to check on the validity of the deed of appointment and then altering the register under the Land Registration Act 1925, s.47.

provision to the contrary therein contained, operate as if it had contained such a declaration by the appointor extending to all the estates interests and rights with respect to which a declaration could have been made.

(2) Where by a deed a retiring trustee is discharged under the statutory power without a new trustee being appointed, then—

(*a*) if the deed contains such a declaration as aforesaid by the retiring and continuing trustees, and by the other person, if any, empowered to appoint trustees, the deed shall, without any conveyance or assignment, operate to vest in the continuing trustees alone, as joint tenants, and for the purposes of the trust, the estate, interest, or right to which the declaration relates; and

(*b*) if the deed is made after the commencement of this Act and does not contain such a declaration, the deed shall, subject to any express provision to the contrary therein contained, operate as if it had contained such a declaration by such persons as aforesaid extending to all the estates, interests and rights with respect to which a declaration could have been made.

(3) An express vesting declaration, whether made before or after the commencement of this Act, shall, notwithstanding that the estate, interest or right to be vested is not expressly referred to, and provided that the other statutory requirements were or are complied with, operate and be deemed always to have operated (but without prejudice to any express provision to the contrary contained in the deed of appointment on discharge) to vest in the persons respectively referred to in subsections (1) and (2) of this section, as the case may require, such estates, interests and rights as are capable of being and ought to be vested in those persons.

(4) This section does not extend—

(*a*) to land conveyed by way of mortgage for securing money subject to the trust, except land conveyed on trust for securing debentures or debenture stock;

(*b*) to land held under a lease which contains any covenant, condition or agreement against assignment or disposing of the land without licence or consent, unless, prior to the execution of the deed containing expressly or impliedly the vesting declaration, the requisite licence or consent has been obtained, or unless, by virtue of any statute or rule of law, the vesting declaration, express or implied, would not operate as a breach of covenant or give rise to a forfeiture;

(*c*) to any share, stock, annuity or property which is only transferable in books kept by a company or other body, or in manner directed by or under an Act of Parliament.

In this subsection "lease" includes an underlease and an agreement for a lease or underlease.

(5) For purposes of registration of the deed in any registry, the person or persons making the declaration expressly or impliedly, shall be deemed the conveying party or parties, and the conveyance shall be deemed to be made by him or them under a power conferred by this Act.

(6) This section applies to deeds of appointment or discharge executed on or after the first day of January, eighteen hundred and eighty-two.

## Section 2. Retirement of Trustees

Where a trustee retires and a new trustee is appointed[37] to fill the vacancy, the retirement and new appointment are effected under section 36(1) of the Trustee Act 1925, *supra*. Where a new trustee is not appointed to fill the vacancy, the retirement is effected under section 39, *infra*.

### The Trustee Act 1925

Section 39.[38]—(1) Where a trustee is desirous of being discharged from the trust, and after his discharge there will be either a trust corporation or at least two individuals to act as trustees to perform the trust, then, if such trustee as aforesaid by deed declares that he is desirous of being discharged from the trust, and if his co-trustees and such other person, if any, as is empowered to appoint trustees, by deed consent to the discharge of the trustee, and to the vesting in the co-trustees alone of the trust property, the trustee desirous of being discharged shall be deemed to have retired from the trust, and shall, by the deed, be discharged therefrom under this Act, without any new trustee being appointed in his place.

(2) Any assurance or thing requisite for vesting the trust property in the continuing trustees alone shall be executed or done.

## Section 3. Disclaimer by Trustees

A person appointed trustee may naturally *disclaim*, for "a man cannot have an estate put into him in spite of his teeth." The disclaimer of a trust by a person appointed trustee—

  (i) ought to be in writing (or by deed); but it may be
     (a) oral[39];
     (b) by conduct[40];
     (c) by mere inactivity (*semble*)[41];
     (d) signified on behalf of the person appointed trustee by counsel at the Bar[42];
 (ii) must be a disclaimer of the whole trust; it cannot be partial.[43]

If a person is appointed both executor and trustee and he proves the will, he thereby accepts the trust. But if he renounces probate, he does not thereby necessarily disclaim the trust.[44]

---

[37] If no one else can be found the Public Trustee will usually be willing to act.
[38] Independently of statute a trustee may retire (i) under a power of retirement contained in the trust instrument: *Camoys* v. *Best* (1854) 19 Beav. 414; (ii) by the consent of all the beneficiaries, the latter being *sui juris*: *Wilkinson* v. *Parry* (1828) 4 Russ. 472, 476; (iii) by authority of the court, to which the trustee has a right to apply to be discharged from the trust; but costs will depend on whether he has reasonable grounds for desiring to be discharged: *Gardiner* v. *Dounes* (1856) 22 Beav. 395; *Barker* v. *Peile* (1865) 2 Dr. & Sm. 340; *Re Chetwynd* [1902] 1 Ch. 692.
[39] *Bingham* v. *Clanmorris* (1828) 2 Moll. 253; *dubitante* Wood V.-C. in *Re Ellison* (1856) 2 Jur. 62.
[40] *Stacey* v. *Elph* (1883) 1 My. & K. 195; *Re Birchall* (1889) 40 Ch.D. 436.
[41] *Re Clout and Frewer* [1924] 2 Ch. 230.
[42] *Landbroke* v. *Bleaden* (1852) 16 Jur.(O.S.) 630; *Foster* v. *Dawber* (1860) 8 W.R. 646.
[43] *Re Lord and Fullerton* [1896] 1 Ch. 228.
[44] *Mucklow* v. *Fuller* (1821) Jac. 198; *Ward* v. *Butler* (1824) 2 Moll. 533; Romilly M.R. in *Dix* v. *Burford* (1854) 19 Beav. 409, 412.

## Section 4. Removal of Trustees

The trust instrument may confer a power of removal, though if it is conferred on a majority of the trustees it seems that notice of the meeting of trustees to consider exercising such power must be given to the trustee the majority wish to remove or the removal will be ineffective.[45]

The court has a jurisdiction, independent of statute, to remove trustees (*Letterstedt* v. *Broers, infra*) and under section 41 on appointing a new trustee it may remove a trustee.[46] On appointment of a new trustee under section 36 the appointors may remove a trustee. If hostility between trustees prevents them from acting unanimously (as they must do unless the trust instrument authorises otherwise) then one or all should be removed and replaced.[47]

In an emergency trustees may be removed on an *ex parte* interlocutory application and a receiver appointed of the trust assets until appointment of new trustees at an *inter partes* hearing.[48]

## LETTERSTEDT v. BROERS

Privy Council (1884) 9 App.Cas. 371; 51 L.T. 169 (Lord Blackburn, Sir Robert P. Collier, Sir Richard Couch and Sir Arthur Hobhouse)

The Board of Executors of Cape Town were the sole surviving executors and trustees of a will under which the appellant was a beneficiary. The appellant alleged misconduct in the administration of the trust, and claimed that the Board were unfit to be entrusted with the management of the estate and should be removed in favour of a new appointment. The Supreme Court of the Cape of Good Hope had refused the application to remove the Board. The beneficiary appealed successfully.

LORD BLACKBURN: " . . . The whole of the matters which have been complained of, and the whole that, if this judgment stands, may yet have to be done by the Board, are matters which they had to do, as having accepted the burden of carrying out the trusts which on the true construction of the will were imposed upon them, and so become trustees. What they had to do as executors merely, such as paying debts, collecting assets, etc., have long ago been over, and by the terms of the compromise the plaintiff cannot now say they have not been done properly. There may be some peculiarity in the Dutch colonial law, which made it proper to make the prayer in the way in which it was done to remove them from the office of executor; if so, it has not been brought to their Lordships' notice; the whole case has been argued here, and, as far as their Lordships can perceive, in the court below, as depending on the principles which should guide an English court of equity when called upon to remove old trustees and substitute new ones. It is not disputed that there is a

---

[45] *Gibbs* v. *Stanners*, 1975 S.L.T.(Notes) 30.
[46] If there is a dispute as to fact then instead of taking out a summons under section 41 a writ should be issued for administration or execution of the trusts invoking the inherent jurisdiction to remove trustees: *Re Henderson* [1940] Ch. 764.
[47] *Re Consigli's Trusts (No. 1)* (1973) 36 D.L.R. (3d) 658.
[48] *Clarke* v. *Heathfield* (1985) 82 Law Soc.Gaz. 599, [1985] I.C.R. 203.

jurisdiction 'in cases requiring such a remedy,' as is said in Story's *Equity Jurisprudence*, s.1287, but there is very little to be found to guide us in saying what are the cases requiring such a remedy; so little that their Lordships are compelled to have recourse to general principles.

"Story says, section 1289: 'But in cases of positive misconduct, courts of equity have no difficulty in interposing to remove trustees who have abused their trust; it is not indeed every mistake or neglect of duty, or inaccuracy of conduct of trustees, which will induce courts of equity to adopt such a course. But the acts or omissions must be such as to endanger the trust property or to show a want of honesty, or a want of proper capacity to execute the duties, or a want of reasonable fidelity.'

"It seems to their Lordships that the jurisdiction which a court of equity has no difficulty in exercising under the circumstances indicated by Story is merely ancillary to its principal duty, to see that the trusts are properly executed. This duty is constantly being performed by the substitution of new trustees in the place of original trustees for a variety of reasons in non-contentious cases. And therefore, though it should appear that the charges of misconduct were either not made out, or were greatly exaggerated, so that the trustee was justified in resisting them, and the court might consider that in awarding costs, yet if satisfied that the continuance of the trustee would prevent the trusts being properly executed, the trustee might be removed. It must always be borne in mind that trustees exist for the benefit of those to whom the creator of the trust has given the trust estate.

"The reason why there is so little to be found in the books on this subject is probably that suggested by Mr. Davey in his argument. As soon as all questions of character are as far settled as the nature of the case admits, if it appears clear that the continuance of the trustee would be detrimental to the execution of the trusts, even if for no other reason than that human infirmity would prevent those beneficially interested, or those who act for them, from working in harmony with the trustee, and if there is no reason to the contrary from the intentions of the framer of the trust to give this trustee a benefit or otherwise, the trustee is always advised by his own counsel to resign, and does so. If, without any reasonable ground, he refused to do so, it seems to their Lordships that the court might think it proper to remove him; but cases involving the necessity of deciding this, if they ever arise, do so without getting reported. It is to be lamented that the case was not considered in this light by the parties in the court below, for, as far as their Lordships can see, the Board would have little or no profit from continuing to be trustees, and as such coming into continual conflict with the appellant and her legal advisers, and would probably have been glad to resign, and get out of an onerous and disagreeable position. But the case was not so treated.

"In exercising so delicate a jurisdiction as that of removing trustees, their Lords do not venture to lay down any general rule beyond the very broad principle above enunciated, that their main guide must be the welfare of the beneficiaries. Probably it is not possible to lay down any more definite rule in a matter so essentially dependent on details often of great nicety.[49] . . .

"It is quite true that friction or hostility between trustees and the immediate possessor of the trust estate is not of itself a reason for the removal of the

---

[49] "You must find," said Warrington J. in *Re Wrightson* [1908] 1 Ch. 789, 803, "something which induces the court to think either that the trust property will not be safe, or that the trust will not properly be executed in the interests of the beneficiaries."

trustees. But where the hostility is grounded on the mode in which the trust has been administered, where it has been caused wholly or partially by substantial overcharges against the trust estate, it is certainly not to be disregarded.

"Looking, therefore, at the whole circumstances of this very peculiar case, the complete change of position, the unfortunate hostility that has arisen, and the difficult and delicate duties that may yet have to be performed, their Lordships can come to no other conclusion than that it is necessary, for the welfare of the beneficiaries, that the Board should no longer be trustees.

"Probably if it had been put in this way below they would have consented. But for the benefit of the trust they should cease to be trustees, whether they consent or not. . . . "

The charge of misconduct was not proved: no costs were awarded.

## Section 5. Special Types of Trustee

*Custodian trustees*[50]

These are distinct from the usual managing trustees. They hold the trust property and the trust documents (*e.g.* title deeds, share certificates) and all sums payable to or out of the income or capital of the trust property are paid to or by them except that dividends and other income derived from the trust property may be paid to such other persons as they direct, *e.g.* the managing trustees or a beneficiary.[51] The day-to-day running of the trust is left to the managing trustees. The following may be appointed custodian trustees: the Public Trustee, the Official Custodian for Charities and trust corporations.[52] A trustee cannot be custodian trustee and managing trustee of the same trust.[53]

*Trust corporations*

A trust corporation can act alone where otherwise two trustees would be required, *e.g.* receipt of capital moneys on a sale of land. The following are trust corporations[54]: the Public Trustee, the Treasury Solicitor, the Official Solicitor, certain charitable corporations and corporations either appointed by the court in any particular case or entitled to act as custodian trustees under the Public Trustee Act 1906. Corporations so entitled include those constituted under United Kingdom law or the law of an EEC state and having a place of business in the United Kingdom and empowered to undertake trust business, which are either incorporated by special Act or Royal Charter or else registered United Kingdom or EEC-state companies with an issued

---

[50] Generally see S. G. Maurice (1960) 24 Conv.(N.S.) 196; P. Pearce (1972) 36 Conv.(N.S.) 260–261; Keeton's *Modern Developments in the Law of Trusts*, Chap. 3.

[51] Public Trustee Act, s.4(2).

[52] Public Trustee Rules 1912 r. 30, as substituted by the Public Trustee (Custodian Trustees) Rules 1975, S.I. 1975 No. 1189 and amended by S.I. 1976 No. 836, S.I. 1981 No. 358, S.I. 1984 No. 109, S.I. 1985 No. 132.

[53] *Forster* v. *Williams Deacon's Bank Ltd.* [1935] Ch. 359; *Arning* v. *James* [1936] Ch. 58.

[54] See n. 52, *supra*.

capital of at least £250,000 (or its foreign equivalent) of which at least £100,000 (or its equivalent) has been paid up in cash.

### The Public Trustee[55]

He was established in 1906 as a corporation sole available to deal with the difficulty persons might have in finding someone willing to act as trustee. However, he cannot accept charitable trusts, insolvent estates or, normally, trusts involving the carrying on of a business. He can act as personal representative, ordinary managing trustee, custodian trustee or judicial trustee.

### Judicial trustee

The Judicial Trustees Act 1896 established judicial trustees in order "to provide a middle course in cases where the administration of the estate by the ordinary trustees had broken down and it was not desired to put the estate to the expense of a full administration" by the court.[56] Judicial trustees can only be appointed by the court upon a summons in existing proceedings or an originating summons if there are no existing proceedings. Trouble-shooting accountants are often appointed to sort out the muddled situation. The judicial trustee is an officer of the court so that he can at any time obtain the court's directions as to the way in which he should act without the necessity of a formal application by summons though he has as much authority as ordinary trustees to act on his own initiative, and, for example, compromise claims.[57]

### Section 6. Trusts do not fail for want of Trustees

If the settlor or testator failed to appoint trustees or if the trustees appointed refuse or are unable to act or have ceased to exist the trust does not fail (unless its operation was conditional upon a specific trustee undertaking the trust[58]). The property reverts to the settlor or remains in the personal representatives of the testator to be held upon the trusts of the settlement or the will as the case may be.[59]

On the death of a sole or sole surviving trustee the trust property vests in his personal representatives subject to the trusts and by the Trustee Act 1925, s.18(2), they are capable of exercising or performing any power or trust which the deceased trustee could have exercised or performed. They are not bound to accept the position and duties of

---

[55] The Hutton Committee of Enquiry into the Public Trustee Office (1972) Cmnd. 4913 recommended that it be wound up and merged with the Official Solicitor's Department. In July 1974 the Lord Chancellor announced that the government do not propose to take any action on the Committee's recommendations. The office has been renamed "The Public Trust Office."

[56] Per Jenkins J. in *Re Ridsdell* [1947] Ch. 597, 605.

[57] *Re Willis* [1921] 1 Ch. 44; *Re Armitage* [1972] Ch. 438; *Re Morrison* (1967) 111 S.J. 758.

[58] *Re Lysaght* [1966] 1 Ch. 191.

[59] *Mallot* v. *Wilson* [1903] 2 Ch. 494. P. Matthews [1981] *Conv.* 141 contends that disclaimer of an *inter vivos* transfer to a trustee should make the transfer void and the trust fail; but one may treat the transferor as constructive trustee on *Re Rose* [1952] Ch. 499 principles and *Tett* v. *Phoenix* [1984] B.C.L.C. 599: p. 225, *supra*.

trustees and may exercise their power of appointing new trustees under s.36 with a right to payment of the costs thereof from the trust moneys.[60] If need be the court may appoint new trustees under section 41[61] or itself execute the trust.[62]

Where a deceased trustee's powers have devolved upon his personal representative who then dies (without having appointed new trustees) it seems that if he accepted the trustee role under s.18(2) then he should himself be treated as a trustee for his powers to devolve under s.18(2) to his own personal representative.[63] If he was executor of the deceased trustee and himself appointed an executor then his executor would be executor by representation of the trustee[64] and so have the s.18(2) powers in any event.

---

[60] *Re Benett* [1906] 1 Ch. 216.
[61] *Jones* v. *Jones* (1874) 31 L.T. 538.
[62] *McPhail* v. *Doulton* [1971] A.C. 424, 457, *supra*, p. 154; (A. J. Hawkins) (1967) 31 (Conv.(N.S.) 117).
[63] P. W. Smith (1977) 41 Conv. 423; *Williams on Title* (4th ed.), p. 490.
[64] Administration of Estates Act 1925, s.7.

# Chapter 9

# THE ADMINISTRATION OF A TRUST

## Section 1. General Introduction[1]

THE office of trustee is onerous. Equity imposes many duties upon a trustee. Unless these duties are abrogated or relaxed by the trust instrument they must all be strictly discharged with the utmost diligence in order to escape liability to account for any *loss* sustained by the trust as a result of any breach of the duties or liability to account for *profits* made by the trustee personally in breach of his duties. A trustee often has more discretions than duties but in exercising those discretions the trustee merely has to act bona fide using as much diligence as "a man of ordinary prudence would exercise in the management of his own private affairs"[2] except that in the investment sphere he must take as much care as a prudent man would take in making an investment for persons for whom he felt morally obliged to provide and so ignore speculative investments which a prudent man might take a chance on occasionally.[3] If the appropriate standard of care is honestly taken but loss occurs the trustee will not be liable (*e.g.* for the dramatic depreciation of a trust holding of Rolls-Royce or Polly Peck shares) nor will he be liable for profits that the trust would have made if he had been more dynamic and skilful (*e.g.* in manipulating a significant minority shareholding in a private company so as either to sell at a very high price or to take over the company and strip it of its assets).

If any doubts arise then the trustee should apply by originating summons to the Chancery Division for directions. As a last resort the trustee may under section 61 of the Trustee Act be excused liability wholly or partly for breach of trust if he acted "honestly and reasonably, and ought fairly to be excused for the breach of trust *and* for omitting to obtain the directions of the court in the matter in which he committed such breach." A paid trustee will be less likely to be excused than an unpaid trustee.[4]

Where there is more than one trustee, as is usually the case, each trustee is personally responsible for the acts performed in the administration of the trust and so should personally consider each act

---

[1] On trust administration generally it is useful to read Sladen's *Practical Trust Administration*.

[2] *Learoyd* v. *Whiteley* (1887) 12 App.Cas. 727, 737, *per* Lord Watson; see also *Re Lucking's W.T.* [1968] 1 W.L.R. 866, 875; *Speight* v. *Gaunt* (1883) 22 Ch.D. 727 affd. (1883) 9 App.Cas. 1.

[3] *Learoyd* v. *Whiteley* (*supra*); *Cowan* v. *Scargill* [1985] Ch. 270.

[4] *Re Rosenthal* [1972] 1 W.L.R. 1273; *Re Pauling's S.T.* [1964] Ch. 303, 338, 339; *National Trustee Co. of Australasia* v. *General Finance Co.* [1905] A.C. 373. See p. 781, *infra*.

requiring to be done: it is no defence that one was a "sleeping trustee" blindly relying on one's co-trustees.[5] It is not possible to delegate a trustee's duties except where authorised under the trust instrument or by statute.[6] The trustees must act unanimously except where the settlement or the court otherwise directs or in the case of charitable trusts where the trustees may act by a majority.[7] It follows that if there is a trust to sell with power to postpone sale then the power is only effective so long as all trustees wish to postpone sale: once one wishes a sale the trust to sell must be carried out, all the trustees being under a duty to sell so long as the power to postpone sale is not effectively exercised unanimously.[8]

Upon accepting[9] trusteeship in order to safeguard himself against claims for breach of trust the new trustee should ascertain the terms of the trust and check that he has been properly appointed. He should inspect all trust documents and ensure that all trust property is properly invested and is in the joint names of himself and his co-trustees.[10] It is often best to have title deeds or share certificates deposited at a bank in the joint names but in the absence of special circumstances the court will not order one trustee who has possession of the documents so to deposit them.[11] If appointed new trustee of an existing trust then it is necessary to investigate any suspicious circumstances which indicate a prior breach of trust so that action may be taken to recoup the trust fund if necessary.[12]

Equity is seen at its strictest in the duty it imposes upon a trustee not to allow himself to be put in a position where there may be a conflict between his position as trustee and his personal interest—as the next section shows. This overriding duty of loyalty to the trust must always be borne in mind by trustees.

---

[5] *Bahin* v. *Hughes* (1886) 31 Ch.D. 390; *Munch* v. *Cockerell* (1840) 5 Myl. & Cr. 178; *Re Turner* [1897] 1 Ch. 536; *Head* v. *Gould* [1898] 2 Ch. 250. There is no automatic vicarious liability for co-trustees' breaches, *e.g. Re Lucking's W.T.* [1968] 1 W.L.R. 866.

[6] See pp. 636–640, *infra*.

[7] *Luke* v. *South Kensington Hotel Ltd.* (1879) 11 Ch.D. 121; Charities Act 1960, ss.28, 34; *Re Butlin's S.T.* [1976] Ch. 251 (rectification to allow majority decisions).

[8] *Re Mayo* [1943] Ch. 302. However, the letter of the trust will not be enforced if so to do would defeat the spirit of the trust: *Jones* v. *Challenger* [1961] 1 Q.B. 176.

[9] Of course, no one is bound to accept office as trustee and office should be refused if one wishes to buy property owned by the trust, or run a business likely to compete with a business owned by the trust, or if one is likely to be in a position where it might be said that profits had been made through advantage being taken of the office.

[10] *Hallows* v. *Lloyd* (1888) 39 Ch.D 686, 691; *Harvey* v. *Olliver* (1887) 57 L.T. 239; *Tiger* v. *Barclays Bank* [1952] W.N. 38; *Lewis* v. *Nobbs* (1878) 8 Ch.D. 591. For those classes of property not vesting in the new trustee under Trustee Act 1925, s.40, the ordinary modes of transferring the property will have to be utilised.

[11] *Re Sisson's Settlements* [1903] 1 Ch. 262. Bearer securities have to be deposited in the custody of a banker: Trustee Act 1925, s.7.

[12] *Re Strahan* (1856) 8 De G.M. & G. 291; *Re Forest of Dean Coal Co.* (1878) 10 Ch.D. 250.

## Section 2. Conflict of Interest and Duty[13]

### 1. PURCHASE OF TRUST PROPERTY BY TRUSTEES

A purchase of trust property by a trustee is voidable *ex debito justitiae,* however fair the price, at the instance of any beneficiary, unless authorised by the trust instrument, or by the court, or by section 68 of the Settled Land Act 1925 (purchases by tenant for life[14]), or made pursuant to a contract or option[15] arising before the trusteeship arose, or acquiesced in by the beneficiary or very special circumstances exist as in *Holder* v. *Holder*. Here it was held by the Court of Appeal, boldly examining the mischief underlying the supposed arbitrary rule, that a renouncing executor who remained executor owing to technical acts of intermeddling and who acquired no special knowledge as executor and who took no part in preparing for a sale by public auction took a valid title as the highest bidder. He had never acted as executor in a way which could be taken to amount to acceptance of a duty to act in the interests of the beneficiaries under the will.

### HOLDER v. HOLDER

Court of Appeal [1968] Ch. 353; [1968] 2 W.L.R. 237; [1968] 1 All E.R. 665

The plaintiff beneficiary sought to rescind the sale of trust property to the third defendant in circumstances sufficiently appearing from the following extracts of the reserved judgments of Harman, Danckwerts and Sachs L.JJ.

HARMAN L.J.: "The cross-appeal raises far more difficult questions, and they are broadly three. First, whether the actions of the third defendant before probate made his renunciation ineffective. Second, whether on that footing he was disentitled from bidding at the sale. Third, whether the plaintiff is disentitled from taking this point because of his acquiescence.

"It was admitted at the Bar in the court below that the acts of the third defendant were enough to constitute intermeddling with the estate and that his renunciation was ineffective. On this footing he remained a personal representative even after probate had been granted to his co-executors and could have been obliged by a creditor or a beneficiary to re-assume the duties of an executor. The judge decided in favour of the plaintiff on this point because the third defendant at the time of the sale was himself still in a fiduciary position and, like any other trustee, could not purchase the trust property. I feel the force of this argument, but doubt its validity in the very special circumstances of this case. The reason for the rule is that a man may not be both vendor and purchaser; but the third defendant was never in that position here. He took no part in instructing the valuer who fixed the reserves or in the preparations for the auction. Everyone in the family knew that he was not a seller but a buyer. In this case the third defendant never assumed the duties of an executor. It is

---

13 See A. W. Scott, "The Trustee's Duty of Loyalty" (1936) 49 H.L.R. 521; Marshall, "Conflict of Interest and Duty" (1955) 8 C.L.P. 91; Gareth Jones, "Unjust Enrichment and the Fiduciary's Duty of Loyalty" (1968) 84 L.Q.R. 472.
14 *Re Pennant's W.T.* [1970] Ch. 75.
15 *Re Mulholland's W.T.* [1949] 1 All E.R. 460.

true that he concurred in signing a few cheques for trivial sums and endorsing a few insurance policies, but he never so far as appears interfered in any way with the administration of the estate. It is true he managed the farms, but he did that as tenant and not as executor. He acquired no special knowledge as executor. What he knew he knew as tenant of the farms.

"Another reason lying behind the rule is that there must never be a conflict of duty and interest, but in fact there was none here in the case of the third defendant, who made no secret throughout that he intended to buy. There is of course ample authority that a trustee cannot purchase. The leading cases are decisions of Lord Eldon L.C.—*Ex p. Lacey*[16] and *Ex p. James.*[17] In the former case Lord Eldon L.C. expressed himself thus[18]:

> 'The rule I take to be this: not, that a trustee cannot buy from his *cestui que trust*, but, that he shall not buy from himself. . . . A trustee, who is entrusted to sell and manage for others, undertakes in the same moment, in which he becomes a trustee, not to manage for the benefit and advantage of himself.'

"In *Ex p. James* Lord Eldon L.C. said this[19]:

> 'This doctrine as to purchases by trustees, assignees, and persons having a confidential character, stands much more upon general principle than upon the circumstances of any individual case. It rests upon this, that the purchase is not permitted in any case, however honest the circumstances, the general interests of justice requiring it to be destroyed in every instance.'

These are no doubt strong words, but it is to be observed that Lord Eldon was dealing with cases where the purchaser was at the time of sale acting for the vendors. In this case the third defendant was not so acting: his interference with the administration of the estate was of a minimal character, and the last cheque that he signed was in August before he executed the deed of renunciation. He took no part in the instructions for probate, nor in the valuations or fixing of the reserves. Everyone concerned knew of the renunciation and of the reason for it, namely that he wished to be a purchaser. Equally, everyone including the three firms of solicitors engaged assumed that the renunciation was effective and entitled the third defendant to bid. I feel great doubt whether the admission made at the Bar was correct, as did the judge, but assuming that it was right, the acts were only technically acts of intermeddling and I find no case where the circumstances are parallel. Of course, I feel the force of the judge's reasoning that if the third defendant remained an executor he is within the rule, but in a case where the reasons behind the rule do not exist I do not feel bound to apply it. My reasons are that the beneficiaries never looked to the third defendant to protect their interests. They all knew he was in the market as purchaser; that the price paid was a good one and probably higher than anyone not a sitting tenant would give. Further, the first two defendants alone acted as executors and sellers: they alone could convey: they were not influenced by the third defendant in connection with the sales.

---

[16] (1802) 6 Ves. 625.
[17] (1803) 8 Ves. 337.
[18] (1802) 6 Ves. 625, 626.
[19] (1803) 8 Ves. 337, 344.

"I hold, therefore, that the rule does not apply in order to disentitle the third defendant to bid at the auction, as he did."

DANCKWERTS L.J.: "There is no allegation of fraud in the present case. The third defendant acted in complete innocence and did not know that he was regarded as debarred from purchasing the farms. He bought them at a public auction, in respect of which he took no part in regard to the arrangements for the auction, and the judge found[20] that the prices that he paid were good prices. They were well above the reserve prices. The third defendant and the two proving executors were at arm's length. There was no question of knowledge which the third defendant might have acquired as an executor. He had a great amount of knowledge of the farms acquired by him, while he was a tenant or when he helped his father in the carrying on of the farms, and he was the obvious person to purchase these farms and likely to offer the best price. I agree with Harman L.J. that there was no reason why he should not bid at the auction and purchase the farms.

"The subject is dealt with in Snell's *Equity* (26th edn.), at p. 259, where it is pointed out that the true rule is not that a trustee may not purchase trust property; it is that a purchase of trust property by a trustee is voidable within a reasonable time at the instance of any beneficiary.

"It is said that it makes no difference, even though the sale may be fair and honest and may be made at a public auction (see Snell's *Equity*, p. 260); but the court may sanction such a purchase and, if the court can do that (see Snell, p. 219), there can be no more than a practice that the court should not allow a trustee to bid. In my view it is a matter for the discretion of the judge."

### The Width of the "Self-dealing" Rule

In *Movitex Ltd.* v. *Bulfield*[21] Vinelott J. stated, "The self-dealing rule is founded on and exemplifies the wider principle that 'no one who has a duty to perform shall place himself in a situation to have his interests conflicting with that duty.'[22] To that should be added for completeness 'nor to have his duty to one conflicting with his duty to another.'[23] So, the fiduciary owes a duty to the person whose interest he is bound to protect not to place himself in a position in which duty and interest or duty and duty are in conflict."[24]

The prohibition against purchase by the trustee applies whether or not he himself fixes the price. Thus in *Wright* v. *Morgan*,[25] a testator left land on trust for sale with power to postpone sale for seven years and provided that it should be offered at a price to be fixed by valuers to one of his sons, X, who was one of the trustees. X assigned his right (which was treated as an option and not a right of pre-emption) to his brother, Y, who was also one of the trustees but who was not authorised to purchase by the terms of the will. Y arranged for the sale to himself, retired from the trust and purchased at a price fixed by the

---

20 [1966] 3 W.L.R. 229, 237.
21 [1988] BCLC 104, 117.
22 *Broughton* v. *Broughton* (1855) 5 De G.M. & G. 160, 164.
23 *Re Haslam & Hier-Evans* [1902] 1 Ch. 765.
24 See also *Chan* v. *Zachariah* (1984) 154 C.L.R. 178, *supra*, p. 452.
25 [1926] A.C. 788.

valuers, and it was held that the sale could be set aside. After all, Y as a trustee was one of those responsible for determining when the land was first to be offered for sale (and prices could fluctuate over the years) and for determining the terms of payment, *e.g.* cash or instalments with interest payable. If X had assigned to a stranger, Z, then assuming the right was assignable and not personal to X, Z could quite properly have purchased the land. Of course, if X had exercised his right and had the land conveyed to him, then a subsequent conveyance to Y would have been proper.

The prohibition against purchase by the trustee is applicable where the sale is conducted at an auction held by the trustee himself,[26] since the trustee is in a position to discourage bidders. Further, where the sale is conducted, not by the trustee, but a third party, as, for example, where a trustee holds trust property subject to a mortgage and the mortgagee sells under his power of sale, the trustee is nevertheless not allowed to buy the property, since to hold otherwise might be to permit him to prefer his own interest to his duty,[27] and this is so whether or not he could have prevented the sale.[28] The rule is a strong one and is not circumvented by the device of the trustee selling to a third party to hold on trust for him.[29] But if there is no prior agreement and the sale is in all respects bona fide there is no objection to the trustee subsequently buying the trust property from the person to whom he sold it,[30] though if the trustee contracts to sell the property to X, a stranger, and before the conveyance is made he purchases the benefit of the contract from X, the contract can be set aside.[31] Further, if the trustee has retired from the trust with a view to purchasing the property the sale can be avoided,[32] but it is otherwise if at the date of his retirement he had no idea of making the purchase, unless the circumstances show that when he made the purchase he used information acquired by him while a trustee.[33] But a trustee who has disclaimed is not caught by the rule.[34]

Moreover, the rule is sufficiently strong and elastic to prevent a trustee from selling the trust property to a company of which he is the

---

[26] *Whelpdale* v. *Cookson* (1747) 1 Ves.Sen. 9; *Campbell* v. *Walker* (1800) 5 Ves. 678, 682.
[27] A. W. Scott, "The Trustee's Duty of Loyalty" (1936) 49 H.L.R. 521, 529–530.
[28] *Griffith* v. *Owen* [1907] 1 Ch. 195, where it was held that the tenant for life of an equity of redemption could not purchase the property for himself from the mortgagee selling under his power of sale.
[29] *Michoud* v. *Girod* (1846) 4 How. 503 (U.S.).
[30] *Re Postlethwaite* (1888) 37 W.R. 200.
[31] *Williams* v. *Scott* [1900] A.C. 499.
[32] *Wright* v. *Morgan* [1926] A.C. 788.
[33] *Re Boles and British Land Co.'s Contract* [1902] 1 Ch. 244.
[34] *Stacey* v. *Elph* (1833) 1 Myl. & K. 195; *cf. Clark* v. *Clark* (1884) 9 App.Cas. 733, 737 (P.C.).

principal shareholder,[35] managing director or other principal officer,[36] or to a partnership of which he is a member.[37] Of course, the rule applies to corporate trustees, so that a trust corporation cannot in the absence of authorisation by the trust instrument or consent of the beneficiaries or approval of the court sell the trust property either to itself or to its subsidiaries.[38]

Where a sale takes place in breach of the rules outlined above, the beneficiaries have a number of remedies open to them. Thus they may claim any profit made by the trustee on a resale of the property. If the property has not been resold they can insist on a reconveyance or alternatively they can demand that it be offered for sale again. If on this occasion a higher price is bid than which the trustee paid, it will be sold at that price. If not, the trustee may at the option of the beneficiaries be allowed to retain the property, and in the nature of things the beneficiaries will confer this doubtful favour upon him where the property has fallen in value since he purchased it.[39] The right which the beneficiaries have to avoid the sale is an equitable one, and as such is liable to be lost through laches, but for laches to apply the beneficiaries must have full knowledge of the facts and must acquiesce in the situation for an unreasonably long period.[40] Further, the right to have the sale set aside may be lost if the court in the exercise of its inherent jurisdiction sets the seal of its approval on the transaction, and it seems that not only may the court authorise a sale which is about to take place, but in a suitable case it may ratify one which has already occurred.[41]

The above presupposes that the sale has taken place without the consent of the beneficiaries. Where, however, the beneficiaries are *sui juris* they may authorise the sale, which will then stand, provided that the trustee made a full disclosure, and did not induce the sale by taking advantage of his relation to the beneficiaries or by other improper conduct, and the transaction was in all respects fair and reasonable.[42]

---

[35] *Silkstone & Haigh Moor Coal Co.* v. *Edey* [1900] 1 Ch. 167; *Farrars* v. *Farrars Ltd.* (1888) 40 Ch.D. 395. Sale to a trustee's wife is risky (see *Ferraby* v. *Hobson* (1847) 2 Ph. 255, 261) but perhaps not absolutely prohibited (see *Burrell* v. *Burrell's Trustees*, 1915 S.C. 33; (1949) 13 Conv.(N.S.) 248; *Re King's W.T.* (1959) 173 Est.Gaz. 627; *Tito* v. *Waddell* (*No. 2*) [1977] 3 All E.R. 129, 241) though see *Re McNally* [1967] N.Z.L.R. 521. A mortgagee can exercise his power of sale in favour of a company in which he is interested only if he shows he acted in good faith and took all reasonable steps to obtain the best price reasonably obtainable: *Tse Kwong Lam* v. *Wong Chit Sen* [1983] 3 All. E.R. 54.

[36] *Eberhardt* v. *Christiana Window Glass Co.* (1911) 9 Del.Ch. 284 (U.S.).

[37] *Colgate's Executor* v. *Colgate* (1873) 23 N.J.Eq. 372 (U.S.). The self-dealing rule extends to cases where a trustee concurs in a transaction which cannot be effected without his consent and where he also has an interest in, or holds a fiduciary duty to another in relation to, the same transaction: *Re Thompson* [1985] 2 All E.R. 720.

[38] *Purchase* v. *Atlantic Safe Deposit and Trust Co.* (1913) 81 N.J.Eq. 334 (U.S.).

[39] For further details, see *Holder* v. *Holder* [1966] 2 All E.R. 116, 130, *per* Cross J.

[40] *Infra*, p. 792; *Holder* v. *Holder* [1968] Ch. 353.

[41] *Farmer* v. *Dean* (1863) 32 Beav. 327; *Campbell* v. *Walker* (1800) 5 Ves. 678.

[42] *Coles* v. *Trecothick* (1804) 9 Ves. 234; *Morse* v. *Royal* (1806) 12 Ves. 355; *Gibson* v. *Jeyes* (1801) 6 Ves. 266; *cf. Fox* v. *Mackreth* (1788) 2 Bro.C.C. 400. These factors can make it difficult for the trustee to find a purchaser when he himself wishes to sell, as a purchaser will be bound by a beneficiary's equity to set aside the transaction if he has actual or constructive notice.

The onus of proof is on the trustee to show affirmatively that these conditions existed, but there is no objection to the consent of the beneficiaries being obtained after the sale to the trustees.[43]

### The "fair dealing" rule

Of course, a trustee may purchase his beneficiary's equitable interest under the trust (subject to making full disclosure and negativing undue influence) so as to acquire the trust property itself when he has acquired all the equitable interests. In *Tito* v. *Waddell (No. 2)*[44] Megarry V.-C. categorised this as subject to the "fair-dealing" rule that "if a trustee purchases the beneficial interest of any of his beneficiaries, the transaction is not voidable *ex debito justitiae*, however fair the transaction, [as under the 'self-dealing' rule] but can be set aside by the beneficiary unless the trustee can show that he has taken no advantage of his position and has made full disclosure to the beneficiary, and that the transaction is fair and honest."

### II. PROFITS INCIDENTAL TO TRUSTEESHIP

In order to maintain confidence in the trust institution by maintaining high standards of conduct in the trustee role equity has developed the rule that a trustee may not place himself in a position where his trusteeship duties and his personal interest may possibly conflict.[45] It follows that he is strictly liable to account for any profit made by using trust property or his position as trustee. Except where he obtains a secret commission or bribe[46] the court, if need be, will be prepared to find that the profit is held on constructive trust[47] for the trust beneficiaries and that the equitable tracing remedy is available. Of course, an injunction may also lie against any trustee who is in breach of or is about to break his duties to the trust.

The rules applicable to trustees have been extended to all persons in a fiduciary relationship.[48] The categories of fiduciary relationships are not closed. The following relationships have been held to be fiduciary: director,[49] senior management employee,[50] promoter[51] and the company; solicitor and client[52]; agent (including a self-appointed agent[53])

---

[43] T. B. Ruoff, "Purchases in Breach of Trust: A Suggested Cure" (1954) 18 Conv.(N.S.) 528.
[44] [1977] 3 All E.R. 129, 241. A mortgagee may purchase the mortgagor's equity of redemption by a subsequent transaction independent of and separate from the mortgage: *Alec Lobb Garages Ltd.* v. *Total Oil* [1983] 1 All E.R. 944, 965.
[45] See p. 446, *supra*; *Bray* v. *Ford* [1896] A.C. 44, 51; *Parker* v. *McKenna* (1874) L.R. 10 Ch.App. 96, 124–125; *Boardman* v. *Phipps* [1967] 2 A.C. 46. Generally see Goff & Jones, Chap. 34; Oakley, Chap. 3. In *Swain* v. *Law Society* [1981] 3 All E.R. 797, 813 Oliver L.J. preferred to consider the rule "as an application of the principle that that which is the fruit of trust property or of the trusteeship is itself trust property."
[46] *Lister* v. *Stubbs* (1890) 45 Ch.D. 1 and see pp. 442–446, *supra*.
[47] See Chap. 7, s.1, pp. 446–466, *supra*.
[48] Generally see P. D. Finn, *Fiduciary Obligations*.
[49] *Regal (Hastings) Ltd.* v. *Gulliver* [1967] 2 A.C. 134; L. S. Sealy [1967] C.L.J. 83.
[50] *Canadian Aero Services Ltd.* v. *O'Malley* (1973) 40 D.L.R. (3d) 371, 381.
[51] *Lydney Iron Ore Co.* v. *Bird* (1886) 33 Ch.D. 85, 94.
[52] *McMaster* v. *Byrne* [1952] 1 All E.R. 1362.
[53] *English* v. *Dedham Vale Properties Ltd.* [1978] 1 All E.R. 382.

and principal[54]; partner and co-partner[55]; mortgagee and mortgagor.[56] Once a fiduciary relationship has been established it is necessary to ascertain the scope and ambit of the fiduciary's duties. Then one can examine whether or not the fiduciary has placed himself in a position where his personal interest may possibly conflict with those duties. If so, then he is accountable for all profits made from acting within the scope and ambit of those duties[57] whether the profit arises before or after his resignation, retirement or dismissal from his fiduciary post, *e.g.* where information concerning certain economic opportunities has been gained *qua* fiduciary which leads to the fiduciary resigning his post so that *he* can profit from the opportunity rather than his principal.[58]

The English courts have retained a strict deterrent approach to fiduciaries. *Boardman* v. *Phipps* (*supra,* p. 457) establishes that the fiduciary must disgorge any benefit obtained by him "even though he acted honestly and in his principal's best interest, even though his principal benefited as well as he from his conduct, even though his principal could not otherwise have obtained the benefit and even though the benefit was obtained through the use of the fiduciary's own assets and in consequence of his personal skill and judgment."[59]

As will be seen from reading *Boardman* v. *Phipps* the majority thought there was a feasible possibility of conflict, since the trustees might have sought Boardman's advice on an application to the court to acquire power to purchase the outstanding shares in the company, when there would be required not just legal advice but practical advice as to the likelihood of the assured success of the proposed takeover and reorganisation of the company. Boardman would hardly have been able to give unprejudiced advice if, when his plans were well advanced, he had been consulted by the trustees as to whether they should then try to take advantage of what he had done so as to obtain profits otherwise passing to him. However, the minority considered that a reasonable man would not think there was a real sensible possibility of conflict.

*Regal (Hastings) Ltd.* v. *Gulliver*[60] discussed pp. 601–603, *infra,* is another important case, though dealing with the director-company relationship. Similarly, in *Cook* v. *Deeks*[61] where directors diverted to

---

[54] *Lowther* v. *Lowther* (1806) 13 Ves. 95, 103; *Parker* v. *McKenna* (1874) 10 Ch.App. 96, 124–125. To the extent the agent-principal relationship is a debtor-creditor relationship no constructive trusteeship or tracing can be allowed.

[55] *Bentley* v. *Craven* (1853) 18 Beav. 75.

[56] *Farrars* v. *Farrars Ltd.* (1888) 40 Ch.D. 395.

[57] *Boardman* v. *Phipps* [1967] 2 A.C. 46, 128–129, *per* Lord Upjohn; *Patel* v. *Patel* [1982] 1 All E.R. 68 (no breach of trust and so no accountability where trustees live in a house held on trust for young children adopted by trustees on death of their parents).

[58] *Industrial Development Consultants Ltd.* v. *Cooley* [1972] 1 W.L.R. 443; *Canadian Aero Services Ltd.* v. *O'Malley* (1973) 40 D.L.R. (3d) 371; *Abbey Glen Pty. Co.* v. *Stumborg* (1978) 85 D.L.R. (3d) 35. Contrast *Queensland Mines* v. *Hudson* (1978) 18 A.L.R. 1.

[59] (1968) 84 L.Q.R. 472, 474, Prof. G. H. Jones.

[60] [1967] 2 A.C. 134.

[61] [1916] 1 A.C. 554.

themselves contracts which they should have taken up on behalf of the company, the Privy Council found the directors held the benefit of the contracts on constructive trust for the company. In *Industrial Development Consultants v. Cooley*[62] the managing director of the plaintiff company was held constructive trustee of the benefit of a contract with the Eastern Gas Board and made liable to account for the profits thereof. The Gas Board had privately told him he would not obtain a contract from them for the benefit of his company but that he would have a good chance of privately obtaining the contract for himself if he left the company. Pretending poor health and concealing his true reason, he secured his release from his employment with the company. He then personally obtained the contract with the Gas Board which he had tried unsuccessfully to obtain for the company. He was held liable to account for all the profit, though the chance of his persuading the Gas Board to contract with the company was estimated by the judge as no greater than 10 per cent.

In *English v. Dedham Vale Properties*[63] self-appointed agents were held liable to account for profits. The plaintiff sold her property to the defendant for £7,750. However, seven days before contracts were exchanged the defendant had applied for planning permission, making the application in the plaintiff's name and signed by the defendant as agent for the plaintiff. Under the Planning Acts the plaintiff did not then need to be notified of the application or informed of its outcome. Planning permission was granted after exchange of contracts but before completion. When, after completion, the plaintiff discovered the position she successfully claimed an account of profits since Slade J. was prepared to treat the defendant as a fiduciary who should have disclosed the planning application to the plaintiff before the contract and the price had been concluded.

In *Swain v. Law Society*[64] a solicitor sought to make the Law Society accountable for commission received by it from an insurance company in respect of premiums paid by solicitors under the Solicitors' Indemnity Insurance Scheme which the Law Society had negotiated with the company. Oliver L.J. stated[65]:

> "What one has to do is to ascertain first of all whether there was a fiduciary relationship and, if there was, from what it arose and what, if there was any, was the trust property; and then to inquire whether that of which an account is claimed either arose, directly or indirectly, from the trust property itself or was acquired not only in the course of, but by reason of, the fiduciary relationship."

On appeal, Lord Brightman (with whom the other Law Lords agreed) endorsed[66] this approach but held that no fiduciary relationship

---

[62] [1972] 1 W.L.R. 443. For Canadian cases where directors were liable see *Canadian Aero Services Ltd. v. O'Malley* (1973) 40 D.L.R. (3d) 371 noted (1974) 37 M.L.R. 464; *Abbey Glen Pty. Co. v. Stumborg* (1978) 85 D.L.R. (3d) 35 noted (1979) 42 M.L.R. 215; (1975) 51 Can.B.R. 771 (Beck).
[63] [1978] 1 All E.R. 382.
[64] [1982] 1 W.L.R. 17; reversed [1982] 2 All E.R. 827; [1983] 1 A.C. 598.
[65] [1982] 1 W.L.R. 17, 37.
[66] [1982] 2 All E.R. 827, 838; [1983] A.C. 598, 619.

existed since the Law Society was performing a public duty under section 37 of the Solicitors Act 1974.

In *Queensland Mines Ltd.* v. *Hudson*[67] the Privy Council took a liberal view on a case of unusual merits to produce a decision that is out of line with earlier strict cases. Queensland was formed to exploit the anticipated award of mining licences: its managing director was Hudson. At the last minute Queensland's financial backing collapsed so Hudson took the licences in his own name in 1961 and resigned as managing director, though remaining a director for a further 10 years. At a 1962 board meeting Hudson admitted he held the licences for Queensland and candidly warned of the risks attendant on exploiting the licences. So the board resolved Queensland would not pursue the matter further, so Hudson was free to go it alone. It was held that Hudson was not liable for his profits for either of two reasons since the board had (1) given their fully informed consent, and (2) placed the licences venture outside the scope of the fiduciary relationship of director and company. As to (1) the consent of the board is not enough: one needs the consent of the majority vote of shareholders at a general meeting at the very least,[68] if not the consent of all the shareholders.[69] As to (2) to allow fiduciary managers to define the scope of their own fiduciary obligations, and so immunise themselves from liability, is startling when there will be such a conflict of interest involved if the directors can then acquire for themselves what they have rejected on behalf of the company. The decision seems rather weak when contrasted with the House of Lords decisions in *Regal (Hastings)*[70] and in *Boardman*.[71] The Privy Council were over-influenced by the fact that Hudson seemed a good chap who had worked hard and risked all, while Queensland had risked nothing, and watched him becoming very successful and then had tried to take away everything he had worked for.

## Defences

It will be a defence to show that the conduct generating the profit was authorised by the trust instrument,[72] or by the contract of agency, or the deed of partnership, or the articles of a company,[73] or by the court.[74] A further defence is to show the informed consent of all the beneficiaries being each *sui juris* and between them absolutely entitled to the trust property.[75] A partner will need the consent of the other partners; a director the consent of all the members of the company for

[67] (1978) 18 A.L.R. 1, well criticised by G. R. Sullivan (1979) 42 M.L.R. 711.
[68] *Imperial Credit Association* v. *Coleman* (1871) 6 Ch.App. 556, 557; *Regal (Hastings) Ltd.* v. *Gulliver* [1967] 2 A.C. 134, 150, 154; Gower's *Company Law* (4th ed.), pp. 617–618.
[69] *Cook* v. *Deeks* [1916] 1 A.C. 554; *Daniels* v. *Daniels* [1978] 2 All E.R. 89, 95.
[70] [1967] 2 A.C. 134.
[71] [1967] 2 A.C. 46.
[72] *Re Llewellin* [1949] Ch. 225.
[73] *Movitex Ltd.* v. *Bulfield* [1988] BCLC 104.
[74] *e.g.* Trustee Act, s.42; R.S.C., Ord. 85, r. 2.
[75] *Boardman* v. *Phipps* [1967] 2 A.C. 46.

it will be a fraud on the minority to expropriate property held on a constructive trust for the company.[76] It would seem that someone employed by trustees in a fiduciary position (*e.g.* a solicitor or accountant) or a beneficiary acquiring special information while purportedly representing the trust so as to be treated as a fiduciary, may have a defence if obtaining the informed consent of independent trustees.[77]

The fact that a fiduciary could have avoided problems by obtaining an informed consent or court approval before entering into the profit-making situation and the practical problems in the way of the principal finding out for himself what exactly the fiduciary was involved in suggest that the strict deterrent approach is likely to be maintained.

## The equitable obligation of confidence

This equitable right of confidentiality is still in course of development.[78] It is usually protected by the grant of an injunction to prevent disclosure of the confidence or by damages in lieu of an injunction under Lord Cairns's Act or by making the confidant liable to account to the confider for profits made from exploiting the confidence or, perhaps, by making a *quantum meruit* award. The right "depends on the broad principle of equity that he who has received information in confidence shall not take unfair advantage of it. He must not make use of it to the prejudice of him who gave it without obtaining his consent": *Seager* v. *Copydex*[79] *infra*. Thus the information must have the necessary quality of confidentiality, must have been imparted in circumstances importing an obligation of confidence, and there must have been unauthorised use of the information.[80] If the circumstances are such that any reasonable man, standing in the shoes of the recipient of the information, would have realised that upon reasonable grounds the information was being given to him in confidence, then this should suffice to impose upon him the equitable obligation of

---

[76] *Cook* v. *Deeks* [1916] 1 A.C. 554; *Borland's Trustees* v. *Steel Bros. Ltd.* [1901] Ch. 279. In contrast a majority by resolution in general meeting may waive a director's personal liability to account if they consider he acted in the company's best interests: Gower's *Company Law*, (4th ed.), pp. 618–620.

[77] *Regal (Hastings) Ltd.* v. *Gulliver* [1967] 2 A.C. 134 (solicitor not liable though closely involved with the directors as emerges from *Luxor (Eastbourne) Ltd.* v. *Cooper* [1941] A.C. 108, especially [1939] 4 All E.R. at 414–417); *Boardman* v. *Phipps* [1967] 2 A.C. 46, 93, 117 and implicit in Lord Upjohn's speech 130–133; *Anson* v. *Potter* (1879) 13 Ch.D. 141. The trustees should be independent just like company directors must be if disclosure to them is to protect a promoter: *Gluckstein* v. *Barnes* [1900] A.C. 240. If to the fiduciary's knowledge a fund is distributable under a bare trust because the beneficiaries are each *sui juris* and between them absolutely entitled to call for the capital then according to Lord Cohen in *Boardman* v. *Phipps* [1967] 2 A.C. 46, 104, the informed consent of the beneficiaries is required. Presumably, trustees can employ an agent to exploit information on terms he receives as fee a percentage of the profit.

[78] See *Malone* v. *Commissioner of Police (No. 2)* [1979] 2 All E.R. 620, 633; Goff & Jones, Chap. 35; Law Commission Working Paper No. 58; Meagher, Gummow & Lehane, Chap. 41, and especially, F. Gurry's *Breach of Confidence* (Clarendon, 1984).

[79] [1967] 1 W.L.R. 923, 931. For insider trading criminal sanctions see Company Securities (Insider Dealing) Act 1985.

[80] See *Coco* v. *Clark (Engineers) Ltd.* [1969] R.P.C. 41, 47; *Att.-Gen.* v. *Jonathan Cape* [1975] 3 All E.R. 484, 494; *Dunford & Elliott Ltd.* v. *Johnson* [1977] 1 Lloyd's Rep. 505; *Fraser* v. *Thames Television* [1983] 2 All E.R. 101, 116. See also Braithwaite (1979) 42 M.L.R. 94.

confidence.[81] It will be a defence to show that disclosure was in the public interest.[82] By analogy with the restraint of trade doctrine Lord Denning considers,[83] "The court will not enforce a stipulation for confidence if it was not reasonable at the time of making it, nor if afterwards, owing to subsequent happenings it became unreasonable that it should be enforced."

If the confidant consciously breaks the plaintiff's confidence the court will grant an injunction and direct an account of profits, treating the confidant as constructive trustee of the profits or any patent or copyright which is the product of the confidential information.[84] If the confidant acted honestly but foolishly in believing that he was not breaching confidence then damages[85] under Lord Cairns's Act[86] or a *quantum meruit*[87] will be awarded, at least if the information had only partially contributed to the product marketed to produce the profits. If the information were the *sine qua non* and the confidant was foolish in thinking he was not breaching the plaintiff's confidence the confidant should be liable to account for his unjust enrichment.[88] If a person uses information without having reason to think that it had been imparted to him in breach of another's confidence, and later discovers the truth of the matter, he should not be liable for use of the information in the prior period.[89] Thereafter he should be liable whether he be a volunteer or a purchaser,[90] so that if he continues with a project with the informant he should be liable to be restrained as participating in a dishonest design in breach of confidence.[91]

---

[81] *Coco* v. *Clark (Engineers) Ltd.* [1969] R.P.C. 41, 48; *Att.-Gen.* v. *Guardian Newspapers (No. 2)* [1988] 3 All E.R. 545.

[82] *Initial Services Ltd.* v. *Putterill* [1968] 1 Q.B. 396, 405; *Lion Laboratories Ltd.* v. *Evans* [1984] 2 All E.R. 417; *Francome* v. *Mirror Group Newspapers* [1984] 2 All E.R. 408.

[83] *Dunford & Elliott Ltd.* v. *Johnson* [1977] 1 Lloyd's Rep. 505, 509.

[84] *Peter Pan Manufacturing Co.* v. *Corsets Silhouette Ltd.* [1964] 1 W.L.R. 96; *British Syphon Co.* v. *Homewood* [1956] 1 W.L.R. 1190; *Att.-Gen.* v. *Guardian Newspapers (No. 2)* [1988] 3 All E.R. 545; *Nanus Asia Co. Inc.* v. *Standard Chartered Bank* [1990] Hong Kong L.R. 396 holding that even a tippee may be constructive trustee of his profits.

[85] For principles of assessment see *Seager* v. *Copydex (No. 2)* [1969] 1 W.L.R. 809 and *Dowson & Mason Ltd.* v. *Potter* [1986] 2 All E.R. 418. If the plaintiff is a manufacturer loss of manufacturing profits is an appropriate basis but not if the plaintiff instead intended to exploit the information by licensing it to others when the value to the plaintiff of the information is an appropriate basis.

[86] The damages were treated as in lieu of an injunction under Lord Cairns's Act 1858 by Slade J. in *English* v. *Dedham Vale Properties Ltd.* [1978] 1 All E.R. 382, 399, and Megarry V.-C. in *Malone* v. *Commissioner of Police (No. 2)* [1979] 2 All E.R. 620, 633. It is arguable that Lord Cairns's Act is concerned purely with damages in aid of legal rights and that where the plaintiff has suffered a loss and seeks relief within the exclusive jurisdiction of equity he is entitled to restitutionary compensation (see pp. 772–773, *infra*) so that the court should award this restitutionary remedy and not damages: Meagher, Gummow & Lehane, p. 841.

[87] See Goff & Jones, pp. 517–518.

[88] Prof. G. H. Jones (1970) 86 L.Q.R. 463, 476.

[89] "It may be a reason for limiting the account of profits to the period subsequent to the date at which he becomes aware of the true facts": *Att.-Gen.* v. *Spalding* (1915) 32 R.P.C. 273, 283.

[90] The defence of bona fide purchaser for value without notice does not apply since the equitable obligation is not a property right, *e.g. Oxford* v. *Moss* (1978) 68 Cr.App.R. 183; [1979] Crim. L.R. 119. Even if the property analogy were adopted the equitable nature of the right would mean that the confider's claim would prevail as being the equitable right first in time.

[91] *Cf.* the constructive trusteeship imposed on strangers to a trust to make them accountable: Chap. 7, section 2, *supra; Wheatley* v. *Bell* [1982] 2 N.S.W.L.R. 544; [1984] F.S.R. 16; J. D. Davies (1984) 4 Ox.J.L.S. 142; *Malone* v. *Commissioner of Police* [1979] 2 All E.R. 620, 634.

*Use of information acquired qua fiduciary*

Information acquired by a trustee in the course of his duties as such may be used by him for his own benefit or for the benefit of other trusts unless its use would place him in a position where his duty and his interest might possibly conflict or it was imparted to him in circumstances placing an obligation of confidence upon him.[92] Thus if A is trustee of S1 and of S2 and as trustee of S1 learns facts that make him and his co-trustees wish to sell X Co. shares he cannot use this knowledge for S2 until S1's X Co. shares have been sold, for a prior sale of S2's shares could well drive down the price of X Co. shares. If A as trustee of S1 learnt encouraging facts about Y Co. shares and his S2 co-trustees were thinking of selling Y Co. shares then A could tell them this would be unsatisfactory unless S1 was thinking of purchasing more Y Co. shares. If A obtains as trustee of S2 information subject to the equitable obligation of confidence then he cannot use it for the benefit of S1 and, it seems, even if he became trustee of S1 before he became trustee of S2, he cannot be sued by the S1 beneficiaries for breach of trust for failing to take advantage of the confidential information obtained *qua* S2 trustee.[93]

A partner may make a profit from information obtained in the course of the partnership business where he does so in another firm with business outside the scope of the partnership business.[94] As Lord Hodson stated in *Boardman* v. *Phipps*,[95] "Partnership is special in that a partner is the principal as well as the agent of the other partners and works in a defined area of business so that it can normally be determined whether the particular transaction is within or without the scope of the partnership. It is otherwise in the case of a general trusteeship or fiduciary position such as was occupied by Mr. Boardman the limits of which are not readily defined."

The scope of a trustee's duties to the trust is unclear where he acquired useful information privately but not in circumstances placing him under the equitable obligation of confidence. Obviously, he can first make as much use of the information for himself as he likes. If he uses the information to make a profit for himself should he not also go on to use it for the benefit of the trust if an ordinary prudent man of business with such information should be expected so to act?[96] If use of the information could enable the shares to be sold quickly before the share price drops dramatically should he not use such information to save the trust suffering a loss?

---

[92] *Boardman* v. *Phipps* [1967] 2 A.C. 46, 128–129, *per* Lord Upjohn who also provides the next two examples.

[93] *Cf. North & South Trust Co.* v. *Berkeley* [1971] 1 W.L.R. 470 and see B. A. K. Rider [1978] Conv. 114.

[94] *Aas* v. *Benham* [1891] 2 Ch. 244.

[95] [1967] 2 A.C. 46, 108. For companies see *Queensland Mines*, above.

[96] See what approximates to a trustee's duty to gazump in *Buttle* v. *Saunders* [1950] 2 All E.R. 193. Is there a distinction between a profit-making situation when there are so many different ways of investing money for profit and a loss-making situation when there is only one way of avoiding the loss, *viz.* selling the shares as soon as possible?

## RE GEE, WOOD AND OTHERS v. STAPLES AND OTHERS

Chancery Division [1948] Ch. 284; [1948] 1 All E.R. 498

The capital of a private company, Gee & Co. (Publishers) Ltd., was £5,000 in £1 shares. Alfred Lionel Gee ("the testator") was the registered owner of 4,996 shares, of which he held 1,996 in his own right and 3,000 as sole surviving executor of his father's will upon the trusts relating thereto. The remaining four shares were held, one each, by the testator's sister, Miss Gee; his second wife, who remarried after his death and at the time of this action had become Mrs. Haynes; his daughter, Mrs. Hunter; and Mr. Staples.

The testator appointed Mrs. Haynes, Mrs. Hunter and Mr. Staples to be the executors and trustees of his will. After the death of the testator Mr. Staples was appointed managing director of the company by unanimous agreement of the executors and Miss Gee, who together constituted all the registered shareholders. The appointment and remuneration of Mr. Staples were subsequently confirmed by an annual general meeting.

The testator's will was proved on March 24, 1939, by all three executors, and the 3,000 shares, previously vested in the testator as executor of his father's will, were registered in the names of the beneficiaries entitled under that will. The testator was himself so entitled to 334 shares.

Mr. Staples received £15,721 as remuneration between the date of the testator's death and March 31, 1947. Some of the beneficiaries under the testator's will claimed that Mr. Staples was liable to account.

HARMAN J.: " . . . [The claim] raises in a complicated form the vexed question of the liability of trustees who become salaried officers of companies in which their testator's estate is largely interested. . . .

"The allegation made against Mr. Staples is that he made use of his position of trust under the testator's will to obtain his remuneration, and it is this which needs examination. The cases on the subject are not numerous, nor do I find them very helpful. None of them deals with a position where more than one trust estate is involved. The principle that a trustee, in the absence of a special contract, cannot make a profit out of his trust, nor be paid for his time and trouble, is an old one, and is spoken of as established in *Robinson* v. *Pett.*[97] It is most clearly stated by Lord Herschell in *Bray* v. *Ford*[98] in these words: 'It is an inflexible rule of a court of equity that a person in a fiduciary position . . . is not, unless otherwise expressly provided, entitled to make a profit; he is not allowed to put himself in a position where his interest and duty conflict.' The difficulty of applying this principle arises where the payment is made not directly out of the trust estate, but by a third party or body, and, in particular, by a limited company. The modern cases begin with *Re Francis*,[99] from which it appears that Kekewich J. declined to allow trustees to retain for their own use remuneration received by them from a company in which the testator held substantially all the shares. The remuneration was voted at a general meeting, and appears to have been procured by the trustees by the exercise of the voting powers attached to the trust shares which had become registered in their names. This case was not cited in *Re Dover Extension Ltd.*,[1] which has been

---

97 (1734) 3 P.Wms. 250, 261.
98 [1896] A.C. 44, 51.
99 (1905) 74 L.J.Ch. 198.
1 [1908] 1 Ch. 65.

sometimes thought to be inconsistent with it.[2] This, however, in my judgment is not so. The *Dover* case appears, when examined, to have been what Cozens-Hardy M.R. called it,[3] 'a very plain case.' The trustees there had become directors before they held any trust shares. The trust shares were, by their own procurement, registered in their names in order to qualify them to continue as directors, but it was not by virtue of the use of these shares that they either became entitled or continued to earn their fees. Warrington J., however, in this case does suggest[4], that remuneration paid for acting as director of a company can never be a profit for which a trustee needs to account, and it is this expression of opinion which is reflected in the headnote and has given rise to a good deal of misconception about the case. This view was not necessary to the decision and may be regarded as mere *obiter dictum*. It is, in my judgment, too wide, if applied to a case where either the use of the trust shares brings about the appointment, or there is no independent board of the employing company to strike a proper bargain with the employed trustee. Moreover, it leaves out of account the second leg of the principle stated by Lord Herschell in *Bray* v. *Ford.*[5] The beneficiaries are entitled to the advantage of the unfettered use by the trustee of his judgment as to the government of the company in which they are interested. This they do not get if his judgment is clouded by the prospect of the pecuniary advantage he may acquire if he makes use of the trust shares to obtain for himself a directorship carrying remuneration. *Re Lewis*[6] is again an instance where the trustee did not receive the remuneration by virtue of the use of his position as a trustee, but by an independent bargain with the firm employing him.

"There follow two cases on the other side of the line, first, *Williams* v. *Barton*[7] where one of the trustees, a half-commission agent in the Stock Exchange, had persuaded his co-trustees to employ his firm to value the trust securities, thus increasing his commission from his firm and making a profit directly by the use of his position as a trustee. Russell J. held him accountable. Last, there is the decision of Cohen J. in *Re Macadam*,[8] where the cases are reviewed. There certain trustees had a power as such, and by virtue of the articles of the company, to appoint two directors of it. By the exercise of this power they appointed themselves and were held liable to account for the remuneration they received because they had acquired it by the direct use of their trust powers. Cohen J. felt (and I respectfully concur) that he ought to do nothing to weaken the principle, and he expressed the view that[9] 'the root of the matter . . . is: Did the trustee acquire the position in respect of which he drew the remuneration by virtue of his position as trustee?' The judge also held[10] that the liability to account for a profit could not 'be confined to cases where the profit is derived directly from the trust estate.'

"I conclude from this review that a trustee who either uses a power vested in him as such to obtain a benefit, as in *Re Macadam*, or who (as in *Barton's* case) procures his co-trustees, to give him, or those associated with him,

---

[2] See, *e.g. Underhill on Trusts*, (9th ed.), p. 353.
[3] [1908] 1 Ch. 65, 69.
[4] [1907] 2 Ch. 76, 83.
[5] [1896] A.C. 44, 51.
[6] (1910) 103 L.T. 495.
[7] [1927] 2 Ch. 9.
[8] [1946] Ch. 73.
[9] *Ibid.* 82.
[10] *Ibid.*

remunerative employment, must account for the benefit obtained. Further, it appears to me that a trustee, who has the power, by the use of trust votes, to control his own appointment to a remunerative position, and refrains from using them, with the result that he is elected to the position of profit, would also be accountable. On the other hand, it appears not to be the law that every man who becomes a trustee, holding, as such, shares in a limited company, is made *ipso facto* accountable for remuneration received from that company independently of any use by him of the trust holding, whether by voting or refraining from doing so. For instance, A, who holds the majority of the shares in a limited company, becomes the trustee of the estate of B, a holder of a minority interest. This cannot, I think, disentitle A to use his own shares to procure his appointment as an officer of the company, nor compel him to disgorge the remuneration he so receives, for he cannot be disentitled to the use of his own voting powers, nor could the use of the trust votes in a contrary sense prevent the majority prevailing. Many other instances could be given of a similar kind of these, *Re Dover Coalfield Extension Ltd.* is really one. There the trustees did not earn their fees by virtue of the trust shares, though, no doubt, the holding of those shares was a qualification necessary for the continued earning of the fees. In so far as Warrington J. goes further than this, as he seems to do by suggesting that remuneration paid by a company could not be a 'profit,' it being a mere wage equivalent in value to the work done for it, I feel he goes too far. Certainly this view was not taken in *Re Macadam*. It would gravely encroach on the principle which Cohen J. [in that case] and Russell J. in *Williams* v. *Barton* felt to be so important.

"I turn now to an examination of the facts in this case to see what (if any) use was made of the trust shares in the appointment of Mr. Staples. In my judgment, when the facts are examined, no such use was made. After the death of the testator, only four persons remained on the register of this company, and they alone could attend meetings of it. As I have said before, the meeting [at which Mr. Staples was appointed managing director] was attended by all the corporators. Each of them held one share, and, as the resolutions were passed unanimously, they must be supposed to have voted in favour by the use of that share. If the corporators, as I think, held their shares beneficially, they were entitled to vote as they chose. If, on the other hand, they were nominees of the testator, there were still three of them whose votes outweighed the vote of Mr. Staples if it was his duty to vote against his own interest. In neither event did the trust shares come into the picture at all. If this be too narrow a view to take, and it is right for this purpose to look behind the register at the beneficial interests in the shares of the company, then it will be seen that the majority interest belonged to the estate of [the testator's father] and that the persons entitled to have his shares registered in their names . . . were in favour of the appointment and the payment of the stipulated remuneration. If then the shares in which the testator's estate was interested had all been used against the resolutions, they would still have been carried, and, therefore, the appointment was not procured by the use of the trust interest vested in the defendant executors, or any of them, by the will of the testator, in which alone the plaintiffs are interested. On the evidence tendered to me, I think it is clear that the persons present at this meeting had no notion that they were using trust votes, or that trust votes controlled the company. They merely met as the four corporators to decide the company's

future and were entitled to come to the conclusion at which they arrived. . . .
"11

### Gareth Jones (1968) 84 L.Q.R. 472

"*Manufacturers Trust Co.* v. *Becker*[12] concerned the fate of claims made on the liquidation of a corporation. Directors of the corporation[13] had acquired debentures at a discount, at prices varying from 3 per cent. to 14 per cent. of their face value. At the time of their purchase the corporation was a going concern but the market value of its property was insufficient to pay its outstanding debts.[14] The referee found that the purchases were made 'without overreaching or failure to disclose any material fact to the selling bond holders,' that the purchases 'were not unfair to debtor, that at the time of respondents' purchases debtor was not in the field to settle its indebtedness on the debentures, and that the assistance rendered to debtor by respondents materially aided [it] in its grave financial situation.'[15] The trustee for the debenture holders objected to the claims on the ground that the holders, being directors, could not profit from the purchase of claims against an insolvent corporation. The Supreme Court dismissed the trustee's objection, and allowed the claims in full.

"Justice Clark, who delivered the opinion of the court, recognised 'that equity must apply not only the doctrines of unjust enrichment when fiduciaries have yielded to the temptation of self-interest but also a standard of loyalty which will prevent a conflict of interests from arising.'[16] It was true that there was a possibility of 'an inherent conflict of interest. . . . It may [have been] necessary for them [the directors] to choose between a corporate policy of reorganisation which might be best for the corporation and one of liquidation which might yield more certain profits to them as note holding directors.'[17] On the other hand, the directors had acted in the utmost good faith with the interests of the corporation at heart. There was 'nothing to suggest that had the debentures been acquired by the *Becker* directors, they would have been unjustly enriched.'[18] Against 'this potentiality of conflict' the court balanced the desirability of permitting the directors, in the circumstances of the case, to reinforce the financial position of the insolvent company; and concluded that the latter policy should prevail.[19]

---

[11] See also *Re Llewellin* [1949] Ch. 225 (testator authorised trustees to use trust shares to secure appointment as directors: *held* he must be deemed to have authorised them to retain directors' fees).

[12] 338 U.S. 304, 70 S.Ct. 127 (1949).

[13] The facts of the case have been simplified in the text. The claims had in fact been bought by close relatives and an office associate of the directors. But the Supreme Court treated the acquisition as having been made by the directors themselves: see 338 U.S. 304, 310. And see *post*, n. 19 for a further comment on this point.

[14] This distinction is fundamental to the court's decision. If the corporation has been in liquidation the court would have had to "reject any claim that would not be fair and equitable to other creditors": see *Pepper* v. *Litton*, 308 U.S. 295, 60 S.Ct. 238 (1939). On going into liquidation, the company's assets are held on trust for its creditors and contributors: see *R. S. Hollins* v. *The Brierfield Coal & Iron Co.*, 150 U.S. 371, 383, *per* Justice Brewer (1893); *Re Calton Crescent Inc.*, 173 F. 2d 944, 950, *per* Swan J. (1949); cited *post*, p. 600. And *cf.* the English case of *I.R.C.* v. *Olive Mill Ltd.* [1963] 1 W.L.R. 712.

[15] 338 U.S. 304, 309.

[16] 338 U.S. 304, 312.

[17] This quotation is in fact taken from Justice Burton's dissenting opinion: 338 U.S. 304, 316. In his view, there was such a conflict.

[18] 338 U.S. 304, 311.

[19] If the court had held the other way, the question would have arisen as to the extent (if any) to which the relatives and the office associate should be identified with the directors: see *Re Franklin Building Co.*, 178 F. 2d 805 (1950), cert. denied 339 U.S. 978 (1950).

"In the *Becker* case, the fiduciaries, the directors, had acted in good faith, with the firm intention of assisting the corporation. By pumping money into the corporation at a critical time in its history and thereby encouraging public confidence in its future, they acted in what was reasonably thought to be its best interests.[20] Moreover, the profit was made not at the expense of the corporation, which always remained liable for the face value of the bonds to the holders whoever they might be, but at the expense of the selling bond holders. The corporation suffered no real loss. This consideration weighed heavily with the judges of the Federal Court of Appeals, Second Circuit, from whose judgment the trustee-in-bankruptcy had appealed.[21]

"As Judge Swan said[22]:

> 'After insolvency it may be said that the directors are fiduciaries for the group of creditors who will share in the insolvent's estate. But the creditors who have retained their claims will suffer nothing whether or not the director is allowed to make a profit from his purchases. If a wrong has been done to any of the group of *cestuis*, it is to those who sold their claims at a price less than the dividend they would have received had they retained them. If they were suing for the wrong done them, they would have to show something equivalent to a fraudulent non-disclosure. . . . Plainly if the contest for the director's profits was between the wronged *cestuis* and the unwronged *cestuis*, the former should prevail. Where it is between the unwronged *cestuis* and a director, if the former are allowed to prevail it can only be as a disciplinary measure against the director for wronging someone who has not complained of the wrong. . . .
>
> 'In the case at Bar, where there was no overreaching of the sellers, we are not convinced that the circumstances are such as to require imposition of the sanction.'

"Both the Supreme Court and the Court of Appeals refused, therefore, to create a conflict of interest where none in fact existed and, on the particular facts, to impose a penal liability on a fiduciary whose enrichment could not be said to be unjust.

"In *Phipps* v. *Boardman*,[23] however, the majority of the House of Lords imposed such a liability on fiduciaries who had acted in the best interests of their principal, without inquiring whether it was necessary to do so. . . .

"In Canada, the Supreme Court has recently refused to declare that a director who had acted honestly and in perfect good faith was a trustee of a mining claim for his corporation, where the board of which he was a member had previously refused to take it up.[24] As Bull J.A. said in the lower court[25]:

> 'In this modern day and country when it is accepted as commonplace that substantially all business and commercial undertakings, regardless of

---

[20] *Cf. McGeoch Building Co.* v. *Dick & Reuteman Co.*, 253 Wis. 166, 33 N.W. 2d 252 (1948).

[21] *Sub nom. Re Calton Crescent Inc.*, 173 F. 2d 944 (1949).

[22] At p. 950.

[23] [1967] 2 A.C. 46 (*sub nom.* Boardman v. Phipps); affirming the decision of the Court of Appeal ([1965] Ch. 992).

[24] *Peso Silver Mines Ltd.* v. *Cropper* (1966) 58 D.L.R. (2d) 1; affirming the judgment of the British Columbia Court of Appeal: 56 D.L.R. (2d) 117; 54 W.W.R. 329. *cf. Lincoln Stores* v. *Grant*, 309 Mass. 417, 34 N.E. 2d 704 (1941), and *Canadian Western National Gas Co.* v. *Central Gas Utilities, Ltd.* (1966) 58 W.W.R. 155. Now see *Queensland Mines* v. *Hudson* (1978) 18 A.L.R. 1.

[25] (1966) 56 D.L.R. (2d) 117, 154–155.

size or importance, are carried on through the corporate vehicle with the attendant complexities involved by interlocking, subsidiary and associated corporations, I do not consider it enlightened to extend the application of these principles beyond their present limits. That the principles, and the strict rules applicable to trustees upon which they are based, are salutary cannot be disputed, but care should be taken to interpret them in the light of modern practice and way of life.'

Similar reasoning persuaded the Michigan court to allow a director to retain a tax title when it would have been *ultra vires* the corporation to have bought it.[26]

"*Regal (Hastings) Ltd.* v. *Gulliver*[27] is a good illustration of the approach of the English courts. The appellant company owned a cinema in Hastings and wanted to acquire two more cinemas, with a view to selling the property of the company as a going concern. For the purpose of acquiring the cinemas a subsidiary company was formed. The landlord was prepared to offer a lease of these properties but required the directors to guarantee the rent unless the paid-up capital of the subsidiary was £5,000. The appellant company, which was to hold all the shares of the subsidiary company, could only afford to subscribe for 2,000 shares; and the directors did not want to give personal guarantees for the rest. Accordingly the directors (on their own behalf and on behalf of certain third parties) and the company solicitor arranged to finance the transaction by personally taking up the other 3,000 shares. This arrangement was formalised by a resolution at a board meeting at which the solicitor was present, and the shares were duly paid up and allotted. The trial judge found that the directors and the solicitor had acted in perfect good faith and in the best interests of the appellant company. Shortly afterwards the proposed sale and purchase of the three cinemas as going concerns fell through. But it was replaced by another proposal which involved a sale of the shares in the appellant company and its subsidiary. This proposal was accepted. From the sale of their shares in the subsidiary, the directors and the solicitor made a profit of £2 16s. 1d. per share. In this action the appellant company, now controlled by the purchasers, sought to recover this profit from the former directors and the solicitor.

"The House of Lords held that the directors, but not the solicitor, must disgorge their profits to the company, for the opportunity and special knowledge to acquire the shares had come to them *qua* fiduciaries. As Lord Russell of Killowen said[28]:

> 'The rule of equity which insists on those who by use of a fiduciary position make a profit, being liable to account for that profit, in no way depends on fraud, or absence of bona fides: or upon such questions or considerations as whether the profit would or should otherwise have gone to the plaintiff, or whether the profiteer was under a duty to obtain the source of the profit for the plaintiff, or whether he took a risk or acted as he did for the benefit of the plaintiff, or whether the plaintiff has in fact been damaged or benefited by his action. The liability arises from the mere fact of a profit having, in the stated circumstances, been made. The profiteer, however honest and well intentioned, cannot escape the risk of being called upon to account. . . .

---

[26] *Thilco Timber* v. *Sawyer*, 236 Mich. 401 (1926). But *cf. Fine Industrial Commodities Ltd.* v. *Powling* (1954) 71 R.P.C. 253.

[27] The decision has now been reproduced in the *Law Reports*: [1967] 2 A.C. 134n.

[28] [1967] 2 A.C. 134, 145, 149.

'I am of the opinion that the directors' standing in a fiduciary relationship to Regal [the appellant company] in regard to the exercise of their powers as directors, and having obtained these shares by reason and only by reason of the fact that they were directors of Regal and in the course of the execution of that office, are accountable for the profits which they have made out of them. The equitable rule laid down in *Keech* v. *Sandford* . . . and similar authorities applies to them in full force. It was contended that these cases were distinguishable by reason of the fact that it was impossible for Regal to get the shares owing to lack of funds, and that the directors in taking the shares were really acting as members of the public. I cannot accept this argument. It was impossible for the *cestui que trust* in *Keech* v. *Sandford* to obtain the lease, nevertheless the trustee was accountable. The suggestion that the directors were applying simply as members of the public is a travesty of the facts.'

"The solicitor, however, was not in a fiduciary position.[29] Because he had taken the shares at the directors' request, he was not compelled to account for his profits. The chairman of the company who had bought his shares only as a nominee of the third parties was also not liable to account to the appellant company. 'Neither the shares nor the profit ever belonged to [him].'[30]

"The company's claim lacked all merit.[31] As a result of the House of Lords' decision, the purchasers of the shares 'receive[d] in one hand part of the sum which ha[d] been paid by the other.' For the shares in Amalgamated [the subsidiary] they paid £3 16s. 1d. per share, yet part of that sum may be returned to the group, though not necessarily to the individual shareholders by reason of the enhancement in the value of the shares in Regal—an enhancement brought about as a result of the receipt by the company of the profit made by some of its former directors on the sale of Amalgamated shares."[32] Only Lord Porter, from whose speech this quotation is taken, chose to mention this point. He recognised that Regal, and hence its purchasers, had received an 'unexpected windfall.' But, he concluded,[33]

'whether it be so or not, the principle that a person occupying a fiduciary relationship shall not make a profit by reason thereof is of such vital importance that the possible consequence in the present case is in fact as it is in law an immaterial consideration.'

"But did the House too easily assume that principle to be of 'vital importance'? The critical issue was whether directors, acting in good faith, should be allowed to retain profits made from the sale of shares in circumstances where the company wanted to acquire them but was financially unable to do so. It may well be necessary in such a case to impose a prophylactic rule. As Judge Swan of the Court of Appeals, Second Circuit, pointed out in *Irving Trust Co.* v. *Deutsch*,[34] if directors could justify their conduct on the theory that their corporation was financially unable to undertake their venture,

---

[29] He was rather lucky to escape liability: see *Luxor (Eastbourne) Ltd.* v. *Cooper* [1939] 4 All E.R. 414–417 for his close involvement with the directors.
[30] At p. 151, *per* Lord Russell of Killowen.
[31] L. C. B. Gower, *Modern Company Law* (2nd ed., London 1957), p. 487.
[32] [1967] 2 A.C. 134, 152, *per* Lord Porter.
[33] At p. 152.
[34] 73 F. 2d 121, 124 (1934). But *cf. Zeckendorf* v. *Steinfeld*, 12 Ariz. 245, 100 P. 784 (1909); *Beaumont* v. *Folsom*, 136 Neb. 235, 285 N.W. 547 (1939).

'there will be a temptation to refrain from exerting their strongest efforts on behalf of the corporation since, if it does not meet the obligations, an opportunity of profit will be open to them [the directors] personally. . . .

'If the directors are uncertain whether the corporation can make the necessary outlays, they need not embark it upon the venture; if they do, they may not substitute themselves for the corporation any place along the line and divert possible benefits into their own pockets.'

"But directors are business men. In the Court of Appeal in *Regal (Hastings) Ltd.* v. *Gulliver*,[35] Lord Greene sympathised with the dilemma of the Regal directors:

'[A]s a matter of business . . . there was only one way left of raising the money, and that was putting it up themselves. . . . That being so, the only way in which [they] could secure that benefit for the company was by putting up the money themselves. Once that decision is held to be a bona fide one and fraud drops out of the case, it seems to me that there is only one conclusion, namely, that the [company's] appeal must be dismissed with costs.'

"The House of Lords rejected Lord Green's reasoning and followed *Keech* v. *Sandford*.[36] Yet it is not easy to see why because Lord King decided in 1726 that a trustee could not renew a trust lease for his own benefit, it *must* follow that the Regal directors, acting honestly and in the best interests of the company should disgorge the profit from the sale of the shares. The relevant policy considerations were delicately balanced. But the House of Lords' unquestioning adherence to the inexorable rule of equity meant that they were never properly weighed against each other."

## SEAGER v. COPYDEX

Court of Appeal [1967] 1 W.L.R. 923; [1967] 2 All E.R. 415 (Lord Denning M.R., Salmon and Winn L.JJ.)

LORD DENNING M.R. (in a reserved judgment): "Summarised, the facts are these—

"(i) The plaintiff invented the 'Klent' carpet grip and took out a patent for it. He manufactured this grip and sold it. He was looking for a selling organisation to market it.

"(ii) The plaintiff negotiated with the defendant company with a view to their marketing the 'Klent' grip. These negotiations were with Mr. Preston, the assistant manager, and Mr. Boon, the sales manager. These negotiations lasted more than a year, but came to nothing.

"(iii) In the course of those negotiations, the plaintiff disclosed to Mr. Preston and Mr. Boon all the features of the 'Klent' grip. He also told them of an idea of his for an alternative carpet grip with a 'V' tang and strong point. But they rejected it, saying that they were only interested in the 'Klent' grip.

"(iv) Both Mr. Preston and Mr. Boon realised that the information was given to them in confidence. Neither of them had any engineering skills, nor had invented anything.

---

[35] The decision of the Court of Appeal is not reported. This quotation from Lord Greene's judgment was cited by Viscount Sankey in his speech in the House of Lords (at p. 381). It was adopted and followed in *Peso Silver Mines Ltd. (N.P.L.)* v. *Cropper* (1966) 58 D.L.R. (2d) 1.

[36] (1726) Cas.temp. King 61.

"(v) As soon as the negotiations looked like coming to nothing, the defendant company decided to make a carpet grip of their own, which was to be basically similar to the 'Klent' grip, but with spikes which would not infringe the plaintiff's patent.

"(vi) The defendant company did in fact make a carpet grip which did not infringe the plaintiff's patent for a 'Klent' grip. But it embodied the very idea of an alternative grip (of a 'V-tang' with strong point) which the plaintiff mentioned to them in the course of the negotiations. They made an application to patent it, and gave the name of Mr. Preston as the true and first inventor.

"(vii) The defendant company gave this carpet grip the name 'Invisigrip' which was the very name which the plaintiff says that he mentioned to Mr. Preston and Mr. Boon in the course of the negotiations.

"(viii) The defendant company say that their alternative grip was the result of their own ideas and was not derived in any way from any information given to them by the plaintiff. They say also that the name of 'Invisigrip' was their own spontaneous idea.

"(ix) I have no doubt that the defendant company honestly believed the alternative grip was their own idea; but I think that they must unconsciously have made use of the information which the plaintiff gave them. The coincidences are too strong to permit of any other explanation.

"*The Law*. I start with one sentence in the judgment of Lord Greene M.R. in *Saltman Engineering Co. Ltd.* v. *Campbell Engineering Co. Ltd.*[37]:

> 'If a defendant is proved to have used confidential information, directly or indirectly obtained from the plaintiff, without the consent, express or implied, of the plaintiff, he will be guilty of an infringement of the plaintiff's rights.'

To this I add a sentence from the judgment of Roxburgh J. in *Terrapin Ltd.* v. *Builders' Supply Co. (Hayes) Ltd.*,[38] which was quoted and adopted as correct by Roskill J. in *Cranleigh Precision Engineering Co. Ltd.* v. *Bryant*[39]:

> 'As I understand it, the essence of this branch of the law, whatever the origin of it may be, is that a person who has obtained information in confidence is not allowed to use it as a springboard for activities detrimental to the person who made the confidential communication, and springboard it remains even when all the features have been published or can be ascertained by actual inspection by any member of the public.'

The law on this subject does not depend on any implied contract. It depends on the broad principle of equity that he who has received information in confidence shall not take unfair advantage of it. He must not make use of it to the prejudice of him who gave it without obtaining his consent. The principle is clear enough when the whole of the information is private. The difficulty arises when the information is in part public and in part private. As for instance in this case. A good deal of the information which the plaintiff gave to the defendant company was available to the public, such as the patent specification in the Patent Office, or the 'Klent' grip, which he sold to anyone who asked.

37 [1963] 3 All E.R. 413, 414.
38 [1960] R.P.C. 130.
39 [1965] 1 W.L.R. 1293.

But there was a good deal of other information which was private, such as, the difficulties which had to be overcome in making a satisfactory grip; the necessity for a strong, sharp tooth; the alternative forms of tooth; and the like. When the information is mixed, being partly public and partly private, then the recipient must take special care to use only the material which is in the public domain. He should go to the public source and get it: or, at any rate, not be in a better position than if he had gone to the public source. He should not get a start over others by using the information which he received in confidence. At any rate, he should not get a start without paying for it. It may not be a case for injunction but only for damages, depending on the worth of the confidential information to him in saving him time and trouble.

"*Conclusion.* Applying these principles, I think that the plaintiff should succeed. On the facts which I have stated, he told the defendant company a lot about the making of a satisfactory carpet grip which was not in the public domain. They would not have got going so quickly except for what they had learned in their discussions with him. They got to know in particular that it was possible to make an alternative grip in the form of a 'V-tang,' provided the tooth was sharp enough and strong enough, and they were told about the special shape required. The judge thought that the information was not significant. But I think it was. It was the springboard which enabled them to go on to devise the 'Invisigrip' and to apply for a patent for it. They were quite innocent of any intention to take advantage of him. They thought that, as long as they did not infringe his patent, they were exempt. In this they were in error. They were not aware of the law as to confidential information.

"I would allow the appeal and give judgment to the plaintiff for damages to be assessed. . . .

"The court grants neither an account of profits, nor an injunction, but only damages to be assessed by the master. Damages should be assessed on the basis of reasonable compensation for the use of the confidential information which was given to the defendant company."[40]

### III. COMPETITION WITH THE TRUST

The general rule is that a trustee may not, after accepting a trust which comprises a business, set up a private business which competes or may compete with the business of the trust since, if he did so, his interest would conflict with his duty. Thus in *Re Thomson*,[41] the testator's estate included a yachtbroker's business which he bequeathed to his executors on trust to continue it. One of the executors claimed the right to set up a similar business in competition with the trust, but the court granted an injunction to restrain him. On the other hand, in the Irish case of *Moore* v. *M'Glynn*, [42] the court refused to restrain a

---

[40] In *Seager* v. *Copydex (No. 2)* [1969] 1 W.L.R. 809 the measure of damages was held to be a consultant's fee, if the information could have been acquired by employing a consultant, or the sale price between a willing seller and buyer if the information was of a special inventive nature using damages for conversion as an analogy.

[41] [1930] 1 Ch. 203. Where at p. 215 Clauson J. said, "An executor and trustee having duties to discharge of a fiduciary nature towards the beneficiaries under the will shall not be allowed to enter into any engagement in which he has or can have a personal interest conflicting or which possibly may conflict with the interests of those whom he is bound to protect."

[42] [1894] 1 I.R. 74.

trustee from setting up a competing business, but considered that it would be a good ground for removing him from his trusteeship. Chatterton V.-C. observed[43]: "I have not been referred to, nor am I aware of, any case deciding that an executor or trustee of a will carrying on the business of his testator is disabled from setting up a similar business in the same locality on his own account. . . . I am not prepared to hold that a trustee is guilty of a breach of trust in setting up for himself in a similar line of business in the neighbourhood, provided that he does not resort to deception or solicitation of custom from persons dealing at the old shop." A distinction between this case and *Re Thomson* is that in the latter the business was highly specialised and the locality was very small so that the competition was inevitable whether or not there was solicitation of custom.

Any profits made in breach of duty should be held on trust for the beneficiaries as the profits are their profits which have been lost by the trustee's competition.[44] Whilst partners are under a statutory obligation[45] not to engage in a competing business it seems that non-service directors are not so obliged (unless their contract so provides) but they must be very careful as to the information they disclose to rival companies[46] since confidential information must not be disclosed.

## IV. GRATUITOUS ADMINSTRATION OF TRUST[47]

Trustees must, in the absence of some special dispensation, administer the trust gratuitously for otherwise "the trust estate might be loaded and made of little value."[48]

The cases in which the trustee is entitled to payment for his services are as follows.

First, in a suitable case the court has an inherent jurisdiction to be excercised sparingly to authorise a trustee to receive remuneration prospectively or retrospectively and it may increase the remuneration authorised by the trust instrument: *Re Duke of Norfolk's S.T. infra*, p. 608. In order to do so the court must be satisfied that the services of the particular trustee will be or have been of exceptional benefit to the estate.[49] The court, when appointing a *corporation* (other than the

---

43 *Ibid.* p. 89.
44 Goff and Jones, p. 650 citing *Somerville* v. *Mackay* (1810) 16 Ves. 382; *Dean* v. *MacDowell* (1877) 8 Ch.D. 345, 353; *Trimble* v. *Goldberg* [1906] A.C. 494; Restatement of Restitution, para. 199.
45 Partnership Act 1890, s.30.
46 *London & Mashonaland Exploration Co.* v. *New Mashonaland Exploration Co.* [1891] W.N. 165 approved by Lord Blanesburgh in *Bell* v. *Lever Bros.* [1932] A.C. 161, 195; Gower's *Company Law*, 4th ed. pp. 599–600; *Aubanel & Alabaster Ltd.* v. *Aubanel* (1949) 66 R.P.C. 343.
47 Generally see Bishop & Prentice (1983) 46 M.L.R. 289; Parry [1984] Conv. 275.
48 *Robinson* v. *Pett* (1734) 3 P.Wms. 249, 251.
49 *Marshall* v. *Holloway* (1820) 2 Swans. 432; *Docker* v. *Somes* (1834) 2 My. & K. 655; *Re Freeman* (1887) 37 Ch.D. 148; *Re Masters* [1953] 1 W.L.R. 81; *Re Macadam* [1946] Ch. 73; *Boardman* v. *Phipps* [1967] 2 A.C. 46; *Re Barbour's Settlement* [1974] 1 All E.R. 1188, 1192; *Re Keeler's S.T.* [1981] 1 All E.R. 888 (though it overlooks *Re Llewellin's W.T.* [1949] Ch. 225); *Re Duke of Norfolk's S.T.* [1982] Ch. 61. Even a wrongdoer may benefit: *O'Sullivan* v. *Management Agency & Music Ltd.* [1985] 3 All E.R. 351; *John* v. *James* [1986] S.T.C. 352, 358.

Public Trustee) to act, also has a statutory jurisdiction[50] under section 42 of the Trustee Act 1925 to authorise it to charge for its services.

Secondly, if the settlement authorises the trustee to charge for his services he is entitled to be paid, but charging clauses are construed strictly in the sense that the onus is on the trustee to show that the charge which he proposes to make is covered by the terms of the settlement. Thus, if a solicitor-trustee is authorised to make "professional charges," even where the words "for his time and trouble" are added, he will not be allowed to charge for time and trouble expended other than in his position as solicitor.[51] But where a will authorises the solicitor-trustee to make "the usual professional or *other proper and reasonable* charges for all business done and time expended in relation to the trusts of the will, *whether such business is usually within the business of a solicitor or not*," the solicitor is permitted to charge for business not strictly of a professional nature transacted by him in relation to the trust,[52] though, apparently, not for work altogether outside his professional vocation.[53] Even if not needed at first it is important always to insert a charging clause so that a professional trustee may be appointed if need be at some stage. The Law Reform Committee would like to see a presumption that a clause authorising a trustee to charge should cover work that could reasonably be done by a person of his expertise, even though it could also be done by a layman, if an ordinary prudent man of business would expect a trustee to do this work. An executor remunerated under a charging clause cannot retain such remuneration against creditors if the estate turns out to be insolvent. The Law Reform Committee recommend that an executor should be able to claim such remuneration as an administration expense in priority to creditors so far as properly incurred. Currently, if an executor has doubts over the solvency of the estate he may appoint an outside professional under section 23 of the Trustee Act and the costs thereof will be proper administration expenses.

Thirdly, if the beneficiaries are all *sui juris* and between them absolutely entitled to the trust estate, they may authorise the trustee to be paid. If the beneficiaries then sue the trustee for breach of trust in

---

[50] The Public Trustee has a statutory right to charge under the Public Trustee Act 1906, s.9, as have custodian trustees acting as custodian trustees *only* under the Public Trustee Act 1906, s.4: *Forster* v. *Williams Deacon's Bank* [1935] Ch. 359. Judicial trustees may charge under Judicial Trustees Act 1896, s.1.

[51] *Re Chapple* (1884) 27 Ch.D. 584; *Re Orwell* [1982] 3 All E.R. 177.

[52] *Re Ames* (1883) 25 Ch.D. 72.

[53] *Clarkson* v. *Robinson* [1900] 2 Ch. 722. See clause 8(c) in settlement in Chap. 1 to ensure that a trustee may charge for matters which a layman is able to do personally. It should be noted that if a will appoints a solicitor-trustee and there is a charging clause the charges are treated as a legacy—except for tax purposes when they are earned income: *Dale* v. *I.R.C.* [1954] A.C. 11. It follows that the solicitor must not be an attesting witness (Wills Act 1837, s.15) and that if the assets are insufficient the "legacy" will abate proportionately with the other legacies unless there is some provision giving it priority. The Law Reform Committee have recommended that sums due to executors under charging clauses should rank as administration expenses so far as incurred properly: 1982 Cmnd. 8733, para. 3.45. They also recommend that a beneficiary should be entitled to obtain a remuneration certificate from the Law Society to establish that the charges made by a solicitor-trustee under a charging clause are reasonable. (para. 3.50).

paying trust moneys to himself the trustee has their acquiescence as a defence unless undue influence was exercised by him.

Fourthly, the general rule of gratuitous service is particularly severe in the case of solicitor-trustees. Thus in *Christophers* v. *White*,[54] it was held that a solicitor-trustee's firm was not entitled to charge for professional services rendered to the trust by a partner in the firm even though the partner was not one of the trustees.[55] But where a solicitor-trustee employed his partner, as distinct from his firm, under an *express* agreement that the partner should be individually entitled to charges, these were allowed on the ground that where such an agreement is carried out there is no infringement of the rule that a trustee may not make his office a source of remuneration.[56] Moreover, the severity of the rule has been relaxed by the case of *Cradock* v. *Piper*,[57] in which a solicitor-trustee acted as solicitor for himself and his co-trustees in legal proceedings relating to the trust, and was held to be entitled to his usual charges. The rule is that unlike a sole trustee acting as solicitor to the trust, a solicitor-trustee acting in legal proceedings[58] for a body of trustees, of whom he himself is one, is entitled to his usual charges if the fact of his appearing for himself and his co-trustees jointly has not increased the costs which would have been incurred if he had appeared for those co-trustees only.

Fifthly, where the trust property is situate abroad and the law of the foreign country permits payment, the trustee is entitled to keep any remuneration which he has received. Thus in *Re Northcote*,[59] a testator who left assets both in this country and in the United States died domiciled in England, and the principal forum of administration was therefore English. The executors took out an English grant, and on doing so they were put on terms by the Revenue, the English effects being insufficient to pay the English duty, to undertake themselves personally to obtain a grant in New York in respect of the American assets. In due course they obtained such a grant, and got in the assets. Under the law of New York they were entitled to commission for so doing, and Harman J. held that they were under no duty to account for it to the beneficiaries.

### RE DUKE OF NORFOLK'S SETTLEMENT TRUSTS

Court of Appeal [1982] Ch. 61; [1981] 3 All E.R. 220 (Fox, Brightman, Cumming- Bruce L.JJ.).

Fox L.J.: "I conclude that the court has an inherent jurisdiction to authorise the payment of remuneration of trustees and that that jurisdiction extends to

---

54 (1847) 10 Beav. 523.
55 See also *Re Gates* [1933] Ch. 913 and *Re Hill* [1934] Ch. 623.
56 *Clack* v. *Carlon* (1861) 30 L.J.Ch. 639.
57 (1850) 1 Mac. & G. 664.
58 Legal proceedings need not necessarily be hostile litigation but may be friendly proceedings in chambers: *Re Corsellis* (1887) 34 Ch.D. 675. It must be work in connection with a writ or an originating summons rather than general advisory work not relating to legal proceedings.
59 [1949] 1 All E.R. 442; see also *Chambers* v. *Goldwin* (1802) 9 Ves. 271.

increasing the remuneration authorised by the trust instrument. In exercising that jurisdiction the court has to balance two influences which are to some extent in conflict. The first is that the office of trustee is, as such, gratuitous; the court will accordingly be careful to protect the interests of the beneficiaries against claims by the trustees. The second is that it is of great importance to the beneficiaries that the trust should be well administered. If therefore the court concludes, having regard to the nature of the trust, to the experience and skill of a particular trustee and to the amounts which he seeks to charge when compared with what other trustees might require to be paid for their services and to all the other circumstances of the case, that it would be in the interests of the beneficiaries to increase the remuneration, then the court may properly do so.

"Having regard to the view which I take as to the inherent jurisdiction, it is not necessary to consider the extent of the court's jurisdiction under section 57 of the Trustee Act 1925 or otherwise.

"I would allow the appeal, and make the declaration sought by the amended summons so far as it relates to the inherent jurisdiction. The matter should, I think, be remitted to the Chancery Division to enable the trustees to make such application and on such further evidence as they think fit."

BRIGHTMAN L.J.: "I entirely agree with the judgment of Fox L.J. . . .

"In this appeal we are concerned with the power of the High Court to authorise a trust corporation, which has been in office for some 20 years, to charge fees for its future services in excess of those laid down in the trust instrument. In his admirable submissions in the unwelcome role of advocatus diaboli which this court imposed on him, counsel for the sixth and seventh defendants confined himself to that narrow issue. He did not dispute that the High Court can, in the exercise of its inherent jurisdiction, authorise a trustee to retain remuneration where none is provided by the terms of the trust. What the court has no jurisdiction to do, he submitted, was to authorise an increase in the general level of remuneration of a paid trustee by way of addition to the remuneration which is allowed by the trust, once the trust has been unconditionally accepted.

"Where the court appoints a trust corporation to be a trustee, it has a statutory power to authorise it to charge remuneration: see the Trustee Act 1925, s.42. The inherent power of the court to authorise a prospective trustee to charge remuneration is exemplified by such cases as *Re Freeman's Settlement Trusts* (1887) 37 Ch.D., 148. The inherent power to authorise an unpaid trustee to charge remuneration, notwithstanding prior acceptance of the unpaid office, was regarded by Lord Langdale M.R. in *Bainbrigge* v. *Blair* (1845) 8 Beav. 588 as undoubted.

"If the court has an inherent power to authorise a prospective trustee to take remuneration for future services, and has a similar power in relation to an unpaid trustee who has already accepted office and embarked on his fiduciary duties on a voluntary basis, I have some difficulty in appreciating the logic of the principle that the court has no power to increase or otherwise vary the future remuneration of a trustee who has already accepted office. It would mean that, if the remuneration specified in the trust instrument were lower than was acceptable to the incumbent trustee or any substitute who could be found, the court would have jurisdiction to authorise a substitute to charge an acceptable level of remuneration, but would have no jurisdiction to authorise the incumbent to charge precisely the same level of remuneration. Such a result appears to me bizarre, and to call in question the validity of the principle on which it is supposedly based.

"Two foundations for the principle are suggested. One is that the right to remuneration is based on contract, and the court has no power to vary the terms of a contract. The contractual conception suffers from the difficulties explained in the judgment of Fox L.J. It also seems to me, in the context of the present debate, to give little weight to the fact that a trustee, whether paid or unpaid, is under no obligation, contractual or otherwise, to provide future services to the trust. He can at any time express his desire to be discharged from the trust and in that case a new trustee will in due course be appointed under section 36 or section 41 of the 1925 Act. The practical effect therefore of increasing the remuneration of the trustee (if the contractual conception is correct) will merely be to amend for the future, in favour of a trustee, the terms of a contract which the trustee has a unilateral right to determine. The interference of the court in such circumstances can hardly be said, in any real sense, to derogate from the contractual rights of the settlor or the beneficiaries if he or they are to be regarded as entitled to the benefit of the contract.

"The other foundation suggested for the supposed principle is that the remuneration allowed to a trustee under the terms of the trust is a beneficial interest, and the court has no inherent jurisdiction to vary that beneficial interest save in special circumstances not here material (see *Chapman* v. *Chapman* [1954] A.C. 429). I agree that the remuneration given to a trustee by a will is an 'interest' within the meaning of section 15 of the Wills Act 1837, that it is a 'gift' on a condition for the purposes of the legislation which formerly charged legacy duty on testamentary gifts and that an executor or trustee remunerated by the will cannot retain such remuneration against creditors if the estate turns out to be insolvent. There are obvious arguments why a testator should not be able to circumvent the provisions of the Wills Act 1837, or avoid legacy duty, or defeat his creditors, by the award of remuneration to his executors or trustees. It does not follow that a remunerated trustee is to be considered as a cestui que trust for the purposes of the principles laid down in *Chapman* v. *Chapman*. If he were it is difficult, as Fox L.J. says, to see what right the court would have to authorise remuneration to be charged by a prospective trustee, since such authority will have the inevitable effect of adding a new beneficiary to the trust at the expense of the existing beneficiaries.

"I would allow the appeal." *Appeal allowed. Declaration granted. Summons to be remitted to the Chancery Division for further application by trustees.*

## Section 3. Investment of Trust Funds

A fundamental function of the trustees is to invest the trust fund so that there is adequate income or capital available for the beneficiaries. First, the trustees must familiarise themselves with their powers of investment so that they know which investments are *intra vires* and which are *ultra vires*. Secondly, in deciding whether to sell or purchase *intra vires* investments, the trustees must comply with further duties.

### I. THE RANGE OF INVESTMENTS

Trustees are under a fundamental duty to invest the trust funds in investments authorised expressly or impliedly by the trust instrument or by the court[60] or in default by the Trustee Investments Act 1961. A properly drafted trust instrument will contain very extensive powers of investment so that there is no need to apply to the court for wider powers or otherwise be restricted to the unsatisfactory range of investments permitted by the 1961 Act. If a testator by specific bequest leaves certain investments (*e.g.* shares in a particular private company) to trustees for A for life, then B absolutely, this impliedly authorises the trustees to retain such investments but not to purchase any more.[61] If personal representatives appropriate property to trustees under section 41 of the Administration of Estates Act 1925, then such property is by such section thereafter treated as an authorised investment for purposes of retention but not for purchasing more of the same.

If an express investment power is void for uncertainty[62] (*e.g.* to invest in blue chip shares and such other investments as my trustees know I would approve of) then the trustees are relegated to the powers under the 1961 Act unless they obtain wider powers from the court.

## II. DUTIES WHEN INVESTING

### To act prudently and safely

A trustee must "take such care as an ordinary prudent man would take if he were minded to make an investment for the benefit of other people for whom he felt morally obliged to provide,"[63] *e.g.* widows and orphans whom he would feel he would personally have to support if the trust fund were decimated by unsatisfactory investment. Thus, a trustee should not purchase speculative investments that he might as a prudent businessman buy for himself. "Safety first" should be his motto. However, as Hoffman J. stated in *Nestle* v. *National Westminster Bank*,[64] "Modern trustees acting within their investment powers are entitled to be judged by the standards of current portfolio theory, which emphasises the risk level of the entire portfolio rather than the risk attaching to each investment taken in isolation." The emphasis has thus changed, in line with increasing sophistication, from evaluating a specific investment and its performance to evaluating a package of different investments and its performance. It is the performance of the portfolio rather than the performance of its individual components that matters. This should diminish risks. Take shares in the manufacturers, Oil Heaters Ltd. and Gas Heaters Ltd. If oil prices increase, share prices in the former company will decline but share prices in the latter will increase. Conversely, if gas prices rise shares in the latter will

---

[60] The court's powers are in Trustee Act 1925, s.57 and the Variation of Trusts Act 1958.
[61] *Re Pugh* [1887] W.N. 143; *Re Whitfield* (1920) 125 L.T. 61. A residuary bequest of unauthorised property gives rise to a *Howe* v. *Dartmouth* trust for sale: see p. 667, *infra*.
[62] *Re Kolb's W.T.* [1962] Ch. 531.
[63] *Re Whiteley* (1886) 33 Ch.D. 347, 355, *Cowan* v. *Scargill* [1985] Ch. 270.
[64] June 29, 1988, unreported.

decline in value and shares in the former will increase in value. Because the share price of each company share is offset by the price movement of the other share, the aggregate risk of a portfolio containing both shares will be lower than the average of the risks of both shares.

If the trustees lack investment knowledge then the duty to act prudently and safely requires them to seek professional advice and on receiving that advice to act with the same degree of prudence.[65] If they have power to delegate[66] their discretionary duties of investment then they may delegate such duties to a professional portfolio manager,[67] subject to guiding him as to their aims concerning income and capital growth and subject to regular reviews of his performance and of the income and capital needs of the beneficiaries.

### To act fairly

A "trustee must act fairly in making investment decisions which may have different consequences for differing classes of beneficiaries,"[68] *e.g.* life tenant and remainderman.

> "The trustees have a wide discretion. They are, for example, entitled to take into account the income needs of the tenant for life or the fact that the tenant for life was a person known to the settlor and a primary object of the trust whereas the remainderman is a remoter relative or stranger. Of course, these cannot be allowed to become the overriding considerations but the concept of fairness between classes of beneficiaries does not require them to be excluded. It would be an inhuman rule which required trustees to adhere to some mechanical rule for preserving the real value of the capital when the tenant for life was the testator's widow who had fallen upon hard times and the remainderman was young and well-off."[69]

### To do the best they can financially for the beneficiaries

If trustees have agreed to sell Blackacre so as to be morally bound but not yet bound by a legally enforceable contract, they are under a duty to gazump (*i.e.* negotiate with someone putting in a serious higher offer) so as to obtain a higher price for the beneficiaries, even if as honourable men they would prefer to implement the bargain to which they felt in honour bound: *Buttle* v. *Saunders*.[70] If they have strong opinions against alcohol or investment in South Africa then if such investments would be likely to be more beneficial financially than other proposed investments they must purchase those investments despite

---

[65] *Cowan v. Scargill* [1985] Ch. 270; *Martin* v. *Edinburgh D.C.* [1989] 1 Pensions L.R. 9.
[66] See p. 635, *infra.*
[67] Authorised to carry on investment business under the Financial Services Act 1986.
[68] *Nestlé* v. *National Westminster Bank*, June 29, 1988, unreported.
[69] *Ibid.*
[70] [1950] 2 All E.R. 193.

finding them disagreeable.[71] However, if trustees obtain professional advice that particular investments other than in alcohol or in South Africa are equally satisfactory for the portfolio from the financial point of view then, of course, they can proceed to purchase those other investments. Thus, "all things being equal," trustees can refuse to invest in companies whose products or policies they find disagreeable.[72]

A settlor, of course, can always restrict the trustees' powers of investment by excluding certain types of investments and can always reduce the duties owed by the trustees, *e.g.* by permitting or directing the trustees to invest only in companies whose products or policies are ecologically more beneficial than those of other competing companies in the opinion of the trustees and by exempting[73] the trustees from liability so long as they acted in good faith.

In the case of charitable trusts, the trustees must consider whether a particular investment is consistent with its charitable purposes so that, for example, it would not be proper for a trust concerned to rehabilitate alcoholics and prevent alcoholism to invest in companies manufacturing and distributing alcoholic drinks.[74]

### Statutory duty to consider diversification and suitability

By section 6(1) of the Trustee Investments Act 1961 a trustee must have regard:

"(a)  to the need for diversification of investments of the trust in so far as is appropriate to the circumstances of the trust;

(b)  to the suitability to the trust of investments of the description of investment proposed and of the investment proposed as an investment of that description."

This seems to spell out what a trustee acting prudently and safely should be doing in any event, taking account of the size of the trust fund, the beneficiaries' needs and their tax position (in light of their income and their residence).

### Extent of liability

Liability will normally be to account for a loss caused by purchasing an *ultra vires* investment or by purchasing a wholly inappropriate *intra vires* investment.[75] Exceptionally, it may be possible to make out a case that the trustee should be liable to account for a profit that ought to have been made. However, as Hoffmann J. said,[76] "In reviewing the conduct of trustees over a period of more than 60 years, one must be careful not to endow the prudent trustee with prophetic vision or

---

[71] *Cowan v. Scargill* [1985] Ch. 270.
[72] See R. E. Megarry in *Equity Fiduciaries and Trusts* (T. G. Youdan ed.), pp. 149–159.
[73] On exemption clauses see *infra.*
[74] *Martin* v. *Edinburgh D.C.* [1989] 1 Pensions L.R. 9.
[75] See pp. 759 *et seq. infra.*
[76] *Nestlé* v. *National Westminster Bank*, June 29, 1988, unreported.

expect him to have ignored the received wisdom of his time," *e.g.* as to the balance between gilt-edged securities and company shares.

## COWAN v. SCARGILL

Chancery Division [1985] Ch. 270; [1984] 2 All E.R. 750; [1984] 3 W.L.R. 501

MEGARRY V.-C.: "I turn to the law. The starting point is the duty of trustees to exercise their powers in the best interests of the present and future beneficiaries of the trust, holding the scales impartially between different classes of beneficiaries. This duty of the trustees towards their beneficiaries is paramount. They must, of course, obey the law; but subject to that, they must put the interests of their beneficiaries first. When the purpose of the trust is to provide financial benefits for the beneficiaries, as is usually the case, the best interests of the beneficiaries are normally their best financial interests. In the case of a power of investment, as in the present case, the power must be exercised so as to yield the best return for the beneficiaries, judged in relation to the risks of the investments in question; and the prospects for the yield of income and capital appreciation both have to be considered in judging the return from the investment.

"The legal memorandum that the union obtained from their solicitors is generally in accord with these views. In considering the possibility of invest-ment for 'socially beneficial reason which may result in lower returns to the fund,' the memorandum states that 'the trustees only concern is to ensure that the return is the maximum possible consistent with security'; and then it refers to the need for diversification. However, it continues by saying that:

> 'Trustees cannot be criticised for failing to make a particular invest-ment for social or political reasons, such as in South African stock for example, but may be held liable for investing in assets which yield a poor return or for disinvesting in stock at inappropriate times for non-financial criteria.'

This last sentence must be considered in the light of subsequent passages in the memorandum which indicate that the sale of South African securities by trustees might be justified on the ground of doubts about political stability in South Africa and the long-term financial soundness of its economy, whereas trustees could not properly support motions at a company meeting dealing with pay levels in South Africa, work accidents, pollution control, employment conditions for minorities, military contracting and consumer protection. The assertion that trustees could not be criticised for failing to make a particular investment for social or political reasons is one that I would not accept in its full width. If the investment in fact made is equally beneficial to the beneficiaries, then criticism would be difficult to sustain in practice, whatever the position in theory. But if the investment in fact made is less beneficial, then both in theory and in practice the trustees would normally be open to criticism.

"This leads me to the second point, which is a corollary of the first. In considering what investments to make trustees must put on one side their own personal interests and views. Trustees may have strongly held social or political views. They may be firmly opposed to any investment in South Africa or other countries, or they may object to any form of investment in companies concerned with alcohol, tobacco, armaments or many other things. In the conduct of their own affairs, of course, they are free to abstain from making any such investments. Yet under a trust, if investments of this type would be more beneficial to the beneficiaries than other investments, the trustees must not refrain from making the investments by reasons of the views that they hold.

"Trustees may even have to act dishonourably (though not illegally) if the interests of their beneficiaries require it. Thus where trustees for sale had struck a bargain for the sale of trust property but had not bound themselves by a legally enforceable contract, they were held to be under a duty to consider and explore a better offer that they received, and not to carry through the bargain to which they felt in honour bound: see *Buttle* v. *Saunders* [1950] 2 All E.R. 193. In other words, the duty of trustees to their beneficiaries may include a duty to 'gazump,' however honourable the trustees. As Wynn-Parry J. said (at 195), trustees 'have an overriding duty to obtain the best price which they can for their beneficiaries.' In applying this to an Official Receiver, Templeman J. said in *Re Wyvern Developments Ltd.* [1974] 1 W.L.R. 1097 at 1106 that he—

' . . . must do his best by his creditors and contributories. He is in a fiduciary capacity and cannot make moral gestures, nor can the court authorise him to do so.'

In the words of Wigram V.-C. in *Balls* v. *Strutt* (1841) 1 Hare 146 at 149:

'It is a principle in this court that a trustee shall not be permitted to use the powers which the trust may confer upon him at law, except for the legitimate purposes of his trust.'

Powers must be exercised fairly and honestly for the purposes for which they are given and not so as to accomplish any ulterior purpose, whether for the benefit of the trustees or otherwise: see *Duke of Portland* v. *Topham* (1864) 11 H.L. Cas. 32 a case on a power of appointment that must apply a fortiori to a power given to trustees as such.

"Third, by way of a caveat I should say that I am not asserting that the benefit of the beneficiaries which a trustee must make his paramount concern inevitably and solely means their financial benefit, even if the only object of the trust is to provide financial benefits. Thus if the only actual or potential beneficiaries of a trust are all adults with very strict views on moral and social matters, condemning all forms of alcohol, tobacco and popular entertainment, as well as armaments, I can well understand that it might not be for the 'benefit' of such beneficiaries to know that they are obtaining rather larger financial returns under the trust by reason of investments in those activities than they would have received if the trustees had invested the trust funds in other investments. The beneficiaries might well consider that it was far better to receive less than to receive more money from what they consider to be evil and tainted sources. 'Benefit' is a word with a very wide meaning, and there are circumstances in which arrangements which work to the financial disadvantage of a beneficiary may yet be for his benefit: see, for example, *Re Towler's Settlement Trusts* [1964] Ch. 158; *Re C L* [1969] 1 Ch. 587. But I would emphasise that such cases are likely to be very rare, and in any case I think that under a trust for the provision of financial benefits the burden would rest, and rest heavy, on him who asserts that it is for the benefit of the beneficiaries as a whole to receive less by reason of the exclusion of some of the possibly more profitable forms of investment. Plainly the present case is not one of this rare type of case. Subject to such matters, under a trust for the provision of financial benefits, the paramount duty of the trustees is to provide the greatest financial benefits for the present and future beneficiaries.

"Fourth, the standard required of a trustee in exercising his powers of investment is that he must—

' . . . take such care as an ordinary prudent man would take if he were minded to make an investment for the benefit of other people for whom he felt morally bound to provide.'

See *Re Whiteley* (1886) 33 Ch.D. 347 at 355 *per* Lindley L.J. and see also at 350, 358; *Learoyd* v. *Whiteley* (1887) 12 App. Cas. 727. That duty includes the duty to seek advice on matters which the trustee does not understand, such as the making of investments, and on receiving that advice to act with the same degree of prudence. This requirement is not discharged merely by showing that the trustee has acted in good faith and with sincerity. Honesty and sincerity are not the same as prudence and reasonableness. Some of the most sincere people are the most unreasonable; and Mr. Scargill told me that he had met quite a few of them. Accordingly, although a trustee who takes advice on investments is not bound to accept and act on that advice, he is not entitled to reject it merely because he sincerely disagrees with it, unless in addition to being sincere he is acting as an ordinary prudent man would act.

"Fifth, trustees have a duty to consider the need for diversification of investments. By section 6(1) of the Trustee Investments Act 1961:

'In the exercise of his powers of investment a trustee shall have regard—(a) to the need for diversification of investments of the trust, in so far as is appropriate to the circumstances of the trust; (b) to the suitability to the trust of investments of the description of investment proposed and of the investment proposed as an investment of that description.'

The reference to the "circumstances of the trust" plainly includes matters such as the size of the trust funds: the degree of diversification that is practicable and desirable for a large fund may plainly be impracticable or undesirable (or both) in the case of a small fund.

"In the case before me, it is not in issue that there ought to be diversification of the investments held by the fund. The contention of the defendants, put very shortly, is that there can be a sufficient degree of diversification without any investment overseas or in oil, and that in any case there is no need to increase the level of overseas investments beyond the existing level. Other pension funds got on well enough without overseas investments, it was said, and in particular the NUM's own scheme had, in 1982, produced better results than the scheme here in question. This was not so, said Mr. Jenkins, if you compared like with like, and excluded investments in property, which figure substantially in the mineworkers' scheme but not at all in the NUM scheme: and in any case the latter scheme was much smaller, being of the order of £7m.

"I shall not pursue this matter. Even if other funds in one particular year, or in many years, had done better than the scheme which is before me, that does not begin to show that it is beneficial to this scheme to be shorn of the the ability to invest overseas. . . .

"Sixth, there is the question whether the principles that I have been stating apply, with or without modification, to trusts of pension funds. Counsel for the plaintiffs asserted that they applied without modification, and that it made no difference that some of the funds came from the members of the pension scheme, or that the funds were often of a very substantial size. Mr. Scargill did not in terms assert the contrary. He merely said that this was one of the questions to be decided, and that pension funds may be subject to different rules. I was somewhat unsuccessful in my attempts to find out from him why this was so, and what the differences were. What it came down to, I think, was that the rules for trusts had been laid down for private and family trusts and wills a long time ago; that pension funds were very large and affected large numbers of people; that in the present case the well-being of all within the coal industry was affected; and that there was no authority on the point except *Evans* v. *London Co-op Society Ltd. The Times*, July 6, 1976 and certain overseas cases. . . .

"I can see no reason for holding that different principles apply to pension fund trusts from those which apply to other trusts. Of course, there are many provisions in pension schemes which are not to be found in private trusts, and to these the general law of trusts will be subordinated. But subject to that, I think that the trusts of pension funds are subject to the same rules as other trusts. The large size of pension funds emphasises the need for diversification, rather than lessening it, and the fact that much of the fund has been contributed by members of the scheme seems to me to make it even more important that the trustees should exercise their powers in the best interests of the beneficiaries. In a private trust, most, if not all, of the beneficiaries are the recipients of the bounty of the settlor, whereas under the trusts of a pension fund many (though not all) of the beneficiaries are those who, as members, contributed to the funds so that in due time they would receive pensions. It is thus all the more important that the interests of the beneficiaries should be paramount, so that they may receive the benefits which in part they have paid for. I can see no justification for holding that the benefits to them should run the risk of being lessened because the trustees were pursuing an investment policy intended to assist the industry that the pensioners have left, or their union. . . .

"*Blankenship* v. *Boyle* 329 F.Supp. 1089 (1971) was a case heard in the U.S. district court for the District of Columbia by Judge Gesell. The trustees of a pension fund had allowed large sums of money to remain in bank accounts bearing no interest at a bank controlled by the union. Over an 18-year period, varying sums between $14m. and $75m., representing between 14 per cent. and 44 per cent. of the fund's total resources, had been left in this way. The fund was established for the benefit of employees of coal operators, their families and dependants, and over 95 per cent. of the members of the fund were also members of the union. It was contended that the trustees could properly consider not only the interests of the beneficiaries but also collateral matters such as increasing the tonnage of union-mined coal; but this was rejected. The court reaffirmed the duty of undivided loyalty to the beneficiaries that a trustee owes, and did not accept that regard should also be paid to the union or its members who generated some of the income of the fund, or to the industry as a whole. That seems to me to be plainly right.

"*Withers* v. *Teachers' Retirement System of the City of New York* 447 F.Supp. 1248 (1978) arose out of the impending insolvency of the City of New York in 1975. The Teachers' Retirement System (TRS) and four other New York pension funds agreed to purchase $2,530m. unmarketable and highly speculative New York City bonds over the next two and a half years in an attempt to stave off the imminent bankruptcy of the city; the share contributed by TRS was $860m. TRS was an unfunded scheme, and the evidence was that if the city ceased to make its massive contributions to the scheme, the reserves would be exhausted in some eight to ten years, even if the contributions by employees continued and there was a constant rate of retirement of teachers. In the U.S. District Court for the Southern District of New York, Judge Conner considered and accepted *Blankenship* v. *Boyle* and the traditional rules of equity, but held that the trustees had been justified in purchasing the bonds since they had done so in the best interest of the beneficiaries, and not out of concern for the general public welfare or the protection of the jobs of city teachers. The object of the trustees, who had imposed stringent conditions in an attempt to protect the TRS, had been to ensure the continuance of the city's major contributions to the scheme, and preserve the city's position as the ultimate guarantor of the payment of pension benefits; and this was in the best interests of the beneficiaries. This differed from the position in *Blankenship* v. *Boyle*, where—

> ' . . . the trustees pursued policies which may incidentally have aided the beneficiaries of the fund but which were intended, primarily, to enhance the position of the Union and the welfare of its members, presumably, through the creation and/or preservation of jobs in the coal industry.'

(See 447 F.Supp. 1248 at 1256.) Apart from the expression 'and/or', I would agree.

"The American cases do not, of course, bind me; but they seem, if I may say so, to be soundly based on equitable principles which are common to England and most jurisdictions in the United States, and they accord with the conclusion that I would have reached in the absence of authority. Accordingly, on principle and on the two American cases, I reach the unhesitating conclusion that the trusts of pension funds are in general governed by the ordinary law of trusts, subject to any contrary provision in the rules or other provisions which govern the trust. In particular, the trustees of a pension fund are subject to the overriding duty to do the best that they can for the beneficiaries, the duty that in the United States is known as 'the duty of undivided loyalty to the beneficiaries' (see *Blankenship* v. *Boyle* 329 F.Supp. 1089 at 1095).

"In considering that duty, it must be remembered that very many of the beneficiaries will not in any way be directly affected by the prosperity of the mining industry or the union. Miners who have retired, and the widows and children of deceased miners, will continue to receive their benefits from the fund even if the mining industry shrinks: for the scheme is fully funded, and the fund does not depend on further contributions to it being made. If the board fell on hard times, it might be unable to continue its voluntary payments to meet cost-of-living increases, quite apart from the statement about this made by Mr Cowan at the forty-seventh committee meeting on November 14, 1983. The impact of that remote possibility falls short of the imminent disaster facing the City of New York and TRS in the *Withers* case; and I cannot regard any policy designed to ensure the general prosperity of coal mining as being a policy which is directed to obtaining the best possible results for the beneficiaries, most of whom are no longer engaged in the industry, and some of whom never were. The connection is far too remote and insubstantial. Further, the assets of even so large a pension fund as this are nowhere near the size at which there could be expected to be any perceptible impact from the adoption of the policies for which Mr. Scargill contends. . . . "

### III. THE TRUSTEE INVESTMENTS ACT 1961

*New powers of investment of trustees*

Section 1.—(1) A trustee may invest any property in his hands, whether at the time in a state of investment or not, in any manner specified in Part I or II of the First Schedule to this Act or, subject to the next following section, in any manner specified in Part III of that Schedule, and may also from time to time vary any such investments.

(2) The supplemental provisions contained in Part IV of that Schedule shall have effect for the interpretation and for restricting the operation of the said Parts I to III.

(3) No provision relating to the powers of the trustee contained in any instrument (not being an enactment or an instrument made under an enactment) made before the passing of the Act shall limit the powers conferred by this section, but those powers are exercisable only in so far as a contrary intention is not expressed in any Act or instrument made under an enactment whenever passed or made, and so relating or in any other instrument so relating which is made after the passing of this Act.

The new powers conferred by this Act are available to trustees unless a *contrary intention* is expressed in any statute or statutory instrument, whenever made, relating to the powers of trustees or in any other instrument so relating made after August 3, 1961.]

(4) In this Act "narrower-range investment" means an investment falling within Part I or II of the First Schedule to this Act and "wider-range investment" means an investment falling within Part III of that Schedule.

*Restrictions on wider-range investment*

Section 2.—(1) A trustee shall not have power by virtue of the foregoing section to make or retain any wider-range investment unless the trust fund has been divided into two parts (hereinafter referred to as the narrower-range part and the wider-range part), the parts being, subject to the provisions of this Act, equal in value at the time of the division; and where such a division has been made no subsequent division of the same fund shall be made for the purposes of this section, and no property shall be transferred from one part of the fund to the other unless either—

(*a*) the transfer is authorised or required by the following provisions of this Act, or

(*b*) a compensating transfer is made at the same time.

In this section "compensating transfer", in relation to any transferred property, means a transfer in the opposite direction of property of equal value.

(2) Property belonging to the narrower-range part of a trust fund shall not by virtue of the foregoing section be invested except in narrower-range investments, and any property invested in any other manner which is or becomes comprised in that part of the trust fund shall either be transferred to the wider-range part of the fund, with a compensating transfer, or be reinvested in narrower-range investments as soon as may be.

[Trustees *may* invest in wider-range investments, subject to two conditions: (a) the trust fund must have been divided into two parts of equal value without taking into account the "special range" part of the fund (as to which, see section 3(3) and Schedule 2, *infra*); (b) the trustees must obtain and consider written expert advice about the particular investments (as to which, see, section 6(2)—(5), *infra*). But even after such division trustees *may* invest the wider-range part in narrower-range investments: on the other hand they *must* always invest the narrower-range part in narrower-range investments or arrange for a compensating transfer.]

(3) Where any property accrues to a trust fund after the fund has been divided in pursuance of subsection (1) of this section, then—

(*a*) if the property accrues to the trustees as owner or former owner of property comprised in either part of the fund, it shall be treated as belonging to that part of the fund;

(*b*) in any other case, the trustee shall secure, by apportionment of the accruing property or the transfer of property from one part of the fund to the other, or both, that the value of each part of the fund is increased by the same amount.

Where a trustee acquires property in consideration of a money payment the acquisition of the property shall be treated for the purposes of this section as investment and not as the accrual of property to the trust fund, notwithstanding that the amount of the consideration is less than the value of the property acquired; and paragraph (*a*) of this subsection shall not include the case of a dividend or interest becoming part of a trust fund.

[Thus (i) bonus issue in respect of shares in the wider-range part accrues to that part; (ii) a "rights" issue taken up by the trustees constitutes a new investment and the new shares belong to that part of the fund which paid for them; (iii) accumulations of income and gifts to the trustees on the trusts of the settlement have to be apportioned between the two parts of the fund.]

(4) Where in the exercise of any power or duty of a trustee property falls to be taken out of the trust fund, nothing in this section shall restrict his discretion as to the choice of property to be taken out.

[This enables a trustee to reduce the narrower range part effectively.]

*Relationship between Act and other powers of investment*

Section 3.—(1) The powers conferred by section one of this Act are in addition to and not in derogation from any power conferred otherwise than by this Act of investment or postponing conversion exercisable by a trustee (hereinafter referred to as a "special power").

(2) Any special power (however expressed) to invest property in any investment for the time being authorised by law for the investment of trust property being a power conferred on a trustee before the passing of this Act or conferred on him under any enactment passed before the passing of this Act, shall have effect as a power to invest property in like manner and subject to the like provisions as under the foregoing provisions of this Act.

(3) In relation to property, including wider-range but not including narrower-range investments,—

(*a*) which a trustee is authorised to hold apart from—

(i) the provisions of section one of this Act or any of the provisions of Part I of the Trustee Act 1925 or any of the provisions of the Trusts (Scotland) Act 1921, or

(ii) any such power to invest in authorised investments as is mentioned in the foregoing subsection, or (*b*) which became part of a trust fund in consequence of the exercise by the trustee, as owner of property falling within this subsection, of any power conferred by subsection (3) or (4) of section ten of the Trustee Act 1925 or paragraph (*o*) or (*p*) of subsection (1) of section four of the Trusts (Scotland) Act 1921,

the foregoing section shall have effect subject to the modifications set out in the Second Schedule to this Act.

[Subsections (1)–(3) of this section and Schedule 2, *infra*, contain the main rules where the trust includes "special-range" property. A trustee with a wide special power of investment (*e.g.* to invest in all respects as if he was the beneficial owner of the trust fund) may not wish to use the Act at all. On the other hand a trustee with a limited special power of investment (*e.g.*, to invest in certain ordinary or preference shares not authorised under the Act, or in the purchase of land) may also wish to make use of the powers of investment conferred by the Act. If he does so wish, then in dividing the fund he will ignore the value of the special-range property (*e.g.*, preference shares) which will be carried to a separate part of the fund. If he sells other investments and buys preference shares, they also become special-range property: it appears that he may purchase them entirely out of the proceeds of sale of narrower-range investments or wider-range investments or partly one and partly the other in his absolute discretion. If he sells the preference shares he can put the proceeds of sale either in narrower-range or wider-range investments or partly in one and partly in the other but he must comply with the requirement that the values of each of these two parts of the fund must be increased by the same amount. Suppose the trustees sell the preference shares for £2,000 and at that date the value of the narrower-range part of the fund is £4,000 and of the wider-range part £5,000, including £1,000 worth of narrower-range investments. The trustees can *either* split the £2,000 and invest £1,000 in narrower-range investments in the narrower-range part of the fund and the other £1,000 in wider-range investments in the wider-range part of the fund, *or* invest the whole £2,000 in wider-range investments and transfer the £1,000 worth of narrower-range investments from the wider-range part of the fund *or* invest £1,500 in wider-range investments and £500 in narrower-range investments together with a transfer to the narrower range part of £500 worth of the narrower-range investments in the wider-range part of the fund.]

(4) The foregoing subsection shall not apply where the powers of the trustee to invest or postpone conversion have been conferred or varied—

(*a*) by an order of any court made within the period of ten years ending with the passing of this Act, or

(*b*) by any enactment passed, or instrument having effect under an enactment made, within that period, being an enactment or instrument relating specifically to the trusts in question, or

(*c*) by an enactment contained in a local Act of the present Session;

but the provisions of the Third Schedule to this Act shall have effect in a case falling within this subsection.

[One effect of this is that if the court has, within the period mentioned in the subsection, extended the powers of investment of the trustees, the extended powers are not to be regarded as special so as to constitute investments made by virtue of their exercise "special-range" property, and leave the remainder of the fund available for division into a narrower-range part and a wider-range part under the Act. Another effect can be illustrated by the following example: In 1958 the court authorised trustees to invest in shares of a kind now authorised by the Act. On August 3, 1961, the value of the trust fund was £10,000, of which the shares constituted £6,000. If the fund was divided, the narrower-range part would include £1,000 worth of shares, *i.e.* wider-range investments. So long as that situation continued, the trustee could not use the powers under the Act (*e.g.* to invest in units of a unit trust) but they could go on using the extended powers given them by the court.]

*Interpretation of references to trust property and trust funds*

Section 4.—(1) In this Act "property" includes real or personal property of any description, including money and things in action:

Provided that it does not include an interest in expectancy, but the falling into possession of such an interest, or the receipt of proceeds of the sale thereof, shall be treated for the purposes of this Act as an accrual of property to the trust fund.

(2) So much of the property in the hands of a trustee shall for the purposes of this Act constitute one trust fund as is held on trusts which (as respects the beneficiaries or their respective interests or the purposes of the trust or as respects the powers of the trustee) are not identical with those on which any other property in his hands is held.

(3) Where property is taken out of a trust fund by way of appropriation so as to form a separate fund, and at the time of the appropriation the trust fund had (as to the whole or a part thereof) been divided in pursuance of subsection (1) of section two of this Act, or that subsection as modified by the Second Schedule to this Act, then if the separate fund is so divided the narrower-range and wider-range parts of the separate fund may be constituted so as either to be equal, or to bear to each other the same proportion as the two corresponding parts of the fund out of which it was so appropriated (the values of those parts of those funds being ascertained as at the time of appropriation), or some intermediate proportion.

[The following is an example. T1 and T2 hold a trust fund worth £10,000 on trust for X for life, with remainder to Y. T1 and T2 divide the fund into two equal parts and some years later decide to make an advancement in favour of Y in the form of a marriage settlement. At that date the narrower-range part of the fund has depreciated to £4,000 and the wider-range part has appreciated to £8,000. The amount to be advanced is £2,000. This sum could be drawn from the two parts of the parent fund either equally or in the proportions 1:2 or in any intermediate proportions.]

*Certain valuations to be conclusive for purposes of division of trust fund*

Section 5.—(1) If for the purposes of section two or four of this Act or the Second Schedule thereto a trustee obtains, from a person reasonably believed by the trustee to be qualified to make it, a valuation in writing of any property, the valuation shall be conclusive in determining whether the division of the trust fund in pursuance of subsection (1) of the said section two, or any transfer or apportionment of property under that section or the said Second Schedule, has been duly made.

(2) The foregoing subsection applies to any such valuation notwithstanding that it is made by a person in the course of his employment as an officer or servant.

*Duty of trustees in choosing investments*

Section 6.—(1) In the exercise of his powers of investment a trustee shall have regard—

(a) to the need for diversification of investments of the trust, in so far as is appropriate to the circumstances of the trust;

(b) to the suitability to the trust of investments of the description of investment proposed and of the investment proposed as an investment of that description.

[In *Learoyd* v. *Whiteley*[77] Lord Watson stated the general equitable position thus " . . . the law requires of a trustee no higher degree of diligence in the execution of his office than a man of ordinary prudence would exercise in the management of his own private affairs. Yet he is not allowed the same discretion in investing the moneys of the trust as if he were a person *sui juris* dealing with his own estate. Business men of ordinary prudence may, and frequently do, select investments which are more or less of a speculative character; but it is the duty of a trustee to confine himself to the class of investments which are permitted by the trust, and likewise to avoid all investments of that class which are attended with hazard. So, so long as he acts in the honest observance of these limitations, the general rule already stated will apply."]

(2) Before exercising any power conferred *by section one* of this Act to invest in a manner specified in Part II or III of the First Schedule to this Act, or before investing in any such manner in the exercise of a power *falling within subsection (2)* of section three of this Act, a trustee shall obtain and consider[78] proper advice on the question whether the investment is satisfactory having regard to the matter mentioned in paragraphs (a) and (b) of the foregoing subsection.

(3) A trustee retaining any investment made in the exercise of such a power as aforesaid shall determine at what intervals the circumstances, and in particular the nature of the investment, make it desirable to obtain such advice as aforesaid, and shall obtain and consider such advice accordingly.

(4) For the purposes of the two foregoing subsections, proper advice is the advice of a person who is reasonably believed by the trustee to be qualified by his ability in and practical experience of financial matters; and such advice may be given by a person notwithstanding that he gives it in the course of his employment as an officer or servant.

(5) A trustee shall not be treated as having complied with subsection (2) or (3) of this section unless the advice was given or has been subsequently confirmed in writing.

(6) Subsections (2) and (3) of this section shall not apply to one of two or more trustees where he is the person giving the advice required by this section to his co-trustee or co-trustees, and shall not apply where powers of a trustee are lawfully exercised by an officer or servant competent under subsection (4) of this section to give proper advice.

---

[77] (1887) 12 App.Cas. 727, 733, and see p. 611, *supra*.
[78] They must exercise their own judgment but in practice it may be difficult for them to justify refusing to follow the advice. Note the italicised words indicating the statutory duties do not apply when exercising special range powers or an express power conferred after the Act to invest in investments authorised by law.

(7) Without prejudice to section eight of the Trustee Act 1925 or section thirty of the Trusts (Scotland) Act 1921 (which relate to valuation, and the proportion of the value to be lent, where a trustee lends on the security of property) the advice required by this section shall not include, in the case of a loan on the security of freehold or leasehold property in England and Wales or Northern Ireland or on heritable security in Scotland, advice on the suitability of the particular loan.

[For section 8 of the Trustee Act 1925, see *infra*, p. 630.]

### Saving for powers of court

Section 15. The enlargement of the investment powers of trustees by this Act shall not lessen any power of a court to confer wider powers of investment in trustees, or affect the extent to which any such power is to be exercised.

[In a series of cases decided shortly after the 1961 Act the courts indicated that they would not confer investment powers wider than those contained in the Act, unless there are special circumstances. However in *British Museum Trustees* v. *Att.-Gen.*,[79] Megarry V.-C. held that this approach should no longer be followed since conditions had changed greatly over the last 20 years as recognised by the reforms proposed by the Law Reform Committee in 1982, though the approach would be revived if a new Act replaced the 1961 Act. Until then the court should be ready to grant suitable applications taking them on their merits].

## FIRST SCHEDULE

## MANNER OF INVESTMENT

## PART I

### NARROWER-RANGE INVESTMENTS NOT REQUIRING ADVICE

1. In Defence Bonds, National Savings Certificates and Ulster Savings Certificates, Ulster Development Bonds, National Development Bonds, British Savings Bonds, National Savings Income Bonds, National Savings Deposit Bonds, National Savings Indexed Income Bonds, National Savings Capital Bonds.

2. In deposits in the National Savings Bank, and deposits in a bank or department thereof certified under subsection (3) of section 9 of the Finance Act 1956.

## PART II

### NARROWER-RANGE INVESTMENTS REQUIRING ADVICE

1. In securities issued by Her Majesty's Government in the United Kingdom, the Government of Northern Ireland or the Government of the Isle of

---

79 [1984] 1 All E.R. 337. See also *Steel* v. *Wellcome Custodian Trustees* [1988] 1 W.L.R. 167.

Man, not being securities falling within Part I of this Schedule and being fixed-interest securities registered in the United Kingdom or the Isle of Man, Treasury Bills or Tax Reserve Certificates or any variable interest securities issued by H.M. Government in the U.K. and registered in the U.K.

2. In any securities the payment of interest on which is guaranteed by Her Majesty's Government in the United Kingdom or the Government of Northern Ireland.

3. In fixed-interest securities issued in the United Kingdom by any public authority or nationalised industry or undertaking in the United Kingdom.

4. In fixed-interest securities issued in the United Kingdom by the government of any overseas territory within the Commonwealth or by any public or local authority within such a territory, being securities registered in the United Kingdom.

References in this paragraph to an overseas territory or to the government of such a territory shall be construed as if they occurred in the Overseas Service Act 1958.

4A. In securities issued in the United Kingdom by the government of an overseas territory within the Commonwealth or by any public or local authority within such a territory, being securities registered in the United Kingdom and in respect of which the rate of interest is variable by reference to one or more of the following:

(*a*) the Bank of England's minimum lending rate;
(*b*) the average rate of discount on allotment on 91 day Treasury Bills;
(*c*) a yield on 91 day Treasury Bills;
(*d*) a London sterling inter-bank offered rate;
(*e*) a London sterling certificate of deposit rate.

5. In fixed-interest securities issued in the United Kingdom by the African Development Bank, the Asian Development Bank, the Caribbean Development Bank, the International Finance Corporation, the International Monetary Fund or by the International Bank for Reconstruction and Development, being securities registered in the United Kingdom [*also* fixed interest securities issued by the Inter-American Development Bank or by the European Economic Community or the European Atomic Energy Community or by the European Investment Bank or by the European Coal and Steel Community].

5A. In securities issued in the U.K. by

(i) the International Bank for Reconstruction and Development or by the European Investment Bank or by the European Coal and Steel Community, being securities registered in the U.K. or

(ii) the Inter-American Development Bank being securities in respect of which the rate of interest is variable by reference to one or more of the following:

(*a*) the Bank of England minimum lending rate;
(*b*) the average rate of discount on 91 day Treasury Bills;
(*c*) a yield on 91 day Treasury Bills;
(*d*) a London sterling inter-bank offered rate;
(*e*) a London sterling certificate of deposit rate.

5B. In securities issued in the U.K. by the African Development Bank, the Asian Development Bank, the Caribbean Development Bank, the European Atomic Energy Community, the EEC, the International Finance Corporation or the IMF being securities registered in the U.K. and in respect of which the interest is variable by reference to one or more of the following:

(*a*)  the average rate of discount on allotment on 91 day Treasury Bills;
(*b*)  a yield on 91 day Treasury Bills;
(*c*)  a London sterling inter-bank offered rate;
(*d*)  a London sterling certificate of deposit rate.

6. In debentures issued in the United Kingdom by a company incorporated in the United Kingdom, being debentures registered in the United Kingdom.

7. In stock of the Bank of Ireland and in Bank of Ireland 7 per cent. Loan Stock 1986/1991.

8. In debentures issued by the Agricultural Mortgage Corporation Limited or the Scottish Agricultural Securities Corporation Limited.

9. In loans to any authority to which this paragraph applies charged on all or any of the revenues of the authority or on a fund into which all or any of those revenues are payable, in any fixed-interest securities issued in the United Kingdom by any such authority for the purpose of borrowing money so charged, and in deposits with any such authority by way of temporary loan made on the giving of a receipt for the loan by the treasurer or other similar officer of the authority and on the giving of an undertaking by the authority that, if requested to charge the loan as aforesaid, it will either comply with the request or repay the loan.

This paragraph applies to the following authorities, that is to say:

(*a*)  any local authority in the United Kingdom;
(*b*)  any authority all the members of which are appointed or elected by one or more local authorities in the United Kingdom;
(*c*)  any authority the majority of the members of which are appointed or elected by one or more local authorities in the United Kingdom, being an authority which by virtue of any enactment has power to issue a precept to a local authority in England and Wales, or a requisition to a local authority in Scotland, or to the expenses of which, by virtue of any enactment, a local authority in the United Kingdom is or can be required to contribute;
(*d*)  the Receiver for the Metropolitan Police District or a combined police authority (within the meaning of the Police Act 1946);
(*e*)  the Belfast City and District Water Commissioners;
(*f*)  the Great Ouse Water Authority;
(*g*)  any district council in Northern Ireland.
(*h*)  the Inner London Education Authority;
(*i*)  any residuary body established by section 57 of the Local Government Act 1985.

9A. In any securities issued in the U.K. by any authority to which paragraph 9 applies for the purpose of borrowing money charged on all or any of the revenues of the authority or on a fund into which all or any of those revenues are payable and being securities in respect of which the rate of interest is variable by reference to one or more of the following:

(*a*)  the Bank of England's minimum lending rate;
(*b*)  the average rate of discount on allotment of 91 day Treasury Bills;
(*c*)  a yield on 91 day Treasury Bills;
(*d*)  a London sterling inter-bank offered rate;
(*e*)  a London sterling certificate of deposit rate.

10. In debentures or in the guaranteed or preference stock of any incorporated company, being statutory water undertakers within the meaning of the

Water Act 1945, or any corresponding enactment in force in Northern Ireland, and having during each of the ten years immediately preceding the calendar year in which the investment was made paid a dividend of not less than three and a half per cent. on its ordinary shares.

10A. In any units, or other shares of the investments subject to the trusts of a unit trust scheme which, at the time of investment, is an authorised unit trust, within the meaning of subsection (1) of section 468 of the Income and Corporation Taxes Act 1988, in relation to which that subsection does not, by virtue of subsection (5) of that section, apply [*i.e.* gilt-edged unit trusts].

12. In deposits with a building society within the meaning of the Building Societies Act 1986.

13. In mortgages of freehold property in England and Wales or Northern Ireland and of leasehold property in those countries of which the unexpired term at the time of investment is not less than sixty years, and in loans on heritable security in Scotland.

14. In perpetual rent-charges charged on land in England and Wales or Northern Ireland and fee-farm rents (not being rent-charges) issuing out of such land, and in feu-duties or ground annuals in Scotland.

15. In certificates of Tax Deposit.

## PART III

### WIDER-RANGE INVESTMENTS

1. In any securities issued in the United Kingdom by a company incorporated in the United Kingdom, being securities registered in the United Kingdom and not being securities falling within Part II of this Schedule.

2. In shares in a building society within the meaning of the Building Societies Act 1986.

3. In any units of an authorised unit trust scheme within the meaning of the Financial Services Act 1986.

## PART IV

### SUPPLEMENTAL

1. The securities mentioned in Parts I to III of this Schedule do not include any securities where the holder can be required to accept repayment of the principal, or the payment of any interest, otherwise than in sterling.

2. The securities mentioned in paragraphs 1 to 8 of Part II, other than Treasury Bills or Tax Reserve Certificates, securities issued before the passing of this Act by the Government of the Isle of Man, securities falling within paragraph 4 of the said Part II issued before the passing of this Act or securities falling within paragraph 9 of that Part, and the securities mentioned in paragraph 1 of Part III of the Schedule do not include—

(a) securities the price of which is not quoted on a recognised investment exchange within the meaning of the Financial Services Act 1986;

(b) shares or debenture stock not fully paid up (except shares or debenture stock which by the terms of issue are required to be fully paid up within nine months of the date of issue).

3. The securities mentioned in paragraph 6 of Part II and paragraph 1 of Part III of this Schedule do not include—

(a) shares or debentures of an incorporated company of which the total issued and paid up share capital is less than one million pounds;

(b) shares or debentures of an incorporated company which has not in each of the five years immediately preceding the calendar year in which the investment is made paid a dividend on all the shares issued by the company, excluding any shares issued after the dividend was declared and any shares which by their terms of issue did not rank for the dividend for that year.

For the purposes of sub-paragraph (b) of this paragraph a company formed—

(i) to take over the business of another company or other companies,

(ii) or to acquire the securities of, or control of, another company or other companies,

or for either of those purposes and for other purposes shall be deemed to have paid a dividend as mentioned in that sub-paragraph in any year in which such a dividend has been paid by the other company or all the other companies, as the case may be.

4. In this Schedule, unless the context otherwise requires, the following expressions have the meanings hereby respectively assigned to them, that is to say—

"debenture" includes debenture stock and bonds, whether constituting a charge on assets or not, and loan stock or notes;

"enactment" includes an enactment of the Parliament of Northern Ireland;

"fixed-interest securities" means securities which under their terms of issue bear a fixed rate of interest;

"local authority" in relation to the United Kingdom, means any of the following authorities—

(a) in England and Wales, the council of a county, a borough, an urban or rural district or a parish, the Common council of the City of London the Greater London Council and the Council of the Isles of Scilly;

(b) in Scotland, a local authority within the meaning of the Local Government (Scotland) Act 1947;

"securities" includes shares, debentures, Treasury Bills and Tax Reserve Certificates;

"share" includes stock;

"Treasury Bills" includes Exchequer bills and other bills issued by Her Majesty's Government in the United Kingdom and Northern Ireland Treasury Bills.

## SECOND SCHEDULE

## MODIFICATION OF S.2 IN RELATION TO PROPERTY FALLING WITHIN s.3(3)

1. In this Schedule "special-range property" means property falling within subsection (3) of section three of this Act.

2.—(1) Where a trust fund includes special-range property, subsection (1) of section two of this Act shall have effect as if references to the trust fund were references to so much thereof as does not consist of special-range property, and the special-range property shall be carried to a separate part of the fund.

(2) Any property which—

(*a*) being property belonging to the narrower-range or wider-range part of a trust fund, is converted into special-range property, or

(*b*) being special-range property, accrues to a trust fund after the division of the fund or part thereof in pursuance of subsection (1) of section two of this Act or of that subsection as modified by sub-paragraph (1) of this paragraph,

shall be carried to such a separate part of the fund as aforesaid; and subsections (2) and (3) of the said section two shall have effect subject to this sub-paragraph.

3. Where property carried to such a separate part as aforesaid is converted into property other than special-range property,—

(*a*) it shall be transferred to the narrower-range part of the fund or the wider-range part of the fund or apportioned between them, and

(*b*) any transfer of property from one of those parts to the other shall be made which is necessary to secure that the value of each of those parts of the fund is increased by the same amount.

## THIRD SCHEDULE

### PROVISIONS SUPPLEMENTARY TO S.3(4)

1. Where in a case falling within subsection (4) of section three of this Act, property belonging to the narrower-range part of a trust fund—

(*a*) is invested otherwise than in a narrower-range investment, or

(*b*) being so invested, is retained and not transferred or as soon as may be reinvested as mentioned in subsection (2) of section two of this Act,

then, so long as the property continues so invested and comprised in the narrow-range part of the fund, section one of this Act shall not authorise the making or retention of any wider-range investment.

2. Section four of the Trustee Act 1925 or section thirty-three of the Trusts (Scotland) Act 1921 (which relieve a trustee from liability for retaining an investment which has ceased to be authorised) shall not apply where an investment ceases to be authorised in consequence of the foregoing paragraph.

## IV. INVESTMENT IN MORTGAGES OF LAND

For the power, see paragraph 13 of Part II of Schedule 1 to the Trustee Investments Act 1961; *supra*, p. 627. It is doubtful whether this power has swept away the old restrictions prohibiting either a second, an equitable or a contributory mortgage so a prudent trustee should refuse to advance money on such types of mortgage. It would seem that a simple power to invest upon mortgage is not taken at its face value by courts of equity.[80]

---

[80] Underhill & Hayton, p. 533 and Law Reform Committee 1982 Cmnd. 8733, para. 3–12.

## The Trustee Act 1925

*Loans and investments by trustees not chargeable as breaches of trust*

Section 8.[81]—(1) A trustee lending money on the security of any property on which he can properly lend[82] shall not be chargeable with breach of trust by reason only of the proportion borne by the amount of the loan to the value of the property at the time when the loan was made, if it appears to the court—

  (*a*)  that in making the loan the trustee was acting upon a report as to the value of the property made by a person whom he reasonably believed to be an able practical surveyor or valuer instructed and employed independently of any owner of the property, whether such surveyor or valuer carried on business in the locality where the property is situate or elsewhere; and

  (*b*)  that the amount of the loan does not exceed two third parts of the value of the property as stated in the report; and

  (*c*)  that the loan was made under the advice of the surveyor or valuer expressed in the report.

(2) A trustee lending money on the security of any leasehold property shall not be chargeable with breach of trust only upon the ground that in making such loan he dispensed either wholly or partly with the production or investigation of the lessor's title.

(3) A trustee shall not be chargeable with breach of trust only upon the ground that in effecting the purchase, or in lending money upon the security, of any property he has accepted a shorter title than the title which a purchaser is, in the absence of a special contract, entitled to require, if in the opinion of the court the title accepted be such as a person acting with prudence and caution would have accepted.

(4) This section applies to transfers of existing securities as well as to new securities and to investments made before as well as after the commencement of this Act.

*Liability for loss by reason of improper investment*

Section 9.[83]—(1) Where a trustee improperly advances trust money on a mortgage security which would at the time of the investment be a proper investment in all respects for a smaller sum than is actually advanced thereon, the security shall be deemed an authorised investment for the smaller sum, and the trustee shall only be liable to make good the sum advanced in excess thereof with interest.

(2) This section applies to investments made before as well as after the commencement of this Act.

## RE SOLOMON

Chancery Division [1912] 1 Ch. 261

---

[81] Re-enacting the Trustee Act 1893, s.8, which re-enacted the Trustee Act 1888, s.4. This section is not affected by the Trustee Investment Act 1961: see s.6(7), *supra*, p. 624.

[82] On a sale of trust property trustees may leave on legal mortgage not more than two-thirds of the purchase price without having first obtained a report and without being liable for any loss incurred by reason only of the security being insufficient at the date of the legal mortgage: Trustee Act 1925, s.10.

[83] Re-enacting the Trustee Act 1893, s.9, which re-enacted the Trustee Act 1888, s.5. In *Re Walker* (1890) 59 L.J.Ch. 386 Kekewich J. emphasised that the trustee must first establish the propriety of the investment independently of value before being able to take advantage of s.9 for the impropriety consisting in the amount invested.

The judgment of Warrington J. brings out the following points in relation to section 8 of the Trustee Act 1925.

(1) "By reason only of the proportion borne by the amount of the loan to the value of the property." As to this, Warrington J. said[84]: "Translated into simpler language, that means and means only, it seems to me, that they shall not be chargeable by reason only of their investing on an insufficient security."

(2) "Instructed and employed independently of any owner of the property." As to this, Warrington J. said[85]: "What is meant by 'instructed and employed independently of any owner of the property'? I think it means this: that the relation existing between employer and employed must exist as between the trustees and the valuer, and between them only—that the valuer must be entitled to look for his remuneration to the person who employs him, and, on the other hand, must be responsible to that person and to that person only for the due performance of his duty as valuer. When you have that, he is instructed and employed by the trustee, and he is instructed and employed by him independently of the owner."[86]

(3) "That the loan was made under the advice of the surveyor or valuer expressed in the report." The learned judge said[87]: "It is said that the condition has not been complied with because the surveyor and valuer in this case did not in so many words say 'I advise the trustees to advance so much money.' In my opinion, to so hold would be to cast away the substance for the shadow." The condition is satisfied if the surveyor indicates that the property is a sufficient security for the amount advanced.

(4) The business of taking into account the circumstances which affect the value of the property is the business of the valuer. "I agree," said Warrington J.,[88] "with what Parker J. said in *Shaw* v. *Cates*,[89] that it is the business of the expert to determine what are the facts and circumstances connected with the property which it is necessary for him to take into account in arriving at his valuation, and it will be properly assumed that, when the expert is directed to report on the value of the property, he will discover for himself those circumstances which bear on its value and will make his valuation in accordance with those circumstances."

(5) It is the valuer's duty to advise the trustee not only as to the actual value of the property, but also as to what proportion of that value may with safety be advanced.[90]

Warrington J. also questions[91] whether the valuer must *in fact* be instructed and employed independently of any owner of the property, or whether it is sufficient that the trustee reasonably believed him to be so instructed and employed. Kekewich J. had held, however, in *Re Walker*,[92] and had considered *obiter* in *Re Somerset*,[93] that the surveyor or valuer must in fact be instructed and employed independently.

If a trustee does not comply with all the requirements of the section, the effect is that he cannot claim the relief it affords; he is not thereby prevented

---

[84] [1912] 1 Ch. 261, 279.
[85] *Ibid.* 281.
[86] See also *Smith* v. *Stoneham* [1886] W.N. 178.
[87] [1912] 1 Ch. 261, 283.
[88] *Ibid.* 274.
[89] [1909] 1 Ch. 389, 398.
[90] [1912] 1 Ch. 261, 282.
[91] *Ibid.* 281. Similarly *Re Stuart* [1897] 2 Ch. 583, 592; *Shaw* v. *Cates* [1909] 1 Ch. 389, 403.
[92] (1890) 62 L.T. 449, 452.
[93] [1894] 1 Ch. 231, 253.

from falling back on the general law or deprived of the benefit of some other
statutory provision like section 9.[94] "Section 8," observed Eve J. in *Palmer* v.
*Emerson*,[95] "is really a relieving section, and not a section which imposes
further obligations upon trustees." The section does, however, in the case of
investment of trust funds on mortgage, constitute a standard by which
reasonable conduct is to be judged.[96]

## V. INVESTMENTS IN PURCHASE OF LAND

There is no power to invest in land unless expressly authorised by the
trust instrument or the settlement is of land under the Settled Land
Act or held on trust for sale. An express power to invest in land does
not authorise the purchase of a house for the occupation of a
beneficiary since "investment" requires income-yielding property to be
purchased.[97]

### The Settled Land Act 1925

Section 73.—(1) Capital money arising under this Act, subject to payment of
claims properly payable thereout and to the application thereof for any special
authorised object for which the capital money was raised, shall, when received,
be invested or otherwise applied[98] wholly in one, or partly in one and partly in
another or others, of the following modes (namely): . . .

(xi) In purchase of land in fee simple, or of leasehold land held for sixty
years or more unexpired at the time of purchase, subject or not to any
exception or reservation of or in respect of mines or minerals therein,
or of or in respect of rights or powers relative to the working of mines
therein, or in other land.

### The Law of Property Act 1925

Section 28.—(1) Trustees for sale shall, in relation to land or to manorial
incidents and to the proceeds of sale, have all the powers of a tenant for life
and the trustees of a settlement under the Settled Land Act 1925, including in
relation to the land the powers of management conferred by that Act during a
minority; and (subject to any express trust to the contrary) all capital money
arising under the said powers shall, unless paid or applied for any purpose
authorised by the Settled Land Act 1925, be applicable in the same manner as
if the money represented proceeds of sale arising under the trust for sale.

All land required under this subsection shall be conveyed to the trustees on
trust for sale.

The powers conferred by this subsection shall be exercised with such
consents (if any) as would have been required on a sale under the trust for
sale, and when exercised shall operate to overreach any equitable interests or
powers which are by virtue of this Act or otherwise made to attach to the net
proceeds of sale as if created by a trust affecting those proceeds.

---

94 See *Re Dive* [1909] 1 Ch. 328, 342, *Shaw* v. *Cates* [1909] 1 Ch. 389.
95 [1911] 1 Ch. 758, 769.
96 *Re Stuart* [1897] 2 Ch. 583.
97 *Re Power's W.T.* [1947] Ch. 572.
98 At the direction of the tenant for life who can direct that he has rent-free occupation: S.L.A. 1925,
s.75(2). *Re Wellsted's W.T.* [1949] Ch. 296.

[Trustees for sale of land have power to invest the proceeds of sale in the purchase of other land provided they have not ceased to be trustees for sale by selling all their land: *Re Wakeman*.[99] Proceeds of sale of land remain such so long as they can be traced. Thus, if trustees hold Blackacre on trust for sale and sell part of it for £5,000, which they invest in shares, they can realise the shares and reinvest in the purchase of land: *Re Wellsted's W.T.*[1]]

## VI. REFORM PROPOSED BY LAW REFORM COMMITTEE (1982 Cmnd. 8733)

### Powers and Duties of Investment (paragraphs 3.1–3.25)

(a) *Investment in Land* (paragraphs 3.1–3.14)

6. Trustees' powers to purchase freehold and leasehold land should be widened as follows:—

   (i) all trustees should have the power to buy freehold property as an investment, subject to their first obtaining favourable professional advice; (paragraph 3.2)
   (ii) all trustees should be empowered to invest in leasehold land, provided that appropriate advice is taken; (paragraph 3.3)
   (iii) the absolute prohibition on the purchase of leaseholds with less than sixty years to run should be removed; (paragraph 3.4)
   (iv) the decision in *re Power* should be reversed and a new statutory power introduced enabling trustees to purchase a residence for occupation by the person entitled to the income on the moneys laid out in the purchase or eligible to have it applied for his benefit; (paragraph 3.5)

7. Trustees should be empowered to make purchases under recommendation 6(iv) above on mortgage. (paragraph 3.11)

8. Trustees' powers to invest in mortgages should be widened so as to permit them to invest in second mortgages. (paragraphs 3.12–3.13)

9. The 10-year limit on the exercise of options should be abolished and trustees should be empowered to stipulate that the purchase price may be calculated by reference to the market value of the property at the time of the exercise of the option. (paragraph 3.14)

(b) *The Trustee Investments Act 1961* (paragraphs 3.15–3.25)

10. The statutory powers contained in the Trustee Investments Act 1961 are out of date and ought now to be revised. We recommend that the 1961 Act be repealed and the following new powers be conferred upon trustees:—

   (i) investments should be divided into those which can be made without advice and those which can be made only with advice; (paragraph 3.21)
   (ii) the former category should comprise those investments presently known as narrower-range securities and listed in Parts I and II of the 1961 Act and also unit trusts and investment trusts, as defined in section 359 of the Income and Corporation Taxes Act 1970; (paragraph 3.21)

---

[99] [1945] Ch. 177. Whether or not trustees ceased to be trustees for sale of land within s.205(1) (xxix) ("trustees for sale" means the persons holding land on trust for sale) upon sale of all trust land was expressly reserved by Cohen L.J. in *Re Wellsted's W.T.* [1949] Ch. 296, 319.
[1] [1949] Ch. 296, 305, 315 (C.A.).

   (iii)  the latter category should comprise any other investment quoted on the English Stock Exchange; (paragraph 3.21)

   (iv)  trustees should be free to invest in such proportions as they choose; (paragraph 3.21)

   (v)  the provisions on advice presently contained in section 6 of the 1961 Act should be retained; (paragraph 3.22)

   (vi)  express reference should be made in the new statutory provision to the duty of trustees to maintain a balance between income and capital so as to protect all those interested under the trust fund; (paragraph 3.22)

  (vii)  the requirement in section 6(1)(*a*) of the 1961 Act which compels trustees to have regard to the need for diversification of investments in so far as is appropriate to the circumstances of the trust is sufficient and further restrictions on the trustees' discretion are not required; (paragraph 3.23)

 (viii)  investments in foreign securities should not be made unless expressly authorised by the trust instrument; (paragraph 3.24)

  (ix)  trustees should continue to be able to apply to the court under section 57 of the Trustee Act 1925 to make otherwise unauthorised investments; (paragraph 3.25)

   (x)  since section 57 is concerned only with the authorisation of specific dealings trustees should be entitled to make an application under the Variation of Trusts Act to ask the court to widen their investment powers generally.

## VII. Interpretation of Investment Clauses

The modern approach to interpreting investment clauses appears from *Re Harari's S.T., infra*, p. 635 applied in *Re Peczenik's Settlement*.[2] The court will not be astute to limit the express clause by implying some limitation to statutory authorised investments if the natural and proper meaning of the clause allows for wider investment powers. However "investment" is treated as requiring the purchase of property to produce some income yield so as not to cover the purchase of a house with vacant possession for occupation by beneficiaries.[3] It takes a very clear express provision to authorise lending merely on the security of a personal promise of the borrower to repay, since this is no security at all.[4] Furthermore, in the absence of a clear express provision the trustees cannot "gear" up the trust fund by borrowing on the security of trust property in order to acquire further property (*e.g.* land) for the trust.[5] The trustees cannot delegate their power of

---

[2] [1964] 1 W.L.R. 720. See also *Re Douglas' W.T.* [1959] 1 W.L.R. 1212: "securities" held to include stocks and shares and not confined to secured investments.

[3] *Re Power's W.T.* [1947] Ch. 576; 63 L.Q.R. 421 (R.E.M.): "All moneys requiring to be invested may be invested by the trustee in any manner which he may in his absolute discretion think fit in all respects as if he were the sole beneficial owner of such moneys including the purchase of freehold property in England and Wales." *Quaere* would the result have been different if the clause had authorised "investment or other application of the money whether by way of investment or not"? The conferment of the power to act as if he were sole beneficial owner does not exempt the trustee from the duty of care required by *Learoyd* v. *Whiteley* (1887) 12 App.Cas. 727, and Trustee Investments Act 1961, s.6(1). *cf. Re Maberly* (1886) 33 Ch.D. 455, 458, *Bartlett* v. *Barclays Bank Trust Co.* [1980] 1 All E.R. 139, 154.

[4] [1934] A.C. 529.

[5] *Re Suenson-Taylor's S.T.* [1974] 1 W.L.R. 1280.

investment to a fund manager unless expressly authorised by the trust instrument or under the Powers of Attorney Act 1971 amendment of the Trustee Act 1925, s.25, *infra*, p. 639.[6]

### RE HARARI'S SETTLEMENT TRUSTS

Chancery Division [1949] 1 All E.R. 430; [1949] W.N. 79.

By a settlement dated June 16, 1938, the settlor, Sir Victor Harari, Pasha, transferred certain securities, none of them on the Trustee List, to trustees and directed: "The trustees shall hold the said investments so transferred to them as aforesaid upon trust that they may either allow the same to remain in their present state of investment so long as the trustees may think fit or may at any time or times with the consent of the daughter [a beneficiary under the trust] realise the said investments or any of them or any part thereof respectively and shall with the like consent invest the money produced thereby and also all capital moneys which may be or become subject to the trusts of this settlement in the names or under the control of the trustees in or upon such investments as to them may seem fit with power with such consent to vary or transpose any investments for or into others . . . "

JENKINS J.: "I have to decide whether, on the true construction of the few words in the settlement referring to investment, the trustees have an unrestricted discretion to invest in such investments as they think fit, whether they are or are not of a kind authorised by law for the investment of trust funds, or whether such discretion as they have should be construed as limited in its operation to the trustee range of investments. . . .

"The question turns primarily on the meaning to be attached to the words 'in or upon such investments as to them may seem fit.' Prima facie those words mean what they say—that the trustees are not to be limited in any way by any statutory range of investments, but can invest in any investment which they may select as seeming to them a fit one for the money subject to the trusts of the settlement. There is, however, a good deal of authority, which must be borne in mind, to the effect that investment clauses should be strictly construed and should not be construed as authorising investments outside the trustee range unless they clearly and unambiguously indicate an intention to that effect. [He referred to these authorities and continued.]

"That, I think, is a representative collection of the authorities bearing on this topic, and, having given them the best consideration I can, it seems to me that I am left free to construe this settlement according to what I consider to be the natural and proper meaning of the words used in their context, and, so construing the words 'in or upon such investments as to them may seem fit,' I see no justification for implying any restriction. I think the trustees have power, under the plain meaning of those words, to invest in any investments which, to adopt Kekewich J.'s observation, they 'honestly think' are desirable investments for the investment of moneys subject to the trusts of the settlement. To hold otherwise would really be to read words into the settlement which are not there. The wide construction which the words themselves are, in my view, sufficient to bear is, I think, to some extent,

---

[6] See Section 4, *infra*. It imposes automatic vicarious liability. Hence see clause 7(1) of the Trust Precedent p. 20, *supra*.

supported by the fact that the investments brought in, in the first place, are non-trustee investments, and also to some small extent by the reference in paragraph 2 [of the settlement] to 'investment money or property representing' the trust fund. There is nothing in those words that one can say is really inconsistent with a limitation on the range of investment to trustee investments, but there is, perhaps, more likelihood of something which in common parlance would be described as 'property' rather than an 'investment' coming into the hands of the trustees in the course of exercising their powers of investment if the range is the unrestricted one rather than the narrow one. The real ground, however, for my decision is the plain and ordinary meaning of the words 'in or upon such investments as to them may seem fit.' Having found nothing in the authorities to constrain me to construe those words otherwise than in accordance with their plain meaning, that is the meaning I propose to place on them.

"For these reasons, I will declare that the power given by the settlement in question to the trustees to invest trust moneys, with the consent therein mentioned, in or upon such investments as to them may seem fit, with power to vary or transpose any investments for or into others, enables investments to be made in any investments which seem fit to the trustees, whether or not they are investments authorised by law for the investment of trust funds." *Declaration accordingly*.

### Section 4. Delegation by a Trustee

#### (a) *Employment of agents to do specified acts*

The general rule of equity is *delegatus non potest delegare*. "I must observe," said Langdale M.R. in *Turner* v. *Corney*[7] "that trustees who take on themselves the management of property for the benefit of others have no right to shift their duty on other persons; and if they employ an agent, they remain subject to the responsibility towards their *cestuis que trust*, for whom they have undertaken the duty" so that they were liable for the acts of such agents. The trustee was, however, justified in delegating if, in the circumstances, delegation was either reasonably necessary or in the ordinary course of affairs: *Ex p. Belchier*.[8] But even in cases where the employment of an agent to do specific acts was justified, the trustee had to be prudent in his selection and supervision of his agent. He had to exercise the care of a reasonable man of business in his choice of the agent and he could not employ an agent to do an act outside the scope of the agent's business: *Fry* v. *Tapson*,[9] *Rowland* v. *Witherden*.[10] If these conditions were satisfied the trustee would not be responsible for a loss arising through the default of the agent, provided he exercised a proper supervision over the agent: *Matthews* v. *Brise*.[11] In this respect an express or

---

[7] (1841) 5 Beav. 515, 517.
[8] (1754) Amb. 218, applied in *Speight* v. *Gaunt* (1883) 22 Ch.D. 727, 9 App.Cas. 1.
[9] (1884) 28 Ch.D. 268.
[10] *Ibid.*
[11] (1845) 10 Jur.(O.S.) 105.

statutory provision[12] authorising a wide use of agents in ministerial matters and exempting a trustee from liability for loss caused by the acts or defaults of an agent unless the loss occurred through the trustee's 'wilful default' did not relieve the trustee of his duty to show the care of the reasonable man of business both in the selection and in the supervision of agents: *Re Brier.*[13] A trustee was thus only liable for his own acts or defaults, *e.g.* negligent selection, or negligent supervision. There was no automatic vicarious liability for the agent's acts or defaults in those cases where delegation to agents was permissible.

*Re Vickery, infra,* p. 645 is a decision to the effect that section 23(1) of the Trustee Act 1925, *infra,* has reversed the old law of delegation. Whereas formerly a trustee could not delegate unless it was either reasonably necessary or in the ordinary course of affairs, today he can delegate whether there is any necessity for it or not, even, it seems, where he personally could have effected the transaction himself. The Law Reform Committee would like to limit this so that a trustee should only be entitled to such charges and expenses of delegation as are reasonably incurred taking into account the trustee's knowledge, qualifications and experience and the level of remuneration received by him.[14]

In so far as *Re Vickery* purports to decide more than this, and, in particular, that a trustee is no longer liable if he fails to exercise any supervision over the acts of his agents, it has been severely criticised, notably by Professor Gareth Jones.[15]

In *Re Lucking's Will Trusts,*[16] Cross J. (as he then was) *obiter* treated *Re Vickery* as only deciding (a) that section 23(1) empowered the trustee's appointment of the solicitor as agent and (b) that the trustee would be excused liability by virtue of section 30(1) unless guilty of "wilful default" which he was not in the circumstances. So restricted, *Re Vickery* is unexceptional except for its interpretation of "wilful default," uncritically accepted by Cross J. In *Re Lucking's Will Trusts* where a company of which the trustee was a director with a substantial interest, honestly appointed the trustee's old army friend, Lt.-Col. Dewar O.B.E., to manage the company's business. Since the manager was appointed by the company and not by the trustees section 23(1) and section 30(1) were inapplicable. On *Speight* v. *Gaunt*[17] principles the trustee was liable in the events that happened for failing to supervise the manager properly.

Section 30(1) specifically excuses a trustee for losses of moneys or securities deposited with agents unless the loss happened through the

---

[12] *Underwood* v. *Stevens* (1816) 1 Mer. 712; s.30(1) of the Trustee Act 1925, replacing s.24 of the Trustee Act 1893, replacing s.31 of the Law of Property Amendment Act 1859.

[13] (1884) 26 Ch.D. 238, 243 (*per* Lord Selborne L.C.). Also *Re Chapman* [1896] 2 Ch. 763, 776, *per* Lindley L.J., "Wilful default which includes want of ordinary prudence on the part of the trustees must be proved"; and in *Speight* v. *Gaunt* (1883) 9 App.Cas. 1, 13–15, 22–23 the Lords treated wilful default as including want of ordinary prudence.

[14] 1982 Cmnd. 8733, para. 4.6. A trustee will thus have to pay for his laziness.

[15] (1959) 22 M.L.R. 381; see also J. E. Stannard [1979] Conv. 345.

[16] [1968] 1 W.L.R. 866.

[17] (1883) 9 App.Cas. 1, p. 640, *infra.*

trustee's own wilful default. "Wilful default" exemption clauses in earlier express trust provisions or in the statutory predecessors to section 30(1) had been strictly interpreted against trustees as including not just intentional or reckless breach of duty but also want of ordinary prudence on the part of the trustees.[18] Section 30(1) should have been similarly interpreted though Maughan J. in *Re Vickery* utilised the meaning of "wilful default" in company law cases for protecting directors[19] to treat "wilful default" in section 30(1) as meaning just intentional or reckless breach of duty. These company law cases were not cited to him by counsel but were discovered by his own researches over the Christmas vacation and he gave the defendant's counsel no opportunity to deal with this before delivering judgment. This may well be because in all the circumstances the defendant did not seem to have failed to exercise ordinary prudence in his supervision of the solicitor-agent.

Section 23(1) allows trustees to use and pay agents for specific acts whenever they wish and states they are not to be responsible for an agent's defaults "if employed in good faith." There must be a presumption that an honest appointment of an agent cannot exempt the trustee from his traditional personal duty to exercise common prudence in the *selection* of an agent within the scope of his expertise and in the *supervision* thereafter of the agent unless very clear words are used. Can this personal duty not be left untouched on the basis that the final part of section 23(1) was added to emphasise that the *benefit* of the revolutionary wide statutory power of appointment of agents was not to be counterbalanced by *burdening* the trustee with automatic vicarious liability for agents appointed in good faith?[20] The trustee remains personally liable for his *own* acts, neglects and defaults if not exhibiting ordinary prudence, and under section 30(1) he is not liable for *agents'* acts, etc., with regard to moneys or securities in their possession unless himself guilty of "wilful default" which should include want of ordinary prudence, *e.g.* in leaving the agents in possession for too long. The Law Reform Committee propose that the

---

18 *Underwood* v. *Stevens* (1816) 1 Mer. 712; *Re Brier* (1884) 26 Ch.D. 238, 243; *Re Chapman* [1896] 2 Ch. 763, 776, *Speight* v. *Gaunt* (1883) 9 App.Cas. 1, 13–15, 22–23. A trustee may still be able to be relieved from liability under the Trustee Act 1925, s.61, *infra*, p. 780.

19 *Re City Equitable Fire Insurance* [1925] Ch. 407, 439; *cf. Re Munton* [1927] 1 Ch. 262, 274. See Prof. G. H. Jones's views pp. 770–772, *infra.* J. E. Stannard [1979] Conv. 345 also emphasises the difference between the technical equitable meaning of wilful default as including failure to do what is reasonable and the contractual common-law meaning where the parties are taken to intend that "wilful default" means intentional misconduct. In *Bartlett* v. *Barclays Bank Trust Co. (No. 2)* [1980] 2 All E.R. 92, 97 Brightman L.J. said that wilful default covers "a passive breach of trust, an omission to do something which, as a prudent trustee, he ought to have done."

20 This reflects the equitable principles manifested in *Speight* v. *Gaunt* (1883) 9 App.Cas. 1, 4; (1883) 22 Ch.D. 727, 762, that a trustee is not automatically vicariously liable for agents appointed in good faith in those circumstances where equity allowed such appointments. If s.23(1) provided an umbrella even for honest fools then ss.23(2) and (3) are unnecessary and s.30(1) with the traditional equitable meaning of "wilful default" would be inconsistent with s.23(1). If one overlooks the historical development of sections 23 and 30 it is too easy to take the simple literal view that a s.23 appointment in good faith confers complete exemption from liability (*cf.* ss.15 and 22(1)) as assumed without argument by Hoffmann J. in *Steel* v. *Wellcome Custodian Trustees Ltd.* [1988] 1 W.L.R. 167, 174.

final clause of section 23(1) should be replaced by a provision enabling a trustee to escape liability for the default of his agent only *where it was reasonable for him to employ an agent*, where he has taken reasonable steps to ensure that the agent is competent and to ensure that the agent's work has been done competently: Cmnd. 8733. para. 4.11. The italicised words seem unjustifiable.[21]

(b) *Delegation of discretions enabling delegates to decide what to do*

Discretions may now be delegated under section 23(2) (for things to be done outside the United Kingdom) and under section 25 as substantially amended by section 9 of the Powers of Attorney Act 1971 (allowing a general power to delegate for a year whereas previously it was dependent on the trustee leaving the United Kingdom for more than one month).[22] A delegate to whom a trustee has delegated his discretions under section 25 is the *alter ego* of the trustee and will be entitled to attend meetings of the trustees. It seems that he will not be entitled to remuneration unless trustees are authorised to be remunerated by the trust instrument. Whereas under section 25(5) a trustee is automatically vicariously liable for the acts or defaults of his agent a trustee's liability is personal only under section 23(2). In the former case relief under section 61 may be a serious possibility.

Under section 29 of the Law of Property Act 1925 trustees for sale of land may revocably in writing delegate the powers of leasing, accepting surrenders of leases and management to any person of full age beneficially entitled in possession to the net rents and profits.[23] By section 29(3) the trustees are under no automatic vicarious liability for the beneficiary's acts or defaults: their personal liability, however, remains, *e.g.* if they do not revoke the delegation when it has become obvious that the beneficiary is completely unfitted to exercise the powers revocably delegated to him.

(c) *Delegation of investment decisions*

Trustees can delegate their investment decisions for a year[24] at a time under section 25 to anyone other than the only other co-trustee of the delegating trustee. Trustees thus cannot delegate their decisions to one

---

[21] C. T. Emery (1983) 133 New L.J. 1096.

[22] The Law Reform Committee propose that the section should state that trustees are entitled to be allowed any expenses reasonably incurred in remunerating a delegate under s.25: Cmnd. 8733, para. 4.19. Trustees cannot delegate power to execute a conveyance or transfer of land by general power of attorney under Powers of Attorney Act 1971, s.10(1): see s.10(2) and *Walia* v. *Naughton* [1985] 1 W.L.R. 1115.

[23] Such a person may obtain the court's assistance under the Law of Property Act 1925, s.30, to compel a delegation.

[24] At face value Enduring Powers of Attorney Act 1985, s.3(3) allows the attorney to take over all his donor's trusteeships without limit of time. This would be odd when s.2(8) of the 1985 Act expressly provides that a power of attorney delegating trustees' functions under s.25 of the Trustee Act cannot be an enduring power under the 1985 Act. The subsection was introduced to deal with *Walia* v. *Michael Naughton Ltd.* [1985] 1 W.L.R. 1115 and the situation where A and B (or A) hold property like a house for A and B as co-owners and not for persons with successive (as opposed to concurrent) interests.

of their number alone, unless of course the trust instrument specifically authorises this. A well-drafted trust instrument should authorise the trustees to delegate investment management to a discretionary port-folio manager upon the same terms as if they were themselves absolutely beneficially entitled to the trust fund. Otherwise, trustees have problems in delegating investment management and in the terms of the Customer Agreement with their portfolio manager[25]: see p. 647, *infra*. In selecting a discretionary portfolio manager to fulfil their rôle and in agreeing the terms of his appointment it seems likely that the trustees need to show as much care as a prudent man of business would take in appointing a manager of a trust fund for persons for whom he feels morally obliged to provide.[26]

## SPEIGHT v. GAUNT

Court of Appeal (1883) 22 Ch.D. 727 (Jessel M.R., Lindley and Bowen L.JJ.) affirmed, 9 App.Cas. 1; 53 L.J.Ch. 419; 50 L.T. 330; (Earl of Selborne L.C., Lords Blackburn, Watson and Fitzgerald)

The defendant trustee employed a broker (Mr. Cooke) for the purpose of investing £15,000 of trust funds in corporation stocks. Cooke (who was chosen as the broker on the suggestion of the beneficiaries) had previously been in partnership with his late father under the name of John Cooke & Son, a firm of high repute. The broker brought the trustee a bought-note stating that he required the money to pay for the corporation stocks on the following day, which was the next settling-day. Cheques for the necessary amount were drawn in favour of and handed to the broker, who left the bought-note with the trustee's cashier. Four days later the trustee asked the broker whether the securities had been acquired, to which the broker answered that there had not been time; and when the trustee made inquiries of the broker on further occasions he was from time to time put off with similar excuses. The broker had in fact appropriated the cheques to his own use a day or two after they had been handed to him; and a month afterwards he filed a petition on which he was adjudicated bankrupt.

The *cestuis que trust* claimed a declaration that the defendant trustee had committed a breach of trust with respect to this transaction and was personally liable to make good the loss. They argued that the trust funds handed to the broker should have been paid to the corporations' bankers pending the acquisition of the securities, instead of being made payable to the broker by means of cheques drawn in his favour. The defendant contended that he could not be fixed with liability unless it were shown that he had not acted as a prudent man of business would have acted on his own behalf; that it was the regular course of business for investors, on receiving the bought-note, to give their broker a cheque for the amount, the cheque being retained by the broker in the interval between purchase and transfer; and that he, the defendant, had followed the regular course of business. Evidence was given that the form of the bought-note would indicate to brokers, but probably not to the public in general, that the securities were to be acquired not in the market but direct from the corporations.

---

[25] See (1990) 106 L.Q.R. 88–93 (D. J. Hayton).
[26] On this standard of care see above.

BACON V.-C. held the trustee liable to make good the loss, inasmuch as he had not acted prudently in drawing cheques in favour of the broker (instead of in favour of the corporations) on the strength of a "scrap of paper" (the bought-note). The trustee appealed.

JESSEL M.R.: " . . . In the first place, I think we ought to consider what is the liability of a trustee who undertakes an office which requires him to make an investment on behalf of his *cestui que trust*. It seems to me that on general principles a trustee ought to conduct the business of the trust in the same manner that an ordinary prudent man of business would conduct his own, and that beyond that there is no liability or obligation on the trustee. In other words, a trustee is not bound because he is a trustee to conduct business in other than the ordinary and usual way in which similar business is conducted by mankind in transactions of their own. It never could be reasonable to make a trustee adopt further and better precautions than an ordinary prudent man of business would adopt, or to conduct the business in any other way. If it were otherwise, no one would be a trustee at all. He is not paid for it. He says, 'I take all reasonable precautions, and all the precautions which are deemed reasonable by prudent men of business, and beyond that I am not required to go.' Now what are the usual precautions taken by men of business when they make an investment? If the investment is an investment made on the Stock Exchange through a stockbroker, the ordinary course of business is for the investor to select a stockbroker in good credit and in a good position, having regard to the sum to be invested, and to direct him to make the investment— that is, to purchase on the Stock Exchange of a jobber or another broker the investment required. In the ordinary course, all that the broker can do is to enter into a contract—usually it is for the next account-day. Of course you may, by special bargain, make it for cash or for any other day, but the ordinary course is for the next account-day. Before the account-day arrives the purchasing stockbroker requests his principal to pay him the money, because on the account-day he is himself liable to pay over the money to the vendor, whether a jobber or broker, and therefore he must have it ready for the account-day, and according to the usual course of business he sends a copy of the purchasing note to the principal stating when the money is required to be paid, and he obtains the money from him a day or two before the account-day. When he gets it he pays it over, if it is a single transaction, to the vendor, and if it is one of a number of transactions he makes out an account with his vendor and pays over or receives from him the balance on the transactions. It by no means follows, therefore, that he pays over to the vendor the sum received, indeed there may be a number of transactions, and if the balance is the other way, then he has to receive money on the account, but he must in any case have the money in order to keep himself out of cash advances. It is after payment, and very often a considerable time after payment, that is, several days, that he gets the securities perfected. If they are shares or stock in a company, or railway or other company, it may be a considerable time before the transfers are lodged at the office, and it is not until the matter is ready for completion that he gets the transfer and the certificates. But in all cases, except in the case of consols, and a few other such stocks, there is some interval between the payment of the purchase-money and the obtaining of the security, or of the investment purchased.

"If, therefore, a trustee has made a proper selection of a broker, and has paid him the money on the bought-note, and, by reason of the default of the broker, the money is lost, it does not appear to me in that case that the trustee can be liable. Indeed it was not argued in this court that he would be liable, and I have said what I have said upon the subject more on account of an observation reported to have been made by Vice-Chancellor Bacon in the court below than because of any argument that was addressed to us upon the point . . . "

He then held that the trustee did not know nor could reasonably be expected to know from the form of the bought-note that the securities were to be acquired not in the market but from the corporations. It was thus proper for the trustee in accordance with normal practice to make out his cheque to the broker. Failure to obtain the securities within a month did not reveal a lack of care on the trustee's part, such a delay being common. Jessel M.R. stated:

"You are to endeavour as far as possible, having regard to the whole transaction, to avoid making an honest man *who is not paid* for the performance of an unthankful office liable for the failure of other people from whom he receives no benefit."[27]

*Held*, by the Court of Appeal, that the trustee was not liable, inasmuch as he had acted in accordance with the regular course of business. The beneficiaries' appeal to the House of Lords was dismissed.[28]

## The Trustee Act 1925

### Power to employ agents

Section 23.—(1) Trustees or personal representatives may, instead of acting personally, employ and pay an agent, whether a solicitor, banker, stockbroker, or any other person, to transact any business or do any act required to be transacted or done in the execution of the trust, or the administration of the testator's or intestate's estate, including the receipt and payment of money, and shall be entitled to be allowed and paid all charges and expenses so incurred, and shall not be responsible for the default of any such agent if employed in good faith.[29]

(2) Trustees or personal representatives may appoint any person to act as their agent or attorney for the purpose of selling, converting, collecting, getting in, and executing and perfecting assurances of, or managing or cultivating, or otherwise administering any property real or personal, moveable or immoveable, subject to the trust or forming part of the testator's or intestate's estate, in any place outside the United Kingdom or executing or exercising any discretion or trust or power vested in them in relation to any such property, with such ancillary powers, and with and subject to such provisions and restrictions as they may think fit, including a power to appoint substitutes, and shall not, by reason only of their having made such appointment, be responsible for any loss arising thereby.[30]

---

[27] Bowen L.J. expressly left this point open: (1883) 22 Ch.D. 727, 766. In the House of Lords, Lord Fitzgerald did not accept Jessel M.R.'s view: (1883) 9 App.Cas. 1, 31.

[28] Modern cases which illustrate the application of the principle of *Speight* v. *Gaunt*; *Re Lucking's W.T.* [1968] 1 W.L.R. 866, *Bartlett* v. *Barclays Bank Trust Co.* [1980] 1 All E.R. 139, *infra*, p. 764.

[29] In *Green* v. *Whitehead* [1930] 1 Ch. 38, X and Y were trustees for sale of land, which they contracted to sell to Z. Y gave A a power to sell and convey "my property." Z refused to take a conveyance from X and A. Eve J. held that Z's refusal was justified: Y had made a complete delegation of the office of trustee which was not possible under s.23(1). His decision was affirmed by the Court of Appeal on the grounds that the power conferred by Y upon A extended only to property of which Y was beneficial owner; Hanworth M.R. thought that but for this, the delegation would have been valid: see Jones (1959) 22 M.L.R. 381, 387, citing the report at 46 T.L.R. 11.

[30] This subsection is new. It was not applicable in *Green* v. *Whitehead, supra*, because the property in that case was situated in England.

(3) Without prejudice to such general power of appointing agents as aforesaid—

(*a*) A trustee may appoint a solicitor to be his agent to receive and give a discharge for any money or valuable consideration or property receivable by the trustee under the trust, by permitting the solicitor to have custody of, and to produce, a deed having in the body thereof or endorsed thereon a receipt for such money or valuable consideration or property, the deed being executed, or the endorsed receipt being signed, by the person entitled to give a receipt for that consideration;

(*b*) A trustee shall not be chargeable with breach of trust by reason only of his having made or concurred in making any such appointment; and the production of any such deed by the solicitor shall have the same statutory validity and effect as if the person appointing the solicitor had not been a trustee;

(*c*) A trustee may appoint a banker or solicitor to be his agent to receive and give a discharge for any money payable to the trustee under or by virtue of a policy of insurance, by permitting the banker or solicitor to have the custody of and to produce the policy of insurance with a receipt signed by the trustee and a trustee shall not be chargeable with a breach of trust by reason only of his having made or concurred in making any such appointment:

Provided that nothing in this subsection shall exempt a trustee from any liability which he would have incurred if this Act and any enactment replaced by this Act had not been passed, in case he permits any such money, valuable consideration, or property to remain in the hands or under the control of the banker or solicitor for a period longer than is reasonably necessary to enable the banker or solicitor, as the case may be, to pay or transfer the same to the trustee.

This subsection applies whether the money or valuable consideration or property was or is received before or after the commencement of this Act.

*Power to delegate trusts*

25.[31]—(1) Notwithstanding any rule of law or equity to the contrary, a trustee may, by power of attorney, delegate for a period not exceeding twelve months[32] the execution or exercise of all or any of the trusts, powers and discretions vested in him as trustee either alone or jointly with any other person or persons.

(2) The persons who may be donees of a power of attorney under this section include a trust corporation but not (unless a trust corporation) the only other co-trustee of the donor of the power[33]

---

[31] By the powers of Attorney Act 1971, s.2, no instrument creating a power of attorney, and no copy of any such instrument shall be deposited or filed at the central office of the Supreme Court or at the Land Registry under this section, although any right to search for, inspect, copy, or obtain an office copy of, any such document deposited or filed before October 1, 1971, remains unaffected. Similarly, s.9 applies whenever the trusts, powers or discretions in question arose but does not invalidate anything done by virtue of this section. A section 25 power is not an enduring power for the purposes of the Enduring Powers of Attorney Act 1985 dealing with donors subsequently suffering from mental incapacity.

[32] If no period at all were specified would the power be valid for one year from its date applying the *Mogridge* v. *Clapp* [1892] 3. Ch. 382 principle applied in *Re Pennant's W.T.* [1970] Ch. 75?

[33] On this see [1978] Conv. 85 (J. T. Farrand).

(3) An instrument creating a power of attorney under this section shall be attested by at least one witness.

(4) Before or within seven days after giving a power of attorney under this section the donor shall give written notice thereof (specifying the date on which the power comes into operation and its duration, the donee of the power, the reason why the power is given and, where some only are delegated, the trusts, the powers and discretions delegated) to—

(*a*) each person (other than himself) if any, who under any instrument creating the trust has power (whether alone or jointly) to appoint a new trustee; and

(*b*) each of the other trustees, if any;

but failure to comply with this subsection shall not, in favour of a person dealing with the donee of the power, invalidate any act done or instrument executed by the donee.

(5) The donor of a power of attorney given under this section shall be liable for the acts or defaults of the donee in the same manner as if they were the acts or defaults of the donor.

(6) For the purpose of executing or exercising the trusts or powers delegated to him, the donee may exercise any of the powers conferred on the donor as trustee by statute or by the instrument creating the trust, including power, for the purpose of the transfer of any inscribed stock, himself to delegate to an attorney power to transfer but not including the power of delegation conferred by this section.

(7) The fact that it appears from any power of attorney given under this section, or from any evidence required for the purposes of any such power of attorney or otherwise, that in dealing with any stock the donee of the power is acting in the execution of a trust shall not be deemed for any purpose to affect any person in whose books the stock is inscribed or registered with any notice of the trust.

(8) This section applies to a personal representative, tenant for life and statutory owner as it applies to a trustee except that subsection (4) shall apply as if it required the notice there mentioned to be given—

(*a*) in the case of a personal representative, to each of the other personal representatives, if any, except any executor who has renounced probate;

(*b*) in the case of a tenant for life, to the trustees of the settlement and to each person, if any, who together with the person giving the notice constitutes the tenant for life;

(*c*) in the case of a statutory owner, to each of the persons, if any, who together with the person giving the notice constitute the statutory owner and, in the case of a statutory owner by virtue of section 23(1)(*a*) of the Settled Land Act 1925, to the trustees of the settlement.

## Implied indemnity of trustees

Section 30.—(1) A trustee shall be chargeable only for money and securities actually received by him notwithstanding his signing any receipt for the sake of conformity, and shall be answerable and accountable only for his own acts, receipts, neglects, or defaults, and not for those of any other trustee, nor for any banker, broker, or other person with whom any trust money or securities may be deposited, nor for the insufficiency or deficiency of any securities, nor for any loss,[34] unless the same happens through his own wilful default.

## RE VICKERY, VICKERY v. STEPHENS

Chancery Division [1931] 1 Ch. 572; 100 L.J.Ch. 138

The plaintiffs were the two sons of a testatrix, entitled in equal shares to her estate undisposed of by her will, including £214 14s. 5d. in the Post Office Savings Bank and £62 4s. in Savings Certificates. The defendant, a missionary, as sole executor of the testatrix, employed in May 1927 to wind up her estate a solicitor Mr. Jennens who, unknown to him, had at one time been suspended from practice, and who obtained from the first plaintiff the Post Office Savings Bank deposit book and the Savings Certificates. The defendant heard for the first time of the solicitor's suspension approximately three months later, when the first plaintiff told him of it. Under the defendant's written authority, a warrant valued at £62 4s. had been issued [in respect of the Savings Certificates] in favour of the solicitor's firm, and the first plaintiff wrote to the defendant objecting to his having taken that course. Later, the first plaintiff asked the defendant to employ another solicitor, but the defendant did not do so, as the solicitor was then promising to settle the matter. Ultimately the solicitor absconded, and the sums of £214 14s. 5d. and £62 4s. were not recovered.[35]

In this action the plaintiffs claimed a declaration that the defendant had committed a breach of trust in allowing the two sums to be received and retained for over a month by the solicitor, and that he was liable to replace the loss with interest. The defendant relied mainly on sections 23(1) and 30(1) of the Trustee Act 1925.

MAUGHAM J. (after stating the facts): "The question that arises is whether in the circumstances, and in view of my findings as to the facts, the defendant is liable to make good these sums with interest by reason of his negligence either in employing Jennens to receive the sums, or in permitting those sums to remain in his hands, in the circumstances of this case, for a longer period than was necessary.

"In considering this question the court has to bear in mind in particular two sections of the Trustee Act 1925. Section 23(1) is as follows: [His Lordship read the subsection, and continued:] This subsection is new and, in my opinion, authorised the defendant in signing the authorities to Jennens & Jennens to collect the two sums in question,[36] for I do not think it can be doubted that the defendant acted in good faith in employing Jennens for the purpose. It will be observed that the subsection has no proviso or qualification to it such as we find in relation to section 23(3). It is hardly too much to say that it revolutionises the position of a trustee or an executor so far as regards the employment of agents. He is no longer required to do any actual work

---

[34] The *ejusdem generis* rule applies to this as appears from *Eaves* v. *Hickson* (1861) 30 Beav. 136 and as made clear by Maugham J. in *Re Vickery, infra,* so that the loss must flow from the depositing of trust money or securities: a person employed by a trustee to manage an unincorporated business owned by the trust is not a person with whom trust money or securities are deposited within the meaning of s.30: *Re Lucking's W.T.* [1968] 1 W.L.R. 866.

[35] The defendant put the matter in the hands of another solicitor in December 1927.

[36] It is not definitely stated in any other part of the report that the defendant had signed more than one authority.

himself, but he may employ a solicitor or other agent to do it, *whether there is any real necessity for the employment or not.* No doubt he should use his discretion in selecting an agent, and should employ him only to do acts within the scope of the usual business of the agent; but, as will be seen, a question arises whether even in these respects he is personally liable for a loss due to the employment of the agent unless he has been guilty of wilful default.

"Section 23(3) is in the following terms: [His Lordship read the subsection, and continued:] This subsection is a reproduction with amendments of section 17 of the Trustee Act 1893, which replaced section 2 of the Trustee Act 1888. It will be observed that paragraph (a) of the subsection relates to the production of a deed having endorsed thereon a receipt for money or other property, and that paragraph (c) refers to the receipt of money payable to the trustee under a policy of insurance.[37] In these cases, no doubt, there is no reason why the banker or solicitor should do anything more than receive the money and pay the same to the trustee or as he shall direct. The proviso must, I think, be limited to these two cases; and, of course, it is not intended to preclude a trustee from keeping trust funds at his bank pending investment or other proper use of them; and it has nothing to do, in my opinion, with the case I have to decide, in which the powers given by paragraphs (a) and (c) were not utilised by the defendant. There was no doubt a good reason for not making the proviso extend to subsection (1) of section 23, since in many cases, where, for example, a banker or other agent is employed by a trustee to receive money, the money cannot at once be conveniently paid to the trustee, but has to be employed by the banker or other agent in a number of ways.

"I have now to consider section 30(1) of the Trustee Act 1925, a section which replaces section 24 of the Trustee Act 1893, which in its turn re-enacted Lord Cranworth's Act,[38] s.31. It is in the following terms: [His Lordship read the subsection, and continued:] Reliance has been placed on the words concluding the subsection, 'nor for any other loss, unless the same happens through his own wilful default.' To avoid misconception I wish to say that, having regard to the numerous decisions since the enactment of Lord Cranworth's Act in relation to the liability of trustees for innocent breaches of trust, it is impossible now to hold that the words 'for any other loss' are quite general, with the result that no trustee is ever liable for breach of trust unless the breach is occasioned by his own wilful default. In my opinion the words are confined to losses for which it is sought to make the trustee liable, occasioned by his signing receipts for the sake of conformity, or by reason of the wrongful acts or defaults of another trustee or of an agent with whom trust money or securities have been deposited, or for the insufficiency or deficiency of securities or some other analogous loss. It may be noted that if the phrase is not so limited it is difficult to see how there could have been any need for section 3 of the Judicial Trustees Act 1896, now re-enacted as section 61 of the Trustee Act 1925, or for section 29 of that Act[39]; nor would it be possible to explain the numerous cases before 1896 where trustees were made liable for honest mistakes either of construction or fact: see, for example *Learoyd* v. *Whiteley*,[40] *National Trustees Co. of Australasia* v. *General Finance Co. of Australasia*,[41] and cases there cited.

---

[37] On the subsection referred to, see *Re Sheppard* [1911] 1 Ch. 50 and *Wyman* v. *Paterson* [1900] A.C. 271, 280–281.

[38] Law of Property Amendment Act 1859.

[39] Exoneration of trustees in respect of certain powers of attorney.

[40] (1887) 12 App.Cas. 727.

[41] [1905] A.C. 373.

"On the other hand, since section 30(1) expressly refers to the defaults of bankers, brokers, or other persons with whom any trust money or other securities may be deposited, I am unable—dealing here with the more limited case—to escape the conclusion that the trustee cannot be made liable for the default of such a person unless the loss happens through the 'wilful default' of the trustee. Before considering the meaning of the words 'wilful default' in this connection I would observe that in the case of *Re Brier*[42] the Court of Appeal, consisting of Lord Selborne L.C. and Cotton and Fry L.JJ., gave effect to Lord Cranworth's Act, s.31, and held the trustees and executors not liable inasmuch as it had not been established that the loss occasioned by the agent's insolvency (in a case where, as the law then required, it was shown that the employment of the agent was a proper one) was due to the wilful default of the trustees and executors.

"Now the meaning of the phrase 'wilful default' has been expounded by the Court of Appeal in the case of *Re Trusts of Leeds City Brewery Ltd.'s Deed*[43] and in the case of *Re City Equitable Fire Insurance Co.*[44] It should be noted that in both those cases the indemnity, given to the trustees in the first case and to the directors and officers of the company in the second case, was worded in a general form, so that it could not be contended that they were liable for any matter or thing done or omitted unless it could be shown that the loss so occasioned arose from their own wilful default. This, as I have said, is not true of an ordinary executor or trustee; but the exposition of the phrase 'wilful default' is not the less valuable. The Court of Appeal held, following in the case of *Re City Equitable Fire Insurance Co.* the decision of Romer J., that a person is not guilty of wilful neglect or default unless he is conscious that, in doing the act which is complained of or in omitting to do the act which it is said he ought to have done, he is committing a breach of his duty, or is recklessly careless whether it is a breach of his duty or not. I accept with respect what Warrington L.J. said—namely, that in the case of trustees there are definite and precise rules of law as to what a trustee may or may not do in the execution of his trust, and that a trustee in general is not excused in relation to a loss occasioned by a breach of trust merely because he honestly believed that he was justified in doing the act in question. But for the reasons which I have given I think that, where an executor employs a solicitor or other agent to receive money belonging to the estate in reliance on section 23(1) of the Trustee Act 1925, he will not be liable for a loss of the money occasioned by the misconduct of the agent unless the loss happens through the wilful default of the executor, using those words as implying, as the Court of Appeal have decided, either a consciousness of negligence or breach of duty, or a recklessness in the performance of a duty . . . "

After reviewing the circumstances, his Lordship came to the conclusion that the defendant had been guilty only of an error of judgment, and held, therefore, that he was not liable.

## INVESTMENT MANAGEMENT PROBLEMS

D. J. HAYTON (1990) 106 L.Q.R. 89–93

Assuming that there is a proper delegation to an investment manager, can the trustees, in the absence of express authority in the trust instrument, accept

---

[42] (1884) 26 Ch.D. 238.
[43] [1925] Ch. 532n.
[44] [1925] Ch. 407.

in the Customer Agreement terms allowing the manager to retain custody of investment scrip, to place securities in the name of itself or of a nominee, to place trust money with its own money and that of other customers and aggregate transactions of the trust with those of itself or other customers, to make a profit by selling its own securities to the trust or by purchasing securities from the trust for itself, and to be exempt from liability for negligence?

A delegate under section 25 of the Trustee Act 1925 can obviously register securities in his name and have custody of scrip; but the trustees remain vicariously liable. Section 21 of the 1925 Act generally authorises deposit "with any banker or banking company or any other company whose business includes the undertaking of the safe custody of documents." The difficulty is that a company carrying on the business of investment management may not be carrying on the business of charging for the undertaking of the safe custody of documents, so that the incidental retention of scrip to facilitate the business of investment management would seem to fall outside the wording.

Can it be argued that where a trust instrument expressly authorises employment of an investment manager and such a manager either requires or has a strong preference for securities to be registered in the name of itself or of its nominee and for scrip to be retained accordingly, then implicit in such express authority must be authority to follow that requisite or preferred practice? The answer depends on the proper application of the well-established rule[45] that in the investment sphere a trustee has to act, not as a prudent man of business might act on his own behalf, but as a prudent man of business would act when acting for persons for whom he feels morally obliged to provide. His primary concern is thus the safety of the trust fund and the avoiding of risk so far as possible. In this investment sphere, Equity may be regarded as a mother hen clucking over the nest-egg of her beneficiaries.

Traditionalists will argue that the dangers inherent in allowing a manager to have trust securities vested in it, when it may fraudulently or negligently deal with them and become insolvent, are such that trustees should only employ a portfolio manager which is prepared to register securities in the trustees' names. So long as there are such managers it will therefore be a breach of trust to employ other managers. To support their argument they would invoke the considerations that led Parliament out of caution to enact section 5 of the Stock Exchange (Completion of Bargains) Act 1976, which reads:

> "A trustee or personal representative shall not be liable by reason only of the fact that
>
> (a) he has for the purpose of acquiring securities . . . paid for them under arrangements which provide for them to be transferred to him . . . but not to be so transferred until after payment of the price, or
>
> (b) he has for the purpose of disposing of securities transferred them . . . under arrangements which provide that the price is not to be paid to him until after the transfer."

Modernists will argue that if the requisite or preferred practice of most investment managers is registration of securities in their names or those of

---

[45] *Re Whiteley* (1886) 33 Ch.D. 347, affd. *sub nom. Learoyd* v. *Whiteley* (1887) 12 A.C. 727; *Cowan* v. *Scargill* [1985] Ch. 270. He must minimise risk but maximise profit, as in *Buttle* v. *Saunders* [1950] 2 All E.R. 193, [1950] W.N. 255 (trustees' duty to "gazump").

their nominees, such registration is impliedly authorised by the express power to employ such managers. While there is much to be said for this pragmatic approach it cannot be said with any certainty that the purist, traditional approach will not prevail. Of course, the risks will be more theoretical than practical if a manager is chosen who has substantial assets and reputation. Matters would however be much improved if new legislation expressly and retrospectively authorised trustees to place investments in the name of, and scrip in the custody of, a person authorised under the Financial Services Act 1986.

Greater problems arise where a Customer Agreement purports to allow the investment manager as a market-maker to sell its own shares to the trust or purchase shares from the trust for itself and to pool trust money with its own and aggregate transactions of the trust with its own so as to average the cost of purchases and sales. The extent to which trustees can authorise such breaches of the "self-dealing" rule and exempt the manager from his fiduciary disabilities is uncertain, except that such authorisation and exemption seems impossible where a delegation is made under section 25 of the Trustee Act to a delegate treated as the *alter ego* of the trustees.

It is clear from *Boardman* v. *Phipps*[46] that trustees can give prior, specific authority to a third party to break what would otherwise be fiduciary obligations, so long as they are given full disclosure of all relevant details pertaining to the projected transaction and so long as their decision satisfies the prudent man test already discussed. Such a test clearly could not be satisfied if a prior general authority were given, since such *carte blanche* would give the manager leeway for blind robbery. The inherent dangers of any prior general authority are such that it can be argued that no such authority can ever be granted.

However, what if the prior general authority is limited to granting to an investment manager authorised under the Financial Services Act

(a) general authority to "self-deal" so long as it undertakes to obtain the best price reasonably available in the circumstances; and

(b) general authority to pool funds or aggregate transactions with those of other customers and itself as authorised by rules made by the relevant regulatory bodies under the Financial Services Act?

There are obvious dangers in the scope for abuse in the timing of a self-dealing transaction, in the length of the period for pooling funds and aggregating transactions and in the allocation of transactions carried out in different periods. However, the detailed records required to be kept by the manager under Chapter IV of the Investment Management Regulatory Organisation ("I.M.R.O.") Rulebook should enable there to be some sort of retrospective checking, assuming that those records are properly kept. The difficulty is that the evidence required to prove abuse by the fiduciary manager is peculiarly within the knowledge and control of the manager, which puts the beneficiaries at a serious disadvantage. This, of course, is the major justification for the general prohibition on self-dealing and similar activities which involve a possible conflict of fiduciary duty and self-interest.

Despite this, if the best management services or best advisory executory services are available only where such prior, but limited, general authority is

---

[46] [1964] 1 W.L.R. 993 at pp. 1012–1013 (Wilberforce J.); [1965] Ch. 992 at p. 1031 (C.A.).

given, so that the trustees are prudently maximising the performance of the trust fund and minimising their costs, a seriously arguable, pragmatic case can be made for the validity of such authority if the trustees consciously decide that a prudent man of business would so act when acting for persons for whom he feels morally obliged to provide and so is primarily concerned with the safety of the trust fund.

Since it is dubious whether the courts would accept this bold view, trustees are in such an unenviable situation that statute should retrospectively endorse it. Indeed, it seems that any legislation needs to go further and automatically validate such prior limited general authority to a person authorised under the Financial Services Act, thus creating an irrebuttable presumption that it satisfies the "prudent man" test. It is not sufficient to say that the court can always grant relief to the trustees under section 61 of the Trustee Act, for no professional trustee wants to have to rely on this expensive and public last resort.

Where a draft Customer Agreement has a term providing exemption from liability for negligence the trustees must weigh up the risk of the trust fund's value being halved or worse by the manager's negligence against the alleged advantages of employing his services. Indeed, if the manager is so good, why should the exemption clause not be deleted and slightly more paid for his services? The test of the prudent man of business primarily concerned with the safety of the trust fund is likely to require that trustees should normally reject such a clause: the difficult onus of proving a special case for accepting such a clause will then lie on the trustees.

Since so many trustees have already entered into agreements containing exemption clauses there is a strong case for statute retrospectively validating such conduct of trustees, at any rate where the agreements were entered into before January 1, 1989. Since then Chapter III Rule 2.08 of the I.M.R.O. Rulebook has prohibited exemption clauses where the customer is a private, *i.e.* ordinary investor as opposed to a business, professional or experienced investor. It can be argued that if ordinary investors are protected in this way, then trustees who are business or professional or experienced investors should have been alerted to the fact that prima facie they should protect their ordinary beneficiaries by refusing to agree to exemption clauses.

### Section 5. Deviations from the Terms of a Trust

In case it is overlooked it is, of course, possible to change the structure of fixed or discretionary interests under a settlement if there is an overriding power of appointment in this behalf conferred by the settlement, *e.g.* upon the trustees, or the life-tenant (or settlor).

### I. WHERE THE BENEFICIARIES ARE SUI JURIS

If property is given not contingently but absolutely to a person of full age *any* restriction on his enjoyment of it is inconsistent with his absolute interest.[47] Hence a beneficiary *sui juris* and entitled *absolutely* can call for a transfer: *Saunders* v. *Vautier, infra*; and he may do so

---

[47] *Weatherall* v. *Thornburgh* (1878) 8 Ch.D. 261, 270 (Cotton L.J.).

even if the settlor purports to remove this right.[48] So also *several* beneficiaries who are all *sui juris* and between them entitled absolutely may call for a transfer, if they act together.[49] Even beneficiaries who are entitled *in succession* can combine to call for a transfer, provided they are *sui juris* and are collectively entitled absolutely.[50] The rule in *Saunders* v. *Vautier, infra,* operates also in favour of a charity.[51] But it does not apply where other persons have an interest in the accumulations of income which the beneficiaries are seeking to stop.[52] Nor does it give beneficiaries the right to control the trustee in the exercise of any discretion conferred upon him by statute or the trust instrument.[53]

In the case of income accruing to a closed class of discretionary trust beneficiaries the sole member of the class for the time being can claim an entitlement to that income. If such class were open such sole member cannot claim such entitlement so long as it is possible for another member of the class to come into existence before a reasonable time for the distribution of the accrued income has elapsed.[54]

One must distinguish between the rights of the beneficial interest holders collectively and the rights of one of the co-owners: the latter are much more restricted as appears from *Stephenson* v. *Barclays Bank, infra,* p. 652.

### SAUNDERS v. VAUTIER

Master of the Rolls (1841) 4 Beav. 115; Cr. & Ph. 240; 10 L.J.Ch. 354

A testator bequeathed his stock on trust to accumulate the dividends until V. should attain the age of twenty-five, and then to transfer the principal, together with the accumulated dividends, to V. V., having attained twenty-one, claimed to have the fund transferred to him. It was contended for him that he had "a vested interest, and that as the accumulation and postponement of payment was for his benefit alone, he might waive it and call for an immediate transfer of the fund."

LORD LANGDALE M.R.: "I think that principle has been repeatedly acted upon; and where a legacy is directed to accumulate for a certain period, or where the payment is postponed the legatee, if he has an absolute indefeasible interest in the legacy, is not bound to wait until the expiration of that period, but may require payment the moment he is competent to give a valid discharge."

On a question raised, with reference to a previous order for maintenance, as to whether there was a vested interest in V. before he attained twenty-five, the petition stood over, with liberty to apply to the Lord Chancellor.

---

[48] *Stokes* v. *Cheek* (1860) 28 Beav. 620.
[49] *Re Sandeman* [1937] 1 All E.R. 368; *Magrath* v. *Morehead* (1871) L.R. 12 Eq. 491; *Re Smith* [1928] Ch. 915, *supra,* p. 261.
[50] *Haynes* v. *Haynes* (1866) 35 L.J.Ch. 303; *Re Millner* (1872) L.R. 14 Eq. 245; *Anson* v. *Potter* (1879) 13 Ch.D. 141; *Re White* [1901] 1 Ch. 570; *Re Bowes* [1896] 1 Ch. 507.
[51] *Wharton* v. *Masterman* [1895] A.C. 186; but see *Re Levy* [1960] Ch. 346. Whilst an indefinite gift of income to an individual carries the right to the capital, this is not necessarily so in the case of a similar gift to charity, for such a gift can be enjoyed by the charity in perpetuity.
[52] *Berry* v. *Green* [1938] A.C. 575.
[53] *Re Brockbank* [1948] Ch. 206; *Re George Whichelow Ltd.* [1954] 1 W.L.R. 5; *cf. Butt* v. *Kelson* [1952] Ch. 197, 207.
[54] *Re Trafford's Settlement* [1984] 1 All E.R. 1108; *Re Weir's Settlement* [1971] Ch. 145.

*Held*, by the Lord Chancellor, the fund was intended wholly for the benefit of V., although the enjoyment of it was postponed: it vested immediately, and he could now claim the transfer.[55]

## STEPHENSON v. BARCLAYS BANK

Chancery Division [1975] 1 All E.R. 625; [1975] 1 W.L.R. 88

WALTON J.: "I think it may be desirable to state what I conceive to be certain elementary principles. (1) In a case where the persons who between them hold the entirety of the beneficial interests in any particular trust fund are all *sui juris* and acting together ('the beneficial interest holders'), they are entitled to direct the trustees how the trust fund may be dealt with. (2) This does not mean, however, that they can at one and the same time override the pre-existing trusts and keep them in existence. Thus, in *Re Brockbank*[56] itself the beneficial interest holders were entitled to override the pre-existing trusts by, for example, directing the trustees to transfer the trust fund to X and Y, whether X and Y were the trustees of some other trust or not, but they were not entitled to direct the existing trustees to appoint their own nominee as a new trustee of the existing trust. By so doing they would be pursuing inconsistent rights. (3) Nor, I think, are the beneficial interest holders entitled to direct the trustees as to the particular investment they should make of the trust fund. I think this follows for the same reasons as the above. Moreover, it appears to me that once the beneficial interest holders have determined to end the trust they are not entitled, unless by agreement, to the further services of the trustees. Those trustees can of course be compelled to hand over the entire trust assets to any person or persons selected by the beneficiaries against a proper discharge, but they cannot be compelled, unless they are in fact willing to comply with the directions, to do anything else with the trust fund which they are not in fact willing to do. (4) Of course, the rights of the beneficial interest holders are always subject to the right of the trustees to be fully protected against such matters as duty, taxes, costs or other outgoings; for example, the rent under a lease which the trustees have properly accepted as part of the trust property.

"So much for the rights of the beneficial interest holders collectively. When the situation is that a single person who is *sui juris* has an absolutely vested beneficial interest in a share of the trust fund, his rights are not, I think, quite as extensive as those of the beneficial interest holders as a body. In general, he is entitled to have transferred to him (subject, of course, always to the same rights of the trustees as I have already mentioned above) an aliquot share of each and every asset of the trust fund which presents no difficulty so far as division is concerned. This will apply to such items as cash, money at the bank or an unsecured loan, stock exchange securities and the like. However, as regards land, certainly, in all cases, as regards shares in a private company in very special circumstances (see *Re Weiner's Will Trusts*[57]) and possibly

---

[55] Joyce J., in *Re Couturier* [1907] 1 Ch. 470, 473, points out the distinction between giving a person a *vested* interest and postponing the enjoyment to a certain age, and giving him an interest *contingent* on his attaining a certain age.

[56] [1948] Ch. 206.

[57] [1956] 1 W.L.R. 579. Now see *Lloyds Bank* v. *Duker* [1987] 1 W.L.R. 1324 where a beneficiary entitled to 46/80 of the testator's residuary estate claimed therefore to have 574 of 999 shares in a private company transferred to her. Such a majority shareholding was worth much more than 46/80 of the proceeds of sale of the whole 999 shares. It was held that the duty to maintain an even hand or fair balance between the beneficiaries prevailed so that the shares must be sold and the claimant beneficiary receive 46/80 of the proceeds.

(although the logic of the addition in facts escapes me[58]) mortgage debts (see *Re Marshall*[59] per Cozens-Hardy M.R.) the situation is not so simple, and even a person with a vested interest in possession in an aliquot share of the trust fund may have to wait until the land is sold, and so forth, before being able to call on the trustees as of right to account to him for his share of the assets."

## II. WHERE THE BENEFICIARIES ARE NOT SUI JURIS

### A. *Introductory*[60]

The decision of the House of Lords in *Chapman* v. *Chapman*[61] in 1954 made it clear that the court did not possess plenary powers to alter a trust because alteration was thought to be advantageous to infant or unborn beneficiaries except in certain limited cases. Some of these exceptions related to acts done by the trustees in regard to the trust property in the administration of the trust, while others went beyond this and conferred a limited power to remould the beneficial interests when this was to the advantage of the beneficiaries.

### (a) *Exceptions relating to acts done in administration of trust*

(i) *Salvage.* This group of cases involved the alienation of infants' property and established the proposition that the court could sanction a mortgage or sale of part of an infant's beneficial interest for the benefit of the part retained in cases of absolute necessity.[62]

(ii) *Emergency.* This exception can be regarded as an extension of the salvage cases. The salvage cases required proof of absolute necessity. The principle of the emergency cases was somewhat wider and enabled the court to sanction departure from the terms of a trust where an emergency had arisen which the settlor had not foreseen and which required to be dealt with by the conferment of extraordinary powers on the trustees.[63]

(iii) *Expediency*—Section 57 of the Trustee Act 1925. Section 57 of the Trustee Act 1925 rested the jurisdiction on expediency—a basis which, it is conceived, is wider than that of salvage or emergency. The section provides:

> "Where in the management or administration of any property vested in trustees, any sale, lease, mortgage, surrender, release or other disposition or any purchase, investment, acquisition, expenditure, or other transaction is in the opinion of the court expedient, but the same

---

[58] In *Crowe* v. *Appleby* [1975] 3 All E.R. 529, 537, Goff J. endorsed Walton J.'s views and pointed out "the logic of the addition of mortgages is that they include not only the debt but the estate and powers of the mortgagee."

[59] [1914] 1 Ch. 192, 199.

[60] See O. R. Marshall (1954) 17 M.L.R. 420; (1957) 21 Conv.(N.S.) 448.

[61] [1954] A.C. 429. The variation of the trust in that case was later effected under the Variation of Trusts Act 1958, *infra*, p. 657: see *Re Chapman's Settlement Trusts (No. 2)* [1959] 1 W.L.R. 372.

[62] See *Re Jackson* (1882) 21 Ch.D. 786; *Conway* v. *Fenton* (1888) 40 Ch.D. 512; *cf. Re De Teissier* [1893] 1 Ch. 153; *Re Montagu* [1897] 2 Ch. 8.

[63] *Re New* [1901] 1 Ch. 534; *Re Tollemache* [1903] 1 Ch. 457.

cannot be effected by reason of the absence of any power for that purpose vested in the trustees by the trust instrument, if any, or by law, the court may by order confer upon the trustees, either generally or in any particular instance, the necessary power for the purpose, in such terms, and subject to such provisions and conditions, if any, as the court may think fit and may direct in what manner any money authorised to be expended, and the costs of any transaction, are to be paid or borne as between capital and income."

The object of the section is to enable the court to authorise specific dealings with the trust property which it might not have been able to do on the basis of salvage or emergency, but it was no part of the legislative aim to disturb the rule that the court will not rewrite a trust.[64]

This is an overriding section, the provisions of which are read into every settlement.[65] The powers of the court are limited only by expediency, though the proposed transaction must be for the benefit not of one beneficiary but of the whole trust.[66] The power has been used to authorise the sale of chattels settled on trusts which prevent sale,[67] the sale of land where a consent requisite to sale has been refused,[68] the partitioning of land where there was no power to partition,[69] and the blending of two charitable funds into one.[70] Apparently, trustees could not obtain from the court a general extension of their investment powers, although they could apply for a particular investment to be specially authorised.[71]

(b) *Exceptions relating to the remoulding of the beneficial interests*

(i) *Maintenance.*[72] Where a settlor made a provision for a family but postponed the enjoyment, either for a particular purpose or generally for the increase of the estate, it was assumed that he did not intend that the children should be left unprovided for, or in a state of such moderate means that they could not be educated properly for the position which he intended them to have, and the court accordingly

---

[64] *Re Downshire* [1953] Ch. 218.
[65] *Re Mair* [1935] Ch. 562.
[66] *Re Craven's Estate (No. 2)* [1937] Ch. 431.
[67] *Re Hope's Will Trust* [1929] 2 Ch. 136.
[68] *Re Beale's Settlement Trusts* [1932] 2 Ch. 15.
[69] *Re Thomas* [1930] 1 Ch. 194.
[70] *Re Harvey* [1941] 3 All E.R. 284; for other cases on s.57, see *Municipal and General Securities Ltd. v. Lloyds Bank Ltd.* [1950] Ch. 212; *Re Pratt* [1943] 2 All E.R. 375.
[71] See *Re Powell-Cotton's Resettlement* [1956] 1 W.L.R. 23. The court had an inherent jurisdiction to authorise a general extension in case of trustees of charity. See *Re Royal Society's Charitable Trusts* [1956] Ch. 87; 19 M.L.R. 94 (S. F. C. Milsom); cf. *Re Shipwrecked Fishermen and Mariners' Royal Benevolent Society* [1959] Ch. 220. Since the coming into force of the Variation of Trusts Act 1958, *infra*, all trustees seeking extended investment powers should apply under that Act though it is also possible to do so under s.57 of the Trustee Act, *supra*; see *Mason* v. *Farbrother* [1983] 2 All E.R. 1078. Investment powers may now be enlarged relatively readily for circumstances have much changed since the passing of the Trustee Investments Act 1961; *supra*, p. 624.
[72] *Havelock* v. *Havelock* (1880) 17 Ch.D. 807; *Re Collins* (1886) Ch.D. 229; *Re Walker* [1901] 1 Ch. 879; *Greenwell* v. *Greenwell* (1800) 5 Ves. 194; *Errat* v. *Barlow* (1807) 14 Ves. 202.

broke in upon the accumulation and provided maintenance for the children. The exercise of this jurisdiction resulted in an alteration of beneficial interests since income was applied in maintaining beneficiaries notwithstanding the fact that the settlor had directed that it should be accumulated or applied in reduction of incumbrances. The jurisdiction was not confined to cases of emergency or necessity.[73]

(ii) *Compromise.* It has long been clear that where the rights of the beneficiaries under a trust are the subject of doubt or dispute, the court has jurisdiction on behalf of all interested parties, whether adult, infant or unborn, to sanction a compromise by substituting certainty for doubt.[74] The issue in *Re Downshire, Re Blackwell* and *Re Chapman* before the Court of Appeal,[75] and in the last-named case[76] before the House of Lords, was whether the court had jurisdiction to do the same with regard to rights which were admittedly not in dispute. Their Lordships emphatically rejected the view that the courts had so ample a jurisdiction; but Lord Cohen, alone, was prepared to give an extended meaning to the word "compromise." In his opinion, even where there was no dispute, the court could sanction arrangements between tenants for life on the one hand and remaindermen on the other; but it could not vary the rights of a class *inter se* which the settlor had directed should be treated in a particular way.

(iii) *Section 64 of the Settled Land Act* 1925. Section 64(1) of the Settled Land Act 1925 provides that any transaction affecting or concerning the settled land, or any part thereof, or any other land (not being a transaction otherwise authorised by the Act, or by the settlement) which in the opinion of the court would be for the benefit of the settled land, or any part thereof, or the persons interested under the settlement, may, under an order of the court, be effected by a tenant for life, if it is one which could have been validly effected by an absolute owner. "Transaction" is defined by subsection (2) to include "any sale, extinguishment of manorial incidents, exchange, assurance, grant, lease, surrender, reconveyance, release, reservation or other disposition, any purchase or other acquisition, any covenant, contract, or option, and any application of capital money . . . and any compromise or other dealing or arrangement. . . . "

Roxburgh J. in *Re Downshire*[77] thought that the section did nothing more than authorise, with the sanction of the court, the carrying out of transactions in the nature of practical steps of an administrative character; it did not authorise the remoulding of beneficial interests. On appeal Lord Evershed M.R. and Romer L.J. expressed the view

---

[73] See *Haley* v. *Bannister* (1820) 4 Madd. 275.
[74] *Brooke* v. *Mostyn* (1864) 2 De G.J. & S. 415; *Re Barbour's Settlement* [1974] 1 All E.R. 1188.
[75] [1953] Ch. 218.
[76] [1954] A.C. 429. In *Mason* v. *Farbrother* [1983] 2 All E.R. 1078 it was held that doubts over the scope of narrow investment powers should not be compromised in the court's discretion by insertion of a new wide investment clause.
[77] Sub nom. *Re D's Settled Estates* [1952] W.N. 428, 432.

that the jurisdiction conferred by the section was more ample.[78] "Transaction" is a word of very wide import, and is defined by the section itself to include "compromise, and any other dealing or other arrangement." Practical steps of an administrative character are provided for by section 71 of the Settled Land Act. Therefore it was improbable that section 64 was meant to act merely as a supplement to section 71. Nor was the fact that the transaction has to be effected by the tenant for life an indication that a restricted meaning should be given to the word "transaction," since section 75(2) of the Act permitted the tenant for life to give directions to the trustees with regard to the application of capital moneys. The factors limiting the scope of the section were, first, that the transaction must be for the benefit either of the settled land or of the persons interested under the settlement, though not necessarily of both; secondly, it must affect or concern the settled land, or any other land whether settled or not, and whether within or without England; and, thirdly, when it concerns settled land, it must have an effect which is real and substantial by ordinary common-sense standards as distinct from one which is oblique or remote and merely incidental.[79] It has since been held that the powers conferred by section 64 are also available to trustees for sale.[80]

(iv) *Section 53 of the Trustee Act* 1925. Section 53 of the Trustee Act provides that where an infant is beneficially entitled to *any* property the court may with a view to the *application* of the capital or income thereof for the maintenance, education or *benefit* of the infant make an order appointing a person to convey such property upon such terms as the court may think fit. The effect of this section may be summarised as follows:

Where—

    (a) an infant is beneficially entitled to any interest in property, whether real or personal;

    (b) the interest itself is not under the settlement applicable for his maintenance, education or benefit, nor is it producing any income which is so applicable;

    (c) a proposal is made that the court should authorise a "conveyance"[81] of the infant's interest with a view to the application of the capital or income, arising out of such conveyance, for the maintenance, education or benefit of the infant;

then the court has jurisdiction to sanction the proposal upon such terms as it thinks fit. Thus the sale of an infant's contingent reversionary interest to the life-tenant in order to minimise liability to estate duty was made with a view to, and was, an application of the proceeds

78 [1953] Ch. 218.
79 See also *Re Scarisbrick* [1944] Ch. 229; *Re Mount Edgcumbe* [1950] Ch. 615; *Re White-Popham* [1936] Ch. 725.
80 *Re Simmons's Trusts* [1956] Ch. 125.
81 Including a mortgage: *Re Gower's Settlement* [1934] Ch. 365; *Re Bristol's Settled Estates* [1965] 1 W.L.R. 469.

of sale for the infant's benefit, where they amounted to more than he would have been likely to receive if no sale had taken place, and they were to be settled upon[82] and not paid outright to him.[83]

### B. The Variation of Trusts Act 1958[84]

The decision in *Chapman* v. *Chapman*[85] was criticised by the Law Reform Committee whose report[86] led to the passing of the Variation of Trusts Act 1958, *infra.*

Essentially, the Act enables the court on behalf of persons who cannot themselves give their approval (*e.g.* because unborn, unascertainable or minors) to approve arrangements varying or revoking beneficial and administrative provisions under trusts so long as such arrangements are for the benefit of the individual persons in question. Exceptionally, in the case of persons with contingent discretionary interests under protective trusts, where the interest of the protected beneficiary has not failed or determined, the court can give an approval on behalf of (and against the will of) ascertained adults and no benefit to them is required.[87] Jurisdiction extends to foreign settlements where the property and the trustees are within the physical jurisdiction[88] and the foreign law governing validity of the trust allows variation of the trust.[89] It also extends to the approval of an arrangement substituting a foreign settlement for an English one[90] if the beneficiaries have a genuine foreign connection.[91] The Act is useful for saving tax by exporting trusts and by a partition of the trust fund between the life tenant (who might have a protected interest) and the remaindermen (who might be minors, unborn or unascertained).

### *Variation cannot be resettlement*

The Act does not extend beyond a variation to a completely new resettlement as pointed out by Megarry J. in *Re Holt's Settlement.*[92]

---

[82] *Re Meux's Will Trusts* [1957] 3 W.L.R. 377; *Re Lansdowne's W.T.* [1967] 1 All E.R. 888.
[83] *Re Heyworth's Contingent Reversionary Interest* [1956] Ch. 364. Other exceptions under this head which are outside the scope of this note are the *cy-près* jurisdiction of the court in relation to charitable trusts, the statutory jurisdiction of the court in regard to mental patients' settlements under the Mental Health Act 1983, s.96, and the statutory jurisdiction of the Family Division of the High Court to vary ante-nuptial and post-nuptial settlements. See Matrimonial Causes Act 1973, ss.24, 31.
[84] See Harris, *Variation of Trusts* (Sweet and Maxwell 1975).
[85] [1954] A.C. 429.
[86] (1957) Cmnd. 310; [1958] C.L.J. 1 (S. J. Bailey).
[87] s.1(1)(*d*) and proviso thereto in Variation of Trusts Act 1958. The settlor's intentions must still be considered: *Re Steed's W.T.* [1960] Ch. 407.
[88] *Re Ker's S.T.* [1963] Ch. 553; *Re Paget's Settlement* [1965] 1 W.L.R. 1046, 1050.
[89] Recognition of Trusts Act 1987 incorporating Article 8 of The Hague Convention on The Law Applicable to Trusts and on their Recognition, *infra*, p. 817.
[90] *Re Seale's Settlement* [1961] Ch. 574; *Re Windeat's W.T.* [1969] 1 W.L.R. 692.
[91] *Re Weston's Settlement* [1969] 1 Ch. 224 where the Court of Appeal refused to make the settlement a Jersey settlement for the reason *inter alia* that it doubted whether the beneficiaries, having only moved to Jersey three months before making the application, would stay in Jersey very long after the approval of the arrangement, if approved, and the saving of the liability to capital gains tax of £163,000. Also see *Re Chamberlain* unreported but discussed in (1976) 126 N.L.J. 1034 (J. B. Morcom): see p. 570, *supra.*
[92] [1969] 1 Ch. 100.

Later, in *Re Ball's Settlement*[93] Megarry J. enunciated a substratum test for ascertaining upon which side of this jurisdictional line a proposed arrangement falls[94]: "If an arrangement changes the whole substratum of the trust, then it may well be that it cannot be regarded merely as varying that trust. But if, an arrangement, whilst leaving the substratum, effectuates the purpose of the trust by other means, it may still be possible to regard that arrangement as merely varying the original trusts, even though the means employed are wholly different and even though the form is completely changed." In the case a settlement conferred a life interest on the settlor (subject to a power of appointment in favour of his sons and grandchildren) and the capital was in default of appointment to be divided between the two sons of the settlor or their issue *per stirpes* if either son predeceased the settlor. The approved arrangement revoked the beneficial and administrative provisions of the settlement and replaced them with new provisions whereby each half of the trust fund was held on trust for one of the sons for life and, subject thereto, for such of that son's children equally as were born before a certain date. This jurisdictional limit is thus unlikely in practice to cause much difficulty.

### Benefit

"Benefit" may be financial, moral or social[95] or the facilitation of the administration of the settlement.[96] Unfortunately, the reported cases all too often show, as one commentator puts it,[97] "that benefit and the measure of it is simply what the court says it is." An extreme case is *Re Remnant's W.T.*[98] where the children of two sisters, Dawn and Merrial, had contingent interests under a testamentary trust which contained a forfeiture provision in respect of any child who practised Roman Catholicism or was married to a Catholic at the time of vesting, with an accruer provision in favour of the children of the other sister. Dawn's children were Protestant whilst Merrial's children were Catholic. In the interests of family harmony an application was made *inter alia* for deletion of the forfeiture provision. Pennycuick J. acceded to the application in the interests of family harmony and freedom of marital choice, though defeating the testator's clear intentions[99] and though financially disadvantageous to Dawn's children who otherwise had a good chance of gaining under the accruer clause. *Re Tinker's Settlement*[1] was not cited where Russell J. had refused approval to

---

[93] [1968] 1 W.L.R. 899; (1968) 84 L.Q.R. 458.
[94] [1968] 1 W.L.R. 899, 904.
[95] *Re Towler's S.T.* [1964] Ch. 158; *Re Holt's Settlement* [1969] 1 Ch. 100; *Re Weston's Settlement* [1969] 1 Ch. 224; *Re Remnant's S.T.* [1970] 1 Ch. 560, but *cf. Re Tinker's Settlement* [1960] 1 W.L.R. 1011. See also G. R. Bretten (1968) 32 Conv.(N.S.) 194.
[96] *Re University of London Charitable Trusts* [1964] Ch. 282; *Re Seale's Marriage Settlement* [1961] Ch. 574.
[97] R. B. M. Cotterell (1971) 34 M.L.R. 98.
[98] [1970] 1 Ch. 560.
[99] In *Re Steed's W.T.* [1960] Ch. 407 (not cited in *Re Remnant*) the Court of Appeal placed much emphasis on not frustrating the testator's intentions.
[1] [1960] 1 W.L.R. 1011.

inserting a provision (omitted in error) which would have taken away a sister's children's chance of obtaining property under an accruer clause on the brother's death under 30. Further, Pennycuick J. did not consider whether the Protestant children, when adult, would in all probability be happy to forgo a larger share in the trust fund resulting from their cousins' Catholicism, this being the test taken by Cross J. in *Re C.L.*[2] to distinguish *Re Tinker* from *Re C.L.*, where he approved a mental patient giving up certain life interests in favour of her adopted daughters with interests in remainder. Perhaps one may artificially reconcile *Re Remnant's W.T.* with *Re Tinker's Settlement* on the basis that in the former both sides of the family could benefit in theory while in the latter only one side of the family could benefit.[3]

The court may sanction a proposed arrangement which involves an element of risk to infant or unborn beneficiaries if the risk is one which an adult might well be prepared to take.[4] It will not sanction an arrangement involving an appointment made under a special power considered to be a fraud on the power.[5]

### Parties to the application

Application is by originating summons supported by affidavits to which a draft scheme of arrangement will be exhibited. The proper plaintiffs are the adult beneficiaries and not the trustees.[6] The trustees are supposed to be "watch-dogs" concerned with the interests of those who may possibly be adversely affected by the arrangement proposed. The defendant should be the trustees, the settlor, any beneficiary not a plaintiff, and any person who may become entitled to an interest under the trusts as being at a future date or on the happening of a future event a person of any specified description or a member of any specified class (*e.g.* next-of-kin of S, still alive) who would be of that description or of that class if the said date had fallen or the said event had happened (*e.g.* S's death) at the date of the application to the court.[7] No other persons who might eventually fulfil that description or be members of that class (*e.g.* distant relatives who might be next-of-kin if the nearer relatives conveniently died) need be made parties, nor need possible objects of a power of appointment which has not actually been exercised in their favour, or persons whose only interest is under discretionary trusts in a protective trust where the interest of the protected beneficiary has not failed or determined. A person who has

---

2 [1969] 1 Ch. 587.

3 P. J. Clarke [1987] Conv. 69.

4 *Re Cohen's W.T.* [1959] 1 W.L.R. 865; (1960) 76 L.Q.R.(R.E.M.); *Re Holt's Settlement* [1969] 1 Ch. 100; *Re Robinson's S.T.* [1976] 1 W.L.R. 806.

5 *Re Brook's Settlement* [1968] 1 W.L.R. 1661, *infra*, p. 720; S. M. Cretney (1969) 32 M.L.R. 317.

6 *Re Druce's S.T.* [1962] 1 W.L.R. 363; trustees should only act as plaintiffs where they are satisfied that the proposed arrangement is beneficial and that no beneficiary is willing to make the application.

7 Rules of Supreme Court, Order 93. For infants or unborn beneficiaries evidence must show that their guardians *ad litem* or the trustees support the arrangement as in their interests and exhibit counsel's opinion to this effect; Practice Direction [1976] 3 All E.R. 160.

an actual interest conferred directly on him by a settlement, however remote or contingent, has been held not to be a person who *may* become entitled to an interest so the court cannot approve on his behalf: *Knocker* v. *Youle, infra*, p. 662.

## The effect of approval by the court

The variation takes effect as soon as the order of the court is made without any further instrument,[8] and the order may be liable to stamp duty.[9]

A fundamental question is whether it is the order of the court or the arrangement which that order approves which has the effect of varying the trusts. The former view was taken in *Re Hambleden's W.T.*.[10] The latter view is supported by dicta of Lords Reid and Wilberforce in *Re Holmden's Settlement.*[11] In particular, Lord Reid said[12]:

> "Under the Variation of Trusts Act 1958 the court does not itself amend or vary the trusts of the original settlement. The beneficiaries are not bound by variations because a court has made the variation. Each beneficiary is bound because he has consented to the variation. If he was not of full age when the arrangement was made he is bound because the court was authorised by the Act of 1958 to approve of it on his behalf and did so by making an order. If he was of full age and did not in fact consent he is not affected by the order of the court and he is not bound. So the arrangement must be regarded as an arrangement made by the beneficiaries themselves. The court merely acted on behalf of or as representing those beneficiaries who were not in a position to give their own consent and approval."

In *Re Holt's Settlement*,[13] decided before *Re Holmden's Settlement*[14] was reported, Megarry J. rejected the view taken in *Re Hambleden's W.T.*, canvassed the difficulties arising from such rejection and accepted counsel's submission that,[15] "when the adults by their counsel assented to the arrangement and the court on behalf of the infants by order approved the arrangement then there was an arrangement which varied the trusts." The variation is thus effected by the consent of all parties on *Saunders* v. *Vautier*[16] principles, the court supplying the consents of the unborn, the unascertained and infants, and new trusts replace the old so that since July 16, 1964, the Perpetuities and Accumulations Act 1964 has been available to provide new perpetuity and accumulation periods for trusts varied under the Variation of Trusts Act.[17]

---

[8] *Re Holmden's Settlement* [1968] A.C. 685; *Re Holt's Settlement* [1969] 1 Ch. 100.
[9] Practice Note [1966] 1 W.L.R. 345; *Re Holt's Settlement, supra*; *Thorn* v. *I.R.C.* [1976] 1 W.L.R. 915, though *ad valorem* duty on gifts abolished by Finance Act 1985, s.82.
[10] [1960] 1 W.L.R. 82.
[11] [1968] A.C. 685, 701, 702, 710, 713.
[12] *Ibid.* at 701–702.
[13] [1969] 1 Ch. 100.
[14] [1968] A.C. 685.
[15] [1969] 1 Ch. 100, 115.
[16] *Supra*, p. 651.
[17] So held in *Re Holt's Settlement* [1969] 1 Ch. 100. It is thought that as it is the court that orders variations under Matrimonial Causes Act 1973, s.24 such orders in the Family Division, like the exercise of special powers, are subject to the periods laid down in the original settlement.

Adult beneficiaries who give their own consents to the variation would seem to be *pro tanto* disposing of their subsisting equitable interests so that signed writing is required by section 53(1)(c) of the Law of Property Act 1925. However, in *Re Holt's Settlement*[18] Megarry J. held that the court's power under the 1958 Act was to approve arrangements that actually did vary the trusts effectively so the court's order approving the arrangement makes it effective irrespective of whether there is any signed writing provided by the consenting adults. The 1958 Act by implication ousted section 53(1)(c). Furthermore, where the arrangement consisted of a specifically enforceable contract the beneficial interests would have passed under a constructive trust to the purchasers, such a trust being effective under section 53(2) without signed writing.

### Variation of Trusts Act 1958

Section 1.—(1) Where property, whether real or personal, is held on trusts arising, whether before or after the passing of this Act, under any will, settlement or other disposition, the court may if it thinks fit by order approve on behalf of—

(a) any person having, directly or indirectly, an interest, whether vested or contingent, under the trusts who by reason of infancy or other incapacity is incapable of assenting,[19] or

(b) any person (whether ascertained or not) who may[20] become entitled, directly or indirectly, to an interest under the trusts as being at a future date or on the happening of a future event a person of any specified description[21] or a member of any specified class of persons, so however that this paragraph shall not include any person[22] who would be of that description, or a member of that class, as the case may be, if the said date had fallen or the said event had happened at the date of the application to the court,[23] or

(c) any person unborn, or

(d) any person[24] in respect of any discretionary interest of his under protective trusts where the interest of the principal beneficiary has not failed or determined,

any arrangement (by whomsoever proposed,[25] and whether or not there is any other person beneficially interested who is capable of assenting thereto)

---

[18] [1969] 1 Ch. 100, 115–116.
[19] Objects of a discretionary trust are treated as included: *Re Clitheroe's S.T.* [1959] 3 All E.R. 784.
[20] See *Knocker* v. *Youle* [1986] 2 All E.R. 914, *infra*, p. 662.
[21] Unascertained future spouses are included: *Re Steed's W.T.* [1960] Ch. 407.
[22] This is tacitly assumed to cover only "ascertained" persons so as not to cover all females who may possibly marry a bachelor beneficiary and so become a beneficiary.
[23] This refers *inter alia* to the potential next-of-kin of a living person, who must make up their own minds whether or not to give their consent: *Re Suffert's Settlement* [1961] Ch. 1.
[24] Including an unascertained or unborn person: *Re Turner's Will Trusts* [1960] Ch. 122; (1959) 75 L.Q.R. 541 (R.E.M.). This approval may be given without the need to show "benefit."
[25] The arrangement need not be in the nature of a contract between parties: *Re Steed's W.T.* [1959] Ch. 354; but must not amount to a completely new settlement: *Re T's S.T.* [1964] Ch. 158; *Re Ball's S.T.* [1968] 1 W.L.R. 899; and it must be practical and businesslike: *Re Van Jenisen's W.T.* [1964] 1 W.L.R. 449.

varying or revoking all or any of the trusts, or enlarging[26] the powers of the trustees of managing or administering any of the property subject to the trusts:

Providing that except[27] by virtue of paragraph (*d*) of this subsection the court shall not approve an arrangement on behalf of any person unless the carrying out thereof would be for the benefit[28] of that person.

(2) In the foregoing subsection "protective trusts" means the trusts specified in paragraphs (i) and (ii) of subsection (1) of section thirty-three of the Trustee Act 1925 or any like trusts, "the principal beneficiary" has the same meaning as in the said subsection (1) and "discretionary interest" means an interest arising under the trust specified in paragraph (ii) of the said subsection (1) or any like trust.[29]

(3) The jurisdiction conferred by subsection (1) of this section shall be exercisable by the High Court, except that the question whether the carrying out of any arrangement would be for the benefit of a person falling within paragraph (*a*) of the said subsection (1) shall be determined by order of the authority having jurisdiction under Part VII of the Mental Health Act 1983 if that person is a patient within the meaning of the said Part VII.

(5) Nothing in the foregoing provisions of this section shall apply to trusts affecting property settled by Act of Parliament.

(6) Nothing in this section shall be taken to limit the powers conferred by section sixty-four of the Settled Land Act 1925, section fifty-seven of the Trustee Act 1925, or the powers of the authority having jurisdiction under Part VII of the Mental Health Act 1983.

## KNOCKER v. YOULE

Chancery Division [1986] 2 All E.R. 914; [1986] 1 W.L.R. 934

WARNER J. "I have before me three originating summonses under the Variation of Trusts Act 1958 which are interconnected. The first relates to the trusts of a settlement made by the late Charles McMahon Knocker, whom I will call 'the settlor,' on 25 November 1932, as varied by three subsequent deeds; the second relates to the trusts of a settlement made by the settlor on 22 December 1937; and the third relates to the trusts of the will and codicil of the settlor.

---

[26] *e.g.* conferring wider investment powers: see *Re Coates's Trusts* [1959] 1 W.L.R. 375; *Re Byng's Will Trusts* [1959] 1 W.L.R. 375; *Re Allen's Settlement Trusts* [1960] 1 W.L.R. 6; *Re Royal Naval and Royal Marine Children's Homes, Portsmouth* [1959] 1 W.L.R. 755.

[27] Even in the excepted case the court must exercise its discretion judicially: *Re Burney's Settlement* [1961] 1 W.L.R. 545; *Re Baker's S.T.* [1964] 1 W.L.R. 336.

[28] In *Re Cohen's W.T.* [1959] 1 W.L.R. 865, 868 Danckwerts J. said that the court could take a risk on behalf of an infant if it was a risk an adult would be prepared to take. This was criticised at (1960) 76 L.Q.R. 22 (R. E. M.). In a case of the same name [1965] 1 W.L.R. 1229, Stamp J. stressed, however, that (i) the court had to be satisfied that there was a benefit in the case of each individual infant and not merely of the whole class to which the infant belonged; and (ii) while the court need not be satisfied that each individual infant is bound to be better off than he would otherwise have been, it must be sure that he is making a bargain which is a reasonable one which an adult would be prepared to make. The court may take a broad reasonable view but not a galloping gambling view: *Re Robinson's S.T.* [1976] 1 W.L.R. 806. The court will not approve an arrangement which is a fraud on a power (*Re Robertson's W.T.* [1960] 1 W.L.R. 1050) or is contrary to public policy (*Re Michelham's W.T.* [1964] Ch. 550). Nor will the court use the Act as a justification for rectifying a settlement on the basis of mistake (*Re Tinker's Settlement* [1960] 1 W.L.R. 1011) or for making an order which can be made without the aid of the Act (*Re Pettifor's W.T.* [1966] Ch. 257 where the female beneficiary was 70 years old and so well past child-bearing age.)

[29] For "like" trusts, see *Re Wallace's Settlement* [1968] 1 W.L.R. 711, 716.

"The settlor had three children: a daughter Augusta, who was born in 1932 and who is now Mrs Youle, a daughter Ann, who was born in 1933 and died unmarried, without issue, in 1977, and a son Charles Cyprian Knocker, who was born in 1936 and whom I will call 'Mr Knocker.' Mrs Youle has three children, all now of age. Mr Knocker has two children, both still minors. The plaintiffs, in the case of each of the originating summonses, are Mr Knocker and Mrs Youle.

"A problem has arisen which particularly affects the second settlement, that dated 22 December 1937. The trusts of that settlement were unusual and are now effectively these. In the case of a share of the trust fund settled on Mrs Youle (referred to in the settlement as 'Augusta') cl. 3(2) provides:

'*If* Augusta shall attain the age of twenty-one years [which of course she did long ago] the Trustees shall thereafter pay the income of the first share to Augusta during the reminder of her life and after her death shall hold such share and the future income thereof in trust for such person or persons for such purposes and in such manner as Augusta shall by Will or Codicil appoint.'

"In default of appointment there is an accruer clause to a share of the trust fund settled on Mr Knocker. The trusts of that share are, *mutatis mutandis*, the same. Then there is, in cl. 7, an ultimate trust in these terms:

'IN the event of the failure or determination of the trusts hereinbefore declared concerning the Trust Fund and subject to the trusts powers and provisions hereinbefore declared and contained concerning the same and to every or any exercise of such powers and to any statutory provisions which may be applicable the Trustees shall hold the Trust Fund upon trust to pay the income thereof to the Settlor's Wife Mildred Alice Knocker for her life or until she remarries and subject thereto shall hold the Trust Fund and the income thereof in trust for such of the Settlor's four sisters Emily Mills the said Ada Florence Potter Annie Maude Leveaux and Alice Augusta Baker as shall be living at the time of such failure or determination and the issue then living and attaining the age of twenty-one years of such of the said four sisters as shall then be dead in equal shares per stirpes.'

"The settlor's wife, Mildred Alice Knocker, and his four named sisters have all long since died. The problem is this. None of the issue of the four sisters, whom I will call, for convenience, 'the cousins,' has been made a party to any of these originating summonses. They are very numerous and some of them live in Australia. It is not practicable to get their approval of the proposed arrangement. There are 17 of them who, if the failure or determination of the prior trusts had occurred at the date of the issue of the originating summonses, would have been members of the class of issue entitled to take under the ultimate trust in cl. 7 of the settlement.

"What is said by counsel is that I have power under s.1(1)(*b*) of the Variation of Trusts Act 1958 to approve the arrangement on behalf of the cousins.

"There are two difficulties. First, it is not strictly accurate to describe the cousins as persons 'who may become entitled . . . to an interest under the trusts.' There is no doubt of course that they are members of a 'specified class.' Each of them is, however, entitled now to an interest under the trusts, albeit a contingent one (in the case of those who are under 21, a doubly contingent one) and albeit also that it is an interest that is defeasible on the exercise of the general testamentary powers of appointment vested in Mrs Youle and Mr Knocker. None the less, it is properly described in legal language as an interest, and it seems to me plain that in this Act the word 'interest' is used in its technical, legal sense. Otherwise, the words 'whether vested or contingent' in para. (*a*) of s.1(1) would be out of place.

"What counsel invited me to do was in effect to interpret the word 'interest' in s.1(1) loosely, as a layman might, so as not to include an interest that was remote. I was referred to two authorities: *Re Moncrieff's Settlement Trusts* [1962] 1 W.L.R. 1344 and the earlier case of *Re Suffert's Settlement* [1961] Ch. 1. In both those cases, however, the class in question was a class of prospective next of kin, and, of course it is trite law that the prospective or presumptive next of kin of a living person do not have an interest. They have only a *spes successionis*, a hope of succeeding, and quite certainly they are the typical category of persons who fall within s.1(1)(*b*). Another familiar example of a person falling within that provision is a potential future spouse. It seems to me, however, that a person who has an actual interest directly conferred on him or her by a settlement, albeit a remote interest, cannot properly be described as one who 'may become' entitled to an interest.

"The second difficulty (if one could think of a way of overcoming the first) is that there are, as I indicated earlier, 17 cousins who, if the failure or determination of the earlier trusts declared by the settlement had occurred at the date of the application to the court, would have been members of the specified class, in that they were then living and over 21. Therefore, they are *prima facie* excluded from s.1(1)(*b*) by what has been conveniently called the proviso to it, that is to say the part beginning 'so however that this paragraph shall not include . . . ' They are in the same boat, if I may express it in that way, as the first cousins in *Re Suffert's Settlement* and the adopted son in *Re Moncrieff's Settlement Trusts*. The court cannot approve the arrangement on their behalf; only they themselves can do so.

"Counsel for the plaintiffs suggested that I could distinguish *Re Suffert's Settlement* and *Re Moncrieff's Settlement Trusts* in that respect for two reasons.

"First, he suggested that the proviso applied only if there was a single event on the happening of which one could ascertain the class. Here, he said, both Mr Knocker and Mrs Youle must die without exercising their general testamentary powers of appointment to the full before any of the cousins could take anything. But it seems to me that what the proviso is referring to is the event on which the class becomes ascertainable, and that that is a single event. It is, in this case, the death of the survivor of Mrs Youle and Mr Knocker, neither of them having exercised the power to the full; in the words of cl. 7 of the settlement, it is 'the failure or determination of the trusts hereinbefore declared concerning the trust fund.'

"The second reason suggested why I should distinguish the earlier authorities was that the event hypothesised in the proviso was the death of the survivor of Mr Knocker and Mrs Youle on the date when the originating summonses were issued, that is to say on 6 January 1984. There is evidence that on that day there were in existence wills of both of them exercising their testamentary powers to the full. The difficulty about that is that the proviso does not say ' . . . so however that this paragraph shall not include any person who would have become entitled if the said event has happened at the date of the application to the court.' It says:

   ' . . . so however that this paragraph shall not include any person who would be of that description, or a member of that class, as the case may be, if the said date had fallen or the said event had happened at the date of the application to the court.'

"So the proviso is designed to identify the presumptive members of the class at the date of the application to the court and does not advert to the question whether at that date they would or would not have become entitled.

"I was reminded by counsel of the principle that one must construe Acts of Parliament having regard to their purpose, and it was suggested that the purpose here was to exclude the need to join as parties to applications under the Variation of Trusts Act 1958 people whose interests were remote. In my view, however, that principle does not enable me to take the sort of liberty with the language of this statute that I was invited to take. It is noteworthy that remoteness does not seem to be the test if one thinks in terms of presumptive statutory next of kin. The healthy issue of an elderly widow who is on her deathbed, and who has not made a will, have an expectation of succeeding to her estate; that could hardly be described as remote. Yet they are a category of persons on whose behalf the court could, subject of course to the proviso, approve an arrangement under this Act. On the other hand, people in the position of the cousins in this case have an interest that is extremely remote. None the less, it is an interest, and the distinction between an expectation and an interest is one which I do not think that I am entitled to blur. So, with regret, having regard to the particular circumstances of this case, I have to say that I do not think that I have jurisdiction to approve these arrangements on behalf of the cousins."

### Section 6. The Trustee's Duty of Impartiality

It is the trustees' duty to balance the conflicting interests of life-tenants interested in income and remaindermen interested in capital and certain rules have evolved to guide trustees and, in some cases, to provide what is to be done if the rules have been broken.[30] In an exceptional case it may even be necessary for them to balance fairly the interests of beneficiaries entitled to capital. Thus, they can reject the claim of a beneficiary entitled to 46/80 of a trust fund to have 574 of the 999 shares in a private company owned by the trust where such majority shareholding is worth much more than 46/80 of the proceeds of sale of the 999 shares.[31] To maintain an even hand or fair balance between the beneficiaries the shares should be sold and the proceeds divided in the relevant fractions between the beneficiaries. In making investments we have already seen[32] that the trustees must act fairly in making decisions which may have different consequences for different classes of beneficiaries.

### I. THE RULE IN ALLHUSEN *v.* WHITTELL[33]

Take a case where a testator has left his residuary estate to A for life remainder to B absolutely and in accordance with the general law

---

[30] Generally, see Josling's *Apportionments for Executors and Trustees* (Oyez Publications); also the chapter by John Flower in *Debits, Credits, Finance & Profits* edited by Edey and Yamey (Sweet & Maxwell, 1974).

[31] *Lloyds Bank plc* v. *Duker* [1987] 1 W.L.R. 1324.

[32] *Supra*, p. 612.

[33] (1887) L.R. 4 Eq. 295. For a good general statement of the rule see *per* Romer L.J. in *Corbett* v. *I.R.C.* [1938] 1 K.B. 567.

debts, funeral and testamentary expenses and legacies have to be paid out of the residue. It would be unfair to apply all the income of the gross residue towards payment of debts, expenses and legacies, so favouring B. Similarly, it would be unfair to apply capital only towards such payments, so favouring A. The rule in *Allhusen* v. *Whittell* thus treats the payments as coming partly from income and partly from capital. It requires that sum to be ascertained which together with interest for the year succeeding death would amount to the total expended on payment of debts, expenses and legacies: the sum so ascertained will be borne by B and the excess of the total expenditure over that sum will be borne by A. The rate of interest to be taken depends on the ratio subsisting between the actual net income after tax[34] for the year succeeding death and the gross capital of the estate. The rule assumes payment at the end of the executor's year and should be modified if payment is significantly before or after that year.[35] Exact calculations are not required: rough and ready bona fide calculations will suffice.[36] In practice many wills exclude the rule (as any contrary intention displaces it).[37] Moreover, the rule is often ignored, especially as few beneficiaries know about the rule and most beneficiaries are so pleased to receive the testator's bounty that they do not "look a gift horse in the mouth."[38]

## II. THE DUTY TO CONVERT

Once the net residue to which A and B are successively entitled has been ascertained there are still further problems. The residue may comprise wasting, hazardous or other unauthorised investments producing a high income for A and making B worry whether the capital will have depreciated considerably by the time he receives it. Alternatively, the residue may comprise some reversionary (or other non-income-producing asset) such that A receives no income whilst the capital value of the reversionary interest increases all the time as the life-tenant grows older and poorer.

Four questions then have to be borne in mind:

(1) is there a duty to convert property from its present state into an authorised investment;
(2) *if so*, is there a duty to apportion income pending conversion;
(3) *if so*, what is the method of apportionment;
(4) what is the position of leaseholds?

A duty to convert arises: (a) if the trust instrument so directs whether by an express trust for sale or by other indications that the

---

[34] *Re Oldham* [1927] W.N. 113.
[35] *Re McEwen* [1913] 2 Ch. 704; *Re Wills* [1915] 1 Ch. 769.
[36] *Re Wills* [1915] 1 Ch. 769, 779.
[37] *Re Ullswater* [1952] Ch. 105 holding that a common form clause for excluding the rule in *Howe* v. *Dartmouth* failed to exclude the rule in *Allhusen* v. *Whittell*.
[38] (1946) 10 Conv.(N.S.) 125 (George and George).

property must be sold or (b) if the rule in *Howe* v. *Dartmouth*[39] applies. This rule ensures that where a *will*[40] contains a *residuary*[41] bequest of *personal*[42] property to be enjoyed by persons in succession then unauthorised investments (*e.g.* wasting and hazardous assets, reversionary interests and other non-income-producing assets) are held upon an implied trust to sell them and invest the proceeds in authorised investments unless (since the rule is based upon presumed intention) the will reveals an intention that no such sale is to take place.

There is a clear contrary intention where the testator indicates that there is to be no trust or duty to sell at all as where the trustees are given the right to decide to sell only if they see fit since such right not to sell but to retain is inconsistent with any duty to sell.[43] A contrary intent is also present if there is an express duty to sell at some future date (*e.g.* the death of the life-tenant), where there is nothing else to oust the implication that there is no duty to sell till then but rather a duty to retain.[44] A mere provision that the residue is to be divided between certain persons after the life-tenant's death does not exclude *Howe* v. *Dartmouth* since the division may be of the residue as converted under *Howe* v. *Dartmouth: Re Evans*.[45]

Where the trustees have a power to decide *when* to sell, rather than a right to decide *if* to sell, this presupposes a sale is intended to occur so this situation is really not an instance of an implied *Howe* v. *Dartmouth* trust for sale but an instance of the will itself expressly or impliedly imposing a duty to convert.

Where a contrary intention is present so that there is no duty to convert then obviously the life-tenant will be entitled to the income actually produced by the property—no more, no less.[46]

### III. DUTY TO APPORTION

Even if there is a duty to convert it does not follow that pending conversion the tenant for life will get an apportioned part of the income only. The duty to apportion may itself be excluded by an

---

[39] (1802) 7 Ves. 137; generally see L. A. Sheridan (1952) 16 Conv. 349. The "rule in *Howe* v. *Dartmouth*" is confusingly used sometimes not just for the duty to convert but compendiously for the apportionment rules where there is an express or a *Howe* v. *Dartmouth* trust for sale.

[40] Deeds necessarily deal with specific authorised property: *Re Van Straubenzee* [1901] 2 Ch. 779. On an intestacy a statutory trust for sale arises: Administration of Estates Act 1925, s.33.

[41] A specific bequest of assets makes them authorised for the purposes of retention but not for further purchases: see p. 611, *supra*.

[42] Realty is presumed meant to be enjoyed *in specie*: *Re Woodhouse* [1941] Ch. 332; *Lottman* v. *Stanford* (1980) 107 D.L.R. (3d) 28. Since L.P.A. 1925, s.28(2) income from land is in any event treated as income passing to the life-tenant even where the land is not settled land within S.L.A. 1925.

[43] *Re Sewell* (1870) L.R. 11 Eq. 80; *Re Pitcairn* [1896] 2 Ch. 199; *Re Bates* [1907] 1 Ch. 22 pointing out that another way of regarding the matter is to view the right to retain shares, for example, as making them authorised investments.

[44] *Alcock* v. *Sloper* (1833) 2 My. & K. 699; *Rowe* v. *Rowe* (1861) 29 Beav. 276; *Re North* [1909] 1 Ch. 625.

[45] [1921] 2 Ch. 309.

[46] *Re Pitcairn* [1896] 2 Ch. 199; *Rowlls* v. *Bebb* [1900] 2 Ch. 107.

intention of specific enjoyment of income pending conversion. The rules are:

(i) If the property is realty so that a duty to convert can only exist under an express trust for sale the tenant for life gets the actual income,[47] unless the will directs an apportionment, or there is an improper postponement of conversion: *Wentworth* v. *Wentworth*.[48]

(ii) If the property is personalty of the prescribed kind[49] and the will is treated as indicating expressly or impliedly that there is an express trust for conversion the tenant for life gets an apportionment only unless the will expressly or impliedly gives him the actual income: *Re Chaytor*.[50] A mere trust for conversion with an ancillary power to postpone conversion does not of itself give the income of the property before conversion *in specie* to the life-tenant.[51] More is required in the way of showing an intention that the power was intended not for the more convenient realisation of the estate but for the special benefit of the life-tenant.[52] Even then until the trustees consciously exercise this power for the life-tenant's benefit the life-tenant is entitled to an apportioned income and not the actual income.[53]

(iii) If the property is personalty of the prescribed kind and there is an implied trust for conversion under the rule in *Howe* v. *Dartmouth* there will be an apportionment.

There is, of course, no duty to apportion income of property invested in authorised investments: the life-tenant takes all such income. The extension by the 1961 Act of the powers of investment might have been expected to narrow the scope of the rule in *Howe* v. *Dartmouth*. It seems clear that the rule does not apply to special-range property, narrower-range property not requiring advice, and narrower-range and wider-range property requiring advice for the period *after* advice to retain them has been properly obtained and followed. However, on a strict view it may be that the rule applies to narrower-range and wider-range property requiring advice for the period before the trust fund has been divided into the narrower-range and wider-range parts, and before advice to retain them has been properly

---

[47] The Law of Property Act 1925, s.28(2).

[48] [1900] A.C. 163: testator gave trustees power to postpone sale of realty for 21 years. Trustees improperly postponed for longer. *Held* by the Privy Council the tenant for life entitled to a reasonable percentage yield based upon the value of the property estimated as at the expiration of the period of 21 years.

[49] Residuary comprising wasting, hazardous or unauthorised investments or reversionary interests.

[50] [1905] 1 Ch. 233.

[51] *Re Chaytor* [1905] 1 Ch. 233; *Re Slater* (1915) 113 L.T. 691, 693; *Re Berry* [1962] Ch. 97 pointing out deficiencies in *Re Fisher* [1943] Ch. 377.

[52] *Re Inman* [1915] 1 Ch. 187.

[53] *Rowlls* v. *Bebb* [1900] 2 Ch. 107; *Re Fisher* [1943] Ch. 377 (intestacy trust for sale); *Re Hey's S.T.* [1945] Ch. 294; *Re Guinness's Settlement* [1966] 1 W.L.R. 1355.

obtained and followed. If the trustees follow advice to sell and reinvest such property it would seem the rule applies until such sale.

## IV. THE METHOD OF APPORTIONMENT

If the tenant for life is entitled to an apportionment only it will be calculated[54] as follows:

(a) Where there is for the benefit of the estate as a whole[55] a power to postpone conversion and the trustees postpone:

(i) The subject-matter being wasting or unauthorised property, the tenant for life is entitled, as from the testator's death, to the current percentage[56] of the value of the property estimated as at the death, plus the income from investing the difference[57] (if any) between that percentage and the income actually produced: *Re Owen,*[58] *Re Parry.*[59] Valuation is at the date of death as no other date is appropriate in view of the power to postpone sale.

(ii) The subject-matter being reversionary interests or other non-income-producing property (*e.g.* a 10-year interest-free loan to a charity), the mode of apportionment is that adopted in *Re Chesterfield's Trusts, infra.*

(b) Where there is no power to postpone sale but an immediate sale would be disadvantageous to the estate:

(i) The subject-matter being wasting or unauthorised property, the tenant for life is entitled, as from the testator's death to the current percentage[60] of the value of the property estimated as at the expiration of the executor's year, *i.e.*[61] one year from the death, plus the income from investing the difference (if any) between that percentage and the income actually produced: *Re Fawcett, infra.*

---

[54] For calculations see J. F. Josling's *Apportionments for Executors and Trustees*; Rowland's *Trust Account*; Ranking Spicer & Pegler's *Executorship Law and Accounts.*

[55] If given exceptionally to benefit the life-tenant then he takes the income *in specie* so no question of apportionment arises: *Re Inman* [1915] 1 Ch. 187.

[56] It is surprising that no one has asked for directions from the court as to whether or not a higher rate than 4 per cent. is now proper since an intestate's statutory legacies now carry 6 per cent. In *Bartlett* v. *Barclays Bank Trust Co.* [1980] Ch. 515, 547 the rate applied to compensation for breach of trust was that allowed on the court's short-term investment account under Administration of Justice Act 1965, s.6(1), *infra*, p. 779, though where this is a high rate such as 12 per cent. this reflects compensation for loss of capital value because of inflation so Brightman L.J. said, "It seems arguable that a proportion of the interest should be added to capital in order to help maintain the value of the corpus of the trust estate." The current percentage is intended to represent a fair yield so why not take the mean between the "higher rate" and the "lower rate" prescribed by the Treasury under Inheritance Tax Act 1984, s.50(3) to prevent manipulation of artificial values for I.H.T.? The higher rate is that shown in the F.T. Actuaries Share Indices for British Government Stocks and the lower rate is the current gross dividend yield on the F.T. Actuaries All-Share Index.

[57] The difference is authorised capital to the income of which the life-tenant is entitled.

[58] [1912] 1 Ch. 519.

[59] [1947] Ch. 23.

[60] See n. 56, *supra.*

[61] If sale takes place before the end of the executor's year then the actual sale price is taken: *Re Fawcett, infra.*

(ii) The subject-matter being reversionary interests or other non-income-producing property, the mode of apportionment is as in *Re Chesterfield's Trusts, infra,* once the apportionable capital figure has materialised either on sale of the interest or on the property coming into hand, *e.g.* on the life-tenant's death.

## RE FAWCETT

Chancery Division [1940] Ch. 402; 109 L.J.Ch. 124

The testatrix bequeathed her residuary estate, which comprised several unauthorised investments, to trustees upon trust to invest it and divide the income equally among her nephews and nieces for their respective lives and then for their children.

FARWELL J. (in a reserved judgment): "The rule in *Howe* v. *Lord Dartmouth*[62] is founded in the judgment of Lord Eldon L.C. in the case of that name. It was made for the purpose of holding, as far as possible, an even hand between those whose interests are in capital and those whose interests are in income, in respect of investments which are not authorised by law for the investment of trust funds. In the present case, so far as the construction of this will is concerned, it is, I think, clear that there is a trust for sale so far as the unauthorised investments are concerned. There is no express trust for sale but there is a trust to invest and that must mean to invest in trustee securities. Accordingly there is an implied trust for sale of any investments which are not authorised by law for the investment of trust funds. It is also to be noticed that there is no power to postpone the sale in question. The rule in *Howe* v. *Lord Dartmouth,* in my judgment, was based upon the equitable idea of treating that which ought to be done as having been done, and accordingly in the early cases the general rule was that the tenant for life was entitled to whatever the investments, if they were sold and re-invested in Consols, would produce. To that extent, and to that extent only, he was entitled to payment on account of income. In more recent years the practice has generally been to give to the tenant for life interest at 4 per cent. upon the capital value of the unauthorised investment. The reason for the alteration in the rule was, I think, due to the fact that the range of authorised investments has been very greatly extended in comparatively recent years, and accordingly the court took the view that a rate of interest which might be higher than that which was produced by Consols would be a reasonable rate to allow to tenants for life, since there was, at any rate, some possibility that trust funds could be invested in securities returning such income. The general, although not the universal, rule is now to allow 4 per cent. and I see no reason in the present case to depart from that modern practice. In order to give effect to the rule it appears to me that in a case of this kind it is the duty of the trustees to have the unauthorised investments valued as at the end of the first year after the testatrix's death. During that year the executors are given time to deal with the estate as a whole. At the end of it comes the time when, in my judgment, any unauthorised investments which they still retain should be valued and the tenant for life becomes entitled to be paid 4 per cent. on the valuation of the whole of the unauthorised investments. To that extent these tenants for life are entitled to receive income

---

[62] (1802) 7 Ves. 137.

in each year and that income, 4 per cent. on the capital value of the unauthorised investments, must be paid out of the actual income received from the unauthorised investments; that is to say, the trustees will receive the whole of the dividends which the unauthorised investments pay and there will be no apportionment. Those dividends will be applied in the first instance in paying, so far as they go, 4 per cent. on the capital value of the unauthorised investments. If the income received on the unauthorised investments is more than sufficient to pay the 4 per cent., then the balance will be added to the capital and it will form part of the whole fund in the hands of the trustees. If, on the other hand, the income actually received from the unauthorised investments is not sufficient to pay 4 per cent. in each year to the tenants for life, they will not be entitled to immediate recoupment out of the capital, but when the unauthorised investments are sold the trustees will then have in their hands a fund representing the proceeds of sale of the unauthorised investments, together with any surplus income which may have accrued in the earlier years; out of those proceeds of sale the tenants for life will be entitled to be recouped so as to provide them with the full 4 per cent. during the whole period and they will be entitled to be refunded the deficit calculated at 4 per cent. simple interest but less tax. In that way it appears to me the rule can be worked out satisfactorily as between capital and income and the balance will be held as evenly as possible between the two opposing interests. No doubt the duty of the trustees is to realise the unauthorised securities as soon as conveniently may be, but until that has been done that, in my view, is the right way of dealing with the matter. The fact that there may be some investments which are of little or no value and which produce no income does not affect the position if the whole of the unauthorised investments are treated as one whole, and the value of the whole of those investments is ascertained and the income received from the whole of those investments is received by the trustees and applied in the way which I have stated.

"That being the general principle upon which, in my view, the trustees should act in this case, I think the questions raised in the summons can be answered without much difficulty.

"I should add this. It must be observed that in the present case, as I have already pointed out, there is no power to postpone the sale, and the judgment which I have given does not necessarily apply in a case where there is an express power to postpone; other considerations may arise in such a case, but where there is no power to postpone and there is a trust for sale and re-investment in trustee securities the judgment which I have given indicates the right way in which the administration of the estate should be proceeded with.

"Accordingly I will make a declaration, in answer to question 1 of the summons, that on the true construction of the will of the testatrix there was and is a trust for sale as to all unauthorised investments and that the rule in *Howe* v. *Lord Dartmouth* ought to have been and ought to be applied with reference to her residuary estate as between capital and income.

"In answer to question 2 of the summons I will make a declaration that (*a*) in the case of unauthorised investments which were still retained unsold at the end of one year from the death of the testatrix the life tenants were and are entitled to interest at the rate of 4 per cent. per annum on the value of such investments taken at the end of such year but commencing from the date of the death and running on until the realisation of such investments respectively; (*b*) in the case of unauthorised investments realised during the first year after the death of the testatrix the life tenants are entitled to interest at the rate aforesaid on the net proceeds of such realisation respectively from the date of the death down to the respective dates of completions of such realisations; (c) the unauthorised investments for the time being unsold ought to be taken en bloc as one aggregate for the purposes of the rule in *Howe* v. *Lord Dartmouth*; (d) in applying that rule the Apportionment Act 1870 ought not to be applied in the income accounts at the death of the testatrix or at the beginning or end of any accounting period with reference to the income of unauthorised investments; (e) any excess of income from unauthorised investments beyond the interest payable in respect of such investments to the life tenants ought to be invested in authorised investments as part of the capital with the other authorised investments, and accordingly the whole of the actual subsequent income of such invested excess income is payable as income; (f) the interest so payable in respect of unauthorised investments was and is payable out of moneys being income from unauthorised investments or, so far as such income is insufficient, being proceeds of realisation of such investments, and any interest so payable for the time being in arrear is payable (but calculated as simple interest only) out of subsequent income from unauthorised investments which are for the time being retained and out of the proceeds of sale of such investments as and when realised, but neither any excess income from unauthorised investments, which at the end of any accounting period is available under head (e) for investment in authorised investments, nor any proceeds of realisation of unauthorised investments not required at the date of realisation to pay interest payable as aforesaid for the time being in arrear and accordingly available to be invested in authorised investments, were or are applicable towards payment of subsequently accruing interest as aforesaid in respect of unauthorised investments then still retained."

*Note*

Assume that the testator died on January 1, 1990, and that it is now January 1, 1992. It is estimated that a sale of the unauthorised securities at the death of the testator would have produced £1,000. The tenant for life is entitled for two years to the current percentage—say, 4 per cent.—of that sum, *i.e.* £80. The income in fact produced during the two years is £200. The difference of £120—being the difference between the percentage on the notional conversion and the income actually produced—forms part of the capital. The interest or income on that £120 when invested henceforth goes to income. If the tenant for life actually received the whole of the £200, he has received £120 more than he was entitled to, so that an adjustment will be made out of subsequent payments; and if the tenant for life dies before a complete adjustment, the balance may apparently be recouped out of his estate.[63]

The difference might also be the other way round. The percentage on the notional conversion is £80, but the income actually produced and actually received by the tenant for life might have been only £50, so that he has received £30 *less* than the sum he was entitled to. Here also an adjustment will be made. The deficiency in the income payable

[63] *Cf. Hood* v. *Clapham* (1854) 19 Beav. 90.

to the tenant for life is primarily payable out of any excess income produced by the unauthorised assets in a subsequent accounting period, and, failing that, out of the proceeds of sale of the unauthorised assets. Any excess income received in a previous year cannot be resorted to in order to make good the deficiency, as such excess income must be regarded as capital and invested accordingly.[64]

## RE EARL OF CHESTERFIELD'S TRUSTS

Chancery Division (1883) 24 Ch.D. 643; 52 L.J.Ch. 958; 49 L.T. 261

A testator who died on December 1, 1871, devised and bequeathed his residuary estate to trustees on trust for conversion, with a discretionary power to postpone conversion, for the benefit of one for life, with remainders over. This residue included outstanding personal estate consisting of (*inter alia*) a mortgage debt with arrears of interest. The trustees postponed the conversion of the outstanding estate, which eventually fell in (with interest) a number of years later.

*Held*, following *Beavan* v. *Beavan*,[65] that the property was to be apportioned between capital and income "by ascertaining the respective sums which, put out at £4 per cent. per annum on December 1, 1871 . . . and accumulating at compound interest calculated at that rate with yearly rests, and deducting income tax, would, with the accumulations of interest, have produced, at the respective dates of receipt, the amounts actually received; and that the aggregate of the sums so ascertained ought to be treated as principal and be applied accordingly, and the residue should be treated as income."[66]

### Note

A testator who dies on December 1, 1990, bequeaths his residuary personalty on trust for conversion, with a power of postponement, for A for life, remainder to B. Part of this residue consists of a reversionary interest under a marriage settlement of which the tenant for life is the testator's wife, and the remainderman the testator. The testator's trustees postpone, and it is assumed, in order to eliminate the necessity of calculating with yearly rests (compound interest), that the wife dies exactly one year after the testator, whereupon the reversionary interest falls in and produces £1,030. Of this sum £1,000 goes to capital for B, and £30 goes to income for A; for the sum which, with interest at 4 per cent. from December 1, 1984, to December 1, 1985, minus income tax at 25p in the pound, would produce £1,030 is £1,000. Henceforth A receives the income of this £1,000 when invested. Calculation becomes involved if a lengthy period has elapsed between the testator's death and the apportionment, for after the first year of calculation there is interest upon interest. The position would be the same if the trustees had sold the reversionary interest at the end of the year for £1,030. As

---

[64] See *Re Fawcett* [1940] Ch. 402.
[65] (1883) 24 Ch.D. 649n.
[66] So also *Re Morley* [1895] 2 Ch. 738; *Rowells* v. *Bebb* [1900] 2 Ch. 107; *Re Hollebone* [1919] 2 Ch. 93; *Re Hey's S.T.* [1945] Ch. 294; *Re Guinness's Settlement* [1966] 1 W.L.R. 1355; *cf. Re Hengler* [1893] 1 Ch. 586; *Re Chance* [1962] Ch. 593.

the £30 passing to A is part of the £1,030 capital it is not liable to income tax: the notional tax deducted in the calculation enures for B's benefit. As reversionary interests fetch relatively little owing to the imponderable factors involved, it is best if possible to wait till they fall into possession.[67]

The same method of apportionment applies to a *contingent* reversionary interest.[68] But it does not apply where the interest is vested in possession, but the income therefrom is temporarily charged in favour of a third party,[69] and it does not apply to realty.[70] On the other hand, it can apply where the sum to be apportioned includes both principal and interest.[71]

## V. APPORTIONMENT IN RELATION TO LEASEHOLDS

In the case of land settled on trust for sale or under the Settled Land Act 1925 leaseholds for 60 years or more unexpired are authorised investments,[72] so no question of apportionment arises. Lesser leaseholds are unauthorised so there will be a duty to convert under the rule in *Howe* v. *Dartmouth* unless there is some positive indication in the will ousting such duty by indicating that the rents are to be enjoyed *in specie*. In *Re Trollope's W.T.*[73] Tomlin J. said *obiter* that "so far as leaseholds held in trust for sale are concerned the rule of *Howe* v. *Dartmouth* is gone" but, as that quotation shows,[74] he was presupposing the existence of a trust for sale which is the very concept implied by an application of the *Howe* v. *Dartmouth* rule. His reference to *Howe* v. *Dartmouth* (like the references of so many judges)[75] seems to be a reference not to the duty to convert under *Howe* v. *Dartmouth* but to the apportionment rules that apply once a trust for sale has arisen.

The apportionment rules for leaseholds have been altered by subsection (2) of section 28 of the Law of Property Act 1925: "Subject to any direction to the contrary in the *disposition on trust for sale* or in the *settlement of the proceeds of sale*, the net rents and profits of the land until sale . . . shall be paid or applied . . . in like manner as the income of investments representing the purchase money would be payable or applicable if a sale had been made and the proceeds had been duly invested." Thus, in the case of a disposition on trust for sale of land or a settlement of the proceeds of sale of land, the tenant for life is, pending conversion, entitled *in specie*, unless there is a contrary

---

[67] As administrators are directed to do under an intestacy by the Administration of Estates Act 1925, s.33(1).
[68] *Re Hobson* (1885) 55 L.J.Ch. 422.
[69] *Re Holliday* [1947] Ch. 402.
[70] *Re Woodhouse* [1941] Ch. 332; *Lottman* v. *Stanford* (1980) 107 D.L.R. (3d) 28.
[71] *Re Chance's W.T.* [1962] Ch. 593 (the aggregate of principal sums payable out of the compensation fund established under the Town and Country Planning Act 1947, as subsequently amended, together with the interest thereon held to be apportionable in accordance with the rule).
[72] *Re Gough* [1957] Ch. 323; Settled Land Act 1925, s.73(xi); Law of Property Act 1925, s.28(1).
[73] [1927] 1 Ch. 596, 601.
[74] Also the preceding paragraph of his judgment.
[75] *e.g.* Clauson L.J. in *Re Berton* [1939] Ch. 200; Pennycuick J. in *Re Berry* [1962] Ch. 97.

direction. By subsection (5) of the section it is provided: "This section applies to dispositions on trust for sale coming into operation either before or after the commencement or by virtue of this Act." Accordingly, in *Re Brooker*,[76] Lawrence J. held that where a residuary bequest in 1903 upon express trust for sale included leaseholds the life-tenants were entitled to the rent, *in specie* as from January 1, 1926. Furthermore, in *Re Berton*[77] Clauson L.J. (sitting at first instance) held that where a residuary bequest of leaseholds was made directly to two persons equally for their respective lives so as to take effect by virtue of sections 34 and 35 of the Law of Property Act 1925 as a trust for sale for the persons as tenants in common, then section 28(2) applied to entitle the life-tenants to the rents *in specie*. Since section 28(2) applies in the case of express trusts for sale and trusts for sale implied by statute it seems[78] that it should apply to trusts for sale implied by *Howe* v. *Dartmouth*.[79]

## VI. OVERRIDING DUTY TO ACT FAIRLY

In case it might be thought that section 28(2) scandalously enables a life-tenant to receive all rents during the last 10 or 12 years of an unauthorised lease, leaving nothing for the remainderman, it should be remembered that the trustees have an overriding duty to keep an even hand between the beneficiaries. They would be in breach of this duty[80] if they retained the leases till they expired or for any longer period than reasonably necessary to sell the depreciating leases. It would also seem that the remainderman could specifically invoke section 30 of the Law of Property Act for the court to compel the trustees to sell or he could take advantage of his inherent right to call for conversion.[81]

Hoffmann J. has pointed out[82] that the duty to keep an even hand between the beneficiaries in making or retaining investments is more appropriately the less mechanical duty to act fairly. His approach

---

[76] [1926] W.N. 93.
[77] [1939] Ch. 200. S. J. Bailey, "Leaseholds and the Rule in *Howe* v. *The Earl of Dartmouth*"(1932) 4 C.L.J. 357; 164 L.T.J. 326.
[78] Pettit, p. 369; Hanbury & Maudsley, p. 515.
[79] It is no longer considered that the courts will accept the narrow technical approach of Professor Sir Roy Marshall in the 5th ed. hereof, p. 418, where it was stated: "A *Howe* v. *Dartmouth* trust for sale is probably not a 'disposition on trust for sale' within s.28 notwithstanding that by s.205(1)(ii) of the Act the word 'disposition' in the Act includes a bequest of property contained in a will; for a *Howe* v. *Dartmouth* trust for sale is not a bequest of property on trust for sale, but a bequest of property on which a trust for sale is engrafted by operation of law. Again, a 'settlement of the proceeds of sale' presupposes an *express* trust for sale. It is submitted, therefore, that s.28 does not affect the *Howe* v. *Dartmouth* rule."
[80] *e.g. Beauclerk* v. *Ashburnham* (1845) 8 Beav. 322; 14 L.J.Ch. 241 where trustees were *authorised and required* by and with the consent and direction in writing of the life-tenant to invest in leaseholds. Obviously, the trustees could not object to investment in leaseholds as such, but they had a discretion whether or not to agree to a particular investment proposed "because it must be agreed at once that it would not be fit for them to lay out the trust moneys in a low, bad and deteriorating situation," *per* Lord Langdale M.R. at 8 Beav. 328. It should be noted that executors in realising the estate and paying off liabilities have a duty to consider the interest of the estate as a whole and are under no duty to consider the effect between the beneficiaries so as to hold the balance evenly between them: *Re Hayes's W.T.* [1971] 1 W.L.R. 758.
[81] *Thornton* v. *Ellis* (1852) 15 Beav. 193; *Wightwick* v. *Lord* (1857) 6 H.L.C. 217.
[82] *Nestlé* v. *National Westminster Bank, supra*, p. 612.

indicates that English courts would reach the same result as the Ontario Court of Appeal in *Re Smith*[83] circumstances. The trust property comprised only Imperial Oil Co. stock held on trust for S's mother for life, remainder to S. From the outset there was only an average dividend of 2½ per cent. when returns of 8 to 10 per cent. were available in respect of good quality bonds and mortgages. S did not want the stock sold and the trustee was happy to agree with this and ignore the life tenant's requests to obtain a higher income for her. The Court of Appeal upheld the judge's finding that the trustee was in breach of trust and should be removed and replaced by a new trustee.

## QUESTION

What is the purpose and effect of the following clause in a will?

"I give all my property of whatsoever kind and wheresoever situate of which I have any power of testamentary disposition and not otherwise disposed of by this my will or by any codicil hereto to my trustees upon the following trusts:

Upon trust to sell, call in and convert the same into money with power to postpone such sale, calling in and conversion for so long as they in the exercise of their absolute discretion shall think fit without being liable for loss and so that the income of my real, leasehold and personal estate howsoever constituted and invested (including the income of property required for the payment of debts and other payments in due course of administration in payment whereof the proceeds of such sale, calling in and conversion are hereinafter directed to be applied) shall as from my death be treated as income and that a reversionary or future interest shall not be sold prior to falling into possession unless my trustees shall see special reason for such earlier sale and that the net rents and profits of my real and leasehold estate for the time being remaining unsold after payment thereout of all outgoings which my trustees shall consider to be properly payable out of income shall go and be applied as if the same were income of authorised investments of such proceeds of an actual sale thereof and no property not actually producing income shall be treated as producing income."

## VII. Proposals of Law Reform Committee

3.31 Our experience, confirmed by the evidence we received, is that in practice the rules of apportionment are in well-drawn settlements almost always excluded. It is quite clear that in present-day investment conditions the rules both of conversion and apportionment pending conversion have little if any relevance. When they do apply they require, in effect, the sale of equities, other than those authorised by the Trustee Investments Act 1961, and re-investment in gilt-edged securities. At a time when investment in equities may be the only way in which the capital value of the fund can in fact be maintained the traditional theory that re-investment is necessary to protect those interested in the capital no longer holds good. Conversely, the yield on fixed interest investments is now such as to provide the tenant for life with an income which is as high and may be higher than the average yield on

---

[83] (1971) 16 D.L.R. (3d) 130; 18 D.L.R. (3d) 405.

unauthorised equities. The second reason why the equitable rules are frequently excluded in practice is that the calculations they require are so complex that the costs and administrative difficulties involved are quite out of proportion to any advantage that they might, in very exceptional cases, confer. Nearly all our witnesses took particular exception to the rule in *Allhusen* v. *Whittell*, which was described as complex, fiddlesome and resulting in a disproportionate amount of work and expense. It was suggested that where not excluded it was often simply ignored. . . .

3.36 After careful consideration, we agree that the best solution would be for the rules both as to conversion and apportionment in *Howe* v. *The Earl of Dartmouth*, *Re Chesterfield* and *Allhusen* v. *Whittell* to be subsumed in a new statutory duty to hold a fair balance between the beneficiaries, in particular those entitled to capital and those entitled to income. Coupled with such a general duty should be an express power for such purposes to convert income into capital and vice-versa. In compliance with such a general duty to act impartially and to protect the various interests in the trust, the trustees could, if they thought fit, continue to convert investments and to apportion pending conversion. But in deciding whether or not this was necessary, trustees would be able to have regard to the whole investment policy of the trust. Where they decided that apportionment was desirable or where it was required by virtue of an express duty to convert, the existing rules would not have to be rigidly applied although, where their application was the best way of achieving justice between the beneficiaries, they would continue to be used. To provide for conversion and apportionment in this way within the context of a statutory duty to hold an even hand would, we think, make it clear to trustees that they must consider whether or not apportionment is necessary whilst at the same time allowing them a sufficient degree of flexibility.

3.37 Clearly it should be open to the beneficiaries to ensure that this general duty is fulfilled and we therefore recommend that any beneficiary should be entitled to apply to the court for an order directing the trustees either to make or to adjust an apportionment. The onus would, however, be upon the beneficiary seeking such an order to show that the trustees' exercise of their discretion had substantially prejudiced his interests. This would mean, for example, that trustees would not be bound to apportion in accordance with the existing equitable rules if satisfied that a fair result could be achieved in some other way. But on the application of a beneficiary, the court would be empowered to order the application of the existing rules if it were shown that this would make a substantial difference to the result. What is "substantial" would clearly depend upon the size of the trust. On such an application, the court would have to examine the overall administration of the trust fund and, bearing in mind the vast choice of investments available to trustees, in practice it would be exceptional for it to conclude that they had not held an even balance. The practical importance of the existing apportionment rules would be diminished although, in as much as they are an attempt by equity to do exact mathematical justice, they might continue to be applied in exceptional cases. Should the court order an adjustment of the division between the beneficiaries, trustees should not, we think, be open to an action for breach of trust, provided that they acted in good faith throughout.

## VIII. OTHER APPORTIONMENT INSTANCES[84]

*Losses on realisation of authorised securities, e.g.* mortgages, debentures. Where a trust security turns out to be insufficient, then the proceeds of the security are divisible between income and capital in shares bearing the same proportion to each other as the arrears of interest and capital: *Re Atkinson.*[85]

*Losses on realisation of unauthorised investments made by the trustees.* If the personal remedy against the trustees is worthless, then the life tenant cannot be compelled to refund income received by him over the current percentage to make up the capital.[86] Otherwise, the loss is borne rateably by dividing the sum realised (including both the proceeds of sale and any income received before sale) in the proportion which the income which the life tenant ought to have received had the unauthorised investment not been made bears to the value of the sum wrongly invested, but the life tenant must bring into hotchpot[87] all the income actually received during the currency of the unauthorised investment: *Re Bird.* If no loss of capital has been sustained, then the remainderman is not entitled to have the capital increased by adding to it the difference between the income actually paid to the life tenant and the current percentage.[88]

*General apportionment rule.* By section 2 of the Apportionment Act 1870 "all rents, annuities, dividends and other periodical payments in the nature of income . . . shall . . . be considered as accruing from day to day and shall be apportionable in respect of time accordingly." The Law Reform Committee (Cmnd. 8733, para. 3.40) recommend that subject to express contrary intention, the 1870 Act should not apply on any death where a settlement arises as a result of that death, and where it does apply to a trust it should be amended so that income is treated as belonging to the person entitled to the income of the trust on the date when that income falls due.

*Stocks or shares bought or sold cum dividend.* By the rule in *Bulkeley* v. *Stephens*[89] there is no apportionment here unless a really glaring injustice would otherwise be caused.

*Capitalised profits of companies.* Where a company instead of distributing its profits by way of dividend capitalises those profits by issuing bonus shares, debentures or redeemable loan stock, the company's decision binds those interested under trusts so that those interested in capital benefit: *Bouch* v. *Sproule.*[90] Of course, if the issue

---

[84] Generally see Josling's *Apportionments for Executors and Trustees.*
[85] [1904] 2 Ch. 160; *Re Morris's W.T.* [1960] 1 W.L.R. 1210. For the position where trustee mortgagees foreclose, see Law of Property Act 1925, s.31; *Re Horn's Estate* [1924] 2 Ch. 222.
[86] *Re Bird* [1901] 1 Ch. 916. For the current percentage see p. 669, *supra,* n. 56.
[87] *Stroud* v. *Gwyer* (1860) 28 Beav. 130, 141; *Re Appleby* [1903] 1 Ch. 565.
[88] *Slade* v. *Chaine* [1908] 1 Ch. 522; *Re Hoyles* [1912] 1 Ch. 67.
[89] [1896] 2 Ch. 241; *Re Henderson* [1940] Ch. 368.
[90] (1887) 12 App.Cas. 385; *Hill* v. *Permanent Trustee Co. of New South Wales Ltd.* [1930] A.C. 720; *Re Maclaren's S.T.* [1951] 2 All E.R. 414; *Re Outen's W.T.* [1963] Ch. 291.

of shares is a rights issue (entitling current shareholders to subscribe new capital in proportion to their existing share holdings) the new shares, being bought with capital moneys, form part of capital.

## IX. THE CAPITAL-INCOME DISTINCTION

J. Flower, "A Note on Capital and Income in the Law of Trusts" in H. C. Edey and B. S. Yamey (eds.), *Debits, Credits, Finance and Profits* (1974), pp. 85–7

"The courts developed a concept of capital which is fundamentally different from that used by the economist as exemplified by the famous definition of Hicks: 'Income is the maximum amount the individual can consume in a week and still expect to be as well off at the end of the week as he was at the beginning' (J. R. Hicks, *Value and Capital* (1938), p. 172).

"Suppose that X's capital at the start of 1972 is £20,000; under the Hicksian definition he will have maintained his capital, as measured by disposable wealth, intact if he finishes the year with assets worth £20,000 (given constancy of the general price level). Any increase will be income. The composition of the assets is immaterial—only their total value is taken into account.

"The lawyer's normal concept of capital in the context of a trust is different. To him, if X's capital at January 1, 1972 was 1,000 shares in a company, X will have maintained his capital intact if he finishes the year with the same 1,000 shares. If he sells some shares, the money that he receives in exchange is regarded as the equivalent capital asset. Any increase in the value of the assets whether realised or unrealised is not part of income. If a capital asset is sold for a value greater than its initial value, the extra value has indeed to be recorded, but it is called a 'capital gain' to differentiate it from income.

"Lawyers have thus tended to regard a capital asset as a *res* or a 'thing.' Seltzer in a fascinating chapter has traced this concept to the practice of entailing landed estates in eighteenth-century England. (L. H. Seltzer, *The Nature and Tax Treatment of Capital Gains and Losses*, (1951) Ch. 2). The person to whom a life interest in the estate was granted, was entitled to receive the income of the estate but had no right to spend the capital. The courts often had to decide what was in fact the income of the estate and therefore belonged to the life-tenant, as opposed to what was capital. Not unnaturally they took the view that the capital was the land itself and the income was the annual harvest. The life-tenant was entitled to the annual harvest, which could be disposed of without affecting the physical existence of the land.

"Over the next two hundred years estates came to consist more and more of financial securities—shares, bonds, etc.—but the courts applied the same principles to these assets as to land. The capital to be maintained was the bond itself, not its money value. A rise or fall in the market value of the bond did not change the physical character of the bond; it was not therefore regarded as an element of income. If the bond were sold, the entire proceeds of the sale retained the character of a capital asset as did any assets acquired with the money. Any surplus arising on the sale was of course capital; the life-tenant had no right to it. It was described as a capital gain to emphasise this point. Thus the practice developed of recording capital gains when they were 'realised,' *i.e.* on the sale of the assets. Unrealised capital gains were ignored. The income of the bond was its annual 'harvest'—that 'which is periodically detached and periodically recurs,' *i.e.* the annual interest payment.

"The reason for the courts adopting the *res* principle seems to have been largely pragmatic. To have applied a Hicksian 'value' principle consistently and accurately would have required regular revaluations of all the assets of the estate. This would not only have entailed considerable extra work but would have provided endless opportunities for disputes between life-tenants and remaindermen. . . .

"There is clearly a world of difference between the lawyer's and the economist's concept. The lawyer's realised capital gain would be classified by an economist as income if it were expected; it would be a capital gain from the point of view of economic analysis only in so far as it was unexpected, and this concept, unlike the laywer's, would have nothing to do with respective property rights. Many of the lawyer's capital gains can be clearly shown to be expected. A person who in December 1972 buys £100 of 3 per cent. Savings Bonds at 89 which are due to be redeemed at 100 in 1975 is clearly expecting to make a gain on redemption of £11. The economist would regard this as income, the lawyer would call it a capital gain."

To escape the influence of the legal concepts of capital and income and the concomitant apportionment rules some foreign jurisdictions have developed the "percentage trust" or "uni-trust." The trustees are directed to value all the trust assets annually, such assets being the capital plus the income arising therefrom (on land, accumulated and accrued) on the valuation day. The trustee must then pay only a percentage of that valuation, say 4 per cent., instead of all the income to the person with an interest in possession or to discretionary beneficiaries. This percentage payment will be made from income arising during the accounting year, and, so far as income is insufficient, from capital; any income arising in excess of the percentage payment is accumulated and added to capital. To encourage such trusts in England the accumulation period should be extended from 21 to 80 years to match the perpetuity period allowed in the Perpetuities and Accumulations Act 1964. After all, such trusts fulfil a sensible need and their benefits are equally valid in times of inflation or deflation.

## Section 7. The Trust Property

### I. REDUCTION OF TRUST PROPERTY INTO POSSESSION

#### *The Trustee Act 1925*

*Power to compound liabilities*
Section 15. A personal representative or two or more trustees acting together, subject to the restrictions[91] imposed in regard to receipts by a sole trustee not being a trust corporation, a sole acting trustee where by the instrument, if any, creating the trust, or by statute, a sole trustee is authorised to execute the trusts and powers reposed in him, may, if and as he or they think fit—

    (*a*) accept any property, real or personal, before the time at which it is made transferable or payable; or

---

[91] See s.27 of the Law of Property Act 1925; s.14 of the Trustee Act 1925.

(*b*)  sever and apportion any blended trust funds or property; or

(*c*)  pay or allow any debt or claim on any evidence that he or they think sufficient; or

(*d*)  accept any composition or any security, real or personal, for any debt or for any property, real or personal, claimed; or

(*e*)  allow any time of payment of any debt; or

(*f*)  compromise, compound, abandon, submit to arbitration, or otherwise settle any debt, account, claim or thing whatever relating to the testator's or intestate's estate or to the trust[92];

and for any of those purposes may enter into, give, execute, and do such agreements, instruments of composition or arrangement, releases, and other things as to him or them seem expedient, without being responsible for any loss occasioned by any act or thing so done by him or them in good faith.

[This section replaces, with amendments and additions, section 21 of the Trustee Act 1893 which replaced section 37 of the Conveyancing Act 1881. In *Re Brogden*[93] the Court of Appeal laid it down that trustees must demand payment of funds due to the trust, and take legal proceedings, if necessary, to enforce payment if the demand is not complied with within a reasonable time, unless they reasonably believe that such action would be fruitless. In this case the breach of trust occurred before the Conveyancing Act 1881 came into force. In *Re Owens*[94] Jessel M.R. said *obiter*: "[Section 37 of the Conveyancing Act 1881] may have a revolutionary effect on this branch of the law. It looks as if the only question left would be whether the executors [or trustees] have acted in good faith or not." But Eve J. in *Re Greenwood*[95] put a strict interpretation on the section by holding that it involved the exercise of an *active discretion* on the part of the trustee, with the result that if loss arises from the neglect, carelessness or supineness of the trustee, the case is outside the section altogether.]

*Reversionary interests, valuations and audit*

Section 22.—(1) Where trust property includes any share or interest in property not vested in the trustees, or the proceeds of the sale of any such property, or any other thing in action, the trustees on the same falling into possession, or becoming payable or transferable may—

(*a*)  agree or ascertain the amount or value thereof or any part thereof in such manner as they may think fit;

(*b*)  accept in or towards satisfaction thereof, at the market or current value, or upon any valuation or estimate of value which they may think fit, any authorised investments;

(*c*)  allow any deductions for duties, costs, charges and expenses which they may think proper or reasonable;

(*d*)  execute any release in respect of the premises so as effectually to discharge all accountable parties from all liability in respect of any matter coming within the scope of such release;

without being responsible in any such case for any loss occasioned by any act or thing so done by them in good faith.

---

[92] See *Re Earl of Stafford* [1979] 1 All E.R. 513 for a useful examination of the scope of this.

[93] (1888) 38 Ch.D. 546.

[94] (1882) 47 L.T. 61, 64.

[95] (1911) 105 L.T. 509.

(2) The trustees shall not be under any obligation and shall not be chargeable with any breach of trust by reason of any omission—

(*a*) to place any distringas notice or apply for any stop or other like order upon any securities or other property out of or on which such share or interest or other thing in action as aforesaid is derived, payable or charged; or

(*b*) to take any proceedings on account of any act, default, or neglect on the part of the persons in whom such securities or other property or any of them or any part thereof are for the time being, or had at any time been, vested;

unless and until required in writing so to do by some person, or the guardian of some person, beneficially interested under the trust, and unless also due provision is made to their satisfaction for payment of the costs of any proceedings required to be taken:

Provided that nothing in this subsection shall relieve the trustees of the obligation to get in and obtain payment or transfer of such share or interest or other thing in action on the same falling into possession.

(3) Trustees may, for the purpose of giving effect to the trust, or any of the provisions of the instrument, if any, creating the trust or of any statute, from time to time (by duly qualified agents) ascertain and fix the value of any trust property in such manner as they think proper, and any valuation so made in good faith shall be binding upon all persons interested under the trust.

(4) Trustees may, in their absolute discretion, from time to time, but not more than once in every three years unless the nature of the trust or any special dealings with the trust property make a more frequent exercise of the right reasonable, cause the accounts of the trust property to be examined or audited by an independent accountant, and shall, for that purpose, produce such vouchers and give such information to him as he may require; and the costs of such examination or audit, including the fee of the auditor, shall be paid out of the capital or income of the trust property, or partly in one way and partly in the other, as the trustees, in their absolute discretion, think fit, but, in default of any direction by the trustees to the contrary in any special case, costs attributable to capital shall be borne by capital and those attributable to income by income.

### *Public Trustee Act 1906*

Investigation and audit of trust accounts

Section 13.—(1) Subject to rules under this Act and unless the court otherwise orders, the condition and accounts of any trust shall, on an application being made and notice thereof given in the prescribed manner by any trustee or beneficiary, be investigated and audited by such solicitor or public accountant as may be agreed on by the applicant and the trustees or, in default of agreement, by the public trustee or some person appointed by him:

Provided that (except with the leave of the court) such an investigation or audit shall not be required within twelve months after any such previous investigation or audit, and that a trustee or beneficiary shall not be appointed under this section to make an investigation or audit.

(2) The person making the investigation or audit (hereinafter called the auditor) shall have a right of access to the books, accounts, and vouchers of the trustees, and to any securities and documents of title held by them on

account of the trust, and may require from them such information and explanation as may be necessary for the performance of his duties and upon the completion of the investigation and audit shall forward to the applicant and to every trustee a copy of the accounts, together with a report thereon, and a certificate signed by him to the effect that the accounts exhibit a true view of the state of the affairs of the trust and that he has had the securities of the trust fund investments produced to and verified by him (or as the case may be) that such accounts are deficient in such respects as may be specified in such certificate.

(3) Every beneficiary under the trust shall, subject to rules under this Act, be entitled at all reasonable times to inspect and take copies of the accounts, report, and certificate, and, at his own expense, to be furnished with copies thereof or extracts therefrom.

[Trustees must keep proper accounts and have them ready for inspection and examination.[96] If a trustee causes expense through neglect or refusal to furnish or keep accounts he has to bear that expense personally.[97] In general, beneficiaries have a right to investigate the accounts of their trustees.[98]

The Law Reform Committee (Cmnd. 8733, para. 4.48) recommend that Public Trustee Act 1906, s.13 be repealed: there are no powers to enforce the Public Trustee's findings and Trustee Act 1925, s.22(4) provides adequate protection.]

## II. Duty to Account and Give Information

The fundamental obligation of a trustee is to account for losses and profits arising in the course of his trusteeship: he is not liable to damages, he is liable to account.[99] The beneficiary principle fundamental to the existence of a trust requires that there are beneficiaries able to enforce their rights against the trustees[1]: this cannot be done unless the beneficiaries can compel the trustees to account for what they have done with the trust property. Inherent in the trust relationship is thus the duty to keep trust accounts. Even a discretionary beneficiary is entitled to access to the trust accounts and to information concerning the management of the trust fund.[2]

However, this right is limited because of the need to ensure that sensitive discretions of the trustees can be exercised without interference or inhibition and with impartiality and circumspection: *Re Londonderry's Settlement, infra,* p. 684. After all, trustees who exercise a discretion are not obliged to give reasons for such exercise

---

[96] *Eglin* v. *Sanderson* (1862) 3 Giff. 434, 440; *Pearse* v. *Green* (1819) 1 Jac. & W. 135, 140. Where funds are given to parents to provide for the maintenance and education of their infant children the parents are under no duty to keep accounts to show the precise manner in which the funds have been spent provided that the infants have been maintained by the parents: *Browne* v. *Paull* (1850) 1 Sim.(N.S.) 92; *Re Rogers* [1944] Ch. 297 revealing that in such cases the funds are treated as a beneficial gift to the parents subject to an equitable charge for the maintenance and education of the infant children.

[97] *Re Skinner* [1904] 1 Ch. 289. *Cf. Heugh* v. *Scard* (1875) 33 L.T. 659.

[98] *Re Fish* [1893] 2 Ch. 413, 425, *infra*, p. 683.

[99] See p. 772, *infra*.

[1] See pp. 185–197, *supra*.

[2] *Chaine-Nickson* v. *Bank of Ireland* [1976] I.R. 393, *Spellson* v. *George* (1987) 11 New South Wales L.R. 300, 315–316, *Jones* v. *Shipping Federation of British Columbia* (1963) 37 D.L.R. (2d) 273.

(unless so required by the terms of the trust instrument). Thus, access will not be permitted to documents closely connected with the exercise of the trustees' discretion, *e.g.* agenda and minutes of their meetings, correspondence with beneficiaries or a person whose consent is required for the exercise of a discretion.[3]

Exceptionally, if a beneficiary bona fide commences hostile litigation against the trustees then he is entitled to discovery of any document which may fairly lead him to a train of inquiry that may either directly or indirectly enable him to advance his own case or to damage the trustees' case.[4]

The terms of the trust instrument must be considered because they can to some extent control a beneficiary's right of access to information.[5] Thus, a wealthy man upon taking up a political or public position can entrust management of his wealth to trustees for beneficiaries of whom he may be one and prohibit the trustees from revealing the investment policy to him until he has given up the position. This safeguards him against allegations that he used his position to enhance his personal fortune. However, it is considered that any blanket clause purporting to prohibit beneficiaries' rights of access to accounts and information would be held to be ineffective as inconsistent with the existence of any intended trustee beneficiary relationship.

Finally, it should be noted that trustees are under a duty to inform each beneficiary of full age and capacity of his rights under the trust.[6]

## RE LONDONDERRY'S SETTLEMENT, PEAT AND OTHERS v. WALSH

Court of Appeal [1965] Ch. 918; [1965] 2 W.L.R. 229; [1964] 3 All E.R. 855
(Harman, Danckwerts and Salmon L.JJ.)

On December 5, 1934, the seventh Marquess of Londonderry settled a trust fund upon trusts as to the capital for members of a specified class in such shares and generally in such manner as the trustees with the consent of certain named persons, called "the appointors," might in writing from time to time appoint. There were provisions in default of that appointment.

The settlement then directed the trustees to hold the income until disposal of the capital upon trust for such member or members of the same class as the trustees might from time to time within twelve months after the receipt of such income with the written consent of the appointors determine and subject thereto upon trust to pay an annuity of £5,000 to the settlor's wife and subject thereto to pay the income to the settlor's eldest son and after his death to the settlor's other children.

The settlor's wife and eldest son having died, the settlor's daughter, Lady Helen Maglona Walsh, became entitled to share in the income of the trust

---

[3] *Re Londonderry's Settlement* [1965] Ch. 918, though too much emphasis is placed on equitable proprietary interests as the foundation for the right to inspect instead of the duty to account and give information.
[4] See R. E. Megarry, p. 688, *infra.*
[5] *Tierney* v. *King* [1983] 2 Queensland R. 580.
[6] *Hawkesley* v. *May* [1956] 1 Q.B. 304, *Burrows* v. *Walls* (1855) 5 De G.M. & G. 233, 253, *Brittlebank* v. *Goodwin* (1868) L.R. 5 Eq. 545, 550.

fund under the above gift of income in default of appointment. There were other children of the marriage.

The trustees had from time to time appointed considerable sums to various beneficiaries and in December 1962 they unanimously decided with the consent of the appointors to make further substantial appointments of capital with a view to bringing the settlement to an end. The settlor's daughter was dissatisfied with the amounts proposed to be appointed to her and asked the trustees to supply her with copies of various documents relating to the settlement. The trustees supplied copies of the appointments and of the accounts up to date but refused to disclose any other documents. The settlor's daughter remained dissatisfied.

Accordingly on January 30, 1964, the trustees issued a summons, to which the settlor's daughter was defendant, asking which, if any, of the following documents the trustees were bound to disclose: (a) the minutes of the meetings of the trustees of the settlement; (b) agendas and other documents prepared for the purposes of the meetings or otherwise for the consideration of the trustees; (c) correspondence relating to the administration of the trust property or otherwise to the execution of the trusts and passing between (i) the trustees and the appointors; (ii) the trustees and the appointors on the one hand and the solicitors to the trustees on the other; and (iii) the trustees and the appointors on the one hand and the beneficiaries on the other.

Plowman J.[7] made a declaration that the trustees were bound to disclose all the documents in the categories set out above.

HARMAN L.J.: "I have found this a difficult case. It raises what in my judgment is a novel question on which there is no authority exactly in point although several cases have been cited to us somewhere near it. The court is really required here to resolve two principles that come into conflict, or at least apparent conflict. The first is that . . . trustees exercising a discretionary power are not bound to disclose to their beneficiaries the reasons actuating them in coming to a decision. This is a long-standing principle and rests largely, I think, on the view that nobody could be called upon to accept a trusteeship involving the exercise of a discretion unless, in the absence of bad faith, he were not liable to have his motives or his reasons called in question either by the beneficiaries or by the court. To this there is added a rider, namely, that if trustees do give reasons, their soundness can be considered by the court. . . .

"It would seem on the face of it that there is no reason why this principle should be confined to decisions orally arrived at and should not extend to a case, like the present, where, owing to the complexity of the trust and the large sums involved, the trustees, who act subject to the consent of another body called the appointors, have brought into existence various written documents, including, in particular, agenda for and minutes of their meetings from time to time held in order to consider distributions made of the fund and its income. It is here that the conflicting principle is said to emerge. All these documents, it is argued, came into existence for the purposes of the trust and are in the possession of the trustees as such and are, therefore, trust documents, the property of the beneficiaries, and as such open to them to inspect. . . .

"The judge, though he felt the strength of the trustees' submission that it was undesirable to wash family linen in public which would be productive only of family strife and also odium for the trustees and embarrassment in the performance of their duties, felt constrained by a decision of Kindersley V.-C. in *Talbot* v. *Marshfield*.[8] It now appears, however, in the light of documents obtained from the Record Office and the other reports of the case, notably in the *Weekly Reporter*[9] and *Law Reports* 4 *Equity*,[10] that this case was not at all in point. It was an action by beneficiaries against trustees who had a discretionary power, by making advancements to the tenants for life, to deprive the remaindermen. The matter came on first as a motion for an order on the trustees to pay into court. In the course of the hearing of that motion, the trustees stated their reasons for the action they proposed to take and were cross-examined. The court refused to order payment into court, whereupon the trustees distributed and the action proceeded as an action to administer the estate upon the footing of wilful default. There was an application for discovery and it was upon the hearing of this application that Kindersley V.-C. gave his decision. He ordered[11] the trustees to disclose a case to counsel and opinion taken by the trustees before the action was started and also a number of letters showing the trustees' intentions and their action in distributing other parts of the fund.

"The case and opinion were, of course, trust papers, having come into existence *ante litem motam*. Counsel was advising the trustees as to their rights and duties and every beneficiary must be entitled to seek advice of that sort. It is paid for out of the trust money and is the property of the beneficiaries. As to the letters, the trustees' objection seems to have been that as they were with beneficiaries of other shares in which the plaintiff was not interested, they were not relevant and need not be disclosed. This was overruled, as is not surprising, for the action was an action to administer the estate and the dealings of the trustees with all the shares was called in question. No point was taken that the trustees' exercise of their discretion was confidential. They had in fact already been cross-examined about it. I find nothing in this decision which helps us here.

"Apart from this, the defendant relied on certain observations in *O'Rourke* v. *Darbishire*.[12] The decision was that the plaintiff was not entitled to the production of what were called the 'trust documents,' and I find Lord Parmoor making this observation[13]: 'A *cestui que trust*, in an action against his trustees, is generally entitled to the production for inspection of all documents relating to the affairs of the trust. It is not material for the present purpose whether this right is to be regarded as a paramount proprietary right in the *cestui que trust*, or as a right to be enforced under the law of discovery.' Lord Wrenbury says[14]: 'If the plaintiff is right in saying that he is a beneficiary, and if the documents are documents belonging to the executors as executors, he has a right to access to the documents which he desires to inspect upon what has been called in the judgments in this case a proprietary right. The beneficiary is entitled to see all the trust documents because they are trust documents and because he is a beneficiary. They are in a sense his own. Action or no action,

---

8 (1865) 2 Drew. & Sm. 549.
9 13 W.R. 885.
10 (1867) L.R. 4 Eq. 661.
11 13 W.R. 885, 886.
12 [1920] A.C. 581.
13 *Ibid.* p. 619.
14 *Ibid.* p. 626.

he is entitled to access to them. This has nothing to do with discovery. The right to discovery is a right to see someone else's documents. A proprietary right is a right to access to documents which are your own. No question of professional privilege arises in such a case. Documents containing professional advice taken by the executors as trustees contain advice taken by trustees for their *cestuis que trust*, and the beneficiaries are entitled to see them because they are beneficiaries.'

"General observations of this sort give very little guidance, for first they beg the question what are trust documents, and secondly their Lordships were not considering the point here that papers are asked for which bear on the question of the exercise of the trustees' discretion. In my judgment category (a) . . . *viz.*, the minutes of the meetings of the trustees . . . ; and part of (b), *viz.*, agenda prepared for trustees' meetings, are, in the absence of an action impugning the trustees' good faith, documents which a beneficiary cannot claim the right to inspect. If the defendant is allowed to examine these, she will know at once the very matters which the trustees are not bound to disclose to her, namely, their motives and reasons. Trustees who wish to preserve their rights in this respect must either commit nothing to paper or destroy everything from meeting to meeting. Indeed, if the defendant be right, I doubt that if the last course is open, for she must succeed, if at all, on the ground that the papers belong to her, and if so, the trustees have no right to destroy them.

"I would hold that even if documents of this type ought properly to be described as trust documents, they are protected for the special reason which protects the trustees' deliberations on a discretionary matter from disclosure. If necessary, I hold that this principle over-rides the ordinary rule. This is, in my judgment, no less in the true interest of the beneficiary than of the trustees. Again, if one of the trustees commits to paper his suggestions and circulates them among his co-trustees; or if inquiries are made in writing as to the circumstances of a member of the class; I decline to hold that such documents are trust documents the property of the beneficiaries. . . . On the other hand, if the solicitor advising the trustees commits to paper an *aide-mémoire* summarising the state of the fund or of the family and reminding the trustees of past distributions and future possibilities, I think that must be a document which any beneficiary must be at liberty to inspect. It seems to me, therefore, that category (b) [as set out *supra*, p. 666] embraces documents on both sides of the line.

"As to (c) I cannot think that communications passing between individual trustees and appointors are documents in which beneficiaries have a proprietary right. On the other hand, as to category (ii) in general the letters of the trustees' solicitors to the trustees do seem to me to be trust documents in which the beneficiaries have a property. As to category (iii) I do not think letters to or from an individual beneficiary ought to be open to inspection by another beneficiary. . . . "[15]

SALMON L.J.: "The category of trust documents has never been comprehensively defined. Nor could it be—certainly not by me. Trust documents do, however, have these characteristics in common: (1) they are documents in the possession of the trustees as trustees; (2) they contain information about the

---

[15] See also *Re Cowin* (1886) 33 Ch.D. 179; *Re Bosworth* (1889) 55 L.J.Ch. 432; *Re Dartnall* [1895] 1 Ch. 474; *Tiger* v. *Barclays Bank Ltd.* [1952] W.N. 38; *Hawkesley* v. *May* [1956] 1 Q.B. 304; generally (1965) 81 L.Q.R. 192 (R.E.M.).

trust which the beneficiaries are entitled to know; (3) the beneficiaries have a proprietary interest in the documents and, accordingly, are entitled to see them. If any parts of a document contain information which the beneficiaries are not entitled to know, I doubt whether such parts can truly be said to be integral parts of a trust document. Accordingly, any part of a document that lacked the second characteristic to which I have referred would automatically be excluded from the document in its character as a trust document.

"I agree with my Lords that the appeal should be allowed."

### R. E. Megarry (1965) 81 L.Q.R. 196

"It seems safe to say that the last of *Re Londonderry's Settlement* has not been heard. Perhaps the most obvious point which may arise is whether a beneficiary who is determined to discover all he can about the grounds upon which a discretion has been exercised may not achieve this by instituting litigation alleging that the trustees have exercised their discretion in some improper way, and then obtaining discovery of documents in those proceedings, as in *Talbot* v. *Marshfield* (1865) 2 Drew. & Sm. 549. Will the courts permit the bonds of secrecy to be invaded by the simple process of commencing hostile litigation against the trustees? It is not easy to see how the courts can prevent this. True, questions of relevance may obviously arise; but on discovery the test of relevance is wide. The classical statement is that of Brett L.J.: an applicant is entitled to discovery of any document 'which may fairly lead him to a train of inquiry' that may 'either directly or indirectly enable the party requiring the affidavit either to advance his own case or to damage the case of his adversary' (*Compagnie Financière et Commerciale du Pacifique* v. *Peruvian Guano Co.* (1882) 11 Q.B.D. 55 at 63). Indeed, the formal order of the court, . . . seems to recognise this possibility.

"The other main point which plainly needs further exploration is the ambit of the term 'trust documents.' The negative proposition is now plain: not all documents held by trustees as such are 'trust documents.' But even after a detailed examination of the judgments it is difficult to frame any positive proposition with any degree of confidence. Nor does the formal order of the court (see at p. 938) lessen the difficulty; indeed, it contributes its own quota of problems. The order states that without prejudice to any right of the defendant to discovery in any subsequent proceedings against the trustees, and subject to any order of the court in any particular circumstances, there are four categories of documents which the trustees are not bound to disclose to the defendant. The first of these categories is 'The agenda of the meetings of the trustees of the settlement'; the second and third categories consist of correspondence of the trustees *inter se* and with the beneficiaries; and the fourth category consists of minutes of the meetings of the trustees and other documents disclosing their deliberations as to the manner in which they should exercise their discretion or disclosing their reasons for any particular exercise of their discretion, or the materials therefor. It is thus only the minutes and the other documents in the fourth category which appear to be qualified by words relating to disclosure of the trustees' reasons for exercising their discretion in a particular way; the freedom from disclosure seems to apply to all agenda and correspondence, whether or not they would reveal any such reasons or the material on which they were based. Nor does the order make it plain how it applies to documents in the fourth category which not only disclose confidential matters but also deal with other points as well; the inclusion of any confidential matter seems to confer exemption upon the entire document, and not merely upon the confidential matter. The order did, however, declare that the trustees were bound to disclose to the defendant any written advice from their solicitors or counsel as to the manner in which the trustees were in law entitled to exercise their discretion.

"Putting all the material together, it seems at present to be difficult to say more than that all documents held by trustees *qua* trustees are prima facie trust documents, but that there is a class of exceptions from this rule which is ill-defined but includes confidential documents which the beneficiaries ought not to see. For greater precision than that we must await further decisions by the courts. The Court of Appeal has taken a firm step in the right direction; but that is all."

## III. DISTRIBUTION OF TRUST PROPERTY

### A. Maintenance

The statutory power of maintenance in the Trustee Act 1925, section 31 is of fundamental importance in the administration of trusts for the assistance it may provide to minors, for the taxation repercussions flowing from the way in which it can convert what are vested interests under the terms of the trust into contingent interests and also flowing from a beneficiary's entitlement to income at eighteen years of age, and for the apportionment problems it creates where there is a class of beneficiaries.

The trustees must be aware of these points and they must consciously exercise their discretion. In *Wilson* v. *Turner*[16] they automatically paid over the income to the minor's father without any request from him and without any attempt to ascertain whether any income was required for the minor's maintenance: the father was ordered to repay the income. Trustees should particularly review the situation a month or two before the minor attains eighteen years since the statutory power to apply income and its accumulations over the years expires on his eighteenth birthday.

Under the statutory power, so long as income is legally available,[17] there is a *duty* to accumulate the income, so far as not used under a *power* to apply it for the maintenance education or benefit of the beneficiary, for the period of the beneficiary's minority. During such period accumulations may be used as if they were current income despite having accrued to the capital.[18] Once the beneficiary attains eighteen the trustees *must* pay the income from the capital (including the accumulations which become part of the capital) to the beneficiary even if the beneficiary's interest is still contingent under the trust terms, *e.g.* to B if he attains 25 years.[19]

---

[16] (1883) 22 Ch.D. 521.

[17] A trust instrument may oust s.31 expressly or by necessary implication and s.31 only applies in the case of a contingent interest if the interest carries the intermediate income: see p. 693, *infra*.

[18] s.31(2).

[19] This gives the beneficiary an interest in possession which has much significance for inheritance tax purposes: Inheritance Tax Act 1984, ss.49–53 and p. 29, *supra*. Also see *Swales* v. *I.R.C.* [1984] 3 All E.R. 16, 24.

Section 31(2) may convert what appear to be indefeasible vested interests into defeasible or contingent interests[20] since accumulations of income will not pass to a beneficiary with a vested interest in income under the terms of the trust unless he satisfies a contingency within section 31(2)(i) or unless he is entitled not just to income but also to the capital to which the accumulations automatically accrue, as where personalty is settled on a minor absolutely (s.31(2)(ii)). The contingencies within section 31(2)(i) are (a) attaining the age of eighteen or marrying thereunder when having a vested interest in income during his infancy and (b) attaining the age of eighteen or marrying thereunder when thereupon becoming entitled to the capital from which the income arose in fee simple absolute or determinable[21] (realty) or absolutely and indefeasibly[22] (personalty) or for an entailed interest (realty and personalty). Thus, if B is an unmarried minor and under a trust an apparently indefeasible vested interest is conferred on him (*e.g.* to B for life) in substance B's interest in income is defeasible or contingent[23] since he has no right to income as it arises (the trustees being under a duty to accumulate it in so far as not exercising their power to use it if they see fit for B's maintenance, education or benefit) and he has no right to accumulated income unless he attains eighteen or marries thereunder.[24]

The Apportionment Act 1870 requiring apportionment of income on a day to day basis has an odd effect when a beneficiary attains eighteen. Take dividends received after the eighteenth birthday in respect of a period before and after the birthday. The income apportioned to the pre-birthday period "cannot be applied for maintenance, etc., because the trustees cannot exercise their discretion in advance so as to affect the income when it is received and they cannot apply it in arrear because the infancy will have ceased."[25]

The 1870 Act also applies when a class member dies or is born. So much of a particular beneficiary's share of income that is not used for his maintenance but accumulated must be allocated to him and kept separate from the other beneficiaries' allocations. The particular share of income will vary with births or deaths of class members. If a minor dies before obtaining a vested interest the income provisionally accumulated and allocated to him is treated as an accretion to the capital of the whole fund, divisible among all beneficiaries ultimately

---

[20] Thus making 35 per cent. income tax payable under Finance Act 1973, s.16: see p. 26, *supra*.

[21] *Re Sharp's S.T.* [1973] Ch. 331 treats this as a determinable fee in the strict sense distinct from a fee simple on condition though the Settled Land Act 1925, s.117(1)(iv) (not cited) treats "determinable fee" as meaning a fee determinable whether by limitation or condition. Consider Trustees Act 1925, s.68(1) (18).

[22] The interest will not be absolute if defeasible by an overriding power or a condition: *Re Sharp's S.T.* (*supra*).

[23] *Stanley* v. *I.R.C.* [1944] K.B. 255, *Re Delamere's S.T.* [1984] 1 All E.R. 584.

[24] The Finance Act 1973, ss.16–18 applies to tax the income at 35 per cent. instead of at basic rate.

[25] *Re Joel's W.T.* [1967] Ch. 14, 29. The Law Reform Committee (Cmnd. 8733, para. 3.41) recommend replacing time apportionment by apportionment between the class of beneficiaries as constituted on the date the income is received by the trustees.

becoming entitled to capital even if not alive during the period when such accumulation occurred.[26]

Section 31 may be ousted wholly or partly by a contrary intention expressed directly or indirectly in the trust instrument. Its provisions will be inapplicable if on a fair reading of the instrument in question one can say that such application would be inconsistent with the purport of the instrument.[27]

### The Trustee Act 1925

*Power to apply income for maintenance[28] and to accumulate surplus income during a minority*

Section 31.—(1) Where any property is held by trustees in trust for any person for any interest whatsoever, whether vested or contingent, then, subject to any prior interests[29] or charges affecting that property—

 (i) during the infancy of any such person, if his interest so long continues, the trustees may, at their sole discretion, pay to his parent or guardian, if any, or otherwise apply for or towards his maintenance, education, or benefit, the whole or such part, if any, of the income of that property as may, in all the circumstances, be reasonable, whether or not there is—

 (*a*) any other fund applicable to the same purpose; or

 (*b*) any person bound by law to provide for his maintenance or education; and

 (ii) if such person on attaining the age of [eighteen][30] years has not a vested[31] interest in such income, the trustees shall[32] thenceforth pay the income of that property and of any accretion thereto under subsection (2) of this section to him, until he either attains a vested interest therein or dies, or until failure of his interest:

Provided that, in deciding whether the whole or any part of the income of the property is during a minority to be paid or applied for the purposes

---

[26] *Re Joel's W.T.* [1967] Ch. 14. If trustees hold property on discretionary trusts and allocate income absolutely to a minor beneficiary such income does not fall within s.31 (though income arising from such income will): *Re Vestey's Settlement* [1951] Ch. 209.

[27] *I.R.C.* v. *Bernstein* [1961] Ch. 399, 412; *Re Delamere's S.T.* [1984] 1 All E.R. 584, 588.

[28] See B. S. Ker, "Trustees' Power of Maintenance" (1953) 17 Conv.(N.S.) 273 and Wolstenholme & Cherry's *Conveyancing Statutes* Vol. 4 (13th ed., by J. T. Farrand).

[29] If there is a prior direction to set apart and accumulate income, the trustees have no power to apply intermediate income for maintenance under this section: *Re Reade-Revell* [1930] 1 Ch. 52, but the court may do so under its inherent jurisdiction: *Re Walker* [1901] 1 Ch. 879; *supra*, p. 654.

[30] Substituted by the Family Law Reform Act 1969, s.1(3), Sched. 1, Pt. I. For interests under any instruments made before Jan. 1, 1970, 21 years remain the relevant age: Sched. III, para. 5(1). In such a case money may be paid direct to the beneficiary once he attains 18 instead of to his parent or guardian, Sched. III, para. 5(2). For appointments made after 1969 under a pre-1970 settlement the relevant age is 18: *Re Delamere's S.T.* [1984] 1 All E.R. 584, 588.

[31] The section does not apply if the person has a vested interest, even if it is liable to be divested: *Re McGeorge* [1963] Ch. 544.

[32] The word "shall" prima facie imports a "duty" as distinct from a "power." In this context, however, it imports a "power" which can be overridden by the expression of a contrary intention: see s.69(2) of the Trustee Act 1925; *Re Turner's Will Trusts* [1937] Ch. 15. Provisions made by the settlor or testator if inconsistent with the statutory power amount to contrary intention, *e.g.* a direction to accumulate: *Re Erskine's S.T.* [1971] 1 W.L.R. 162, *Re Henderson's Trusts* [1969] 1 W.L.R. 651, 659. But if there is no contrary intention the trustees are under a duty to pay the income to the beneficiary on his attaining the age of 18: *Re Jones' Will Trusts* [1947] Ch. 48. Even though the beneficiary may not be entitled to the capital till attaining 30 years of age the fact that he is entitled to the income will give him an interest in possession for inheritance tax purposes.

aforesaid, the trustees shall have regard to the age of the infant and his requirements and generally to the circumstances of the case, and in particular to what other income, if any, is applicable for the same purposes; and where trustees have notice that the income of more than one fund is applicable for those purposes, then, so far as practicable, unless the entire income of the funds is paid or applied as aforesaid or the court otherwise directs, a proportionate part only of the income of each fund shall be so paid or applied.

(2) During the infancy of any such person, if his interest so long continues, the trustees shall accumulate[33] all the residue of that income in the way of compound interest by investing the same and the resulting income thereof from time to time in authorised investments, and shall hold those accumulations as follows:

    (i) If any such person—

        (a) attains the age of [eighteen][34] years, or marries under that age, and his interest in such income during his infancy or until his marriage is a vested interest; or

        (b) on attaining the age of [eighteen][35] years or on marriage under that age becomes entitled to the property from which such income arose in fee simple, absolute or determinable,[36] or absolutely,[37] or for an entailed interest;

    the trustees shall hold the accumulations in trust for such person absolutely, but without prejudice to any provision with respect thereto contained in any settlement by him made under any statutory powers during his infancy, and so that the receipt of such person after marriage, and though still an infant, shall be a good discharge; and

    (ii) In any other case the trustees shall,[38] notwithstanding that such person had a vested interest in such income, hold the accumulations as an accretion to the capital of the property from which such accumulations arose,[39] and as one fund with such capital for all purposes, and so that, if such property is settled land, such accumulations shall be held upon the same trusts as if the same were capital money arising therefrom;

but the trustees may, at any time during the infancy of such person if his interest so long continues, apply those accumulations, or any part thereof, as if they were income arising in the then current year.

(3) This section applies in the case of a contingent interest only if the limitation or trust carries the intermediate income[40] of the property, but it applies to a future or contingent legacy by the parent of, or a person standing in *loco parentis* to, the legatee, if and for such period as, under the general

---

[33] See A. M. Prichard [1973] C.L.J. 246.

[34] See n. 30, *supra*.

[35] See n. 30, *supra*.

[36] See n. 22, *supra*.

[37] This applies exclusively to personalty and requires the interest in personalty to be indefeasible so that there is an odd distinction between realty and personalty: *Re Sharp's S.T.* [1973] Ch. 331.

[38] This may be excluded if its application would be inconsistent with the purport of the instrument in question, *e.g.* where an appointment of income to six minors "in equal shares *absolutely*" reveals in context an intention that each was to take an indefeasible share even if dying before attaining 18: *Re Delamere's S.T.* [1984] 1 All E.R. 584.

[39] Thus accumulations subject to an overriding power of appointment form an accretion to the respective shares of the beneficiaries subject to the overriding power: *Re Sharp's S.T.* [1973] Ch. 331 following *Re Joel's W.T.* [1967] Ch. 14.

[40] As to this, see s.175 of the Law of Property Act 1925, *infra* p. 693; (1963) 79 L.Q.R. 184 (P.V.B.).

law, the legacy carries interest for the maintenance of the legatee, and in any such case as last aforesaid the rate of interest shall (if the income available is sufficient, and subject to any rules of court to the contrary[41]) be five pounds per centum per annum.

(4) This section applies to a vested annuity in like manner as if the annuity were the income of property held by trustees in trust to pay the income thereof to the annuitant for the same period for which the annuity is payable, save that in any case accumulations made during the infancy of the annuitant shall be held in trust for the annuitant or his personal representatives absolutely.

(5) This section does not apply where the instrument, if any, under which the interest arises came into operation before the commencement of this Act.[42]

## The Law of Property Act 1925

*Contingent and future testamentary gifts carry intermediate income*

Section 175.—(1) A contingent or future specific devise or bequest of property, whether real or personal, and a contingent residuary devise of freehold land, and a specific or residuary devise of freehold land to trustees upon trust for persons whose interests are contingent or executory shall, subject to the statutory provisions relating to accumulations, carry the intermediate income of that property from the death of the testator, except so far as such income, or part thereof, may be otherwise expressly disposed of.

(2) This section applies only to wills coming into operation after the commencement of this Act.

## Need for available income or interest

In the case of an infant with a vested interest section 31 of the Trustee Act 1925, *supra*, requires income to be accumulated except so far as it is applied for the maintenance of the infant unless the income is disposed of in favour of someone else or directed only to be accumulated.[43] But if the infant's interest is contingent, by section 31(3) income is not so required to be dealt with unless the limitation or trust carries the intermediate income. The rules in regard to this are as follows (subject to any contrary intention):

1. A contingent gift by will of residuary personalty carries with it all the income which it produces after the testator's death: *Re Adams*.[44] If the income is accumulated until the contingency occurs, the rules in sections 164–166 of the Law of Property Act 1925, and section 13 of the Perpetuities and Accumulations Act 1964, which limit the period of accumulation, must be complied with: *Countess of Bective* v. *Hodgson*.[45] On the other hand, a residuary bequest, whether vested or contingent, which is expressly deferred to a future date does not carry

---

[41] 6 per cent. is now prescribed by R.S.C. O. 44 r. 10.
[42] The section applies to an appointment made after 1925 under a power created before 1926: *Re Dickinson's Settlements* [1939] Ch. 27. S. 43 of the Conveyancing Act 1881, which was more limited in its scope than the present section, applies to instruments coming into operation before 1926.
[43] *Re Turner's W.T.* [1937] Ch. 15; *Re Ransome* [1957] Ch. 348; *Re Reade-Revell* [1930] 1 Ch. 52; *Re Stapleton* [1946] 1 All E.R. 323.
[44] [1893] 1 Ch. 329, 334.
[45] (1864) 10 H.L.C. 656.

intermediate income: *Re Oliver*[46]; *Re Gillett's Will Trusts*[47]; *Re Geering.*[48]

2. A contingent residuary devise of freehold land and a residuary devise of freehold land to trustees upon trust for persons, whose interests are contingent, carry the intermediate income which they produce: s.175 of the Law of Property Act 1925, *supra*.

3. A contingent or future specific bequest of personalty carries the intermediate income: *ibid*.

4. So does a contingent or future specific devise of realty: *Re McGeorge, infra*, p. 695.

5. An *inter vivos* contingent interest will be of specific property and will carry the intermediate income (unless the income is disposed of in favour of someone else or directed to be accumulated).

6. Where a testator directs that a general or pecuniary contingent legacy (*e.g.* "a thousand ICI plc shares" or "£15,000") be set apart from the rest of his estate for the benefit of the minor contingent legatee this will carry the intermediate income produced by such separate fund.[49]

Section 31(3) further makes section 31 apply to a future or contingent legacy by a parent or person *in loco parentis* so far as under the general law the legacy *carries interest* for the maintenance of the legatee. Where a future or contingent legacy has not been directed to be set apart so as itself to produce intermediate income, it will be paid in due course at the appropriate time out of the residuary estate, and usually the legatee just receives the legacy without being allowed any interest for the period before the legacy became payable.[50] Exceptionally, a legacy carries 6 per cent. interest[51] payable from the testator's death out of the residuary estate income if the testator was the parent or *in loco parentis* to the minor legatee, the legacy was direct to the minor and not to trustees for him,[52] no other fund was set aside for the maintenance of the minor,[53] and, if the legacy was contingent, the contingency related to the legatee's minority and so was not the attaining of an age greater than the age of majority.[54] In this exceptional case the provisions of section 31 apply.

There is a further exceptional case where a contingent legacy carries 6 per cent. interest before it becomes payable: where the testator's will reveals an intention that the legacy should carry interest from the

---

[46] [1947] 2 All E.R. 162, 166.
[47] [1950] Ch. 102.
[48] [1964] Ch. 136.
[49] *Re Medlock* (1886) 55 L.J. Ch. 738, *Re Woodin* [1895] 2 Ch. 309, *Re Couturier* [1907] 1 Ch. 470. Income will be carried from the end of the executor's year unless intended to provide for the maintenance of a minor legatee as from the testator's death.
[50] *Re Raine* [1929] 1 Ch. 716.
[51] Trustee Act 1925, s.31(3), R.S.C. O. 44 r. 10.
[52] *Re Pollock* [1943] Ch. 338.
[53] *Re West* [1913] 2 Ch. 345.
[54] *Re Abrahams* [1911] 1 Ch. 108.

testator's death for the maintenance of the minor.[55] Here the testator need not be the parent of or *in loco parentis* to the minor and the contingency may be the attainment of an age exceeding majority.[56] It would seem that this was overlooked so that, strictly, section 31 is inapplicable, so that there must be used for the maintenance of the legatee interest at 6 per cent. rather than the higher actual income produced if, on winding up the testator's estate, the executors for convenience sake set aside the capital to which the legatee will be entitled on attaining, say, 25 years of age. It will be troublesome that the balance of income over the sum representing 6 per cent. interest will fall into residue. However, it would probably strain section 31(3) too much to construe "contingent interest" which "carries the intermediate income" to include contingent legacies to the extent they indirectly (via interest payable out of the residuary estate income) carry intermediate income so as to cover this further exceptional case,[57] especially when the latter half of the subsection deals with legacies which carry interest for maintenance.

Tax considerations should always be borne in mind. Income applied for an infant unmarried child of the settlor is treated as the settlor's income.[58] Moreover, any sum paid out of trust funds to the settlor's child is treated as income and not capital to an amount equal to the total undistributed income of the trust to that date.[59]

### RE McGEORGE

Chancery Division [1963] Ch. 544; [1963] 2 W.L.R. 767; [1963] 1 All E.R. 519

A testator devised land to his daughter and declared that "the devise . . . shall not take effect until after the death of my wife should she survive me." The testator also provided that if the daughter should die during the lifetime of the wife leaving issue, then the issue on attaining twenty-one were to "take by substitution the aforesaid devise in favour of" the daughter. The testator bequeathed his residuary estate on trust for his wife for life and after her death to be divided equally between his son and daughter.

CROSS J. held that the declaration that the devise should not take effect until a future time deferred its vesting in possession until that time but not its vesting in interest, read the terms of section 175 of the Law of Property Act 1925, *supra*, p. 693, and continued:

"The devise is, it is said, a future specific devise within the meaning of the section; the testator has not made any express disposition of the income accruing from it between his death and the death of his widow, and so that income is carried by the gift. At first sight it is hard to see how Parliament

---

[55] *Re Churchill* [1909] 2 Ch. 431 (intention implied from a power to apply the whole or any part of the contingent legacy for the advancement or otherwise for the benefit of the legatee at any time before attaining 21 years of age, which clearly authorised payments for the minor's maintenance), *Re Selby Walker* [1949] 2 All E.R. 178.

[56] *Re Jones* [1932] 1 Ch. 108 (beware the incorrect headnote).

[57] But see B. S. Ker (1953) 17 Conv. 273, 279, 283–284.

[58] The Income and Corporation Taxes Act 1988, ss.663, 664.

[59] s.664(2)(3) (*ibid.*). See p. 25, *supra*.

could have enacted a section which produces such a result. If a testator gives property to A after the death of B, then whether or not he disposes of the income accruing during B's life he is at all events showing clearly that A is not to have it. Yet if the future gift to A is absolute and the intermediate income is carried with it by force of this section, A can claim to have the property transferred to him at once, since no one else can be interested in it. The section, that is to say, will have converted a gift in remainder into a gift in possession in defiance of the testator's wishes. The explanation for the section taking the form which it does is, I think, probably as follows. It has long been established that a gift of residuary personalty to a legatee in being on a contingency or to an unborn person at birth carried the intermediate income so far as the law would allow it to be accumulated, but that rule had been held, for reasons depending on the old land law, not to apply to gifts of real property, and it was apparently never applied to specific dispositions of personalty. Section 175 of the Law of Property Act 1925 was plainly intended to extend the rule to residuary devises and to specific gifts whether of realty or of personalty. It is now established, at all events so far as courts of first instance are concerned, that the old rule does not apply to residuary bequests whether vested or contingent which are expressly deferred to a future date which must come sooner or later (see *Re Oliver*,[60] *Re Gillett's Will Trusts*[61] and *Re Geering*[62]). There is a good reason for this distinction. If a testator gives property to X contingently on his attaining the age of thirty it is reasonable to assume, in the absence of a direction to the contrary, that the testator would wish X, if he attains thirty, to have the income produced by the property between the testator's death and the happening of the contingency. If, on the other hand, he gives property to X for any sort of interest after the death of A, it is reasonable to assume that he does not wish X to have the income accruing during A's lifetime unless he directs that he is to have it. This distinction between an immediate gift on a contingency and a gift which is expressly deferred was not drawn until after the Law of Property Act 1925 was passed. There were statements in textbooks and even in judgments to the effect that the rule applied to deferred as well as to contingent gifts of residuary personalty.[63] The legislature, when it extended this rule to residuary devises and specific gifts, must, I think, have adopted this erroneous view of the law. I would have liked, if I could, to construe the reference to 'future specific devises' and 'executory interest' in section 175(1) of the Act of 1925 in such a way as to make it consistent with the recent cases on the scope of the old rule applicable to residuary bequests. To do that, however, would be to rectify the Act, not to construe it, and I see no escape from the conclusion that whereas before 1926 a specific gift or a residuary devise which was not vested in possession did not prima facie carry intermediate income at all, now such a gift may carry intermediate income in circumstances in which a residuary bequest would not carry it.

"It was argued in this case that the fact that the will contained a residuary gift constituted an express disposition of the income of the land in question which prevented the section from applying. I am afraid that I cannot accept this submission. I have little doubt that the testator expected the income of the

60 [1947] 2 All E.R. 162.
61 [1950] Ch. 102.
62 [1964] Ch. 136.
63 See *Jarman on Wills* (7th ed.), p. 1006.

land to form part of the income of residue during his widow's lifetime, but he has made no express disposition of it. I agree with what was said in this connection by Eve J. in *Re Raine*.[64] As the devise is not vested indefeasibly in the daughter but is subject to defeasance during the mother's lifetime the intermediate income which the gift carries by virtue of section 175 ought prima facie to be accumulated to see who eventually becomes entitled to it. It was, however, submitted by counsel for the daughter that she could claim payment of it under section 31(1) of the Trustee Act 1925. [His Lordship summarised the subsection, and continued:] There are, as I see it, two answers to the daughter's claim. The first—and narrower—answer is that her interest in the income of the devised land is a vested interest. It is a future interest liable to be divested but it is not contingent. Therefore section 31(1) does not apply to it. The second—and wider—answer is that the whole framework of section 31 shows that it is inapplicable to a future gift of this sort and that a will containing such a gift expresses a contrary intention within section 69(2) which prevents the subsection from applying. By deferring the enjoyment of the devise until after the widow's death the testator has expressed the intention that the daughter shall not have the immediate income. It is true that as he has not expressly disposed of it in any other way, section 175 of the Law of Property Act 1925 defeats that intention to the extent of making the future devise carry the income, so that the daughter will get it eventually, if she survives her mother or dies before her leaving no children to take by substitution. Even if, however, the words of section 31(1) of the Trustee Act 1925 fitted the case, there would be no warrant for defeating the testator's intention still further by reading section 31(1) into the will and thus giving the daughter an interest in possession in the income during her mother's lifetime. In the result, the income . . . must be accumulated, in my judgment, for twenty-one years if the widow so long lives."

### B. Advancement[65]

Trustees must be particularly careful in exercising the statutory power of advancement in order to "benefit" a beneficiary, for a mistake will mean that both capital and income disappear, probably for good. Danckwerts J. has said,[66] " 'benefit' is the widest possible word one could have and it must include payment direct to the beneficiary but that does not absolve the trustees from making up their minds whether the payment in the particular manner which they contemplate is for the benefit of the beneficiary." Viscount Radcliffe has said,[67] it "means any use of money which will improve the material situation of the beneficiary." In *Re Clore's S.T.*[68] making a donation to a charity at a wealthy beneficiary's request to discharge what he felt to be a moral obligation was held an advancement for his benefit.

*Re Pauling's S.T.*[69] provides a sorry, salutary story for compulsory reading before trustees exercise their power of advancement. It is a

---

[64] [1929] 1 Ch. 716, 719.

[65] See Wolstenholme & Cherry's *Conveyancing Statutes*, Vol. 4 (13th ed. by J. T. Farrand).

[66] *Re Moxon's W.T.* [1958] 1 W.L.R. 165. For "benefit" under an express clause see *Re Buckinghamshire's S.T., The Times*, March 29, 1977.

[67] *Pilkington* v. *I.R.C.* [1964] A.C. 612, 635.

[68] [1966] 1 W.L.R. 955.

[69] [1964] Ch. 303.

fascinating but overlengthy case to set out in any detail. Essentially, the father of the beneficiaries was so charming and forceful that the trustees frittered away much of the capital in ways that enabled the wife's overdraft to be paid off, a house to be bought for the father and his wife absolutely and an overly high standard of living to be maintained for the family. The lessons to be drawn are that requests for advancements from young adults unemancipated from the undue influence of their parents must be treated with caution and the moneys requested applied by the trustees themselves for a particular purpose if previous experience indicates that otherwise the purported purpose is unlikely to be effected.

An advancement may be by way of settlement that benefits someone other than the beneficiary so long as the beneficiary receives significant benefit,[70] *e.g.* receiving a life interest in the advanced moneys, remainder to his widow for life, remainder to his children equally. However, unless the power of advancement is expressly extended to permit delegation of duties and discretions the resettlement must not be by way of discretionary trusts or by way of protective trusts which may end up after forfeiture as discretionary trusts.[71] It is also necessary to ensure that the rule against remoteness is not infringed, for the perpetuity period relevant to the exercise of the power of advancement runs from the date of the settlement and not from the date of the exercise of the power[72]: *Pilkington* v. *I.R.C., infra*, p. 701. If part of the exercise of the power of advancement is void for remoteness *and* the resultant effect of the intended advancement is such that it could not reasonably be regarded as being beneficial to the beneficiary intended to be advanced, then the advancement fails for it cannot be authorised as within the powers of the trustees under section 32: otherwise the part of the advancement not void for remoteness will stand as within the trustees' powers,[73] *e.g.* C's life interest stands where the advancement is to trustees for C for life with remainders to his issue where the remainders are void for remoteness. The fact that in such a case no effective beneficial trusts of capital are created does not mean that there has been no payment or application of capital as required by section 32: the transfer of capital to the trustees of the settlement for C for life is an application of capital within section 32.[74]

[70] *Pilkington* v. *I.R.C.* [1964] A.C. 612, *Re Hampden* [1977] T.R. 177.

[71] *Re Wills' Trusts* [1959] Ch. 1; *Re Morris* [1951] 2 All E.R. 528; *Re Hunter's W.T.* [1963] Ch. 372, *Re Hay's S.T.* [1982] 1 W.L.R. 202 *supra*, p. 163.

[72] The exercise of a power of advancement is treated as the exercise of a special power so that the Perpetuities and Accumulations Act 1964 is of no avail unless the original settlement was created after July 15, 1964: s.15(5) of the Perpetuities and Accumulations Act 1964.

[73] *Re Abraham's W.T.* [1969] 1 Ch. 463 as cut down by the interpretation of the Court of Appeal in *Re Hastings-Bass* [1975] Ch. 25 explored in *Mettoy Pension Trustees* v. *Evans* [1991] 2 All E.R. 513.

[74] *Re Hastings-Bass* [1975] Ch. 25. At p. 203 the court laid down the general proposition, "where by the terms of a trust (as under s.32) a trustee is given a discretion as to some matter under which he acts in good faith, the court should not interfere with his action notwithstanding that it does not have the full effect intended unless (1) what he has achieved is unauthorised by the power conferred on him or (2) it is clear that he would not have acted as he did (a) had he not taken into account considerations which he should not have taken into account or (b) had he not failed to take into account considerations which he ought to have taken into account."

A capital gains tax charge arises not only on an advance to a beneficiary absolutely but also where the advancement is on new trusts even where T1 and T2 appropriate the property on new trusts and are themselves trustees of the appropriated property.[75] No capital gains tax charge will arise if the trustees instead of creating a new separate settlement merely sub-settle some trust assets. To help distinguish between a new settlement and a sub-settlement the Revenue issued a Statement of Practice as follows:

"It is now clear that a deemed disposal under C.G.T.A. 1979, section 54(1) cannot arise unless the power exercised by the trustees, or the instrument conferring the power, expressly or by necessary implication, confers on the trustees authority to remove assets from the original settlement by subjecting them to the trusts of a different settlement. Such powers (which may be powers of advancement or appointment) are referred to by the Court of Appeal as 'powers in the wider form.' However, the Board considers that a deemed disposal will not arise when such a power is exercised and trusts are declared in circumstances such that:
(a) the appointment is revocable, or
(b) the trusts declared of the advanced or appointed funds are not exhaustive so that there exists a possibility at the time when the advancement or appointment is made that the funds covered by it will on the occasion of some event cease to be held upon such trusts and once again come to be held upon the original trusts of the settlement.
Further, when such a power is exercised the Board considers it unlikely that a deemed disposal will arise when trusts are declared if duties in regard to the appointed assets still fall to the trustees of the original settlement in their capacity as trustees of that settlement, bearing in mind the provision in CGTA 1979 section 52(1) that the trustees of a settlement form a single and continuing body (distinct from the persons who may from time to time be the trustees).
Finally, the Board accept that a power of appointment or advancement can be exercised over only part of the settled property and that the above consequences would apply to that part."

When advances are brought into account they are accounted for at their value at the time of the advance and not at their value prevailing at the time of the final distribution.[76] This is unjust in these inflationary times so the Law Reform Committee (Cmnd. 8733, para. 4.47) recommend that advances should be accounted for at their value at the time of the advance multiplied by any increase in the retail price index up to the time of the final distribution.

---

[75] *Hart* v. *Briscoe* [1979] Ch. 110; *Roome* v. *Edwards* [1981] 1 All E.R. 736; *Bond* v. *Pickford* [1983] S.T.C. 517; Capital Gains Tax Act 1979, s.54.
[76] *Re Gollins' Declaration of Trust* [1969] 3 All E.R. 1591, but trustees may get a beneficiary to consent to his advancement being treated as of a fraction of the fund: *Re Leigh's S.T.* [1981] C.L.Y. 2453.

## The Trustee Act 1925

Section 32.—(1) Trustees may[77] at any time or times pay or apply any capital money[78] subject to a trust, for the advancement or benefit, in such manner as they may, in their absolute discretion, think fit, of any person entitled to the capital[79] of the trust property or of any share thereof, whether absolutely or contingently on his attaining any specified age or on the occurrence of any other event, or subject to a gift over on his death under any specified age or on the occurrence of any other event, and whether in possession or in remainder or reversion, and such payment or application may be made notwithstanding that the interest of such person is liable to be defeated by the exercise of a power of appointment or revocation, or to be diminished by the increase of the class to which he belongs:

Provided that—

(a) the money so paid or applied for the advancement or benefit of any person shall not exceed altogether in amount *one-half*[80] of the presumptive or vested share or interest of that person in the trust property; and

(b) if that person is or becomes absolutely and indefeasibly entitled to a share in the trust property the money so paid or applied shall be brought into account as part of such share; and

(c) *no such payment or application shall be made so as to prejudice any person entitled to any prior life or other interest,*[81] whether vested or contingent, in the money paid or applied *unless* such person is in existence and of full age and *consents in writing* to such payment or application.

(2) This section applies only where the trust property consists of money or securities or of property held upon trust for sale calling in and conversion, and

---

[77] The section confers a power: it does not impose a duty: hence it cannot be utilised if the settlement contains a contrary intention: see *Inland Revenue Commissioners* v. *Bernstein* [1960] Ch. 444 (Danckwerts J.); [1961] Ch. 399 (C.A.); *Re Henderson's Trusts* [1969] 1 W.L.R. 651; *Re Evans' Settlement* [1967] 1 W.L.R. 1294. Whilst a duty to accumulate is necessarily inconsistent with the power of maintenance it is not necessarily inconsistent with the power of advancement: *I.R.C.* v. *Bernstein* [1961] Ch. 399.

[78] Assets can be transferred *in specie*: *Re Collard's W.T.* [1961] Ch. 293 noted (1961) 77 L.Q.R. 161. When brought into account on final distribution of the trust property they will be taken into account as of their cash value when originally received: *Re Gollins' Declaration of Trust* [1969] 3 All E.R. 1591.

[79] The section does not apply where the beneficiary is given only an interest in income: *Re Winch's Settlement* [1917] 1 Ch. 633.

[80] If A and B are the two beneficiaries contingently equally entitled to a trust fund of £200,000 and B receives the maximum advancement of £50,000 does this mean that the power can no longer be exercised in his favour or if the fund remaining appreciates to £250,000 can B maintain that the fund is now notionally worth £250,000 plus his advanced £50,000 so that an advancement of half of half of £300,000, *i.e.*, £75,000, may be made to him so that he may receive a further £25,000 on top of the £50,000 he has already received? Consider s.32(1) proviso (b) and *Re Marquess of Abergavenny's Estate Act Trusts* [1981] 2 All E.R. 643 (trustees had express power to advance to the life tenant "any part or parts not exceeding in all one half in value of the settled fund." Goulding J. held an advance of half the value of the settled fund exhausted the exercise of the power so that it ceased to be exercisable in the future even though the retained assets had later increased in value).

[81] An object of a discretionary trust is not entitled to such a prior interest as to render his consent requisite: *Re Beckett's Settlement* [1940] Ch. 279 but where income is held on the protective trusts in Trustee Act 1925, s.33, and there has been no forfeiture the "principal beneficiary" has a prior interest within para. (c) his consent not incurring a forfeiture: *Re Harris' Settlement* (1940) 162 L.T. 358; *Re Rees' W.T.* [1954] Ch. 202. Further see *I.R.C.* v. *Bernstein* [1960] Ch. 444; [1961] Ch. 399. Often the power to advance is extended to the whole, rather than half, of the prospective share but the life tenant's consent remains requisite: *Henley* v. *Wardell, The Times*, January 29, 1988.

such money or securities, or the proceeds of such sale calling in and conversion are not by statute or in equity considered as land, or applicable as capital money for the purposes of the Settled Land Act 1925.

(3) This section does not apply to trusts constituted or created before the commencement of this Act.[82]

## PILKINGTON AND ANOTHER v. INLAND REVENUE COMMISSIONERS

House of Lords [1964] A.C. 612; [1962] 3 W.L.R. 1051; [1962] 3 All E.R. 622; 40 T.C. 416 (Viscount Radcliffe, Lords Reid, Jenkins, Hodson and Devlin)

By his will the testator left his residuary estate to trustees on trust, for his nephew, Richard Godfrey Pilkington (hereinafter called "Richard"), upon protective trusts during his life with a provision that any consent which he might give to the exercise of any applicable form of advancement should not cause a forfeiture of his life interest. After Richard's death the trustees were to hold the residuary estate upon trust for such of Richard's children or remoter issue at such age in such shares and with such trusts for their respective benefit and such provisions for their respective advancement and maintenance and education as Richard should by deed or will without transgressing the rule against perpetuities appoint. In default of appointment the trustees were to hold the residuary estate on trust for such of Richard's children as, being male, attained the age of twenty-one, or, being female, attained that age or married under it, and, if more than one, in equal shares.

The testator's will did not confer any express power of advancement upon the trustees, but, by implication, the power of advancement under section 32 of the Trustee Act 1925, *supra*, was applicable.

Richard had three children, of whom the defendant Penelope Margaret Pilkington (hereinafter called "Miss Penelope") was one.

Richard's father, Guy Reginald Pilkington (hereinafter called "the settlor"), proposed to make a settlement, to be executed by himself, Richard and the trustees of the testator's will, upon the following trusts: (i) Until Miss Penelope attained the age of twenty-one the trustees of the settlement were to have power to apply income for her maintenance whether or not there was any other income available for that purpose and were to accumulate and capitalise surplus income; (ii) If Miss Penelope attained the age of twenty-one the trustees were to be under a duty to pay the income to her until she reached the age of thirty or died under that age; (iii) If Miss Penelope attained the age of thirty the trustees were to hold the capital of the trust fund upon trust for her absolutely; (iv) If Miss Penelope died under the age of thirty, leaving a child or children who attained the age of twenty-one, the trustees were to hold the trust fund and the income thereof in trust for such child or children, and, if more than one, in equal shares.

Subject to these trusts, the trustees of the settlement were to hold the trust fund in trust equally for all of Richard's children (other than Miss Penelope) who, being male, attained the age of twenty-one, or, being female, attained the age or married under it.

---

[82] If the trust is a testamentary one and the testator dies after 1925, the power contained in s.32 of the Act, *supra*, is available to the trustees: *Re Taylor's Will Trusts* (1950) 66 T.L.R.(Pt. 2) 507. *Aliter* if the trusts arose under a special power of appointment created before 1926 but exercised after 1925: *Re Batty* [1952] Ch. 280; criticised (1952) 68 L.Q.R. 319 (J. H. C. M., citing *Re Stimpson* [1931] 2 Ch. 77).

In the case of the failure of the trust, the fund was to be held on the trusts of the testator's will which would take effect after Richard's death as if he had died without having been married.

The proposed settlement provided that the power of maintenance contained in Section 31 of the Trustee Act 1925, subject to certain modifications, and the power of advancement contained in section 32 of the Act in an unmodified form, should be available to the trustees.

The trustees of the testator's will took out an originating summons for the determination of the question whether they as such trustees could lawfully exercise the powers conferred on them in relation to the expectant interest of the defendant Miss Penelope, in the testator's residuary estate by applying (with the consent of the defendant Richard, her father) some part not exceeding one-half of the capital of such interest in such manner as to make it subject to the trusts, powers and provisions of the settlement proposed to be executed by the plaintiff, the settlor, or whether such application would be improper and unauthorised. Danckwerts J.[83] held that the exercise of the power of advancement in this way would not be objectionable; but his decision was reversed by the Court of Appeal.[84] Richard and Miss Penelope appealed.

VISCOUNT RADCLIFFE: "The word 'advancement' itself meant in this context the establishment in life of the beneficiary who was the object of the power or at any rate some step that would contribute to the furtherance of his establishment. Thus it was found in such phrases as 'preferment or advancement' (*Lowther* v. *Bentinck*[85]), 'business, profession, or employment or . . . advancement or preferment in the world' (*Roper-Curzon* v. *Roper-Curzon*[86]) and 'placing out or advancement in life' (*Re Breeds' Will*[87]). Typical instances of expenditure for such purposes under the social conditions of the nineteenth century were an apprenticeship or the purchase of a commission in the Army or of an interest in business. In the case of a girl there could be advancement on marriage (*Lloyd* v. *Cocker*[88]). Advancement had, however, to some extent a limited range of meaning, since it was thought to convey the idea of some step in life of permanent significance, and accordingly, to prevent uncertainties about the permitted range of objects for which moneys could be raised and made available, such words as 'or otherwise for his or her benefit' were often added to the word 'advancement'. It was always recognised that these added words were 'large words' (see Jessel M.R. in *Re Breeds' Will*[89]) and indeed in another case (*Lowther* v. *Bentinck*[90]) the same judge spoke of preferment and advancement as being 'both large words' but of 'benefit' as being the 'largest of all.' So, too, Kay J. in *Re Brittlebank*.[91] Recent judges have spoken in the same terms—see Farwell J. in *Re Halsted's Will Trusts*[92] and Danckwerts J. in *Re Moxon's Will Trusts*.[93] This wide construction of the range of the power, which evidently did not stand upon niceties of distinction provided that the proposed

[83] [1959] Ch. 699.
[84] [1961] Ch. 466.
[85] (1874) L.R. 19 Eq. 166.
[86] (1871) L.R. 11 Eq. 452.
[87] (1875) 1 Ch.D. 226.
[88] (1860) 27 Beav. 645.
[89] (1875) 1 Ch.D. 226, 228.
[90] (1874) L.R. 19 Eq. 166, 169.
[91] (1881) 30 W.R. 99, 100.
[92] [1937] 2 All E.R. 570, 571.
[93] [1958] 1 W.L.R. 165, 168.

application could fairly be regarded as for the benefit of the beneficiary who was the object of the power, must have been carried into the statutory power created by section 32, since it adopts without qualification the accustomed wording 'for the advancement or benefit in such manner as they may in their absolute discretion think fit.'

"So much for 'advancement,' which I now use for brevity to cover the combined phrase 'advancement or benefit.' It means any use of the money which will improve the material situation of the beneficiary. It is important, however, not to confuse the idea of 'advancement' with the idea of advancing the money out of the beneficiary's expectant interest. The two things have only a casual connection with each other. The one refers to the operation of finding money by way of anticipation of an interest not yet absolutely vested in possession or, if so vested, belonging to an infant: the other refers to the status of the beneficiary and the improvement of his situation. The power to carry out the operation of anticipating an interest is not conferred by the word 'advancement' but by those other words of the section which expressly authorise the payment or application of capital money for the benefit of a person entitled 'whether absolutely or contingently on his attaining any specified age or on the occurrence of any other event, or subject to a gift over on his death under any specified age or on the occurrence of any other event, and whether in possession or in remainder or reversion,' etc.

"I think, with all respect to the Commissioners, a good deal of their argument is infected with some of this confusion. To say, for instance, that there cannot be a valid exercise of a power of advancement that results in a deferment of the vesting of the beneficiary's absolute title (Miss Penelope, it will be remembered, is to take at thirty under the proposed settlement instead of at twenty-one under the will) is in my opinion to play upon words. The element of anticipation consists in the raising of money for her now before she has any right to receive anything under the existing trusts: the advancement consists in the application of that money to form a trust fund, the provisions of which are thought to be for her benefit.

"I have not been able to find in the words of section 32, to which I have now referred, anything which in terms or by implication restricts the width of the manner or purpose of advancement. It is true that, if this settlement is made, Miss Penelope's children, who are not objects of the power, are given a possible interest in the event of her dying under thirty leaving surviving issue. But if the disposition itself, by which I mean the whole provision made, is for her benefit, it is no objection to the exercise of the power that other persons benefit incidentally as a result of the exercise. Thus a man's creditors may in certain cases get the most immediate advantage from an advancement made for the purpose of paying them off, as in *Lowther* v. *Bentinck*; and a power to raise money for the advancement of a wife may cover a payment made direct to her husband in order to set him up in business (*Re Kershaw's Trusts*[94]). The exercise will not be bad, therefore, on this ground.

"Nor in my opinion will it be bad merely because the moneys are to be tied up in the proposed settlement. If it could be said that the payment or application permitted by section 32 cannot take the form of a settlement in any form but must somehow pass direct into or through the hands of the object of the power, I could appreciate the principle upon which the Commissioners'

---

[94] (1868) L.R. 6 Eq. 322.

objection was founded. But can that principle be asserted? Anyone can see, I think, that there can be circumstances in which, while it is very desirable that some money should be raised at once for the benefit of an owner of an expectant or contingent interest, it would be very undesirable that the money should not be secured to him under some arrangement that will prevent him having the absolute disposition of it. I find it very difficult to think that there is something at the back of section 32 which makes such an advancement impossible. Certainly neither Danckwerts J. nor the members of the Court of Appeal in this case took the view. Both Lord Evershed M.R. and Upjohn L.J.[95] explicitly accept the possibility of a settlement being made in exercise of a power of advancement. Farwell J. authorised one in *Re Halsted's Will Trusts*,[96] a case in which the trustees had left their discretion to the court. The trustees should raise the money and 'have' it 'settled,' he said. So, too, Harman J. in *Re Ropner's Settlement Trusts*[97] authorised the settlement of an advance provided for an infant, saying that the child could not 'consent or request the trustees to make the advance, but the transfer of a part of his contingent share to the trustees of a settlement for him must advance his interest and thus be for his benefit . . . ' All this must be wrong in principle if a power of advancement cannot cover an application of the moneys by way of settlement.

"The truth is, I think, that the propriety of requiring a settlement of moneys found for advancement was recognised as long ago as 1871 in *Roper-Curzon* v. *Roper-Curzon* and, so far as I know, it has not been impugned since. Lord Romilly M.R.'s decision passed into the textbooks and it must have formed the basis of a good deal of subsequent practice. True enough, as counsel for the Commissioners has reminded us, the beneficiary in that case was an adult who was offering to execute the post-nuptial settlement required: but I find it impossible to read Lord Romilly's words as amounting to anything less than a decision that he would permit an advancement under the power only on the terms that the money was to be secured by settlement. That was what the case was about. If, then, it is a proper exercise of a power of advancement for trustees to stipulate that the money shall be settled, I cannot see any difference between having it settled that way and having it settled by themselves paying it to trustees of a settlement which is in the desired form.

"The Commissioners' objections seem to be concentrated upon such propositions as that the proposed transaction is 'nothing less than a resettlement' and that a power of advancement cannot be used so as to alter or vary the trusts created by the settlement from which it is derived. Such a transaction, they say, amounts to using the power of advancement as a way of appointing or declaring new trusts different from those of the settlement. The reason why I do not find that these propositions have any compulsive effect upon my mind is that they seem to me merely vivid ways of describing the substantial effect of that which is proposed to be done and they do not in themselves amount to convincing arguments against doing it. Of course, whenever money is raised for advancement on terms that it is to be settled on the beneficiary, the money only passes from one settlement to be caught up in the other. It is therefore the same thing as a resettlement. But, unless one is to say that such moneys

---

[95] [1961] Ch. 466, 481, 486.
[96] [1937] 2 All E.R. 570, 572.
[97] [1956] 1 W.L.R. 902, 906.

can never be applied by way of settlement, an argument which, as I have shown, has few supporters and is contrary to authority, it merely describes the inevitable effect of such an advancement to say that it is nothing less than a resettlement. Similarly, if it is part of the trusts and powers created by one settlement that the trustees of it should have power to raise money and make it available for a beneficiary upon new trusts approved by them, then they are in substance given power to free the money from one trust and to subject it to another. So be it: but, unless they cannot require a settlement of it at all, the transaction they carry out is the same thing in effect as an appointment of new trusts.

"In the same way I am unconvinced by the argument that the trustees would be improperly delegating their trust by allowing the money raised to pass over to new trustees under a settlement conferring new powers on the latter. In fact I think that the whole issue of delegation is here beside the mark. The law is not that trustees cannot delegate: it is that trustees cannot delegate unless they have authority to do so. If the power of advancement which they possess is so read as to allow them to raise money for the purpose of having it settled, they do have the necessary authority to let the money pass out of the old settlement into the new trusts. No question of delegation of their powers or trusts arises. If, on the other hand, their power of advancement is read so as to exclude settled advances, *cadit quaestio*.

"I ought to note for the record (1) that the transaction envisaged does not actually involve the raising of money, since the trustees propose to appropriate a block of shares in the family's private limited company as the trust investment, and (2) there will not be any actual transfer, since the trustees of the proposed settlement and the will trustees are the same persons. As I have already said, I do not attach any importance to these factors, nor, I think, do the Commissioners. To transfer or appropriate outright is only to do by short cut what could be done in a more roundabout way by selling the shares to a consenting party, paying the money over to the new settlement with appropriate instructions and arranging for it to be used in buying back the shares as the trust investment. It cannot make any difference to follow the course taken in *Re Collard's Will Trusts*[98] and deal with the property direct. On the other point, so long as there are separate trusts, the property effectually passes out of the old settlement into the new one, and it is of no relevance that, at any rate for the time being, the persons administering the new trusts are the same individuals.

"I have not yet referred to the ground which was taken by the Court of Appeal as their reason for saying that the proposed settlement was not permissible. To put it shortly, they held that the statutory power of advancement could not be exercised unless the benefit to be conferred was 'personal to the person concerned, in the sense of being related to his or her own real or personal needs.'[99] Or, to use other words of the learned Master of the Rolls,[1] the exercise of the power 'must be an exercise done to meet the circumstances as they present themselves in regard to a person within the scope of the section, whose circumstances call for that to be done which the trustees think fit to do.' Upjohn L.J.[2] expressed himself in virtually the same terms.

---

[98] [1961] Ch. 293.
[99] *Ibid.* p. 484.
[1] [1961] Ch. 466, 481.
[2] *Ibid.*

"My Lords, I differ with reluctance from the views of judges so learned and experienced in matters of this sort: but I do not find it possible to import such restrictions into the words of the statutory power which itself does not contain them. First, the suggested qualification, that the considerations or circumstances must be 'personal' to the beneficiary, seems to me uncontrollably vague as a guide to general administration. What distinguishes a personal need from any other need to which the trustees in their discretion think it right to attend in the beneficiary's interest? And, if the advantage of preserving the funds of a beneficiary from the incidence of death duty is not an advantage personal to that beneficiary, I do not see what is. Death duty is a present risk that attaches to the settled property in which Miss Penelope has her expectant interest, and even accepting the validity of the supposed limitation, I would not have supposed that there was anything either impersonal or unduly remote in the advantage to be conferred upon her of some exemption from that risk. I do not think, therefore, that I can support the interpretation of the power of advancement that has commended itself to the Court of Appeal, and, with great respect, I think that the judgments really amount to little more than a decision that in the opinion of the members of that court this was not a case in which there was any occasion to exercise the power. That would be a proper answer from a court to which trustees had referred their discretion with a request for its directions; but it does not really solve any question where, as here, they retain their discretion and merely ask whether it is impossible for them to exercise it.

"To conclude, therefore, on this issue, I am of opinion that there is no maintainable reason for introducing into the statutory power of advancement a qualification that would exclude the exercise in the case now before us. It would not be candid to omit to say that, though I think that that is what the law requires, I am uneasy at some of the possible applications of this liberty, when advancements are made for the purposes of settlement or on terms that there is to be a settlement. It is quite true, as the Commissioners have pointed out, that you might have really extravagant cases of resettlements being forced on beneficiaries in the name of advancement, even a few months before an absolute vesting in possession would have destroyed the power. I have tried to give due weight to such possibilities, but when all is said I do not think that they ought to compel us to introduce a limitation of which no one, with all respect, can produce a satisfactory definition. First, I do not believe that it is wise to try to cut down an admittedly wide and discretionary power, enacted for general use, through fear of its being abused in certain hypothetical instances. And moreover, as regards this fear, I think that it must be remembered that we are speaking of a power intended to be in the hands of trustees chosen by a settlor because of his confidence in their discretion and good sense and subject to the external check that no exercise can take place without the consent of a prior life-tenant; and that there does remain at all times a residual power in the court to restrain or correct any purported exercise that can be shown to be merely wanton or capricious and not to be attributable to a genuine discretion. I think, therefore, that, although extravagant possibilities exist, they may be more menacing in argument than in real life. . . . "

[However, their Lordships also held that the power of advancement under section 32 was to be regarded in the same way as a special power of appointment so far as the application of the rule against perpetuities was concerned so that the proposed advancement would be void.]

### C. *Payment of Trust Funds to Beneficiaries*

Trustees must pay trust moneys to the right beneficiaries, for otherwise it is a breach of trust. In *Eaves* v. *Hickson*,[3] trustees were induced by a forgery to pay trust funds to persons not entitled, and Romilly M.R. held that, as between trustee and beneficiary, the loss fell on the former.[4]

Section 61 of the Trustee Act 1925, *infra*, is now available as a defence to a trustee who honestly and reasonably makes a wrongful payment through circumstances similar to those in *Eaves* v. *Hickson*, or through an erroneous construction of the trust instrument,[5] but section 30(1) of the Act, *supra*, p. 644 is not.[6]

Before paying trust funds to an alleged *assignee* from a beneficiary a trustee must investigate the assignee's title. If he relies merely on the alleged assignee's statement, he is not acting reasonably. If the assignee happens also to be solicitor to the trust the trustee will still be liable[7] unless excused under section 61 of the Trustee Act.[8] But although the trustee must investigate the assignee's title, he cannot require actual delivery up to him of the assignee's document of title.[9]

If a trustee, through inadvertence or a mistake of construction or of fact, has overpaid one beneficiary at the expense of another, and the court is administering the estate, it will adjust accounts out of future payments.[10] If the estate is not being administered by the court, an adjustment can be made with the court's assistance; and might presumably be made without any application to the court. If the underpaid beneficiary can identify the fund erroneously paid, he has, in addition, the remedy of tracing it into the hands of the overpaid beneficiary or an assignee (except a bona fide purchaser),[11] and if beneficiary under a will, or probably under a trust also, he may also have a personal action against a recipient under *Ministry of Health* v. *Simpson* principles.[12]

But if a *trustee-beneficiary* underpays *himself*, then, as held in *Re Horne*,[13] he suffers by his mistake.

The Law Reform Committee (Cmnd. 8733, para. 5.4) have made the following recommendation: "where it appears that the cost of taking out a summons is out of all proportion to the amount at stake, trustees should be empowered to take the advice of counsel (in the

---

[3] (1861) 30 Beav. 136. However, only if the forger or the wrong recipients could not compensate the beneficiary.
[4] See also *Ashby* v. *Blackwell* (1765) 2 Eden 299, 302; *Sheridan* v. *Joyce* (1844) 7 Ir.Eq.R. 115; *Boulton* v. *Beard* (1853) 3 De G.M. & G. 608; *Sporle* v. *Barnaby* (1864) 10 Jur. 1142.
[5] *Re Smith, Smith* v. *Thompson* (1902) 71 L.J.Ch. 411; *National Trustees' Case* [1905] A.C. 381; *Re Allsop* [1914] 1 Ch. 1.
[6] *Re Windsor Co.* [1929] 1 Ch. 151, 161, 166, 170.
[7] *Davis* v. *Hutchings* [1907] 1 Ch. 356.
[8] *Re Allsop* [1914] 1 Ch. 1.
[9] *Re Palmer* [1907] 1 Ch. 486; see *Warter* v. *Anderson* (1853) 11 Hare 301.
[10] *Dibbs* v. *Goren* (1849) 11 Beav. 483; *Re Musgrave* [1916] 2 Ch. 417.
[11] *Re Diplock* [1948] Ch. 465.
[12] [1951] A.C. 251, see p. 549, *supra*.
[13] [1905] 1 Ch. 76.

case of trusts having adult beneficiaries only) or Chancery Queens Counsel or conveyancing counsel of the court (where there are infant beneficiaries) and to distribute on the basis of that advice if no adult beneficiary starts proceedings within three months of being sent a copy of the relevant opinion." As a half-way measure section 48 of the Administration of Justice Act 1985 gives the court power to authorise action to be taken in reliance on counsel's opinion concerning the construction of a will or trust.

## IV. STATUTORY AND JUDICIAL PROTECTION OF TRUSTEES IN RESPECT OF THE DISTRIBUTION OF THE TRUST PROPERTY

### The Trustee Act 1925

*Protection against liability in respect of rents and covenants*

Section 26.—(1) Where a personal representative or trustee liable as such[14] for—

(a) any rent, covenant, or agreement reserved by or contained in any lease; or

(b) any rent, covenant or agreement payable under or contained in any grant made in consideration of a rentcharge; or

(c) any indemnity given in respect of any rent, covenant or agreement referred to in either of the foregoing paragraphs:

satisfies all liabilities under the lease or grant which may have accrued, or been claimed, up to the date of the conveyance hereinafter mentioned, and where necessary, sets apart a sufficient fund to answer any future claim that may be made in respect of any fixed and ascertained sum which the lessee or grantee agreed to lay out on the property demised or granted, although the period for laying out the same may not have arrived, then and in any such case the personal representative or trustee may convey the property demised or granted to a purchaser, legatee, devisee or other person entitled to call for a conveyance thereof and thereafter—

(i) he may distribute the residuary real and personal estate of the deceased testator or intestate, or, as the case may be, the trust estate (other than the fund, if any, set apart as aforesaid) to or amongst the persons entitled thereto, without appropriating any part, or any further part, as the case may be, of the estate of the deceased or of the trust estate to meet any future liability under the said lease or grant;

(ii) notwithstanding such distribution, he shall not be personally liable in respect of any subsequent claim under the said lease or grant.

(2) This section operates without prejudice to the right of the lessor or grantor, or the persons deriving title under the lessor or grantor, to follow the assets of the deceased or the trust property into the hands of the persons amongst whom the same may have been respectively distributed, and applies

---

14 The protection of the section avails a personal representative or trustee in respect of his liability *as such*. Personal liability, unprotected by the section, is incurred if the personal representative or trustee takes possession of the leaseholds: *Re Owers (No. 2)* [1941] Ch. 389; *Re Bennett* [1943] 1 All E.R. 467; *Youngmin* v. *Heath* [1974] 1 W.L.R. 135, 138.

notwithstanding anything to the contrary in the will or other instrument, if any, creating the trust.

(3) In this section "lease" includes an underlease and an agreement for a lease or underlease and any instrument giving any such indemnity as aforesaid or varying the liabilities under the lease; "grant" applies to a grant whether the rent is created by limitation, grant, reservation, or otherwise, and includes an agreement for a grant and any instrument giving any such indemnity as aforesaid or varying the liabilities under the grant; "lessee" and "grantee" include persons respectively deriving title under them.

### Protection by means of advertisements

Section 27.[15]—(1) With a view to the conveyance to or distribution among the persons entitled to any real or personal property, the trustees of a settlement or of a disposition on trust for sale or personal representatives, may give notice by advertisement in the Gazette, and in a daily London newspaper, and also, if the property includes land not situated in London in a daily or weekly newspaper circulating in the district in which the land is situated, and such other like notices, including notices elsewhere than in England and Wales, as would, in any special case, have been directed by a court of competent jurisdiction in an action for administration, of their intention to make such conveyance or distribution as aforesaid, and requiring any person interested[16] to send to the trustees or personal representatives within the time, not being less than two months, fixed in the notice or, where more than one notice is given, in the last of the notices, particulars of his claim in respect of the property or any part thereof to which the notice relates.

(2) At the expiration of the time fixed by the notice the trustees or personal representatives may convey or distribute the property or any part thereof to which the notice relates, to or among the persons entitled thereto, having regard only to the claims, whether formal or not, of which the trustees or personal representatives then had notice[17] and shall not, as respects the property so conveyed or distributed, be liable to any person of whose claim the trustees or personal representatives have not had notice[18] at the time of conveyance or distribution; but nothing in this section—

(a) prejudices the right of any person to follow the property, or any property representing the same, into the hands of any person, other than a purchaser, who may have received it; or

(b) frees the trustees or personal representatives from any obligation to make searches or obtain official certificates of search similar to those which an intending purchaser would be advised to make or obtain.

(3) This section applies notwithstanding anything to the contrary in the will or other instrument, if any, creating the trust.

---

[15] For the form which the advertisement should take, see *Re Aldhous* [1955] 1 W.L.R. 459.
[16] Protection is afforded against belated claims of creditors, next of kin or beneficiaries under a will: *Re Aldhous* [1955] 1 W.L.R. 459, 462.
[17] The Law Reform Committee (Cmnd. 873, para. 5.1) recommend that trustees should be empowered to write to any potential creditors, enclosing a copy of counsel's opinion, informing them they should make their claim within three months of receiving the opinion. If no claim is then made the trustees should be free to make the proposed distributions without liability, but without prejudice to the creditor's right to follow the trust assets.
[18] In view of s.27(2)(b) this may well cover constructive notice as well as actual notice. See also Law Com. No. 157 (Illegitimacy) 1986 para. 3.10, n. 22.

*Payment into court by trustees*

Section 63.[19]—(1) Trustees, or the majority of trustees, having in their hands or under their control money or securities belonging to a trust, may pay the same into court; and the same shall, subject to rules of court, be dealt with according to the orders of the court.

(2) The receipt or certificate of the proper officer shall be a sufficient discharge to trustees for the money or securities so paid into court.

(3) Where money or securities are vested in any persons as trustees, and the majority are desirous of paying the same into court, but the concurrence of the other or others cannot be obtained, the court may order the payment into court to be made by the majority without the concurrence of the other or others.

(4) Where any such money or securities are deposited with any banker, broker, or other depositary, the court may order payment or delivery of the money or securities to the majority of the trustees for the purpose of payment into court.

(5) Every transfer payment and delivery made in pursuance of any such order shall be valid and take effect as if the same had been made on the authority by the act of all the persons entitled to the money and securities so transferred, paid, or delivered.

*Miscellaneous statutory protection*

Trustees and personal representatives have protection under the Adoption Act 1976, s.45 and the Legitimacy Act 1976, s.7, if they do not have notice of illegitimate or legitimated or adopted persons where the existence of such persons affects entitlement to the trust property. However, protection under section 27 of the Trustee Act may be sufficient.[20]

*Rules of Supreme Court, Order 85*

*Administration and Similar Actions*

## Interpretation (O. 85, r. 1).

1. In this Order "administration action" means an action for the administration under the direction of the Court of the estate of a deceased person or for the execution under the direction of the Court of a trust.

## Determination of questions, etc., without administration (O. 85, r. 2)

2.—(1) An action may be brought for the determination of any question or for any relief which could be determined or granted, as the case may be, in an administration action and a claim need not be made in the action for the administration or execution under the direction of the Court of the estate or trust in connection with which the question arises or the relief is sought.

---

[19] This section replaces s.42 of the Trustee Act 1893, which replaced s.1 and s.2 of the Trustees' Relief Act 1847. Unless trustees have reasonable cause, they may be made liable for the costs of paying funds into, and getting them out of, court. In case of doubt as to the claim, share or identity of a beneficiary the practice today is to submit the matter to the court for determination by an originating summons under Ord. 85, r. 2, and Ord. 5, r. 1 and r. 4, of the Rules of the Supreme Court. See A. J. Hawkins (1968) 84 L.Q.R. 65.

[20] See repeal of Family Law Reform Act 1969, s.17 by s.20 F.L.R.A. 1987 and comments of G. Miller [1988] Conv. 410, 417–419.

(2) Without prejudice to the generality of paragraph (1), an action may be brought for the determination of any of the following questions:—

    (*a*) any question arising in the administration of the estate of a deceased person or in the execution of a trust;

    (*b*) any question as to the composition of any class of persons having a claim against the estate of a deceased person or a beneficial interest in the estate of such a person or in any property subject to a trust;

    (*c*) any question as to the rights or interests of a person claiming to be a creditor of the estate of a deceased person or to be entitled under a will or on the intestacy of a deceased person or to be beneficially entitled under a trust.

(3) Without prejudice to the generality of paragraph (1), an action may be brought for any of the following reliefs:—

    (*a*) an order requiring an executor, administrator or trustee to furnish and, if necessary, verify accounts;

    (*b*) an order requiring the payment into court of money held by a person in his capacity as executor, administrator or trustee;

    (*c*) an order directing a person to do or abstain from doing a particular act in his capacity as executor, administrator or trustee;

    (*d*) an order approving any sale, purchase, compromise or other transaction by a person in his capacity as executor, administrator or trustee;

    (*e*) an order directing any act to be done in the administration of the estate of a deceased person or in the execution of a trust which the Court could order to be done if the estate or trust were being administered or executed, as the case may be, under the direction of the Court.

**Parties**

(3).—(1) All the executors or administrators of the estate or trustees of the trust, as the case may be, to which an administration action or such an action as is referred to in rule 2 relates must be parties to the action, and where the action is brought by executors, administrators or trustees, any of them who does not consent to being joined as a plaintiff must be made a defendant.

(2) Notwithstanding anything in Order 15, rule 4(2), and without prejudice to the powers of the Court under that Order, all the persons having a beneficial interest in or claim against the estate or having a beneficial interest under the trust, as the case may be, to which such an action as is mentioned in paragraph (1) relates need not be parties to the action; but the plaintiff may make such of those persons, whether all or any one or more of them, parties as, having regard to the nature of the relief or remedy claimed in the action, he thinks fit.

R. E. Megarry (1966) 82 L.Q.R. 306

"The facts in *Re Allen-Meyrick's Will Trusts* ([1966] 1 W.L.R. 499; [1966] 1 All E.R. 740), were simple and elegant. A testratrix gave her residue to trustees in trust to apply the income thereof 'in their absolute discretion for the maintenance of my . . . husband,' and subject to the exercise of this discretion, she gave the residue in trust for her two godchildren equally. The trustees had made certain payments for the benefit of the husband, who was bankrupt, but had been unable to agree whether any further income should be so applied. In these circumstances the trustees sought to surrender their discretion to the court, and also sought to have it determined whether their discretion still existed in relation to past accumulations of income.

"It is well settled that trustees confronted by a particular problem may surrender their discretion to the court, and so be relieved both of the agony of decision and the responsibility for the result. But it is another matter where it is sought to surrender discretion which is not merely present and confined but prospective and indefinite. The Court of Chancery had a long history of administrative jurisdiction; but it exercised this jurisdiction not on its own investigations but on facts duly put before it in evidence by those concerned. It is not surprising, therefore, that Buckley, J. refused to accept the proffered general surrender of discretion. Whenever a specific problem arose upon specific facts, the aid of the court could be sought; but that was all. As regards past accumulations of income, the position was simple. The whole of the property, capital and income, belonged to the two godchildren except in so far as the trustees had effectually exercised their discretionary power to apply income to the husband. Trustees must, of course, be unanimous in exercising any powers vested in them, and so if within a reasonable time of receiving any income they had failed to exercise their discretion in favour of the husband, it ceased to be exercisable, and the godchildren became entitled to it. The principles are old, the facts new, and the result satisfactory."

It might be added that in cases where it is likely that there will be further disagreements necessitating expensive applications to the court it is best for the trustees to retire to allow the appointment of more compatible trustees.

### Section 8. Judicial Control of Trustees

Wherever trustees have a discretion to exercise, the question arises as to the extent to which the court can control the exercise of the discretion at the behest of a complaining beneficiary. The discretion may be a dispositive discretion (under a discretionary trust or a power of appointment or of maintenance or of advancement) or an administrative discretion (under a power of investment, for example).

*Dispositive discretions*

Under a discretionary trust the trustees, of course, have a duty to exercise their discretion by distributing income (or, ultimately, capital) in some sort of amounts to some of the beneficiaries (unless, under a power to accumulate, they have decided to accumulate income). If the trustees neglect or refuse to discharge their duty, then the court will let them remedy this[21] or will have the settlor's intentions carried out "by appointing new trustees or by authorising or directing representative persons of the classes of beneficiaries to prepare a scheme for distribution, or even, should the proper basis for distribution appear, by itself directing the trustees so to distribute."[22]

---

[21] *Re Locker's S.T.* [1978] 1 All E.R. 216, *supra*, p. 129.
[22] *McPhail* v. *Doulton* [1971] A.C. 424, 451, A. J. Hawkins (1967) 31 Conv.(N.S.) 117.

In the case of dispositive powers of appointment, advancement or maintenance, the trustees have a duty to consider from time to time whether or not to exercise the power but they need not exercise the power.[23] Thus, if a power to distribute income to X instead of to trust beneficiaries is not exercised within a reasonable period (in default of an expressly specified period) the power lapses in respect of that income so that the income devolves on the trust beneficiaries entitled in default of a valid exercise of the power.[24]

If a trustee's attitude is that he is not going to bother about using any powers to benefit B as B does not deserve any consideration, (*e.g.* because B married without his consent) the court will intervene to remove the trustee or direct a payment that no trustee could refuse to make unless being spiteful or malicious: *Klug* v. *Klug*.[25] In that case legacy duty had to be paid by a beneficiary in four equal instalments but the beneficiary's income was insufficient to pay these instalments. Neville J. said,[26] "When the summons was previously before me, I decided that the trustees could in the exercise of their discretion under the powers of advancement, if they thought fit, advance out of capital a sum sufficient to pay this legacy duty. The public trustee thinks that their discretion should be so exercised, but his co-trustee, the mother, declines to join him in so doing, not because she has considered whether or not it would be for her daughter's welfare, that the advance should be made, but because her daughter has married without her consent, and her letters show, in my opinion, that she has not exercised her discretion at all. . . . In such circumstances, it is the duty of the court to interfere and to direct a sum to be raised out of capital sufficient to pay off . . . the legacy duty."

Once powers are consciously[27] exercised, then the court will not intervene[28] unless it can be shown that the particular purported exercise of the powers is unauthorised by the powers or that the trustees acted in bad faith, oppressively, corruptly or with improper motive or for reasons which can be said to be irrelevant to any sensible

---

[23] *Re Hay's S.T.* [1981] 3 All E.R. 786, 792–793, *supra*, p. 163.
[24] *Re Allen-Meyrick's W.T.* [1966] 1 W.L.R. 499.
[25] [1918] 2 Ch. 67. See *Re Lofthouse* (1885) 29 Ch.D. 921 (where trustees had refused to pay maintenance under a discretionary power and Bacon V.-C. ordered £400 p.a. to be paid; on appeal his order was discharged without more ado since the trustees were agreeable to pay £250 p.a.). There is an out-dated interventionist attitude in some 19th century cases, especially if the beneficiary was a ward of court: *Re Hodges* (1878) 7 Ch.D. 754, *Re Roper's Trusts* (1879) 11 Ch.D. 271.
[26] *Ibid.* at 71. In *Mettoy Pension Trustees Ltd.* v. *Evans* [1991] 2 All E.R. 513 the Court decided to exercise an insolvent corporate trustee's fiduciary power.
[27] *Wilson* v. *Turner* (1883) 22 Ch.D. 521 (no conscious exercise of discretion so recipient liable to repay); *Turner* v. *Turner* [1983] 2 All E.R. 745 (deed of appointment void since trustees signed it at settlor's behest without understanding they had a discretion to exercise).
[28] *Re Beloved Wilkes' Charity* (1851) 3 Mac. & G. 440; *Re Charteris* [1917] 2 Ch. 379; *Re Steed's W.T.* [1960] Ch. 407; *Re Hastings-Bass* [1974] 2 All E.R. 193 which indicates in its interpretation of *Re Abraham's W.T.* [1969] 1 Ch. 463 that in the special case where some rule of law (*e.g.*, rule against remoteness) has altered the consequences of the exercise of a power of the trustees so drastically that the trustees cannot reasonably be supposed to have addressed their minds to the questions relevant to the true effect of the transaction then the exercise of the power will be void.

expectation of the settlor[29] or if it can be shown that they considered the wrong question or that, although they purported to consider the right question they did not really consider the right question.[30] The court's intervention will be negative in restraining the exercise of a power or declaring a purported exercise void: it may have some indirect positive effect if it indicates that a trustee's refusal to join in the exercise of a power in a particular way could lead to removal of the trustee if it appeared that no trustee could so refuse except on some spiteful or other improper ground.

One must also consider the doctrine of a fraud on a power[31] if the donee of a special power of appointment (*e.g.* A, where there is a trust for A for life then to such of his children as he shall appoint and in default of appointment for his children equally) exercises it other than bona fide for the purpose for which it was given him, *e.g.* if he exercises it for a corrupt or foreign purpose or pursuant to a bargain to benefit non-objects of the power. The doctrine in modern times has become particularly relevant where for fiscal reasons the life tenant donee of the power has wished to appoint to certain adult (or infant) beneficiaries in order that the trust property can then be divided up between them. The strict view is laid down in *Re Brook's Settlement*[32]: "an appointment made partly for the purpose of enabling part of the capital of the appointed fund, however small, to be put in the pocket of the appointor is a fraud on the power." However, certain judges[33] have taken a more liberal line in answering the question of fact "was the appointment made for the ulterior purpose, or partly for the ulterior purpose, of enabling a division of the trust fund?" If a fraud on the power is involved then the appointment is void but the appointor can still make a fresh appointment.[34] Purchasers from appointees to whom "fraudulent" appointments have been made have a limited amount of protection under section 157 of the Law of Property Act 1925.

The doctrine of fraud on a power does not apply to releases of powers as they simply benefit those entitled in default of appointment, who have all along had the property vested in them subject only to divestment upon an exercise of the power. Thus in *Re Somes*[35] where a

---

[29] *Re Lofthouse* (1885) 29 Ch.D. 921, 930; *Re Manisty's Settlement* [1973] 2 All E.R. 1203, 1210. This is very difficult to prove especially if the trustees, as they are entitled to do, refuse to give any reasons for their acts: see *Re Londonderry's Settlement, supra*, p. 684 and comment of R.E.M. thereon (1965) 81 L.Q.R. 196. It would seem that trustees do not need to observe the rules of natural justice by allowing a beneficiary entitled in default of appointment to make representations to them before exercising their power of appointment: *Karger* v. *Paul* [1984] V.L.R. 161, 186.

[30] *Dundee General Hospitals* v. *Walker* [1952] 1 All E.R. 896, 905, a Scots case in the House of Lords. Further see N. M. B. Parry [1989] Conv. 244.

[31] Snell, pp. 549–553, Hardingham & Baxt, *Discretionary Trusts* (2nd ed), pp. 102–110, Maclean; *Trusts and Powers*, pp. 85–126.

[32] [1968] 1 W.L.R. 1661, *infra*, p. 720.

[33] *e.g.* Megarry J. in *Re Wallace's Settlements* [1968] 1 W.L.R. 711. See also S. M. Cretney (1969) 32 M.L.R. 317, J. G. Monroe [1968] B.T.R. 424.

[34] *Topham* v. *Duke of Portland* (1869) 5 Ch.App. 40; *Re Chadwick's Trusts* [1939] 1 All E.R. 850.

[35] [1896] 1 Ch. 250.

father had a power of appointment in favour of a daughter or her issue, the daughter also being entitled in default of appointment, the father was able to release his power so that his daughter could mortgage the property to secure a sum of £10,000 to be paid to the father for his own purposes.[36]

It should be noted that whilst powers[37] given to individuals in their private capacity can be released (or exercised spitefully), powers given to trustees as fiduciaries cannot be released[38] (except under an express authority in the trust instrument or under the Variation of Trusts Act 1958) though the beneficiaries can validly release the trustees from their duties towards them, *e.g.* so as even to cease to be objects of a discretionary trust: *Re Gulbenkian's Trusts (No. 2).*[39]

## Administrative discretions

Questions concerning the exercise of trustees' administrative discretions can often arise in the investment sphere. Here it has been seen[40] that trustees are *inter alia* under a duty to act fairly as between beneficiaries interested in income and beneficiaries interested in capital and to exhibit the standard of care that a prudent man of business would take if investing for persons for whom he feels morally obliged to provide.

In *Tempest* v. *Lord Camoys, infra*, p. 718, the trustees on selling real estate had to purchase real estate "in their absolute discretion." One trustee wanted to purchase particular real estate for £60,000 with £30,000 borrowed on mortgage pursuant to the trustees' power to raise money by mortgage "at their absolute discretion." The other trustee refused to concur in the purchase, considering it not to be a prudent exercise of the power. The Court of Appeal held that it could not interfere with the dissenting trustee's discretion. Jessel M.R. pointed out that all the court will do is prevent the trustees from exercising their power "improperly." Cotton L.J. said,[41] "No doubt it [the court] will prevent trustees from exercising their discretion in any way which is wrong or unreasonable."

As Slade L.J. said,[42] "In other words the court was of opinion that even a power expressed in terms that it should be exercisable at the trustees' absolute discretion was subject to the implicit restriction that it should be exercised properly within the limits of the general law."

---

[36] Similarly the doctrine of fraud on a power does not apply to the revocation of a revocable appointment even though the revoking appointor thereby intends to obtain a benefit: *Re Greaves* [1954] Ch. 434.

[37] Also note a life tenant is under no duty to consent to an advancement to a remainderman.

[38] This is basically the position but the borderlines are difficult to draw though an attempt was made in *Re Wills' Trust Deeds* [1964] Ch. 219. See A. J. Hawkins (1968) 84 L.Q.R. 64.

[39] [1970] Ch. 408.

[40] See pp. 611–614, *supra*. To protect himself a trustee may surrender his discretion to the court upon putting all relevant information before it: *Marley* v. *Mutual Security Merchant Bank* [1991] 3 All E.R. 198.

[41] (1882) 21 Ch.D. 571, 580.

[42] *Bishop* v. *Bonham* [1988] 1 W.L.R. 742, 751–752; also see *Elder's Trustee and Executor Co. Ltd.* v. *Higgins* (1965) 113 C.L.R. 426, 448.

Because trustees must act unanimously[43] (unless otherwise provided by the trust instrument) any trustee with some fairly slight basis for doubt about the proposed exercise of a discretion can prevent such an exercise. A beneficiary can obtain an injunction against a proposed exercise of an investment discretion only if such exercise is plainly improper or not in accordance with the trustees' duty of safe investment. If the beneficiary does not find out about an improper or unsafe investment until after the event, then his remedy will be to have the investment sold and to make the trustees liable to account for losses that arise.

Exceptionally, where the trustees are trustees for sale of land then the court has a vast positive discretion under section 30 of the Law of Property Act though it will not enforce the letter of a trust for sale if so to do would defeat the spirit or purpose of the trust.[44] The section provides: "If the trustees for sale refuse to sell or to exercise any of the powers conferred by either of the last two sections,[45] or any requisite[46] consent cannot be obtained, any person interested may apply to the court for a vesting or other order for giving effect to the proposed transaction or for an order directing the trustees for sale to give effect thereto, and the court may make such order as it thinks fit."

### Exemption clauses

It should first be noted that the jurisdiction of the court as to matters of law cannot be ousted by provisions in the trust instrument giving the trustees power to determine all questions arising in the execution of the trusts under the instrument.[47]

Exemption clauses, whether excluding trustees' liabilities for breach of trust or negating positive duties so that no liabilities arise, are not allowed by the courts to protect a trustee who commits what would otherwise be a breach of trust in bad faith or intentionally or with reckless indifference to the beneficiaries' interests.[48] Such clauses are also construed strictly against the trustee.[49]

---

[43] *Luke* v. *South Kensington Hotel Ltd.* (1879) 11 Ch.D. 121, *supra*, p. 583.

[44] *Jones* v. *Challenger* [1961] 1 Q.B. 176. This is generally treated as a land law topic so see Megarry & Wade (5th ed.), pp. 441–442, Gray's *Elements of Land Law*, pp. 820–827. In bankruptcy cases see the Insolvency Act 1986, ss.336, 337.

[45] Section 28 confers very wide powers equivalent to those of a tenant for life under the Settled Land Act 1925 whilst s.29 enables the trustees to delegate their powers of management and leasing and accepting surrenders of leases.

[46] Like that of an equitable co-tenant: *Bull* v. *Bull* [1955] 1 Q.B. 234.

[47] *Re Wynn* [1952] Ch. 271; *Re Coxen* [1948] Ch. 747 especially 761, 762; *Re Jones* [1953] Ch. 125; *Re Wright's W.T.* [1981] L.S.Gaz. 841; *cf. Dundee General Hospitals Board* v. *Walker* [1952] 1 All E.R. 896.

[48] *Wilkins* v. *Hogg* (1861) L.J.Ch. 41; *Knox* v. *Mackinnon* (1888) 13 App.Cas. 753; *Rae* v. *Meek* (1889) 14 App.Cas. 558; *Boe* v. *Alexander* (1988) 41 D.L.R.(4th) 518; P. Matthews [1989] Conv. 42. Some cases like *Wyman* v. *Patterson* [1900] A.C. 271, 286 and *Re Poche* 6 D.L.R.(4th) 40, 55 suggest an exemption clause cannot excuse gross negligence falling short of reckless indifference but it is difficult to justify this. Indeed, the *Re Vickery* [1931] 1 Ch. 572, 583 view that "wilful default" in the statutory exemption clause in Trustee Act 1925, s.30(1) extends only to deliberate or reckless conduct means that s.30(1) can excuse gross negligence. Only where a trustee has *mens rea* (a guilty mind) should he be prevented from relying on an exemption clause.

[49] *Bartlett* v. *Barclays Bank Trust Co. Ltd.* [1980] 1 All E.R. 139, 154; *Bishop* v. *Bonham* [1988] 1 W.L.R. 742; *Re Brier* (1884) 26 Ch.D. 238.

As revealed in discussing the beneficiary principle[50] and beneficiaries' rights to accounts and information,[51] fundamental to the trust institution are the rights of beneficiaries and the corresponding duties of trustees. Thus, if "trustees" owe no duties to the "beneficiaries" due to an enormously wide exemption clause then the transferor's transfer of property to them will be treated as a beneficial gift to them or as creating an agency relationship between him and them. However, it seems perfectly possible for a settlor to make what would otherwise be burdensome duties into light duties,[52] *e.g.* to convert a duty to diversify investments into a duty to invest only in one or two specific companies or to convert a duty to take as much care as, objectively, a prudent man of business would take investing for persons for whom he feels morally obliged to provide into a duty to take as much care as the trustee would subjectively take if investing on his own behalf a windfall of an amount equal in value to the trust fund. Similarly, it seems that a settlor, by an appropriately worded clause in the trust instrument, can convert a trustee's inability to profit from his position into an ability to profit from his position if so authorised by his co-trustees not being fewer than two in number, though such safeguarding qualification is not essential.[53]

As between the settlor and the original trustees it may well be that the Unfair Contract Terms Act 1977 applies so that all exemption clauses are subject to the test of reasonableness.[54] However, the rights of trustees subsequently appointed by the original trustees are not regarded as contractual[55] so that there is no scope for the 1977 Act.

Finally, section 192 of the Companies Act 1985 specifically intervenes where there is a trust deed for securing an issue of debentures. In such a deed a borrower, which is a company, charges some of its property by way of fixed or floating charges in favour of the trustees as security for money lent. The trustees hold these secured rights on trust for the debenture holders who hold debenture stock in proportion to the amounts provided by them by way of loan. This device is very useful for raising a large sum of money from a large number of people. The deed states when the security will become enforceable and confers much discretion on the trustees subject to varying degrees of control by the debenture holders. Any provision in the deed is void under section 192 "in so far as it would have the effect of exempting a trustee of the deed from, or indemnifying him against, liability for breach of trust where he fails to show the degree of care and diligence required

---

[50] *Supra*, p. 185.
[51] *Supra*, p. 683.
[52] *Hayim* v. *Citibank* [1987] A.C. 730.
[53] *Re Beatty's W.T.* [1990] 3 All E.R. 844.
[54] W. Goodhart [1980] Conv. 333; *cf.* P. Kenny (1982) 126 S.J. 631, 632.
[55] *Re Duke of Norfolk's S.T.* [1982] Ch. 61, 77, *supra*, p. 608. Any equity that the settlor may have to rectify an exemption clause or a remuneration clause for undue influence will only bind subsequent trustees if they are the *alter ego* of the original trustee or if they have notice which could arise from the outrageous terms of such a clause.

of him as trustee, having regard to the provisions of the trust deed conferring on him any powers, authorities or discretions." Section 192(2) makes it clear that subsection (1) does not invalidate any release given to a trustee for things done or undone under a power for a three-quarters majority of debenture holders to give such a release. For authorised unit trusts section 84 of the Financial Services Act 1986 makes any provision void so far as it would have the effect of exempting the manager or trustee from liability for failing to exercise due care and diligence.

### TEMPEST v. LORD CAMOYS[56]

Court of Appeal (1882) 21 Ch.D. 571; 51 L.J.Ch. 785; 48 L.T. 13; (Jessel M.R., Brett and Cotton L.JJ.)

The headnote summarises the facts as follows: "A testator gave his trustees a power to be exercised at their absolute discretion of selling real estates, with a declaration that the proceeds should be applied, at the like discretion, in the purchase of other real estates. He also gave them power at their absolute discretion to raise money by mortgage for the purchase of real estates. A suit having been instituted for the execution of the trusts of the will, and a sum of money, the proceeds of the sale of real estate, having been paid into court, one of the trustees proposed to purchase a large estate and to apply the fund in court in part-payment of the purchase-money, and to raise the remainder of the purchase-money by mortgage of the purchased estate. The other trustee refused to concur in the purchase."

Some of the beneficiaries being in favour of the proposal, a petition was presented for the purpose of having the purchase carried out. It was contended that it was desirable to purchase at a moderate price—£60,000, there being some £30,000 in court—an estate which had previously been in the family for a long while. The dissentient trustee, Mr. Fleming, objected that the transaction would not be a prudent exercise of the power. Chitty J. held, in accordance with *Gisborne* v. *Gisborne*,[57] that the court had no power to interfere with Mr. Fleming's bona fide exercise of his discretion. The petitioners appealed.

JESSEL M.R.: "It is very important that the law of the court on this subject should be understood. It is settled law that when a testator has given a pure discretion to trustees as to the exercise of a power, the court does not enforce the exercise of a power against the wish of the trustees, but it does prevent them from exercising it improperly. The court says that the power, if exercised at all, is to be properly exercised. This may be illustrated by the case of persons having a power of appointing new trustees. Even after a decree in a suit for administering the trusts has been made they may still exercise the power, but the court will see that they do not appoint improper persons.

"But in all cases where there is a trust or duty coupled with the power the court will then compel the trustees to carry it out in a proper manner and within a reasonable time. In the present case there was a power which amounts to a trust to invest the fund in question in the purchase of land. The trustees

---

[56] See also *Gisborne* v. *Gisborne* (1877) 2 App.Cas. 300; *Camden* v. *Murray* (1880) 16 Ch.D. 161, 170; *Re Blake* (1885) 29 Ch.D. 913, 917; *Re Courtier* (1886) 34 Ch.D. 136; *Re Horsnaill* [1909] 1 Ch. 631; *Re Kipping* [1914] 1 Ch. 62; *Re Charteris* [1917] 2 Ch. 379, 391.
[57] (1877) 2 App.Cas. 300.

would not be allowed by the court to disregard that trust, and if Mr. Fleming had refused to invest the money in land at all the court would have found no difficulty in interfering. But that is a very different thing from saying that the court ought to take from the trustees their uncontrolled discretion as to the particular time for the investment and the particular property which should be purchased. In this particular case it appears to me that the testator in his will has carefully distinguished between what is to be at the discretion of his trustees and what is obligatory on them.

"There is another difficulty in this case. The estate proposed to be purchased will cost £60,000, and only £30,000 is available for the purchase, and the trustees will have to borrow the remaining £30,000. There is power to raise money by mortgage at the absolute discretion of the trustees, and assuming that such a transaction as this is within the power, and that the trustees can mortgage the estate before they have actually bought it, there is no trust to mortgage, it is purely discretionary. The court cannot force Mr. Fleming to take the view that it is proper to mortgage the estate in this way; he may well have a different opinion from the other trustee. Here again the court cannot interfere with his discretion. The appeal must therefore be dismissed." *Appeal dismissed.*

## RE BELOVED WILKES'S CHARITY

Lord Chancellor (1851) 3 Mac. & G. 440

Charitable trustees had to select a boy to be educated at Oxford for the Anglican ministry, preference to be given to boys from four named parishes if in the trustees' judgment a fit and proper candidate therefrom could be found. Without giving any reasons, but stating that they had acted impartially, the trustees selected Charles Joyce who did not come from the named parishes but who had a brother who was a minister who had put forward Charles's merits to the trustees. The court was asked to set aside the selection, and to select William Gale, whose father was a respectable farmer residing in one of the specified parishes.

*Held.* In the absence of evidence that the trustees had exercised their discretion unfairly or dishonestly, the court would not interfere.

LORD TRURO L.C.: "The question, therefore, is, whether it was the duty of the trustees to enter into particulars, or whether the law is not, that trustees who are appointed to execute a trust according to discretion, that discretion to be influenced by a variety of circumstances (as, in this instance, by those particular circumstances which should be connected with the fitness of a lad to be brought up as a minister of the Church of England), are not bound to go into a detail of the grounds upon which they come to their conclusion, their duty being satisfied by shewing that they have considered the circumstances of the case, and have come to their conclusion accordingly. Without occupying time by going into a lengthened examination of the decisions, the result of them appears to me so clear and reasonable, that it will be sufficient to state my conclusion in point of law to be, that in such cases as I have mentioned it is to the discretion of the trustees that the execution of the trust is confided, that discretion being exercised with an entire absence of indirect motive, with honesty of intention, and with a fair consideration of the subject. The duty of supervision on the part of this Court will thus be confined to the question of the honesty, integrity, and fairness with which the deliberation has been conducted, and will not be extended to the accuracy of the conclusion arrived at, except in particular cases. If, however, as stated by Lord Ellenborough in *The King* v. *The Archbishop of Canterbury* ((1812) 15 East 117), trustees think fit to state a reason, and the reason is one which does not justify their conclusion, then the Court may say that they have acted by mistake and in error, and that it will correct their decision; but if, without entering into details, they simply state, as in many cases it would be most prudent and judicious for them to do, that they have met and considered and come to a conclusion, the court has then no means of saying that they have failed in their duty, or to consider the accuracy of their conclusion.[58] It seems, therefore, to me, that having in the present case to look to the motives of the trustees as developed in the affidavits, no ground exists for imputing bad motives. The Petitioners, indeed, candidly state, on the face of their petition, that they do not impute such motives, they merely charge the trustees with a miscarriage as regards the duty which they had to perform. I cannot, therefore, deal with the case as if the petition had contained a statement of a different kind, and if I could, still I should say, having read the affidavits, that I see nothing whatever which can lay the foundation for any judicial conclusion that the trustees intentionally and from bad motives failed in their duty, if they failed at all."

## RE BROOK'S SETTLEMENT

Chancery Division [1968] 1 W.L.R. 1661; [1968] 3 All E.R. 416

STAMP J. read the following judgment: "By the originating summons which was issued under the Variation of Trusts Act, 1958, on February 28, 1968, the plaintiff asks that the court may approve on behalf of the infant defendant, Ann Brook, and on behalf of all persons who may become interested under the discretionary trust to arise in the event of a forfeiture of the plaintiff's life interest, a variation of the trust of the settlement affecting the fund constituting the plaintiff's share. By the effect of the proposed variation a part of the fund would be held on trust for the plaintiff absolutely, the *quid pro quo* being in effect the release of the remainder of the fund from the protected life interest of the plaintiff and the consequent acceleration of the interests of those entitled in reversion expectant on the determination of that protected life interest.

"The proposed variation, however, and this is the point at which the difficulty arises, proceeds on the footing that the two existing children are alone entitled to a share in the capital of the fund and the part of the fund which is to be freed from the protected life interest of the plaintiff is, under the proposed variation, to be held on trust, in effect, for them to the exclusion of after-born children. The court is not asked to approve the variation on behalf of after-born children. Plainly this would not do because even if the court could properly have approved the variation on the ground that it was for the benefit of Miss Ann Brook, the interest of after-born children would not be bound and the trustees could not have given effect to the variation. Nor could this court have bound the interest of after-born children because as the proposed variation stood, and still stands, they are to take nothing. When the plaintiff's counsel considered the matter a few days before the hearing he, of course, appreciated the difficulty; and in reliance, perhaps, on a recent

---

[58] See *Re Londonderry's Settlement* [1965] Ch. 918, *supra*, p. 684.

decision of this court in *Re Wallace's Settlements*[59] an appointment was executed by the plaintiff of the whole of the plaintiff's share in favour of his two existing children. The question then arises was this appointment an effective appointment or was it a fraud on the power of appointment? This is a question which must be decided because, until it is decided, the trustees of the settlement will not know to whom the fund belongs; and counsel for the trustees in accordance with his duty on behalf of the trustees, was bound to argue, as he did, that the appointment was a fraud on the power.

"I observe first that the question whether an appointment is made for the ulterior purpose, or partly for the ulterior purpose, of enabling a division of a trust fund or without any such ulterior purpose is one of fact; secondly, that the protestation that the appointor had no such ulterior purpose but that the appointment was a separate and independent transaction made irrespective of the scheme of division, is more easily acceptable if the apparent ulterior purpose—here a division of the trust fund under which the appointor takes part—could from the appointor's point of view have been better or equally well achieved had there been no appointment. In the present case counsel for the infant defendant, found no difficulty in submitting that the division proposed is one which is for her benefit; but had there been no appointment it is at least less clear, because after-born children will not have the same advantage of acceleration, that the proposed division, under which the plaintiff is to have a half share of the fund, could have been supported as beneficial to any after-born child of the plaintiff. It appears, moreover, from what counsel told me, that in the course of the negotiations and discussions leading up to the formulation of the proposed variation it became apparent, as in my experience is very often the case, that the plaintiff wished to obtain as much as he could fairly do on the division and the fact that he might be able to receive less if there was no appointment was very present in the minds of his advisers.

"It was, however, submitted in reliance on *Re Wallace's Settlements*, that where you find that under the scheme for the division of the fund contemplated by the appointing tenant for life and the appointee, the tenant for life is to take no more than the equivalent of the market value of his life interest, there is no such benefit to the tenant for life as to render the appointment *ipso facto* a fraud on the power. It was for the purpose of considering the implications of this submission that I reserved my judgment.

"The facts in *Re Wallace's Settlements* were not quite the same as the facts of this case, but there is a clear finding in *Re Wallace's Settlements* that the appointments there in question were not fraudulent. The considerations which led Megarry J. to conclude that the extent to which the appointments there had become embrangled with the arrangements for the variation of the trusts had not tainted the appointments, were I think these: first, that as regards such advantages as there might be in the certainty and flexibility of capital as opposed to the limitations of an inalienable and defeasible life interest, the judge was satisfied that in relation to other material circumstances of life tenants there was no real advantage to either of them: secondly, that, on the facts of the cases there before him, the prospects of the life interests determining in the lifetime of either life tenant seemed to him to be negligible; and, thirdly, the excess of the actuarial value of the protected life interests, which was what each life tenant was to receive under the division, over the

[59] [1968] 1 W.L.R. 711.

market value of the life interests, had those life interests not been protected, was negligible; so that the life tenants under the two settlements were receiving no more than the value to them of their life interests. In effect, therefore, Megarry J. took the view that the receipt by the life tenant of part of the capital of the appointed fund, if of no more value to him than the market value of his protected life interest if sold as an unprotected life interest, was not a benefit to the tenant for life, or at least not such a benefit as was referred to by Lord St. Leonards in *Duke of Portland* v. *Lady Topham*.[60] In so holding, the judge followed decisions of the Court of Session to which he referred and in which the Court of Session placed reliance on a late decision of Lord Romilly M.R., in *Re Huish's Charity*.[61]

"Consistently with *Portland* v. *Topham*[62] and *Vatcher* v. *Paull*,[63] *Re Wallace's Settlements* and the cases in the Court of Session which it followed, can in my judgment go no further than this: that if you find an appointment such as is here in question and, on the contemplated division of the fund, the appointor takes no more of the appointed fund than the value of his life interest, the appointment is not invalidated by the mere fact that it is made in contemplation of the division. It does not in my judgment, however follow that an appointment made by one entitled to a life interest not with an entire and single object of benefiting the appointee, but with a view also to having part of the capital of the appointed fund to spend, would be unobjectionable if the capital to be received was less than the market value of the life interest. The question must be one of fact. If my view of the earlier high authorities is correct and it is the purpose and the object of the appointment which is the test of its validity or invalidity, it must, I think, follow that, an appointment made partly for the purpose of enabling part of the capital of the appointed fund, however small, to be put in the pocket of the appointor is a fraud on the power: for if that be part of the motive for the appointment there is not the absence of an ulterior object necessary to support it. Nor do I find it easy to accept that, in an age when income tax and surtax rests so heavily on the recipients of income, the advantage of having the capital equivalent of the value of a life interest is not a benefit, or may not prompt an appointment which would not otherwise be made thereby excluding other objects of the power and those entitled in default of appointment. If, however, one finds that just before the issue of the originating summons or, as in this case, just before its hearing, that an appointment has been made and that the court is being invited to approve on behalf of some person a variation of the trusts of a settlement under which part of the appointed fund is to be paid or transferred to the appointor, then in the absence of evidence that the appointment was a separate transaction or would have been made irrespective of the division, it may be—for I find nothing in *Re Wallace's Settlements* to suggest that this is not so—that the proper prima facie inference is that the appointment was not made 'with the entire and single view' that the appointee should have the property. Suppose a fund be settled on A for life and after his death on trust for such of his three children in such shares as he shall appoint and in default of appointment on trust for those same named children in equal shares. Then suppose that the tenant for life partly in order to avoid estate duty, partly in

60 (1864) 11 H.L.Cas. 32, 55.
61 (1870) L.R. 10 Eq. 5.
62 (1864) 11 H.L.Cas. 32, 55.
63 [1915] A.C. 372.

order to put a capital sum into his own pocket and partly in order to benefit one of the three children, makes an appointment in favour of that child with a view to a division of the fund between himself and that child. I cannot doubt that in that case the appointment constitutes a fraudulent appointment as against the other two children who might have been willing to give him only a lesser price. Moreover in my view it would be none the less a fraudulent appointment if the amount received by the tenant for life was less than the amount which he could have obtained by selling his life interest on the market. I have come to the conclusion, however, in accordance with the recent authorities, that the mere fact that the tenant for life makes the appointment as part of a scheme for the division of the appointed fund does not *ipso facto* show that the appointment was made for an ulterior purpose not permitted by the instrument creating the power; at least in a case where the part of the appointed fund to be taken by the appointor is not more valuable than the life interest which the appointor gives up. If that were the position here I would, but subject to the caution at the end of this judgment, hold that the appointment which I have to consider was not a fraud on the power and make the order asked for.

"The facts of this case are, however, in my judgment clearly distinguishable from the facts in *Re Wallace's Settlements* and the cases on which Megarry J. rested his judgment in that case: for here, first, the known effect of the appointment was to produce, by defeating the interests of future children, a state of affairs under which the court might be expected to approve a division more favourable to the tenant for life than would have been the case if the division had had to be shown to be for the benefit of the after-born children: and secondly, because of the fact that the tenant for life here was anxious to obtain all he could on the division. As counsel for the trustees pointed out, prima facie an appointment should be treated as made for the object which it achieved and I am constrained to hold that one of the objects of this appointment was to obtain a benefit for the appointor which he might not otherwise have had, and was a fraud on the power."

## BOE v. ALEXANDER

Court of Appeal British Columbia (1988) 41 D.L.R. (4th) 518 (Taggart, Macdonald and Wallace JJ.A.)

A non-contributory pension fund agreement included as para. 10:

> 10. Subject to the provisions of this agreement the Trustees shall have full authority to determine all questions of coverage, elibility and methods of providing or arranging for provision of benefits and all other related matters. The Trustees shall have the power to construe the provisions of this agreement and the terms used herein. Any such determination and any such construction adopted by the Trustees in good faith shall be binding upon all parties hereto and the beneficiaries hereof.

Macdonald J.A. (delivering the court's judgment): "Embarking on the issue of judicial review, the judge emphasized that there was no evidence of dishonest motivation or intention on the part of any trustee with respect to any of the disputed contributions. He cited and quoted from a number of cases: *Gisborne et al.* v. *Gisborne et al.* (1877), 2 App. Cas. 300; *Re Sayers et al. and*

*Philip* (1973), 38 D.L.R. (3d) 602; *Re Blow* (1977), 82 D.L.R. (3d) 721; *Re Wynn's Will Trusts* [1952] 1 All E.R. 341; *Re Jeffery*, [1948] 4 D.L.R. 704; *Re Bronson* (1958), 14 D.L.R. (2d) 51; *Cowan et al.* v. *Scargill et al.*, [1984] 2 All E.R. 750; and *Re Floyd* (1961), 26 D.L.R. (2d) 66.

"The judge then decided the issue saying [at pp. 271–2]:

> 'From a consideration of these cases, it is in my view clear that the jurisdiction of the Court to review the exercise of a trustee's discretion cannot be displaced by even the broadest language creating the discretion. The law imposes overriding duties on trustees, breach of which will call for the Court's intervention. Without attempting an exhaustive list of the circumstances which will justify judicial intervention, I will summarize my conclusions from the authorities cited above, insofar as they are relevant to the facts before me.
>
> A privative clause protecting the exercise of a trustee's discretion will not be effective to prevent judicial review whenever the trustees:
>
> 1. have failed to exercise the discretion at all (*Re Floyd, Re Blow,* and *Re Sayers and Philip*);
> 2. have acted dishonestly (*Gisborne, Re Sayers and Philip, Cowan* v. *Scargill, Re Floyd*);
> 3. have failed to exercise the level of prudence to be expected from a reasonable businessman (*Re Sayers and Philip, Cowan* v. *Scargill*); and
> 4. have failed to hold the balance evenly between beneficiaries, or have acted in a manner prejudicial to the interests of a beneficiary (*Re Jeffery, Re Sayers and Philip*).
>
> These requirements are all examples of the general requirement that trustees act reasonably. I find support for that requirement in the language of Lord Penzance and Lord O'Hagan quoted above from *Gisborne*.
>
> I am therefore of the view that a breach by the trustees of the duties described above will permit judicial review, and that the language of para. 10 will not prevent that review, even where there has been no bad faith, in the sense of dishonesty. In my view, the words "good faith" in para. 10 neither add to, nor subtract from, the powers which the trustees may lawfully exercise; nor do they limit or impair the power of the Court to intervene where the trustees have acted in breach of their duty.'

"In my opinion the judge drew the correct principles from the cases. I intend to refer particularly only to the judgment of Wells J. in *Re Jeffery*. At p. 710, after observing that the trustees were given very wide discretionary powers by the settlor, he said:

> 'If this provision were given its full extent it would, I think, be clear that the trustees were a law unto themselves and that the Court had no jurisdiction to interpret the documents. The Court, however, has never recognized such an exclusion of its authority by any of His Majesty's subjects, and while wide discretion may be given to trustees they cannot be placed outside their obligations as trustees under the instrument appointing them and under the general law of the land.'

And, on p. 711 he continued:

> 'It is therefore, I think, quite clear that, while the trustees had a very wide discretion, they were not freed of their responsibility of carrying

out the trusts imposed on them in accordance with the terms of the settlement and the ordinary principles of law relating to trusts. Trustees are still responsible to the Court even in the circumstances attempted to be set up by those advising the late Mrs. Jeffery.

It is I think a primary principle, which need not be laboured by me, that one of the trustees' first duties was to hold the balance evenly between the beneficiaries and various groups of beneficiaries and to try to interpret the document and carry out its provisions in the spirit and letter in which it was expressed. They were not, nor are they now, entitled to favour one group of beneficiaries in any way as against another. They were obliged to treat all beneficiaries with fairness and impartiality, always attempting to carry out the expressed intention of the settlor.'

"Further, I am of opinion that the judge was right in finding that there is power of judicial review in this case notwithstanding paragraph 10."

## Section 9. The Control of Pension Funds

### THE BACKGROUND

British pension funds are worth about £275 billion, the top 10 funds alone being responsible for the best part of £60 billion. An individual's pension rights are very significant private assets. The nature and extent of these rights is determined usually by two documents, the Trust Deed and the Rules of the Scheme, by principles of trust law, by contractual principles of employment law, and by statutory intervention, *e.g.* Social Security Acts 1973 and 1990, Social Security Pensions Act 1975.

Pensions are often provided by a final salary scheme (otherwise known as a defined benefit plan) determining a pension by a formula related to an employee's earnings on retirement and the number of years worked, *e.g.* one-sixtieth of final pensionable salary for each year worked, not exceeding 40 years. In advance, the employee and the employer contribute money to trustees of the trust fund so that assets will be available safe from the employer's creditors if the employer has financial problems. Benefits may be provided for the employee's dependants despite the absence of privity of contract between such persons and the employer.

In the 1980s a surplus developed in most of these trust funds, a surplus being the amount by which the actuarially determined value of the assets of a pension scheme exceeds the actuarially determined value of the liabilities to the employees and other beneficiaries of the scheme. The surpluses arose because of greater than anticipated investment returns, many employees leaving before reaching retirement age, overly conservative assumptions made by actuaries in determining the amount of funding required, and employers for tax reasons (or out of ignorance) contributing more than was necessary. The question of ownership of the surplus became a crucial concern on the liquidation of the employer or on the taking over of the employer by a predator.[64]

Such surpluses did not arise in the rarer case of pensions being provided by a money purchase scheme (otherwise known as a defined contribution plan). Here, the level of an employee's contribution is fixed in the scheme and the benefit depends upon the interest and bonuses allocated to the employee each year depending upon how well the fund containing his contribution performs. It will also depend on the level of annuity rates at the time of retirement when an annuity is purchased with the available capital amount. The employee is like a person having an endowment assurance policy in that the amount of contributions is certain but the ultimate benefit is speculative. Indeed, the employer will normally place the contributions with a life assurance company.

Contributions to, and investments of, pension funds attract exceptional tax advantages if the pension scheme is approved by the Superannuation Funds Office of the Inland Revenue. The S.F.O. will not approve schemes if they do not satisfy the requirements of the Occupational Pensions Board set up under the Social Security Act 1973. Indeed, new schemes seeking approval are submitted via the O.P.B. The O.P.B. vets the rules and financial arrangements of schemes contracting out of the State Pension Scheme and supervises such schemes. It also has the function of authorising or ordering the modification of schemes if certain conditions are satisfied, *e.g.* so that the scheme can satisfy new S.F.O. requirements if it is to remain an approved scheme or so that surplus may be paid back to the employer.

### SPECIAL FEATURES OF PENSION TRUSTS

Apart from the special function of the O.P.B., the size of a pension trust fund has long been regarded as a special feature so that it may have something of a public element in it and so that investment powers can justifiably be very wide-ranging indeed, entitling a court under the Variation of Trusts Act 1958 to confer such wide powers if so requested.[65] However, some pension funds are small, being restricted to fewer than 12 members and being established wholly or partly for directors with shareholdings of at least 20 per cent. in their company. The trustees are directors who invest the funds with an eye to assisting the companies and themselves, though conflicts of interest can arise between the trustee-rôle and the director-rôle. As a result, in the case of these small self-administered schemes, known as pensioneer trusts, the S.F.O. will not normally approve such a scheme unless there is an independent external trustee approved by the S.F.O.

---

[64] *e.g. Davis* v. *Richards and Wallington Ltd.* [1990] 1 W.L.R. 1511; *Re Courage Group's Pension Scheme* [1987] 1 W.L.R. 495.
[65] *Mason* v. *Farbrother* [1983] 2 All E.R. 1078, 1087. For problems caused by too narrow powers of investment see the Monaghan Report on the Superannuation Fund Investment Trust (Australian Government Publishing Service, Canberra, 1984).

Indeed, the public interest in safeguarding pension benefits has led to the Social Security Act 1990[66] introducing a regulation-making power to restrict the proportion of an occupational pension scheme's resources which may be invested in "employer-related investments." These include shares or securities issued by the employer or any person connected with the employer; land occupied or used by, or subject to a lease in favour of, the employer or a connected person; and loans to the employer or a connected person. It is likely that a regulation will be made to prohibit schemes from having more than 5 per cent. invested in employer-related investments other than land after a transitional period of a year or so. Even the European Commission is now taking an interest. It is likely to lay down rules for the proper balance of the investment portfolio of a pension fund. As things stand, the O.P.B. requires proper audited accounts and disclosure to the scheme members in the trustees' annual report of particular investments comprising at least 5 per cent. of the scheme's assets. The Disclosure of Information Regulations (S.I. 1986 No. 1046) amount to a recognition that ordinary trust law rules are inadequate for providing sufficient information to the beneficiary-employees. Similarly, approved pension schemes are not subject to the perpetuity rules (S.I. 1990 No. 1143 Perpetuity Regulations).

A key feature of pension fund trusts is that they normally contain broad flexible powers, if the employer consents, to increase or reduce the benefits or the range of beneficiaries or to alter the trust deed to cope with mergers or take-overs involving the employer. On the other hand, the scheme members are not in the position of volunteers under a discretionary trust absolutely at the mercy of the trustees. Their rights derive from a commercial contractual origin: they earn their pension rights as deferred remuneration.[67] They may well have expectations or hopes that if a surplus materialises then it should be used to reduce employees' contributions or provide a contributions "holiday" or to keep in line with inflation if possible the value of retired employees' pensions of half or two-thirds of final salary.

However, the employer may regard the surplus as belonging to it so that it can have a contributions holiday or have the surplus paid over. A company taking over the employer might want to merge the surplus with its own less profitable pension fund and then even sell on the employer with a reduced pension fund of an amount lowly valued on the past service reserve basis.[68] The decision on using surplus will usually be that of the trustees or of a management committee (whose wishes the trustees, like custodian trustees, must follow) but normally

---

[66] Sched. 4, para. 3 inserting s.57A of the Social Security Pensions Act 1975.
[67] See *Kerr* v. *British Leyland (Staff) Trustees Ltd.* and *Mihlenstedt* v. *Barclays Bank International Ltd.* [1989] I.R.L.R. 522 cited in *Davis* v. *Richards & Wallington* [1990] 1 W.L.R. 1511, 1538 cited *infra*, p. 738; *Swan* v. *Charlesworth* [1987] I.C.R. 288; *Mettoy Pension Trustees Ltd.* v. *Evans* [1991] 2 All E.R. 513.
[68] *Cf. Re Courage Group's Pension Scheme* [1987] 1 W.L.R. 495.

such decision can only be taken if the employer consents.[69] This power
to withhold consent may not need to be exercised if the trustees or the
management committee are appointed and dismissed by the employer,
especially if such persons as employees may be dismissed or not
promoted if they do not comply with the employer's wishes. Many
conflicts of interest and duty may arise! To help trustees and committee members to stand firm they may need the protection of seeking the
guidance and instruction of the court.

As fiduciaries they are under a duty to act honestly and in good
faith, to act fairly between the different classes of beneficiaries, to
consider from to time whether or not to exercise a fiduciary power and
to ascertain the relevant facts to enable such duty and any discretion to
be properly exercised, and a duty to act in the interests of the
beneficiaries by exercising the fiduciary power for its proper purposes
and upon relevant (as opposed to irrational or perverse or irrelevant)
considerations.[70] A fiduciary cannot exercise his power so as to benefit
himself unless expressly allowed or unless there is a very necessary
implication from the trust deed.

A person who is not a trustee but who has a power, *e.g.* to withhold
consent, will be treated prima facie as having a merely personal, as
opposed to a fiduciary, power so that he can act spitefully and for his
personal benefit. However, it is necessarily implicit in the contract of
employment that the employer will duly discharge its pensions scheme
rights and powers in good faith: *Imperial Group Pension Trust Ltd.* v.
*Imperial Tobacco Ltd.*,[71] *infra.* It can have regard to its own financial
interests in any surplus but only to the extent that in so doing it does
not breach the obligation of good faith to its employees: this is the
obligation not to conduct itself in a manner likely seriously to damage
the relationship of confidence between employer and employee.

SURPLUSES

*Introduction*
In balance of costs schemes where the employers make up the
necessary money so far as the employees' fixed proportions of their
salaries are insufficient, the problem was one of deficits until the 1980s
produced major surpluses for the reasons already mentioned. Indeed,
the Revenue became so concerned that pension funds were deliberately being used as a tax shelter that the Finance Act 1986[72] required

---

[69] Assuming that he is not a trustee.
[70] *Re Hay's S.T.* [1981] 3 All E.R. 786, 792–793; *Dundee General Hospital* v. *Walker* [1952] 1 All
E.R. 896, 905; *Mills* v. *Mills* (1938) 60 C.L.R. 150; *Nestlé* v. *National Westminster Bank* discussed
*supra*, p. 611.
[71] [1991] 2 All E.R. 597. Also see *Mihlenstedt* v. *Barclays Bank International Ltd.* [1989] I.R.L.R.
522 where Nourse L.J. states, "It is necessarily implicit in the contract of employment that the
Bank agrees with the employee that it will duly discharge those functions [it has under the pension
scheme] in good faith."
[72] Now see Income and Corporation Taxes Act 1988, ss.601–603, Sched. 22.

reduction of surplus of assets over liabilities to not more than 5 per cent. Surplus can be reduced by improving benefits, reducing or suspending contributions for up to five years by employers or employees, or by making a payment to the employer. If surplus is not maintained at less than 5 per cent. tax exemptions on investment income are lost. Surplus returned to the employer is taxed at 40 per cent.

A major problem arose where the trust deed did not provide the trustees with the necessary power to pay surplus to the employer (especially if the other methods of reducing surplus were inadequate to reduce surplus only to 5 per cent.), the S.F.O. for years having required schemes to contain provisions prohibiting returns to the employer. The O.P.B. now has power[73] to make modification orders enabling schemes to reduce surplus by returning it to the employer if the proposal is approved by the S.F.O., if the trustees or managers are satisfied that it is in the interests of the beneficiaries, if annual pension increases (in accordance with the increase in the Retail Price Index up to a ceiling of 5 per cent. per annum) are already provided for or are included in the package for reducing the surplus, and if the O.P.B. is satisfied that it is reasonable in all the circumstances to make the order.

The application to the O.P.B. must state whether the trustees have taken independent advice in reaching their decision and enclose a copy of the notice given to employees informing them of the O.P.B. application and their opportunity to make representations to the O.P.B. There will thus need to be co-operation between employer and employees: the *quid pro quo* for paying some surplus to the employer should be generous treatment for employees and pensioners, so helping to maintain good industrial relations with the workforce. The destination of surplus after satisfying employees' legitimate expectations is thus the employer but it is left to a bargaining process to determine exactly what expectations are legitimate.

*Surpluses on liquidation of employer*

Where the trust deed as amended deals fully with entitlement to the surplus there are no loose ends, and where the company employer is a going concern the powers of the O.P.B. should be available to amend the trust deed so as to obviate problems, especially that of the surplus being regarded as *bona vacantia*. After all, if the employer has no entitlement to surplus due to a prohibition in the trust deed and if the employees are regarded as having contractual rights simply to two-thirds of final salary at the date of retirement then such contractual rights exclude the possibility of a resulting trust so that the surplus must pass to the Crown as *bona vacantia* on liquidation of the company employer.[74]

---

[73] See S.I. 1990 No. 2021 the Occupational Pension Schemes (Modification) Regulations 1990.
[74] *Palmer* v. *Abney Park Cemetery Co. Ltd.* (unreported) cited in *Davis* v. *Richards and Wallington Ltd.* [1990] 1 W.L.R. 1511, 1539, *infra*, p. 738.

This seems harsh on the employees. They are settlors of the trust fund as well as beneficiaries. Why should an employee just because he is a beneficiary be precluded from asserting his rights as a settlor to the return of his contributions? Alternatively, should the pension scheme for members not be regarded as analogous to a club for members, between whom the assets would be distributed on the dissolution of the club as indicated by Walton J. in *Re Bucks Constabulary Fund Friendly Society*?[75]

On liquidation of a company its pension fund trust deed may deal comprehensively with the position, so ousting any question of *bona vacantia*. However, if the company is a trustee with power to pay surplus to the company (and therefore to its creditors) or to use it to augment employees' pensions there is an obvious conflict of interest, but this could be authorised by the trust deed expressly authorising the exercising of discretionary powers notwithstanding any personal interest of the exerciser.[76] Accordingly, the Social Security Act 1990[77] now requires that if there is not at least one independent trustee then the insolvency practitioner liquidating the company must appoint an independent trustee. If the discretionary power to augment benefits is vested not in the trustees but in the employer as such, then Warner J. has held[78] that this is a fiduciary power so that it cannot be exercised on the company's behalf by a receiver or liquidator (whose duties are owed to the creditors alone) or, if it is a solvent voluntary winding-up, by the directors (when the only class of members whose interests can be considered are the employees[79]). The discretionary power thus has to be exercised by the court.

How should such power be exercised by the court or by the independent trustees? The starting point could be the view that the surplus belongs morally to the employer for the reasons given by Millett J., as follows[80]:

> "Employees are obliged to contribute a fixed proportion of their salaries or such lesser sum as the employer may from time to time determine. They cannot be required to pay more, even if the fund is in deficit; and they cannot demand a reduction or suspension of their own contributions if it is in surplus. The employer, by way of contrast, is obliged only to make such contributions if any as may be required to meet the liabilities of the scheme. If the fund is in deficit, the employer is bound to make it good; if it is in surplus, the employer has no obligation to pay anything. Employees have no right to complain if, while the fund is in surplus, the employer should require them to continue their contributions while itself contributing nothing. If the employer chooses to reduce or suspend their contributions, it does so ex gratia and in the interests of maintaining good industrial relations.

---

75 [1979] 1 W.L.R. 936, *supra*, p. 419.
76 *cf. Icarus (Hertford) Ltd.* v. *Driscoll* [1990] Pensions L.R. 1.
77 Sched. 4, para. 1 inserting ss.57C, 57D of the Social Security Pensions Act 1975.
78 *Mettoy Pension Trustees Ltd.* v. *Evans* [1991] 2 All E.R. 513.
79 See *Parke* v. *Daily News Ltd.* [1962] Ch. 927 as modified by Companies Act 1980, s.74.
80 *Re Courage Group's Pension Scheme* [1987] 1 All E.R. 528, 545.

From this, two consequences follow. First, employees have no legal
right to a 'a contributions holiday.' Second, any surplus arises from past
overfunding not by the employer and the employees pro rata to their
respective contributions but by the employer alone to the full extent of
its past contributions and only subject thereto by the employees."

The employer is then in a position similar to that of a person entitled
in default of the exercise of a power of appointment[81] in favour of the
employees. Even if the power is regarded as for the purpose of holding
a fair balance between the employees and the employer, can it be
unfair to return to the employer the surplus generated by the
employer's over-funding? If an independent trustee ascertained the
relevant facts concerning employees and the employer's liabilities and
in good faith then decided to pay the surplus to the employer's
liquidator why should the decision not to favour the employee-objects
of the power be impeachable? The employees' hopes may not mater-
ialise but that is the common fate for the objects of discretionary
powers.

However, Warner J. has stated[82]:

"One cannot in my opinion, in construing a provision in the rules of a
'balance of cost' pension scheme relating to surplus, start from the
assumption that any surplus belongs morally to the employer . . . in
deciding whether the employer owed a duty to the objects of the power,
one must have regard to the fact that the beneficiaries under a pension
scheme are not volunteers . . . their rights are derived from the contract
of employment as well as from the trust instrument. Those rights have
been earned by the service of the members under those contracts as well
as by their contributions . . . In construing the trust instrument one must
bear in mind as an important part of the background the origins of the
beneficiaries' rights under it."

Thus, the discretionary power is a fiduciary one requiring regard to be
had to the interests of the employee-members of the scheme; but this
is a weak duty leaving it open to the power-exerciser to consider them
but still pay the surplus to the employer's liquidator.[83] It is arguable
that the courts should go further and require the power to be exercised
according to the purpose of advancing the interests of the employee-
beneficiaries as much as possible,[84] and treat failure to exercise the
power (so as to benefit third parties at the expense of the beneficiaries)
as a breach of duty to the employee-beneficiaries.

It will thus be seen that even if the rules of the scheme are not
comprehensive there should be no question of the surplus on liquida-

---

[81] The fraud on a power doctrine (see p. 714, *supra*) does not apply if an appointment is not made:
*Re Somes* [1896] 1 Ch. 250; *Vatcher* v. *Paull* [1915] A.C. 372, 279.

[82] *Mettoy Pension Trustees Ltd.* v. *Evans* [1991] 2 All E.R. 513, 549.

[83] See R. Nobles (1990) 53 M.L.R. 377–380 discussing *Mettoy* and *Icarus (Hertford) Ltd.* v. *Driscoll*
[1990] Pensions L.R. 1.

[84] Millett J. in *Re Courage Group's Pension Scheme* [1987] 1 All E.R. 528, 541 stated, "A pension
scheme is established, not for the benefit of a particular company, but *for the benefit of those
employed* in a commercial undertaking."

tion of the company going to the Crown as *bona vacantia* unless the trust deed excludes any right to surplus of the company or its employees. Scott J. considered the position recently in *Davies* v. *Richards and Wallington Industries Ltd.*[85] where the employer went into liquidation before the execution of a definitive trust deed dealing with distribution of surplus funds. He held that a definitive deed executed after liquidation was effective in the circumstances but that even if it had been ineffective its inefficacy could have been remedied by treating an interim deed as constituting an executory trust which would be executed by a court order bringing into effect provisions corresponding to those in the definitive deed. Thus the trustees, using the discretion conferred on them by the definitive deed, could use the surplus for the purpose of augmenting members' benefits.

In *obiter dicta* (*infra*, pp. 737–743) he considered the situation where the scheme did not prohibit the return of surplus money to the employer and opined that a resulting trust did arise in favour of the employer, the surplus being regarded as primarily arising from over-funding by the employer. However, so far as part of the surplus derived from employees' contributions he opined that it devolved as *bona vacantia*.

He considered that where a trust deed is silent as to destination of a surplus the law will supply a resulting trust in favour of the provider of the funds in question and that it is only where it is "absolutely clear,"[86] expressly or by necessary implication, that in no circumstances is a resulting trust to arise that such trust will be excluded. Indeed, if a contributor's intention is that a resulting trust should not apply it would not be right for the law to contradict that intention. "Therefore, the fact that a payment to a fund has been made under a contract and that the payer has obtained all that he or she bargained for under the contract is not necessarily a decisive argument against a resulting trust."[87]

Surprisingly, Scott J. then discovered that the employee-contributors intended that there should be no resulting trust in their favour. Why was this "absolutely clear"? First, because an intention to have a resulting trust would be "unworkable," the employees' entitlements (taking benefits received into account) being so various. Secondly, because an intention to have a resulting trust would give them more than the legislature intended in its legislative requirements for benefits under exempt approved schemes. These two reasons are not at all convincing: would these thoughts have crossed the employees' minds? Each employee would probably expect to be able to work out what he was entitled to[88] and why should the *legislature's* intention provide

---

[85] [1990] 1 W.L.R. 1511.
[86] [1990] 1 W.L.R. 1511, 1541, endorsing Knox J. in *Re ABC T.V. Pension Scheme* (unreported).
[87] *Ibid.* 1541–1542.
[88] Distribution of the surplus could be proportionate to the amounts contributed by employees and pensioners.

evidence of the *employees'* intention (though if the legislation clearly prevents a resulting trust arising in favour of the employees then *cadit quaestio*, regardless of the employees' intentions)? One may also note that Scott J. treated as gospel truth the *bona vacantia* findings of Goff J. in the *West Sussex Constabulary* case[89] whereas, as has been seen,[90] such findings are probably incorrect in view of Walton J.'s later reasoning in the *Bucks Constabulary* case[91] applied in subsequent members' club cases with which an analogy may be drawn for members' pension fund schemes.

## Sale of employer and related pension fund

Problems involving ownership of surplus pension moneys also arise where a controlling company sells a subsidiary company to a purchaser. Where the trust deed provides for a portion of the group pension fund to be transferred to the purchaser of the subsidiary company and for the amount of the portion to be determined by an appointed actuary then the court cannot intervene with the actuary's expert decision in the absence of bad faith.[92] Thus a valuation made by him on the past service reserve method (the amount required to meet pension benefits for service rendered to date) with allowance for future pay and pension increases was unimpeachable. Indeed, the judge regarded such approach more appropriate than the higher valued share of fund basis, the notional temporary surplus being capable of being dealt with by the employer, primarily responsible for the surplus, in various ways which could lead to disappearance of the surplus over a period without the surplus necessarily being used for the benefit of the relevant employees even if they stayed within the scheme. On transfers the past service reserve method is now regularly used.

The Hanson Group tried to take advantage of this when buying the Imperial Group and selling its Courage brewing division to Elders. The Courage division had its own pension fund surplus so Hanson tried to merge the Courage scheme (with its £80 million surplus) into the Imperial Group scheme, substituting Hanson for the Imperial Group as principal employer under a purported power in that behalf, so that the Courage brewing division could then be sold on to Elders with a pension fund of an amount based only on the past service reserve method, so that £70 million of the surplus would remain in the main Imperial Group Scheme controlled by Hanson.

Hanson took advantage of a provision allowing the trust deed to be varied, if it did not have the effect of altering the main purpose of the fund, to add a broad power to substitute the employer company by

---

[89] [1971] Ch. 1. Scott J. also held that if any part of the surplus was derived from funds transferred from the pension schemes of other companies such transfers were outright transfers, excluding any resulting trust possibility, so that any surplus therefrom was *bona vacantia*, but why could such surplus not accrue to the shares of the employees and the employer?

[90] *Supra*, p. 417.

[91] [1979] 1 W.L.R. 936.

[92] *Re Imperial Foods Ltd. Pension Scheme* [1986] 1 W.L.R. 717.

another company. Millett J. held[93] that the addition of such power was *ultra vires* but, even if it were not, the exercise of such power in the circumstances was for a purpose foreign to the purpose for which the power could be conferred and so was invalid. He explained that he did not base his decision on the ground that Hanson's proposals would deprive the employees of an accrued legal entitlement to surplus because the surplus derives from past overfunding by the employer. He further said[94]:

> "It will, however, only be in rare cases that the employer will have any legal right to repayment of any part of the surplus. Regulations are expected to confer power on the Occupational Pensions Board to authorise modifications to pension schemes in order to allow repayment to employers. Repayment will, however, still normally require amendment to the scheme, and thus co-operation between the employer and the trustees or committee of management. Where the employer seeks repayment, the trustees or committee can be expected to press for generous treatment of employees and pensioners, and the employer to be influenced by a desire to maintain good industrial relations with its workforce.
>
> It is, therefore, precisely in relation to a surplus that the relationship between 'the company' as the employer and the members as its present or past employees can be seen to be an essential feature of a pension scheme. In the present case, the members of these schemes object to being compulsorily transferred to a new scheme of which they know nothing except that it has a relatively small surplus. While they have no legal right to participate in the surpluses in the existing schemes, they are entitled to have them dealt with by consultation and negotiation between their employers with a continuing responsibility towards them and the committee of management with a discretion to exercise on their behalf, and not to be irrevocably parted from these surpluses by the unilateral decision of a take-over raider with only a transitory interest in the share capital of the companies which employ them."

## THE SOCIAL SECURITY ACT 1990

The Act provides for a register of occupational and personal pension schemes[95] and, most significantly, creates[96] the post of Pensions Ombudsman with retrospective powers involving matters arising before the 1990 Act came into force. This will enable employee-beneficiaries to challenge trustees or managers of pension schemes more easily and cheaply than before, when recourse had to be made to the courts. Section 11 further requires final salary schemes to provide increases in line with retail price index increases up to a maximum of 5 per cent. per annum in respect of future pensionable service and also for past pensionable service out of any surpluses which may occur

---

93 *Re Courage Group's Pension Scheme* [1987] 1 All E.R. 528.
94 *Ibid.* 545.
95 s.13.
96 s.12.

following actuarial valuations. Indeed, from August 17, 1990 such schemes are precluded from making payments (with some exceptions) to the employer until provision has been made in the scheme rules for every current and future pension to be increased to the above level.

The restriction on investment in employer-related investments[97] and the need for an independent trustee on the liquidation of the company-employer[98] have already been mentioned.

### THE EUROPEAN COMMUNITY DIMENSION

In *Barber* v. *Guardian Royal Exchange Assurance Group*[99] the European Court of Justice held that occupational pension schemes fall within Article 119 of the EEC Treaty of Rome requiring the application of the principle that men and women should receive equal pay for equal work. "Pay" includes the wage or salary "and any other consideration which the worker receives, directly or indirectly, in respect of his employment from his employer" and so the Court held that pension rights of the employee or his dependants constitute "pay," albeit deferred pay. It may well be that the *Barber* judgment only applies prospectively[1] to rights *earned* by virtue of pensionable service in pay periods after 17 May, 1990, but it is possible that it extends to rights *claimed* after 17 May, and in respect of the whole of pensionable service before and after 17 May.[2] To clarify matters the Government is supporting a test case arising out of the liquidation of Coloroll involving the Trustees of the Coloroll Group Pension Schemes.

As already mentioned, the European Commission is currently considering laying down balance of portfolio guidelines for pension funds. It is likely to go on to consider giving employees rights to representation on the body of trustees or the management committee.

### IMPERIAL GROUP PENSION TRUST LTD. v. IMPERIAL TOBACCO LTD.

Chancery Division *The Times* December 6, 1990. (also [1991] 2 All E.R. 597).

BROWNE-WILKINSON V.-C. said that the Imperial Tobacco Pension Fund had a surplus of at least £130 million. Under the present rules of the pension fund, the company had no right to any of that surplus.

The present management of the company wished the members of the fund to transfer their rights and assets to a different fund, RBS. This was an open fund in which the company would be entitled to surplus.

From the early 1970s pensions were increased broadly in line with inflation. Although there was no express provision for that in the rules, the increases were awarded each year at the discretion of the committee of management and with the consent of the company by virtue of a power of amendment in clause

---

[97] See p. 727, *supra*.
[98] See p. 730, *supra*.
[99] [1990] 2 All E.R. 660, discussed (1991) 54 M.L.R. 271.
[1] *Cf. Defrenne* v. *Sabena* [1976] E.C.R. 455.
[2] See Art. 7(1) of Council Directive 79/7/EEC of December 19, 1978 and Art. 9(a) of Directive 86/378/EEC of July 24, 1986.

36 of the trust deed dated April 4, 1929 by which the fund was originally established.

In 1985, when a takeover of the company by Hanson plc was imminent, the committee of management made two amendments under clause 36 with the consent of the company: (i) provision that the fund would be automatically closed to new members in the event of a hostile takeover; (ii) a guarantee of at least a 5 per cent. annual increase under a new rule 64A.

Hanson took over the company and the fund duly closed. Since the takeover by Hanson the company had refused to consent to any further increase in pensions over that guaranteed by rule 64A. The committee of management wished to increase pensions in line with inflation which exceeded 5 per cent.

The first argument of the pensioners was that the words "at least" in rule 64A in themselves conferred power on the committee of management to increase pensions by more than 5 per cent. without the consent of the company. His Lordship rejected that argument. Increases of over 5 per cent. could only be effected by amending the trust deed and rules with the company's consent.

That raised the question of whether the company in granting or withholding its consent was under any fiduciary or other duty to consider the interests of members and not merely the company's own interests.

That was a point of fundamental importance not only in relation to this pension fund but in relation to all pension schemes.

Clause 36 contained no express limitation on the company's right to give or withhold consent, for example, that such consent should not be unreasonably withheld. Accordingly, if this were a traditional private family trust there could be no question of any such limitation.

But pension schemes trusts were of quite a different nature to traditional trusts. The traditional trust was one under which the settlor, by way of bounty, transferred property to trustees to be administered for the beneficiaries as objects of his bounty.

Normally, there was no legal relationship between the parties apart from the trust. The beneficiaries had given no consideration for what they had received. The settlor, as donor, could impose such limits on his bounty as he chose, including imposing a requirement that the consent of himself or some other person should be required to the exercise of the powers.

A pension scheme was quite different. Pension benefits were part of the consideration which an employee received in return for the rendering of his services.

In many cases, including the present, membership of the pension scheme was a requirement of employment. In his Lordship's judgment, the scheme was established against the background for such employment and fell to be interpreted against that background.

In every contract of employment there was an implied term that the employer would not, without reasonable and proper cause, conduct himself in a manner calculated or likely to destroy or seriously damage the relationship of confidence and trust between employer and employee: "the implied obligation of good faith."

In his Lordship's judgment, that obligation of an employer applied as much to the exercise of his rights and powers under a pension scheme as they did to the other rights and powers of an employer.

Applying that test to the present case, the company could have regard to its own financial interests but only to the extent that, in so doing, it did not breach the obligation of good faith to its employees.

If the sole purpose of withholding consent to increase benefits out of the fund was to force its present and past employees to give up their accrued right in an existing fund so as to confer on the company benefits that it could not enjoy unless the members gave up such rights, that conflicted with the company's duty to act fairly and in good faith to its employees.

There were apparently no financial or other reasons why the company should not provide non-contributory pensions and guaranteed inflation linking up to a maximum of 15 per cent. subject to an obligation on the members to surrender part of their initial pension; those were the very benefits which the company was offering to all the members of the fund if they transferred to the RBS taking with them their share of the fund.

His Lordship had asked why the company was seeking to induce members of the fund to give up their rights in the fund and transfer to the RBS rather than consent to alteration of the rules of the fund on several occasions but had received no answer.

The pensioners suspected that the only reason why the benefits were not being provided in the fund as opposed to the RBS was the company's wish to transfer the surplus of the fund (to which the members of the fund were entitled) to the RBS where the surplus would belong to the company.

His Lordship considered, in the absence of any other explanation, that that was a fair inference. If correct, it indicated that the company was using its right to withhold consent not for the purpose of continuing to use the assets currently applicable exclusively for pensions for employees of the company but for some other collateral purpose. If so, the company would be acting unlawfully.

Accordingly, his Lordship would declare that the company's right to give or withhold its consent was subject only to the restriction that such right was not validly exercisable in breach of the obligation of good faith.

See *Woods* v. *WM Car Services (Peterborough) Ltd.* [1989] I.R.L.R. 347 and *Lewis* v. *Motorworld Garages Ltd.* [1985] I.R.L.R. 465.

## DAVIS v. RICHARDS & WALLINGTON LTD.

Chancery Division [1990] 1 W.L.R. 1511

SCOTT J.: "Finally, I must address myself to the arguments on resulting trust. These arguments arise only if the definitive deed was ineffective and its inefficacy cannot be remedied by the execution of the executory trust.

"Mr. Charles, arguing for *bona vacantia*, drew a distinction between payments made under contract and payments made under a trust. He suggested that rights arising under pension schemes were, basically, rights of a contractual character rather than equitable rights arising under a trust. As I understood the argument, if the context in which the rights arise is mainly or exclusively contractual, then a resulting trust will be excluded; but if the context is mainly or exclusively that of trust, a resulting trust may apply. Unincorporated associations, he said, were based in contract, a pension scheme was a species of unincorporated association, the contributions to pension schemes by employees and employers alike were made under contract with one another; so there was no room for any resulting trust to apply to the surplus produced by the contributions. Mr. Charles' analysis of rights under pension schemes as being based on contract has some authority to support it. In *Kerr* v. *British Leyland (Staff) Trustees Ltd.* Court of Appeal (Civil Division) Transcript No. 286 of 1986, Fox L.J., referring to the trusts of a pension scheme, said:

'Now this is not a case of a trust where the beneficiaries are simply volunteers. The beneficiaries here are not volunteers. Their rights derive from contractual and commercial origins. They have purchased their rights as part of their terms of employment.'

"In *Mihlenstedt* v. *Barclays Bank International Ltd.*, Court of Appeal (Civil Division) Transcript No. 817 of 1989, Nourse L.J., referring to a rule relating to an ill-health pension scheme that enabled the bank 'at its discretion after consulting its medical adviser . . . [to] vary or suspend any such pension,' said:

'If therefore the matter had rested on the trust deed and the rules alone, I would have held that the bank was under no obligation in regard to the plaintiff's application for an ill-health pension. But it was a term of her contract of employment with the bank that she should be entitled to membership of the pension scheme and to the benefits thereunder. From that it must follow, as a matter of necessary implication, that the bank became contractually bound, so far as it lay within its power, to procure for the plaintiff the benefits to which she was entitled under the scheme.'

"Mr. Charles drew attention to the emphasis placed by Nourse L.J. on the contractual nature of the claimant's rights *vis-à-vis* the bank, his employer. However, Nourse L.J. continued:

'If, on the material which is before it, the court can see that the trustee's opinion has been formed dishonestly or on an erroneous basis, it could not be doubted that a court of equity would be able to grant the relief above suggested. And since the fusion of law and equity the granting of such relief cannot sensibly be held to depend on whether the underlying obligation arises out of trust or in contract.'

"Neither of these Court of Appeal decisions was concerned with the question of whether a resulting trust applied to the surplus of a fund. But that question did arise in *Palmer* v. *Abney Park Cemetery Co. Ltd.* (unreported), July 4, 1985. Judge Blackett-Ord Q.C., sitting as a judge of the Chancery Division, said:

'The nature of the scheme in the present case is not primarily a trust, but primarily a matter of contract. The contributions of members and the contributions of the company were paid irrevocably into the common pool to be applied by the trustees in accordance with the deed and the rules. Under the deed and the rules the company was entitled to no return or benefit other than that of goodwill with its employees, and the members were entitled only to what they contracted for. That they have obtained. And on that ground it seems to me that the balance of the fund can only pass to the Crown as *bona vacantia*.'

"This reasoning was adopted by Mr. Charles in the present case. In my opinion, the contractual origin of rights under a pension scheme, although relevant to the question whether a resulting trust applies to surplus, is not conclusive. There are a number of authorities where the courts have had to deal with the question whether the assets of a defunct association or the surplus assets of a pension scheme had become *bona vacantia* or were held on resulting trusts for the subscribers or members.

"I can start with *In re West Sussex Constabulary's Widows, Children and Benevolent (1930) Fund Trusts* [1971] Ch. 1. The case concerned a benevolent

fund raised from various sources, including raffles, sweepstakes, street collections, legacies and donations. The fund had to be wound up and the question
was its destination. Goff J. held that so much of the fund as derived from
raffles, sweepstakes, street collections and the like was not the subject of any
resulting trust and was *bona vacantia*, but that there was a resulting trust in
respect of the legacies and donations. As to the proceeds of the raffles and
sweepstakes, Goff J. said:

> 'it appears to me to be impossible to apply the doctrine of resulting trust
> to the proceeds of entertainments and sweepstakes and suchlike money-
> raising operations for two reasons: first, the relationship is one of
> contract and not of trust; the purchaser of a ticket may have the motive
> of aiding the cause or he may not; he may purchase a ticket merely
> because he wishes to attend the particular entertainment or to try for the
> prize, but whichever it be, he pays his money as the price of what is
> offered and what he receives . . . '

"Mr. Charles drew attention to the reference to contract. As to the proceeds
of the collecting-boxes, Goff J. said [1971] Ch. 1, 13:

> 'I agree that all who put their money into collecting-boxes should be
> taken to have the same intention, but why should they not all be
> regarded as intending to part with their money out and out absolutely in
> all circumstances?'

"On that ground he held that a resulting trust did not apply to the proceeds of
collecting-boxes and that the proceeds were *bona vacantia*. He declined,
however, when dealing with legacies and donations to draw the same inference
of intention to part out and out with the money that he had drawn in respect of
the collecting-boxes and held that a resulting trust applied to the part of the
fund attributable to legacies and donations.

"The principles to be applied in deciding between a resulting trust and *bona
vacantia* were considered by Knox J. in *Jones* v. *Williams* (unreported), March
15, 1988. He said:

> 'The general rule is well settled that where the owner of property
> conveys it to another to be held on certain trusts which fail, either in
> whole or in part, the beneficial interest comes back to the person who
> conveyed the property: see *Snell's Principles of Equity* (29th ed.),
> p. 102. The basis of this doctrine is often described as an implied trust
> based on the original provider's presumed intention. Mr. Charles for the
> Treasury Solicitor submitted that such an intention was excluded in those
> cases where it would be unrealistic for such an intention to be imputed to
> the provider. He pointed to the passages in the *West Sussex Constabul-
> ary* case [1971] Ch. 1, in which Goff J. set out the differing views
> expressed in relation to the intentions to be imputed to persons who put
> coins in collecting-boxes and similar transactions. One view expressed by
> P. O. Lawrence in *In re Welsh Hospital (Netley) Fund* [1921] 1 Ch. 655
> and adopted by Upjohn J. in *In re Hillier's Trusts* [1945] 1 W.L.R. 9, is
> that such contributors must be taken to have parted out and out with
> their contributions because, in the words of Upjohn J. "The circum-
> stances in which the money was given negative the idea that the donor
> ever intended that he should receive any of that money back." The other
> view was expressed by Harman J. in *In re Gillingham Bus Disaster Fund*

[1958] Ch. 300, who held that there is a resulting trust in respect of the surplus of collections, and specifically he said, in a passage quoted by Goff J. in the *West Sussex Constabulary* case: "This doctrine does not, in my judgment, rest on any evidence of the state of mind of the settlor, for in the vast majority of cases no doubt he does not expect to see his money back: he has created a trust which so far as he can see will absorb the whole of it. The resulting trust arises where that expectation is for some unforeseen reason cheated of fruition, and is an inference of law based on after-knowledge of the event." Goff J. preferred and followed the view of Upjohn J. in *In re Hillier's Trusts*, saying [1971] Ch. 1, [1954] 1 W.L.R. 9, 14: "That commends itself to my humble judgment, and I therefore prefer and follow the judgment of Upjohn J. in *In re Hillier's Trusts*." He then continued to say that that did not appear to transgress the principle that Harman J. had laid down in the *Gillingham* case, which I have just read. This particular problem does not arise in the present case, but the decisions throw light on the limitations on the doctrine of resulting trusts. Whether it is a proper implication to make in relation to contributions to collecting boxes and the like is not a matter which falls for decision by me, but I am satisfied that it is possible for a disposition of property to be made on terms which make it plain that the transferor affirmatively desires to exclude all possibility of a resulting trust in his favour. The presumption of law is against this and such an expression needs to be clear and unambiguous more especially as the likely result is that the property concerned, if there is such a failure as would normally give rise to a resulting trust, will pass as bona vacantia and that is a result which should not lightly be imputed to any transferor.'

"Knox J. then referred to *In re A.B.C. Television Pension Scheme*, May 22, 1973, where the rules of the pension scheme under review had provided, inter alia, that 'No moneys which at any time have been contributed by the principal company shall in any circumstances be repayable to the principal company' and where Foster J. had held that 'this paragraph negatives the possibility of implying a resulting trust.' Knox J. agreed and said:

'Where a trust deed is silent as to the destination of a surplus the law will supply a resulting trust in favour of the provider of the funds in question. That is something which arises outside the trust deed as an implication of law. The trust deed may include a clause which prevents a resulting trust from operating and in that case it will operate according to its terms.'

"But, later, he said: 'it is only where it is absolutely clear that in no circumstances is a resulting trust to arise that it will be excluded.'

"I respectfully agree with Knox J.'s approach. I would, however, venture one qualification. The provision in a trust deed necessary to exclude a resulting trust need not, in my opinion, be express. In the absence of an express provision it would, I think, often be very difficult for a sufficiently clear intention to exclude a resulting trust to be established. But, in general, any term that can be expressed can also, in suitable circumstances, be implied. In my opinion, a resulting trust will be excluded not only by an express provision but also if its exclusion is to be implied. If the intention of a contributor that a resulting trust should not apply is the proper conclusion, it would not be right, in my opinion, for the law to contradict that intention. In my judgment, therefore, the fact that a payment to a fund has been made under contract and that the payer has obtained all that he or she bargained for under the contract is not necessarily a decisive argument against resulting trust.

"I must apply these principles to the surplus in the present case. The fund was, as I have said, fed from three sources: employee's contributions, transfers from other pension schemes and employers' contributions. The employees' contributions were made under contract. Employees were obliged to contribute 5 per cent. of salary. They were entitled, in return, to the specified pension and other benefits. The funds from other pension schemes, too, were transferred under contract. There would have been three parties to all these contracts, namely, the trustees of the transferor scheme, the trustees of the 1975 scheme and the transferring members themselves. Perhaps the employer company would have been a party as well. The transfer would certainly have been made with its consent. Under these contracts, by implication if not expressly, the transferor trustees would have been discharged from liability in respect of the transferred funds, whether liability to the transferring employee members or liability to the employer company. Finally there are the employers. They, too, made their contributions under contract; they made them under the contracts of employment between themselves and their employees. But there is a very important difference between the contractual obligation of the employees and that of the employers. The employees' contractual obligation was specific in amount—5 per cent. of salary. The employers' contractual obligation was conceptually certain but the amount was inherently uncertain. The obligation was to pay whatever was necessary to fund the scheme. The terms of rule 3 of the 1975 rules describe accurately the contractual obligation of the employers:

> 'The employer will pay to the trustees such amounts as many from time to time be necessary to enable the trustees to maintain the benefits . . . '

"In practice, the amount of the employers' contributions in respect of each employee was actuarially calculated. The calculations were based on assumptions as to the time when the benefits would become payable and as to the amount of the employee's final salary at that time. If the scheme should terminate before that time, the amount paid would be bound to have been more than needed to have been paid in order to fund the employee's benefits as at the date of termination.

"Two separate questions seem to me to require to be answered. First, to what extent should the surplus, the £3m.-odd, be regarded as derived from each of these three sources? One possible answer is that there should be a calculation of the total amount of the employees' contributions, the total amount of funds transferred from other companies' pension schemes and the total amount of employees' contributions, and that the surplus should be regarded as derived from these three sources in the same proportions as the three totals bear to one another. I do not accept that this is right. It ignores the different bases on which these contributions were paid. Since the employers' obligation was to pay whatever was from time to time necessary to fund the various scheme benefits and since the employees' 5 per cent. contributions and the amount of the transferred funds constituted the base from which the amount of the employers' contributions would from time to time have to be assessed, it is logical, in my judgment, to treat the scheme benefits as funded first by the employees' contributions and the transferred funds, and only secondarily by the employers' contributions, and, correspondingly, to treat the surplus as provided first by the employers' contributions and only secondarily by the employees' contributions and the transferred funds.

"There are two possible factual situations to be considered. It is possible (although, I think, very unlikely) that the employees' contributions and the funds transferred from the pension schemes of other companies would, without there having been any contribution at all from the employers, have been sufficient to provide in full for all the scheme benefits and, perhaps, still to have left some surplus. If that is the position, it would follow that, with the advantage of hindsight, the employers need not have made any contributions at all in order to have funded the benefits. This situation would, in my judgment, require that that surplus (which would be bound, I think, to be very small) should be regarded as derived from the employees' contributions and the transferred funds and that the balance of the surplus should be regarded as derived from the employers' contributions.

"The much more likely situation is that some contribution at least was required from the employers in order to produce assets sufficient to provide all the scheme benefits to which employees became entitled on July 31, 1982. In that event the whole of the surplus, in my judgment, should be regarded as derived from the employers' contributions. This conclusion is, to my mind, in accordance both with logic and with equity. The actuarial calculations on which the employers' actual contributions were based were themselves based upon a series of assumptions. The termination of the scheme invalidated the assumptions. The employers had, in the event, made payments exceeding the amount necessary to discharge their obligation to fund the benefits to which the employees eventually became entitled. There is a well established equity that enables accounts drawn up under a mistake to be reopened: see Goff & Jones, *The Law of Restitution* (3rd ed., 1986), p. 199. In cases such as the present there was no mistake at the time the contributions were assessed and paid. The actuarial calculations were, I am sure, impeccable. But subsequent events having invalidated some of the assumptions underlying the calculations, the case is, in my opinion, strongly analogous to that of an account drawn up under a mistake. In my opinion, equity should treat the employers as entitled to claim the surplus, or so much of it as derived from the overpayments.

"The second question is whether a resulting trust applies to the surplus, or to so much of the surplus as was derived from each of the three sources to which I have referred. As to the surplus derived from the employers' contributions, I can see no basis on which the resulting trust can be excluded. The equity to which I referred in the previous paragraph demands, in my judgment, the conclusion that the trustees hold the surplus derived from the employers' contributions upon trust for the employers. There is no express provision excluding a resulting trust and no circumstances from which, in my opinion, an implication to that effect could be drawn. On the other hand, in my judgment, the circumstances of the case seem to me to point firmly and clearly to the conclusion that a resulting trust in favour of the employees is excluded.

"The circumstances are these. (i) Each employee paid his or her contributions in return for specific financial benefits from the fund. The value of these benefits would be different for each employee, depending on how long he had served, how old he was when he joined and how old he was when he left. Two employees might have paid identical sums in contributions but have become entitled to benefits of a very different value. The point is particularly striking in respect of the employees (and there were several of them) who exercised their option to a refund of contributions. How can a resulting trust work as between the various employees inter se? I do not think it can and I do not see why equity should impute to them an intention that would lead to an unworkable result. (ii) The scheme was established to take advantage of the legislation relevant to an exempt approved scheme and a contracted-out scheme. The legislative requirements placed a maximum on the financial return from the fund to which each employee would become entitled. The proposed rules would have preserved the statutory requirements. A resulting trust cannot do so. In my judgment, the relevant legislative requirements prevent imputing to the employees an intention that the surplus of the fund derived from their contributions should be returned to them under a resulting trust.

"In my judgment, therefore, there is no resulting trust for the employees.

"Finally, there are the transferred funds. The intention, in my judgment, appears sufficiently clear from the documents by which the transfers were effected and from the surrounding circumstances that the trustees of the transferred schemes were divesting themselves once and for all of the transferred funds. So far as the employee members of the transferee schemes were concerned there could not, for the same reasons as those I have already given, be a resulting trust in favour of them. So far as the employer contributors to those funds were concerned, i.e. the companies whose shares had been taken over, they were not all in the same position *vis-à-vis* the transferred funds. Some of the transferor schemes expressly excluded any refund of assets to the employer contributors. Those employers could not, therefore, assert any resulting trust. As to the others, it is possible to regard the transferred funds as being subject to some contingent resulting trust of surplus in favour of employer contributors. But, as I understand the evidence, it would be virtually impossible now to identify the part of the £3m.-odd surplus that represented the surplus (if there was one) inherent in any of the transferred funds. In my judgment, it is reasonable in the circumstances to regard the employer contributors to the transferred funds, as well as the employee contributors, as intending that the funds should vest in the 1975 scheme trustees to the entire exclusion of any claim under the transferor scheme, whether under the rules thereof or by way of resulting trust. Here again, I do not think equity should impute to the parties an impracticable and unworkable intention.

"Accordingly, in my judgment, if any part of the surplus has derived from employees' contributions or from the funds transferred from the pension schemes of other companies, that part of the surplus devolves as *bona vacantia*. Subject thereto, the surplus is, in my judgment, held upon trust for the employer contributors."

## Section 10. Indemnity of Trustees[3]

### I. INDEMNITY AGAINST THE TRUST PROPERTY[4]

By section 30(2) of the Trustee Act 1925 "A trustee may reimburse himself or pay or discharge out of the trust premises all expenses incurred in or about the execution of the trusts or powers."[5] This confirms what has always been the rule of equity in respect of expenses properly incurred[6] in the administration of the trust: *Stott* v. *Milne, infra*. Of course, there is no such right in respect of expenses or costs improperly incurred through unreasonable conduct on the part of the trustee: *Re Chapman*.[7] Exceptionally, if an unauthorised liability has been incurred by the trustee acting in good faith and this has conferred a benefit on the trust property, he will have a right of indemnity up to the amount of such benefit.[8] If litigation is contemplated trustees should safeguard themselves by obtaining a Beddoe's Order from the court: this entitles them to be reimbursed the costs no matter how the litigation results.[9] The right of indemnity gives the trustee an equitable lien over the trust property which gives him a right to retain trust property until the right of indemnity is satisfied and if necessary to sell it.[10] It will bind an assignee of a beneficiary.[11]

A trustee's right of indemnity depends ultimately on the state of accounts between him and the beneficiaries and is limited to the balance, if any, in his favour.[12] Thus, if he has committed a breach of trust occasioning loss to the trust he will have no right of indemnity until accounts have been taken and a balance in his favour emerges.

---

[3] See generally A. W. Scott, "Liabilities Incurred in the Administration of Trusts" (1915) 28 H.L.R. 725; Stone, "A Theory of Liability of Trust Estates for the Contracts and Torts of the Trustee" (1922) 22 Col.L.R. 527; A. J. Hawkins, "The Personal Liability of Charity Trustees" (1979) 95 L.Q.R. 99. As to a trustee's indemnity (a) in respect of liabilities incurred in carrying on (with authority) his testator's business, see Murray, "Indemnity of Executor" (1893) 9 L.Q.R. 331; *Re Oxley* [1914] 1 Ch. 604; (b) in respect of damages he has paid for a tort committed in the course of the administration of the trust, see *Bennett* v. *Wyndham* (1862) 4 De G.F. & J. 259; *Re Raybould* [1900] 1 Ch. 199.

[4] For indemnity against the beneficiaries personally, see Part II of this section, *infra*, p. 746; for indemnity against the beneficiary's beneficial interest under s.62 of the Trustee Act 1925, see *infra*, p. 783; for a trustee's indemnity against his co-trustee, see *infra*, p. 797.

[5] This subsection replaces s.24 of the Trustee Act 1893. See also s.11(2) of the Trustee Act 1925 and s.100 of the Settled Land Act 1925.

[6] The trustee need not satisfy the liability before claiming indemnity; he may in the first instance discharge the liability by making the payments direct from the trust estate: see *Lacey* v. *Hill* (1874) L.R. 18 Eq. 182; *Re National Financial Co.* (1868) L.R. 3 Ch. 791; *Hobbs* v. *Wayet* (1887) 36 Ch.D. 256; *Re Blundell* (1888) 40 Ch.D. 370, 377.

[7] (1895) 72 L.T. 66. A trustee is also not entitled to an indemnity where he is a party to proceedings not really as a trustee but in some other capacity, *e.g.* landlord's agent holding maintenance fund as trustee: *Holding & Management Ltd.* v. *Property Holdings plc* [1988] 2 All E.R. 702.

[8] *Vyse* v. *Foster* (1872) L.R. 8 Ch.App. 309; *Re Leslie* (1883) 23 Ch.D. 552; *Re Smith's Estate* [1937] Ch. 636.

[9] *Re Beddoe* [1893] 1 Ch. 541; *Re Yorke* [1911] Ch. 370; *Re England's S.T.* [1918] 1 Ch. 24.

[10] *Re Exhall Coal Co. Ltd.* (1866) 35 Beav. 449; *Re Chennel* (1877) 8 Ch.D. 492, 503; *Jennings* v. *Mather* [1901] 1 Q.B. 108, 113–114.

[11] *Re Knapman* (1881) 18 Ch.D. 300.

[12] *Re Johnson* (1880) 15 Ch.D. 548; *Re Evans* (1887) 34 Ch.D. 597, 601; *Jennings* v. *Mather* [1901] 1 Q.B. 113, 114; *Re British Power Traction & Lighting Co. Ltd.* [1910] 2 Ch. 470.

The trustee's right of indemnity may be wholly or partly excluded[13] as may occur if he has a liberal right to remuneration under a charging clause so that limited reasonable expenses will still leave the trustee in pocket.

As Lord Templeman stated in *Carver* v. *Duncan*[14]: "Trustees are entitled to be indemnified out of the capital and income of their trust fund against all obligations incurred by the trustees in the due performance of their duties and the due exercise of their powers. The trustees must then debit each item of expenditure either against income or against capital. The general rule is that income must bear all ordinary outgoings of a recurrent nature, such as rates and taxes and interest on charges and incumbrances. Capital must bear all costs, charges and expenses incurred for the benefit of the whole estate."

## STOTT v. MILNE[15]

Court of Appeal (1884) 25 Ch.D. 710; 50 L.T. 742 (Lord Selborne L.C., Cotton and Lindley L.JJ.)

The defendant trustees had brought two actions, on the advice of counsel and without the knowledge of the plaintiff beneficiary, against third parties for wrongs alleged to have been done to the trust estate. The actions were compromised before trial. The trustees found themselves out of pocket after having paid, from the income of the trust, the balance of the costs in one of the actions. The plaintiff (tenant for life) brought the present action, before the Vice-Chancellor of the Lancaster Palatine Court, claiming payment to him of income received by the trustees, he being willing to concur in an arrangement to pay costs (if satisfied that they were properly chargeable) out of corpus only.

*Held,* by the Vice-Chancellor, that the actions having been brought by the trustees without the concurrence or knowledge of the beneficiary, the costs were not chargeable against income. Secondly, the actions having been brought on the advice of counsel, costs were chargeable against corpus. Thirdly, the trustees must pay the plaintiff his cost of the present action.

This decision was reversed by the Court of Appeal on the first and third points, and affirmed on the second, but on the following grounds:

EARL OF SELBORNE L.C.: "I feel no doubt that the trustees acted bona fide and reasonably in bringing the actions. The property was peculiarly circumstanced, it was not large, but was available for building purposes, and anything done by tenants or neighbours which would give any other persons rights over it might cause a material depreciation in its value. The trustees therefore had an anxious duty to perform, which was not rendered less anxious by the course taken by the plaintiff. In 1872, he, being desirous of avoiding actions, gave the trustees an indemnity for not bringing any; but he afterwards changed his mind, withdrew the indemnity, and gave the trustees notice that he should

---

[13] *Ex p. Chippendale, Re German Mining Co.* (1854) 4 De G.M. & G. 19, 52; Trustee Act 1925, s.69(2); *R.W.G. Management Ltd.* v. *Commissioner of Corporate Affairs* [1985] V.R. 385; *McLean* v. *Burns Philp Trustee Co. Pty. Ltd.* [1985] 2 N.S.W.L.R. 623 (the right to indemnity will be excluded in unit trusts so as not to affect the marketability of units).

[14] [1985] S.T.C. 356, 363; [1985] 2 All E.R. 645, 652.

[15] See also *Rowley* v. *Ginnever* [1897] 2 Ch. 503; *Jennings* v. *Mather* [1902] 1 K.B. 1.

hold them liable if they did not take proper steps to protect the estate. Under these circumstances we ought to be clearly satisfied that the actions were improper before we reverse the decisions that the cost of them were properly payable out of the estate. I think, however, that the reason given in the decree for allowing them is not sufficient, and ought to be varied, because it states merely that they were commenced under the advice of counsel. Now, I cannot say that because an action is advised by counsel it is always and necessarily one which trustees may properly bring. The advice of counsel is not an absolute indemnity to trustees in bringing an action, though it may go a long way towards it. The actions were compromised before trial. That the result of the first action was beneficial to the estate is clear. Whether the estate was benefited by the second action is disputed, but I am disposed to think that it was. Looking at the whole circumstances, at the manifest bona fides of the trustees, and at the opinion of the Vice-Chancellor that the costs ought to be allowed, I am of opinion that the direction for payment of them out of the corpus must be sustained.

"Then as to the second appeal, the Vice-Chancellor has ordered the trustees to pay the costs up to the hearing. This is a severe order, which can only be justified by misconduct on their part, and I cannot find any misconduct which would justify it. The only thing urged against them is that they retained the cost of the actions out of the income, and they are alleged also to have insisted that the tenant for life should bear them. But did they so insist in any such way as to amount to misconduct? I think not. On referring to the correspondence, we find that the trustees before this action expressed themselves ready to concur in any reasonable arrangement as to the raising and paying the costs. Under these circumstances it would be very harsh to make them pay costs because they refused to part with the income until the costs of the former actions had been paid. If they had had no right to retain their costs out of the income the case would have stood very differently, and perhaps the Vice-Chancellor thought that they had not; but if he was of that opinion I cannot agree with him. The right of trustees to indemnity against all costs and expenses properly incurred by them in the execution of the trust is a first charge on all the trust property, both income and corpus. The trustees, therefore, had a right to retain the costs out of the income until provision could be made for raising them out of the corpus. I am of opinion that their costs of this action ought to be raised and paid out of the estate in the same way as the costs of the former actions."

## II. INDEMNITY AGAINST THE BENEFICIARY PERSONALLY

A trustee's right of indemnity in respect of expenses properly incurred—*e.g.* in respect of costs, a call on shares, solicitor's, stockbroker's or auctioneer's charges—is a right of indemnity against the trust *estate*, not *against* the beneficiary. Hence, the trustees of an ordinary club are entitled to be indemnified out of the club property, not by the club members,[16] unless, as is often the case, the club rules allow this. But in the following circumstances a trustee's indemnity extends beyond the estate to the *beneficiary* personally:

---

16 *Wise* v. *Perpetual Trustee Co.* [1903] A.C. 139.

First, where he (the trustee) accepted the trust at the request of the settlor who is also a beneficiary so as to raise an implied contract of indemnity[17] and secondly, where the beneficiary is a *sole* beneficiary *sui juris* and entitled absolutely[18] or there are *several* beneficiaries, provided they are *sui juris* and between them collectively entitled absolutely.[19] This can prove very useful where a trustee for such beneficiaries properly borrows money to carry out authorised trading or investing and the borrowings exceed the assets when things go dreadfully wrong as occurred in *J.W. Broomhead (Vic.) Pty. Ltd. (in liq.)* v. *J.W. Broomhead Pty. Ltd.*[20] where McGarvie J. held "where there are several beneficiaries entitled to separate benefits, a beneficiary who gets a proportion of the benefit of the property should bear that proportion of its burdens unless he can show why the trustee should bear the proportion of them himself." He further held that where a beneficiary is insolvent the loss in respect of his proportion falls on the trustee and not the other beneficiaries. He also accepted that "a request from a beneficiary to the trustee to assume the office of trustee or to incur liabilities obviously justifies the imposition of a personal liability to indemnify on the beneficiary and this should be so even if the beneficiary has only a limited interest."

## Section 11: Third Parties and Trustees

In carrying out the trusts or powers a trustee is personally liable for debts, contracts, torts or taxes arising in respect of his acts or omissions as trustee. After all, the trust property is not an entity that can be regarded as a person to be made liable. Having transferred his property, usually by way of gift, to the trustees the settlor has disappeared from the picture. The trustees are not agents for the beneficiaries nor are they in a partnership with them so there is no legal connection between the beneficiaries and any creditors.

As a matter of contract law a trustee and a third party may agree that the trustee may limit or exclude his personal liability and that the trustee shall pay the debt out of the trust property under his statutory right of indemnity.[21] The onus lies on the trustee to displace the strong

---

[17] *Ex p. Chippendale* (1854) 4 De G.M. & G. 19, 54; *Jervis* v. *Wolferstan* (1874) L.R. 18 Eq. 18 as explained by Lord Blackburn in *Fraser* v. *Murdoch* (1881) 6 App.Cas. 855, 872; *Matthews* v. *Ruggles-Brise* [1911] 1 Ch. 194. In that case it was also held that where a beneficiary is personally liable to indemnify his trustee, an assignment by him of his beneficial interest does not affect that liability as it stood at the date of the assignment.

[18] *Hardoon* v. *Belilios* [1901] A.C. 118.

[19] *Buchan* v. *Ayre* [1915] 2 Ch. 474, 477; *Re Reid* (1971) 17 D.L.R. (3d) 199. Often the two categories will overlap since X and Y may well ask A and B to hold property on trust for X and Y.

[20] [1985] V.R. 891, 936–939.

[21] *Muir* v. *City of Glasgow Bank* (1879) 4 App.Cas. 337, 355. It is possible for the trustee, if authorised, to go further and charge the trust property with payment of the debt: such an intention to create a charge is not likely to be inferred merely from an agreement that the creditor is to look to the trust property and not to the trustee for payment: *cf. Swiss Bank Corporation* v. *Lloyds Bank* [1980] 2 All E.R. 419, 426; affd. [1981] 2 All E.R. 449. See also Law Reform Committee's proposals at p. 750, *infra*.

presumption of personal liability so that contracting descriptively "as trustee" is not sufficient,[22] but contracting "as trustee and not otherwise" will suffice since the phrase would be meaningless if not excluding personal liability.[23]

Where a trustee does not pay a creditor out of his own moneys or out of trust moneys available under his statutory right of indemnity the creditor may have a claim by way of subrogation to the trustee's right of indemnity.[24] The problem is that the creditor's right is derivative: he stands in the shoes of the trustee and has no better right than the trustee.[25] Thus, for the creditor to be paid out of the trust assets he will need to show that the right of indemnity was not excluded by the trust instrument, that the debt was properly incurred in the authorised carrying-on of the trust, and that the state of accounts between the trustee and the beneficiaries (taking into account any losses caused by any breach of trust on the trustee's part) is such that there is some balance in the trustee's favour to which the right of indemnity may attach.[26] Where there are two or more trustees and one of them does not have a clear account (*e.g.* because of an outstanding claim against him for a breach of trust) the creditor can rely on the right to indemnity enjoyed by the other trustee.[27]

In addition to his proprietary right of indemnity, a trustee in some limited circumstances[28] may have a personal right of indemnity against a beneficiary personally. The right of subrogation in respect of the proprietary right of a trustee to an indemnity from the trust property arose out of the Court of Chancery's practice in administration of trust estates in an administration action. There was no similar practice for allowing a right of subrogation in respect of a trustee's right of indemnity against a beneficiary personally but, in principle, it seems there should be such a right of subrogation.

The protection afforded third parties by the personal liability of the trustee to the extent of his whole fortune disappears if the trustee is a worthless company and if no subrogation claim can be made whether against the trust assets or the beneficiaries who set up the trust or who between them are *sui juris* and absolutely entitled to the trust

---

22 *Watling* v. *Lewis* [1911] 1 Ch. 414, 424.
23 *Re Robinson's Settlement* [1912] 1 Ch. 717, 729; *Muir* v. *City of Glasgow Bank* (1879) 4 App.Cas. 337, 362.
24 *Re Johnson* (1880) 15 Ch.D. 548, 552; *Re Blundell* (1889) 44 Ch.D. 1, 11; *Vacuum Oil Pty. Ltd.* v. *Wiltshire* (1945) 72 C.L.R. 319, 325, 336; *Re Raybould* [1900] 1 Ch. 199. He may bring an action under R.S.C., Ord. 85, r. 2 (*supra*, p. 710) if a judgment against the trustee would be fruitless, *e.g.* if he seems insolvent.
25 *Ex p. Edmonds* (1862) 4 De G.F. & J. 488, 498; *Re Johnson* (*supra*).
26 See section 10, *supra*, p. 744.
27 *Re Frith* [1902] 1 Ch. 342, 346; "The indemnity is not to the trustees as a body but to each of the trustees. Each of them who has acted properly is entitled to be indemnified against the debts properly incurred by him in the performance of the trusts. The Court prevents a trustee from insisting upon that right unless he comes in with clear accounts; but if he comes in with clear accounts he is not the less entitled to be indemnified because he has a co-trustee who has run away with certain moneys. I am, of course, excluding the case where a trustee who has a clear account is responsible for a co-trustee who has not."
28 See section 10, *supra*, p. 747.

property. However, directors or "shadow" directors involved in the fraudulent or wrongful carrying on of business by the company may be made personally liable for all or any part of the debts and liabilities as the court may direct.[29] Criminal charges relating to deception, fraud or conspiracy may also be brought against those involved.

Where no subrogation claim lies because it is alleged that the trustee's statutory right of indemnity has been excluded under the general authorisation in section 69(2) of the Trustee Act, it seems clear that to the extent that the settlor is himself a beneficiary under the trust he will not be allowed to resist the subrogation claim.[30] In the case of other beneficiaries who are volunteers under the trust it may be that a court of equity will not permit the beneficiaries to invoke section 69(2) for ignoring the statutory right of indemnity in section 30(2) in order to perpetrate a fraud[31]: they should take the benefit and the burden.

If the trustee company had contractually excluded its personal liability by agreeing with the creditor that his debt should be paid only out of the trust property, but the trustee company was indebted to the beneficiaries for breach of trust so as to have no right of indemnity then the creditor can have no derivative subrogation claim. It can be argued,[32] however, that he should have a direct claim to be paid out of the trust property since from the outset there was no possibility of a derivative subrogation claim. From the outset the trustee company was not personally liable and so could have no personal claim against the trust property to which the creditor could be subrogated. Thus, the trustee company's power to pay the debt out of the trust property is not affected by the personal state of account between the trustee and the beneficiaries.

Any right against the trust property will be worthless if the trust property is worthless. If this is because it consists of borrowed money it may well be that the trustee company was wrongfully or fraudulently trading so that those involved therein may be personally liable[33] and may be liable to criminal charges. If any suit against the trustee company is worthless and the trust fund is empty and worthless because trust property has recently been distributed amongst the beneficiaries, it would seem that the creditor has "something very like a lien"[34] upon the trust property exercisable against the beneficiaries

---

[29] Insolvency Act 1986, ss.213, 214.
[30] See *Re Johnson* (1880) 15 Ch.D. 548, 550, *per* Jessel M.R.: "The trust assets having been devoted to carrying on the trade, it would not be right that the *cestui que* trust should get the benefit of the trade without paying the liabilities; therefore the court says to him 'You shall not set up a trustee who may be a man of straw and make him a bankrupt to avoid the responsibility of the assets for carrying on the trade': the court puts the creditors, so to speak, in the place of the trustee" *cf. Re Burroughs-Fowler* [1916] 2 Ch. 251, *supra*, p. 271 and *McLean* v. *Burns Philp Trustee Co. Pty. Ltd.* [1985] 2 N.S.W.L.R. 623, 641.
[31] See Chap. 2. *supra*, p. 56.
[32] Stone (1922) 22 Col.L.R. 527.
[33] Insolvency Act 1986, ss.213, 214. Beneficiaries may also be personally liable under *Hardoon* v. *Belilios* principles, *supra*, p. 747 and creditors may have a right of subrogation (*supra*, p. 748).
[34] *Ex p. Garland* (1803) 10 Ves.Jun. 111, 120, *per* Lord Eldon.

or, perhaps, a sufficient interest to enable him to bring a personal claim against the beneficiaries along the lines of the claim in *Ministry of Health* v. *Simpson*.[35]

Where a deceased's estate includes a business, special problems arise since it is necessary to consider not just the beneficiaries interested in the estate, but also the claims of creditors of the deceased and the claims of creditors of the business carried on by the deceased's executors. The applicable principles appear most clearly from a judgment of the High Court of Australia in *Vacuum Oil Company Pty. Ltd.* v. *Wiltshire, infra.*

In dealing with third parties, especially in borrowing money, it is useful if the trustees have power to create a charge over the trust *fund* (as distinct from particular assets happening at the time to be comprised in the trust fund) so to provide security for third parties. The Law Reform Committee (Cmnd. 8733) have discussed this issue as follows:

"2.20 . . . our conclusion is that where the trust is of such a kind that the trustees are likely to wish to engage in commercial operations such as large scale borrowing, the right solution would be for the trust deed to confer upon the trustees a power to create a charge upon the trust fund in favour of a creditor. The effect of such a charge would be to make the third party, in whose favour it was created, a *cestui que trust*. His rights as chargee would be analogous to those conferred by a floating charge, just as the rights of any other *cestui que trust* subsist in the assets from time to time comprised in the trust fund. The trustees would retain all their powers of dealing with the trust fund although they would, of course, have to exercise them with due regard for the interests of the chargee as of any other beneficiary.

2.21 We see no reason to doubt that a trust instrument could be so worded under the present law as to confer on trustees just the sort of power that we have in mind. Trustees can be, and frequently are, given power to appoint beneficial interests without consideration and we think it would in fact be possible to empower them to create beneficial interests for valuable consideration, the consideration being part of the trust fund in which the beneficial interest will thereafter subsist. However, because there is some doubt whether this would be permissible under the present law, we think that legislation is needed to make it clear that a power to create a charge upon the trust fund as a continuing entity can be conferred upon trustees by the trust deed, thus enabling them to give the maximum possible security to third parties. However, we do not think that the trustees of an existing trust should be able to make use of this new statutory provision: in our view it would not be right to allow the imposition of such a power on an existing trust where the settlor had not envisaged it would be needed. If the power is needed, it will always be possible for a trustee in this position to apply to the court under the Variation of Trusts Act 1958 . . .

---

[35] See pp. 549–556, *supra.* Trading via limited companies as trustees hardly happens in the U.K. so that the above solutions to the problems posed can only be proposed on principle rather than be propounded by precedents. For Australian literature see *Essays in Equity* (ed. P. Finn), Chap. 8; H. A. J. Ford (1981) 13 Melbourne U.L.R; D. R. Williams (1983) 57 A.L.J. 233; *Equity and Commercial Relationships* (P. Finn ed.), Chap. 3, and for Canada see *Equity, Fiduciaries and Trusts* (T. G. Youdan ed.), Chap. 8.

2.24 Whilst the form of any legislation following our report is, of course, a matter for Parliamentary Counsel to determine, we do not think that it should be necessary to define or in any way to limit the nature of the power that we envisage. The suggested new clause below, which is no doubt capable of a good deal of improvement, is intended simply to draw attention to the fact that trustees can, under existing law, be given the sort of powers we have in mind:

*Charges for value on trust funds*

(1) Where under the terms of any trust instrument the trustees have power to charge the trust fund or any part thereof (as distinct from any assets for the time being comprised in the trust fund) to secure obligations created by them for valuable consideration, the persons in whose favour such obligations are created shall take equitable interests in the trust fund or part with such priority and subject to such conditions and provisions as the trustees have power under the trust instrument and are expressed by the instrument creating the charge to create.

(2) Subject to subsection (4) of this section, a person in whose favour such a charge is created may require that
   (a) a memorandum of the charge be endorsed, written on or permanently annexed to the instrument creating the trust;
   (b) the instrument be produced to him by the person having the possession or custody thereof to prove that a sufficient memorandum has been placed thereon or annexed thereto.
   Without prejudice to any other manner in which persons dealing with trustees may acquire notice of such a charge, such memorandum shall, as respects priorities, be deemed to constitute actual notice to all persons and for all purposes of the matters therein stated.

(3) Subsections (5) and (6) of section 137 of the Law of Property Act 1925 shall apply in relation to any memorandum authorised by this section.

(4) Section 138 of the Law of Property Act 1925 (power to nominate a trust corporation to receive notices) shall apply for the purposes of this section with the omission of subsection (7), and the obligation imposed on the trust corporation by subsection (9) shall extend to any person authorised by the trustees to inspect and take copies of the register and notices held by the trust corporation."

## RE RAYBOULD

Chancery Division [1900] 1 Ch. 199, 69 L.J. Ch. 249

The surviving trustee and executor of a deceased's estate properly worked one of the testator's collieries. Earthworks caused a subsidence damaging the buildings and machinery of the adjoining owners, Roberts & Cooper. They obtained a judgment against the trustee for damages and costs. In the present proceedings they sought an order that this amount and costs be paid out of the testator's estate.

BYRNE J.: "The first question I have to consider is whether the same principle ought to be applied to the case of a trustee claiming a right to indemnity for liability for damages for a tort, as is applied to the simpler case of claims made against a trustee by ordinary business creditors, where they have been allowed the benefit of his right to indemnity, by proving directly against the assets: the kind of case of which *Dowse* v. *Gorton* [1891] A.C. 190 is a recent illustration. It has been argued that there is no authority to justify me in holding that, where damages have been recovered against a trustee in respect of a tort, the person so recovering can avail himself of the trustee's right to indemnity, and so go direct against the trust estate; but the authority of *Bennett* v. *Wyndham* (1862) 4 D.F. & J. 259 goes to shew that if a trustee in the course of the ordinary management of his testator's estate, either by himself or his agent, does some act whereby some third person is injured, and that third person recovers damages against the trustee in an action for tort, the trustee, if he has acted with due diligence and reasonably, is entitled to be indemnified out of his testator's estate. When once a trustee is entitled to be thus indemnified out of his trust estate, I cannot myself see why the person who has recovered judgment against the trustee should not have the benefit of this right to indemnity and go direct against the trust estate or the assets, as the case may be, just as an ordinary creditor of a business carried on by a trustee or executor has been allowed to do, instead of having to go through the double process of suing the trustee, recovering the damages from him and leaving the trustee to recoup himself out of the trust estate. I have the parties interested in defending the trust estate before me, and I have also the trustee, and he claims indemnity, and, assuming that a proper case for indemnifying him is made out by the evidence, I think his claim should be allowed.

"The next question I have to decide is whether this trustee has worked the colliery in such a way as to be entitled to be indemnified. Having considered all the evidence, I am not prepared to say that the injury done to the applicants' land was occasioned by reckless or improper working, or otherwise than by the ordinary and reasonable management of the colliery; and I therefore come to the conclusion that the trustee is entitled to be indemnified out of the assets against the damages and costs which he has been ordered to pay to Messrs. Roberts & Cooper. It follows, therefore, for the reasons already given, that Messrs. Roberts & Cooper are entitled to stand in the trustee's place for the purpose of obtaining this indemnity direct from this testator's estate. The result, therefore, is that this summons succeeds. . . . "

### VACUUM OIL COMPANY PTY. LTD. v. WILTSHIRE

High Court of Australia (1945) 72 C.L.R. 319

Questions arose as to the priority of the claims of creditors of a testator (such as Vacuum Oil) and creditors of the business carried on by the testator's executor, in the course of administration of the testator's bankrupt estate.

LATHAM C.J.: "In the first place I refer to the general principles of law which have been developed in relation to the rights and liabilities of the parties concerned when an executor carries on the business of his testator. These parties are the executor, the beneficiaries who claim under the will, the creditors of the testator (who may be called estate creditors) and the creditors to whom debts have been incurred in the course of trading by the executor (who may be called trading creditors).

"1. An executor is entitled (apart from any express authority given by the will) as against both beneficiaries and estate creditors to carry on the business of his testator for the purpose of realisation, but only for that purpose (*Collinson* v. *Lister* (1855) 20 Beav. 356). In respect of debts incurred by him in so carrying on the business he is personally liable to the trading creditors—

the debts are his debts, and not the debts of his testator (*Labouchere* v. *Tupper* (1857) 11 Moo.P.C. 198; *Ex p. Garland* (1804) 10 Ves. Jun. 110). But as against beneficiaries and both classes of creditors he is entitled to indemnity in respect of those debts out of the assets of the estate (*Dowse* v. *Gorton* [1891] A.C. 190 at 199).

"2. If an executor is authorised by the will to carry on the business not merely for the purpose of realisation, then it is still the case that debts incurred by him are his debts for which he is liable to the new creditors. The authority given by the testator is part of his disposition of his estate and binds beneficiaries under his will. Thus, as against the beneficiaries in such a case the executor is entitled to an indemnity against the new debts out of the assets of the estate which the testator authorised to be used for the purpose of carrying on the business and out of any assets acquired in the course of carrying on (*Ex p. Garland*).

"But the testator cannot by his will prejudice the rights of his own creditors (*Re Oxley* [1914] 1 Ch. 604 at 613). They may insist upon payment of the debts and upon realisation of the assets of the estate in due course in order to obtain payment, notwithstanding any provisions in the will with respect to the carrying on of the business. They can make the executor account upon the basis of the assets which came to his hands or which he has subsequently acquired as executor, leaving the new creditors to get such remedy as they can against the executor himself, but with the added right of subrogation to his indemnity against the estate—an indemnity which will be worth nothing if the old creditors exhaust the estate (*Dowse* v. *Gorton*).

"3. If an executor carries on a business otherwise than for the purpose of realisation and without authority given by the will of his testator, he acts at his own risk, the debts which he incurs are his debts, and he has no authority as against either beneficiaries or creditors to come upon the assets of the estate for the purpose of meeting them (*Labouchere* v. *Tupper*).

"4. But if a beneficiary actually authorises him to carry on the business, he is entitled as against that beneficiary to indemnity out of the estate in respect of the debts which, in the course of such carrying on, he incurs to the trading creditors. Similarly, if a creditor of the testator actually authorises him to carry on the business he is entitled as against that creditor to a similar indemnity, which in each case enures by subrogation for the benefit of the new creditors (*Dowse* v. *Gorton*).

"5. The position is the same if a creditor of the testator *actively* and positively *assents* to the executor carrying on the business, but it is not easy to determine, on the authorities, what kind of conduct should be held to amount to the necessary active and positive assent. The principle upon which the right of the executor in such a case to indemnity out of assets of the estate as against an estate creditor has been variously stated. In *Dowse* v. *Gorton* (at 208), Lord Macnaghten said: 'If the business is carried on by the executors at the instance of the creditors without regard to the terms of the will, the executors, I suppose, have the ordinary rights of agents against their principals.' In *Re Millard; Ex p. Yates* (1895) 72 L.T. 823, Smith L.J. referred to the words of Lord Macnaghten and applied the principle suggested by him. In the same case, however, Lord Esher M.R. pointed out that it could hardly be said that the executor in such a case was the agent of the creditors, because, if he were, the creditors would be undisclosed principals in the business and would be liable to new creditors for goods supplied to the business. The law, however, had held otherwise. Lord Esher took the view that the executor carrying on was in the position of a trustee for the creditors and that Lord Herschell in *Dowse* v. *Gorton* had based his judgment in that case upon the view that the executor was such a trustee. Upon either view the result followed that the executor was entitled to an indemnity as against the estate creditors—in one case the indemnity to which an agent is entitled against his principal and in the other case the indemnity which a *cestui que trust* is bound to give to his trustee against liabilities reasonably incurred in performing the trust—to use the words of Lord Esher M.R. in *Millard's* case.

"There are difficulties in adopting the theory of agency (as pointed out by Lord Esher) and there is no clear binding decision of any court (as distinct from *obiter dicta*) that the executor is a trustee in respect of creditors who have assented to the carrying on, but is not a trustee in the same sense with respect to creditors who have not assented to the carrying on.

"6. The principle which has been developed in the cases appears to be *sui generis*. It was decided in *Dowse* v. *Gorton* that knowledge by estate creditors that the business is being carried on otherwise than for purposes of realisation does not amount to such an assent as to entitle the executors to an indemnity out of assets of the estate as against those creditors. There must be something more than mere knowledge and inaction—more than 'standing by' with knowledge.

"7. But the principle which has been applied is not an example of the application of the equitable doctrine of acquiescence. A person may lose his rights by acquiescence, that is, by quiescence in such circumstances that assent to an infringement of his rights which is taking place may reasonably be inferred. Acquiescence is an instance of estoppel by words or conduct. (*De Bussche* v. *Alt* (1878) 8 Ch.D. 286 at 314). A person who so acquiesces is not allowed in equity to complain of the violation of his right because he has really induced the person infringing his right to pursue a course of action from which the latter person might otherwise have abstained. It is a condition, however, of the application of the doctrine of acquiescence that the person who acts in infringement of the right should be acting under a mistake as to his own rights. If he knows that he is infringing the right of another person he takes the risk of those rights being asserted against him (*Ramsden* v. *Dyson* (1866) L.R. 1 H.L. 129 at 141). Further, the person whose rights are infringed must know that the other person is acting under a mistaken belief (*Ramsden* v. *Dyson*; *Russell* v. *Watts* (1883) 25 Ch.D. 559 at 576). A case of acquiescence by an estate creditor in this sense in the executor trading might be made out in some cases. But there is no evidence of such acquiescence in the present case—no evidence of any such mistake or inducement—and I therefore set the equitable doctrine of acquiescence on one side.

"8. There is one other matter to which reference may be made before endeavouring to apply the law to the present case. In *Dowse* v. *Gorton*, Lord Macnaghten expressed the opinion that estate creditors could not claim the assets of the business which had been acquired after the death of the testator and then refuse the executors indemnity in respect of liabilities incurred in carrying on the business. If they so acted, it was said, they would be reprobating after approbating. The same view is expressed in *Re Oxley*, by Cozens-Hardy M.R. at 610 and by Buckley L.J. at 614. These observations were not necessary for the decision of either case, because Lord Macnaghten in *Dowse* v. *Gorton* and the majority in *Re Oxley* held that the creditors were not making any claim in respect of assets acquired subsequently to the death of the testator. I find much difficulty in reconciling these observations with the clearly established rule of law that assets acquired by an executor in carrying on the business of his testator are assets of the testator's estate in every respect in the same way as the testator's assets which came to the hands of the executor at the time of his testator's death. See the statement of the law by Herschell L.C. in *Dowse* v. *Gorton* (at 198) and the many cases cited in *Williams on Executors & Administrators* (11th ed., 1921), Vol. 2, 1271 *et seq.*, where the law is stated as it existed before the Administration of Estates Act 1925 (Imp.). When an estate creditor sues an executor for his debt or takes an administration order the assets upon which execution can be levied under a judgment *de bonis testatoris* or which can be administered in the suit are all the assets which the executor has obtained in his capacity as executor. A creditor so suing does not 'claim against' any particular part of the assets. He is entitled as of course to the application to estate liabilities of all the estate assets, including assets acquired after the death. He may not have known that the business had been carried on. It would be a remarkable thing if the result of such a creditor taking the only possible steps to compel payment of his debt should be that he must be taken to have assented to the carrying on so as to be postponed to the trading creditors.

"9. In the present case the testator's estate is being administered in bankruptcy under the provisions of section 155 of the Bankruptcy Act. It is clear that all the assets in the hands of the executor as executor will be administered and that no distinction will be drawn between assets which belonged to the testator and assets which have been subsequently acquired by the executor in the course of carrying on the business. Thus all the estate creditors in the present case are, simply because they have lodged proofs of debt, claiming against all the assets. If the *obiter dicta* in *Dowse* v. *Gorton* and *Oxley's* case to which I have referred were to be taken as accurately stating the relevant law the result would be that all the estate creditors, independently of any assent by them in fact to the business being carried on, would be treated as having assented on the ground that they could not 'approbate' the business being carried on by claiming the after-acquired assets, and 'reprobate' by refusing to allow the executor an indemnity out of those assets. If this were the law, then the result would be that all the estate creditors would be deemed to have assented because they have made claims to the satisfaction of which any assets in the executor's hands can be applied, even though some of them may have been completely unaware that the business had been carried on. The statements to which I have referred were not necessary for the decision of the cases mentioned and should not, I think, be regarded as an authoritative statement of the law.

"10. Strictly it would appear, the trading creditors, whose debts are owed only by the executor personally, should not be admitted as creditors in the administration under the Bankruptcy Act section 155 of the estate of the testator. They are not creditors of the testator's estate. But, as the executor may have a right of indemnity out of the estate assets in respect of the trading debts against some beneficiaries or some estate creditors, the trading creditors will be entitled to the benefit of his indemnity, and so will be entitled, through him, though not directly, to the application of estate assets to the satisfaction of their debts in priority to the claims of such beneficiaries or creditors. It is only in this way that the claims of trading creditors can come into consideration in these proceedings."

## PROBLEMS

1. David, Eric and Ferdinand are trustees of a fund whose portfolio of investments includes some 10,000 shares out of an issued 30,000 shares in a private company. The fund is held upon protective trusts for Ferdinand during his life and after his death for George and Harry equally. Ian, who is the trustees' solicitor, discussed with them the possibility of their acquiring a sufficient number of shares in the company to give them a majority holding. The trustees refused for though they had power to retain their existing shares they had no power to invest in further shares in any private companies. Ian told them that they had a chance of applying successfully to the court for such a power but the trustees considered that it would not be worth it. In consideration of Ian agreeing not to charge legal fees for his unbilled work for the preceding year they told Ian that if he wished he could personally go ahead and try to obtain control for himself for as far as they could see this could only enhance the value of the trust's shareholding.

Ian then acquired all the remaining shares in the company, disposed of some of its assets, reorganised the business and increased the value of the shares from £1 each to £4 each. In the meantime, Ferdinand had become bankrupt and David and Eric removed him from his trusteeship on the ground of his unfitness to act (without replacing him) and refused to apply any income for his benefit.

How far is Ian entitled to keep the profit on these transactions?

How far is the conduct of David and Eric legally justified?

Can Ferdinand call for the correspondence which passed between David and Eric, on the one hand, and Ian, on the other, relating to his removal from office and to the decision not to pay him any money?

2. Terence died having bequeathed all his residuary personalty to his executors and trustees upon trust for Arthur for life, remainder to Brian absolutely. A charging clause in the will authorised any executor or trustee thereof being a person engaged in any profession to be paid all usual professional charges for services performed in connection with proving the will and executing the trusts.

Advise the executors and trustees, who happen to be stockbrokers, as to the scope of the charging clause and their responsibilities towards Arthur and Brian in relation to:

   (i) the incidence of debts, expenses and legacies;
   (ii) some shares in a private company which form part of Terence's residuary personalty;
   (iii) a leasehold flat held on a lease with only seven years to run which is sub-let to a weekly tenant at £38 per week;
   (iv) a reversionary interest in a fund of personalty which is held on trust for Terence's mother (still alive) for life and thereafter for Terence absolutely.

3. David Rockechild is beneficially interested under a will trust of his grandfather who died on April 1, 1980. Sir Malcolm Place and Sir Frank Haddock are the trustees of the settlement (with the broadest possible powers of investment) currently holding investments worth about £600,000 upon trust for Alan Rockechild for life, with overriding power for the trustees to appoint that upon or before Alan Rockechild's death the capital be distributed to any one or more of Alan's children in such shares as the trustees in their absolute

discretion may think fit, but with remainder in default of appointment to Alan's three children, Brian, Charles and David equally if they attain 30 years of age.

The trustees have recently refused to pay an already agreed advancement of money to David in the following circumstances. David is a qualified pharmacist and he was offered the opportunity to buy his way into a good chemist's shop for £50,000. His father and the trustees recognised that this was a very worthwhile opportunity so arrangements were made for David to call upon the trustees to receive the moneys under an exercise of the statutory power of advancement and David gave three months' notice of leaving his present job.

When David arrived he was told that he would have to sign a particular document before he could have the moneys. Upon examining the document he discovered it to be a deed already signed by his father and his brothers consenting to certain share transactions carried out in 1981 and authorising the trustees to retain any profits made by them in respect of those transactions.

Apparently, at tea at the 1981 Annual General Meeting of Quickgains Ltd. attended by the trustees as representatives of the settlement, which had a not insubstantial shareholding, the trustees had obtained some information about some prospective profitable contracts, that might lead to a take-over bid in a year or so, from one of the directors who was an old friend of theirs. The trustees discussed this information with Alan, Brian and Charles (for David, then aged 15 years and the youngest son by 5 years, was away at boarding school) and they all agreed that it would be worth risking investing a further £20,000 (but no more) of trust moneys in the company and that the trustees could spend as much of their moneys as they wished once the £20,000 trust moneys had been invested.

The trustees invested the £20,000 and then their own moneys and the shares had quadrupled in value between 1981 and 1986 when the trust shareholding was sold upon the written advice of the trust's stockbrokers.

When pressed by David the trustees refused to disclose how much of their own moneys had been invested in Quickgains Ltd., how much profit they had made or when or if they had sold their shares. The trustees merely pointed out that David should be very grateful for the profits which they had enabled the trust to make. However, David refused to sign the deed whereupon the trustees refused to advance any moneys to him. They also pointed out that if he did not be sensible like his father and his brothers and sign the deed, then it might well be that the power of appointment might be exercised in a way that might not be favourable to him. Two days later David received a letter from his father saying that as the father's personal circumstances had changed he was no longer prepared to consent to any advancement being made to David. Instructing solicitors imagine that the trustees put the father up to this.

Consider what courses of action may be available to David.

4. Theo died recently, leaving a will which states: "I leave my ordinary shares in Splendiferous Ltd. to such of my sons Roger and Saul as shall attain 30 years of age. I leave my residuary estate (after payment of debts expenses and taxes) to my executors Alan and Brian upon trust for Lucy for life remainder to Roger and Saul absolutely."

His residuary estate consists of 2,000 Barclays Bank p.l.c. shares, 1,000 preference shares in Splendiferous Ltd., an unquoted private company, a freehold house, Coseynook, a 21 year lease (with 14 years unexpired) of a cottage, Seaview, sublet on a yearly tenancy at £1,000 p.a., and some cash.

Lucy, Roger and Saul are aged 55, 21 and 17 years respectively.

Advise Alan and Brian how they should deal with the above assets and the income therefrom. Is there any way in which they can transfer capital to Lucy, Roger or Saul or sell Coseynook to Alan?

5. In September 1987 Tim died, bequeathing his coin collection and £300,000 to his executor and trustee, Eric, on trust for his widow for life, remainder to his children Alan, Brian and Charles equally. The children were then aged 30, 25 and 15 years respectively. Since then, Charles has become mentally handicapped as a result of a road accident. The will contained various administrative provisions including wide powers of investment.

Although Eric was himself an experienced investor, upon winding up Tim's estate in February 1988 he gave the £300,000 for investment to Whizz Kid & Co. which specialises in discretionary portfolio management for clients and for itself. Eric signed the Company's current Customer Agreement in 1988. Its terms enable the Company *inter alia* to sell its own shares to the trust at a price no higher than that generally available at the time and to purchase for itself the trust's shares at a price no lower than that generally available at the time and provide that the Company shall not be liable for any loss arising from its negligence. The Company reports back to Eric every six months and follows his instructions concerning going for higher income or for greater capital growth.

The investments are now only worth £150,000. At the end of 1988 the Company sold £30,000 of its own ABC plc shares to the trust and these shares are now only worth £5,000. In 1989 the Company bought from the trust for £20,000 XYZ plc shares now worth £80,000. About £75,000 of the loss is due to the negligence of Jason, an employee of the Company, who is addicted to cocaine. He is the son of the managing director of the Company who knew about Jason's addiction but did not tell Jason's immediate superior about it.

A year ago Eric gave the coin collection to Donald, an apparently reputable dealer in coins, to sell as soon as someone was found prepared to pay about £25,000 for the collection. At first Eric phoned Donald every new month to see if a purchaser had materialised. After four months Donald told Eric not to bother phoning because he would phone Eric if a sale occurred. Last week Eric tried to phone Donald and discovered that Donald had sold the collection for £22,500 six months ago, had used the proceeds in his business and then been made bankrupt a month ago.

Advise Tim's widow, who would also like to have the trust property sold up and its proceeds divided between her and her children.

# Chapter 10

# LIABILITY FOR BREACH OF TRUST

THIS chapter is concerned with the personal liability of a trustee for breach of trust. In some circumstances the beneficiaries may have an equitable proprietary tracing remedy against trust property and its product in the hands of all but a bona fide purchaser for value of the legal interest without notice of the trust.[1] Then the beneficiaries seem to be able to choose whether to sue the trustees or trace against the person in possession of the property.[2] If the beneficiaries choose to sue the trustees, *e.g.* because the trustees are responsible, wealthy people it would seem in principle that if the trustees' breach of trust was innocent, (*e.g.* a mistake of law as in *Re Diplock*), they should be subrogated to the beneficiaries' rights and recoup what they have paid from the person possessing the property which the beneficiaries could have traced, so as to prevent the unjust enrichment of such person.[3]

## Section 1. The Test of Liability

A trustee is liable for a breach of trust if he fails to do what his duty as trustee requires or if he does what as trustee he is not entitled to do. As Lindley L.J. stated,[4] "The conduct of trustees ought to be regarded with reference to the facts and circumstances existing at the time when they had to act and which were known or ought to have been known by them at the time." Breaches may be grossly fraudulent or innocently technical.[5] A beneficiary must prove a causal connection between the breach of duty and the resulting loss: there is no principle that once a breach of duty is shown the burden falls on the defaulting trustee to show that the loss did not result from the breach.[6] "A trustee is not a surety nor is he an insurer; he is only liable for some wrong done by himself, and loss of trust money is not *per se* proof of such wrong."[7]

It will be necessary to see if the trust instrument contains any clause qualifying the extent of the trustee's duties or otherwise exempting him from liability unless guilty of some dishonesty. Any such clause is strictly construed against any trustee attempting to rely upon it.[8]

---

[1] See Chap. 7, section 5.
[2] Denning J. (as he then was) in (1949) 65 L.Q.R. at p. 44.
[3] *Cf. Eaves* v. *Hickson* (1861) 30 Beav. 136; Goff & Jones (3rd ed.), p. 128, favouring recovery unless the recipient can rely on change of position or estoppel or the payment was in satisfaction of an honest claim. s.61 of the Trustee Act may protect trustees.
[4] *Re Chapman* [1986] 2 Ch. 763, 774.
[5] For these latter breaches relief may be available under the Trustee Act 1925, s.61, *infra*, p. 781.
[6] *Re Miller's Deed Trusts* [1978] L.S.Gaz. 454.
[7] *Re Hurst* (1892) 67 L.T. 96, 99.
[8] *Brumridge* v. *Brumridge* (1858) 27 Beav. 5; *Re Brier* (1884) 26 Ch.D. 238; *Bartlett* v. *Barclays Bank Trust Co. Ltd.* [1980] 1 All E.R. 139, 154. See p. 716, *supra*.

The major problem will often be in ascertaining whether in all the circumstances the trustee exhibited that degree of reasonable care required of a prudent man of business,[9] a higher standard it seems being required in the case of a paid professional trustee unless altered by the trust instrument.[10] Paid trustees usually ensure that the trust instrument is so drawn up that they can only be liable in the most extreme cases, *e.g.* if actual dishonesty is involved.

Problems can arise where there is a link between a family trust and a family company or between a company pension fund trust and the company.[11] First, one must ascertain whether the family trust or pension fund had power to lend money to the company and then whether it was proper to exercise such a power, especially if the interest rate is authorised to be well below market rates. Then, one must ask for how long was it proper to leave outstanding such debt at such interest? If the trustees are also directors of the company there will be quite a conflict of interest. Even if the trustees are independent what are they to do if, *e.g.* the family trust has a significant shareholding in the family company, which also employs some of the beneficiaries' and some of the beneficiaries' parents, and where not calling in the debt might either see the company through a difficult period or lose the debt on the company's subsequent liquidation, whilst calling in the debt might occasion some benefit to the trust in obtaining the money but might precipitate events leading to liquidation of the company?

At least in the case of leaving a debt outstanding the Trustee Act 1925, s.15(*e*) affords some protection.[12] More problems can arise where the trust does not sell shares in the company for fear of encouraging others to sell so that the trust is left with shares with minimal value after many others have sold, or where the trust has continually bought shares in the company from prospective vendors in order to try to keep up the company's share price and the creditworthiness of the company and of the trust (which may have borrowed on the security of the shares).

*Evans* v. *London Co-operative Society*[13] is an interesting, though inadequately reported, case. The London Co-operative Society Ltd. was a trustee of the London Co-operative Society Ltd. Employees' Superannuation Fund. Under a 1933 rule of the Fund, "The moneys from time to time in the hands of the Trustees upon the Trusts hereof, and not presently required for making any payment pursuant thereto,

---

9 "There is no rule of law which compels the Court to hold that an honest trustee is liable to make good loss sustained by retaining an authorised security in a falling market if he did so prudently and honestly in the belief it was the best course to take in the interests of all parties": *Re Chapman* [1896] Ch. 763, 776.

10 *Re Waterman's W.T.* [1952] 2 All E.R. 1054, 1055; *Bartlett* v. *Barclays Bank Trust Co.* [1980] 1 All E.R. 139, 152.

11 *Evans* v. *London Co-operative Society, The Times*, July 6, 1976; *Re Hurst* (1892) 67 L.T. 96; *Ward* v. *Ward* (1843) 2 H.L.Cas. 777, 784.

12 See p. 680, *supra.*

13 *The Times*, July 6, 1976.

shall, if and so far as the Society shall be willing to accept the same, be advanced to the Society by way of loan repayable on demand and carrying interest at such rate as may be agreed upon by the Society and the Pension Committee, providing that it be not less than 3³/₄ per cent. per annum and the Society may at any time pay off any moneys so advanced, and any moneys which the society shall be unwilling to accept on loan may be invested in any investments permitted by law to trustees." The Society borrowed all available moneys (in the region of 10 million pounds) at 3³/₄ per cent.

Brightman J. held that the rule empowered the Society to borrow money from the Fund (and therefore make a profit from use of such money though being a trustee) at a rate of interest (which could be less than the market rate) genuinely agreed between the Society and the Pensions Committee but there had to be a properly negotiated agreement. The Committee members had never directed their minds towards considering how they should exercise their discretion since they thought they were forced to accept the 3³/₄ per cent. rate unless they could persuade the Society out of the goodness of its heart to raise the rate or not to borrow the moneys so that other more profitable investments could be made. Thus, the Committee was in breach of trust and the Society had fully participated therein since its Board knew precisely what was happening. Therefore, the Society had to compensate the Fund by making up the difference between the 3³/₄ per cent. it had paid and a proper rate of interest which the learned judge considered to be 5 per cent. for 1956–64 inclusive, 6 per cent. for 1965–67 inclusive and 7 per cent. for 1968–69 inclusive. He did not consider that it was the *Wallersteiner* v. *Moir (No. 2)*[14] sort of case where a full commercial rate of interest should be presumed to have been obtained and therefore debited against the defendant.

### Liability for Co-trustees

Here, apart from miscellaneous instances, the cases seem to revolve mainly around four sets of circumstances in which a trustee is guilty of an act or a default prejudicial to the trust:

1. If he leaves a matter in the hands of his co-trustee without inquiry.[15]

2. If he stands by while a breach of trust, of the facts of which he is cognisant, is being committed by his co-trustee.[16] In the words of Lord Cottenham in *Styles* v. *Guy*,[17] it is the duty of executors and trustees "to watch over, and, if necessary, to correct, the conduct of each other."

3. If he allows trust funds to remain in the sole control of his co-trustee.[18] "The duty of trustees," said Kay J. in *Re Flower*,[19] "is to

---

14 [1975] Q.B. 373; see p. 780, *infra*.
15 *Wynne* v. *Tempest* (1897) 13 T.L.R. 360; *Second East Dulwich* (1899) 68 L.J.Ch. 196; *Re Lucking's W.T.* [1968] 1 W.L.R. 866.
16 *Booth* v. *Booth* (1838) 1 Beav. 125; *Gough* v. *Smith* [1872] W.N. 18.
17 (1849) 1 Mac. & G. 422, 433.
18 *Williams* v. *Higgins* (1868) 17 L.T. 525; *Lewis* v. *Nobbs* (1878) 8 Ch.D. 591.
19 (1884) 27 Ch.D. 592, 597.

prevent one of themselves having the exclusive control over the money, and certainly not, by any act of theirs, to enable one of themselves to have the exclusive control of it."

4. Apparently also if, becoming aware of a breach of trust committed or contemplated by his co-trustee, he takes no steps to obtain redress.[20]

The general principle of these decisions in which a trustee is held liable for a breach of trust when the active hand was not his own, but that of his co-trustee, appears to be that he is *himself* guilty of an act or a default prejudicial to the trust. It is in fact a rule of equity that a trustee is not automatically vicariously liable for the acts or defaults of his co-trustee: he is liable for *his own* acts or defaults, *his own* acts of commission *or of omission*; for in the eye of equity there is no difference in substance between an active and a passive breach of trust.[21] But the rule seems always to have been a somewhat poor measure of protection, for a trustee himself can be guilty, in many unsuspected ways, of an act or a default which in the eye of equity constitutes a breach of trust. It is only an *exceptionally strong* protective clause in the instrument of trust which will keep him outside the range of equitable liability.[22]

A trustee is not liable for breach of trust merely by retiring from the trust in circumstances in which he is aware that his retirement will facilitate the commission of a breach of trust by his successor in office. To make him liable in such a case it must be shown that he retired *with the object of* facilitating that breach of trust which was in fact committed by his successor.[23]

The question now arises whether legislation has affected the law represented by the cases cited above. Section 30(1) of the Trustee Act 1925 provides, "A trustee shall be chargeable only for money and securities actually received by him notwithstanding his signing any receipt for the sake of conformity, and shall be answerable and accountable only for his own acts, receipts, neglects or defaults, and not for those of any other trustee, nor for any banker, broker or other person with whom any trust money or securities may be deposited, nor for the insufficiency or deficiency of any securities nor for any other loss, *unless the same happens through his own wilful default.*" Prima facie section 30 of the Act of 1925 (replacing s.31 of the 1859 Act) diminishes the area of equitable liability. Against this, however, it is arguable, first, that since the statute was not pleaded in any of the cases which were decided after 1859—with the exception of *Re Munton*[24]—the reason must presumably have been that it would not have made any difference if it had been pleaded. Secondly, there is in

---

[20] *Boardman* v. *Mosman* (1779) 1 Bro.C.C. 68; *Wilkins* v. *Hogg* (1861) 8 Jur. 25, 26.
[21] See Lord Langdale's observations in *Ghost* v. *Waller* (1846) 9 Beav. 497, 499, 500.
[22] See *Wilkins* v. *Hogg* (1861) 8 Jur. 25; *Pass* v. *Dundas* (1880) 43 L.T. 665, *supra*, p. 716.
[23] *Head* v. *Gould* [1898] 2 Ch. 250; *Kingdom* v. *Castleman* (1877) 36 L.T. 141.
[24] [1927] 1 Ch. 262.

*Re Brier*[25] a statement of Lord Selbourne on section 31 of the Act of 1859 which appears (so far) to settle the matter: "The statute incorporated, generally, into instruments creating trusts the common indemnity clause which was usually inserted in such instruments. *It does not substantially alter the law as it was administered by courts of equity.*" Section 31 of the Act of 1859 was in fact merely a reproduction of the common indemnity clause, which was present in many of the cases cited above, but seems to have been a poor measure of protection: so poor, indeed, that one is tempted to believe that its practical value lay in beguiling a prospective trustee into accepting the trust. A good example will be found in *Underwood* v. *Stevens*,[26] where a clause in a will which provided that the executor-trustees should not be responsible for any loss unless it occurred through their "wilful default" was not even *mentioned* in a judgment which made one of the executor-trustees liable for a breach of trust in having, in good faith, allowed trust funds to be in the sole control of his co-executor-trustee; *and* notwithstanding misrepresentations by that co-executor-trustee as to the circumstances attending the transactions in question. It appears true to say, in fact, that the common indemnity clause did not shield a trustee from the passive innocent breach of trust; and if all that the statute has done is to incorporate the clause into instruments of trust, it would seem to follow that the general law is unaltered.[27]

However, the interpretation put upon the expression "wilful default" in *Re Vickery*[28] as meaning a consciousness of committing a breach of duty or a recklessness as to whether or not a breach was being committed turns the scales in favour of trustees where losses occur within section 30 of the Trustee Act 1925.[29] It is doubtful whether such an interpretation will stand a determined onslaught in future litigation as the interpretation is based on company law cases and is out of line with the pre-1925 trust cases which establish that "wilful default includes want of ordinary prudence."[30]

Most surprisingly, the Law Reform Committee,[31] without referring to the criticism of the *Re Vickery* interpretation of "wilful default," expressed themselves satisfied with the "wilful default" test saying: "A trustee should be liable for loss caused by the actions of another where the trustee has connived at those actions in some way: in other words where his default has been wilful." This view that a trustee shall only be liable for his own wilful default in conniving at (*i.e.* at least turning a blind eye to) the other's actions not only ignores well-documented

---

[25] (1884) 26 Ch.D. 238, 243.
[26] (1816) 1 Mer. 712.
[27] See Bogert (1921) 34 Harvard L.R. 483, 496; *supra*, pp. 636–638.
[28] [1931] 1 Ch. 572; *supra*, p. 645.
[29] "Nor for any other loss" is restrictively interpreted under the *eiusdem generis* rule to losses involving persons with whom trust money or securities are deposited; *Re Lucking's W.T.* [1968] 1 W.L.R. 866.
[30] *Re Chapman* [1896] 2 Ch. 763, 776, *per* Lindley L.J.; Gareth Jones (1959) 22 M.L.R. 381, p. 770, *infra*; J. Stannard [1979] Conv. 345.
[31] Cmnd. 8733, paras. 4.10, 4.15 criticised by C. T. Emery (1983) 133 New L.J. 1096.

criticism but is inconsistent with the Committee's recommendations that a trustee should be responsible for his agent's defaults unless he took the care of a prudent businessman (*e.g.* in taking reasonable steps to ensure that the agent's work was done competently).

Trustees liable for a breach of trust are liable jointly and severally. This means that the beneficiaries may call upon any two of the trustees jointly, or any one of them severally (separately), to discharge the liability.[32]

Ordinarily, between trustees who are jointly and severally liable for a breach of trust there is a right of contribution.[33] That is, as between the trustees themselves the liability must be shared. But where there "has existed a relation between a trustee and his co-trustee which will justify the court in treating his co-trustee as solely liable"—as where he acted under the *guidance* of his *solicitor* co-trustee—or where his co-trustee "has himself got the benefit of the breach of trust," a right of *indemnity* against that co-trustee comes into play. That is, as between the trustee and his co-trustee the former can, in these special circumstances, shift the entire liability onto the shoulders of his co-trustee. Contribution and indemnity are thus mutually exclusive; contribution between trustees exists ordinarily: indemnity between them arises only in special circumstances.[34]

## BARTLETT v. BARCLAYS BANK TRUST CO. LTD.

Chancery Division [1980] Ch. 515; [1980] 1 All E.R. 139

The plaintiff sued the trustees for failing to exercise proper supervision over the management of a family company, "BTL," which they controlled through having a 99.8 per cent. shareholding. Subsequently BTL became a wholly-owned subsidiary of "BTH" which the trustees controlled through a 99.8 per cent. shareholding. The trustees' failure to supervise BTL and then BTH led to the company losing over £½ million in a disastrous property speculation.

BRIGHTMAN J.: "The situation may be summed up as follows. BTH made a large loss as a result of the involvement of itself and BTL in the Old Bailey project. This loss reduced the value of the BTH shares and thereby caused a loss to the trust fund of the 1920 settlement. The bank, had it acted in time, could by reason of its shareholding have stopped the board of BTL embarking on the Old Bailey project; and, had it acted in time, could have stopped the board of BTL and later the board of BTH (it is unnecessary to differentiate) from continuing with the project; and could, had it acted in time, have required BTH to sell its interest in Far [a company interested in the Old Bailey site] to Stock Conversion on the no-loss or small-loss terms which (as I find) were available for the asking. This would not have necessitated the draconian course of threatening to remove, or actually removing, the board in favour of compliant directors. The members of the board were reasonable persons, and would (as I find) have followed any reasonable policy desired by the bank had

---

[32] See *Edwards* v. *Hood-Barrs* [1905] 1 Ch. 20; *Re Ingham* (1885) 52 L.T. 714.
[33] See p. 797, *infra*.
[34] See p. 797, *infra*.

the bank's wishes been indicated to the board. The loss to the trust fund could have been avoided (as I find) without difficulty or disruption had the bank been prepared to lead, in a broad sense, rather than to follow.

"What, then was the duty of the bank and did the bank fail in its duty? It does not follow that because a trustee could have prevented a loss it is therefore liable for the loss. The questions which I must ask myself are: (1) what was the duty of the bank as the holder of 99.8 per cent. of the shares of BTL and BTH? (2) was the bank in breach of duty in any and if so what respect? (3) if so, did that breach of duty cause the loss which was suffered by the trust estate? (4) if so, to what extent is the bank liable to make good that loss? In approaching these questions, I bear in mind that the attack on the bank is based, not on wrongful facts, but on wrongful omissions, that is to say, non-feasance not misfeasance.

"The cases establish that it is the duty of a trustee to conduct the business of the trust with the same care as an ordinary prudent man of business would extend towards his own affairs: see *Re Speight*[35] per Jessel M.R. and Bowen L.J. (affirmed on appeal[36] and see Lord Blackburn[37]). In applying this principle, Lindley L.J. added in *Re Whiteley*[38]:

> '. . . care must be taken not to lose sight of the fact that the business of the trustee, and the business which the ordinary prudent man is supposed to be conducting himself, is the business of investing money for the benefit of persons who are to enjoy it at some future time, and not for the sole benefit of the person entitled to the present income. The duty of a trustee is not to take such care only as a prudent man would take if he had only himself to consider; the duty rather is to take such care as an ordinary prudent man would take if he were minded to make an investment for the benefit of other people for whom he felt morally bound to provide. That is the kind of business the ordinary prudent man is supposed to be engaged in; and unless this is borne in mind the standard of a trustee's duty will be fixed too low; lower than it has ever yet been fixed, and lower certainly than the House of Lords or this court endeavoured to fix it in *Speight* v. *Gaunt*.'[39]

On appeal Lord Watson added[40]:

> 'Business men of ordinary prudence may, and frequently do, select investments which are more or less of a speculative character; but it is the duty of a trustee to confine himself to the class of investments which are permitted by the trust, and likewise to avoid all investments of that class which are attended with hazard.'

That does not mean that the trustee is bound to avoid all risk and in effect act as an insurer of the trust fund: in *Re Godfrey*[41] Bacon V.-C. said:

> 'No doubt it is the duty of a trustee, in administering the trusts of a will, to deal with property entrusted into his care exactly as any prudent

---

[35] (1883) 22 Ch.D. 727 at 739, 762.
[36] (1883) 9 App.Cas. 1.
[37] 9 App.Cas. 1 at 19.
[38] (1886) 33 Ch.D. 347, 355.
[39] (1883) 22 Ch.D. 727, 9 App.Cas. 1.
[40] (1887) 12 App.Cas. 727 at 733.
[41] (1883) 23 Ch.D. 483 at 493.

man would deal with his own property. But the words in which the rule is expressed must not be strained beyond their meaning. Prudent businessmen in their dealings incur risk. That may and must happen in almost all human affairs.'

The distinction is between a prudent degree of risk on the one hand, and hazard on the other. Nor must the court be astute to fix liability on a trustee who has committed no more than an error of judgment, from which no business man, however prudent, can expect to be immune: in *Re Chapman*[42] Lopes L.J. said:

> 'A trustee who is honest and reasonably competent is not to be held responsible for a mere error in judgment when the question which he has to consider is whether a security of a class authorised, but depreciated in value, should be retained or realised, provided he acts with reasonable care, prudence, and circumspection.'

"If the trust had existed without the incorporation of BTL, so that the bank held the freehold and leasehold properties and other assets of BTL directly on the trusts of the settlement, it would in my opinion have been a clear breach of trust for the bank to have hazarded trust money in the Old Bailey development project in partnership with Stock Conversion. The Old Bailey project was a gamble, because it involved buying into the site at prices in excess of the investment values of the properties, with no certainty or probability, with no more than a chance, that planning permission could be obtained for a financially viable redevelopment, that the numerous proprietors would agree to sell out or join in the scheme, that finance would be available on acceptable terms, and that the development would be completed, or at least become a marketable asset, before the time came to start winding up the trust. However one looks at it, the project was a hazardous speculation on which no trustee could properly have ventured without explicit authority in the trust instrument. I therefore hold that the entire expenditure in the Old Bailey project would have been incurred in breach of trust, had the money been spent by the bank itself. The fact that it was a risk acceptable to the board of a wealthy company like Stock Conversion has little relevance.

"I turn to the question, what was the duty of the bank as the holder of shares in BTL and BTH? I will first answer this question without regard to the position of the bank as a specialist trustee, to which I shall advert later. The bank, as trustee, was bound to act in relation to the shares and to the controlling position which they conferred, in the same manner as a prudent man of business. The prudent man of business will act in such manner as is necessary to safeguard his investment. He will do this in two ways. If facts come to his knowledge which tell him that the company's affairs are not being conducted as they should be, or which put him on enquiry, he will take appropriate action. Appropriate action will no doubt consist in the first instance of enquiry of and consultation with the directors, and in the last but most unlikely resort, the convening of a general meeting to replace one or more directors. What the prudent man of business will *not* do is to content himself with the receipt of such information on the affairs of the company as a shareholder ordinarily receives at annual general meetings. Since he has the

---

power to do so, he will go further and see that he has sufficient information to enable him to make a responsible decision from time to time either to let matters proceed as they are proceeding, or to intervene if he is dissatisfied. This topic was considered by Cross J. in *Re Lucking's Will Trusts*.[43] In that case nearly 70 per cent. of the shares in the company were held by two trustees, L and B, as part of the estate of the deceased; about 29 per cent. belonged to L in his own right, and 1 per cent. belonged to L's wife. The directors in 1954 were Mr. and Mrs. L and D, who was the manager of the business. In 1956 B was appointed trustee to act jointly with L. The company was engaged in the manufacture and sale of shoe accessories. It had a small factory employing about 20 people, and one or two travellers. It also had an agency in France. D wrongfully drew some £15,000 from the company's bank account[44] in excess of his remuneration, and later became bankrupt. The money wa lost. Cross J. said this:

> 'The conduct of the defendant trustees is, I think, to be judged by the standard applied in *Speight* v. *Gaunt*,[45] namely, that a trustee is only bound to conduct the business of the trust in such a way as an ordinary prudent man would conduct a business of his own. Now, what steps, if any, does a reasonably prudent man who finds himself a majority shareholder in a private company take with regard to the management of the company's affairs? He does not, I think, content himself with such information as to the management of the company's affairs as he is entitled to as shareholder, but ensures that he is represented on the board. He may be prepared to run the business himself as managing director or, at least, to become a non-executive director while having the business managed by someone else. Alternatively, he may find someone who will act as his nominee on the board and report to him from time to time as to the company's affairs. In the same way, as it seems to me, trustees holding a controlling interest ought to ensure so far as they can that they have such information as to the progress of the company's affairs as directors would have. If they sit back and allow the company to be run by the minority shareholder and receive no more information than shareholders are entitled to, they do so at their risk if things go wrong.'

"I do not understand Cross J. to have been saying that in every case where trustees have a controlling interest in a company it is their duty to ensure that one of their number is a director or that they have a nominee on the board who will report from time to time on the affairs of the company. He was merely outlining convenient methods by which a prudent man of business (as also a trustee) with a controlling interest in a private company, can place himself in a position to make an informed decision whether any action is appropriate to be taken for the protection of his asset. Other methods may be equally satisfactory and convenient, depending on the circumstances of the individual case. Alternatives which spring to mind are the receipt of the copies of the agenda and minutes of board meetings if regularly held, the receipt of monthly management accounts in the case of a trading concern, or quarterly

---

[43] [1968] 1 W.L.R. 866.
[44] [1968] 1 W.L.R. 866 at 874–875.
[45] (1883) 22 Ch.D. 727.

reports. Every case will depend on its own facts. The possibilities are endless. It would be useless, indeed misleading, to seek to lay down a general rule. The purpose to be achieved is not that of monitoring every move of the directors, but of making it reasonably probable, so far as circumstances permit, that the trustee (or as in *Re Lucking's Will Trusts*[46]) one of them will receive an adequate flow of information in time to enable the trustees to make use of their controlling interest should this be necessary for the protection of their trust asset, namely the shareholding. The obtaining of information is not an end in itself, but merely a means of enabling the trustees to safeguard the interests of their beneficiaries.

"The principle enunciated in *Re Lucking's Will Trusts* appears to have been applied in *Re Miller's Deed Trusts* decided by Oliver J. No transcript of the judgment is available but the case is briefly noted in a journal of the Law Society.[47] There are also a number of American decisions proceeding on the same lines, to which counsel has helpfully referred me.

"So far, I have applied the test of the ordinary prudent man of business. Although I am not aware that the point has previously been considered, except briefly in *Re Waterman's Will Trusts*,[48] I am of opinion that a higher duty of care is plainly due from someone like a trust corporation which carries on a specialised business of trust management. A trust corporation holds itself out in its advertising literature as being above ordinary mortals. With a specialist staff of trained trust officers and managers, with ready access to financial information and professional advice, dealing with and solving trust problems day after day, the trust corporation holds itself out, and rightly, as capable of providing an expertise which it would be unrealistic to expect and unjust to demand from the ordinary prudent man or woman who accepts, probably unpaid and sometimes reluctantly from a sense of family duty, the burdens of trusteeship. Just as, under the law of contract, a professional person possessed of a particular skill is liable for breach of contract if he neglects to use the skill and experience which he professes, so I think that a professional corporate trustee is liable for breach of trust if loss is caused to the trust fund because it neglects to exercise the special care and skill which it professes to have. The advertising literature of the bank was not in evidence (other than the scale of fees) but counsel for the bank did not dispute that trust corporations, including the bank, hold themselves out as possessing a superior ability for the conduct of trust business, and in any event I would take judicial notice of that fact. Having expressed my view of the higher duty required from a trust corporation, I should add that the bank's counsel did not dispute the proposition.

"In my judgment the bank wrongfully and in breach of trust neglected to ensure that it received an adequate flow of information concerning the intentions and activities of the boards of BTL and BTH. It was not proper for the bank to confine itself to the receipt of the annual balance sheet and profit and loss account, detailed annual financial statements and the chairman's report and statement, and to attendance at the annual general meetings and the luncheons that followed, which were the limits of the bank's regular sources of information. Had the bank been in receipt of more frequent information it would have been able to step in and stop, and ought to have

---

[46] [1968] 1 W.L.R. 866.
[47] [1978] L.S.Gaz. 454.
[48] [1952] 2 All E.R. 1054.

stopped, Mr Roberts and the board embarking on the Old Bailey project. That project was imprudent and hazardous and wholly unsuitable for a trust whether undertaken by the bank direct or through the medium of its wholly owned company. Even without the regular flow of information which the bank ought to have had, it knew enough to put it on enquiry. There were enough obvious points at which the bank should have intervened and asked questions. Assuming, as I do, that the questions would have been answered truthfully, the bank would have discovered the gamble on which Mr Roberts and his board were about to embark in relation to the Old Bailey site, and it could have, and should have, stopped the initial move towards disaster, and later on arrested further progress towards disaster. I have indicated in the course of this judgment a number of obvious points at which the bank should have intervened, and it would be repetitive to summarise them.

"I hold that the bank failed in its duty whether it is judged by the standard of the prudent man of business or of the skilled trust corporation. The bank's breach of duty caused the loss which was suffered by the trust estate. If the bank had intervened as it could and should have, that loss would not have been incurred. By 'loss,' I mean the depreciation which took place in the market value of the BTL and BTH shares, by comparison with the value which the shares would have commanded if the loss of the Old Bailey project had not been incurred, and reduction of dividends through loss of income. The bank is liable for the loss so suffered by the trust estate, except to the extent that I shall hereafter indicate. . . .

"The bank also relies on clause 18 of the settlement. Clause 18 entitled the bank to—

'  . . . act in relation to [BTL] or any other company and the shares securities and properties thereof in such way as it shall think best calculated to benefit the trust premises and as if it was the absolute owner of such shares securities and property.'

In my judgment this is a clause which confers on the bank power to engage in a transaction which might otherwise be outside the scope of its authority; it is not an indemnity protecting the bank against liability for a transaction which is a breach of trust because it is one that a prudent man of business would have eschewed. . . .

"Section 61 of the Trustee Act 1925 is pleaded. There is no doubt that the bank acted honestly. I do not think it acted reasonably. Nor do I think it would be fair to excuse the bank at the expense of the beneficiaries.

"There remains this defence, which I take from paragraph 26 of the amended pleading:

'In about 1963 the Old Company purchased a site at Woodbridge Road, Guildford, pursuant to the policy pleaded in paragraph 19 hereof, for the sum of £79,000 and re-sold the same for £350,000 to MEPC Ltd. in 1973. The net profit resulting from such sale was £271,000. If, which is denied, the Defendant is liable for breach of trust, whether as alleged in the amended Statement of Claim or otherwise, the Defendant claims credit for such sum of £271,000 or other sum found to be gained in taking any accounts or inquiries.'

"The general rule as stated in all the textbooks, with some reservations, is that where a trustee is liable in respect of distinct breaches of trust, one of which has resulted in a loss and the other in a gain, he is not entitled to set off the gain against the loss, unless they arise in the same transaction. The relevant cases are, however, not altogether easy to reconcile. All are centenarians and none is quite like the present. The Guildford development stemmed from exactly the same policy and (to a lesser degree because it proceeded less far) exemplified the same folly as the Old Bailey project. Part of the profit was in fact used to finance the Old Bailey disaster. By sheer luck the gamble paid off handsomely, on capital account. I think it would be unjust to deprive the bank of this element of salvage in the course of assessing the cost of the shipwreck. My order will therefore reflect the bank's right to an appropriate set-off. . . . "

Gareth Jones (1959) 22 M.L.R. 390

"The learned judge's definition in *Re Vickery*[49] of 'wilful default' as a conscious or reckless breach of duty on the part of the trustee cannot be supported; the words should have been construed, in their pre-1926 sense, so as to include want of reasonable care. His Lordship purported to follow the judgment of Romer J. in the *Re City Equitable* case. In that decision, Romer J. was called upon, *inter alia*, to construe a set of articles of association, and in particular, a clause which was in terms similar to the indemnity clause (s.24) of the Trustee Act 1893. It was inevitable, therefore, that counsel should rely[50] on the *Re Brier*[51] line of cases, which had impliedly interpreted 'wilful default' to include lack of reasonable care, as well as a conscious act of omission or recklessness on the part of the trustee. Romer J. rejected this argument. He pointed out that these cases did not involve a consideration of these precise words and that, in the *Re Brier* line of cases, the court was concerned with the 'law as to the employment of agents by trustees.'[52] Directors and auditors were not trustees in the strict sense of the word and there is little resemblance between their duties and the 'duties of a trustee of a will or a marriage settlement.' His Lordship preferred to follow a number of company law decisions, which were authority for a *Derry* v. *Peek*[53] definition of 'wilful default.'

> 'An act, or an omission to do an act, is wilful where the person of whom we are speaking knows what he is doing and intends to do what he is doing. But if that act or omission amounts to a breach of his duty, and therefore to negligence, is the person guilty of wilful negligence? In my opinion that question must be answered in the negative unless he knows that he is committing, and intends to commit, a breach of this duty, or is recklessly careless in the sense of not caring whether his act or omission is or is not a breach of duty.'[54]

"This definition was later accepted by Astbury J. in *Re Munton*,[55] a decision which was concerned with the liability of a trustee for the acts or defaults of his agent. The learned judge held that a retiring trustee was not guilty of a breach of trust in executing a power of attorney authorising a broker to sell stock and receive the purchase price, the broker having, without authority, handed over

---

[49] [1931] 1 Ch. 572, *supra*, p. 622.
[50] *Re City Equitable* [1925] Ch. 407, 424.
[51] (1884) 26 Ch.D. 238.
[52] At p. 439. Maugham J. in *Re Vickery* recognised this distinction but found the exposition of Romer J. of "wilful default" none the less valuable (at p. 583).
[53] (1889) 14 App.Cas. 337.
[54] At p. 434.
[55] [1927] 1 Ch. 262.

the proceeds of sale to a co-trustee who had misappropriated them. The reasoning of the learned judge is, with respect, a little difficult to follow. The following passage is significant:

> 'The indemnity clauses, containing the exception of wilful default, in the Trustee Acts, may or may not have added anything to the previous law, but in *Re City Equitable Fire Insurance Co. Ltd.*, the whole question of wilful default as regards a fiduciary agent is dealt with at great length. Warrington L.J. says: "Romer J. was quite right in arriving at the conclusion that a person is guilty of 'wilful neglect or default' unless he is conscious that in doing the act which is complained of, or in omitting to do the act which it is said he ought to have done, he is committing breach of his duty, and also, as he said, recklessly careless whether it is a breach of the duty or not. . . . '

> 'The plaintiff's counsel say that the *City Equitable* case has made no change in the law as regards an ordinary trustee's liability. I do not propose to discuss that. I have read the passage representing the general result of the decision and it seems to me to apply to the present case.'[56]

"The question was not raised in the Court of Appeal and their Lordships did not comment on these observations of Astbury J.

"It is submitted, with respect, that the translation of the definition of 'wilful default' in *Re City Equitable* to section 30(1) of the Trustee Act 1925 was completely unjustified. Romer J. was construing a particular set of articles of association and the decision on the facts of *Re City Equitable* was to have no application to the case of trustees, *stricto sensu*. This, indeed, was the view of Warrington L.J., in the Court of Appeal, in that case, and his approval of Romer J.'s definition, quoted by Astbury J. in the above passage, was a strictly limited approval. The following extract from the learned Lord Justice's judgment is relevant.[57]

> 'With all respect to counsel who cited those trustees cases to us, I think there is great danger of being misled if we attempt to apply decisions as to the duties of trustees to a case as to the conduct of persons in the position of auditors in this case. In the case of trustees there are certain definite and precise rules of law as to what a trustee may or may not do in the execution of his trust, and it is no answer for a trustee to say, if, for example, he invests the trust property in his hands in a security which the law regards as an unauthorised security: "I honestly believed that I was justified in doing that." No honest belief will justify him in committing that which is a breach of such a rule of law, and therefore the question which we have to determine in expressing a view on the construction of such words in a contract like the present is not solved by seeing how the question has been determined in a case relating to the duties of a trustee.'

"In effect, neither Romer J. nor the Court of Appeal in *Re City Equitable* intended to derogate from the pre-1926 decisions, which, impliedly if not expressly interpreted the words 'wilful default,' within section 24 of the 1893 Act, so as to include lack of reasonable care. Section 30(1) is a mere re-

---

[56] At p. 274.
[57] *Re City Equitable, loc. cit.*, pp. 523–524.

enactment of section 24 of the Trustee Act 1893 and like that section should, it is submitted, render the trustee liable if he failed to act with reasonable care."

## Section 2. Extent of Liability

A trustee is not liable for damages like those at common law for breach of contract (or for tort[58]). "The Court of Chancery never entertained a suit for damages occasioned by fraudulent conduct or for breach of trust. . . . It was a suit for the restitution of the money or thing, or value of the thing, of which the cheated party had been cheated."[59] The measure of liability for breach of trust is to account for profits made or to account for and so replace the loss caused to the estate.[60] The liability to replace the loss is of a restitutionary character so that the principles applicable to contractual or tortious damages are of no relevance. Indeed, no deduction should be made for the tax that would have been payable but for the breach of trust.[61] The tax liabilities of beneficiaries do not enter into the picture because they arise not at the point of restitution to the trust estate but at the point of distribution of capital or income out of the trust estate. A trustee cannot set off profits made on breaches of trust against losses made on breaches of trust except where they may be regarded as flowing from the same breach of trust.[62] A manager of a unit trust who fulfils the investment function normally accorded to trustees will be treated like a trustee in this regard. A purchaser of high-priced units in the trust just before the manager's breach of fiduciary duty was discovered could well suffer if the then forced sale of unauthorised investments (*e.g.* Japanese warrants in excess of 5 per cent. of the fund's value) leads to a large loss, reflected in the lower price of the units when sold on, but balanced by earlier gains flowing from the same policy of unauthorised investment so that the manager does not have to compensate the fund. The purchaser will have to fall back on such rights as he may have against the manager under section 62 of the Financial Services Act 1986.

### RE DAWSON

[1966] 2 N.S.W.R. 211, 214–216 endorsed by Brightman L.J. in *Bartlett* v. *Barclays Bank Trust Co. Ltd. (No. 2)* [1980] Ch. 515, 543

STREET J.: "The obligation of a defaulting trustee is essentially one of effecting a restitution to the estate. The obligation is of a personal character

---

[58] Beneficiaries cannot sue their trustee for negligence in tort: *Parker-Tweedale* v. *Dunbar Bank* [1990] 2 All E.R. 577, 582–583.

[59] *Re Collie* (1878) 8 Ch.D. 807, 819; *Erlanger* v. *New Sombrero Phosphate Co.* (1878) 3 App.Cas. 1218, 1278; *Uphoff* v. *International Energy Trading Ltd., The Times*, February 4, 1989; Underhill & Hayton, pp. 732–734.

[60] For profits see Chap. 7, section 1 and Chap. 9, section 2, *supra.*

[61] *Bartlett* v. *Barclays Bank Trust Co. Ltd. (No. 2)* [1980] Ch. 515, 545; *Re Bell's Indenture* [1980] 1 W.L.R. 1217; *John* v. *James* [1986] S.T.C. 352.

[62] *Dimes* v. *Scott* (1828) 4 Russ. 195; *cf. Fletcher* v. *Green* (1864) 33 Beav. 426; *Bartlett* v. *Barclays Bank Trust Co. Ltd.* [1980] Ch. 515, *supra*, p. 764.

and its extent is not to be limited by common law principles governing remoteness of damage. In *Caffrey* v. *Darby*,[63] trustees were charged with neglect in failing to recover possession of part of the trust assets. The assets were lost and it was argued by the trustees that the loss was not attributable to their neglect. The Master of the Rolls, in stating his reasons, asked 'will they be relieved from that by the circumstance that the loss has ultimately happened by something that is not a direct and immediate consequence of their negligence?' His answer to this question was that, even supposing that 'they could not look to the possibility' of the actual event which occasioned the loss, 'yet, if they have already been guilty of negligence they must be responsible for any loss in any way to that property; for whatever may be the immediate cause the property would not have been in a situation to sustain that loss if it had not been for their negligence. If they had taken possession of the property it would not have been in his possession. If the loss had happened by fire, lightning, or any other accident, that would not be an excuse for them, if guilty of previous negligence. That was their fault.' *Caffrey* v. *Darby* is consistent with the proposition that if a breach has been committed then the trustee is liable to place the trust estate in the same position as it would have been in if no breach had been committed. Considerations of causation, foreseeability and remoteness do not readily enter into the matter. To the same effect is the case of *Clough* v. *Bond*.[64] It was argued before Lord Cottenham L.C. that 'the principle of the court is to charge persons in the situation of trustees as parties to a breach of trust, wherever they have acted irregularly, and the irregularity, however well intended, has in the result enabled their co-trustees to commit a breach of trust, or has been, however remotely, the origin of the loss.' . . . The principles embodied in this approach do not appear to involve any inquiry as to whether the loss was caused by or flowed from the breach. Rather the inquiry in each instance would appear to be whether the loss would have happened if there had been no breach. . . . The cases to which I have referred demonstrate that the obligation to make restitution, which courts of equity have from very early times imposed on defaulting trustees and other fiduciaries, is of a more absolute nature than the common-law obligation to pay damages for tort or breach of contract. It is on this fundamental ground that I regard the principles in *Tomkinson's Case*[65] as distinguishable. Moreover the distinction between common law damages and relief against a defaulting trustee is strikingly demonstrated by reference to the actual form of relief granted in equity in respect of breaches of trust. The form of relief is couched in terms appropriate to require the defaulting trustee to restore to the estate the assets of which he deprived it. Increases in market values between the date of breach and the date of recoupment are for the trustee's account: the effect of such increases would, at common law, be excluded from the computation of damages but in equity a defaulting trustee must make good the loss by restoring to the estate the assets of which he deprived it notwithstanding that market values may have increased in the meantime. The obligation to restore to the estate the assets of which he deprived it necessarily connotes that, where a monetary compensation is to be paid in lieu of restoring assets, that compensation is to be assessed by reference to the value of the assets at the date of restoration and not at the

---

[63] (1801) 6 Ves. 488.
[64] (1838) 3 My. & Cr. 490.
[65] [1961] A.C. 1007.

date of deprivation. In this sense the obligation is a continuing one and ordinarily, if the assets are for some reason not restored *in specie*, it will fall for quantification at the date when recoupment is to be effected, and not before."

## I. MAKING UNAUTHORISED INVESTMENTS

Where trustees make an unauthorised investment they are liable for all loss incurred when it is realised.

### KNOTT v. COTTEE

Master of the Rolls (1852) 16 Beav. 77; 16 Jur.(O.S.) 752

A testator who died in January 1844 directed his executor-trustees to invest in "the public or Government stocks or funds of Great Britain, or upon real security in England and Wales." In 1845 and 1846, the defendant executor-trustee invested part of the estate in Exchequer bills, which in 1846 were ordered into court, and in the same year sold at a loss. By a decree made in 1848, the court declared that the investment in Exchequer bills was improper. If, however, the investment had been retained, its realisation at the time of the decree of 1848 would have resulted in a profit.

*Held*, "that the executor ought to be charged with the *amount improperly invested*, and credited with the produce of the Exchequer bills in 1846." Thus he was liable for the loss incurred when the unauthorised investments were realised.

ROMILLY M.R.: "Here is an executor who had a direct and positive trust to perform, which was, to invest the money upon government stocks or funds, or upon real securities, and accumulate at compound interest all the balances after maintaining the children. He has made certain investments, which the court has declared to be improper. The case must either be treated as if these investments had not been made, or had been made for his own benefit out of his own moneys, and that he had at the same time retained moneys of the testator in his hands. I think, therefore, that there must be a reference back, to ascertain what balances the executor retained from time to time, it being clear that he has retained some balances. . . .

"I cannot concur in the argument that the court must charge him as if the money had been invested in consols. If that were so, the court must charge him the other way where the funds have fallen, which it never does. There was a conflict of decision as to how a trustee was to be charged, where the investment might either be made in the funds or on real security. The decision of Lord Langdale and Sir John Leach were opposed.[66] The case, however, of *Robinson* v. *Robinson*[67] has settled the rule, and I have adopted it in a former case. I stated my reasons for doing so.

"As to the mode of charging the executor in respect of the Exchequer bills, I treat the laying out in Exchequer bills in this way: The persons interested were entitled to earmark them, as being bought with the testator's assets, in the same manner as if the executor had bought a house with the trust funds; and

---

66 See an examination of authorities in *Robinson* v. *Robinson* (1851) 1 De G.M. & G. 247.
67 (1851) 1 De G.M. & G. 247.

though they do not recognise the investment, they had a right to make it available for what was due; and though part of the property of the executor, it was specifically applicable to the payment. When the Exchequer bills were sold and produced £3,955, the court must consider the produce as a sum of money refunded by the executor to the testator's estate on that day; and on taking the account, the master must give credit for this amount as on the day on which the Exchequer bills were sold. . . . "[68]

If a trustee of a trust to which the rule in *Howe* v. *Earl of Dartmouth, supra*, p. 667 does *not apply* invests in an unauthorised investment, and pays the income therefrom to the tenant for life, and the capital is intact or has been replaced, the remainderman has no equity to make the trustee pay into capital any excess of income actually received over income which would have been received on an authorised investment.[69] In the words of Cozens-Hardy M.R. in *Slade* v. *Chaine*,[70] there is neither a loss to the capital of a trust, nor a profit to the trustee by the breach of trust. It is immaterial that the trustee happens also to be himself the tenant for life.[71] Suppose, however, that the capital has diminished, and the trustee could not replace the whole of the balance. "If the trustee were not solvent, the reduced amount which he was able to pay and did pay would no doubt have to be apportioned as between corpus and income."[72] These cases also illustrate the proposition that a technical breach of trust grounds no liability unless there is actual loss.

If a trustee makes an unauthorised investment, the beneficiaries may, if they choose, and if they are all *sui juris*, adopt the investment as part of the trust.[73] The difficulty is as to the *extent* of their remedy. If they decide to adopt the investment, but it has caused a loss to the estate, can they also require the trustee to replace that loss? According to *Re Lake*,[74] they apparently can. But Wood V.-C. in *Thornton* v. *Stokill*[75] seems to have held that if they adopt the investment, it settles the matter. To play safe the beneficiaries should refuse to authorise or adopt the investment but accept the investment *in specie* as part satisfaction of the trustees' personal liability.

Where the unauthorised investment has not or cannot be adopted (*e.g.* where the beneficiaries are not each *sui juris*) the beneficiaries have a lien over it until the trust fund loss is made up, whether by the trustees using their own resources to replace the loss so that they can take over the investment themselves, or by the sale of the investment

---

[68] Where an investment is improper only in so far as it is an over-investment in a mortgage otherwise proper, see s.9 of the Trustee Act 1925, *supra*, p. 630.
[69] *Stroud* v. *Gwyer* (1860) 28 Beav. 130; *Re Appleby* [1903] 1 Ch. 565, 566; *Slade* v. *Chaine* [1908] 1 Ch. 522. See *supra*, p. 678.
[70] [1908] 1 Ch. 522, 533.
[71] *Re Hoyles* [1912] 1 Ch. 67.
[72] Buckley L.J. in *Slade* v. *Chaine* [1908] 1 Ch. 522, 536; *Re Bird* [1901] 1 Ch. 916, *supra*, p. 678.
[73] *Re Patten* (1883) 52 L.J.Ch. 787; *Re Jenkins* [1903] 2 Ch. 362; *Wright* v. *Morgan* [1926] A.C. 788, 799.
[74] [1903] 1 K.B. 439; and see *Ex p. Biddulph* (1849) 3 De. G. & Sm. 587.
[75] (1855) 1 Jur. 751. See also *Re Cape Breton* (1885) 29 Ch.D. 795.

with the balance to make up the loss coming from the trustees' own resources. Of course, if the investment is of an *authorised* nature, the beneficiaries have no option of adopting or rejecting it, for it is necessarily part of the trust.[76]

## II. IMPROPER RETENTION OF UNAUTHORISED INVESTMENTS[77]

Where trustees retain an unauthorised investment they are liable for the difference between the price obtainable on sale at the proper time and the proceeds of sale of the unauthorised investment when eventually sold.

### FRY v. FRY

Master of the Rolls (1859) 27 Beav. 144; 28 L.J.Ch. 591; 34 L.T.(o.s.) 51; 5 Jur. 1047

A testator who died in March 1834, after devising his residuary real estate to two trustees on trust to pay the rents (except those of the Langford Inn) to his wife during her widowhood, with remainder over, and bequeathing his residuary personal estate upon trust for conversion for his wife during her widowhood, with remainder over, directed the trustees: "And as for and concerning all that messuage or dwelling-house called Langford Inn . . . upon trust, as soon as convenient after his decease, to sell and dispose of the same, either by auction or private sale, and for the most money that could be reasonably obtained for the same." In April 1836 the trustees advertised the Langford Inn for sale for £1,000. They refused an offer of £900, made in 1837. One of the trustees died in 1842. A railway opened in 1843 caused the property to depreciate in value through the diversion of traffic. The property was again advertised for sale in 1845, but no offer was received. The other trustee died in 1856. Langford Inn was still unsold and could not be sold except at a low price.

*Held*, by Romilly M.R., the trustees had committed a breach of trust by reason of their negligence in not selling the property for so many years, that the property must be sold, and that the estates of the trustees were "liable to make good the deficiency between the amount which should be produced by the sale of the inn and the sum of £900, in case the purchase-money thereof should not amount to that sum."[78]

It was held by the Court of Appeal in *Re Chapman*[79] and in *Rawsthorne* v. *Rowley*,[80] that a trustee is not liable for a loss arising through the retention of an *authorised* investment unless he was guilty

---

[76] *Re Salmon* (1889) 42 Ch.D. 351.

[77] The assumption being that the investment has depreciated; otherwise any gain belongs of course to the trust. See Arden M.R. in *Piety* v. *Stace* (1799) 4 Ves. 620, 622, 623.

[78] See also *Grayburn* v. *Clarkson* (1868) 3 Ch.App. 605; *Dunning* v. *Gainsborough* (1885) 54 L.J.Ch. 891. Where the proper time during which the unauthorised investments, *e.g.* shares, should have been sold is a period during which fluctuations occur in the value of the shares one may take half the sum of the lowest and highest prices at which the shares might have been sold in the period commencing when the shares could first have been sold to advantage and ending at the date by which they should reasonably have been sold: *Fales* v. *Canada Permanent Trust Co.* (1976) 70 D.L.R. (3d) 257, 274.

[79] [1896] 2 Ch. 763.

[80] [1909] 1 Ch. 409n.

of *wilful default*.[81] This requires proof of want of ordinary prudence on the part of the trustee.[82]

Section 4 of the Trustee Act 1925 provides: "A trustee shall not be liable for breach of trust by reason *only* of his continuing to hold an investment which has ceased to be an investment authorised by the trust instrument or by the general law." This provision is inapplicable in cases governed by section 3(4) of the Trustee Investments Act 1961. Moreover, where investments requiring advice are made under that Act, the trustees must from time to time obtain and consider advice on whether retention of the investment is satisfactory having regard to the need for diversification and the suitability of the investments.[83]

### III. IMPROPER REALISATION OF PROPER INVESTMENTS

It is clearly a breach of trust if trustees sell an authorised investment for the purpose of investing in an unauthorised investment or for the purpose of paying the proceeds to the life-tenant in breach of trust. In such cases the trustees are liable to replace the authorised investment or the proceeds of sale of the authorised investment, whichever is the greater burden. Replacement of the authorised investment will be at its value at the date it is actually replaced or at the date of the court judgment if not earlier replaced or, exceptionally, at the date the authorised investment would, in any event, have been sold.[84]

### PHILLIPSON v. GATTY

Vice-Chancellor (1848) 6 Hare 26; affirmed (1850) 7 Hare 516; 2 H. & Tw. 459; 12 L.T.(O.S.) 445; 13 Jur.(O.S.) 318

The trustees of a sum of consols, who had power to convert and reinvest in the public funds or upon real security, realised part of the stock and invested it in an *un*authorised investment.

WIGRAM V.-C.: " . . . Then comes another material question—are the trustees to replace the stock, or the money produced by the sale? Mr. Wood argued that they were liable to make good the money only, distinguishing the sale, which he said was lawful, from the investment, which I have decided to have been a breach of trust. My opinion is, that the trustees must replace the stock. There was no authority to sell, except with a view to the reinvestment; and here the sale was made with a view to the investment I have condemned. It was all one transaction, and the sale and investment must stand or fall together. . . . "

*Held*, therefore, the trustees must replace the stock improperly realised. *Affirmed on appeal.*[85]

---

[81] See also *Baud* v. *Fardell* (1855) 4 W.R. 40; *Henderson* v. *Hunter* (1843) 1 L.T.(O.S.) 359, 385; *Robinson* v. *Murdoch* (1881) 45 L.T. 417; Joyce J. in *Re Oddy* (1910) 104 L.T. 128, 131; *Re Godwin* (1918) 87 L.J.Ch. 645.

[82] *Per* Lindley L.J. in *Re Chapman* [1896] 2 Ch. 763, 776.

[83] s.6(3), (4), (5) of the Trustee Investment Act 1961; *supra*, p. 623.

[84] *Re Bell's Indenture* [1980] 3 All E.R. 425, 437–439, pointing out that in *Re Massingberd* (1890) 63 L.T. 296 the reference to the date of the writ for ascertaining the value of the property sold in breach of trust was *per incuriam* and should be the date of the judgment.

[85] Followed in *Re Massingberd* (1890) 63 L.T. 296.

## IV. NON-INVESTMENT OF TRUST FUNDS

A trustee ought not to leave trust moneys uninvested for an unreasonable length of time. If he unnecessarily retains trust moneys which he ought to have invested, he is chargeable with interest.[86]

While an investment is being sought, however, a trustee has a statutory power to pay trust moneys into a deposit or other account.[87] Cases prior to the Act, and decided under the general law, have held that the moneys must not be left in the bank for an unreasonable length of time.[88]

If a trustee, having been *directed* to invest in a *specific* investment, *makes no investment at all*, and the price of the specified investment rises, he may be required to purchase so much of that investment as would have been obtained by a purchase at the proper time.[89] This applies equally where he is directed to invest in a specific investment and he makes some investment other than the one specified.[90] But if he is directed to invest in a specified *range* of investments, and he makes no investment at all, he is chargeable only with the trust fund itself, and not with the amount of one or other of the investments which might have been purchased.[91] The reason was stated by Wigram V.-C in *Shepherd* v. *Mouls*[92] as follows: "The discretion given to the trustees to select an investment among several securities makes it impossible to ascertain the amount of the loss (if any) which has arisen to the trust from the omission to invest, except, perhaps, in the possible case (which has not occurred here) of a particular security having been offered to the trustees, in conformity with the terms of the trust."

## V. TRUST FUNDS IN TRADE

If a trustee in breach of trust lends funds to a third party who knows they are trust funds but not that the loan is a breach of trust and employs the trust funds in trade, the beneficiaries cannot claim from the third party a share of the profits. For example, a trustee in breach of trust lends £1,000 of trust moneys to X, who employs the fund in his trade. The agreement between the trustee and X provides that X is to pay interest at the rate of 15 per cent. By employing this fund of £1,000 in his trade, X makes a profit during the first year of £300. The beneficiaries cannot claim from X a share of that profit; all that they can require is that he replace, with interest, the fund which he borrowed. What is the position if X knew, not merely that the funds were trust funds, but also *that the loan was itself a breach of trust*? In this latter case, it would seem that X is a constructive trustee, that he

---

86 *Stafford* v. *Fiddon* (1857) 23 Beav. 386; *Re Jones, Jones* v. *Searle* (1883) 49 L.T. 91.
87 Trustee Act 1925, s.11(1).
88 *Moyle* v. *Moyle* (1831) 2 Russ. & M. 710; *Cann* v. *Cann* (1884) 33 W.R. 40.
89 *Byrchall* v. *Bradford* (1822) 6 Madd. 235.
90 *Pride* v. *Fooks* (1840) 2 Beav. 430, 432.
91 *Shepherd* v. *Mouls* (1845) 4 Hare 500; *Robinson* v. *Robinson* (1851) 1 De G.M. & G. 247.
92 *Ibid.* p. 504.

may not "traffic in his trust," and must therefore account for his profit.[93] Of course, if the instrument of trust authorises a loan of trust funds to a third party, and such a loan is made, the beneficiaries have no right to claim profits.[94]

On the other hand, if it is the trustee himself who in breach of trust employs trust funds in *his own* trade, the beneficiaries may, instead of taking interest, require him to account for the profit. Thus, if in breach of trust he employs £1,000 of trust moneys in his own trade and thereby makes a profit during the first year of £200, the beneficiaries (on calling upon him to replace the fund of £1,000), may, instead of taking interest on that sum, claim the profit of £200.[95]

Even if the trust funds so employed by the trustee in his own trade were mixed up with his private moneys, so that the fund used by him was a mixed one, the beneficiaries may still claim a proportionate share of the profits.[96] But it is either the one or the other, *either* interest *or* profit. They cannot, even if they find it advantageous to do so, claim interest for part of the time and profit for the other part.[97]

## VI. SUMMARY OF INCOME POSITION

If the life-tenant has lost income owing to the trustee's default he is entitled to interest on the capital moneys at what one may term the "trustees' rate" or, exceptionally, at a higher rate. In the nineteenth century the trustees' rate was 4 per cent., with 5 per cent. in cases of fraud or active misconduct.

The rate depends on the court's discretion but trustees' rate now seems the rate of the court's special account replacing the short-term investment account,[98] reflecting the rate a trust fund would have earned if invested in authorised securities.

However, a higher rate will be charged:

(i) where the trustee actually received a higher rate—when the life tenant takes the actual interest;[99]

---

[93] See Chap. 8, section 3 and *Stroud* v. *Gwyer* (1860) 25 Beav. 130; *Vyse* v. *Foster* (1872) 8 Ch.App. 309, 334; *Belmont Finance Co. Ltd.* v. *Williams Furniture Ltd.* [1979] Ch. 250.

[94] *Parker* v. *Bloxam* (1855) 20 Beav. 295, 302–304; *Evans* v. *London Co-operative Society Ltd., The Times*, July 6, 1976.

[95] *Jones* v. *Foxall* (1852) 15 Beav. 388; *Williams* v. *Powell* (1852) 15 Beav. 461; *Townsend* v. *Townsend* (1859) 1 Giff. 201; *Re Davis* [1902] 2 Ch. 314.

[96] *Docker* v. *Somes* (1834) 2 My. & K. 655; *Edinburgh T.C.* v. *Lord Advocate* (1879) 4 App.Cas. 823. Indeed, if the trust funds were the *sine qua non* of the purchase of a valuable asset later sold at a profit it is arguable that the trust should take the whole profit for to allow the trustee a proportion for himself would be to allow him to profit from his position.

[97] *Heathcote* v. *Hume* (1819) 1 Jac. & W. 122.

[98] *Bartlett* v. *Barclays Bank Trust Co. Ltd.* [1980] Ch. 515, 547 where Brightman L.J. further stated: "To some extent the high interest rates payable on money lent reflect and compensate for the continued erosion in the value of money by reason of inflation. It seems arguable that if a high rate of interest is payable in such circumstances a proportion of such interest should be added to capital in order to help maintain the value of the corpus. It may be there will have to be some adjustment as between life tenant and remaindermen. I do not decide this point and I express no view upon it." The Court Fund Rules 1987, rules 26, 27 deal with special account rates for funds invested with the court.

[99] *Re Emmet's Estate* (1881) 17 Ch.D. 142. This should include the case where the trustee has used the money to reduce his overdraft and to save paying an actual interest rate: *Farnell* v. *Cox* (1898) 19 L.R.(N.S.W.)Eq. 142.

(ii) where the trustee ought to have received a higher rate (*e.g.* if he realised an authorised investment bearing 15 per cent. and bought an unauthorised investment bearing 5 per cent.[1]) when the life-tenant is entitled to interest at that higher rate;

(iii) where the trustee is presumed to have received a commercial rate as where he has made unauthorised use of trust moneys for his own purposes and the profits actually made by the trustee are unascertainable[2] or are less than the amount produced by applying the commercial rate—when the life-tenant is entitled to interest at the commercial rate instead of the actual interest or profit.[3] The commercial rate that is now presumed is 1 per cent. above the London and Scottish clearing banks' base lending rate now that Bank of England minimum lending rate no longer exists.[4] Exceptionally, interest will be compounded with yearly rests where the trustee has been guilty of active and deliberate fraud in using trust money for his own purposes.[5]

### Section 3. Impounding the Trustee's Beneficial Interest; Rule in *Re Dacre*[6]

If a beneficiary is also trustee, but is in default to the estate in his character of trustee, he is not entitled to receive any further part of his beneficial interest until his default is made good. His beneficial interest may also be applied in satisfaction of his liability. X is a trustee, for himself for life, remainder to Y. X commits a breach of trust, and has not yet satisfied his liability. Until he does so, he cannot receive any further part of his beneficial interest, and that interest may be applied in satisfaction of his liability. The rule holds good where X's beneficial interest is *derivative* as well as where it is original. For example, X holds on trust for several beneficiaries, of which he is not himself one. He is in default to the estate in his character of trustee. One of the beneficiaries dies, and then X becomes entitled to that beneficiary's share as intestate successor or as legatee or devisee. X is now derivatively a beneficiary, and the rule applies as stated above.

What is the position of an *assignee* from the trustee-beneficiary X? The assignee is in the same position as his assignor, *i.e.* he takes subject to the equity available against the trustee-beneficiary.[7] He

---

[1] *Jones* v. *Foxall* (1852) 15 Beav. 388; *Att.-Gen.* v. *Alford* (1855) 4 De G.M. & G. 843 explained in *Mayor of Berwick* v. *Murray* (1857) 7 De G.M. & G. 497.

[2] *Wallersteiner* v. *Moir (No. 2)* [1975] Q.B. 373.

[3] *Burdick* v. *Garrick* (1870) 5 Ch.App. 233; *Vyse* v. *Foster* (1872) 8 Ch.App. 309, 329 (affd. L.R. 7 H.L. 318); *Gordon* v. *Gonda* [1955] 1 W.L.R. 885; *O'Sullivan* v. *Management Agency Ltd.* [1985] Q.B. 428.

[4] *Belmont Finance Ltd.* v. *Williams Furniture Ltd. (No. 2)* [1980] 1 All E.R. 393; *O'Sullivan* v. *Management Agency Ltd.* [1985] Q.B. 428; *John* v. *James* [1986] S.T.C. 352, 363; *Shearson Lehman Inc.* v. *Maclaine Watson & Co. Ltd.* [1990] 3 All E.R. 723, 732–734.

[5] *Jones* v. *Foxall* (1852) 15 Beav. 388; *Re Barclay* [1899] 1 Ch. 674; *Burdick* v. *Garrick* (1870) 5 Ch.App. 233; *O'Sullivan* v. *Management Agency Ltd.* [1985] Q.B. 428; *John* v. *James* [1986] S.T.C. 352, 363–364. Compound interest will also be charged where there was a duty to accumulate income: *Re Barclay* [1899] 1 Ch. 674; *Wallersteiner* v. *Moir (No. 2)* [1975] Q.B. 373.

[6] [1916] 1 Ch. 344; *Jacubs* v. *Rylance* (1874) L.R. 17 Eq. 341; *Re Brown* (1886) 32 Ch.D. 597.

[7] *Irby* v. *Irby (No. 3)* (1858) 25 Beav. 632.

takes subject to that equity even if the trustee-beneficiary's default to the estate was *subsequent* to the assignment.[8]

It can, in fact, be most unsafe to take an assignment of the beneficial interest of a trustee-beneficiary, especially if that interest is reversionary. But it was held in *Re Towndrow*[9] that the rule does not apply to a case in which the trustee-beneficiary's liability relates to one trust and his beneficial interest is derived from another trust, even though he is trustee of both trusts and both trusts are created by the same instrument. The rule in *Re Dacre* therefore applies only where the default relates to, and the beneficial interest is derived from, the same trust.

## Section 4. Relief of Trustees

### I. POWER OF THE COURT TO RELIEVE TRUSTEES FROM PERSONAL LIABILITY

Section 61[10] of the Trustee Act 1925 states, "If it appears to the court that a trustee, whether appointed by the court or otherwise, is or may be[11] personally liable for any breach of trust, whether the transaction alleged to be a breach of trust occurred before or after the commencement of this Act, but has acted honestly and reasonably, and ought fairly to be excused for the breach of trust and for omitting to obtain the directions of the court in the matter in which he committed such a breach, then the court *may* relieve him either wholly or partly from personal liability for the same." This enables the court to excuse not just breaches of trust in the management of trust property but also payments to the wrong persons.[12] The question of fairness should be considered separately from whether the trustee acted honestly and reasonably: is it fair for the trustee to be excused when the inevitable result is to deny compensation to the beneficiaries? The burden is on the trustee[13] to satisfy the threefold obligation[14] of proving he acted honestly, reasonably and ought fairly to be excused.

The court is rather reluctant to grant relief to a paid trustee but may do so in special circumstances.[15] The taking of legal advice will be a significant consideration if such advice is followed but a breach of trust

---

[8] *Doering* v. *Doering* (1889) 42 Ch.D. 203; *Re Knapman* (1881) 18 Ch.D. 300, 307.

[9] [1911] 1 Ch. 662.

[10] Re-enacting s.3 of the Judicial Trustees Act 1896. See Sheridan, "Excusable Breaches of Trust" (1955) 19 Conv.(N.S.) 420; Lord Maugham, "Excusable Breaches of Trust" (1898) 14 L.Q.R. 159. For other examples of statutory protection, see the Trustee Act 1925, ss.8 and 9, *supra* pp. 630–631. For similar protection of officers of a company, see s.727 of the Companies Act 1985.

[11] This does not authorise relief in respect of future anticipated breaches of trust: it relates to an existing situation where the trustee may or may not be liable for breach of trust: *Re Rosenthal* [1972] 1 W.L.R. 1273.

[12] *Re Alsop* [1914] 1 Ch. 1.

[13] *Re Stuart* [1897] 2 Ch. 583.

[14] *Marsden* v. *Regan* [1954] 1 W.L.R. 423, 434–435, *per* Evershed M.R.

[15] *National Trustees Co. of Australasia* v. *General Finance Co.* [1905] A.C. 373; *Re Windsor Steam Coal Co.* [1929] 1 Ch. 151; *Hawkesley* v. *May* [1956] 1 Q.B. 304; *Re Pauling's S.T.* [1964] Ch. 303; *Re Rosenthal* [1972] 1 W.L.R. 1273.

occurs because the advice was erroneous: the standing of the legal adviser and the value of the property affected by the advice will be relevant considerations.[16] If the adviser were a negligent solicitor then the trustee should sue the solicitor to recover the loss for the trust and it seems hardly likely that the court would excuse the trustee if he failed to sue.[17] One must distinguish between trustees obtaining advice on behalf of the trust beneficiaries and trustees obtaining advice for their own personal protection and benefit. In the former case any cause of action arising from negligent advice will be a trust asset so that, if not barred by the limitation period, the beneficiaries could sue for themselves on joining the trustees as co-defendants with the adviser if the trustees refused to sue; in the latter case the beneficiaries have no rights against the adviser, being able only to sue the trustees for any breach of trust.[18]

## II. AN INSTIGATING OR CONSENTING BENEFICIARY CANNOT SUE THE TRUSTEE AND THE COURT HAS POWER TO MAKE SUCH BENEFICIARY INDEMNIFY TRUSTEE FOR BREACH OF TRUST

A beneficiary[19] who is *sui juris*[20] and knowingly[21] concurs in a breach of trust cannot afterwards complain of it against the trustees[22] unless they knew or ought to have known that the beneficiary's concurrence was the result of undue influence.[23] The position is summarised by Wilberforce J.[24] (as he then was) in a passage approved by the Court of Appeal[25]: "The court has to consider all the circumstances in which the concurrence of the *cestui que trust* was given with a view to seeing whether it is fair and equitable that, having given his concurrence, he should afterwards turn round and sue the trustees: that, subject to this, it is not necessary that he should know that what he is concurring in is a breach of trust, provided that he fully understands what he is concurring in, and that it is not necessary that he should himself have directly benefited by the breach of trust." It would thus seem that if B consents to an act which the trustees know to be unauthorised but refrain from so telling B then B may still sue the trustees. The trustees

---

[16] *National Trustees Co. of Australasia, supra*; *Re Allsop* [1914] 1 Ch. 1, 13; *Marsden* v. *Regan* [1954] 1 All E.R. 475, 482.

[17] *National Trustees Co. of Australasia, supra.*

[18] *Wills* v. *Cooke* (1979) 76 L.S.G. 706 (Slade J.); *Parker-Tweedale* v. *Dunbar Bank plc* [1990] 2 All E.R. 577, 583.

[19] In charitable trusts only the Attorney-General can consent or acquiesce in a breach of trust: *Re Freeston's Charity* [1978] 1 All E.R. 481, 490, though the Court of Appeal found it unnecessary to say anything on this point: [1979] 1 All E.R. 51, 63.

[20] *Wilkinson* v. *Parry* (1828) 4 Russ. 272, 276; *Montford* v. *Cadogan* (1816) 19 Ves. 635. He may not fraudulently misrepresent his age to obtain money and then claim the money again on majority: *Overton* v. *Banister* (1844) Hare 503.

[21] *Phipps* v. *Boardman* [1964] 2 All E.R. 187, 204–205, 207; the point was not appealed.

[22] *Fletcher* v. *Collis* [1905] 2 Ch. 24, *infra*, p. 784. If he instigates or requests the breach then *a fortiori* he cannot sue.

[23] *Re Pauling's S.T.* [1964] Ch. 303, 338. Trustees must take special care in the case of young adults living with their parents.

[24] *Re Pauling's S.T.* [1962] 1 W.L.R. 86, 108.

[25] *Holder* v. *Holder* [1968] Ch. 353; *Re Freeston's Charity* [1978] 1 W.L.R. 741.

must put the beneficiaries fully in the picture and must not withhold crucial information.[26] If they themselves do not appreciate that what they propose is a breach of trust and B fully understands and agrees with the proposal then B should not be able to sue them if things turn out badly.

The above equitable principles apply whether the beneficiary's consent or acquiescence is before or after the breach of trust. They operate to prevent that particular beneficiary from suing for breach of trust, whether or not he benefited from consenting to such breach: *Fletcher* v. *Collis, infra.*

Where the beneficiary instigated, requested or consented to a breach of trust which the trustees then committed and another beneficiary called upon the trustee to make good the breach of trust, the court has always had jurisdiction to order the trustee to be indemnified out of the interest of the beneficiary who, being *sui juris*, either instigated, requested or concurred in the breach. A motive of personal benefit on the part of the beneficiary was sufficient to invoke the jurisdiction in cases of instigation[27] or request[28]; but personal benefit actually derived by the beneficiary was necessary in cases of concurrence.[29] In order to succeed in claiming an indemnity, the trustee had to show that the beneficiary knew the facts which constituted the breach of trust although it was not necessary to show that the beneficiary knew that these facts amounted in law to a breach of trust: *Re Somerset, infra.*[30]

Section 62 of the Trustee Act 1925[31] enlarges the jurisdiction as follows: "Where a trustee commits a breach of trust at the instigation or request or with the consent in writing[32] of a beneficiary, the court may if it thinks fit make such order as to the court seems just for impounding all or any part of the interest of the beneficiary in the trust estate by way of indemnity to the trustee[33] or persons claiming through him."[34] However, the factors of motive and actual benefit are likely to continue to influence the court in exercising its discretion.

The section provides for impounding the interest of the "beneficiary in the trust estate." In *Ricketts* v. *Ricketts*[35] there was a marriage

---

[26] *Phipps* v. *Boardman* [1964] 2 All E.R. 187, 204–205.

[27] *Trafford* v. *Boehm* (1746) 3 Atk. 440, 442; *Raby* v. *Ridehalgh* (1855) 7 De G.M. & G. 104.

[28] *M'Gachen* v. *Dew* (1851) 15 Beav. 84; *Hanchett* v. *Briscoe* (1856) 22 Beav. 496.

[29] *Cocker* v. *Quayle* (1830) 1 Russ. & M. 535, 538; *Booth* v. *Booth* (1838) 1 Beav. 125, 130; *Blyth* v. *Fladgate* [1891] 1 Ch. 337, 363. It makes no difference that the concurring beneficiary became a beneficiary after the date of his concurrence; *Evans* v. *Benyon* (1887) 37 Ch.D. 329, 344. These factors of motive and actual benefit may still influence the exercise of discretion of the court determining whether all or any part of the beneficial interest should be impounded: *Bolton* v. *Curre* [1895] 1 Ch. 544, 549; *Re Somerset* [1894] Ch. 231, 275.

[30] See also *Rehden* v. *Wesley* (1861) 29 Beav. 213, 215.

[31] Replacing Trustee Act 1893, s.45 replacing Trustee Act 1888, s.6.

[32] The requirement of writing only refers to consent and not instigation or request: *Re Somerset* [1894] 1 Ch. 231.

[33] An order for indemnity can be made in favour of a former trustee: *Re Pauling's S.T. (No. 2)* [1963] Ch. 576.

[34] Would the section be available if the sole trustee had fled the country leaving only trust assets behind and the remaindermen claimed to be subrogated to the trustee's right to impound the instigating life-tenant's income?

[35] (1891) 64 L.T. 263.

settlement for a mother for her life, remainder to her son. The son, on his marriage, assigned his reversionary interest under that settlement to the trustees of his own marriage settlement, under which latter settlement he was a beneficiary for life. Notice of the assignment was given to the trustees of the first settlement. By that assignment the son divested himself of his character of beneficiary under the first settlement, and substituted in his place the trustees of the second settlement. Afterwards the son instigated the trustees of the first settlement to commit a breach of trust in his favour by applying trust capital in discharging his debts, and when those trustees proceeded against him under the section for an indemnity, they discovered that he was not a beneficiary against whom they could proceed. Their beneficiary was now to be found in the trustees of the second settlement, who were trustees for the son who instigated the breach of trust to pay off his debts. He was not a "beneficiary in the trust estate."

## FLETCHER v. COLLIS

Court of Appeal [1905] 2 Ch. 24; (Vaughan Williams, Romer and Stirling L.JJ)

Securities were settled on trust for the husband for life, remainder to the wife for life, remainder to children. At the request of the wife and with the (written) consent of the husband, the trustee in 1885 sold out the whole of the trust fund and handed the proceeds to the wife, who spent them. In June 1891 the husband was adjudicated bankrupt. In August 1891 the present action was commenced by the *remaindermen* against the trustee to make him replace the loss, but proceedings were stayed on an undertaking by the trustee, on the security of (*inter alia*) certain policies on his life, to make good the trust fund. By means of payments by the trustee and of the policies which fell in on his death in 1902, the whole of the trust fund was replaced, together with interest from August 1891.

The personal representative of the deceased trustee then took out a summons in this action for a declaration that she was entitled, during the life of the husband, to the income of the trust fund replaced by the deceased trustee. It was argued for her (before the Court of Appeal) that a beneficiary who concurs in a breach of trust cannot afterwards complain of it against his trustee. The capital had in fact been replaced by the trustee at the instance of the remaindermen, but since the husband himself had by virtue of his concurrence no claim against the trustee, the income of the capital so replaced should (during the life of the husband) go to her as personal representative of the trustee who replaced it.

For the husband's trustee in bankruptcy, who resisted the claim of the personal representative, it was contended that the authorities showed that mere concurrence by a beneficiary does not preclude him from complaining against his trustee: it must be shown that he (the beneficiary) also derived a personal benefit from the breach of trust, which was not the case here.

ROMER L.J.: "There was one proposition of law urged by the counsel on behalf of the respondents before us to which I accede. It is this: If a beneficiary claiming under a trust does not *instigate* or *request* a breach of trust, is not the active moving party towards it, but merely *consents* to it, *and* he obtains no personal benefit from it, then his interest in the trust estate would not be impoundable in order to indemnify the trustee liable to make good loss occasioned by the breach. I think this is what was meant and referred to by Chitty J. in his judgment in *Sawyer* v. *Sawyer*,[36] where he says: 'It strikes me as a novelty in law, and a proposition not founded on principle, to say that the person who merely consents is bound to do more than what he says he consents to do. It does not mean that he makes himself personally liable, nor does he render any property liable to make it good.' But that proposition of law must be taken to be subject to the following right of the trustee as between himself and the beneficiaries. In the case I have before referred to in respect to the general proposition, the beneficiary who knowingly consented to the breach could not, if of full contracting age and capacity, and in the absence of special circumstances, afterwards be heard to say that the conduct of the trustee in committing the breach of trust was, as against him the particular beneficiary, improper, so as to make the trustee liable to the beneficiary for any damage suffered in respect of that beneficiary's interest in the trust estate by reason of the loss occasioned by the breach, and of course if satisfactorily proved the consent of the beneficiary to the breach need not be in writing.

"I will illustrate what I have said by a concrete case, not only to make my meaning perfectly plain, but also because the illustration will have a bearing upon the case now before us. Take a simple case of a trust under a settlement, say, of £3,000, for a tenant for life, and after the death of the tenant for life for certain remaindermen. Suppose the trustee commits a breach of trust and sells out £1,000, and pays it over to some third person, so that the *cestui que trust* does not benefit by it himself, and suppose that the tenant for life, being of full age and *sui juris*, knows of that act of the trustee and consents to it. What would be the position of the trustee in reference to that breach of trust if he were made liable at the instance of the remaindermen for the loss accruing to the trust estate by the breach of trust, assuming the £1,000 to have been lost? The remaindermen would have the right of saying, so far as their interest in remainder is concerned, the capital must be made good by the trustee; but the tenant for life who consented could not himself have brought an action against the trustee to make him liable for the loss of income suffered by the tenant for life by reason of the breach of trust as to the £1,000. On the other hand, the trustee would not have had a right, as against the *cestui que trust*, the tenant for life, to have impounded the tenant for life's interest on the remaining £2,000 of the trust fund in order to indemnify himself. Now suppose the remaindermen having brought an action to make good the breach of trust against the trustee, and the tenant for life is a co-plaintiff, a defence is put in by the trustee raising his right as against the tenant for life seeking relief in respect of the loss of income, but admitting the right of the remaindermen: what would the court in such a case do if the question between the tenant for life and the trustee had to be tried out, and the tenant for life was found to have consented knowingly to the breach of trust? To my mind the right thing for the court to do would have been clear. It might order the £1,000 to be paid into court by the trustee; but, pending the life of the tenant for life, it might also order the income to be paid to the trustee, because the income of the £1,000 would have been out of the pocket of the trustee just as much as the corpus from which it proceeded, and not to have given that relief to the trustee

[36] (1885) 28 Ch.D. 595, 598.

would have been to ignore his right, and to have acceded to the claim of the tenant for life in the action by him that I have indicated. Now suppose that the tenant for life is not a plaintiff, but co-defendant with the trustee, so that the question cannot be tried out at the trial as between the tenant for life and the trustee: what might the court do, if so advised, in that case? It might order the £1,000 to be paid into court by the trustee, and it might reserve the question of the right as between the tenant for life and the trustee to the income to be determined at some later period. It will be found that that illustration is pertinent to the case that is now before us. In such a case when the question as to income arose the trustee would be able to say: 'The remaindermen are clearly not entitled to the income on the trust fund I have replaced, if the tenant for life is not entitled to it as against me. I replaced it; it is my money, and I am entitled to it'; and, therefore, when the question came to be tried out ultimately as between the tenant for life and the trustee, if that income was still under the control of the court, the court would again have the right to say to the trustee who replaced the corpus: 'The income is yours in the absence of the right of the beneficiary, the tenant for life, to claim as against you to make you liable for that income.'

"Now that right of a trustee which I have been dealing with, the right to resist the claim by the beneficiary to make good as against him the income, has clearly not been affected either by section 6 of the Trustee Act of 1888, or by section 45 of the Trustee Act of 1893. As I pointed out in *Bolton* v. *Curre*,[37] those sections were intended to and did *extend* the powers of the court for the benefit of the trustee. They clearly extended the powers of court so far as concerns the case of a married woman restrained from anticipation; but they also extended them in another respect by giving power to the court to impound any part of the interest in the trust property of any beneficiary who consented to a breach of trust, provided that consent was in writing. But clearly there was nothing in those sections which was intended to, and nothing in my opinion which operated so as to, deprive the trustee of the right I previously indicated, namely, the right of saying as against a beneficiary who has consented to a breach of trust that the beneficiary cannot make him, the trustee, personally liable to recoup, to the beneficiary who consented, the loss accruing to that beneficiary by the breach of trust committed with his consent. The beneficiary, if he consented to the breach of trust, could not be heard to make that a ground of complaint or a ground of action as against the trustee. Of course, the right I have indicated of a trustee as against the consenting beneficiary might possibly be lost if not raised by the trustee before it was too late. Probably—I say probably, for I have not to decide the question—if a trustee in such a case were to hand over the funds out of his own pocket to new trustees without reserving his right in any way as against the tenant for life, it might be—I will say no more—that he might be held to have lost his right to claim the income after he had parted with the fund. It might be so, and other cases might be given; but so long as his right can be claimed by him it is a right which must be recognised by the court, and given full effect to when it is insisted upon at the proper time.

"Now that being the law, so far as it is necessary to deal with it for the purpose of the present case, I will say a few words about the facts of this case; and I ask myself, looking at those facts, this question: Is not this matter that

37 [1895] 1 Ch. 544, 549.

we have to deal with on this appeal in substance one where a beneficiary who has consented to a breach of trust is now for his own benefit calling upon the trustee to make good the loss accruing to the beneficiary by reason of the breach? I think it is. . . . "

*Held*, therefore, by the Court of Appeal that the personal representative of the deceased trustee was entitled, during the life of the husband tenant for life, to the income of the fund replaced by the trustee.

## HOLDER v. HOLDER

Court of Appeal [1968] Ch. 353; [1968] 2 W.L.R. 237; [1968] 1 All E.R. 665

The plaintiff was seeking to set aside a sale made to the third defendant by the first two defendant trustees when the third defendant was technically a trustee. The facts have already been set out at p. 584 and Harman L.J. with whom Danckwerts and Sachs L.JJ. expressly agreed on this point dealt as follows with the defence of the plaintiff's consent or acquiescence.

HARMAN L.J.: " . . . There arises a further defence, namely, that of acquiescence, and this requires some further recital of the facts.

"Completion of the sale was due for Michaelmas, 1961, but by that time the third defendant was not in a position to find the purchase money. The proving executors served a notice to complete in October, 1961, and, the validity of this notice being questioned, served a further notice in December. In February 1962 the plaintiff's solicitor pressed the defendants to forfeit the third defendant's deposit and this was a right given by the contract of sale and is an affirmation of it. Further, in May, 1962, the plaintiff issued a writ for a common decree of administration against the proving executors, seeking thus to press them to complete the contract and wind up the estate. The contract was in fact completed in June, 1962, and in the same month £2,000 on account was paid to and accepted by the plaintiff as his share and he thereupon took no further steps with his action. In order to complete, the third defendant borrowed £21,000 from the Agricultural Mortgage Corporation with interest at $7^{1}/_{2}$ per cent. He also borrowed £3,000 from his mother with interest at $6^{1}/_{2}$ per cent., and a like sum from his sister at a similar rate of interest. In November 1962 the third defendant demanded possession of Glebe Farm house from the plaintiff, who at that time changed his solicitors, and it was suggested by the new solicitors in February 1963 that the third defendant was disqualified from bidding at the auction. This was the first time any such suggestion had been made by anyone. The writ was not issued till a year later.

"I have found this question a difficult one. The plaintiff knew all the relevant facts but he did not realise nor was he advised till 1963 that the legal result might be that he could object to his brother's purchase because he continued to be a personal representative. There is no doubt strong authority for the proposition that a man is not bound by acquiescences until he knows his legal rights. In *Cockerell* v. *Cholmeley*[38] Sir John Leach M.R. said this:

> 'It has been argued that the defendant, being aware of the facts of the case in the lifetime of Sir Henry Englefield has, by his silence, and by being a party to the application to Parliament, confirmed the title of the plaintiffs. In equity it is considered, as good sense requires it should be,

---

[38] (1830) 1 Russ. & M. 418, 425.

that no man can be held by any act of his to confirm a title, unless he was fully aware at the time, not only of the fact upon which the effect of title depends, but of the consequence in point of law; and there is no proof that the defendant, at the time of the acts referred to, was aware of the law on the subject. . . . '

There, however, the judge was asked to set aside a legal right. In *Wilmott* v. *Barber*[39] Fry J. said this:

'A man is not to be deprived of his legal rights unless he has acted in such a way as would make it fraudulent for him to set up those rights. What, then, are the elements or requisites necessary to constitute fraud of that description? In the first place the plaintiff must have made a mistake as to his legal rights. Secondly, the plaintiff must have expended some money or must have done some act (not necessarily upon the defendant's land) on the faith of his mistaken belief. Thirdly, the defendant, the possessor of the legal right, must know of the existence of his own right which is inconsistent with the right claimed by the plaintiff. If he does not know of it he is in the same position as the plaintiff, and the doctrine of acquiescence is founded upon conduct with a knowledge of your legal rights.'

On the other hand, in *Stafford* v. *Stafford*[40] Knight Bruce L.J. said this:

'Generally, when the facts are known from which a right arises, the right is presumed to be known. . . . '

"Like the judge, I should desire to follow the conclusion of Wilberforce J. who reviewed the authorities in *Re Pauling's Settlement Trusts*[41]; and this passage was mentioned without dissent in the same case in the Court of Appeal[42]:

'The result of these authorities appears to me to be that the court has to consider all the circumstances in which the concurrence of the *cestui que trust* was given with a view to seeing whether it is fair and equitable that, having given his concurrence, he should afterwards turn round and sue the trustees: that, subject to this, it is not necessary that he should know that what he is concurring in is a breach of trust, provided that he fully understands what he is concurring in, and that it is not necessary that he should himself have directly benefited by the breach of trust.'

There is, therefore, no hard and fast rule that ignorance of a legal right is a bar, but the whole of the circumstances must be looked at to see whether it is just that the complaining beneficiary should succeed against the trustee.[43]

"On the whole I am of the opinion that in the circumstances of this case it would not be right to allow the plaintiff to assert his right (assuming he had one) because with full knowledge of the facts he affirmed the sale. He has had

---

[39] (1880) 15 Ch.D. 96, 105.
[40] (1857) 1 De G. & J. 193, 202.
[41] [1961] 3 All E.R. 713, 730.
[42] [1964] Ch. 303.
[43] Endorsed in *Re Freeston's Charity* [1979] 1 All E.R. 51, 62. The third proposition of Fry J. in *Wilmott* v. *Barber* (1880) 15 Ch.D. 96, 105 has also been rejected in *Taylor Fashions Ltd.* v. *Liverpool Victoria Trustees Co. Ltd.* [1981] 1 All E.R. 897, 915–918 and *Habib Bank Ltd.* v. *Habib Bank A.G. Zurich* [1981] 2 All E.R. 650, 666, 668. See p. 60, *supra.*

£2,000 as a result. He has caused the third defendant to embark on liabilities which he cannot recoup. There can in fact be no *restitutio in integrum* which is a necessary element in rescission.

"The plaintiff is asserting an equitable and not a legal remedy. He has by his conduct disentitled himself to it. It is extremely doubtful whether the order if worked out would benefit anyone, I think we should not assent to it, on general equitable principles."

## RE SOMERSET, SOMERSET v. EARL POULETT

Court of Appeal [1894] 1 Ch. 231; (Lindley, A. L. Smith and Davey L.JJ.)

Kekewich J. held that a £34,612 mortgage was a proper investment except in so far as the trustees had advanced too much, so that they were liable for a breach of trust in respect only of the amount excessively advanced: Trustee Act 1888, s.5.[44] He considered that the largest sum which in the circumstances the trustees could properly have advanced was £26,000. He further held that the trustees were entitled to have the plaintiff's life interest impounded by way of indemnity under the Trustee Act 1888, s.6; as to which the plaintiff appealed.

LINDLEY L.J.: " . . . The second question is whether, in order to indemnify the trustees, the court ought to impound the income of the trust funds during the life of the appellant. This question turns on the construction of section 6, and on the conduct of the parties. [Section 6 is now Trustee Act 1925, s.62.]

"Did the trustees commit the breach of trust for which they have been made liable at the instigation or request, or with the consent in writing, of the appellant? The section is intended to protect trustees, and ought to be construed so as to carry out that intention. But the section ought not, in my opinion, to be construed as if the word 'investment' had been inserted instead of 'breach of trust.' An enactment to that effect would produce great injustice in many cases. In order to bring a case within this section the *cestui que trust* must instigate, or request or consent in writing to some act or omission which is itself a breach of trust and not to some act or omission which only becomes a breach of trust by reason of want of care on the part of the trustees. If a *cestui que trust* instigates, requests or consents in writing to an investment not in terms authorised by the power of investment, he clearly falls within the section; and in such a case his ignorance or forgetfulness of the terms of power would not, I think, protect him—at all events, not unless he could give some good reason why it should, *e.g.*, that it was caused by the trustee. But if all that a *cestui que trust* does is to instigate, request or consent in writing to an investment which is authorised by the terms of the power, the case is, I think, very different. He has a right to expect that the trustees will act with proper care in making the investment, and if they do not they cannot throw the consquences on him unless they can show that he instigated, requested or consented in writing to their non-performance of their duty in this respect. This is, in my opinion, the true construction of this section.

"As regards the necessity for a writing, I agree with the decision of Mr. Justice Kekewich in *Griffith* v. *Hughes*,[45] that an instigation or request need not be in writing, and that the words 'in writing' apply only to the consent.

[44] s.9 of the Act of 1925; *supra*, p. 630.
[45] [1892] 3 Ch. 105.

"I pass now to the facts. It is, in my opinion, perfectly clear that the appellant instigated, requested and consented in writing to the investment by the trustees of the trust money on a mortgage of Lord Hill's estate. This, indeed, was not disputed. But the evidence does not, that I can see, go further than this. He certainly never instigated, requested or consented in writing to an investment on the property without inquiry; still less, if upon inquiry the rents payable in respect of the lands mortgaged were found to be less than the interest payable on the mortgage.

"Whether the appellant knew the rental is a very important question. Mr. Justice Kekewich has found that he did. But the evidence does not, in my opinion, warrant this inference. The appellant certainly knew a good deal about the property; and Colonel Hill [his father-in-law], to whom he very must trusted, more likely knew more than the appellant himself. There was also a proposal from Lord Hill, which the appellant once had, but which was lost. This might have shown the rental. But the appellant positively denies that he knew the rental, and says that Mr. Haste, the mortgagor's agent, told him it was £1,700 a year, whilst in fact it was only £1,070 net. It was contended that Messrs. Wilde, Berger & Co., who were the solicitors of the mortgagor and of the trustees, were also the solicitors of the appellant, and that through them he must be treated as having known of the valuation and the rental, and all other material facts. But to affect him with this notice would be extremely unjust, for the facts, a knowledge of which the court is asked to impute to him, were clearly kept from him. The solicitors obtained the valuation for and on behalf of the trustees; they obtained the second opinion of the valuers for the benefit of the borrower, and for the protection of the trustees. In obtaining the valuation and opinion the solicitors were not acting for or on behalf of the appellant; and considering that they never disclosed the valuation or opinion to the appellant, and never informed him of their effect, he cannot, in my opinion, be held to have known them. It is important to observe that the statute does not make a *cestui que trust* responsible for a breach of trust simply because he had actual or constructive notice of it; he must have instigated or requested it, or have consented to it in writing. Even if the knowledge of his solicitors could be imputed to him for some purposes, it is not true in fact that the appellant did by himself or his agent instigate, request or consent in writing to a breach of trust.[46] Even if the appellant had constructive notice through his solicitors of the valuation, the court, in exercising the power conferred on it by the statute, would, in my opinion, be acting unjustly, and not justly, if, under the circumstances of this case, it held the appellant liable to indemnify the trustees. The court would be treating the appellant as having done more than he did, and I can see no justification for such a course. It must be borne in mind that the plaintiff was not seeking to benefit himself at the expense of the remaindermen as in *Raby* v. *Ridehalgh*.[47] He was seeking a better security for the trust money for the benefit of everyone interested in it . . . "

---

[46] On this point, A. L. Smith L.J. observed (at p. 270): "In my opinion, upon the true reading of this section, a trustee, in order to obtain the benefit conferred thereby, must establish that the beneficiary knew the facts which rendered what he was instigating, requesting or consenting to in writing a breach of trust." Davey L.J. observed (at p. 274): " . . . in order to bring the case within the section the beneficiary must have requested the trustee to depart from and go outside the terms of his trust. It is not, of course, necessary that the beneficiary should know the investment to be in law a breach of trust."

[47] (1855) 7 De G.M. & G. 104.

*Held*, therefore, by the Court of Appeal that the defendants were not entitled to have the plaintiff's life interest impounded by way of indemnity.[48]

## RE PAULING'S SETTLEMENT TRUST (NO. 2)

Chancery Division [1963] Ch. 576; [1963] 2 W.L.R. 838; [1963] 1 All E.R. 857

Coutts & Co. were held liable for breach of trust in respect of a number of advances of capital to the children of a life tenant, Mrs. Younghusband. The bank claimed to be entitled to impound the life interest. The plaintiffs sought the appointment of two new trustees in place of the bank who opposed this as it might negate their right to impound.

Wilberforce J. appointed new trustees as this would not affect the right to impound.

WILBERFORCE J.: . . . "Next I come to a separate series of objections which raise some difficult questions of law. The defendants, as I have already mentioned, have a claim to impound the life interest of Mrs. Younghusband now vested in the Guardian Assurance Co. Ltd. in order to recoup themselves against any money which they may be ordered to repay. What is said by the defendants is that that right to impound would be prejudiced if new trustees were appointed now and the trust fund handed over to them. That involves a consideration as to what is the nature of the right to impound which exists in favour of a trustee who has committed a breach of trust at the instigation of a beneficiary. I have to consider both the ordinary right which exists in equity apart from statute and also the further statutory right which has been conferred by section 62 of the Trustee Act 1925 both of which are invoked by the defendants as plaintiffs in the Chancery action now pending. It seems to me that it is not possible to maintain, as is the defendants' contention here, that a trustee, having committed a breach of trust, is entitled to remain as a trustee until it has exercised its right to impound the income of the beneficiary in order to recoup itself. That seems to me an impossible proposition. It is quite true that, in the reported authorities, there is no case where the right to impound has been exercised by a former trustee as distinct from an existing trustee, but it seems to me in principle that it is impossible to contend that the right to impound is limited to the case where the trustee seeking the right is an actual trustee. The nature of the right to impound seems to me to turn on two things: first, that the money paid back to capital is in its origin the money of the trustee, and that when it comes to considering who should get the income of it, the trustee who has provided the money has a better right to it than the tenant for life who has instigated the breach of trust. The alternative way of putting the matter is that the trustee in breach of trust is in some way subrogated to the rights of the beneficiary. He stands in his position in order that he may be indemnified. That seems to me the way in which it was put by the Lords Justices in *Raby* v. *Ridehalgh*.[49] It does not seem to me that there is any support in authority or in principle for saying that the right depends upon the actual possession of the trust fund, and it appears to me that the analogy

---

[48] In accordance with this case is *Mara* v. *Browne* [1892] 2 Ch. 69, 92–93, where North J. held that the trustee was not entitled to impound the interest of the beneficiary because the beneficiary, though she had consented in writing, had not consented to those acts which constituted the breach of trust. On appeal [1896] 1 Ch. 199 the point did not arise.

[49] (1855) 7 De G.M. & G. 104.

which has been sought to be drawn with the executor's right to retain is a false one and does not apply to this case. So much for the equitable right to impound as opposed to the statutory right.

"As regards the statutory right, that depends on the language of section 62 of the Trustee Act 1925, and at first sight it might look as if that right only exists in favour of a person who is actually a trustee. But, on consideration, that seems to me to be a misconstruction of the section. In the first place, the same objection against limiting the right in that way applies to the statutory jurisdiction. It seems to me an absurdity that it is required as a condition of exercising the right to obtain an impounding order, that the trustee who, *ex hypothesi*, is in breach of trust, must remain the trustee in order to acquire a right of indemnity. Further, it seems to me on the authorities, and, indeed, on the very terms of the section, that the section is giving an additional right, among other things, to deal with the case of a married woman beneficiary; that the statutory right is extending the equitable right and not limiting it, and that it is not right to read the section so as to apply only to a person who was formerly a trustee. The section begins with the words: 'Where a trustee commits a breach of trust,' thereby indicating that at the time the breach of trust is committed the person in question must be a trustee. Then further down in the section there is a reference to a trustee and that appears to me to be merely a reference back to the same person as the person who committed the breach of trust and not as an indication that the person in question must be a trustee at the date of the order. I would add to that, that here the writ which has been issued in the Chancery Division was issued at a time when the defendants were trustees, and, therefore, at the date of the writ the requirement of being a trustee was fulfilled. So that, although I entirely appreciate that the defendants may be anxious not to lose their right to impound the income of the tenant for life, that right could not, in my view, be prejudiced by appointing new trustees at this stage."

### III. STATUTES OF LIMITATION

#### Equitable rules

The doctrine of "laches" is expressly preserved by the Limitation Act 1980, section 36 of which provides that "nothing in the Act shall affect any equitable jurisdiction to refuse relief on the ground of acquiescence or otherwise." The doctrine is available "where it would be practically unjust to give a remedy, either because the party has, by his conduct, done that which might fairly be regarded as equivalent to a waiver of it, or where by his conduct and neglect he has, though perhaps not waiving that remedy, yet put the other party in a situation in which it would not be reasonable to place him if the remedy were afterwards asserted."[50] The doctrine really consists of a substantial lapse of time coupled with the existence of circumstances which make it inequitable to enforce the plaintiff's claim.

The field of operation of the doctrine has been narrowed by statute.[51] Nowadays, it is the statutory six-year period which operates

---

[50] *Per* Lord Selborne L.C. in *Lindsay Petroleum Co.* v. *Hurd* (1874) L.R. 5 P.C. 221, 239–240. See also *Weld* v. *Petre* [1929] 1 Ch. 33, 51–52; *Holder* v. *Holder* [1968] Ch. 353.
[51] Trustee Act 1888, s.8, Limitation Act 1939 replaced by Limitation Act 1980.

against a beneficiary in respect of a claim against the trustee for a breach of trust[52] and not the equitable doctrine of "laches." But there are cases outside the Act (*e.g.* frequent claims against trustees who have purchased trust property or beneficial interests therein[53] and claims simply for a fiduciary to account without any claim for any breaches of duty[54]) and cases under the Act[55] in which the liability of the trustee is subject to no *statutory* period of limitation at all (*e.g.* a claim against trustees for property or proceeds thereof retained by them). In such a case the right of the beneficiary will only be barred by an unreasonably long period of delay amounting to laches.[56]

The ability of equity to act by analogy to the statute is expressly recognised and preserved, for section 36(1) of the 1980 Act provides that the six-year period which it lays down is not to apply to "any claim for specific performance of a contract or for an injunction or for *other equitable relief*" save in so far as a court of equity may apply it by analogy.[57] But the analogous application of section 36(1) is limited to claims for which no express provision is to be found elsewhere in the statute.[58]

Thus it was held in *Re Diplock*[59] that even if the claims in equity were analogous to the common law action for money had and received (which they were not), they were also "actions in respect of a claim to the personal estate of a deceased person" for which under section 20 of the 1939 Act (now s.22 of the 1980 Act) the relevant period of limitation was one of 12 years from the date when the right to receive the share or interest accrued; accordingly, there was no scope for applying any other period by way of analogy or otherwise.

The equitable rule that time would not run against the plaintiff in cases of fraud and mistake is adopted by the 1980 Act (replacing and amending s.26 of the 1939 Act) which provides:

"Where in the case of any action for which a period of limitation is prescribed by this Act, either:

(*a*) the action is based upon the fraud of the defendant or his agent or of any person through whom he claims or his agent, or

---

[52] See Limitation Act 1939, s.19(2) replaced by Limitation Act 1980, s.21(3), *infra*, p. 795; *Re Pauling's S.T.* [1964] Ch. 303.

[53] *Tito* v. *Waddell (No. 2)* [1977] Ch. 106, 250.

[54] *Att.-Gen.* v. *Cocke* [1988] Ch. 414.

[55] Limitation Act 1980, s.21(1), *infra*, p. 794.

[56] See *McDonnell* v. *White* (1865) 11 H.L.C. 271; *Sleeman* v. *Wilson* (1871) L.R. 13 Eq. 36; *Tito* v. *Waddell (No. 2)* [1977] Ch. 106, 248–250.

[57] On this and actions for accounts, see *Tito* v. *Waddell (No. 2)* [1977] Ch. 106, 250–252 discussing Limitation Act 1939, s.2(7) replaced by Limitation Act 1980, s.36(1). An equitable claim for an account is usually ancillary to another claim in which the period applicable to the main claim should also apply to the ancillary claim, but if the claim is only for an account no period of limitation applies: *Att.-Gen.* v. *Cocke* [1988] Ch. 414.

[58] A case like *Re Robinson* [1911] 1 Ch. 502 would be decided today in accordance with the provisions of s.21(3) of the Limitation Act 1980 and not by the use of any analogy to the statute.

[59] [1948] Ch. 465, 502–516; when the case reached the House of Lords, *sub nom. Ministry of Health* v. *Simpson* [1951] A.C. 251, their Lordships approved the views of the Court of Appeal on the applicability of s.20 of the Limitation Act 1939 (now s.22 of the 1980 Act) and it therefore became unnecessary to express an opinion on the applicability of s.26 thereof (now s.32 of the 1980 Act). It seems s.22 of the 1980 Act applies even after the personal representatives have become trustees.

(*b*) any fact relevant to the plaintiff's right of action has been deliberately concealed from him by any such person as aforesaid, or

(*c*) the action is for relief from the consequences of mistake,

the period of limitation shall not begin to run until the plaintiff has discovered the fraud concealment or mistake, as the case may be, or could with reasonable diligence have discovered it."[60] Subsection (3) goes on to protect purchasers taking under transactions without notice of the fraud having been committed or the mistake having been made, as the case may be. "Deliberate commission of a breach of duty in circumstances in which it is unlikely to be discovered for some time amounts to deliberate concealment of the facts involved in that breach of duty."[61]

It was decided in *Phillips-Higgins* v. *Harper*[62] that section 26(*c*) of the 1939 Act does not apply to the case of a right of action concealed from the plaintiff by a mistake. Its scope is limited to actions where a mistake has been made and has had certain consequences and the plaintiff is seeking to be relieved from those consequences, *e.g.* actions to recover money paid under a mistake; to rescind or rectify contracts on the ground of mistake; to reopen accounts settled in consequence of mistakes. It applies, in fact, only where mistake is an essential ingredient of the cause of action, and it does not help a plaintiff to ascertain the amount still due to him after the ordinary period of limitation has expired. The anomalous result is that a person who has by mistake paid too much can take advantage of the section, but the person who has by mistake received too little cannot avail himself of it.

*Statutory rules affording little protection to trustees*

Section 21 of the Act reads as follows:

"(1) No period of limitation prescribed by this Act shall apply to an action by a beneficiary under a trust, being an action—

(*a*) in respect of any fraud or fraudulent breach of trust to which the trustee was a party or privy[63]; or

(*b*) to recover from the trustee trust property or the proceeds thereof in the possession of the trustee, or previously received by the trustee and converted to his use.

(2) Where a trustee who is also a beneficiary under the trust receives or retains trust property or its proceeds as his share on a distribution of trust

---

[60] See *Kitchen* v. *R.A.F. Association* [1958] 1 W.L.R. 563 (C.A.) (solicitor's negligence); *Baker* v. *Medway Supplies* [1958] 1 W.L.R. 1216 (fraudulent conversion of money); *Bartlett* v. *Barclays Bank Trust Co.* [1980] 1 All E.R. 139, 154; *Peco Arts Inc.* v. *Hazlitt Gallery Ltd.* [1983] 3 All E.R. 193 (reasonable diligence in discovering drawing not an original).

[61] *King* v. *Victor Parsons & Co.* [1973] 1 W.L.R. 29, 33, *per* Lord Denning M.R. This reflects the old case law on (*b*) when it was known as fraudulent concealment in Limitation Act 1939, s.26.

[62] [1954] 1 Q.B. 411.

[63] Does this apply both to proceedings against a trustee who has been guilty of fraud and to a person who was not the original trustee but who acquired the trust property or payment which was fraudulently made out of the trust property? *Semble* it applies to both: *Baker* v. *Medway Supplies* [1958] 1 W.L.R. 1216.

property under the trust, his liability in any action brought by virtue of subsection (1)(*b*) above to recover that property or its proceeds after the expiration of the period of limitation prescribed by this Act for bringing an action to recover trust property shall be limited to the excess over his proper share.

This subsection only applies if the trustee acted honestly and reasonably in making the distribution.

(3) Subject to the preceding provisions of this section an action by a beneficiary to recover trust property or in respect of any breach of trust, not being an action for which a period of limitation is prescribed by any other provision of this Act,[64] shall not be brought after the expiration of six years from the date on which the right of action accrued. For the purposes of this subsection the right of action shall not be treated as having accrued to any beneficiary entitled to a future interest in the trust property until the interest fell into possession.

(4) No beneficiary as against whom there would be a good defence under this Act shall derive any greater or other benefit from a judgment or order obtained by any other beneficiary than he could have obtained if he had brought the action and this Act had been pleaded in defence."

The following observations may be made upon the effect of the section.

Since the Limitation Act 1939 there has no longer been any distinction drawn between express and other trustees, since the word "trustee" is defined by reference to section 68(17) of the Trustee Act 1925. This definition excludes the duties incident to an estate conveyed by way of mortgage,[65] but includes implied and constructive trusts and personal representatives. It has been held to include the directors of a company,[66] but not trustees in bankruptcy[67] nor apparently the liquidators of companies in voluntary liquidation.[68]

The section is limited to actions by *beneficiaries* in respect of trust property. It is thought, however, that a newly-appointed trustee would have the same rights as the beneficiaries themselves against the surviving trustees.[69] A claim by the Attorney-General against trustees of a charitable trust (which has no beneficiary) is outside the section.[70]

Perpetual liability is confined under this section as under the 1888 Act to cases of (a) fraudulent[71] breaches of trust and (b) of retention or

---

[64] Where personal representatives have become trustees upon completing administration of an estate the relationship between s.21(3) and s.22 is unclear. It would seem that the breadth of s.22 (formerly s.20 of the 1939 Act) makes the 12-year period applicable: *Re Diplock* [1948] Ch. 465, 511–513; *Ministry of Health* v. *Simpson* [1951] A.C. 251, 276–277.

[65] But a prior mortgagee of land exercising his power of sale is a trustee of the surplus for subsequent mortgagees after meeting his own claims. See *Thorne* v. *Heard* [1894] 1 Ch. 599; the Law of Property Act 1925, s.105.

[66] *Re Lands Allotments Co.* [1894] 1 Ch. 616, 631, 638, 643 and *Whitwam* v. *Watkin* (1898) 78 L.T. 188.

[67] *Re Cornish* [1896] 1 Q.B. 99.

[68] *Re Windsor Steam Coal Co. (1901) Ltd.* [1928] Ch. 609; affd. on a different ground [1929] 1 Ch. 151.

[69] See *Re Bowden* (1890) 45 Ch.D. 444, a case decided under the 1888 Act which was not limited to actions by beneficiaries.

[70] *Att.-Gen.* v. *Cocke* [1988] Ch. 414.

[71] See *North American Land Co.* v. *Watkins* [1904] 1 Ch. 242; [1904] 2 Ch. 233; *Vane* v. *Vane* (1872) L.R. 8 Ch. 383.

conversion of the trust property. It appears from *Thorne* v. *Heard*[72] that the negligence of a trustee, resulting in his solicitor embezzling the trust funds, was insufficient to render the trustee "party or privy" to the fraud.

The section speaks of property "previously received by the trustee and converted to his use." In *Re Howlett*[73] it was contended that this referred to an *actual* receipt of property, but Danckwerts J. held that it included a *notional* receipt, and so he was able to charge a trustee who had occupied trust property for some 20 years with an occupation rent. To fall foul of section 21(1) a trustee's retention or conversion must be some wrongful application in his own favour.[74]

Exceptionally, he has some protection under section 21(2) so that if he had distributed one-third of the trust property to himself, honestly and reasonably believing that only three beneficiaries existed, he will be liable to a fourth beneficiary turning up after six years not for a quarter share but only for the one-twelfth difference between the one-third share he took and the one-quarter share which was truly his.

Section 21(3) of the Act prescribes a six-year period of limitation for breach of trust[75] cases not falling within section 21(1) or (2) or within any other provision of the Act. Thus, if a trustee can show that an innocent or negligent breach of trust led him to part with the trust property the six-year period is the appropriate one to limit his liability. The recipient retaining such property or its product will be subject to a perpetual liability unless he is a bona fide purchaser for value without notice. The six-year period will also be appropriate if the trust funds were dissipated by a co-trustee.[76]

The last sentence of section 21(3) protects reversionary interests by enacting that time shall not run against a beneficiary until his interest has fallen into possession.[77] Even before that date a remainderman can sue for breach of trust. In such a case if the prior beneficiary is himself barred the trustees must nevertheless replace the fund at the suit of the remainderman, but during the continuance of the prior beneficiary's interest they will be entitled to the income of the property: for a judgment recovered by one beneficiary is not to improve the position of one who is already barred.[78]

### Section 5. Liability of Trustees *inter se*

Since trustees are jointly and severally liable one trustee may be compelled to replace the whole loss or more than his share of the

---

[72] [1895] A.C. 495.

[73] [1949] Ch. 767.

[74] *Re Gurney* [1893] 1 Ch. 590; *Re Page* [1893] 1 Ch. 304; *Re Fountaine* [1909] 2 Ch. 382.

[75] Purchases by a trustee (or other fiduciary) of trust property or beneficial interests therein are not breaches of trust for this purpose but fall within a general disability of fiduciaries: *Tito* v. *Waddell (No. 2)* [1977] Ch. 106, 248–250 revealing the doctrine of laches applies.

[76] *Re Tufnell* (1902) 18 T.L.R. 705; *Re Fountaine* [1909] 2 Ch. 382.

[77] Consent by a life-tenant to an advance in favour of a remainderman does not amount to a release of the life interest so as to convert the remainderman's interest into an interest in possession: *Re Pauling's S.T.* [1964] Ch. 303.

[78] *Re Somerset* [1894] 1 Ch. 231; s.19(3) of the Limitation Act 1939 and s.21(4) of the 1980 Act; *Mara* v. *Browne* [1895] 2 Ch. 69 reversed on another point [1896] 1 Ch. 199.

loss.[79] In such a case he will have a right of contribution from the others unless he was a fraudulent trustee.[80] Exceptionally, a trustee can obtain a complete indemnity so as to throw the whole loss on his co-trustee if (a) his co-trustee has exclusively benefited from the breach of trust as by using trust money for his own purposes when he would be unjustly enriched if he could obtain contribution from his co-trustees or (b) his co-trustee is someone with special qualifications on whom he could reasonably be expected to rely, such as a solicitor[81] whose advice and control caused his passive participation in the breach of trust or (c) his co-trustee has a beneficial interest liable to impounding under general equitable principles or section 62 of the Trustee Act which is large enough to satisfy the loss: *Chillingworth* v. *Chambers.*[82] In respect of an unsatisfied loss in this last instance the trustee is left to his right of contribution against the co-trustee.

If, *e.g.* the trustees are a professional corporate trustee and a private person and the beneficiaries sue only the corporate trustee then it may bring in the private trustee as a party to the proceedings. If the beneficiaries recover the whole sum from the corporate trustee it may claim half from the private trustee except to the extent the court may relieve him under the Trustee Act 1925, s.61.[83]

The Civil Liability (Contribution) Act 1978 (*infra*, pp. 802–804) effective from January 1, 1979, has superseded the equitable right of contribution but not the right to an indemnity. It gives the court a vast discretion to fix the contribution anywhere between 1 and 99 per cent. However, in the case of trustees it is considered that the court's discretion will be exercised along the old equitable guidelines. It would need to be a very special case indeed for unequal treatment to be accorded to co-trustees (except in indemnity cases) since the sanction of equal liability serves a useful salutary function for breach of what is a joint obligation *par excellence*.

### BAHIN v. HUGHES

Court of Appeal (1886) 31 Ch.D. 390; 55 L.J.Ch. 472; 54 L.T. 188; 34 W.R. 311; 2 T.L.R. 276 (Cotton, Bowen and Fry L.JJ.)

A testator, Robert Hughes, bequeathed a legacy of £2,000 to his three daughters—Eliza Hughes, Mrs. Burden and Mrs. Edwards—on trust to invest in specified securities and in real securities in England and Wales. Eliza Hughes, who was the active trustee, and Mr. Burden invested the fund on the

---

[79] A trustee may take proceedings against his co-trustee who derived all the benefit from the breach to make good the loss to the trust estate: *Baynard* v. *Woolley* (1855) 20 Beav. 583; *Elwes* v. *Barnard* (1865) 13 L.T. 426; 11 Jur.(N.S.) 1035.

[80] *Att.-Gen.* v. *Wilson* (1840) Cr. & Ph. 1, 28.

[81] As in *Re Partington* (1887) 57 L.T. 654. What about Chancery barristers, bank managers, professional trustees? See broad dicta of Cotton L.J. in *Bahin* v. *Hughes* (1886) 31 Ch.D. 390, *infra*, p. 797.

[82] [1896] 1 Ch. 685, *infra*, pp. 801–802.

[83] *Wohleben* v. *Canada Permanent Trust Co. & Wohleben* (1976) 70 D.L.R. (3d) 257 totally relieving the private trustee, commented on by D. W. M. Waters (1977) 55 Can. Bar Rev. 342.

(unauthorised) security of leasehold properties, an investment discovered by Mr. Burden. Mrs Edwards had been informed of the proposal, but her concurrence was not obtained. The security proving insufficient, the tenant for life and remaindermen brought this action against Eliza Hughes, Mr. Edwards (whose wife had died) and Mr. and Mrs. Burden, claiming that the defendants were liable to make good the trust fund.[84] Edwards served a third-party notice on Eliza Hughes claiming to be indemnified by her, on the ground that she had assumed the role of sole trustee, that the investment had been made at her instigation, and that she had represented to Mrs. Edwards that the mortgage was a proper and sufficient security.

*Held*, by Kay J., that the defendants were jointly and severally liable to replace the £2,000, and that the defendant Edwards had no right of indemnity against Eliza Hughes. Edwards appealed.

COTTON L.J.: " . . . On going into the authorities, there are very few cases in which one trustee, who has been guilty with a co-trustee of breach of trust and held answerable, has successfully sought indemnity as against his co-trustee. In *Lockhart* v. *Reilly*[85] it appears from the report of the case in the *Law Journal* that the trustee by whom the loss was sustained had been not only trustee, but had been and was a solicitor, and acting as solicitor for his self and his co-trustee, and it was on his advice that Lockhart had relied in making the investment which gave rise to the action of the *cestui que trust*. The Lord Chancellor (Lord Cranworth) refers to the fact that he was a solicitor, and makes the remark: 'The whole thing was trusted to him. He was the solicitor, and, independently of the consideration that one cannot help seeing it was done with a view of favouring his own family, yet if that had not been so, the co-trustee leaves it with the solicitor-trustee, by whose negligence (I use no harsher word) all this evil, in a great degree, has arisen.' Therefore the Lord Chancellor, in giving his decision, relies upon the fact of the trustee being a solicitor. In *Thompson* v. *Finch*[86] a right was conceded to prove against the estate of the deceased trustee for the full loss sustained; but it appears that in this case also he was a solicitor, and that he really took this money to himself, for he mixed it with his own money, and invested it on a mortgage; and therefore it was held that the trustee was entitled to indemnity from the estate of the co-trustee, who was a solicitor. This was affirmed in the Court of Appeal; and the Court of Appeal took so strong a view of the conduct of the solicitor that both of the judges concurred in thinking that he ought to be called on to show cause why he should not be struck off the rolls. Of course, where one trustee has got the money into his own hands, and made use of it, he will be liable to his co-trustee to give him an indemnity. Now I think it wrong to lay down any limitation of the circumstances under which one trustee would be held liable to the other for indemnity, both having been held liable to the *cestui que trust*; but so far as cases have gone at present, relief has only been granted against a trustee who has himself got the benefit of the breach of trust, or between whom and his co-trustees there has existed a relation which will justify the court in treating him solely liable for the breach of trust. . . .

---

84 Prior to s.18 of the Married Women's Property Act of 1882 (which did not apply to the present case) a married woman could not act as trustee without the participation of her husband (Mr. Edwards); he was necessarily a trustee through her trusteeship, and was responsible for her breaches of trust.

85 (1856) 25 L.J.Ch. 697, 702.

86 (1856) 25 L.J.Ch. 681.

"Miss Hughes was the active trustee and Mr. Edwards did nothing, and in my opinion it would be laying down a wrong rule that where one trustee acts honestly, though erroneously, the other trustee is to be held entitled to indemnity who by doing nothing neglects his duty more than the acting trustee. That Miss Hughes made an improper investment is true, but she acted honestly, and intended to do the best she could, and believed that the property was sufficient security for the money, although she made no inquiries about their being leasehold houses. In my opinion the money was lost just as much by the default of Mr. Edwards as by the innocent though erroneous action of his co-trustee, Miss Hughes. All the trustees were in the wrong, and every one is equally liable to indemnify the beneficiaries."

FRY L.J.: " . . . I also agree with my brother Lord Justice Cotton. This part of the appeal is based upon some notion that one trustee is liable to indemnify his co-trustee against loss or injury from his acts, but I cannot think that such liability exists, for if it did exist the books would be full of authorities bearing upon the point, and the courts would be crowded with litigation on the subject. It is well known that the authorities are extremely few, and the authorities which do exist do not favour the appellant's contention. It has been pointed out by Lord Justice Cotton that in each of the two cases cited the trustee who was held to be secondarily liable, and who had a right of indemnity, had been misled by his co-trustee, who was the solicitor to the trust, and had been proved to have been guilty of negligence in his duty as such solicitor. In my judgment the courts ought to be very jealous of raising any such implied liability as is insisted on, because if such existed it would act as an opiate upon the consciences of the trustees; so that instead of the *cestui que trust* having the benefit of several acting trustees, each trustee would be looking to the other or others for a right of indemnity, and so neglect the performance of his duties. Such a doctrine would be against the policy of the court in relation to trusts.

"In the present case, in my judgment, the loss which has happened is the result of the combination of the action of Miss Hughes with the inaction of Mr. Edwards. If Miss Hughes has made a mistake, it was through simple ignorance and want of knowledge, and if on the other hand Mr. Edwards had used all the diligence which he ought to have done, I doubt whether any loss would have been incurred. The money might have been recovered before the property went down in value. I think, therefore, that it is not possible for Mr. Edwards to obtain any relief, and I concur with my brethren that this appeal must be dismissed with costs." *Appeal dismissed.*

## HEAD v. GOULD

Chancery Division [1898] 2 Ch. 250; 67 L.J.Ch. 480; 78 L.T. 739

Several points fell to be decided in this case, but for the purposes of a trustee's claim of indemnity against his co-trustee the facts may be sufficiently stated as follows:

Miss Head and Mr. Gould were appointed new trustees of certain marriage settlements (the beneficial interests being the same under both settlements), and thenceforth Gould acted as solicitor to the trusts. Miss Head was one of the remaindermen under these settlements, the tenant for life being her mother. The new trustees sold a house forming part of the trust, and in breach of trust handed the proceeds of sale to the tenant for life. Part of the trust property consisted also of certain policies on the life of Mrs. Head, policies which Mrs. Head had mortgaged to the trust by way of security for advances of trust capital which the former trustees had made to her at her urgent request for the purpose of assisting the family. These policies were (in breach of trust) surrendered by the new trustees with the concurrence of Mrs. Head.

Miss Head claimed to be indemnified by her co-trustee, Gould, under circumstances which appear from the judgment:

KEKEWICH J.: " . . . It will be convenient here at once to deal with the claim made by Miss Head against her co-trustee, Gould. By her third party notice she seeks to be indemnified by him against loss by reason of the breaches of trust, on the ground that the loss and misapplication (if any) of the trust funds, or any part thereof, were occasioned entirely by his acts or defaults, and that he assumed to act as solicitor to the trust estate and as the sole trustee thereof, and exercised control of the administration of the trust funds, and that whatever was done by herself in connection with the trust was at his instigation and in reliance upon his advice.

"This is a serious charge, and if it had been proved would have entitled her to the relief claimed according to well-known and well-recognised principles. Mr. Gover, in support of the claim, relied on the decision of Byrne J. in *Re Turner*[87]; but it is to be observed that the learned judge did no more than follow *Lockhart* v. *Reilly*,[88] and act upon the principles there enunciated and to which I have alluded. There is before me no evidence bringing the case within those principles, or showing that the charge which is correctly formulated on them is consistent with the facts. My conclusion from such evidence as there is before the court is distinctly adverse to the claim. I know that, before the appointment of herself and Gould as trustees, Miss Head was an active party to the importunities of her mother which induced the former trustees to commit a breach of trust for their benefit, and that she looked to the change of trustees as a means of, in some way or other, obtaining further advances. I know, further, that she was well acquainted with the position of the trust, and that it was all-important to maintain the policies and to appropriate the rents of the house to that purpose. She now affects to ignore all that has been done since her appointment, and professes not to remember having executed the several instruments which must have been executed by her for the sale of the house and the surrender of the policies, or the receipt of moneys arising therefrom. With regret, and under a painful sense of duty, I am bound to say that I do not credit her testimony. True it is that the defendant, Gould, is a solicitor, and that he was appointed a trustee for that very reason. True no doubt, also, that the legal business was managed by him, and I do not propose to absolve him from any responsibility attaching to him on that ground; but I do not myself think that Byrne J. or any other judge ever intended to hold that a man is bound to indemnify his co-trustee against loss *merely* because he was a solicitor, when that co-trustee was an active participator in the breach of trust complained of, and is not proved to have participated merely in consequence of the *advice and control* of the solicitor. . . . "

*Held* therefore, the trustee, Miss Head, had no claim of indemnity against her co-trustee.[89]

---

[87] [1897] 1 Ch. 536.
[88] (1856) 25 L.J.Ch. 697.
[89] On indemnity between trustees, see also *Blyth* v. *Fladgate* [1891] 1 Ch. 337, 364, 365; *Re Turner* [1897] 1 Ch. 536, 544; *Re Linsley* [1904] 2 Ch. 785.

## *Chillingworth* v. *Chambers*[90]

The decision of the Court of Appeal in the above case has been said to lie on the border between contribution and indemnity. It is to the effect that a *trustee-beneficiary* who has participated in, and, as between himself and his co-trustee, benefited exclusively, by a breach of trust for which he and his co-trustee are equally to blame must indemnify his co-trustee to the extent of his beneficial interest. X and Y were trustees. X was also a beneficiary, his share being (say) £500. X and Y, with the object of increasing the rate of dividend, invested trust funds in a mortgage which was held to be a breach of trust. As between X and Y, X benefited exclusively by this breach of trust; at any rate, he was so treated by the Court of Appeal. The mortgage was eventually realised at a loss of £400, the whole of which was in fact made good out of X's beneficial share (the trust fund now being in court). X's claim of contribution against Y, that Y should share the loss with him, failed; for X was held liable to indemnify his co-trustee Y to the extent of his beneficial interest. Since X's beneficial interest (£500) exceeded the actual loss (£400), the result was that Y managed to shift the whole of that loss on to X. Strictly speaking, Y did not shift the loss on to X; he shifted it on to X's beneficial interest.

Lindley L.J. summed up the position between X and Y as follows[91]: "To the extent to which the [trustee-beneficiary's] right as trustee is neutralised by his obligation as *cestui que trust* he will have no right to contribution." The trustee-beneficiary's right as trustee is a right of contribution from his co-trustee. His obligation as beneficiary is to indemnify that trustee out of his beneficial interest, for where a beneficiary is an active party in a breach of trust committed with a view towards his benefit he is liable to indemnify his trustee out of his beneficial interest.[92]

Lindley L.J. continued: "But except so far as it is thus neutralised his right of contribution will remain." If, therefore, X's beneficial interest had been £300, and not £500, that £300 would have been used up in indemnifying Y as to three-quarters of the loss of £400 for which they are jointly and severally liable, but the remaining £100 would have been shared between them.

In considering *Chillingworth* v. *Chambers*[93] it is of advantage to approach the matter in three stages:

First, the set of circumstances which brings it into operation, *viz.*, a trustee-beneficiary and his co-trustee have between them committed a breach of trust from which the former benefited and the latter did not;

Secondly, the trustee-beneficiary's obligation to indemnify which arises from his character of beneficiary, the rule being that a benefici-

---

[90] [1896] 1 Ch. 385. See *Re Dacre* [1916] 1 Ch. 344, *supra*, p. 780.
[91] *Ibid.* 698.
[92] *Supra*, pp. 749–751.
[93] [1896] 1 Ch. 685.

ary who participates in a breach of trust committed with a view towards his benefit must indemnify his trustees out of his beneficial interest; and

Thirdly, the trustee-beneficiary's right of contribution which arises from his character of trustee.

It would seem that, in order to bring the rule in *Chillingworth* v. *Chambers* into operation, it is not necessary that the trustee-beneficiary *actually benefit* from the breach of trust. The decisions on this particular point establish that it is quite sufficient if a beneficiary actively participates in a breach of trust with *a motive of personal benefit*.[94] Thus simplified, the decision in *Chillingworth* v. *Chambers* decides only one new point, *viz.*, that where a right of contribution *qua* trustee conflicts with an obligation to indemnify *qua* beneficiary, the obligation to indemnify must be discharged before the right of contribution may be exercised.

Just as *Chillingworth* v. *Chambers* was based on liability *qua* beneficiary to have a beneficial interest impounded under the old law so it would appear that its principles have been extended by section 62 of the Trustee Act 1925 which extends the law on impounding beneficial interests.

In *Chillingworth* v. *Chambers* it was also held that it made no difference that the trustee-beneficiary was not a beneficiary at the time the breach of trust was committed, but became a beneficiary *after* that date. This part of the decision was based on the analogy of *Evans* v. *Benyon*,[95] where it was held that the rule that a beneficiary who concurs in a breach of trust cannot complain of it against his trustee holds good even if the beneficiary was not a beneficiary at the time of his concurrence, but became a beneficiary after that date.

## CIVIL LIABILITY (CONTRIBUTION) ACT 1978

1.—(1) Subject to the following provisions of this section, any person liable in respect of any damage suffered by another person may recover contribution from any other person liable in respect of the same damage (whether jointly with him or otherwise).

(2) A person shall be entitled to recover contribution by virtue of subsection (1) above notwithstanding that he has ceased to be liable in respect of the damage in question since the time when the damage occurred, provided that he was so liable immediately before he made or was ordered or agreed to make the payment in respect of which the contribution is sought.

(3) A person shall be liable to make contribution by virtue of subsection (1) above notwithstanding that he has ceased to be liable in respect of the damage in question since the time when the damage occurred, unless he ceased to be

---

94 *Supra*, p. 783; and see s.62 of the Trustee Act 1925. In *Chillingworth* v. *Chambers* Lindley L.J. at 700 considered personal benefit immaterial though Kay L.J. at 707 was not prepared so to commit himself as the plaintiff in the circumstances had received a personal benefit. They were concerned only with liability to impound on general equitable principles as the action was pending before section 6 of the Trustee Act 1888 was enacted: see *per* Kay L.J. at 707.
95 (1887) 37 Ch.D. 329, 344; *supra*, p. 783, n. 29.

liable by virtue of an expiry of a period of limitation or prescription which extinguished the right on which the claim against him in respect of the damage was based.

(4) A person who has made or agreed to make any payment in bona fide settlement or compromise of any claim made against him in respect of any damage (including a payment into court which has been accepted) shall be entitled to recover contribution in accordance with this section without regard to whether or not he himself is or ever was liable in respect of the damage, provided, however, that he would have been liable assuming that the factual basis of the claim against him could be established.

(5) A judgment given in any action brought in any part of the United Kingdom by or on behalf of the person who suffered the damage in question against any person from whom contribution is sought under this section shall be conclusive in the proceedings for contribution as to any issue determined by that judgment in favour of the person from whom the contribution is sought.

2.—(1) Subject to subsection (3) below, in any proceedings for contribution under section 1 above the amount of the contribution recoverable from any person shall be such as may be found by the court to be just and equitable having regard to the extent of that person's responsibility for the damage in question.

(2) Subject to subsection (3) below, the court shall have power in any such proceedings to exempt any person from liability to make contribution, or to direct that the contribution to be recovered from any person shall amount to a complete indemnity.

(3) Where the amount of the damages which have or might have been awarded in respect of the damage in question in any action brought in England and Wales by or on behalf of the person who suffered it against the person from whom the contribution is sought was or would have been subject to—

    (*a*)  any limit imposed by or under any enactment or by any agreement made before the damage occurred;

    (*b*)  any reduction by virtue of section 1 of the Law Reform (Contributory Negligence) Act 1945 or section 5 of the Fatal Accidents Act 1976; or

    (*c*)  any corresponding limit or reduction under the law of a country outside England and Wales;

the person from whom the contribution is sought shall not by virtue of any contribution awarded under section 1 above be required to pay in respect of the damage a greater amount than the amount of those damages as so limited or reduced.

6.—(1) A person is liable in respect of any damage for the purposes of this Act if the person who suffered it (or anyone representing his estate or dependants) is entitled to recover compensation from him in respect of that damage (whatever is the legal basis of his liability, whether tort, breach of contract, breach of trust or otherwise).

7.—(1) Nothing in this Act shall affect any case where the debt in question became due or (as the case may be) the damage in question occurred before the date on which it comes into force [January 1, 1979].

(2) A person shall not be entitled to recover contribution or liable to make contribution in accordance with section 1 above by reference to any liability based on breach of any obligation assumed by him before the date on which this Act comes into force.[96]

---

[96] Persons becoming trustees before 1979 thus are excluded from the Act: *Lampitt* v. *Poole B.C.* [1990] 2 All E.R. 887, 892.

(3) The right to recover contribution in accordance with section 1 above supersedes any right, other than an express contractual right, to recover contribution (as distinct from indemnity) otherwise than under this Act in corresponding circumstances; but nothing in this Act shall affect—

   (*a*)  any express or implied contractual or other right to indemnity; or
   (*b*)  any express contractual provision regulating or excluding contribution;

which would be enforceable apart from this Act (or render enforceable any agreement for indemnity or contribution which would not be enforceable apart from this Act).

## PROBLEMS

1. Ted and Tom are trustees of a £500,000 fund held on trust for Ted himself, Arthur, Brian, Charles and David in equal shares contingent upon each attaining 30 years of age. To allay any suspicions of the other beneficiaries Ted takes little part in running the trust affairs, relying to a large extent on Tom, a 50-year old solicitor.

Tom and Arthur consider that it would be desirable to buy shares in Exploration Syndicate Co. Ltd. but realise that the trustees have no power to do so under the Trustees Investments Act 1961, the will creating the trust conferring no express powers of investment. Nevertheless, Tom writes to Ted telling him that his City connections lead him to consider it a very good idea to buy shares in Exploration Syndicate Co. Ltd. For this purpose they can call in £30,000 deposited with the Countrywide Building Society bringing in a gross 11 per cent. interest. Ted replies by letter, "If you wish us to invest that £30,000 in the Exploration Syndicate Co. Ltd. that is all right by me."

Tom then wrote to Brian, Charles and David, "Ted and I as trustees are considering investing £30,000 of the trust funds in buying shares in the Exploration Syndicate Co. Ltd. That is quite a lot of money but we would consider it well spent on such shares. However, before we go ahead we would like to have your consent. Arthur has already consented and we look forward to receiving replies from you and the other beneficiaries quite soon."

Brian and David replied briefly consenting. Charles replied, "I am quite happy for the £30,000 to be invested in the shares proposed. Of course, I assume they are authorised investments." The beneficiaries, Ted, Arthur, Brian, Charles and David were then respectively aged 29, 27, 25, 23 and 17 years. After the replies had been received the £30,000 was invested in buying the proposed shares.

Three years later the company collapsed and the whole £30,000 was lost, the shares only having produced a gross 3 per cent. yield in the first year and nothing thereafter.

Advise the trustees of their position *vis-à-vis* (1) the beneficiaries and (2) themselves.

2. Frank Shoal is a grandchild-beneficiary under a discretionary trust of income and capital set up in 1970 by Simon Shoal for his three sons Alan, Brian, and Charles, their spouses and their children.

Simon Shoal, Frank's grandfather, settled his 75 per cent. shareholding in Shoal Fishing Co. Ltd. (of which he was founder and managing director) along with other investments. The settlement conferred upon the trustees power to appoint capital amongst the beneficiaries as the trustees saw fit from time to time (Clause 4), power to add/or subtract persons (other than the settlor or his spouse) to or from the class of beneficiaries (Clause 5), and power "to invest or otherwise use or apply moneys as if they were absolutely entitled thereto beneficially, so long as the settlor or his spouse do not benefit in any way thereby" (Clause 6). Clause 8 provided that "any Trustee may exercise any power or discretion notwithstanding that he may have a direct or other personal interest in the mode or result of exercising the same," and by Clause 9, "No Trustee shall be liable for any loss to the Trust unless the same happens through his own wilful default."

The original trustees were Simon Shoal, his solicitor, Sebastian Shallow and his accountant, Nigel Nexus. In 1974 Nexus died and Simon Shoal retired from the trust, being replaced by Alan and Brian Shoal. The third brother, Charles, held no interest in the family fishing company and had left in 1960 to seek his fortune in Australia. Simon Shoal died in 1976 and Shallow in 1980.

In 1987 the family company was in difficult straits. Alan and Brian, who had taken over from their father as joint managing directors, reckoned that they had either to contract the size of the business significantly or expand to obtain the economies afforded by larger-scale operations. They considered the latter alternative preferable and raised the money for expansion by a rights issue, which involved the settlement in paying up £150,000 to take up its entitlement to further shares in the family company. After this the settlement's shares in the family company were valued at £225,000, whilst its other investments were valued at £120,000.

Owing to industrial troubles and the international situation things unfortunately went from bad to worse. In January 1989 in a last-ditch attempt to save the family company, Alan and Brian on behalf of the settlement lent the company £50,000 at 4 per cent. interest. Even this failed to save the company which went into liquidation in January 1990. The company shares are worthless and the settlement has lost its £50,000 loan.

Alan and Brian were adjudicated bankrupt in March 1990, having used their own assets in their attempt to save the company, but in January 1990 they had exercised their powers under Clause 4 of the settlement to appoint £60,000 of capital to each of their respective wives to provide *inter alia* new matrimonial homes secure from grasping creditors. In September 1990 Brian won £130,000 on the football pools and used £61,288 to pay off all his debts in full, and so have his bankruptcy adjudication annulled.

Charles died a widower in Australia in 1974 but his only son, Frank, aged 26, has just come to England and discovered the above facts. He seeks to have the settlement losses made good. However, the trustees, Alan and Brian, have told him he has nothing to gain in pursuing the matter since they did their best in difficult circumstances and are fully protected by the terms of the settlement under which he must bear in mind both Clause 5 and the fact that he is merely a discretionary beneficiary.

# Chapter 11

# TRUSTS AND THE CONFLICT OF LAWS

The conflict of laws is that part of the private law of the English and Welsh system of law which deals with issues which concern elements connected with other legal systems, *e.g.* of Scotland, Northern Ireland, the Republic of Ireland, Jersey, the Isle of Man, each of the American and Australian states, each of the Canadian provinces. A settlor of British nationality domiciled[1] in California may create a trust of assets, half of which are in Bermuda and half in Ontario, and appoint four trustees, one habitually resident in Bermuda, one habitually resident in Ontario and two habitually resident in England. One-third of the beneficiaries may be habitually resident in California, one-third in England and one-third in Jersey. The trust instrument may specify Californian law as governing the validity of the trust, and Bermudan law as governing administration of trust assets there and Ontario law as governing administration of the assets there. It may also confer express powers on the trustees to change the law governing the validity of the trust and to change the place of administration and the law governing administration. An alleged breach of trust may lead the beneficiaries to bring an action against the trustees before the Chancery Division of the English High Court.

The two questions that arise are (1) does the English court have jurisdiction to hear the case, and, if so, (2) what system of law shall apply to each point in issue? Sometimes, the case may be an exceptional one where, though the English court technically has jurisdiction, it will stay or strike out the proceedings on the ground of *forum non conveniens*, because the defendant shows there is another forum to whose jurisdiction he is amenable, in which justice can be done at substantially less inconvenience and expense, and where the plaintiff will not be deprived of a legitimate personal or juridical advantage which would be available to him under the English jurisdiction. Sometimes, the question arises whether the English court will recognise or enforce a foreign judgment purporting to determine an issue that relates to the action before the court.

Questions of jurisdiction, of *forum non conveniens*, and of recognition or enforcement of foreign judgments are best left to the major works on conflict of laws.[2] It is the choice of law issue—determining

---

1 Domicile is a technical concept: it does not mean habitual residence. No one can be without a domicile since it is this that connects him with some legal system for conflict of laws purposes. A person has a domicile of origin at birth, a domicile of dependency when the infant's parents change domicile and may acquire a domicile of choice by the *factum* of permanent residence with the *animus* of residing there permanently.
2 Dicey and Morris on *Conflict of Laws*, Cheshire & North on *Private International Law*. On conflict of laws there is a very useful chapter in Honoré's *Law of Trusts in South Africa*.

806

the law applicable to the matter in question—that will be examined. However, as will be seen, there are some situations where if the English court has jurisdiction it will apply English domestic law. One is used to this in family matters relating to divorce, separation and maintenance, and guardianship, custody and adoption of children, but in *Chellaram* v. *Chellaram, infra*, Scott J. has recently held that the machinery for the enforcement of beneficiaries' rights determined under the proper law, particularly the removal of trustees and the appointment of new ones, is a matter to be governed by English law where the English court has jurisdiction to hear the case, even though the proper law governing the validity of the trust may not be English but Indian and regardless of whether the law governing administration may be English or Indian.[3] He was strongly influenced by the maxim "Equity acts *in personam*" enabling the court to make orders effective against trustees within the jurisdiction of the court.

### Background Matters

A distinction needs to be made between the testator's will or the settlor's trust document, which may be considered as the "rocket-launcher" on the one hand, and the trust itself—the "rocket"—on the other hand.[4] The law that governs whether or not the property of the testator or settlor is vested under a valid will or other instrument in personal representatives or trustees, free or not from third-party rights (*e.g.* under *légitim* regimes,[5] matrimonial property regimes[6] or bankruptcy laws) may be different from the law that governs the trust provisions once the intended trust property has wholly or partly survived the application of the law, or laws, relating to the preliminary issues.

There is an important distinction in conflict of laws between immovables and movables since, naturally and practically, the *lex situs* must be very significant for immovables. This distinction is not the same as that between real property and personal property. Leasehold interests in land, though personal property, are immovables,[7] whilst land directed to be sold under a trust for sale, though personalty under the doctrine of conversion, is an immovable in its unsold state.[8] Where Settled Land Act 1925 capital moneys have been invested in stocks and shares but by section 75(5) such capital moneys and investments therewith are regarded as "land" then the stocks and shares are immovables.[9]

---

[3] Essentially, Scott J. seems to be regarding the enforcement of beneficiaries' rights as a matter of procedure and so governed by the *lex fori*. Also see *Stirling-Maxwell* v. *Cartwright* (1879) 11 Ch.D. 5, 22; *Re Lord Cable* [1976] 3 All E.R. 417, 431–432.

[4] *Re Lord Cable* [1976] 3 All E.R. 417, 431. *Att.-Gen.* v. *Campbell* (1872) L.R. 5 H.L. 524, Article 4 of Hague Convention *infra*, p. 817.

[5] *e.g.* under Scots law and French law a deceased's children have rights to part of his estate so that he may only freely dispose of, say, one-third of his estate; *Re Annesley* [1926] Ch. 692, *Re Adams* [1967] I.R. 424.

[6] *e.g.* a husband cannot dispose of property within the matrimonial regime without his wife's participation.

[7] *Freke* v. *Carberry* (1873) L.R. 16 Eq. 461.

[8] *Re Berchtold* [1923] 1 Ch. 192.

[9] *Re Cutcliffe's W.T.* [1940] Ch. 565.

General equitable principles of the Court of Chancery have a significant role, especially the maxim "Equity acts *in personam*."[10] Other maxims that may be applicable are, for example, "equity will do nothing in vain" and "equity will not require persons to do acts illegal by the law of the place where the acts are to be performed," *e.g.* where foreign exchange laws prevent trustees from getting money out of the country for the beneficiaries.[11]

### Choice of Applicable Law

As provided by Articles 6 and 7 of The Hague Convention, implemented by the Recognition of Trusts Act 1987, a trust is governed by the law expressly or impliedly chosen by the settlor, or in the absence of such choice, by the law with which the trust is most closely connected. It is easy to assume that there can be only one applicable law governing the trust except where the trust assets are physically situate in two or more countries where different applicable laws may be chosen to cover the assets situate in different countries. Upon a little reflection it can be seen that there may well be one law governing the validity of the trust provisions, often referred to as the "proper" law, and one law governing the administration of the trust. Upon further reflection, quite apart from preliminary issues concerning form or capacity with respect to the instrument creating the trust, there may be questions relating to formal validity of the trust itself[12] or capacity to act as trustee,[13] as well as questions relating to the substantive (or essential) validity of the trust provisions or questions affecting the interpretation (or construction) of such provisions. A settlor might thus state that his trust is to be governed by English law except that Queensland law is to govern matters of interpretation[14] and Cayman Isles law is to govern matters of administration.

Where there is an express choice[15] the position is clear enough, except for the finer points of the distinction between matters of validity

---

[10] See also *Cook Industries Ltd.* v. *Galliher* [1979] Ch. 439, *Derby & Co. Ltd.* v. *Weldon (No. 2)* [1989] 1 All E.R. 1002.

[11] *Re Lord Cable* [1976] 3 All E.R. 417, for analogous contracts, see *Kahler* v. *Midland Bank Ltd.* [1950] A.C. 24. See Articles 15 and 16, Hague Convention, *infra*, p. 818.

[12] *e.g.* if the proper law applicable to the transfer of property allowed it to be done by conduct or by writing, whilst the proper law applicable to the creation of a trust of such property required use of a deed.

[13] *e.g.* if the proper law applicable to the transfer of property allowed transfer to any person *sui juris* but the proper law applicable to the creation of a trust requires a trustee to be an official trust corporation or a male over 35 years of age.

[14] At first sight a Chancery lawyer might wonder how substantive validity and interpretation can be governed by different laws: validity almost inevitably depends on interpretation or construction. However, a trust provision may be valid whatever the interpretation, *e.g.* if "children" is legitimate children or children whether legitimate or illegitimate. Even if a trust provision would have been void under the old rule against remoteness if "issue" meant "descendants" and not just "children" the meaning of "issue" may be determined by the law expressly chosen by the testator even if different from the law governing validity. A testator may create his own dictionary of meanings whether by using specific foreign legal phrases or, generally incorporating a foreign law to govern interpretation: *Studd* v. *Cook* (1883) 8 App.Cas. 577.

[15] For split laws in a contractual context see *Forsikrings Vesta* v. *Butcher* [1986] 2 All E.R. 488, 504–505; *Libyan Arab Bank* v. *Bankers Trust Co.* [1989] 3 All E.R. 252, 267, and the Contracts (Applicable Law) Act 1990 implementing the 1980 Rome Convention, especially Articles 3 and 4.

and matters of administration and except for any rule of public policy that might invalidate such choice. Leaving these aside for the moment, it seems that a settlor may expressly go further and empower his trustees to change the law governing the validity of the trust (so far as it does not invalidate the rights of the beneficiaries under the original law governing validity) and to change the law governing the administration of the trust, with or without changing the principal place of administration of the trust. It would seem that the law governing validity at the time of the disputed issue should determine whether that issue was a matter for the law governing validity or for the law governing administration and should, indeed, determine whether or not and by what formal methods the law governing administration may be replaced by another law.[16] This last point is particularly significant where there is no express power to change the law governing administration.

This leads one to implied choice of law for matters of validity or matters of administration and to implied powers to change the law governing administration. If the addresses of the settlor and the trustees are English and the trust instrument refers to the English Trustee Act 1925 (*e.g.* in extending the powers in sections 31 and 32 thereof) then there will be an implied choice of English law as the applicable law governing the trust in all its aspects. At some stage implied subjective intent shades off into an imputed objective intent that the trust shall be governed by the law with which it is most closely connected at the time of its creation.[17] In ascertaining such objective law various factors are taken into account, with the weight to be attached to each factor varying according to the particular circumstances. In a testamentary trust the domicile of the testator at his death has traditionally had much significance.[18] In the case of an *inter vivos* trust the domicile or habitual residence of the settlor at the time he created the trust has some significance as well as the place of execution of the trust instrument. Regard will also be had to the trustee's place of residence or business, though it must not be overlooked that trustees (other than professional corporate trustees) are often chosen for their personal qualities irrespective of where they live or work.

---

[16] In England we consider the law governing validity as the "mother" law to which the law governing administration is attached by an umbilical cord: *cf. Marlborough* v. *Att.-Gen.* [1945] Ch. 78, 85, *Iveagh* v. *I.R.C.* [1954] Ch. 364, 370, *Fattorini* v. *Johannesburg Trust* (1948) 4 S.A.L.R. 806, 812. So far, this seems the position in Australia and Canada. In the U.S.A. their greater experience of having different laws governing administration and of changing the place of and law of administration from time to time, has led them to consider the law governing validity as an "elder brother" and the law governing administration as a "younger brother": matters of administration are determined by the law governing administration but a change of the law governing administration cannot derogate from the beneficiaries' interests as established under the law governing validity. See Article 10, Hague Convention *infra*, p. 818.

[17] *Iveagh* v. *I.R.C.* [1954] Ch. 364.

[18] *Re Lord Cable* [1976] 3 All E.R. 417, 431. Older cases tended to assume that the law of the testator's domicile because it governed the validity of the will must govern trust dispositions in that will: this may happen to be the case but such does not necessarily follow: *Chelleram* v. *Chelleram*, *infra*.

Thus, if the testator or settlor expressly designates where the trust is to be administered this will be a more significant factor. Account will also be taken of the *situs* of the trust assets and the objects of the trust and the places where they are to be fulfilled.[19]

It seems there will be a presumption in favour of one implied or imputed applicable law governing all aspects of the trust,[20] the onus being upon he who alleges that one law governs validity and another law governs administration. After all, if a trustee remains out of the United Kingdom for more than 12 months, this in the absence of contrary intention in the trust deed, is a ground for removing him under section 36 of the Trustee Act 1925 and appointing a United Kingdom trustee in his place. If the original trustees appointed to administer the trust are foreign there will usually be other foreign elements and rarely will there be no express choice of the applicable law—in such rare case if there is a preponderant connection with one foreign system of law it is very likely that such law will govern both validity and administration and not just administration. If the trust instrument authorises the trustees to retire in favour of foreign trustees and to transfer the assets to such foreign trustees it seems likely that this power to change the place of administration impliedly carries with it the power to change the law governing administration to the law with which those foreign trustees are familiar, so far as this will be the law of a state that has its own internal law of trusts. For the law governing validity to be changed as well, it seems that the authority to transfer assets to foreign trustees will need to state that this is so so that such assets shall thereafter be exclusively governed by such foreign law, the "mother" law governing validity not being capable of change or exclusion except by clearly expressed intention.

### Matters of Validity Contrasted with Matters of Administration

Where there is an express power to change the law governing administration a wise settlor will specify what are matters of administration since there is precious little case law guidance on what amounts to matters of administration as opposed to matters of validity.

Some guidance may be found in *Pearson* v. *I.R.C., supra,* p. 35, which was concerned with "dispositive" powers of trustees that prevent a beneficiary having an interest in possession and "administrative" powers that do not. After all, dispositive powers affect the nature or *quantum* of a beneficiary's beneficial interest and so would appear not to be matters of administration. From *obiter dicta* in *Chellaram* v. *Chellaram, infra,* p. 827, it appears that the rights of the beneficiaries are matters of validity so that the corresponding duties of the trustees must also be matters of validity. This is obviously true where the beneficial interests are concerned but not as concerns the beneficiaries'

---

[19] *Fordyce* v. *Bridges* (1848) 2 Ph. 497; *Re Mitchner* [1922] St.R.Qd. 252. Article 7, Hague Convention *infra*, p. 817.
[20] *Chelleram* v. *Chelleram* [1985] Ch. 409.

rights and the trustees' duties relating to investments authorised only under the 1961 Trustee Investments Act. Matters of investment are clearly matters of administration. If the law governing administration changes so that the trustees may invest as they wish without being liable for loss unless acting dishonestly, it seems that if the trustees cause loss by acting without common prudence they will escape liability since their duty will only be a duty not to act dishonestly.[21]

Matters of administration, it seems, must include the powers of trustees to administer and dispose and acquire trust assets, their powers of investment, their powers of delegation, their powers to pay debts and expenses and compromise claims, their rights to remuneration, their rights to contribution and indemnity between themselves, the appointment, retirement and removal of trustees and the devolution of trusteeship, the distinction between capital and income, the powers of the court to give advice and to confer powers upon trustees.

Powers of maintenance and advancement can affect the nature and extent of beneficiaries' interests, *e.g.* if the law of administration is changed to a foreign law which allows up to three-quarters of a beneficiary's contingent share to be advanced to him or gives no right to income at the age of 18 years to a beneficiary whose interest in capital is contingent on acquiring a greater age such as 30 years.[22] Thus sections 31 and 32 of the English Trustee Act should continue to apply even if the place and law of administration are changed to a different system of law, unless the clause that empowers such change can be broadly construed as authorising the foreign state's Trustee Act to apply to the exclusion of the English Act.

Matters pertaining to the original validity of the trust provisions (*e.g.* the rules against remoteness, accumulations and inalienability and prohibiting purpose trusts unless charitable trusts) are for the law governing validity. However, if an English testator in his will directs his executors to transfer some Scottish property, whether movable or immovable, that he himself had earlier inherited to two Scottish trustees on public but non-charitable trusts (valid according to Scots law but not English law) then although the law governing the testator's will and other trust dispositions in it may be English it should be Scots law that governs and upholds the validity of the public trusts.[23]

The Variation of Trusts Act position is special. Most jurisdictions have such Acts. Since the legislation can drastically alter the nature

---

[21] Settlors should be careful because if the law governing administration may be changed it is possible that this could occur, so enabling the trustees to charge twice the maximum possible rate of remuneration under English law and enabling the trustees to reduce their English duty to administer the trust assets with common prudence to a new duty merely not to act dishonestly. Such considerations must make the courts reluctant to find an implied power to change the law governing administration.

[22] He will only be entitled to income on attaining the specified age in some jurisdictions. Some jurisdictions, indeed, exclude a beneficiary's rights under *Saunders* v. *Vautier* either altogether or only with the court's leave.

[23] *Cf. Jewish National Fund* v. *Royal Trust Co.* (1965) 53 D.L.R. (2d) 577. The courts tend, where possible, to choose as the applicable law one which will sustain the validity of the trust: *Dicey & Morris*, p. 675.

and extent of beneficiaries' interests one might have expected that the court's jurisdiction should be restricted to those trusts whose validity is governed by the *lex fori*. However, the English courts have arrogated to themselves unlimited jurisdiction in the absence of restricting words in the Variation of Trusts Act 1958.[24] "However, where there are substantial foreign elements in the case, the court must consider carefully whether it is proper to exercise the jurisdiction. If, for example, the court were asked to vary a settlement which was plainly a Scottish settlement, it might well hesitate to exercise its jurisdiction to vary the trusts simply because some of, or even all, the trustees and beneficiaries were in this country. It may well be that the judge would say that the Court of Session was the appropriate tribunal to deal with the case."[25] In the light of Article 8(2)(h) of the Hague Convention it is very likely that an English court will decline jurisdiction for trusts governed by a foreign law. One must remember that all the parties before the court will be anxious for the jurisdiction to be exercised for family or for taxation reasons and that the interests of infant or unborn beneficiaries will hardly ever[26] be prejudiced by any variation. However, the taxation authorities in a particular country may take the point that the variation is ineffective except to the extent that adult beneficiaries are estopped from reverting to the pre-variation position.

*Limitations upon Free Choice of Law*

Obvious problems exist where immovables are concerned. Take land in Spain (which does not have the trust concept within its code of law) or in Jersey (which allows trusts so long as they are not of land in Jersey). There are practical problems if recourse has to be had to Spanish or Jersey courts and so far as title to the land is concerned the trustees would appear as ordinary private beneficial owners. However, if the land comprised say one-twentieth of the aggregate of property subjected to trusts with an English proper law why should the English trustees not be under valid *in personam* trusteeship obligations to the English beneficiaries in respect of the land, *e.g.* to pay rents over to the beneficiaries and to keep the premises in reasonable repair?[27]

A settlor has total freedom of choice of law unless such choice is manifestly incompatible with public policy.[28] Article 13 of the Hague Convention affords a discretion to refuse to recognise a trust if its

---

[24] *Re Ker's Settlement* [1963] Ch. 553; *Re Paget's Settlement* [1965] 1 W.L.R. 1046. The same has happened in Alberta and in Western Australia: *Commercial Trust Co.* v. *Laing* unreported (Waters, p. 1134); *Faye* v. *Faye* [1973] W.A.R. 66.

[25] *Re Paget's Settlement* [1965] 1 W.L.R. 1046, 1050, *per* Cross J.

[26] See *Re Remnant's W.T.* [1970] 1 Ch. 560.

[27] *cf. Re Fitzgerald* [1904] 1 Ch. 573. Sufficient scope is afforded to the *lex situs* to govern preliminary or policy issues, *e.g. Re Ross* [1930] 1 Ch. 377 (*legitima portio*), *Re Hoyles* [1911] 1 Ch. 179, *Duncan* v. *Lawson* (1889) 41 Ch.D. 394 (Mortmain Acts), *Freke* v. *Carberry* (1873) L.R. 16 Eq. 461 (perpetuities and accumulations), *Re Pearse's Settlement* [1909] 1 Ch. 304 (Jersey land could not be conveyed by a married woman to someone except for adequate pecuniary compensation so that her after-acquired property covenant in an English settlement was construed as not intended to include after-acquired Jersey land within the scope of the covenant).

[28] See Articles 6 and 18 but note the safeguards in Articles 15 and 16 of The Hague Convention.

significant elements, except for the choice of law, the place of administration and the habitual residence of the trustee, are more closely connected with a non-trust-State. The United Kingdom considered it unnecessary and unhelpful for its courts to have such a discretion and so the Recognition of Trusts Act 1987 deliberately omits Article 13.

If, in what would otherwise be a trust governed by English law, an Englishman purports to create a trust of English land but expressly chooses a foreign law with the intent of enabling the land to be held for ever on valid public but non-charitable purpose trusts it is clear that the trust will be void. The English court will have to give effect to the English policy rules as to the administration of land within the jurisdiction. Indeed, the policy rules recognising the unenforceability of purpose trusts, where no one has *locus standi* to apply to the court to have the purposes positively carried out, would prevent the trust being effective even if the property was not land.

If, however, it was movable or immovable property in Scotland subjected to public non-charitable purpose trusts expressed to be subject to Scots law then there seems no policy reason for the English court to invalidate such trusts of an English testator in his English will.

One should note that a choice of law (*e.g.* English law) to govern a trust makes that law govern the relationship between the trustees and the beneficiaries: that law governs the "internal" aspects of the trust. As far as the trustees' "external" relations with third parties are concerned, *e.g.* in contracting with them or transferring property to them one has to apply the conflict of laws rules applicable to contracts or to the transfer of property. Thus, a trustee of a trust governed by the law of Jersey may rely when contracting in Jersey on Article 32(1) of the Trusts Jersey Law 1983, "Where in any transaction or matter affecting a trust a trustee informs a third party that he is acting as trustee a claim by such third party in relation thereto shall extend only to the trust property." If the trustee contracts in England under English law (not expressly choosing Jersey law to govern the contract) he will be personally liable since any person contracting under English law is personally liable except to the extent he expressly restricts liability, for example to trust property to which he has a right of recourse for paying trust expenses.[29]

## THE RECOGNITION OF TRUSTS ACT 1987

Since August 1, 1987, Articles 1 to 18 (except 13 and 16 para. 2) and 22 of The Hague Trusts Convention, *infra*, have been in force in the United Kingdom in respect of trusts whenever created, but this does not affect the law to be applied to anything done or omitted before August 1, 1987.[30] Section 1(2) extends the Convention's provisions to

---

[29] See p. 747, *supra*.
[30] S.I. 1987 No. 1177. The Convention is regarded as clarifying the common law position (on which see Wallace (1987) 36 I.C.L.Q. 454) but the non-retrospective provision was inverted in s.1(5) of the 1987 Act *ex abundante cautela*.

any other trusts of property arising (*e.g.* orally or by statute) under the law of any part of the United Kingdom or by virtue of a judicial decision in the United Kingdom or elsewhere.

## LIMITED SCOPE OF TRUSTS CONVENTION

1. This (private international law) Convention does not introduce the trust into the internal private law of States that do not have the concept of the trust; it simply makes foreign States recognise trusts of property as a matter of private international law.

2. This (private international law) Convention does not affect the internal private law of States that have the trust concept: the extent to which the applicable law can be expressly or impliedly changed and the distinction between matters of validity and matters of administration may vary according to the appropriate applicable law because State A's internal trust rules may differ from such rules of State B.

3. The Convention applies only to a trust ("the rocket") and not to the instrument launching the trust ("the rocket-launcher"). Antecedent preliminary issues that may affect the validity of wills, deeds or other acts by which property is allegedly subjected to a trust fall outside the Convention: Article 4. The Convention only applies if whatever is the applicable law governing capacity or formal or substantive validity of wills or *inter vivos* declarations of trust by the settlor or transfers of property to trustees has not operated to prevent the relevant property being available to be subjected to trusts.

4. While the Convention recognises the equitable proprietary right to trace trust property and its traceable product in States that have the trust concept, it does not introduce such proprietary right into States that do not have the trust concept and so have no concept of equitable proprietary interest in their fixed scheme of property interests. If trust property is transferred in such a State to X the *lex situs* will govern the effect of such transfer and deny the existence of any equitable proprietary interest except to the extent that any actual knowledge by X of a breach of trust may make it possible to take advantage of any *lex situs* rules on fraud. See the last sentence of Article 11 paragraph 3(d) and also Article 15(d)(f) and paragraph 113 of the Von Overbeck Official Report on the Trusts Convention.

5. Article 15 ensures the application of the internal mandatory rules of a State whose law is applicable according to the conflicts rules of the forum, irrespective of the law applicable to the trust. A forum will have choice of law rules in areas such as succession, property, bankruptcy, matrimonial property regimes. Mandatory succession rules (reserve legale, legitima portio, pflichtteil) have special significance, especially if a settlor's trust assets are found in the civil law forum of a forced heir who seeks such assets: *Holzberg* v. *Sasson* 1986 Rev. crit. de dr. int. pr. 685. Choice of law rules may lead to the *lex successionis, lex situs* or *lex fori* being invoked so as wholly or partly to undo the effects of a trust. While an English court should characterise

a Frenchman's transfer of assets in England to English trustees as a straightforward *inter vivos* transfer of property governed by the English *lex situs* and then by the English applicable law of the trust, a French court will characterise such transfer as pertaining to the French *lex successionis* so far as it affects property subject to reserve legale. So long as the trust property remains in England (or another common law country) it will remain intact but if the property is found in France (or a sympathetic civil law country) then the heirs may claim it in satisfaction of their reserves legales.

6. Under the first paragraph of Article 16 the *lex fori* court must of course apply its own international mandatory rules, *e.g.* if a beneficiary is suing the trustee for failure to export to the beneficiary some thing or animal whose export is prohibited by the *lex fori*.

Under the second paragraph the *lex fori* court has a discretion, to be exercised only in the most exceptional case, to apply the international mandatory rules of some other State with a sufficiently close connection with the case, where the State's law is neither the *lex fori* nor the law applicable to the trust as such.

Trust States find it difficult to appreciate the need for such a provision since a Court of Equity will do nothing in vain (*i.e.* will not make orders which cannot be carried out as where foreign immovables are concerned) and will not require a person to do an act that is illegal in the place where it is to be done. Thus, if the law of the trust is that of State A, the law of the forum that of State B, and the law of State C makes it illegal to take certain sorts of assets out of State C, any action by a beneficiary against the trustees for not getting such assets out to the beneficiary will fail, regardless of the second paragraph. The uncertain ambit of the paragraph is also unsatisfactory for lawyers and for courts. The United Kingdom government therefore made the reservation allowed by the third paragraph.

7. By Article 13 a court in a trust or non-trust State has a discretionary power to refuse to recognise a trust if the significant elements of the trust (*e.g.* situs of assets, settlor's and beneficiaries' habitual residence) are more closely connected with non-trust than with trust States, except for the choice of the applicable law, the place of administration and the habitual residence of the trustee. It seems that it is up to the court to decide in a particular case what are the significant elements which connect the trust closely to a non-trust State. The relevant time for these significant elements to be so connected seems to be the time of the events occasioning the claim for recognition and not the time of creation of the trust. The United Kingdom Recognition of Trusts Act 1987 deliberately omitted Article 13 because it was considered unnecessary for such a discretion to be available.

8. The Convention is only concerned with trusts of property and not with the imposition of constructive trusteeship upon a defendant so that he is personally liable to account as a constructive trustee if he

knowingly assisted in a breach of trust, whether or not any trust property was ever in his hands. Where a defendant cannot be made personally liable in tort or contract but has acted with want of probity equity constructively treats him as if he had been a trustee as a formula for an equitable personal (as opposed to proprietary) remedy, which will be of no assistance if the defendant is deeply insolvent. A defendant in a State not having the trust and any equitable jurisdiction can never be liable as a constructive trustee in that State.

## CONVENTION ON THE LAW APPLICABLE TO TRUSTS AND ON THEIR RECOGNITION[31]

The States signatory to the present Convention,

Considering that the trust, as developed in courts of equity in common law jurisdictions and adopted with some modifications in other jurisdictions, is a unique legal institution,

Desiring to establish common provisions on the law applicable to trusts and to deal with the most important issues concerning the recognition of trusts,

Have resolved to conclude a Convention to this effect, and have agreed upon the following provisions—

### CHAPTER I—SCOPE

*Article 1*
This Convention specifies the law applicable to trusts and governs their recognition.

*Article 2*
For the purposes of this Convention, the term "trust" refers to the legal relationships created—*inter vivos* or on death—by a person, the settlor, when assets have been placed under the control of a trustee for the benefit of a beneficiary or for a specified purpose.
A trust has the following characteristics—

*a* the assets constitute a separate fund and are not a part of the trustee's own estate;
*b* title to the trust assets stands in the name of the trustee or in the name of another person on behalf of the trustee;
*c* the trustee has the power and the duty, in respect of which he is accountable, to manage, employ or dispose of the assets in accordance with the terms of the trust and the special duties imposed upon him by law.

The reservation by the settlor of certain rights and powers and the fact that the trustee may himself have rights as a beneficiary, are not necessarily inconsistent with the existence of a trust.

*Article 3*
The Convention applies only to trusts created voluntarily and evidenced in writing.

---

[31] Generally see Explanatory Report by A. E. von Overbeck published by Permanent Bureau of The Hague Conference in Acts and Documents of the 15th Session of the Hague Conference pp. 370 *et seq.* and D. J. Hayton (1987) 36 I.C.L.Q. 260.

## Article 4

The Convention does not apply to preliminary issues relating to the validity of wills or of other acts by virtue of which assets are transferred to the trustee.

## Article 5

The Convention does not apply to the extent that the law specified by Chapter II does not provide for trusts or the category of trusts involved.

## CHAPTER II—APPLICABLE LAW

## Article 6

A trust shall be governed by the law chosen by the settlor. The choice must be express or be implied in the terms of the instrument creating or the writing evidencing the trust, interpreted, if necessary, in the light of circumstances of the case.

Where the law chosen under the previous paragraph does not provide for trusts or the category of trust involved, the choice shall not be effective and the law specified in Article 7 shall apply.

## Article 7

Where no applicable law has been chosen, a trust shall be governed by the law with which it is most closely connected.

In ascertaining the law with which a trust is most closely connected reference shall be made in particular to—

*a* the place of administration of the trust designated by the settlor;
*b* the situs of the assets of the trust;
*c* the place of residence or business of the trustee;
*d* the objects of the trust and the places where they are to be fulfilled.

## Article 8

The law specified by Article 6 or 7 shall govern the validity of the trust, its construction, its effects, and the administration of the trust.
In particular that law shall govern—

*a* the appointment, resignation and removal of trustees, the capacity to act as a trustee, and the devolution of the office or trustee;
*b* the rights and duties of trustees among themselves;
*c* the right of trustees to delegate in whole or in part the discharge of their duties or the exercise of their powers;
*d* the power of trustees to administer or to dispose of trust assets, to create security interests in the trust assets, or to acquire new assets;
*e* the powers of investment of trustees;
*f* restrictions upon the duration of the trust, and upon the power to accumulate the income of the trust;
*g* the relationships between the trustees and the beneficiaries including the personal liability of the trustees to the beneficiaries;
*h* the variation or termination of the trust;
*i* the distribution of the trust assets;
*j* the duty of trustees to account for their administration.

## Article 9

In applying this Chapter a severable aspect of the trust, particularly matters of administration, may be governed by a different law.

*Article 10*
The law applicable to the validity of the trust shall determine whether that law or the law governing the severable aspect of the trust may be replaced by another law.

## Chapter III—Recognition

*Article 11*
A trust created in accordance with the law specified by the preceding Chapter shall be recognized as a trust. Such recognition shall imply, as a minimum, that the trust property constitutes a separate fund, that the trustee may sue and be sued in his capacity as trustee, and that he may appear or act in this capacity before a notary or any person acting in an official capacity.

In so far as the law applicable to a trust requires or provides, such recognition shall imply, in particular—

*a* that personal creditors of the trustee shall have no recourse against the trust assets;
*b* that the trust assets shall not form part of the trustee's estate upon his insolvency or bankruptcy;
*c* that the trust assets shall not form part of the matrimonial property of the trustee or his spouse nor part of the trustee's estate upon his death;
*d* that the trust assets may be recovered when the trustee, in breach of trust, has mingled trust assets with his own property or has alienated trust assets. However, the rights and obligations of any third party holder of the assets shall remain subject to the law determined by the choice of law rules of the forum.

*Article 12*
Where the trustee desires to register assets, movable or immovable, or documents of title to them, he shall be entitled, in so far as this is not prohibited by or inconsistent with the law of the State where registration is sought, to do so in his capacity as trustee or in such other way that the existence of the trust is disclosed.

*Article 13*
No State shall be bound to recognize a trust the significant elements of which, except for the choice of the applicable law, the place of administration and the habitual residence of the trustee, are more closely connected with States which do not have the institution of the trust or the category of trust involved.

*Article 14*
The Convention shall not prevent the application of rules of law more favourable to the recognition of trusts.

## Chapter IV—General Clauses

*Article 15*
The Convention does not prevent the application of provisions of the law designated by the conflicts rules of the forum, in so far as those provisions cannot be derogated from by voluntary act, relating in particular to the following matters—

*a* the protection of minors and incapable parties;

*b* the personal and proprietary effects of marriage;

*c* succession rights, testate and intestate, especially the indefeasible shares of spouses and relatives;

*d* the transfer of title to property and security interests in property;

*e* the protection of creditors in matters of insolvency;

*f* the protection, in other respects, of third parties acting in good faith.

If recognition of a trust is prevented by application of the preceding paragraph, the court shall try to give effect to the objects of the trust by other means.

### Article 16

The Convention does not prevent the application of those provisions of the law of the forum which must be applied even to international situations, irrespective of rules of conflict of laws.

If another State has a sufficiently close connection with a case then, in exceptional circumstances, effect may also be given to rules of that State which have the same character as mentioned in the preceding paragraph.

Any Contracting State may, by way of reservation, declare that it will not apply the second paragraph of this article.

### Article 17

In the Convention the word "law" means the rules of law in force in a State other than its rules of conflict of laws.

### Article 18

The provisions of the Convention may be disregarded when their application would be manifestly incompatible with public policy (*ordre public*).

### Article 19

Nothing in the Convention shall prejudice the powers of States in fiscal matters.

### Article 20

Any Contracting State may, at any time, declare that the provisions of the Convention will be extended to trusts declared by judicial decisions.

This declaration shall be notified to the Ministry of Foreign Affairs of the Kingdom of the Netherlands and will come into effect on the day when this notification is received.

Article 31 is applicable to the withdrawal of this declaration in the same way as it applies to a denunciation of the Convention.

### Article 21

Any Contracting State may reserve the right to apply the provisions of Chapter III only to trusts the validity of which is governed by the law of a Contracting State.

### Article 22

The Convention applies to trusts regardless of the date on which they were created.

However, a Contracting State may reserve the right not to apply the Convention to trusts created before the date on which, in relation to that State, the Convention enters into force.

*Article 23*

For the purpose of identifying the law applicable under the Convention, where a State comprises several territorial units each of which has its own rules of law in respect of trusts, any reference to the law of that State is to be construed as referring to the law in force in the territorial unit in question.

## CHELLARAM v. CHELLARAM

Chancery Division [1985] 1 All E.R. 1043; [1985] Ch. 409

SCOTT J.: "The bedrock of counsel for the defendants' case is that these two settlements are foreign settlements, the proper law of which is the law of India. Counsel for the plaintiffs contends, on the contrary, that the proper law is the law of England.

"It is important to be clear at the outset as to the relevance of this issue on the present application. The application seeks to prevent the plaintiffs from prosecuting in England a claim for the removal of the trustees and for the appointment of new trustees. Counsel for the defendants argues that the law by which the proposition that the trustees should be removed must be tested, and by which the question of who should be appointed in their places must be answered, is the proper law of the settlement. Counsel for the plaintiffs submits, however, that it is not the proper law of the settlement but the law of the place of administration that should govern such issues as removal of trustees and appointment of new ones. The place of administration, he submits, is London.

"The proper law of the settlement is, *per* Lord Greene M.R. in *Duke of Marlborough* v. *A.-G. (No. 1)* [1945] Ch. 78 at 83, the law which governs the settlement. He went on:

'This law can only be the law by reference to which the settlement was made and which was intended by the parties to govern their rights and liabilities.'

In Dicey and Morris on the *Conflict of Laws* (10th ed., 1980), p. 678, r. 120 states:

'The validity, the interpretation and the effect of an *inter vivos* trust of movables are governed by its proper law, that is, in the absence of any express or implied selection of the proper law by the settlor, the system of law with which the trust has its closest and most real connection.'

"When counsel for the defendants first opened the case to me, I was strongly inclined to regard the law of India as the obvious proper law of these two settlements, but as argument progressed I found myself progressively less certain. The beneficiaries are an Indian family. The trustees were all Indian in origin although one or other may have held a British passport. The settlements were drawn up in Bombay by Mr. Advani, an Indian practitioner, acting apparently in the course of his profession. The settlors were Indian in origin and Indian-domiciled at the date of the settlement. All these factors point, and I think point strongly, to the law of India being the proper law.

"Mr. Advani has sworn an affirmation in which he has stated in terms that he intended Indian law to apply to these settlements which he drafted. This evidence is inadmissible as evidence of the intentions of the parties to the settlements, but I may, I think, take it as indicating that the settlements are appropriate in form for the purposes of Indian law. Nevertheless, I am left with doubts. The trust property was Bermudian. The underlying assets, in the form of the operating companies, were all situated outside India. The purpose of the settlements was, it seems, in part to escape Indian taxation and, in part, to escape Indian exchange control regulations. But most important of all, it seems to me, is the identity of the three original trustees. Two, Mr. Rupchand and Mr. Bharwani, were permanently resident in England. The third, Ram Chellaram, was the member of the family who, in 1975, appeared to have the closest connection with England. The inference is inescapable that the parties to the settlements contemplated that administration thereof would take place in London. Indeed, counsel for the defendants accepted that this was an inference which was open to be drawn.

"The question why, if the parties intended the settlements to be governed by Indian law they should have arranged for an English administration, is a difficult one to answer. The parties' contemplation of an English administration seems to me to point strongly in favour of an English proper law. For the moment, however, I propose to leave the question open and to assume that counsel for the defendants is right that the law of India is the proper law of the settlement and to see where that leads. It leads, counsel for the defendants submitted, to the conclusion that the English courts should have nothing to do with the plaintiffs' claim for the removal of the trustees. You cannot have, he said, English courts removing foreign trustees of foreign settlements any more than you can have foreign courts removing English trustees of English settlements. Tied up in this *cri de coeur* are, in my view, three separate points. First, there is the question of jurisdiction. Does an English court have jurisdiction to entertain such a claim? Second, there is the question of power. If an English court does have jurisdiction, can it make an effective order removing foreign trustees of foreign settlements? Third, there is the *forum conveniens* point. Is this an action which an English court ought to be trying?

"I start with jurisdiction. In a sense, there is no doubt at all but that the court has jurisdiction. Each of the defendants was either served personally or service was effected on Norton Rose Botterell & Roche who had authority to accept service. By reason of due service of the writ, the court has jurisdiction over each of the defendants in respect of each of the issues raised by the writ.

"As to subject matter, also there is in my judgment no doubt that the court has jurisdiction. In *Ewing* v. *Orr Ewing* (1883) 9 App.Cas. 34 it was held by the House of Lords that the English courts had jurisdiction to administer the trusts of the will of a testator who died domiciled in Scotland. The will was proved in Scotland by executors, some of whom resided in Scotland and some in England. The assets, the subject of the trusts, consisted mainly of hereditable and personal property in Scotland. An infant beneficiary resident in England brought an action in England for the administration of the trusts of the will by the English courts. It was clear that the proper law of the trusts was the law of Scotland. None the less, the House of Lords, affirming the Court of Appeal, upheld the jurisdiction of the English courts. The Earl of Selborne L.C. said (at 40–41):

> ' . . . the jurisdiction of the English Court is established upon elementary principles. The Courts of Equity in England are, and always have been, Courts of conscience, operating *in personam* and not *in rem*; and in exercise of this personal jurisdiction that have always been accustomed to compel the performance of contracts and trusts as to

subjects which were not either locally or *ratione domicilii* within their jurisdiction. They have done so as to land, in Scotland, in Ireland, in the Colonies, in foreign countries. . . . A jurisdiction against trustees, which is not excluded *ratione legis rei sitae* as to land, cannot be excluded as to movables, because the author of the trust may have had a foreign domicil; and for this purpose it makes no difference whether the trust is constituted *inter vivos*, or by a will, or *mortis causâ* deed.'

Lord Blackburn agreed (at 46):

'The jurisdiction of the Court of Chancery is *in personam*. It acts upon the person whom it finds within its jurisdiction and compels him to perform the duty which he owes to the plaintiff.'

Both the Earl of Selborne L.C. and Lord Blackburn went on to say that the jurisdiction of the court to administer the foreign trust was not truly discretionary and that the plaintiff was entitled to the order sought *ex debito justitae* (see 9 App.Cas. 34 at 41–42, 47–48).

"That view cannot, in my judgment, stand with more recent pronouncements in the House of Lords (see *e.g.* Lord Diplock in *The Abidin Daver* [1984] A.C. 398 at 411–412. Current authority establishes that the court does have a discretion to decline jurisdiction on *forum non conveniens* grounds. But the principle that the English court has jurisdiction to administer the trusts of foreign settlements remains unshaken. The jurisdiction is *in personam*, is exercised against the trustees on whom the foreign trust obligations lie, and is exercised so as to enforce against the trustees the obligations which bind their conscience.

"The jurisdiction which I hold the court enjoys embraces, in my view, jurisdiction to remove trustees and appoint new ones. In *Letterstedt* v. *Broers* (1884) 9 App.Cas. 371 at 385–386, Lord Blackburn referred to a passage in Story's *Equity Jurisprudence* (12th ed., 1877), section 1289, which reads:

' . . . Courts of equity have no difficulty in interposing to remove trustees who have abused their trust. . . . '

Lord Blackburn then continued:

'It seems to their Lordships that the jurisdiction which a Court of Equity has no difficulty in exercising under the circumstances indicated by Story is merely ancillary to its principal duty, to see that the trusts are properly executed.'

Accordingly, in my judgment, the courts of this country, having jurisdiction to administer the trusts of the two settlements, have jurisdiction ancillary thereto to remove the trustees.

"The argument of counsel for the defendants that the court did not have jurisdiction to remove the trustees of a foreign settlement was based in part on the proposition that an order of removal would be ineffective to divest the present trustees of the fiduciary duties they owed under the proper law of the settlements. To some extent, this submission was based on the form of the relief sought in paragraph 4 of the writ. It seeks:

'An order removing the defendants as trustees of Mohan's Settlement and Harish's Settlement and appointing some fit and proper persons to be trustees in their place.'

An order in that form would not of itself, however, divest existing trustees and vest trust property in new trustees. Consequently, such an order would usually be accompanied by a vesting order under section 44 (in the case of land) section 51 (in the case of stocks and shares) of the Trustee Act 1925. It could not, in my opinion, sensibly be suggested (and counsel for the plaintiffs has not suggested) that a vesting order under section 51 could divest the defendants of the trust shares in the Bermudan holding companies or could vest those shares in new trustees. A vesting effect could be achieved by a vesting order only in respect of stocks and shares situated within the territorial jurisdiction of the court. Further, so long as the trust shares remain vested in the defendant trustees, their fiduciary obligations in respect thereof must remain. So, counsel for the defendants submitted, the court lacks the power to grant relief sought by paragraph 4 of the writ.

"This argument is, in my judgment, based on a point of form and not of substance. The jurisdiction of the court to administer trusts, to which the jurisdiction to remove trustees and appoint new ones is ancillary, is an *in personam* jurisdiction. In the exercise of it, the court will inquire what personal obligations are binding on the trustees and will enforce those obligations. If the obligations are owed in respect of trust assets abroad, the enforcement will be, and can only be, by *in personam* orders made against the trustees. The trustees can be ordered to pay, to sell, to buy, to invest, whatever may be necessary to give effect to the rights of the beneficiaries, which are binding on them. If the court is satisfied that, in order to give effect to or to protect the rights of the beneficiaries, the trustees ought to be replaced by others, I can see no reason in principle why the court should not make *in personam* orders against the trustees requiring them to resign and to vest the trust assets in the new trustees. The power of the court to remove trustees and to appoint new ones, owes its origin to an inherent jurisdiction and not to statute, and it must follow that the court has power to make such *in personam* orders as may be necessary to achieve the vesting of the trust assets in the new trustees. This is so, in my judgment, whether or not the trust assets are situated in England, and whether or not the proper law of the trusts in question is English law. It requires only that the individual trustee should be subject to the jurisdiction of the English courts. It does not matter, in my view, whether they have become subject to the jurisdiction by reason of service of process in England or because they have submitted to the jurisdiction, or because under R.S.C., Ord. 11 the court has assumed jurisdiction. In every case, orders *in personam* are made by the courts on the footing that those against whom they are made will obey them.

"Accordingly, and for these reasons, I do not accept counsel for the defendants' submission that the English courts have no power to remove the defendants as trustees of these two settlements. Since, however, such removal would have to be effected by *in personam* orders, the plaintiffs have put before me an amended statement of claim which seeks such orders. In my judgment, the court would have power, if it thought it right to do so, to make those orders.

"There are two other associated points which I should now deal with. As an adjunct to his submission that the English courts lack the power to remove trustees of foreign settlements, counsel for the defendants submitted that if such an order in the *in personam* form were made the defendants could not safely obey the order without first obtaining confirmation from the Indian courts that it would be proper for them to do so. Further, he submitted, his clients ought not to be subjected to such an order unless it were clear that

Indian law would regard them, if they did obey, as discharged from their fiduciary obligations under the settlement.

"It would be a matter entirely for the defendants and their advisers what steps they take in the Indian courts, but for my part I am not impressed by the proposition that such confirmation would be necessary. The English courts have jurisdiction over these defendants. An objection to the exercise of jurisdiction on *forum conveniens* grounds has been taken and I must deal with it, but, if in the end the case continues in England, I would expect that the Indian courts, for reasons of comity would afford the same respect to orders of this court as in like circumstances and for the same reasons English courts would afford to theirs.

"Counsel for the defendants suggested to me that I would give short shrift to an order of a foreign court removing a trustee of an English trust; but if the English trustee had been subject to the jurisdiction of the foreign court exercised in like circumstances to those in which English courts claim and exercise jurisdiction, I can see no reason why I should recoil from an order *in personam* made by the foreign court against an English trustee. And if the order had been given effect to by, for example, the trustee transferring trust assets in England into the names of new trustees, I see no reason why an English court should question the efficacy of the transfer. All of this assumes, of course, that there were no vitiating features in the manner in which the foreign order was obtained.

"As to the point that the defendants might, notwithstanding that they had transferred the Bermudan shares to new trustees, still owe fiduciary duties under the settlements, there is, in my view, no substance to that point. Firstly, no party to the English action could so contend. Mohan and Lachmibai Chellaram are not parties to the action but could easily be joined, as also could any of the sisters who wished to be joined. This does not therefore seem to me to be a practical problem. Secondly, the point could be raised as a defence to the plaintiffs' claim for the removal of trustees, and, if the court were satisfied that the point was a sound one, I cannot imagine that the defendants would be ordered to transfer the shares. Thirdly, the status of trustee and the burden of the fiduciary obligations arising therefrom have, as it seems to me, no reality except in relation to assets which are vested in or under the control of the trustee. If a trustee is divested of the trust assets, I do not understand how it can be supposed that he can retain any fiduciary obligation thereafter in respect of those assets or in respect of the income derived from them.

"I do not, therefore, think, there is anything in counsel for the defendants' objections to the efficacy of the *in personam* orders, if such orders were made.

"I have dealt with counsel for the defendants' submission on jurisdiction and on the power of an English court to make the orders sought on the footing that Indian law is the proper law of the settlements. As an adjunct to his arguments on those matters, counsel for the defendants submitted that, if Indian law was the proper law of the settlements, then Indian law was the system of law which ought to be applied to the matter of removal of trustees of the settlements and to the appointment of new ones. He drew my attention to the relevant provisions of the Indian Trusts Act 1882, as amended up to 1969, and commented, rightly in my opinion, that the various provisions in that Act relevant to the removal and appointment of trustees by the Indian court could not be applied by an English court in the present case.

"Counsel for the defendants wielded this point as part of his argument on jurisdiction and also as relevant to his *forum conveniens* point. Counsel for the plaintiffs has contended that the proper law of the settlement is English law but he has submitted that, even if that is wrong, England is the place where the trusts were intended to be administered and the place where, in fact, the trusts have been administered, that the administration of a trust is governed not by the proper law of the trust but by the law of the place where administration takes place, and that the removal of trustees and the appointment of new ones is a matter of administration. It is a feature of the history of these settlements that there has been remarkably little administration. The reason for this is that the trust property has been represented simply by shares in Bermudan holding companies, and no trust income has been derived therefrom. Until recently, when in response to the plaintiffs' demand trust accounts were prepared, there were no such accounts. However, counsel for the plaintiffs is, in my view, right in pointing out that such administration as there has been has taken place in London. It was in London that the deeds of retirement and appointment of new trustees were prepared and executed; such legal advice as has been taken by the trustees seems to have been taken by Mr. Advani from Norton Rose Botterell & Roche in London, and there seems to me to be no room for any real doubt that the parties to the settlement contemplated that the administration would take place in London.

"Accordingly, in my judgment, the factual basis on which counsel for the plaintiffs makes his submission is sound. As to law, counsel for the plaintiffs relies on the proposition stated in *Dicey and Morris*, p. 683, r. 121 that:

> 'The administration of a trust is governed (*semble*) by the law of its place of administration.'

Among the matters classified in the notes to rule 121 as matters of administration is 'the question who can appoint a trustee and what persons may be so appointed.' If this rule correctly states the law, it would seem to follow that the issue regarding removal of the trustees of these settlements should be governed by the law of the place of administration of the settlements. However, the tentative manner in which the rule is expressed is justified, in my view, by the lack of clear authority provided by the cases cited in the footnotes.

"There are two categories of case which must be distinguished from cases as the present case. Firstly, there are cases which establish that the administrative powers conferred on personal representatives by the Administration of Estates Act 1925 can be exercised by English personal representatives in relation to assets in England, whether or not the deceased died domiciled in England (see *Re Wilks*, [1935] Ch. 645). These cases exemplify the well-settled proposition that the administration of a deceased's assets is governed by the law of the country from which the administrator derives his authority.

"Secondly, there are cases which support the view that the provisions of English trust legislation apply to trust property situated in England whether or not the trusts on which the trust property is held are the trusts of foreign settlements (see *Re Kehr (decd.)*, *Martin* v. *Foges* [1952] Ch. 26, although Danckwerts J. doubted 'whether trustees constituted by the law of a foreign country would have the powers conferred on trustees regulated by English law' (see [1952] Ch. 26 at 30); see also *Re Ker's Settlement Trusts* [1963] Ch. 553. But neither of these lines of cases supports the proposition in *Dicey and Morris*, r. 121 when applied to a foreign settlement which is being administered in England but where the trust property is not in England.

"More cogent support is provided by *Re Pollak's Estate* [1937] T.P.D. 91. In that case the testator was domiciled in the Transvaal. He left movables in

England and in South Africa as well as in other countries. By his will he appointed as his executor and trustee an English bank which had no branch in South Africa and left his residuary estate on trust for beneficiaries, the majority of whom were domiciled in England. A number of questions were raised for the decision of the Transvaal court, including a question as to the law which should determine the rights and duties of the bank as trustee in the execution of the testamentary trust. Since the testator was domiciled in the Transvaal, South African law governed the construction of the will, but the court concluded that the testator had intended the trust to be administered in England, and Davis J., with whose judgment Greenberg J. concurred, said (at 101):

> 'I have no doubt that in appointing an English bank . . . to administer a trust fund wherein the great majority of the persons interested were at the time domiciled in England, the testator . . . intended English law to govern.'

He cited with approval this passage in the American Law Institute's Restatement of the Law of Conflict of Laws (see [1937] T.P.D. 91 at 101–102):

> 'If the testator appoints as trustee a trust company of another state, presumptively his intention is that the trust should be administered in the latter state; the trust will therefore be administered according to the law of the latter state.'

Accordingly, the court held that the rights and duties of the bank as trustee were to be governed by English law, notwithstanding that the essential validity of the trust and the construction of the will were governed by the law of South Africa, the domicile of the testator. The reasoning which led the Transvaal court to this decision I respectfully accept. The court concluded that the testator in establishing a settlement to be administered in England must have intended English law to govern its administration. The court gave effect to that intention. But it does not follow from *Re Pollak's Estate* that the law of the place of the administration of a trust would govern the rights and duties of the trustee in a case where the circumstances did not enable the inference to be drawn that such was the testator's or settlor's intention. *Re Pollak's Estate* was a case of testamentary trust. It is well-established English law that the essential validity of a testamentary trust of movables is governed by the law of the testator's domicile. But there is no reason why a testator should not by will establish a trust to be governed by some law other than the law of his domicile. His ability to create the trust may be subject to the law of his domicile but subject thereto he is, in my view, as able by will to make a foreign settlement as he is able to do so *inter vivos*. *Re Pollak's Estate* supports the proposition that a testator can do so. It does not, in my view, support anything further and does not really support rule 121.

"As a matter of principle, I find myself unable to accept the distinction drawn by rules 120 and 121 in *Dicey and Morris* between 'validity, interpretation and effect' on the one hand and 'administration' on the other hand.[32] The rights and duties of trustees, for example, may be regarded as matters of

---

[32] Dicey & Morris, *Conflict of Laws* (11th ed., 3rd cum. supp.), Rule 157 now reads, "The validity, construction, effects and administration of a trust are governed by the law chosen by the settlor, or, in the absence of any such choice, by the law with which the trust is most closely connected."

administration but they also concern the effect of the settlement. The rights of the trustees are enjoyed as against the beneficiaries; the duties of the trustees are owed to the beneficiaries. If the rights of the beneficiaries are to be ascertained by applying the proper law of the settlement, I do not understand how the duties of the trustees can be ascertained by applying a different law, and vice versa. In my judgment, a conclusion that the law of the place of administration of a settlement governs such matters as the rights and duties of the trustees can only be right if that law is the proper law governing the settlement.

"But the right of beneficiaries to have trustees removed and new ones appointed is a right of a rather special nature. It is not, at least in the usual case, a right conferred by the settlement. If it were the case that a settlement conferred on particular beneficiaries or on a particular person such as the settlor the right to remove trustees and appoint new ones, that right (like any other rights conferred by the settlement on beneficiaries or trustees) would, in my view, require to be given effect in accordance with the proper law of the settlement. That would, in my view, be so, regardless of where the settlement was being administered. But no such right is conferred by the two settlements with which I am concerned.

"The plaintiffs' claim for the removal of trustees and the appointment of new ones is, in this case, as in most cases, not an attempt to enforce a corresponding right conferred by the settlements, but is an appeal to the inherent jurisdiction of the court to which Lord Blackburn referred in *Letterstedt* v. *Broers* (1884) 9 App.Cas. 371 at 385–386. The function of English courts in trust litigation is to enforce or protect the rights of the beneficiaries which bind the conscience of the trustee defendants. The identification and extent of those rights is a matter for the proper law of the settlement, but the manner of enforcement is, in my view, a matter of machinery which depends on the powers enjoyed by the English courts. Among the powers available to English courts is the power to order the removal of trustees and the appointment of new ones. This power is, in my view, machinery which, under English domestic law, can be exercised by English courts where necessary in order to enable the rights of beneficiaries to be enforced or protected. The exercise of the domestic power does not, in my view, depend on whether the rights of the beneficiaries are enjoyed under domestic settlements or foreign settlements, or on whether the trust property is situated in England or abroad. The locality of the trust property will, however, determine whether the removal can be achieved by an *in rem* order or whether an *in personam* order is appropriate. Accordingly, except where rights conferred by the settlement are under consideration, the removal of trustees and the appointment of new ones are not, in my judgment, a matter to be governed by the proper law of the settlement. Nor, in my opinion, is it a matter governed by the law of the place where the administration of the settlement has taken place. It is, in my judgment, a matter to be governed by the law of the country whose courts have assumed jurisdiction to administer the trusts of the settlement in question.

"In the view of the matter I take, therefore, I do not think that the identification of the proper law of the settlement is a critical issue on this application. Any court before which the plaintiffs' case is litigated will have to consider the rights of the beneficiaries under these discretionary settlements in order to form an opinion whether the enforcement or protection of those rights requires the removal of the present trustees but no one has suggested that the nature of those rights is going to be different if tested under Indian law than if tested under English law. Any such difference is likely to be marginal only and to be immaterial for the purposes of the plaintiffs' claim for the removal of the trustees.

"It is, therefore, not necessary for me to decide on this application whether Indian law or English law is the proper law of the settlements. I am dealing with an interlocutory application. The relevant evidence has not been tested by cross-examination. In these circumstances, I would, I think, be unwise to express a conclusion on the proper law question and I do not do so.

"I have held, contrary to counsel for the defendants' submission, that the English courts have both jurisdiction and power to deal with the plaintiffs' claim for the removal of trustees and for the appointment of new ones. In that event, counsel for the defendants submits that the court ought nevertheless to decline to exercise that jurisdiction on the ground, shortly stated, that there is another competent jurisdiction, India, in which justice can be done between the parties, and that by comparison with India, England is a *forum non conveniens*. . . .

"In my judgment, the defendants have failed to cast England as a *forum non conveniens*. It is settled on authority that the onus lies on the defendants to satisfy me that I ought, in my discretion, to grant a stay. They have not done so, and I therefore refuse a stay and dismiss their application." *Application dismissed.*

## QUESTION

S, an Englishman domiciled in England, visits Dublin in 1988 and pays 100 Irish punts to A and B as trustees on specified trusts which confer on the trustees a power to accumulate income for 100 years or until the expiry of 20 years from the death of the last survivor of all the descendants of Queen Elizabeth II living at the date of his trust instrument which expressly makes Irish law govern the trust (so the accumulation power is valid).

On his return to his London residence S has £1 million transferred to A and B in Dublin who then use it to purchase shares in English companies for £500,000 and an English house for £500,000. A month later S transfers English company shares worth £1 million to A and B as well as English shop premises worth £1 million.

Twenty-one years later a beneficiary claims that the trustees can no longer exercise their power of accumulation in respect of income from the above assets. Advise the trustees.

Would your advice differ if S had stayed in London and paid £100 to London resident trustees, though still creating such an extensive power of accumulation and expressly choosing Irish law to govern the trust and subsequently transferring the above assets to such English trustees?

# INDEX